UNIVERSITY CASEBOOK SERIES®

MERGERS AND ACQUISITIONS

CASES AND MATERIALS

FOURTH EDITION

WILLIAM J. CARNEY
Charles Howard Candler Professor Emeritus
Emory University School of Law

FOUNDATION
PRESS

University Casebook Series is a trademark registered in the U.S. Patent and Trademark Office.

© 2000 FOUNDATION PRESS
© 2007, 2011 THOMSON REUTERS/FOUNDATION PRESS
© 2016 LEG, Inc. d/b/a West Academic
    444 Cedar Street, Suite 700
    St. Paul, MN 55101
    1-877-888-1330

Printed in the United States of America

ISBN: 978-1-68328-075-0

To Jane

PREFACE

This book's goal is to introduce students to transactional lawyering in the context of mergers and acquisitions. The core of the book remains introducing the reader to the rich complexities of doing acquisitions in the shadow of a large and complex body of law. As in the prior editions, areas that merit entire courses, such as tax reorganization and antitrust, are given short shrift, as are areas such as environmental law, labor law, securities law (except the Williams Act) and products liability. The emphasis in the book is on managing risk—which is what good transactional lawyers do. And they manage it by contracting in the shadow of the law, which represents the book's approach to this area. The law chosen in the corporate area is overwhelmingly that of Delaware, which presents a problem. While Delaware law is richly textured and provides important limits on the discretion of its corporate fiduciaries, it is not the entire universe. Yet to do justice to the other "half" of that universe would unduly extend the book. So instead I have chosen a few state cases that offer sharp contrasts with Delaware law. Some note material attempts to describe other variations in approaches. It remains the case that where local corporate law on this subject is less well developed many practitioners will advise corporate clients on the basis of Delaware law, probably on the theory that local law is highly unlikely to provide greater restrictions on their discretion.

Lest this be thought to be a cookbook for young lawyers to enable them to begin billing their time without discounts for learning technical material, the book retains its brief reviews of finance and economic materials. Some of the older materials retain their value, because of their correct understandings of theories and markets. One observation is that the more things change the more they remain the same—the hostile leveraged buyouts of the 1980s have become the negotiated private equity deals of the twenty-first century, also financed with huge amounts of debt. In both cases these eras were followed by periods of reckoning and remorse.

Students will find the cases involving hostile acquisitions introduce an entirely new jargon. They are encouraged to use the Glossary in Appendix A to clarify these terms.

WILLIAM J. CARNEY

July 15, 2016

ACKNOWLEDGMENTS

I thank my wife Jane for her patience and support during the preparation of this edition.

With appreciation, this acknowledgment is made for the publishers and authors who gave permission for the reproduction of excerpts from the following materials:

AEI Press

Roberta Romano, THE GENIUS OF AMERICAN CORPORATE LAW (1993)

William T. Allen, Jack B. Jacobs and Leo F. Strine

"Function Over Form: A Reassessment of Standards of Review in Delaware Corporate Law," Vol. 55, The Business Lawyer, p. 1287, 1306—1308 (2001)

American Law Institute—American Bar Association Committee on Continuing Professional Education

Jere D. McGaffey, BUYING, SELLING AND MERGING BUSINESSES, p. 15–26 (2d ed. 1989)

Catholic University Law Review

William J. Carney, "Signalling and Causation in Insider Trading," Vol. 36 Catholic University Law Review, p. 863, 877–883 (1987)

University of Chicago Press

Henry G. Manne, "Mergers and the Market for Corporate Control," Vol. 73 Journal of Political Economy, pp. 110–119 (1965)

Columbia University Press

Edward Ross Aranow and Herbert A. Einhorn, TENDER OFFERS FOR CORPORATE CONTROL (1973).

E. Allan Farnsworth, "Precontractual Liability and Preliminary Agreements: Fair Dealing and Failed Negotiations," Vol. 87 Columbia Law Review p. 217, 288–89 (1987)

Reinier Kraakman, "Taking Discounts Seriously: The Implications of 'Discounted' Share Prices as an Acquisition Motive," Vol. 88 Columbia Law Review p. 891, 898–902, 908–909 (1988)

Journal of Applied Corporate Finance (Wiley–Blackwell)

William J. Carney, "Two–Tier Tender Offers and Shark Repellents," Vol. 4, No. 2 Midland Corporate Finance Journal, p. 48, 49 (1986)

Journal of Financial Economics (Elsevier)

Clifford W. Smith and Jerold B. Warner, "On Financial Contracting: An Analysis of Bond Covenants," Vol. 7, Journal of Financial Economics p. 117 (1979)

James C. Freund, THE ACQUISITION MATING DANCE AND OTHER ESSAYS ON NEGOTIATING (1987)

Robert R. Kibby, A List of Transaction Show–Stoppers

Morris Manning & Martin

Teressa Tarpley, "Solving Valuation Issues with Earnouts–Clever or Stupid?"

University of Notre Dame

William J. Carney and Leonard A. Silverstein, "The Illusory Protections of the Poison Pill," Vol. 79 Notre Dame L. Rev., p. 183–191 (2003)

University of Pennsylvania Law Review

William J. Carney and Mark Heimendinger, Appraising The Non–Existent: The Delaware Courts' Struggle With Control Premiums, Vol. 152 University of Pennsylvania Law Review, p. 845 (2003)

RiskMetrics Group

2010 U.S. Proxy Voting Guidelines Summary

Stanford Law Review

Bernard Black, "Bidder Overpayment in Takeovers," Vol. 41, p. 597, 599–600, 602–604 (1989)

Thompson-West

Kevin A. Miller, "The ConEd Decision—One Year Later: Significant Implications for Public Company Mergers Appear Largely Ignored," Vol. 10 No. 9 The M & A Lawyer 1 (Oct., 2006)

Widener University School of Law

William J. Carney, Toward a More Perfect Market for Corporate Control, Vol. 9, Delaware Journal of Corporate Law 593 (1984) Jeffrey L. Silberman, "How Do Pennsylvania Directors Spell Relief? Act 36," Vol. 17, Delaware Journal of Corporate Finance, 115 (1991)

William F. Wynne Jr., "Corporate Review in Connection with Mergers and Acquisitions," in CORPORATE COUNSEL'S GUIDE TO ACQUISITIONS & DIVESTITURES, p. 7.008–.010 (1994)

SUMMARY OF CONTENTS

TABLE OF CONTENTS

PART IV. REGULATION OF ACQUISITIONS

TABLE OF CASES

The principal cases are in bold type.

UNIVERSITY CASEBOOK SERIES®

MERGERS AND ACQUISITIONS

CASES AND MATERIALS

FOURTH EDITION

PART I

THE SOURCES OF GAIN IN BUSINESS COMBINATIONS

CHAPTER ONE

THE HISTORY OF BUSINESS COMBINATIONS

1. INTRODUCTION

American business history and law have been influenced in part by the great waves of merger and acquisition activity that have swept through the economy periodically. For the lawyer handling a friendly negotiated transaction, these changes may seem isolated and irrelevant, but they have shaped the institutional background in which the lawyer works. No doubt they will continue to do so. This chapter provides a brief look at the theories of why acquisitions occur and a look at the modern history of this phenomenon.

2. THEORIES ABOUT MOTIVATIONS FOR ACQUISITIONS

Mergers and the Market for Corporate Control
Henry G. Manne.
73 Journal of Political Economy 110—119 (1965).[*]

In recent years many of the traditional economic justifications of our antitrust laws have been seriously questioned. A new sophistication has developed, and economic activities frequently held illegal by the courts are now thought by many to be consistent with our antitrust goals. The rules against tie-ins, vertical mergers, predatory competition, among others, have to a greater or lesser degree had their theoretical foundations considerably weakened. Recently even cartels, the most venerable victim of American antitrust laws, have found their near champion.

One practice, however, remains generally condemned in both the economic literature and the most recent Supreme Court rulings. Mergers among competitors would seem to have no important saving grace. The position has gained considerable legal currency that any merger between competing firms is at least suspect and perhaps per se illegal. The latter result seems especially likely when one of the combining firms already occupies a substantial position in the relevant market. Antitrust problems in the merger field seem more and more to be confined to discussions of relevant product and geographic markets and perhaps to the issue of quantitative substantiality.

---

[*]   This is the seminal article in the literature on this subject. For an article discussing its historical importance, *see* Carney, The Legacy of "The Market for Corporate Control" and the Origins of the Theory of the Firm, 50 CASE WES. RES. L. REV. 215 (1999).—Ed.

Presumably there is still a so-called failing-company defense to an illegal merger charge. The announced justification for this doctrine was that, if indeed the merged company was failing, then it was not actually a competitor in the industry. But there are strong suggestions that even that defense may be unavailable when a large corporation is making the acquisition, or when there is any chance of absorption by a non-competing firm, or when the acquired company has not "failed" enough.

There is general agreement among economists that the courts' approach to horizontal mergers is correct. Professor Donald Dewey, who appears slightly regretful about the severe treatment of mergers by our courts and administrative agencies, concedes that no important economies can be attained through a merger which cannot be gained either by internal growth or, at worst, by a cartel, if that were legal. But Dewey is certainly not as severe in his personal indictment of horizontal mergers as most other economists. He has argued that most mergers "have virtually nothing to do with either the creation of market power or the realization of scale economies. They are merely a civilized alternative to bankruptcy or the voluntary liquidation that transfers assets from failing to rising firms."

Consistent with his alternative-to-bankruptcy explanation of mergers, Dewey points out that, "[i]f the capital market were perfect and a merger conferred no monopoly power, a rising firm would be indifferent between the two forms of expansion." Thus a rapidly expanding industry with a relatively short life cycle of its firms would be characterized by substantial internal growth of successful firms. Mergers then would "most commonly indicate not the decline of competition but its undoubted vigor."

Dewey's argument is, however, only a partial redemption of mergers, since a great many have occurred in industries in which the life cycle of firms is not as short as in the southern textile industry, which he mentions as his example. Further, Dewey's defense of mergers seems to be limited to those cases in which bankruptcy or liquidation is imminent. But, if a merger can be justified at this stage of the firm's life, presumably it is also desirable before bankruptcy becomes imminent in order to avoid that eventuality. If, as Dewey suggests, mergers actually are superior to bankruptcy as a method of "shifting assets from failing to rising firms," and if mergers were completely legal, we should anticipate relatively few actual bankruptcy proceedings in any industry which was not itself contracting. The function so wastefully performed by bankruptcies and liquidations would be economically performed by mergers at a much earlier stage in a firm's life.

THE CORPORATE-CONTROL MARKET

The conventional approach to a merger problem takes corporations merely as decision-making units or firms within the classical market framework. This approach dictates a ban on many horizontal mergers almost by definition. The basic proposition advanced in this paper is that the control of corporations may constitute a valuable asset; that this asset exists independent of any interest in either economies of scale or monopoly profits; that an active market for corporate control exists; and that a great many mergers are probably the result of the successful workings of this special market.

Basically this paper will constitute an introduction to a study of the market for corporation control. The emphasis will be placed on the antitrust implications of this market, but the analysis to follow has important implications for a variety of economic questions. Perhaps the most important implications are those for the alleged separation of ownership and control in large corporations. So long as we are unable to discern any control relationship between small shareholders and corporate management, the thrust of Berle and Means' famous phrase remains strong. But, as will be explained below, the market for corporate control gives to these shareholders both power and protection commensurate with their interest in corporate affairs.

A fundamental premise underlying the market for corporate control is the existence of a high positive correlation between corporate managerial efficiency and the market price of shares of that company. As an existing company is poorly managed—in the sense of not making as great a return for the shareholders as could be accomplished under other feasible managements—the market price of the shares declines relative to the shares of other companies in the same industry or relative to the market as a whole. This phenomenon has a dual importance for the market for corporate control.

In the first place, a lower share price facilitates any effort to take over high-paying managerial positions. The compensation from these positions may take the usual forms of salary, bonuses, pensions, expense accounts, and stock options. Perhaps more important, it may take the form of information useful in trading in the company's shares; or, if that is illegal, information may be exchanged and the trading done in other companies' shares. But it is extremely doubtful that the full compensation recoverable by executives for managing their corporations explains more than a fraction of outsider attempts to take over control. Take-overs of corporations are too expensive generally to make the "purchase" of management compensation an attractive proposition.

It is far more likely that a second kind of reward provides the primary motivation for most take-over attempts. The market price of shares does more than measure the price at which the normal compensation of executives can be "sold" to new individuals. Share price, or that part reflecting managerial efficiency, also measures the potential capital gain inherent in the corporate stock. The lower the stock price, relative to what it could be with more efficient management, the more attractive the take-over becomes to those who believe that they can manage the company more efficiently. And the potential return from the successful take-over and revitalization of a poorly run company can be enormous.

Additional leverage in this operation can be obtained by borrowing the funds with which the shares are purchased, although American commercial banks are generally forbidden to lend money for this purpose. A comparable advantage can be had from using other shares rather than cash as the exchange medium. Given the fact of special tax treatment for capital gains, we can see how this mechanism for taking over control of badly run corporations is one of the most important "get-rich-quick" opportunities in our economy today.

But the greatest benefits of the take-over scheme probably inure to those least conscious of it. Apart from the stock market, we have no objective standard of managerial efficiency. Courts, as indicated by the so-called business-judgment rule, are loath to second-guess business decisions or remove directors from office. Only the take-over scheme provides some assurance of competitive efficiency among corporate managers and therefore affords strong protection to the interests of vast numbers of small, non-controlling shareholders. Compared to this mechanism, the efforts of the SEC and the courts to protect shareholders through the development of a fiduciary duty concept and the shareholder's derivative suit seem small indeed. It is true that sales by dissatisfied shareholders are necessary to trigger the mechanism and that these shareholders may suffer considerable losses. On the other hand, even greater capital losses are prevented by the existence of a competitive market for corporate control.

There are several mechanisms for taking over the control of corporations. The three basic techniques are the proxy fight, direct purchase of shares, and the merger. The costs, practical difficulties, and legal consequences of these approaches vary widely. The selection of one or another or some combination of these techniques frequently represents a difficult strategy decision. An attempt will be made in this paper to analyze some of the considerations involved in a selection of one device over another.

PROXY FIGHTS

The most dramatic and publicized of the take-over devices is the proxy fight; it is also the most expensive, the most uncertain, and the least used of the various techniques. Indeed it is somewhat difficult to describe the necessary conditions under which a proxy fight rather than some other take-over form will be indicated. At first blush, the proxy fight appears to be inexpensive since one does not have to own a large number of shares (or for that matter any shares) in order to wage a fight. But this fact is most relevant when the take-over is for the purpose of gaining the incumbents' compensation. If the outsider wants capital gains, he will be interested in owning more, not fewer, shares. This suggests that proxy fights will be relatively more often used when the issue is not one of management policies but of distribution of insiders' compensation.*

Even as a device for settling internal power struggles, actual proxy fights constitute only a small percentage of threatened fights. The parties will generally prefer to negotiate a settlement in accordance with their respective strengths than incur the costs of soliciting proxies. The more reliable the information about relative strengths available, the more will settlement be likely to occur. This suggests that proxy fights will be relatively more common when there is widespread distribution of the company's shares than when there are relatively large holdings.

In a number of cases the outsider would probably like to own more shares and take over control without waging or threatening a proxy fight. But if he is unable to accumulate sufficient capital to purchase control directly, he may settle for half a loaf. In effect he indicates his willingness to share the capital-gain potential with all other shareholders in exchange for enough of their votes to put him into control.

When a proxy fight is announced, the shares tend to rise in price, reflecting a rise in both the market value of the vote and the discounted value of potential gain in the underlying share interest if the outsider wins. Other outsiders will find it in their interest to retain their shares or purchase shares, to vote for the outsider seeking control, and to share in the capital appreciation. It may be cheaper to elicit the support of these voters through expenditures on persuasion than through outright purchase of the shares. But to the outsider seeking control, every voter represents another person with whom he must share the potential gain resulting from his more efficient management. These voters are analogous to, or substitutes for, the capital or credit with which the outsider would otherwise purchase control directly.

Proxy-fight expenses have always included direct expenses of mailings, advertising, telephone calls, and visits to large shareholders. But since the Securities Exchange Act of 1934, the cost of waging a proxy fight has probably increased substantially. Prior to the act, the proxy system operated largely through broker intermediaries acting as full agents for the beneficial owners of the shares. To the brokers was delegated not merely the ministerial job of voting but the more important responsibility of deciding how to vote. That practice has been largely replaced because of the SEC philosophy that the proxy system should duplicate actual meetings of shareholders as closely as possible. Thus,

---

* [Ed.] By the end of the 1990s over 60% of all shares listed on the New York Stock Exchange were owned by financial institutions. A good many of these shares were held by institutions that followed the "indexing" approach to investing, in which they attempt to assure that their portfolio is representative of the entire stock market, or some portion of it, perhaps one represented by an index of stock performance, such as the Standard & Poor's 500 Stock Index. For these institutions, neither selling a stock that performs badly nor buying more of it are viable strategies, since to do either destroys the indexed nature of their portfolios. For these institutions, a proxy fight may be the only means available to effect changes in control designed to enhance the value of a company's shares.

today, "giving a proxy" is really tantamount to voting. And, since the shareholder himself is voting, it is also felt that he should be fully and truthfully informed about all aspects of the corporation's affairs. This has tremendously increased the cost of soliciting proxies. But while the incumbents finance the bulk of their proxy solicitation expenses from corporate funds, the outsider will have this advantage only if he wins.

DIRECT PURCHASE OF SHARES

The second mechanism for taking over control of a corporation is the direct purchase of the requisite number of shares of the corporations. There are several techniques that may be used in the direct purchase of shares. The most obvious is the outright purchase on the open market of the requisite percentage of shares. The outsider might also try to buy the shares from large individual owners, thus preserving secrecy and allowing negotiation on price. Finally, he may make a bid for tenders, that is, a request that shareholders make an offer to sell their shares to him at a certain price, usually above the market. This last form of direct purchase is most apposite when the shares are widely held and there is a chance of a fast increase in market price if the news spreads that there is a heavy buyer in the market for the company's shares. A tender bid is usually stated to be effective only if a minimum percentage of shares is offered at the announced price. Also, the bid will ordinarily be for less than 100 per cent of the shares in order to avoid the problem of many individual shareholders trying to be the sole hold-out. In practice, private negotiation for large blocks of shares may be combined with either open-market purchases or a tender bid.

There are few serious legal problems with any of the direct purchase techniques. In fact, about the only one which has arisen with any regularity in recent years results from Professor Adolf A. Berle's contention that control is a corporate asset. The implications of this notion is that any premium received by an individual for a sale of control belongs in equity to all of the shareholders. As a general proposition, the courts have refused to follow this thesis; and there are numerous judicial statements to the effect that one may claim a premium for control.

A number of legal writers, following Berle, continue to press for a rule of equality in share purchase price when an outsider buys control in a corporation. The economic results of such a rule could be most unfortunate. Many holders of control blocks of shares would refuse to sell at a share price which did not pay them a premium at least sufficient to compensate them for the loss of net values presently being received from their position in the corporation. If all non-controlling shareholders must accordingly be paid a premium over the market price of their shares, then in a substantial number of cases the purchaser will not conclude the bargain. This further suggests that, if control is securely held in one block, the "market price" of traded shares is the price for an underlying share interest without an aliquot portion of control. That is, if one person owns 51 per cent of the shares of a company, nothing will be paid for the vote attached to the other shares, no matter how actively the shares may be traded on the market. The less securely control is held in one block, the more likely are non-controlling shareholders to participate in the "premium," and the less will an outsider be willing to pay any one shareholder for control. Both proxy fights and competitive tender bids are more likely to occur under these conditions, since each of them gives shareholders the power to sell their votes at a premium.

MERGERS

The third major mechanism for taking over control of the corporation is the merger. Here, by definition, the acquiring concern will be a corporation and not an individual, and the medium of exchange used to buy control will typically be shares of the acquiring corporation rather than cash.* Another major difference between the merger and other take-over forms is that, almost without exception, a merger requires the explicit approval of those already in control of the corporation. And most statutes require more than a simple majority vote by shareholders to effectuate a merger.** If the merger occurs after an acquisition of shares in a tender bid, then the tender bid and not the merger is the actual mechanism for changing control.

The requirement of management's approval for a merger generates some peculiar results. Generally speaking, managers' incentives and interests coincide with those of their shareholders in every particular except one: they have no incentive, as managers, to buy management services for the company at the lowest possible price. Even if the market for corporate control is working perfectly, so long as the cost to the corporation of the incumbent managers' inefficiency is below the cost to an outsider of taking over control, the insiders will remain secure in the positions with protected high salaries.

In the case of tender bids, as we have seen, a premium for control may be paid; and in the proxy fight situation, in one sense, at least, the premium is paid in the form of expenditures necessary to persuade shareholders to vote a certain way. But the merger has considerable cost advantages over the other two forms of take-over, not the least being the ability to use shares rather than cash as the purchasing medium.

The shareholders should ordinarily be willing to accept any offer of a tax-free exchange of new marketable shares worth more than their old shares. But the managers are in a position to claim almost the full

---

*   [Ed.] Subsequent to this article most corporate statutes were amended to permit the consideration in a merger to consist of cash or other assets, in addition to shares. With the advent of junk bond financing in the 1980's, the consideration in mergers frequently consisted of cash, borrowed on the security of the acquired corporation's assets.

**   [Ed.] By 1990 most statutes required only a simple majority vote of shareholders to approve a merger. The Model Act now requires only a majority of a quorum for approval, but many states have adopted special antitakeover statutes that allowed corporations to opt in or out of special voting rules for mergers that set much higher voting requirements, unless relaxed by the acquired firm's board of directors.

market value of control, since they have it in their power to block the merger by voting against it. When we find incumbents recommending a control change, it is generally safe to assume that some side payment is occurring.

Side payments are not simple transactions at law because of the rule that directors and officers may not sell their positions shorn of the share interest necessary to insure a transfer of control. The most obvious kind of side payment to managers is a position within the new structure either paying a salary or making them privy to valuable market information. This arrangement, easily established with mergers, can look like normal business expediency, since the argument can always be made that the old management provides continuity and a link with the past experience of the corporation.

There is still another very important reason why mergers may be more desirable than proxy fights or take-over bids as a way of operating in the corporate-control market. This is a market in which reliable information about valuable opportunities will be extremely difficult to discover. For reasons already mentioned, the corporate insiders will generally have no incentive to advertise this kind of information. Blatant cases will, of course, be evident from casual observation of industrial affairs and the stock market.

The great problem in the corporate-control market is finding reliable information about new opportunities. There have generally been a few individual operators in this market, and perhaps they have found the more obvious cases of bad management. But to guarantee effective competition in the market for corporate control, it seems clear that corporations must be allowed to function therein. Managers of a competing firm, unlike free-wheeling individual participants in the market for corporate control, almost automatically know a great deal of the kind of information crucial to a take-over decision. Careful analysis of cost conditions in their own firm and the market price of shares of other corporations in the same industry will provide information that can be relied upon with some degree of confidence.

Since, in a world of uncertainty, profitable transactions will be entered into more often by those whose information is relatively more reliable, it should not surprise us that mergers within the same industry have been a principal form of changing corporate control. Reliable information is often available to suppliers and customers as well. Thus many vertical mergers may be of the control take-over variety rather than of the "foreclosure of competitors" or scale-economies type. Undoubtedly many more mergers, both horizontal and vertical, would have occurred but for our antitrust laws. The managers of corporations have considerable incentive to exploit such opportunities for their corporation, just as they are motivated to find any good new investment opportunity. And there are both legal and practical barriers to the individuals' utilizing such opportunities for themselves.

―――――――

3. MOTIVATIONS FOR MERGERS

Much of modern law of mergers and acquisitions was made during the 1980s, and is a product of particular market conditions and motivations of buyers. From the end of World War II until the late 1970s, much of American industry was insulated from global competition. The U.S. had the largest common market, and many American companies felt content to concentrate on business within the U.S. Our large manufacturing plants were seen as efficient, and continuing growth in the economy fueled the view that these industries were efficiently managed. In 1933 Adolph A. Berle and Gardiner Means argued in PRIVATE PROPERTY AND THE MODERN CORPORATION (1933) that most large U.S. companies had considerable market power, to restrict output and raise prices, and collect some form of monopoly or at least oligopoly profits. Further, it was popularized by the economist John Kenneth Galbraith, in THE AFFLUENT SOCIETY (1958) that these companies could manipulate consumer preferences and cause them to keep buying an unending stream of new products, whether truly useful or not. The final part of this lore was that corporate managers were no longer accountable to widely dispersed and apathetic shareholders, and could dispense their monopoly profits at their discretion, paying shareholders just enough to keep them satisfied, while employing the rest for excessive compensation and perquisites.

Many corporate managers acted as if they believed this story, with two important consequences. First, some attempted to "manage" reported earnings so they grew steadily, if not spectacularly, from year to year. Seeking this growth might mean retaining earnings to invest in new production capacity, or, in many cases, buying other businesses. Second it might involve setting growth targets for lower-level managers to meet, and effectively communicating to them that if they had profits above the target in one year, it might be better to hold back some of those gains for the following year, to assure that the manager could meet ever-rising targets.

The 1960s and 1970s witnessed the growth of the so-called conglomerate firm. Growth through acquisition of competitors ("horizontal integration") became problematic under stricter enforcement of the antitrust laws in the 1950s and 1960s. Even acquiring suppliers or customers ("vertical integration") became more difficult under these laws. For the manager eager to reinvest earnings to grow the revenues and profits of the company, the only route (other than increasing sales of existing products or reducing their cost) was to acquire businesses that had no particular relationship to the existing business, but which could contribute to revenues and profits. This was most easily accomplished when a company could acquire another firm with a lower price-earnings ratio. This meant that the market value of shares of the acquired company were lower for each dollar of earnings than those of the buyer. By "buying" those earnings, the buying company could add more earnings dollars per share of stock issued in the merger than it had available from its existing business.* By increasing earnings per share, these companies continued to show steady earnings growth. In some cases acquiring companies borrowed funds to finance the purchase, increasing still further the earnings per share. None of these manipulations were likely to increase real values. Indeed, by the early 1970s there were signs that some conglomerates were failing, and even falling into bankruptcy, due in part to heavy debt loads and poor performance of their many businesses.

Expectations of improved performance had been high during the 1960s, as managers and business schools persuaded themselves that the new breed of managers, armed with MBAs, were far better trained (and perhaps even smarter) than their predecessors. The truly foolish thought they could acquire any type of business and learn how to manage it effectively. Professor Oliver Williamson described the organization of these firms as "M-form," involving decentralized management of each division, supervised by upper level management, which made strategic decisions. In this model, the firm created its own "internal capital market," in which top management allocated retained earnings to those managers who competed most successfully to obtain them. In some cases the allocative efficiency was limited by top management's ignorance of some divisions, or favoritism among managers. The results, ultimately, were a decline in performance and profitability of these firms.

At the same time, other forces drove acquisitions in many industries. As the OPEC cartel reduced oil production and raised prices, consumer demand did not grow at the rapid rates previously experienced, and the oil industry found itself with excess capacity, which led to mergers that would allow use of the most efficient refineries. The increasing sophistication of data processing technology led to the availability of economies of scale in banking that drove consolidations, which continue to this day. Brokerage firms combined in some cases to eliminate failing firms, while in others brokerage firms and other financial service firms combined in the belief that they could cross-market products to the other's customers. Not all of these experiments were successful, and some were later divested. Some of these transactions were hostile, meaning uninvited by the management of the company to be acquired, as early as the 1960s, and led to the passage of the Williams Act amendments to the

---

* This assumes markets are inefficient, and that investors will continue to value the combination at the earnings multiple of the acquiring firm, rather than at the weighted average of the multiples of both firms. Much of this kind of acquisition occurred before the Efficient Capital Markets Hypothesis (ECMH) became widely accepted. (See Chapter Two, Part 2.)

Securities Exchange Act in 1968. But hostile takeovers carried a negative aura. The most prestigious brokerage firms refused to work for hostile bidders until Morgan Stanley broke ranks in 1974 to advise on a hostile bid for International Nickel.

It should come as no surprise that as foreign economies recovered from the devastation of World War II their industries, often rebuilt with U.S. aid, would become strong competitors on a global scale. Aging U.S. steel plants, with high-wage workers, were unable to compete with much more modern plants, often in developing economies. Japanese cars first trickled into the U.S., and then with the creation of OPEC and a quantum leap in gasoline prices, flooded in, meeting very little U.S. competition for smaller more efficient automobiles. Japanese electronic products virtually wiped out American manufacturers in this area. Oil companies, awash in profits from increasing oil prices during the 1970s, repeated the earlier mistakes in other industries, investing retained earnings in the purchase of a typewriter company, just as IBM introduced its personal computer, in the now-defunct Montgomery Ward chain of department stores, and in increasing drilling and exploration in areas that were high cost and had only remote possibilities of returning a profit.

There is no disaster that does not also provide some opportunities, of the kind Manne described. With the end of the 1970s came the development of a new acquisition technique and of a new financial market. Michael Miliken, of the small brokerage firm of Drexel Burnham Lambert, had read studies that showed that corporate bonds that were not rated "investment grade" by the dominant rating services yielded a return that more than compensated investors for the additional risk of default associated with these bonds. At the same time investors developed a tremendous appetite for higher yields on corporate debt. This was fueled by two industries that were facing insolvency—casualty insurance and savings and loan associations, or thrifts, which concentrated on long-term real estate mortgage lending. As inflation increased during the late 1970s and early 1980s, thrifts were forced to seek deposits at increasingly higher interest rates, exceeding 12% in some cases. At the same time their investments, real estate loans with thirty year maturities made during a lower-interest rate period, were paying much lower interest rates. Casualty insurers had enjoyed some years of high stock market returns, and had not raised insurance premiums for some period of time. Both sought the higher returns available from high risk corporate bonds. Drexel Burnham Lambert developed this market, serving as the intermediary between borrowers willing to pay high rates and investors desperate to earn them. Many of the borrowers were small public companies that could not access the public markets for corporate debt, which was focused on investment grade debt. Their bonds were sold by Drexel Burnham Lambert in private offerings to these financial institutions and other sophisticated investors prepared to take the risk.

By the 1980s the hostile takeover had become commonplace. While financing acquisitions was not an insuperable problem for larger companies, the development of the junk bond market opened new opportunities. One of the early leaders in the use of junk bonds was T. Boone Pickens, the CEO of Mesa Petroleum Co., a small oil and gas producer located in West Texas. Pickens was convinced that the major oil companies were wasting surplus cash by reinvesting excessive profits in drilling for new oil and gas reserves, at a time when demand was weakening and the prospects for successful drilling were deteriorating. He argued that the majors should pay out all of their free cash flow to their shareholders, a suggestion that did not receive a warm reception with these oil companies. Pickens then began a series of hostile tender offers for companies much larger than Mesa. Mesa made hostile bids for Gulf Oil in 1984, for Phillips Petroleum, and later for Unocal Corporation, a case chronicled in Chapter Six. In each case Mesa failed to achieve control, but it was able to sell its holdings in the target at a premium, thus gaining the name "greenmailer" for Pickens—for threatening control unless management paid off Mesa to go away.

The other mode of acquisition that developed was the "leveraged buyout," where buyers would use huge amounts of borrowed funds to purchase control of public companies at a premium. The buyers in these cases were investment vehicles organized by private investment banks such as Kohlberg Kravis Robert ("KKR") and Forstmann Little & Co. These firms would assemble risk capital from large institutional investors seeking high returns, and fund the balance of the purchase price, sometimes over 90%, with borrowings, largely in the junk bond market raised by Drexel Burnham Lambert. These buyers often engaged in a rapid sell-off of the divisions or subsidiaries of the acquired firm, especially in the case of a conglomerate. The result was that the pieces of the former conglomerate were worth more than the whole. The pieces would be sold to buyers able to manage them better than the former management, in many cases because the buyers were focused on a single business. The gains in the LBO of Safeway were reported to have been more than $5 billion on an equity investment of $130 million, while KKR's investors in the buyout of Beatrice Foods were estimated to have earned a 43% return on their investments. Tony Ablum & Mary Beth Burgis, *Leveraged Buyouts: The Ever Changing Landscape*, 13 DEPAUL BUS. L.J. 109, 113–14 (2000). These buyers are characterized as "financial buyers," as opposed to "strategic buyers," that are operating businesses before the acquisition.

Where the buyers did not immediately sell the entire company, large gains were still possible. In many cases the buyers invited target company management to participate in the purchase (sometimes called a management buyout, or MBO). In these cases managers were expected to invest most of their wealth in a heavily leveraged company with pressing obligations to reduce its debt to gain relief from the high interest rates associated with high leverage. Together with close monitoring from the LBO firm, this provided strong incentives to reduce costs and sell off non-performing divisions. In the LBO of RJR Nabisco, the lavish expenditures of its former CEO, F. Ross Johnson, which included a fleet of corporate jets that were sometimes employed to fly his pet dog to his current location, were among the first to be eliminated.

The results were often remarkable. One article reported that shareholders who sold in LBO transactions during the 1980s received premiums of 40% to 50% over the pre-bid market price. The operating cash flows of the acquired businesses increased by about 40% over the next two to four years after the buyout. In some cases, where the LBO investors either sold the company to another buyer or reoffered its shares to the public, the gains in value, adjusted for movements in the market, averaged 96%. Joel M. Stern, G. Bennett Stewart III, and Donald H. Chew, 8, No. 2 Bank of America Journal of Applied Corporate Finance 32 (1995).

Like all good things, LBOs were overdone, and used to acquire enterprises that were not suitable for such high leverage. A series of defaults followed, which reduce the popularity of this form of financing. The failure of many savings & loan associations (now known as "thrifts") in the 1980s led to federal regulation prohibiting their investment in junk bonds, and dumping huge amounts of them into the market when buyers were reluctant to buy, thus driving bond prices down and yields up. By the late 1980s the SEC had begun an investigation of Drexel Burham Lambert which ultimately led to a very large fine and the withdrawal of capital by Michael Miliken, both of which pushed the privately held firm into bankruptcy, and destroyed the principal market-maker for junk bonds. As a consequence, LBOs underwent a sharp decline during the early 1990s. But LBOs have made a resurgence. Weak stock market returns during the early years of the current century, following a market crash in 2001, led some institutional buyers to seek higher returns though what are now called "private equity funds." These funds assemble capital, often to purchase public companies, and use large amounts of borrowings to finance the acquisitions.

The financially motivated acquisitions of private equity firms in the twenty-first century were driven not by taking over inefficiently managed firms and improving them, but by the availability of credit on historically cheap terms. The Federal Reserve kept interest rates near zero for much of this time, so the amount of funds available to lenders increased. This activity explained both the subprime mortgage bubble and its later collapse, as well as the boom in acquisition activity. With the collapse of the subprime mortgage and derivative securities market, easy credit for acquisitions dried up. The table below summarizes the ups and downs of acquisition activity over the past several decades.

Acquisition & Tender Offer Activity, 1984–2014

Year	All Deals	Value ($billions)*	Tender Offers**	Hostile Tender Offers	Success Rate
1984	2,255	$152.3	79	18	56%
1985	1,728	$148.4	84	32	44%
1986	2,521	$220.1	150	40	38%
1987	2,513	$194.8	116	31	58%
1988	3,008	$271.5	217	46	59%
1989	3,798	$311.0	132	28	77%
1990	4,287	$200.4	56	8	38%
1991	3,513	$138.3	20	2	100%
1992	3,678	$124.8	18	2	50%
1993	3,930	$168.7	32	3	67%
1994	5,301	$282.8	70	10	60%
1995	6,712	$390.5	85	11	55%
1996	7,839	$570.4	166	8	25%
1997	9,115	$782.8	160	14	36%

---

*   Source for All Deals and Value: 28 Mergers & Acquisitions 48 (May-June 1994) and 2002 M & A Almanac 15. These numbers differ somewhat from those provided by Mergerstat. See http://www.mergerstat.com/new/free_reports_m_and_a_activity.asp. Source for 2002 Tender Offers: 2003 M & A Almanac 55. Source for 2006 deal value, 2006 M & A Profile, Mergers & Acquisitions, 46 (Feb. 2007). Source for 2007 deals and values, 2008 M & A Profile, Mergers & Acquisitions, 50 (Feb. 2009) and similar articles through 2012.

**   Source for Tender Offers: 1989 Mergerstat Review 74; 1996 Mergerstat Review 38, 2002 Mergerstat Review 39, and 2008 Mergerstat Review 6; 2015 Mergerstat Review, 58.. Success rate refers to contested tender offers.

1998	10,806	$1,373.3	179	22	59%
1999	9,608	$1,433.7	204	16	50%
2000	9,293	$1,792.2	184	14	50%
2001	6,499	$1,148.4	106	7	57%
2002	5,488	$612.6	126	5	20%
2003	6,246	$531.6	79	13	54%
2004	7373	$607.6	87	10	80%
2005	7857	$806.6	103	17	53%
2006	8,203	$1,371.2	112	24	67%
2007	9,477	$1,803.4	129	12	67%
2008	7,623	$994.2	122	13	38%
2009	5,862	$721.4	95	7	57%
2010	7,309	$812.4	72	9	44%
2011	7,413	$987.5	117	12	67%
2012	7,433	$918.2	110	10	60%
2013	10,162	$962.8	84	4	50%
2014	6,870	$792.4	107	11	82%
2015	N/A	$2,500	102	8	75%

2015 was a record year for M & A activity. There is speculation that companies hoarded cash during the 2008 recession and the weak years that followed, and with signs of a modest recovery in the economy cash-rich firms are not finding profitable growth opportunities in their own businesses and have turned to acquisitions to grow.

Hostile tender offers have been replaced by negotiated transactions to a very large extent over this period. One possible explanation is that takeover defenses, especially the poison pill, have become so effective that it is extremely difficult to succeed against an unwilling target. The author believes that a more likely explanation is a cultural change in boards of directors, largely brought about by Delaware court decisions, but also by increased pressure from the financial institutions that dominate stock ownership in the U.S. Corporate directors are very aware of their duties to shareholders, and their obligation to maximize shareholder wealth. One other possibility is that the SEC's changed regulations governing mergers were designed to level the regulatory playing field between mergers and tender offers, thus making mergers relatively more attractive. At least one SEC regulation, the "best price rule," discouraged the use of tender offers in connection with acquisitions, until the SEC changed its interpretation of the rule.

In the 1980s many acquisitions were financed largely with borrowed funds—the so-called "leveraged buyout," or "LBO." The debt issued in these financings was necessarily high-risk, and carried higher interest rates than more conventional corporate debt. It was typically rated less than investment grade by the rating services, such as Moodys and Standard and Poors, and was often called "junk bonds." The development of this market was driven by Michael Milken at Drexel Burnham Lambert, and turned Drexel Burnham into a powerhouse in corporate finance. Regulatory changes and charges of securities fraud brought this dominance to a close by the end of the 1980s, and with it the use of leveraged buyouts and high yield securities declined.

The foregoing explanation of acquisitions is focused on the driving financial forces of many of the acquisitions of the recent past. It does not address many of the traditional reasons for acquisitions that have existed before and exist after the dramatic events of the 1980s. These reasons drive acquisition activity through economic cycles, regardless of the legal background for hostile takeovers.

Economies of Scale. In many businesses there are enormous economies to be achieved from large size. Where the capital costs of tooling up to produce goods is high, very long runs allow the manufacturer to recover these costs over large numbers of units. The automobile industry is an example of these economies, with most plants in the United States designed to produce 200,000 units per year, and in some cases manufacturers have several plants producing the same cars, or very similar models under different model names. Mergers have occurred in the auto industry over a very long period of time. General Motors and Chrysler are both the result of acquisitions, in many cases taking over smaller producers no longer able to compete effectively on their own. Chrysler acquired American Motors, which, in turn, was a combination of Willys Overland (Jeep) and Nash. Chrysler was acquired by Daimler-Benz in what might described as one of the worst deals of all time, since Daimler later sold most of Chrysler to a private equity firm. (Since that time Chrysler has gone through Chapter 11 bankruptcy reorganization and been purchased by Fiat.) Exxon's acquisition of Mobil has been characterized as a return to John D. Rockefeller's Standard Oil (the predecessor of both companies), which may be apt, because the acquisition appears to be inspired by a decline in oil prices accompanied by overcapacity. It is expected that the acquisition will result in some job losses as duplication is eliminated.

In some cases acquisitions allow two firms in difficulty to economize, and thus to survive. In the 1990s, as defense spending declined, defense contractors began combining. Airlines have been engaged in similarly motivated combinations in the twenty-first century. This allowed them to reduce overhead by eliminating duplication and spreading overhead costs over greater numbers of units. This is not a new reason for acquisitions. John D. Rockefeller's creation of the Standard Oil Company is largely explained not by predatory activities, but by the reduction of capacity in an industry characterized by overcapacity. Rockefeller profited by acquiring many small producers, and then closing down the inefficient plants, operating at full capacity with the most efficient ones. Indeed, the cycle has been repeating itself in recent years, as oil companies once again engage in mergers.

Economies of Scope. Economies of scope often explain mergers involving firms that make different but related products. Many food and beverage combinations of the 1980s were explainable on this basis. Food producers with well-known brand names and many products are able to secure more shelf space in supermarkets because of their market power. In other cases, the economies may be at the other end of the spectrum. When Bendix Corporation made a hostile takeover bid in the early 1980s for Martin-Marietta Corporation, a defense contractor with different products, one explanation given by the President of Bendix was the attraction of having 10,000 engineers in a single company, whose ideas could be applied across a vast array of products.

Synergies. Since the 1990s many businesses in computer software, cable television, telephones, entertainment and even computer hardware have been acquiring related businesses in the hope of gaining competitive advantages in developing the "information highway." These companies assume that businesses either providing access to or products for the information highway will require a wide range of know-how, which can only be obtained by combining with companies in these related industries. These acquisitions represent the essence of entrepreneurship, since none of the executives involved in making these decisions have any certainty about how the information highway will look and operate in a few years.

Market Share. For many companies, holding a large if not dominant market share is viewed as the key to earning above normal profits. Well recognized brand names often command a premium price. Accordingly, these companies are often willing to purchase smaller competitors whenever they become available. In turn, smaller companies are often put up for sale because they are privately held, and the founder or the chief executive is reaching retirement age, with no successor in sight, and no way to provide liquidity for retirement. Substantial family-owned businesses form a significant share of the companies sold in any year, although their sale rarely makes the headlines. Market share acquisitions can run into conflict with the antitrust laws.

Diversification. Investors do not need companies to diversify, because they can do it for themselves at relatively low cost, either through mutual funds or on their own. Nevertheless, diversification has played a role in acquisitions at various stages in our economic history. Diversification enables a company to stabilize its income and cash flows, and should reduce the riskiness of both its debt and equity. While investors can achieve the same results on their own, managers cannot always do so for themselves. Managers often have most of their wealth invested in a single company, in the form of expected income and capital investments, in the company's stock. To the extent that managers hold an undiversified, and therefore unnecessarily risky, portfolio, they are tempted to reduce their personal risks through corporate diversifications.

Acquisition of New Technology. Technological change has occurred with amazing rapidity in many industries. This author recalls his original pc, which (with an upgrade) had 128k of ram, two 5¼" floppy drives holding 256K, and no hard drive. All of this cost nearly $3,000 around 1980. IBM has not been the sole driver of technological change in computers, and has itself acquired software companies. Software companies have been born, either died or succeeded, and either offered their stock to the public or been acquired by larger companies. Telecommunications has changed rapidly over the past twenty years, and new pharmaceuticals have been developed that provide new solutions and cures for old diseases. Particularly in pharmaceuticals, larger companies that have had huge shares of the market have not always been the innovators—they have turned to smaller companies that succeed with new drugs, and either licensed them or acquired the smaller company. The larger companies have existing marketing capability which often would be too costly for smaller companies to develop on their own. In some cases rather than engage in an acquisition, a joint venture may be developed through a licensing agreement, as a substitute for an acquisition.

The legal climate for mergers under the antitrust laws has changed over time. The Sherman Antitrust Act prohibits combinations in restraint of trade and monopolizing or attempting to monopolize interstate commerce. 15 U.S.C. §§ 1 & 2. The Clayton Antitrust Act was passed in 1914, and in 1955 section 7 of that act was amended to prohibit corporate acquisitions "where . . . the effect of such acquisition may be substantially to lessen competition or to tend to create a monopoly." 15 U.S.C. § 18. These statutes were applied not only to mergers among competitors, where the Government was highly successful, but also to mergers among suppliers and customers (vertical integration) and to conglomerate acquisitions. As one observer stated, "[b]y the late 1960s . . . the Supreme Court had in effect made all corporate mergers illegal if attacked by the Government."* In 1968 the Justice Department issued merger guidelines suggesting when it would take action. These guidelines suggested that market share was the critical question, so that in markets where the four largest firms represented less than 75% of output, it would ordinarily challenge the acquisition of a firm with 4 percent of the market by a firm with 4 percent. Over the next decade a rich economic literature began to develop about competition in industries with few competitors, suggesting that monopoly was less of a problem than previously thought. The leaders in this literature came from the so-called "Chicago school" and were led by George Stigler, Yale Brozen and Harold Demsetz. The result was that the Department of Justice issued new merger guidelines in 1982. They recognized what economists of the Chicago School have come to call "rivalrous competition." The 1982 guidelines contained a footnote stating that "there is some evidence that, where one or two firms dominate a market, the creation of a strong third firm enhances competition." The 1982 guidelines omit discussion of the major theory for attacking vertical combinations—foreclosure of competition, and omit any mention of conglomerates, and the major theory used to attack them—reciprocal buying. A new set of guidelines for measuring concentration was applied, the Herfindahl-Hirschman index. The result was that fewer mergers were challenged after adoption of the 1982 guidelines. The election of President Obama in 2008 has led to some increase in antitrust enforcement.

Section 7A was added to the Clayton Act in 1976, requiring premerger notification to the Government of all mergers above a minimum size. Waiting periods are imposed before a merger can be completed.

4. THE HISTORY OF SECURITIES LAWS AND ACQUISITIONS

The early focus of the securities laws was on regulating sellers rather than buyers. Sellers were the focus of the early blue sky laws, beginning with Kansas in 1911. While some of these laws simply prohibited fraud, most imposed a registration requirement before securities could be offered or sold. In some states, such as Kansas, registration was on a merit basis; that is, securities could only be offered and sold after a

---

*   Rockefeller, Antitrust Counseling for the 1980's 141 (1983).

determination that the offering would be fair, just and equitable to investors. In other states, registration was purely a disclosure process.

The Securities Act of 1933 adopted the disclosure philosophy with respect to offers and sales of securities. It required the filing of a registration statement before any offers could be made, and "effectiveness" of the registration statement before sales. Effectiveness depended upon a Securities and Exchange Commission ("SEC") staff determination that the registration statement was complete and not misleading on its face. No effort was made by the staff to verify the truth of the statements contained in the registration statement. Truthfulness was assured by civil liabilities and criminal sanctions for the willful violation of the securities laws. A series of exemptions from the costly registration process were provided for those offerings where other regulatory schemes gave investors protection, or where the costs of regulation exceeded the benefits to the public, as in small and private offerings.

Nothing in the Securities Act of 1933 was expressly designed to regulate purchasers of securities, except to the extent that purchasers resold their securities, and became underwriters for issuers. But the regulation of purchases did extend to two sets of acquisition transactions. First, coverage occurred because the acquiring firm proposed to issue its securities in the acquisition. Thus, where bidders proposed to exchange their own securities for the securities of the target, the bidder was required to register its securities under Federal law.* Registration is a public process, and involves a waiting period that can extend for up to four months before effectiveness. The result was that exchange offers required long waits for completion. The time delay had two negative features for bidders. First, if target management was resisting the offer, it provided a lengthy period within which to design defenses. Second, it provided a long period during which an auction may develop, and any bidder with cash would be able to make and close a cash tender offer before the first bidder's registration statement became effective. The SEC revised these rules in 1999 to place exchange offers on a more even footing with cash tender offers. This is described in Chapter Eleven. The former disparity of regulatory treatment partly explains the growth of the cash tender offer.

The Securities Exchange Act of 1934 was interpreted to cover mergers as involving the sale of securities from a relatively early date. This took place under Rule 10b–5, which prohibits fraud in connection with the purchase or sale of securities. While the usual focus was on a fraudulent issuer, it was possible to invoke the rule in connection with a fraudulent purchase of securities for cash. But there were no separate

---

* Federal law now preempts parallel registration requirements under state securities laws. Securities Act of 1933, § 18, 15 U.S.C. § 77r.

filing or registration requirements in connection with corporate acquisitions under the § 34 Act.

Thus the cash tender offer was left essentially unregulated prior to 1968. It was generally agreed that in the case of a hostile tender offer, the bidder owed no disclosure duties to target shareholders under Rule 10b–5. The bidder was not an insider in the target firm, and was not privy to any material nonpublic information about the target. Further, to the extent that the subject was considered in the 1960's, it was clear that the bidder's relationship with target shareholders was adversary, not fiduciary. Thus the cash bidder was not seen to owe any disclosure duties about itself, its financing, or its plans for the target after completion of the acquisition. Fraudulent statements made in soliciting shareholders to tender their shares were, of course, subject to the provisions of Rule 10b–5.

The following traces both the history of the development of federal regulation of tender offers, and presents a popular view of the reasons for hostile takeovers that would be rejected by most modern observers as providing any real explanation for them. But stock markets have a history of developing speculative "bubbles." Was the takeover boom of the 1960s one of them?

Tender Offers for Corporate Control

Edward Ross Aranow and Herbert A. Einhorn.
64–68 (1973).

Federal regulation of cash tender offers was originally proposed in October 1965 by Senator Harrison Williams of New Jersey for the ostensible purpose of protecting incumbent management from "industrial sabotage" resulting from what were deemed to be reckless corporate raids on "proud old companies." Such regulation, unique in that it represented perhaps the first attempt to enact securities regulation designed primarily for the benefit of the issuer rather than the investor, was inspired by the conglomerate merger mania of the early and mid 1960s. During this period, the cash tender offer, which had previously been resorted to only on infrequent occasions in the United States, emerged with frenetic abandon.[5] The following have been suggested as some of the underlying reasons for the rapid growth of the tender offer phenomenon in this country:

1. Increased corporate liquidity and readily available credit;

2. Comparatively depressed price/earnings ratios, book values, and cash or quick assets ratios, making acquisition via the tender offer more attractive.

---

[5] In 1960 there were only eight cash tender offers involving companies with securities listed on national securities exchanges as compared to 107 in 1966. In 1960 there were tender offers for $200 million of listed securities as compared to approximately $1 billion in 1965. * * *

3. Greater recognition, sophistication, and knowledge with respect to the takeover via tender technique;

4. Lack of extensive federal or state regulation of tender offers;

5. Quicker and more successful results when compared with a full-dress proxy contest;

6. Greater flexibility—the ability to hedge by reserving certain options against a final and irrevocable commitment;

7. Psychology—the appeal to shareholders in straight dollars and cents language, eliminating the need, as in a proxy contest, to convince the shareholder that the insurgent can do a more efficient job;

8. Notwithstanding the actual capital investment, the reduced costs of effecting a tender offer when compared with a proxy contest;

9. A new "respectability" for cash tender offers.

While no hearings were held on the original Williams Bill, many of its proposals formed the basis for a second bill introduced by Senator Williams in 1967. By the time this second bill was introduced, however, there was a greater recognition of the desirability of providing investors confronted with a tender offer with certain basic substantive protections together with full disclosure of the terms, conditions, and financing of the offer as well as the identity and pertinent background information regarding the offeror. In addition, there was a growing recognition that tender offers might in some cases promote the best interests of society by providing an effective method of removing entrenched but inefficient management. Nonetheless, the view persisted that the motives behind many tender offers did not reflect a desire to improve the management of companies and were but disguised forms of industrial sabotage. References by a co-sponsor of the legislation to attempted takeovers by undisclosed principals financed by Swiss banks, to the "corporate raider," and to the "takeover pirate" helped to generate hearty Congressional support for the second Williams Bill. [This irrational response, attributing major economic activity to destructive forces without a theory about how raiders profited, parallels some of the frenetic legislative activity surrounding the later adoption of the Sarbanes-Oxley Act in 2002.—Ed.]

While the bill was embraced by the SEC and supported by several managements that had recently fought off cash takeover bids, there were others who opposed such legislation. Opposition to the bill was based primarily on the contention that the legislation was weighted so as to give incumbent management an unfair advantage in defending against a cash takeover bid and would therefore help to promote inefficient management. One commentator went so far as to suggest that the purpose of the legislation was to enhance the powers of the SEC rather than to protect the legitimate interests of the investing public. In addition, it was argued that a tender offer was in essence an open-market transaction and that traditional market forces, powered by individual self-interest, would best promote the interests of investors and our corporate system as a whole.

These objections notwithstanding, the final version of the second Williams Bill, which took the form of amendments to the Securities Exchange Act of 1934, became law on July 29, 1968 and was ostensibly designed to provide investors with full disclosure and other substantive protections within a statutory framework favoring neither the tender offeror nor the management of the target company. To insure adequate disclosure as well as the continued integrity of the securities markets in connection with acquisitions of securities which might cause or affect changes in control of public corporations, the bill also granted the SEC authority to regulate corporate repurchases of their own securities and imposed detailed disclosure requirements on persons acquiring more than 10 percent of certain equity securities other than pursuant to a tender offer. The Commission immediately adopted "temporary regulations" to effectuate those sections of the statute which were not self-operative. These regulations were amended a month later and are still in effect.

In 1970, the Williams Act was amended, primarily to expand SEC rule-making authority and to extend the coverage of the law to certain types of offers previously exempt from regulation. These amendments, designed for the benefit of the public investor and referred to as "consumer protection" legislation, provided for the following:

1. Reduction of the percentage of stock ownership needed to trigger the disclosure requirements of the Act from 10 percent to 5 percent in an effort to provide public disclosure at a more meaningful level;

2. Extension of the Act to cover exchange tender offers in order to provide investors subject to such offers with the substantive protections of the Act;

3. Extension of the Act to cover tender offers for insurance companies;

4. Rule-making power for the SEC under the anti-fraud provisions of the Act to enable it to deal more effectively with fraudulent practices; and

5. Rule-making power for the SEC to create flexibility in regulation of persons in a control relationship with the issuer.

5. STATE RESPONSES TO ACQUISITIONS—FROM ENABLING CORPORATION LAWS TO ANTITAKEOVER STATUTES

Until the 1970s state law was characterized by its silence on business acquisitions and takeovers. State corporation laws provided procedures for fundamental corporate changes such as mergers, consolidations and sales of substantially all assets not in the ordinary course of business. The shareholder protection features of this legislation were generally to require shareholder votes on these transactions, and to afford appraisal rights to dissenting shareholders. When shareholders dealt in their own shares, corporation statutes were generally silent, recognizing the primacy of property rights and market transactions.

After the passage of the Williams Act states rushed to pass their own takeover statutes. The first generation of these statutes took a form generally similar to that of the Williams Act, with some notable twists. Some of them called for disclosure filings in advance of a tender offer; others provided for review by state securities commissioners of the adequacy of the disclosures. Still others called for securities commission review of the substantive fairness and adequacy of the bid. Jurisdiction was asserted aggressively; in many cases not only did these statutes cover corporations incorporated within the state, but also corporations with substantial operations within the state or a substantial percentage of their shares held by residents of the state. The result was that a bid might be subject to several of these statutes, and conflicts might develop. The Illinois statute, representative of many others, was declared unconstitutional in Edgar v. MITE Corp., 457 U.S. 624 (1982), as a burden on interstate commerce.

The second and later generations of state takeover statutes have been developed as an extension of state corporation law rather than securities law. The "internal affairs" doctrine of conflicts of laws grants each state full power to set the terms under which corporations organized in that state shall operate. As a result, these later statutes focus on voting rules for take-out mergers, the voting power of large shareholders, and the right of minority shareholders to "put" their shares to a bidder who has acquired control. These statutes have generally withstood constitutional challenge, as will be developed in Chapter Seven.

These statutes are notable examples of special interest legislation. In most states they have been promoted by one or two large local corporations, or a body, such as a chamber of commerce, representing them. See Romano, The Political Economy of Takeover Statutes, 73 Va. L. Rev. 111 (1987).

6. EPILOGUE AND HOT TIPS

Corporate lawyers and even law teachers are expected by students and others to have special insights about the next big thing. A former colleague recently sent the author some hot information on expected future deals. Should you have any cash left after paying for books, be aware of the next expected mergers so that you can get in on the ground floor and make some BIG bucks.

Watch for these consolidations later on this year:

1.) Hale Business Systems, Mary Kay Cosmetics, Fuller Brush, and W R. Grace Co. will merge and become: Hale, Mary, Fuller, Grace.

2.) Polygram Records, Warner Bros., and Zesta Crackers join forces and become: Poly, Warner Cracker.

3.) 3M will merge with Goodyear and become: MMMGood.

4.) Zippo Manufacturing, Audi Motors, Dofasco, and Dakota Mining will merge and become: ZipAudiDoDa.

5.) FedEx is expected to join its competitor, UPS, and become: FedUP.

6.) Fairchild Electronics and Honeywell Computers will become: Fairwell Honeychild.

7.) Grey Poupon and Docker Pants are expected to become: PouponPants.

8.) Knotts Berry Farm and the National Organization of Women will become: Knott NOW.

And finally . . .

9.) Victoria's Secret and Smith & Wesson will merge under the new name: TittyTittyBangBang.

Some of you may be relieved to know that there are no other attempts at humor in this book.

CHAPTER TWO

VALUATION AND PRICING OF ACQUISITIONS

1. VALUATION

This Chapter provides some background for thinking about how businesses are valued. It is not a short corporate finance course, but only an outline of the major themes in valuation theory. For the purposes of this book, the importance of the material is to allow the reader to grasp intuitively how financial economists measure the market value of a particular announcement by a company—adoption of a takeover defense, an agreement to be acquired, etc. These are called "event studies," and a number of them are referred to throughout the text.

Business acquisition negotiations often center around price. A business is generally a combination of several assets. First, there are hard tangible assets that have been purchased in order to provide goods or services that the business can sell. What are they worth? In some cases the answer is easy: there may be a ready market for them. A car rental company, for example, owns a fleet of late model automobiles that can readily be sold in the used car market. There are publications that regularly survey the selling prices of used cars, both wholesale and retail, that can provide reasonably reliable information about the value of the fleet. In other cases assets are unique, as in the case of real estate and buildings. What is the value of an abandoned factory? It may depend on how readily adaptable it is to uses other than its former use, or whether there are other buyers who could operate it in its current use. How many such prospective buyers are there? Not as many as for used cars. And perhaps the prospective buyers have just completed construction or acquisition of their own new factories, and thus have no need for this one in the foreseeable future. Finally, the assets may be specific to the business or its location. A high speed newspaper press, weighing many tons, affixed to a concrete pad inside a building, may be useless unless there is another newspaper in the same area that requires increased press capacity. Refinery tanks may be useless to others if a refinery is to be closed. On the other hand, some real estate can be readily valued because its uses are varied and there are many prospective buyers for it. Thus, office buildings and warehouses are of general use to all types of businesses, and are sold with enough frequency that an informed appraiser can make an intelligent estimate of what such real property would bring in a sale.

The courts frequently refer to "book value" as a measure of the value of a firm. Book value is an accounting artifact that frequently has no relationship to the economic value of a business. The book value of a company is a function of the value of its assets as recorded in its accounting records. Typically book value begins with the price paid for assets in arm's length transactions. In some cases, funds spent by the firm to create assets will be assigned as the book value of the asset thus created. At the moment of an arm's length purchase, there is generally good reason to believe that book value reflects fair market value for the acquired asset. But frequently book value begins to deviate from fair market value immediately after purchase. In some cases this is because the market value of such assets changes. The longer the asset has been held, the more likely such changes are to occur. Further, with inflation, all price levels rise, and the value of assets frequently rises above the original acquisition price. Depreciation offers another explanation for why asset values may diverge from market values. Many assets have a finite useful life, such as plant or equipment. They are either worn out or become economically obsolete over time. Depreciation is an annual charge designed to reflect that loss of value over the useful life of the asset. For a variety of reasons, this depreciation may not fairly reflect the actual loss of value.

Book value is a concept often extended from individual assets to the entire firm, and then to the shares of the firm. Thus, the book values of the individual assets may be summed up, and the firm's debts subtracted from them. The remaining value is described as the book value of the firm, which reflects the book value of the shareholders' claims on these assets. When the number of outstanding shares is divided into the book value of the firm, the number is described as book value per share. (This explanation ignores adjustments necessary if preferred shares are outstanding.)

In addition to its hard assets, a business has a series of relationships that may generate value. It may be a computer software company with a large team of highly skilled and innovative software designers and programmers. If the business is sold, what assurance does the buyer have that these valuable assets, with their human capital, will not walk out the door? A small drug development company has net book value of assets of approximately $125 million, while the market value of its stock is about $800 million. The difference of $675 million is apparently accounted for by its pipeline of drugs in development and the talent and skills of its employees, which don't show up on a balance sheet. Or a clothing company may have a loyal clientele. If the business is sold, will these customers go elsewhere? Does it depend on whether the sales people remain on the job? These are questions that sometimes are ignored by executives eager to make a deal.

In valuing a business, one question that might be asked is how cheaply could the buyer duplicate the business? Would it be expensive to assemble the land, buildings, equipment, personnel and management systems required to do the same thing? This element is sometimes called "going concern" value.

Why would one want to buy assets or relationships? The obvious answer is not for the intrinsic pleasure of ownership or relationships in most cases. Business assets are frequently not intrinsically beautiful. Even if we hire an appraiser who can tell us the value of an office building or warehouse, we still need to ask why someone would pay that sum for it. The answer, in the case of all business assets, is because of the amount of cash it can produce for its owner, net of expenses, over time. Here we must emphasize that business assets in most cases don't produce cash for their owners in just one period (which in accounting terms is usually a year). In many cases their lives will extend over a long period of time, and they will help the business earn money over their lifetime.

In a business acquisition, buyers typically value all of the assets assembled to operate the business, including employees, as a whole. Thus the question becomes, "how much cash will this business produce, net of expenses, over its lifetime?" A related question is how long will the business survive? A final, and most important question, is when will it produce that cash, sooner or later? A dollar received in ten years is not worth as much to me as a dollar received today. If, for example, I have 38.6 cents and invest it today earning 10% interest compounded annually, I will have a dollar in ten years. The flip side of this relationship is a promise of one dollar to be paid to me in ten years is worth 38.6 cents to me now—that is its "present value." We determine this present value by "discounting the sum, which involves dividing it by one plus the relevant 'discount rate'" for the appropriate number of years.

An important extension of this method of compounding is to provide the value of a perpetuity. Here we assume that the income stream will go on to infinity. Why would anyone care about a perpetuity? There are two reasons. First, although I will die some day, before I die I could sell my perpetuity for a lump sum to a much younger person who can receive the income stream for many years. And that person, in turn, could do the same. Second, using a perpetuity calculation is a useful tool for calculating the value of shares in a business. Most large publicly held corporations have no plans to shut down at a time certain. Their managers intend to reinvest enough profits to keep the business running for the indefinite future. While some businesses will fail, that risk is accounted for in the interest rate demanded by investors on their investments (and in the corresponding discount rate).

Perpetuity calculations are simple. We simply divide the expected annual payment by the appropriate discount rate. Thus, if the expected annual payment is $1.00, and the appropriate discount (or capitalization) rate is 10%, the calculation is:

$$\text{Present value} = \frac{\$1.00}{.10} = \$10.00$$

or, more formally, where PV = present value, A = expected payment, and r = capitalization rate:

$$PV = \frac{A}{r}$$

Stocks are often described as selling for "ten times earnings" if they bear the relationship to the most recently reported twelve months' earnings described above. This is a useful shorthand for saying that the company's most recent earnings are being capitalized at 10%. The calculation only is slightly more complicated if a company's earnings are growing. If we expect earnings to grow at 3% per year indefinitely, we simply subtract the growth rate, g, from the capitalization rate in our formula, which becomes:

$$PV = \frac{A}{r-g}$$

In our previous example, this becomes:

$$PV = \frac{\$1.00}{.10 - .03} = PV = \frac{\$1.00}{.07} = \$14.29$$

In many cases analysts are unwilling to assume that earnings will grow indefinitely. This is particularly true where growth rates are very high, reflecting a young industry. As it matures, competitors will enter the field, driving prices and earnings down, until earnings stabilize at a competitive level. In these cases the valuation process is a two-step one. First, the analyst will calculate the present value of earnings with a growth rate for a finite period, perhaps 5–7 years. Then the analyst will calculate the discounted present value of a stable earnings stream beginning in the year following the growth period, and add the two values.

Thus far we have spoken of "expected value" without definition. Expected value is simply the weighted average of the best guesses about future payments to be received from an investment. Guesses can be uncertain. The author experienced a situation where the prospective seller projected future revenues from a new drug at one price, and after the sale the buyer priced the drug at more than double the seller's projected price.

In the context of business acquisitions, these are the basic tools needed to value a business. The basis for the calculations, of course, is a determination of the payments expected to be produced by the business. While this analysis begins with financial statements, sophisticated business executives are aware that accounting treatment of several items can vary, and that even where it does not vary, it may be misleading in terms of calculating the payments available to owners of the business. See George Benston, Accounting Numbers and Economic Values, 27 ANTITRUST BULLETIN 161 (1982).

The remaining question is how discount or interest rates are set. One can readily observe that interest rates have two components; one is compensation for the time value of money—for consumption deferred by the lender or investor. Generally we can isolate this by looking at the return on risk-free investments, such as short term Treasury bills. (This rate must also compensate for inflation.) One major study showed that the nominal average interest rate before inflation on Treasury Bills was 3.5% for the period 1926–2014. The real rate of return, after adjusting for inflation, was 0.6% on Treasury bills.[*]

Higher rates of return are demanded by investors for risky investments. The same study showed the following rates of return through 2014[**]:

Asset Class	Nominal Return	Real Return	Std. Deviation of Annual Returns	Risk Premium over Treasury Bills
Short-term Treasury Bills	3.5%	0.6%	3.1%	0%
Intermediate-Term Treasury Bonds	5.3%	2.4%	5.6%	1.8%
Long-Term Treasury Bonds	5.7%	2.8%	10.0%	2.2%

---

[*]   Ibbotson SBBI, MARKET RESULTS, STOCKS, BONDS, BILLS AND INFLATION: 2015 CLASSIC YEARBOOK, Table 2–1, at 40.

[**]   *Id.* All of the data except risk premium and real return is taken from Table 2–1, p. 40. The inflation rate is reported as 2.9% at id., and real returns are inferred by this author.

Asset Class	Nominal Return	Real Return	Std. Deviation of Annual Returns	Risk Premium over Treasury Bills
Long-Term Corporate Bonds	6.1%	3.2%	8.4%	2.6%
Large-Company Stocks (S&P) 500	10.1%	7.2%	20.1%	6.6%
Small-Company Stocks*	12.2%	9.3%	32.1%	8.7%

Some stocks are riskier than others. Thus investors might be expected to demand higher rates of return on riskier stocks. Individual companies are subject to the particular risks that attend their particular circumstances: the quality of their management, the stability of their customers, the extent to which raw material prices may be more volatile than finished good prices, the exposure to new competition and new products, to name a few. But even with a group of high risk securities, risk can be reduced through diversification. Thus, if one holds a portfolio of thirty securities, each with the same high degree of risk, it is likely that the portfolio will be less risky than the individual securities. This is because the performance of all stocks in the portfolio will not move exactly together. That is, their performance will not be perfectly (and positively) correlated.

If a sufficiently large number of stocks are held in the portfolio, the risk associated with individual firms can be nearly completely eliminated. Firm risk, or unique risk, also called nonsystematic risk, stems from the fact that many of the perils that face an individual company are not faced by all other companies. Indeed, what is risk for one company may be an opportunity for another. For example, the risk of higher gasoline prices threatens sales of large vehicles such as SUVs, but it's an opportunity for oil companies. Thus, in a properly diversified portfolio, individual firm risk, often called unsystematic risk, is irrelevant. Hence this risk will have no impact on the market price of a security.

---

*   The author used the reported geometric rather than arithmetic mean.

But there are also risks that are general to all securities, that are associated with the performance of the economy generally, and in the case of stocks, with the performance of the stock market. This risk, called systematic risk because it is associated with the economic system, cannot be eliminated through diversification. All stocks are subject to this risk. Thus market risk is important in valuing securities.

Not all stocks are similarly affected by market risk. Some stocks are relatively immune to the fluctuations of the business cycle, while others are severely impacted by it. Thus an investor must consider market risk when selecting the stocks that will comprise a portfolio. The sensitivity of an individual stock's return to market movements is called its beta. This is measured over time by measuring the returns to the particular stock against returns to a broad market portfolio, such as the Standard & Poor's 500 Stock Index, or the New York Stock Exchange Index.

Beta is measured by its relationship to market moves. Thus, if a stock's return is perfectly correlated with that of the market portfolio, it is said to have a beta of one. If the stock moves up (or down) in its return exactly one-half as much as the market portfolio moves, it has a beta of .5. Similarly, if its returns increase (or decrease) twice as much as those of the market, it has a beta of two. With this knowledge of the beta of particular securities, an investor can select exactly the degree of market risk he or she wishes. Beta is measured over time, by plotting the price movements of a broad market average, and then plotting the movements of individual stocks at each point. The beta is then estimated by using a straight regression, by using a standard least-squares regression program to find the best fit between the points on a chart showing the price moves of the particular stock against the market.

The final part of the story involves how returns to risk are set. We begin with the notion that two points on a graph are set—the return on a risk-free portfolio, consisting of government securities (Treasury Bills), and the return on a stock market portfolio, consisting of either the entire market or some portfolio large enough to represent the market. The previous table shows that the risk premium over Treasury Bills paid on common stocks is somewhere between 6.6% and 8.7% over the long term. This spread is not the result of a mathematical formula; it is simply a reflection of the prices investors demand for accepting risk.

This principle of substituting risk-free and risky investments can best be understood by examining the rates of return obtainable through substitution. The following example illustrates expected returns, assuming the risk-free Long-Term Treasury Bond rate is 5% and the return on large-company stocks is 10%:

% Treasury Bonds	Rate of Return	Weighted Return	% Common Stocks	Rate of Return	Weighted Return	Total Return
100	5%	5%	0	0%	0	5%
75	5%	3.75%	25	10%	2.5%	6.25%
50	5%	2.5%	50	10%	5%	7.5%
25	5%	1.25%	75	10%	7.5%	8.75%
0	5%	0%	100	10%	10%	10%

Note that an investor can choose any set of expected returns between the risk-free rate and the market rate simply by mixing risky and risk-free investments in a portfolio. In doing so, the investor who moves from 100% Treasury Bills to a diversified common stock portfolio will move the expected returns along a straight line between the two points we have defined. As risk moves up, expected returns also move up in a linear relationship. If an investor chooses a portfolio of common stocks that do not replicate the entire stock market, but are, for example, less risky, the investor's expected returns will decline in the same linear relationship. Thus, if the investor's portfolio has only 75% as much market risk as the entire market (a beta of 0.75), then the return the investor can expect is the same as that on a portfolio invested in 75% of a broad market portfolio and 25% in risk-free treasuries. Why is this so? Because financial markets are generally viewed as efficient, and if the stock portfolio with a beta of 0.75 returns more than the comparable mixed portfolio, investors will sell Treasuries and buy stocks with betas of 0.75, thus bidding up their prices until their expected returns decline to restore an equilibrium.

If investors can borrow at the risk-free rate, they can "leverage" their investments in risky stocks, and achieve returns higher than those offered by the market portfolio. This is easy to see: if an investor can borrow at 5% and invest at 10%, the 5% increment represents an increase in the total rate of return on the investors' own funds. If an investor can build a portfolio with funds borrowed at rates below the expected return on stocks, this provides an alternative to investing in stocks with greater market risk (beta). This substitute portfolio thus sets the ceiling and floor for expected returns on higher-beta stocks.

This can be illustrated by extending the previous table to show the results of investing borrowed money:

Stocks	% Return	Return on Equity	% Borrowed Funds	Interest Rate	Interest Expense	Net Return
100	10%	10%	0	5%	0	10%
125	10%	12.5	25%	5%	1.25%	11.25%
150	10%	15%	50%	5%	2.5%	12.5%
175	10%	17.5%	75%	5%	3.75%	13.75%
200	10%	20%	100%	5%	5%	15%

Placed together and extended, these tables illustrate all of the possible combinations of risk and return. Overall, this line, called the "security market line" reflects a straight line from the risk-free rate of return to the return on the riskiest stocks available in the market. While the notion of borrowing at the risk-free rate is somewhat artificial, there appear to be enough borrowers who can obtain rates close to the risk-free rate, because stock prices do seem to be distributed along this security market line, which slopes upward and to the right. The Capital Asset Pricing Model ("CAPM") is illustrated in the following figure, where the diagonal line represents the security market line. The logic of the model, combining risky and risk-free investments and borrowing as substitutes, suggests that all stocks must be priced along the security market line.

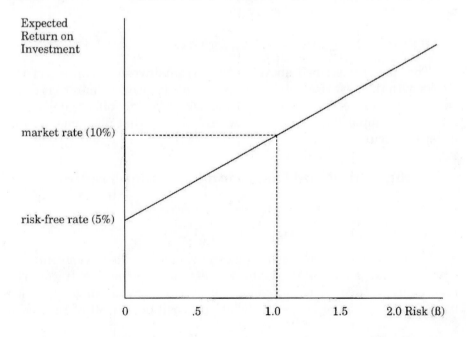

The capital asset pricing model thus predicts that all expected returns will lie along the diagonal line in the above figure. Early empirical studies have confirmed that actual returns lie approximately along this line. See, e.g., E. F. Fama and J. D. MacBeth, Risk, Return, and Equilibrium: Empirical Tests, 81 J. Political Economy 607 (1973). Subsequent work has challenged this model, primarily by showing other relationships that influence stock valuations. More recently at least one study suggests these relationships have weakened or disappeared in the last thirty years, to be replaced by multiple variables. Fama and French, The Cross-Section of Expected Stock Returns, 47 Journal of Finance 427 (1992).

In the model shown above, the risk premium over the risk-free rate for holding the market portfolio is 5%. (Obviously the historical risk premium has been much greater, as shown by the earlier table.) This enables us to predict the cost of equity capital for any company, if we know its beta. The formula is simply that the expected risk premium on a stock equals its beta times the expected market risk premium. Thus, for a company with a beta of 1.5, the risk premium is 1.5 x %, or 7.5%. The company's cost of capital will thus be 12.5%, because it must also include the risk-free rate of return.

Experience with the bull market of the late 1990s and early 21st century has reduced expected returns to stocks, as stock prices have risen more rapidly than expected returns on stocks. Some observers believe this represents a speculative "bubble" that will eventually collapse, returning stock prices to levels where expected risk premia are closer to historical averages. Other observers believe there has been a permanent change in the market, and that the risk premium for stocks (the "equity premium") has been permanently reduced.

2. EFFICIENT CAPITAL MARKETS

The model described above assumes that investors can select the stocks with the best risk-return relationships. It also assumes that these choices will drive the prices of other securities to offer comparable returns to comparable risks. We now explore why that phenomenon will generally occur.

Signalling and Causation in Insider Trading
William J. Carney.
36 Cath. U. L. Rev. 863, 877–883 (1987).

A.   Efficient Capital Market Theory

Theories and evidence about investor choices and behavior center on how participants in capital markets process new information. It would be redundant to repeat all of the evidence in support of what Michael Jensen has called one of the best established propositions in all of the social sciences: the Efficient Capital Markets Hypothesis. Beginning with research that established that stock price movements are unpredictable, researchers were able to infer that stock markets were efficient in a weak form—that nothing in the sequence of past stock prices enabled us to predict future price movements. From that, researchers proceeded to test stronger claims of market efficiency. The semi-strong form asserted that all publicly available information about issuers was reflected in stock prices, while the strong form asserted that all such information, public or not, was reflected.

Tests of the semi-strong form provide voluminous support for the hypothesis. There is, nevertheless, some contradictory evidence. Thus far, evidence does not support an alternative theory. Those who make general challenges to the semi-strong form may make anecdotal arguments, or argue that market participants sometimes play sub-games so that some stock prices inaccurately reflect "intrinsic values," or that bargains can be found in supposedly efficient markets. The most recent criticism, that of Gordon and Kornhauser, appears merely to be that the tools used to test market efficiency are not necessarily accurate. But none of these studies challenge the general proposition that markets are effective, if not perfect, processors of information about the value of firms. Further, little evidence challenges the conclusion that markets are unbiased predictors of future values, and that is the most important feature of this literature for purposes of this Article.

The strong form of the Efficient Capital Markets Hypothesis argues that stock prices reflect all available information about firms, so that gains are unavailable even to insiders. However, empirical tests have demonstrated that insiders do indeed earn above-normal returns on their trading. On the other hand, the semi-strong form now appears supported by this evidence, since the most recent study shows that it is unlikely that outsiders can gain from emulating insiders' trades.

The significance of these findings can be stated simply. Where stock markets are efficient, public announcements will immediately affect the price of a security, without the necessity of any trading, as traders rapidly adjust reservation prices to reflect the new information. Sophisticated traders will realize that there is little reason to trade on the basis of this announcement, to the extent the information contained in these filings is unambiguous in its significance to investors. Ambiguous information that is publicly available may have trading value, but it may require expenditures of considerable resources to enable traders to extract significance (and therefore value) from it.

Only unsophisticated traders might believe that they can win at this stage by "beating the market." They are naive to hold this belief, and can hardly be described as "prudent" in expending resources to trade on information that has no value. Sophisticated traders, on the other hand, can confidently alter their portfolios knowing that the market reflects all of this information. Indeed, that has been one of the goals of the securities laws—to build confidence in the securities markets.

B.   The Mechanisms of Market Efficiency

The point here is not to test whether or not capital markets are efficient, but to examine the processes by which prices reflect information of various types. This Article will follow the model of Gilson and Kraakman, which attempted to link the three forms of the Efficient Capital Markets Hypothesis with the mechanisms used to distribute information. As these authors pointed out, to say that sooner or later prices will reflect certain information is not by itself very interesting; the most critical question is "How long does it take?"

Weak form market efficiency presumes that information is readily available to all traders. This includes old information, such as price histories, as well as information about current events, such as important news items. Indeed, even news stories about particular firms affect prices too rapidly to support trading profits. In these instances, no particular trading seems required to move stock prices to adjust to new widely distributed information. Thus, public announcements of Federal Reserve Board policy changes can be met with instantaneous changes in the reservation prices of traders, just as major company announcements can. Gilson and Kraakman point out that where news is incomplete, uncertainty about future prospects will remain until events or announcements resolve the uncertainty. During this period, a certain amount of trading activity will occur to fine-tune the price to reflect the consensus of traders' assessments.

Semi-strong form market efficiency shifts from "publicly distributed" information to "publicly available" information that is not known to all market participants. For example, experts pore over government filings by issuers, such as SEC reports, to analyze this information. The resulting market insights might be available only to such experts. Studies support the assertion that stock markets also reflect this information with such rapidity that no extraordinary trading profits are generally available. Since virtually all such disclosures are historical rather than forward-looking, they provide only weak insights about the future performance of a firm. Because this information is not readily available to all traders (at least in a useful form), price adjustments to such information rely on trading by a minority of market traders— informed professionals. Gilson and Kraakman explain this in terms of the trading volume controlled by market professionals, but volume arguments, standing alone, raise serious questions about market efficiency. The evidence to date suggests that all stocks with similar beta coefficients are treated as fungible by investors, so demand for any given security is perfectly elastic, absent special information about an issuer. In this context, volume is relevant to price only to the extent that it signals traders that someone is apparently acting on superior information.

Thus far, this Article has described the forms of market efficiency generally accepted by the SEC when designing an integrated disclosure system and rules governing shelf registrations. Here, there seems to be a consensus among lawyers and economists that markets are fully informed about the data disclosed. Investors can confidently rely on this information when trading in securities in efficient markets, without undertaking further analysis on their own. With respect to this data, at least, stocks are assumed to be fairly priced, in the sense that there is no systematic bias. Insiders who are aware of this information can trade freely on it, confident that the courts will not find any unlawful informational advantage over other market participants.

Moving from information that is publicly available to firm-specific information not formally announced or released, price adjustments become more complex, and less well documented. Market participants act as if markets are not efficient, and as if information can produce gains. This has been described as the paradox of efficient markets; in order for them to function, participants must disbelieve in the hypothesis. Expenditures on securities research may provide more or less perfect substitutes for much inside information. There are reports that traders and analysts spend as much as $600 million seeking information. Securities analysts attempt to duplicate inside information by researching sources identical or similar to those providing insiders with their insights. Suppliers, customers, and competitors are all potential sources.

Acquisitions normally involve the payment of some premium over pre-bid market prices to shareholders of an acquired firm. This raises the question of whether stocks are efficiently priced, if reasonable buyers are willing to pay above-market prices to acquire companies. The next section explores various theories that may reconcile premiums and ideas of market efficiency. At the end, however, they leave one question: if there is obvious value to be gained from acquiring a firm, why didn't investors recognize that and drive the price of the target's stock up to reflect that value?

3. EVENT STUDIES

Starting in the 1960s financial economists began to put this learning to use to assess the market's reaction to various pieces of news about corporations with publicly traded stocks. These studies use an "event study" methodology pioneered by Eugene Fama, Lawrence Fisher, Michael Jensen and Richard Roll, in "The Adjustment of Stock Prices to New Information," 10 International Economic Review 1 (1969). The method begins with the market model of stock pricing developed earlier. It assumes that stock markets are efficient in the semi-strong form; that prices rapidly reflect all publicly available information. It further assumes that stock prices are a function of the beta of a stock and the risk-free rate of return. Thus, in efficient markets, a stock with a beta of one will earn the market rate of return, absent any special information. This is the "normal" rate of return on such a stock. Similarly, a stock with a beta of .5 will earn the risk-free rate plus one-half the difference between the market rate and the risk-free rate, and so forth.

When an event is announced that affects firm value, we can expect stock prices to adjust rapidly to the news. That adjustment adds to an investor's actual return on the stock (whether positively or negatively) when compared to the expected return, which is derived from the movement of a broad market average, adjusted for the beta of the particular stock. That adjustment is called an "abnormal" return on the stock, because it cannot be predicted from overall market movements. Because of leakage of information before a public announcement, or insider trading, stock prices sometimes begin their adjustment before the public announcement date. And where the information is complex and takes some time for analysts to digest, the full price adjustment may not occur immediately after announcement. For these reasons it is common for event studies to look at abnormal returns for a period surrounding the announcement date, often two days or ten days. These abnormal returns over the study period are summed as the Cumulative Abnormal Return, or "CAR." These cumulative abnormal returns tell us how much unexpected price movement occurred in this period that cannot be explained by the market's general movement.

If, for example, a company announced a new product, how did the market value that news? Assume for the moment that the announcement was clear and credible, and that sophisticated financial analysts and investors could understand the potential value of the new product. Now assume that the stock's price rose on the day of the announcement and for several days thereafter. Is that price rise all attributable to the product announcement? Not necessarily. Recall that stocks are valued largely on the basis of their beta—what contribution they make to a diversified portfolio. Once we know a stock's beta, given the behavior of the relevant market index, financial economists can predict how the particular stock's price would behave, all other things being equal. The difference between the predicted stock price and the observed stock price is the measure of how much the market valued the announced news. In a market that is semi-strong form efficient, we should expect the price to reflect that news within a very short period of time, on a single day. But if the news is more complex, such that the idea of the new product initially puzzles some analysts and investors about how much value to attach to it, the market may react for more than one day. As a result, event studies, that measure the stock price movement not explained by the firm's beta, often report market movements for one-day windows as well as slightly longer windows.

No such measure is perfect in all cases. In some cases more than one piece of news may have affected a stock's price during the relevant period. In other cases, where the news is complex, or about novel events, traders may not be able to make an accurate assessment of its true impact on the value of the firm. Nevertheless, where large numbers of similar events are studied, these studies are relied on as the best information we can currently develop about the value attached by impersonal markets to particular types of announcements. You will encounter reports of academic studies in this book that employ the event study methodology.

4. EFFICIENT MARKETS AND THE PARADOX OF THE SEARCH FOR BARGAINS

The teaching of the Efficient Capital Markets Hypothesis is that all stocks are fairly priced in relation to each other, given the publicly available information about each company traded in this market. If that is so, how can one corporate management describe another corporation as a "bargain"? Yet in many cases this explanation has been offered for acquisitions. Value is to be obtained, according to this explanation, because the seller's shareholders are willing to accept less than the company is "worth." On its face, this explanation flies in the face of the Efficient Capital Markets Hypothesis.

One response has been offered by Sanford Grossman and Joseph Stiglitz.* Their explanation is more general than explaining corporate acquisitions; it is addressed to the search for investment bargains by investors and traders. If markets were perfectly efficient at all times, they argue, traders would have no incentives to engage in research about particular companies. They could invest confidently in any company, knowing that its stock was fairly priced with respect to all others, based on all publicly available information. But it is the very act of research that produces valuable information about companies, that allows some investors to earn above-normal returns from their trading. That information, in turn, moves stock prices. If no research were undertaken, then stock prices would quickly become inefficient, and opportunities for trading profits on superior information would rapidly increase. At this point researchers could earn larger than normal profits, providing superior returns to their research activities. Grossman and Stiglitz describe a world in which prices cycled between efficiency, when traders were actively engaged in research, and inefficiency, when traders ceased their research activity because all publicly available information was fully reflected in prices. But in the real world, of course, traders never stop hoping that there are market inefficiencies to be exploited, and

---

* Sanford Grossman and Joseph Stiglitz, On the Impossibility of Informationally Efficient Markets, 70 Am. Econ. Rev. 393 (1980).

valuable information to be discovered and traded on. Accordingly, it is the activity of non-believers in market efficiency who continue to make stock markets as efficient as they are.

In the past two decades a growing body of literature by "behavioralist" economists has argued that markets are not so efficient at pricing stocks, and that this creates the possibility of bargains. Based on the findings of behavioral psychologists that individuals do not always calculate risks rationally because they use a series of simplified models, or heuristics, to calculate probable future outcomes, they argue that such miscalculations can cause stocks to be mispriced. The argument about individual miscalculations is extended by observations of herd behavior, as investors chase trends. According to these theorists, professional investors are either influenced by the same biases or lack sufficient capital to overcome the price effects created by misguided herds. While controversy surrounds these theories, they offer another possible reason why bargains may exist in stock markets.

There are at least two explanations given for the possibility of bidders' belief in bargains. One is the exploitation of target company shareholders, and the other involves bidder management overestimation of values. The shareholder exploitation story points toward target shareholders receiving "too little" for their stock, while bidders profit. The bidder management overestimation story points in the opposite direction—that target shareholders are generously compensated at the expense of shareholders of the bidder.

There are two ways in which it is said that shareholders may be exploited. The first involves problems of shareholder coordination of their responses to takeover bids. The second involves questions of information asymmetries, where the bidder has superior information to that of target company shareholders.

The problem of shareholder coordination arises because of the dispersed nature of share ownership of large American corporations. Before regulation of tender offers under the Williams Act, bidders could simply announce an offer for a majority of the stock of a company at a premium over the current market price, with disclosure that those shareholders who remained as minority shareholders would be poorly (although legally) treated. The threats involved de-listing of shares from exchanges, de-registration under the Securities Exchange Act (and the consequent destruction of a market for the shares), or a take-out merger at a price below the cash tender offer price. These bids were often on a "first come, first served" basis, thereby creating a rush among shareholders to accept and avoid the consequences of being left behind as a minority shareholder. The Williams Act ameliorated the problem for shareholders by requiring that bids be kept open for a period of time, and that if the bid was oversubscribed during that time period, that shares be taken pro rata from all who tendered. Nevertheless, the shareholder who held out for a higher price, or higher expected future values from his company, was left behind if the bid was successful, and ran the risk of receiving less than his fellow shareholders who tendered. These pressures meant that some shareholders might tender even if they thought a better price could be obtained, if they believed that their fellow shareholders would tender and cause the bid to succeed. Modern takeover defenses, to be covered in Chapter Six, also serve to ameliorate (or overreact to) this problem.

A second theory of shareholder exploitation involves information asymmetries, in which bidder corporations have superior information about the value of a firm's assets than its own shareholders. They exploit current shareholders when market values for shares fall below true values. As Professor Reinier Kraakman has observed, short of hiring informers, hostile acquirers lack access to inside information about targets. In addition, information that unsuccessful bids fail to increase the share prices of target firms over the long run suggests that hostile bids do not release key inside information. Reinier Kraakman, Taking Discounts Seriously: The Implications of "Discounted" Share Prices as an "Acquisition Motive," 88 Colum. L. Rev. 891, 895–95 (1988). Professor Kraakman cites, among other studies, Bradley, Desai & Kim, The Rationale Behind Interfirm Tender Offers: Information or Synergy?, 11 J. Fin. Econ. 183 (1983), which found that share prices of target firms gradually fall to pre-bid levels within five years after unsuccessful takeover bids. Further evidence that bidders do not exploit private information arises, surprisingly, in the context of management buyouts, where one might expect incumbent management to have an informational advantage over shareholders. A study by Jeffry Davis and Kenneth Lehn found that managers appeared to pay premiums as high as third parties when engaging in buyouts of public shareholders. Davis & Lehn, Information Asymmetries, Rule 13e–3, and Premiums in Going-Private Transactions, 70 Wash. U. L. Q. 587 (1992).

Two other theories remain to be explored. First, are stock prices distorted from true value of the underlying assets in some way that creates bargains for bidders, who can then pay premia, regardless of cost savings or synergies? Second, do bidders simply overpay for target firms? The following articles explore these topics.

Taking Discounts Seriously: The Implications of "Discounted" Share Prices as an Acquisition Motive

Reinier Kraakman.
88 Columbia Law Review 891, 898–902, 908–909 (1988).

* * *

The alternative discount hypothesis—the market hypothesis—fits less easily with standard accounts of the securities market. In this view, share prices may discount asset values for reasons endogenous to the formation of market prices. Financial economics conventionally assumes that share prices are best estimates, given available information, of the present value of expected corporate cash flows available for distribution to shareholders. Thus, share prices should fully capitalize the value of corporate assets in the hands of existing managers. In real markets, this assumption is an approximation; it is unlikely to be either precisely correct or, given the sensitivity of share prices to new information, wholly misguided. It is a very good approximation in the standard view. By contrast, the market hypothesis asserts that discounts arise because share prices are sometimes very poor estimates of the expected value of corporate assets.

Modern objections to identifying share prices with asset values typically fall into two classes. The first class includes "valuation" challenges that question whether a single valuation model can apply across the markets for shares and firms or within the share market itself. Even if traders in both the asset and share markets value corporate assets similarly, share prices might nonetheless discount asset values simply because assets and shares differ in ways that matter to traders. For example, the share prices of firms holding liquid assets might discount asset values if traders placed an intrinsic value on the right to liquidate firms in the asset market—a right that minority shareholders in these firms would necessarily lack. Alternatively, overlapping clienteles of traders within the securities market might have heterogeneous demands for timing, magnitude, or tax attributes of shareholder distributions. In this case, shares might sell at either a discount or a premium relative to asset values.

The second and more prominent class of objections to equating share prices with asset values challenges the price setting role of informed traders. Thus, there is a growing theoretical literature on "mispricing" behavior, which argues that uninformed traders may introduce persistent biases or cumulative noise into share prices or that speculative trading might lead to positive or negative price "bubbles." Large-scale noise trading—arising from misconceived strategies, erroneous valuation assumptions, fashion and fads, or simple pleasure in trading—might distort share prices and generate discounts or premia through the sheer pressure of trading. In addition, some commentators suggest that noise trading further distorts share prices by encouraging informed traders to speculate on noise and by imposing "noise trader risk" on all traders in a noisy market. Finally, noise theorists find evidence of mispricing in the long-term price behavior of both individual firms and the entire market.

For present purposes, however, the important point does not involve a particular model of noisy prices, but rather the uncertainty, generated by a wide range of recent research, about the extent and persistence of mispricing behavior. Few observers would assert that mispricing never occurs, just as few would deny that share prices rapidly reflect information bearing on future corporate prospects. What remains uncertain is how effectively share prices estimate the full present value of corporate cash flows, as distinct from predicting near-term share prices, and how large residual mispricing effects are likely to be. The market hypothesis simply asserts that recurrent discrepancies between share prices and asset values can explain major portions of at least some acquisition premia.

Stepping back from the market hypothesis, then, it is apparent that neither this account nor the misinvestment theory of acquisition gains is easily evaluated. Unlike traditional gains hypotheses such as synergy or private information, discount hypotheses turn on far-reaching and sharply divergent narratives about the securities market. The misinvestment hypothesis implies that prices sensitively anticipate future management decisions, while the dominant market hypothesis holds that prices may be systematically depressed (or inflated) by noise trading. The fact that both hypotheses can be further particularized in diverse ways makes their evaluation even more formidable. Fortunately, however, one task does not require such an evaluation: namely, examining the discount claim in its own right as a motive for acquisitions. Evidence of discounts can support either hypothesis. But equally important, such evidence can also support a unitary account of acquisition behavior that does not immediately force us to choose between discount hypotheses.

II. THE CASE FOR DISCOUNTS

Market discounts must satisfy three conditions to be meaningful. First, potential acquirers and market professionals must be able to form reliable asset or break up values for the firm "as is;" that is, as its component assets are already managed and deployed. Asset values in this sense are particularly credible when assets can be separated from the functions of top management. Thus, natural resources or established corporate divisions may lend themselves to reliable valuation, while start-up projects or undeveloped investment opportunities might be impossible to value with confidence. Second, share prices must fall significantly below asset values. And third, potential acquirers must accept appraisals within the consensus range as useful—perhaps as minimal—estimates of what target assets will be worth to themselves and competing bidders.

Although these conditions are difficult to test, the case for discounts is nonetheless persuasive. Certain specialized firms that hold easily priced assets provide direct evidence of discounting. In addition, pervasive discounting can explain much recent acquisition behavior, including breakup acquisitions, management buyouts, and the sheer size of takeover premia. Finally, support for discounts can be found in many forms of corporate restructuring, including the wave of share repurchases and recapitalizations that swept American corporations during the mid-1980s.

* * *

Nevertheless, difficulty in observing discounts across all categories of firms does not diminish the significance of their presence on closed-end funds and natural resource firms. These examples create a presumption in favor of the discount claim. They cannot be ignored unless they can be explained or distinguished as anomalous by some still undiscovered characteristic of the securities market. This is a methodological point at bottom, for closed-end funds are corporate oddities only if the dominant conjecture—the norm of "no discounts"—prevails for other firms. In the absence of other data, extrapolating from the evidence at hand seems to be the most reasonable course. Why suppose that discounts perversely exist only where they can be seen and nowhere else?

B. Acquisition Behavior

Given a basic presumption in favor of discounts, the discount claim becomes an intuitively attractive explanation over a broad spectrum of corporate activity. In particular, it accords well with at least two aspects of acquisition behavior where traditional hypotheses falter. One is the sheer size of premia in hostile acquisitions and management buyouts. The other is the recent prominence of break up acquisitions that exploit perceived differences between the share prices and asset values of conglomerate firms.

Consider first the size of acquisition premia. In recent years, premia have averaged about 50% of share value in management buyouts and 50% or more in hostile acquisitions. Most studies suggest that acquisitions of all kinds are either zero or positive net present value transactions on average. Thus, assuming that most acquirers reasonably expect to recover their premia costs, the obvious question is: How can they be so sure? Apart from possible tax gains, which few commentators believe to dominate premia, we are left to choose among market discounts and the usual suspects including the displacement of inefficient management, synergy gains, or the exploitation of private information. The fact that these various sources of premia and gain are not mutually exclusive makes this choice more difficult. Yet we can learn which sources of gain dominate in which transactions and, in particular, whether discounts yield significant gains at all. Absent better information, our only handle is the plausibility of the assumptions underlying each source of gain.

QUESTIONS

1. If we accept Professor Kraakman's hypothesis that stocks may be discounted from their true value in some way, what reason do we have to believe that all stocks are not equally discounted?

2. Why would an acquiring firm not expect the target's discount to carry over to the bidder if an acquisition is made at a premium?

3. How can an acquiring firm be sure that its own assets are not subject to a similar or even greater discount than the target's? Keep in mind the difficulty observers such as Professor Kraakman and others have in observing such discounts outside the simplest settings, where the values of assets are ascertainable on markets nearly as efficient as securities markets.

Bidder Overpayment in Takeovers

Bernard S. Black.
41 Stanford Law Review 597, 599–60, 602–604 (1989).

In this paper, I advance the hypothesis (the "Overpayment Hypothesis") that, for many takeovers, target shareholders gain partly because the bidder pays too much. These overpayments don't cause bidder stock prices to drop because investors already expect the bidder to waste the money, one way or another.

This hypothesis, I will argue, is plausible theoretically and consistent with the evidence on takeovers in the late 1970s and the 1980s. It is not intended to describe earlier periods, when bidders generally realized substantial stock price gains from takeover bids.

A simple example may illustrate the hypothesis. In 1982, U.S. Steel paid $6.4 billion to acquire Marathon Oil. This was a premium of 70 percent, or $2.5 billion, over Marathon's pretakeover market value. U.S. Steel's market value was almost unchanged. Where did the $2.5 billion net gain come from? Misvaluation by the market was unlikely, because Marathon was a fairly simple company whose chief asset was the Yates oil field, on which good data were publicly available. There were no operating synergies from the acquisition. Nor could U.S. Steel, with no experience in the oil business and a long history of poor performance in the steel business, be expected to greatly improve Marathon's management.

Part of the gain was tax-related. After writing up Marathon's assets to market value, U.S. Steel would pay less tax than Marathon on the same pretax cash flow. Moreover, U.S. Steel's tax losses and tax credits from its steel operations could further shield Marathon's income from tax. But taxes cannot explain the whole premium.

The gain arose in large part, I believe, because U.S. Steel's shareholders had expected its management to reinvest its cash flow in the steel business, where the returns were poor to nonexistent. In contrast, overpaying for an oil company didn't look so bad. For U.S. Steel's shareholders, the takeover's value equaled the sum of (i) the present value of the expected future cash flows from Marathon; plus (ii) the negative net present value of U.S. Steel's most likely alternative investments (whether in steel or something else), which would now be forgone.

* * *

All [event] studies [of stock market returns to bidding firms] report bidder losses, on average, when a narrow window is used. In several, the abnormal returns are statistically significant . . . more than half of all bidders also suffer stock price declines, and binomial sign tests show that this result is statistically significant.

Returns over a wider window may be a better measure of investor reactions, because they allow time for uncertainty about the bid's success and final price to be resolved. Accordingly, Panel B of Table 1 reports bidder returns for 11 to 41 day windows around the announcement date. Most of these studies also report negative bidder returns, although the abnormal returns are statistically significant in only one study. Taken as a whole, the data in Table 1 suggest that since 1975, takeover bidders have earned at best a zero, and perhaps a slightly negative, net-of-market return.

The studies reported in Table 1 are unable to measure returns to privately held bidders. This may be a significant shortcoming in the 1980s, with the emergence of leveraged buyouts ("LBOs") and highly leveraged "raiders," often privately held, as a factor in many takeovers.

Acquiring firms in divestitures appear to gain slightly, on average. The available studies show positive mean CARs of 0.3 to 2.1 percent, which are statistically significant in several cases. Why buying only part of another company is more profitable than buying all of it is as yet unexplored.

There has also been a strong secular trend toward lower bidder returns. Abnormal returns have dropped from roughly 4 percent in the 1960s to 1 to 2 percent in the 1970s taken as a whole, and zero percent or a bit less in the 1980s. This drop could reflect greater competition in the market for corporate control, learning by shareholders about the unprofitability of prior deals, other secular changes in the corporate control market, or a combination of these factors.

An unanswered puzzle is why bidder returns are so low. Put another way, why don't bidders earn a share of the gains from trade? The usual explanation stresses competition in the market for corporate control. If there are many fungible bidders for any one target, excess returns will be competed away. This explanation is consistent with the hypothesis that bidders maximize firm value and (the occasional mistake aside) avoid negative net present value projects.

The "competitive market" explanation has problems, however. The corporate control market does not seem perfectly competitive. Target managers often go to extreme lengths to avoid an auction, and most takeovers do not involve an explicit auction. Moreover, targets and bidders aren't always fungible. Where the target is uniquely valuable to a particular bidder, the bidder and target ought to share the gains from trade.

In addition, in a perfectly competitive market, expected bidder abnormal returns, as reflected in stock price, should cluster closely around zero. Instead, there is a lot of scatter—many cases in which the bidder's stock price rises, suggesting positive expected returns that were not competed away, and many others in which the bidder's stock price falls by 5 percent or more, suggesting substantial overpayment. There are also many anecdotal examples of apparent overpayment—cases in which investors marked down the bidder's stock when the deal was announced, and the acquisition later proved to have major problems. Examples include Kennecott Copper-Carborundum, Exxon-Reliance, Mobil-Montgomery Ward, and Atlantic Richfield-Anaconda.

Moreover, if average bidder returns are even slightly negative (as many of the studies in Table 1 suggest), then competition among value-maximizing bidders can't be the whole story. Competition can drive stock price returns to zero, but not beyond.

The Warren Buffett Phenomenon

There have been some investors who have beaten market averages by significant amounts over long periods of years. There are two possible explanations for this. One is that if you have a billion people engaged in a coin-flipping contest, only one will be the ultimate winner. We could call this person either the most skilled coin-flipper in the world or just plain lucky. But what are the odds of the same person winning the contest year after year, if it's a game of luck? Warren Buffett is one of a very few investment managers to achieve long-run success in beating the market. Among others are John Maynard Keynes, who managed the endowment for King's College Cambridge through the great Depression and achieved positive returns during a period when the market overall had declined, Phil Fisher, Charlie Munger (who managed an investment partnership before becoming Buffett's colleague at Berkshire-

Hathaway), Lou Simpson, who managed GEICO's investments, William Ruane who managed the Sequoia Fund and William Miller, who managed the Legg Mason Value Trust. One author describes these legendary investors as members of Graham and Doddsville, after legendary finance teacher Benjamin Graham and his successor and co-author David Dodd, at Columbia University.* From them Buffett and the others learned their basic approach to investing.

Buffett describes his approach as one of intensive examination of a company in which he is considering investing, which he calls "focus investing." Rather than hold the widely diversified portfolio of many financial managers, which generally underperform market averages and index funds because of transaction costs and the taxable nature of gains on frequent sales of stock, Buffett and his peers prefer a close examination to find companies (not stocks) they really like, and limiting their portfolios to a handful of such stocks. In each instance, these investors value each company independent of market valuations. They do this by looking for businesses that are simple and understandable (Buffett avoided the dot.com crash of the early 2000s by adhering to this principle). They look for a consistent operating history and good long-term prospects. Second, they look for capable and rational managers who are candid with shareholders about mistakes, and who avoid the pressure of mutual fund managers to produce short-term quarterly results. They look for companies with high profit margins, which often mean dominating their market. They focus on the return on equity, rather than earnings per share, and want assurance that each dollar of earnings reinvested has a positive net present value—that is, a return in excess of the cost of capital.

In determining the cost of capital, these investors use the weighted average cost of capital. They do not use CAPM to determine cost of capital, because CAPM is primarily focused on stock correlations with market variance. Their view is that short-term cyclical variances are not a proper measure of risk, because of their long-term investment horizons. Instead, they focus on non-systematic risk of the particular firm. This is a more challenging and less mechanical method that requires a deeper understanding of each company, its market and the risks anticipated to be found in the particular instance. Judging risks that have not yet occurred involves not variance but uncertainty—sometimes called the "unknown unknown." From this comes a personal judgment about the appropriate cost of capital for the company. Only then can the company be valued based on discounting expected future cash flows by this cost of capital. This represents the intrinsic value of the company.

Once this valuation of the company is achieved, the managers then must ask if the market is currently undervaluing the company. These

---

* Much of this account is drawn from Robert G. Hagstrom, THE WARREN BUFFETT PORTFOLIO (1999).

investors believe that many price fluctuations in the overall market are caused by irrational changes in investor sentiment. After the speculative dot.com bubble burst in 2000, the NASDAQ index, where most of these stocks were traded, fell from a high of 4,300 in January 2000 to a low of 1,160 in September 2002, a loss of 73%. This was accompanied by a loss of nearly 30% on the Dow, where few dot.coms were traded. Both of course, were negatively influenced by the World Trade Center attack on 9/11/2001. After Lehman Brothers filed for bankruptcy in September, 2009, the Dow Jones Index dropped from 13,000 to 7,350 by March 31, 2009, a drop of over 43% in six months. This reflected investor fears of a financial collapse by large financial institutions that could wreak havoc on the economy. At this writing in 2015 the Dow is above 17,000. These managers believe that this reflects investor panic in 2008–2009, and irrational selling, followed by irrational buying as the stock market began to hit new highs—a form of "buy high, sell low" behavior. For them, these events represent a buying opportunity for long-term investors, when good companies are at least temporarily undervalued. If corporate managers take a similar approach to valuation in considering potential acquisitions, one can begin to understand why acquiring firms can justify paying a premium over the market price for target companies.

Not all companies are as successful as Warren Buffett in their analysis. When Bristol Myers Squibb took a pass at an invitation to bid for a Hepatitis C drug later acquired by Gilead Scientific for a record $11 billion in 2012, Bristol offered $2.5 billion to acquire Inhibitex, which an early stage drug in the same class. By August of 2012 Bristol announced it was abandoning this drug because of dangerous side effects. It wrote off $1.8 billion of its investment as a result. Gilead's drug, on the other hand, became the biggest first year seller of all time. Oh well, you win some and you lose some.

PART II

AN OVERVIEW

CHAPTER THREE

AN OVERVIEW OF DEALS

This Chapter provides a road map of the basic structure of modern acquisition transactions. In that sense it is formalistic, providing the reader with information about the basic forms. What it does not provide will be left for Chapter Four—exactly what strategies are employed to get the deal done, the consequences of choice, and how this affects the choice of form.

1. GETTING STARTED

Who does acquisitions, and how do they get started? They start for all of the reasons mentioned in Chapter Two, and one not mentioned there. Many successful closely held businesses are run by their founders. As they near retirement age, unless younger family members are interested in and have the ability to continue running the business, the time may come when founders need to plan for their own retirement by considering a sale. In other cases the burden of estate taxes may require a sale, if the founders lack enough life insurance or other liquid assets to cover these taxes while passing ownership along to the next generation.

Prospective buyers may consider either privately or publicly held firms as potential targets. The buyers' executives may already know the major and even minor players in their own industry, if the expansion is to be horizontal. Knowledge may come from past competition, perhaps from joint ventures or just through membership in trade associations. If the buyer is expanding horizontally, its executives may already have a good idea about these potential candidates, including the quality of their products or services, their competitive position within the industry, and the quality of their management. In many fields there are business brokers who, for a fee, will attempt to identify likely targets for acquisition. Typically their work ends at the time of an introduction of the two parties, and buyer and seller are left to their own negotiations. The other major source is the mergers & acquisition department of brokerage firms. Many of these firms will employ analysts who specialize in particular industries, and can provide some insights on the likelihood that certain firms' managers will be amenable to negotiations. Credit reporting services such as Dun & Bradstreet may have current financial information on privately owned companies. Company web sites often provide further information. A good reference librarian is capable of locating many news stories about the potential target, all of which may provide a reasonably full picture on which to make preliminary judgments about which target firms to approach.

Where the targets are public companies, the sources of information are even better. All publicly traded companies must file massive disclosures with the SEC. Publicly traded companies are governed by the periodic reporting requirements of § 13 of the Securities Exchange Act. The central reporting requirement under that Act is Form 10–K, the annual report that must be filed with the SEC, the essence of which must be delivered to shareholders. Item 8 of Form 10–K requires audited financial statements meeting the requirements of Regulation S-X, 17 C.F.R. § 210.1 et seq., the SEC's accounting regulation. Rules 3.01, 3.02, 3.04 of Regulation S-X require filings to include balance sheets for the two most recent fiscal years, audited statements of income and cash flows for the three most recent fiscal years, and a statement of changes in stockholders' equity in periods between income statements required to be presented. Public companies' web sites frequently contain their financial statements. Many also link to the SEC's site that contains the financial reports of all companies filing reports with the SEC. These documents are filed electronically, on the SEC's Electronic Data Gathering and Retrieval ("EDGAR") system. Here one can identify major shareholders that might be inclined to sell. You can locate it at: http://www.sec.gov/edgar/searchedgar/webusers.htm. You can also locate these filings on most companies' web pages under "investor information" or "SEC reports."

Once a target has been identified, both sides will generally employ both legal and financial advisers. Valuation in negotiations is a problem that requires expert advice in many cases. Even where the target is a public company with a quoted market price for its stock, the question remains about the magnitude of any "control premium" if the entire company is put up for sale. Where the target is privately held, valuation issues are even more challenging. If the bidder intends to use its own securities as the consideration in the transaction, it needs early advice about compliance with the securities laws. Deal structure may depend on tax issues, which also need an early exploration by the bidder. The target will want to obtain a nondisclosure agreement from the bidder at the start of negotiations, to assure that sensitive private information won't be revealed to competitors or customers. In the case of a publicly held target, it may also seek a "stand-still agreement," that it won't unilaterally make an offer directly to the target's shareholders, without first reaching agreement on price with target management. If the bidder intends to use its own securities for the consideration, the target will want to do its own investigation of the bidder's business and finances, in which case the bidder will seek a reciprocal nondisclosure agreement.

Target company management frequently plays a significant role in the acquisition process. In the negotiated acquisition setting for a closely held firm, management and ownership may be identical. A sale may be occurring because the owners are reaching retirement age and have no obvious succession within the family group that owns the company. In these cases the buyer may be negotiating to have the management team stay on for a while, to assure a smooth transition to new management.

Or perhaps a growing business run by younger entrepreneurs is seeking a sale either because it lacks the management depth and experience to continue to grow profitably, or because the owners seek a new source of capital, and the greater personal liquidity that comes from being stockholders in a larger and public corporation. In these cases both sides may be seeking assurances of a continuing employment relationship. In other cases, where target management is not being retained, the buyer may want covenants not to complete from key target executives.

The setting in the acquisition of publicly-held companies is quite different. Whether the transaction is in the form of an uninvited ("hostile") tender offer or negotiations, management of the target firm is aware that in many cases their jobs will be eliminated, or at the very least, their management powers restricted, if their company is acquired. Where the takeover bid is "hostile" (at least from management's perspective), management can be expected, at the very least, to urge shareholders to reject the bid. Indeed, under Rule 14e–2, adopted under the Williams Act, management of the target company is required to inform shareholders of its position on the bid within ten business days.

Frequently management resists bids in order to assure that the price obtained by shareholders is the highest possible price. One such defense involves eliminating the sting of the two-tier bid, where a bidder offers a relatively high price for shares sufficient to gain control, with the threat or promise of a cash-out merger at a lower price for the remaining shares. This is accomplished by asking shareholders to amend the articles of incorporation to amend the voting rules of the corporation to make it difficult for a bidder that gains a majority of the company's shares to undertake a cash-out merger at a price below the cash tender offer. Where shareholders were unlikely to consent to such a defense, many states adopted statutes allowing boards to either opt in or opt out of "fair price" rules that imposed very high voting requirements for second step take-out mergers unless the take-out price was as high as the front end price. We will cover these statutes in Chapter 7. Beginning in the mid-1980s, boards of directors adopted "poison pill" plans. Generally these plans involve the issuance by the board of rights to purchase additional shares of stock of the company at a bargain price, which become exercisable only when a bidder gains a significant ownership position. These rights are void in the hands of the bidder. This has the effect of reducing the value of the bidder's shares as large numbers of new shares are issued at lower prices ("dilution"), and have been thought to be highly effective at stopping hostile tender offers, a view we will examine in Chapter Six. In other cases target firms may seek other preferred buyers for the company ("white knights"), or may seek to emulate the bidder's strategy, by repurchasing company shares with borrowed money, hoping to drive share prices above the tender offer price.

The boards of directors of both companies will be involved at the negotiating stage, and they will be kept advised of the progress of negotiations as they precede. In many cases the seller won't want to permit much investigation of its affairs ("due diligence") before receiving at least an indication of the kind of price and terms the bidder has in mind. This is because news that a company may be sold may be unsettling for many employees, and they may begin to look for other employment. The more the seller's business depends on human capital, such as technology companies, the more critical this issue becomes. Accordingly, at an early stage the buyer may have to indicate the price it is currently prepared to pay if due diligence confirms the initial view of the business, and the form that consideration will take—cash at the closing, an initial cash payment, with the prospect of an additional payment later if the acquired business does as well as expected (an "earn-out" provision), or a stock for stock merger, or some combination of stock and cash. If a preliminary agreement can be reached on price and structure, this is often memorialized in a term sheet or a letter of intent, which is typically non-binding on most of its provisions, and is regarded as an indication of a good faith intent to proceed to the next stage. The letter of intent may have a provision that the seller will negotiate exclusively with this buyer for a period of time (a "no-talk" clause), subject to an exception if a third party makes a "superior proposal" that the seller's board believes its fiduciary duties require it to accept (a "fiduciary out").

At this point due diligence begins in earnest. Typically it proceeds in tandem with negotiation of the definitive agreement. As you will see in Chapter Five, the definitive agreement is the document that forces full disclosure, at least by the seller in a cash deal, and by both sides if the buyer's securities are being used. Each party makes a series of elaborate representations and warranties about its business and financial condition, which refer in most cases to schedules of documents to allow the other party to examine all relevant documents. Typically these representations and warranties take the form of a statement by the party that "other than as disclosed in schedule x, there are no other agreements obligating the seller to its employees." Thus the burden is on the seller to make certain that all such documents are revealed in the schedules. The buyer will then obtain copies of all of the scheduled documents and examine them. At the same time, the buyer's accountants are typically engaged to review the financial statements and the judgments made by the auditors in certifying them. The target may engage in the same kind of due diligence concerning the buyer if the buyer's stock is being used as the consideration.

In many contracts, if the representations are discovered to be untrue after the closing, the other party can bring suit, either for damages for false representations, or, in some cases, rescission. But consider the following problem: The seller's financial statements turn out to be materially false. For example, in one case, the seller had recorded as sales contracts to sell its goods, but officers of the seller had concealed the fact that they had given side letters to the customers that they could terminate these contracts for any reason without liability. The deal was a stock-for-stock merger, in which the buyer's stock was the consideration, and the seller was merged into a subsidiary of the buyer. Because the seller was publicly held, it had thousands of innocent shareholders who received the merger consideration. When the financial fraud was revealed months later, the value of the buyer's stock plummeted nearly 50%, imposing huge losses on its innocent stockholders. Who can the buyer sue? The seller has been merged into a wholly-owned subsidiary of the buyer. Can the buyer rescind? The business has now been integrated into the buyer's business. Can the buyer sue all of the seller's shareholders for unjust enrichment? They were innocent of any knowledge of the fraud. While the buyer can sue those officers of the seller who were actively involved in the fraud, it is highly unlikely that they can respond in damages in the amounts required to make the seller whole. Lest you think the author is making this up, this is essentially the story of the acquisition of HBO & Co., a healthcare software provider, by McKesson Corporation in 1998. In effect, the value of any representations and warranties expires with the expiration of the corporate life of the selling corporation. For this reason buyers regard it as critically important to verify all of the representations and warranties in the agreement before the closing takes place.

When due diligence is complete and the parties are satisfied with the definitive agreement, the next step is approval by the boards of directors of both companies. We reserve the details of this approval for Chapter Four. Board approval authorizes the officers of the companies to execute the agreement, and begins the process of seeking shareholder approval, also delineated later in Chapter Four. There may also be regulatory approvals required, such as by antitrust authorities in horizontal mergers, that will be conditions precedent to the obligation to close and pay the merger consideration.

2. TAX AND ACCOUNTING ISSUES

Tax and accounting issues form perhaps the most important background for decisions about which form of acquisition to employ. Because a transaction can be taxable or non-taxable, the form may have a great deal to do with how much a buyer will have to pay to persuade owners of a target to part with their company. Because these issues are sufficiently complex, it is important for clients to understand them as they negotiate the price and structure of the acquisition. It is also important to recognize that the following description is much simplified, and is by no means a substitute for in depth knowledge of these issues.

A. TAX ISSUES

While taxation of corporate acquisitions is often the subject of a separate law school course, it is important for those who do not take that course to have at least a basic understanding of the issues involved.* This section must begin with a distinction between acquisitions—a generic term—and reorganizations—which generally covers only those transactions where no taxable event is recognized.** It must also note the distinction between acquisitive "reorganizations," the subject of this book, and bankruptcy "reorganizations."

Shareholders of a target company would, in many cases, prefer a tax-free reorganization, because this allows them to defer recognition of taxable gain until they dispose of the consideration (normally equity securities of the buyer) received in the reorganization. There may be cases where this is not a major consideration, and cash, which is fully taxable, would be more appealing. This may occur when the target corporation's shares have not appreciated significantly over a long period of time, so many shareholders will not recognize significant gains if they sell in a taxable transaction.

Under modern accounting for acquisitions, buyers will have to record assets acquired either through a merger or asset purchase on their books at fair market value. In many cases this value may be well above the book value at which the assets were carried on the seller's books. Writing up assets to their fair market value increases the buyer's depreciation expense and lowers reported earnings. To the extent that the buyer can keep the asset valuation lower, it can record the balance of the purchase price as goodwill, which is not subject to depreciation or amortization. Sellers also prefer not to have much of the purchase price allocated to depreciable assets, because they may suffer depreciation recapture to the extent the purchase price exceeds the depreciated book value of the assets, which leads to payment of taxes on these gains at ordinary income rates. Sellers would prefer allocation to non-depreciable assets, such as land or goodwill, which permits capital gain treatment, taxable at a lower rate.*** Because of the two levels of taxation that a seller will face in a taxable asset sale, at both the corporate level and then at the shareholder level if the selling firm is liquidated and the sale proceeds distributed to shareholders, this method is generally employed only where a company is selling off one of several business operations, continuing to operate others.

---

* Good brief reviews of this topic can be found in Howard E. Abrams and Richard L. Doernberg, Federal Corporate Taxation, 7th ed. (2013), Chaps. 9–10 and in Barnet Phillips, IV and Robert P. Rothman, Structuring Corporate Acquisitions—Tax Aspects, Tax Management Portfolio No. 770.

** Tax-free reorganizations are covered in Internal Revenue Code of 1986, 26 U.S.C. § 368 (hereinafter "Code").

*** This subject is governed by Code § 1060 in the event the agreement does not allocate the purchase price.

The buyer's consideration of the preferable form of acquisition may be altered by the presence of tax Net Operating Loss carryforwards ("NOLs") in the selling corporation. A corporation that has suffered a series of tax losses may carry those losses forward as an offset against future taxable income. If the buying corporation acquires the shares of the target and keeps it as a separate entity, these NOLs will remain available to offset future income of the acquired corporation, and of its parent if tax returns are filed on a consolidated basis.* A purchase of all the assets of the target in a taxable transaction does not transfer the NOLs, while a purchase of assets in a tax-free reorganization does transfer them, as does any form of tax-free reorganization that meets certain requirements.**

The result of these incentives is that choice of form can have a significant influence on the ultimate price of the transaction. Selling shareholders may demand a higher price in a taxable transaction, and a buyer seeking tax benefits from increased depreciation deductions may be willing to pay more in cash.***

i.   TAXABLE TRANSACTIONS

Asset purchases in a taxable transaction involve a bidder purchasing the assets of a target for cash and the subsequent liquidation of the target, which often distributes the cash to its shareholders. In this case the transaction would be subject to taxation at two levels. If the sale price of the assets exceeds their basis, the selling corporation has recognized taxable income to this extent, taxable at its current rate. When the selling corporation liquidates, the shareholders are again taxed on this distribution, to the extent it exceeds their basis in their shares.**** This result can't be avoided by first liquidating through an in-kind distribution to shareholders, who then sell the assets to the purchasing corporation.*****

Share purchases for cash involve only one level of taxation for the target corporation and its shareholders—the gain received by

---

*   26 C.F.R. 1.1502–11 (hereinafter "Regs."). The availability of a share exchange under § 11.03 of the Model Business Corporation Act facilitates such transactions.

**   Code § 381(a)(2). There are, however, limitations on the use of net operating loss carryforwards by the acquiring or surviving corporation. Among other things, there must be satisfaction of continuity of business requirements. (Code § 382(c)) Additionally, the amount of NOLs that a buyer may use annually is limited to the acquisition price times the current long-term tax exempt bond rate. (Code § 382(a)). For other limitations, see Code § 383.

***   This is borne out by some empirical studies, which show weighted average abnormal returns to target shareholders of 7.7% in mergers, while similar returns for shareholders in tender offers (which are always for cash), averaged 29.1%. The early evidence is summarized in Michael C. Jensen & Richard S. Ruback, The Market for Corporate Control: The Scientific Evidence, 11 J. Fin. Econ. 5, 10–14 (1983).

****   Code §§ 331 and 1001.

*****   On liquidation, the corporation would recognize a gain under Code § 336, and the shareholders would be taxed on the difference between the fair market value of the assets and their basis in their stock under Code § 334(a). For an example, see Abrams & Doernberg, *supra* note 1 at § 9.01.

shareholders, measured by the excess of the purchase price over their individual bases in shares.* Similarly, a merger in which target shareholders received cash or debt is a taxable transaction, triggering capital gains treatment for target shareholders. At present there is a tax of 23.4% on long-term capital gains.**

Acquiring corporations in taxable acquisitions recognize no taxable income in an acquisition of either assets or stock. They have a basis in either the assets or stock equal to the price paid.*** However, if stock is purchased, the value of the assets is not stepped up to the amount of the purchase price, because the assets remain in the same corporation.

ii.   TAX-FREE REORGANIZATIONS

General. Shareholders who dispose of shares in a tax-free reorganization do not recognize gain or loss to the extent they receive "qualifying consideration (stock rather than cash or debt)."**** Similarly, the target corporation in a tax-free reorganization recognizes no gain or loss.***** The buying corporation acquires shares in a tax-free reorganization at the same basis as the selling shareholders.****** It acquires assets from the target in a tax-free reorganization at the same basis as the selling corporation's basis.******* There are three important types of tax-free reorganizations, discussed below.

"A" Reorganizations. The statutory merger or consolidation—the "A" reorganization—is the most flexible form of reorganization. Any form of consideration may be used—provided the continuity of interest doctrine—discussed below—is satisfied. The only disadvantage of this form is that the merger must be between the acquiring and acquired corporations.******** This creates difficulties for many acquiring firms, because the triangular merger—between a subsidiary of the acquiring firm and the target—is often preferred, for reasons discussed in Part 3 of this chapter. In a triangular merger (the "(a)(2)(D) transaction"), the consideration paid is often shares of the parent corporation, but this triggers special rules not applicable when the merger is directly between the bidder and the target. In triangular mergers of this type, only stock of the parent, and not of the acquisition subsidiary, may be used to satisfy the continuity of interest requirement discussed below. Different rules apply to "reverse triangular" mergers, which are not discussed here. An "A" reorganization need not involve solely stock of the acquiring corporation as the consideration, although a significant amount—

---

*   Code § 1001.
**   Code § 1(h). This includes a 3.8% Medicare tax.
***   Code § 1012.
****   Code § 354.
*****   Code § 361(a) & (b).
****** Code § 362(b).
******* *Id.*
******** Code § 368(a)(1)(A).

discussed below under the continuity of interest concept—must be stock. The balance is "boot." Shareholders in the selling corporation are subject to taxation on boot received, but only to the extent of their gains on the entire transaction.* Within the limits of the continuity of interest rules this permits bidders to offer target shareholders a choice between the bidder's stock and cash.

"B" Reorganizations. The exchange of voting stock of the target constituting control of 80% of the outstanding voting stock plus 80% of all nonvoting classes of stock solely for voting stock of the acquiring corporation or its parent is perhaps the least flexible form of reorganization.** Whether the acquisition is "solely" for voting stock of the buyer may turn on whether the buyer has previously purchased any of the target's shares for cash, and whether these purchases should be integrated with the exchange.*** Receipt of any non-qualifying consideration ("boot") destroys the tax-free status of the reorganization.**** Thus, the bidder's assumption of a target corporation liability guaranteed by a shareholder constitutes boot that violates the "solely" requirement.***** Because so many transactions involving publicly traded companies involve the bidder's prior acquisition of some target stock for cash, the use of "B" reorganizations seems to be largely confined to the acquisition of closely held corporations. Until the 1980s, share exchanges were purely voluntary transactions, but the 1984 revision of the Model Business Corporation Act provides for share exchanges by corporate action.****** Thus, if the required vote is obtained from the shareholders as a class, the exchange will be effected for all shares in the class. But this does not make it easier to use a share exchange for public corporations, because each shareholder has the right to dissent from the share exchange and be paid the fair value of his or her shares, thus destroying the "B" reorganization.*******

"C" Reorganizations. The last major form of reorganization is the exchange of substantially all of a corporation's assets solely for voting stock of the acquirer.******** But the interpretation of "solely for voting stock" of the buyer is much more flexible than in "B" reorganizations. Virtually all active businesses have some debt obligations; the inability

---

*   Code § 356(a). While the general rule is that any gain recognized is taxable as capital gain, boot will be taxed as a dividend at ordinary income rates to the extent of retained earnings in the target corporation, if the exchange "has the effect of the distribution of a dividend."

**   Code § 368(a)(1)(B).

***   Most cases have held that earlier cash purchases absolutely violate the "solely for" requirement. See, e.g., Howard v. Commissioner, 238 F.2d 943 (7th Cir.1956); Chapman v. Commissioner, 618 F.2d 856 (1st Cir.1980), cert. dismissed 451 U.S. 1012 (1981) and Heverly v. Commissioner, 621 F.2d 1227 (3d Cir.1980).

****   Turnbow v. Commissioner, 368 U.S. 337 (1961).

*****   Rev. Rul. 79–4, 1979–1 C.B. 483.

******   Model Bus. Corp. Act ("MBCA") § 11.02

*******   MBCA § 13.02.

********   Code § 368(a)(1)(c).

of a buyer to assume these obligations in the course of a reorganization would render this form virtually useless. Accordingly, assumption of seller corporation debt is disregarded in a "C" reorganization. Further, up to 20% of the total consideration paid in a "C" reorganization may be in a form other than common stock of the buyer ("boot"). As previously discussed under "A" reorganizations, receipt of "boot" will be taxable to the shareholder. However, for purposes of determining how much "boot" has been paid, the value of seller corporation indebtedness assumed must be included in the calculation of "boot." Because there will be many cases where the debt assumed exceeds 20% of the total purchase price, the use of boot may be effectively precluded. The final requirement for a "C" reorganization is that the plan of reorganization must require the selling corporation to liquidate and distribute the stock and other consideration received, plus any remaining assets, to its shareholders.[*]

Continuity of Interest. In order for a transaction to qualify as a tax-free "reorganization," a substantial portion of the consideration paid must be in the form of stock of the acquiring corporation or its parent, with the rules spelled out with more specificity with respect to "B" and "C" reorganizations, as discussed above.[**] The stock may be either preferred or common, voting or non-voting, or participating or non-participating preferred.[***] In "A" reorganizations, there is no specific statutory requirement, and one case held that if 38% of the consideration were stock, that satisfied the continuity of interest requirement.[****] In both "B" and "C" reorganizations, the Code provides that 100% of the consideration must be voting stock of the issuer, subject to the "boot" allowed in a "C" reorganization.[*****] These rules represent a codification of previous judicial rulings that for all acquisitive reorganizations, the shareholders of the target corporation retain a significant equity interest in the corporation following the transaction. The focus is on the stock received as a proportion of total consideration received—not on the proportion of the bidder's stock held by target shareholders.[******] If the target shareholders intend to sell the bidder's stock in the market immediately after closing, the continuity of interest requirement will not be met, because of the "step transaction" doctrine that folds together all planned steps into a single transaction.

Business Purpose. Regulations requiring the existence of a business purpose (other than tax avoidance) for the acquisition codify

---

[*]   Code § 268(a)(2)(G).

[**]   Regs. § 1.368–2(a).

[***]   See John A. Nelson Co. v. Helvering, 296 U.S. 374 (1935). "Participating" preferred stock is preferred which, after payment of its fixed dividend, shares in additional dividends on some basis with the common stock.

[****] Nelson v. Helvering, *supra*.

[*****] Code §§ 368(a)(1)(B) and 368(a)(1)(C).

[******] See, e.g., Helvering v. Minnesota Tea Co., 296 U.S. 378 (1935).

earlier judicial decisions in this area.* This requirement is normally not difficult to satisfy where the acquisition is on an arms' length basis, and is most frequently problematic where the corporations are under common ownership or control.

Continuity of Business Enterprise. The regulations require that the acquiring corporation must either continue a line of the target's historic business or use a significant part of the target's assets in any business.** This is one way in which the Code prevents the acquisition of a corporation simply to take advantage of its net operating loss carryforwards, and "trafficking in net operating losses."

B. ACCOUNTING ISSUES

Today acquisitions are accounted for by the "purchase method" of accounting, described below. Until 2001, there were two methods of accounting for the results of an acquisition. Because they had dramatically different impacts on both the balance sheet and the income statement of the surviving corporation, corporate managers attached great importance to the accounting treatment of acquisitions, in the belief that stated earnings mattered greatly in the market's determination of stock value, even if there are no real differences in the company. The source of these rules was the Accounting Principles Board ("APB") of the American Institute of Certified Public Accountants ("AICPA"). The APB was replaced in 1973 by the Financial Accounting Standards Board ("FASB"), which is independent of the AICPA. The rules governing accounting for acquisitions were promulgated in APB Opinion No. 16, in 1970, and remained in effect until June 30, 2001, when they were replaced by Statements of Financial Accounting Standards Nos. 141 ("Business Combinations") and 142 ("Goodwill and Other Intangible Assets.") This text describes the older rules because in some cases they had dramatic consequences for reported earnings of companies after acquisitions, and in some cases they explained bidder's strategies.

Pooling of Interests. In general, this method treated a business combination transaction as a combination of two ongoing businesses in which the owners of the separate entities combine their ownership through common stock. In the prototypical example, the shareholders of two separate entities would each receive common stock of an entirely new entity. In this case the accounting treatment assumed that there have been no changes in the entities other than a simple combination. The balance sheets of the two companies were simply combined, with no change in the book values of any assets. To qualify for pooling of interest accounting treatment, a set of specific conditions had to be met. Pooling was allowed only if all conditions were met. These conditions addressed (1) the attributes of the combining companies, (2) the manner of

---

*   Regs. §§ 1.368–1(b), 1.368–1(c) and 1.368–2(g).

**   Regs. § 1.368–1(d)

combining ownership interests, and (3) the absence of planned transactions to dispose of shares. Acquiring firm managers preferred this method because it produced no changes in the value of assets in the combined firm, or in the depreciation charges against earnings. Pooling of interest treatment was eliminated by the 2001 changes.

Purchase Method. The surviving method of accounting for acquisitions is called the purchase method. In general, it assumes that one company is buying another out. In the prototypical example, an acquiring company would pay cash for the assets and goodwill of a selling corporation. In this case, the purchasing corporation would account for the purchased assets at their actual cost—the full price paid for them. Where the price paid for tangible assets exceeds the seller's book value, these assets will be "written up" on the buyer's books to the full purchase price. One result of this was an increase in depreciation charges for the combined firm. Where the total purchase price for all assets exceeds the fair market value of the tangible assets, the tangible assets will be assigned their fair market value on the buyer's books, and the balance of the purchase price will be assigned to an intangible asset—good will. Until 2001 good will had to be amortized—that is, written off the books through annual expense entries over the expected useful life of the asset. The purchase method of accounting was the default method for accounting for acquisitions. Unless the transaction met all the criteria for the other method, purchase accounting must be used. Today it is the only method.

When FASB first proposed to eliminate pooling of interest accounting, it was opposed by much of the business community. Spokesmen complained that because purchase accounting created goodwill that must be amortized (and might also require write-ups of assets to their market value, thus increasing depreciation expense), purchase accounting would reduce reported income for acquiring companies, and thus discourage merger activity. The solution, political or otherwise, was for FASB to eliminate the requirement that goodwill be amortized. Instead, the 2001 accounting rules simply require that goodwill can remain on the acquiring corporation's books as long as it is not "impaired." As Statement of Financial Accounting Standards No. 142 explains, "Opinion 17 presumed that goodwill and all other intangible assets were wasting assets (that is, finite lived), and thus the amounts assigned to them should be amortized in determining net income. . . . This Statement does not presume that those assets are wasting assets. Instead, goodwill and intangible assets that have indefinite useful lives will not be amortized but rather will be tested at least annually for impairment."

In 2007 FASB issued SFAS No. 141 to clarify some issues remaining from the 2001 revision. Even in mergers of equals, it requires recognition of one entity as the acquiring firm. It provides greater specificity about measurement of value of assets acquired, requires valuation of certain contingent liabilities and assets, requires measurement of contingent payments and inclusion of those amounts in calculating the purchase price. It also provides that as new information becomes available during the fiscal year about values as of the closing date, adjustments are to be made (excluding new developments or events). In the case of a bargain purchase, where the seller is under some duress, it recognizes the concept of "negative goodwill" to the extent the net value of the assets acquired exceeds the purchase price. Such "negative goodwill is recognized by the buyer in income in the year of the acquisition.

Accounting for Partial Acquisitions. There are three possible methods to account for acquisitions that are less than complete acquisitions. They are the cost method, the equity method, and consolidation of financial statements of subsidiaries.

The cost method is the only method available where the acquiring firm does not acquire a large enough interest to exercise significant influence over the target, normally less than 20% of the target's stock. In the cost method, the investing corporation records its investment at cost, as it would with any other asset. APR Opinion No. 18, paragraph 6. In this case, the acquiring firm recognizes income from its investment only to the extent it receives dividends, like any other shareholder.

The equity method is available only for investments where the buyer holds enough stock to have the ability to exercise significant influence, normally 20% or more of the stock of the target. Under the equity method, the investor recognizes its pro rata share of the earnings or losses of the target firm in the period for which they are reported by the target. Where the target is profitable, this will normally have the effect of allowing the acquiring firm to report a larger amount of earnings, because most companies do not distribute all of their profits in the year earned.

Finally, where the investment exceeds 50% of the stock of the target, it is deemed to be a "subsidiary," in which case its financial reports may be consolidated with those of the parent corporation. Where there are minority interests, adjustments must be made for them.

3. CORPORATE DEALS

Virtually all transactions involving public companies occur at the corporate level. Closely held firms may be acquired by purchasing all of their stock, which has no effect on the corporate financial statements or corporate structure or governance. Chapter One demonstrated how the number of tender offers has declined. Hostile tender offers have always been a small fraction of all acquisitions, vastly outnumbered by the negotiated transactions. Typically, as you will see, the majority of tender offers are part of a negotiated transaction. Because SEC rules created some legal uncertainty about how one could compensate executives of the acquired corporation and still come within the "best price" rules, 17 CFR 240–14d–10, tender offers were sometimes avoided in negotiated acquisitions. The SEC has modified this rule to simplify compliance and to reduce uncertainty, as discussed in Part 3.D of Chapter Eleven.

A. MERGERS

Model Business Corporation Act, §§ 10.04, 11.01 to 11.08; 12.01 to 12.02; 13.02; Delaware General Corporation Law, §§ 251, 259 and 262.

The vast majority of all acquisitions are negotiated transactions, usually between top executives of two companies, with board authorization followed by shareholder approval. Mergers involve corporate action, rather than the individual actions that are at the heart of tender offers. In the prototypical conception of a merger, Corporation A, by virtue of corporate action, "becomes" part of Corporation B (the "surviving corporation"), which also must undertake similar corporate action. The shareholders of Corporation A, by operation of law, become shareholders of Corporation B, as a result of the merger. In the words of Bayless Manning, this wonderful abstraction means that a man who owned a horse suddenly finds that he owns a cow.* Corporation A disappeared by operation of the merger laws, and in its place stood only Corporation B. Corporation B succeeded to the legal title to all assets of Corporation A, and inherited all of its obligations as well.

Corporation statutes spell out the procedures for such mergers in detail. First, the boards of directors of the merging corporations must approve an agreed-upon plan of merger. After giving sufficient advance notice as required by the statute, the shareholders must approve the plan of merger. If they do so, and if the merger is not abandoned by the board of directors, a power reserved in virtually all statutes, the merger is consummated upon the filing of "articles of merger" with the appropriate state authority, usually the Secretary of State. While Corporation A shareholders may continue to hold their stock certificates that state they own shares in Corporation A, by operation of law they now own shares in Corporation B.

Typically the shareholder votes required for mergers are higher than those required for ordinary actions. While in most states action can be taken by a majority of a quorum of voting shares (with a quorum often set at a simple majority), mergers often require higher votes. These votes are usually set at the same level as those for other "fundamental corporate changes," such as amendments to the articles of incorporation, authorizing the sale of all assets, or dissolution. The Model Act formerly set the required vote at a majority of all votes entitled to be cast. Some states still provide for higher votes, such as two-thirds, a vestige of 19th

---

* Bayless Manning, The Shareholder's Appraisal Remedy: An Essay for Frank Coker, 72 Yale L. J. 223, 246 (1962).

century voting, when unanimous consent was usually required to amend a corporate charter, because it was seen as a contract among all shareholders, which could only be changed with the consent of all contracting parties. Recent changes to § 11.04(e) of the Model Act now permit such approval by a majority vote if a quorum is present. It remains to be seen how quickly this change will be adopted by the states.

Contracting still plays a role in setting voting rules for mergers. In many cases where there is more than one class of shares, or where there are series of shares within a preferred class, these shares may have different (or no) voting rights on ordinary matters such as election of directors. But in many instances these classes will be granted voting rights on mergers, because a merger may radically alter the economic situation facing differing classes, either because their contract rights in the surviving corporation may be different, or because owning shares, even with the same contract rights, in a different company may impose different levels of risk on the shareholders. Most statutes now provide basic voting rights for all shares, regardless of their contract rights. The Model Business Corporation Act provides such rights in § 10.04, whenever charter amendments threaten to change fundamental economic rights of a particular class. These rights provide for voting as a separate voting group, the approval of which is required for the change. In other words, holders of a small class have a veto power over changes to the terms of their contract, that cannot be overridden by the common stockholders. The Model Act provides similar rights to these classes to vote separately as a class on mergers. Model Business Corporation Act § 11.04(f). While Delaware provides similar voting rights for charter amendments under § 242(2) of its corporation law, it does not provide separate class voting rights in mergers as a matter of law, although they can be contracted for.

Shareholders who are outvoted in a merger are given the right to dissent from the merger, and demand payment of the fair value of their shares. A shareholder seeking appraisal rights must notify the corporation of his or her intent to dissent, and thereafter the statutes generally set a strict timetable within which both the corporation and the shareholder must proceed. Under most statutes shareholders must be notified of their appraisal rights at the time their proxies are solicited to approve the transaction, or in the notice of the meeting or, in some cases (short form mergers), notice that action approving the merger has been taken without their approval. Where public company shareholders will receive stock in another public company, both Delaware and the Model Act deny appraisal rights, although the Model Act restores them where the merger involves a controlling shareholder.

There are enormous variations possible from this classical concept of the merger. First, shareholders in Corporation A need not receive shares in Corporation B under modern statutes. Section 11.02(c)(3) of the Model

Business Corporation Act permits conversion of the A shares "into shares or other securities, eligible interests, obligations, rights to acquire shares, other securities or eligible interests, cash, other property or any combination of the foregoing." Del. G.C.L. § 251(b) contains similar language. These statutes, which first appeared in the 1960s, permit the cash-out merger, discussed in Chapter Nine and elsewhere. The reference to securities without limitation on the identity of the issuing entity also permits the triangular merger. In a triangular merger, the shareholders of Corporation A may receive shares in Corporation C, which is the parent of Corporation B, the acquisition subsidiary. Of course they may receive other securities of Corporation C as well.

Another form of merger involves the "leveraged buyout" or "LBO." Technically, nothing in the LBO differs from the descriptions of mergers set out above. But the form became distinct enough during the 1980s to be given its own title. LBOs worked best with firms that had both stable cash flows and assets that could readily be pledged to secure loans, such as real estate, inventory or accounts receivable, and thus were able safely to assume a great deal of indebtedness. A buyer wishing to acquire control of a target under these circumstances would secure loan and investment commitments to provide the vast majority of the purchase price, perhaps as much as 90%, in the form of preferred stock, secured loans and unsecured, often subordinated debt. In other cases buyers during the 1980s financed these purchases by borrowing money in the public markets, issuing high-yield, high-risk bonds and debentures, known as "junk bonds." The borrower, using a separate acquisition corporation, caused the acquisition corporation to agree to borrow these funds and to secure them with pledges of all the assets it was about to acquire. At the closing of the merger transaction, the target's assets became those of the surviving buyer, and became subject to the debts of the buyer. Because of the pledges of all of the assets of the surviving corporation, these claims became superior to those of the unsecured creditors of the target, who now found themselves holding much riskier obligations.

B. SHORT FORM MERGERS

Generally under the Model Business Corporation Act shareholders of both corporations that are parties to a statutory merger must vote to approve the merger. One exception appears in Model Act § 11.05, for "short form" mergers of parents and 90% owned subsidiaries, where only the board of the parent corporation must approve the transaction. Section 253 of the Delaware General Corporation Law ("GCL") is substantially similar. Note that Model Act § 11.04(g) excuses shareholder votes for acquiring corporations that are the surviving corporations under certain conditions—where the articles of incorporation are unchanged, the shareholders' rights are unchanged, and the number of voting shares outstanding immediately after the merger does not exceed those outstanding before the merger by more than 20%. See also Delaware GCL§ 251(f), which contains a comparable exception. Companies traded on the New York Stock Exchange will be required to provide a shareholder vote if the newly issued shares exceed 20% of the outstanding shares, under New York Stock Exchange Listed Company Guide § 312.00. In contrast, Georgia has provided that if all of the other conditions are met, no shareholder vote is required if the shares outstanding after the merger do not exceed the previously authorized shares of the corporation. Official Code of Ga. Ann. § 14–2–1103(h). The comments to the Georgia provision state "Public policy does not require a shareholder vote to acquire another business by merger or share exchange where the board possessed authority to issue the same number of shares for cash to finance the same acquisition." Is this a wise rule?

In 2013 Delaware amended section 251(h) to allow mergers to be approved by a majority of the outstanding shares where another corporation had acquired such a majority by a tender offer upon terms previously agreed to with the subject corporation. The reasoning presumably was that the outcome of a shareholder vote was a foregone conclusion. As of this writing the Corporate Laws Committee of the ABA Business Law Section has proposed similar amendments to MBCA § 11.04(j).

C. TRIANGULAR MERGERS

Section 11.02(c)(3) of the Model Business Corporation Act permits conversion of a merging corporation's shares "into shares or other securities, eligible interests, obligations, rights to acquire shares, other securities or eligible interests, cash, other property or any combination of the foregoing." This permits a parent corporation to create an acquisition subsidiary, which it wholly owns, and which becomes the party to the merger. The shareholders of the acquired firm may receive parent company securities or other consideration from the parent, in what is known as the triangular merger. The triangular merger has become a very common feature of the M & A landscape. There is a variant of this called the "reverse triangular merger," in which the target corporation is the surviving corporation. The merger agreement will provide that the shareholders of the acquisition subsidiary will be the shareholders of the surviving corporation, and that the target shareholders will either receive securities or other consideration from the parent corporation. This form is used when there are reasons to preserve Corporation A as an ongoing legal entity, perhaps because it has goodwill in its current corporate name, or has licenses or other privileges that might be jeopardized if it merged into another corporation, but which remain intact if Corporation A is the surviving corporation. This is, as the reader can see, the height of legal formalism, but this is an area where forms are often critical. Bidders in hostile takeovers often create an "acquisition subsidiary" in which the bidder owns 100% of the stock.

In these cases the acquisition subsidiary actually acquires shares in the tender offer (using the parent's funds) and then merges with the target corporation.

D. ASSET PURCHASES

Model Business Corporation Act, §§ 12.01 to 12.02; 13.02; Delaware General Corporation Law, § 271.

The other major form of acquisition involves the purchase of all (or substantially all) of the assets of the target corporation. This must necessarily be a negotiated transaction. The procedures to be followed are very much like those for a merger. First the sale must be approved by the board of directors, and then submitted to the shareholders, after notice required by statute, for their approval. In most states separate voting rights are not provided for separate classes of shares, and the only shares entitled to vote are those entitled by the articles of incorporation. In most states such an asset sale also triggers appraisal rights, although it does not in Delaware.

Asset sales differ from mergers in two significant ways in most cases. First, a bidder buying assets does not assume the liabilities of the selling corporation, with a few exceptions to be discussed in Chapter Four. Where liabilities are uncertain, perhaps because the seller is facing lawsuits, this provides a means for the buyer to be far more certain about the value of what it is acquiring than it could in a merger where it would assume those liabilities. Second, asset sales are taxable events, while most mergers will not necessarily be recognized as taxable events. Because of this adverse tax distinction, asset purchases of entire corporations are rare. What remains are asset sales of divisions of companies, which are much more frequent.

4. DEALS WITH SHAREHOLDERS

A. PRIVATELY NEGOTIATED DEALS

Ordinary investments in the shares of a corporation raise few questions of corporate or securities law, except for the availability of exemptions from the registration requirements of both state and federal securities laws. Shareholders obtain their rights by virtue of the contracts that create the corporation, including the background rules of state corporation law. In negotiated acquisitions of non-public corporations a buyer may find itself negotiating primarily with a single large shareholder or with a small group of such shareholders. If these shareholders have a majority of the shares their collective decision will determine the outcome of the acquisition effort, and their cooperation will assure that the target corporation will take whatever corporate action is necessary for the particular form of the transaction, including approvals by the board of directors and shareholders, if necessary.

B. TENDER OFFERS AND EXCHANGE OFFERS

Securities Exchange Act, §§ 13(d) & (e); 14(d) & (e).

Acquiring securities that are traded in public markets raised few issues under the securities laws prior to 1968.* This regime changed markedly with the adoption of the Williams Act amendments to the Securities Exchange Act ("Exchange Act" or "§ 34 Act") that became effective in 1968. Thereafter, whenever an investor purchased more than 10% (now 5%) of a class of equity securities registered under the Exchange Act, the investor was required by Section 13(d) to file a disclosure document with the issuer and the SEC within ten days after the acquisition. The buyer had to identify itself and its allies, its holdings, its source of funding for the investment, and its purposes in making the acquisition in this filing, on Schedule 13D.

Typically an announcement by a buyer that it intends to seek control of a corporation causes the target corporation's stock price to rise, as traders recognize that it will require a premium over the pre-bid market price to persuade the holders of a large amount of a company's shares to sell. In effect, the supply curve for the shares of that company shifts upward at the time traders realize a bid will be forthcoming. A bidder seeking control, therefore, will prefer to accumulate as much stock as it can in the market place before announcing its plans. Accordingly, bidders generally seek to acquire target shares as quietly as possible. Bidders may acquire these shares through several brokers, in order to disguise the fact that so many orders are coming from a single buyer, although this creates the risk that two brokers working for the same buyer will compete against each other in the marketplace. These purchases usually cease before the bidder reaches the 10% level, because any person holding more than 10% of the stock of a company becomes a statutory insider for purposes of section 16 of the Exchange Act. Once such insider status attaches, if the bidder proceeds to sell shares within six months of any purchases, those profits belong to the target under section 16(b), with minor exceptions. Because a bidder typically realizes that it may be outbid if a bidding contest develops, it realizes that it may wish to sell out to the high bidder in the reasonably near future.

A tender offer developed from the English "invitation for tenders," in which target shareholders are invited to tender their shares to the bidder for purchase. Typically a tender offer involves certain conditions that must be met before the bidder will obligate itself to purchase the tendered shares. The most common condition is that a sufficient number of shares be tendered to give the bidder control, which normally will be a majority of all the voting shares. Other conditions may include antitrust

---

*   Fraudulent, deceptive and manipulative acts or practices in connection with the purchase or sale of securities were covered by section 10(b) and Rule 10b–5 of the Securities Exchange Act, and section 16(b) precluded certain short-swing trading by named insiders in a company.

clearances, regulatory approvals, relaxation of takeover defenses by target management (including redemption of poison pills) and the like. A tender offer begins with a public announcement of the terms of the offer in which the bidder has provided a means of acceptance, which must, under section 14(d) of the Exchange Act, be filed with the SEC and the issuer at the time of announcement. The disclosure requirements are similar to those under section 13(d), but of course they also include requirements of full disclosure of the terms of the tender offer. Announcements of plans to make a tender offer do not trigger the same disclosure requirements, although the announcement must be filed with the SEC and the target company. Under regulations adopted under the antifraud provisions of section 14(e) of the Exchange Act, tender offers must be kept open for at least 20 business days from the time of announcement.

Typically tender offers are made at prices that include a substantial premium over the market price, in order to persuade shareholders to tender. Where the tender offer is a surprise to the market, the market price rises toward the tender offer price. Why are shareholders selling at this time rather than tendering? They do this in part because the tender offer may not be successful, and the stock price may drop toward its pre-bid price if this happens. Shareholders who sell into this market typically are selling to so-called "risk arbitrageurs," who intend to tender to the bid. These "arbs" thus bear the risk of failure, in return for an "insurance premium" represented by the difference between the tender offer price and the lower price they pay for shares. These arbitrageurs may also bear a second risk in some cases: the risk of oversubscription. Some bids are announced as bids for only just enough stock to give the bidder control. In the event the bid is oversubscribed, the bidder is required by section 14(d)(6) of the Exchange Act to take up the shares *pro rata* from all tendering shareholders. Thus an arbitrageur may only earn the bid premium on some fraction of its entire stake in the target corporation. A third explanation for market discounts from the tender offer price may involve the time value of money. Even if a tender offer is for any and all shares, and is certain to succeed, closing may be delayed for some time as regulatory approvals or other conditions are met. That delay makes the discounted present value of the expected tender offer payment something less than its face value.

A bidder beginning a tender offer may face a "free rider" problem, discussed further in Chapter Six. If target company shareholders believe the bidder will improve the value of the company through better management, or economies of scale achieved through combination with another company, or for other reasons, they may prefer to hold on to their shares and share in the resulting gains. After all, if the bidder is willing to pay such a handsome price in the tender offer, the bidder must believe that the company can be made even more valuable in the future. Before the Williams Act, bidders dealt with this problem through bids on a "first-come, first-served" basis, with a hint (or perhaps even a promise) that things would get worse for those shareholders who did not tender. This practice ended in part in 1968, because Williams Act regulations require bids to be kept open for minimum time periods, and require bidders to take *pro rata* from all tendering shareholders. A bidder can also "coerce" (in the words of some commentators) target shareholders into tendering by promising that the remaining shareholders will be "cashed out" of their shares at a lower price in a "takeout merger" once the bidder has gained control of the company. See Chapter Six. This is known as the "two-tier bid."

Target company management frequently plays a significant role in the acquisition process. Whether the transaction is in the form of an uninvited ("hostile") tender offer or negotiations, management of the target firm is aware that in many cases their jobs will be eliminated, or at the very least, their management powers restricted, if their company is acquired. Where the takeover bid is "hostile" (at least from management's perspective), management can be expected, at the very least, to urge shareholders to reject the bid. Indeed, under Rule 14e–2, adopted under the Williams Act, management of the target company is required to inform shareholders of its position on the bid within ten business days.

Frequently management resists bids to assure that the price obtained by shareholders is the highest possible price. One such defense involves eliminating the sting of the two-tier bid. This is accomplished by asking shareholders to amend the articles of incorporation to amend the voting rules of the corporation to make it difficult for a bidder that gains a majority of the company's shares to undertake a cash-out merger at a price below the cash tender offer. Beginning in the mid-1980s, boards of directors adopted "poison pill" plans. Generally these plans involve the issuance by the board of rights to purchase additional shares of stock of the company at a bargain price, which become exercisable only when a bidder gains a significant ownership position. These rights are void in the hands of the bidder. This has the effect of reducing the value of the bidder's shares as large numbers of new shares are issued at lower prices, and has been thought to be highly effective at stopping hostile tender offers, a view we will examine in Chapter Six. In other cases target firms may seek other preferred buyers for the company ("white knights"), or may seek to emulate the bidder's strategy, by repurchasing company shares with borrowed money, hoping to drive share prices above the tender offer price.

Because poison pills have been viewed as such effective defenses, in the late 1980s and thereafter bidders have frequently coupled their bids with proxy solicitations, in which they seek to elect their own slate to replace existing directors. This strategy has been successful in a number of cases, where shareholders wish to sell but managers do not. One management response to the threat of a proxy fight is to ask shareholders to vote to provide a staggered board, in which only one-third of the directors are elected annually, and in which existing directors can only be removed for cause. The prospect of waiting for two annual meetings to elect a majority of the board has been enough to discourage most proxy fights by bidders where this defense has been adopted.

Once a bidder has gained a controlling interest in a firm, the bidder typically proceeds to acquire the remaining interest in the target through a cash-out merger or similar reorganization.

CHAPTER FOUR

Deal Structure and Getting Consent

Acquisition lawyers will be expected to make an early determination of the most desirable form for an acquisition. Among the questions that the lawyer must consider are whether the consent of the board of directors or the shareholders will be required, or whether both will be. Where time is important, it may be desirable to structure the transaction to avoid a shareholder vote, if possible. On the other hand, where management is likely to resist a change of control, a direct appeal to the shareholders in the form of a tender offer may provide the only chance of success. As the cases below will illustrate, the lawyer can generally achieve the same ultimate result using a variety of forms of transactions

The ability to achieve the same results using different forms raises a difficult question for legislators and courts. Should the requirements for each transaction be essentially identical, in order to protect whatever interests these bodies determine merit protection? In other words, should substance rather than form govern legal requirements for the transaction? While this can be accomplished by corporate statutes that make the requirements identical for each form of transaction, this has not been the general approach of state corporation statutes. Accordingly, the question is frequently raised whether the courts should recast a transaction that formally complies with statutory requirements in order to impose certain requirements or liabilities upon the participants. The 1984 revision of the Model Business Corporation Act goes further toward uniformity than most prior statutes except California, which has a unified treatment of all transactions falling into a broad category of "reorganizations." See Cal. Corp. Code §§ 181, 1200–1203. Delaware, in contrast, has distinctive rules for different forms.

These issues raise difficult questions about the function of corporate law. Those who would impose identical requirements on all forms of transactions appear to view corporate law as performing a regulatory function. Those who oppose this view see the different forms as a menu of choices for corporate participants, who are given the freedom to contract as they wish using these forms. For readings on this issue see Symposium: Contractual Freedom in Corporate Law, 89 Colum. L. Rev. 1395 (1989).

From a tactical viewpoint, shareholder voting rules can be used defensively by corporations reluctant to engage in business combinations, whether in the form of a merger, share exchange, or asset purchase. In some cases a veto power may be provided to holders of a relatively small class or series of shares, either by corporate law or by provisions of the articles of incorporation. In other cases special voting rules are provided where a hostile bidder has acquired a significant block of shares before proposing a business combination. While the general topic of restrictive voting rules will be treated in this chapter, further consideration is provided in Chapter 6, Part 2.D.

This chapter expands on the overview in the previous chapter, providing more detail on voting requirements for transactions. Much of the chapter is devoted to the complexities of shareholder voting rules in asset sales, and problems of successor liability in these transactions.

1. MERGERS

A. THE STATUTES

Model Business Corporation Act, §§ 10.04, 11.01–11.08; 13.02; Delaware General Corporation Law, §§ 251, 259, 262.

New York Stock Exchange Listed Company Manual

312.03(c)   Shareholder Approval

(c) Shareholder approval is required prior to the issuance of common stock, or of securities convertible into or exercisable for common stock, in any transaction or series of related transactions if:

(1)   the common stock has, or will have upon issuance, voting power equal to or in excess of 20 percent of the voting power outstanding before the issuance of such stock or of securities convertible into or exercisable for common stock; or

(2)   the number of shares of common stock to be issued is, or will be upon issuance, equal to or in excess of 20 percent of the number of shares of common stock outstanding before the issuance of the common stock or of securities convertible into or exercisable for common stock.

However, shareholder approval will not be required for any such issuance involving:

- any public offering for cash;

* * *

(d) Shareholder approval is required prior to an issuance that will result in a change of control of the issuer.

NASDAQ Marketplace Rule 5635

5635.   Shareholder Approval

This Rule sets forth the circumstances under which shareholder approval is required prior to an issuance of securities in connection with: (i) the acquisition of the stock or assets of another company; (ii) equity-based compensation of officers, directors, employees or consultants; (iii) a change of control; and (iv) private placements. General provisions relating to shareholder approval are set forth in Rule 5635(e), and the financial viability exception to the shareholder approval requirement is set forth in Rule 5635(f). Nasdaq-listed Companies and their representatives are encouraged to use the interpretative letter process described in Rule 5602.

(a) Acquisition of Stock or Assets of Another Company

Shareholder approval is required prior to the issuance of securities in connection with the acquisition of the stock or assets of another company if:

(1) where, due to the present or potential issuance of common stock, including shares issued pursuant to an earn-out provision or similar type of provision, or securities convertible into or exercisable for common stock, other than a public offering for cash:

(A) the common stock has or will have upon issuance voting power equal to or in excess of 20% of the voting power outstanding before the issuance of stock or securities convertible into or exercisable for common stock; or

(B) the number of shares of common stock to be issued is or will be equal to or in excess of 20% of the number of shares of common stock outstanding before the issuance of the stock or securities; or

(2) any director, officer or Substantial Shareholder (as defined by Rule 5635(e)(3)) of the Company has a 5% or greater interest (or such persons collectively have a 10% or greater interest), directly or indirectly, in the Company or assets to be acquired or in the consideration to be paid in the transaction or series of related transactions and the present or potential issuance of common stock, or securities convertible into or exercisable for common stock, could result in an increase in outstanding common shares or voting power of 5% or more; or

(b) Change of Control

Shareholder approval is required prior to the issuance of securities when the issuance or potential issuance will result in a change of control of the Company.

Located at: http://nasdaq.cchwallstreet.com/nasdaqtools/platformviewer. asp?selectednode=chp-1-1-4-2&manual=®nasdaq®main®nasdaq"equity rules®.

B. Variations in Voting Rules

At an early stage in the development of American corporate law there were no variations in voting rules depending on the nature of the transaction. Corporate charters were obtained by special grant from the legislature, and were seen as contracts among the incorporators, the corporate entity, and the state. Trustees of Dartmouth College v. Woodward, 17 U.S. (4 Wheat.) 518 (1819). Because grants from the sovereign were seen as carrying with them some of the sovereign's power, they were narrowly construed (leading to carefully drawn purpose clauses, among other things). And because they were contractual, alteration required consent of all of the parties to the contract, which implied unanimous consent of the shareholders, as successors to the incorporators. This was the universal rule in the first half of the 19th century, whether the matter involved a merger, sale of assets, or dissolution. As a result, a single holdout among the shareholders could block action desired by the vast majority. For a tracing of this history see Carney, Fundamental Corporate Changes, Minority Shareholders, and Business Purposes, 1980 Am. Bar Found. Res. J. 69.

In the first half of the nineteenth century, as increasing numbers of corporations were formed and the pace of the industrial revolution accelerated, the number of business combinations began to increase. This first occurred in the railroad industry, as short lines consolidated into longer lines, such as the New York Central System. The benefits from such consolidations were obvious, and state legislatures readily consented to them. This led to increasing dissatisfaction with the rule of unanimous shareholder consent to approve such mergers, liquidations and asset sales.

The courts ultimately solved the holdout problem by altering the property rights of shareholders. States began reserving the right to amend charters unilaterally in response to Justice Story's suggestion in his concurring opinion in the Dartmouth College Case that states that issued charters as sovereigns could, as part of the contract, reserve this right.

Statutory change continued even after the adoption of general merger statutes in the late 19th century. While early acts often provided for an 'extraordinary' vote of shareholders to approve fundamental changes (usually two-thirds), recent amendments have generally lowered the required vote to a simple majority.* Adoption of short-form merger statutes, which allow mergers between parents and subsidiaries that are more than 90 percent owned by the parent, have eliminated the requirement of any shareholder vote or approval by the board of the subsidiary, leaving the matter entirely to the discretion of the parent's board of directors.**

---

   *   Perhaps representative of this shift is the Model Act, which reduced the requirement from two-thirds to a majority of the total shares entitled to vote in 1962. 2 ABA Model Bus. Corp. Act Ann.2d §§ 78, 79 2 (1971). More recently it has shifted to a majority of a quorum. MBCA §§ 11.04(e) and 7.25(a). Delaware shifted from a two-thirds to majority of shares entitled to vote requirement in 1967. Del. code Ann.2d tit. 8, § 251(c) (Cum. Supp. 1978); Ernest L. Folk III, The Delaware General Corporation Law: A Commentary and Analysis 381 (Boston: Little Brown & Co., 1972).

   **   See, e.g., ABA-ALI Model Bus. Corp. Act § 75 (1979); Del. Code Ann. tit. 8, § 253 (1974 & Cum. Supp. 1978). The history of the Delaware statute is traced in Coyne v. Park & Tilford Distillers Corp., 38 Del.Ch. 514, 154 A.2d 893, 894 (Sup. Ct. 1959). The Model Act short-form provision was added in 1957. Elvin R. Latty, Some Miscellaneous Novelties in the New Corporation Statutes, 23 Law & Contemp. Prob. 363, 392 (1958). Recently, where a merger agreement expressly permits a short form merger and a corporation consummates a tender or

As of 2015, forty jurisdictions required a majority vote of shares entitled to vote to approve a merger; nine jurisdictions required approval by 2/3 of the shares entitled to vote.* The Model Act now requires only approval by shareholders at a meeting at which a quorum of at least a majority of votes entitled to be cast exists. MBCA § 11.04(d). In some cases, these rules require approval by non-voting as well as voting shares. Many states, like Delaware, have adopted anti-takeover statutes that require very high votes from all shares not held by a party to the business combination. See Del. G.C.L. § 203. These statutes only apply to publicly held corporations, and can be relaxed under specified circumstances. These statutes are described in Chapter Seven. Special provisions in the articles of incorporation may raise the required votes for mergers. They are also described in Chapter Six, Part 2.C.

Holders of options to purchase shares or debt instruments convertible into shares are not treated as shareholders for purposes of voting on mergers, share exchanges, or other fundamental changes under corporate laws.

Preferred shares represent a special problem. The default rule is that all shares possess voting rights on a one share, one vote basis unless these rights are denied in the articles of incorporation. Rev. Model Bus. Corp. Act § 7.21(a); Del. Gen. Corp. L. § 212(a). Typically voting rights are limited or denied to preferred shares in the articles of incorporation, with some exceptions.** In some cases preferred shares may be allowed to elect a minority of directors; in others voting rights to elect directors are granted when dividends are passed; in part because of stock exchange requirements. See N.Y. Stock Exchange Listed Company Manual § 313.00(c) (preferred to have the right to elect a minimum of two directors when six quarterly dividends have been passed). Because voting rights are creatures of contract (although subject to mandatory class veto rights under the Model Act for actions that adversely affect their rights), charter provisions may provide small classes of preferred with a veto power over actions desired by the common, as in the following case.

Two crucial questions are whether, in mergers, asset sales or other fundamental changes, preferred shareholders who have no contract rights to vote shall be allowed to vote at all; and if they are allowed, whether their votes will be aggregated with those of the common, or will be voted separately as a class, the approval of which is a requirement for the transaction to proceed.

---

exchange offer for any and all shares that achieves a majority of all voting stock sufficient to approve a long form merger (which generally will be a simple majority. Del. Code Ann. § 251(h).

* The states requiring a two-thirds vote are Alaska, Illinois, Maryland, Massachusetts, Missouri, South Carolina, Texas, Virginia and Washington.

** Venture capitalists typically bargain for convertible preferred stock with voting rights equal to the common shares into which they are convertible. Thus in a sale or merger of a venture capital financed company these shareholders will have a veto power, because they also obtain the right to vote separately as a class.

The question of whether voting is required at all for non-voting shares in mergers and other business combinations could have been left as a matter of private contract, to be covered in the articles of incorporation, or as a default rule, which operated in the absence of contract, or as a regulation. The general approach has been regulatory, as in Rev. Model Bus. Corp. Act § 11.04(f), which ties the voting rights of nonvoting shares to those cases where an amendment of the articles of incorporation affecting their rights would require a vote of that class. All but Delaware, Georgia, Kansas, Maryland, Missouri, Oklahoma and Puerto Rico require separate class voting on a plan of merger.

Where corporations have multiple classes or series of preferred stock with voting rights as separate voting groups, investors with a relatively small stake in the corporation can prevent mergers and other reorganizations that may be beneficial for the common stockholders. The older the corporation, the more likely that it will have multiple classes or series. Public utility corporations are likely candidates for this type of capital structure. In some cases older classes or series may represent a relatively small amount of a firm's capital, because the firm has grown considerably since the original issue of the class or series of preferred. In some cases series of preferred have been issued at least partly for the purpose of placing a veto power in friendly hands, to make hostile acquisitions by others more difficult.

The SEC plays a role in governing the procedures for shareholder votes in its proxy regulations under Section 14(a) of the Securities Exchange Act. Rule 14a–4 sets out the required forms of proxies for shareholder voting, and section 14a–4(a)(3 provides that proxy statements shall identify each matter to be voted on at a meeting. In 2014 the SEC published new guidance about this provision, requiring that various provisions in a proxy statement must be broken out, or unbundled, to allow shareholders to accept or reject each material change. In a merger transaction, the SEC gives, as examples, matters that "substantively effect shareholder rights," such as matters dealing with classified boards, limitations on removal of directors, supermajority voting, delaying an annual meeting for more than a year, eliminating the ability to act by written consent, and changing minimum quorum requirements—in effect, matters dealing with takeover defenses covered in Chapter Six, *infra*. https://www.sec.gov/interps/telephone/phone supplement5.htm.

Schreiber v. Carney

447 A.2d 17 (Del. Ch. 1982).

■ HARTNETT, VICE CHANCELLOR.

In this stockholder's derivative action, Leonard I. Schreiber, the plaintiff, brought suit on behalf of defendant—Texas International

Airlines, Inc. ("Texas International"), a Delaware corporation, challenging the propriety of a loan from Texas International to defendant Jet Capital Corporation ("Jet Capital"), the holder of 35% of the shares of stock of Texas International. Also joined as individual defendants were Texas International's board of directors—several of whom also served on Jet Capital's board of directors. The matter is presently before the Court on cross-motions for summary judgment. Defendants' motion is based on their contention that there has been no showing of waste and that plaintiff lacks standing to bring this suit. Plaintiff's motion is based on his contention that the transaction was tainted by vote-buying and is therefore void. For the reasons set forth below, both motions must be denied.

I

The essential facts are undisputed. The lawsuit arises out of the corporate restructuring of Texas International which occurred on June 11, 1980. The restructuring was accomplished by way of a share for share merger between Texas International and Texas Air Corporation ("Texas Air"), a holding company formed for the purpose of effectuating the proposed reorganization. Texas Air is also a Delaware corporation. At the annual meeting held on June 11, 1980 the shareholders voted overwhelmingly in favor of the proposal. As a result the shareholders of Texas International were eliminated as such and received in trade for their stock an equal number of shares in Texas Air. Texas International in turn became a wholly-owned subsidiary of Texas Air.

Prior to the merger Texas International was engaged in the airline business servicing the cities of Houston and Dallas, Texas. All concede that the purpose of the merger was to enable Texas International—under a new corporate structure—to diversify, to strengthen itself financially and in general to be transformed into a more viable and aggressive enterprise. According to the proxy statement issued in connection with the merger, management indicated that although there were no commitments at that time, it was actively considering the possibility of acquiring other companies engaged in both related as well as unrelated fields.

During the formulation of the reorganization plan, management was confronted with an obstacle, the resolution of which forms the basis for this lawsuit, because Jet Capital, the owner of the largest block of Texas International's stock, threatened to block the merger. Jet Capital's veto power resulted from a provision in Texas International's Certificate of Incorporation which required that each of its four classes of stock participate in the approval of a merger. At that time, Texas International's four classes of outstanding stock consisted of 4,669,182 shares of common stock and three series of convertible preferred stock; 32,318 shares of Series A stock, 66,075 shares of Series B stock and 2,040,000 shares of Series C stock. According to the Certificate of

Incorporation a majority vote was required of both the common stockholders and the Series A preferred stockholders voting as separate classes. Similarly, a majority vote was required of the Series B and Series C preferred stockholders, but voting together as a single class. Because Jet Capital owned all of the Series C preferred stock—the larger class— it was in a position to block the merger proposal. Jet Capital indicated that although the proposal was indeed beneficial to Texas International and the other shareholders, it was nevertheless compelled to vote against it because the merger, if approved, would impose an intolerable income tax burden on it. This was so because the merger had an adverse impact on Jet Capital's position as the holder of certain warrants to purchase Texas International's common stock which would expire in 1982. There were warrants outstanding for the purchase of 1,029,531 shares of Texas International common stock at $4.18 per share and, of these, Jet Capital owned sufficient warrants to acquire 799,880 shares of Texas International's common shares. As the holder of these warrants, Jet Capital was faced with three alternatives.

The first alternative for Jet Capital was for it to participate in the merger and exchange its Texas International warrants for Texas Air warrants. However, according to an Internal Revenue Service ruling obtained by management, each holder of an unexercised Texas International warrant would be deemed to have realized taxable income from the merger as if the warrant had been exercised. Thus, it was estimated that Jet Capital would incur an $800,000 federal income tax liability. Because Jet Capital was a publicly held company, its management could not justify the assumption of such a tax liability and, therefore, did not consider this a viable alternative.

The second alternative was for Jet Capital to exercise the warrants prematurely. The merger would then be tax free to it as it would be to the other shareholders. This, however, was also not deemed to be feasible because Jet Capital lacked the approximately three million dollars necessary to exercise the warrants. Jet Capital's assets—other than its Texas International stock—were worth only $200,000. In addition, borrowing money at the prevailing interest rates in order to finance an early exercise of the warrants was deemed prohibitively expensive by the management of Jet Capital.* In any event, this alternative was considered to be imprudent because the early exercise of the warrants posed an unnecessary market risk because the market value of Texas International's stock on the date of the early exercise might prove to be higher than that on the expiration date. As a result, this alternative was also not considered viable.

---

* In early 1980 the prime rate, charged by banks to their best customers, reached a high of 18%, as inflation raged at a 21% rate for a short time.—Ed.

The third and final alternative was for Jet Capital to vote against the merger and thus preclude it. Given these alternatives, Jet Capital obviously chose to oppose the restructuring.

In order to overcome this impasse, it was proposed that Texas International and Jet Capital explore the possibility of a loan by Texas International to Jet Capital in order to fund an early exercise of the warrants. Because Texas International and Jet Capital had several common directors, the defendants recognized the conflict of interest and endeavored to find a way to remove any taint or appearance of impropriety. It was, therefore, decided that a special independent committee would be formed to consider and resolve the matter. The three Texas International directors who had no interest in or connection with Jet Capital were chosen to head up the committee. After its formation, the committee's first act was to hire independent counsel. Next, the committee examined the proposed merger and, based upon advice rendered by an independent investment banker, the merger was again found to be both a prudent and feasible business decision. The committee then confronted the "Jet Capital obstacle" by considering viable options for both Texas International and Jet Capital and, as a result, the committee determined that a loan was the best solution.

After negotiating at arm's length, both Texas International and Jet Capital agreed that Texas International would loan to Jet Capital $3,335,000 at 5% interest per annum for the period up to the scheduled 1982 expiration date for the warrants. After this period, the interest rate would equal the then prevailing prime interest rate. The 5% interest rate was recommended by an independent investment banker as the rate necessary to reimburse Texas International for any dividends paid out during this period. Given this provision for anticipated dividends and the fact that the advanced money would be immediately paid back to Texas International upon the exercise of the warrants, the loan transaction had virtually no impact on Texas International's cash position.

As security Jet Capital was required to pledge all of its Series C preferred stock having a market value of approximately 150% of the amount of the loan. In addition, Jet Capital was expected to apply to the prepayment of the loan any after tax proceeds received from the sale of any stock acquired by Jet Capital as a result of the exercise of the 1982 warrants.

The directors of Texas International unanimously approved the proposal as recommended by the committee and submitted it to the stockholders for approval—requiring as a condition of approval that a majority of all outstanding shares and a majority of the shares voted by the stockholders other than Jet Capital or its officers or directors be voted in favor of the proposal. After receiving a detailed proxy statement, the shareholders voted overwhelmingly in favor of the proposal. There is no allegation that the proxy statement did not fully disclose all the germane facts with complete candor.

The complaint attacks the loan transaction on two theories. First, it is alleged that the loan transaction constituted vote-buying and was therefore void. Secondly, the complaint asserts that the loan was corporate waste. In essence, plaintiff argues that even if the loan was permissible and even if it was the best available option, it would have been wiser for Texas International to have loaned Jet Capital only $800,000—the amount of the increased tax liability—because this would have minimized Texas International's capital commitment and also would have prevented Jet Capital from increasing its control in Texas International on allegedly discriminatory and wasteful terms. Plaintiff also points out that the 5% interest rate on the loan was only equal to the amount of dividends Texas International would have been expected to pay during the period between the time of the early exercise and the date the warrants expired. Jet Capital, therefore in effect it is urged, received an interest free loan for the nearly two-year period preceding the 1982 warrant expiration date.

* * *

IV

* * *

It is clear that the loan constituted vote-buying as that term has been defined by the courts. Vote-buying, despite its negative connotation, is simply a voting agreement supported by consideration personal to the stockholder, whereby the stockholder divorces his discretionary voting power and votes as directed by the offeror. The record clearly indicates that Texas International purchased or "removed" the obstacle of Jet Capital's opposition. Indeed, this is tacitly conceded by the defendants. However, defendants contend that the analysis of the transaction should not end here because the legality of vote-buying depends on whether its object or purpose is to defraud or in some manner disenfranchise the other stockholders. Defendants contend that because the loan did not defraud or disenfranchise any group of shareholders, but rather enfranchised the other shareholders by giving them a determinative vote in the proposed merger, it is not illegal per se. Defendants, in effect, contend that vote-buying is not void per se because the end justified the means. Whether this is valid depends upon the status of the law.

The Delaware decisions dealing with vote-buying leave the question unanswered. In each of these decisions, the Court summarily voided the challenged votes as being purchased and thus contrary to public policy and in fraud of the other stockholders. However, the facts in each case indicated that fraud or disenfranchisement was the obvious purpose of the vote-buying.

* * *

The present case presents a peculiar factual setting in that the proposed vote-buying consideration was conditional upon the approval of a majority of the disinterested stockholders after a full disclosure to them of all pertinent facts and was purportedly for the best interests of all Texas International stockholders. It is therefore necessary to do more than merely consider the fact that Jet Capital saw fit to vote for the transaction after a loan was made to it by Texas International. As stated in Oceanic Exploration Co. v. Grynberg, Del. Supr., 428 A.2d 1 (1981), a case involving an analogous situation, to do otherwise would be tantamount to "[d]eciding the case on . . . an abstraction divorced from the facts of the case and the intent of the law." 428 A.2d at 5.

A review of the present controversy, therefore, must go beyond a reading of Macht v. Merchants Mortgage & Credit Co., *supra*, and consider the cases cited therein. . . . There are essentially two principles which appear in these cases. The first is that vote-buying is illegal per se if its object or purpose is to defraud or disenfranchise the other stockholders. A fraudulent purpose is as defined at common law, as a deceit which operates prejudicially upon the property rights of another.

The second principle which appears in these old cases is that vote-buying is illegal per se as a matter of public policy, the reason being that each stockholder should be entitled to rely upon the independent judgment of his fellow stockholders. Thus, the underlying basis for this latter principle is again fraud but as viewed from a sense of duty owed by all stockholders to one another. The apparent rationale is that by requiring each stockholder to exercise his individual judgment as to all matters presented, "[t]he security of the small stockholders is found in the natural disposition of each stockholder to promote the best interests of all, in order to promote his individual interests." Cone v. Russell, N.J. Ch., 21 A. 847, 849 (1891). In essence, while self interest motivates a stockholder's vote, theoretically, it is also advancing the interests of the other stockholders. Thus, any agreement entered into for personal gain, whereby a stockholder separates his voting right from his property right was considered a fraud upon this community of interests.

The often cited case of Brady v. Bean, 221 Ill. App. 279 (1921), is particularly enlightening. In that case, the plaintiff—an apparently influential stockholder—voiced his opposition to the corporation's proposed sale of assets. The plaintiff feared that his investment would be wiped out because the consideration for the sale appeared only sufficient enough to satisfy the corporation's creditors. As a result and without the knowledge of the other stockholders, the defendant, also a stockholder as well as a director and substantial creditor of the company, offered to the plaintiff in exchange for the withdrawal of his opposition, a sharing in defendant's claims against the corporation. In an action to enforce this contract against the defendant's estate, the Court refused relief stating:

"Appellant being a stockholder in the company, any contract entered into by him whereby he was to receive a personal consideration in return for either his action or his inaction in a matter such as a sale of all the company's assets, involving, as it did, the interests of all the stockholders, was contrary to public policy and void, it being admitted that such contract was not known by or assented to by the other stockholders. The purpose and effect of the contract was apparently to influence appellant, in his decision of a question affecting the rights and interests of his associate stockholders, by a consideration which was foreign to those rights and interests and would likely to induce him to disregard the consideration he owed them and the contract must, therefore, be regarded as a fraud upon them. Such an agreement will not be enforced, as being against public policy. Teich v. Kaufman, 174 Ill. App. 306; Guernsey v. Cook, 120 Mass. 501; Palmbaum v. Magulsky, 217 Mass. 306." (emphasis added) 221 Ill. App. at 283.

In addition to the deceit obviously practiced upon the other stockholders, the Court was clearly concerned with the rights and interests of the other stockholders. Thus, the potential injury or prejudicial impact which might flow to other stockholders as a result of such an agreement forms the heart of the rationale underlying the breach of public policy doctrine.

An automatic application of this rationale to the facts in the present case, however, would be to ignore an essential element of the transaction. The agreement in question was entered into primarily to further the interests of Texas International's other shareholders. Indeed, the shareholders, after reviewing a detailed proxy statement, voted overwhelmingly in favor of the loan agreement. Thus, the underlying rationale for the argument that vote-buying is illegal per se, as a matter of public policy, ceases to exist when measured against the undisputed reason for the transaction.

Moreover, the rationale that vote-buying is, as a matter of public policy, illegal per se is founded upon considerations of policy which are now outmoded as a necessary result of an evolving corporate environment. According to 5 Fletcher Cyclopedia Corporation (Perm. Ed.) § 2066:

"The theory that each stockholder is entitled to the personal judgment of each other stockholder expressed in his vote, and that any agreement among stockholders frustrating it was invalid, is obsolete because it is both impracticable and impossible of application to modern corporations with many widely scattered stockholders, and the courts have gradually abandoned it."

In addition, Delaware law has for quite some time permitted stockholders wide latitude in decisions affecting the restriction or transfer of voting rights. In Ringling Bros., Etc., Shows, Inc. v. Ringling, Del. Supr., 53 A.2d 441 (1947), the Delaware Supreme Court adopted a liberal approach to voting agreements which, prior to that time, were viewed with disfavor and were often considered void as a matter of public policy. In upholding a voting agreement the Court stated:

> "Generally speaking, a shareholder may exercise wide liberality of judgment in the matter of voting, and it is not objectionable that his motives may be for personal profit, or determined by whims or caprice, so long as he violates no duty owed his fellow stockholders." (citation omitted)

The Court's rationale was later codified in 8 Del. C. § 218(c), which [permits shareholder voting agreements]. . . .

Recently, in Oceanic Exploration Co. v. Grynberg, Del. Supr., 428 A.2d 1 (1981), the Delaware Supreme Court applied this approach to voting trusts. The Court also indicated, with approval, the liberal approach to all contractual arrangements limiting the incidents of stock ownership. Significantly, Oceanic involved the giving up of voting rights in exchange for personal gain. There, the stockholder, by way of a voting trust, gave up his right to vote on all corporate matters over a period of years in return for "valuable benefits including indemnity for large liabilities." 428 A.2d at 5.

Given the holdings in Ringling and Oceanic it is clear that Delaware has discarded the presumptions against voting agreements. Thus, under our present law, an agreement involving the transfer of stock voting rights without the transfer of ownership is not necessarily illegal and each arrangement must be examined in light of its object or purpose. To hold otherwise would be to exalt form over substance. As indicated in Oceanic more than the mere form of an agreement relating to voting must be considered and voting agreements in whatever form, therefore, should not be considered to be illegal per se unless the object or purpose is to defraud or in some way disenfranchise the other stockholders. This is not to say, however, that vote-buying accomplished for some laudable purpose is automatically free from challenge. Because vote-buying is so easily susceptible of abuse it must be viewed as a voidable transaction subject to a test for intrinsic fairness.

V

Apparently anticipating this finding, plaintiff also attempts to cast the loan agreement as one seeking to accomplish a fraudulent purpose. As indicative of fraud, plaintiff points to the fact that no other warrant holder was given a similar loan to enable an early exercise of the warrants. However, despite this contention, I am satisfied that, based on the record, there is no evidence from which an inference of a fraudulent object or purpose can be drawn.

As to the other warrant holders who did not get a loan, they were merely the holders of an expectant and contingent interest and, as such, were owed no duty by Texas International except as set forth in the warrant certificates. FOLK, The Delaware General Corporation Law, Little, Brown (1972) § 155, p. 126. In any event, the record fails to show any evidence that Texas International's ultimate decision to fund Jet Capital's early exercise of the warrants was motivated and accomplished except with the best interests of all Texas International stockholders in mind.

VI

I therefore hold that the agreement, whereby Jet Capital withdrew its opposition to the proposed merger in exchange for a loan to fund the early exercise of its warrants was not void per se because the object and purpose of the agreement was not to defraud or disenfranchise the other stockholders but rather was for the purpose of furthering the interest of all Texas International stockholders. The agreement, however, was a voidable act. Because the loan agreement was voidable it was susceptible to cure by shareholder approval. Michelson v. Duncan, Del. Supr., 407 A.2d 211 (1979). Consequently, the subsequent ratification of the transaction by a majority of the independent stockholders, after a full disclosure of all germane facts with complete candor precludes any further judicial inquiry of it.

* * *

VIII

In summary plaintiff's motion for summary judgment on the grounds that the transaction before the Court was permeated by vote-buying and was therefore void or voidable is denied. Defendants' motion for summary judgment on the grounds that plaintiff lacks standing to bring this suit or on the grounds that there is no factual basis for a claim of waste is denied.

It is so ordered.

QUESTIONS

1. What if the preferred in Texas International were held by a hostile investor, unlikely to approve the merger? Is this a barrier to an acquisition?

2. Would this approach work under the Model Act and the Delaware Act?

3. In Section IV of its opinion, the Schreiber court discussed the holding in Brady v. Bean, 221 Ill. App. 279 (1921), where a shareholder who was also a creditor of the corporation, seeking to cause the corporation to sell its assets, offered to share his gains as a creditor with another shareholder if he would drop his opposition and vote in favor of the

dissolution. The court characterizes this as causing a potential injury to other shareholders, because the motivating force was a creditor's claim, "a consideration which was foreign to those rights and interests [of the other stockholders]." How does this differ from the interests of Jet Capital? Are warrants to purchase stock claims that are foreign to the rights of the shareholders? Are they foreign if the warrant-holder can purchase shares at a price below the current market price, and thus would dilute the investment of the existing shareholders?

4. Can a prospective buyer of the corporation enter into an agreement with a major stockholder that it will vote in favor of a merger with the buyer, if the consideration is that the major stockholder will receive a premium over the merger price, in the form of either cash or buyer securities?

5. Assume that a bidding war has developed between two buyers for control of a target corporation. Can one bidder contract with a major shareholder for it to vote against a merger with its competitor, in return for an agreement to pay it a control premium for its shares after defeat of the merger?

6. How would the Schreiber court have decided Brady v. Bean? Why?

7. Recall that the Revised Model Business Corporation Act gives separate voting rights as a voting group to classes or series of stock in certain mergers. Could you restructure the transaction that Texas International wishes to engage in under the Model Act, using a share exchange, to avoid Jet Capital's veto power?

8. Delaware has recently added a provision allowing holding company mergers without a shareholder vote at all, in 8 Del. L. § 251(g). Would it have allowed Texas International to avoid the vote of the preferred?

NOTE

In Crown EMAK Partners LLC v. Kurz, 992 A.2d 377 (Del. 2010), the Delaware Supreme Court dealt with the sale of shares at a premium by a shareholder who knew he was selling the swing votes in a proxy contest. The Court affirmed the holding by the Chancery Court that this was not illegal vote buying, although it also held that the shares could not be lawfully sold because they were restricted as to transfer at the time. The opinion stated:

No Improper Vote Buying

For many years, Delaware decisions have expressed consistent concerns about transactions that create a misalignment between the voting interest and the economic interest of shares. As then Vice-Chancellor (now Chief Justice) Steele explained, "[g]enerally speaking, courts closely scrutinize vote-buying because a shareholder who divorces property interest from voting interest [ ] fails to serve the 'community of interest' among all shareholders, since the 'bought' shareholder votes may not reflect rational, economic self-interest arguably common to all shareholders."

Again, in this case, the Court of Chancery recognized that "[w]hat legitimizes the stockholder vote as a decision-making mechanism is the premise that stockholders with economic ownership are expressing their collective view as to whether a particular course of action serves the corporate goal of stockholder wealth maximization."[1]

Accordingly, the Court of Chancery held that "[p]olicing third-party vote buying does not rest on the outdated notion that every stockholder owes every other stockholder a duty to use its best judgment while voting. It flows instead from the legitimating conditions necessary for meaningful stockholder voting. . . ." The Court of Chancery concluded that:

> Because transactions in which economic interests are fully aligned with voting rights do not raise concern, Delaware law does not restrict a soliciting party from buying shares and getting a proxy to bolster the solicitation's chance of success. Delaware law presumes that in the sale of the underlying stock, the seller sells and assigns all of its rights, title and interest, "including its right to grant a consent or a revocation with respect to a past record date. . . ." Commonwealth Assocs. v. Providence Health Care, 641 A.2d at 158. Delaware law further presumes that "upon request the seller will, in good faith, take such ministerial steps as are necessary (*e.g.*, granting proxies) to effectuate the transfer." *Id.* Such transactions are common. John C. Wilcox, John J. Purcell III, & Hye-Won Choi, *"Street Name" Registration & The Proxy Solicitation Process*, at 10–26 in Amy Goodman, et al., *A Practical Guide to SEC Proxy and Compensation Rules* (4th Ed. 2007 & 2008 Supp.) ("[O]ver the course of a proxy contest, it is not uncommon for contestants to attempt to increase their voting power by purchasing additional shares. . . ."); Robert B. Thompson & Paul H. Edelman, *Corporate Voting*, 62 Vand. L. Rev. 129, 130 (2009) ("A corporate voter who has intense feelings about the matter to be determined can influence, if not control, the outcome by purchasing shares.").

Guided by these principles, the Court of Chancery scrutinized the Purchase Agreement as follows:

> I find no evidence of fraud in the transaction. The record indicates that Boutros was fully informed about the ongoing consent solicitations. Both factions had made multiple attempts to get him to commit to their side. Although there is no direct evidence establishing that Boutros knew his shares

---

[1] A Delaware public policy of guarding against the decoupling of economic ownership from voting power can be seen in the 2009 amendment to section 213(a), which now authorizes a board to set one record date for purposes of giving notice of a meeting of stockholders and a second, later record date for determining which stockholders can vote at the meeting. Del. Code Ann. tit. 8, § 213(a) (West Supp. 2010).

were the swing shares, I conclude that he must have been cognizant of this fact. He cut his deal with Kurz over the weekend before the Monday on which the TBE Consent Solicitation ended. At a time when EMAK's stock was trading on the pink sheets for less than a dollar, Boutros asked for $2.25 per share and received $1.50 per share. Boutros was advised by counsel and bargained to obtain specific terms for the deal, including an absence of representations and warranties and contractual indemnification from Kurz. These are the hallmarks of a transaction in which Boutros understood what he was selling, the circumstances under which he was selling it, and what he was getting in return.

This brings me to the *alignment of interests*. Although Kurz did not take title to the 150,000 shares that Boutros owned, and although I assume the Restricted Stock Grant Agreement prohibits Boutros from transferring title to Kurz until March 3, 2011, Boutros nevertheless transferred to Kurz, and *Kurz now bears, 100% of the economic risk* from the 150,000 shares. If the value of EMAK's shares drops further, then Kurz will suffer. If EMAK goes bankrupt and its shares become worthless, then Kurz will have a paper souvenir. Conversely, if EMAK turns itself around and prospers, then Kurz will benefit. Kurz has already paid Boutros. Kurz's only interest lies in how EMAK performs.

Because Kurz now holds the economic interest in the shares, Delaware law presumes that he should and will exercise the right to vote. Commonwealth Assocs. v. Providence Health Care, 641 A.2d at 158; *see* Len v. Fuller, 1997 Del. Ch. LEXIS 78, 1997 WL 305833, at *5 (Del. Ch. May 30, 1997) (barring record holder from voting shares by written consent after corporation exercised option to acquire shares); Freeman v. Fabiniak, 1985 Del. Ch. LEXIS 486, 1985 WL 11583, at *7 (Del. Ch. Aug. 15, 1985) ("[I]t would be inequitable to allow a holder of record who holds mere legal title to stock to act by consent in a manner contrary to the wishes of the true owner."). The proxy Boutros granted to Kurz under the Purchase Agreement comports with what our law expects. *See generally* John C. Wilcox, John J. Purcell III, & Hye-Won Choi, *"Street Name" Registration & The Proxy Solicitation Process* at 10–27 in Amy Goodman, et al., *A Practical Guide to SEC Proxy and Compensation Rules* 10–3 (4th ed. 2007 & 2008 Supp.) (explaining that a purchaser typically obtains an irrevocable proxy when shares are acquired from a registered holder).

We hold that the Court of Chancery correctly concluded that there was no improper vote buying, because the economic interests and the voting interests of the shares remained aligned since both sets of interests were transferred from Boutros to Kurz by the Purchase Agreement.

In Goldman v. Postal Telegraph, Inc., 52 F.Supp. 763 (D. Del.1943), the court sustained what was in effect a payment to holders of common stock to secure their consent to a liquidating asset sale. The suit was brought by a holder of preferred stock, who complained that the proceeds of the sale were less than the liquidation claims of the preferred, but that, in the vote submitted to the shareholders to approve the sale, it was proposed to amend the company's charter to provide that the preferred stockholders would receive stock of the buyer at a formula that left approximately 16% of the sale proceeds for the common stockholders. If the company had been liquidated, the plaintiff complained, the common stockholders would have received nothing. Accordingly, he argued that this amendment was simply a payment to the common stockholders to secure their votes, which were necessary to approve the sale. The court dismissed the complaint, stating:

> "The reality of the situation confronting Postal's management called for some inducement to be offered the common stockholders to secure their favorable vote for the plan. * * * The fact is something had to induce the common stockholders to come along. This court and the Delaware courts have recognized the strategic position of common stock to hamper the desires of the real owners of the equity of a corporation, and the tribute which common stock exacts for its vote under reclassification and reorganization."

NOTE ON CHOICE OF LAW FOR CALIFORNIA-BASED FOREIGN CORPORATIONS

Voting rules in mergers become confusing when one of the entities is based in California but incorporated elsewhere. California, unlike virtually all other states, does not strictly follow the Internal Affairs Doctrine of choice of law, which dictates that the law of the state of incorporation will govern relationships among the officers, directors, shareholders and the corporation. This rule is codified in MBCA § 15.05(c). The difficulties for transactional lawyers began with Western Air Lines, Inc. v. Sobieski, 191 Cal. App.2d 399, 12 Cal. Rptr. 719 (1961). Western, a Delaware corporation (subsequently acquired by Delta Air Lines), had 30% of its shares held by California residents and its operational center in California. Western's board proposed to eliminate cumulative voting after an insurgent group sought board seats, and prepared to solicit proxies from its shareholders to approve the amendment to its certificate of incorporation. Sobieski, the Corporations Commissioner of California, asserted that elimination of cumulative voting constituted an exchange of a new class of shares for the outstanding shares, which subjected the transaction to the California Securities Act, which gave the Commissioner authority to determine whether an exchange was "fair, just or equitable." He determined that it was not fair and denied a permit for the transaction. On appeal his position was sustained by the California Court of Appeals. Western argued that this amendment and the vote to obtain its approval were part of the internal affairs of the corporation, and thus subject only to Delaware law. The court conceded that California had no jurisdiction over the internal affairs of a Delaware corporation, but that it had jurisdiction over a sale or exchange of stock in California. The Commissioner and the court characterized Western as "pseudo-foreign corporation," because of its significant contacts with the state.

California has codified this doctrine, expanding it from its basis under the California Securities Act, to cover "pseudo-foreign corporations" under various provisions of California law, including mergers and asset sales. Cal. Corp. Code § 2115, with an exclusion for corporations with shares traded on the New York or American stock exchanges or on the NASDAQ National Market. Pseudo-foreign corporations are defined as those that conduct half their business in California as measured by a formula weighing property, payroll and sales located in California, and more than 50% of its shares are held in California. The California courts have consistently upheld the validity of these provisions against challenges under the full faith and credit clause, the commerce clause and the equal protection clause, generally finding that what was mandatory under California law was a permitted option under the law of the state of incorporation.

Delaware courts recently have taken a different view of this conflict. Examen, Inc. was a privately owned Delaware corporation headquartered in California that apparently met the "pseudo-foreign corporation" standards of California law. Examen entered into a merger agreement with Reed Elsevier, Inc., which Examen's board approved on Feb. 15, 2005 that expired on April 15, 2005. Examen had a class of preferred stock outstanding that had no separate class voting rights in its certificate of incorporation, meaning that all shares would vote as a single group under Del. GCL § 251(c). VantagePoint Venture Partners 1996, owns 83% of the preferred stock, convertible into 1.6 million common shares, in addition to the 8.6 million common shares already outstanding. On March 3, 2006, Examen filed suit in the Delaware Chancery Court seeking a declaratory judgment that its merger vote is subject only to Delaware law, and that California law does not govern. In response, on March 8 VantagePoint sued in the California courts seeking discovery to establish that Examen is subject to Cal. Corp. Code § 2115, and that if it is, that separate class voting is required, which would give VantagePoint a veto power over the merger. Following the lead of the California decisions, VantagePoint argued that there was no irreconcilable conflict between the two laws, and that California law, just like the rules of stock exchanges, simply gave stockholders an additional layer of protection that is not inconsistent with Delaware law. The Chancery Court noted that VantagePoint's argument was weakened by the language of § 2115(b), which provided that the listed provisions of California law "shall apply to a foreign corporation as defined in subdivision (a) (*to the exclusion of the law of the jurisdiction in which it is incorporated*). . . ." (Emphasis supplied.) VantagePoint responded that Delaware law permits separate class voting; it simply doesn't mandate it. The Chancery Court rejected this argument, noting that application of California law would be "in derogation of the rights of Examen's other stockholders," so that the court could not enforce both Delaware and California law. The Chancery Court treated this as a question of choice of law, and applied the internal affairs doctrine of choice of law of Delaware to hold that the law of Delaware, and not that of California, applies to a Delaware corporation.

On expedited appeal, the Delaware Supreme Court affirmed. Citing *dicta* in a case involving the validity of takeover defenses under the Commerce Clause, CTS Corp. v. Dynamics Corp. of America, 481 U.S. 69 (1987) [see page 514, *infra*], in which Justice Powell noted that the court had struck down statutes that imposed inconsistent regulations on activities. But it was not content to affirm simply on the choice of law grounds. The court noted that California's attempt to supplant the law of the state of incorporation for a pseudo-foreign corporation might apply in one year when the criteria were met, but not apply in a subsequent year, leaving a corporation uncertain about the governing law. The court held that under the Due Process Clause "directors and officers of corporations 'have a significant right to know what law will apply to their actions' and 'stockholders . . . have a right to know by what standards of accountability they may hold those managing the corporation's business and affairs," and that the internal affairs doctrine is mandated by constitutional principles. The opinion went on, gratuitously, to suggest that the California courts would likely agree with this analysis in light of cases such as CTS. VantagePoint Venture Partners 1996 v. Examen, Inc., 871 A.2d 1108 (2005).

---

2. SHORT FORM MERGERS

Revised Model Business Corporation Act § 11.05; Delaware General Corporation Law §§ 251(f) and (h) and 253.

Generally under the Model Business Corporation Act shareholders of both corporations that are parties to a statutory merger must vote to approve the merger. One exception appears in Model Act § 11.05, for "short form" mergers of parents and subsidiaries, where only the board (and possibly the shareholders) of the parent corporation must approve the transaction. Delaware General Corporation Law § 253 contains a comparable provision. While the Model Act limits this power to corporations where the parent owns at least 90% of the subsidiary's shares, Delaware GCL § 251(h) was added in 2013 to permit short form mergers when the parent controls a majority of the stock under certain conditions. Section 251(h) is set forth below:

> (h) Notwithstanding the requirements of subsection (c) of this section, unless expressly required by its certificate of incorporation, no vote of stockholders of a constituent corporation whose shares are listed on a national securities exchange or held of record by more than 2,000 holders immediately prior to the execution of the agreement of merger by such constituent corporation shall be necessary to authorize a merger if:

(1) The agreement of merger, which must be entered into on or after August 1, 2013, expressly provides that such merger shall be governed by this subsection and shall be effected as soon as practicable following the consummation of the offer referred to in paragraph (h)(2) of this section;

(2) A corporation consummates a tender or exchange offer for any and all of the outstanding stock of such constituent corporation on the terms provided in such agreement of merger that, absent this subsection, would be entitled to vote on the adoption or rejection of the agreement of merger;

(3) Following the consummation of such offer, the consummating corporation owns at least such percentage of the stock, and of each class or series thereof, of such constituent corporation that, absent this subsection, would be required to adopt the agreement of merger by this chapter and by the certificate of incorporation of such constituent corporation;

(4) At the time such constituent corporation's board of directors approves the agreement of merger, no other party to such agreement is an "interested stockholder" (as defined in § 203(c) of this title) of such constituent corporation;

(5) The corporation consummating the offer described in paragraph (h)(2) of this section merges with or into such constituent corporation pursuant to such agreement; and

(6) The outstanding shares of each class or series of stock of the constituent corporation not to be canceled in the merger are to be converted in such merger into, or into the right to receive, the same amount and kind of cash, property, rights or securities paid for shares of such class or series of stock of such constituent corporation upon consummation of the offer referred to in paragraph (h)(2) of this section.

If an agreement of merger is adopted without the vote of stockholders of a corporation pursuant to this subsection, the secretary or assistant secretary of the surviving corporation shall certify on the agreement that the agreement has been adopted pursuant to this subsection and that the conditions specified in this subsection (other than the condition listed in paragraph (h)(5) of this section) have been satisfied; provided that such certification on the agreement shall not be required if a certificate of merger is filed in lieu of filing the agreement. The agreement so adopted and certified shall then be filed and shall become effective, in accordance with § 103 of this title. Such filing shall constitute a representation by the person who executes the agreement that the facts stated in the certificate remain true immediately prior to such filing.

3. TRIANGULAR MERGERS

"Straight" mergers ("A" reorganizations) frequently involve a vote of the shareholders of the acquiring corporation, with its attendant expense and delays. Where the target is a closely held corporation where shareholder consent can be obtained quickly, the costs and delays of obtaining shareholder approval for the buyer can become a major irritant and expense. There are some exceptions from this voting requirement Thus, if the acquired firm is relatively small compared to the acquiring firm, it may be that the number of shares of common stock to be offered will be sufficiently small so that no shareholder vote will be required to increase the authorized but unissued shares. Rev. Model Bus. Corp. Act § 11.04(g) excuses a vote by the shareholders of the surviving corporation if its conditions are met: (1) there is no change in the articles of incorporation of the surviving corporation; (2) there is no change in the rights of the existing shareholders (except for dilution); and (3) the number of shares of common stock outstanding will not increase by more than 20%. Similar rules appear in Del. Gen. Corp. L. § 251(f). But even where state law does not require a shareholder vote, other authorities may. Companies with shares listed on the New York Stock Exchange are required to seek shareholder approval if the shares issued will increase outstanding stock by 20% or more. New York Stock Exchange Listed Company Manual, § 312.03(c). See also NASDAQ Marketplace Rule 5635. Thus a cash merger frequently will not require a shareholder vote for the acquiring corporation, if the charter is not changed.

The triangular merger offers another way to avoid a shareholder vote for the acquiring firm in some cases. The triangular merger is a development of 1967 revisions of both Delaware law and the Model Business Corporation Act that permitted the consideration in a merger to consist of "shares or other securities, eligible interests, obligations, rights to acquire shares, other securities or eligible interests, cash, other property or any combination of the foregoing." Rev. Model Bus. Corp. Act § 11.02(c)(3); see also Del. Laws tit. 8, § 251(b)(5). The effect of these revisions is to allow the acquiring corporation to use a subsidiary corporation as the merger vehicle.

(1) In this situation the acquiring corporation typically creates an acquisition subsidiary, which issues all of its outstanding common stock to its parent. The merger agreement then involves three parties: the acquiring corporation, its acquisition subsidiary, and the selling corporation.

(2) The acquisition subsidiary then merges with the target corporation.

(3) The shares of the target corporation are canceled in the merger, and former target shareholders receive the merger consideration from the acquiring firm, which is the parent of the acquisition subsidiary. The requisite shareholder vote on the buyer's side is by the shareholder of the acquisition subsidiary. The Merger Agreement and Plan of Reorganization in Appendix C is an example of a triangular merger. The following chart illustrates a reverse triangular merger, in which the Target is the surviving corporation.

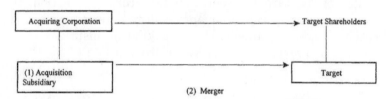

The acquisition lawyer may consider alternatives to "straight" statutory mergers for several reasons. First, a triangular merger isolates the target's liabilities from the parent corporation, which may be important where contingent liabilities, such as product liabilities or environmental liabilities are a risk. Second, it also has the effect of separating the labor forces of the two businesses. If the parent is subject to a union collective bargaining agreement and the target is not, keeping the target separate may avoid the obligation to include the target's employees in the collective bargaining unit.

Third, the triangular merger is a more flexible means of accomplishing a tax-free reorganization (as an "A" reorganization) than most other means. In stock or asset acquisitions, there are severe restrictions on using anything but the acquiring corporation's common stock as consideration. In a "B" reorganization, the bidder must offer its voting stock for at least 80% of the target's stock. In a "C" reorganization, the bidder must offer its voting stock for the assets of the target corporation (although some non-stock consideration, or "boot" is permitted). A triangular merger, in order to qualify as an "A" reorganization, only requires approximately 50% of the consideration to be the bidder's voting stock, while the remainder can be cash or other securities.

A reverse triangular merger involves creation and funding of the acquisition subsidiary in the same manner as in a triangular merger. The only difference is that the target corporation is the surviving corporation. Not only does this preserve the corporate identity of the target, it offers the other advantages of the triangular merger. Preserving the target may be important for a variety of reasons. Its name may carry considerable good will that can best be preserved by preserving both the entity and its name. In some circumstances it may be that no additional regulatory approvals will be required for existing leases, loan agreements, licenses or franchises if the target is preserved. See, e.g., Meso Scale Diagnostics, LLC v. Roche Diagnostics GMBH, 62 A.3d 62 (Del. Ch. 2013) (holding that anti-assignment clauses in a license were not violated by a reverse triangular merger). For an extended discussion of the advantages of the triangular merger see Note, Three-Party Mergers: The Fourth Form of Corporate Acquisition, 57 Va. L. Rev. 1242 (1971). The merger agreement in Appendix C contemplates a reverse triangular merger.

Changes in the Model Act have created a substitute for the reverse triangular merger in the share exchange. In a share exchange shareholders of the target corporation take corporate action, through board resolution and shareholder approval, to determine whether they wish to exchange their shares for the same kind of consideration that can be offered in a merger. Rev. Model Bus. Corp. Act § 11.03.

California Corporation Code § 1201; Rev. Model Bus. Corp. Act § 11.04(f) & (g); Del. Gen. Corp. L. § 251(f).

The following case illustrates a way to avoid a preferred stock veto by using a reverse triangular merger.

Kirschner Brothers Oil, Inc. v. Natomas Company

185 Cal. App.3d 784, 229 Cal. Rptr. 899 (Ct. App. 1986).

■ SCOTT, ASSOCIATE JUSTICE.

Plaintiffs, all holders of Natomas Company (Natomas) preferred stock, filed similar actions against Natomas, one of its directors, and Diamond Shamrock Corporation. Plaintiffs sought to enjoin a proposed merger, as well as damages for breach of fiduciary duty. After a preliminary injunction was denied, the merger or reorganization was effected. According to its terms, each share of Natomas preferred was exchanged for a share of the preferred stock of another corporation, New Diamond. Subsequently summary judgment was entered in favor of defendants. Plaintiffs, now all former Natomas preferred shareholders, have appealed. The merger triggered several lawsuits, and this is the third such case which this court has recently considered.

I

Natomas is a California corporation. In 1980, 2.5 million Natomas $4 "Series C" cumulative convertible preferred shares were issued. The rights of the preferred shareholders were specified in a certificate of determination issued by the Natomas board of directors.

In May 1983, Diamond Shamrock Corporation, through a wholly owned subsidiary, commenced a hostile tender offer for Natomas common stock and stated its intention to propose a merger between Natomas and the subsidiary. Shortly thereafter, the boards of Diamond Shamrock and

Natomas approved a plan and agreement of reorganization between the two companies, and the tender offer was terminated.

According to the plan, a new holding company, New Diamond, was to be formed, which in turn would form two wholly owned subsidiaries, D Sub, Inc., and N Sub, Inc. In two reverse triangular "phantom" mergers, D Sub, Inc., would merge into Diamond Shamrock, and N Sub, Inc., into Natomas; New Diamond would issue New Diamond common shares to common shareholders of Natomas and Diamond Shamrock in exchange for their shares. New Diamond would thus become the sole shareholder of Natomas' common shares.

* * *

The agreement was to be submitted to Natomas common and preferred shareholders, voting as separate classes. Upon the approval of each class, the Natomas common shares would be converted into New Diamond common shares and the Natomas preferred into New Diamond preferred, convertible into New Diamond common. Failure to obtain the approval of the Natomas preferred shareholders would not prevent consummation of the merger, however, and it is that feature of the reorganization plan which is at the heart of this litigation. If a majority of Natomas common shareholders approved the agreement but its preferred shareholders did not, the reorganization would still take place. The Natomas common shares would be converted into New Diamond common, but the Natomas preferred would remain outstanding and continue to be convertible into Natomas common.

Between the date of the initial hostile tender offer by Diamond Shamrock and the announcement of the reorganization agreement, Kirschner Brothers Oil, Inc., and others (the Kirschner plaintiffs) purchased 6,000 Natomas preferred shares. On July 8, 1983, the Kirschner plaintiffs filed a class action against Natomas, its president and chief executive officer, Dorman L. Commons, and Diamond Shamrock, seeking damages and an order enjoining the proposed reorganization. Among their allegations was that consummation of the merger without an affirmative vote of a majority of the preferred shareholders would violate Corporations Code section 1201 and the certificate of determination specifying the rights of Natomas preferred shareholders; they also alleged a breach of the fiduciary duty owed by Natomas and Dorman L. Commons to the preferred shareholders. A similar complaint was filed by David R. Kotok and the Cumberland Growth Fund, Inc., other holders of Natomas preferred shares.

The actions were consolidated and on August 1, 1983, in a written opinion, the trial court denied a preliminary injunction. On August 30, 1983, at a special meeting of Natomas common and preferred shareholders, a majority of each class of shareholders voted to approve the reorganization plan which provided for the conversion of Natomas common shares into New Diamond common and Natomas preferred into

New Diamond preferred, and the mergers were carried out. In mid-1984, defendants' motions for summary judgment were granted and judgments were entered in their favor.[3] Both groups of plaintiffs appealed, and their appeals have been consolidated in this court.

II

* * *

a.

We consider plaintiffs' first contention that defendants breached their fiduciary duties by abridging the preferred shareholders' statutory right under section 1201, subdivision (a), to vote on the Natomas merger.

The Corporations Code recognizes several methods of reorganization whereby two or more corporations are combined into a single business enterprise. (§ 181; 2 Marsh's Cal. Corporation Law, *supra*, § 18.1–18.15, pp. 478–507.) Section 1201 spells out when a vote by the shareholders of any corporation involved in a reorganization is required. Subdivision (a) of section 1201 provides in pertinent part: "The principal terms of a reorganization shall be approved by the outstanding shares . . . of each class of each corporation the approval of whose board is required under Section 1200 . . . except that (unless otherwise provided in the articles) no approval of any class of outstanding preferred shares of the surviving or acquiring corporation or parent party shall be required if the rights, preferences, privileges and restrictions granted to or imposed upon such class of shares remain unchanged. . . ." (Italics added.)

Plaintiffs contend that despite the appearance of the transaction at issue, in reality Natomas was acquired by Diamond Shamrock. Therefore, plaintiffs reason, Natomas was not a "surviving corporation" under either reorganization alternative and the preferred shareholders' approval was required by section 1201, subdivision (a), for either to become effective.

Ignoring for the moment the fact that a majority of the preferred shareholders did approve the reorganization, we consider the argument unpersuasive. The reorganization at issue here was structured as a "reverse triangular 'phantom' merger," well-recognized as a method of reorganization which preserves the existing corporate entity of the target corporation. Notwithstanding the fact that the parent holding company, New Diamond, would wholly own Natomas, it is still undisputed that N Sub, Inc., corporation merged into Natomas, leaving the latter intact as a legal entity. Similarly, D Sub, Inc., merged into Diamond Shamrock, which also remained a legal entity. The Corporations Code defines a "surviving corporation" simply as "a corporation into which one or more

---

[3] One needs a scorecard to keep track of the corporate name changes in this case. After the reorganization, Diamond Shamrock Corporation changed its name to Diamond Chemicals Company, but will be referred to as Diamond Shamrock in this opinion. New Diamond, the holding company, changed its name to Diamond Shamrock Corporation, but will be referred to in this opinion as New Diamond.

other corporations are merged." (§ 190.) In another case which arose out of this same corporate reorganization, Gaillard v. Natomas Co. (1985) 173 Cal. App.3d 410 [219 Cal. Rptr. 74], this court has already recognized the continued existence of Natomas after the reorganization. (*Id.*, at p. 336.)

* * *

b.

Plaintiffs also contend that even if Natomas was a surviving corporation, their vote was required under section 1201, subdivision (a), because their rights were being changed. They argue that the reorganization plan unlawfully deprived them of rights guaranteed by the certificate of determination under which their preferred shares were issued. As we understand this contention, it is identical to that unsuccessfully urged below in support of the motion for preliminary injunction. There, plaintiffs argued that the second alternative proposal, which would have permitted merger without their vote and left them with Natomas preferred, would have adversely affected their right to a public market for Natomas common and preferred shares. In other words, under that alternative, the preferred's rights, preferences and privileges would not have remained unchanged; thus reorganization under that alternative without their vote would have violated section 1201, subdivision (a).

The trial court rejected the argument that the preferred had a right to a public market for their shares and denied the injunction. Thereafter, as already discussed, a majority of both the common and preferred shareholders voted to approve the plan which gave them New Diamond shares for their shares. On appeal, if this "right to a public market" argument survives even though the preferred shareholders voted to approve the reorganization, it does so because plaintiffs now argue that their affirmative vote was unlawfully coerced. Plaintiffs insist that the preferred had no real choice but to approve the merger. Plaintiffs reason that the reorganization plan made it economically unfeasible for the preferred shareholders to remain as shareholders of Natomas because as a practical matter the conversion value and marketability of their Natomas shares would vanish with the merger. The preferred shareholders were thus forced to approve the reorganization and accept the alternative which granted them preferred shares in New Diamond.

Plaintiffs' rights and privileges argument before the trial court rested on the premise that as preferred shareholders, they had a right to the continued existence of a public market for their shares, but no authority cited then or now supports that proposition, and Kessler v. General Cable Corp. (1979) 92 Cal. App.3d 531 [155 Cal. Rptr. 94] holds otherwise.

* * *

III

Plaintiffs contend that there is a triable issue of fact as to whether defendants breached their fiduciary duty to the preferred shareholders by structuring the merger to the detriment of those shareholders and by "negotiating for themselves" while failing to protect or enhance the interests of those shareholders.

In support of this contention, plaintiffs focus primarily on Jones v. H. F. Ahmanson & Co., *supra*, 1 Cal.3d 93.* Although the issue in Ahmanson was the fiduciary duty of majority to minority shareholders, the court also spoke in strong language of a director's fiduciary duty. It cautioned that a director must not use his power for his personal advantage and to the detriment of the stockholders no matter how absolute in terms that power may be and no matter how meticulous he is to satisfy technical requirements. (*Id.*, at pp. 108–109.) Relying on Ahmanson, plaintiffs urge that in negotiating the reorganization, defendants did not protect the interests and rights of the preferred shareholders.

* * *

Next, holding that the complaint stated a cause of action, the court [in Jones v. Ahmanson] spoke more precisely about the parameters of the duty of majority shareholders in the context of the facts alleged. "[W]e do not suggest that the duties of corporate fiduciaries include in all cases an obligation to make a market for and to facilitate public trading in the stock of the corporation. But when, as here, no market exists, the controlling shareholders may not use their power to control the corporation for the purpose of promoting a marketing scheme that benefits themselves alone to the detriment of the minority." (Jones v. H. F. Ahmanson & Co., *supra*, 1 Cal.3d at p. 106.)

In this case, relying on the sweep of the court's language in Ahmanson, plaintiffs argue that defendants' fiduciary duties were broader than their contractual and statutory obligations to the preferred shareholders. Nevertheless, what plaintiffs overlook is that after

---

*   In Jones v. H. F. Ahmanson & Co., 1 Cal.3d 93, 460 P.2d 464 (Cal. 1969), the defendants, the majority shareholders in United Savings and Loan Association, a corporation the shares of which were not publicly traded, exchanged their Association shares for shares in a newly incorporated holding company. The holding company then engaged in a public offering and created a public market for its shares. Because the holding company owned 85% of the savings and loan association's shares, the remaining shares of the savings and loan association were rendered unmarketable, in the view of the court. Subsequently, the holding company offered to exchange its shares for the remaining stock of the savings and loan association, but on less favorable terms than the majority shareholders had received. Plaintiff sued on the basis that the majority shareholders had breached a fiduciary duty owed to the minority. Chief Justice Traynor noted that the association's management had made no effort to make its stock marketable, and that the defendants, rather than choosing this course that would have benefitted all shareholders, chose to create a holding company that benefitted the majority to the exclusion of (and damage to) the minority. The court held that they breached their duty when "they used their control of the Association to obtain an advantage not made available to all stockholders."—Ed.

discussing the rule of inherent fairness in general terms, the Ahmanson court carefully related that rule to the facts alleged. Plaintiffs in this case ignore that step. They fail to explain with any specificity what they, as preferred shareholders, might have been entitled to that they did not receive, or how defendants violated the rule of "inherent fairness." Nor do they address the obligations owed by the directors to the common shareholders under the facts involved here.

Preferred shares are those which have a preference over other shares either as to distribution of assets on liquidation or as to payment of dividends, or some other combination of rights, preferences, privileges, and restrictions. "Since the relation between the holders of preferred stock and the corporation is contractual, the extent of their right to share in the corporate profits and of their preference over common stockholders depends upon the terms of their contract." In this state, the articles of incorporation and the certificate of determination define the rights, preferences, and privileges granted to preferred shareholders.

Preferred shares have been described as "a distinctive and often unsatisfactory security. They have been compared to debt securities, since practically they represent only a preferential claim to a specified rate of return and return of capital . . . rather than a meaningful ownership interest. . . ." (1 Ballantine & Sterling, Cal. Corporation Laws, *supra*, § 127.03 at p. 7–50, fn. omitted.) Another commentator notes that holders of common stock "can object to and prevent any arrangement or transaction entered into or threatened by the company for the purpose of putting the preferred stockholders on a more favorable footing than is secured to them by their contract." (11 Fletcher, Cyclopedia of Corporations (rev. ed. 1986) Stocks and Stockholders, § 5305, p. 679, fn. omitted.)

As defendants point out, courts in other jurisdictions have generally rejected the claims of preferred shareholders to rights and preferences other than those defined or necessarily implied in their contract. * * *

In light of the foregoing authority, we conclude that in this case, the fiduciary duty of the directors of Natomas did not include the obligation to negotiate or structure the reorganization such that the preferred shareholders would receive rights and privileges in excess of their entitlement under the certificate of determination.

* * *

IV

When the trial court in this case ruled on the motion for summary judgment, it acknowledged the "fairness doctrine," but concluded that its application did not require defendants to obtain something more for the preferred shareholders than they were entitled to by statute or by the "governing corporate documents." The court concluded that plaintiffs were provided with the voting rights to which they were entitled under section 1201 and the certificate of determination. It also concluded that defendants' fiduciary duty to plaintiffs did not encompass the duty to negotiate for some unspecified financial benefits to which plaintiffs were not entitled by statute or the certificate of determination. We agree. Summary judgment was proper.

Judgment is affirmed.

■ WHITE, P. J., and BARRY-DEAL, J., concurred.

_____

QUESTIONS

1. Why isn't the approval of the holders of the preferred stock required for this merger?

2. Why do plaintiffs argue that § 1201 of the California Corporation Code doesn't excuse a vote of preferred shareholders because Natomas was not an acquiring or surviving corporation?

3. What rights of the Natomas Preferred do plaintiffs claim were changed by the merger?

4. What did the plaintiffs mean when they argued that the vote of the preferred approving the merger was coerced?

5. Would it have mattered if the court had concluded that the vote was coerced?

6. Based on this opinion, do directors owe fiduciary duties to preferred shareholders? If there are some fiduciary duties, what is their extent?

7. Are there contract doctrines that would provide the preferred shareholders with some protection of their conversion rights, similar to the fiduciary obligations for which they argue?

8. Would Section 11.04(f) of the Revised Model Business Corporation Act change the outcome in this case, if applicable? If not, what should the drafters of the preferred stock have provided in order to protect against this kind of change without a class vote?

_____

4. ASSET PURCHASES

Model Business Corporation Act, §§ 12.01 & 12.02; Delaware General Corporation Law, § 271.

The purchase of assets rather than a merger is sometimes attractive because the buyer does not take all of the liabilities of the seller (although this is subject to further qualification with respect to certain liabilities). This may be attractive where the purchaser has more difficulties than the seller in valuing the exposure. Asset sales trigger their own sets of rules concerning target shareholder approval of proposed transactions.

In some cases the sales are of less than all assets. Questions then arise about the need for a vote of the common shareholders.

The following case is set at the time of a radical change in oil and gas prices, caused by the formation of the OPEC cartel in 1973 and the tripling of the price of Persian Gulf crude oil in a few months. It is possible that the sale agreement was reached immediately before the formation of OPEC, and the closing was to be after prices had risen. The purchase price is $480 million. As evidence of the rapid change in values at this time, Chancellor Quillen noted that at the board meeting considering the sale, "[i]t appears that there was some review of the per share value of Signal stock and it was determined that, as of the market closing on December 20, the total market value of Signal stock was estimated at 440 million dollars." 316 A.2d at 612.

Gimbel v. The Signal Companies, Inc.

316 A.2d 599 (Del. Ch.1974).

■ QUILLEN, CHANCELLOR:

This action was commenced on December 24, 1973 by plaintiff, a stockholder of the Signal Companies, Inc. ("Signal"). The complaint seeks, among other things, injunctive relief to prevent the consummation of the pending sale by Signal to Burmah Oil Incorporated ("Burmah") of all of the outstanding capital stock of Signal Oil and Gas Company ("Signal Oil"), a wholly-owned subsidiary of Signal. The effective sale price exceeds 480 million dollars. The sale was approved at a special meeting of the Board of Directors of Signal held on December 21, 1973.

* * * This is the Court's decision on plaintiff's application for a preliminary injunction to prevent the sale of Signal Oil to Burmah pending trial on the merits of plaintiff's contentions. * * *

Turning specifically to the pleadings in this case, the complaint contains three separate counts. In Count 1 of the complaint, plaintiff asserts that the special meeting of the Board of Directors of Signal at which the proposed sale was approved and authorized and was not properly noticed and that the proposed sale requires authorization by the majority of the outstanding stock of Signal pursuant to 8 Del. C. § 271(a).

* * *

I turn first to the question of 8 Del. C. § 271(a) which requires majority stockholder approval for the sale of "all or substantially all" of the assets of a Delaware corporation. A sale of less than all or substantially all assets is not covered by negative implication from the statute. Folk, The Delaware General Corporation Law, Section 271, p. 400, ftnt. 3; 8 Del. C. § 141(a).

It is important to note in the first instance that the statute does not speak of a requirement of shareholder approval simply because an independent, important branch of a corporate business is being sold. The plaintiff cites several non-Delaware cases for the proposition that shareholder approval of such a sale is required. But that is not the language of our statute. Similarly, it is not our law that shareholder approval is required upon every "major" restructuring of the corporation. Again, it is not necessary to go beyond the statute. The statute requires shareholder approval upon the sale of "all or substantially all" of the corporation's assets. That is the sole test to be applied. While it is true that test does not lend itself to a strict mathematical standard to be applied in every case, the qualitative factor can be defined to some degree notwithstanding the limited Delaware authority. But the definition must begin with and ultimately necessarily relate to our statutory language.

In interpreting the statute the plaintiff relies on Philadelphia National Bank v. B.S.F. Co., 41 Del. Ch. 509, 199 A.2d 557; (Ch. 1964), rev'd on other grounds, 42 Del. Ch. 106, 204 A.2d 746 (Sup. Ct. 1964). In that case, B.S.F. Company owned stock in two corporations. It sold its stock in one of the corporations, and retained the stock in the other corporation. The Court found that the stock sold was the principal asset B.S.F. Company had available for sale and that the value of the stock retained was declining. The Court rejected the defendant's contention that the stock sold represented only 47.4% of consolidated assets, and looked to the actual value of the stock sold. On this basis, the Court held that the stock constituted at least 75% of the total assets and the sale of the stock was a sale of substantially all assets.

But two things must be noted about the Philadelphia National Bank case. First, even though shareholder approval was obtained under § 271, the case did not arise under § 271 but under an Indenture limiting the activities of B.S.F. for creditor financial security purposes. On appeal, Chief Justice Wolcott was careful to state the following:

> "We are of the opinion that this question is not necessarily to be answered by references to the general law concerning the sale of assets by a corporation. The question before us is the narrow one of what particular language of a contract means and is to be answered in terms of what the parties were intending to guard against or to insure."

42 Del. Ch. at 111–112, 204 A.2d at 750.

Secondly, the Philadelphia National Bank case dealt with the sale of the company's only substantial income producing asset.

The key language in the Court of Chancery opinion in Philadelphia National Bank is the suggestion that "the critical factor in determining the character of a sale of assets is generally considered not the amount of property sold but whether the sale is in fact an unusual transaction or one made in the regular course of business of the seller." (41 Del. Ch. at 515, 199 A.2d at 561). Professor Folk suggests from the opinion that "the statute would be inapplicable if the assets sale is 'one made in furtherance of express corporate objects in the ordinary and regular course of the business'" (referring to language in 41 Del. Ch. at 516, 199 A.2d at 561). Folk, *supra*, Section 271, p. 401.

But any "ordinary and regular course of business" test in this context obviously is not intended to limit the directors to customary daily business activities. Indeed, a question concerning the statute would not arise unless the transaction was somewhat out of the ordinary. While it is true that a transaction in the ordinary course of business does not require shareholder approval, the converse is not true. Every transaction out of normal routine does not necessarily require shareholder approval. The unusual nature of the transaction must strike at the heart of the corporate existence and purpose. As it is written at 6A Fletcher, Encyclopedia Corporations (Perm. Ed. 1968 Rev.) § 2949.2, p. 648:

> "The purpose of the consent statutes is to protect the shareholders from fundamental change, or more specifically to protect the shareholders from the destruction of the means to accomplish the purposes or objects for which the corporation was incorporated and actually performs."

It is in this sense that the "unusual transaction" judgment is to be made and the statute's applicability determined. If the sale is of assets quantitatively vital to the operation of the corporation and is out of the ordinary and substantially affects the existence and purpose of the corporation, then it is beyond the power of the Board of Directors. With these guidelines, I turn to Signal and the transaction in this case.

Signal or its predecessor was incorporated in the oil business in 1922. But, beginning in 1952, Signal diversified its interests. In 1952, Signal acquired a substantial stock interest in American President lines. From 1957 to 1962 Signal was the sole owner of Laura Scudders, a nationwide snack food business. In 1964, Signal acquired Garrett Corporation which is engaged in the aircraft, aerospace, and uranium enrichment business. In 1967, Signal acquired Mack Trucks, Inc., which is engaged in the manufacture and sale of trucks and related equipment. Also in 1968, the oil and gas business was transferred to a separate division and later in 1970 to the Signal Oil subsidiary. Since 1967, Signal has made acquisition of or formed substantial companies none of which are involved or related with the oil and gas industry. As indicated previously, the oil and gas production development of Signal's business is now carried on by Signal Oil, the sale of the stock of which is an issue in this lawsuit.

According to figures published in Signal's last annual report (1972) and the interest quarterly report (September 30, 1973) and certain other internal financial information, the following tables can be constructed:

SIGNAL'S REVENUES (in millions)

	9 Mos. Ended September 30, 1973	December 31, 1972	1971
Truck manufacturing	$655.9	$712.7	$552.5
Aerospace and industrial	407.1	478.2	448.0
Oil and gas	185.8	267.2	314.1
Other	16.4	14.4	14.0

SIGNAL'S PRE-TAX EARNINGS (in millions)

	9 Mos. Ended September 30, 1973	December 31, 1972	1971
Truck manufacturing	$55.8	$65.5	$36.4
Aerospace and industrial	20.7	21.5	19.5
Oil and gas	10.1	12.8	9.9

SIGNAL'S ASSETS (in millions)*

	9 Mos. Ended September 30, 1973	December 31, 1972	1971
Truck manufacturing	$581.4	$506.5	$450.4
Aerospace and industrial	365.2	351.1	331.5
Oil and gas	376.2	368.3	69.9
Other	113.1	102.0	121.6

---

*   Signal had requested Kenneth E. Hill, an expert in the evaluation of oil properties, to undertake an evaluation of the petroleum properties of Signal Oil. Mr. Hill had done so and, as of September 13, 1973, his opinion of the fair market value of the oil properties was $350,000,000. Hill concluded that their worth had reached $410,000,000 by December 21, 1973. Plaintiff's expert estimated the value of the oil and gas properties at $761 million.—Ed.

SIGNAL'S NET WORTH (in millions)

	9 Mos. Ended September 30, 1973	December 31, 1972	1971
Truck manufacturing	$295.0	$269.7	$234.6
Aerospace and industrial	163.5	152.2	139.6
Oil and gas	280.5	273.2	254.4
Other	(55.7)	(42.1)	(2.0)

Based on the company's figures, Signal Oil represents only about 26% of the total assets of Signal. While Signal Oil represents 41% of Signal's total net worth, it produces only about 15% of Signal's revenues and earnings. Moreover, the additional tables shown in Signal's brief from the Chitiea affidavit are also interesting in demonstrating the low rate of return which has been realized recently from the oil and gas operations.

PRE-TAX DOLLAR RETURN
ON VALUE OF ASSETS

	9 Mos. Ended September 30, 1973	1972	1971
Truck manufacturing	12.8%	12.9%	8.1%
Aerospace and industrial	7.5	6.1	5.9
Oil and gas	3.6	3.5	2.7

PRE-TAX DOLLAR RETURN
ON NET WORTH

	9 Mos. Ended September 30, 1973	1972	1971
Truck manufacturing	25.1%	24.2%	15.5%
Aerospace and industrial	16.8	14.1	14.0
Oil and gas	4.8	4.7	3.9

While it is true, based on the experience of the Signal-Burmah transaction and the record in this lawsuit, that Signal Oil is more valuable than shown by the company's books, even if, as plaintiff suggests in his brief, the $761,000,000 value attached to Signal Oil's properties by the plaintiff's expert Paul V. Keyser, Jr., were substituted as the asset figure, the oil and gas properties would still constitute less than half the value of Signal's total assets. Thus, from a straight quantitative approach, I agree with Signal's position that the sale to Burmah does not constitute a sale of "all or substantially all" of Signal's assets.

In addition, if the character of the transaction is examined, the plaintiff's position is also weak. While it is true that Signal's original purpose was oil and gas and while oil and gas is still listed first in the certificate of incorporation, the simple fact is that Signal is now a conglomerate engaged in the aircraft and aerospace business, the manufacture and sale of trucks and related equipment, and other businesses besides oil and gas. The very nature of its business, as it now in fact exists, contemplates the acquisition and disposal of independent branches of its corporate business. Indeed, given the operations since 1952, it can be said that such acquisitions and dispositions have become part of the ordinary course of business. The facts that the oil and gas business was historically first and that authorization for such operations are listed first in the certificate do not prohibit disposal of such interest. As Director Harold M. Williams testified, business history is not "compelling" and "many companies go down the drain because they try to be historic." Williams' deposition, docket number 301, p. 28.

It is perhaps true, as plaintiff has argued, that the advent of multi-business corporations has in one sense emasculated § 271 since one business may be sold without shareholder approval when other substantial business are retained. But it is one thing for a corporation to evolve over a period of years into a multi-business corporation, the operations of which include the purchase and sale of whole businesses, and another for a single business corporation by a one transaction revolution to sell the entire means of operating its business in exchange for money or a separate business. In the former situation, the processes of corporate democracy customarily have had the opportunity to restrain or otherwise control over a period of years. Thus, there is a chance for some shareholder participation. The Signal development illustrates the difference. For example, when Signal, itself formerly called Signal Oil and Gas Company, changed its name in 1968, it was for the announced "need for a new name appropriate to the broadly diversified activities of Signal's multi-industry complex." Walkup affidavit, docket number 34.

The situation is also dramatically illustrated financially in this very case. Independent of the contract with Burmah, the affidavit of Signal's Board Chairman shows that over $200,000,000 of Signal Oil's refining and marketing assets have been sold in the past five years. Walkup affidavit, docket number 34. This activity, prior to the sale at issue here, in itself constitutes a major restructuring of the corporate structure.

I conclude that measured quantitatively and qualitatively, the sale of the stock of Signal Oil by Signal to Burmah does not constitute a sale of "all or substantially all" of Signal's assets. This conclusion is supported by the closet case involving Delaware law which has been cited to the

Court. Wingate v. Bercut, 146 F.2d 725 (9th Cir.1944). Accordingly, insofar as the complaint rests on 8 Del. C. § 271(a), in my judgment, it has no reasonable probability of ultimate success.

QUESTIONS

1. The opinion states, referring to the Chancery Court's opinion in the Philadelphia National Bank case that "the critical factor . . . is generally . . . not the amount of property sold but whether the sale is in fact an unusual transaction. . . ." If a company has had the same ten divisions, of equal size, for the past thirty years, is the sale of one an "unusual transaction" requiring a shareholder vote? What if there are three such divisions? Five?

2. If Signal had waited several years, and the income from the oil & gas division had risen, and it obtained a higher sale price for the same assets, would the outcome be different? What if the oil & gas business constituted 75% of total income, and a proportionate share of market value? If the expected profits from oil and gas operations had just tripled, what effect would this have on Signal's stock price, all other things being equal? Did the court have a means of measuring this aspect of Signal's value?

3. How can a court determine the market value of the entire company, as well as that of the division being sold?

4. What is the source of the court's requirement that the sale be "unusual" rather than quantitatively determined?

5. In the Philadelphia National Bank case the court looked at the actual value of the stock sold to determine whether the sale was of substantially all assets. The court here rejects the use of the alleged value of the oil properties. Why?

6. If a company has been a conglomerate, but has had a stable group of divisions, does a decision to pare down to a "core" business by selling off non-core divisions serially require a shareholder vote?

7. How would a court deal with this case under the Model Business Corporation Act?

NOTE

Another count in the complaint alleged that the purchase price approved by the board was "wholly inadequate" to the point that it demonstrated recklessness by the board. Here Chancellor Quillen first noted the applicability of the business judgment rule, and Delaware authority to the effect that "the business judgment rule weighs in favor of the directors' decision to sell assets unless the complaining shareholders can prove fraud or a clearly inadequate sale price . . . " There were no allegations of conflicts of interest or actual fraud on the part of the Signal board. But the opinion stated: "Actual fraud, whether resulting from self-dealing or otherwise, is not necessary to challenge a sale of assets. And, although the language of 'constructive fraud' or 'badge of fraud' has frequently and almost traditionally been used, such language is not very helpful when fraud admittedly has not been established. There are limits on the business judgment rule which fall short of intentional or inferred fraudulent misconduct and which are based simply on gross inadequacy of price." Such inadequacy of price, the opinion stated, is a "badge of fraud." After receiving valuations of Signal Oil from the most prominent firm in the oil & gas consulting business lower than the prices being discussed, the Signal board finally approved a cash offer of over $480,000,000, which exceeded by approximately $75,000,000 the market value of the total number of Signal shares currently outstanding. But one of plaintiff's experts, concluded that Signal Oil's oil reserves alone could be conservatively valued at $791,875,000; that its total gas reserves are worth another $124,980,000 and that its other properties are worth $98,000,000. This expert discounted the total of these values ($1,014,855,000) by a substantial discount factor of 25% to produce his final fair market value estimate of $761,000,000. Chancellor Quillen stated "I am convinced that the discrepancy between the values is so great that an immediate fuller investigation into this matter of fair value should be had." On that basis he granted a preliminary injunction against completing the sale, but he conditioned it on the posting of a $25 million bond by the plaintiffs to protect Signal from harm. Given the fact that the plaintiffs were major stockholders in Signal, this bond was probably not beyond their financial capacity, although they may have been unwilling to risk the loss of this amount if they did not prevail on the merits and Burmah had withdrawn its offer.

The reader should note that oil prices began to rise in October 1973 when the members of the Organization of Arab Petroleum Exporting Countries (OAPEC, consisting of the Arab members of the OPEC plus Egypt and Syria) proclaimed an oil embargo. By the end of the embargo in March 1974, the price of oil had risen from $3 per barrel to nearly $12. Thus, with the benefit of hindsight, it would be easy for a plaintiff's expert to insist that the oil assets were worth more than the selling price approved by the board.

Katz v. Bregman
431 A.2d 1274 (Del. Ch.1981).

■ MARVEL, CHANCELLOR:

The complaint herein seeks the entry of an order preliminarily enjoining the proposed sale of the Canadian assets of Plant Industries, Inc. to Vulcan Industrial Packaging, Ltd., the plaintiff Hyman Katz allegedly being the owner of approximately 170,000 shares of common stock of the defendant Plant Industries, Inc., on whose behalf he has brought this action, suing not only for his own benefit as a stockholder but for the alleged benefit of all other record owners of common stock of the defendant Plant Industries, Inc. * * *

The complaint alleges that during the last six months of 1980, the board of directors of Plant Industries, Inc., under the guidance of the individual defendant Robert B. Bregman, the present chief executive officer of such corporation, embarked on a course of action which resulted in the disposal of several unprofitable subsidiaries of the corporate defendant located in the United States, namely Louisiana Foliage Inc., a horticultural business, Sunaid Food Products, Inc., a Florida packaging business, and Plant Industries (Texas), Inc., a business concerned with the manufacturer of woven synthetic cloth. As a result of these sales Plant Industries, Inc. by the end of 1980 had disposed of a significant part of its unprofitable assets.

According to the complaint, Mr. Bregman thereupon proceeded on a course of action designed to dispose of a subsidiary of the corporate defendant known as Plant National (Quebec) Ltd., a business which constitutes Plant Industries, Inc.'s entire business operation in Canada and has allegedly constituted Plant's only income producing facility during the past four years. The professed principal purpose of such proposed sale is to raise needed cash and thus improve Plant's balance sheets. * * *

In seeking injunctive relief, as prayed for, plaintiff relies on two principles, one that found in 8 Del. C. § 271 to the effect that a decision of a Delaware corporation to sell " * * * all or substantially all of its property and assets * * * " requires not only the approval of such corporation's board of directors but also a resolution adopted by a majority of the outstanding stockholders of the corporation entitled to vote thereon at a meeting duly called upon at least twenty days' notice.

* * *

Turning to the possible application of 8 Del. C. § 271 to the proposed sale of substantial corporate assets of National to Vulcan, it is stated in Gimbel v. Signal Companies, Inc., Del. Ch., 316 A.2d 599 (1974) as follows:

> "If the sale is of assets quantitatively vital to the operation of the corporation and is out of the ordinary and substantially affects the existence and purpose of the corporation then it is beyond the power of the Board of Directors."

According to Plant's 1980 10K form, it appears that at the end of 1980, Plant's Canadian operations represented 51% of Plant's remaining assets. Defendants also concede that National represents 44.9% of Plant's sales' revenues and 52.4% of its pre-tax net operating income. Furthermore, such report by Plant discloses, in rough figures that while National made a profit in 1978 of $2,900,000, the profit from the United States businesses in that year was only $770,000. In 1979, the Canadian business profit was $3,500,000 while the loss of the United States businesses was $344,000. Furthermore, in 1980, while the Canadian business profit was $5,300,000, the corporate loss in the United States was $4,500,000. And while these figures may be somewhat distorted by the allocation of overhead expenses and taxes, they are significant. In any event, defendants concede that " * * * National accounted for 34.9% of Plant's pre-tax income in 1976, 36.9% in 1977, 42% in 1978, 51% in 1979 and 52.4% in 1980."

While in the case of Philadelphia National Bank v. B.S.F. Co., Del. Ch., 199 A.2d 557 (1964), rev'd on other grounds, Del. Supr., 204 A.2d 746 (1964), the question of whether or not there had been a proposed sale of substantially all corporate assets was tested by provisions of an indenture agreement covering subordinated debentures, the result was the same as if the provisions of 8 Del. C. § 271 had been applicable, the trial Court stating:

> "While no pertinent Pennsylvania case is cited, the critical factor in determining the character of a sale of assets is generally considered not the amount of property sold but whether the sale is in fact an unusual transaction or one made in the regular course of business of the seller. . . ."

Furthermore, in the case of Wingate v. Bercut (CA9) 146 F.2d 725 (1944), in which the Court declined to apply the provisions of 8 Del. C. § 271, it was noted that the transfer of shares of stock there involved, being a dealing in securities, constituted an ordinary business transaction.

In the case at bar, I am first of all satisfied that historically the principal business of Plant Industries, Inc. has not been to buy and sell industrial facilities but rather to manufacture steel drums for use in bulk shipping as well as for the storage of petroleum products, chemicals, food, paint, adhesives and cleaning agents, a business which has been profitably performed by National of Quebec. Furthermore, the proposal, after the sale of National, to embark on the manufacture of plastic drums represents a radical departure from Plant's historically successful line of business, namely steel drums. I therefore conclude that the proposed sale of Plant's Canadian operations, which constitute over 51% of Plant's total assets and in which are generated approximately 45% of Plant's 1980 net sales, would, if consummated, constitute a sale of substantially all of Plant's assets. By way of contrast, the proposed sale of Signal Oil in Gimbel v. Signal Companies, Inc., *supra*, represented only about 26% of the total assets of Signal Companies, Inc. And while Signal Oil represented 41% of Signal Companies, Inc. total net worth, it generated only about 15% of Signal Companies, Inc. revenue and earnings.

I conclude that because the proposed sale of Plant National (Quebec) Ltd. would, if consummated, constitute a sale of substantially all of the assets of Plant Industries, Inc., as presently constituted, that an injunction should issue preventing the consummation of such sale at least until it has been approved by a majority of the outstanding stockholders of Plant Industries, Inc., entitled to vote at a meeting duly called on at least twenty days' notice.

* * *

QUESTIONS

1. How does the sale of the steel drum business, constituting 45% of sales, differ from the sale of Signal Oil? Note that if oil and gas prices had tripled, the oil and gas revenues of Signal would have grown from 15% to 45% of total revenues.

2. Does the presence or absence of multiple divisions of the seller seem to matter? Does it matter that other divisions have already been sold? Did it matter in Signal?

3. If Plant Industries had simply sold the steel drum-making equipment in its factory and replaced it with equipment for making plastic drums, so that the book value of the assets sold was less than half, would the court have required a shareholder vote? The Model Act, § 12.01(1) excludes from shareholder voting transactions in the usual and regular course of business.

4. Assume that a corporation has owned since its inception a manufacturing plant that is not fully utilized, which represents 50% of the book value of its assets. Can the corporation enter into a long-term lease of that plant to another manufacturer, and then lease a smaller plant for its own use, without a shareholder vote? Suppose the lease is for the useful life of the plant, perhaps 20 years? Assume that the lease shifts many of the risks of ownership to the lessee, such as the obligation to maintain the plant, and to pay, as part of the rental, increases calculated to account for increased property taxes and pay both fire and liability insurance premiums on the building?

NOTE ON SALES OF ASSETS

California follows the qualitative approach, notwithstanding the lack of any statutory language referring to sales not in the ordinary course of business, see Jeppi v. Brockman Holding Co., 34 Cal.2d 11, 206 P.2d 847 (1949). Not all courts appear to agree with Delaware's qualitative approach to what constitutes "substantially all" assets, thus requiring a shareholder vote. See, e.g., Walden v. Elrod, 72 F.R.D. 5 (D. Okl.1976) (holding that where "it appears that the sale complained of involves only one half of the corporate assets of the involved corporation", that was not "substantially all" assets). Judge Ralph Winter reached a similar conclusion under a bond indenture in Sharon Steel Corp. v. Chase Manhattan Bank, N.A., 691 F.2d 1039 (2d

Cir.1982), cert. denied, 460 U.S. 1012, 103 S. Ct. 1253, 75 L. Ed.2d 482 (1983), where the operating properties transferred were only 51% of the book value of all of the seller's assets. But where all of the operating assets of a business were transferred, constituting approximately 2/3 of total assets and it retained only certain real estate and stock, a court held that the transfer was of "all or substantially all" assets. Stiles v. Aluminum Products Co., 338 Ill. App. 48, 86 N.E.2d 887 (1949). Experienced practitioners have argued that there is a broad range within which predicting whether a shareholder vote is required in Delaware is extremely difficult. They have argued that it should be clear that if less than 26% of the assets are to be sold, no shareholder approval is needed, while if more than 75% are sold, shareholder approval is clearly needed. Herzel, Sherk & Colling, Sales and Acquisitions of Divisions, 5 Corp. L. Rev. 3, 25 (1982). How comfortable do you feel about advising when a shareholder vote is required in between these limits?

One statutory solution is to provide a bright line. In 1999 § 12.02 of the Model Act was amended to provide a safe harbor, by adopting a bright-line quantitative test, that excluded from shareholder voting requirements transactions that left the seller with a business activity that represented at least 25% of total assets and at least 25% of income before taxes or gross revenues.

NOTE ON HOLLINGER INC. V. HOLLINGER INTERNATIONAL, INC.

In Hollinger Inc. v. Hollinger International, Inc., 858 A.2d 342 (Del. Ch. 2004), Vice Chancellor Strine encountered the ambiguities of the judicial interpretation of section 271 in a proposed sale of the London Daily Telegraph, the flagship newspaper in Hollinger International ("International"). The suit was brought by Hollinger, Inc. ("Inc."), the controlling shareholder of International, to secure a shareholder vote. International was controlled by Lord Conrad Black, a media mogul of considerable stature in both Canada and the United Kingdom, where apparently, the head of the Daily Telegraph was able to "dine with the Queen." International was a newspaper holding company that, like Signal, had engaged in the acquisition and sale of various subsidiaries. Vice Chancellor Strine characterized the issue as whether "the judiciary transmogrified the words 'substantially all' in § 271 of the Delaware General Corporation Law into the words 'approximately half' "? He answered the question negatively, and held that no shareholder vote was required where the sale involved a business that was one of two approximately equal in size, accompanied by other assets remaining in the business that were no more than 10% of total assets. The language below is selected from his opinion:

"I will note, our courts arguably have not always viewed cases involving the interpretation of § 271 through a lens focused by the statute's plain words. Nonetheless, it remains a fundamental principle of Delaware law that the courts of this state should apply a statute in accordance with its plain meaning, as the words that our legislature has used to express its will are the best evidence of its intent. To analyze whether the vote requirement set forth in § 271 applies to a particular asset sale without anchoring that analysis to the statute's own words involves an unavoidable risk that normative preferences of the judiciary will replace those of the General Assembly."

The opinion reviewed dictionary definitions of "substantially" and "all," and concluded that "[a] fair and succinct equivalent to the term 'substantially all' would therefore be 'essentially everything.' "

"In our jurisprudence, however, words of this kind arguably long ago passed from the sight of our judicial rear view mirrors, to be replaced by an inquiry more focused on the judicial gloss put on the statute than on the words of the statute itself. The need for some gloss is understandable, of course. There are various metrics that can be used to determine how important particular assets are in the scheme of things. Should a court look to the percentage of the corporation's potential value as a sales target to measure the statute's application? Or measures of income-generating potential, such as contributions to revenues or operating income? To what extent should the flagship nature of certain assets be taken into account?

* * *

"Our jurisprudence eschewed a definitional approach to § 271 focusing on the interpretation of the words 'substantially all,' in favor of a contextual approach focusing upon whether a transaction involves the sale 'of assets quantitatively vital to the operation of the corporation and is out of the ordinary and substantially affects the existence and purpose of the corporation.' Gimbel v. Signal Cos., Inc., Del. Ch., 316 A.2d 599, 606, *aff'd*, Del. Supr., 316 A.2d 619 (1974). This interpretative choice necessarily involved a policy preference for doing equity in specific cases over the value of providing clear guidelines for transactional lawyers structuring transactions for the corporations they advise. *See* 1 David A. Drexler, et al., *Delaware Corporation Law and Practice* § 37.03 (1999) ("[*Gimbel*] and its progeny represent a clear-cut rejection of the former conventional view that 'substantially all' in Section 271 meant only significantly more than one-half of the corporation's assets.").* It would be less than candid to fail to acknowledge that the § 271 case law provides less than ideal certainty about the application of the statute to particular circumstances. This may result from certain decisions that appear to deviate from the statutory language in a marked way and from others that have dilated perhaps longer than they should in evaluating asset sales that do not seem to come at all close to meeting the statutory trigger for a required stockholder vote. In this latter respect, the seminal § 271 decision, Gimbel v. Signal Cos., may have contributed to the lack of clarity. In the heat of an expedited injunction proceeding, the Chancellor examined in some detail whether the sale of assets comprising only 26% and 41% of the Signal Companies' total and net assets was subject to stockholder approval. Although the assets involved the oldest business line of the Signal Companies, the magnitude involved does

---

*   In re GM Class H Shareholders Litig., 734 A.2d 611, 623 (Del. Ch. 1999).

not seem to approach § 271's gray zone." (citing In re GM Class H
Shareholders Litig., 734 A.2d 611, 623 (Del. Ch. 1999, Strine, V.C.))

"To underscore the point that the test it was articulating was tied
directly to the statute, Gimbel noted that its examination of the quantitative
and qualitative importance of the transaction at issue was intended to
determine whether the transaction implicated the statute because it struck
'at the heart of the corporate existence and purpose,' in the sense that it
involved the 'destruction of the means to accomplish the purposes or objects
for which the corporation was incorporated and actually performs.' It was in
that sense, Gimbel said, that the 'statute's applicability was to be
determined.' "

Having determined that assets that were no more than one-half of total
company assets were not "substantially all from a quantitative perspective,
Vice Chancellor Strine turned to the qualitative part of the test:

"The relationship of the qualitative element of the Gimbel test to the
quantitative element is more than a tad unclear. If the assets to be sold are
not quantitatively vital to the corporation's life, it is not altogether apparent
how they can 'substantially affect the existence and purpose of' the
corporation within the meaning of Gimbel, suggesting either that the two
elements of the test are actually not distinct or that they are redundant. In
other words, if quantitative vitality takes into account factors such as the
cash-flow generating value of assets and not merely book value, then it
necessarily captures qualitative considerations as well. Simply put, the
supposedly bifurcated Gimbel test may be no more bifurcated in substance
than the two-pronged entire fairness test and may simply involve a look at
quantitative and qualitative considerations in order to come up with the
answer to the single statutory question, which is whether a sale involves
substantially all of a corporation's assets. Rather than endeavor to explore
the relationship between these factors, however, I will just dive into my
analysis of the qualitative importance of the *Telegraph* Group to
International."

Here Vice Chancellor Strine examined plaintiff's arguments that the
London Daily Telegraph is one of the world's leading papers, in the same
class as the New York Times, Washington Post and the Wall Street Journal
in the U.S. The plaintiff noted that if you own the Telegraph, "you can have
dinner with the Queen."

"The argument that Inc. makes in its papers misconceives the
qualitative element of Gimbel. That element is not satisfied if the court
merely believes that the economic assets being sold are aesthetically superior
to those being retained; rather, the qualitative element of Gimbel focuses on
economic quality and, at most, on whether the transaction leaves the
stockholders with an investment that in economic terms is qualitatively
different than the one that they now possess. Even with that focus, it must
be remembered that the qualitative element is a gloss on the statutory
language 'substantially all' and not an attempt to identify qualitatively
important transactions but ones that 'strike at the heart of the corporate
existence.'

"The *Telegraph* sale does not strike at International's heart or soul, if that corporation can be thought to have either one. When International went public, it did not own the *Telegraph*. During the course of its existence, International has frequently bought and sold a wide variety of publications. In the CanWest sale, it disposed of a number of major newspapers in Canada—and diminished its assets by half—all without a stockholder vote. That sale came on the heels of its departure from Australia and an American downsizing. Thus, no investor in International would assume that any of its assets were sacrosanct. In the words of Gimbel, it 'can be said that . . . acquisitions and dispositions [of independent branches of International's business] have become part of the [company's] ordinary course of business.'

"Even more importantly, investors in public companies do not invest their money because they derive social status from owning shares in a corporation whose controlling manager can have dinner with the Queen. Whatever the social importance of the *Telegraph* in Great Britain, the economic value of that importance to International as an entity is what matters for the Gimbel test, not how cool it would be to be the *Telegraph's* publisher. The expected cash flows from the *Telegraph* Group take that into account, as do the bids that were received for the *Telegraph* Group. The 'trophy' nature of the *Telegraph* Group means that there are some buyers—including I discern, the Barclays [prospective buyers of the Telegraph], who run a private, not public, company—who are willing to pay a higher price than expected cash flows suggest is prudent, in purely economic terms, in order to own the *Telegraph* and to enjoy the prestige and access to the intelligentsia, the literary and social elite, and high government officials that comes with that control.

"After the *Telegraph* Sale, International's stockholders will remain investors in a publication company with profitable operating assets, a well-regarded tabloid newspaper of good reputation and large circulation, a prestigious newspaper in Israel, and other valuable assets. While important, the sale of the *Telegraph* does not strike a blow to International's heart."

The court denied plaintiff's motion for a preliminary injunction to stop the sale until a shareholder vote could be held.

QUESTIONS

1. How would this case have been treated under the Model Business Corporation Act?

2. In Katz v. Bregman, *supra*, cited critically by Vice Chancellor Strine, the company was selling its steel drum plant so it could shift to the manufacture of plastic drums, which the court characterized as "a radical departure from Plant's historically successful line of business, namely steel drums." Would Vice Chancellor Strine be likely to accord significance to this fact?

3. Could a corporation avoid a shareholder vote by creating a subsidiary to hold these assets, and causing the subsidiary to sell its assets to the acquiring corporation for cash? See Del. Corp. Law § 271 and Revised Model Business Corporation Act § 12.02, Schwadel v. Uchitel, 455 So.2d 401 (Fla. App.1984) and Campbell v. Vose, 515 F.2d 256 (10th Cir.1975). If a shareholder vote is required, who are the shareholders who are entitled to vote? Vice Chancellor Strine discussed this issue in the Hollinger decision, but did not decide it. The Telegraph Group was owned by a sixth tier subsidiary, and the fifth tier subsidiary, its sole shareholder, approved the sale. He noted that there were no grounds for piercing the corporate veil, because the subsidiaries' separate legal existence had been properly observed. In J.P. Griffin Holding Corp. v. Mediatrics, Inc., 1973 WL 651 (Del. Ch. 1973), Vice Chancellor Marvel expressed the view that a parent corporation's vote in favor of selling all of the assets of its wholly owned subsidiary satisfied section 271, but in Leslie v. Telephonics Office Technologies, Inc., 1993 WL 547188 (Del. Ch. 1993), Chancellor Allen noted the possibility that a vote of the parent's shareholders would be required where the subsidiary had functioned merely as the instrumentality or agent of the parent in effecting the asset sale. Vice Chancellor Strine noted that requiring only a vote of the direct shareholder of the selling subsidiary would provide an easy way for corporations to evade section 271's shareholder voting requirement entirely, and noted that in the Hollinger case International had guaranteed the performance of the subsidiary.

The Model Act, § 12.01(1) excludes from shareholder voting transactions in the usual and regular course of business, and § 12.01(3) excludes transfers by a corporation of its assets "to one or more corporations or other entities all of the shares or interests of which are owned by the corporation." Does this mean that a corporation can first transfer its assets to a subsidiary, and then cause the subsidiary to sell all of its assets, with the parent corporation acting as the shareholder to satisfy the shareholder voting requirements of § 12.02? Formerly official comment 2.c provided:

> "Section 12.01 provides that a transfer of property to a wholly owned subsidiary does not require a vote of shareholders. This provision, however, may not be used as a device to avoid a vote of shareholders by a multiple-step transaction."

The 1999 amendments added a new section 12.02(h), which provides:

> "The assets of a direct or indirect consolidated subsidiary shall be deemed the assets of the parent corporation for the purpose of this section."

Does this mean that the parent need not vote as the sole shareholder of a subsidiary selling all of its assets, if they also constitute "substantially all" of the assets of the parent? How does one account for the parent's ownership of the subsidiary's shares, which it will still own after the asset sale?

Delaware added subsection (c) to § 271 in 2005, resolving Vice Chancellor Strine's puzzle.

Query: Suppose the subsidiary merged into the acquiring corporation for cash? Would the parent's board's approval of the merger be sufficient? This problem raises the question of whether the cash merger is a de facto sale. De facto transactions are the subject of the next section of this part.

A. ASSET TRANSACTIONS AND DE FACTO MERGERS

The distinctions between the forms of transactions described above are not always observed by the courts. The next two sections attempt to describe the circumstances under which courts may be willing to recast a transaction to ameliorate what they may view as harsh consequences to one or more constituencies of the corporation. This section deals primarily with the shareholders as a constituency; the next section deals with such constituencies as customers, product users, employees, and neighboring communities.

There are numerous reasons why firms may choose to purchase assets rather than engage in a merger. First, traditional rules leave sellers with their own liabilities; they do not transfer to the buyer, as they do in a merger. Second, subject to stock exchange rules about shareholder votes to authorize issuance of shares and state law rules, the buyer may not need to seek shareholder approval (which can also be achieved through a triangular merger). Third, for Delaware corporations, appraisal is not available under Del. Code Ann. tit. 8 § 262. Fourth, even if a shareholder vote is required for the acquiring corporation, its shareholders will not be entitled to appraisal rights. We begin below with an exploration of this last topic.

Note the formalism involved in choices between asset purchases and mergers. In many cases the results of the two forms are economically identical. The doctrine of independent legal significance in Delaware is the ultimate expression of the enabling act approach to corporation statutes. It began to develop as a result of the great depression of the 1930's, when a great many companies had passed on cumulative preferred dividends. The result was that enormous arrearages had built up that must be paid in full before any dividends could be paid on the common stock. As a result, common stock offerings were extremely difficult, since these companies could offer no promise of dividends for a very long period. In Keller v. Wilson, 21 Del. Ch. 391, 190 A. 115 (1936), the court considered a plan of recapitalization that would exchange old preferred shares and their arrearages for a new class of preferred. A similar arrangement was made for a second class of preferred, called class A. The vote in favor of the recapitalization was approved by the overwhelming vote of each class. The Delaware statute in effect at the time permitted amendments that affected the rights of classes if approved by the holders of a majority of the shares of each affected class. Yet One holder of Class A stock brought suit to enjoin the recapitalization. The court noted the conventional rule that dividends do not become a liability of the corporation until declared (and none of these dividends were declared), and noted the need for corporate flexibility. While conceding that these dividends were not vested property rights because they had not been declared, there were elements of an estoppel theory in the court's opinion—that the cumulative feature of the dividends was an inducement that caused investors to purchase the class. While they could not legally become vested property rights until a fund of retained profits existed from which they could be paid, " . . . it is difficult to perceive the justice of permitting the corporation to destroy the opportunity to create the fund by action under a subsequent amendment to the law which, when the corporation was formed and the stock issued, did not permit of such destruction." 190 A. at 124.

The final passages of the opinion were a ringing defense of property rights:

> "It may be conceded, as a general proposition, that the State, as a matter of public policy, is concerned in the welfare of its corporate creatures to the end that they may have reasonable powers wherewith to advance their interests by permitting adequate financing. It may also be conceded that there has been an increasing departure from the conception which formerly prevailed when the right of individual veto in matters of corporate government operated as a dangerous obstruction to proper functioning. But in determining whether the rights of the complainants herein are such as ought to be regarded a property rights, all aspects of the question must be considered to ascertain what is conducive to the best interests of society. The State is concerned also with the welfare of those who invest their money, the very essence of generation, in corporate enterprises. Some measure of protection should be accorded them. While many interrelations of the State, the corporation, and the shareholders may be changed, there is a limit beyond which the State may not go. Property rights may not be destroyed; and when the nature and character of the right of a holder of cumulative preferred stock to unpaid dividends, which have accrued thereon through passage of time, is examined in a case where that right was accorded protection when the corporation was formed and the stock was issued, a just public policy, which seeks the equal and impartial protection of the interests of all, demands that the right be regarded as a vested right of property secured against the destruction by the Federal and State Constitutions."

190 A. at 124–25. The court enjoined the recapitalization.

This ringing defense of cumulative dividend arrearages as vested property rights lasted four years. Federal United Corporation faced a similar problem, but rather than use a recapitalization, engaged in a merger with a wholly owned subsidiary, as a result of which the old preferred and its arrearages were canceled and replaced by new preferred in the merged entity, together with some common stock. The preferred shareholders were induced to vote for the merger in part by the corporation's promise that dividend payments on the new preferred would begin immediately. The court noted that the preferred shareholders were protected by their appraisal rights, and that the preferred shareholders bought their shares subject to the provisions of Delaware law permitting mergers upon satisfaction of certain conditions. Because of this, there was no vested property right that could permit preferred shareholders to object to a merger, when their financial interests were protected by appraisal. "There is a clear distinction between the situations recognized by the General law and the modes of procedure applicable to each of them; and we think that the strictness of the view of the merger provisions of the law entertained by the Chancellors below was, perhaps, induced by overlooking the distinction, so that it was assumed that to attempt to accomplish by merger that which could not be done by mere charter amendment, was a perversion of the statute in an effort to escape the reach of the decision in the Keller case." Federal United Corporation v. Havender, 24 Del. Ch. 318, 11 A.2d 331, 342–43 (Del. 1940).

The doctrine underlying this decision was articulated more clearly by Judge Leahy in Langfelder v. Universal Laboratories, Inc., 68 F.Supp. 209 (D.Del.1946) (applying Delaware law), involving another merger that eliminated arrearages on cumulative dividends. The opinion stated in part, reconciling the opinions in Keller v. Wilson and Federal United Corporation v. Havender:

> "Under Delaware law, accrued dividends after the passage of time mature into a debt and cannot be eliminated by an amendment to the corporate charter under Sec. 26 of the Delaware Corporation Law. But the right to be paid in full for such dividends, notwithstanding provisions in the charter contract, may be eliminated by means of a merger which meets the standard of fairness. The rationale is that a merger is an act of independent legal significance, and when it meets the requirements of fairness and all other statutory requirements, the merger is valid and not subordinate or dependent upon any other section of the Delaware Corporation Law."

The following case demonstrates how some courts will ignore form in favor of substance.

Farris v. Glen Alden Corporation

393 Pa. 427, 143 A.2d 25 (1958).

■ MR. JUSTICE COHEN.

We are required to determine on this appeal whether, as a result of a "Reorganization Agreements" executed by the officers of Glen Alden Corporation and List Industries Corporation, and approved by the shareholders of the former company, the rights and remedies of a dissenting shareholder accrue to the plaintiff.

Glen Alden is a Pennsylvania corporation engaged principally in the mining of anthracite coal and lately in the manufacture of air conditioning units and firefighting equipment. In recent years the company's operating revenue has declined substantially, and in fact, its coal operations have resulted in tax loss carry overs of approximately $14,000,000. In October 1957, List, a Delaware holding company owning interests in 429 motion picture theaters, textile companies and real estate, and to a lesser extent, in oil and gas operations, warehouses and aluminum piston manufacturing, purchased through a wholly owned subsidiary 38.5% of Glen Alden's outstanding stock. This acquisition enabled List to place three of its directors on the Glen Alden board.

On March 20, 1958, the two corporations entered into a "reorganization agreement," subject to stockholder approval, which contemplated the following actions:

1.   Glen Alden is to acquire all of the assets of List, excepting a small amount of cash reserved for the payment of List's expenses in connection with the transaction. These assets include over $8,000,000 in cash held chiefly in the treasuries of List's wholly owned subsidiaries.

2.   In consideration of the transfer, Glen Alden is to issue 3,621,703 shares of stock to List. List in turn is to distribute the stock to its shareholders at a ratio of five shares of Glen Alden stock for each six shares of List stock. In order to accomplish the necessary distribution, Glen Alden is to increase the authorized number of its shares of capital stock from 2,500,000 shares to 7,500,000 shares without according pre-emptive rights to the present shareholders upon the issuance of any such shares.

3.   Further, Glen Alden is to assume all of List's liabilities including a $5,000,000 note incurred by List in order to purchase Glen Alden stock in 1957, outstanding stock options, incentive stock options plans, and pension obligations.

4.   Glen Alden is to change its corporate name from Glen Alden Corporation to List Alden Corporation.

5.   The present directors of both corporations are to become directors of List Alden.

6.   List is to be dissolved and List Alden is to then carry on the operations of both former corporations.

Two days after the agreement was executed notice of the annual meeting of Glen Alden to be held on April 11, 1958, was mailed to the shareholders together with a proxy statement analyzing the reorganization agreement and recommending its approval as well as approval of certain amendments to Glen Alden's articles of incorporation and bylaws necessary to implement the agreement. At this meeting the holders of a majority of the outstanding shares, (not including those owned by List), voted in favor of a resolution approving the reorganization agreement.

On the day of the shareholders' meeting, plaintiff, a shareholder of Glen Alden, filed a complaint in equity against the corporation and its officers seeking to enjoin them temporarily until final hearing, and perpetually thereafter, from executing and carrying out the agreement.[2]

The gravamen of the complaint was that the notice of the annual shareholders' meeting did not conform to the requirements of the Business Corporation Law in three respects: (1) It did not give notice to the shareholders that the true intent and purpose of the meeting was to effect a merger or consolidation of Glen Alden and List; (2) It failed to give notice to the shareholders of their right to dissent to the plan of merger or consolidation and claim fair value for their shares, and 431 (3) It did not contain copies of the text of certain sections of the Business Corporation Law as required.[3]

* * *

The court below concluded that the reorganization agreement entered into between the two corporations was a plan for a de facto merger, and that therefore the failure of the notice of the annual meeting to conform to the pertinent requirements of the merger provisions of the Business Corporation Law rendered the notice defective and all proceedings in furtherance of the agreement void. Wherefore, the court entered a final decree denying defendants' motion for judgment on the pleadings, entering judgment upon plaintiff's complaint and granting the injunctive relief therein sought. This appeal followed.

When use of the corporate form of business organization first became widespread, it was relatively easy for courts to define a "merger" or a "sale of assets" and to label a particular transaction as one or the other. But prompted by the desire to avoid the impact of adverse, and to obtain

---

[2]   The plaintiff also sought to enjoin the shareholders of Glen Alden from approving the reorganization agreement and from adopting amendments to Glen Alden's articles of incorporation, certificate of incorporation and bylaws in implementation of the agreement. However, apparently because of the shortness of time, this prayer was refused by the Court.

[3]   The proxy statement included the following declaration: "Appraisal Rights.

In the opinion of counsel, the shareholders of neither Glen Alden nor List Industries will have any rights of appraisal or similar rights of dissenters with respect to any matter to be acted upon at their respective meetings."

the benefits of favorable, government regulations, particularly federal tax laws, new accounting and legal techniques were developed by lawyers and accountants which interwove the elements characteristic of each, thereby creating hybrid forms of corporate amalgamation. Thus, it is no longer helpful to consider an individual transaction in the abstract and solely by reference to the various elements therein determine whether it is a "merger" or a "sale". Instead, to determine properly the nature of a corporate transaction, we must refer not only to all the provisions of the agreement, but also to the consequences of the transaction and to the purposes of the provisions of the corporation law said to be applicable. We shall apply this principle to the instant case.

Section 908A of the Pennsylvania Business Corporation Law provides: "If any shareholder of a domestic corporation which becomes a party to a plan of merger or consolidation shall object to such plan of merger or consolidation . . . such shareholder shall be entitled to . . . [the fair value of his shares upon surrender of the share certificate or certificates representing his shares]." Act of May 5, 1933, P.L. 364, as amended, 15 P.S. § 2852–908A.

This provision had its origin in the early decision of this Court in Lauman v. The Lebanon Valley R.R. Co., 30 Pa. 42 (1858). There a shareholder who objected to the consolidation of his company with another was held to have a right in the absence of statute to treat the consolidation as a dissolution of his company and to receive the value of his shares upon their surrender.

The rationale of the Lauman case, and of the present section of the Business Corporation Law based thereon, is that when a corporation combines with another so as to lose its essential nature and alter the original fundamental relationships of the shareholders among themselves and to the corporation, a shareholder who does not wish to continue his membership therein may treat his membership in the original corporation as terminated and have the value of his shares paid to him. See Lauman v. Lebanon Valley R.R. Co., *supra*, 30 Pa. at 46–47.

Does the combination outlined in the present "reorganization" agreement so fundamentally change the corporate character of Glen Alden and the interest of the plaintiff as a shareholder therein, that to refuse him the rights and remedies of a dissenting shareholder would in reality force him to give up his stock in one corporation and against his will accept shares in another? If so, the combination is a merger within the meaning of section 908A of the corporation law.

If the reorganization agreement were consummated, plaintiff would find that the "List Alden" resulting from the amalgamation would be quite a different corporation than the "Glen Alden" in which he is now a shareholder. Instead of continuing primarily as a coal mining company, Glen Alden would be transformed, after amendment of its articles of incorporation, into a diversified holding company whose interests would range from motion picture theaters to textile companies. Plaintiff would find himself a member of a company with assets of $169,000,000 and a long-term debt of $38,000,000 in lieu of a company one-half the size and with but one-seventh the long-term debt.

While the administration of the operations and properties of Glen Alden as well List would be in the hands of management common to both companies, since all executives of List would be retained in List Alden, the control of Glen Alden would pass to the directors of List; for List would hold eleven of the seventeen directorships on the new board of directors.

As an aftermath of the transaction plaintiff's proportionate interest in Glen Alden would have been reduced to only two-fifths of what it presently is because of the issuance of an additional 3,621,703 shares to List which would not be subject to pre-emptive rights. In fact, ownership of Glen Alden would pass to the stockholders of List who would hold 76.5% of the outstanding shares as compared with but 23.5% retained by the present Glen Alden shareholders.

Perhaps the most important consequence to the plaintiff, if he were denied the right to have his shares redeemed at their fair value, would be the serious financial loss suffered upon consummation of the agreement. While the present book value of his stock is $38 a share, after combination it would be worth only $21 a share. In contrast, the shareholders of List who presently hold stock with a total book value of $33,000,000 or $7.50 a share, would receive stock with a book value of $76,000,000, or $21 a share.

Under these circumstances it may well be said that if the proposed combination is allowed to take place without right of dissent, plaintiff would have his stock in Glen Alden taken away from him and the stock of a new company thrust upon him in its place. He would be projected against his will into a new enterprise under terms not of his own choosing. It was to protect dissident shareholders against just such a result that this Court one hundred years ago in the Lauman case, and the legislature thereafter in section 908A, granted the right of dissent. And it is to accord that protection to the plaintiff that we conclude that the combination proposed in the case at hand is a merger within the intendment of section 908A.

* * *

We hold that the combination contemplated by the reorganization agreement, although consummated by contract rather than in accordance with the statutory procedure, is a merger within the protective purview of sections 908A and 515 of the corporation law. The shareholders of Glen Alden should have been notified accordingly and advised of their statutory rights of dissent and appraisal. The failure of the corporate officers to take these steps renders the stockholder approval of the agreement at the 1958 shareholders' meeting invalid. The lower court did not err in enjoining the officers and directors of Glen Alden from carrying out this agreement.[9]

QUESTIONS

1. The court refers to the dilution of book value from $38 to $21 as a "serious financial loss." Is this correct? If so, why did the Glen Alden shareholders approve the reorganization?

2. If you were on the Committee on Corporation Law of the Pennsylvania Bar Association and you wished to deny dissenter's rights in de facto mergers, how would you draft such language after the Glen Alden decision? See the court's recounting of legislative action in the discussion of Terry v. Penn Central Corporation, *infra*, this part, in Note on Independent Legal Significance.

3. Could you restructure this transaction to achieve the same result and yet not have the transaction treated as a merger under Pennsylvania law at the time?

4. Could you accomplish this transaction without a stockholder vote under the merger provisions of the Revised Model Business Corporation Act? See (c) §§ 11.04 and 13.02.

5. Could you avoid dissenters' rights by using a "reverse triangular merger" under the (c)? (This involves the creation of an "acquisition subsidiary" by Glen Alden, and the merger of List into the Glen Alden subsidiary, with the Glen Alden subsidiary surviving, in exchange for common stock of Glen Alden.) How much stock could Glen Alden issue? See (c) § 11.04(g).

Hariton v. Arco Electronics, Inc.

41 Del. Ch. 74, 188 A.2d 123 (Del. 1963).

■ SOUTHERLAND, CHIEF JUSTICE.

This case involves a sale of assets under § 271 of the corporation law, 8 Del. C. It presents for decision the question presented, but not decided, in Heilbrunn v. Sun Chemical Corporation, Del., 150 A.2d 755. It may be stated as follows:

A sale of assets is effected under § 271 in consideration of shares of stock of the purchasing corporation. The agreement of sale embodies also a plan to dissolve the selling corporation and distribute the shares so

---

[9]   Because of our disposition of this appeal, it is unnecessary for us to consider whether the plaintiff had any pre-emptive rights in the proposed issuance of newly authorized shares as payment for the transfer of assets from List, or whether amended sections 908C and 311F of the corporation law may constitutionally be applied to the present transaction to divest the plaintiff of his dissenter's rights.

received to the stockholders of the seller, so as to accomplish the same result as would be accomplished by a merger of the seller into the purchaser. Is the sale legal?

The facts are these:

The defendant Arco and Loral Electronics Corporation, a New York corporation, are both engaged, in somewhat different forms, in the electronic equipment business. In the summer of 1961 they negotiated for an amalgamation of the companies. As of October 27, 1961, they entered into a "Reorganization Agreement and Plan." The provisions of this Plan pertinent here are in substance as follows:

1. Arco agrees to sell all its assets to Loral in consideration (inter alia) of the issuance to it of 283,000 shares of Loral.

2. Arco agrees to call a stockholders meeting for the purpose of approving the Plan and the voluntary dissolution.

3. Arco agrees to distribute to its stockholders all the Loral shares received by it as a part of the complete liquidation of Arco.

At the Arco meeting all the stockholders voting (about 80%) approved the Plan. It was thereafter consummated.

Plaintiff, a stockholder who did not vote at the meeting, sued to enjoin the consummation of the Plan on the grounds (1) that it was illegal, and (2) that it was unfair. The second ground was abandoned. Affidavits and documentary evidence were filed, and defendant moved for summary judgment and dismissal of the complaint. The Vice Chancellor granted the motion and plaintiff appeals.

The question before us we have stated above. Plaintiff's argument that the sale is illegal runs as follows:

The several steps taken here accomplish the same result as a merger of Arco into Loral. In a "true" sale of assets, the stockholder of the seller retains the right to elect whether the selling company shall continue as a holding company. Moreover, the stockholder of the selling company is forced to accept an investment in a new enterprise without the right of appraisal granted under the merger statute. § 271 cannot therefore be legally combined with a dissolution proceeding under § 275 and a consequent distribution of the purchaser's stock. Such a proceeding is a misuse of the power granted under § 271, and a de facto merger results.

The foregoing is a brief summary of plaintiff's contention.

Plaintiff's contention that this sale has achieved the same result as a merger is plainly correct. The same contention was made to us in Heilbrunn v. Sun Chemical Corporation, Del., 150 A.2d 755. Accepting it as correct, we noted that this result is made possible by the overlapping scope of the merger statute and section 271, mentioned in Sterling v. Mayflower Hotel Corporation, 33 Del. Ch. 293, 93 A.2d 107, 38 A.L.R.2d 425. We also adverted to the increased use, in connection with corporate reorganization plans, of § 271 instead of the merger statute. Further, we observed that no Delaware case has held such procedure to be improper, and that two cases appear to assume its legality. Finch v. Warrior Cement Corporation, 16 Del. Ch. 44, 141 A. 54, and Argenbright v. Phoenix Finance Co., 21 Del. Ch. 288, 187 A. 124. But we were not required in the Heilbrunn case to decide the point.

We now hold that the reorganization here accomplished through § 271 and a mandatory plan of dissolution and distribution is legal. This is so because the sale-of-assets statute and the merger statute are independent of each other. They are, so to speak, of equal dignity, and the framers of a reorganization plan may resort to either type of corporate mechanics to achieve the desired end. This is not an anomalous result in our corporation law. As the Vice Chancellor pointed out, the elimination of accrued dividends, though forbidden under a charter amendment (Keller v. Wilson & Co., 21 Del. Ch. 391, 190 A. 115) may be accomplished by a merger. Federal United Corporation v. Havender, 24 Del. Ch. 318, 11 A.2d 331.

In Langfelder v. Universal Laboratories, D.C., 68 F.Supp. 209, Judge Leahy commented upon 'the general theory of the Delaware Corporation Law that action taken pursuant to the authority of the various sections of that law constitute acts of independent legal significance and their validity is not dependent on other sections of the Act." 68 F.Supp. 213, footnote 5.

        * * *

Plaintiff concedes, as we read his brief, that if the several steps taken in this case had been taken separately they would have been legal. That is, he concedes that a sale of assets, followed by a separate proceeding to dissolve and distribute, would be legal, even though the same result would follow. This concession exposes the weakness of his contention. To attempt to make any such distinction between sales under § 271 would be to create uncertainty in the law and invite litigation.

We are in accord with the Vice Chancellor's ruling, and the judgment below is affirmed.

QUESTIONS

1. Can you reconcile this result with the doctrine of Schnell v. Chris-Craft Industries, Inc., 285 A.2d 437, 439 (1971), where Chief Justice (then Justice) Herrmann answered management's claim that strict statutory compliance insulated its action from attack by saying "that inequitable action does not become permissible simply because it is legally possible"?

2. How should the reasoning of this opinion apply in a case like Hollinger, *supra*, if the court had determined that the assets and business of

Telegraph, held by an indirect subsidiary, were in fact substantially all the assets of the International group?

3. Why does the court reject treating each separate step as part of a single integrated transaction?

NOTE

There have been some dicta suggesting that under limited circumstances Delaware courts might recognize the de facto merger doctrine. In Heilbrunn v. Sun Chemical Corporation, 146 A.2d 757 (Del. Ch. 1985), shareholders of Sun challenged an asset purchase by Sun in exchange for its stock, after which the seller dissolved and distributed the Sun stock to its stockholder, with Sun assuming the seller's liabilities and hiring its employees. (This was a twelve-month liquidation under former section 337 of the Internal Revenue Code, which provided favorable tax treatment for such transactions.) Oddly, the court did not cite Hariton v. Arco Electronics, but did cite Faris v. Glen Alden. Nevertheless, the court noted the statutory authority for the share issuance in denying plaintiffs relief. In dicta, the court remarked, "[w]ere this an action brought by a creditor or stockholder of Ansbacher or a case in which the purchasing corporation was in effect to be "acquired" by a "seller" whose business was totally alien to the "buyer's" plaintiffs' arguments would carry greater conviction. In Binder v. Bristol-Myers Squibb Co., 184 F.Supp. 23d 762, 769 (N.D. Ill. 2001), a case involving a de jure merger, the court remarked in *dicta* that the de facto merger doctrine had been recognized in "only very limited circumstances." In another case, the Delaware Supreme Court used the doctrine where a de jure merger was defective, to confirm the intended transaction. Drug, Inc. v. Hunt, 168 A. 87 (1933). In another, the court employed the doctrine where a merger was improperly accomplished to award a pro rata share of value to a shareholder who refused to accept the stock offered. Finch v. Warrior Cement Corp., 141 A. 54 (Del. Ch. 1928).

Relying on those cases and a general statement that the doctrine is recognized in Delaware in only very limited circumstances, a federal court declined to apply the doctrine where it found no fraud in the purchase of assets by Bank of America from a subsidiary, which acquired them in turn by merger from Countrywide Financial Corporation, the defendant in a multi-billion dollar fraud class action. Maine State Retirement System v. Countrywide Financial Corporation, 2011 U.S. Dist. LEXIS 53359 (C.D. Cal. 2011). The opinion stated:

> Second, the SAC does not allege that the asset sale failed to comply with the relevant Delaware statutes governing such a sale. The Delaware Supreme Court allows parties to choose whatever reorganization plan they wish, asset sale or merger, so long as they follow the mechanical guidelines of the statute. Hariton, 188 A.2d at 125. Third, the SAC does not allege that creditors or stockholders have suffered an injury as a result of Bank of America's failure to

comply with the statutory requirements of an asset sale. Heilbrunn, 150 A.2d at 758–59. Fourth, as Bank of America has repeatedly emphasized, the SAC does not allege that the November 2008 asset sale was designed to disadvantage stockholders or creditors.

The Delaware approach was rejected in Rath v. Rath Packing Co., 257 Iowa 1277, 136 N.W.2d 410 (1965). In that case Iowa law required approval of the holders of 2/3 of all outstanding shares to approve a merger, but only a majority vote to approve an amendment to the articles of incorporation. Rather than attempt to obtain the 2/3 vote required for a merger with Needham Packing Co., Rath officials proposed to issue Rath shares in exchange for all of the assets of Needham, to change the name of the company to Rath-Needham, and to elect certain Needham directors to the Rath-Needham board. Because it was necessary to increase the authorized capital stock of the Company and to change its name, as well as to elect new directors, a special shareholders' meeting was called, which approved the amendment by the vote of holders of only 60.1% of the outstanding shares, despite the vigorous solicitation of proxies by company officials. In rejecting the trial court's view that each section of the Iowa corporation statute had independent legal significance, the Iowa Supreme Court noted that only Hariton v. Arco Electronics, Inc. was cited in support of the doctrine. The court stated:

> "We can agree all provisions of our chapter 496A are of equal dignity. But we cannot agree any provisions of the act are legally independent of others if this means that in arriving at the correct interpretation thereof and the legislative intent expressed therein we are not to consider the entire act and, so far as possible, construe its various provisions in the light of their relation to the whole act."

Joint ventures can raise similar questions. Pratt v. Ballman-Cummings Furniture Co., 495 S.W.2d 509 (Ark.1973), held that proof of a joint venture, in which two corporations with interlocking ownership became partners for purposes of selling activities, in which a single individual was appointed general manager, all output was sold to the partnership, and single individuals were in charge of various activities other than sales for both companies, proved a prima facie case of a de facto merger. In contrast, in Good v. Lackawanna Leather Co., 233 A.2d 201 (N.J. Super.1967), one corporation, which was primarily engaged in selling leather hides to a related corporation, found its activities sufficiently unprofitable that it sold 94% of its operating assets, purchased land and built a new plant in a new location, which it leased to a joint venture corporation in which the other shareholder was its customer, was held not to have engaged in a de facto merger. The court noted that the corporation still existed and conducted profitable operations as a lessor of a leather tanning plant, and that there was neither transfer of assets between the two corporations nor exchange of stock in one corporation for that of the other corporation. How would this analysis be affected by the adoption of modern merger statutes that no longer require securities of a surviving corporation to be exchanged for those of constituent corporations?

More recently, the Eleventh Circuit Court of Appeals applied the de facto doctrine in a bankruptcy case. Matter of Munford, 97 F.3d 456 (11th Cir.1996), Chapter Eight, Part 3, holding that a leveraged buyout involved a de facto dividend that was unlawful under Georgia's former statute governing dividends. For a contrary holding see C-T of Virginia, Inc. v. Barrett, 958 F.2d 606 (4th Cir.1992).

The Model Business Corporation Act, § 13.02, provides dissenters' rights both for mergers and sales of substantially all the assets other than in the usual course of business and for certain amendments to the articles of incorporation. California's approach is similar, defining "reorganizations" in Cal. Corp. Code § 181 to include mergers, share exchanges and asset purchases and providing dissenters' rights under § 1300. Does this symmetry eliminate any justification for the de facto merger doctrine, or do asset purchases still provide an argument in favor of the doctrine?

Omitted portions of the Farris opinion involved the court's rejection of the application of 1957 amendments to § 908 of the Pennsylvania Business Corporation Law, which provided:

> "The right of dissenting shareholders . . . shall not apply to the purchase by a corporation of assets whether or not the consideration therefor be money or property, real or personal, including shares or bonds or other evidences of indebtedness of such corporation."

The court also rejected the significance of the commentary of the bar association committee that had drafted the amendment, which made clear the statutory intent to reject the de facto merger doctrine. Instead, it concluded that the Farris transaction was outside the literal language quoted above, because Farris involved an asset purchase followed by a dissolution of the selling corporation and amalgamation of the boards of the two corporations.

In Terry v. The Penn Central Corp., 668 F.2d 188, 193 (3d Cir.1981), the court, declining to apply the de facto merger doctrine, described the remainder of the battle between the courts and the Pennsylvania legislature in the following terms:

> "Farris was the penultimate step in a pas de deux involving the Pennsylvania courts and the Pennsylvania legislature regarding the proper treatment for transactions that reached the same practical result as a merger but avoided the legal form of merger and the concomitant legal obligations. In the 1950s the Pennsylvania courts advanced the doctrine that a transaction having the effect of an amalgamation would be treated as a de facto merger. See, e.g., Bloch v. The Baldwin Locomotive Works, 75 Pa. D. & C. 24 (1951). The legislature responded with efforts to constrict the de facto merger doctrine. Farris, addressing those efforts, held that the doctrine still covered a reorganization

agreement that had the effect of merging a large corporation into a smaller corporation. In a 1959 response to Farris, the legislature made explicit its objection to earlier cases that found certain transactions to be de facto mergers. The legislature enacted a law, modifying inter alia Sections 311 and 908, entitled in part:

> "An Act . . . changing the law as to . . . the acquisition or transfer of corporate assets, the rights of dissenting shareholders, . . . abolishing the doctrine of de facto mergers or consolidation and reversing the rules laid down in Bloch v. Baldwin Locomotive Works, 75 Pa. D. & C. 24, and Marks v. The Autocar Co., 153 F.Supp. 768, . . . Act of November 10, 1959 (P.L. 1406, No. 502).

"Following this explicit statement, the de facto merger doctrine has rarely been invoked by the Pennsylvania courts."

PROBLEM

Consider, under §§ 12.01 & 12.02 of the Model Business Corporation Act or § 271 of the Delaware Act, whether a corporation can avoid a shareholder vote in a business combination by using the following strategy:

1. The corporation will create a wholly owned subsidiary, and transfer substantially all of its assets to the subsidiary, in return for all of its shares, leaving the corporation as a holding company.

2. The holding company will cause the subsidiary to merge into the acquiring corporation for cash.

Will a shareholder vote be required for transaction 1?

Who are the shareholders entitled to vote in transaction 2?

B. SUCCESSOR LIABILITY IN ASSET PURCHASES

Merger statutes generally provide that the surviving corporation succeeds to all the rights and liabilities of the constituent corporations. MBCA § 11.07(a)(4); Del. Gen. Corp. L. § 259. Generally this is not a problem for the acquiring corporation, if the target's liabilities are clearly understood. The size of these liabilities simply affects the consideration target shareholders will receive. But where liabilities are uncertain, it becomes more costly for the buyer to ascertain their expected size, and the calculation is infected with the risk that the ultimate liabilities may be much larger than previously thought. These circumstances are most likely to arise with contingent liabilities, where the ultimate amount and probability of liability is highly uncertain. Thus, where employees have worked under hazardous conditions, the target corporation may have serious contingent liabilities to them. Further, if the selling corporation has operated in a manner that created toxic wastes on the property, the liability for clean-up may be extremely difficult to estimate. The writer is familiar with one case where the buyer purchased all of the operating assets of a business and leased the plant from the target, leaving the seller's shareholders to bear the risk of liability for clean-up under Comprehensive Environmental Response, Compensation and Liability Act of 1980 ("CERCLA" or "Superfund legislation"). Similar problems may exist with respect to potential product liabilities. One solution, of course, is to purchase assets, and avoid the successor liability provisions of the merger statutes. This presumably leaves the seller with sufficient cash to be responsible for its own liabilities. To the extent that assets are subject to liens, either the seller must see to their payment at the closing to secure the release of liens, or the buyer must assume the obligations and take the assets subject to the liens. Normally assuming liabilities of this kind does not create problems for a buyer, because the assumed liabilities are well known and carefully specified.

This is the black-letter analysis of the problem; but it creates the risk that the seller will not be fully responsible for its existing or contingent obligations. If the seller remains in existence and proceeds to carry on another line of business, it remains available for suits involving torts it committed or product liabilities incurred while carrying on its earlier line of business. Where once sales of all assets were frequently followed by liquidation, this is far less likely since tax changes in 1986 that impose taxes on gains realized by the selling corporate entity as well as by the shareholders receiving the proceeds of the liquidation.

Where sellers proceed to liquidate after an asset sale, several protections are provided by corporate law to creditors. Corporate dissolution requires corporate action similar to that for other fundamental changes—approval by the board of directors, followed by a shareholder vote. Del. G.C.L. § 275; Model Act §§ 14.02–14.03. In each case a filing with the Secretary of State is required to record this action. Del. G.C.L. § 275(d); Model Act § 14.03. But filing the certificate or articles of dissolution is not corporate death; it only begins the process of winding up the business and affairs of the corporation, which includes payment of creditors. For these purposes the corporate existence continues, and claims against it are not terminated by dissolution, nor are pending lawsuits abated or terminated by it. Del. G.C.L. § 278; Model Act § 14.05. Both statutes require dissolved corporations to give notice to known creditors, giving them periods ranging from 60 to 120 days after notice to file their claims and demand payment. Del. G.C.L. § 280; Model Act § 14.06. If claimants who have been notified fail to do so, or if their claims are rejected by the corporation and they do not begin suit within either 120 or 90 days, their claims are barred. Del. G.C.L. § 280(a)(4); Model Act § 14.06(c)(2).

The more difficult cases involve claims that are contingent at the time of dissolution, including unknown claims, such as product liability claims that may only occur after the expiration of these notice periods. Delaware law provides a procedure for a corporation in dissolution to petition a court for a determination of the likely amount of contingent claims and may set aside an amount to pay them. The corporation may also petition the court to determine the amount that will be sufficient to pay claims currently unknown to the corporation or that have not arisen, but are likely to arise or become known within the next five years after the date of dissolution, or some longer period as the court may determine, not to exceed ten years. Del. G.C.L. § 280(c). The Model Act takes a slightly different approach. It allows a corporation to protect itself from unknown or contingent claims by publishing a newspaper notice of its dissolution stating that such claims will be barred unless filed within three years of the publication of the notice. Claims filed in a timely manner may be enforced either against the corporate assets or, if already distributed, against each shareholder to the extent of the assets received in dissolution. Model Act § 14.07.

The following is the official comment to section 14.07:

"Earlier versions of the Model Act did not recognize the serious problem created by possible claims that might arise long after the dissolution process was completed and the corporate assets distributed to shareholders. Most of these claims were based on personal injuries occurring after dissolution but caused by allegedly defective products sold before dissolution, but they also involved negligence for which the statute of limitations did not begin to run until the negligence was discovered (e.g., a surgical instrument left inside the patient). The application of the Model Act provision (and of the state dissolution statutes phrased in different terms) to this problem led to confusing and inconsistent results. See generally Friedlander and Gilbert, 'Post Dissolution Liabilities of Shareholders and Directors for Claims Against Dissolved Corporations,' 31 Vand. L. Rev. 1363 (1978). The problems raised by this type of litigation are intractable; on the one hand, the application of a mechanical two-year limitation period to a claim for injury that occurs after the period has expired involves obvious injustice to the plaintiff. On the other hand, to permit these suits generally makes it impossible ever to complete the winding up of the corporation, make suitable provisions for creditors, and distribute the balance of the corporate assets to the shareholders.

"In some circumstances a tort law concept of transferee liability, sometimes characterized as 'de facto merger,' has been applied to allow plaintiffs incurring post dissolution injuries to bring suit against the person that acquired the corporate assets. See the Official Comment to section 11.01. Some courts have refused to apply this doctrine, particularly when the purchaser of the corporate assets has not continued the business of the dissolved corporation. In these cases, the remedy of the plaintiff is limited to claims against the dissolved corporation and its shareholders receiving the assets pursuant to the dissolution.

"The solution adopted in section 14.07 is to continue liability of a dissolved corporation for subsequent claims for a period of [three] years after it publishes notice of dissolution. It is recognized that a [three] year cut-off is itself arbitrary, but it is believed that the great bulk of post dissolution claims will arise during this period.* This provision is therefore believed to be a reasonable compromise between the competing considerations of providing a remedy to injured plaintiffs and providing a period of repose after which assets distributed by dissolved corporations to their shareholders are free of all claims and shareholders may hold them secure in the knowledge that they may not be reclaimed."

Fraudulent transfer laws provide another means by which the law deals with this problem. These statutes, which began with the statute of 13 Elizabeth in 1571, were designed to deal with the problem of the debtor who, upon seeing the sheriff approaching to levy on his goods, conveyed them all to a family member for nominal consideration in order to escape the judgment. Fraudulent conveyance statutes, discussed in Chapter Eight, part 3, provide one means by which debtors can set aside asset transfers made for inadequate consideration in fraud of creditors. The material which follows in this part demonstrates how other parts of the law deal with these issues. Buyers may face the prospect that the assets they purchase will remain subject to the claims of the seller's creditors.

For the moment, our focus is on those claims never contemplated by drafters of earlier laws. Products liability rules have expanded liability enormously during the 20th century. Within the last three decades liabilities for environmental pollution and disposal of waste materials have expanded in ways not anticipated by drafters of earlier laws. Claims of workers who suffer health problems as a result of employment conditions have also expanded. In some cases the seller of a business may be aware of the potential liability; in other cases it may be that neither seller nor buyer could know of the risk at the time of the sale of a business. Typically no funds will be reserved to honor such unknown and contingent claims in a sale of a business.

None of this would matter if the seller remained in business; it would ultimately bear the full cost of all claims against it. But where the seller is a corporate entity selling its entire business with an intent to liquidate, the differences become critical. From the tort claimant's perspective, liquidation of the selling corporation may be a fraudulent conveyance, since typically funds are distributed to shareholders for no additional

---

*   Formerly the Model Act had a five-year cut-off for claims against dissolved corporations. Ed.

consideration. That, of course, may be of small comfort, especially where share holdings were widely dispersed, so that no single shareholder received a large enough distribution to satisfy the claims (especially in class actions). From the acquiring firm's perspective, a representation and warranty that there are no other claims, contingent or otherwise, beyond those disclosed in a schedule of the seller's creditors, may provide no protection. Typically acquisition agreements provide that warranties expire after a fixed period of time. Second, where the warranty is given by a corporate entity that intends to liquidate, how does a buyer enforce a breach of warranty claim? In closely held businesses the principal shareholders who are active in the business may be asked to join in the selling corporation's warranties. In publicly held corporations this will not be a practical solution, since no shareholder will be knowledgeable enough about the business, or have enough at stake to be willing to enter into such a warranty.

Traditional rules governing the sale of assets thus permitted the seller to externalize some costs of operating its business. In effect, the seller received a purchase price as if it were selling a business with no contingent liabilities, which would be a higher price than the buyer would have been willing to pay in a merger where these liabilities would have been assumed by operation of law.

i.   DE FACTO MERGERS REVISITED

The concept of a de facto merger is a useful device for activist courts not only in recasting transactions to obtain certain results for dissenting shareholders, but also for creditors of the firm. In Knapp v. North American Rockwell Corp., 506 F.2d 361 (3d Cir.1974) an employee injured while using a machine manufactured by Textile Machine Works ("TMW") sued Rockwell, which had purchased the assets of TMW some time after the machine had been made and sold to the plaintiff's employer. As in the case of most purchasers of assets, Rockwell did not assume TMW's liabilities for which TMW carried insurance. Rockwell paid for the assets with its own stock. Probably for tax reasons, TMW committed to liquidate and distribute the Rockwell stock to its shareholders. Apparently Knapp was injured within two years of TMW's dissolution, which meant he could have brought suit against TMW. But the court emphasized the fact that had Knapp been injured more than two years after the dissolution, his claim against TMW would have been barred. In applying the doctrine of Farris v. Glen Alden Corp., 393 Pa. 427, 143 A.2d 25 (1958), *supra*, part 4.B of this chapter, the court stated in part that "denying Knapp the right to sue Rockwell because of the barren continuation of TMW after the exchange with Rockwell would allow a formality to defeat Knapp's recovery. Although TMW technically existed as an independent corporation, it had no substance." The court then noted that as a matter of public policy, the Pennsylvania Supreme Court had considered which of two parties is better able to spread the loss. It conceded that neither Knapp nor Rockwell was in a position to prevent the loss, and rested its decision to treat the asset sale as a de facto merger solely on the greater loss-spreading ability of Rockwell. In Terry v. Penn Central Corp., 668 F.2d 188 (3d Cir.1981) the same court declined to apply the de facto merger doctrine to protect shareholders' voting rights in an asset purchase for stock, noting the 1959 amendments of the Pennsylvania corporate statute following Farris v. Glen Alden. While the Terry court did not overrule the Knapp decision, it declined to apply the doctrine in the setting of a shareholders' suit.

The de facto merger doctrine has been applied in a variety of other settings: Arnold Graphics Indus. v. Independent Agent Center, Inc., 775 F.2d 38 (2d Cir.1985) (judgment creditor can sue successor); Wilson v. Fare Well Corp., 140 N.J. Super. 476, 356 A.2d 458 (Law Div. 1976); Shannon v. Samuel Langston Co., 379 F.Supp. 797 (W.D. Mich.1974); Atlas Tool Co. Inc. v. Commissioner Internal Revenue, 614 F.2d 860 (3d Cir.1980) (successor liable for tax obligations of liquidated company); and Syenergy Methods, Inc. v. Kelly Energy Systems, 695 F.Supp. 1362 (D.R.I.1988). The doctrine has been rejected in Bud Antle, Inc. v. Eastern Foods, Inc., 758 F.2d 1451 (11th Cir.1985); John Mohr & Sons v. Apex Terminal Warehouses, Inc., 422 F.2d 638 (7th Cir.1970); and R. Renaissance Inc. v. Rohm & Haas Co. 674 F.Supp. 591 (S.D .Ohio 1987). A comprehensive analysis of successor liability under the de facto merger doctrine and other doctrines treated here appears in George W. Kuney, A Taxonomy and Evaluation of Successor Liability (Revisited), at http:// papers.ssrn.com/sol3/papers.cfm?abstract_id=2307190. An earlier version appears in 6 Fla. St. U. Bus. L. Rev. 9 (2007).

One question frequently left unaddressed by these decisions is the extent to which the corporate law of the state of incorporation, with its own rules about formal separation of mergers from asset sales, should govern courts in other states dealing with tort liabilities.

QUESTIONS

1. Prior to 1986 Section 337 of the Internal Revenue Code permitted a corporation to sell its assets without recognition of gain when a plan of complete liquidation was adopted, and, within a twelve month period beginning on the date of the adoption of the plan, all of the corporation's assets, except those reserved to meet claims, are distributed in liquidation. The Tax Reform Act of 1986 repealed Section 337. Thus a contractual commitment by a selling corporation to liquidate within twelve months in connection with a sale of all its assets no longer has any tax advantages. Would the absence of such a provision in the acquisition agreement defeat a plaintiff's argument that a de facto merger had taken place?

2. What alternatives would be available to a careful drafter to avoid creating a de facto merger?

3. Would it help avoid the de facto merger doctrine if the purchase were for cash rather than for the buyer's stock? What about using debt securities of the buyer convertible into stock?

---

ii.   PRODUCT LINE LIABILITIES

To some extent imposition of liability upon buyers under the de facto merger doctrine depends on the formalities of the transaction, which are subject to the control of the parties. There is a certain irony in a doctrine designed to elevate substance over form that relies on certain forms to achieve its goal. Other courts have taken other approaches to successor liabilities. The following opinion describes the development of the "product line" doctrine.

Ramirez v. Amsted Industries, Inc.
86 N.J. 332, 431 A.2d 811 (N.J. 1981).

■ The opinion of the Court was delivered by CLIFFORD, J.

This products liability case implicates principles of successor corporation liability. We are called upon to formulate a general rule governing the strict tort liability of a successor corporation for damages caused by defects in products manufactured and distributed by its predecessor. The Appellate Division, in an opinion reported at 171 N.J. SUPER. 261 (1979), devised the following test, based essentially on the holding of the Supreme Court of California in Ray v. Alad Corp., 19 Cal.3d 22, 560 P.2d 3, 136 Cal. Rptr. 574 (Cal.1977):

> [W]here, as in the present case, the successor corporation acquires all or substantially all the assets of the predecessor corporation for cash and continues essentially the same manufacturing operation as the predecessor corporation the successor remains liable for the product liability claims of its predecessor. [171 N.J. SUPER. at 278.]

In affirming the judgment below we adopt substantially this test for determining successor corporation liability in the factual context presented.

I

On August 18, 1975 plaintiff Efrain Ramirez was injured while operating an allegedly defective power press on the premises of his employer, Zamax Manufacturing Company, in Belleville, New Jersey. The machine involved, known as a Johnson Model 5, sixty-ton punch press, was manufactured by Johnson Machine and Press Company (Johnson) in 1948 or 1949. As a result of the injuries sustained plaintiffs filed suit against Amsted Industries, Inc. (Amsted) as a successor corporation to Johnson, seeking to recover damages on theories of negligence, breach of warranty and strict liability in tort for defective design and manufacturing.

[The trial court granted summary judgment for the defendant, which was reversed by the Appellate Division.]

II

[The machine that caused the injury was manufactured in 1948 or 1949 by Johnson Machine and Press Company. In 1956 Johnson transferred all its assets and liabilities to Bontrager Construction Co., which continued the business. In 1962 Amsted purchased all of the assets of Bontrager for cash, including the right to use the trade name "Johnson Machine and Press Corporation." The contract expressly provided:

> "It is understood and agreed that Purchaser shall not assume or be liable for any liability or obligations other than those expressly assumed by Purchaser.

> * * *

> "Defective Products. All machines sold by Seller on or prior to the Closing Date shall be deemed for the purpose of this Section 8 to be products of Seller, and Seller alone shall be responsible, to the extent of the warranties heretofore given by Seller to its customers, for all liability for the correction and repair of defects in material or workmanship thereof involving costs and expenses in excess of $50 per machine. Purchaser agrees to perform the necessary work to correct and repair the defects involved in such claims for and on behalf of Seller, and Seller agrees to assume and pay for the costs and expenses occasioned by such work to the extent of the warranties heretofore given by Seller to its customers * * * ."

In 1975 Amsted sold the business to South Bend Lathe Co., and agreed to indemnify the buyer for any losses arising from products made and sold prior to the closing. It was by virtue of this agreement that Amsted would be held liable for any liability against South Bend.]

III

Amsted urges this Court to judge its potential liability for defective Johnson products on the basis of the traditional analysis of corporate successor liability. Although not heretofore treated by this Court the general principle has been accepted in New Jersey that "where one company sells or otherwise transfers all its assets to another company the latter is not liable for the debts and liabilities of the transferor, including those arising out of the latter's tortious conduct." Menacho v. Adamson United Co., 420 F.Supp. 128, 131 (D.N.J.1976) (applying New Jersey law); * * * Courts applying this traditional corporate law approach have examined the nature and consequences of the asset acquisition in order to determine whether successor liability can be imposed upon the purchasing corporation under one or more of the exceptions to the general rule of nonliability.

In recent years, however, the traditional corporate approach has been sharply criticized as being inconsistent with the rapidly developing principles of strict liability in tort and unresponsive to the legitimate interests of the products liability plaintiff. Courts have come to recognize that the traditional rule of nonliability was developed not in response to the interests of parties to products liability actions, but rather to protect the rights of commercial creditors and dissenting shareholders following corporate acquisitions, as well as to determine successor corporation liability for tax assessments and contractual obligations of the predecessor.

Strict interpretation of the traditional corporate law approach leads to a narrow application of the exceptions to nonliability, and places unwarranted emphasis on the form rather than the practical effect of a particular corporate transaction. The principal exceptions to nonliability outlined in McKee, [McKee v. Harris-Seybold Co., 109 N.J. Super. 555 (Law Div.1970), aff'd 118 N.J. Super. 480 (App. Div.1972)] *supra*, condition successor liability on a determination of whether the transaction can be labeled as a merger or a de facto merger, or whether the purchasing corporation can be described as a mere continuation of the selling corporation. Traditionally, the triggering of the "de facto merger" exception has been held to depend on whether the assets were transferred to the acquiring corporation for shares of stock or for cash— that is, whether the stockholders of the selling corporation become the stockholders of the purchasing corporation. Under a narrow application of the McKee exception of de facto merger no liability is imposed where the purchasing corporation paid for the acquired assets principally in cash.

In like manner, narrow application of McKee's "continuation" exception causes liability vel non to depend on whether the plaintiff is able to establish that there is continuity in management, shareholders, personnel, physical location, assets and general business operation between selling and purchasing corporations following the asset acquisition. Where the commonality of corporate management or ownership cannot be shown, there is deemed to have been no continuation of the seller's corporate entity.

When viewed in this light, narrow application of the McKee approach to corporate successor liability is indeed inconsistent with the developing principles of strict products liability and unresponsive to the interests of persons injured by defective products in the stream of commerce. * * *

We likewise refuse to decide this case through a narrow application of McKee. The form of the corporate transaction by which Amsted acquired the manufacturing assets of Bontrager should not be controlling as to Amsted's liability for the serious injury suffered by plaintiff some thirteen years after that transaction. We therefore must consider the alternative approaches to successor corporation liability that have been adopted by other reviewing courts in an effort to arrive at the standard most consistent with the principles underlying the New Jersey law of strict products liability.

IV

In an effort to make the traditional corporate approach more responsive to the problems associated with the developing law of strict products liability several courts have broadened the McKee exceptions of "de facto merger" and "mere continuation" in order to expand corporate successor liability in certain situations.

The "mere continuation" exception was first expounded by a federal court applying New Hampshire law in Cyr v. B. Offen & Co., Inc., *supra*, Cyr v. B. Offen & Co., Inc., 501 F.2d [1145,] at 1152–54 [(1st Cir.1974)]. In Cyr, two printing press employees were seriously injured in 1969 by the drying ovens of a machine manufactured in 1959 by B. Offen & Company, a sole proprietorship. In 1963 a group of employees of the original manufacturer had formed the defendant corporation, B. Offen & Company, Inc., and had purchased for cash the drying system of the presses from the executor of the estate of the sole proprietor. The contract of sale between the successor corporation and the predecessor's estate provided for the purchase of the predecessor's good will, contract and service obligations, and the continued operation of the predecessor's business without substantial change. 501 F.2d at 1151. The contract expressly disclaimed successor corporation liability for costs incurred by the torts of the predecessor. *Id.* The court held that there was sufficient justification for a jury to treat the successor corporation as the mere continuation of its predecessor for the purposes of imposing tort liability for injuries caused by defective products. *Id.* at 1153–54. It found that the successor corporation continued to produce the same product, through the same employees, in the same physical plant, and under the same supervision as its predecessor, and that by use of essentially the same name held itself out to the world as the same enterprise.

The Cyr court based the justification for its holding on the public policy considerations underlying strict products liability. It recognized that the successor corporation, not being the original manufacturer, is not the specific legal entity that placed the defective product in the stream of commerce or made implied representations as to its safety. Nonetheless, there were several other policy justifications for imposing strict products liability on the successor. The first was in essence the risk-spreading approach:

> The very existence of strict liability for manufacturers implies a basic judgment that the hazards of predicting and

insuring for risk from defective products are better borne by the manufacturer than by the consumer. The manufacturer's successor, carrying over the experience and expertise of the manufacturer, is likewise in a better position than the consumer to gauge the risks and the costs of meeting them. The successor knows the product, is as able to calculate the risk of defects as the predecessor, is in position to insure therefor and reflect such cost in sale negotiations, and is the only entity capable of improving the quality of the product.

[*Id.* at 1154.] The court also reasoned that the successor corporation, having reaped the benefits of continuing its predecessor's product line, exploiting its accumulated good will and enjoying the patronage of its established customers, should be made to bear some of the burdens of continuity, namely, liability for injuries caused by its defective products.

Perhaps the most significant decision expanding the "mere continuation" exception to the traditional rule of corporate successor nonliability is Turner v. Bituminous Cas. Co., 397 Mich. 406, 244 N.W.2d 873 (Mich. 1976). The defendant in Turner contended that where manufacturing assets are acquired by a purchasing corporation for cash rather than for stock, there is no continuity of shareholders and therefore no corporate successor liability. *Id.* at 879. However, the court looked upon the kind of consideration paid for assets as but "one factor to use to determine whether there exists a sufficient nexus between the successor and predecessor corporations to establish successor liability." *Id.* at 880. It reasoned that there was no practical basis for treating a cash purchase of corporate assets any differently from an acquisition of assets for stock, concluding that "[i]t would make better sense if the law had a common result and allowed products liability recovery is each case." *Id.*

Accordingly, the Turner court held that in applying the "mere continuation" exception to situations involving the sale of corporate assets for cash, continuity of shareholders between selling and purchasing corporations is not a relevant criterion for the purposes of determining successor liability for injury caused by defective products. Rather, it adopted a less stringent version of the "mere continuation" exception in the sale-of-assets-for-cash context, jettisoning the criterion of continuity of shareholders and emphasizing continuity of the enterprise of the predecessor corporation. 244 N.W.2d at 883. Applying the rule it had adopted to the record before it, the court concluded that all relevant elements of continuation were present.

In the instant case plaintiffs contend that Amsted can be held responsible for liability arising out of defective Johnson products based upon Turner's expanded "continuation" approach. To support this line of attack they rely on Korzetz v. Amsted Industries, Inc., 472 F.Supp. 136 (E.D.Mich.1979). In Korzetz, a federal court in Michigan applied the Turner analysis to the very same corporate succession involved in the instant case (Johnson to Bontrager to Amsted), and determined that Amsted could be held liable for injuries caused by presses manufactured by Johnson well before Amsted acquired the Johnson assets from Bontrager. The court found "strong and convincing evidence of continuity of enterprise" from Johnson to Bontrager to Amsted, not significantly diluted by the facts that Amsted changed its corporate name rather than continue the official corporate names "Johnson" or "Bontrager," that Bontrager continued to exist as a shell for more than two years following the sale of assets to Amsted, that Bontrager's period of ownership intervened between Johnson's and Amsted's, and that Amsted expressly refused to assume liability for breach of warranties on the Johnson machines it purchased from Bontrager. 472 F.Supp. at 144. Rather, the court in Korzetz emphasized the following evidence of continuity:

> Amsted purchased all of Bontrager's assets: plants, lands, designs, inventories, work in progress, patents, trademark, and customer lists. Also sales representative contracts were to be maintained as well as other then existing contracts. Amsted secured a covenant not to compete for five years from Bontrager's shareholders; Bontrager was to maintain inventory supplies in accordance with prior practice, and real property was transferred with the stipulation that it was to be used for continuing operations; Amsted was to make best effort to take on all of Bontrager's employees with the exception of three management level personnel. We believe this evidence convincingly establishes the type of relationship or continuity of interest envisioned by Turner. [*Id.*]

Also of relevance to the court was the fact that Amsted represented its presses as "Johnson Presses" in advertising campaigns and made further efforts "to exploit the Johnson goodwill, name and market." *Id.* Korzetz concluded that Amsted was a mere continuation of the manufacturing enterprise that Johnson established, despite the intervening ownership of Bontrager. *Id.* at 144–45.

We agree with plaintiffs that under Turner, which simply expands the "continuation" exception to the traditional McKee approach, ante at 815, Amsted may be held to be the mere continuation of Johnson for the purpose of imposing corporate successor liability for injuries caused by defective Johnson products. However, the Appellate Division actually based its decision below and its ultimate test of successor corporation liability not on the Turner analysis but rather on the so-called "product line exception" developed by the California Supreme Court in Ray v. Alad Corp., 19 Cal.3d 22, 560 P.2d 3, 136 Cal. Rptr. 574 (1977). . . . There are fundamental practical and analytical differences between Turner's expanded "mere continuation" exception and Ray's "product line" approach. Turner merely broadens the inroads into the traditional principles of corporate successor nonliability expressed in McKee and related cases, while Ray completely abandons the traditional rule and its exceptions, utilizing instead the policies underlying strict liability in tort for injuries caused by defective products. Whereas the Turner variation on continuation of the enterprise contemplates such factors as the ownership and management of the successor's corporate entity, its personnel, physical location, assets, trade name, and general business operation, the Ray test is concerned not with the continuation of the corporate entity as such but rather with the successor's undertaking to manufacture essentially the same line of products as the predecessor.

Because we believe that the focus in cases involving corporate successor liability for injuries caused by defective products should be on the successor's continuation of the actual manufacturing operation and not on commonality of ownership and management between the predecessor's and successor's corporate entities, and because the traditional corporate approach, even as broadened by Turner and its progeny, renders inconsistent results,* we adopt substantially Ray's product line analysis.

V

* * *

[In Ray v. Alad, t]he California Supreme Court reversed a trial court's summary judgment in favor of Alad II. It determined that none of the four stated exceptions to the general rule of nonliability under the traditional corporate law approach was sufficient basis for imposing liability on the purchasing corporation, Alad II. 19 Cal.3d at 29, 560 P.2d at 7, 136 Cal. Rptr. at 578. Nevertheless, the court determined that a special departure from that traditional approach was called for by the policies underlying strict tort liability for injuries caused by defective products. Rather than adopt the expanded "mere continuation" exception to the corporate law approach as developed in Cyr, *supra*, and Turner, *supra*, the Ray court abandoned the traditional analysis. *Id.* at 30, 560 P.2d at 8, 136 Cal. Rptr. at 579. It developed instead the following formulation, which has since come to be known as the "product line"

---

*   For example, in Hernandez v. Johnson Press Corp., 70 Ill. App.3d 664, 388 N.E.2d 778 (App.Ct.1979), an Illinois appellate court applied the Turner analysis to the very same corporate genealogy as involved herein, and determined that there was no de facto merger between Johnson and Amsted. The court's findings of fact, however, indicate that the plaintiff presented a shamefully weak record, as the court was unable to point to facts indicating continuity of management, personnel, physical location, assets and general business operation. 388 N.E.2d at 780. In Korzetz, supra, Turner's continuity rationale was applied to the identical factual situation and the court found "strong and convincing evidence of continuity of enterprise" from Johnson to Amsted, emphasizing continuity of personnel, physical location, assets, trade name, sales contract, customer lists, and general business operations. 462 F.Supp. at 144. While the record in the present case clearly supports the Korzetz court's result, the point is that the Turner analysis lends itself to inconsistency and ambiguity. Ray's product line analysis, focusing primarily on the continuation of the general business operations, not only can be applied with greater consistency, but better reflects the underlying policy in New Jersey that liability for defective products attaches to the manufacturing enterprise.

approach to successor corporation liability for injuries caused by defective products:

> We * * * conclude that a party which acquires a manufacturing business and continues the output of its line of products under the circumstances here presented assumes strict tort liability for defects in units of the same product line previously manufactured and distributed by the entity from which the business was acquired. [19 Cal.3d at 34, 560 P.2d at 11, 136 Cal. Rptr. at 582.]

The Ray court offered a three-fold justification for its imposition of potential liability upon a successor corporation that acquires the assets and continues the manufacturing operation of the predecessor:

> (1) the virtual destruction of the plaintiff's remedies against the original manufacturer caused by the successor's acquisition of the business, (2) the successor's ability to assume the original manufacturer's risk spreading role, and (3) the fairness of requiring the successor to assume a responsibility for defective products that was a burden necessarily attached to the original manufacturer's good will being enjoyed by the successor in the continued operation of the business. [19 Cal.3d at 31, 560 P.2d at 9, 136 Cal. Rptr. at 580.]

In our view these policy considerations likewise justify the imposition of potential strict tort liability on Amsted under the circumstances here presented. First, the plaintiff's potential remedy against Johnson, the original manufacturer of the allegedly defective press, was destroyed by the purchase of the Johnson assets, trade name and good will, and Johnson's resulting dissolution. It is true that there was an intermediate transaction involved, namely, the acquisition of the Johnson assets by Bontrager in 1956. But the acquisition of these assets by Amsted in 1962 directly brought about the ultimate dissolution of Bontrager's corporate existence. Accordingly, the Bontrager acquisition destroyed whatever remedy plaintiff might have had against Johnson, and the Amsted acquisition destroyed the plaintiff's potential cause of action against Bontrager. What is most important, however, is that there was continuity in the manufacturing of the Johnson product line throughout the history of these asset acquisitions.

Second, the imposition of successor corporation liability upon Amsted is consistent with the public policy of spreading the risk to society at large for the cost of injuries from defective products. * * *

In essence, Amsted contends that because it had no physical control over the allegedly defective Johnson press when it was placed into the stream of commerce, it is not the maker of the product who put it in the channels of trade. But to argue that a successor corporation can not be liable for injuries arising out of defects in certain products because it is not the same corporate entity that actually manufactured or distributed those products is to beg the underlying question involved in downstream corporate liability cases in the products liability context. No one asserts that Amsted was responsible for actually placing the allegedly defective press into the commercial stream. This was done by Johnson, the original manufacturer. But the injured plaintiff obviously cannot look to Johnson for a recovery of the damages occasioned by the accident involving the defective press. Rather, he looks to a viable successor corporation that continued to manufacture and sell the line of products that injured him. Strict liability for injuries caused by defective products placed into the stream of commerce is "an enterprise liability" Santor, *supra*, 44 N.J. at 65, one that continues so long as the defective product is present on the market. See Suter, *supra*, 81 N.J. at 169; Santor, *supra*, 44 N.J. at 65. The successor corporation that continues the manufacturing enterprise of its predecessor may not have had the means available for avoiding the risk of placing a defective product into the stream of commerce initially, but it does have the means available for avoiding the risk of harm caused by its predecessor's defective products still present on the market.

As stated by Justice Schreiber for the Court in Suter, *supra*:

> Strict liability in a sense is but an attempt to minimize the cost of accidents and to consider who should bear those costs. See the discussion in Calabresi & Hirschoff, "Toward a Test for Strict Liability in Torts," 81 Yale L.J. 1055 (1972), in which the authors suggest that the strict liability issue is to decide which party is the "cheapest cost avoider" or who is in the best position to make the cost-benefit analysis between accident costs and accident avoidance costs and to act on that decision once it is made. *Id.* at 1060. Using this approach, it is obvious that the manufacturer rather than the factory employee is "in the better position both to judge whether avoidance costs would exceed foreseeable accident costs and to act on that judgment." *Id.* [81 N.J. at 173–74.]

Similarly, because the manufacturer transfers to its successor corporation "the resources that had previously been available to [the manufacturer] for meeting its responsibilities to persons injured by defects in [products] it had produced," Ray v. Alad, *supra*, 19 Cal.3d at 33, 560 P.2d at 10, 136 Cal. Rptr. at 581, the successor rather than the user of the product is in the better position to bear accident-avoidance costs. By the terms of the 1962 purchase agreement with Bontrager, Amsted acquired the Johnson trade name, physical plant, manufacturing equipment, inventory, records of manufacturing designs, patents and customer lists. Amsted also sought the continued employment of the factory personnel that had manufactured the Johnson presses for Bontrager. "With these facilities and sources of information, [Amsted] had virtually the same capacity as [Johnson] to estimate the risks of claims for injuries from defects in previously manufactured [presses] for purposes of obtaining [liability] insurance coverage or planning self-insurance." *Id.* at 33, 560 P.2d at 10, 136 Cal. Rptr. at 581. Amsted was in the same position as its predecessors to avoid the costs and to spread the risk of accident injuries to users of defective Johnson power presses.

Third, the imposition upon Amsted of responsibility to answer claims of liability for injuries allegedly caused by defective Johnson presses is justified as a burden necessarily attached to its enjoyment of Johnson's trade name, good will and the continuation of an established manufacturing enterprise. See Ray v. Alad, *supra*, 19 Cal.3d at 33–34, 560 P.2d at 10–11, 136 Cal. Rptr. at 581–82. Through acquisition of the Johnson trade name, plant, employees, manufacturing equipment, designs and customer lists, and by holding itself out to potential customers as the manufacturer of the same line of Johnson power presses, Amsted benefited substantially from the legitimate exploitation of the accumulated good will earned by the Johnson product line. See Korzetz, *supra*, 472 F.Supp. at 144. Public policy requires that having received the substantial benefits of the continuing manufacturing enterprise, the successor corporation should also be made to bear the burden of the operating costs that other established business operations must ordinarily bear. See Cyr, *supra*, 501 F.2d at 1154; Shannon, *supra*, 379 F.Supp. at 802; Ray v. Alad, *supra*, 19 Cal.3d at 34, 560 P.2d at 11, 136 Cal. Rptr. at 581. By acquiring all of the Johnson assets and continuing the established business of manufacturing and selling Johnson presses, Amsted "became 'an integral part of the overall producing and marketing enterprise that should bear the cost of injuries resulting from defective products.'" *Id.* at 34, 560 P.2d at 11, 136 Cal. Rptr. at 582 (quoting Vandermark v. Ford Motor., 61 Cal.2d 256, 262, 391 P.2d 168, 171, 37 Cal. Rptr. 896, 899 (1964)).

VI

Defendant contends that the imposition of strict products liability on corporations that purchase manufacturing assets for cash will have a chilling—even a crippling—effect on the ability of the small manufacturer to transfer ownership of its business assets for a fair purchase price rather than be forced into liquidation proceedings. Business planners for prospective purchasing corporations will be hesitant to acquire "a potential can of worms that will open with untold contingent products liability claims." In order to divest itself of its business assets, the small manufacturing corporation will be forced to sacrifice such a substantial deduction from a fair purchase price that it would lose the ability to net a sum consistent with the true worth of the business assets.

These contentions raise legitimate concerns. We do not look upon them as "cassandrian arguments," see Turner, *supra*, 397 Mich. at 428, 244 N.W.2d at 883; Juenger & Schulman, Assets Sales and Products Liability, 22 Wayne L. Rev. 39, 57 (1975). However, in light of the social policy underlying the law of products liability, the true worth of a predecessor corporation must reflect the potential liability that the shareholders have escaped through the sale of their corporation. Thus, a reduction of the sale price by an amount calculated to compensate the successor corporation for the potential liability it has assumed is a more, not less, accurate measure of the true worth of the business.

Furthermore, a corporation planning the acquisition of another corporation's manufacturing assets has certain protective devices available to insulate it from the full costs of accidents arising out of defects in its predecessor's products. In addition to making adjustments to the purchase price, thereby spreading the potential costs of liability between predecessor and successor corporations, it can obtain products liability insurance for contingent liability claims, and it can enter into full or partial indemnification or escrow agreements with the selling corporation. True, the parties may experience difficulties in calculating a purchase price that fairly reflects the measure of risk of potential liabilities for the predecessor's defective products present in the market at the time of the asset acquisition. Likewise do we acknowledge that small manufacturing corporations may not find readily available adequate and affordable insurance coverage for liability arising out of injuries caused by the predecessor's defective products. However, these concerns, genuine as they may be, cannot be permitted to overshadow the basic social policy, now so well-entrenched in our jurisprudence, that favors imposition of the costs of injuries from defective products on the manufacturing enterprise and consuming public rather than on the innocent injured party. In time, the risk-spreading and cost avoidance measures adverted to above should become a normal part of business planning in connection with the corporate acquisition of the assets of a manufacturing enterprise. See Turner, *Supra*, 397 Mich. at 428, 244 N.W.2d at 883.

VII

Defendant further asserts that it is unfair to impose on it liability defects in a predecessor's product manufactured and placed into the stream of commerce twenty eight years and two corporate transactions before the accidental injury occurred. This argument, however, goes essentially to a question of repose, namely, whether there should be a limitation on the time period during which a party may bring suit for injury arising out of a defective product. As the Appellate Division correctly concluded, only the legislature is authorized to establish a limitation on the period during which suit may be commenced against a manufacturer, its successor, or seller of allegedly defective products. 171 N.J. SUPER. at 277.

* * *

Affirmed.

QUESTIONS

1. If stock is employed as the consideration for an asset purchase, what is the likelihood that the seller will retain that stock and remain in existence? Consider the consequences of continuing to hold the buyer's stock if the Investment Company Act of 1940 requires companies whose business is ownership of securities to register if they have more than 100 shareholders? See Investment Company Act of 1940, § 3(c)(1), 15 U.S.C. § 80a–3(c)(1). Note that a corporation regulated under this act cannot advertise itself as a diversified investment company unless at least 75% of its assets are limited to an amount no greater than 5% of total assets and not more than 10% of the total voting securities of any issuer. Investment Company Act of 1940, 15 U.S.C. § 80a–5. If an investment company fails to comply with these diversification requirements, it will not qualify as a "regulated investment company" under Subchapter M of the Internal Revenue Code of 1986, and will not qualify for pass-through tax treatment of its income. Internal Revenue Code of 1986, 26 U.S.C. § 851(b)(4). The result of a failure to diversify in this manner would be triple taxation—at the portfolio firm, the investment company, and then, when distributed, in the hands of its shareholders. See Chapter Ten, Part 7. Does this increase the risk that the transaction will be treated as a de facto merger or that the buyer will be treated as a mere continuation?

2. What can a buyer do to avoid having an asset purchase treated as a mere continuation of the seller's business? Is a notice to the seller's creditors helpful in this respect?

3. How useful is a hold harmless agreement obtained from a seller in situations like those in Amsted?

4. The Amsted court argued that a buyer could "obtain products liability insurance for contingent liability claims. . . ." Could it obtain an assignment of the seller's liability insurance? Consider the following:

    > "Liability policies are generally regarded as highly personalized contracts, wherein the insurer has carefully selected its risks with regard to the moral hazard involved. Accordingly, it has been uniformly held that such policies cannot be assigned so as to bind the insurer thereto, without the consent of the latter."

    > * * *

    > "Moreover, after a loss has occurred and rights under the policy have accrued, an assignment may be made without the consent of the insurer, even though the policy prohibits assignment. Under such circumstances, the assignment of a

right under the policy is not regarded as a transfer of the policy itself, but rather of a chose in action."

6B Appleman, Insurance Law and Practice § 4269 (1979).

5. What difference would it make if the selling corporation were in a Revised Model Business Corporation Act state, where RMBC § 14.07 expressly addresses the issue of products liability? If the injury from a previously manufactured product occurs in New Jersey, what effect will this statute have on the successor's liability?

6. One of the justifications for "mere continuation" liability given in the Cyr case, quoted by the Amsted court, was that the manufacturer's successor, carrying over the experience and expertise of the manufacturer, is in a better position than the consumer to gauge the risks and costs of meeting them. Is this true where the purchase is at arm's length by a buyer that has not previously engaged in the business, and which deals with the seller's management as adversaries, at least until the closing? Does it matter if the jurisdiction has adopted the "product line" theory of liability? Where the risk of defects stems from negligent supervision of the manufacturing process, is the successor able to assess the level and quality of monitoring over many years prior to its purchase of the assets?

7. The Ramirez court also justified successor "mere continuation" liability on the basis that "having received the substantial benefits of the continuing manufacturing enterprise, the successor corporation should also be made to bear the burden of the operating costs that other established business operations must ordinarily bear." Suppose the acquisition agreement expressly disclaims the purchase of goodwill, and assigns all of the purchase price to tangible assets? If the business is highly competitive and sells a product for which there are many substitutes, would this make a difference?

NOTE ON PRODUCT LINE SUCCESSOR LIABILITY

The product line exception has been considered and rejected in Bernard v. Kee Mfg. Co., 409 So.2d 1047 (Fla.1982); Hernandez v. Johnson Press Corp., 388 N.E.2d 778 (Ill. App.1979); Stratton v. Garvey Int., Inc., 676 P.2d 1290 (Kan. App.1984); Domine v. Fulton Iron Works, 76 Ill. App.3d 253, 257, 395 N.E.2d 19, 23 (1979), Jones v. Johnson Machine and Press Co., 320 N.W.2d 481 (Neb.1982); Schumacher v. Richards Shear Co., Inc., 59 N.Y.2d 239, 245, 451 N.E.2d 195, 198, 464 N.Y.S.2d 437, 440 (1983) Downtowner, Inc. v. Acrometal Products, Inc., 347 N.W.2d 118 (N.D.1984); and Fish v. Amsted Industries, Inc., 126 Wis.2d 293, 376 N.W.2d 820 (Wis. 1985). Alabama, Pennsylvania and Washington have adopted the product line exception. Rivers v. Stihl, 434 So.2d 766 (Ala.1983); Dawejko v. Jorgensen Steel Co., 290 Pa. Super. 15, 26, 434 A.2d 106, 111 (1981); Martin v. Abbott Laboratories, 102 Wash.2d 581, 689 P.2d 368 (1984); and Hall v. Armstrong Cork, Inc., 103 Wash.2d 258, 692 P.2d 787 (1984). Hickman v. Thomas C.

Thompson Co., 592 F.Supp. 1282 (D. Colo.1984) held that the Colorado courts would also adopt the product line exception. Other federal courts have generally held that the states the law of which they were applying would not adopt the rule. Dayton v. Peck, Stow and Wilcox Co., 739 F.2d 690, 694 (1st Cir.1984) (applying Mass. law); Tucker v. Paxson Mach. Co., 645 F.2d 620, 625 (8th Cir.1981) (applying Mo. law); Rhynes v. Branick Mfg. Corp., 629 F.2d 409, 410 (5th Cir.1980) (applying Tex. law); Travis v. Harris Corp., 565 F.2d 443, 448 (7th Cir.1977) (applying Ohio and Ind. laws); Leannais v. Cincinnati, Inc., 565 F.2d 437, 441 (7th Cir.1977) (applying Wis. law).

Schecter, Acquiring Corporate Assets Without Successor Liability: A Myth?, 30 Corp. Prac. Commen. 486, 498 (1988–89) described a situation where an English company wished to purchase the assets of a U.S. corporation that had manufactured a product containing asbestos during the 1950's and 60's, and was currently a defendant, although not the primary defendant, in litigation with maximum potential liability of $60 million. The buyer created an acquisition subsidiary which was adequately capitalized to avoid having the corporate veil pierced to reach the parent corporation, which limited the parent's total risk to its investment in the acquired business. "The English company was then able to secure through a New York insurance broker what was termed a 'sleep easy' insurance policy. It was a policy specially written by Lloyd's of London that covered the amount of the English company's initial investment in its American subsidiary. Assuming that the sleep easy policy stands up, the end result should be that all the English company ultimately has at risk is the profits to be earned by the American subsidiary."

For an extensive description of the doctrines of successor liability generally, see Philip I. Blumberg, The Continuity of the Enterprise Doctrine: Corporate Successorship, 10 Fla. J. Int'l L. 365 (1996). Professor Blumberg states that "[a]lthough the product line doctrine has been adopted in California, New Jersey, Pennsylvania, and Washington, it has been rejected by most jurisdictions and remains a highly controversial minority view. Most jurisdictions reject any expansion of successorship liability beyond the confined limits of the traditional exceptions to the classic doctrine. In addition, these jurisdictions that have been ready to broaden the traditional law seem to prefer to rely on the 'continuation of the enterprise' doctrine instead of the product line doctrine. The product line doctrine is not apt to win any new converts." *Id.* at 373.

For a case rejecting the products line doctrine, see Griggs v. Capitol Machine Works, Inc., 690 S.W.2d 287 (Tex. App.), affirmed per curiam, 701 S.W.2d 238 (Tex.1985). The court demonstrated the slippery slope nature of the products line theory of liability. It noted that Ramirez v. Amsted Industries, Inc., 86 N.J. 332, 431 A.2d 811 (1981), *supra*, argued that policies of imposing costs of defective products on makers of products were furthered by imposing liability on successors because they can buy insurance, and because buyers of businesses are presumed to be aware of the hazards of the products when they purchase the assets and good will of the seller's business. Because the buyer benefits from the good will of the business, it should bear the costs associated with the defective products of that business. But, the Griggs court argued, if awareness of hazards and benefit from the seller's good will are the basis for liability, then limited liability should be ignored, and employees, officers and directors, who are all aware of the defects and benefit from the good will, should also be liable. The Texas Legislature has rejected the de facto merger doctrine and limited successor liability to express provisions for it in another statute. Tex. Bus. Corp. Act Ann. art. 5.10B (Vernon 1980).

Some academic writers have called for a rejection of limited liability for shareholders, particularly where corporations have created catastrophic liability, through widespread dissemination of dangerous products. See, e.g., Henry Hansmann and Reinier Kraakman, Toward Unlimited Shareholder Liability for Corporate Torts, 100 Yale L. J. 1879 (1991) and David W. Leebron, Limited Liability, Tort Victims, and Creditors, 91 Colum. L. Rev. 1565 (1991). Further, the Griggs court argued, it imposes liability upon persons for breach of a duty of care they could not perform.

The Griggs court relied in part or Restatement (Second) of Torts, § 402A, in the following discussion:

"§ 402A. Special Liability of Seller of Product for Physical Harm to User or Consumer

"(1) *One who sells any product* in a defective condition unreasonably dangerous to the user or consumer or to his property is *subject to liability* for physical harm *thereby caused* to the ultimate user or consumer, or to his property, if

"(a) the seller is engaged in the business of selling such product, and

"(b) it is expected to and does reach the user or consumer without substantial change in the condition in which it is sold.

"(2) The rule stated in Subsection (1) applies although

"(a) the seller has exercised all possible care in the preparation and sale of his product, and

"(b) the user or consumer has not bought the product from or entered into any contractual relation with the seller.

"(emphasis supplied). The emphasized words highlight the theory of the section, wherein liability may be imposed upon a seller without his being at 'fault.' But the scope of possible liability is not without limits and the limits are explicitly set forth in the section itself. First and foremost, the theory of the section is to make *one who sells* a product *subject to liability* for physical harm *thereby caused* to the ultimate consumer or user. The phrase 'one who sells' implies, of course, that any liability under the section fastens upon the one who places the article in commerce. More importantly for our purposes, however, the phrase 'subject to liability' also circumscribes the scope of possible liability. In comment a under § 5 of the Restatement, wherein the phrase is defined, we find the following summary of the phrase 'subject to liability': 'The phrase thus deals with so much of the circumstances and events *preceding a plaintiff's injury* as are within the defendant's *exclusive ability to control*' (emphasis added). The 'product line' theory thus contradicts, by definition, this fundamental limitation which the Restatement imposes upon the doctrine of 'products liability.' "

Does imposition of successor liability have any deterrent effect on product manufacturers, if they realize that the ultimate sale price of the business will be depressed by the discounted expected cost of future liabilities? Does the time horizon matter here?

For a legislative response to the use of the de facto merger doctrine in the product liability area, see Rev. Model Bus. Corp. Act § 14.07, discussed above, which cuts off contingent or unknown claims against dissolved corporations three years after publication of a notice of dissolution.

---

iii. ASSUMED LIABILITIES

Antiphon, Inc. v. LEP Transport, Inc.

183 Mich. App. 377, 454 N.W.2d 222 (Ct. App.1990).

■ GLENN S. ALLEN, JR., J.

Plaintiff Antiphon, Inc., appeals as of right from an October 28, 1988 entry of a judgment of cause of action in favor of defendant LEP Transport, Inc., following a one-day bench trial in the Wayne Circuit Court. Antiphon sought the recovery of monies allegedly wrongfully paid to LEP under theories of breach of contract, interference with an advantageous economic and business relationship and unjust enrichment. * * * We affirm.

The material facts are not in serious dispute According to its complaint, Antiphon is a Connecticut corporation; wholly owned by Perstorp, Inc., a corporation located in Massachusetts, which in turn is wholly owned by Perstorp A.B., a corporation located in Sweden. Antiphon imports and sells sound-deadening materials primarily from Sweden. Antiphon also manufactures and markets felt-based "dampening pads" which are used as interior roof liners in automobiles. LEP is a New York corporation engaged in the business of customs brokering and international freight forwarding. It has an office in Detroit.

In May, 1986, Antiphon A.B. forwarded to National Auto Radiator, a company located in Windsor, Ontario, Canada, pallets of high temperature steel via the vessel Can Mar Europe. Antiphon paid all invoiced charges directly related to the shipment. However, LEP notified Antiphon that it would not release the shipment to National Auto Radiator until Antiphon paid an additional $34,029.61 LEP claimed it was owed from previous shipments. Rather than lose the business of National Auto Radiator, Antiphon paid the amount LEP alleged it was owed. It did so, however, under protest.

LEP claimed that the $34,029.61 was due from Antiphon as a result of a debt owed to LEP by a company known as Seamco, Inc. Seamco operated three manufacturing plants in Indiana, one each in Fort Wayne, Kendallville and South Whitley. For an unidentified period of time prior to July 1985, Seamco produced sound dampening products pursuant to a licensing agreement with Antiphon at its Fort Wayne, Indiana plant. Seamco also obtained the right to use the name "Antiphon" under the terms of the licensing agreement and thereafter formed an Indiana corporation known as Antiphon-Seamco, Inc. Both Seamco and Antiphon-Seamco employed LEP as a customs broker and freight forwarder for shipments of felt from Europe, primarily Finland.

At some point in time, Seamco spun off a subsidiary corporation known as Seamco Enterprises, Inc. This subsidiary corporation then acquired the assets associated with Seamco's Fort Wayne manufacturing plant and in turn sold same to Antiphon II, a corporation formed by Perstorp, Inc., for the apparent sole purpose of acquiring the Fort Wayne manufacturing plant. Seamco Enterprises, Inc., then dissolved. Thereafter Antiphon II merged with Antiphon and also dissolved. Seamco's creditors were not notified of the sales. On July 1, 1985, Antiphon began production at the Fort Wayne plant. At no time was there any common ownership of Seamco and Antiphon.

On November 19, 1986, Antiphon filed its complaint in the instant action. In its answer, LEP pled that Antiphon's post-purchase behavior led LEP to conclude that Antiphon was somehow related to Seamco and responsible for Seamco's obligations. Among the affirmative defenses pled by LEP were noncompliance with the bulk sales provisions of the Uniform Commercial Code, MCL 440.6102; MSA 19.6102, and estoppel.* The parties waived jury trial and the case was tried on September 29, 1988. Only two witnesses testified: Staffan Cedergren, vice-president of finance and administration for Antiphon and Michael Forward, former Detroit branch office manager of LEP.

Following proofs, the trial court ruled from the bench that "as between Seamco and Antiphon, there appears to be an agreement to pay whatever came up after the closing of that sale." The court also ruled "that Plaintiff and/or its predecessor corporation at the time of the sale owed a duty to Defendant to notify them of the sale of the assets and the various mergers . . . [and that] there is no evidence that Defendant was notified of the changes due to the sale of the assets." The court then concluded:

---

*   Formerly the Uniform Commercial Code contained an Article 6, which required notice to seller's creditors where inventory held for sale was involved. This article has been repealed by the authors of the UCC, and repealed by virtually all states.—Ed.

There was clearly an unbroken line of doing business between the Defendant and the various entities which preceded Plaintiff and the Plaintiff [sic], which means that $28,196.39 is their bill, which they may collect from Seamco.

* * *

* * * We must determine whether Antiphon may be held responsible for the debts incurred by Seamco where neither Seamco nor Antiphon informed Seamco's creditors, in this case LEP, of the sale of some or all of the Seamco Enterprises' assets and where Seamco and Antiphon engaged in activities that could reasonably lead LEP to believe that the two companies were either related or that Antiphon had assumed responsibility for the liabilities incurred by Seamco. We conclude that Antiphon may be held liable.

Generally, when one corporation sells its assets to another, the purchaser is not responsible for the debts and liabilities of the selling corporation. Stevens, *supra*, 371. However, as with any general rule, there are exceptions:

> The law is well settled in regard to liability of the consolidated or purchasing corporation for the debts and liabilities of the consolidating or selling corporation. Such obligations are assumed (1) when two or more corporations consolidate and form a new corporation, making no provision for the payment of the obligations of the old; (2) when by agreement, express or implied, a purchasing corporation promises to pay the debts of the selling corporation; (3) when the new corporation is a mere continuance of the old; (4) when the sale is fraudulent, and the property of the old corporation, liable for its debts, can be followed into the hands of the purchaser.

The trial court in the instant case did not expressly state which, if any, of the above-enumerated exceptions it found applicable. A review of the trial court's opinion leads us to conclude that the court based its finding of successor liability on the equitable doctrine of estoppel[5] and thus adopted a defense asserted by LEP. The question before us then becomes whether the doctrine of estoppel may be harmonized with any of the exceptions to the general rule against successor liability.

In Wiersma v. Michigan Bell Telephone Co., 156 Mich.App. 176, 184–185, 401 N.W.2d 265 (1986), a panel of this Court stated:

> An equitable estoppel arises where: (1) a party by representations, admissions or silence induces another party to believe facts; (2) the other party detrimentally relies and acts on this belief; and (3) the other party will be prejudiced if the first

---

[5] Antiphon asserts that the trial court predicated its finding of liability on a violation of the bulk sales provisions of MCL 440.6102; MSA 19.6102. We do not read the court's opinion as reaching such a conclusion, either explicitly or implicitly.

party is allowed to deny the existence of the facts. West Bay
Exploration Co. v. Amoco Production Co., 148 Mich. App. 197,
207, 384 N.W.2d 407 (1986).

The panel also noted that a party "may be estopped by its acts, conduct,
silence and acquiescence." *Id.* at 185.

In the realm of corporate successor liability, a successor corporation
may be held responsible for the liabilities incurred by its predecessor
where the facts demonstrate that there existed an implied agreement to
assume liability. Although there is no precise rule governing the finding
of implied liability, there is authority that suggests such a finding may
be made where the conduct or representations relied upon by the party
assuming liability indicates an intention on the part of the buyer to pay
the debts of the seller. Whether such an intent exists must be determined
from the facts and circumstances of each case. The factors to consider are:
(1) the effect of the transfer on the creditors of the predecessor
corporation; and (2) admissions of liability on the part of officers or other
spokespersons of the successor corporation.

We believe that the rationale underlying an application of the
doctrine of estoppel and the implied agreement to assume liability
exception are the same—that rationale being that a party may not, by its
conduct or silence, assume a position that if not maintained would result
in an injustice to another. Accordingly, we conclude that when the trial
court found that Antiphon was estopped from denying successor liability
it, in actuality, was deciding that Antiphon's conduct gave rise to an
implied acceptance of liability and that LEP was reasonable in relying on
this implied acceptance to its detriment. The trial court's ruling falls
within the parameters of the second enumerated exception set forth in
Chase, *supra.*

We also conclude that the trial court's finding of liability was
supported by the evidence adduced at trial. The conduct of Seamco and
Antiphon, combined with their silence about the sale, could have led LEP
to reasonably believe that the two companies were either related or that
Antiphon had assumed the liabilities of Seamco.

A review of the evidentiary record reveals that the last group of
invoices paid by Seamco was by check dated June 28, 1985, bearing the
name "Seamco, Inc.", and the address "Kendallville, Indiana."
Thereafter, LEP sent invoices to "Seamco Enterprises, Inc., Fort Wayne,
Indiana," and "Antiphon-Seamco" at that same address and on eight
occasions through November 20, 1985 the invoices were paid by checks
bearing the name "Antiphon-Seamco, Inc., Fort Wayne, Indiana."
Moreover, invoices for May and June, 1985 for costs incurred prior to the
sale were paid by Antiphon-Seamco after the sale. In December, 1985,
"Antiphon II, Inc., Fort Wayne, Indiana" sent LEP three checks in
payment of a number of invoices sent to "Antiphon-Seamco, Inc., Fort
Wayne, Indiana." Finally, three invoices sent to "Antiphon, Inc., Fort

Wayne, Indiana" were paid by Antiphon by check dated February 12, 1986.

Additionally, the record reveals that during the same period of time LEP dealt with the same personnel, that the orders were placed in the same manner, that the business operations were conducted in the same manner and that neither Seamco nor any of its subsequent reincarnations ever informed LEP of the change in ownership of the Fort Wayne plant. Moreover, as a result of Seamco-Antiphon's silence, LEP forewent its other creditor's remedies against Seamco before Seamco became uncollectible.

On these facts, we conclude that the trial court correctly found that Antiphon was estopped from denying liability by the existence of an implied agreement to assume the liabilities of Seamco.

_____

QUESTIONS

1. What is the source of Antiphon's duty to notify Seamco's creditors of the sale?

2. Could LEP have collected from Seamco's shareholders or directors under sections 6.40, 8.33, 14.06 and 14.07 of the Model Business Corporation Act? If so, where is the detrimental reliance in this case?

_____

iv. ENVIRONMENTAL LAW LIABILITIES

Purchasers of assets may be presented with another unpleasant surprise. Under the "Superfund" legislation, Comprehensive Environmental Response, Compensation, and Liability Act of 1980, 42 U.S.C. § 9601 ("CERCLA"), when hazardous waste is found on a site, liability for clean-up costs may be imposed on any of the following four entities: (1) the owner/operator of the site at the time of disposal; (2) the generator of the waste that arranged for the disposal; (3) those who transported the waste; and (4) the present owners of the site. Landowner liability is imposed even though the present landowner was not involved in the disposal in any way. There is no way to contract out of this liability. Under § 9607(b), there are only three limited defenses to this liability: "(1) an act of God, (2) an act of war, and (3) 'an act or omission of a third party other than an employee or agent of the defendant, or [other] than one whose act or omission occurs in connection with a contractual relationship, existing directly or indirectly, with the defendant . . . if the defendant establishes by a preponderance of the evidence that (a) he exercised due care with respect to the hazardous substance concerned . . . and (b) he took precautions against foreseeable acts or omissions of any such third party and the consequences that could foreseeably result from such acts or omissions.' "

Under this language, the courts held innocent landowners liable for clean-up costs, without regard to their culpability. See, e.g., New York v. Shore Realty Corp., 759 F.2d 1032 (2d Cir.1985). The defendant landowner asserted the "third party" defense of § 9607(b)(3) above, but it was rejected by the Court of Appeals, which held that a prior owner could not be a third party, "since the acts or omissions referred to in the statute are doubtless those occurring during the ownership or operation of the defendant." One commentator has observed that courts creating successor liability under CERCLA have resorted to the product line and continuity of enterprise doctrines developed in the product liability area, although the Department of Justice has shown some reluctance in recent years to pursue cases on these theories. Light, "Product Line" and "Continuity of Enterprise" Theories of Corporate Successor Liability Under CERCLA, 11 Miss. Coll. L. Rev. 63 (1990).

In 1986 Congress created the "innocent landowner" defense in § 9601(35)(A), which defines "contractual relationship" referred to in § 9607(b)(3), quoted above, to include:

"land contracts, deeds or other instruments transferring title or possession, unless the real property on which the facility concerned is located was acquired by the defendant after the disposal or placement of the hazardous substance on, in, or at the facility, and one or more of the circumstances described [below] is also established by the defendant by a preponderance of the evidence:

"(i) At the time the defendant acquired the facility the defendant did not know and had no reason to know that any hazardous substance which is the subject of the release or threatened release was disposed of on, in, or at the facility . . .

"(B) To establish that the defendant had no reason to know, as provided in clause (i) of subparagraph (A) of this paragraph, the defendant must have undertaken, at the time of acquisition, all appropriate inquiry into the previous ownership and uses of the property consistent with good commercial or customary practice in an effort to minimize liability. For purposes of the preceding sentence the court shall take into account any specialized knowledge or experience on the part of the defendant, the relationship of the purchase price to the value of the property if uncontaminated, commonly known or reasonably ascertainable information about the property, the obviousness of the presence or likely presence of contamination at the property, and the ability to detect such contamination by appropriate inspection."

How much "due diligence" is enough to avail a landowner of this defense is not yet settled. A 1991 study found only two cases in which the innocent landowner defense was upheld. Aaron Gershonowitz and Miguel Padilla, Superfund's Innocent Landowner Defense: Elusive or Illusory?, 6 Toxics L. Rep. (BNA) 626 (Oct. 16, 1991). A 1989 bill that would have amended CERCLA, "The Innocent Landowner Defense Amendment of 1989," would have provided a "safe harbor" for the innocent purchaser defense, if the purchaser conducted an environmental audit that included at least (1) a review of recorded chain of title documents; (2) a review of aerial photographs available from state and local governments that may reflect prior uses of the property; (3) a determination whether there are any existing environmental cleanup liens against the property that have arisen under federal, state or local laws; (4) a review of reasonably obtainable federal, state and local records of sites or facilities when there have been, and are likely to be, further releases of hazardous substances, including reports and environmental records concerning landfills, underground storage tanks and activities that are likely to cause or contribute to the release of hazardous substances; and (5) a visual site inspection of real property, its improvements and adjacent real property. Leland, Environmental Audit Should Become Part of Merger Checklist, The National Law Journal, Feb. 5, 1990, pp. S10, S12. These procedures have become a common part of a due diligence investigation. Edward B. Witte and Mark L. Prager, "Environmental Lender Liability: Searching for Safe Harbors in the Wake of Kelley v. EPA, 1 Wis. Envtl. L.J. 1 (1994). They are similar to those recommended by the American Society for Testing and Materials (ASTM) in Standard E.50.02.02, "Phase I Environmental Site Assessment Process."

In an active M & A market, there may be competition for a prospective seller. This allows the seller to set a short deadline for offers, and limits the amount of due diligence possible for buyers. One writer suggested that under these circumstances the buyers need to focus on the materiality of various risks, and, instead of waiting for one comprehensive environmental report at the end of the diligence process, should request environmental counsel and consultants to provide more frequent oral briefings and shorter periodic written summaries, allowing a focus on material risks. Peggy Otum, Practical Considerations for Environmental Due Diligence in a Competitive M & A Market, Business Law Today, February, 2016, at http://www.americanbar.org/publications /blt/2016/02/05_otum.html.

If an environmental audit discloses a polluted site, what are the possible responses? In return for a reduction in the price, the purchaser may be willing to assume the cost of cleanup. Thus the purchaser may accept the property "as is." But see Wiegmann & Rose International Corp. v. NL Industries, 735 F.Supp. 957 (N.D. Cal.1990), where a court declined to interpret an "as is" clause in a deed as waiving the buyer's claims against the seller with respect to CERCLA liabilities. The court held that only the defenses enumerated in the statute were available to those made liable in the statute. The court was influenced by the fact that the buyer was unaware of the environmental problem at the time of sale, and that CERCLA had not yet been enacted. In Mardan v. C.G.C. Music, Ltd., 804 F.2d 1454 (9th Cir.1986), parties to an asset sale both knew about the hazardous waste contained in a settling pond at the time of sale, and at the time of execution of a "General Settlement and Release" two years after the sale, purporting to resolve all claims of the purchaser against the seller. The court held that the parties had clearly intended the settlement agreement to include all possible claims relating to the property, including claims under CERCLA.

Aerovox, Inc. acquired all of the assets of Belleville Industries, Inc., and agreed to assume all of Belleville's balance sheet liabilities and to perform all of its contracts, except that Aerovox specifically disclaimed any liability arising out of Belleville's use of PCBs. The court held that the disclaimer was ineffective against the United States as a defense to an action asserting liability for cleanup of the PCBs in the adjacent river and harbor. In re Acushnet River and New Bedford Harbor Proceedings re Alleged PCB Pollution, 712 F.Supp. 1010 (D. Mass. 1989). The court also relied on the de facto merger doctrine to find the current owner potentially liable for the preceding owner's discharges.

A buyer that discovers polluted property that will require cleanup may obtain an indemnification agreement from the seller by which the seller agrees to indemnify the buyer for any cleanup costs or other liabilities. These agreements are expressly permitted by CERCLA. 42 U.S.C. § 9607(e), as are contribution actions. Where the seller proposes to dissolve immediately after the sale, of what use are such indemnification agreements? The de facto merger doctrine has been used to impose liability where the seller did not sell all its assets to the buyer of the polluted site, but sold its remaining assets to another corporation. Philadelphia Electric Co. v. Hercules, Inc., 762 F.2d 303 (3d Cir.1985). In another case the selling corporation's corporate existence was revived by the Secretary of State for the limited purpose of defending superfund litigation. In re Acushnet River and New Bedford Harbor Proceedings re Alleged PCB Pollution, 712 F.Supp. 1010 (D. Mass. 1989).

Another possibility is to exclude the polluted site from the sale, if it is not essential to the continued operations the buyer intends to conduct. In one case with which the author is familiar, the buyer declined to purchase the polluted site, even though it contained the manufacturing plant owned by the business. The buyer entered into a long-term lease, and required the seller to place part of the sale proceeds in escrow for future clean-up expenses. Will this avoid purchaser liability under successorship doctrines? For a critical view of the successor liability doctrine, particularly the product line theory, see Barnard, EPA's Policy of Successor Liability under CERCLA, 6 Stan. Environmental L. J. 78, 95–97 (1986).

Could a buyer use a newly created subsidiary corporation as the purchaser of assets, in order to protect other assets from the possibility of calamitous liability for clean-up? There are two theories under which a parent might be held liable for the subsidiary's liabilities. First, under traditional common law doctrines, "the corporate veil may be pierced and the shareholder held liable for the corporation's conduct when, inter alia, the corporate form would otherwise be misused to accomplish certain wrongful purposes, most notably fraud, on the shareholder's behalf." United States v. Bestfoods, 524 U.S. 51, 118 S.Ct. 1876, 141 L.Ed.2d 43, 56 (1998). The Supreme Court did not decide whether state veil-piercing principles should be employed or whether the federal courts should instead apply a federal common law of veil piercing. New York v. National Services Industries, Inc., 352 F.3d 201 (2d Cir. 2006) held that "substantial continuity" was not a common law test, and thus could not create successor liability under CERCLA. *See also* Mickowski v. Visi-Trak Worldwide, LLC, 415 F.3d 501 (6th Cir. 2005); *Contra*: Laborers' Pension Fund v. Lay-Com, Inc., 455 F.Supp.2d 773 (N.D. Ill. 2006).

A corporate seller may be held directly liable under CERCLA if it "operated" the property under section 107(a)(2) of CERCLA. This broadening of liability means that buyers must inquire not only about owned properties, but also about those the seller has operated in the past. The doctrines of successor liability explored in the products liability section come into play here as well. Federal courts may treat an asset sale as a de facto merger or may determine that the purchaser's business is a mere continuation of the seller's business. A buyer may expressly agree to assume the environmental liabilities of the seller, or the court may find that the transaction is for the fraudulent purpose of escaping liability, as where the seller is left insolvent and received inadequate consideration for the assets. Most courts have concluded that a federal law of successor liability should apply in order to develop uniform federal rules in this area. *See, e.g.*, United States v. General Battery Corporation, Inc., 423 F.3d 294 (3d Cir. 2005), reaffirming an earlier decision applying federal common law of successor liability on policy grounds. For a discussion of these doctrines in the CERCLA context see Kenneth K. Kilbert, Successor Liability under CERCLA: Whither Substantial Continuity?, 14 Penn. St. Envtl. L. Rev. 1 (2005).

v. LABOR RELATIONS OBLIGATIONS

It is not surprising that the courts would hold that a surviving corporation in a merger assumes some, if not all, of the obligations of an acquired corporation to recognize an employees' union and its prior collective bargaining agreement. John Wiley & Sons, Inc. v. Livingston, 376 U.S. 543 (1964). But the Supreme Court has taken essentially the same position, although in a more limited manner, in cases involving asset transfers, in NLRB v. Burns International Security Services, Inc., 406 U.S. 272 (1972). Burns replaced another security firm, Wackenhut, in supplying security protection for Lockheed Aircraft. Burns hired 27 of Wackenhut's former guards at this location, and added 15 of its present employees to perform guard duties at the plant. Thus a majority of the guards at the plant were former Wackenhut employees. Burns then found itself in a jurisdictional dispute between the American Federation of Guards, which represented Burns' employees, and the United Plant Guards, which had represented Wackenhut's employees. The Supreme Court held that while the NLRB could not force Burns to adopt the Wackenhut collective bargaining agreement, it could require Burns to bargain with the Wackenhut union once it had completed its hiring, despite the absence of a merger agreement. The court found "substantial continuity" in the business enterprise, especially that a majority of the work force were former Wackenhut employees. The court held that the obligation did not begin at the hiring stage—that Burns was free to set the initial terms and conditions of employment without bargaining with the Wackenhut union, but once it had hired a unit consisting of a majority of Wackenhut employees, the obligation arose. The importance of this distinction became clear in Howard Johnson Co. v. Detroit Local Joint Executive Board, Hotel and Restaurant Employees & Bartenders International Union AFL-CIO, 417 U.S. 249 (1974), where Howard Johnson purchased the assets of a motor lodge from another company. Howard Johnson refused to recognize the union or assume the seller's collective bargaining agreements, which provided by their terms that they would be binding on the employer's "successors, assigns, purchasers, lessees or transferees." Howard Johnson began to hire new workers, rather than the seller's employees. The Supreme Court held that Howard Johnson was neither obliged to hire the previous employees nor to arbitrate its alleged responsibility to do so. Because only a minority of the new work force consisted of the seller's former employees, the Court held that there was insufficient continuity in the work force to justify arbitration under the seller's labor agreements.

In early 1982 Sterlingwale Corp., a New England textile manufacturer, fell on hard times, and laid off its entire work force and closed down its business entirely. A former executive formed Fall River Dyeing & Finishing Corp., and purchased the assets and inventory of Sterlingwale. Operations began seven months after Sterlingwale's operations were closed down. A month after Fall River began operating, the Textile Workers local that had represented Sterlingwale's employees requested recognition from Fall River. At the startup stage, and even after operations were manned more substantially, a majority of Fall River's employees were former Sterlingwale employees, although once full production was reached, former Sterlingwale employees were no longer in the majority. But because the union demand was made at a time when Fall River had hired a "substantial and representative complement" of employees that included a majority of former employees, it was required to recognize the union as their representative.

The NLRB has identified the following criteria that govern whether a buyer will be treated as a successor for purpose of union recognition:

1. Has there been a substantial continuity of the same business operations?

2. Does the new employer use the same plant?

3. Does the alleged successor have the same or substantially the same work force?

4. Do the same jobs exist under the same working conditions?

5. Does the new employer employ the same supervisors?

6. Does the new employer use the same machinery, equipment, and methods of production?

7. Does the new employer manufacture the same product or offer the same services?

Miles & Sons Trucking, 269 NLRB 7, 13 (1984). For a general discussions of the successorship doctrine in employee relations law, see Fasman & Fischler, Labor Relations Consequences of Mergers and Acquisitions, 13 Employee Relations L. J. 14 (1987). In addition, a successor employer may have an obligation to remedy a predecessor's unfair labor practices. Golden State Bottling Co. v. NLRB, 414 U.S. 168 (1973), required a successor employer to reinstate an employee who had been wrongfully discharged by the predecessor employer. See DuRoss, Increasing the Labor-Related Costs of Business Transfers and Acquisitions—The Specter of Per Se Liability for New Owners, 67 Wash. U. L.Q. 375 (1989). Indeed, as the author suggested, it has been extended to a seller's unpaid contributions to a multi-employer retirement plan covered by ERISA, in Einhorn v. M. L. Ruberton Construction Co., 632 F.3d 89 (3d Cir. 2011). In this case the court added another factor to the list set out above: Did the purchaser know of the liability, and was there a sufficient continuity of operations and workforce?

This ruling may extend to many other areas of employment as well, including civil rights liabilities, liabilities under the Federal Coal Mining Safety and Health Act, and liabilities under the Fair Labor Standards Act. Indeed, the Seventh Circuit has extended it to final judgments under settlement agreements for violations of the Fair Labor Standards Act in Teed v. Thomas & Betts Power Solutions, L.L.C., 711 F.3d 763 (7th Cir. 2013). Betts had purchased the assets of J. T. Packard Associates in an agreement that made the purchase "free and clear of all liabilities." Judge Posner wrote:

> Most states limit such liability, with exceptions irrelevant to this case, to sales in which a buyer (the successor) expressly or implicitly assumes the seller's liabilities. Wisconsin, the state whose law would apply if the underlying claim were based on state law, is such a state.

But when liability is based on a violation of a federal statute relating to labor relations or employment, a federal common law standard of successor liability is applied that is more favorable to plaintiffs than most state-law standards to which the court might otherwise look. [Citing John Wiley & Sons, *supra.*]

Judge Posner's broad language suggests that federal successor doctrines will generally preempt state law in labor and employment matters, under a more liberal standard of successor liability. He stated that the following factors would be used in determining successor liability:

1. Whether the successor had notice of the pending liability;

2. Whether the predecessor would have been able to pay the relief sought before the sale—if not, that favors no successor liability;

3. Whether the predecessor could have provided relief after the sale—if not, that favors successor liability;

4. Whether the successor can provide the relief sought, which favors successor liability;

5. Whether there is continuity between the operations and work force of the predecessor and successor, which favors successor liability.

Courts have thus saddled buyers with a variety of liabilities they did not contractually assume, including: products liability, environmental liabilities, labor, employment and benefits liabilities, liabilities to trade creditors, and even liabilities arising under seller's agreements not assumed by the buyer. A multi-factor test increases buyers' uncertainty about the risk of liability, despite language in the agreement. It is also difficult to predict not only what theory of successor liability might be imposed, but what state's laws might be applicable to a successor liability claim. Courts may disregard the choice of law provision in the asset purchase agreement will be relevant to the choice of law in a successor liability case. Berg Chilling Systems, Inc. v. Hull Corp., 435 F.3d 455 (3rd Cir., 2006) (contractual choice of law provision inapplicable to successor liability claim, the majority reasoning that the *de facto* merger doctrine, by its very nature, looks beyond the form of the contract to its substance and that a claimant not a party to the contract should not be bound by its choice of law provision); *see also* Ruiz v. Blentech Corp., 89 F.3d 320 (7th Cir., 1996) (in a products liability case, the law of the state wherein the injured party resides governs the successor liability analysis). For these reasons, some buyers conclude that successor liability is an unavoidable risk, to be insured against to the extent possible and cost effective.

PART III

THE MATING DANCE

CHAPTER FIVE

GETTING WHAT YOU PAY FOR: THE BUYER'S SEARCH FOR INFORMATION

Introduction

Acquiring and valuing a large business enterprise is a complex task. Any going concern is a mix of tangible assets, assembled to perform particular tasks as efficiently as possible, and intangible assets, such as patents, copyrights, customer goodwill, employee relations and the like, which permit the efficient and profitable production of whatever goods and services the seller produces. Financial relationships, both with creditors and debtors, also contribute importantly to value. A buyer initially approaching the prospective purchase of a business must know that a good deal of investigation will be necessary in order to assure that real value is present in the enterprise. The task facing the buyer's team is two-fold; to investigate all of these matters to determine what the business really owns, the nature of the relationships that contribute to its success, all of the claims against (contingent or otherwise) and liabilities of the seller, and to get the seller and those who should know to represent that things are as they appear. The last chapter on buyers' liabilities in asset sales illustrates some of the areas of risk facing buyers in both mergers and assets purchases.

Professor Ronald Gilson has described the role of the business lawyer in this setting as that of an information specialist, or a "transaction cost engineer."* While some clients will only engage in a single acquisition transaction, the acquisition lawyer is a specialist in such transactions. While even the executives of clients inexperienced at acquisitions will know what it takes to constitute a successful and valuable business in the client's own field, if the client's own business is well managed, these executives may not be aware of all of the ways in which appearances can be deceiving. The lawyer, trained to worry about deceptive appearances, often serves the function of eliciting information about the seller's assets and liabilities that provides valuable assistance to the buyer. The center of the acquisition agreement becomes the representations and warranties given by the seller. Here the seller is expected to describe all of the assets being conveyed—both tangible

---

* Ronald J. Gilson, Value Creation by Business Lawyers: Legal Skills and Asset Pricing, 94 Yale L.J. 239 (1984). But see Stephen Schwarcz, Explaining the Value of Transactional Lawyering, 12 Stanford J. of L., Bus. & Fin. 486 (2007), arguing that lawyers primarily serve as technicians. See also William J. Carney, Ronald J. Gilson and George W. Dent, Jr., Discussion: What Does a Transactional Lawyer Do?, 12 Transactions 175 (2011).

assets, and intangibles, such as leases, employment agreements, patents, and others that are being assigned to the buyer. These descriptions are typically found in schedules attached to the acquisition agreement, which are incorporated in the agreement by reference. The seller will typically warrant ownership of these assets, and either warrant that there are no liens against them, or fully describe all of the existing liens and burdens on these assets. Similarly, the seller will describe all of the claims of creditors against the business, and typically warrant that there are no others. These representations and warranties on liabilities typically begin with the disclaimer, "there are no other claims or liabilities other than those described in Exhibit x." Much of this process occurs in the form of representations and warranties about the seller's financial statements. Not only do these statements attach a book value to all assets and liabilities, but they make claims abthe profitability of the seller's business, which are critical to a determination of its value. (Where the transaction involves a stock merger, the seller will see itself as making an investment in the buyer, and will be equally interested in reciprocal disclosures, representations and warranties by the buyer.)

Much of the rest of the acquisition agreement surrounds these critical representations and warranties. The initial agreement on price, for example, may be conditioned upon their truthfulness and accuracy. Frequently price adjustments are provided, so the transaction will close, but at a higher or lower price, especially in the acquisition of closely held firms. In some cases these clauses provide that minor deviations will not be considered "material" to the transaction, and will neither justify a refusal to close or a price adjustment, There may be formulas for adjusting the price if the business turns out to be worth less (or sometimes more) than the representations and warranties suggest. On the other hand, the continued truthfulness and accuracy of the representations and warranties may be a condition of the buyer's obligation to close, and to pay for the acquired business. There is nearly always a time lag between the signing of the definitive acquisition agreement and the closing, for a variety of reasons. Some may relate to preparation of a registration statement if the transaction is a stock-for-stock merger or involves the buyer's debt securities as consideration. Others may relate to tax rulings, or to approval of the Justice Department or the Federal Trade Commission (depending upon the industry) under the Hart-Scott-Rodino Antitrust Improvements Act. These delays call for a set of covenants that the business will continue to remain as valuable at the closing as it was at the signing. For example, the covenants may call for working capital to be maintained at some minimum level, or may call for inventories (or their proceeds) to continue at certain levels until the closing. Another means for the buyer to protect itself is to insist that there be no material adverse changes in the seller's business or prospects prior to the closing. A failure to comply with these covenants may be treated not only as a breach of covenant, but as a justification for the buyer to decline to close the transaction. Finally, the lawyers must consider remedies for each side if things don't go as expected.

The attorney's job begins with assignment of tasks to various members of the acquisition team at the beginning of the negotiation process. At the same time, requests for documents will be made to the seller. In cases where the seller initiates the process, the seller may have provided an electronic room that contains all documents the seller can anticipate being required. There are many checklists published for these tasks, and the buyer's attorney should be certain that he or she is aware of all of the facts that need to be ascertained, and all of the records that need to be inspected, or in some cases verified, as part of the process. A sample checklist appears in Appendix B.* The seller's preparation of schedules of assets, material contracts and liabilities as part of the drafting of the acquisition agreement often provides much of the base information about which documents require inspection. In many cases the attorney's due diligence process culminates in a "due diligence memo," which memorializes the matters investigated and identifies any problems discovered during the process, and perhaps any curative steps that have been taken. In smaller transactions the buyer may wish to avoid the expense of this due diligence memo, but in most cases the preparatory work does not differ, whether the memo is prepared or not. Due diligence continues up to the time of closing, often with buyers insisting on receipt of various certificates to assure the buyer that the facts remain as they first appeared. Some of these will be from officers of the seller, but others may be from third parties, such as landlords or licensors, who will certify that the seller is not in breach of any terms of the lease or license as of the closing.

One might reasonably ask why such due diligence is required, when the seller must represent and warrant to all material facts about itself and its business. Aren't damage suits good enough, if some representation turns out to be inaccurate, incomplete and misleading? After all, having these representations warranted eliminates any problems of proof about the seller's state of mind or intent to deceive (scienter, as required for a fraud claim), or the level of care exercised by the seller in making its representations (as in a suit for negligent misrepresentation). If the statement was untrue, that's really the end of the litigation under a breach of warranty claim. This ignores the difficulties the buyer might face in proving damages. The buyer might simply prefer to cancel the entire transaction if the representations and warranties are not true at the closing, and walk away from the transaction, or renegotiate the price. Perhaps the more critical issue is whether there will be a seller in existence after the closing. If there's a

---

*   For a more complete treatment of the subject, see Section of Business Law, American Bar Association, MANUAL ON ACQUISITION REVIEW (1995).

merger, the seller has disappeared into the buyer or its acquisition subsidiary, and the seller's shareholders have walked away with the merger consideration. If a company sells all its assets and then liquidates (a fairly unusual scenario under the current tax laws), the same is true. For these reasons, the last chance a buyer may get to protect itself is prior to the closing, and the due diligence is the critical activity in implementing that protection. In the acquisition of privately held companies, there are opportunities to hold shareholders responsible through indemnification provisions.

The seller's attorney may have at least one area in which he or she must engage in due diligence as well. The buyer may insist on an opinion of seller's attorney, addressed to the buyer, that the execution of the Merger Agreement was properly authorized by the corporation's board, that it is enforceable against the seller according to its terms (with specified exceptions), will not violate any agreements to which the company is a party, nor any laws to which the company is subject. In recent years this practice has begun to disappear, and in other cases lawyers are now cautioned not to ask for any opinions they would not be prepared to give themselves. Standard forms of opinion letters have addressed these issues.

The Acquisition Mating Dance and Other Essays on Negotiating

James C. Freund.
119–123 (1987).

[O]ne of the real keys to how the bargaining comes out in this situation is which party wants the deal more. And, in many cases, it's the *buyer*. Consider, for example, this typical scenario.

The seller is about to part with "his baby"—the business that he built up from nothing over 30 years. He's bound to have mixed emotions about selling. And we've all seen how someone who really doesn't want to do something—whether his feelings have already surfaced or are still unconscious—can come up with lots of reasons justifying inaction.

For example, this seller may become mesmerized by his own swollen asking price, and then use the buyer's unwillingness to pay it as the excuse to break off negotiations—reckoning that he'll get top dollar from another buyer, or convincing himself he's unwilling to sell at a lesser price. Or he may dig in his heels (and even end the talks) if he perceives the buyer—or the buyer's lawyer!—as negotiating too hard for the kind of protection that buyers commonly think they need.

Meanwhile, examine the buyer in the same scenario. While the seller ends up with just money or paper (pretty prosaic stuff), the buyer is out there trying to acquire a dream, to breathe life into a fantasy—buying a company that's a perfect fit with his other businesses, or that gives him a toehold in a long-sought marketplace. And there's a ready rationalization for such a buyer in shelling out more dollars' he's paying so much already, what's a few extra bucks?—particularly when (unlike a refrigerator) there's no price tag hanging from the item being purchased. Or, why not give in on some of those protections he's been seeking? That's all lawyer stuff, anyway, and none of those eventualities is likely to come to pass. . . .

Now, on the other hand, there may be instances when it's the *seller* who wants the deal more. Perhaps he really needs the money, prosaic though cash may be. Or, he sees black clouds on the horizon (the Japanese have duplicated his technology) and wants to get out before the deluge. Or, he realizes that this buyer is nibbling at a top-dollar price, and he doesn't want to let him off the hook—particularly since there may not be other bidders for a basically unique business that's unlikely to fit into many buyers' plans.

The *buyer*, in this second scenario, may be a little more cautious. After all, the price seems quite high, the horizon is murky, the seller appears anxious. . . .

Who Moves . . . and Who Stands Firm?

The determination of who wants it more is most relevant to the bargaining over price. To state the obvious, the seller generally wishes to receive more than the buyer would like to pay; the buyer wants to pay less than the seller would like to receive. They start off some distance apart; to make a deal, there has to be movement toward the middle. Usually, both parties move at least some of the way, since no one wants to do a deal in which he's been unable to bargain for *anything* off (or over) his adversary's initial proposal. The real question is, who will move *more*? And conversely, who will—at a point when he seems to have too little (or too much) on the table to make the deal—stand firm?

So, for instance, assume you're advising the seller. There have been several rounds of movement toward the center; the last was made by the buyer. Now, it's the seller's turn. You assess the situation. Your client doesn't have to do the deal. His initial asking price wasn't outrageous, and he's made some meaningful concessions as the bargaining has progressed. The buyer, on the other hand, gives every sign of badly wanting the deal—and doesn't appear tapped out in terms of funds.

Well, this might be an ideal point to advise the seller to pause, stand firm, and see if he can get the buyer to bid against himself.

The same process applies in terms of other negotiable items, once the price is resolved. Let's say you represent the buyer this time. A battle is raging over a certain protection your client would like to have—though you reckon that, in the final analysis, he could do without it.

You size things up. The seller has achieved a nifty price that he's unlikely to duplicate elsewhere. You have a hunch he's under some financial pressure. The issue being debated involves a contingency that may or may not happen; the buyer's position isn't unreasonable. And—of prime importance—you feel that, despite the emotion he's displaying over this issue, the seller is basically a rational individual, who's likely to behave in accordance with his economic best interests.

Well, it's not a bad place for the buyer to draw the line. People rarely give up a deal over non-price issues, unless the other party's position is totally egregious, or unless they don't care that much about the deal in the first place. This seller cares; the buyer's position isn't that extreme; the seller can't take a chance that you just might mean business. The buyer can stick, with reasonable confidence that the seller will come around.

Candor with the Client

Sometimes, though, the assessment goes the other way; and you, as the objective counselor, face the difficult task of advising your client that *he's* the party who wants or needs the deal more—and consequently, that he ought to go up (or down) on price, or collapse on some other hotly contested issue. Of course, you can't really tell your client how badly he wants something. What you can do is help him arrive at that realization on his own, by putting the particular issue—be it price or whatever—in context. ("I know it's painful, Paul, but think of it this way: The increment they're demanding is less than two percent of what you're already prepared to pay. If the decision to buy is a good one at $10 million, does another $180,000 make it wrong?")

You can also help your client size up the guy on the other side. Presumably, you've been listening to what's been said, peering behind the words, assessing the action (more important than the words), piecing together the clues. What's the net? ("Bottom line, Paul, it's my feeling that the seller is very ambivalent on doing this deal; in fact, he may be looking for an excuse to call it off. The $180,000 may furnish him with just that excuse. . . .")

1.   THE DUE DILIGENCE PROCESS FOR BUYERS

The discussion of due diligence should be prefaced by noting that sellers will always insist on execution of a confidentiality agreement or a nondisclosure agreement ("NDA") by the prospective buyer, in order to protect private business information. (See Appendix D) Generally these agreements begin with a commitment to disclose none of the seller's information, and then expressly carve out information already in the public domain, such as SEC filings. Even in a company subject to the disclosure rules of the Securities Exchange Act, there will be trade secrets, business plans and other matters not required to be disclosed. A seller should not disclose confidential information about its business, especially to a competitor, without limitations on the potential buyer's use of the information if the transaction does not occur. Indeed, where a buyer is acquiring a competitor, all personnel involved in due diligence should be cautioned about the need to avoid discussions of coordinating sales efforts, allocating customers or territories and other matters that might constitute a per se violation of the antitrust laws.

A confidentiality agreement may contain additional restrictions such as the agreement of the potential buyer not to solicit the seller's employees and customers for a period after termination of the negotiations (a "no-poaching" covenant), as well as agreement to keep confidential the negotiations (including the fact that negotiations are occurring). An agreement not to disclose the existence of negotiations may be important to a public company because premature disclosure could make customers nervous, attract hostile bidders or affect trading in the seller's stock. In addition, because information being disclosed may include "inside information," confidentiality agreements signed by bidders of publicly traded targets may restrict a potential buyer from trading in the company's stock for a period of time until the information becomes stale or is publicly disclosed. The agreement may also contain other provisions which prevent the potential buyer from taking actions that would be deemed hostile by the board. The buyer, on the other hand, will want to be protected from liability for using or disclosing information it had legitimately obtained from other sources. A form of confidentiality agreement is found in Appendix D. Note that it also contains a "standstill" agreement, preventing the prospective buyer from mounting an uninvited takeover attempt for three years after negotiations terminate, on the theory that the buyer would have an informational advantage over other prospective bidders resulting from its review of confidential information. See Chapter 6, section 6.2.G.

In August 2011 Hewlett Packard Co. (HP) bought Autonomy Corp., a British software company that had been reporting rapid growth, for $11 billion. In November 2012, HP wrote down the value of this investment by $8.8 billion. Approximately $5.5 billion was related to accounting misstatements. How could such inaccuracies be missed? On the accounting side, Autonomy refused to hand over copies of financial documents supporting its audits, leaving HP to rely on publicly reported financial statements and about 25 sales contracts, according to pleadings in pending litigation. At this point little is known about other problems that caused the balance of the write-down. But the point is clear: serious due diligence really matters.

In 1999 McKesson acquired HBO & Co. for $13.9 billion, only to discover that some HBO officers had committed extensive financial fraud. McKesson's CEO resigned, and his successor reported that the market value of McKesson's stock declined by approximately the amount of the purchase. See http://www.forbes.com/2010/07/15/healthcare-acquisition-fraud-intelligent-technology-mckesson.html.

Less than 8 months after Bristol-Myers Squibb bought out Inhibitex and its lead hepatitis C drug for $2.5 billion in 20122, the company wrote off the therapy as a complete waste of money and a potential threat to human safety. Bristol-Myers took a $1.8 billion charge for Inhibitex's drug, a key part of its plan to develop an all-oral therapy for hepatitis C. Clinical trials were halted when one patient under treatment died and others were hospitalized. One can only wonder if more thorough due diligence would have made a difference.

Buying, Selling and Merging Businesses

Jere D. McGaffey.
15–26 (2d ed. 1989).

§ 1.03   The Purchase Investigation

The nature of the purchase investigation will vary depending upon the individual circumstances of each transaction. The investigation may have a variety of purposes and involve many different personnel; it should certainly involve, however, a business history of the seller, its legal structure, current liabilities, and financial commitments.

Purchase investigations involve various steps occurring over a period of time. What investigations occur prior to arriving at a price, prior to a letter of intent, prior to a definitive agreement, and prior to closing all depend upon the circumstances. The extent of these investigations prior to closing is dependent, in part, upon the nature of the representations and warranties, whether they survive the closing, and the strength of any indemnification. The purchase may be one in which the representations are not going to survive the closing or in which no effective indemnification exists. If the purchase is of a public corporation that will liquidate after the transaction, if it is likely that the seller may dissipate a substantial portion of the funds, or if creditors will obtain most of what is realized in the purchase, such a result may be reached through negotiations. In such a case, the degree of investigation may be of greater significance than in a situation in which it is reasonable for the purchaser to rely upon the indemnification provisions and the representations and warranties.

* * *

Normally, an investigation of the business will not be permitted by the seller until the prospective buyer has made a fairly strong commitment to the purchase. This is because the seller is unwilling to disclose confidential business information and because the investigation may have a disruptive effect upon the seller's personnel. An exception to this general policy occurs when the corporation is known to be for sale and is trying to attract a number of bidders. Some substantial investigation may at times be required when the transaction is still confidential and is being withheld from most employees. This fact may substantially limit the nature of the inquiry.* Letters of intent [or term sheets] are often entered into and [sometimes] announced in order to lay the groundwork for further investigation—the letters being evidence that a reasonable commitment has occurred.

The seller should be sure to make a disclosure of all problems and offer an adequate evaluation of any potential risks. Seldom will the purchaser fail to go through with the transaction based upon disclosures of this type. Moreover, disclosure may avoid later indemnification. If the same officers who worked for the seller continue to work for the purchaser and if the problem occurs, they can point out that they did mention the potential for this type of problem and avoid the embarrassing position of not having mentioned it at the time of purchase. In this connection owners who are no longer going to be active in the business must recognize that their employees may have various conflicting reactions to the proposed sale. If employees are going to continue in the business, they will want to impress the new owner of the business as well as to be loyal to the old owner.

§ 1.03(a) Purpose of the Purchase Investigation

The principal purpose of the purchase investigation is to determine whether or not the acquisition should, in fact, be made. It is also important that those conducting the investigation have a clear idea of the purpose and goals of the investigation.

* * *

Prior to the purchase investigation, the principals will normally have an interest in arriving at a price range based upon historical financial statements adjusted by assumptions as to future performance. The purpose of the purchase investigation is to verify these assumptions in order to determine whether or not the transaction is to proceed.**

* * *

It is important that the individuals conducting the investigation have a clear idea of what they are attempting to determine in this investigation. It may be a simple question of whether or not a substantial number of undisclosed liabilities exist. On the other hand, it may be much more complicated and involve the future marketing and production capabilities; whether certain plants can be closed or expanded, whether a different system of marketing can be used, and whether the seller's business can be integrated with the purchaser's operations.

---

*   Since the date of this article sellers often establish electronic data "rooms" with virtually all relevant documents available in digital form, protected by passwords only given to prospective buyers that have executed non-disclosure agreements.—Ed.

**   Except, as note, where the target has determine to conduct an auction to determin the best price attainable.—Ed.

§ 1.03(b) Organization

The purchase investigation should be carefully organized in regard to its method, the personnel employed, the information desired, and the scope of the investigation.

* * *

Although a variety of desirable methods exist, the initial purchase investigation normally takes place after the agreement on price has been reached, and it is conducted by two or three individuals, usually an accountant and a lawyer, who may be either corporate personnel or outside consultants, and a representative from the business side. It is helpful to have more than one individual involved in the investigation so that ideas can be shared. Care must be taken, however, to divide up the duties and to make sure that the same items are not being investigated by several individuals.

If an audit or a major examination of financial statements is to be conducted by an accounting firm, more extensive examination and personnel will be required.

Prior to the visit to the seller's business, materials should be gathered and analyzed. If the seller is a public corporation, a beginning point for the investigation is to obtain all the public material, including all periodic filings with the Securities and Exchange Commission for a number of years, the annual reports, and any prospectuses issued in recent years. It may also be helpful to obtain any reports on the corporation made by analysts, since these may describe the business in greater detail than filed documents and discuss the strengths and weaknesses of the corporation.* The number of years to be examined may vary with the corporation, and the emphasis must certainly be placed on the later years; however, at least a five-year period should be considered.

In the case of private corporations, financial statements for a number of years should be obtained. These may have substantial detail in footnotes on in supplementary schedules depending upon the form of the accountants' reports. It is desirable to obtain an adequate supply of financial statements to be distributed to all individuals involved in the transaction.

* * *

In large acquisitions in which a number of individuals are working, control over documents and adequate communication are important. One person should be made responsible for maintaining files on all documents obtained and for supplying all personnel with the documents and information they need. Generally the results of these purchase

---

*   The buyer's representatives may also want to examine credit ratings for the seller's debt. Publicly issued corporate bonds are typically rated by a small group of companies, such as Moody's Investor Services, Standard & Poors, and Fitch Investors Service. Private companies that have issued debt may be rated by Dun & Bradstreet. Ed.

investigations are not written up in detailed reports, although summaries of material information should be exchanged among all parties working on the transaction. In major transactions involving a number of parties, the communication of various pieces of information is an important factor. Often much information is informally exchanged among the various personnel conducting the investigation during meals. The attorney responsible for drafting the agreement must be either the principal one involved in the purchase investigation or one who is very closely linked with the individuals who are so involved in order that the attorney may draft the agreement to reflect the knowledge obtained from the seller.

§ 1.03(c) Liabilities and Commitments Investigated.

The purchase investigation should also be a thorough examination of all aspects of the business operation under consideration. Financial history, assets and liabilities, collections, leases, retirement plans, and labor contracts are among those areas to be carefully scrutinized.

The purchase investigation involves examination of various documents, short conferences with the personnel in charge of particular areas, and discussions with outside lawyers and accountants for the seller. A tour of the operations is often helpful to form a better idea of the nature of the business. Catalogs and any business policy bulletins may also prove helpful in gaining an understanding of the business.

A history of the seller from a business viewpoint and the legal structure of his organization should be obtained. This may lead to a need for further investigation of past years. Experience indicates that it may be desirable to check the discussions of past events and their timing with the written record as reprinted in the SEC filings and annual reports, since the time sequence is often blurred in the minds of the executives of a corporation, and particular details may have been forgotten. The annual reports may also give a better indication of the thinking at a particular time regarding what was occurring and what seemed likely to present new avenues to the corporation—all of which may in later years have taken on a different emphasis or deemphasis as a result of what in fact took place.

Information should be obtained regarding subsidiaries, including capital structure, articles of incorporation, by-laws, any other shareholders, and lists of officers and directors.

If the seller is a corporation with a number of subsidiaries, an examination of the history of the corporate structure and its various attributes must be considered. This includes determining whether all of the subsidiaries are wholly owned and whether any agreement calls for sale of stock of any of the subsidiaries to employees or lenders. The tax basis of the stock of the subsidiaries must be determined as well as the tax basis of the assets. Are there any net operating losses in any of the subsidiaries? The status of intercompany obligations among the subsidiaries should be determined and their history noted. Are there losses in any of the subsidiaries for state tax purposes that are not available for federal tax purposes because of the use of consolidated returns? The capital structure of the subsidiaries should be determined. This may have significance in the event of a liquidation of one of the subsidiaries and a determination to take a worthless-security deduction under Section 165(g) of the Internal Revenue Code.

Any securities held by the seller other than those in subsidiaries will normally have a historical significance, and a decision as to their future disposition should be made.

Similarly, life insurance policies with cash surrender value should be examined to determine whether they should be continued, offered to the insured for their cash surrender value, or surrendered.

The investigation of contingent liabilities may be carried out from the accounting side by discussions with accounting personnel and outside auditors, from the legal side by investigating various contractual documents, and in all cases by discussing with pertinent personnel the activities involved in their areas. All pending litigation in which the corporation is involved should be reviewed both with the personnel inside the corporation and with the outside counsel for the corporation (in the case of material litigation). The nature of the investigation will, of course, depend upon the nature of the suits. Discussions should be held with the individual responsible for the insurance programs of the corporation as well as with the individuals handling product liability claims to determine what claims exist, what kinds of potential problems may occur in the future, what claims have occurred in the past, and what payments have been made on these kind of claims. Concern must be given to past product lines that have been discontinued as well as to existing product lines. Each corporation's potential for product liability varies. The detail with which this is investigated must also vary with regard to determining ways to reduce present liability, estimated probable future liability, and allocating the liability between the purchaser and seller. Potential environmental liability should be carefully investigated. An environmental audit may be desirable.

Detailed schedules of insurance coverage, including carriers, premiums, expiration dates, and provisions for retrospective premiums should be developed and evaluated by the purchaser's insurance department to determine what the future potential insurance requirements may be, whether there are advantages in combining it with the purchaser's operation, and whether the coverage is adequate. This investigation may also be a source of information concerning the locations at which the business is being done and should be checked against the information given with respect to real estate, both leased and owned.

Discussions should be held with the credit manager concerning collections on receivables. The investigator should explore whether, when suits are commenced for collection, countersuits are normally brought and, if so, what types of claims are made in these suits. Determination should be made regarding whether or not the distributors of the customers could, in fact, continue to pay off existing accounts-receivable balances if sales were no longer made to them. Arrangements with customers or distributors, if in written form, should be obtained, as should any types of business forms used in either purchasing or selling. Contracts involving purchases and sales should be examined to ascertain what long term commitments have been made. If the seller has a chance of declines in price, how adversely would this affect his competitive position? If sales are made on long-term fixed-price commitments, how vulnerable are the seller's profits to cost escalation? Any contracts with purchasers of a significant amount should be investigated, and special attention should be given to any government contracts.

Questions should be asked with respect to possible sensitive payments being made to customer personnel, and this matter should be investigated with respect to the nature of the particular business and the prevalence of this practice in the industry.

Leases of a material nature should be examined to determine whether or not there are options for renewal or purchase. The ability to sublet or assign and the ability to transfer these leases to a related corporation should be considered. Real estate title evidence should be reviewed.

All borrowing by the corporation should be investigated with respect to terms, ability to prepay, whether or not loan amounts become due upon the type of transaction that is proposed, security arrangements for the debts, and covenants that are included.* Covenants should be investigated to determine the need for delivering audited financial statements of the seller. If separate audited financial statements are required of the seller after the transaction, additional expense may be incurred; industrial revenue bonds should be particularly investigated in this regard.

All employee contracts and benefit plans should be reviewed. Minutes for the last few years should at least be scanned to seek out evidence of such commitments to employees or of other types of commitments. The effect of a change of ownership upon the employee benefit plan, the need for revisions, and how these are to be integrated into the purchaser's overall plan should be considered. Questions should be asked with respect to informal pension arrangements with retired employees who may not have been covered by qualified plans.

---

*   Loan agreements should be reviewed for change of control provisions, that make loans immediately due and payable in the event of a change of control. Ed.

Documentation with respect to qualified plans should be reviewed; and, in the case of pension plans, actuarial studies should be analyzed to determine the nature of the liabilities to be expected. This area is one requiring expertise and may involve a substantial expenditure. The terminology should be clearly understood by all individuals involved. If the plans are substantially different from the purchaser's own plans or if the accounting or funding means are different, it will be important that those differences be explained to top management so that they do not have any misunderstanding concerning the commitments undertaken. The mere fact that assets are sufficient for all vested liabilities does not preclude the existence of substantial potential liability to fund the obligations of those individuals who are not vested; and, although current benefits may be funded, past service obligations and improvements that have been made to the pension plan may be funded over a number of years. It must be recognized that substantial dollars will go into the plans, which, in a sense, relate to the activities of the employees prior to the time of the change of ownership. The investigation is made to gain an understanding of these items so that any need for negotiation concerning their effect on price may be made. If there are any multiemployer plans, they must be carefully investigated for potential liability.

All labor contracts should be reviewed, particularly for termination pay and expiration dates. The labor relations experience of the seller must be considered to anticipate likely needed salary increases at the time expiration occurs, the potential for strikes, and the adverse impact upon the corporation in the event of a strike.*

All contracts that involve significant amounts or major time-period obligations should be reviewed. The review should determine whether the other party can be relieved of the obligation if it so desires and what possibilities of renewal exist if the contract is advantageous. Each contract must also be reviewed to ascertain what the liabilities would be if the seller wished to discontinue the contract and how long the seller is obligated under the contract. Consideration must also be given to the effect on the contract of the transaction or of any subsequent assignment of the contract to a related corporation. Whether the acquisition of the business would have an impact that would make some of the basic fundamentals of the contract no longer sensible should also be considered. For example, in a contract in which the price is made dependent upon the costs of the seller, is it going to be practical to make such a determination if the seller's operation is going to be combined with the purchaser's? Employment contracts that have consideration based upon the corporation's stock are examples of contracts that will require revision in the event of the acquisition. Any agreements with respect to patents must be investigated; so must the significance of the patent

---

* The author once had a partner who specialized in examining the files of former employees of sellers to determine if there were any patterns of employer misbehavior that might lead to contingent liabilities or other labor problems. Ed.

position of the seller and the potential liability for any infringements on patents of others.

State taxes should be investigated by interviewing the individuals involved in making the necessary filings. Particular consideration should be given to the possible liability for sale, use, income and personal property in states in which no filing is being made. This can be determined by talking to the individual involved, by determining in what states the filings are being made, and by examining the contracts in states in which no filings are being made. In the case of sales that are exempt from sales tax upon filing resale certificates, review of the policy of obtaining these resale certificates should be considered. Questions raised in past audits by state tax officials should also be evaluated.

Federal income tax liability should be investigated. Past reports of revenue agents should be examined to ascertain what types of issues have arisen. Consideration should be given to the tax reserve and to the potential liabilities that are being reserved against. A general discussion should be held with the tax and accounting personnel about possible liabilities and aggressive positions that have been taken. Examination should be made of any potential withholding or FICA tax liability. Payments made on a regular basis to individuals that are not considered employees should be reviewed to determine whether there is any potential for them being taxed as employees.

The seller's record of compliance with various government regulations, such as ERISA in its pension plans, pollution control provisions, wage and hour provisions, and OSHA, should be studied.* Investigations by governmental authorities and their reports should be explored. Often as part of the purchase investigation and the obtaining of documentation, the seller may learn more about the business than previously known, and this may be the one time when the purchaser gets a good chance to accumulate a substantial bit of information and to gain some idea of operations at the divisions or subsidiaries of the business.

The amount of sales commissions to salesmen should be determined. Although salesmen may be independent contractors, a person who is accounting for a substantial portion of the total sales and is receiving large commissions may be a very important individual in the total business operation. This fact should be known and given due weight in the purchase.

---

* The buyer should also determine whether regulatory permission for a transfer of control will be required. Ed.

Due Diligence in the Digital Age: What We've Lost

Marita A. Makinen, Corporate Counsel.
December 10, 2015.

M & A professionals of a certain vintage fondly recall the due diligence trips of their youth. These offered the enthusiastic M & A warrior the opportunity to visit cultural meccas such as warehouses in Orlando, tanneries in upstate New York and nameless office parks across the Midwest. With a plane ticket in hand, young law firm associates would be transformed into members of an elite cross-disciplinary strike force including accountants, bankers and clients.

The target was the data room—this citadel would be guarded by a young Harvard Business School banker posing as a well-dressed librarian, checking documents in and out on a sheet clamped to a clipboard and watching over the data room prisoners. For the lucky ones, a visit to the company's offices and filing cabinets might be in store. Imagine the excitement of a young associate facing a wall of file drawers and being told "what you need is in there." Hours of sifting through hundreds of badly labeled folders to find unexecuted or incomplete documents followed. Copying of documents was not allowed, and phones back then did not take pictures, so the young professional had to read as fast as possible and focus only on what was important.

There were highlights in this process. One was the camaraderie of the team members at the end of the day. While the lawyers may have longed to bill hours all night, the guardians of the data room usually took a dim view of this. At closing time, well-organized clients would download with the team. Each of the reviewers, no matter how junior, would offer their commentary to the group. Listening to the reports, law firm associates would have the opportunity to hear about valuation models, tax returns and financial statement issues. The client would receive immediate feedback on the issues of the day and instruct the group's activities for the day to come. At the end of it all, the group could enjoy the best local food and drink available and bond for a few hours before it started all over again.

Fast forward 20 years . . .

The in-person data room is now extinct. Intralinks Dealspace and its kin are the new rulers of the virtual diligence realm. The new realm has its advantages, including better organization of documents, no travel expense and presumably fewer expenses and wasted "down time." The M & A professionals are now free to work at diligence at their own pace, in their own offices or homes and at all hours of the day and night.

However, virtual due diligence comes with some often-unacknowledged downsides. Consider the following:

- *Out of Focus:* In the past, data room participants often sat together, without computers, and did not take calls or respond to emails during data room hours. The time with the documents was limited and they were the sole focus during the day. Now, associates must multitask on several transactions and competing demands during the day. The presence of computers (and privacy) also introduces other potential distractions.

- *Out of Touch:* In the data room, multiple opportunities to connect with clients and financial and accounting professionals arose during the day. Questions and concerns could be addressed in real-time in conversation. Now, there is a greater risk that concerns are held back for a final report.

- *Out of Order:* Documents could not leave the data room and mindless summaries were not an option due to time constraints and writing or typing fatigue. Now, the ability to review hundreds of documents on command, at any time of day or night, lessens the need to prioritize and not waste time.

- *Out of Time:* Less exposure of junior lawyers to other diligence participants (bankers, lawyers, accountants, clients) is driven by today's cost pressures and increasing specialization in the legal field. We have lost the "town square" for communication that was the diligence trip. While it may seem cost effective to have a team member only spend time with his narrower area of expertise, losing the big picture lessens the overall quality of the work and lessens the ability to focus on the most important issues.

- *Out of Context:* With electronic media, it is easier to "cut and paste" excessive amounts of uninteresting, routine material into a diligence report. This material has the tendency to bury what is important.

- *Out of Bounds:* Working with a group in a data room means that a collective direction can be taken. A junior lawyer can easily "get lost" in the woods of a virtual data room. Given that the professional is sitting in her office, alone, it is less likely that someone will notice that she has gotten lost in a timely manner.

Despite some reservations, the virtual diligence model offers efficiencies, better access to information and is here to stay. Accordingly, we all need to recognize and address the downfalls. I'd like to share a few suggestions that I have found helpful:

- *Understand the Plan:* All members of the team must ensure they understand not only the basic deal structure, but also why the client wants to do the deal and what is planned for the business post-closing. How will synergies or growth be achieved and what needs to change in the current business to make this happen? If no one explains this to you, please ask.

- *Know the Valuation:* It is never too early for younger lawyers to start learning the basics of accounting and valuation. The diligence team needs to set materiality thresholds understanding the multiples of revenue and/or EBITDA that the client is paying. In a 9X EBITDA transaction, not unusual in today's market, an undiscovered million-dollar expense item becomes a $9 million valuation issue. Don't be the team that misses this issue, or worse, sees it but doesn't understand its importance.

- *Scope the Work:* Before the whole team dives into the virtual data room, before a single document is reviewed, a work plan needs to be agreed on with the client. Is any outside help needed to review data room materials? Are languages or areas of law not covered by the firm presented in the data room? These issues should be addressed on day one. For clients frequently engaging in M & A, a standard diligence scope expectations document can be maintained and provided to outside counsel.

- *Hold Team Meetings:* Periodic team meetings should be scheduled at the start of the diligence process. The meetings can provide a framework for checking that sufficient progress is being made, and to provide and adjust direction midstream. Findings can also be reviewed in a format that encourages real-time questions and answers.

- *Communicate Informally, Frequently:* Supervising attorneys should check in more frequently with team members performing diligence to minimize wheel-spinning, answer questions as they arise and provide clear direction. More frequent contact between client and outside counsel (in advance of the delivery of a diligence report) is also a good idea. Pick up the phone and chat about updates on a more frequent basis. If a serious item arises, the outside lawyer should send an email right away with a summary so that the client can circulate it to others internally.

- *Stay Abreast:* Know what other professionals are finding in their diligence and how it ties in to your part of the job. Ask to see the tax, accounting and any other relevant due diligence summaries. The senior lawyer should ensure that, in turn, legal findings are fully reviewed and understood by the persons performing finance and accounting due diligence.

- *Don't Summarize:* The most common issue with diligence reports is that they regurgitate summaries of documents reviewed without applying the facts to the client's deal structure, post-closing plans or valuation model. Don't summarize, explain "why" something is important and how problems can be fixed. Clients can help to avoid this issue by providing their diligence report expectations up-front.

- *Explore Technology:* Some downsides of the virtual data room can be overcome by other technology. While a virtual data room can create the risk of attorneys "getting lost" in a sea of immaterial agreements, search tools can be a life saver (think store leases or customer subscription agreements). Kira Diligence Engine provides a search engine and contract term aggregation tool that saves on manual review time. Everyone's goal should be to spend the diligence hours in the budget to analyze the impact of contracts on a client's business plan (explaining the "why") rather than in preparing summaries. Other tools can lessen the risk of virtual data room isolation by facilitating communication among team members, allowing reports and documents to be shared and annotated securely among internal and external team members. The leading provider of board portals, Diligent Corporation, recently introduced its Diligent Teams product, with exciting potential future application in M & A transactions.

While the virtual data room has changed the landscape of diligence dramatically over the past decade, it is important to remember "how things used to be" and to try to replicate the best of the past. As legal advisors with ever quicker and better access to data, we need to resist the temptations of information overload. We must not function as mere reporters of legal terms—this job, ultimately, will be performed by technology—but as analytic, value-additive team members who support the client with our legal expertise in the valuation and business planning process.

Marita A. Makinen is a partner at Lowenstein Sandler in New York, and is chair of the mergers and acquisitions practice as well as cochair of the transactions and advisory group. She has a focus on strategic acquisitions and divestitures by public and growth-stage private companies.

Source: http://www.corpcounsel.com/printerfriendly/id=1202744547 175.

Due Diligence Checklists

The due diligence checklist in Appendix B is illustrative of the areas with which the purchaser's team must concern itself during the course of the investigation. More detailed checklists are frequently used. Part A focuses particularly on the lawyer's tasks. It does not distinguish between mergers and asset purchases. For a more detailed checklist and a discussion of the tasks involved, see Subcommittee on Acquisition Review of the Committee on Negotiated Acquisitions, Section on Business Law, American Bar Association, MANUAL ON ACQUISITION REVIEW (1995).

A List of Common M & A Transaction Showstoppers

Robert R. Kibby, Munsch Hardt Kopf & Harr, P.C.

The following is a list of typical "showstoppers" that can derail an M & A transaction or result in a reduction of the purchase price. * * *

Stock/equity ownership issues. If the buyer is acquiring the stock/equity of the seller, the buyer's counsel will do a thorough investigation of the seller's capital structure to attempt to spot any of the following:

- Commitments to grant equity that haven't been recorded in the ownership records
- Equity ownership records that aren't clear or are inconsistent with other company records
- Agreements to issue equity interests with unusual antidilution or other rights
- Agreements or obligations to issue securities haven't been complied with
- Equity ownership records that conflict with information in Secretary of State filings
- Stock certificates that are lost or misplaced
- Owners who can't be located
- Company repurchases of equity where state laws haven't been followed
- Owners who are uncooperative
- Issuances of equity in transactions that are not clearly exempt from securities registration requirements
- Use of unregistered broker to conduct private securities offerings
- Issues with financial statements or accounting records.

- Financial statements don't reflect all financial transactions

- Because buyers typically analyze the performance of a business based on the seller's financial statements, exceptions from generally accepted accounting principles (GAAP) need to be identified. Revenue recognition and inventory valuation are commonly recurring issues.

- Personal financial transactions are run through the business and mingled with business transactions.

Intellectual property (IP) ownership issues. These types of issues commonly arise from the following:

- Employees haven't signed confidentiality agreements that protect customer lists, trade secrets, technology, etc.

- Independent contractors have developed software or other technology but haven't assigned their rights to the company, which could create joint ownership of the IP.

- Company uses IP that appears to infringe upon another's IP rights.

- Key employees aren't bound by non-competition/non-solicitation agreements, which could enable them to leave and raid customers or employees or set up a competing business.

Contracts with terms that a buyer won't want to assume. Examples include:

- Pricing is substantially below market and can't be modified; there are substantial limitations on the ability to raise prices; or "most favored nations" clauses require seller to give specified customers the best deal offered to any customer.

- Contract provides for substantial future payments when no future benefits will be realized to the buyer. One example of this is a referral fee agreement that provides for "perpetual" payments to the referral source, far beyond the initial customer introduction.

- Contracts contain "no assignment" clauses or require consent of the contract counterparties to assign, which makes an asset sale difficult to consummate.

Tax risks. There are many tax issues that can derail a transaction, and buyers will typically conduct substantial tax due diligence. One way a seller can anticipate these issues and solve issues before they occur is to have its accounting firm weigh in on substantial tax issues as they are encountered instead of waiting until an M & A transaction is in view.

Customer issues. Because buyers will want to talk to your key customers, you'll need to make sure that your relationships with them are good and that any outstanding issues have been addressed. It's best not to have any surprises here.

Employee claims. This can be a particular problem with recently terminated employees who smell an opportunity to make a claim and get a quick settlement. Substantial liabilities can also result if the company doesn't comply with OSHA requirements or facilities do not comply with access requirements for the disabled.

Immigration matters. Potential issues often arise with companies that use a significant number of unskilled workers. Buyers will often ask to review copies of Social Security "no match" letters the seller has received. This review will help potential buyers assess whether the company has a substantial risk of government raids or fines.

Regulatory issues. The particular issue depends on the industry in which seller operates and could include failure to possess the necessary licenses or the failure to comply with regulatory requirements that would expose the company to fines or penalties.

Issues with key creditors. If the seller's business is substantially dependent upon its relationships with key creditors, the buyer will be interested in the quality of those relationships. If the seller is experiencing financial difficulties, the buyer will want to assess whether the seller's lender will continue to advance funds until the closing.

Litigation, claims and contingent liabilities. Buyer's counsel will do substantial due diligence to find and assess potential problems, and a buyer will typically expect the seller to continue to be responsible for claims that aren't insured. Claims often come out of the woodwork when a transaction is in view, and it often pays to try to resolve any claims and potential claims before a transaction arises.

Environmental conditions or liabilities. Buyers typically don't want to assume environmental liabilities, so it's often best to have a game plan to address environmental liabilities and risks if the seller's business lends itself to those types of risks.

Joint ventures/strategic partner relationships. Although sellers might view joint venture and similar agreements as being similar to other types of business contracts, they do present special risks and will require the buyer to do substantial due diligence. Buyers will pay special attention to ongoing capital contribution requirements, tax issues, potential liabilities, and the reputation and competitive position of the other venture party.

ERISA/Employee Benefits. Issues often arise in the following areas:

- Failure of compensation plans and benefit plans (including qualified plans, option plans, etc.) or their operation to comply with legal requirements

- Underfunded pension plan liabilities
- Employment or severance contracts provide for substantial payments or obligations to terminated employees, including golden parachute payments, health benefits, perks, etc.

The Due Diligence Review Memorandum: Corporate Review in Connection with Mergers and Acquisitions

William F. Wynne, Jr.
CORPORATE COUNSEL'S GUIDE TO ACQUISITIONS
& DIVESTITURES (1994), pp. 7.008–.010.

After the review of all requested documents has been completed, the reviewing attorney should compare the information reviewed to the information contained in the Acquisition Agreement and the Exhibits and Schedules thereto. The purpose of the comparison is to determine whether any material matter that should have been disclosed in the Acquisition Agreement or the Exhibits and Schedules thereto has been omitted, and whether, based on the results of the corporate review, the information provided by Purchaser as the basis for its acquisition decision is consistent with the information and documents reviewed.

The reviewing attorney should prepare a memorandum providing the following information:

(a) the date and place of the review and specific identification of the documents reviewed;

(b) names of the persons contacted with regard to information about the documents of the Company;

(c) a general review of the history of the Company and its subsidiaries including the place and date of incorporation, any foreign qualifications and predecessor companies;

(d) a general discussion of the securities of the Company, due authorization, etc.;

(e) general discussion of outstanding debt and material contracts, including material leases;

(f) specific description and discussion of consents, authorizations or approvals required by the terms of the documents reviewed or other problems, rights or forfeitures triggered by the proposed acquisition and specific recommendations for dealing with such matters;

(g) specific discussion of all pending material legal proceedings to which the Company or any of its subsidiaries is a party or to which any of their property is subject;

(h) specific discussion of any variance between the material reviewed and the information contained in the Acquisition Agreement and the Exhibits and Schedules thereto; and

(i) any other information the reviewer deems relevant to the client in assessing the acquisition.

If you have any questions regarding the information reviewed or cannot understand the significance of information provided in the Exhibits or Schedules in response to a representation or warranty, you should include such questions or information in the memorandum.

Significant problems capable of resolution and discovered in the course of the corporate review should be raised, in writing, with the Company as soon as possible. Required consents, authorizations, or approvals, whether governmental or third party, are best handled in a cooperative fashion to avoid postponement of the completion of the acquisition. If, in the course of the corporate review, you discover a transaction-threatening issue, for instance a certain antitrust obstacle, a material undisclosed liability or any other matter which would jeopardize or preclude the Company's satisfaction of the conditions precedent to the closing of the transaction, you should bring the issue to the attention of the partner on the transaction or to the client so that an appropriate strategy dealing with the issue may be developed.

Certain deficiencies in the corporate records can be corrected; suggestions for such corrections include

(a) if minutes are missing, a certificate should be obtained from officers of the Company setting forth the reason for the unavailability of the minutes and describing any material action believed to have been taken (and setting forth for certain key events, e.g., share authorizations, were not addressed at the meeting) during the period for which the minutes are unavailable;

(b) if there were required authorizations by the Board of Directors or the shareholders for specific transactions which were not obtained, or which authorizations appear, on their face, to be inadequate, the action taken should be ratified by a vote of the Board of Directors or shareholders, as the case may be. The ratification sought should be as specific as would ordinarily be required for the original authorization; a blanket authorization of all prior transactions without specific identification should be resisted; and

(c) mechanical omissions such as signatures on minutes and waivers of notice should be cured to the extent the persons needed to sign are available. If such signatories are not available, an affidavit of the persons present at the meeting setting forth the business transacted will be sufficient.

This is obviously not an exhaustive description of possible corrective measures in the event of deficiencies in the documents or records reviewed.

Where corrective measures are taken to clean up matters such as those described above, the reviewing attorney should prepare and distribute a supplemental memorandum to Purchaser prior to the closing of the acquisition.

A Due Diligence Horror Story

In August 2011 Hewlett Packard Co. (HP) bought Autonomy Corp, a British software company that had been reporting rapid growth, for $11 billion. In November 2012, HP wrote down the value of this investment by $8.8 billion. Approximately $5.5 billion was related to accounting misstatements. How could such inaccuracies be missed? On the accounting side, Autonomy refused to hand over copies of financial documents supporting its audits, leaving HP to rely on publicly reported financial statements and about 25 sales contracts, according to pleadings in pending litigation. At this point little is known about other problems that caused the balance of the write-down. But the point is clear: serious due diligence really matters. The following is taken from the May 5, 2015 issue of the GUARDIAN, reciting the claims from pleadings in the case Hewlett Packard filed against Autonomy's founder, Mike Lynch and the finance director, Sushovan Hussain, in London's High Court. This has been edited to focus primarily on Hewlett Packard's claims.

"HP, which bought Autonomy in 2011 for $11bn, has filed a claim against Lynch and his finance director, Sushovan Hussain, in the high court in London, alleging they engaged in improper transactions with software resellers and in questionable accounting practices.

"HP claims that Lynch and Hussain breached their fiduciary duties as directors, that Lynch breached his contractual duties as an employee of Autonomy, and that Hussain repeatedly misled the Autonomy audit committee.

"The dispute has seen the HP chief executive, Meg Whitman, who joined the company after its disastrous Autonomy deal, lock horns with Britain's most successful software boss.

* * *

"Between the first quarter of 2009 and the second quarter of 2011, the Cambridge-based company reported revenues totaling more than $2bn. HP claims that a third of that was wrongly reported, misleading Autonomy's shareholders on the London Stock Exchange and later HP.

"This conduct by Lynch and Hussain was systematic and was sustained for more than two years prior to the acquisition of Autonomy by HP," the Californian software group said. "Its purpose was to ensure that the Autonomy group's financial performance . . . appeared to be that of a rapidly growing pure software company . . . The reality was that the group was experiencing little or no growth, it was losing market share, and its true financial performance consistently fell far short of market expectations.

"HP's lawyers have outlined five main sources of allegedly wrongly claimed income:

"$194m of supposedly hidden hardware sales. HP said it found Autonomy resold hardware such as servers made by other companies, often at a loss, and claims its directors allowed investors to believe this was software revenue.

"$196m in apparently wrongly reported sales of Autonomy's core software product, IDOL, to other software companies.

"$205m in supposedly questionable transactions with software resellers.

"$80m of claimed incorrectly reported hosting deals, in which Autonomy renegotiated contracts to host other companies' data on its own servers.

"$33m in other alleged improper transactions.

"Of particular interest are 37 deals with small IT contractors that bought Autonomy's software. Deals with these outfits, known in the industry as "value added resellers", were key to Autonomy's ability to present itself as a fast-growing software business.

"The resellers were presented as acquiring the rights to sell on Autonomy software to end users including UBS bank, General Motors, the Vatican library, accounting firm KPMG and even Hewlett Packard itself. But HP claims many of these deals were fictional in that no agreement with an end user was ever concluded, and that the resellers were simply warehousing Autonomy's software.

"Other deals were recorded as revenue too early, before the end user had agreed to buy the Autonomy products.

"The resellers involved were located in countries including the US, Italy and the UK, but most of the questioned deals involved five companies.

"HP says three in particular, MicroTech, DiscoverTech and Capax Discovery, claimed about $7.7m in "marketing fees" from Autonomy. These fees were improper, HP claims, because the reseller was either not involved in negotiations with the intended end user or the whole deal was eventually written off.

* * *

"HP also claims to have identified circular or round-trip transactions involving resellers, where the smaller businesses agreed to buy Autonomy software, while simultaneously selling products and services to Autonomy of similar value.

* * *

"HP has also questioned revenue claimed from data hosting deals. Autonomy bought a business called Zantaz, which specialized in storing data for companies on its own servers. The money for these contracts was typically collected in instalments over a number of years. Autonomy says the deals were renegotiated for a lower overall fee in exchange for a bigger upfront payment." http://www.hitc.com/en-gb/2015/05/06/Hewlett Packard-unveils-details-of-5bn-autonomy-fraud-case/ (last visited 7/11/ 2015).

Note that many of the claims involve false treatment of financial data. One might think that responsibility for these failure would rest solely with HP financial staff and accountants. The following case is usually featured in Securities Regulation casebooks. Because the due diligence issues are essentially the same in securities offerings and acquisitions, it is featured here, with editing designed to highlight due diligence issues sometimes slighted in securities casebooks, and with less emphasis on the application of the federal securities laws. The emphasis is on the due diligence of the professionals involved, both inside and outside the company, although discussions of those inside professionals who knew about and concealed damaging facts are omitted. The facts are extensively treated here and the law is only lightly touched upon. The significance of this case is to illustrate how many ways things can go wrong during an investigation of a company, and what role lawyers might play in these failures. We emphasize the places where lawyers might have done more, rather than relying exclusively on the accountants.

In this case, the problem facing the professionals involved is that a registration statement is filed with the Securities Exchange Commission well in advance of the time when the securities can actually be sold. There is a "waiting period" during which the SEC staff reviews the filing for misstatements or omissions that appear on the face of the document. During this time the underwriters and selling securities dealers can circulate a "preliminary prospectus" to prospective buyers for their review, but they cannot accept binding purchase orders. With a company that is new to the public securities markets, the delay between the initial filing of the registration statement and satisfactory conclusion of the SEC's review may be between one and three months. When the review is completed, the SEC permits the registration statement to become "effective," at which time sales can be made, although they must be accompanied by the final form of the prospectus approved by the SEC.

This final form must be true, complete and not misleading as of the effective date, under Section 11 of the Securities Act. Consequently, not only must careful investigation precede the filing of the registration statement, but it must also precede the effective date.

In a suit against the company, the underwriter, and officers and directors of an issuer, the issuer is strictly liable under Section 11 for anything that is materially inaccurate or misleading in the registration statement as of the effective date. The underwriter and the other individual defendants have a "due diligence" defense available, if they are able to sustain the burden of proof: that they "had, after reasonable investigation, reasonable ground to believe and did believe, at the time such part of the registration statement became effective, that the statements therein were true and that there was no omission to state a material fact required to be stated therein or necessary to make the statements therein not misleading." With respect to portions of the registration statement prepared on the authority of an expert, a defendant only need show that "he had no reasonable ground to believe and did not believe, at the time such part of the registration statement became effective, that the statements therein were untrue or that there was an omission to state a material fact required to be stated therein or necessary to make the statements therein not misleading." Experts are held to the same standard of care with respect to the expertised portion of the registration statement as are non-experts with respect to the non-expertised portions.

Escott v. BarChris Construction Corporation
283 F.Supp. 643 (S.D.N.Y.1968).

■ McLean, District Judge.

This is an action by purchasers of 5½ per cent convertible subordinated fifteen year debentures of BarChris Construction Corporation (BarChris). Plaintiffs purport to sue on their own behalf and "on behalf of all other and present and former holders" of the debentures. When the action was begun on October 25, 1962, there were nine plaintiffs. Others were subsequently permitted to intervene. At the time of the trial, there were over sixty.

The action is brought under Section 11 of the Securities Act of 1933 (15 U.S.C. § 77k). Plaintiffs allege that the registration statement with respect to these debentures filed with the Securities and Exchange Commission, which became effective on May 16, 1961, contained material false statements and material omissions.

Defendants fall into three categories: (1) the persons who signed the registration statement; (2) the underwriters, consisting of eight investment banking firms, led by Drexel & Co. (Drexel); and (3) BarChris's auditors, Peat, Marwick, Mitchell & Co. (Peat, Marwick).

The signers, in addition to BarChris itself, were the nine directors of BarChris, plus its controller, defendant Trilling, who was not a director. Of the nine directors, five were officers of BarChris, i.e., defendants Vitolo, president; Russo, executive vice president; Pugliese, vice president; Kircher, treasurer; and Birnbaum, secretary. Of the remaining four, defendant Grant was a member of the firm of Perkins, Daniels, McCormack & Collins, BarChris's attorneys. * * *

Defendants, in addition to denying that the registration statement was false, have pleaded the defenses open to them under Section 11 of the Act, plus certain additional defenses, including the statute of limitations. * * *

This opinion will not concern itself with the cross-claims or with issues peculiar to any particular plaintiff. These matters are reserved for later decision. On the main issue of liability, the questions to be decided are (1) did the registration statement contain false statements of fact, or did it omit to state facts which should have been stated in order to prevent it from being misleading; (2) if so, were the facts which were falsely stated or omitted "material" within the meaning of the Act; (3) if so, have defendants established their affirmative defenses?

Before discussing these questions, some background facts should be mentioned. At the time relevant here, BarChris was engaged primarily in the construction of bowling alleys, somewhat euphemistically referred to as "bowling centers." These were rather elaborate affairs. They contained not only a number of alleys or "lanes," but also, in most cases, bar and restaurant facilities.

BarChris was an outgrowth of a business started as a partnership by Vitolo and Pugliese in 1946. The business was incorporated in New York in 1955 under the name of B & C Bowling Alley Builders, Inc. Its name was subsequently changed to BarChris Construction Corporation.

The introduction of automatic pin setting machines in 1952 gave a marked stimulus to bowling. It rapidly became a popular sport, with the result that "bowling centers" began to appear throughout the country in rapidly increasing numbers. BarChris benefitted from this increased interest in bowling. Its construction operations expanded rapidly. * * *

BarChris's sales increased dramatically from 1956 to 1960. According to the prospectus, net sales, in round figures, in 1956 were some $800,000, in 1957 $1,300,000, in 1958 $1,700,000. In 1959 they increased to over $3,300,000, and by 1960 they had leaped to over $9,165,000.

* * *

In general, BarChris's method of operation was to enter into a contract with a customer, receive from him at that time a comparatively small down payment on the purchase price, and proceed to construct and equip the bowling alley. When the work was finished and the building delivered, the customer paid the balance of the contract price in notes, payable in installments over a period of years. BarChris discounted these notes with a factor and received part of their face amount in cash. The factor held back part as a reserve.

In 1960 BarChris began a practice which has been referred to throughout this case as the "alternative method of financing." In substance this was a sale and leaseback arrangement. It involved a distinction between the "interior" of a building and the building itself, i.e., the outer shell. In instances in which this method applied, BarChris would build and install what it referred to as the "interior package." Actually this amounted to constructing and installing the equipment in a building. When it was completed, it would sell the interior to a factor, James Talcott Inc. (Talcott), who would pay BarChris the full contract price therefor. The factor then proceeded to lease the interior either directly to BarChris's customer or back to a subsidiary of BarChris. In the latter case, the subsidiary in turn would lease it to the customer.

Under either financing method, BarChris was compelled to expend considerable sums in defraying the cost of construction before it received reimbursement.[4] As a consequence, BarChris was in constant need of cash to finance its operations, a need which grew more pressing as operations expanded.

In December 1959, BarChris sold 560,000 shares of common stock to the public at $3.00 per share. This issue was underwritten by Peter Morgan & Company, one of the present defendants.

By early 1961, BarChris needed additional working capital. The proceeds of the sale of the debentures involved in this action were to be devoted, in part at least, to fill that need.

The registration statement of the debentures, in preliminary form, was filed with the Securities and Exchange Commission on March 30, 1961. A first amendment was filed on May 11 and a second on May 16. The registration statement became effective on May 16. The closing of the financing took place on May 24. On that day BarChris received the net proceeds of the financing.

By that time BarChris was experiencing difficulties in collecting amounts due from some of its customers. Some of them were in arrears in payments due to factors on their discounted notes. As time went on those difficulties increased. Although BarChris continued to build alleys in 1961 and 1962, it became increasingly apparent that the industry was overbuilt. Operators of alleys, often inadequately financed, began to fail. Precisely when the tide turned is a matter of dispute, but at any rate, it was painfully apparent in 1962.

---

[4]   Under the sale and leaseback arrangement, Talcott paid part of the price to BarChris as the work progressed.

In May of that year BarChris made an abortive attempt to raise more money by the sale of common stock. It filed with the Securities and Exchange Commission a registration statement for the stock issue which it later withdrew. In October 1962 BarChris came to the end of the road. On October 29, 1962, it filed in this court a petition for an arrangement under Chapter XI of the Bankruptcy Act.[5] BarChris defaulted in the payment of the interest due on November 1, 1962 on the debentures.

The Debenture Registration Statement

In preparing the registration statement for the debentures, Grant acted for BarChris. He had previously represented BarChris in preparing the registration statement for the common stock issue. In connection with the sale of common stock, BarChris had issued purchase warrants. In January 1961 a second registration statement was filed in order to update the information pertaining to these warrants. Grant had prepared that statement as well.

Some of the basic information needed for the debenture registration statement was contained in the registration statements previously filed with respect to the common stock and warrants. Grant used these old registration statements as a model in preparing the new one, making the changes which he considered necessary in order to meet the new situation.

The underwriters were represented by the Philadelphia law firm of Drinker, Biddle & Reath. John A. Ballard, a member of that firm, was in charge of that work, assisted by a young associate named Stanton.

Peat, Marwick, BarChris's auditors, who had previously audited BarChris's annual balance sheet and earnings figures for 1958 and 1959, did the same for 1960. These figures were set forth in the registration statement. In addition, Peat, Marwick undertook a so-called "S-1 review," the proper scope of which is one of the matters debated here.

The registration statement in its final form contained a prospectus as well as other information. Plaintiffs' claims of falsities and omissions pertain solely to the prospectus, not to the additional data.

The prospectus contained, among other things, a description of BarChris's business, a description of its real property, some material pertaining to certain of its subsidiaries, and remarks about various other aspects of its affairs. It also contained financial information. It included a consolidated balance sheet as of December 31, 1960, with elaborate explanatory notes. These figures had been audited by Peat, Marwick. It also contained unaudited figures as to net sales, gross profit and net earnings for the first quarter ended March 31, 1961, as compared with

---

[5] The Chapter XI proceeding was converted into a straight bankruptcy in March 1963. Thereafter the adjudication in bankruptcy was vacated and in November 1963 BarChris was placed in reorganization under Chapter X of the Bankruptcy Act. That proceeding is still pending. BarChris's trustees have appeared for it in this action.

the similar quarter for 1960. In addition, it set forth figures as to the company's backlog of unfilled orders as of March 31, 1961, as compared with March 31, 1960, and figures as to BarChris's contingent liability, as of April 30, 1961, on customers' notes discounted and its contingent liability under the so-called alternative method of financing.

Plaintiffs challenge the accuracy of a number of these figures. They also charge that the text of the prospectus, apart from the figures, was false in a number of respects, and that material information was omitted. Each of these contentions, after eliminating duplications, will be separately considered.

1960 Net Sales, Net Operating Income and Earnings per Share

The earnings figure set forth at page 4 of the prospectus shows net sales for the calendar year 1960 of $9,165,320. Plaintiffs claim that this figure was overstated by $2,525,350. They assert that it necessarily follows that the figure of $1,742,801 shown in the prospectus as net operating income for 1960, and the figure of earnings per share of $.75, were also incorrect.

* * *

Alleys in Process on December 31, 1960
* * *

Unsold Alleys

We come now to items of more importance, namely, the inclusion in 1960 sales of the contract price of completed alleys which in fact were not sold by BarChris.

Capitol Lanes

Capitol was also known as Heavenly Lanes.[7] The premises were located in East Haven, Connecticut.

Heavenly Lanes was listed in the 1960 computations as a completed contract. The contract price of $330,000 was included in 1960 sales.

BarChris originally had a contract to construct Heavenly Lanes for an outside customer. Despite all the testimony on this subject, the date of the contract and the name of the customer never emerged. In any event, it is clear that that customer did not go through with the contract.

On July 29, 1960, BarChris entered into a contract with its wholly-owned subsidiary, BarChris Leasing Corporation, described in the contract as the purchaser, to build this alley. BarChris went ahead and constructed the alley and completed it before December 31, 1960. It never sold it to any outside interest. Purely as a financing mechanism, it sold the alley to Talcott, a factor, who leased it back to Capitol Lanes, Inc., a

---

[7] It appears that alleys often had more than one name. For example, in addition to Capitol-Heavenly, Federal Lanes was also called Betsytown, Bridge Lanes was sometimes referred to as Whitestone, etc. In dealing with accounting problems as complex as BarChris's, this double nomenclature was a fertile source of confusion.

new corporation organized by BarChris in December 1960, the stock of which was owned by Sanpark Realty Corp., itself a wholly owned subsidiary of BarChris.

Capitol Lanes, Inc. operated the alley beginning in December 1960. BarChris's minutes show that BarChris contemplated its operation as early as November 22, 1960. There is no doubt that nothing should have been included in the 1960 sales figure for this alley. Consequently, the sales figure was inflated by $330,000.

Howard Lanes Annex

On January 15, 1960, BarChris entered into a contract with Howard Lanes Company, a Connecticut partnership, to build an alley in Greenwich, Connecticut, for $320,000. It was to contain tenpin lanes. This alley was built and sold and no question is raised as to the propriety of including the $320,000 in 1960 sales.

Prior to the end of 1960, the purchaser decided that it also wanted an annex to be constructed to house duckpin lanes. The contract price for the annex was $150,000. This sum was also included in the 1960 sales figures.

BarChris agreed to build the annex and eventually did build it. But it did not sell it to Howard Lanes. Instead, it retained title through a subsidiary and leased the annex to Howard. Although there was some testimony to the effect that Howard had an option to buy the property, this was not established by any documentary evidence, for the lease was never produced. The testimony on the subject is not sufficiently definite to be credible.

Some of the documents on this subject are dated in the spring of 1961. * * *

Although the fact that these documents were executed in March 1961 rather than in 1960 has a bearing upon whether Peat, Marwick should have discovered them in the course of its 1960 audit, that is not the present question. It is clear for present purposes that the $150,000 should not have been included in 1960 sales because the annex was not sold. Consequently, the sales figure was overstated by that amount.

* * *

Summary

To recapitulate, I find that the 1960 sales figure of $9,165,320, as stated in page 4 of the prospectus, was inaccurate in that it included the following amounts which should not have been included:

Worcester	$101,200
Atlas-Bedford	47,700
Burke	25,000
Capitol	330,000

Howard Lane Annex	150,000
Total	$653,900

The total figure, instead of $9,165,320, should have been $8,511,420.

It necessarily follows that the figure for net operating income for 1960 appearing on page 4 of the prospectus was also incorrect. The extent to which it was incorrect depends upon the extent to which the incorrect sales figure for the five alleys in question was carried into profits.

* * *

It follows that profit, and consequently net operating income, was overstated in the following amounts:

Capitol	$ 89,773
Howard Lanes Annex	72,846
Burke	25,000
Worcester	36,280
Atlas-Bedford	22,706
Total	$246,605

The net operating income, instead of $1,742,801, should have been $1,496,196.

Since the net operating income figure was incorrect, it necessarily follows that the ultimate result of the entire table, i.e., the earnings per share figure, was incorrect. The evidence does not permit precise determination of the amount of this error. Since the net operating income figure as restated is approximately 14 per cent less than the figure stated in the prospectus, it would seem to be true, speaking roughly, that the earnings per share figure should be reduced by approximately the same percentage. To do so would produce an earnings per share figure of approximately 65 cents per share rather than 75 cents.

1960 Balance Sheet

The prospectus contained a balance sheet as of December 31, 1960 of BarChris and consolidated subsidiaries. This was audited by Peat, Marwick. Plaintiffs attack its accuracy on a variety of grounds.

* * *

Contingent Liabilities as of December 31, 1960

* * *

I turn now to the alternative method of financing with Talcott. This is complicated by the fact that these sale and leaseback arrangements with Talcott took two forms. BarChris's contingent liability was not the same in each.

The first form (referred to for convenience as Type A) involved the sale of the "interior" of an alley by BarChris to Talcott and the leasing of the interior by Talcott directly to BarChris's customer. The second (Type B) involved the sale of the interior by BarChris to Talcott, the leasing back of the interior by Talcott to a BarChris subsidiary, BarChris Leasing Corporation, and the lease of the interior by BarChris Leasing Corporation to the customer.

As to each Type A arrangement, BarChris signed and delivered to Talcott a written guaranty of the customer's, i.e., the lessee's, performance under the lease from Talcott. In each instance, this guaranty contained a limitation of BarChris's liability thereunder to a specified dollar amount. Although the guaranties did not expressly so state, in fact this dollar amount, in each instance, was 25 per cent of the customer's total obligation under the lease.

In Type B arrangements, BarChris executed and delivered to Talcott a written guaranty of the performance of BarChris Leasing Corporation under its lease from Talcott. The obligation of BarChris under its guaranty was not limited in any way. Thus, BarChris was contingently liable to the extent of 100 per cent for the performance by BarChris Leasing Corporation of its obligation under its lease.

Footnote 9 to the balance sheet, in stating that BarChris's contingent liability as of December 31, 1960 under the alternative method of financing was approximately $750,000, failed to take account of this difference. The $750,000 figure was computed on the basis of 25 per cent of the lessee's obligation under the lease, regardless of whether the lessee was a customer or was BarChris Leasing Corporation.

There were three Type B leases included in this computation, those involving Asbury Lanes, Yankee Lanes (Torrington), and Capitol (Heavenly). The obligation of Torrington was $320,627.50 and of Asbury $288,766.68, a total of $609,394.18. This was the amount of BarChris's contingent liability on these two leases, not 25 per cent thereof, or $152,348.54. BarChris's contingent liability was thus understated as to these two leases by $457,045.64.

The situation as to Capitol (Heavenly) is different and worse. The amount of its lease obligation was $325,000. Capitol was not leased by BarChris Leasing Corporation to an outside customer. It was leased to a BarChris subsidiary. This was an inter-company transaction. Consequently, in this instance BarChris, on a consolidated basis, was directly, not contingently, liable. Hence, instead of including 25 per cent of this $325,000 in contingent liabilities in a footnote, the full $325,000 should have been reflected in the balance sheet as a direct liability of BarChris.

* * *

Hence, instead of $750,000, the contingent liability figure under the alternative method of financing should have been $1,125,795. Capitol should have been shown as a direct liability in the amount of $325,000.

* * *

The 1961 Figures

The prospectus sets forth on page 4 the amount of BarChris's net sales, gross profits and net earnings for the three months ended March 31, 1961, in the amounts of $2,138,455, $483,121, and $125,699, respectively. These figures were unaudited, as the prospectus stated. On page 6 the prospectus set forth $5,101,351 as the amount of BarChris's contingent liability as of April 30, 1961 on customers' notes discounted, and "approximately $825,000" as its contingent liability under the alternative method of financing. Plaintiffs challenge the accuracy of these figures.

* * *

Net Sales, Gross Profit and Net Earnings

Plaintiffs correctly contend that the net sales of $2,138,455 for the three months ended March 31, 1961 were overstated.

This figure included $269,810 for Bridge Lanes. I have previously noted that the stock of the original customer for this alley, Biel Land & Development Company, was acquired by BarChris in the spring of 1961. The date of acquisition was March 24, 1961. Subsequently, BarChris operated this alley through a subsidiary. Once it began to operate it, it did not sell it at any time thereafter, as far as appears. There is no doubt that by March 31, 1961, this transaction had become an intercompany one. It should not have been included in first quarter 1961 sales.

Yonkers Lanes is in the same category. The amount included in sales for this alley was $250,000. On May 4, 1961, BarChris organized a subsidiary, Yonkers Lanes, Inc., which eventually operated this alley. Whether BarChris originally had intended to operate it, or whether at the outset it had a customer for it, is not clear from the testimony. However, the minutes of a meeting of BarChris's executive committee held on March 18, 1961 show that as of that date BarChris had no contract with a customer for this alley. It seems clear that by March 31, 1961 this was an intercompany transaction and should not have been included in first quarter sales.

* * *

The net result is that the March 31, 1961 net sales figure was overstated as follows:

Bridge Lanes	$269,810
Yonkers Lanes	250,000
Total	$519,810

The net sales figure, therefore, should have been $1,618,645, not $2,138,455.

* * *

"Backlog" as of March 31, 1961

The prospectus stated on page 5:

"The Company as of March 31, 1960, had $2,875,000 in unfilled orders on its books. As of March 31, 1961, the comparable amount was approximately $6,905,000. Substantially all of the latter orders are scheduled and are expected to be completed in 1961."

Plaintiffs contend that the figure of $6,905,000 was erroneous. There is no doubt that it was, to a substantial extent. It is impossible to determine, however, precisely what the figure should have been.

The difficulty results from the fact that BarChris's books did not contain a record of unfilled orders as of March 31, 1961. Russo testified that he prepared a list of them which was the basis for the figure in the prospectus. The list was never produced. Its absence gave rise to controversy as to what alleys were on the list and what were not. Despite all the testimony and argument on this subject, the matter was never completely settled.

Out of all this testimony, however, some things clearly emerge. Although it is not possible to specify each and every alley which was included in the total of $6,905,000, there is no dispute about the fact that certain alleys were included. And it is clear that alleys were included for which BarChris, as of March 31, 1961, held no valid enforceable contracts.

T-Bowl

I shall first consider the group of six alleys referred to as the "T-Bowl" group. The principal figure in these transactions was August E. Tumminello. In December 1960 or January 1961, he, at the urging of Vitolo, signed six undated documents on BarChris's printed form of purchase contract. The name of the purchaser at the head of the respective documents was stated as "T-Bowl, Groton," "T-Bowl, Milford," "T-Bowl, No. Attleboro," "T-Bowl Baltimore," "T-Bowl Saverna Park," and "T-Bowl Odenton." On five of the six documents the same name appeared after the word "Purchaser" at the bottom, followed by the signature, "August E. Tumminello Pres." On the sixth, that pertaining to North Attleboro, nothing appeared at the bottom after the word "Purchaser" except Tumminello's signature as "Pres."

In fact, there were no corporations entitled T-Bowl Groton, T-Bowl Milford, etc. These names were merely designations of the geographical area of the proposed alley.

Each of these "purchase contracts" purported to be for the "interior" of an alley. Each stated that the "purchaser" agreed to purchase "the equipment set forth below." Nothing was set forth below. Each document stated that "specifications are attached." No specifications were attached.

Each recited that a specific part of the purchase price had been paid upon the signing of the contract. Nothing was paid at that time.

Birnbaum, BarChris's secretary and house counsel, advised his fellow officers that these documents were not legally enforceable contracts. The minutes of BarChris's executive committee meeting of March 18, 1961 included each of these alleys in a list of "jobs which are presently being constructed, or will soon be commenced, and on which no contracts with customers have been written."

On May 2, 1961, a corporation known as T-Bowl International Inc. was organized. Tumminello was its president. Russo was a director. This corporation sold common stock to the public in September 1961. The issue was underwritten by Peter Morgan & Company, one of the underwriting group in the BarChris debenture issue involved here. The T-Bowl prospectus stated:

> "At June 30, 1961, T-Bowl had consolidated negative working capital of $229,058.79. . . ."

This financing appears to have succeeded. Out of its proceeds T-Bowl International Inc. finally made the down payments to BarChris with respect to the six T-Bowl jobs. Birnbaum caused a line to be drawn through the name of the purchaser on each of the six documents, i.e., T-Bowl Groton, etc., and the words "T-Bowl International Inc." to be written in ink. The documents were not re-executed.

Five of the six alleys were eventually built by BarChris, long after May 16, 1961. One, Severna Park, was never built because its site was condemned for a highway.

It is undisputed that the total contract price of these six alleys, $2,205,000, was included in the backlog figure. I find that it was inaccurate and misleading to include it.

* * *

Customers Delinquencies in 1961

After describing BarChris's practice of discounting notes with factors, the prospectus stated on page 5:

> "Since 1955, the Company has been required to repurchase less than ½ of 1% of such promissory notes discounted by such unaffiliated financial institutions."

Plaintiffs contend that this statement was false, and that in any event the prospectus was misleading because of its failure to advert to the difficulties which confronted BarChris in May 1961 by reason of the failure of some of its customers to pay their notes which BarChris had discounted with Talcott. The relevant facts are as follows.

The customer delinquency problem was much more serious in May 1961 than it had been in December 1960. It had been growing more serious for some time. At a BarChris executive committee meeting on

February 27, 1961, Russo not only mentioned his troubles with Federal Lanes, a perennial delinquent, but he also pointed out that Stratford Bowl was four months in arrears on its payments to Talcott, that six notes of Northford Lanes were due and unpaid, that Leader Lanes was six months behind in its payments, and that the owners of Howard Lanes had said that they could not pay any more notes.

Russo frequently discussed these problems with Talcott and attempted to allay any apprehensions that Talcott might have. By April, Talcott was no longer willing to content itself with sending to BarChris periodic notices of its customers' arrears. On April 21, 1961, Talcott wrote to Russo confirming their discussions as to four of the worst offenders, Dreyfuss Bowl (Harlem), Stratford, Leader and Federal. As to Dreyfuss, the letter stated that Talcott would retain counsel on BarChris's behalf to repossess the alley and that in the meantime BarChris must pay Talcott $9,737.41 "as a special reserve toward the repurchase of this account." As to Stratford, BarChris was to pay $22,100 as a similar reserve against repurchase. As to Leader, Talcott would expect BarChris to repossess the alley unless Leader paid $11,266.64 by April 24. As to Federal, Talcott stated that if $5,000 were not received by April 24, BarChris must repossess the alley.

This letter further expressed Talcott's understanding, based on conversations with Russo, that BarChris intended to form an operating company to operate these four alleys, plus a fifth, Hart Lanes, and to make, on their behalf, the payments due from them currently to Talcott. The letter pointed out that this would deviate from Talcott standard procedure of requiring the repurchase of delinquent accounts, i.e., requiring BarChris to repurchase all the notes of a defaulting customer. Talcott refused to commit itself not to insist on this standard procedure.

Thus, by April 21, 1961, BarChris knew that it might be faced with a demand to repurchase all the notes of Dreyfuss, Stratford, Leader and Federal. These aggregated more than $1,350,000. Obviously, BarChris was in no position to comply with any such demand.

Further discussions and negotiations ensued. It is clear that Russo informed Talcott of the forthcoming debenture financing and it is highly probable that he emphasized to Talcott the improvement which the consummation of this financing would bring about in BarChris's cash situation.

On May 5, 1961, Talcott wrote to Russo stating that four accounts, Dreyfuss, Stratford, Leader and Federal, "are eligible for repurchase under the terms of our agreement," that Talcott wanted to receive the sums mentioned in its letter of April 21 "as a token beginning toward eventual repurchase in full of the accounts in question," and that Talcott "cannot condone any further delays in starting a reasonable program to clear these defaulted accounts."

Russo continued to negotiate. He and Kircher met with Talcott on May 16, 1961 (the very day that the registration statement became effective). The results were embodied in Talcott's letter of May 17. That letter was mainly devoted to Stratford and Dreyfuss. As to Stratford, Talcott agreed to refrain from demanding that BarChris repurchase all Stratford's notes provided that BarChris took over the operation of Stratford and paid to Talcott all Stratford's arrears. As to Dreyfuss, Talcott agreed "to forego a request for immediate repurchase," provided that BarChris paid all arrears plus a specified reserve. Talcott expressed its feeling that "if the Dreyfuss situation is not turned around by August 15," BarChris should repurchase all Dreyfuss' notes.

The net amount demanded by Talcott in this letter, after giving certain credits to BarChris, was $34,329.78. On May 26 Russo called Talcott to tell Talcott that BarChris "had gotten their money on May 24." On June 5 BarChris paid the $34,329.78 to Talcott.

Talcott advised Russo that Talcott did not "want any more metropolitan bowling paper," but that it "would look at deals elsewhere in the nation." In fact, Talcott did not discount any more notes of BarChris's customers, metropolitan or otherwise, after April 1961.

Dreyfuss went into bankruptcy in May 1961. Stratford and Federal also went into bankruptcy. BarChris eventually repossessed these alleys and a number of others, including Leader. By May 1962 BarChris was operating thirteen alleys, some of which it had repossessed from defaulting customers and others of which, such as Capitol, Bridge, Woonsocket, etc., it had operated from the beginning.

* * *

[Judge McLean concluded that these misrepresentations and omissions were material—that is, that a reasonable investor would be influenced by them in making an investment decision.]

The "Due Diligence" Defenses

Section 11(b) of the Act provides that:

" . . . no person, other than the issuer, shall be liable . . . who shall sustain the burden of proof— * * *

(3) that (A) as regards any part of the registration statement not purporting to be made on the authority of an expert . . . he had, after reasonable investigation, reasonable ground to believe and did believe, at the time such part of the registration statement became effective, that the statements therein were true and that there was no omission to state a material fact required to be stated therein or necessary to make the statements therein not misleading; . . . and (c) as regards any part of the registration statement purporting to be made on the authority of an expert (other than himself) . . . he had no

reasonable ground to believe and did not believe, at the time such part of the registration statement became effective, that the statements therein were untrue or that there was an omission to state a material fact required to be stated therein or necessary to make the statements therein not misleading. . . . "

Section 11(c) defines "reasonable investigation" as follows:

"In determining, for the purpose of paragraph (3) of subsection (b) of this section, what constitutes reasonable investigation and reasonable ground for belief, the standard of reasonableness shall be that required of a prudent man in the management of his own property."

* * *

Grant

Grant became a director of BarChris in October 1960. His law firm was counsel to BarChris in matters pertaining to the registration of securities. Grant drafted the registration statement for the stock issue in 1959 and for the warrants in January 1961. He also drafted the registration statement for the debentures. In the preliminary division of work between him and Ballard, the underwriters' counsel, Grant took initial responsibility for preparing the registration statement, while Ballard devoted his efforts in the first instance to preparing the indenture.

* * *

There is no valid basis for plaintiffs' accusation that Grant knew that the prospectus was false in some respects and incomplete and misleading in others. Having seen him testify at length, I am satisfied as to his integrity. I find that Grant honestly believed that the registration statement was true and that no material facts had been omitted from it.

In this belief he was mistaken, and the fact is that for all his work, he never discovered any of the errors or omissions which have been recounted at length in this opinion, with the single exception of Capitol Lanes. He knew that BarChris had not sold this alley and intended to operate it, but he appears to have been under the erroneous impression that Peat, Marwick had knowingly sanctioned its inclusion in sales because of the allegedly temporary nature of the operation.

* * *

There were things which Grant could readily have checked which he did not check. For example, he was unaware of the provisions of the agreements between BarChris and Talcott. He never read them. Thus, he did not know, although he readily could have ascertained, that BarChris's contingent liability on Type B leaseback arrangements was 100 per cent, not 25 per cent. He did not appreciate that if BarChris defaulted in repurchasing delinquent customers' notes upon Talcott's demand, Talcott could accelerate all the customer paper in its hands, which amounted to over $3,000,000.

As to the backlog figure, Grant appreciated that scheduled unfilled orders on the company's books meant firm commitments, but he never asked to see the contracts which, according to the prospectus, added up to $6,905,000. Thus, he did not know that this figure was overstated by some $4,490,000.

Grant was unaware of the fact that BarChris was about to operate Bridge and Yonkers. He did not read the minutes of those subsidiaries which would have revealed that fact to him. On the subject of minutes, Grant knew that minutes of certain meetings of the BarChris executive committee held in 1961 had not been written up. Kircher, who had acted as secretary at those meetings, had complete notes of them. Kircher told Grant that there was no point in writing up the minutes because the matters discussed at those meetings were purely routine. Grant did not insist that the minutes be written up, nor did he look at Kircher's notes. If he had, he would have learned that on February 27, 1961 there was an extended discussion in the executive committee meeting about customers' delinquencies, that on March 8, 1961 the committee had discussed the pros and cons of alley operation by BarChris, that on March 18, 1961 the committee was informed that BarChris was constructing or about to begin constructing twelve alleys for which it had no contracts, and that on May 13, 1961 Dreyfuss, one of the worst delinquents, had filed a petition in Chapter X.

* * *

The application of proceeds language in the prospectus was drafted by Kircher back in January. It may well have expressed his intent at that time, but his intent, and that of the other principal officers of BarChris, was very different in May. Grant did not appreciate that the earlier language was no longer appropriate. He never learned of the situation which the company faced in May. He knew that BarChris was short of cash, but he had no idea how short. He did not know that BarChris was withholding delivery of checks already drawn and signed because there was not enough money in the bank to pay them. He did not know that the officers of the company intended to use immediately approximately one-third of the financing proceeds in a manner not disclosed in the prospectus, including approximately $1,000,000 in paying old debts.

In this connection, mention should be made of a fact which has previously been referred to only in passing. The "negative cash balance" in BarChris's Lafayette National Bank account in May 1961 included a check dated April 10, 1961 to the order of Grant's firm, Perkins, Daniels, McCormack & Collins, in the amount of $8,711. This check was not deposited by Perkins, Daniels until June 1, after the financing proceeds had been received by BarChris. Of course, if Grant had knowingly withheld deposit of this check until that time, he would be in a position similar to Russo, Vitolo and Pugliese. I do not believe, however, that that was the case. I find that the check was not delivered by BarChris to Perkins, Daniels until shortly before June 1.

This incident is worthy of mention, however, for another reason. The prospectus stated on page 10 that Perkins, Daniels had "received fees aggregating $13,000" from BarChris. This check for $8,711 was one of those fees. It had not been received by Perkins, Daniels prior to May 16. Grant was unaware of this. In approving this erroneous statement in the prospectus, he did not consult his own bookkeeper to ascertain whether it was correct. Kircher told him that the bill had been paid and Grant took his word for it. If he had inquired and had found that this representation was untrue, this discovery might well have led him to a realization of the true state of BarChris's finances in May 1961.

As far as customers' delinquencies is concerned, although Grant discussed this with Kircher, he again accepted the assurances of Kircher and Russo that no serious problem existed. He did not examine the records as to delinquencies, although BarChris maintained such a record. Any inquiry on his part of Talcott or an examination of BarChris's correspondence with Talcott in April and May 1961 would have apprised him of the true facts. It would have led him to appreciate that the statement in this prospectus, carried over from earlier prospectuses, to the effect that since 1955 BarChris had been required to repurchase less than one-half of one per cent of discounted customers' notes could no longer properly be made without further explanation.

Grant was entitled to rely on Peat, Marwick for the 1960 figures. He had no reasonable ground to believe them to be inaccurate. But the matters which I have mentioned were not within the expertised portion of the prospectus. As to this, Grant was obliged to make a reasonable investigation. I am forced to find that he did not make one. After making all due allowances for the fact that BarChris's officers misled him, there are too many instances in which Grant failed to make an inquiry which he could easily have made which, if pursued, would have put him on his guard. In my opinion, this finding on the evidence in this case does not establish an unreasonably high standard in other cases for company counsel who are also directors. Each case must rest on its own facts. I conclude that Grant has not established his due diligence defenses except as to the audited 1960 figures.

The Underwriters and Coleman

The underwriters other than Drexel made no investigation of the accuracy of the prospectus. One of them, Peter Morgan, had underwritten the 1959 stock issue and had been a director of BarChris. He thus had some general familiarity with its affairs, but he knew no more than the other underwriters about the debenture prospectus. They all relied upon Drexel as the "lead" underwriter.

Drexel did make an investigation. The work was in charge of Coleman, a partner of the firm, assisted by Casperson, an associate. Drexel's attorneys acted as attorneys for the entire group of underwriters. Ballard did the work, assisted by Stanton.

* * *

In April 1961 Ballard instructed Stanton to examine BarChris's minutes for the past five years and also to look at "the major contracts of the company."[23] Stanton went to BarChris's office for that purpose on April 24. He asked Birnbaum for the minute books. He read the minutes of the board of directors and discovered interleaved in them a few minutes of executive committee meetings in 1960. He asked Kircher if there were any others. Kircher said that there had been other executive committee meetings but that the minutes had not been written up.

Stanton read the minutes of a few BarChris subsidiaries. His testimony was vague as to which ones. He had no recollection of seeing the minutes of Capitol Lanes, Inc. or Biel or Parkway Lanes, Inc. He did not discover that BarChris was operating Capitol or that it planned to operate Bridge and Yonkers.

As to the "major contracts," all that Stanton could remember seeing was an insurance policy. Birnbaum told him that there was no file of major contracts. Stanton did not examine the agreements with Talcott. He did not examine the contracts with customers. He did not look to see what contracts comprised the backlog figure. Stanton examined no accounting records of BarChris. His visit, which lasted one day, was devoted primarily to reading the directors' minutes.

On April 25 Ballard wrote to Grant about certain matters which Stanton had noted on his visit to BarChris the day before, none of which Ballard considered "very earth shaking." As far as relevant here, these were (1) Russo's remark as recorded in the executive committee minutes of November 3, 1960 to the effect that because of customers' defaults, BarChris might find itself in the business of operating alleys; (2) the fact that the minutes of Sanpark Realty Corporation were incomplete; and (3) the fact that minutes of the executive committee were missing.

On May 9, 1961, Ballard came to New York and conferred with Grant and Kircher. They discussed the Securities and Exchange Commission's deficiency letter of May 4, 1961 which required the inclusion in the prospectus of certain additional information, notably net sales, gross profits and net earnings figures for the first quarter of 1961. They also discussed the points raised in Ballard's letter to Grant of April 25. As to the latter, most of the conversation related to what Russo had meant by his remark on November 3, 1960. Kircher said that the delinquency problem was less severe now than it had been back in November 1960,

---

[23] Stanton was a very junior associate. He had been admitted to the bar in January 1961, some three months before. This was the first registration statement he had ever worked on.

that no alleys had been repossessed, and that although he was "worried about one alley in Harlem" (Dreyfuss), that was a "special situation." Grant reported that Russo had told him that his statement on November 3, 1960 was "merely hypothetical." On the strength of this conversation, Ballard was satisfied that the one-half of one per cent figure in the prospectus did not need qualification or elaboration.

As to the missing minutes, Kircher said that those of Sanpark were not significant and that the executive committee meetings for which there were no written minutes were concerned only with "routine matters."

It must be remembered that this conference took place only one week before the registration statement became effective. Ballard did nothing else in the way of checking during that intervening week.

Ballard did not insist that the executive committee minutes be written up so that he could inspect them, although he testified that he knew from experience that executive committee minutes may be extremely important. If he had insisted, he would have found the minutes highly informative, as has previously been pointed out (supra at p. 217). Ballard did not ask to see BarChris's schedule of delinquencies or Talcott's notices of delinquencies, or BarChris's correspondence with Talcott.

Ballard did not examine BarChris's contracts with Talcott. He did not appreciate what Talcott's rights were under those financing agreements or how serious the effect would be upon BarChris of any exercise of those rights.

Ballard did not investigate the composition of the backlog figure to be sure that it was not "puffy." He made no inquiry after March about any new officers' loans, although he knew that Kircher had insisted on a provision in the indenture which gave loans from individuals priority over the debentures. He was unaware of the seriousness of BarChris's cash position and of how BarChris's officers intended to use a large part of the proceeds. He did not know that BarChris was operating Capitol Lanes.[24]

Like Grant, Ballard, without checking, relied on the information which he got from Kircher. He also relied on Grant who, as company counsel, presumably was familiar with its affairs.

* * *

In any event, it is clear that no effectual attempt at verification was made. The question is whether due diligence required that it be made. Stated another way, is it sufficient to ask questions, to obtain answers which, if true, would be thought satisfactory, and to let it go at that,

---

[24] Stanton was also unaware of this, although there was a reference to it in the minutes of the board of directors' meeting of November 22, 1960, which he presumably read.

without seeking to ascertain from the records whether the answers in fact are true and complete?

I have already held that this procedure is not sufficient in Grant's case. Are underwriters in a different position, as far as due diligence is concerned?

[After a lengthy discussion, the court concluded that the underwriters were not entitled to rely upon the officers and directors of the issuer, because the underwriter's position is adverse to that of the issuer in examining an issuer.]

It is impossible to lay down a rigid rule suitable for every case defining the extent to which such verification must go. It is a question of degree, a matter of judgment in each case. In the present case, the underwriters' counsel made almost no attempt to verify management's representations. I hold that that was insufficient.

QUESTIONS

1. Why were the net sales figures for 1960 for Capitol Lanes and the Howard Lanes Annex in error? Should this have come to the attention of Grant, Ballard or Stanton, the attorneys? Examine the Merger Agreement and Plan of Reorganization, Section 4.1(m), in Appendix C. Would this help a buyer of BarChris avoid these problems?

2. What were the differences between Type A and Type B alternative financing? Why were Type B contingent liabilities understated? Should Grant, Ballard or Stanton have caught this, or was this exclusively the accountants' responsibility?

3. Why were the net sales figures for the three months ending March 31, 1961 for Bridge Lanes and Yonkers Lanes in error? Was this solely the responsibility of the accountants, or should the attorneys, Grant, Ballard and Stanton, have been aware of this problem?

4. Why were the T-Bowl contracts erroneously included in backlog? Among the outside professionals (including Grant), who should have been aware of this? Examine the Merger Agreement and Plan of Reorganization, Section 4.1(l), in Appendix C. Would this help a buyer of BarChris avoid these problems?

5. Should the lawyers involved (Grant, Ballard & Stanton) have learned about the customer delinquencies in the Spring of 1961, or was this a matter exclusively for the accountants?

6. Grant was counsel to BarChris as well as director. He had drafted the registration statement for the issue of stock in 1959 as well as for the warrants in 1961.

   (a) Assuming that Grant was not familiar with accounting records, what could he have done to discover accounting deficiencies?

(b) What were the specific contracts and other documents that Grant should have examined?

7. How does the underwriters' "due diligence" responsibility differ, if at all, from that of Grant?

   (a) How much investigatory work should the lead underwriter delegate to its legal counsel? Is this similar to what a buyer delegates to its counsel? Is there a difference between the role of seller's counsel and Grant's role in the underwriting that would suggest differences in how much a buyer's counsel might be willing to rely on seller's counsel?

   (b) What kind of formal legal opinion to the client should the underwriter's counsel prepare? Would you expect a similar opinion from buyer's counsel to the buyer?

   (c) Assume that BarChris was about to be acquired by another corporation in exchange for stock of the acquiring firm. Under SEC rules the acquiring firm would have to prepare and file a registration statement, which would be employed to solicit the votes of BarChris' shareholders to approve the merger. This registration statement will be required to describe both corporations, and, through "pro forma" financial statements, what the combined companies' financial statements would have looked like had they already been combined. If Ballard were the senior attorney for the acquiring firm and Grant represented BarChris, what would Ballard's responsibilities be to engage in due diligence with respect to BarChris? Would Ballard's client have obtained any legal protection from Securities Act Rule 409, which is quoted in the note following these questions?

   (d) Ballard, the senior attorney for the underwriters, sent his junior associate, Stanton, to examine Bar Chris' minute books and major contracts. Is that a proper procedure? Is this a job which should be delegated only to very senior associates? How could Stanton have demonstrated due diligence? Which of the misleading statements in the registration statement would have been uncovered by a careful reading of the minute books and major contracts? In this context, consider the following comments about the appropriateness of using inexperienced associates to perform due diligence:

   > "3. Why use junior associates when more senior associates would seem to have more due diligence experience?

   > "3.1 You have to start sometime.

   > "3.2 Unless the purpose of the due diligence review is to analyze the viability of a very discreet structuring issue, the due diligence review is generally designed to obtain a complete picture of the

target/issuer. A more senior associate's review may be too focused so that if a deal structure changes mid-stream, it is important to have analyzed all aspects of a company so that the team will have a road map, rather than just one that is limited in scope.

"3.3 Once a bright, committed first year has familiarized him or herself with the business of the target/issuer . . . it is generally more cost effective to staff a due diligence review with younger associates."

Mark Schonberger and Vasiliki B. Tsaganos, "Top Twelve Most Frequently Asked Questions by Junior Associates Conducting Due Diligence," in CONDUCTING DUE DILIGENCE 1997 (Practising Law Institute Course Handbook No. B–991, 1997).

8.   Assume now that we are discussing the relationship between a buyer and its legal counsel:

(a) How much investigatory work should a purchasing corporation delegate to its legal counsel?

(b) Is it appropriate for legal counsel to send a junior associate with the instruction to look for "important" matters? What other instructions would you like to have if you were sent on such a task?

(c) What kind of formal legal opinion to the client should the purchaser's counsel prepare?

NOTE

In a hostile acquisition, a bidder may not be able to obtain information about a target corporation without the cooperation of the target's management. The problem is not so difficult with a target that is a public corporation, where regular reports are filed with the SEC and are available to the bidder. If the proposal calls for an exchange of bidder's securities for those of the target, and for corporate action in the form of a merger or share exchange, the transaction will require registration under the Securities Act, as an offer of securities of the bidder to the public, probably under Form S-4. This requires pro forma financial statements that reflect the hypothetical results of the proposed business combination had it existed in a combined fashion in the past. See Form S-4, Item 5. It also requires considerable detail about the target corporation's business, securities, finances, and target management's discussion and analysis of the results of operations and expected trends in its business. Form S-4, Item 17. The dilemma of an uncooperative target management is dealt with in Securities Act Rule 409:

"**Rule 409. Information Unknown or Not Reasonably Available**

"Information required need be given only insofar as it is known or reasonably available to the registrant. If any required information is unknown and not reasonably available to the registrant, either because the obtaining thereof would involve unreasonable effort or expense, or because it rests peculiarly within the knowledge of another person not affiliated with the registrant, the information may be omitted, subject to the following conditions:

"(a) The registrant shall give such information on the subject as it possesses or can acquire without unreasonable effort or expenses, together with the sources thereof,

"(b) The registrant shall include a statement either showing that unreasonable effort or expense would be involved or indicating the absence of any affiliation with the person within whose knowledge the information rests and stating the result of a request made to such persons for the information."

For an interesting decision on the bidder's disclosure obligations prior to the adoption of this rule, see Feit v. Leasco Data Processing Equipment Corp., 332 F.Supp. 544 (E.D.N.Y.1971). Judge Weinstein held that a bidder that originally was hostile no longer had an excuse for nondisclosure of inside details about a target once the bidder and target reached a rapprochement, achieved in part through a generous compensation package for the Target's CEO. In this case the information was somewhat "soft" and evaluative, in the sense that it involved estimates of the amount of capital surplus that could be freed from regulatory reserves through a takeover, and put to more profitable use elsewhere.

Similar discussions and guidance are provided with respect to each other standard part of such an opinion, such as qualification to do business in foreign jurisdictions, the corporate powers, the authority of those acting on behalf of the corporation in this transaction, that performing the contract will not violate any applicable law, regulation or contractual obligation; that no consents of others are required for the corporation to perform, and an opinion that the agreement will be enforceable against the corporation according to its terms. There important qualifications and hedges on many of these matters, and an attorney preparing such an opinion needs to review the guidance in documents such as this with great care.

---

2. THE ACQUISITION AGREEMENT

The Merger Agreement and Plan of Reorganization set out in Appendix C is a comparison of a buyer's strong form and the final negotiated agreement to allow the reader to compare positions that might be taken by buyers and sellers during the course of negotiations. This agreement involves a reverse triangular merger, because that form of acquisition is so common, but most of its terms would be equally applicable to a "straight" merger or even to an asset purchase agreement.

A. THE PRICE TERM

To the extent that due diligence discovers problems with the Seller, these are often dealt with in a price adjustment. Conversely, where a Seller's bold claims about future prospects for the business are not accepted at face value by the Buyer, one solution is to use the price term to make upward adjustments should the Seller's rosy projections turn out to be true.

i.   PRIVATELY HELD SELLERS

Closely held corporations often raise more difficult questions about value than publicly held firms. Closely held firms are not subject to the reporting requirements of the Securities Exchange Act and the rigorous accounting control requirements of section 404 of the Sarbanes-Oxley Act. Public companies are accustomed to providing audited financial statements, and post Sarbanes-Oxley, the company is required to report on the adequacy of the internal controls in its accounting system designed to assure fair and accurate reporting. Any deficiencies in these controls must be disclosed in public filings. The company's auditors then must examine these controls, and provide their own opinion on their adequacy. Public companies' officials are generally acutely aware of the risk of class action fraud suits by investors if things go wrong—including any need to restate past financial statements. The public reports of these companies also contain a section entitled "Management's Discussion and Analysis," which provides a detailed review of financial results, with explanations of changes from prior periods and, where appropriate, warnings about known trends that may result in future changes in these results. Many public companies voluntarily provide analysts and investors with projections of future results, generally for the next quarter and probably for the remainder of the fiscal year. A failure to meet projected earnings often results in a sell-off of the stock by money managers, as their analysts dislike such disappointments intensely. The result is a steady flow of information that is closely reviewed by investment professionals, and monitored for its accuracy. Published analysts' reports on many companies provide more detailed analysis of companies, including their products' prospects, the competitive environment, and other information of value to prospective buyers. Many public companies are relatively large, have a variety of products or services for sale to diversify against the risk of disappointment in any single line, and many sell in markets in which they are either dominant or well-established competitors.

Contrast this with the successful privately owned company. Apart from the lack of detailed reports under the Securities Exchange Act, these companies may not have audited financial statements. Relatively simple accounting systems may provide the current owners with sufficient information on which to make business decisions, given their intimate knowledge of the business. Internal controls are far less likely to be as elaborate as those now required for public companies. Written internal analyses of the business, its prospects and risks may be non-existent. One brokerage firm advises private sellers to prepare a detailed financial model that examines historical and projected growth on each line of business, and the equivalent of "Management's Discussion and Analysis" of past financial results to explain fluctuations, a capital budget that shows capital needs for both maintenance and growth, and a marketing analysis of how the company's products are positioned in their markets, and what levels of protection might exist, such as patents or proprietary information. Even with all of this information, buyers may be concerned that if the current owners exit from management at the time of a sale, it may be more costly to replace them, since owners may take smaller salaries and bonuses than an outsider would require, thus leaving more funds in the corporation to grow the business. Further, to the extent the business depends on relationships, how much will it suffer from the loss of current management, no matter how competent the replacements? Note that a number of the provisions discussed below are covered in the Merger Agreement in Appendix C.

Fixed Price With Adjustments Keyed to Financial Statements. Where the price is keyed to a balance sheet, and the seller lacks a current audited statement, some transactions call for adjustments based on the seller's net worth, either on the closing date or a specified date prior to the closing, such as the close of a fiscal year or quarter. If the price is a multiple of balance sheet net worth, the adjustment can be by the same multiple, both upward and downward from the initially agreed price. This protects the buyer from large cash withdrawals by the seller prior to the closing, once the price has been agreed on. In other cases, where earnings represent the primary consideration in valuing the business, an adjustment in the purchase price can be required based on how much actual earnings exceed either the most recent twelve-month earnings or those for the prior fiscal year. Purchase prices using earnings are almost always a significant multiple of annual earnings. Whenever prices are based on financial statements, the parties must recognize the potential for disagreements, even where auditors are involved. Provision should be made for resolution of such disputes, either through arbitration or some similar device. One such device is for the buyer to get its own auditor to make a determination of the matter in dispute, and if the buyer's and seller's auditor disagree, to turn to a third auditor for resolution. (None of this is inexpensive, but it will always be cheaper than litigation.) Where price adjustments are to be made based on financial statements as of the closing date, this may call for the creation of an escrow account into which some part of the purchase price will be deposited until the final determination of the amount. In some cases the parties may want to limit this "adjustment amount" by a cap, so there is an upper limit on the amount to be paid to the buyer, or by a "floor," which is a lower limit on this amount. Where both devices are used, this is called a "collar." The use of a fairly small range in such a collar brings the range of possible prices closer to the original fixed price stated in the agreement. It is important to consider what this means in terms of assignment of risks in a deal. A small downward adjustment limit leaves the buyer bearing the risk that net worth or earnings may be substantially less than expected, while a small upward adjustment limit leaves the seller bearing the risk that if the business does quite well in the period before the closing, the seller may not be fully compensated for that improvement. A study found that 67% of acquisitions of 420 private companies resulted in post-acquisition claims in 2012, which involved purchase price adjustments, indemnification claims and even fraud. WALL STREET JOURNAL, April 30, 2013, p. B7, reporting a study by Shareholder Representative Services.

Earn-outs. Earn-outs serve several purposes. First, the valuation of a business involves considerable uncertainty, and buyer and seller may find that they both want to do the transaction, but have quite different (and firmly held) views about the future prospects of the business. Young entrepreneurs with a growing high tech business that needs the cash support of a larger company may believe that they have found a market niche that will allow the business to grow rapidly and profitably for many years, while a buyer may be less bullish on the long-term prospects of the business. Even many younger technology companies with long development paths may be publicly held before their products are ready for the market, as in the case of drug development. If the buyer is willing to pay seller's asking price if things turn out to be as rosy as the seller projects, there is ground for a deal. The buyer may agree to pay its valuation of the business as it stands now in the buyer's estimation, and agree to pay more if earnings increase as the seller projects. After all, it's the prospect of future earnings that the buyer is purchasing, so if they turn out to be much higher, a higher price is still a good deal.

The other purpose for an earn-out may be to keep the founders of the company, whose skills and relationships may be critical to its success, involved as dedicated employees after the closing. After all, whose vision was it that got it this far? And it may take several years or more before others can successfully take over the management of the business without disrupting either employee relations or customer relations. In addition to execution of an employment agreement and payment of a salary, the buyer can motivate the founders with the prospect of a much larger payment for the business if all goes as well as the founders have said it will. A promise of a large additional payment based on increasing earnings in future years can provide the motivation, as well as a way to bridge the gap in valuations.

Once again, the drafting attorney cannot ignore accounting issues. Once the business is sold, will the buyer impose its own accounting conventions, which may differ from those in use now? Will this have the effect of increasing or decreasing reported earnings? Buyers can keep reported earnings down by assigning the buyer's expenses of purchase to the selling corporation, or by increasing administrative charges from the buyer to the newly acquired corporation, by increasing employee fringe benefits to provide for uniform treatment of all employees, by shortening the useful lives of assets so annual depreciation expenses rise. A buyer may prefer that the earn-out be based on gross income of the business, to avoid these problems, on the assumption that the seller will have no incentive to reduce sales. But even recognition of income may be adjusted, where large contracts are involved with income paid only upon completion. Should the corporation recognize income on a percentage of completion basis, or only recognize income when it has a legal right to receive full payment from its customer? From a seller's perspective, it is probably important to begin with a statement that the accounting methods currently in use by the seller will continue to govern, and force the buyer to disclose any accounting changes that it wishes to make. In pharmaceutical acquisitions, often of early-stage companies still in clinical testing of promising drugs, earnouts tied to the progress and ultimate success of the trials are used in most transactions. What happens if the buyer subsequently decides to discontinue some line of business or to sell it to a third party? The sale may be at an advantageous price to our buyer, but it reduces the income earned by what remains of the seller's business. One solution to this is for the buyer to covenant that it will use its best efforts to continue to operate the entire business for the earn-out period. Of course this restricts the buyer's flexibility. In one case a buyer subject to a gross sales earn-out discovered that increasing competition meant declining prices and margins, so it lost money on every sale. Thus, the more it sold, the more it lost. See Bloor v. Falstaff Brewing Corp., 454 F.Supp. 258 (S.D.N.Y. 1978). One result of this case is that more buyers are only willing to commit to use "commercially reasonable" efforts to meet the targets that trigger contingent payments. At least one court has held that both "best efforts" and "commercially reasonable efforts" are so vague as to be unenforceable. One solution to this problem is to tie the standard to the existing development efforts of either the seller or the buyer.

In many cases the contingent amount will be represented by notes of the buyer, payment of which is contingent on meeting profit goals. In other cases funds may be placed in escrow, although the longer the contingency period, the less attractive this becomes, since the buyer's capital will be tied up during a longer period. Tax rules governing recognition of income on contingent notes are complex, and we will ignore them here.

O'Tool v. Genmar Holdings, Inc.

387 F.3d 1188 (10th Cir. 2004).

■ BRISCO, CIRCUIT JUDGE.

[This is an appeal by Genmar from a judgment in favor of plaintiffs for breach of an implied covenant of good faith, and breach of employment contracts.]

Geoffrey Pepper had started a company, Horizon Marine LC, to build aluminum jon boats (flat-bottomed utility boats) that were popular in the southern states. His daughter and son-in-law, Cassandra and John O'Tool, were investors in the business and worked in it as well. Production began in the Fall of 1997, and the company struggled, although Pepper expected it would become profitable by the summer of 1998.

[Genmar, the world's largest producer of recreational boats, did not produce the type of boats being built by Pepper's company, instead building boats with a "v" shaped hull favored by northern fishermen. Genmar viewed Pepper's operation as a potential future competitor in the southern market, and as providing a plant where it could enter the southern market more quickly.]

Negotiations culminated in the sale of Horizon to Genmar in December 1998. Under the terms of the parties' written purchase agreement, Genmar created a new subsidiary, defendant Genmar Manufacturing of Kansas, LLC (GMK), that assumed all of the assets and liabilities of Horizon. GMK also offered written employment agreements to Pepper, who assumed the presidency of GMK, and to Pepper's daughter and son-in-law, both of whom assumed managerial positions with GMK similar to the ones they held with Horizon.

The purchase price paid by Genmar for Horizon was comprised of two components: (1) cash consideration of $2.3 million dollars; and (2) "earn-out consideration." Exh.55 at 3. The purchase agreement detailed how the "earn-out consideration" was to be calculated:

> For a period of five (5) years from and after the Closing, Purchaser agrees to remit to Seller as additional consideration and part of the aggregate Purchase Price hereunder an amount equal to a percentage of all annual gross revenues ("Annual Gross Revenues"), subject to achieving certain gross profit percentages [13% or more in the first year of GMK's operation, and 14% or more thereafter], from the sale of (i) Seller's Horizon (or any direct successor) brand boats, trailers, pre-rigging, parts and accessories (collectively the "Seller Products") and (ii) the manufacture of Purchaser's boats (Genmar Holdings' brands) in Seller's Junction City, Kansas plant facility after the Closing Date, in each case of (i) and (ii) above based upon the annual

published dealer list price to a maximum of $5,200,000 (the "Earn-Out Consideration").

At closing, Genmar made an advance payment of $200,000 of earn-out consideration to Horizon, which amount was to be deducted from earn-out consideration payments due to Horizon after the second quarter of 1999.

Pepper's understanding of the earn-out provision was that production of Horizon boats and accessories would afford GMK the most potential for achieving gross revenues and in turn maximizing the earn-out consideration. This was because, in addition to receiving a dealer list price for each Horizon boat sold to a dealer, GMK would receive gross revenues for engines, trailers, and other accessories that were sold with the Horizon boats. Pepper was confident he could achieve the maximum earn-out consideration because, in part, Genmar executives had assured him that Horizon boats would "be the champion of the [GMK] facility."

Pepper's expectations and assumptions for GMK's operations were challenged almost immediately after the deal was closed. In early 1999, Pepper was informed by Genmar of a possible trademark conflict with the Horizon brand name[1] and the Horizon brand of boats was renamed "Nova" (one of two trademark names already registered by Genmar). Further, and more problematically for Pepper, it became evident in early 1999 that two of Genmar's own brands of boats, Ranger and Crestliner, would become the priority of the GMK facility. Specifically, Genmar instructed Pepper that, in the event of production conflicts, GMK should give priority to production of Crestliner boats. Genmar also instructed Pepper to focus all of GMK's engineering efforts on developing fifteen new Ranger boat designs.

[Thereafter Genmar set a fixed price that it would pay GMK for building boats, which turned out to below GMK's cost. The expansion required Pepper to hire more employees in a community with no employees with experience at boat-building, further raising GMK's costs, resulting in operating losses. Pepper protested to Genmar superiors that this shift in emphasis and production was frustrating his ability to cause GMK to meet its profit goals and achieve the earn-out payments. Ultimately Pepper's control over GMK was terminated, and production of the Horizon jon boats was discontinued. In April of 2000 Pepper and the O'Tools were terminated by Genmar.]

At trial a verdict in favor of Pepper on claims of breach of the implied covenant of good faith and fair dealing under Delaware law (the law specified in the acquisition agreement) was entered in the amount of $2.5 million, and the O'Tools recovered on their claims of breach of their employment contracts.]

---

[1] According to Pepper, when he first started Horizon, he hired an attorney who advised him that the Horizon brand name did not present any potential trademark conflicts.

III.

Judgment as a matter of law—breach of contract claim

Defendants contend the district court erred in denying their motion for judgment as a matter of law on the breach of contract claim asserted by plaintiffs Horizon and Pepper.

* * *

During the district court proceedings, Pepper and Horizon asserted alternative theories in support of their breach of contract claim: (1) that defendants breached the express terms of the parties' written purchase agreement; and (2) that defendants breached the implied covenant of good faith and fair dealing associated with the agreement. Defendants challenged both theories in their motion for JMOL. In denying defendants' motion, the district court concluded "there was ample evidence presented at trial to support" the implied covenant theory, and accordingly "declined to address" the breach of express terms theory. On appeal, the parties likewise focus almost exclusively on plaintiffs' implied covenant theory.

"Under Delaware law, an implied covenant of good faith and fair dealing inheres in every contract." Chamison v. Healthtrust, Inc., 735 A.2d 912, 920 (Del.Ch. 1999). "As such, a party to a contract has made an implied covenant to interpret and to act reasonably upon contractual language that is on its face reasonable." Id. "This implied covenant is a judicial convention designed to protect the spirit of an agreement when, without violating an express term of the agreement, one side uses oppressive or underhanded tactics to deny the other side the fruits of the parties' bargain." Id. "It requires the [finder of fact] to extrapolate the spirit of the agreement from its express terms and based on that 'spirit,' determine the terms that the parties would have bargained for to govern the dispute had they foreseen the circumstances under which their dispute arose." Id. at 920–21. The "extrapolated term" is then "implied . . . into the express agreement as an implied covenant," and its breach is treated "as a breach of the contract." Id. "The implied covenant cannot contravene the parties' express agreement and cannot be used to forge a new agreement beyond the scope of the written contract." Id.

The overarching theme of the breach of implied covenant theory asserted by Pepper and Horizon is "that Genmar's entire course of conduct frustrated and impaired [their] realization of the Earn-Out" provided in the parties' agreement. In particular, Pepper and Horizon point to the following actions taken by Genmar following its acquisition of Horizon: (1) changing the brand name of the boats from Horizon to Nova; (2) immediately shifting GMK's production priority from Horizon/Nova boats to Ranger and Crestliner boats; (3) requiring GMK, rather than Ranger or another subsidiary, to bear the costs of designing and producing the new line of Ranger boats; (4) failing to give Pepper operational control over GMK; (5) reimbursing GMK only at "standard cost" for the manufacture of Ranger and Crestliner boats, thereby impairing realization of the earn-out triggers; (6) discontinuing the Horizon/Nova brand of boats; (7) "flipping" Horizon/Nova dealers to other Genmar brands; and (8) shutting down the GMK facility.

Defendants contend all of these actions were expressly contemplated under the terms of the parties' agreement and thus could not form the basis for a violation of the implied covenant of good faith and fair dealing. For reasons discussed below, we disagree.

Changing name of boats from Horizon to Nova. The earn-out provision of the parties' agreement stated, in pertinent part, that calculation of earn-out consideration would be based on the sale of "Horizon (or any direct successor) brand boats." According to defendants, this language "specifically contemplated" the change from the Horizon brand name to the Nova brand name. Defendants further argue that the brand name change occurred at the same time the agreement was finalized, and thus "was part of the agreement, not a violation of it."

We reject defendants' arguments. Although it is true the agreement was broadly worded to encompass GMK's sales of any successor brands of boats, there is otherwise no discussion in the agreement of when or how this might occur. Further, in light of the evidence presented at trial, we conclude the jury reasonably could have inferred that defendants fully intended, prior to signing the agreement with Pepper and Horizon, to change the brand name of the Horizon boats, yet failed to reveal that fact to Pepper and Horizon in a timely fashion (i.e., in time to allow Pepper and Horizon to consider it as part of the contract negotiations). Thus, we conclude the immediate brand name change was not expressly contemplated by the terms of the agreement and could have been considered under plaintiffs' breach of implied covenant theory.

Giving production priority to non-Horizon boats. The parties' agreement does, as noted by defendants, make reference to GMK producing other Genmar boat brands. For example, the earn-out provision of the agreement indicates that Pepper and Horizon were to receive credit for sales "of Purchaser's boats (Genmar Holdings' brands)." Importantly, however, the agreement is otherwise silent with respect to which brand of boats was to receive production priority from GMK. Thus, we conclude defendants' immediate post-acquisition decision to emphasize the production of Ranger and Crestliner boats over the production of Horizon/Nova boats was not expressly contemplated by the terms of the parties' agreement.

Design and production costs of Ranger boats. The parties' agreement contains no mention of the fact that GMK would be required to bear the costs of designing and producing a new line of Ranger boats, and defendants do not suggest otherwise.

Failure to give Pepper operational control over GMK. Again, the parties' agreement contains no mention of precisely how management decisions at GMK would be made, and defendants do not suggest otherwise. Defendants, however, point to language in Pepper's employment contract specifying that he would be "subject to the general supervision," and would act "pursuant to the orders, advice, and direction," of Genmar. Although this language states the obvious, i.e., that Pepper was required to answer to and follow the directions of Genmar, it does not expressly address the issue raised by plaintiffs, i.e., how much authority Pepper retained to determine production priorities for the GMK facility.

"Flipping" Horizon/Nova dealers to other Genmar brands. Nothing in the parties' agreement addresses defendants' authority to "flip" Horizon/Nova dealers to other Genmar brands, and defendants do not assert otherwise.

Closing GMK facility. Finally, nothing in the parties' agreement directly addresses the possible closing of the GMK facility. Thus, defendants' decision to close the GMK facility was not expressly covered or authorized under the terms of the agreement.

Defendants also argue that plaintiffs' "implied covenant claim . . . fails because there is no evidence the parties would have agreed to the obligations the District Court imposed by implication." For example, defendants contend there is no "basis to find that the parties 'would have agreed' that Pepper would have complete discretion to refuse to manufacture Ranger and Crestliner boats." "Nor," defendants argue, "is there any basis to find that the parties 'would have agreed' to maintain the Horizon name."

Defendants' arguments, in our view, ignore the spirit of the parties' agreement. As noted, the agreement expressly stated the purchase price paid by defendants to Pepper/Horizon would be comprised of two components: (1) cash consideration upon closing; and (2) earn-out consideration, based upon GMK meeting or exceeding certain gross revenue goals, for five years following closing. The obvious spirit of this latter component was that Pepper, as president of GMK, would be given a fair opportunity to operate the company in such a fashion as to maximize the earn-out consideration available under the agreement (approximately $5.2 million dollars over five years).

With that spirit in mind, we conclude a reasonable finder of fact could have concluded the parties (had they actually thought about it) would not have simultaneously included within the agreement provisions expressly allowing Genmar to: (1) immediately change the brand name of the boats designed and produced by GMK; (2) set production schedules or priorities that effectively reduced the maximum earn-out consideration available to Pepper; (3) impose significant design and production costs upon GMK for other Genmar brands of boats, while simultaneously limiting the amount of reimbursement GMK could obtain for actually producing other Genmar brands of boats to the "standard cost" of production; or (4) "flip" Horizon dealers to other brands of Genmar boats. See generally Katz v. Oak Indus., Inc., 508 A.2d 873, 880 (Del.Ch. 1986) (stating the legal test for implying contractual obligations is whether it was "clear from what was expressly agreed upon that the parties who negotiated the express terms of the contract would have agreed to proscribe the act later complained of as a breach of the implied covenant of good faith—had they thought to negotiate with respect to that matter").

Lastly, defendants contend there was no evidence that Genmar acted with the intent to harm plaintiffs, i.e., "to injure plaintiff's contractual rights." Instead, defendants contend, "the decisions [plaintiffs] claim[ ] breached an implied duty constitute nothing other than Genmar's reasonable (although ultimately unsuccessful) business efforts to make the Junction City facility profitable for the first time in its operating life."

In denying defendants' post-trial motion, the district court rejected an identical argument. In particular, the court noted that "copious evidence was presented at trial demonstrating that defendants acted with . . . 'dishonest purpose' or 'furtive design.' " For example, the district court noted that "ample evidence" was presented "that defendants had ulterior motives for acquiring Horizon . . . , including the desire to remove a potentially significant competitor from the market and the desire to obtain a facility in the 'southern' market dedicated primarily to the production of Ranger boats." Reduced to its essence, the district court concluded

> the evidence was sufficient to support the conclusion that defendants believed (but were ultimately incorrect) that they could still turn a profit through the production of Ranger and Crestliner boats at Genmar Kansas while simultaneously preventing Mr. Pepper from realizing any earn-out by stifling the production of Horizon boats and reimbursing Genmar Kansas only at standard cost for the production of other boats.

After carefully reviewing the trial transcript, we conclude the district court's summary of the evidence is accurate and sufficient to rebut defendants' assertion that there was no evidence they intended to harm plaintiffs. The district court properly denied defendants' motion for JMOL.

* * *

AFFIRMED.

QUESTIONS

1. Apparently Genmar began making its change shortly after it acquired Horizon. Would it surprise you that a new owner might institute

changes? If Genmar owned the Horizon business and Pepper knew from the agreement that he worked under the general supervision and control of Genmar personnel, what should he conclude about Genmar's power to change production and priorities?

2. Apparently the objectionable changes occurred soon after the acquisition in 1998, suggesting that Genmar had these changes in mind at the time of the closing, although they are not discussed in the contract. If they had occurred more gradually, would Genmar's actions have been more defensible?

3. If you were representing Pepper in negotiating the contract, could you have provided express terms that would have prevented the kind of misunderstandings (assuming that's what they were) that occurred here?

4. Apparently none of the changes of which Pepper complained were expressly contemplated in the agreement. That's another way of saying they weren't expressly prohibited in the agreement. In applying covenants of good faith and fair dealing, most courts decline to provide parties with contract rights not already specified. Has the court done so here?

Lazard Technology Partners, LLC v. Qinetiq N. Am. Operations LLC

2015 Del. LEXIS 201 (Del. 2015).

■ STRINE, CHIEF JUSTICE:

This is an appeal in an earn-out dispute arising from a merger. The appellant represents former stockholders of Cyveillance, Inc., a cyber technology company (the "company"), whom we refer to as the "seller" for the sake of clarity. The appellee (the "buyer") paid $40 million up-front to the company and promised to pay up to another $40 million if the company's revenues reached a certain level. Section 5.4 of the merger agreement prohibited the buyer from "tak[ing] any action to divert or defer [revenue] with the intent of reducing or limiting the Earn-Out Payment." When the earn-out period ended, the revenues had not reached the level required to generate an earn-out.

The seller filed suit in the Court of Chancery, arguing that the buyer breached Section 5.4 of the merger agreement. The seller also argued that the buyer violated the merger agreement's implied covenant of good faith and fair dealing by failing to take certain actions that the seller contended would have resulted in the achievement of revenue sufficient to generate an earn-out.

After a trial, extensive briefing, and post-trial oral argument, the Court of Chancery issued a bench decision reviewing the factual circumstances the seller alleged amounted to a breach of Section 5.4 of the merger agreement and the implied covenant. In that decision, the Court of Chancery found that the merger agreement meant what it said, which is that in order for the buyer to breach Section 5.4, it had to have acted with the "intent of reducing or limiting the Earn-out Payment." After reviewing each of the seller's theories as to how the buyer had acted with the requisite intent, the Court of Chancery found that the seller had not proven that any business decision of the buyer was motivated by a desire to avoid an earn-out payment.

Likewise, the Court of Chancery rejected the seller's implied covenant claim. The Court of Chancery held that the merger agreement was complex and required a number of actions, including actions that would occur post-closing. It thus found that the merger agreement's express terms were supplemented by an implied covenant. But as to whether conduct not prohibited under the contract was precluded because it might result in a reduced or no earn-out payment, the Court of Chancery held that, consistent with the language of Section 5.4, the buyer had a duty to refrain from that conduct only if it was taken with the intent to reduce or avoid an earn-out altogether.

On appeal, the seller argues that the Court of Chancery misinterpreted the merger agreement in both respects, and also that its factual conclusions warrant no deference because they were made in a succinct bench ruling.

As to the first argument, the seller argues that the Court of Chancery erred because it should have recognized that Section 5.4 precluded any conduct by the buyer that it knew would have the effect of compromising the seller's ability to receive an earn-out. It also claims that the Court of Chancery erred when it held that the implied covenant must be read consistently with Section 5.4 because the specific standard in that contractual term reflected the parties' agreement about how the seller would be protected from post-closing conduct that could jeopardize an earn-out payment.

The seller's arguments are without merit. The Court of Chancery acted properly in giving Section 5.4 its plain meaning. By its unambiguous terms, that term only limited the buyer from taking action intended to reduce or limit an earn-out payment. Intent is a well-understood concept that the Court of Chancery properly applied.[8] The

---

[8] "Intent" is most often defined and analyzed in the criminal law context. "[T]he modern [criminal law] approach is to define separately the mental states of knowledge and intent ([which is] sometimes referred to as purpose)." Wayne R. LaFave, 1 Subst. Crim. L. § 5.2 (2d ed. 2014). Most modern codes, including the Model Penal Code, "provide[ ] that one acts 'purposely' when 'it is his conscious object . . . to cause [ ] a result.' " *Id.* (quoting Model Penal Code § 2.02(2)(a)(i)); see also United States v. Falstaff Brewing Corp., 410 U.S. 526, 570 n.22, 93 S. Ct. 1096, 35 L. Ed. 2d 475 (1973) (noting that "the oldest rule of evidence" is "that a man is presumed to intend the natural and probable consequences of his acts") (Marshall, J., concurring); Coverdale v. State, 531 A.2d 1235 (Del. 1987) (Table) ("Intent is a design, resolve or determination with which persons act. Intent in the legal sense is purpose to use particular means to effect a certain result."); Black's Law Dictionary (10th ed. 2014) ("[I]ntent is the mental resolution or determination to do [an act].").

seller seeks to avoid its own contractual bargain by claiming that Section 5.4 used a knowledge standard, preventing the buyer from taking actions simply because it knew those actions would reduce the likelihood that an earn-out would be due. As Section 5.4 is written, it only barred the buyer from taking action specifically motivated by a desire to avoid the earn-out.[9] Contrary to the seller's argument, the Court of Chancery never said that avoiding the earn-out had to the buyer's *sole* intent, but properly held that the buyer's action had to be motivated at least in part by that intention.

Likewise, the seller's argument that it could rely on the implied covenant of good faith and fair dealing to avoid the burden to prove that the buyer intentionally violated Section 5.4 is without merit. Section 5.4 specifically addressed the requirements for an earn-out payment and left the buyer free to conduct its business post-closing in any way it chose so long as it did not act with the intent to reduce or limit the earn-out payment. And as the Court of Chancery found, "[the seller] attempted to negotiate for a range of additional affirmative post-closing obligations, but [the buyer] rejected all of them. . . . Instead of the various affirmative obligations, the agreement provided only that [the buyer] could not take action with the intent of reducing or undermining the earnout payment."[11] Accordingly, the Court of Chancery was very generous in assuming that the implied covenant of good faith and fair dealing operated at all as to decisions affecting the earn-out, given the specificity of the merger agreement on that subject, and the negotiating history that showed that the seller had sought objective standards for limiting the buyer's conduct but lost at the bargaining table.[12] Therefore, the Court of

---

   9   See Cincinnati SMSA Ltd. P'ship v. Cincinnati Bell Cellular Sys. Co., 708 A.2d 989, 992 (Del. 1998) ("Delaware observes the well-established general principle that . . . it is not the proper role of a court to rewrite or supply omitted provisions to a written agreement."); Rhone-Poulenc Basic Chems. Co. v. Am. Motorists Ins. Co. 616 A.2d 1192, 1195–96 (Del. 1992) (Clear and unambiguous language in [a contract] should be given its ordinary and usual meaning. Absent some ambiguity, Delaware courts will not destroy or twist policy language under the guise of construing it. [W]en the language of a contract is clear and unequivocal, a party will be bound by its plain meaning because creating an ambiguity where none exists could, in effect, create a new contract with rights, liabilities and duties to which the parties had not assented.") (internal citations and quotations omitted).

   11   Bench Opinion at 79. The affirmative post-closing covenants that the seller sought but did not obtain at the bargaining table included obligations to "act in good faith to maintain existing or greater levels of business, to preserve relationships of customers . . . and cause the Surviving Corporation to have adequate amounts of capital required to achieve the Earn-Out Payments[,] make reasonable commercial efforts to recruit and employ sufficient employees to achieve the Earn-Out Payments[,] market and bid for new contracts consistent with past practice[,] and [ ] not divert any contracts or business opportunities from the Surviving Corporation to any other entity." App. to Opening Br. at 422 (Merger Agreement Redline Comparing Apr. 3 Draft with Apr. 11 Draft).

   12   See Nemec v. Shrader, 991 A.2d 1120, 1125 (Del. 2010) ("The implied covenant of good faith and fair dealing involves a cautious enterprise, inferring contractual terms to handle developments or contractual gaps that the asserting party pleads neither party anticipated. . . . When conducting this analysis, we must assess the parties' reasonable expectations at the time of contracting and not rewrite the contract to appease a party who later wishes to rewrite a contract he now believes to have been a bad deal. Parties have a right to enter into good and bad contracts, the law enforces both.") (internal quotations omitted); Winshall v. Viacom Int'l, Inc., 55 A.3d 629, 636–37 (Del. Ch. 2011) ("[T]he implied covenant of good faith and fair dealing

Chancery correctly concluded that the implied covenant did not inhibit the buyer's conduct unless the buyer acted with the intent to deprive the seller of an earn-out payment.

Finally, we reject the seller's argument that the Court of Chancery's factual determinations should not be given deference because they were set forth in a bench ruling. That bench ruling dealt with the key factual contentions of the seller and did so clearly. The ruling explained that the Court of Chancery was not persuaded that the buyer had acted with the requisite intent that would allow the seller to prevail on its breach of contract claim.

The Court of Chancery is a busy court charged with giving parties answers to complicated questions in a range of cases, often on an expedited basis. One of the ways in which the judges of that court handle their demanding caseload is by issuing prompt bench decisions on the basis of settled law when they believe they can do so responsibly. That is what the Vice Chancellor did here, and his decision is well grounded in the facts of record and entitled to our deference.

For these reasons, we conclude that the seller's appeal is without merit and that the judgment of dismissal entered for the buyer should be AFFIRMED.

QUESTIONS

1. Footnote 11 in the opinion describes the buyers proposed covenants that were rejected by the purchaser. If, as a seller's attorney, you could get just one of these provisions, which would you prefer?

2. Should this have alerted the seller that the earnout was in jeopardy?

3. If you represented by purchaser, how would you explain your client's rejection of these clauses?

4. Should Mr. Pepper have sought similar protections from Genmar?

---

should not be applied to give plaintiffs contractual protections that they failed to secure for themselves at the bargaining table. . . . [T]he implied covenant is not a license to rewrite contractual language. . . . Rather, a party may only invoke the protections of the covenant when it is clear from the underlying contract that the contracting parties would have agreed to proscribe the act later complained of had they thought to negotiate with respect to that matter.") (internal citations and quotations omitted), aff'd, 76 A.3d 808 (Del. 2013); Aspen Advisors LLC v. United Artists Theatre Co., 843 A.2d 697, 707 (Del. Ch. 2004) ("When, as is the case here, the relevant contracts expressly grant the plaintiffs certain rights, . . . the court cannot read the contracts as also including an implied covenant to grant the plaintiff additional unspecified rights. . . . To do so would be to grant the plaintiffs, by judicial fiat, contractual protections that they failed to secure for themselves at the bargaining table."); Katz v. Oak Indus., 508 A.2d 873, 880 (Del. Ch. 1986) ("[T]he appropriate legal test [for an implied contractual obligation] is [whether] it [is] clear from what was expressly agreed upon that the parties who negotiated the express terms of the contract would have agreed to proscribe the act later complained of as a breach of the implied covenant of good faith-had they thought to negotiate with respect to that matter. If the answer to this question is yes, then . . . a court is justified in concluding that such act constitutes a breach of the implied covenant of good faith.").

5.   The court says that the agreement "only limited the buyer from taking action intended to reduce or limit an earn-out payment." It also says "it only barred the buyer from taking action specifically motivated by a desire to avoid the earn-out." But in footnote 8 it quotes the U.S. Supreme Court that "the oldest rule of evidence" is "that a man is presumed to intend the natural and probable consequences of his acts." Is the court saying that the subsequent actions of the buyer weren't intentional? Is there a narrower reading of Chief Justice Strine's words?

NOTE ON EARN-OUT PROVISIONS

The O'Tool case highlights some of the perils of earn-out clauses. A sophisticated seller will want to specify a number of protections. A recent law firm memo discusses some of the problems that can arise:

Solving Valuation Issues with Earnouts—Clever or Stupid?*

By Teresa R. Tarpley, Morris Manning & Martin LLP

Who keeps control of the business during the earnout period

The main arguments that arise in an earnout situation are over control. If a seller has a large payment coming to them that is contingent upon the target achieving a certain milestone, then eventually it will occur to the seller that the buyer may take actions to minimize the earnout payment. The buyer will argue that both parties have the same goal going forward—to make the business successful—so the seller should not concern itself about this issue, but a sophisticated seller immediately sees through this argument. Earnouts are never set up to measure the "success" of the company as a whole. They are set up with respect to very particular metrics. If a buyer can manipulate the operations to minimize the earnout payment without affecting the overall health of the enterprise, it would be in the buyer's best interest to do so. Moreover, once a transaction is closed, the target likely will be part of a larger organization that may have a different future in mind for the target and a different measure of "success" than that envisioned by the seller.

Accordingly, a sophisticated seller will start asking for certain rights and covenants, which will essentially amount to giving the seller some control over post-closing operations. This control can be asserted outright (by the seller insisting that they stay in actual control of the operations following the closing pursuant to a specified budget) or indirectly (by the seller asking the buyer to agree to a host of affirmative and negative covenants). With respect to an EBITDA earnout hurdle, for example, a seller may be focused initially on broad issues that may affect the probability of the receipt of the earnout payment, such as the state of the economy and the risk that customers may be lost due to the deal, but their focus will need to shift quickly to detailed questions, such as:

---

*   LEXOLOGY, by Association of Corporate Counsel, at http://www.lexology.com/library/detail.aspx?g=7408df4c–702d–4f50–8277–4b5a28fd3400 (last visited June 1, 2009)

- Will the company be required to maintain any sort of advertising budget?

- Will the company be required to continue to employ any particular number of sales people?

- Will the company have to avoid extraordinary expenses?

- Will the company have to engage in certain specified collection efforts with respect to accounts?

- Will the allocation of intercompany expenses to the target be disallowed?

- Will price changes or discounts, certain marketing promotions or certain types of contracts be disallowed?

* * *

A seller has to think through and deal with almost every aspect of the historical business and the business during the earnout period in order to properly set up an earnout.

From the buyer's viewpoint, the buyer's objective is to own the target, and the buyer will quickly point out that it is bearing most of the risk if the target's business fails (because the earnout is generally a minority of the purchase price). Therefore, a buyer is very reluctant to give a seller continuing control over the business or to place significant restrictions on the business going forward. In addition, the buyer doesn't want to be held liable for making reasonable business decisions, even if they have the effect of reducing the earnout. Finding an acceptable balance between the seller's desire to be protected and the buyer's desire to be able to run the business as it sees fit is extremely difficult.

So, whereas in a typical sale transaction the seller wants to sell the company and walk away and the buyer wants to acquire the company and assume control, an earnout frustrates both of these goals. As an advisor in the transaction, you need to block out a significant amount of time to walk through these issues with your client. You should also show them how the earnout discussions are likely to progress and the hard choices they are going to have to make in the end. Often, the seller ends up with far less protection than they would like, and late in the negotiations they are faced with a decision as to whether to take a leap of faith or walk from the deal. Sometimes, after parties have considered these issues carefully, they decide to forego an earnout in favor of a simpler, more certain structure.

———————

There are other perils as well. If the consideration is in buyer shares, should there be a cap on the earnout, to protect against a seller's windfall if the buyer's stock appreciates more than anticipated during the earnout period? If the seller's product is sold as a bundle with the buyer's product and the bundle is sold at a discount, how should the sales price be divided? See, e.g., AmerisourceBergen Corp. v. LaPoint, 956 A.2d 642 (Del. 2008).

———————

ii. PUBLICLY TRADED SELLERS

Earnouts can also be used in public companies to bridge opinions about value. One area of great uncertainty and potential disagreement involves drugs still in clinical testing, or where the owner is applying for Food and Drug Administration (FDA) approval for use of the drug to treat a new disease, where the potential market is large and lucrative. An example involved Celgene Corporation's acquisition of Abraxis BioScience, in a merger agreement announced June 30, 2010. In addition to cash and stock, Abraxis shareholders were to receive one "Contingent Value Right" for each share of Abraxis stock. Payments were to be made to holders upon FDA approval of new uses of ABRAXANE® and related drugs, and upon net sales of these drugs that exceeded certain targets. Portions of the Contingent Value Rights are set forth below. The document takes the form of an indenture of trust that purports to comply with the Trust Indenture Act.

"*CVR Payment*" means any Net Sales Payment and any Milestone Payment.

"*Milestone #1*" means U.S. Regulatory Approval of the Product described in clause (a) of the definition of "Product" for use in the treatment of non-small cell lung cancer (NSCLC), which U.S. Regulatory Approval permits the Company to market such Product under a label that includes a progression free survival claim, but only if the foregoing milestone is achieved no later than the Milestone Target Date. For the avoidance of doubt, an "approvable letter" or similar communication published by the FDA shall not constitute approval for purposes of the foregoing.

"*Milestone #2*" means U.S. Regulatory Approval of the Product described in clause (a) of the definition of "Product" for use in the treatment of pancreatic cancer, which U.S. Regulatory Approval permits the Company to market such Product under a label that includes an overall survival claim, but only if the foregoing milestone is achieved no later than the Milestone Target Date. For the avoidance of doubt, an "approvable letter" or similar communication published by the FDA shall not constitute approval for purposes of the foregoing.

"*Milestone Payment*" means, as applicable, (i) two hundred fifty million dollars ($250,000,000), with respect to the achievement of Milestone #1; and (ii) (a) four hundred million dollars ($400,000,000), with respect to the achievement of Milestone #2 if Milestone #2 is achieved no later than April 1, 2013, and (b) three hundred million dollars ($300,000,000), with respect to the achievement of Milestone #2 if Milestone #2 is achieved after April 1, 2013 but no later than the Milestone Target Date.

"*Net Sales*" means, for each Net Sales Measuring Period, the sum of, without any duplication: (i) the gross amounts invoiced for the Products sold by the Company, its Affiliates or its licensees (other than licensees under Existing Licenses) to third parties (other than the Company, its Affiliates or its licensees) during such Net Sales Measuring Period, including wholesale distributors, less deductions from such amounts calculated in accordance with Accounting Standards so as to arrive at "net sales" under Accounting Standards as reported by the Company, its Affiliate or its licensee, as applicable, in such Person's financial statements, and further reduced by write-offs of accounts receivables or increased for collection of accounts that were previously written off; plus (ii) (A) the amount of royalties and profit split payments received by the Company or its Affiliates from their respective licensees under Existing Licenses for sales (but not the supply) of Products sold by such licensees to third parties (other than the Company or its Affiliates) during such Net Sales Measuring Period, and (B) the amount of any milestone payments received during such Net Sales Measuring Period by the Company or its Affiliates from their licensees under Existing Licenses with respect to the Products.

"Net Sales Measuring Period" means the one-year period beginning January 1st of each year during the term of this CVR Agreement and ending December 31st of each year during the term of this CVR Agreement; provided that the first Net Sales Measuring Period will begin on January 1, 2011 and end on December 31, 2011.

"Net Sales Payment" means, with respect to any Net Sales Measuring Period, an amount equal to (i) two and one-half percent (2.5%) of that portion of Net Sales of the Products that exceeds one billion dollars ($1,000,000,000) but is less than or equal to two billion dollars ($2,000,000,000) for such period, plus (ii) an additional amount equal to five percent (5.0%) of that portion of Net Sales of the Products that exceeds two billion dollars ($2,000,000,000) but is less than or equal to three billion dollars ($3,000,000,000) for such period, plus (iii) an additional amount equal to ten percent (10.0%) of that portion of Net Sales of the Products that exceeds three billion dollars ($3,000,000,000) for such period; provided that no Net Sales Payments will be due following a Net Sales Payment Termination Date.

"Net Sales Payment Dates" means the fifteenth (15th) day after the date the Company is required to provide the Net Sales Statement pursuant to Section 5.4 for the Net Sales Measuring Period in respect of which a Net Sales Payment is due.

"Net Sales Payment Termination Date" means the last day of the Net Sales Measuring Period ending on December 31, 2025; provided that, if Net Sales of the Products for the Net Sales Measuring Period ending on December 31, 2025 are equal to or greater than one billion dollars ($1,000,000,000), then the Net Sales Payment Termination Date shall be extended until the earlier of (a) the last day of the first Net Sales Measuring Period subsequent to December 31, 2025 during which Net

Sales of the Products are less than one billion dollars ($1,000,000,000) and (b) December 31, 2030.

See: http://www.sec.gov/Archives/edgar/data/816284/0000950123100632 23/c03090exv10w1.htm.

Another problem with publicly traded companies is that a closing may be deferred for some period of time, either to allow for completion of due diligence, to complete SEC filings, or to secure regulatory approvals. Stock prices of both buyer and seller may vary between the time of the execution of the agreement and the closing. If the deal is for cash, it's very likely no adjustment will be provided, and the cash offer will provide a floor that will keep the buyer's stock from sinking much below the merger consideration. The more difficult problems involve the stock for stock merger, where both stocks may vary, and in some ways will be positively correlated. If a fixed exchange ratio is used, and the buyer's stock declines in value, this will in all likelihood cause a similar decline in the value of the seller's stock. Both CVRs and earnouts must be valued at fair value as consideration in the sale or merger at the time of closing, and thus are subject to taxation perhaps before the event occurs that triggers the payment, or perhaps even if no further payments are ever received by the sellers. See FAS 141®.

In some cases no adjustment is provided in case of a decline in the buyer's stock price. In the merger agreement of AT & T and Bell South in March of 2006, no adjustment was proposed—there was simply an exchange ratio. In this case both companies were engaged in the same line of business, and even shared joint ownership of a cellular service, Cingular. Both companies were subject to the same competitive pressures from broadband services and other cellular companies, and subject to the same type of regulation. Since both were large companies with mature products in traditional phone service, their prospects were well known, and were likely to be positively correlated.

In other cases the latter is true—the buyer may be in a volatile, highly competitive industry where large drops in its stock price could occur. Sellers may want some price protection, so that selling shareholders will continue to receive a price reasonably close to (if not above) the originally contemplated market value of Buyer shares. This means that if the Buyer's shares decline in value, the exchange ratio will be adjusted to increase the number of Buyer shares received for each Seller share. In an adjustment clause, the parties may specify an exchange ratio based on the stock prices at the time of the deal, perhaps 0.5 Buyer shares for each Seller share. The agreement will then specify that the final exchange ratio will be determined on the basis of stock prices a few days before either the Seller's shareholder vote or the closing date. (Typically this is an average price over as much as 20 trading days, to reduce the possibility that a Buyer might manipulate its own stock price upward.) The agreement will provide that if the Buyer's share price drops substantially, the exchange ratio will increase. Thus, if the Buyer's stock were to drop by 50% in value, the ratio would be increased, so the selling shareholders will receive twice as many Buyer shares as originally contemplated, with the originally contemplated value. Buyers will argue that there must be a limit to this adjustment, on the theory that the Buyer cannot afford to pay that number of its own shares for the Seller without diluting the investment of its own shareholders. To accomplish this, a cap may be placed on the exchange ratio, such as 0.8 Buyer shares for each Seller share. Correspondingly, if the Buyer's stock rises in value prior to the measuring date, the Buyer will argue for a reduction in the exchange ratio, so that Selling shareholders don't receive a windfall gain, and consideration in excess of the real value of their shares. Thus, if the Buyer's shares were to double in value, the Buyer will argue that the exchange ratio should be cut in half, to 0.25 Buyer shares for each Seller share. Seller's representatives will be concerned that such an increase in the value of Seller's shares may be attributable at least in part to a rise in general market prices, so that Seller's shareholders should not be required to bear the entire reduction such a formula suggests, and might put a floor on the exchange ratio at 0.35 Buyer shares for each Seller share. This combination of a cap and a floor on the exchange ratio is called a "collar."

Another type of exchange ratio begins by calculating the cash value to be received by selling shareholders in the aggregate, and adding to it any additional cash received by Seller from the exercise of stock options prior the closing. This amount is then divided by the product of the "Determination Price" for Buyer's shares over a 20—day period by the number of Seller shares issued and outstanding, to produce the number of Buyer shares to be received for each Seller share. Thus the Seller's shareholders will receive an amount of Buyer common stock with a predetermined market value. A collar is then imposed on the exchange ratio, with a floor of 1.3 shares and a cap of 1.7 shares. Absent the collar, the Buyer bears the entire market risk of a decline in its stock price. With the collar, the Seller's shareholders also bear some of that risk.

PROBLEM

Assume you represent a corporation negotiating to purchase BarChris Construction Corp. in the Spring of 1961. You know that the bowling alley business is becoming saturated, and that there is some risk of an earnings decline. At this point in the negotiations, no due diligence has been performed. Nevertheless, negotiations on price are proceeding, based on BarChris' financial statements, which include the statements for the period ending March 31, 1961. Examine the discussion of price adjustment clauses in Part 2A.1 of this chapter. Which type of provision would you recommend to your client for the determination of the consideration?

B. PROTECTION FROM SURPRISES

i. MATERIAL ADVERSE CHANGES

John Borders v. KRLB, Inc.

727 S.W.2d 357 (Tex.App.–Amarillo 1987).

■ RICHARD N. COUNTISS, JUSTICE.

This is a contract case. Appealing from a judgment awarding damages, interest and attorney's fees to appellee KRLB, Inc., appellant John Borders says the trial court erroneously ignored a jury finding and applied the wrong measure of damages. We affirm.

In January 1984, Borders contracted to purchase KRLB, a Lubbock radio station for $1,400,000.00. At that time, the station had an Arbitron* rating of 9.8. Shortly after the contract was signed, new Arbitron ratings were released and the rating of KRLB fell to 4.2, indicating that the station had lost over half its audience. When he learned about the ratings plunge, Borders notified KRLB that he would not abide by the contract, and demanded the return of $25,000.00 he had placed in escrow. KRLB refused to return the money and sued Borders for breach of contract. Borders responded with a counterclaim charging KRLB with breach.

The case was tried before a jury. Consistent with the jury's findings, the trial court entered judgment awarding KRLB $350,000.00 for damages caused by Borders' breach, plus interest and attorney's fees. In doing so, however, the trial court disregarded the jury's response to special issue number eleven:

SPECIAL ISSUE NO. 11

Do you find from a preponderance of the evidence there were any material adverse changes in the business, operations, properties and other assets of KRLB which would impair the operation of radio station KRLB FM and KRLB AM between November 3, 1983, and the date of repudiation by Borders?

ANSWER: "There were" or "There were not."

ANSWER: There were.

By his first four points, Borders says the foregoing finding entitled him to judgment because the finding was supported by the evidence and established an unfulfilled condition precedent to the closing of the sale. In order to resolve the points, we must determine at the outset, and as a question of law, whether a drop in Arbitron ratings was an event under

---

* Arbitron is the primary market research company for radio stations. The ratings indicate the share of the listening market held by a station and are critical to the sale of advertising.—Ed.

the contract that would allow Borders to repudiate the contract. If it was not, then the trial court correctly ignored special issue eleven, because the evidence of the drop in Arbitron ratings is the only evidence that supports the finding. If it was, however, the finding mandated entry of judgment for Borders.

The special issue is based on paragraph 3.5 of the contract which says:

3.5. Operations. Since November 3, 1983, there have not been any material adverse changes in the business, operations, properties and other assets of KRLB which would impair the operation of radio station KRLB-FM and KRLB-AM and since such date the business of KRLB has been conducted in the usual, regular and ordinary manner and shall continue, through and including the Closing Date, to be conducted in such manner, unless prior written approval for any variation therefrom shall have first been secured from Borders. Since said date, KRLB has not, except as indicated on Schedule 7 attached hereto and incorporated herein by this reference, directly or indirectly:

(a) Made any loans or advances to any officer, director, shareholder or employee not exceeding $1,000 in the aggregate;

(b) Declared or paid any dividends on its capital stock or purchased or otherwise acquired any shares of its capital stock, other than those purchased from Ed Wilkes;

(c) Subjected any of the Purchased Assets to any mortgage, deed of trust, lien, pledge, conditional sales contract, lease, encumbrance or charge;

(d) Sold, leased or otherwise transferred any of the Purchased Assets other than in the ordinary course of business;

(e) Entered into any agreements, other than standard purchase orders for materials sold or purchased in the ordinary course of business either not in the ordinary course of business or involving consideration given by KRLB in amounts in excess of One Thousand Dollars ($1,000.00);

(f) Modified, amended or terminated any agreement, or waived or released any right, other than in the ordinary course of business;

(g) Incurred any obligation or liability for borrowed money, or incurred any other obligation or liability except in the ordinary course of business that constitute a lien on the Purchased Assets or which Borders will be obligated to assume;

(h) [sic] Increased the salary, fringe benefits or other compensation of, or paid any bonus or similar compensation to, any of its officers or directors; or

(i) Agreed to do any of the things described in the preceding clauses (a) through (h).

KRLB admits that section 3 of the contract establishes various conditions precedent and Borders admits that the contract does not specifically mention Arbitron ratings. Thus, in order to determine whether KRLB was required to maintain its Arbitron rating, we must construe the contract.

Our primary goal when construing an instrument is to give effect to the intent of the parties. We ascertain that intent from the language of the contract, R & P Enterprises v. LaGuarta, Gavrel & Kirk, 596 S.W.2d 517, 519 (Tex.1980), as a matter of law and without resort to parol evidence unless the contract is ambiguous. Parenthetically, we observe that when, as here, neither party contends the instrument is ambiguous, its construction must be resolved as a question of law. In construing the instrument, we must consider and attempt to give effect to all of it, Southland Royalty Co. v. Pan American Petro. Corp., 378 S.W.2d 50, 57 (Tex.1964), while mindful of the intentions existing when it was executed. The ultimate restraint is that a court cannot, through the construction process, make a new contract for the parties, one they did not make.

When we apply those principles to the contract in question, we conclude that the drop in Arbitron ratings did not justify Borders' refusal to close the transaction. First, examining the entire contract, we find no mention of Arbitron ratings and no language guaranteeing or promising Borders that the station would maintain its audience share between November 8, 1983, and closing.

Second, all parties agree that if such an obligation is to be supplied by necessary implication, it must come from paragraph 3.5 quoted above. It is apparent, however, that paragraph 3.5 is designed to prohibit KRLB management from raiding the corporation or seriously damaging its ability to function as a business entity, by incurring debt, selling assets, or taking money, i.e., impairing its operation. The paragraph contemplates deliberate adverse action by management. We cannot reasonably construe the paragraph to include an event over which management has little control. Certainly there is nothing to indicate that KRLB aided, abetted, or encouraged the ratings decline.

We have examined the entire contract to determine whether KRLB agreed, either expressly or by implication, that the Arbitron ratings would not fall after November 3, 1983. We find no such agreement and to supply one would be to make a new contract for the parties. It follows that the trial court correctly disregarded special issue number eleven because, within the context of this record, there was no evidence to support it. Points of error one, two, three, and four are overruled.

* * *

The judgment is affirmed.

QUESTIONS

1. Why does the court not treat a 50% drop in ratings and audience as a "material adverse change in the business [and] operations . . . of KRLB"?

2. How would this court treat the destruction of the radio station's tower, without insurance to replace it, under this clause?

3. How would this court treat the loss of the station's FCC license under this clause?

4. If a purchase agreement containing the language in paragraph 3.5 were executed to acquire BarChris in March, 1961, would a buyer have had grounds for refusing to proceed with a closing if it had learned of defaults by lessees of bowling alleys and Talcott's demand that BarChris make the lease payments and operate the alleys?

5. Are there any rules of contract construction that justify this reading of the contract?

6. How would you draft a material adverse change provision to protect the buyer from a revenue decline of the kind that the drop in Arbitron ratings will cause? Does the Merger Agreement and Plan of Reorganization in Appendix C provide a solution? (Hint: this is called a "come Hell or high water" agreement.) Why not just make no change in the Arbitron ratings a condition of Border's obligation to close?

7. Would the language in sections 4.1(b) and 6.1 of the Agreement and Plan of in Appendix C have allowed a buyer to refuse to close the purchase of BarChris under the Merger circumstances mentioned in Question 4? If not, how could a buyer obtain such protection, and why would a sophisticated buyer not insist on it?

Esplanade Oil & Gas, Inc. v. Templeton
Energy Income Corporation
889 F.2d 621 (5th Cir.1989).

■ CLARK, CHIEF JUDGE.

I.

Esplanade Oil & Gas, Inc. (Esplanade) appeals the denial of relief from Templeton Energy Income Corporation's (Templeton) alleged breach of a letter agreement to purchase certain oil and gas properties. The district court concluded that Templeton was justified in refusing to complete the purchase because a condition precedent contained in the letter agreement was not fulfilled. Templeton cross-appeals the district court's adverse ruling on three other conditions precedent. We reverse on direct appeal and affirm on cross appeal.

II.

[Esplanade and Templeton entered into a letter agreement by which Esplanade would sell Templeton certain oil and gas properties for $385,000.]

The letter agreement contained, among other things, the purchase price, a description of the Properties, and seven conditions precedent to closing. One condition, condition 4(c), stated that "there shall occur no adverse material change to the Properties or [Esplanade's] interest therein from the date of this letter to Closing." Templeton drafted the provision, and the parties never discussed it. Another condition, condition 4(b), required the parties to execute a "mutually acceptable definitive Purchase and Sale Agreement. . . ."

Later that month, the price of oil on the spot market dropped from approximately $28.85 to $20.35 per barrel. Neither of the parties had foreseen this development. On February 6, Templeton advised Esplanade that it was no longer willing to close the purchase under the terms of the letter agreement because of the "precipitous drop in the price of oil." The next day, Esplanade wrote a letter to Templeton stating that Esplanade still considered the letter agreement in force and was prepared to go forward with the closing. Templeton responded that the precipitous drop in the price of oil had, in its opinion, "adversely affected" the Properties and that Templeton did not consider it "feasible" to negotiate a definitive purchase and sale agreement as required by the letter agreement. Templeton ceased negotiating.

* * *

In July of 1987, the issue of liability was tried before the district court. Templeton defended against Esplanade's claim by asserting that five of the seven conditions precedent contained in the letter agreement had not been fulfilled. The district court rejected all but one of Templeton's contentions. The court ruled that the phrase "adverse material change to the Properties" in condition 4(c) was ambiguous and that Templeton's expert testimony placing the risk of an oil price decline on the seller by industry custom was more credible than the expert testimony offered by Esplanade. The court also ruled that, under the circumstances, the term "adverse material change to the Properties" reasonably encompassed a "dramatic decline in the price of oil." The court thus concluded that the letter agreement did not require Templeton to purchase the Properties and entered judgment dismissing Esplanade's suit.

Esplanade now appeals, contending that the phrase "adverse material change to the Properties" referred to changes to the Properties themselves and not to a decline in the value of the Properties resulting from a drop in the market price of oil. It asserts that the letter agreement was binding on the parties and required Templeton to purchase the Properties for no less than the agreed price of $385,000. Because the district court misconstrued the "adverse material change" clause of condition 4(c), we reverse. Templeton cross-appeals, contending that the district court erroneously concluded that three other conditions precedent were fulfilled or should be deemed fulfilled. These correct rulings are affirmed.

III.

The "interpretation of a contract is the determination of the common intent of the parties." La.Civ.Code art. 2045. When the words of the contract are clear and unambiguous and lead to no absurd consequences, no further inquiry may be made into the parties' intent. *Id.* art. 2046. The fact that one party can, in hindsight, create a dispute about the meaning of a contractual provision does not render the provision ambiguous. The court must give effect to the ordinary meaning of the words and may not create an ambiguity where none exists. See Commercial Union Ins. Co. v. Advance Coating Co., 351 So.2d 1183, 1185 (La.1977).

In this case, the district court found an ambiguity where none exists. The letter agreement provides for the purchase of the "Properties" by Templeton. The agreement explicitly defines the term "Properties" as follows:

> All of Seller's right, title and interest in various oil and gas properties listed in Exhibit "A" including, but not limited to, Seller's working interest and net revenue interest in the respective properties stated in Exhibit "A", together with an identical right, title and interest in and to all leasehold estates, contracts, contract rights, materials, production facilities, salt water disposal systems, pipelines, gathering lines and other fixtures, equipment and personal or real property, easements, rights-of-way, and any and all other rights and privileges of Seller associated with the use, ownership and operation thereof. . . .

Exhibit "A" consists of a list of wells and mineral leases with Esplanade's corresponding working interests and net revenue percentages. The letter agreement then states that "there shall occur no adverse material change to the Properties . . . prior to Closing" (emphasis added).

The plain meaning of this language is that no adverse material changes were to occur to Esplanade's right, title and interest in the mineral leases and equipment listed in the letter agreement. The district court expressly found that no such changes occurred:

> It was undisputed at trial that these properties never physically changed, nor did Esplanade's interest in those properties change. The leases remained in effect, the wells continued to

produce oil, and the physical equipment located on the wells remained in the same condition at all times pertinent hereto as they were on January 14, 1986. (emphasis in original)

Nothing in the letter agreement itself hints of any other construction. Nor does the plain meaning of the words lead to absurd consequences. The essential purpose of the price agreement was to fix the value at which the trade would later be finalized. If increases or decreases in market value were to govern, the price term would have been redundant. Therefore, Templeton's attempt to pour new content into the language of condition 4(c) in an effort to avoid what market fluctuations caused to be an economically unwise business decision is unavailing. We conclude that condition precedent 4(c) was fulfilled.

IV.

Templeton nevertheless argues on cross appeal that the district court erred in concluding that three other conditions precedent were fulfilled or are deemed fulfilled. Templeton urges this court to affirm the district court's judgment of dismissal, based on the non-fulfillment of these other conditions.

Templeton contends that the letter agreement was non-binding because the parties failed to execute a "mutually definitive Purchase and Sale Agreement . . . which contains the usual terms and provisions for the purchase and sale of oil and gas producing properties," as required by condition 4(b). Templeton asserts that Esplanade would not have been able to execute such an agreement because Templeton's final form contract would have required Esplanade to warrant that the Properties had the same value at closing as they had when the letter agreement was executed. We disagree.

"A condition is regarded as fulfilled when it is not fulfilled because of the fault of a party with an interest contrary to the fulfillment." La.Civ.Code art. 1772; see also Moss v. Guarisco, 459 So. 2d 1, 5 (La. App.Ct. 1984), writ denied, 462 So. 2d 1247 (La.1985). In this case, Templeton had "an interest contrary to the fulfillment" of condition 4(b) because the letter agreement required Templeton to purchase the Properties at a fixed price under what later became adverse market conditions. Also, the district court found that "it was Templeton, not Esplanade, which refused to enter into, or even negotiate a definitive purchase and sale agreement." Therefore, condition 4(b) is deemed fulfilled.

Moreover, Templeton's refusal to negotiate and enter into a final contract cannot be justified on the basis of a disagreement about the form of the final contract. Templeton's breach was based on its dissatisfaction with prevailing market conditions and the purchase price that was unambiguously specified in the letter agreement. It was not based on a dispute about the form of the final contract. While certain matters relating to the closing might have been settled one way or the other,

Templeton could not reasonably have tendered any final contract that did not call for the price specified in the underlying letter agreement. For these reasons, Templeton cannot assert the nonfulfillment of condition 4(b) as a defense to its breach, and condition 4(b) is regarded as fulfilled.

* * *

V.

We conclude that the letter agreement was binding on the parties and required Templeton to purchase the Properties for the agreed price of $385,000. We also conclude that Templeton breached the letter agreement by refusing to close the transaction. We therefore reverse on direct appeal, affirm on cross appeal, and remand with directions to determine damages and enter judgment for appellant.

Reversed in part, affirmed in part, and remanded with directions.

_____

QUESTIONS

1. Why does the court not give effect to the letter agreement's unfulfilled conditions to Templeton's obligation to buy? Is there evidence that the parties intended to be bound by this letter agreement, rather than only by a definitive agreement?

2. How would you draft a material adverse change provision in this letter agreement to protect the buyer from a decline in oil and gas prices?

3. How would you draft the agreement to allow Templeton to withdraw because of the failure to deliver documents, even if the decline in oil and gas prices was the real reason? Does anything in section 7(e) of the Merger Agreement and Plan of Reorganization in Appendix C address this issue?

_____

NOTE ON IN RE IBP, INC. SHAREHOLDERS LITIGATION AND IBP, INC. V. TYSON FOODS, INC.

789 A.2d 14 (Del.Ch. 2001).

IBP, formerly known as Iowa Beef Packers, was the nation's number one beef packer and number two pork distributor. Tyson, on the other hand, was the nation's leading chicken distributor. While Tyson was a leader in packaging meats in the more profitable ready-to-eat and ready-to-heat business, IBP was much slower in moving into this business. In 1998 IBP purchased a specialty meat business that produced hors d'oervres, kosher foods and airline food. The President and owner, Zahn, was given an employment contract to stay on with IBP in its new business, now called "DFG" within IBP, and an earn-out provision in the purchase agreement. DFG was a small part of IBP's huge meat business, accounting for less than 1% of its sales. When Zahn left in 2000, he took a sizeable earn-out payment with him. It was only later that IBP discovered that Zahn had falsified accounting records to achieve the earnings that resulted in his payment, and began an audit to discover the size of the problem. The first estimate was that the DFG business was overvalued on IBP's books by $9 million, but as time went on IBP management discovered the problems were worse. The next estimate was that they were worse by at least $20 million, and by the end of 2000 IBP management believed the charges to earnings had risen to $30 to $35 million. The number rose to $50 million by mid January 2001, and ended at $108 million by late February.

IBP management was frustrated by the market's valuation of its stock, and was receptive when an investment bank proposed a leveraged buyout. As an investor group was assembled, IBP prepared itself for sale, and, at the request of the group, prepared five-year projections, which projected growth in its Foodbrands division, in which DFG was located. Subsequently the IBP special committee of the board reached an agreement with the LBO group on a buyout at $22.25 per share, which was announced on October 2, 2000. This spurred two industry giants to make their own bids. Smithfield Foods, the nation's number one pork processor, offered $25 in Smithfield stock, which wasn't welcomed by IBP management because of a cold relationship between these competitors. Tyson had apparently been contemplating an acquisition of IBP for some time, believing that its skills in packaged meat business could add value to IBP. Tyson management, led by Don Tyson, the founder and former CEO met with IBP management in what the court called a "lovefest." On December 4, Tyson offered $26 in a half cash, half stock bid, and argued that its bid was more likely to succeed because it wouldn't face the antitrust problems that Smithfield would. Tyson immediately began due diligence and learned of the growing realization of the size of the write-off problem caused by DFG. Tyson representatives were informed of the cyclical nature of the beef business, which suggested IBP's five year projections might not be met. As Tyson began a tender offer for IBP stock in early December, it learned that IBP now expected lower earnings for 2000 than its five-year projections had indicated. Nevertheless, Tyson raised its tender offer to $27.00 cash. As more bad news was received from Tyson about the growing size of the DFG problem, Tyson management became less trusting of IBP management. Nevertheless, when Smithfield made an all stock bid at $30 on December 29, Tyson countered the next day at $28.50 cash and stock. On December 31 Smithfield countered with a $32 all stock bid, and Tyson responded with a bid of $30, half cash and half stock. IBP agreed to this offer.

The draft merger agreement submitted by IBP to Tyson on December 30 contained a Schedule 5.11, containing a list of all IBP liabilities. Section 5.11 stated:

> Section 5.11. <u>No Undisclosed Material Liabilities</u>. Except as set forth in Schedule 5.11 the Company 10–K or the Company 10–Qs, there are no liabilities of the Company of any Subsidiary of any kind whatsoever, whether accrued, contingent, absolute, determined, determinable or otherwise, and there is no existing

condition, situation or set of circumstances which could reasonably be expected to result in such a liability, other than:

(a)   liabilities disclosed or provided for in the Balance Sheet;

(b)   liabilities incurred in the ordinary course of business consistent with past practice since the Balance Sheet Date or as otherwise specifically contemplated by this Agreement;

(c)   liabilities under this agreement;

(d)   other liabilities which individually or in the aggregate do not and could not reasonably be expected to have a Material Adverse Effect.

Schedule 5.11 itself states:

No Undisclosed Material Liabilities.

Except as to those potential liabilities disclosed in Schedule 5.12, 5.13, 5.16 and 5.19, the Injunction against IBP in the Department of Labor Wage and Hour litigation (requiring compliance with the Wage and Hour laws), and any further liabilities (in addition to IBP's restatement of earnings in its [3]rd Quarter 2000) associated with certain improper accounting practices at DFG Foods, a subsidiary of IBP, there are none.

Annexes to the agreement contained language addressing Tyson's obligation to close both the tender offer and the merger, and stated that Tyson would have no obligation to close if certain events occurred:

(d)   Except as affected by actions specifically permitted by this Agreement, the representations and warranties of the Company contained in this Agreement (x) that are qualified by materiality or Material Adverse Effect shall not be true at and as of the scheduled expiration of the Offer as if made at and as of such time (except in respect of representations and warranties made as of a specified date which shall not be true as of such specified date), and (y) that are not qualified by materiality or Material Adverse Effect shall not be true in all material respects at and as of the scheduled expiration date of the Offer as if made at and as of such time (except in respect of representations and warranties made as of a specific date which shall not be true in all material respects as of such specified date).

IBP warranted that all of its SEC filings and its financial statements were true and complete, with a materiality qualifier. Finally, Section 5.10 of the merger agreement contained a Material Adverse Change provision:

Section 5.10. Absence of Certain Changes. Except as set forth in Schedule 5.10 hereto, the Company 10–K or the Company 10–Qs, since the Balance Sheet Date, the Company and the Subsidiaries have conducted their business in the ordinary course consistent with past practice and there has not been:

(a) any event, occurrence or development of a state of circumstances or facts which has had or reasonably could be expected to have a Material Adverse Effect. . . .

In mid-January of 2001 Tyson's board and shareholders met and approved the merger agreement. At the same time, IBP informed Tyson management that it was unclear if the DFG problems were going to require a restatement of 1999 earnings. Ultimately a restatement of 1999 earnings was necessary, and was announced in mid-February. By this time Tyson management was getting cold feet. Both chicken and beef sales suffered severe decline because of a hard winter. By late March, Tyson wanted out, and announced that it was terminating because of a breach of warranty that the 1999 financial statements were true. The next day IBP filed suit in the Delaware Chancery Court for specific performance of the merger agreement. In defending, Tyson raised not only the problems with the financial statement, but also IBP's disappointing first quarter of 2001, which it characterized as evidence of a Material Adverse effect.

Vice Chancellor Strine rejected Tyson's argument that IBP had flatly warranted its financials, noting the qualifiers in Section 5.11 and Schedule 5.11, which referred to its impending restatements of results because of the DFG problem. While technically the impending DFG disclosures were not "liabilities", it was clear that Tyson was willing to bear the risk of the DFG restatements in Schedule 5.11.

Vice Chancellor Strine thought the Material Adverse Effect question was a much closer one. He noted that the decline in IBP's 2001 first quarter earnings was an industry-wide problem, and that IBP's earnings history showed a cyclical business. "The picture that is revealed from this data is of a company that is consistently profitable, but subject to strong swings in annual EBIT and net earnings. IBP's five-year projections had projected a decline in 2001, although not as large as the one experienced. Vice Chancellor Strine's ruling on this issue follows.

"These negotiating realities bear on the interpretation of § 5.10 and suggest that the contractual language must be read in the larger context in which the parties were transacting. To a short-term speculator, the failure of a company to meet analysts' projected earnings for a quarter could be highly material. Such a failure is less important to an acquiror who seeks to purchase the company as part of a long-term strategy.[151] To such an acquiror, the important thing is whether the company has suffered a Material Adverse Effect in its business or results of operations that is consequential to the company's earnings power over a commercially reasonable period, which one would think would be measured in years rather than months. It is odd to think that a strategic buyer would view a short-term blip in earnings as

---

[151] James C. Freund, Anatomy Of A Merger: Strategies and Techniques for Negotiating Corporate Acquisitions 246 (Law Journals Seminars-Press 1975) ("Whatever the concept of materiality may mean, at the very least it is always relative to the situation.").

material, so long as the target's earnings-generating potential is not materially affected by that blip or the blip's cause.[152]

"In large measure, the resolution of the parties' arguments turns on a difficult policy question. In what direction does the burden of this sort of uncertainty fall: on an acquiror or on the seller? What little New York authority exists is not particularly helpful, and cuts in both directions. One New York case held a buyer to its bargain even when the seller suffered a very severe shock from an extraordinary event, reasoning that the seller realized that it was buying the stock of a sound company that was, however, susceptible to market swings.[153] Another case held that a Material Adverse Effect was evidenced by a short-term drop in sales, but in a commercial context where such a drop was arguably quite critical.[154] The non-New York authorities cited by the parties provide no firmer guidance.

"Practical reasons lead me to conclude that a New York court would incline toward the view that a buyer ought to have to make a strong showing to invoke a Material Adverse Effect exception to its obligation to close. Merger contracts are heavily negotiated and cover a large number of specific risks explicitly. As a result, even where a Material Adverse Effect condition is as broadly written as the one in the Merger Agreement, that provision is best read as a backstop protecting the acquiror from the occurrence of unknown events that substantially threaten the overall earnings potential of the target in a durationally-significant manner.[155] A short-term hiccup in earnings should not suffice; rather the Material Adverse Effect should be material when viewed from the longer-term perspective of a reasonable acquiror. In this regard, it is worth noting that IBP never provided Tyson with quarterly projections.

---

[152] Pine State Creamery Co. v. Land-O-Sun Dairies, Inc., 201 F.3d 437, 1999 WL 1082539, at * 6 (4th Cir. 1999) (per curiam) (whether severe losses during a two month period evidenced a MAC was a jury question where there was evidence that the business was seasonal and that such downturns were expected as part of the earnings cycle of the business).

[153] Bear Stearns Co. v. Jardine Strategic Holdings, No. 31371187, slip. op. (N.Y. Supr. June 17, 1988), aff'd mem., 33 N.Y.S.2d 167 (App. Div. 1988) (Tender offeror who was to purchase 20% of Bear Stearns could not rely on the MAC clause to avoid contract despite $100 million loss suffered by Bear Stearns on Black Monday, October 19, 1997, and the fact that Bear Stearns suffered a $48 million quarterly loss, its first in history. The buyer knew that Bear Stearns was in a volatile cyclical business.).

[154] In Pan Am Corp. v. Delta Airlines, 175 B.R. 438, 492–493 (S.D.N.Y. 1994), Pan Am airlines suffered sharp decline in bookings over a three-month period that was shocking to its management. The court held that a MAC had occurred. It did so, however, in a context where the party relying on the MAC clause was providing funding in a work-out situation, making any further deterioration of Pan Am's already compromised condition quite important.

In another New York case, Katz v. NVF Co., 100 A.D.2d 470, 473 N.Y.S.2d 786 (N.Y. App. Div. 1984), two merger partners agreed that one partner has suffered a material adverse change when its full year results showed a net loss of over $6.3 million, compared to a $2.1 million profit a year before, and steep operating losses due to plant closure. 473 N.Y.S.2d at 788. The Katz case thus presents a negative change of much greater magnitude and duration than exists in this case.

[155] A contrary rule will encourage the negotiation of extremely detailed "MAC" clauses with numerous carve-outs or qualifiers. An approach that reads broad clauses as addressing fundamental events that would materially affect the value of a target to a reasonable acquiror eliminates the need for drafting of that sort.

"When examined from this seller-friendly perspective, the question of whether IBP has suffered a Material Adverse Effect remains a close one. IBP had a very sub-par first quarter. The earnings per share of $.19 it reported exaggerate IBP's success, because part of those earnings were generated from a windfall generated by accounting for its stock option plan, a type of gain that is not likely to recur. On a normalized basis, IBP's first quarter of 2001 earnings from operations ran 64% behind the comparable period in 2000. If IBP had continued to perform on a straight-line basis using its first quarter 2001 performance, it would generate earnings from operations of around $200 million. This sort of annual performance would be consequential to a reasonable acquiror and would deviate materially from the range in which IBP had performed during the recent past.[156]

"Tyson says that this impact must also be coupled with the DFG Impairment Charge of $60.4 million. That Charge represents an indication that DFG is likely to generate far less cash flow than IBP had previously anticipated.[157] At the very least, the Charge is worth between $.50 and $.60 cents per IBP share, which is not trivial. It is worth even more, says Tyson, if one realizes that the Rawhide Projections portrayed Foodbrands as the driver of increased profitability in an era of flat fresh meats profits. This deficiency must be considered in view of the overall poor performance of Foodbrands so far in FY 2001. The Rawhide Projections had targeted Foodbrands to earn $137 million in 2001. In a January 30, 2001 presentation to Tyson, Bond had presented an operating plan that hoped to achieve $145 million from Foodbrands. As of the end of the first quarter, Foodbrands had earned only $2 million, and thus needed another $135 million in the succeeding three quarters to reach its Rawhide Projection. IBP's overall trailing last twelve month's earnings had declined from $488 million as of the end of the third quarter of 2000 to $330 million.

"As a result of these problems, analysts following IBP issued sharply reduced earnings estimates for FY 2001. Originally, analysts were predicting that IBP would exceed the Rawhide Projections in 2001 by a wide margin. After IBP's poor first quarter, some analysts had reduced their estimate from $2.38 per share to $1.44 a share. Even accounting for Tyson's attempts to manipulate the analyst community's perception of IBP, this was a sharp drop.

"Tyson contends that the logical inference to be drawn from the record evidence that is available is that IBP will likely have its worst year since 1997, a year which will be well below the company's average performance for all relevant periods. As important, the company's principal driver of growth is performing at markedly diminished levels, thus compromising the company's future results as it enters what is expected to be a tough few years in the fresh meats business.

---

[156] See Raskin v. Birmingham Steel Corp., 1999 WL 193326, at *5, Allen, C. (Dec. 4, 1990) (while "a reported 50% decline in earnings over two consecutive quarters might not be held to be a material adverse development, it is, I believe unlikely to think that might happen").

[157] The Impairment Charge was, of course, signaled by Shipley's reduced estimate for DFG in FY 2001, and his indication that an impairment study was underway.

"IBP has several responses to Tyson's evidence. IBP initially notes that Tyson's arguments are unaccompanied by expert evidence that identifies the diminution in IBP's value or earnings potential as a result of its first quarter performance.[160] The absence of such proof is significant. Even after Hankins generated extremely pessimistic projections for IBP in order to justify a lower deal price, Merrill Lynch still concluded that a purchase of IBP at $30 per share was still within the range of fairness and a great long-term value for Tyson. The Merrill Lynch analysis casts great doubt on Tyson's assertion that IBP has suffered a Material Adverse Effect.[161]

"IBP also emphasizes the cyclical nature of its businesses. It attributes its poor first quarter to an unexpectedly severe winter. This led ranchers to hold livestock back from market, causing a sharp increase in prices that hurt both the fresh meats business and Foodbrands. Once April was concluded, IBP began to perform more in line with its recent year results, because supplies were increasing and Foodbrands was able to begin to make up its winter margins. Bond testified at trial that he expects IBP to meet or exceed the Rawhide Projection of $1.93 a share in 2001, and the company has publicly indicated that it expects earnings of $1.80 to $2.20 a share. Peterson expressed the same view.

"IBP also notes that any cyclical fall is subject to cure by the Agreement's termination date, which was May 15, 2001. By May 15, IBP had two weeks of strong earnings that signaled a strong quarter ahead. Moreover, by that time, cattle that had been held back from market were being sold, leading to plentiful supplies that were expected to last for most of the year.

"Not only that, IBP notes that not all analyst reporting services had been as pessimistic as Tyson portrays.[162] In March, Morningstar was reporting a mean analyst prediction of $1.70 per share for IBP in 2001. By May, this had grown to a mean of $1.74 a share. Throughout the same period, Morningstar's consensus prediction was an FY 2002 performance of $2.33 range in March, and $2.38 in May. Therefore, according to Morningstar, the analyst community was predicting that IBP would return to historically healthy earnings next year, and that earnings for this year would fall short of the Rawhide Projections by less than $.20 per share.

"IBP also argues that the Impairment Charge does not approach materiality as a big picture item. That Charge is a one-time, non-cash charge, and IBP has taken large charges of that kind as recently as 1999. While IBP does not deny that its decision to buy DFG turned out

---

[160] It has admittedly taken its own payment multiples based on the Rawhide Projections and simply "valued" the effect that way. But IBP never warranted that it would meet those Projections.

[161] Tyson's only expert on this subject testified that a MAE would have occurred in his view even if IBP met the Rawhide Projections, because those Projections were more bearish than the analysts. This academic theory is of somewhat dubious practical utility, as it leaves the enforceability of contracts dependent on whether predictions by third-parties come true.

[162] I take judicial notice of these publicly available estimates, D.R.E. 201, and consider it important to do so given Tyson's heavy reliance on analyst opinion to prove that a Material Adverse Effect has occurred.

disastrously, it reminds me that DFG is but a tiny fraction of IBP's overall business and that a total shut-down of DFG would likely have little effect on the future results of a combined Tyson/IBP. And as a narrow asset issue, the charge is insignificant to IBP as a whole.

"I am confessedly torn about the correct outcome. As Tyson points out, IBP has only pointed to two weeks of truly healthy results in 2001 before the contract termination date of May 15. Even these results are suspect, Tyson contends, due to the fact that IBP expected markedly better results for the second week just days before the actual results come out. In view of IBP's demonstrated incapacity to accurately predict near-term results, Tyson says with some justification that I should be hesitant to give much weight to IBP's assurances that it will perform well for the rest of the year.

"In the end, however, Tyson has not persuaded me that IBP has suffered a Material Adverse Effect. By its own arguments, Tyson has evinced more confidence in stock market analysts than I personally harbor. But its embrace of the analysts is illustrative of why I conclude that Tyson has not met its burden.

"As of May 2001, analysts were predicting that IBP would earn between $1.50 to around $1.74 per share in 2001. The analysts were also predicting that IBP would earn between $2.33 and $2.42 per share in 2002. These numbers are based on reported 'mean' or 'consensus' analyst numbers. Even at the low end of this consensus range, IBP's earnings for the next two years would not be out of line with its historical performance during troughs in the beef cycle. As recently as years 1996–1998, IBP went through a period with a three year average earnings of $1.85 per share. At the high end of the analysts' consensus range, IBP's results would exceed this figure by $.21 per year.

"This predicted range of performance from the source that Tyson vouches for suggests that no Material Adverse Effect has occurred.[170] Rather, the analyst views support the conclusion that IBP remains what the baseline evidence suggests it was—a consistently but erratically profitable company struggling to implement a strategy that will reduce the cyclicality of its earnings. Although IBP may not be performing as well as it and Tyson had hoped, IBP's business appears to be in sound enough shape to deliver results of operations in line with the company's recent historical performance. Tyson's own investment banker still believes IBP is fairly priced at $30 per share. The fact that Foodbrands is not yet delivering on the promise of even better performance for IBP during beef troughs is unavailing to Tyson, since § 5.10 focuses on IBP as a whole and IBP's performance as an entire company is in keeping with its baseline condition.

---

[170] Again, I emphasize that my conclusion is heavily influenced by my temporal perspective, which recognizes that even good businesses do not invariably perform at consistent levels of profitability. If a different policy decision is the correct one, a contrary conclusion could be reached. That different, more short-term approach will, I fear, make merger agreements more difficult to negotiate and lead to Material Adverse Effect clauses of great prolixity.

"Therefore, I conclude that Tyson has not demonstrated a breach of § 5.10. I admit to reaching this conclusion with less than the optimal amount of confidence. The record evidence is not of the type that permits certainty."

Concluding that damages were not an adequate remedy, Vice Chancellor Strine awarded a decree of specific performance to IBP.

Tyson settled with IBP and proceeded to complete the merger. It also settled with a class action brought under state law by IBP shareholders. Thereafter, inexplicably, it sought to have Vice Chancellor Strine vacate his opinion, which was denied. The denial was affirmed in Tyson Foods v. Aetos Corp., 818 A.2d 145 (Del. 2003).

_____

QUESTIONS

1. Why isn't the downturn in the fresh meat business in the first quarter 2001, with its consequent reductions in projected 2001 earnings, a material adverse event?

2. How much would IBP be damaged by its failure to merge with Tyson? What is the nature of IBP's damages?

3. How much would IBP's shareholders be damaged by the failure of the merger? Is the nature of damages to shareholders different in kind from damages to IBP itself?

4. What standing would shareholders have to complain about a contract between IBP and Tyson?

_____

NOTE

Drafters of MAC clauses have learned from the early judicial decisions. Today these clauses may cover material adverse changes in the seller's business, financial condition, results of operations, assets, liabilities, properties, operations and even prospects. For a study on the frequency of these clauses, see Robert T. Miller, Canceling the Deal: Two Models of Material Adverse Change Clauses in Business Combination Agreements, 31 Cardozo L. Rev. 99, 116 (2009). The frequency of use of these clauses is currently the subject of annual studies by the Committee on Negotiated Acquisitions of the Business Law Section of the American Bar Association.

While the use of these specific terms has expanded over time, sellers have resisted, and have negotiated a series of exceptions, for such things as adverse changes in the economy, financial markets, the seller's industry, in applicable laws or regulations, accounting standards, political conditions, war, terrorism or natural disasters—all things out of the control of the seller. In some cases these changes will only provide relief if the seller's change is not disproportionately large compared to the measure—whether the economy as a whole or the seller's industry, for example.

The parties also negotiate hard about the degree of certainty that the event is a MAC required to excuse the buyer. The most stringent term is that a MAC "has occurred" to the seller. The next strongest form is that the event "would reasonably be expected to have been" a MAC for the seller. This suggests that most or all reasonable persons would agree that it is a MAC. The next form is that the event is "could reasonably be expected to have been" a MAC. This allows a seller to withdraw if *any* reasonable person might have thought it was a MAC. Parties bargain hard over these choices for obvious reasons. If courts take this language seriously, it could make a real difference in the degree of harm suffered by the buyer before an escape is possible.

Robert Miller concludes that the courts have largely ignored both the specific types of MACs as well as the probability required. Is that true of Vice Chancellor Strine's discussion of industry conditions in IBP? Miller argues that courts simply look at the financial magnitude of the earnings decline rather than other factors. In Hexion Specialty Chemicals, Inc. v. Huntsman Corp., 965 A.2d 715 (Del. Ch. 2008), Vice Chancellor Lamb referred to "the macroeconomic challenges Huntsman has faced" in explaining why Huntsman had not experienced a MAC. Vice Chancellor Lamb provided an explanation—that the exceptions, such as a general industry decline and no disproportionate drop for the target company, only apply once a MAC-sized event has occurred.

PROBLEM

The following description of an abortive merger between Verizon Communications Inc. and Northpoint Communications Group, Inc. is taken from the decision in a securities class action brought by Northpoint bondholders against Verizon, on a motion to dismiss the complaint. Faulkner v. Verizon Communications, Inc., 156 F.Supp.2d 384 (S.D.N.Y. 2001). NorthPoint's suit against Verizon, in Superior Court in California, was settled in July of 2002 for a payment of $175 million from Verizon.

BACKGROUND

I.   Merger Between NorthPoint and Verizon

* * *

Verizon, the resulting entity of a merger between Bell Atlantic Corporation and GTE Corporation, is the largest provider of wireline and wireless communications and the second largest provider of digital subscriber line ("DSL") services in the United States. It operates in 40 countries, has approximately 2.7 billion shares of outstanding common stock and, in 1999, generated approximately $60 billion in revenues. NorthPoint, formed in 1997, was a national provider of highspeed, local data network services which use DSL technology to transport data over telephone company copper lines 25 times faster than common dial-up modems. As a start-up DSL service provider, it incurred massive losses and negative cash flow. In 1999, it reported net losses of $440 million. In its Form 10–Qs, it reported negative cash flow from operations and investing activities in the amount of $406 million for the six-month period ending June 30, 2000, which increased to $595 million by September 30, 2000. Indeed, NorthPoint reported increasing net losses of $80 million, $112 million and $136 million, for the first, second and third quarters of the 2000 fiscal year. Moreover, in accordance with the securities laws, it repeatedly advised its investors that it expected its operating expenses and losses to increase in the future.

On August 7, 2000, NorthPoint and Verizon entered into a Merger Agreement. Pursuant to the Merger Agreement and the accompanying Funding Agreement, Verizon agreed to contribute $800 million in cash ($450 million to fund NorthPoint's capital expenditures and operations and $350 million to be paid to NorthPoint's shareholders) and more than $500 million of Verizon DSL assets in exchange for a 55% equity interest in NorthPoint. Verizon also agreed to provide interim financing of $200 million by January 1, 2001 and to purchase $150 million of NorthPoint nonvoting 9% convertible preferred stock.

The Merger Agreement contained three relevant provisions. First, Verizon was required to (1) "use all commercially reasonable efforts to obtain in a timely manner all necessary waivers, consents and approvals and to effect all necessary registrations and filings" and (2) "use all commercially reasonable efforts to take, or cause to be taken, all other actions and to do, or cause to be done, all other things necessary, proper or advisable to consummate and make effective as promptly as practicable the transactions contemplated by this [Merger] Agreement." August 7, 2001 was the scheduled termination date. Second, the parties agreed not to "issue any press release or public statement with respect to this [Merger] Agreement or the transactions contemplated hereby . . . without prior consent" of the other entity. Third, Verizon was given the right to terminate only in the case of a Material Adverse Effect, defined as "any fact, event, change or effect having, or which will have, a material adverse effect on the business, operations, properties . . . , financial condition, assets or liabilities of NorthPoint. . . ."

On August 8, 2000, Verizon and NorthPoint jointly announced the proposed merger. In this announcement, Verizon proclaimed, inter alia, that the merger was a "groundbreaking agreement to fundamentally change the dynamics of the broadband industry." Verizon Vice-Chairman, President and Chief Operating Officer Lawrence T. Babbio represented that "this deal combines complementary assets—Verizon's position in the consumer market and NorthPoint's presence with business customers—to provide the scale to fuel growth and deliver the full benefits of high speed connections." Verizon CEO Ivan Seidenberg extolled the merger as one which "will take us a long way toward achieving national scale in our broadband operations and putting another 'piece of the bundle in place.' "

From NorthPoint's perspective, the market reacted relatively well to the news of the merger. Following the August 8, 2000 announcement, the market price of the NorthPoint's $1,000 Notes increased from approximately $600 to approximately par, or $1,000. Conversely, the market value of Verizon's stock plummeted. For example, on August 7, 2000, 5 million Verizon shares were traded, closing at a price of $47 7/8 per share. On August 8, 2000, 33 million shares were traded, closing at a price of $42 ½ per share. On August 9, 2000, 22 million shares were traded, closing at a price of $40 3/8 per share.

Moreover, the merger received negative reactions from analysts. On August 9, 2000, Paine Webber bluntly stated that it did not understand the transaction and remarked that "Verizon gave up too much to get too little." Similarly, on the same day, the New York Times described the merger as a "peculiar structure" and predicted that the merger will dilute "Verizon's per-share earnings growth by about 5 percent."

Nevertheless, in its Form 10–Q filed on August 14, 2000, for the period ending June 30, 2000, Verizon represented that the Merger was expected to be completed in mid-2001. On September 6, 2000, NorthPoint and Verizon issued a joint press release in which they announced that Verizon had funded $150 million through the purchase of preferred stock and that they "expected the deal to close by mid-2001." In the October 2000 edition of Telecommunications, Babbio stated that "the new strategy will expand broadband choice for customers by providing a superior alternative to cable." On October 26, 2000, NorthPoint Chief Executive Officer Liz Fetter stated in a conference call that "the merger with Verizon continues on schedule" and "two months after the announcement, we are even more excited by what the deal holds, not only for NorthPoint, but also for the future of the broadband industry. We continue to be on track for a closing in the first half of 2001 . . . "

On October 26, 2000, NorthPoint filed its Form 10–Q for its third fiscal quarter, reporting operating losses of $106 million and net losses of $125 million on revenues of approximately $30 million, but acknowledged it had opted not to recognize revenues for certain data industry customers in troubled financial condition. In any event, it confirmed, with Verizon's prior approval, that "we continue to be on track with our prior expectation of doing the transaction in the first half of 2001."

Allegedly, during the next two weeks, NorthPoint's management advised Verizon's senior executives that it had decided to revise its previously disclosed third-quarter results and recognize total operating losses in the amount of $118 million and net losses in the amount of $136 million. Verizon gave no indication that a Material Adverse Effect had occurred. Instead, on November 14, 2000, Verizon filed its own Form 10–Q for the period ending September 30, 2000, which stated:

> During August 2000, we announced a merger with Northpoint . . . We expect the Merger to close in 2001. . . . Upon completion of the Merger we will own 55% of Northpoint and will consolidate its results. . . . In addition, we have agreed to make a cash investment in NorthPoint of $450 million. Up to $350 million of this investment will be in the form of financing prior to the closing.

(*Id.*)

On November 20, 2000, NorthPoint, after receiving Verizon's prior consent, issued a press release announcing its revised third-quarter results, but reassured its investors that "we continue to be on track with our prior expectation of closing the Verizon transaction in the first half of 2001." Finally, on November 29, 2000, Verizon announced that it was unilaterally terminating the Merger Agreement, on the basis that NorthPoint's revised third-quarter figures constituted a Material Adverse Effect under the Merger Agreement.

The effects of Verizon's actions were fatal for NorthPoint. Soon after the termination, the market price of NorthPoint's notes plunged from $120 to $150 per Note, or 12–15% of their face value. By January 10, 2001, the Notes traded for less than 10% of their face value. NorthPoint was force to reduce its workforce by 20%. Finally, on January 16, 2001, it filed for bankruptcy pursuant to Chapter 11 of the Bankruptcy Code. Conversely, the market price of Verizon's stock increased, and it received positive reactions from analysts.

Plaintiffs argue that Verizon's stated reasons for terminating the merger were a mere "pretext" for Verizon to avoid its financing obligations which had already had a negative impact on Verizon's near-term earnings. Indeed, plaintiffs allege that no later than November 14, 2000, "Verizon was no longer using commercially reasonable efforts to consummate the Merger, but rather had soured on the deal and was exploring ways to justify terminating the Merger Agreement and its funding obligations" of $200 million prior to January 1, 2001. This was allegedly a result of the negative reaction the merger received from analysts and its concomitant stock price decline. Northpoint argues that Verizon had known of the revised third-quarter results prior to the filing of its November 14, 2000 Form 10–Q as well as its approval of NorthPoint's November 29, 2000 press release. "The truth is that increases in NorthPoint's reported losses and negative cash flow were not contrary to expectations."

II. Lawsuits Commenced by Verizon and NorthPoint

                                  * * *

On December 8, 2000, NorthPoint commenced a lawsuit against Verizon in the California Superior Court, San Francisco County, asserting claims of breach of contract, fraud, negligent misrepresentation, and violation of CAL. BUS. & PROF. CODE § 17200; see NorthPoint Communications Group, Inc. v. Verizon Communications, Inc., No. 317249 (Cal. Super. Ct. Dec.8, 2000). It alleged that Verizon was without a basis to terminate the Merger Agreement and that its purported reasons were merely a pretext designed to free Verizon from its investment obligations and to lift its depressed stock prices. 'In addition, Verizon and its management determined that Verizon could destroy NorthPoint's business by reneging on the merger and could then usurp the DSL business opportunities of Northpoint in Verizon's monopoly territory.' * * * "

The Merger Agreement contained the following definition of a "Material Adverse Effect":

(k) " 'Material Adverse Effect' means

(i)   in the case of NorthPoint or Parent, any fact, event, change or effect having, or which will have, a material adverse effect on the business, operations, properties (including intangible properties), financial condition, assets or liabilities of NorthPoint or Parent, as the case may be, and its Subsidiaries taken as a whole, but shall not include facts, events, changes or effects that are generally applicable to (A) the data industry, (B) the United States economy or (c) the United States securities markets generally or the Nasdaq Technology Index in particular, nor shall it include any fact, event, change or effect caused predominantly by Verizon's involvement in the transactions contemplated by this Agreement; and

(ii)   in the case of the Verizon DSL Business or Verizon, any fact, event, change or effect having, or which will have, a material adverse effect on the business, operations, properties (including intangible properties), financial condition, assets or liabilities of the Verizon DSL Business or Verizon, as the case may be, but shall not include facts, events, changes or effects that are generally applicable to (A) the data industry, (B) the United States economy or (c) the United States securities markets generally or the Nasdaq Technology Index in particular, nor shall it include any fact, event, change or effect caused predominantly by NorthPoint's involvement in the transactions contemplated by this Agreement.

Verizon's obligation to complete the transaction was subject to certain conditions:

Section 8.3 Additional Conditions to Obligations of Verizon. The obligations of Verizon to effect the Merger and the Asset Contribution are also subject to the fulfillment of the following conditions:

* * *

(g)   Material Adverse Effect. There shall not have occurred any Material Adverse Effect on NorthPoint."

———————

Assume now, that in hindsight, you are considering Verizon's position during this transaction.

1.   Would you alter the Material Adverse Effect definition in any way? See C, section 4.1(b) for a recent version of the MAE definition.

2.   When Verizon management decided to terminate the transaction, what would you advise management to say in a press release announcing its decision?

3.   Once suit has been filed, based on the facts given, how would you advise Verizon about its chances? How would your suggested changes have helped?

ii. BEST EFFORTS CLAUSES

Best efforts clauses generally require target boards to use their best efforts to secure shareholder approval of mergers and sales, subject to their fiduciary duties to keep shareholders informed if a better offer appears. We now shift to a different setting for these clauses, typically where the buyer commits to use its best efforts to secure third-party approvals, as from antitrust or other regulatory authorities. Sellers may also commit to use their best efforts to secure consents from various parties with whom the seller is in a contractual relationship, whether a loan agreement, long-term lease, exclusive patent license, or the like. The following case is not a prototypical acquisition, but rather a joint venture agreement in which British Airways invested in financially troubled USAir.

USAirways Group, Inc. v. British Airways PLC

989 F.Supp. 482 (S.D.N.Y.1997).

■ CEDARBAUM, J.

This is an action brought by USAirways Group, Inc. and USAirways, Inc. (collectively "USAir") against British Airways PLC and Britair Acquisition Corp. Inc. (collectively "BA"), and AMR Corporation and American Airlines, Inc. (collectively "AA"). The dispute arises out of an alliance between USAir and BA that began in 1992 and BA's subsequent decision in 1995 to pursue an alliance with AA instead. USAir sues BA for breach of contract, breach of fiduciary duty, and under a respondeat superior theory for acts of the BA directors who are also directors of USAir.

* * *

BA and AA move to dismiss the amended complaint (hereafter simply "the complaint") pursuant to Fed. R. Civ. P. 12(b)(1) and 12(b)(6). For the reasons discussed below, AA's motion to dismiss is granted, and BA's motion to dismiss is granted in part and denied in part.

Allegations of the Complaint

I. *The Nature of the U.S.–U.K. Airline Industry*

Passenger airline service between the United States and the United Kingdom is governed by a bilateral air services agreement known as Bermuda II. Pursuant to Bermuda II, non-stop service to London is permitted from twenty-six gateway cities in the United States. Under Bermuda II, only two U.S. airlines provide such service to Heathrow Airport in London, AA and United Airlines. Demand for slots by air carriers wishing to expand or enter service to Heathrow far exceeds supply. Bermuda II does not, however, restrict U.S. carriers from applying for route authority to service London's Gatwick Airport. The regulatory restrictions of Bermuda II would be removed if the United States and the United Kingdom entered a liberalized air services agreement ("open skies agreement"). The United States already has open skies agreements with several other foreign counties.

II. *The Investment Agreement and the USAir-BA Relationship*

On January 21, 1993, USAir entered into an investment agreement with BA (the "Investment Agreement") which contemplated a series of three investments by BA in USAir totaling $750 million as part of a general plan to integrate and coordinate their operations. Section 2.6(c) of the Investment Agreement requires USAir and BA to use their "best efforts" to obtain Department of Transportation ("DoT") approval of all transactions as promptly as practicable. BA allegedly understood that the key to obtaining DoT approval of Phases Two and Three would be obtaining the British government's consent to liberalization of Bermuda II. Section 6.1(vii) of the Investment Agreement prohibited BA from entering "into any discussion, negotiations, arrangements or understandings with any third party with respect to . . . an extraordinary corporate transaction involving [USAir]." Section 10.1(a) of the Investment Agreement requires USAir and BA to use "reasonable efforts" to consummate all contemplated transactions as soon as practicable.

Pursuant to Phase One, BA paid $300 million for a 20 percent voting interest in USAir, and USAir increased its Board of Directors to sixteen by adding three BA appointed board members. On March 15, 1993, DoT issued an order stating that BA's initial investment of $300 million did not impair USAir's citizenship under applicable law and approved the proposed code sharing agreement and the wet leases. In connection with the Investment Agreement, USAir relinquished its three U.S.–U.K. routes from Charlotte, Baltimore, and Pittsburgh to Gatwick Airport in London. That relinquishment is embodied in a consent decree filed with the United States District Court for the District of Columbia dated September 30, 1993. USAir alleges that it entered into the consent decree while the Department of Justice was considering whether the relinquishment was necessary, because USAir had already acquiesced in BA's insistence that it relinquish those routes. All three of USAir's relinquished routes to Gatwick were subsequently awarded to AA. In a separate wet lease agreement, for a share of the profits, USAir leased its aircrafts and crew used on these U.S.–U.K. routes to BA to service BA's flights to the U.S.

In connection with Phase One, USAir and BA entered into a code sharing agreement on January 21, 1993, pursuant to which BA placed its code on many USAir flights. However, the code sharing agreement did not permit USAir to place its code on BA flights. A coordination team named the Alliance Leadership Group was formed to finalize and implement projects furthering the alliance. In furtherance of the alliance, BA and USAir entered into several collaborative projects including, among other things, a linked frequent flyer program, joint sales and marketing in the United States, consolidated sales and marketing in Canada, joint ground handling arrangements in New York and Frankfurt, integrated fuel purchasing in the United States, and joint marketing of maintenance services.

Phase Two of the Investment Agreement gave BA an option to invest an additional $200 million in USAir. Phase Two involved a comprehensive plan of further integration and cooperation between USAir and BA. Phase Three of the Investment Agreement, which expires on January 21, 1998, gives BA an option to invest an additional $250 million in USAir in exchange for preferred stock. The Investment Agreement also provides that in the event that DoT approval for Phases Two and Three occurs before January 21, 1998, USAir and BA may elect to cause BA to complete Phases Two and Three.

Efforts by USAir during 1994 and 1995 to further strengthen the alliance were unsuccessful. USAir alleges that BA did not take any steps to seek liberalization of Bermuda II during the three-year USAir-BA alliance, although both parties understood that such an agreement was a prerequisite for Phases Two and Three. Moreover, USAir's requests to make the code sharing arrangement reciprocal were rejected by BA, and BA also refused to support USAir's efforts to apply independently for routes between the United States and London. BA had allegedly realized by mid-1994 that further cooperation with USAir was not profitable for BA. According to the complaint, BA realized that Phase One had already provided most of the benefits that BA could enjoy from the BA-USAir alliance.

For that reason, according to the complaint, BA did not exercise its best efforts to obtain DoT approval even though there was a window of opportunity to do so during the summer of 1994. USAir alleges that BA actually discouraged British regulators from making concessions to the United States. BA, however, did not disclose its intention not to pursue the BA-USAir alliance and continued to mislead USAir.

III. *The BA-AA Relationship*

In November of 1994, BA began negotiating a possible alliance with AA. A general outline for such an alliance was developed by January 1, 1995. BA did not inform USAir of the negotiations between BA and AA, which continued through 1995. BA and AA allegedly were conspiring to stifle USAir's efforts to compete in the U.S.–U.K. market. On September 21, 1995, BA finally informed USAir that it had been negotiating a strategic alliance with AA. The directors of BA who sat on USAir's Board of Directors, however, did not inform USAir of the true scope of the alliance. They allegedly assured USAir's Board that BA would not enter into any agreement that was not acceptable to USAir.

In the fall of 1995, USAir and United Airlines began discussions concerning United Airlines' possible acquisition of USAir. In September of 1995, BA and AA allegedly agreed to undermine United Airline's acquisition of USAir. The strategy of BA and AA was to have AA engage in sham negotiations for acquisition of USAir. AA allegedly forced United Airlines to back away from any plans to acquire USAir by informing United Airlines that it would respond to any bid by United Airlines or would protect AA's competitive position "by other means as necessary." On November 13, 1995, United Airlines announced that it would not seek to acquire USAir.

BA and AA allegedly conspired in other ways to prevent USAir from competing in the U.S.–U.K. market. BA allegedly agreed with AA not to seek liberalization of Bermuda II so that USAir would not be able to obtain DoT approval for Phases Two and Three of the Investment Agreement. BA allegedly used its influence to delay ongoing negotiations between the United States and the United Kingdom so that any "open skies" agreement would benefit the BA-AA alliance and not the BA-USAir alliance.

On November 19, 1995, BA informed USAir that BA and AA's proposed alliance included a frequent flyer relationship with terms more favorable than the BA-USAir alliance and a reciprocal code sharing agreement. On January 19, 1996, BA announced that it would not exercise its option under Phase Two of the Investment Agreement. However, BA allegedly continued to reassure USAir that any relationship with AA would be "competitive" and that USAir would benefit from such an agreement. BA allegedly misled USAir about the true nature and scope of the proposed alliance with AA until June 11, 1996, when AA publicly announced the BA-AA alliance. The alliance contemplates the pooling of revenues, profit sharing, coordination of flight schedules, integration of passenger and cargo handling between the U.S. and Europe, extensive reciprocal code sharing, and full reciprocity of frequent flyer programs. The alliance is expressly conditioned on obtaining an order from the DoT conferring antitrust immunity.

Discussion

* * *

II.   *State Law Claims*

A.   *Breach of Contract*

USAir asserts a breach of contract claim against BA. USAir alleges that BA breached the Investment Agreement by failing to use its "best efforts" to obtain DoT approval for Phases Two and Three and for failing to use "reasonable efforts" to effectuate the transactions contemplated by the Investment Agreement. USAir also alleges that BA breached its implied duty of good faith and fair dealing towards USAir.

The "best efforts" provision of the Investment Agreement, Section 2.6(c), provides in relevant part that BA must "use best efforts to obtain, at the earliest practicable date, DoT Approval of all of the transactions and acts contemplated by [the Investment] Agreement." USAir argues that BA breached this provision of the Investment Agreement when it chose to discourage rather than to seek liberalization of Bermuda II, which under the circumstances was understood by all parties as part of the duty to seek DoT approval.

BA argues that the "best efforts" provision of the Investment Agreement is unenforceable because the Investment Agreement does not provide objective criteria by which to measure performance. USAir argues that the factual circumstances surrounding the Investment Agreement give meaning to the "best efforts" provision, and that under the circumstances the duty to use "best efforts" in seeking DoT approval required BA to seek liberalization of Bermuda II.

Under New York law, a contract need not explicitly define "best efforts" for its "best efforts" provision to be enforceable. See Bloor v. Falstaff Brewing Corp., 454 F.Supp. 258, 266–67 (S.D.N.Y.1978), aff'd, 601 F.2d 609, 613 n. 7, 614 (2d Cir.1979). See also, e.g., Pfizer Inc. v. PCS Health Sys., Inc., 234 A.D.2d 18, 19, 650 N.Y.S.2d 164, 165 (1st Dep't 1996) (affirming injunction enforcing defendant's promise "to 'use its best efforts' to promote plaintiff's products and treat them in a 'favorable manner'"); Kroboth v. Brent, 215 A.D.2d 813, 814, 625 N.Y.S.2d 748, 749–750 (3d Dep't 1995) ("best efforts" requires that a party pursue "all reasonable means for obtaining" the promised goal, and whether such an obligation has been fulfilled "will almost invariably . . . involve a question of fact").

Moreover, to the extent that the term "best efforts" in the Investment Agreement is ambiguous, and criteria by which to measure the parties' "best efforts" are lacking, the extrinsic circumstances concerning the parties' understanding of that term may be considered by the finder of fact. McDarren v. Marvel Entertainment Group, Inc., 1995 WL 214482, *4–5 (S.D.N.Y.1995). Accordingly, the precise meaning of the "best efforts" provision, and whether BA breached the provision, are factual issues that cannot be resolved on the face of the complaint. *Id.*

USAir also alleges that by unilaterally and secretly deciding not to pursue Phases Two and Three of the Investment Agreement, BA breached the "reasonable efforts" provision. Section 10.1(a) of the Investment Agreement, the "reasonable efforts" provision, provides in relevant part that BA is obligated to "use all reasonable efforts to promptly take, or cause to be taken, all other actions and do, or cause to be done, all other things necessary, proper or appropriate under applicable laws and regulations . . . to consummate and make effective the transactions and acts contemplated by [the Investment] Agreement as soon as practicable." BA argues that it could not have breached this provision because Article V of the Investment Agreement leaves all transactions contemplated by the "Integration Clause" subject to the ultimate discretion of BA's directors. The general "reasonable efforts" provision, BA argues, cannot trump the discretion afforded to BA under the specific provision in Article V.

USAir challenges BA's interpretation of the Integration Agreement and argues that Article V provided BA only with the discretion to determine the nature and scope of further integration with USAir. It did not provide BA with discretion with respect to using "reasonable efforts" to implement the remainder of the Investment Agreement, including securing approval for Phases Two and Three. USAir notes that BA's discretion under Article V is limited in any event by the covenant of good faith and fair dealing implied in every contract. Article V does not, as a matter of law, resolve the question of whether BA breached the "reasonable efforts" provision. Drawing all reasonable inferences in favor of USAir, USAir may be able to prove that BA breached the "reasonable efforts" provision.

USAir also asserts a breach of BA's duty of good faith and fair dealing. New York law implies a duty of good faith and fair dealing in all contracts. USAir argues that BA breached this implied duty when it secretly decided not advance the BA-USAir alliance while simultaneously pursuing an alliance with AA and when it chose not to seek liberalization of Bermuda II. USAir also argues that BA breached its duty of good faith and fair dealing by misleading USAir about the BA-AA alliance and reassuring USAir that it would not enter into an agreement with AA unless it was acceptable to USAir.

BA argues that it could not have breached the implied duty of good faith because Section 10.7 of the Investment Agreement authorizes other alliances or significant business relationships apart from the BA-USAir alliance. USAir once again disputes BA's interpretation of the Investment Agreement and points out that Section 10.7 does not expressly authorize such transactions, but merely sets out the consequences of an equity investment or business combination—forfeiture of BA's corporate governance rights and its seats on USAir's Board of Directors. Even under BA's interpretation of the contract, USAir may be able to prove that BA breached the implied duty of good faith and fair dealing. In addition to the alliance with AA, BA allegedly made a secret and conscious decision never to complete the transactions contemplated in the Investment Agreement and to otherwise undermine USAir's efforts to pursue the BA-USAir alliance. Accordingly, on the face of the complaint, it cannot be determined that BA did not breach any duty of good faith and fair dealing.

* * *

For the foregoing reasons, all of USAir's claims other than its breach of contract claim against BA are dismissed.

NOTE ON BEST EFFORTS CLAUSES

"Best efforts" clauses are among the most difficult clauses for courts to deal with. See E. Allan Farnsworth, On Trying to Keep One's Promises: The Duty of Best Efforts in Contract Law, 46 U. Pitt. L. Rev. 1 (1984). Indeed, some courts have simply taken the position that they are illusory promises. See, e.g., Kraftco Corp. v. Kolbus, 274 N.E.2d 153 (Ill. App. 1971). Other courts have held that interpretation of the contract language is a matter of fact rather than of law, and have let the jury make the determination. First National Bank of Lake Park v. Gay, 694 So.2d 784 (Fla. App. 1997).

Two cases decided under New York law may provide some guidance. Bloor v. Falstaff Brewing Corp., 454 F.Supp. 258 (S.D.N.Y.1978), affirmed, 601 F.2d 609 (2d Cir. N.Y. 1979), involved Falstaff's purchase of the assets of P. Ballantine & Sons, the brewer of Ballantine beers and ales, in 1972. The agreement provided for the payment of a royalty of 50 cents per barrel for six years, coupled with Falstaff's commitment that it "will use its best efforts to promote and maintain a high volume of sales. . . ." Sales of all regional breweries were declining during this period, and sales of Falstaff and Ballantine beers suffered severe declines. Falstaff claimed to have lost $22 million from its Ballantine operations from 1972–75, after which Falstaff reduced its operating budget, closed four of its six retail distribution centers and replaced them with two small independent distributors incapable of handling the volume of business no longer served directly by Falstaff. In interpreting the "best efforts" covenant, Falstaff argued that it must be judged by what is reasonable for Falstaff, which must take into consideration Falstaff's losses and increasingly perilous financial condition. Plaintiff argued for an objective standard, that of the "average, prudent comparable" brewer. The court took a middle ground—that Falstaff's efforts were not to be judged by what would be "best efforts" for a national brewer, but in light of Falstaff's capabilities. Here the court noted that Falstaff had borrowing capacity, and indeed did borrow, suggesting that simply losing money wasn't enough to excuse continuing sales efforts. Citing a New York decision, the court quoted approvingly that while Falstaff has a right to look at its own interests, "there may be a point where that activity is so manifestly harmful to the [seller] and must have been seen by the [buyer] so to be harmful, as to justify the court in saying there was a breach of the covenant. . . ."

Wayne Wurtsbaugh v. Banc of America Securities LLC, 2006 WL 1683416 (2006) involved a sale of a business, DAFC, owning software to access securities markets to execute trades, to Banc of America. The agreement provided for contingent payments over the following three years, based on the growth of DAFC's business. Banc of America gave the following "best efforts" covenant:

Subject to the terms and conditions of this Agreement, each of the Parties hereto agrees to use all reasonable efforts to take, or cause to be taken, all appropriate action, and to do, or cause to be done, all things necessary, proper or advisable under applicable Laws to consummate and make effective, in the most expeditious manner practicable, the transactions contemplated by this Agreement; provided, however, that nothing in this Agreement shall obligate [Banc of America] or any of its Affiliates to agree (a) to limit or not to exercise any rights of ownership of [DAFC's business], or to divest, dispose of or hold separate all or any portion of the respective businesses, assets or properties or [sic] of [DAFC's businesses] or (b) to limit in any manner whatsoever the ability of such entities (i) to conduct their respective businesses or own such assets or properties or to own and operate [DAFC's business] or (ii) to control their respective businesses or operations of the businesses or operations or [DAFC's business] or its operations.

Thereafter Banc of America liquidated its clearing operations and with it the opportunity of DAFC to link to Banc of America's clearing operation. Plaintiffs further complained that Banc of America interfered in the DAFC business by improperly reclassifying clients from DAFC to Banc of America clients, by reassigning DAFC personnel to service Banc of America clients rather than develop DAFC's business, and by firing the CEO of DAFC, to prevent him from monitoring Banc of America's breaches of its covenants. The Court rejected the best efforts arguments, stating:

The Best Efforts Clause obligates both parties to "use all reasonable efforts to . . . consummate and make effective, in the most expeditious manner practicable, the transactions contemplated by this Agreement." The plaintiffs argue that this language required Banc of America to "promote and assist" the plaintiffs' efforts to increase the division's Non-Prime Client revenues. Plaintiffs contend that defendant has breached this obligation by utilizing the DAF Division personnel and assets in ways that frustrate efforts to generate new Non-Prime Clients and by terminating Wurtsbaugh without cause.

The plaintiffs fail to contend with the limiting language of the Best Efforts Clause, which provides that nothing in the Agreement shall be read "to limit in any manner whatsoever the ability of [Banc of America] to conduct" its "businesses" or "to control" the DAF Division's business or operations. Reading the Best Efforts Clause to require Banc of America to utilize the DAF Division in particular ways or to refrain from terminating Wurtsbaugh, an at-will employee, would impose limitations on both the conduct of Banc of America's business and its control of the DAF Division. The unambiguous language of the clause forbids such a reading, and requires dismissal of the claim based on an alleged breach of the Best Efforts Clause.

In Sonoran Scanners, Inc. v. PerkinsElmer, Inc., 585 F.3d 535 (1st Cir. 2009), the Court of Appeals implied a "reasonable" efforts obligation in a purchase of assets coupled with employment of the seller's owner and earn-out provisions. The court quoted Justice Cardozo's opinion in Wood v. Lucy, Lady Duff-Gordon, 118 N.E. 214, 2015 (N.Y. 1917):

> We are not to suppose that one party was to be placed at the mercy of the other. . . . [The] promise to pay the defendant one-half of the profits and revenues resulting from the exclusive agency and to render accounts monthly was a promise to use reasonable efforts to bring profits and revenues into existence.

The court rejected claims for breach of an implied covenant of good faith and fair dealing, finding no express promises that had been broken, and no bad faith on the part of the buyer.

One commentator suggested that there are steps that can be taken to avoid liability under a best efforts clause. David Shine, "Best Efforts" Standards under New York Law: Legal and Practical Issues, 7 No. 9 The M & A Lawyer 15 (2004):

- Where earn-outs are involved, the buyer should limit its obligation by imposing a loss cap, or providing specific minimum expenditures that will satisfy the requirement;

- Where third-party consents are required, if payments are expected to obtain them, the buyer should cap the payments;

- Where antitrust approvals are required, the buyer should specify whether it will be expected to divest other assets to secure the approval, and if so, the maximum extent of such divestitures;

- Where governmental filings are required, the parties should specify a timetable for them; and

- Specify whether efforts will be measured by the promisor's circumstances, or whether industry standards should be taken into account. Where industry customs suggest reasonable standards, they will be enforced, at least in New York. Joyce Beverage of New York, Inc. v. Royal Crown Cola, 555 F.Supp. 271 (S.D.N.Y. 1983), held that since bottlers usually distributed only a single cola, a commitment to use best efforts to distribute Royal Crown precluded distribution of other colas.

––––––––––

QUESTIONS

1. Your client has agreed to a "merger of equals" with another corporation. In order to make the deal work, both sides have agreed to an arrangement in which there will be co-chief executive officers. Both corporations have agreed to use their "best efforts" to secure shareholder approval for the merger, and to see that conditions precedent to closing

are met, including certain regulatory approvals. After signing the agreement and before shareholder approval and a closing, while awaiting clearance from the Department of Justice under the antitrust laws, the CEO of your client discovers that his style is quite different from that of his counterpart, and cannot imagine working productively with him. He believes the other CEO is acting in a high-handed manner, suggesting that there will not be true equality. It may also be that your client's CEO fears that he will be the loser in any battle for dominance. Assuming that the merger agreement is essentially the same as that in section 5.4 of Appendix C, what advice can you give?

A. Can you advise the CEO about his own rights?

B. What acts during the pre-closing period would be sufficient for the client to refuse to close the merger?

C. What rights would the client have to terminate the merger agreement at the present time?

D. Finally, what disclosure duties does your client have to its shareholders?

2. Part of the purchase price for a business acquisition is an "earn-out" clause, in which the buyer agrees to pay additional compensation to sellers if the sales of the acquired business exceed certain specified targets over the next five years. The buyer has covenanted to use its best efforts to meet those targets. After the closing, the buyer discovers that it can increase sales, but because of increasing competition and declining margins, the more it sells the more it loses. Must the buyer make a serious effort to increase sales under these circumstances? See Bloor v. Falstaff Brewing Corp., 454 F.Supp. 258 (S.D.N.Y.1978). If you represent a buyer negotiating an earn-out with sellers, what would you advise with respect to the terms of the "earn-out" and "best efforts" clauses? Why would a seller prefer contingent payments based on gross sales rather than net profits? Part of the answer is found in the dispute between humorist Art Buchwald and Paramount Pictures. Buchwald authored "Coming to America," made into a successful film starring Eddie Murphy, in return for a share of the profits from the film. After the film had earned large revenues, Paramount informed Buchwald that there were no profits to share. Buchwald sued and prevailed. The trial court held that Paramount used "unconscionable" means of determining how much to pay authors. Paramount claimed, and provided accounting evidence to support the claim, that despite the movie's $288 million in revenues, it had earned no net profit, according to the definition of "net profit" in Buchwald's contract.

---

iii. WHAT CONSTITUTES A BREACH OF A REPRESENTATION AND WARRANTY?

While sellers will give representations and warranties that they state in the acquisition agreement are complete and accurate, they very often want to limit the potential adverse consequences that might occur should things not turn out to be as represented. There are a variety of ways of doing this, which we explore below. These are some of the most heavily negotiated terms in the agreement.

Survival of Representations and Warranties. A buyer may not discover breaches of the representations and warranties, or in some cases of the covenants, until after the closing, no matter how careful the due diligence process is. In a sale of assets the seller may not have paid off some debts that encumber the properties, such as taxes that can ripen into liens on the property. Hazardous wastes in the soil may appear after the closing. Employees may first exhibit symptoms of illnesses contracted in the workplace from years of exposure only after the closing. In the acquisition by merger of a public company there may be no effective remedy for these breaches because the acquired entity is either part of the purchasing corporation, or a wholly-owned subsidiary. Even in a cash purchase of stock of a public company, the proceeds of the acquisition will be disbursed to thousands of shareholders, who are not parties to the acquisition agreement. In effect, the representations, warranties and covenants of the target expire at the closing.

Assuming that there is an identifiable seller that survives the closing, whether a corporation or major shareholders, the buyer will want to assure that the representations and warranties survive the closing, and do not merge into it. Buyer will want the longest possible survival period. For example, while problems with operating assets can probably be determined pretty quickly after the buyer takes over control of the business, and probably no later than the first year's audited financial statements, tax warranties cannot finally be determined until after the applicable statutes of limitations have run, which may be as long as six years. 26 U.S.C. § 6501. Most buyers will want all warranties to survive for a period longer than the production of the first year's financial statements. Normally the buyer should at least seek a reasonable period after completion of an audit (at least four months after the close of the fiscal year) plus some time to evaluate the claim and give the seller notice of a claim. A recent survey of indemnification agreements showed that representations and warranties would survive the closing by periods ranging from fifteen months (the minimum required to obtain audited financials) to two years. Michael J. Hagan, Recent Developments: Trends in Indemnification and Escrow Protection in Private Acquisition Agreements (2012) at http://www.lexology.com/library/detail.aspx?g= d881e54c-d707-4256-ae2d-ebf941d42a0c. See also Steven Glover, Indemnification Provisions: Standard Practice Revisited, 5, No. 9 The M & A Lawyer 1 (March, 2002). A similar result was found by Wilson Chu and Larry Glasgow, You Can't HANDLE the Truth: 4th Annual Deal Points Study, 7, No. 10 The M & A Lawyer 1 (April 2004). Set out below is an example of a survival clause. Coverage of survival provisions is another issue. Survival provisions are most common for tax liabilities, corporate status and share ownership, and least common for intellectual property, no legal conflicts and title to assets. M & A Market Trends Subcommittee of the Committee on Negotiated Acquisitions, Section of Business Law, American Bar Association, 2007 PRIVATE TARGET MERGERS & ACQUISITIONS DEAL POINTS STUDY, slide 52, at http://www.abanet.org/dch/committee.cfm?com=CL560003 (last visited July 8, 2007) ("2007 Private Target Study").

8.1 Survival of representations and Warranties.

8.1.1 All representations, warranties, agreements, covenants and obligations made or undertaken by the Acquired Company and the Shareholders in this Agreement or in any document or instrument executed and delivered pursuant hereto are material, have been relied upon by the Parent and Purchaser, and shall survive the Closing hereunder for the applicable period indicated in Section 8.2.3 hereof (except for the obligations under the Employment Agreements and Covenants Not to Compete which shall survive for the longest period available under applicable laws), and shall not merge in the performance of any obligation by any party hereto. Any examination, inspection or audit of the properties, financial condition or other matters of the Corporation and their businesses conducted pursuant to this Agreement shall in no way limit, affect or impair the ability of Parent and Purchaser to rely upon the representations, warranties, covenants and obligations of the Acquired Company and the Shareholders set forth herein.

Knowledge Clauses. A knowledge clause qualifies an absolute representation and warranty, as in, "to the best of Seller's knowledge, there are no liabilities except those listed in Schedule __." Like all of the representations and warranties, the purpose of knowledge clauses is to allocate the risk between the parties. Buyers would prefer no knowledge qualifications at all, and if they must concede something in this area, want to limit it to specific representations where the seller can make a reasonable argument. One example might involve potential litigation. The seller may reasonably claim that it cannot deliver a blanket warranty that there is no threatened litigation. This may be so because a lower level employee has either received a verbal threat, or a passing reference to the possibility of litigation on some small matter that the employee did not believe justified passing it on to superiors or inside counsel at this stage. Buyers want an unconditional representation that there are no liabilities, whether accrued or contingent or otherwise. Sellers will want to limit this to those required by GAAP, as in "no liabilities of the type required to be disclosed in the liabilities column of a balance sheet prepared in accordance with GAAP." Obviously this would exclude contingent liabilities that might be disclosed in footnotes to the balance sheet.

Sellers will want to define "knowledge" as the actual awareness of a fact, without any duty to investigate. Buyers, on the other hand, will want to define it as knowledge after a reasonable investigation. The next question is who in the seller's organization must have knowledge before it is charged to the seller. The buyer would like to provide that knowledge by any person in the seller's organization constitutes knowledge of the seller. The seller, particularly where there are thousands of employees, may argue to limit knowledge to senior management, those officers and key employees listed on a disclosure schedule. Example of knowledge clauses follow:

"Knowledge" means with respect to Stonepath and Seller, that Robert Arovas, Robert Christensen, Dennis Pellino (solely as to periods from March 5,2002 through October 29, 2004) and Virginia Wei have reviewed the specific representation and warranty and the related portion of Stonepath's Schedules to which such knowledge statement is made, and, in so doing, have exercised reasonable due diligence, and based upon the foregoing, such officers of Stonepath are not aware and have no reason to be aware of any inaccuracies in such specific representation and warranty and related portions of Stonepath's Schedule with respect to which such knowledge statement is made.

"Knowledge" means actual knowledge or awareness as to a specified fact or event of a Person that is an individual or of an executive officer or director of a Person that is a corporation or of a Person in a similar capacity of an entity other than a corporation.

"To the best of Seller's knowledge and belief," "insofar as is known," "aware of" and similar phrases shall mean such level of knowledge or awareness of the matter with respect to which such phrase is used as would be obtained after inquiry reasonable under the circumstances then existing (which circumstances shall be deemed to include the position of the relevant person with Seller), but does not mean knowledge or awareness requiring professional training in law or accounting, although knowledge of such areas as ought reasonably to be possessed by a person in a like position as the position of the relevant person with the Seller is included in such phrases.

Materiality Clauses. Absent some qualifying language, all representations and warranties must be absolutely true and complete. Given the usual "bring-down" clause that makes their continuing accuracy a condition of the buyer's obligation to close, any small omission or minor inaccuracy could give the buyer an excuse to reject the contract. Similarly, after a closing where the representations and warranties survive, the buyer could bring a series of small claims against the seller. In some cases materiality may refer to compliance with laws or agreements, and might state that "seller is in material compliance" with them. In other cases, the materiality clause may refer to the effect of a breach of warranty, so that seller will warrant compliance "except where the failure to comply will not have a material adverse effect on the property, assets or business."

Some agreements contain separate materiality qualifiers, based on threshold amounts. Thus, the list of material contracts might state that there are no other contracts with obligations in excess of $___ or that create obligations lasting more than twelve months. In many cases there will also be an overall materiality qualifier, especially in the "bring-down" clause that makes truthfulness of the representations a condition of buyer's obligation to close. This clause might provide that the representations *in the aggregate* must be true and correct in all material respects. In some cases these clauses require all representations that are qualified as to materiality to be true and correct, and those that are *not* qualified as to materiality must be true and correct in all material respects. This eliminates the ability of a buyer to refuse to close because of an immaterial variation, but preserves the ability of a buyer to seek indemnification for these breaches.

Definitions of materiality are almost uniformly circular. Here is an example:

> For this purpose, "material" shall mean information to which an investor would reasonably attach importance in reaching a decision to buy, sell or hold securities of the Company, which would include any settlement discussions in the Supervisory Goodwill Litigation.

Many of the definitions simply contain a dollar threshold, so that anything above the dollar limit is deemed material. In other respects, drafters seem to be relying on the courts to fill in the blank left by this open term. The definition given by the U.S. Supreme Court in TSC Industries, Inc. v. Northway, Inc., 426 U.S. 438 (1976) is often cited by the courts, that "[an] omitted fact is material if there is a substantial likelihood that a reasonable shareholder would consider it important in deciding how to vote." This appears to be the standard employed in the sample language above. In In re IBP, Inc. Shareholders Litigation, 789 A.2d 14 (Del.Ch. 2001), discussed earlier in this Chapter, at part 2.B.i, Vice Chancellor Strine, in determining whether an earnings decline was a material adverse effect stated that "the contractual language must be read in the larger context in which the parties were contracting. To a short-term speculator, the failure of a company to meet analysts' projected earnings for a quarter could be highly material. Such a failure is less important to an acquiror who seeks to purchase the company as part of a long-term strategy. To such an acquiror, the important thing is whether the company has suffered a Material Adverse Effect in its business or results of operations that is consequential to the company's earnings power over a commercially reasonable period, which one would think would be measured in years rather than months."

Who Makes the Representations? As we have previously noted, representations made by a corporation that disappears at the closing, as in a merger, provide no opportunity for post-closing protection for the buyer. This emphasizes the importance of due diligence and the bring-down clause that requires the representations to be true at the closing. Only when the seller or its controlling persons—a parent corporation or major shareholders—survive the closing, can a buyer find someone to look to for responsibility for a breach of warranty claim. Here the buyer will want the parent corporation selling a subsidiary or a division, or the controlling shareholders of a privately owned corporation, to be responsible for the representations and warranties. These issues are handled in the indemnification provisions described below.

A subject not always covered in indemnification provisions is whether the buyer can obtain indemnification post-closing if the buyer either knew or should have known about the misrepresentation or omission prior to the closing, but closed without objection. Sellers who receive such an indemnification request may feel duped, while the buyer will take the position that it bargained for fully accurate representations and warranties. The buyer could have raised such problems before closing, of course, and sought a price adjustment, but there is at least some risk that this demand would kill the deal. Courts in both New York and Delaware have taken the position that a buyer in such a case need not show reliance on the misrepresentation, which is consistent with the remedies for breach of warranty, rather than the tort of misrepresentation. CBS, Inc. v. Ziff-Davis Publishing Co., 75 N.Y.2d 496 (N.Y. 1990); Interim Healthcare, Inc. v. Spherion Corp., 884 A.2d 513 (Del. Super. 2002).

iv. INDEMNIFICATION PROVISIONS—WHAT HAPPENS AFTER THE CLOSING?

Where assets are purchased from an entity that will continue in existence, as in the sale of a division of a larger company, a seller remains after the closing that can respond in damages. Similarly, where a large company sells the stock of a subsidiary, a seller remains. In the purchase of privately held companies, there are identifiable shareholders who are selling, either directly, in the case of their shares, or indirectly, in the case of a merger. While claims may arise under the securities laws for stock sales, where the shareholders will have direct liability, this is not necessarily the case with corporate action, as in the case of corporate mergers or asset sales. Even if the securities laws are available, claims under the antifraud provisions of the Securities Exchange Act, typically under section 10(b) and Rule 10b–5, require a showing of scienter, which involves either deliberate falsehood or omission, or a reckless disregard for the truth. Proving state of mind is far more difficult than proving a false statement that creates contract liability under a breach of warranty claim, where no intent or negligence need be proven by a plaintiff. Thus the warranties become the crucial basis for a buyer's claims. Under these circumstances, it is common for the Acquisition Agreement to contain some provision for indemnification of the buyer for breach of warranties.

Who Is Liable for Breaches of Warranties? Stock sales are the easiest case for a buyer, because the seller not only survives, but is the contracting party making the representations and warranties. In a closely held corporation, where all of the shareholders are parties to the sale contract, the only question is whether the liability of selling shareholders will be joint and several, which permits the buyer to seek damages from any of the sellers, or pro rata, so the buyer must seek a proportionate share of damages from each shareholder. Where a corporation sells assets, the buyer will want similar indemnification rights against the shareholders. Obviously the buyer would prefer joint and several liability, so it can satisfy any judgment from the assets of the deepest pocket. Buyers will argue that sellers can work out side agreements for cross-indemnification, so each bears its pro rata share of the risk. The alternative is to specify the portion of the liability to be borne by each selling shareholder in the purchase agreement. A recent survey of indemnification agreements showed that where there were multiple shareholders acting as sellers, most of the agreements provided for joint and several liability for indemnification, and did not apportion the liability. Here is an example of a provision holding selling shareholders liable:

8.2 Indemnification by the Acquired Company and the Shareholder.

8.2.1. Subject to the terms and conditions of this Section, 8.2 the Acquired Company and the Shareholders hereby agree, jointly and severally, but only to the extent and in the manner set forth below, to indemnify and hold Parent and Purchaser harmless from and against all liability, loss, damage, or injury and all reasonable costs and expenses (including reasonable counsel fees and costs of any investigation or suit related thereto) arising from (i) any misrepresentation by, or breach of any covenant or warranty of the Acquired Company or the Shareholders contained in this Agreement, or from any misrepresentation in or omissions from any certificate or other instrument, or any breach of any covenant or warranty in any agreement, furnished or to be furnished by the Acquired Company or the Shareholders hereunder, or (ii) from any suit, action, proceeding, claim or investigation pending or threatened against or affecting the Acquired Company which is disclosed on Exhibit P, [FOR ASSET PURCHASES: or (iii) any claim for a debt, obligation or liability which is not specifically assumed by Purchaser pursuant to this Agreement, or (iv) any claim or right, or any alleged claim or right, or third persons by virtue of application of bulk sales laws or otherwise *which may be asserted any of the Assets,] [FOR GUARANTEED NET WORTH TRANSACTIONS:] or (v) any claim against or liability of the Acquired Company, which accrued prior to Closing, to the extent not accrued or reserved against in the calculation of the Closing Date Net Worth as reflected in the balance sheet prepared pursuant to the audit described in Section 2.2 of this Agreement, regardless of whether such claim or liability is disclosed in the notes to the financial statement prepared in such audit.] The maximum aggregate liability of the Acquired Company and the Shareholders for indemnification under this Agreement shall be equal to ___ Dollars ($___) (the "Maximum Aggregate Liability Amount"), and the obligation of the Acquired Company and the Shareholders for indemnification hereunder will terminate when the Maximum Aggregate Liability Amount has been paid; provided, however, that the Maximum Aggregate Liability Amount shall not be charged for or reduced by, nor shall there be any Maximum Aggregate Liability Amount for, any liability, loss damage, injury or claim resulting from a breach of the covenants, representations and warranties contained in the provisions of Section 2.1, 3.1.1, 3.2, 3.3, those provisions of 3.7 and 3.12 relating to collectibility of amounts receivable, 10.2 or 10.5 or from a breach of the covenants contained in Section 2.5.1 to the extent it pertains to the making of a payment described in Section 3.9.8 and 3.9.9. [Each Shareholder shall be liable for indemnification pursuant to this Article VIII of this Agreement up to his Pro Rata Amount of the Maximum Aggregate Liability Amount, but subject to the Minimum Aggregate Liability Amount.] [or: Each Shareholder shall be liable up to his respective Pro Rata Amount for each indemnifiable event pursuant to this Article VIII of this Agreement, up to the Maximum Aggregate Liability Amount and subject to the Minimum Aggregate Liability Amount.] The aggregate obligation of the Acquired Company and the Shareholders for indemnification hereunder will not exceed the Maximum Aggregate Liability Amount and the aggregate obligation of each Shareholder for indemnification hereunder will not exceed such Shareholder's Pro Rata Amount of the Maximum Aggregate Liability Amount. The Pro Rata Amount shall be determined for each Shareholder as a percentage, as follows:*

<u>*Shareholders:*</u>

_____   _____%

_____   _____%

_____   _____%

Since, following the Closing, the Acquired Company will be owned by Purchaser, the parties to this Agreement agree that any recovery against the Acquired Company by Parent or Purchaser after Closing will be against the Shareholders (and such Shareholders will have no right of reimbursement or contribution against the Acquired Company). For all purposes of this Article VIII, if the Closing occurs, any liability, loss, damage or injury and reasonable costs and expenses (including, without limitation, reasonable counsel fees and costs of any investigation or suit related thereto) suffered or incurred by the Acquired Company arising from any such breach of a covenant, representation or warranty by the Acquired Company or the Shareholders as aforesaid against which Parent and Purchaser are indemnified and held harmless hereinabove shall be deemed suffered and incurred by Parent and Purchaser, which shall, either independently or jointly with the Acquired Company, be entitled to enforce such covenants of indemnity.

To What Extent Are Sellers Liable? One question involves a definition of damages. Here is an example of a strong form buyer's provision including consequential damages:

8.2.2 The term "liability, loss, damage or injury" used in this Article VIII shall mean, in the case of undisclosed liabilities of the Acquired Company, the reasonable cost (including reasonable counsel fees and costs of any suit) of satisfying such undisclosed liabilities, and in respect of all other matters, the reasonable costs necessary to place Parent, Purchaser and the Acquired Company in the position they would have been in had the related representation, warranty or covenant been true and correct or fully preformed each in accordance with its terms. The amount of liability, loss, damage or injury (including costs and expenses) for which indemnification may be claimed pursuant, to this Article VIII shall be reduced by the present value of the amount, that (i) there is a reduction in federal and state income taxes, if any, (computed at the then highest marginal federal and state corporate tax rates) that will result to the Acquired Company without reduction for tax credits in one or more of its taxable years from the payment of such liability, loss, damage, or injury (including costs and expenses) exceeds (ii) the amount of federal and state income taxes, if any, (computed at the highest marginal federal and state corporate tax rates) which become payable by the Acquired Company without reduction for tax credits as a result of any indemnity payment made hereunder. [Tax provisions omitted.]

Sellers want to avoid being sued for trivial amounts after the closing, and typically want a minimum amount of damages before a buyer can sue. A "basket" is an agreement between the parties that the buyer will bear the first (specified) dollars of damages claims, aggregated from all breaches of warranties in the agreement. Once the basket is "full," the seller bears the additional liability. If there are also materiality qualifiers, a seller may argue that the basket is in addition to the minimum amounts necessary to meet the materiality standard, so a buyer must be clear that basket qualifications are separate from materiality qualifiers. A seller will argue that the basket must, at a minimum, include the sum of the materiality qualifiers. Some agreements contain thresholds. Once the threshold amount of liability is reached, the seller becomes liable for the entire amount of liability, including the threshold amount. A recent survey of indemnification agreements showed that sellers agreed to indemnify buyers in all of the examined agreements, while buyers agreed to indemnify sellers 58% of the time. Indemnification always covered losses attributable to breaches of representations, warranties and covenants. In half of the deals, sellers agreed to indemnify buyers for liabilities the sellers were retaining, such as litigation. Most of the agreements had a materiality "basket"—that all claims, taken together, must exceed some percentage of the purchase price before indemnification became payable. These percentages ran from 0.1% to 2.9%, with an average of 1%. Steven Glover, Indemnification Provisions: Standard Practice Revisited, 5, No. 9 The M & A Lawyer 1 (March, 2002). A similar study was undertaken in Wilson Chu and Larry Glasgow, You Can't HANDLE the Truth: 4th Annual Deal Points Study, 7, No. 10 The M & A Lawyer 1 (April 2004). The following example provides a basket, but excludes from the basket those items that are easily calculated, such as those relating to the accounts receivable:

8.3 Minimum Aggregate Liability Amount. Parent and Purchaser agree not to seek recourse against, and shall not recover from the Shareholders under this Article VIII on account of any liability, loss, damage, injury or claim until the aggregate amount thereof exceeds $___ (the "Minimum Aggregate Liability Amount"), [at which time claims may be asserted for the excess, and only for the excess, of such claims over the Minimum Aggregate Liability Amount.] [at which time claims may be asserted for the Minimum Aggregate Liability Amount and any excess]. There shall be no Minimum Aggregate Liability Amount for, and the Minimum Aggregate Liability Amount shall not be charged for or reduced by, any liability, loss, damage, injury or claim resulting from the covenants, representations and warranties contained in the provisions of Section 2.1, 3.1.1, 3.2, 3.3, those provisions of 3.7 and 3.12 relating to collectibility of accounts receivable, 10.2 or 10.5 or from a breach of the covenant contained in Section 2.5.1 to the extent it pertains to the making of a payment described in Section 3.9.8 and 3.9.9.

Third, buyers and sellers will negotiate over the survival of the indemnification obligations. This is closely related to the survival of the covenants, set out above. Here is an example:

8.2.3 A claim for indemnification based on the covenants, representations and warranties contained in the provisions of Sections 2.1, 3.1.1, 3.2, 3.3, those provisions of 3.7 and 3.12 relating to collectibility of accounts receivable, 10.2, or 10.5 or from a breach of the covenant contained in Section 2.5.1 to the extent it pertains to the making of a payment described in Section 3.9.8 and 3.9.9 shall survive forever and may be made at any time. Except for such claims, a claim for indemnification hereunder shall be forever barred unless made by notifying the Representative [NOTE: IF MULTIPLE SHAREHOLDERS,

ONE SHOULD BE DESIGNATED AS THE REPRESENTATIVE] (a) in the case of a claim based upon a tax liability of the Acquired Company with respect to any taxable period ending on or prior to the Closing Date (including, without limitation, any claim based upon an assertion that any of the previously filed tax returns of the Acquired Company are inaccurate or incomplete), within the statutory period of limitations under the applicable tax statute, unless such claim is raised by the taxing authority by way of an offset against any claim or suit for refund by or on behalf of the Acquired Company or is allowed to be assessed after the expiration of the applicable statute of limitations pursuant to a validity executed waiver or extension thereof or pursuant to the mitigation provisions contained in the Code, in which case a claim may be made within one year after such offset or assessment, or (b) in all other cases, within ___ years after the Closing Date.

The other side of the coin is whether the liability of sellers to indemnify buyers should be capped. A buyer will want unlimited indemnification for all losses. For example, if undisclosed claims arise against the acquired business, the buyer will want indemnification for the reasonable costs of defense (including attorneys' fees), in addition to the amount required to place the buyer in the same position it would have been in absent the untrue warranty. This creates considerable uncertainty about the extent of liability, where an injunction is issued with respect to a violation of a third party's patent rights, for example. At the least, sellers want to limit indemnifiable losses to the purchase price, presumably on the theory that the buyer received something of net value in the transaction. Where litigation arises over claims based on the seller's operation of the business, the seller may want control over the litigation, on the theory that the buyer's incentives to defend may be weakened by the indemnification rights. In cases where the seller obtains the right to control the defense, the seller may be given the right to join the litigation at its own expense, if it lacks confidence in the ability of the buyer to defend. Further, where the seller insists on the right to control litigation, the buyer may insist that any liability cap be removed. The following is an example of how some of these issues might be resolved:

8.2.4 Parent and Purchaser shall notify the Representative whenever they become actually aware or have actual notice of any event which might give rise to a claim for indemnification hereunder. Following the giving of such notice, [Parent and Purchaser] [the Representative] shall select counsel to defend such claim. Such counsel shall be subject to the approval of [the Representative] [Parent and Purchaser], which approval shall not be unreasonably withheld. [Parent, Purchaser and their] [the Representative and its] counsel shall keep [the Representative] [Parent and Purchaser] informed on all matters with respect to the defense of such claim and no claim shall be paid, settled, or compromised if [the Representative] [Parent and Purchaser] elects to contest the claim in accordance with clause [(b)] [(a)] of this Subsection. [The Shareholders]

[Parent and Purchaser] shall be entitled to be represented by counsel of [the Representative's] [their] choosing at their sole cost and expense. [The Shareholders] [Parent and Purchaser] each agree to cooperate and aid [Parent and Purchaser] [the Shareholder] in the defense of any such claim. In the event there is a dispute between Parent and Purchaser and the Representative concerning whether a claim should be contested, settled or compromised, it shall be settled, compromised or contested in accordance with the next succeeding sentence; provided, however, that Parent, Purchaser, or their respective successors or assigns, shall neither be required to refrain from paying or satisfying any claim which has matured by court judgment or decree, unless appeal is taken thereafter and proper appeal bond posted by the Shareholders, nor shall they be required to refrain from paying or satisfying any claim where such has resulted in an imposition of a lien upon any of the properties or assets then held by Parent, Purchaser or their respective successors and assigns (unless such lien shall have been discharged by the filing of a legally permitted bond by the Shareholders, at their sole expense), or result in a default in a lease or other contract by which any of them is bound, or would materially adversely affect their respective assets, businesses or condition. In the event Parent and Purchaser, on the one hand, or the Representative, on the other hand, has reached a bona fide settlement agreement or compromise, subject only to approval hereunder, with any claimant regarding a matter which may be the subject of indemnification hereunder and desires to settle on the basis of such agreement or compromise, the claim shall be settled or compromised on such basis unless:

(a)   Parent and Purchaser desire to contest the matter, in which case it shall be so contested and the liability of the Shareholders shall be limited as provided in clause (c) below;

(b)   The settlement or compromise would result in a claim for indemnification being made against the Shareholders, in which event it shall be contested if the Representative so requests; provided, however, that the liability of Parent and Purchaser shall be limited as provided in clause (c) below;

(c)   If a matter is contested as provided in clauses (a) or (b) above and is later adjudicated, settled, compromised or otherwise disposed of and such adjudication, compromise, settlement or disposition results in a liability, loss, damages or injury in excess of the amount for which one party desired previously to settle the matter, then the liability of such party shall be limited to such lesser amount and the party contesting the matter shall be solely responsible for such excess amount without regard to any maximum restriction on liability in this Agreement.

A survey of indemnification agreements showed that most agreements provide for a cap on indemnification, although the author concluded that there is no such thing as standard market practice in determining the amount (a claim typically made by lawyers on each side when negotiating). The average cap was set at about 35% of the transaction price, although caps ran from 3% to 100%. Steven Glover, Indemnification Provisions: Standard Practice Revisited, 5, No. 9 The M & A Lawyer 1 (March, 2002). A similar study was undertaken in Wilson Chu and Larry Glasgow, You Can't HANDLE the Truth: 4th Annual Deal Points Study, 7, No. 10 The M & A Lawyer 1 (April 2004). A more recent study found lower caps, in the range of 10 to 20 percent. Michael J. Hagan, Recent Developments: Trends in Indemnification and Escrow Protection in Private Acquisition Agreements (2012) (no longer available). But in private acquisitions higher caps may be employed, and may be secured by the escrow of some of the consideration being received by the sellers. *Id.* Another alternative remedy is the use of earn-out provisions, discussed in Part 2.A.i of this Chapter (before the O'Tool case).

A subject not always covered in indemnification provisions is whether the buyer can obtain indemnification post-closing if the buyer either knew or should have known about the misrepresentation or omission prior to the closing, but closed without objection. Sellers who receive such an indemnification request may feel duped, while the buyer will take the position that it bargained for fully accurate representations and warranties. The buyer could have raised such problems before closing, of course, and sought a price adjustment, but there is at least some risk that this demand would kill the deal. Courts in both New York and Delaware have taken the position that a buyer in such a case need not show reliance on the misrepresentation, which is consistent with the remedies for breach of warranty, rather than the tort of misrepresentation. CBS, Inc. v. Ziff-Davis Publishing Co., 75 N.Y.2d 496 (N.Y. 1990); Interim Healthcare, Inc. v. Spherion Corp., 884 A.2d 513 (Del. Super. 2002).

---

v.   REPRESENTATIONS AND WARRANTIES INSURANCE

Sellers of private companies can reduce the risks of being liable for breaches of representations and warranties under indemnification with representation and warranty insurance. Obviously this comes at price to the seller, but in some cases it is worth it. Absent fraud or other knowing or intentional misrepresentation, this allows shareholders of the seller to get the stated purchase price, less the cost of insurance. The primary coverage of such insurance is over unknown liabilities. Examples might include product liabilities where no product defects had been discovered before the closing. Known risks require special riders, at additional premiums. Coverage for known risks will often involve deductibles (called "retention amounts"), leaving sellers with potential liabilities for specified amounts, in order to protect the insurer from the moral hazard that sellers will be less concerned with the completeness and accuracy of the representations and warranties. In most cases these retention amounts will be reduced after a specified period, usually 12 to 18 months (the "retention drop-down period"). The small retention amounts allow buyers to insist on smaller escrows or hold-backs from sellers to protect against breaches. A recent law firm memo places typical hold-backs at 1.5%—2.0% of the total deal value.*

Commonly, these riders cover such items as regulatory, tax and environmental risk. Where the cost of such coverage is prohibitive or unavailable because no market exists, sellers are left with the protection of the limit on their liability discussed above. These policies only cover representations and warranties, and not breaches of covenants.

Premiums for such insurance are reported to amount to 2–3% of the value of the deal. Generally these policies last for the stated duration of the representations and warranties. There is, of course a risk that if survival of indemnities is keyed to statutes of limitations (note the difficulties where liabilities might arise in multiple jurisdictions), these statutes may be tolled by various circumstances. While policies can be obtained by sellers, the dominant practice is for buyers to negotiate and purchase these policies. Obviously the buyer will consider this cost in making its purchase offer, so the ultimate cost is borne by sellers.

These policies do not issue, and thus provide any protection, until the deal closes and the premium is paid. If the insurer changes the terms of the deal before closing, the seller needs to know of the changes and accept them or terminate the deal. Most acquisition agreements involving representation and warranty insurance will involve sellers obtaining consent rights to any changes in the draft policy furnished to the seller, and the buyer's representation that the draft policy has been furnished to the seller.

---

* Dechert LLP, Representation and Warranty Insurance: No Longer Optional—Deal Terms and Trends, Summer 2015, at http://www.lexology.com/library/detail.aspx?g=ec388d81-1e20-42e7-bff9-251276b3a074.

3. SELLER'S REMEDIES

Consolidated Edison, Inc. v. Northeast Utilities

426 F.3d 524 (2d Cir. 2005).

■ JACOBS, CIRCUIT JUDGE:

On interlocutory appeal from two orders of the United States District Court for the Southern District of New York (Koeltl, J.), we are asked to resolve the following questions: [I] whether shareholders of Northeast Utilities ("NU") were granted a right as third-party beneficiaries to sue Consolidated Edison, Inc. ("CEI") for losses of over $1 billion that they allege resulted from CEI's breach of a contractual undertaking to merge with NU; . . . . We answer the first question in the negative.

BACKGROUND

This case arises from the failed multi-billion dollar merger between CEI and NU. Among the terms and conditions of the underlying merger agreement ("Agreement"), CEI agreed to purchase all of NU's outstanding shares for $3.6 billion—$1.2 billion over the prevailing market price. Consol. Edison, Inc. v. Ne. Utils., 249 F.Supp.2d 387, 390 (S.D.N.Y. 2003) ("Con Ed I"); Consol. Edison, Inc. v. Ne. Utils., 318 F.Supp.2d 181, 183, 185 (S.D.N.Y. 2004) ("Con Ed II").

On March 5, 2001, shortly before the scheduled closing, CEI declared that NU had suffered a material adverse change that "dramatically lowered" NU's valuation, and declined to proceed with the merger unless NU would agree to a lower share price. NU rejected the share-price reduction, treated CEI's demand as an anticipatory repudiation and breach of the Agreement, and declared that the merger was "effectively terminated."

CEI brought suit against NU for (inter alia) breach of contract, fraudulent inducement, and negligent misrepresentation, while NU counterclaimed for breach of contract, alleging that CEI's proposed share-price reduction was attributable to buyer's remorse in a sinking stock market rather than any change in NU's condition. On cross-motions for partial summary judgment, the district court dismissed CEI's claims of fraudulent inducement and negligent misrepresentation, but allowed the dueling breach-of-contract claims to proceed. The substance of those contract claims has little bearing on this appeal; at issue here is whether the $1.2 billion shareholder premium can be claimed as damages arising from CEI's alleged breach of the Agreement.

The district court ruled (at that juncture) that NU could sue on behalf of its shareholders for the $1.2 billion. The court reasoned that [I] the merger agreement expressly designated NU's shareholders as intended third-party beneficiaries; [ii] as third-party beneficiaries, the shareholders could sue CEI for the allegedly wrongful failure to complete the merger, in order to recover the $1.2 billion premium they would have been paid after the merger closed; and [iii] CEI and NU stipulated that NU could sue "on behalf" of its shareholders.

Afterward, Robert Rimkoski intervened as representative of a proposed class of persons holding NU shares on March 5, 2001 (the date of CEI's alleged breach of the Agreement) and asserted the same claim to the same $1.2 billion sought by NU. Rimkoski, who held NU shares on March 5, 2001, but who sold most of those shares thereafter, argued that under New York law: [I] the right to sue CEI for the $1.2 billion accrued on March 5, 2001; [ii] that right was not transferred automatically with any subsequent transfer of shares, Con Ed II, 318 F.Supp.2d at 185–87; and therefore, [iii] Rimkoski (and his proposed class of March 5, 2001 NU shareholders) has the right to sue CEI for the $1.2 billion, and NU— which undertakes to represent only those shareholders holding shares as of the date any judgment is entered against CEI (even if acquired after March 5, 2001)—does not.

The district court agreed with Rimkoski.* However, in light of the novelty of the question and its importance to this litigation, the court authorized NU to seek interlocutory appellate review of its ruling pursuant to 28 U.S.C. § 1292(b). For essentially the same reasons, the district court also authorized CEI to seek an immediate appeal of its earlier ruling that NU shareholders are intended third-party beneficiaries under the Agreement who may sue CEI for the $1.2 billion premium. On October 20, 2004, this Court granted NU and CEI's § 1292(b) applications for review.

DISCUSSION

I

The first question presented is whether any NU shareholders (as of any date) enjoy the right, as third-party beneficiaries, to sue CEI for the $1.2 billion premium that CEI would have paid but for its allegedly wrongful failure to complete the merger.

New York law governs the Agreement. See Agreement, art. VIII, § 8.07. Under New York law, a contractual promise can be enforced by a non-party who is an intended third-party beneficiary of that promise. The question, therefore, is whether CEI and NU intended to confer on NU's shareholders a right to enforce CEI's promise to complete the merger (and thus a claim against CEI for the $1.2 billion premium). The answer is no. Undoubtedly, the merger agreement confers on NU's shareholders certain rights as third-party beneficiaries, so that after the "NU Effective Time," i.e., the moment at which the merger was to be complete, the shareholders could have enforced CEI's contractual obligation to pay them the $1.2 billion premium. However, as the NU Effective Time never arrived, CEI's duty to pay the premium did not arise.

---

* This ruling left NU with its claim for $27 million in corporate losses.

II

Our "fundamental objective" is to determine the intent of the contracting parties "as derived from the language employed in the contract." "Where the contract is clear and unambiguous on its face, the courts must determine the intent of the parties from within the four corners of the instrument." Here, the contract terms are ramified, cross-referenced, and complex, but they are not unclear.

The Agreement treats third-party rights at article VIII, section 8.06. That provision states that there are none, with two exceptions:

> This Agreement . . . (i) constitutes the entire agreement, and supersedes all prior agreements and understandings, both written and oral, among the parties with respect to the subject matter of this Agreement . . . and (ii) except for the provisions of Article II and Article 5.08, [is] not intended to confer upon any person other than the parties any rights or remedies.

One exception to that foreclosure of third-party rights—article V, section 5.08—concerns the personal liability of CEI and NU's trustees, directors, and officers during and after the merger, and has no bearing on this case. The other—Article II—describes what occurs upon the arrival of the NU Effective Time, and is important. In particular, section 2.01(b) states that at the "NU Effective Time" each outstanding NU share "shall be converted into the right to receive" cash or stock in the post-merger company. *Id.*, art. II, § 2.01(b)(ii), (ii)(A)–(B). That consideration would include the shareholder premium at issue here. Reading article VIII's general foreclosure of third-party beneficiary rights together with the exception in article II, section 2.01, we see that the only third-party right conferred on NU's shareholders is a right, arising upon completion of the merger, to receive payment for their shares. Since it is undisputed that the NU Effective Time never arrived, that right never arose.

NU and Rimkoski respond by invoking the principle of New York rule that a party may not avoid performance of a contractual duty by preventing the occurrence of a condition precedent (the so-called "prevention doctrine"). They argue, in a nutshell, that if CEI wrongfully prevented a merger that upon completion would have yielded the shareholder premium, the failure of the merger is no excuse for non-payment, and NU's shareholders may seek to recover the $1.2 billion premium from CEI. The district court relied heavily on the prevention doctrine in ruling that NU's shareholders can sue CEI. We disagree.

To create a third party right to enforce a contract, "the language of the contract" must "clearly evidence[ ] an intent to permit enforcement by the third party[.]" Here, the parties to the Agreement clearly created a third-party right, but just as clearly they took pains to assure that the right was limited to a right to collect the shareholder premium if and when the merger happened, not a right to sue to compel completion of the merger or for damages resulting from a party's refusal to merge. That intent is manifested in article VIII, which confers a third-party right on NU's shareholders in the context of a general foreclosure of such rights, and does so by reference to article II, which says nothing more than that the shareholders' right to payment would arise at the NU Effective Time. See Agreement, art. II, § 2.01(b) ("At the NU Effective Time . . . each issued and outstanding NU Common Share . . . shall be converted into the right to receive [the merger consideration]" (emphasis added)).

NU and Rimkoski are seeking to achieve through the prevention doctrine a right denied to them under the terms of the Agreement. But the prevention doctrine, where it applies, creates nothing more than an implied contractual obligation, similar to—and perhaps rooted in—the implied covenant of good faith and fair dealing. The doctrine therefore exists to serve the intent of the parties, and does not operate at cross-purposes to that intent. NU and Rimkoski ask us to apply the prevention doctrine in a way that would transform a narrow right to secure payment if and when the NU Effective Time arises into a billion-dollar penalty for the failure to merge. We decline.

III

The intent of CEI and NU to limit the third-party right (in the way set out above) is further manifested in the overall context and scheme of the Agreement. The express third-party right of NU shareholders to compel payment of the consideration due to them post-merger implements a contract right that NU could not enforce on their behalf: At and after the NU Effective Time, NU would no longer exist as an independent entity, but CEI would not yet have established the fund from which NU's shareholders would be paid. See Agreement, art. II, § 2.04. NU argues that even without the grant of such a third-party right, the shareholders may have been able to compel payment for their shares through claims of conversion, quasi-contract, implied contract, or accounting. That may be, but the most direct, simple, and potent remedy would be an action at law in contract; and that is exactly what the Agreement provides.

If we were to find a third-party right for shareholders to seek damages for breach of the duty to merge before the NU Effective time, that right would overwhelm the careful arrangements that the Agreement makes for that contingency, and would unduly limit the signatories' own freedom of action to accept or hazard the contractual consequences of non-performance.

Article VII, section 7.01 explains the circumstances under which the Agreement may be "terminated" by either party prior to the merger's completion. Section 7.01(e) provides that NU may terminate:

> if CEI shall have breached or failed to perform in any material respect any of its representations, warranties, covenants or other agreements contained in this Agreement, which breach or failure to perform (A) would give rise to the failure of a condition

set forth in Section 6.03(a) or (b), and (B) is incapable of being cured by CEI or is not cured by CEI within a reasonable period of time following receipt of written notice from NU of such breach or failure to perform.

(emphasis added). If, as NU alleges, CEI unjustifiably refused to complete the merger, CEI breached article VI, section 6.03(b)—which requires that CEI perform "in all material respects all obligations [ ] to be performed by it under this Agreement at or prior to the Closing Date"—and that breach was not cured within a reasonable time (ever, in fact) after NU's notice of breach. Thus, section 7.01(e) covers termination in the event of just such a breach as is alleged by NU.*

The effect of a section 7.01(e) termination is set out in section 7.02. The first part of section 7.02 states:

In the event of termination of this Agreement by either NU or CEI as provided in Section 7.01, this Agreement shall forthwith become null and void and have no effect, without any liability or obligation on the part of CEI or NU, other than the provisions of Section 3.01(q), Section 3.02(o), the penultimate sentence of Section 5.04(a), Section 5.09, this Section 7.02 and Article VIII, which provisions shall survive such termination. . . .

(emphasis added). Termination therefore would result in no "liability or obligation on the part of CEI" except for what is required by the provisions enumerated in section 7.02.

None of those provisions, however, provides support for the shareholders' right to sue CEI under these circumstances. Section 5.09 ("Fees and Expenses") specifies fees and expenses owed by one party to the other. In particular, [I] CEI and NU agreed to share the costs of various regulatory filings and taxes associated with the merger, id. § 5.09(a); [ii] NU agreed to pay CEI a $110 million "Termination Fee" if, under certain circumstances, the Agreement were terminated and NU thereafter entered into an acquisition agreement with a third party, id. § 5.09(b); [iii] NU promised to pay a $20 million "expense reimbursement fee" to CEI if the Agreement were terminated under certain circumstances, id. § 5.09(c), and CEI made a similar promise, id. § 5.09(d); and [iv] NU agreed to cover CEI's costs and expenses if it were to prevail in any suit against NU to procure payment of the Termination Fee or expense reimbursement fee, id. § 5.09(e). None of these provisions contemplate the NU shareholders' right to sue CEI for the lost $1.2 billion premium; and any such right would overwhelm the specified and

---

* NU contends, as it did in the district court, that the Agreement was not technically "terminated," and that article VII is therefore inapplicable. However, the issue here is whether the parties intended NU's shareholders to have a right to sue CEI for failure to complete the merger. Article VII, the only part of the Agreement that describes the effect of a breach, is relevant to that question, whether it technically applies in this case or not.

limited remedies available to each party in the event of breach and termination of the Agreement.

NU and Rimkoski emphasize that, by virtue of section 7.02, article VIII survives termination of the Agreement; and as discussed above, that article includes section 8.06, which refers to article II, which includes section 2.01, which refers to the shareholders' "right to receive" payment for their shares. This leads nowhere, however, for the reasons stated in Part II of this opinion.

That leaves the second part of section 7.02, which states that where "termination results from the willful and material breach by a party of any of its representations, warranties, covenants or agreements set forth in the Agreement":

> such termination shall not relieve any party of any liability or damages resulting from its willful and material breach of this Agreement (including any such case in which a Termination Fee or any expense reimbursement fee is payable pursuant to Section 5.09), to the extent any such liability or damage suffered by the party entitled to such payment exceeds the amount of such payment. . . .

(emphasis added). This wording—which sets out the consequences of a "willful and material breach"—is at the heart of the matter, but this part of section 7.02 applies only to "liability or damage suffered by the party," not by non-parties, and therefore, not by NU's shareholders.

In sum, article VII—which governs breach and termination of the Agreement—provides no support for the shareholders' right to sue CEI for failure to complete the merger. To the contrary, that article reflects the parties' intent [I] to limit the damages resulting from a breach of the Agreement to those owed to each other; and even then, [ii] to liquidate and limit those damages, except in the case of a willful and material breach. By setting out and limiting the consequences of breach, the Agreement affords each party a critical power to abandon the merger if it is willing to suffer the stipulated consequences, a power that would be illusory if such abandonment could trigger a potential billion-dollar liability to the shareholders.

* * *

Because we hold that no NU shareholder may sue CEI, we do not decide whether such a claim would be properly asserted by Rimkoski's proposed class of March 5, 2001 shareholders or NU on behalf of NU's shareholders as of the date any judgment is entered against CEI.

CONCLUSION

For the foregoing reasons, we hold that shareholders of NU have no right to sue CEI for its alleged breach of the Agreement. Accordingly, we reverse the district court's March 21, 2003 opinion and order insofar as it denied CEI's motion for summary judgment as to NU's claim for the shareholder premium. We also reverse the district court's May 15, 2004 opinion and order insofar as it denied NU's motion for summary judgment on its crossclaim against Rimkoski (for declaratory judgment on Rimkoski's claim for the premium). This case is remanded for proceedings consistent with this opinion.

QUESTIONS

1. The court describes shareholders' rights as arising at the closing under Article II, and consisting of the right to receive payment for their shares. The disclaimer in section 8.06, which states that it does not confer any rights or remedies upon any person other than the parties (ConEd and NU), *"except for the provisions of Article II."* Because the alleged breach of contract prevented the closing from occurring, how does the court conclude that the shareholders, who had a right at the closing, have no right to sue for damages caused by ConEd's prevention of the closing? Why doesn't the court hold that the right to sue for damages for a contract breach that deprives them of their right to receive the merger consideration inheres in their third-party beneficiary status?

2. Why does the court conclude that the implied covenant of good faith and fair dealing does not create a right in the shareholders?

3. Is this form over substance? Who is "selling" NU in a merger for cash, in which NU will disappear into an acquisition subsidiary?

4. The court looks to other terms of the contract to conclude that there is no shareholder right to sue for damages for the merger premium. How is NU's right to terminate the agreement if ConEd breaches relevant to questions of who can sue for damages for breach of the shareholders' right to receive merger consideration at a closing?

5. In the event of a termination ConEd agreed to pay NU's expenses associated with the merger, and section 7.02 provided that if termination resulted from a willful breach, the provision of a termination fee and expense reimbursement "shall not relieve any party of any liability or damages resulting from its willful and material breach of this Agreement (including in any such case in which a Termination Fee or any expense reimbursement fee is payable pursuant to Section 50.9), to the extent any such liability or damage suffered by the party entitled to such payment exceeds the amount of such payment." Does the parenthetical necessarily exclude payments to shareholders on the closing?

NOTE

In 2009 17% of deals granted the target corporation the right to pursue damages on behalf of target stockholders. Mergers & Acquisitions Market

Trends Subcommittee of the Mergers & Acquisitions Committee of the American Bar Association's Business Law Sec2009 Strategic Buyer/Public Target M & A Deal Points Study (For Transactions Announced in 2008) at http://www.abanet.org/abanet/common/login/securedarea.cfm?areaType= committee&role=CL560000&url=/buslaw/committees/CL560000/materials/ matrends/2009public_study.pdf ("2009 ABA Study"), slide 95.

As deal values increase over market value, shareholder losses when a deal fails become larger. The low interest rates that prevailed in the first part of the twenty-first century led to a revival of the leveraged buyouts first seen in the 1980s. The buyers were private investors, generally "private equity" firms that assembled capital from institutional investors in limited partnerships. Because interest rates were at historic lows during the early years of the first decade, these investors employed large amounts of borrowings to finance their acquisitions, and to increase the expected returns to equity (in exchange for increased risk). Recognizing the difficulty in enforcing MAC clauses in many cases after IBP, private equity investors, in order to avoid results such as those in the IBP case, provided that if they terminated the purchase agreement without cause they would pay termination fees (liquidated damages) that were often the mirror image of the seller's termination fee commitments. These agreements had the virtue of providing that the agreed payments were the exclusive remedy of the sellers, thus capping the damages to which the buyer was exposed. A 2007 survey by the law firm Paul Hastings Janofsky & Walker revealed that two-thirds of all deals surveyed between January 2006 and May 2007 contained such reverse termination fees. By 2008, when private equity deals had declined in numbers and the financial crisis appeared to have crested, and with it the appetite of private equity funds for highly leveraged deals, only 35% of private equity deals contained such reverse termination fees. 2009 ABA Study, slide 99.

For some sellers, this apparently was not enough. Increasingly, sellers have required buyers to assume all financing risk, whether or not a failure to obtain financing was the buyer's fault. This has carried over from financial to strategic acquisitions. One recent study of larger acquisitions found that none of the agreements contained a financing condition, and that 90% of the deals contained a specific performance obligation on the buyer's part. See Appendix C, section 8.4(b). Correspondingly, buyers will require the seller's cooperation in obtaining and closing financings. See Appendix C, section 513.

Only one of twenty transactions contained a reverse termination fee. Paul. Weiss, Rifkind, Wharton & Garrison LLP, 2011 Review of Selected U.S. Strategic M & A Transactions (2012), 15, found at https://www.paulweiss. com/media/102615/2011_M-A_Survey.pdf.

In other cases sellers have shifted antitrust and regulatory risk to buyers. In NYSE Euronext's agreement to be acquired by Intercontinental Exchange (ICE), if the sale was not approved on antitrust grounds, ICE was obligated to pay a reverse termination fee of 9.1% of the value of the deal. Google agreed to pay a 20% fee if its acquisition of Motorola Mobility were not approved on antitrust grounds. http://dealbook.nytimes.com/2012/12/21/

breakup-fees-in-nyses-deal-with-ice-show-lessons-from-past/?_r=0. In 2016 Haliburton called off a merger agreement with Baker Hughes because of antitrust obstacles, triggering a $3.5 billion reverse termination fee. Haliburton and Baker Hughes Call off $35 Billion Merger, N.Y. Times, May 1, 2016, http://www.nytimes.com/2016/05/02/business/dealbook/halliburton-and-baker-hughes-call-off-35-billion-merger.html?_r=0.

NOTE ON EMPLOYEE CLAIMS AS THIRD PARTY BENEFICIARIES

Acquisition agreements frequently provide assurances that target company employees and retirees will not suffer precipitously as a result of a change of control. Agreements may provide for continuation of employee benefits for the first year after the acquisition and that, thereafter, benefits will be no less favorable that those of employees of the acquiring firm. Employees' seniority may be protected by provisions that target employees will receive credit for their previous service in any plans that require vesting only after specified periods of employment. Some agreements will provide for continuation of severance plans for a specified period following the closing. Some agreements will also provide that annual bonuses for the year of the transition will be calculated and awarded on the basis of the target company's existing bonus plan.

Questions about who can enforce these agreements raise questions similar to those raised about shareholder standing in the Consolidated Edison decision. In Comrie v. Enterasys Networks, Inc., 2004 Del. Ch. LEXIS 196 (Del. Ch. 2004), the acquiring corporation had, pursuant to the merger agreement, provided stock options on its own stock to employees of BIT Management, Inc., the acquired corporation. The acquiring corporation was contemplating an initial public offering ("IPO") of its stock in the near future. The acquisition agreement provided that:

> "In the event that [the parent company] determines not to pursue its current intention to cause [the acquiring firm] to undergo an initial public offering prior to December 31, 2001 or determines not to pursue its current intention to distribute the stock of [the acquiring firm] to the shareholders of [parent] (each a *"Trigger Event"*), within sixty (60) days of the Trigger Event, [the parent] shall either (i) provide equivalent substitute or replacement awards on the same terms and conditions to the former employees of [BIT]; or (ii) pay $4,620,000 in the aggregate for all Options held by the Partners and former employees of [BIT].

A Trigger Event occurred a few months after the closing of the acquisition, and the parent corporation issued replacement options, based on the value of the original options on the date of replacement, rather than on their higher value on the date of the grant of the original options. The partners who were owners of BIT and parties to the acquisition agreement brought suit for breach of contract and prevailed. But over 41% of the options were held by former BIT employees who were not parties to the agreement, which apparently did not contain a prohibition on third-party suits. Thus the employees based their claim on the theory that they were third-party beneficiaries of the contract, and entitled to enforce their rights under it. The court cited former Vice Chancellor (now Justice) Jacobs, in Madison Realty Partners 7, LLC v. AG ISA, LLC, 2001 WL 406268, at *5, for a definition of a third party beneficiary:

> To qualify as a third party beneficiary of a contract, (i) the contracting parties must have intended that the third party beneficiary benefit from the contract, (ii) the benefit must have been intended as a gift or in satisfaction of a pre-existing obligation to that person, and (iii) the intent to benefit the third party must be a material part of the parties' purpose in entering into the contract.

In this case Vice Chancellor Lamb found that the intent to benefit the employees was plain from the face of the acquisition agreement, and that the donative intent was also clear, and was a material part of the agreement. Judgment in favor of some of the employees was entered, while the court held that others were barred by releases they had signed.

Other cases deal with interpretative questions raised clauses providing that the acquisition agreement is not intended to confer any rights upon third parties. In Prouty v. Gores Technology Group, 18 Cal. Rptr.3d 178 (Cal. App. 2004), Hewlett Packard sold a subsidiary to Gores ("GTG") with a provision in section 10.5 of the stock sale agreement that the agreement "is not intended to confer upon any Person other than the Parties hereto, the Company [the H-P subsidiary, VeriFone] [and other entities not relevant here] any rights or remedies hereunder." The agreement also provided that GTG would offer employment to all VeriFone employees upon terms and benefits similar to those paid by VeriFone, except that GTG had no duty to continue any severance pay obligation that Hewlett Packard had previously promised.

Three months later the parties amended the acquisition agreement to provide that GTG would not terminate any Verifone employees in the first 60 days after the closing, and for any employees terminated in the next 90 days would pay the same severance that they would have received from Hewlett Packard. The amendment did not address the "no third-party beneficiary" language of section 10.5. When GTG terminated VeriFone employees in violation of the amendment and the employees sued, the court was faced with the question of whether the "no third-party beneficiary" clause of section 10.5 governed an amendment to the agreement that was clearly intended to benefit VeriFone employees. The court held that the amendment was intended to grant former employees benefits they could enforce, despite the amendment's express incorporation of the "no third-party beneficiary" clause of the original agreement, on the following basis:

> "Sections 10.5 and 8(b) [of the original agreement] state generally no rights or remedies exist under the contract to third persons; section 6 [of the amendment] expressly grants rights to specific third persons regarding their employment with GTG. In this

circumstance, under well established principles of contract interpretation, when a general and a particular provision are inconsistent, the particular and specific provision is paramount to the general provision. [citations omitted] Section 6 of the amendment thus is an exception to section 10.5 of the original contract and section 8(b) of the amendment [incorporating section 10.5], and plaintiffs can enforce it."

Because many retirement and benefit plans are governed by the Employee Retirement Income Security Act of 1974 ("ERISA"), employees may seek to protect their benefits by filing claims under ERISA rather than as third party beneficiaries of an acquisition agreement by which the buyer assumes responsibility for target employee benefits, including for retired employees. When Haliburton Co. acquired Dresser Industries, the acquisition agreement provided that Haliburton would cause its acquisition subsidiary that survived the merger to maintain the Dresser retiree medical plan, except to the extent that changes to the Dresser Plan were consistent with changes in the Haliburton plan. Similarly, the agreement required Haliburton to provide Dresser employees with benefits comparable to those of Haliburton employees for at least three years from the closing. The agreement contained a "no third-party beneficiary" clause, with a specific exception for Dresser-designated directors on the Haliburton board to enforce the provisions on behalf of Dresser's employees (without mention of its retirees). Four years after the closing, Haliburton decided to merge the Dresser retiree's medical plan with its own, and a year later amended the plan to eliminate virtually all medical benefits for Dresser retirees who had reached age 65 and were eligible for Medicare. The former administrator of the Dresser plan wrote the Haliburton board objecting that this violated the merger agreement, because no similar reductions were made for Haliburton retirees.

The Dresser retirees sued to enforce the terms of the merger agreement that no changes would be made to their benefits that were not also made to the Haliburton retirees' benefits. Haliburton raised the "no third-party beneficiary" language of the merger agreement as a bar to the retirees' suit, but the court held that while it might bar their suit under the contract, it did not bar their suit under ERISA, which gave them the right to enforce the terms of the plan. The court held that the plan was effectively amended by the merger to provide the "equal treatment" protection to the Dresser retirees, who prevailed on this claim. Haliburton Company Benefits Committee v. Graves, 463 F.3d 360 (5th Cir. 2006). For a more detailed discussion of these issues, see Michael S. Katzke and David E. Kahan, Recent Court Decisions Permit Employees to Enforce Merger Agreement Compensation and Benefits Covenants 10, No. 10 THE M & A LAWYER 9 (Nov.-Dec. 2006).

––––––––––––

The absence of financing outs, coupled with specific performance clauses, leaves buyers with only limited excuses to escape from a deal when the buyer suffers from buyer's remorse. The following case illustrates the limits on such outs.

Hexion Specialty Chemicals, Inc.
v. Huntsman Corp.
965 A.2d 715 (Del. Ch. 2008).

■ LAMB, VICE CHANCELLOR.

[This dispute arose from a contested takeover battle for Huntsman, a specialty chemical company headquartered in Utah by Hexion, a subsidiary of Apollo, a private equity firm.]

Because the buyer and its parent were eager to be the winning bidder in a competitive bidding situation, they agreed to pay a substantially higher price than the competition and to commit to stringent deal terms, including no "financing out." In other words, if the financing the buyer arranged (or equivalent alternative financing) is not available at the closing, the buyer is not excused from performing under the contract. In that event, and in the absence of a material adverse effect relating to Huntsman's business as a whole, the issue becomes whether the buyer's liability to the seller for failing to close the transaction is limited to $325 million by contract or, instead, is, uncapped.

The answer to that question turns on whether the buyer committed a knowing and intentional breach of any of its covenants found in the merger agreement that caused damages in excess of the contractual limit. Among other things, the buyer covenanted that it would use its reasonable best efforts to take all actions and do all things "necessary, proper or advisable" to consummate the financing on the terms it had negotiated with its banks and further covenanted that it would not take any action "that could be reasonably be expected to materially impair, delay or prevent consummation" of such financing.

While the parties were engaged in obtaining the necessary regulatory approvals, the seller reported several disappointing quarterly results, missing the numbers it projected at the time the deal was signed. After receiving the seller's first quarter 2008 results, the buyer and its parent, through their counsel, began exploring options for extricating the seller from the transaction. At first, this process focused on whether the seller had suffered a material adverse effect. By early May, however, attention shifted to an exploration of the prospective solvency of the combined entity, leading them to retain the services of a well-known valuation firm to explore the possibility of obtaining an opinion that the combined entity would be insolvent. After making a number of changes to the inputs into the deal model that materially and adversely effected the viability of the transaction, and without consulting with the seller about those changes or about other business initiatives that might improve the prospective financial condition of the resulting entity, the buyer succeeded in obtaining an "insolvency" opinion. [The commitment letter with two lending banks required production of a "customary and reasonably satisfactory" solvency certificate from the Chief Financial Officer of Hexion, the Chief Financial Officer of Huntsman, or a reputable valuation firm as a condition to the banks obligation to fund the loan.]

The insolvency opinion was presented to the buyer's board of directors on June 18, 2008, and later published in a press release claiming that the merger could not be consummated because the financing would not be available due to the prospective insolvency of the combined entity and because the seller had suffered a material adverse effect, as defined in the merger agreement. The buyer and a host of its affiliated entities immediately filed the complaint in this action, alleging a belief that the merger cannot be consummated since the financing will not be available.

The complaint alleges financing will be unavailable because, (1) the amounts available under that financing are no longer sufficient to close the transaction and (2) the combined entity would be insolvent. The complaint seeks a declaration that the buyer is not obligated to consummate the merger if the combined company would be insolvent and a further declaration that its liability (and that of its affiliates) to the seller for nonconsummation of the transaction cannot exceed the $325 million termination fee. The complaint also seeks a declaration that the seller suffered a material adverse effect, thus excusing the buyer's obligation to close. The seller answered and filed counterclaims seeking, among other things, an order directing the buyer to specifically perform its obligations under the merger agreement.

The court conducted six days of trial on certain of the claims for declaratory and injunctive relief raised by the pleadings. In this post-trial opinion, the court finds that the seller has not suffered a material adverse effect, as defined in the merger agreement, and further concludes that the buyer has knowingly and intentionally breached numerous of its covenants under that contract. Thus, the court will grant the seller's request for an order specifically enforcing the buyer's contractual obligations to the extent permitted by the merger agreement itself.

The court also determines that it should not now rule on whether the combined entity, however it may ultimately be capitalized, would be solvent or insolvent at closing. In this connection, the court rejects the buyer's argument that it can be excused from performing its freely undertaken contractual obligations simply because its board of directors concluded that the performance of those contractual obligations risked insolvency. Instead, it was the duty of the buyer's board of directors to explore the many available options for mitigating the risk of insolvency while causing the buyer to perform its contractual obligations in good faith. If, at closing, and despite the buyer's best efforts, financing had not been available, the buyer could then have stood on its contract rights and faced no more than the contractually stipulated damages. The buyer and its parent, however, chose a different course.

* * *

Due to the existence of a signed agreement with Basell [the competing bidder] and Apollo's [Hexion's parent] admittedly intense desire for the deal, Huntsman had significant negotiating leverage. As a result, the merger agreement is more than usually favorable to Huntsman. For example, it contains no financing contingency and requires Hexion to use its "reasonable best efforts" to consummate the financing. In addition, the agreement expressly provides for uncapped damages in the case of a "knowing and intentional breach of any covenant" by Hexion and for liquidated damages of $325 million in cases of other enumerated breaches. The narrowly tailored MAE clause is one of the few ways the merger agreement allows Hexion to walk away from the deal without paying Huntsman at least $325 million in liquidated damages.

* * *

III.

Both parties seek declaratory judgment on the subject of knowing and intentional breach. Hexion seeks a declaratory judgment that no "knowing and intentional breach" of the merger agreement has occurred, and therefore its liability for any breach of the merger agreement is capped at $325 million. Huntsman seeks the obverse—a declaratory judgment that Hexion has engaged in a "knowing and intentional breach" of the merger agreement, and therefore it is entitled to full contract damages, not capped or liquidated by the $325 million figure in section 7.3(d) of the merger agreement. For the reasons detailed below, the court concludes that Hexion has engaged in a knowing and intentional breach, and that the liquidated damages clause of section 7.3(d) is therefore inapplicable.

The court first turns to the meaning of "knowing and intentional breach" as it is used in the merger agreement. "Knowing and intentional," a phrase which echoes with notes of criminal and tort law, is not normally associated with contract law. In fact, the term does not appear at all in either WILLISTON ON CONTRACTS or the RESTATEMENT OF THE LAW OF CONTRACTS. Hexion argues in its pretrial brief that a "knowing" breach "requires that Hexion not merely know of its actions, but have *actual knowledge* that such actions *breach* the covenant," and that negligence or a mistake of law or fact will not suffice to establish a knowing breach. Moreover, it argues, for such breach to also be "intentional," Hexion must have "acted 'purposely' with the 'conscious object' of breaching."

Hexion commits the same fundamental error in its analysis of both terms. Hexion interprets the terms "knowing" and "intentional" as modifying the violation of the legal duty supposed, rather than modifying the act which gives rise to the violation. This is simply wrong. Momentarily drawing the analogy to criminal law which Hexion invites makes this immediately clear: it is the rare crime indeed in which knowledge of the criminality of the act is itself an element of the crime. If one man intentionally kills another, it is no defense to a charge of murder to claim that the killer was unaware that killing is unlawful. Similarly, if a man takes another's umbrella from the coat check room, it may be a defense to say he mistakenly believed the umbrella to be his own (a mistake of fact). It is no defense to say he had not realized that stealing was illegal, nor is it a defense that it was not his "purpose" to break the law, but simply to avoid getting wet. Contrary to Hexion's contention, mistake of law virtually never excuses a violation of law.[87] Hexion cites a number of cases in support of its interpretation. However, once this distinction between mistakes of fact and law is plain, it becomes equally plain that the cases Hexion cites in support of its argument are inapposite. Indeed the alternative would make "knowing and intentional breach" synonymous with willful and malicious breach, a concept ultimately having no place in an action sounding in contract rather than tort. It is a fundamental proposition of contract law that damages in contract are solely to give the non-breaching party the "benefit of the bargain," and not to punish the breaching party.[89] It is for this very reason that penalty clauses are unenforceable. Instead, the best definition of "knowing and intentional breach" is the one suggested by Hexion's citation to the entry for "knowing" in Black's Law Dictionary Black's lists "deliberate" as one of its definitions for knowing. Thus a "knowing and intentional" breach is a deliberate one—a breach that is a direct consequence of a deliberate act undertaken by the breaching party, rather than one which results indirectly, or as a result of the breaching party's negligence or unforeseeable misadventure. In other words, a "knowing and intentional" breach, as used in the merger agreement, is the taking of a deliberate act, which act constitutes in and of itself a breach of the merger agreement, even if breaching was not the conscious

---

[87] A mistake of law is an excuse only if the mistake negates one of the elements of the offense. For example, if a law made it a felony to fail to report a crime, it would be a defense to such charge that the defendant was unaware the act he had witnessed was criminal. But it would not be a defense that he was unaware of his obligation to report crimes.

[89] *See 24* WILLISTON ON CONTRACTS § 64:1 (4th ed.):

The fundamental principle that underlies the availability of contract damages is that of compensation. That is, the disappointed promisee is generally entitled to an award of money damages in an amount reasonably calculated to make him or her whole and neither more nor less; any greater sum operates to punish the breaching promisor and results in an unwarranted windfall to the promisee, while any lesser sum rewards the promisor for his or her wrongful act in breaching the contract and fails to provide the promisee with the benefit of the bargain he or she made.

object of the act. It is with this definition in mind that Hexion's actions will be judged.

A. Hexion's Failure to Use Reasonable Best Efforts to Consummate the Financing and Failure to Give Huntsman Notice of its Concerns

Hexion claims that it will be unable to consummate the merger because, if it were to do so, the resulting company would, according to Hexion, be insolvent. The commitment letter requires as a condition precedent to the banks' obligation to fund that the banks receive a solvency certificate or opinion indicating that the combined entity would be solvent.[93] Hexion argues that no qualified party will be able to deliver such an opinion in good faith, and as such the banks will be neither willing nor obligated to fund. Furthermore, Hexion claims, even if it were able to convince the banks to fund under the commitment letter, there would still be insufficient funds available to close the deal. Notably however, such was Apollo and Hexion's ardor for Huntsman in July 2007 that there is no "financing out" in this deal—the conditions precedent to Hexion's obligation to close do not contain any requirement regarding the availability of the financing under the commitment letter. Nor is there a "solvency out," which would make Hexion's obligation to close contingent on the solvency of the combined entity. Nevertheless, as Apollo's desire for Huntsman cooled through the spring of 2008, Apollo and Hexion attempted to use the purported insolvency of the combined entity as an escape hatch to Hexion's obligations under the merger agreement.

Section 5.12(a) of the merger agreement contains Hexion's covenant to use its reasonable best efforts to consummate the financing:

> (a) [Hexion] shall use its reasonable best efforts to take, or cause to be taken, all actions and to do, or cause to be done, all things necessary, proper or advisable to arrange and consummate the Financing on the terms and conditions described in the Commitment Letter, including (i) using reasonable best efforts to (x) satisfy on a timely basis all terms, covenants and conditions set forth in the Commitment Letter; (y) enter into definitive agreements with respect thereto on the terms and conditions contemplated by the Commitment Letter; and (z) consummate the Financing at or prior to Closing; and (ii) seeking to enforce its rights under the Commitment Letter.

---

[93] PX 2 at D–2 P 6. Paragraph 6 of Exhibit D (which exhibit consists of additional conditions precedent to the banks' obligation to fund) reads in pertinent part:

> The [lending banks] shall have received (i) customary and reasonably satisfactory legal opinions, corporate documents and certificates (including a certificate from the chief financial officer of [Hexion] or the chief financial officer of [Huntsman] or an opinion from a reputable valuation firm with respect to solvency (on a consolidated basis) of the [combined company] and its subsidiaries on the Closing Date after giving effect to the Transactions) (all such opinions, documents and certificates mutually agreed to be in form and substance customary for recent financings of this type with portfolio companies controlled by affiliates of or funds managed by [Apollo]). . . .

Parent will furnish correct and complete copies of all such definitive agreements to the Company promptly upon their execution.

Put more simply, to the extent that an act was both commercially reasonable and advisable to enhance the likelihood of consummation of the financing, the onus was on Hexion to take that act. To the extent that Hexion deliberately chose not to act, but instead pursued another path designed to *avoid* the consummation of the financing, Hexion knowingly and intentionally breached this covenant.

Likewise, section 5.12(b) of the merger agreement provides in pertinent part:

(b) [Hexion] shall keep the Company informed with respect to all material activity concerning the status of the Financing contemplated by the Commitment Letter and shall give [Huntsman] prompt notice of any material adverse change with respect to such Financing. Without limiting the foregoing, [Hexion] agrees to notify [Huntsman] promptly, and in any event within two Business Days, if at any time . . . (iii) for any reason [Hexion] no longer believes in good faith that it will be able to obtain all or any portion of the Financing contemplated by the Commitment Letter on the terms described therein.

This provision is equally simple. Hexion covenants that it will let Huntsman know within two business days if it no longer believes in good faith it will be able to draw upon the commitment letter financing.

Sometime in May 2008, Hexion apparently became concerned that the combined entity, after giving effect to the merger agreement and the commitment letter, would be insolvent. At that time a reasonable response to such concerns might have been to approach Huntsman's management to discuss the issue and potential resolutions of it. This would be particularly productive to the extent that such potential insolvency problems rested on the insufficiency of operating liquidity, which could be addressed by a number of different "levers" available to management.[95] This is not what Hexion did. Instead Hexion, through Wachtell Lipton, engaged Duff & Phelps ostensibly to provide them guidance as to whether the combined entity would be in danger of being considered insolvent. At that point, Hexion's actions could not definitively be said to have been in breach of its obligations under section 5.12(a).

By early June, Duff & Phelps reported back to Wachtell Lipton and Hexion that, based on the information they had been provided, the combined company appeared to fail all three of the customary insolvency tests (the failure of any one of which is sufficient to render a company, for the purposes of delivering a solvency opinion, insolvent). By this point

---

[95] Both sides' management testified that there are many "levers" a corporate manager can "pull" to address operating liquidity concerns.

Hexion, assuming *arguendo* it believed in the projections it provided to Duff & Phelps in order to conduct the analysis, would have had a justifiable good faith concern that it would not be able to provide the required solvency certificate, and that the bank financing pursuant to the commitment letter might be imperiled. Hexion was then clearly obligated to approach Huntsman management to discuss the appropriate course to take to mitigate these concerns. Moreover, Hexion's obligations under the notification covenant in section 5.12(b) of the merger agreement was now in play. Because Hexion now had (again giving Hexion the benefit of the doubt) a good faith belief that the combined entity would be insolvent, Hexion had an absolute obligation to notify Huntsman of this concern within two days of coming to this conclusion, *i.e.* within two days of receiving Duff & Phelps's initial report.

But Hexion did nothing to approach Huntsman management, either to discuss ways the solvency problems might be addressed, or even to put Huntsman on notice of its concerns. This choice alone would be sufficient to find that Hexion had knowingly and intentionally breached its covenants under the merger agreement. Hexion in the days that followed would compound its breach further.

B.   Hexion Affirmatively Acts To Scuttle The Financing

Section 5.12(b) of the merger agreement contains more than an affirmative requirement that Hexion provide prompt notice to Huntsman if the financing is imperiled. It also contains a negative covenant:

> *[Hexion] shall not, and shall not* permit any of its Affiliates to, *without the prior written consent of [Huntsman], take or fail to take any action* or enter into any transaction, including any merger, acquisition, joint venture, disposition, lease, contract or debt or equity financing, *that could reasonably be expected to materially impair, delay or prevent consummation of the Financing contemplated by the Commitment Letter* or any Alternate Financing contemplated by any Alternate Financing. (emphasis added).

Hexion's obligation under the covenant here is again quite simple: do nothing without Huntsman's written consent which might reasonably be expected to scuttle or otherwise harm the likelihood or timing of the financing under the commitment letter.

Apparently considering Duff & Phelps's initial determination that the combined entity would likely be insolvent insufficient for its purposes, on June 2, 2008, Hexion engaged a second Duff & Phelps team headed by Wisler, to provide a formal solvency opinion, or, more to the point, a formal insolvency opinion.

The Duff & Phelps formal opinion team eventually delivered a formal insolvency opinion[97] to Hexion on June 18, 2008, which opinion was presented to the Hexion board the same day. Concluding that the board could rely on the opinion, Hexion's did not contact Huntsman to discuss the issue. If Hexion had contacted Huntsman at this point and requested a meeting between Hexion and Huntsman management to discuss strategies to address the apparent insolvency problem, Hexion would once again have been in compliance with its obligations under the covenants in sections 5.12(a) and (b), and any knowing and intentional breach resulting from its earlier failure to notify Huntsman would have been cured, as no prejudice to Huntsman would have occurred by Hexion's delay. But Hexion chose an alternative tack. Upon adopting the findings of the Duff & Phelps insolvency opinion on June 18, the Hexion board approved the filing of this lawsuit, and the initial complaint was filed that day. In that complaint, Hexion publicly raised its claim that the combined entity would be insolvent, thus placing the commitment letter financing in serious peril. The next day, June 19, 2008, Credit Suisse, the lead bank under the commitment letter, received a copy of the Duff & Phelps insolvency opinion from Hexion, all but killing any possibility that the banks would be willing to fund under the commitment letter. Morrison testified on cross-examination that he was well aware that this was virtually certain to be the consequence of delivering the insolvency opinion to the banks[.]

* * *

Given the court's conclusion that a "knowing and intentional" breach must be the deliberate commission of an act that constitutes a breach of a covenant in the merger agreement, Morrison's testimony makes clear that a knowing and intentional breach by Hexion had occurred by June 19, 2008.

Hexion offers two arguments to justify its taking such dramatic and irrevocable action. The first is that it wanted to secure its status as first filer in any lawsuit arising out of the contract in order to ensure for itself a Delaware forum for litigation. Although the merger agreement explicitly lays exclusive jurisdiction over such suits in the Delaware Court of Chancery, Zaken testified at trial that Apollo and Hexion were concerned that Huntsman might choose to bring suit in Texas instead. But this is clearly no defense to a claim that Hexion knowingly and intentionally breached its covenant not to act in any way which could be reasonably expected to harm the likelihood of the consummation of the financing without Huntsman's express written consent. This proposed defense amounts to nothing more than "we were afraid they might breach, so we breached first." Even if Huntsman had filed suit in Texas prior to Hexion's breach of section 5.12(b), to the extent that Huntsman's filing of a suit in Texas might not constitute a material breach of the merger agreement, Hexion's performance under the contract *still* would not be excused and it would have remained obligated to comply with the terms of the covenants under the merger agreement.[99] *A fortiori,* Hexion's obligation under the section 5.12(b) covenant cannot have been excused by Hexion's mere fear that Huntsman would breach the merger agreement by bringing suit in Texas. [The second argument is omitted.— Ed.]

* * *

V.

Huntsman asks the court to enter a judgment ordering Hexion and its merger subsidiary, Nimbus, to specifically perform their covenants and obligations under the merger agreement. For the reasons explained below, the court finds that, under the agreement, Huntsman cannot force Hexion to consummate the merger, but that Huntsman is entitled to a judgment ordering Hexion to specifically perform its other covenants and obligations.

* * *

In view of these provisions, and considering all the circumstances, the court concludes that it is appropriate to require Hexion to specifically perform its obligations under the merger agreement, other than the obligation to close. Hexion does not argue otherwise. When it is known whether the financing contemplated by the commitment letter is available or not, Hexion and its shareholders will thus be placed in the position to make an informed judgment about whether to close the transaction (in light of, among other things, the findings and conclusions in this opinion) and, if so, how to finance the combined operations. As the parties recognize, both Hexion and Huntsman are solvent, profitable businesses. The issues in this case relate principally to the cost of the merger and whether the financing structure Apollo and Hexion arranged in July 2007 is adequate to close the deal and fund the operations of the combined enterprise. The order the court is today issuing will afford the parties the opportunity to resolve those issues in an orderly and sensible fashion.

VI.

For all the foregoing reasons, the court has today entered an Order and Final Judgment granting Huntsman Corporation relief in accordance with the findings of fact and conclusions of law set forth in this Opinion.

QUESTION

1. One commentator suggested that this case and IBP, among others, show that one who instigates the termination is the one that suffers. Could Hexion have achieved the desired result by taking other actions?

2. Would Hexion have been better off just to terminate the agreement and tender the reverse termination fee, as Cerberus did when it terminated its agreement with United Rentals, described *supra* page 297.

The Aftermath

After this decision, Apollo added $540 million to Hexion's capital to try to overcome the insolvency issue. Not surprisingly, the banks refused to fund the loans, and Apollo brought suit against them. Huntsman settled with Hexion and Apollo for $1 billion. Huntsman continued its litigation against Credit Suisse and Deutsche Bank in Texas. Huntsman has argued that the banks conspired with Apollo and interfered with Huntsman's prior merger pact with previous suitor Basell. Huntsman will be able to ask the jury for funds its shareholders would have received had each deal gone through, or $3.6 billion for the Basell deal and $4.6 billion for the Hexion deal. As the case went to trial in 2009 Huntsman settled with the banks. The banks agreed to pay Huntsman $632 million in cash, which includes $12 million for its litigation expenses, plus $1.1 billion in loans and notes, which Huntsman would repay over seven years.

4. ANTIFRAUD RULES AND INTEGRATION CLAUSES

One Communications Corp. v. JP Morgan SBIC LLC
2010 WL 2512306 (2d. Cir. 2010).

Amended Summary Order

Plaintiff-Counter-Defendant-Appellant One Communications Corp. ("OCC") appeals from a March 31, 2009, judgment and a May 1, 2009 order of the United States District Court for the Southern District of New York (Swain, *J.*), dismissing its federal law claims and counterclaims, respectively with prejudice and declining to exercise jurisdiction over the remaining state law claims. OCC argues that Lightship Telecom LLC, a competitive local exchange carrier (together with Lightship Holding, Inc., a corporation holding all of Lightship Telecom's stock, "Lightship"), was operating in violation of its contracts and federal and state telecommunications laws and that the defendants-appellees, who are major shareholders, directors, and high-level employees of Lightship, made misrepresentations during the sale of the company to OCC's predecessor in interest, CTC Communications Group ("CTC"), that violated Sections 10(b), 15 U.S.C. § 78j (b), and 20(a), 15 U.S.C. § 78t(a), of the Securities Exchange Act of 1934, as well as state law. We assume the parties' familiarity with the underlying facts, procedural history, and specification of the issues on appeal.

* * *

In order to state a claim under § 10(b) and Rule 10b–5, which implements it, "[a] plaintiff must allege that in connection with the purchase or sale of securities, the defendant, acting with scienter, made a false material representation or omitted to disclose material information and that plaintiff's reliance on defendant's conduct caused plaintiff injury." A complaint alleging securities fraud is required to satisfy the heightened pleading standard of the Private Litigation Securities Reform Act, Pub.L. No. 104–67, 109 Stat. 737, and Federal Rule of Civil Procedure 9(b); the circumstances constituting the fraud must be stated with particularity http://www.westlaw.com/Find/Default. wl?rs=dfa1.0&vr=2.0&DB=506&FindType=Y&eferencePositionType= S&SerialNum=2012678857&ReferencePosition=99. "A securities fraud complaint based on misstatements must (1) specify the statements that the plaintiff contends were fraudulent, (2) identify the speaker, (3) state where and when the statements were made, and (4) explain why the statements were fraudulent. Allegations that are conclusory or unsupported by factual assertions are insufficient."

* * *

OCC argues with regard to the allegations in its complaint (1) that certain pre-agreement representations made by Lightship and its officers and directors may be the foundation of a § 10(b) claim and were false, (2) that, in any event, the representations in the merger agreement between Lightship and CTC were false and that it so adequately pled in the complaint, (3) that there were post-agreement representations that were not considered by the district court, and (4) that the sellers acted with scienter throughout.

With respect to the pre-agreement representations allegedly made by Lightship, we conclude that the merger agreement foreclosed any reliance by CTC on those representations and that therefore no § 10(b) claim may be brought based on them. The merger agreement itself contained both a merger clause, section 10(c), and a separate provision, section 6(d), specifically disclaiming the ability of CTC to rely on representations or warranties that were "inconsistent with or in addition to the representations and warranties" set forth in the agreement. In assessing whether a plaintiff reasonably relied on a representation, a court must consider the entire context of the transaction, including the sophistication of the parties, the content of written agreements, and the complexity and magnitude of the transaction. "Where the plaintiff is a sophisticated investor and an integrated agreement between the parties does not include the misrepresentation at issue, the plaintiff cannot establish reasonable reliance on that misrepresentation." OCC does not allege that CTC was not a sophisticated investor, and indeed the record reflects that it was such. Section 10(c) of the agreement clearly provides that the agreement is integrated and, in combination with section 6(d), suffices to show that reliance on pre-agreement representations was unwarranted as a matter of law.

* * *

For the foregoing reasons, the March 31, 2009 judgment and May 1, 2009 order of the district court are hereby AFFIRMED.

QUESTIONS

1. Section 29(a) of the Securities Exchange Act, 15 U.S.C. § 78cc(a) provides "Any condition, stipulation, or provision binding any person to waive compliance with any provision of this title or of any rule or regulation thereunder, . . . shall be void." Does the failure to discuss this provision mean that the buyer's reliance was indeed unreasonable, and that the buyer must exercise its own due diligence in a reasonable way? See AES Corp. v. The Dow Chemical Co., 325 F.3d 174 (3d Cir. 2003) (remanding for further findings on whether the buyer's reliance was reasonable in view of similar contract language).

2. Does this holding only apply to pre-agreement statements? Suppose deliberately false statements were made in the merger agreement, or that the financial statements were fraudulent?

NOTE

Language such as Lightship employed is quite effective in common law fraud claims. In Great Lakes Chemical Corp. v. Pharmacia Corp., 788 A.2d 544 (Del.Ch. 2001), the court held that the buyer could not assert fraud claims that were precluded by explicit disclaimers in the contract, which disclaimed sellers' liability not only for any statements or representations outside the contract but also for the accuracy of the information contained in the contract itself. The language was quite broad, e.g., "None of [the sellers] make any express or implied representation or warranty as to the accuracy or completeness of the information contained herein . . ." and "Each of [the sellers] expressly disclaims any and all liability that may be based on such information or errors therein or omissions therefrom." 788 A.2d at 552. In Abry Partners V, L.P. v. F & W Acquisition LLC, 891 A.2d 1032, 1058–59 (Del. Ch. 2006), Vice Chancellor Strine explained the Delaware approach:

> [T]his court has consistently respected the law's traditional abhorrence of fraud in implementing this reasoning. Because of that policy concern, we have not given effect to so-called merger or integration clauses that do not clearly state that the parties disclaim reliance upon extra-contractual statements. Instead, we have held, as in *Kronenberg*, that murky integration clauses, or standard integration clauses without explicit anti-reliance representations, will not relieve a party of its oral and extra-

contractual fraudulent representations. The integration clause must contain "language that . . . can be said to add up to a clear anti-reliance clause by which the plaintiff has contractually promised that it did not rely upon statements outside of the contract's four corners in deciding to sign the contract." This approach achieves a sensible balance between fairness and equity—parties can protect themselves against unfounded fraud claims through explicit anti-reliance language. If parties fail to include unambiguous anti-reliance language, they will not be able to escape responsibility for their own fraudulent representations made outside of the agreement's four corners.

See also Prairie Capital III v. Double E Holding Corp., Case No. D67036 (Del. Ch. Nov. 24, 2015), where the court found the integration clause reflected an affirmative expression by the buyer that it had relied only on the representations and warranties in the purchase agreement.

In FdG Logistics LLC v. A & R Logistics Holdings, Inc., 2016 Del. Ch. LEXIS 31 (2016) Chancellor Bouchard explained that the integration clause was missing "any affirmative expression *by Buyer* of (1) specifically what it was relying on when it decided to enter the Merger Agreement or (2) that it is was [sic] not relying on any representations made outside of the Merger Agreement. Instead, Section 5.27 amounts to a disclaimer *by the selling company* (Old A & R) of what it was and was not representing and warranting."

CHAPTER SIX

THE TARGET BOARD'S DUTIES IN REACTING TO BIDS

1. THE PROBLEM OF THE HOSTILE BID

Hostile tender offers have never accounted for a large proportion of all acquisition activity, but they have garnered a large amount of attention from the public and policy-makers alike. They have been vilified by persons from all walks of life—executives of companies that became unwilling targets of bids, labor representatives who attributed job losses to hostile takeovers, lawyers, economists, journalists and politicians. At the same time they have been praised by a diverse body of commentators, including executives of bidders, investment bankers who profited from this activity, lawyers representing bidders, and economists, to name a few groups.

The reaction of corporate managers to hostile bids is understandable—some studies have shown that after a change of control, fifty percent of the top executives of an acquired firm will have left their employment within three years. As we will see, target managers often behave as loyal representatives of their shareholders in considering uninvited bids to acquire their companies, and appear to seek the best deal for them. Seeking the best deal for shareholders may in some cases call for resisting a takeover bid. This may be because managers have confidential corporate information about the true (higher) value of the company that they cannot reveal without losing some competitive advantage, or because they believe that the market has just ignored their company, and has not valued its shares properly. In some cases a hostile bid may be structured to take advantage of the lack of organization and communication between individual shareholders, as illustrated below.

Assume that a hostile bid is made for a majority of the shares of a company at a low-ball price that target shareholders generally believe is inadequate. Assume a cash bid for half of the shares at $40, when the pre-bid market price was $30. Further assume that the bidder announces an intent, if the cash bid is successful, to engage in a takeout merger at $30. If a simple majority of the shares are taken at the cash bid price and the rest at the take-out price, target shareholders will receive an average ("blended") price of $35. Finally, assume that if the offer fails, the post-bid market price will experience a permanent upward revaluation to $37, an increase which reflects new information about the target's value that is disclosed by the bid itself. That outcome may represent either the expectation or appearance of a higher second bid, disclosure of knowledge about the value of underlying assets that has been ignored by the market, or revelation of value-increasing strategies that can be used by the target firm without a change in control. If the tender offer period is brief and stock holdings are widely dispersed, there will be no real opportunity for target stockholders to communicate with each other and to agree to reject the bid.

We now examine stockholders' collective action problems. Assume that all the stockholders are represented in a two-person game by A and B, who own equal amounts of the stock, with the bidder holding a single share. In this case, either stockholder can tender control and nothing the other stockholder does can alter that outcome.

A's choices must be made on a contingent basis, assessing possible outcomes based on whether or not B tenders. Thus

If B does not tender:

    A will get $37 for not tendering;

    A will get $40 for tendering.

    Thus A will prefer to tender.

If B tenders:

    A will get $30 for not tendering;

    A will get $35 for tendering;

    Thus A will prefer to tender.

B will, of course, face exactly the same decisions. The problem, which is a prisoner's dilemma, can be illustrated by the following matrix:

		B's CHOICES	
		Not Tender	Tender
	Not Tender	A Gets $37	A gets $30
		B gets $37	B gets $40
A's CHOICES			
	Tender	A gets $40	A gets $35
		B gets $30	B gets $35

For most shareholders, the goal is to avoid the worst case—the $30 cash takeout, if the other (greedy) shareholder tenders. Since each stockholder finds that tendering produces a preferable result under either set of assumptions, both will tender and receive an average price of $35. Without prior communication and agreement not to tender, neither can get to the mutually preferred outcome which produces $37. Under these circumstances shareholders may want managers to act as their agents, either to negotiate for a better price for all shareholders, or to resist the bid.

In other cases, resisting a bid may simply be evidence of management entrenchment, to preserve jobs and perquisites. How can one distinguish between these motivations? In either case, managers who resist a bid will claim that they are acting in the best interest of their shareholders. In some cases managers will also claim that it is in the interest of other "constituencies" of the corporation, such as its employees, its suppliers, or the communities in which it operates.

2. THE ROLE OF TAKEOVER DEFENSES

Model Business Corporation Act, §§ 8.30, 8.31, 8.60–8.63; Del. Gen. Corp. L. § 144.

Corporate lawyers are called upon during the course of negotiations to advise boards of directors about the extent of their legal duties of care and loyalty. There is nothing exceptional in this per se. Prior to the 1980s, if directors were operating in good faith and without conflicts of interest, lawyers could advise boards that how they operated was a function of their business judgment, and that courts would defer to that judgment. Two dramatic changes took place in the 1980s that inserted lawyers deeply into the corporate decision-making process. First, the Delaware courts took the lead in undertaking a closer scrutiny of directors' decisions. Second, with the advent of hostile takeovers and the development of sophisticated defenses, directors and their attorneys worked more closely in devising strategies, whether to protect directors' positions or to maximize value for shareholders.

When directors have a sufficient economic interest in a transaction, their approval of the transaction is deemed to be infected by a conflict of interest. These statutes, particularly Model Act § 8.60, specify exactly what decisions involve prohibited conflicts of interest. Delaware GCL § 144 is similar if not as precise. If their decision is not approved by independent decision-makers in the manner specified in the statutes cited above, the burden is on the directors, when their decision is challenged, to prove the entire fairness of the transaction. In contrast to this intrusive standard of review, decisions not involving a conflict of interest are subject to the deference of the Business Judgment Rule. This part deals with an intermediate set of decisions—where directors may receive indirect benefits as a result of their decisions, but do not themselves deal with the corporation. It illustrates the struggle of the Delaware courts to locate an appropriate standard of review. This part focuses on Delaware law not only because it is the most developed body of state law, but also because the Delaware standard of review is perhaps the most intrusive in the nation. In states where the law is less clear, practitioners frequently advise clients on the basis of Delaware law, in the expectation that their jurisdiction will not adopt a stricter standard than Delaware's.

A. STANDARDS OF JUDICIAL REVIEW

The Delaware courts have long recognized that incumbent managers have a strong interest in retaining their positions, and that boards, especially those which consist primarily of top officers of a company, may be unduly responsive to that interest—in short, that they may not always observe their duty of good faith and loyalty to the corporation and its shareholders. The earliest case involving what today would be called the payment of corporate "greenmail" appears to be Kors v. Carey, 158 A.2d 136 (Del.Ch.1960). The managers of Lehn & Fink, a cosmetics manufacturer, learned that United Whelan Corp. had purchased over 10% of Lehn & Fink's outstanding stock, an amount that ultimately increased to 16%. United Whelan owned a chain of drug stores to which Lehn & Fink sold cosmetics, but Lehn & Fink also sold to other retailers such as the Lord & Taylor department store chain. Lehn & Fink knew that Whelan Drug was an aggressive buyer of supplies for its stores, seeking special concessions from manufacturers, and the managers of Lehn & Fink feared that if it were owned by United Whelan that other customers, such as Lord & Taylor, might not want to do business with a competitor. Accordingly, the managers of Lehn & Fink caused the company to repurchase United Whelan's shares for $28.50, when the market price was $25–$26. This was done anonymously through brokerage firms.

The Chancery Court rejected a shareholder challenge to this action. It stated that the use of corporate funds for elimination of a shareholder at odds with management policy "is not illegal as a matter of law." 158 A.2d at 141. The court noted that the board had carefully weighed and evaluated its options, and had consulted outside experts from both the Harvard Business School and Georgeson & Co., a well-known firm of proxy solicitors. The court noted that the premium paid was probably less than the cost of a proxy fight, which the directors would be entitled to conduct with corporate funds in a dispute over corporate policy. As to the charge that managers were only acting to protect their positions, the court rejected this contention, saying:

> "As to plaintiff's contentions that the Lehn & Fink directors were selfishly voting for the retention of their offices and the emoluments thereof, I conclude, having heard the testimony of the principals involved and considered their personal evaluation of the dilemma posed by the existence of their stock in the hands of United Whelan, that plaintiff has not succeeded in overcoming the presumption that directors form their judgment in good faith." 158 A.2d at 141–42.

The Delaware Supreme Court first attempted to grapple with the problems of conflicts of interest in the setting of a transfer of control of a company in Cheff v. Mathes, 199 A.2d 548 (1964). Holland Furnace was criticized in Note, Buying Out Insurgent Shareholders with Corporate

Funds, 70 Yale L. J. 308 (1960). Company manufactured home furnaces, which it sold through numerous door-to-door sales personnel, a unique approach in this business. Effective control was in the Cheff-Landwehr family group, which owned 18.5% of Holland's stock. A family member, Cheff, served as chief executive officer. In the years 1948–1956 Holland's sales declined by approximately 25%, which management attributed to a boom in sales in the period following World War II that could not be sustained. In 1957 Cheff was approached by Mr. Maremont, who owned an automotive parts manufacturing business, and wanted to discuss a merger. Cheff responded negatively, and Maremont then proceeded to acquire approximately 6% of Holland's stock in market transactions. Cheff proceeded to have Maremont investigated, and determined that Maremont's company had operating losses in the most recent operating year, and that Maremont had been involved in the acquisition and liquidation of several companies. When Maremont and Cheff next met, Maremont announced that he now owned over 11% of Holland's stock, and that he believed Holland's method of selling at retail was obsolete, and should be abandoned in favor of sales to wholesalers. Cheff returned to his board, which agreed that Maremont represented a threat to Holland. Cheff later testified that Holland was starting to lose employees because of the threat of a Maremont takeover, and that Maremont had initially deceived him about his intent with respect to his investment in Holland. Accordingly, the Holland board authorized management to cause Holland to repurchase Maremont's shares. Ultimately Holland repurchased Maremont's holdings, which by that time had reached 17.5% of Holland's stock, at a price above the market price for the shares.

The Delaware Supreme Court first had to determine whether the board's decision should be assessed under the business judgment rule. It noted that courts initially presumed that directors made decisions in good faith, but where directors use corporate funds to repurchase shares in order to protect their own control, they are faced with a conflict of interest, citing Bennett v. Propp, 187 A.2d 405 (Del.1962). But the court also concluded that the conflict of interest here is not as severe as that involved where directors are self-dealing directly with their corporation. Accordingly, the court took an intermediate position:

> The question then presented is whether or not defendants satisfied the burden of proof of showing reasonable grounds to believe a danger to corporate policy and effectiveness existed by the presence of the Maremont stock ownership. It is important to remember that the directors satisfy their burden by showing good faith and reasonable investigation; the directors will not be penalized for an honest mistake of judgment, if the judgment appeared reasonable at the time the decision was made.

The court held that the directors held a good faith belief that Maremont represented a threat to the continued existence of Holland, at least in its present form, and thus exonerated the defendant directors. Thus, the result of the case seemed to be that a good faith belief of directors that they were pursuing some purpose—a "business purpose"—that would benefit the corporation was sufficient to rebut any inference of a conflict of interest, and to return the plaintiffs to the position of producing sufficient evidence to overcome the strong presumption of the business judgment rule.

Criticizing this decision, the author has written:

> "Until recently, the Delaware courts have treated defensive responses as involving questions of business judgment, as long as management could demonstrate a colorable business purpose for a defensive response. That approach allowed managers to use the most powerful of defensive weapons . . . as long as they could plausibly claim that investor welfare might be threatened. . . . Because that claim could nearly always be made, the Delaware courts seemed to be closing their eyes to questions of management disloyalty."

Carney, Controlling Management Opportunism in the Market for Corporate Control: An Agency Cost Model, 1988 Wis. L. Rev. 385, 427.

Perhaps the most complete articulation of Delaware's business purpose test appeared in the opinion of former Chancellor Seitz in Johnson v. Trueblood, 629 F.2d 287 (3d Cir.1980). The plaintiffs, 47% shareholders, charged the 53% shareholders who controlled the board with rejecting the plaintiffs' offer of additional financing in favor of that of a third party solely to preserve their own control. In affirming the opinion of the trial court in favor of the defendants, Judge Seitz wrote:

"Next, the plaintiffs argue that the district court improperly charged the jury on their burden in overcoming the business judgment rule. That rule, which admittedly is part of the law of Delaware, provides that directors of a corporation are presumed to exercise their business judgment in the best interest of the corporation. The charge was as follows: [The] desire to retain control of a corporation in and of itself is an improper motive for decision of a director. Therefore, if you find by a preponderance of the evidence that the defendants acted solely or primarily because of a desire to retain control of Penn Eastern, then the presumption of the sound business judgment rule has been rebutted. However, I further instruct you that a director may properly decline to adopt a course of action which would result in a shift of control, so long as his actions can be attributed to a rational business purpose. In other words, so long as other rational business reasons support a director's decision, the mere fact that a business decision involves a retention of control does not constitute a showing of bad faith to rebut the business judgment rule. *That rule is rebutted only where a director's sole or primary purpose for adopting a course of action or refusing to adopt another is to retain control.* (emphasis supplied [by the court]).

"Instead of the emphasized language, the plaintiffs argue that they only needed to prove that control was 'a' motive in the defendants various actions to rebut the business judgment rule. We disagree for two reasons.

"First, the purpose of the business judgment rule belies the plaintiffs' contention. It is frequently said that directors are fiduciaries. Although this statement is true in some senses, it is also obvious that if directors were held to the same standard as ordinary fiduciaries the corporation could not conduct business. For example, an ordinary fiduciary may not have the slightest conflict of interest in any transaction he undertakes on behalf of the trust. Yet by the very nature of corporate life a director has a certain amount of self-interest in everything he does. The very fact that the director wants to enhance corporate profits is in part attributable to his desire to keep shareholders satisfied so that they will not oust him.

"The business judgment rule seeks to alleviate this problem by validating certain situations that otherwise would involve a conflict of interest for the ordinary fiduciary. The rule achieves this purpose by postulating that if actions are arguably taken for the benefit of the corporation, then the directors are presumed to have been exercising their sound business judgment rather than responding to any personal motivations.

"Faced with the presumption raised by the rule, the question is what sort of showing the plaintiff must make to survive a motion for directed verdict. Because the rule presumes that business judgment was exercised, the plaintiff must make a showing from which a fact-finder might infer that impermissible motives predominated in the making of the decision in question.

"The plaintiffs' theory that 'a' motive to control is sufficient to rebut the rule is inconsistent with this purpose. Because the rule is designed to validate certain transactions despite conflicts of interest, the plaintiffs' rule would negate that purpose, at least in many cases. As already noted, control is always arguably 'a' motive in any action taken by a director. Hence plaintiffs could always make this showing and thereby undercut the purpose of the rule.

"Second, the plaintiffs' argument is inconsistent with Delaware case law. Although scholars have argued about how much is required under Delaware law to rebut the business judgment rule, we need not resolve that debate. At a minimum, the Delaware cases require that the plaintiff must show some sort of bad faith on the part of the defendant. We do not think that a showing of 'a' motive to retain control, without more, constitutes bad faith in this context unless we are to ignore the realities of corporate life. Accordingly, unless the plaintiff can tender evidence from which a fact finder might conclude that the defendant's sole or primary motive was to retain control, the presumption of the rule remains.

* * *

"In short, we believe that under Delaware law, at a minimum the plaintiff must make a showing that the sole or primary motive of the defendant was to retain control. If he makes a showing sufficient to survive a directed verdict, the burden then shifts to the defendant to show that the transaction in question had a valid corporate business purpose. Because the charge fairly contains such a standard, we find no error."

Perhaps the most extreme example of the use of the business purpose test is found in Panter v. Marshall Field & Co., 646 F.2d 271 (7th Cir.), certiorari denied 454 U.S. 1092 (1981). Marshall Field was a Delaware corporation, operating Chicago's most famous department store chain. Over a period of years the Field board had been advised by experienced counsel, Joseph Flom, on several occasions when prospective buyers had approached management. Each time Field rejected these proposals on the grounds that they would violate the antitrust laws, either because of a recent acquisition by Field or a proposed acquisition that created a situation where a combination would reduce competition in some market. (This was an era of strict interpretation of the antitrust laws with respect to mergers.) In 1977 Field was in a period of transition, having just appointed a new president from Neiman-Marcus to replace a president who had died unexpectedly. When Field's management was approached by representatives of another chain, Carter Hawley Hale (CHH), its attorneys once again advised rejecting the proposal on antitrust grounds. What followed was a series of bids and responses that illustrated how contentious acquisition activity could become. CHH first offered its own securities worth $36 for each share of Field's stock, then trading at $22. After receiving advice from investment bankers, the Field board rejected the offer as inadequate. Its press release stated that management had faith in the growth of Field, and that it would remain independent in order to continue its growth. Field filed suit against CHH alleging both securities law and antitrust law violations. Just to make certain the antitrust charges would succeed, Field announced that it would expand by adding a store in Houston's Galleria Mall, where CHH also had a store. The feasibility study for this expansion, Field's first outside the Chicago area, was completed in 30 days. Field also sought acquisitions. Negotiations with Dillards, a competitor of CHH in the southwest, fell through, but Field was able to acquire Liberty House, a competitor of CHH in the northwest, after one day's consideration, where the Field board lacked historical financial data at the time of approval. When CHH raised its bid to $42, Field's board declined to consider it, in view of what it now regarded as its illegality under the antitrust laws, given Field's expansion plans for the Galleria. As a result of this aggressive response, CHH announced the withdrawal of its bid. During the bidding Field's stock had traded in the range of $30–34, but when CHH announced its withdrawal, Field's stock declined to $19.

The trial court dismissed plaintiffs' claims on a motion for a directed verdict, finding that there was insufficient evidence of breach of duty by Field's directors to submit the case to a jury. This was affirmed by a divided court of appeals. The majority opinion began by stating that directors are not true fiduciaries, because they inevitably face the conflict of interest of attempting to protect their positions. Nevertheless, the majority argued, they are entitled to a presumption of good faith under the business judgment rule if their actions are *arguably* taken for the benefit of the corporation. In order to rebut the presumption of good faith, the plaintiffs must show that selfish motives dominate the decision, given that a desire to retain control will be present in every decision made by directors. The presumption of good faith was strengthened by the fact that a majority of the Field directors were independent, and not employed by the corporation.

In determining whether self-interest was the primary motive, the majority noted that a desire to build an independent business is rational, and that the board did not determine to resist at any cost. As to the antitrust defenses, the court noted that the antitrust suit filed by Field was begun in good faith on advice of counsel, and plaintiffs had been unable to show that the bringing of the suit was a wrongful act. Judge Cudahy, dissenting, argued that in the case of control battles, courts should be less deferential to management. Here he noted the haste of the board in approving acquisitions that would create antitrust problems. Further, he argued, application of the business judgment rule in this case has the effect of immunizing corporate boards from liability, if they hire experts to advise them who find any business rationale for their actions after the fact.

Decisions such as this were widely criticized as ignoring the real motivations of directors in control battles. See Ronald Gilson, A Structural Approach to Corporations: The Case Against Defensive Tactics in Tender Offers, 33 Stanford L. Rev. 819 (1981). Is the following case a judicial reaction to this criticism?

Unocal Corporation v. Mesa Petroleum Co.

493 A.2d 946 (Del.1985).

■ MOORE, JUSTICE.

We confront an issue of first impression in Delaware—the validity of a corporation's self-tender for its own shares which excludes from participation a stockholder making a hostile tender offer for the company's stock.

The Court of Chancery granted a preliminary injunction to the plaintiffs, Mesa Petroleum Co., Mesa Asset Co., Mesa Partners II, and

Mesa Eastern, Inc. (collectively "Mesa")[1], enjoining an exchange offer of the defendant, Unocal Corporation (Unocal) for its own stock. The trial court concluded that a selective exchange offer, excluding Mesa, was legally impermissible. We cannot agree with such a blanket rule. The factual findings of the Vice Chancellor, fully supported by the record, establish that Unocal's board, consisting of a majority of independent directors, acted in good faith, and after reasonable investigation found that Mesa's tender offer was both inadequate and coercive. Under the circumstances the board had both the power and duty to oppose a bid it perceived to be harmful to the corporate enterprise. On this record we are satisfied that the device Unocal adopted is reasonable in relation to the threat posed, and that the board acted in the proper exercise of sound business judgment. We will not substitute our views for those of the board if the latter's decision can be "attributed to any rational business purpose." Accordingly, we reverse the decision of the Court of Chancery and order the preliminary injunction vacated.

I.

The factual background of this matter bears a significant relationship to its ultimate outcome.

On April 8, 1985, Mesa, the owner of approximately 13% of Unocal's stock, commenced a two-tier "front loaded" cash tender offer for 64 million shares, or approximately 37%, of Unocal's outstanding stock at a price of $54 per share. The "back-end" was designed to eliminate the remaining publicly held shares by an exchange of securities purportedly worth $54 per share. However, pursuant to an order entered by the United States District Court for the Central District of California on April 26, 1985, Mesa issued a supplemental proxy statement to Unocal's stockholders disclosing that the securities offered in the second-step merger would be highly subordinated, and that Unocal's capitalization would differ significantly from its present structure. Unocal has rather aptly termed such securities "junk bonds".

Unocal's board consists of eight independent outside directors and six insiders. It met on April 13, 1985, to consider the Mesa tender offer. Thirteen directors were present, and the meeting lasted nine and one-half hours. The directors were given no agenda or written materials prior to the session. However, detailed presentations were made by legal counsel regarding the board's obligations under both Delaware corporate law and the federal securities laws. The board then received a presentation from Peter Sachs on behalf of Goldman Sachs & Co. (Goldman Sachs) and Dillon, Read & Co. (Dillon Read) discussing the bases for their opinions that the Mesa proposal was wholly inadequate. Mr. Sachs opined that the minimum cash value that could be expected from a sale or orderly liquidation for 100% of Unocal's stock was in excess

---

[1]   T. Boone Pickens, Jr., is President and Chairman of the Board of Mesa Petroleum and President of Mesa Asset and controls the related Mesa entities.

of $60 per share. In making his presentation, Mr. Sachs showed slides outlining the valuation techniques used by the financial advisors, and others, depicting recent business combinations in the oil and gas industry. The Court of Chancery found that the Sachs presentation was designed to apprise the directors of the scope of the analyses performed rather than the facts and numbers used in reaching the conclusion that Mesa's tender offer price was inadequate.

Mr. Sachs also presented various defensive strategies available to the board if it concluded that Mesa's two-step tender offer was inadequate and should be opposed. One of the devices outlined was a self-tender by Unocal for its own stock with a reasonable price range of $70 to $75 per share. The cost of such a proposal would cause the company to incur $6.1–6.5 billion of additional debt, and a presentation was made informing the board of Unocal's ability to handle it. The directors were told that the primary effect of this obligation would be to reduce exploratory drilling, but that the company would nonetheless remain a viable entity.

The eight outside directors, comprising a clear majority of the thirteen members present, then met separately with Unocal's financial advisors and attorneys. Thereafter, they unanimously agreed to advise the board that it should reject Mesa's tender offer as inadequate, and that Unocal should pursue a self-tender to provide the stockholders with a fairly priced alternative to the Mesa proposal. The board then reconvened and unanimously adopted a resolution rejecting as grossly inadequate Mesa's tender offer. Despite the nine and one-half hour length of the meeting, no formal decision was made on the proposed defensive self-tender.

On April 15, the board met again with four of the directors present by telephone and one member still absent. This session lasted two hours. Unocal's Vice President of Finance and its Assistant General Counsel made a detailed presentation of the proposed terms of the exchange offer. A price range between $70 and $80 per share was considered, and ultimately the directors agreed upon $72. The board was also advised about the debt securities that would be issued, and the necessity of placing restrictive covenants upon certain corporate activities until the obligations were paid. The board's decisions were made in reliance on the advice of its investment bankers, including the terms and conditions upon which the securities were to be issued. Based upon this advice, and the board's own deliberations, the directors unanimously approved the exchange offer. Their resolution provided that if Mesa acquired 64 million shares of Unocal stock through its own offer (the Mesa Purchase Condition), Unocal would buy the remaining 49% outstanding for an exchange of debt securities having an aggregate par value of $72 per share. The board resolution also stated that the offer would be subject to other conditions that had been described to the board at the meeting, or which were deemed necessary by Unocal's officers, including the exclusion of Mesa from the proposal (the Mesa exclusion). Any such conditions were required to be in accordance with the "purport and intent" of the offer.

Unocal's exchange offer was commenced on April 17, 1985, and Mesa promptly challenged it by filing this suit in the Court of Chancery. On April 22, the Unocal board met again and was advised by Goldman Sachs and Dillon Read to waive the Mesa Purchase Condition as to 50 million shares. This recommendation was in response to a perceived concern of the shareholders that, if shares were tendered to Unocal, no shares would be purchased by either offeror. The directors were also advised that they should tender their own Unocal stock into the exchange offer as a mark of their confidence in it.

Another focus of the board was the Mesa exclusion. Legal counsel advised that under Delaware law Mesa could only be excluded for what the directors reasonably believed to be a valid corporate purpose. The directors' discussion centered on the objective of adequately compensating shareholders at the "back-end" of Mesa's proposal, which the latter would finance with "junk bonds". To include Mesa would defeat that goal, because under the proration aspect of the exchange offer (49%) every Mesa share accepted by Unocal would displace one held by another stockholder. Further, if Mesa were permitted to tender to Unocal, the latter would in effect be financing Mesa's own inadequate proposal.

On April 24, 1985 Unocal issued a supplement to the exchange offer describing the partial waiver of the Mesa Purchase Condition. On May 1, 1985, in another supplement, Unocal extended the withdrawal, proration and expiration dates of its exchange offer to May 17, 1985.

Meanwhile, on April 22, 1985, Mesa amended its complaint in this action to challenge the Mesa exclusion. * * *

After the May 8 hearing the Vice Chancellor issued an unreported opinion on May 13, 1985 granting Mesa a preliminary injunction. Specifically, the trial court noted that "the parties basically agree that the directors' duty of care extends to protecting the corporation from perceived harm whether it be from third parties or shareholders." The trial court also concluded in response to the second inquiry in the Supreme Court's May 2 order, that "although the facts, . . . do not appear to be sufficient to prove that Mesa's principle objective is to be bought off at a substantial premium, they do justify a reasonable inference to the same effect."

* * *

II.

The issues we address involve these fundamental questions: Did the Unocal board have the power and duty to oppose a takeover threat it reasonably perceived to be harmful to the corporate enterprise, and if so, is its action here entitled to the protection of the business judgment rule?

* * *

III.

We begin with the basic issue of the power of a board of directors of a Delaware corporation to adopt a defensive measure of this type. Absent such authority, all other questions are moot. Neither issues of fairness nor business judgment are pertinent without the basic underpinning of a board's legal power to act.

The board has a large reservoir of authority upon which to draw. Its duties and responsibilities proceed from the inherent powers conferred by 8 Del. C. § 141(a), respecting management of the corporation's "business and affairs". Additionally, the powers here being exercised derive from 8 Del. C. § 160(a), conferring broad authority upon a corporation to deal in its own stock. From this it is now well established that in the acquisition of its shares a Delaware corporation may deal selectively with its stockholders, provided the directors have not acted out of a sole or primary purpose to entrench themselves in office.

Finally, the board's power to act derives from its fundamental duty and obligation to protect the corporate enterprise, which includes stockholders, from harm reasonably perceived, irrespective of its source. Thus, we are satisfied that in the broad context of corporate governance, including issues of fundamental corporate change, a board of directors is not a passive instrumentality.

Given the foregoing principles, we turn to the standards by which director action is to be measured. In Pogostin v. Rice, Del. Supr., 480 A.2d 619 (1984), we held that the business judgment rule, including the standards by which director conduct is judged, is applicable in the context of a takeover. The business judgment rule is a "presumption that in making a business decision the directors of a corporation acted on an informed basis, in good faith and in the honest belief that the action taken was in the best interests of the company." A hallmark of the business judgment rule is that a court will not substitute its judgment for that of the board if the latter's decision can be "attributed to any rational business purpose."

When a board addresses a pending takeover bid it has an obligation to determine whether the offer is in the best interests of the corporation and its shareholders. In that respect a board's duty is no different from any other responsibility it shoulders, and its decisions should be no less entitled to the respect they otherwise would be accorded in the realm of business judgment.[11] See also Johnson v. Trueblood, 629 F.2d 287, 292–

---

[11] This is a subject of intense debate among practicing members of the bar and legal scholars. Excellent examples of these contending views are: Block & Miller, The Responsibilities and Obligations of Corporate Directors in Takeover Contests, 11 Sec. Reg. L.J. 44 (1983); Easterbrook & Fischel, Takeover Bids, Defensive Tactics, and Shareholders' Welfare, 36 Bus.

293 (3d Cir.1980). There are, however, certain caveats to a proper exercise of this function. Because of the omnipresent specter that a board may be acting primarily in its own interests, rather than those of the corporation and its shareholders, there is an enhanced duty which calls for judicial examination at the threshold before the protections of the business judgment rule may be conferred.

This Court has long recognized that:

> We must bear in mind the inherent danger in the purchase of shares with corporate funds to remove a threat to corporate policy when a threat to control is involved. The directors are of necessity confronted with a conflict of interest, and an objective decision is difficult.

Bennett v. Propp, Del. Supr., 41 Del.Ch. 14, 187 A.2d 405, 409 (1962). In the face of this inherent conflict directors must show that they had reasonable grounds for believing that a danger to corporate policy and effectiveness existed because of another person's stock ownership. Cheff v. Mathes, 199 A.2d at 554–55. However, they satisfy that burden "by showing good faith and reasonable investigation. . . ." *Id.* at 555. Furthermore, such proof is materially enhanced, as here, by the approval of a board comprised of a majority of outside independent directors who have acted in accordance with the foregoing standards.

IV.

A.

In the board's exercise of corporate power to forestall a takeover bid our analysis begins with the basic principle that corporate directors have a fiduciary duty to act in the best interests of the corporation's stockholders. As we have noted, their duty of care extends to protecting the corporation and its owners from perceived harm whether a threat originates from third parties or other shareholders. But such powers are not absolute. A corporation does not have unbridled discretion to defeat any perceived threat by any Draconian means available.

The restriction placed upon a selective stock repurchase is that the directors may not have acted solely or primarily out of a desire to perpetuate themselves in office. See Cheff v. Mathes, 199 A.2d at 556; Kors v. Carey, 158 A.2d at 140. Of course, to this is added the further caveat that inequitable action may not be taken under the guise of law. Schnell v. Chris-Craft Industries, Inc., Del. Supr., 285 A.2d 437, 439 (1971). The standard of proof established in Cheff v. Mathes . . . is designed to ensure that a defensive measure to thwart or impede a takeover is indeed motivated by a good faith concern for the welfare of

---

Law. 1733 (1981); Easterbrook & Fischel, The Proper Role of a Target's Management In Responding to a Tender Offer, 94 Harv. L. Rev. 1161 (1981). Herzel, Schmidt & Davis, Why Corporate Directors Have a Right To Resist Tender Offers, 3 Corp. L. Rev. 107 (1980); Lipton, Takeover Bids in the Target's Boardroom, 35 Bus. Law. 101 (1979).

the corporation and its stockholders, which in all circumstances must be free of any fraud or other misconduct. However, this does not end the inquiry.

B.

A further aspect is the element of balance. If a defensive measure is to come within the ambit of the business judgment rule, it must be reasonable in relation to the threat posed. This entails an analysis by the directors of the nature of the takeover bid and its effect on the corporate enterprise. Examples of such concerns may include: inadequacy of the price offered, nature and timing of the offer, questions of illegality, the impact on "constituencies" other than shareholders (i.e., creditors, customers, employees, and perhaps even the community generally), the risk of nonconsummation, and the quality of securities being offered in the exchange. See Lipton and Brownstein, Takeover Responses and Directors' Responsibilities: An Update, p.7, ABA National Institute on the Dynamics of Corporate Control (December 8, 1983). While not a controlling factor, it also seems to us that a board may reasonably consider the basic stockholder interests at stake, including those of short term speculators, whose actions may have fueled the coercive aspect of the offer at the expense of the long term investor. Here, the threat posed was viewed by the Unocal board as a grossly inadequate two-tier coercive tender offer coupled with the threat of greenmail.

Specifically, the Unocal directors had concluded that the value of Unocal was substantially above the $54 per share offered in cash at the front end. Furthermore, they determined that the subordinated securities to be exchanged in Mesa's announced squeeze out of the remaining shareholders in the "back-end" merger were "junk bonds" worth far less than $54. It is now well recognized that such offers are a classic coercive measure designed to stampede shareholders into tendering at the first tier, even if the price is inadequate, out of fear of what they will receive at the back end of the transaction. Wholly beyond the coercive aspect of an inadequate two-tier tender offer, the threat was posed by a corporate raider with a national reputation as a "greenmailer".[15]

In adopting the selective exchange offer, the board stated that its objective was either to defeat the inadequate Mesa offer or, should the offer still succeed, provide the 49% of its stockholders, who would otherwise be forced to accept "junk bonds", with $72 worth of senior debt. We find that both purposes are valid.

---

[15] The term "greenmail" refers to the practice of buying out a takeover bidder's stock at a premium that is not available to other shareholders in order to prevent the takeover. The Chancery Court noted that "Mesa has made tremendous profits from its takeover activities although in the past few years it has not been successful in acquiring any of the target companies on an unfriendly basis." Moreover, the trial court specifically found that the actions of the Unocal board were taken in good faith to eliminate both the inadequacies of the tender offer and to forestall the payment of "greenmail".

However, such efforts would have been thwarted by Mesa's participation in the exchange offer. First, if Mesa could tender its shares, Unocal would effectively be subsidizing the former's continuing effort to buy Unocal stock at $54 per share. Second, Mesa could not, by definition, fit within the class of shareholders being protected from its own coercive and inadequate tender offer.

Thus, we are satisfied that the selective exchange offer is reasonably related to the threats posed. It is consistent with the principle that "the minority stockholder shall receive the substantial equivalent in value of what he had before." Sterling v. Mayflower Hotel Corp., Del. Supr., 33 Del.Ch. 293, 93 A.2d 107, 114 (1952). See also Rosenblatt v. Getty Oil Co., Del. Supr., 493 A.2d 929, 940 (1985). This concept of fairness, while stated in the merger context, is also relevant in the area of tender offer law. Thus, the board's decision to offer what it determined to be the fair value of the corporation to the 49% of its shareholders, who would otherwise be forced to accept highly subordinated "junk bonds", is reasonable and consistent with the directors' duty to ensure that the minority stockholders receive equal value for their shares.

V.

Mesa contends that it is unlawful, and the trial court agreed, for a corporation to discriminate in this fashion against one shareholder. It argues correctly that no case has ever sanctioned a device that precludes a raider from sharing in a benefit available to all other stockholders. However, as we have noted earlier, the principle of selective stock repurchases by a Delaware corporation is neither unknown nor unauthorized. The only difference is that heretofore the approved transaction was the payment of "greenmail" to a raider or dissident posing a threat to the corporate enterprise. All other stockholders were denied such favored treatment, and given Mesa's past history of greenmail, its claims here are rather ironic.

* * *

Thus, while the exchange offer is a form of selective treatment, given the nature of the threat posed here the response is neither unlawful nor unreasonable. If the board of directors is disinterested, has acted in good faith and with due care, its decision in the absence of an abuse of discretion will be upheld as a proper exercise of business judgment.

* * *

Mesa also argues that the exclusion permits the directors to abdicate the fiduciary duties they owe it. However, that is not so. The board continues to owe Mesa the duties of due care and loyalty. But in the face of the destructive threat Mesa's tender offer was perceived to pose, the board had a supervening duty to protect the corporate enterprise, which includes the other shareholders, from threatened harm.

Mesa contends that the basis of this action is punitive, and solely in response to the exercise of its rights of corporate democracy.[16] Nothing precludes Mesa, as a stockholder, from acting in its own self-interest. However, Mesa, while pursuing its own interests, has acted in a manner which a board consisting of a majority of independent directors has reasonably determined to be contrary to the best interests of Unocal and its other shareholders. In this situation, there is no support in Delaware law for the proposition that, when responding to a perceived harm, a corporation must guarantee a benefit to a stockholder who is deliberately provoking the danger being addressed. There is no obligation of self-sacrifice by a corporation and its shareholders in the face of such a challenge.

Here, the Court of Chancery specifically found that the "directors' decision [to oppose the Mesa tender offer] was made in the good faith belief that the Mesa tender offer is inadequate." Given our standard of review under Levitt v. Bouvier, Del. Supr., 287 A.2d 671, 673 (1972), and Application of Delaware Racing Association, Del. Supr., 42 Del.Ch. 406, 213 A.2d 203, 207 (1965), we are satisfied that Unocal's board has met its burden of proof. Cheff v. Mathes, 199 A.2d at 555.

VI.

In conclusion, there was directorial power to oppose the Mesa tender offer, and to undertake a selective stock exchange made in good faith and upon a reasonable investigation pursuant to a clear duty to protect the corporate enterprise. Further, the selective stock repurchase plan chosen by Unocal is reasonable in relation to the threat that the board rationally and reasonably believed was posed by Mesa's inadequate and coercive two-tier tender offer. Under those circumstances the board's action is entitled to be measured by the standards of the business judgment rule. Thus, unless it is shown by a preponderance of the evidence that the directors' decisions were primarily based on perpetuating themselves in office, or some other breach of fiduciary duty such as fraud, overreaching, lack of good faith, or being uninformed, a Court will not substitute its judgment for that of the board.

In this case that protection is not lost merely because Unocal's directors have tendered their shares in the exchange offer. Given the validity of the Mesa exclusion, they are receiving a benefit shared generally by all other stockholders except Mesa. In this circumstance the test of Aronson v. Lewis, 473 A.2d at 812, is satisfied. See also Cheff v. Mathes, 199 A.2d at 554. If the stockholders are displeased with the

---

[16] This seems to be the underlying basis of the trial court's principal reliance on the unreported Chancery decision of Fisher v. Moltz, Del.Ch. No. 6068 (1979), published in 5 Del. J. Corp. L. 530 (1980). However, the facts in Fisher are thoroughly distinguishable. There, a corporation offered to repurchase the shares of its former employees, except those of the plaintiffs, merely because the latter were then engaged in lawful competition with the company. No threat to the enterprise was posed, and at best it can be said that the exclusion was motivated by pique instead of a rational corporate purpose.

action of their elected representatives, the powers of corporate democracy are at their disposal to turn the board out. Aronson v. Lewis, Del. Supr., 473 A.2d 805, 811 (1984). See also 8 Del. C. §§ 141(k) and 211(b).

With the Court of Chancery's findings that the exchange offer was based on the board's good faith belief that the Mesa offer was inadequate, that the board's action was informed and taken with due care, that Mesa's prior activities justify a reasonable inference that its principle objective was greenmail, and implicitly, that the substance of the offer itself was reasonable and fair to the corporation and its stockholders if Mesa were included, we cannot say that the Unocal directors have acted in such a manner as to have passed an "unintelligent and unadvised judgment". Mitchell v. Highland-Western Glass Co., Del.Ch., 19 Del.Ch. 326, 167 A. 831, 833 (1933). The decision of the Court of Chancery is therefore REVERSED, and the preliminary injunction is VACATED.

QUESTIONS

1. What evidence did the board have that Unocal's stock was worth as much as $72? Note that the investment bankers only opined that it was worth more than $60 in a sale or orderly liquidation. Was this an informed business judgment of the kind the court seems to require?

2. What basis could investment bankers have for asserting that a bid above the previous market value for the company was inadequate? Do the readings in chapter 2 provide suggestions?

3. If management employed the investment bankers, is the board entitled to rely on their complete loyalty to the shareholders rather than to management? There are numerous examples of these difficulties. In one merger transaction, an investment banker lowered its estimate of the value of the target and raised its estimate of the value of a bid to justify an exchange ratio. In re Triton Group Ltd. Shareholders Litigation, [1990–91 Decisions] FED. SEC. L. REP. (CCH) ¶ 95,876 (Del.Ch.1991). In a recapitalization transaction the market price of the stock quickly exceeded the investment banker's estimate of fairness, which required an increase in the cash payment to shareholders from $70 to $80. FMC Corp. v. Boesky, 727 F.Supp. 1182, 1186–87 (N. D. Ill.1989). In another case an investment banker added $5 per share to the value of a management recapitalization when a hostile bidder raised its bid. Black & Decker Corp. v. American Standard, Inc., 682 F.Supp. 772, 774–78 (D. Del.1988). In a hostile takeover setting an investment banker set the value of a target at $45 per share to justify resistance, yet reduced its valuation to $38.50 a year later to demonstrate the fairness of a friendly acquisition. Beebe v. Pacific Realty Trust, 578 F.Supp. 1128 (D. Ore.1984). In one famous case investment bankers predicted future prices of $159 to $247 for Time-Warner Communications, when actual prices for the period ranged from $72 to $125, with a closing price of $87.75. Paramount Communications Inc. v. Time Inc., [1989 Decisions]

FED. SEC. L. REP. (CCH) ¶ 94,514, at 93,273 (Del.Ch.), affirmed, 571 A.2d 1140 (Del.1989).

4.   If Mesa's offer of less than $54 for the back end "takeout" merger made the $54 cash tender offer coercive, is Unocal's offer of $72 coercive, if the remaining shares will be worth less than $72? Michael Jensen reported the market value of the remaining Unocal shares was only $35. Michael C. Jensen, When Unocal Won over Pickens, Shareholders and Society Lost, IX, No. 11, Financier 50, 51 (Nov., 1985).

5.   How fair was Unocal's self-tender to those shareholders who did not tender their shares? Michael Jensen reported that holders of 20 million Unocal shares (other than Mesa) suffered total losses of $382 million, based on the difference between $72 and the post-offer stock price of approximately $35, in addition to the loss of $167 million from being denied $54 for all their shares, either in cash or debt securities. Jensen, When Unocal Won Over Pickens, Shareholders and Society Lost, IX, No. 11 FINANCIER 50, 51 (1985).

6.   Is this test more restrictive than that of Cheff v. Mathes, Johnson v. Trueblood, and Panter v. Marshall Field? If so, in what way? Will it make a difference in court?

NOTE

Michael Jensen reported that Unocal's restructuring through its repurchase and issuance of $4.2 billion of debt increased the total value of Unocal to its shareholders by $2.1 billion. Nevertheless, he calculated that this was $1.1 billion less than Unocal shareholders would have received had Mesa been successful (assuming that its debt securities issued in the second stage merger were actually worth $54). Michael C. Jensen, When Unocal Won over Pickens, Shareholders and Society Lost, IX, No. 11, FINANCIER 50 (Nov., 1985). Unocal paid out 59% of its pre-takeover bid equity to shareholders in this restructuring. Mesa would have lost $248 million in this transaction. Rather than suffer the loss, Mesa settled with Unocal by agreeing to resell part of its shares to Unocal at the $72 price (which meant terminating the exclusion in the original bid) in exchange for a 25-year standstill agreement, a promise to vote its remaining Unocal shares in the same proportion as other shares are voted, and constraints on Mesa's rights to sell its remaining shares.

A year later Chancellor Allen faced a similar situation in AC Acquisitions Corp. v. Anderson, Clayton & Co., 519 A.2d 103 (Del.Ch. 1986), infra Part 2.F of this chapter, where a joint venture ("BS/G") made an uninvited bid of $56 cash for any and all shares, with a takeout merger at the same price. Anderson, Clayton then announced a self-tender offer for 60% of its stock at $60 cash, which meant, according to Anderson, Clayton's advisers, that the remaining shares would be valued at between $22 and $31 by one investment bank, and between $37 and $52 by a second investment bank. Chancellor Allen concluded this defense was not a reasonable one in relation to the threat posed, stating:

"I conclude as a factual matter for purposes of this motion that no rational shareholder could afford not to tender into the Company's self-tender offer at least if that transaction is viewed in isolation. The record is uncontradicted that the value of the Company's stock following the effectuation of the Company Transaction will be materially less than $60 per share. The various experts differ only on how much less. Shearson, Lehman opines that the Company's stock will likely trade in a range of $22–$31 per share after consummation of the Company Transaction. First Boston is more hopeful, informally projecting a range of $37–52. What is clear under either view, however, is that a current shareholder who elects not to tender into the self-tender is very likely, upon consummation of the Company Transaction, to experience a substantial loss in market value of his holdings. The only way, within the confines of the Company Transaction, that a shareholder can protect himself from such an immediate financial loss, is to tender into the self-tender so that he receives his pro rata share of the cash distribution that will, in part, cause the expected fall in the market price of the Company's stock.[1]

"I conclude that an Anderson, Clayton stockholder, acting with economic rationality, has no effective choice as between the contending offers as presently constituted. Even if a shareholder would prefer to sell all of his or her holdings at $56 per share in the BS/G offer, he or she may not risk tendering into that proposal and thereby risk being frozen out of the front end of the Company Transaction, should the BS/G offer not close."

Shortly after Unocal the Securities Exchange Commission promulgated Rule 14d–10, the so-called "all holders" rule. Subsection (a) provides that no bidder (including a company bidding for its own shares) shall make a tender offer unless the offer is open to all security holders of the class that is the subject of the tender offer, and requires all members of the class to receive the highest consideration paid to any other security holder during the tender offer.

The decision in Unocal, was important for Unocal because it effectively killed Mesa's hostile takeover attempt. Mesa Corp., as the court pointed out in its first footnote, was headed by famed raider, T. Boone Pickens. With the rise of leveraged buyouts in the early 80's, funded by Michael Millken's junk bond group at Drexel, Burnham & Lambert, Pickens became a menacing force in the world of takeovers. In 1982, he attempted to acquire Cities Service Company of Tulsa, Oklahoma, a company more than twenty times the size of Mesa. Although Pickens lost the battle for control, Mesa was still able to profit by over $30 million after it sold its stock holdings in the company. In 1984, Pickens and his investors pulled off a major coup, pocketing $760 million off the SoCal-Gulf Oil merger after Pickens refused a

---

[1]   As a matter of fairly rudimentary economics it can readily be seen that a self-tender, being for less than all shares, can always be made at a price higher than the highest rational price that can be offered for all of the enterprises stock. See Bradley and Rosenzweig, Defensive Stock Repurchases, 99 Harv. L. Rev. 1378 (May, 1986).

greenmail offer from Gulf Oil's board. These were just some of the many of plays that Pickens made in the early 1980's.

NOTE ON WILLIAMS V. GEIER

671 A.2d 1368 (Del.1996).

Cincinnati Milacron was a machine tool manufacturer with a significant but not majority block of shares held by members of the founding Geier family. When coupled with the employee benefit plans of the company, these holdings amounted to over 50% of the outstanding common stock. (The trustee of the benefit plans had announced his intent to vote for the amendment described below, with respect to the unallocated shares, and the court assumed that former employees with the right to direct the voting of their own shares would also support management).* On advice of investment bankers, the board of Milacron recommended an amendment of the articles of incorporation to adopt a "tenured voting plan" (sometimes called a dual class voting plan), under which all shares would be granted ten votes per share, but upon sale or other transfer these shares would only be entitled to one vote per share. If transferred shares were held for 36 consecutive months, they regained their full voting rights. The shareholders, after what the court held was full and candid disclosure of the antitakeover effects of such a plan, approved adoption of this amendment by the requisite majority. Of the shares not controlled by the Geier family, most of those voting approved the amendment, but the shares voting "no," when coupled with the non-voting shares, exceeded those unaffiliated shares voting "yes."

The plaintiff, Williams, attacked the amendment as a management entrenchment device, and argued that the defendants were subject to the strict standard of review of Unocal. The Delaware Supreme Court rejected this, judging the directors' actions under the Business Judgment Rule, stating:

"A Unocal analysis should be used only when a board unilaterally (i.e., without stockholder approval) adopts defensive measures in reaction to a perceived threat. Unocal, 493 A.2d at 954–55. Unocal is a landmark innovation of the dynamic takeover era of the 1980s. It has stood the test of time, and was recently explicated by this Court in Unitrin, Inc. v. American General Corp., Del. Supr., 651 A.2d 1361 (1995). Yet, it is inapplicable here because there was no unilateral board action." 671 A.2d at 1377.

---

* Employee benefit plans that invest primarily in the employer's stock are called "Employee Stock Ownership Plans," or "ESOPs." Where an ESOP borrows funds to purchase the employer's stock, which loan is typically guaranteed by the employer, it is called a "leveraged ESOP." In these circumstances the employer promises to make annual cash contributions to the ESOP sufficient to allow it to repay the loan. At the same time, shares held by the ESOP vest annually in the individual accounts of employees, who then have the right to direct the voting of their vested shares. Subject to the terms of the ESOP plan, the trustee has the power to vote any shares not yet allocated to individual employees. If the trustee is controlled by management, this can enhance management's voting power. Prior to reforms in the Internal Revenue Code, leveraged ESOPs were a popular takeover defense tool in the 1980s. They are discussed in more detail in Part 2.F of this chapter, following AC Acquisitions Corp. v. Anderson, Clayton & Co..

QUESTIONS

1. What would persuade you, as a shareholder, to vote for a plan that would assure a controlling family group or a management team sufficient votes to defeat any uninvited bidders' attempts to purchase the corporation's shares?

2. If shareholder approval relieves directors from the heightened scrutiny of the Unocal test, what conditions should be imposed on the shareholder vote to assure its integrity? Were these conditions present in this case?

3. In Fliegler v. Lawrence, 361 A.2d 218 (1976), the Delaware Supreme Court rejected the defendants' argument that a conflicting interest transaction was appropriately ratified by shareholders when it was not proven that a majority of the disinterested shareholders approved the transaction. This is consistent with the requirements of Model Business Corporation Act § 8.63. Does Williams v. Geier adopt a more relaxed standard? Can you think of any reasons why the standard should be more relaxed?

NOTE ON STANDARDS OF REVIEW OUTSIDE DELAWARE

Two months after Unocal was decided the previous Delaware standard of review, described in Johnson v. Trueblood, 629 F.2d 287 (3d Cir. 1980), in Part 2.A of this chapter, was employed to review the actions of directors of a New York corporation, without citation to either Unocal or Johnson v. Trueblood. Turner Broadcasting System, Inc. v. CBS, Inc., 627 F.Supp. 901, 910 (N.D. Ga. 1985). Another decision by the same court applied the business judgment rule to the actions of directors of a Georgia corporation that rejected one bid in favor of another transaction. Bonner v. Law Companies Group, Inc., 964 F.Supp. 341, 343 (N.D. Ga. 1997). The Arkansas Supreme Court cited Unocal in a case that ultimately involved self-dealing by the defendant director—officers, but did not apply its standard of review. Hall v. Staha, 858 S.W.2d 672 (Ark. 1993). Kansas has copied the Delaware statute, so it is not entirely surprising that its courts would follow Unocal. In Burcham v. Unison Bancorp, Inc., 77 P.3d 130 (Kan. 2003), the Kansas Supreme Court reviewed the criticisms and commentary about the Unocal rule before applying it. The court stated: "In addition, we note that despite criticism from outside sources, the Delaware courts, and with rare exceptions other jurisdictions, have continued to apply the Unocal test for over 20 years in a variety of fact patterns. A significant body of case law has developed. As our Court of Appeals has noted, 'Kansas follows Delaware's basic principles regarding application of the business judgment rule to insulate board decisions from attack.' Consequently, we adopt the Unocal test as refined by its progeny." 77 P.3d at 149.

B. CONTRACTING FOR LOYALTY

Studies have shown that when there is a change of control at a corporation, over 50% of top managers of the acquired corporation will no longer be employed by it within three years of the change of control.* This job loss is traumatic on several counts. First, it entails loss of a lucrative position, which will be extremely difficult for many senior executives to replace, given the relatively small number of high-level corporate positions and the numerous candidates for them, including those within the firm looking for promotion and those who might be recruited from other firms, as well as displaced executives. Second, expectations of gains from stock options are often disappointed. Stock options normally have a ten-year life, so an employee holding an option can look forward, hopefully, to a long period of growth in the value of the company's stock before exercise. But when a corporation is acquired, many option plans provide that these options are cashed out at the acquisition price, which may cut off years of expected gains. Finally, there are the psychic losses from being terminated. One who is accustomed to command of a large enterprise is often treated well in other settings as a result of that position—by being asked to serve on boards of universities, symphonies, and other organizations, where the executive rubbed elbows with similarly powerful individuals. All of this is likely to disappear with termination. It is small wonder that the author once heard an executive say, "any bidder who wants my job is a hostile bidder." Indeed, as soon as a management team learns that its firm might be vulnerable to a takeover bid, it would not be surprising if some executives began circulating their resumes.

The 1980s saw the development of compensation plans designed to respond to the loyalty problems created by changes of control. They went by various names, management retention agreements, severance agreements, evergreen employment contracts, and, most invidiously, "golden parachutes." The most common form of plan provided that if a manager were terminated without cause after a change of control, the

---

*   One study found that approximately 52% of all top managers will no longer be employed by a target three years after a successful takeover. Perham, Surge in Executive Job Contracts, 32 Dun's Bus. Month 86 (1981). In another study, Jarrell, in The Wealth Effects of Litigation by Targets: Do Interests Diverge in a Merge?, 28 J. Law & Econ. 151, 172 (1985) found 50% attrition rates in one-half of the firms that successfully defeated bids. This figure, he believes, is well above the normal turnover rate of 25%, suggesting that bids are traumatic events for managers regardless of their success. See also Turnover at the Top, Bus. Week, Dec. 19, 1983, at 104; Coff, Merger Mania Adds to Executive Woes, N. Y. Times, Oct. 17, 1982, p. 12. Knoeber, Golden Parachutes, Shark Repellents, and Hostile Tender Offers, 76 Am. Econ. Rev. 155 (1986) Knoeber characterized managers as accepting deferred compensation in many instances, which shareholders can opportunistically capture by accepting a tender offer for control. See also Lambert & Larker, Golden Parachutes, Executive Decision-Making and Shareholder Wealth, 7 J. Acctg. & Econ. 179 (1985). Displacement after a change of control appears to be one of the major risks facing managers. A Business Week survey of 1300 terminated managers was reported to have shown that nearly one-third were terminated after a change of control. Walkling & Long, Strategic Issues in Cash Tender Offers: Predicting Bid Premiums, Probability of Success, and Target Management's response, 4, No. 2 Midland Corp. Fin.J. 57, 64, n.10 (1986).

company or its successor would pay a sum equal to a multiple of the executive's current income upon severance. Recognizing that a new owner might try to evade this benefit, the plans also provided that after a change of control a top executive could voluntarily resign and collect the benefits, if certain conditions were met, such as demotion, relocation, or similar changes that could be seen as an attempt to force the executive out. Note that these payments could be obtained only after a change of control, which had the effect of keeping the executive in office until that event, which led to the name "management retention contract." Another form of agreement that achieved the same result was the "evergreen" employment contract. This involved a multi-year employment agreement with the executive, which was automatically renewed annually, so that it always had the same number of years left. Either party could, of course, give notice of non-renewal, which would lead to the expiration of the term eventually. The result was essentially the same as the severance agreement, since a new owner would have to compensate the executive for the remaining years on termination. Recognizing that new owners might not accept these obligations gladly, but might attempt to escape the obligation by claiming that they were given for no new value, and thus constituted waste, many of these agreements also provided that if the executive had to sue to recover the promised payments, the employer would be liable for the terminated executive's attorney's fees.

Parachute payments have been restricted by punitive taxation in the Internal Revenue Code,* apparently on the basis that contracts for severance pay are simply a form of agents' opportunism.** Because of the large size of severance payments, they were vulnerable to politicians seeking headlines.*** Section 280G of the Internal Revenue Code of 1986 provides for punitive treatment of certain golden parachute payments. "excess parachute payments"—those in excess of three year's compensation for an executive—are likely to be denied a deduction for the employer. The employer can avoid the loss of the deduction if it is able to prove that the payments are reasonable. Further, excess parachute payments are subject to a 20% excise tax when received by the employee. Internal Revenue Code, § 4999(a).

Congress is said to have two motives for adoption of these provisions: it was concerned both that the existence of costly golden parachute contracts created a barrier to takeovers (highly unlikely given the small percentage of total costs represented by these payments) and that the prospect of high payments might encourage management to seek a takeover not in the shareholders' best interests. Susan J. Stabile, Is

---

*   Internal Revenue Code of 1954, § 280G, as amended by Tax Reform Act of 1984, Pub. L. No. 98–369, § 67, 98 Stat. 494 (1984).

**   See generally Executive Compensation: A 1987 Road Map for the Corporate Advisor, 43 Bus. Law. 185, 370–387 (1987).

***   Jensen, in [The] Takeover Controversy: Analysis and Evidence, 4, No. 2 Midland Corp. Fin. J. 6, 23 (1986), kindly states that these contracts have "been vastly misunderstood."

There a Role for Tax law in Policing Executive Compensation?, 72 St. John's L. Rev. 81, 90, n. 35 (1998). This argument is also made by Ronald J. Gilson in Value Creation by Business Lawyers: Legal Skills and Asset Pricing, 94 Yale L.J. 239, 285, n. 114 (1984). Perhaps more significantly, Stabile raises questions about the effectiveness of this law in changing corporate behavior:

"The amount executives have received under golden parachute agreements in the years since the enactment of section 280G provides the ultimate evidence of the limited effect of the statute. As an illustration, the leveraged buyout of RJR Nabisco in 1988 resulted in golden parachute payments of $53,800,000 to Chief Executive Officer F. Ross Johnson, $45,700,000 to Vice Chairman E. A. Horrigan, and $18,200,000 to Executive Vice President John D. Martin.[2] In the same year, the takeover of Primerica by Commercial Credit resulted in golden parachute payments of $46,800,000 to Primerica's Chairman, Gerald Tsai, Jr., and $18,400,000 to its President, Kenneth A. Yarnell.[3]

"There is evidence that not only have many corporations foregone the deduction, but a number have also added a 'gross up' to the compensation paid to executives to take account of the tax imposed by section 280G; that is, they increase the payment made by an amount equal to the taxes that the executive will be required to pay.[4] Thus, instead of eliminating or minimizing golden parachutes, the effect of the tax imposed by section 280G is to make such payments more expensive to the corporations. Therefore, neither with respect to ordinary compensation nor with respect to compensation contingent on a change in control has the Code proven a very meaningful curb on executive compensation.[5]"

---

[2]   See Kevin Phillips, The Politics of Rich and Poor 182 (1991).

[3]   See id.

[4]   See Tate & Lyle v. Staley Continental, Inc., No. CIV. A. 9813, 1988 WL 46064, at *3 (Del.Ch. May 9, 1988) (discussing tax "gross-ups" with the effect of compensating parachute beneficiaries for the federal excise tax and adding $13.8 million in cost to the corporation); Brownstein & Panner, supra note 4, at 34; Martin, supra note 39, at 246 (asserting that there is "no reason to expect that corporations would be unwilling to forego the corporate deduction and increase the payment to corporate officers to offset the excise tax"); Ellen E. Schultz, More-Equal Benefits Go to Some Top Executives, Wall St. J., May 25, 1993, at C1, C17 (stating that companies will restore lost benefits when government puts limits on executive compensation).

[5]   There are several other tax code provisions that have some effect on compensation paid to executives. With respect to pensions, there are limits on the amount of a pension benefit which can be provided to executives under tax-qualified pension plans. The Code limits how much compensation will be considered for purposes of calculating pension benefits, how many benefits may be paid by pension plans and how much executives can save for retirement on a tax-deferred basis. See 26 U.S.C. 415(b) (1994) (imposing limits on contributions to and benefits paid by pension plans); id. 402(g) (imposing limits on elective deferrals an individual can exclude from gross income in any year); id. 401(a)(17) (limiting how much compensation can be considered in the calculation of pension benefits). Additionally, the Code limits the amount of incentive stock options, those which receive favorable tax treatment, that can be exercised in any one year. See 26 U.S.C. 422(d). Although these provisions will have an effect on the individual components of executive compensation, they are not likely to affect the overall level of compensation.

In addition to assuring against management departures during an acquisition, golden parachutes can serve the more important purpose of aligning management's interest with that of the shareholders, in deciding whether the corporation should resist a bid altogether, or simply try to raise the bid price or start an auction. A manager who is fully insured against job loss through a change in control will be more likely to consider maximizing shareholder value. A manager holding a large portion of his or her personal wealth in the form of stock, options to purchase stock, and related benefits, will be more likely to think like a shareholder. Empirical studies support these assertions. First, event studies have shown that stock prices rise when firms adopt Golden parachutes. Lambert & Larcker, *Golden Parachutes, Executive Decision-Making and Shareholders' Wealth*, 7 J. Acct. & Econ. 179 (1985) Second, executives who did not contest tender offers stood to gain 8.2 times their annual salary from a successful bid, while those who contested such offers stood to gain only 1.9 times their annual salary. Walkling & Long, *Strategic Issues in Cash Tender Offers: Predicting Bid Premiums, Probability of Success, and Target Management's Response*, 4, No. 2 Midland Corp. Fin. J. 57, 63–64 (1986); see also Walkling & Long, *Agency Theory, Managerial Welfare, and Takeover Bid Resistance*, 15 Rand J. Econ. 54 (1984).

The following cases take diametrically opposed positions on golden parachutes granted under similar conditions.

Gaillard v. Natomas Company

208 Cal.App.3d 1250; 256 Cal.Rptr. 702 (1989).

■ STRANKMAN, ASSOCIATE JUSTICE.

I

Statement of the Case

These shareholder derivative actions arise from the merger of Natomas Company (Natomas) into Diamond Shamrock Corporation (Diamond), effective August 31, 1983. By their complaints, appellant Tilly Gaillard, a common stockholder of Natomas, and appellant Vincent J. Ashton, a common stockholder of Diamond, challenge the purported "golden parachute" agreements and other benefits provided for five inside directors of Natomas as part of the merger.

Golden parachutes are special termination agreements that shelter executives from the effects of a corporate takeover. Their emergence has been attributed to the dramatic increase in the size of corporate takeovers and the volume of hostile takeovers. Typically, golden parachutes provide senior executives who are dismissed or who, under certain circumstances, resign as a result of a takeover with either continued compensation for a specified period following the executives' departure or with a lump-sum payment. The legality and desirability of this form of executive compensation, which some view as a form of corporate looting, have been the subject of increasing controversy faced by courts and addressed by legal commentators.

Defendants and respondents, who consist of the five inside directors and the twelve outside directors of Natomas at the time of the merger, contend that the golden parachute agreements and other benefits here are protected by California's "business judgment rule," codified in Corporations Code section 309. The trial court agreed with respondents, granted summary judgment in their favor (Code Civ. Proc., § 437c), and dismissed the actions.

We conclude that the business judgment rule does not apply to a judicial review of the conduct of the inside directors, and reverse as to these respondents. We further conclude that, while the business judgment rule applies to the outside directors, there are triable issues of fact as to whether the adoption of the golden parachute agreements constituted a proper exercise of these respondents' "business judgment," and reverse.

II

Facts

A.   *Tender offer and merger negotiations.* In 1983, Natomas was a publicly held California corporation engaged in petroleum and geothermal exploration and production, domestic coal mining, shipping, and real estate. The bulk of its 1982 operating income derived from its Indonesia operations. Natomas's total gross revenues in 1982 were approximately $1.7 billion with assets valued at approximately $2.8 billion. Net income in 1982 was approximately $44 million.

At that time, the Natomas board of directors consisted of the 12 outside directors and Natomas's five principal officers. The 5 officers were respondent Commons, the chairman of the board and chief executive officer; respondent Lee, a vice-president; respondent Reed, the vice-chairman; respondent Seidl, a vice-president and president of Natomas's domestic oil production subsidiary; and respondent Seaton, president and chief operating officer.

Each of the 12 outside directors had a business career independent of Natomas. Most of them had served as a president, vice-president, director, or some similar position for corporate and banking institutions in the past, and many continued to hold such positions. In total, they owned or held an interest in approximately 15 percent of the Natomas common stock.

In May 1983, Diamond initiated a hostile tender offer to acquire 51 percent of Natomas's common stock at $23 per share. Diamond stated in the tender offer that it intended to acquire the remaining shares of Natomas common stock in a later merger in which Natomas stock would be converted into the stock of New Diamond Corporation (the holding company formed for the purpose of merger). After considering various alternative responses to the tender offer, Natomas representatives agreed to meet with Diamond representatives on May 29, 1983.

[Commons, Natomas' CEO, first directed the Compensation Committee of Natomas' board to meet on May 30 to discuss golden parachutes. On May 29, Commons and Bricker, Diamond's CEO, reached agreement on terms of a friendly takeover. After the terms were set, Natomas management met to discuss golden parachutes, and then Commons met with Bricker, and discussed them. Either that day or the following day, Bricker approved the idea, because he wanted everyone to support the deal. Commons instructed Joseph Flom, their attorney advising on the transaction, to draft golden parachutes for the top executives.

On May 30, Flom presented the parachute terms to the Compensation Committee: senior executives could leave their employment during first six months after a change of control for "good reason," and thereafter for any reason, and collect five years' compensation. (This sum would be reduced for time spent on job after 1st 6 months.) (Commons already had a 3–year parachute.)

The Compensation Committee, which was composed of 5 outside directors heard Flom's report.] Flom then discussed the substance of the proposed employment agreements, and Leskin distributed a summary of the material terms. Flom stated that a concern of the directors should be that "management is clearly in place" upon the consummation of the merger, and that the proposed agreements would ensure continuity in management. Flom also stated that the terms of the agreements, as summarized, were acceptable to Bricker of Diamond and that Bricker wanted Natomas's confirmation of the agreements. [The committee approved their terms at the close of a two hour meeting, stating that it was relying on Mr. Flom.

* * *

Later on May 30 the full board considered the parachutes] The Natomas officers present, including Commons, then left and Flom spoke to the board. He stated that in mergers, it was common to adopt arrangements to ensure continuity of management and provide economic protection for those key employees who might be affected. The board meeting minutes reflect that Flom represented that Diamond had agreed that the key Natomas employees should be provided employment arrangements to serve these purposes. Leskin then reviewed for the board the basic terms of the employment agreements.

At the conclusion of the meeting, the board approved the proposed plan and agreement of reorganization to implement the merger, and further approved the amended employment agreements as proposed.

[Prior to the merger Diamond had reached agreement with Natomas that one of its employees, McDoulett, would become the Chief Operating Officer of Natomas. But immediately after shareholder approval of the merger, the Natomas board met and elected one of its own, Reed, as COO. This started a period of difficulties, and Bricker, CEO of Diamond, described this as starting a period of difficulties, which led to an understanding that perhaps the operating philosophies of Natomas and Diamond were so different that they could not work together. Within several months, but well within the first six months, all four key Natomas executives subject to the severance agreements resigned shortly after merger, and were paid approximately $10 million.]

F. *Allegations of complaints.* The first amended complaint of Tilly Gaillard for damages alleges that the adoption and implementation of the golden parachute agreements and the consulting agreement constituted a breach of fiduciary duty by all 19 directors of Natomas, waste and mismanagement, negligence, and conversion. The third amended complaint of Vincent J. Ashton for damages alleges an abdication and breach of the directors' fiduciary duties.

III

Business Judgment Rule

The common law "business judgment rule" refers to a judicial policy of deference to the business judgment of corporate directors in the exercise of their broad discretion in making corporate decisions. The business judgment rule is premised on the notion that those to whom the management of the corporation has been entrusted, and not the courts, are best able to judge whether a particular act or transaction is one which is " . . . helpful to the conduct of corporate affairs or expedient for the attainment of corporate purposes . . . ," and establishes a presumption that directors' decisions are based on sound business judgment. Under this rule, a director is not liable for a mistake in business judgment which is made in good faith and in what he or she believes to be the best interests of the corporation, where no conflict of interest exists.

Notwithstanding the deference to a director's business judgment, the rule does not immunize a director from liability in the case of his or her abdication of corporate responsibilities: " . . . When courts say that they will not interfere in matters of business judgment, it is presupposed that reasonable diligence has in fact been exercised. A director cannot close his eyes to what is going on about him in the conduct of the business of the corporation and have it said that he is exercising business judgment. Courts have properly decided to give directors a wide latitude in the management of the affairs of a corporation provided always that judgment, and that means an honest, unbiased judgment, is reasonably exercised by them. . . ."

* * *

IV

Background on Golden Parachutes

We look at the recognized valid corporate functions served by golden parachutes as well as their recognized potential for executive self-dealing, so that we may review the actions of the directors in the context of these valid functions and the potential for abuse.

Corporate takeovers often threaten the financial and professional security of the managers of target companies. The theoretical purpose of golden parachutes is to shelter senior executives from such threat. To this end, the two principal recognized functions of golden parachutes are (1) to foster executive objectivity toward merger and tender offers; and (2) to attract top executives to companies and industries where the odds of takeover are high. As to the first function, a threatened takeover gives rise to the potential for conflict between executives' personal interests and the interests of shareholders. Golden parachutes align the interests of management more closely with those of shareholders by insuring executives against the possible pecuniary or nonpecuniary losses that may result from a change of control. A properly designed takeover [sic— golden parachute?] will theoretically make its beneficiary indifferent between remaining in control of the corporation and supporting a takeover beneficial to the shareholders.

As to the second function, golden parachutes provide long-term incentives for top quality management executives to enter industries and corporations in which the potential for takeover is above average.

Most commentators agree that, in view of these two functions of golden parachutes, a golden parachute should be negotiated as part of an executive's overall compensation package, and that parachutes enacted in the midst of takeover negotiations should be discouraged. A parachute conferred following a tender offer will likely have little value in creating executive objectivity because the executives generally already will have taken an initial position on the takeover before the golden parachutes are adopted and may not be able to credibly take a different stance at a later time. Further, during a takeover battle, the target corporation has no need for the parachute's executive recruiting functions. For these reasons, parachutes that are adopted in response to actual takeover overtures have been viewed as last minute appropriations of corporate assets or, alternatively, attempts to discourage potential acquirers. One author recommends: "Prohibiting the implementation of golden parachutes during a takeover is probably desirable. During a takeover, executives will have significant bargaining power to demand excessive golden parachutes in return for not opposing the transaction. Moreover, since both the executives and the directors probably will soon be replaced, they will have little concern over how the stockholders may react to the golden parachutes. . . . Prohibiting the implementation of golden parachutes during takeovers creates an incentive for corporations to adopt golden parachutes prior to a takeover, thereby avoiding the above-mentioned problems."

In addition to the timing of the implementation of golden parachutes, their amounts have been challenged as excessive in relation to any possible benefit conferred upon the corporation. Congress's enactment of new tax laws responds in part to this concern. Under the Deficit Reduction Act of 1984 (Int. Rev. Code, §§ 280G, 4999), golden parachutes that give executives payments greater than or equal to three times their total annual compensation are presumed excessive for tax purposes, resulting in the corporation's losing its deduction for the golden parachute payments as well as in the imposition of a 20 percent excise tax on the beneficiaries of the payments.

* * *

VI

*Discussion—Application of Section 309 to golden parachutes and Consulting Agreement**

A.   *Liability of inside directors.* The five inside directors who were the beneficiaries of the golden parachutes and the consulting agreement abstained from voting on their approval, and, accordingly, are not subject to liability on the ground of having approved the amended employment agreements.

* * *

B.   *Liability of outside directors.* We next look to whether the conduct of the outside directors in approving these benefits can withstand judicial scrutiny as a matter of law under section 309.

---

*   Ed.: California Corporation Code § 309 provides:

§ 309. Directors and officers to exercise powers in good faith; Liability

(a) A director shall perform the duties of a director, including duties as a member of any committee of the board upon which the director may serve, in good faith, in a manner such director believes to be in the best interests of the corporation and its shareholders and with such care, including reasonable inquiry, as an ordinarily prudent person in a like position would use under similar circumstances.

(b) In performing the duties of a director, a director shall be entitled to rely on information, opinions, reports or statements, including financial statements and other financial data, in each case prepared or presented by any of the following:

(1) One or more officers or employees of the corporation whom the director believes to be reliable and competent in the matters presented.

(2) Counsel, independent accountants or other persons as to matters which the director believes to be within such person's professional or expert competence.

(3) A committee of the board upon which the director does not serve, as to matters within its designated authority, which committee the director believes to merit confidence, so long as, in any such case, the director acts in good faith, after reasonable inquiry when the need therefor is indicated by the circumstances and without knowledge that would cause such reliance to be unwarranted.

(c)   A person who performs the duties of a director in accordance with subdivisions (a) and (b) shall have no liability based upon any alleged failure to discharge the person's obligations as a director. In addition, the liability of a director for monetary damages may be eliminated or limited in a corporation's articles to the extent provided in paragraph (10) of subdivision (a) of Section 204.

The record does not disclose that the outside directors had any personal interest in the benefits, and does not show any conflict of interest or evidence of bad faith on their part in approving the benefits.

Our inquiry, therefore, is whether the record discloses controverted issues of fact as to whether the outside directors acted in a manner they believed to be in the best interests of Natomas, and with such care, including reasonable inquiry, as an ordinarily prudent person in a like position would use under similar circumstances (§ 309, subd. (a)); and whether, in relying upon various sources, they made reasonable inquiry if the need therefor was indicated by the circumstances (§ 309, subd. (b)). We reach a different conclusion as to the directors' approval of the golden parachutes than we reach as to their approval of Seaton's consulting agreement.

We turn first to the outside directors acting in their capacity as members of the compensation committee. The record shows the compensation committee was persuaded to approve the amended employment agreements for 17 key executives after the initial 2–hour meeting on May 30. The record indicates that the committee members devoted less than two hours to the consideration of these employment agreements, five of which alone would provide for payment of approximately $11 million to executives following the consummation of the merger.

Flom stated that continuity in management should be a concern of the Natomas board and that the golden parachutes would serve that purpose. Flom did not explain, however, how the purported golden parachutes would serve such purpose, and the record does not indicate that any of the committee members requested further explanation of his conclusory opinion or analyzed among themselves how such purpose would be served by the amendments. The director who chaired the meeting indicated that the committee relied entirely upon Flom when agreeing to recommend the agreements.

We find that with the evidence before us, we cannot say as a matter of law that the compensation committee members were justified in relying to the extent that they did upon Flom in approving the golden parachutes, or that the circumstances did not warrant further reasonable inquiry under section 309, subdivision (b). We so conclude for the following reasons.

First, the golden parachutes, by their terms, would not serve the recognized valid functions of golden parachutes discussed ante. Because they were discussed after the terms of the merger had been negotiated and agreed upon, the function of executive objectivity would not be served. Bricker indeed indicated that he agreed to them primarily to keep the level of enthusiasm for the merger high. In addition, because they were provided to existing executives, the function of attracting top-level management obviously was not served. Significantly, the existing employment agreements for Commons and Reed, of which the committee members should have been aware, already provided golden parachutes which served the desirable functions of these forms of compensation. The record provides no explanation why these executives needed to make their benefits more "golden."

Second, Flom asserted that the golden parachutes served the purpose of ensuring continuity of management. Certain respondents at one point therefore refer to the benefits as "golden handcuffs," rather than golden parachutes. The very terms of the amended agreements, however, indicate that the opposite purpose would be served, and that they in fact would encourage the executives to leave Natomas within the six-month period following the merger or shortly thereafter. The testimony of appellants' proposed expert witness explained that typically, a "golden handcuff" is a reward given to an executive for staying with the company in conjunction with a detriment for leaving, but that with the instant agreements, the executives were encouraged to leave as soon as possible.

In deposition, Shumway testified that the purpose of the golden parachutes was to "buy" six months time which would "prevent a hell of a lot of chaos . . . by keeping those key people on the job through the amalgamation of the two entities, learning what the problems are and the like. . . . [para.] . . . [I]t's a small price to pay in a billion dollar deal when you look at the consequences that could result from a fumbled ball in Indonesia or a problem in the North Sea. . . ."

We do not dispute that a trier of fact might find this explanation of the purpose of the golden parachutes to be reasonable, but we find that the evidence would reasonably support an inference to the contrary. Further, the "good reason" condition to leaving Natomas during the six-month period appears to be so broad as to provide the executives with a ready justification to terminate their employment and collect the benefits immediately after the effective date of the merger, before the expiration of the six-month period.

Third, the golden parachutes payable to Commons, Reed, and Lee exceeded the three-year annual salary lump-sum limit under the Deficit Reduction Act, and therefore would be considered excessive for tax purposes under current law. Although these tax provisions, effective in 1984, apparently were not applicable to the 1983 merger, the compensation committee members arguably should have been aware of the pendency of such legislation affecting matters within their purview, and that the lump-sum payments in question would be excessive under the new tax laws.

Fourth, the compensation committee members should have been aware that Commons had proposed the amendment of the employment agreements and that Flom had been acting in accordance with Commons's instructions in preparing drafts of the employment agreements. Evidence of this close connection between Commons, a beneficiary of a golden parachute agreement, and Flom in formulating the terms of the agreements, would support the inference of self-dealing which should have been investigated further by the compensation committee.

A trier of fact could reasonably find that the circumstances warranted a thorough review of the golden parachute agreements by the members of the compensation committee to determine whether they served the best interests of the corporation. Thus, although a trier of fact might conclude that the compensation committee's reliance upon Flom with no further inquiry was reasonable, it could also reasonably find that the members of the compensation committee should have, at the very least, independently reviewed the terms of the golden parachutes to consider whether they served a valid use of corporate funds or constituted executive overreaching.

* * *

We finally turn to the conduct of the outside directors who were not on the compensation committee. Under section 309, these directors were entitled to rely upon the recommendation of the compensation committee, which they believed "to merit confidence" (§ 309, subd. (b)(3)) and were not required to initiate their own independent investigation. However, in this case, the nature of these particular golden parachute agreements and the timing of their proposal create a triable issue of fact as to whether some further inquiry should have been made by the board members who were not on the compensation committee. Even as of the date of the merger, golden parachutes were highly controversial (see Golden Rip-offs, Industry Week (July 25, 1983) p. 46; Those Executive Bailout Deals, Fortune (Dec. 13, 1982) p. 82). The board members, who presumably were appointed to the board because of their business and financial acumen, likely had, or should have had, some knowledge of this controversy. The proposal of the golden parachutes here under somewhat suspicious circumstances, i.e., after the tender offer and in the midst of merger discussions, raises the question of whether these directors should have examined the golden parachutes more attentively.

We perceive that in most cases, directors should be allowed to rely largely upon the recommendation of a board committee as to matters delegated to that committee. Otherwise, the directors' right to rely under subdivision (b) of section 309 would be rendered meaningless, and special committees would be unable to serve any useful function for the board. However, there is a triable issue as to whether the directors' general knowledge of the questionable nature of golden parachutes within the context of takeovers would cause such total reliance to be unwarranted.

We recognize that the amount of benefits provided under the golden parachutes and paid to the executives is not overwhelming in proportion to the net worth of both Natomas and Diamond, and the multi-billion dollar values involved in the merger. Nevertheless, the use of corporate funds for purposes which are not in the best interests of the shareholders cannot be excused simply because the opportunity for such occurs in the course of a takeover or merger which results in an overall financial gain for the shareholders.

* * *

VIII

Disposition

Summary judgment on the Gaillard complaint and summary adjudication of issues on the Ashton complaint in favor of Seaton are reversed. Summary judgment and summary adjudication of issues in favor of the remaining inside directors are reversed. Summary judgment and summary adjudication of issues in favor of the outside directors are reversed, except as to the claim of liability for Seaton's consulting agreement. Appellants are awarded costs on appeal.

Campbell v. Potash Corporation of Saskatchewan, Inc.

238 F.3d 792 (6th Cir. 2001).

■ BOGGS, CIRCUIT JUDGE.

The Potash Corporation of Saskatchewan, Inc. ("PCS") appeals from the district court's partial grant of summary judgment and its judgment after trial in favor of plaintiffs-appellees J. D. Campbell, Peter Kesser, and Alfred Williams, Jr., all former executives of the Arcadian Corporation. Campbell (the former President and CEO), Kesser (the former Vice-President and General Counsel), and Williams (the former Vice-President and CFO) sued PCS for breach of contract approximately two months after its successful March 6, 1997 merger with Arcadian, because PCS refused to make severance payments to the executives triggered under those executives' employment agreements[1] by the change in corporate control of Arcadian and additional "good cause."

* * *

Having received cross-motions for summary judgment, the district court granted partial summary judgment to plaintiffs on August 13, 1998, rejecting PCS's arguments that the severance agreements were void for lacking consideration and for contravening public policy, and holding that the contracts were enforceable against PCS. At the bench trial that began August 17, the court heard testimony regarding the proper construction of the multiplier clause in the severance agreements. The court then rendered a November 18 judgment that accepted the

---

[1]   This opinion will follow the district court in using the terms "employment agreements" and "severance agreements" interchangeably to refer to the executives' agreement with Arcadian.

plaintiffs' interpretation of most aspects of the multiplier clause, and it ordered PCS to pay plaintiffs' attorney's fees and tax penalties. * * * We agree with the district court's judgment concerning the contract consideration and public policy issues; however, we disagree slightly with its damage calculation. Therefore, we will affirm the district court in part, reverse it in part, and remand the case for revisions in the calculation of damages.

I

PCS, a Saskatchewan fertilizer corporation, approached Arcadian, a Tennessee fertilizer corporation, about a possible merger in August 1996. The Arcadian board decided to pursue the overture on August 27, and heard a presentation on proposed severance plans at that time. Over Labor Day weekend, Arcadian and PCS negotiated the terms of the merger and the severance agreements. PCS's Executive Committee and the Arcadian board approved and executed the merger agreement at respective board meetings on September 2. After approving the agreement, the Arcadian board approved employment agreements for nine senior executives that included so-called golden parachutes. Campbell, Kesser, and Williams signed employment agreements containing these parachutes three days later. The "golden parachute" portion of the severance package provided a formula to compensate senior executives in case of a change in corporate control accompanied by a material change in the executive's position at the new company. In such a circumstance, the executive could leave the company and receive an aggregate payment in one lump sum within 30 days of termination, totaling:

> an amount equal to the sum of (A) three (3) times Executive's Base Salary in effect at the time of [the Executive's] termination . . . , (B) three (3) times the average of all bonus, profit sharing and other incentive payments made by the Company to Executive in respect of the two (2) calendar years immediately preceding such termination, and (c) the pro-rata share of Executive's target bonus, profit sharing and other incentive payments for the calendar year in which such termination occurred. . . .

Arcadian's compensation system historically emphasized incentives, enhancing an industry median base salary with supplemental incentive payments for meeting performance targets as well as profit-sharing payments and additional bonuses. * * *

At PCS's insistence during the Labor Day weekend discussions, Arcadian reduced the number of secondary events that could trigger the golden parachutes following a change in corporate control, and devised a formula based on actual compensation for the two calendar years preceding termination rather than on expected compensation for the two years following termination. * * * PCS also requested that the multiplier be limited to salary and bonuses, but Arcadian indicated that its pay structure was too incentive-laden for that to be feasible. [Part of the dispute was over whether the contracts as finally drafted covered incentive payments such as shares of the current year's profit-sharing or bonuses.] * * * Lance [an Arcadian executive] sent PCS copies of all Arcadian benefit plans for due diligence purposes.

* * *

In early November, Lance contacted his counterpart at PCS to call attention to the much higher severance benefit costs that would be entailed by a 1997 closing. Shortly thereafter, PCS told Lance it thought the severance packages should be limited to three times cash compensation, but Lance said that was inconsistent with both his understanding of the terms reached and the language of the employment agreements.

The agreements also contained a provision requiring Arcadian to obtain an assumption agreement from any "direct or indirect" successor agreeing "to expressly assume and agree to perform, by a written agreement in form and substance satisfactory to Executive, all of the obligations of the Company [Arcadian] under this Agreement." Failure by Arcadian to obtain such an agreement from a successor automatically triggered the golden parachutes upon a change in control. PCS and Arcadian filed a Joint Proxy Statement with the SEC on January 28, 1997, laying out the severance formula, including incentive payments, lump-sum pension benefits, and the tax gross-up feature whereby the company increased the golden parachutes to cover related taxes.

PCS continued to resist Arcadian's inclusion of long-term incentives in the formula. Plaintiffs' counsel thus recommended that plaintiffs engage Arthur Anderson to produce a report justifying plaintiffs' interpretation of the golden parachutes, to defend against a possible challenge by PCS. The audit confirmed that the employment agreements were "well within competitive practice." The compensation committee heard the report on February 24, but took no action. Then Arcadian's chairman refused to hear a report to the full board, stating that it was part of PCS's due diligence and "whatever it costs, it costs."

Two days before the March 6, 1997 closing, Kesser demanded that PCS and PCS Nitrogen expressly assume the golden parachute severance agreements signed by plaintiffs. PCS Senior Vice-President and General Counsel John Hampton refused, saying PCS was not the successor to Arcadian's business or assets. Kesser threatened to delay closing on March 6, causing Hampton to have Barry Humphreys, PCS's Senior Vice-President for Finance, sign the assumption agreement on behalf of PCS to avoid delaying closing and incurring difficulties with merger financing. Hampton himself signed on behalf of PCS Nitrogen as its Secretary.

Prior to closing, Campbell and Williams were offered jobs at PCS Nitrogen materially different from their previous ones with Arcadian, so both terminated at closing for good cause. Hampton released Kesser from the new company's employ at the closing. Though PCS acknowledged that it owed some amounts to Campbell, Kesser and Williams, it refused to pay even the undisputed portions of their severance packages within the allotted thirty days, thereby precipitating this suit.

* * *

IV

PCS next argues that the golden parachutes violate public policy, and therefore that the assumption agreement promising them is void.[4] PCS advances this argument even though it offers golden parachutes to its own top managers. Hypocrisy aside, PCS cites no circuit case law supporting its proposition. At most this court has frowned on golden parachutes in past dicta, but we have never held that such severance packages are per se unlawful. Nor does PCS provide much reason to equate this type of executive compensation with contracts prohibited by public policy, such as ones to perform illegal acts. PCS cites a Congressional committee report saying that golden parachutes should be discouraged and notes that there is a heavy excise tax on parachutes over a certain value (exceeded here), but, as Plaintiffs point out, Congress taxed golden parachutes, it did not prohibit them. PCS further argues that these particular golden parachutes violate public policy because they are excessive and have a gross-up feature to compensate the recipient for any tax penalty. These features do not make the golden parachutes violative of public policy, and parachutes with such features have been upheld.

PCS further argues that these golden parachutes violate public policy because they were approved after the merger had been approved, and therefore served no legitimate corporate purpose.[5] Though adopted after the merger was approved, these golden parachutes were authorized later in the same meeting at which the approval occurred. Thus, PCS's

---

[4] There is a rich, albeit somewhat dated, secondary literature discussing the pros and cons of golden parachutes. Whatever else might be gleaned from this material, golden parachutes are not uniformly condemned as offensive to public policy. See, e.g., Kenneth Johnson, Note, Golden Parachutes and the Business Judgment Rule: Toward a Proper Standard of Review, 94 Yale L.J. 909 (1985); John C. Coffee, Jr., Shareholders Versus Managers: The Strain in the Corporate Web, 85 Mich. L. Rev. 1, 76 (1986); Ann Marie Hanrahan, Note, Koenings v. Joseph Schlitz Brewing Co., 126 Wis. 2d 349, 377 N.W.2d 593: The Wisconsin Supreme Court Addresses Executive Termination Benefits in a Golden Parachute Contract, 1987 Wis. L. Rev. 823; Richard P. Bress, Comment, Golden Parachutes: Untangling the Ripcords, 39 Stan. L. Rev. 955 (1987); Drew H. Campbell, Note, Golden Parachutes: Common Sense From the Common Law, 51 Ohio St. L.J. 279 (1990).

[5] Commentators originally objected to the use of golden parachutes as anti-takeover devices where they were crafted as poison pills and triggered automatically by the single trigger of a change in corporate control. More recently, commentators have noted the potential moral hazard entailed by golden parachutes, inasmuch as they may encourage inefficient management to induce a takeover that is lucrative for departing managers. The golden parachutes here were adopted after approval of the merger, so neither of these objections can be made against them. Moreover, they required two triggering events, as termination or a role reduction had to accompany a change in control before the golden parachutes could be demanded. Thus, activation of the parachutes was within PCS's control.

argument that their adoption violated public policy because it came after approval of the merger is somewhat misleading. Moreover, the timing of the adoption of the golden parachute provision fits with the rationale given for their adoption in deposition testimony by Arcadian's then-directors. With a merger pending, the company feared that its top personnel might seek lucrative offers elsewhere. Not only would the company then be deprived of the services of key employees in the interim (and potentially receive less value from a merger if the firm suffered from poor management just prior to closing), but it also risked no longer having the managers who had brought so much profit to Arcadian in the event that the merger was never consummated. To ensure that neither of those situations occurred, Arcadian used golden parachutes to entice nine of its top executives to remain with the company until and unless there was both a change of corporate control and a decline in those executives' respective positions in the company. Five managers stayed with the company for a time after the merger. Four did not, including the three plaintiffs in this case. At least one court has embraced a similar rationale for golden parachutes in the past.[6]

Mixed with its argument about public policy, PCS argues against application of the business judgment rule to this case. Not only did the manner of the golden parachutes' adoption violate public policy, according to PCS, it also violated a duty of care prerequisite to applying the business judgment rule. PCS repeatedly refers to the Gaillard case as similar, but a California appeals court case applying California law is not binding precedent for this circuit's application of Delaware law. See Gaillard v. Natomas Co., 208 Cal. App. 3d 1250, 256 Cal. Rptr. 702 (Cal. Ct. App. 1992). And while the Gaillard case is factually similar in some respects, we do not find its reasoning persuasive. The district court in this case found no gross negligence on the part of the Arcadian board, and our court is less willing than California courts to question a corporate board's business judgment. * * *

Even if we ourselves did not perceive a good rationale for these parachutes, courts should be loath to condemn a business practice simply because they do not perceive a good rationale for a given practice. Condemning poorly understood practices simply for lack of a clear rationale would substitute the court's business judgment for the corporation's. "If what management did was illegal, . . . it should be enjoined. If it wasn't illegal, it should be allowed even if philosophically unpalatable and, if a court cannot tell, it seems . . . that this is what the business judgment rule is all about and the nod should be given to those who are vested with the business decision making responsibility." In

---

[6] Golden parachutes have also been defended as a means of compensating managers for their investments in firm-specific skills. See Daniel R. Fischel, Organized Exchanges and the Regulation of Dual Class Common Stock, 54 U. Chi. L. Rev 119, 137–38 (1987); John C. Coffee, Jr., Shareholders Versus Managers, 85 Mich. L. Rev. at 76.

short, evaluating the costs and benefits of golden parachutes is quintessentially a job for corporate boards, and not for federal courts.

In Delaware, whose law the parties agreed would govern disputes under this contract, a plaintiff must show that the majority of the board acted in a manner that "rises to the level of gross negligence" before a court may second guess its business judgment. PCS argues that the Arcadian board was misled by incomplete slides and presentations made to it about the golden parachutes, and states that the board did not know the total possible cost of the golden parachutes at the time it approved them. As evidence of neglect of the board's duty of care, PCS points to the statements by Arcadian's chairman about the parachutes that "whatever they cost, they cost," and that it would be PCS's responsibility to pay the severance packages anyway. But even if deemed incriminating, these remarks do not show gross negligence by a majority of the board. Board members had a reasonable amount of accurate information about the severance packages before them when they acted. The lack of a completely accurate total outlay estimate before approval does not rise to the level of gross negligence. According to the deposition of independent board member Chester Vanatta, relied on by the district court, the board understood the nature of the benefits, knew that PCS had approved the severance packages, had a rough idea of the cost and knew what was included, wanted to retain the personnel in case the merger failed to go through, and vetted the severance packages through its compensation committee. Finally, PCS also suggests a measure of self-dealing in the approval of these severance packages, but Mr. Campbell is the only plaintiff who was on the board, and he acknowledged his conflict and abstained from the vote.

The Arcadian board therefore exhibited nothing like the lack of knowledge and the swiftness of deliberation condemned in the Van Gorkom or Hanson cases. Nor does this case feature the kind of insider-dealing on a stacked board decried in Ocilla Indus., Inc. v. Katz, 677 F.Supp. 1291, 1299 (E. D. N. Y. 1987). Nor do the severance agreements at issue here approach the possibly wasteful use of corporate assets entailed in the Walt Disney Company's non-fault termination of Michael Ovitz recently adjudicated by the Delaware Supreme Court. See Brehm v. Eisner, 746 A.2d 244, 253 (Del. 2000) (dismissing the action without prejudice on procedural grounds, but observing that "the sheer size of the payout to Ovitz [$140 million for less than 15 months of work] . . . pushes the envelope of judicial respect for the business judgment of directors in making compensation decisions").* If the Ovitz severance payment, which included $39 million in cash, only pushes the envelope under Delaware law, then the smaller sum here spread across three executives

---

* Dismissed on the merits sub nom. In re Walt Disney Co. Deriv. Litig., 907 A.2d 693 (Del.Ch. 2005), aff'd sub nom. Brehm v. Eisner, 906 A.2d 27 (Del. 2006).—Ed.

with longer tenure at their company is well within the confines respected by the business judgment rule.

* * *

VI

PCS has already received the benefit of the bargain it struck concerning golden parachutes (in having an orderly change in corporate control and in insuring Arcadian's health in the event of a failed effort to merge), and it cannot now refuse payment in return. There was consideration for the assumption agreement insofar as it was bound up in the merger obligations. Golden parachutes are not void as against public policy, nor did the Arcadian board exhibit gross negligence in approving the golden parachutes at issue in this case. Finally, although the district court correctly interpreted the multiplier clause's language based on extrinsic evidence gathered at trial, it committed clear error in counting certain incentive payments that were made in respect of more than two years. For these reasons, the judgment of the district court on partial summary judgment and after trial is AFFIRMED in part, REVERSED in part, and REMANDED back to the district court for further proceedings consistent with this opinion.

QUESTIONS

1. Why did the Gaillard court reject the severance agreements granted after a merger agreement was struck? Does this opinion fully address those concerns?

2. If you were charged with rewriting the Natomas golden parachutes in light of the court's decision in that case, what, if anything, would you change?

3. Given the time between the merger agreement's approval by the Arcadian board and the expected closing date, how severe was the risk that Arcadian's top executives would leave in the interim?

4. If the surviving corporation in a merger succeeds by operation of law to all of the obligations of the constituent corporations, of what value is the assumption agreement to the Arcadian executives?

5. Assuming that obtaining an assumption agreement is problematic, what protection could Arcadian have given its executives to assure they received the contemplated severance benefits?

6. What new consideration did PCS receive in return for signing the assumption agreement, given the fact that the merger agreement was approved before the parachute contracts?

NOTE ON RISK METRICS (ISS) GOVERNANCE STANDARDS

Institutional Shareholders Service was organized to capitalize on the shareholder apathy problem of institutional investors. Institutions such as mutual funds, insurance companies and pension funds, to name a few, are managed by stock analysts and traders whose entire focus is on the relative values of companies' shares, and whether buying or selling a particular stock is a good idea. In effect, they generally follow the "Wall Street Rule"—if you don't like the management, sell the stock. Recall Henry Manne's discussion of the free rider problem facing shareholders in Mergers and the Market for Corporate Control in Chapter Two, part 4. Fund managers realize that if they engage in activism to monitor and resist management, they will incur all of the costs and receive only a fraction of the benefits if they should win. Worse, if they fail to win, they simply incur costs that other investors, including competing funds, have not incurred, thus worsening their investment performance.

It should come as no surprise that institutions should arise to fill this gap, and provide information and advice to fund managers about how to vote their shares. Institutional Shareholder Services was one of the earliest companies to provide such services, and is the largest source of voting advice on governance issues to institutional investors. It is now owned by Morgan Stanley Capital International (MSCI), which acquired its parent, Risk Metrics in 2010. ISS not only instructs shareholders on how to vote on particular issues, but also whether to vote for or against incumbent directors if the company's governance does not meet certain ISS standards. ISS also produces a governance index on which it rates publicly traded companies. Its standards for poison pills, which generally had a ten-year life and were adopted exclusively by the board of directors, now limit acceptable pills adopted by a board to a one-year life and require shareholder approval for longer adoptions.

A competitive advisory service, offered by Glass Lewis, advertises that its recommendations are more favorable toward management. A summary of some other standards imposed by ISS is set out below:

Problematic Takeover Defenses:

> The board is classified, and a continuing director responsible for a problematic governance issue at the board/committee level that would warrant a withhold/against vote recommendation is not up for election. All appropriate nominees (except new) may be held accountable.

Director Performance Evaluation:

> The board lacks accountability and oversight, coupled with sustained poor performance relative to peers. Sustained poor performance is measured by one-and three-year total shareholder returns in the bottom half of a company's four-digit GICS industry group (Russell 3000 companies only). Take into consideration the company's five-year total shareholder return and operational metrics. Problematic provisions include but are not limited to:

- A classified board structure;

- A supermajority vote requirement;

- Either a plurality vote standard in uncontested director elections or a majority vote standard with no plurality carve-out for contested elections;

- The inability of shareholders to call special meetings;

- The inability of shareholders to act by written consent;

- A dual-class capital structure; and/or

- A non-shareholder-approved poison pill.

Poison Pills:

- The company's poison pill has a "dead-hand" or "modified dead-hand" feature. Vote against or withhold from nominees every year until this feature is removed;

- The board adopts a poison pill with a term of more than 12 months ("long-term pill"), or renews any existing pill, including any "short-term" pill (12 months or less), without shareholder approval. A commitment or policy that puts a newly adopted pill to a binding shareholder vote may potentially offset an adverse vote recommendation. Review such companies with classified boards every year, and such companies with annually elected boards at least once every three years, and vote against or withhold votes from all nominees if the company still maintains a non-shareholder-approved poison pill; or

- The board makes a material adverse change to an existing poison pill without shareholder approval.

Vote case-by-case on all nominees if:

The board adopts a poison pill with a term of 12 months or less ("short-term pill") without shareholder approval, taking into account the following factors:

- The date of the pill's adoption relative to the date of the next meeting of shareholders—i.e. whether the company had time to put the pill on the ballot for shareholder ratification given the circumstances;

- The issuer's rationale;

- The issuer's governance structure and practices; and

- The issuer's track record of accountability to shareholders http://www.issgovernance.com/file/policy/1_2015-us-summary-voting-guidelines-updated.pdf.

In 2010 Congress passed the Dodd-Frank Wall Street Reform and Consumer Protection Act, which mandates that no less frequently than every three years corporations submit management compensation to a non-binding shareholder advisory vote under § 14A of the Securities Exchange Act. Under

Rule 14a–8 shareholders can request that management adopt certain policies, but where they involve the management of the business, shareholders lack power under corporate statutes to take such actions unilaterally.

Typically shareholder proposals will recommend a policy that caps severance payments, either at two or three times annual compensation. Many of these shareholder proposals are quite brief, and companies that adopt them in the recommended form may well encounter interpretation difficulties. Many severance arrangements involve payments in excess of three times the average annual compensation of an executive who departs after a change of control. As a result, they trigger a 20% excise tax for the receiving executive, in addition to the normal income tax liability. In order to make these "excess parachute payments" similar to those below the threshold, many companies have committed to gross up the payments, with an additional amount necessary to cover the excise tax (plus the additional excise tax generated by the gross-up). Are these gross-ups "benefits" within the meaning of the policy? Typically these policies do not address this issue.

Another area of ambiguity involves payments already earned by but not yet paid to the executive, such as deferred compensation. Some policies exclude these payments from the definition of severance benefits. Where an executive has a bonus agreement, is that part of the severance payments in the year where the executive is paid a pro rata part of his or her earned bonus? Or should it count against average compensation for the measuring period? In some cases executives may be entitled to earn long-term incentives, in the form of shares of the target company. Typically these awards will be for multiple years, with a portion vesting each year. What happens if vesting is accelerated in the year of the change of control? All of these questions create litigation risk for any board interpreting these potentially ambiguous provisions. Hewlett Packard has been the subject of a shareholder class action for its payments in connection with the removal of Carly Fiorina as CEO in 2005.

One of the problems with a policy that requires shareholder approval is its rigidity. Where a company is in negotiations to hire an outside executive who insists on a severance agreement in excess of policy limits, the company may be unable to grant this request without shareholder approval. Ordinarily a company will not have the time to call a special shareholders' meeting to grant an exception or to amend the policy. In 2005 Cendant Corporation declined to implement a golden parachute policy despite support from 65% of the shares voted at its 2005 annual meeting, stating:

> Our board has determined that if it changed our policy to the proposed policy . . . we could be put at a competitive disadvantage because, among other things, the proposal would create uncertainty and delay in finalizing severance arrangements until after the arrangement is approved by our stockholders, which could hinder our flexibility to attract, motivate and retain the best executive talent in today's competitive environment and in the future.

C. SHARK REPELLENTS

Read Model Business Corporation Act § 7.27 and Del. Gen. Corp. L. §§ 102(b)(4), 151(a) & 212.

Two-Tier Tender Offers and Shark Repellents

William J. Carney.

4, No. 2 Midland Corporate Finance Journal 48 (1986).

Stockholder Strategies

The Nature of the Bidding Market

This problem [of "low-ball" bids] fades into insignificance if a competitive auction market for corporate control can respond immediately to a first bid. The user that values the target firm's assets most highly would be expected to make a bid that could not be matched by any other firm. But serious barriers exist to such competition. First, antitrust laws may bar competitors from bidding. Second, transaction costs associated with bids are large, especially if a bidder anticipates target management resistance. Third, the Williams Act imposes mandatory delays on bidders, so a first bidder can close and accept tendered shares while a second bid must remain open.[5] Fourth, large firms may possess economies of scale in capital markets, although the development of junk bond markets may have improved access for smaller firms.[*] Finally, there is a serious "sunk cost" problem for bidders that may deter entry. All expenditures are sunk once made, and have zero salvage value unless the bid is successful. Since the first bidder has already sunk substantial sums in the research, brokerage, financing, legal and accounting costs associated with a bid, a second prospective bidder must decide whether to make an investment of similar costs, knowing that the first bidder must now disregard those costs in deciding whether to raise its bid.[**] Because rational bidders want to avoid games where both sides keep raising the costs in order to salvage their investment, vigorous competition may be discouraged in many situations.[6] Only if the second bidder receives assurances from the target

---

[5]   Subject, of course, to the mandatory 10-day extension of withdrawal rights for an outstanding bid when a second bid appears, under Securities Exchange Act Rule 14d–7.

[*]   While this observation seemed dated by the end of the 1980s, when hostile cash takeover bids financed by high yield debt seemed to disappear, by 2006 private equity funds were acquiring public companies in much the same manner.—Ed.

[**]   There is, of course, the possibility that the second bidder can free ride on the information produced and revealed by the first bidder in its mandatory Williams Act filings on Schedules 13D–1 and TO.—Ed.

[6]   See M. Shubik, "The Dollar Auction Game: A Paradox in Noncooperative Behavior and Escalation," *Journal of Conflict Resolution* 15 (1971), p. 109.

of favored treatment (usually in the form of a lock-up option on shares) is a competing bid likely to develop.

Changing Voting Rules

[Review Part 1 of this Chapter "The Problem of the Hostile Bid."] Stockholder strategies, then, must focus on altering the outcomes expected in the matrix set out above. Target firm managers, fearing displacement if takeover bids are successful, will find it in their interest to call these problems to the attention of stockholders, and to persuade them to take action, since any action will raise the average price stockholders expect to receive closer to the $37 shown in the northwest quadrant of the matrix. To this extent, at least, target managers' interests are aligned with those of stockholders.[7]

Supermajority Voting

The contractual responses to the prisoner's dilemma problem for target shareholders are well known. A rule that alters the usual majority voting rule for corporate mergers is the dominant response. Corporate charters have been amended in large numbers to increase the percentage vote required for stockholder approval of mergers with "related stockholders"—those that already own a substantial percentage of the target's stock. These amendments generally require the approval of at least two-thirds, and sometimes as high as 95 percent, of all of the target's shares for such a merger. The result is obvious: either the bidder must purchase (at the cash bid price) sufficient stock to assure the passage of the merger vote, or must offer a take-out price sufficiently high to persuade some of the remaining shareholders to consent to the takeout merger. In either case the average or "blended" price received for all shares has been increased. The disadvantages for target shareholders are also obvious: if the voting requirement is set too high, stockholders again are tempted to hold out, creating another free rider problem. Bids may be deterred and valuable information about superior uses of the target's assets may not be revealed. [The ISS is hostile toward such proposals:

1. Vote AGAINST proposals to require a supermajority shareholder vote.

2. Vote FOR management or shareholder proposals to reduce supermajority vote requirements. However, for companies with shareholder(s) who have significant ownership levels, vote CASE-BY-CASE, taking into account:

   • Ownership structure;

   • Quorum requirements; and

   • Supermajority vote requirements.]

---

[7]   See my own study, "Shareholder Coordination Costs, Shark Repellents, and Takeout Mergers: The Case Against Fiduciary Duties," *American Bar Foundation Research Journal* (1983), 341.

As a consequence of the dominance of institutional opposition to supermajority voting rules, they only exist in companies that installed them before they first offered their shares to the public.

Independent Stockholder Ratification

A second approach is similar: it requires any takeout merger to be approved by the holders of a specified percentage of all shares not held by the related stockholders. This requirement will affect the terms of the takeout merger and give target stockholders what amounts to an arms'-length negotiating position at the takeout stage. The disadvantage, both for the bidder and the target stockholders, is that the bidder cannot determine what price will be required to assure a complete takeover until the vote is held. This increase in uncertainty for bidders may deter some takeovers that would succeed if attempted, and thus defeat some wealth-creating transactions.

Excusing Voting Requirements

Since compliance with these voting requirements may prevent some wealth-increasing transactions for target stockholders, most shark repellent amendments contain two provisions that waive these rules under certain conditions and allow approval of takeout mergers by the simple majority vote generally provided by state law.

Fair Price Provisions

Many amendments provide that the voting requirements may be excused if the price paid by the bidder in the takeout stage is "fair." Fairness in this context is generally defined as the highest price paid by the successful bidder for any shares of the firm. Generally this will be the cash tender offer price, but it could include a premium paid to a single stockholder. To protect against post-bid manipulations by a successful bidder that would cause stockholders to vote for a takeout at a price below the cash bid price, there are often prohibitions of certain forms of self-dealing, and provisions to encourage a bidder to undertake the second-stage merger, if at all, immediately after a successful bid. While these amendments do not alter voting rules, they do affect the takeout price, and generally bring it in line with the cash bid price. One effect may be to reduce the price the bidder is willing to pay on the front end of a bid. [ISS now provides:

> Vote CASE-BY-CASE on proposals to adopt fair price provisions (provisions that stipulate that an acquirer must pay the same price to acquire all shares as it paid to acquire the control shares), evaluating factors such as the vote required to approve the proposed acquisition, the vote required to repeal the fair price provision, and the mechanism for determining the fair price.

Generally, vote AGAINST fair price provisions with shareholder vote requirements greater than a majority of disinterested shares.]

Board Decisions on Excusing Compliance

Recognizing that all of these requirements may prevent beneficial transactions, many corporations have provided that compliance may be excused by those board members who are not associated with the bidder. The net effect of these provisions may be to delegate bargaining power to sell the firm to the incumbent directors. Incumbent management is in effect given a veto power over certain proposals to acquire the entire firm. Where this occurs, stockholders in effect exchange the coordination costs of the prisoner's dilemma for the "agency costs" associated with management's interest in preserving its own control of the firm.

Seibert v. Gulton Industries, Inc.

1979 WL 2710, 5 Del. J. Corp. L. 514 (Del.Ch. 1979),
affirmed 414 A.2d 822 (Del. 1980).

■ BROWN, VICE-CHANCELLOR.

This suit challenges the validity of an amendment to the certificate of incorporation of a Delaware corporation which would require an 80 per cent vote of shareholders to approve a merger with another person or entity owning 5 per cent or more of the corporation's outstanding voting stock. Plaintiff, a shareholder of the defendant Gulton Industries, Inc. ("Gulton"), contends that such a provision is violative of the Delaware corporation law and cannot be made a part of the corporate charter by amendment even if approved by a majority of the shareholders. Plaintiff says that by failing to advise Gulton's shareholders in the proxy materials for the 1977 annual meeting that the proposed amendment was in violation of Delaware law, Gulton is guilty of having disseminated false and misleading proxy information to its shareholders, as a result of which the amendment must be declared null and void. Gulton has moved to dismiss the complaint pursuant to Rule 12(b)(6) on the grounds that it fails to state a claim upon which relief can be granted.

The charter provision under attack calls for that which is commonly referred to as a "supermajority" vote as to certain types of corporate action. The amendment to Gulton's charter embodying this supermajority provision was approved by a 54 per cent vote of Gulton's shareholders at its annual meeting held on June 21, 1977. In summary, the amendment requires the vote of at least 80 per cent of Gulton's shareholders to approve a merger or consolidation or similar takeover of Gulton by any person or entity that has acquired 5 per cent or more of Gulton's shares prior to its proposed takeover. This 80 per cent requirement is in force unless the directors of Gulton approve its proposed takeover by the other entity prior to the latter's acquisition of its 5 per cent interest in Gulton. However, should Gulton's board of directors approve of the acquisition of Gulton prior to the time that the party acquires its 5 per cent interest, then only a majority vote of Gulton's shareholders is required to approve the takeover.

Plaintiff contends that it is the discretion reposed in the board of directors by this provision that renders it repugnant to Delaware corporation law. She recognizes that under 8 Del. C. § 102(b)(4) a certificate of incorporation can require greater than a majority vote for the approval of designated matters. That portion of § 102 permits the certificate of incorporation to include among other things, the following:

> "(4) Provisions requiring for any corporate action, the vote of a larger portion of the stock or of any class or series thereof, or of any other securities having voting power, or a larger number of directors, than is required by this chapter."

Since 8 Del. C. § 251 provides that an agreement of merger can be approved "[i]f a majority of the outstanding stock of the corporation entitled to vote thereon shall be voted for the adoption of the agreement," plaintiff concedes that it would be permissible for the certificate of incorporation to require an 80 per cent vote for approval of a merger under the authority of § 102(b)(4) as opposed to the simple majority vote required by § 251. This would simply be calling for "the vote of a larger portion of the stock" than is required by other parts of the chapter.

However, plaintiff argues that the statutory language—"larger portion of the stock"—means a fixed percentage greater than a majority. She argues that § 102(b)(4) cannot be read to permit a charter provision which authorizes a shifting vote requirement dependent upon both the percentage stock ownership of the merger or takeover candidate and the ad hoc determination by the board of directors at the time of the takeover candidate's acquisition of a 5 per cent stock interest.

The research of the parties has revealed no Delaware precedent directly on point. * * *

An earlier decision, Sellers v. Joseph Bancroft & Bancroft & Sons Co., Del.Ch., 2 A.2d 108 (1938), deals with the subject of charter-made supermajority voting requirements, although there too the higher vote percentages were fixed at definite figures. In that case, the certificate of incorporation required a 75 per cent vote of preferred shareholders in order to change the designations, preferences and voting powers of the preferred stock. To change the amount to be paid on the preferred shares on dissolution, or to alter the dividend rate or the redemption price, a 100 per cent vote of the class of preferred shareholders was required.

At an annual meeting, by a majority of all shareholders entitled to vote thereon, the certificate of incorporation was amended so as to reduce the 75 per cent requirement as to the preferred stock to 60 per cent, and the 100 per cent requirement to 65 per cent. At the suit of certain holders of the preferred, this amendment was held to be invalid since it constituted an attempt by the common shareholders to take away the contractual preference rights given the preferred shareholders in the charter by a vote which was less than the 75 per cent to which the preferred shareholders were entitled under the charter.

In passing on the matter, the Chancellor noted that the Delaware corporation law permits the certificate of incorporation to require for any corporate action the vote of a larger proportion of the stock or any class thereof than is required by other provisions of the corporation law. As compared to the charter provision in this case, the decision in Sellers v. Joseph Bancroft & Sons Co., seems significant in that it appears to recognize the validity of a charter provision which calls for one percentage vote as to one type of corporate action and another, and differing, percentage vote as to another type of action—both from among the same class of voting shareholders. While it does not recognize a shifting vote on the same subject matter, it does seem to approve differing voting requirements dependent upon the matter being voted upon.

Plaintiff argues that under the statutory scheme, the directors propose and the shareholders vote. She says that Gulton's supermajority provision as to mergers, etc. violates this principle since it impinges on the shareholders' right to vote to the extent that it permits the directors to determine the amount of the vote that will be required for approval of a proposed transaction that could well be of financial benefit to the shareholders. But if the law permits a provision in the certificate of incorporation which calls for a greater or lesser vote dependent upon the particular corporate activity being voted upon, then perhaps the statutory scheme is not governed by how the matter being voted upon comes about.

Under the challenged provision in Gulton's certificate of incorporation, a majority vote is called for as to a proposed transaction with a 5 per cent or more shareholder as to which Gulton's board of directors has given its approval. On the other hand, an 80 per cent vote is required to approve a transaction with a 5 per cent or more shareholder which Gulton's board does not feel to be in the best interests of the corporation and its shareholders. To that extent, Gulton's certificate of incorporation calls for a differing vote from the same class of voting shareholders dependent upon the matter subject to the vote, i.e., a business combination with a 5 per cent shareholder approved by the board of directors or a combination with a 5 per cent shareholder opposed by the board.

I consider this analysis in light of 8 Del. C. § 102(b)(1) which reads as follows:

> "(b) In addition to the matters required to be set forth in the certificate of incorporation by subsection (a) of this section, the

certificate of incorporation may also contain any or all of the following matters—

"(1) Any provision for the management of the business and for the conduct of the affairs of the corporation, and any provision creating, defining, limiting and regulating the powers of the corporation, the directors, and the stockholders, or any class of the stockholders, or the members of a non-stock corporation; if such provisions are not contrary to the laws of this State. Any provision which is required or permitted by any section of this chapter to be stated in the by-laws may instead be stated in the certificate of incorporation;"

In Sterling v. Mayflower Hotel Corp., Del. Supr., 93 A.2d 107, 118 (1952) it is stated as follows:

". . . [S]tockholders of a Delaware corporation may by contract embody in the charter a provision departing from the rules of common law, provided that it does not transgress a statutory enactment or a public policy settled by the common law or implicit in the General Corporation Law itself."

And in Frankel v. Donovan, Del. Ch., 120 A.2d 311, 316 (1956) it is stated that:

"Charter provisions which facilitate corporate action and to which a stockholder assents by becoming a stockholder are normally upheld by the court unless they contravene a principle implicit in statutory or settled decisional law governing corporate management, § 102(b)(1). . . ."

Plaintiff has failed to cite any statute or case precedent which is done violence by the provision in Gulton's certificate of incorporation attacked by her complaint. Nor has she been able to point convincingly to any public policy against the so-called "shifting numbers" where corporate voting rights are concerned. Compare, Providence & Worcester Co. v. Baker, Del. Supr., 378 A.2d 121 (1977). Moreover, various provisions of the corporation law confer discretion upon a board of directors in connection with mergers and other corporate transactions.

As a result of the foregoing considerations, I am convinced that the complaint fails to set forth a claim upon which relief may be granted. Accordingly, the complaint will be dismissed. An appropriate form of order may be submitted.

QUESTIONS

1. How does the court justify giving the board of directors control over the percentage vote required to approve a merger?

2.   What is the relationship between subsections (1) and (4) of section 102(b)?

3.   What are the sources of the board's power to vary the voting rules for shareholders? Is the court evidencing a philosophy about the interpretation of corporate laws?

4.   Review Model Business Corporation Act §§ 2.02(b)(2), 7.21 and 7.27. Would the Gulton Industries voting rule have been enforceable in a Model Act jurisdiction?

NOTE ON SHARK REPELLENTS AND DIFFERENTIAL VOTING

A similar conclusion was reached in Seibert v. Milton Bradley Co., 405 N.E.2d 131 (Mass. 1980).

In Providence and Worcester Co. v. Baker, 378 A.2d 121 (1977), the Delaware Supreme Court addressed another voting scheme. Providence and Worcester's certificate of incorporation had contained the following provision:

> " . . . each stockholder shall be entitled to one vote for every share of the common stock of said company owned by him not exceeding fifty shares, and one vote for every twenty shares more than fifty, owned by him; provided, that no stockholder shall be entitled to vote upon more than one fourth part of the whole number of shares issued and outstanding of the common stock of said company, unless as proxy for other members."

The court held that the validity of this provision was to be determined under Del. Gen. Corp. Law § 212(a), which provided:

> "(a) Unless otherwise provided in the certificate of incorporation and subject to the provisions of § 213 of this title, each stockholder shall be entitled to 1 vote for each share of capital stock held by such stockholder. If the certificate of incorporation provides for more or less than 1 vote for any share, on any matter, every reference in this chapter to a majority or other proportion of stock shall refer to such majority or other proportion of the votes of such stock."

The court rejected the argument that distinctions in voting rights could only be set on the basis of setting rights for an entire class, stating "In the final analysis, these restrictions are limitations upon the voting rights of the stockholder, not variations in the voting powers of the stock *per se*. The voting power of the stock in the hands of a large stockholder is not differentiated from all others in its class; it is the personal right of the stockholder to exercise that power that is altered by the size of his holding. In the hands of smaller stockholders, unrestrained in the exercise of their voting rights, the same stock would have voting power equal to all others in the class. It is reasonable to assume, we think, that if the General Assembly intended to bar the type of restriction on stockholders' voting rights here under review, such prohibition would appear in § 212, which is entitled 'Voting Rights of Stockholders'. . . ." 378 A.2d at 123. The court sustained the charter provisions.

The Model Business Corporation Act is similarly devoid of such restrictions. Section 7.21, entitled "Voting Entitlement of Shares," provides in subsection (a): "Except as provided in subsections (b) and (c) or unless the articles of incorporation provide otherwise, each outstanding share, regardless of class, is entitled to one vote on each matter voted on at a shareholders' meeting."

This device has been used by a number of corporations. MCI Communications Corporation, for example, provided for one one-hundredth of a vote per share for each share owned in excess of 10% of outstanding shares. Winter, Stumpf & Hawkins, Shark Repellents and Golden Parachutes, 346–47. Heights Finance Corporation provides for one-tenth of a vote per share for all shares held in excess of 10%. Banner & Finley, Shark Repellent Charter and Bylaw Provisions, 15th Ann. Inst. Sec. Reg. 629, 667–68. The practice was seriously slowed by the SEC's adoption of Securities Exchange Act Rule 19c–4, which provided in part:

> "(a) The rules of each exchange shall provide as follows: No rule, stated policy, practice, or interpretation of this exchange shall permit the listing, or the continuance of the listing, of any common stock or other equity security of a domestic issuer, if the issuer of such security issues any class of security, or takes other corporate action, with the effect of nullifying, restricting or disparately reducing the per share voting rights of holders of an outstanding class or classes of common stock of such issuer registered pursuant to Section 12 of the Act."

Subsection (b) imposed a similar requirement on national securities associations (NASDAQ). But the rule was held to be invalid, and in excess of the SEC's authority, in The Business Roundtable v. SEC, 905 F.2d 406 (D.C. Cir. 1990). In 1994 the New York Stock Exchange, American Stock Exchange and the National Association of Securities Dealers (NASD) adopted identical rules for the exchanges and the NASDAQ National Market System and Small Cap system. Securities Exchange Act Release 35121 (Dec. 19, 1994). The NYSE policy statement on voting rights mirrors the language of former Rule 19c–4, but it provides a "grandfather clause" for companies with pre-existing dual class voting structures at the time they list with the exchange. NYSE Listed Company Manual § 313.10. See also AMEX Company Guide § 122.01 and NASDAQ Listed Company Manual § 4351 and IM–4351. As a result, many high tech companies that have gone public have done so with dual class voting structures in place, as Google did in 2004.

For a review of the arguments concerning the freedom to amend corporate charters see Bebchuk, The Debate on Contractual Freedom in Corporate Law, 89 Colum. L. Rev. 1395 (1989). For arguments that these amendments can benefit target shareholders, see Baysinger & Butler, Antitakeover Amendments, Managerial Entrenchment and the Contractual Theory of the Corporation, 71 Virginia Law Review 1257 (1985) and Carney,

Shareholder Coordination Costs, Shark Repellents and Takeout Mergers, 1983 American Bar Foundation Research Journal 341. For arguments that these amendments harm investors, see Easterbrook & Fischel, The Proper Role of Target's Management in Responding to a Tender Offer, 94 Harvard Law Review 1161 (1981) and Gilson, The Case Against Shark Repellent Amendments: Structural Limitations on the Enabling Concept, 34 Stanford Law Review 775 (1982). Easterbrook & Fischel argue that any takeover defenses reduce the probability that bids will be made for a target, because, even used in a loyal manner by target managers, they increase the expected cost of a takeover. Implicit in this analysis is the argument that all voluntary economic exchanges involve gains from trade, and the loss of any number of transactions, no matter how small, is society's loss. The arguments that takeover defenses can benefit target shareholders are not directly responsive, because they only consider the gains to target shareholders. In considering only these gains, the magnitude of target shareholder gains must be balanced against the lost opportunities to sell—a much more complex task. For a review of the empirical evidence, see John C. Coates, Takeover Defenses in the Shadow of the Pill: A Critique of the Scientific Evidence, 79 Tex. L. Rev. 271 (2000). Coates argues that shark repellents and some other takeover defenses are no longer very important, because of the development of the poison pill. Part 2.E of this chapter includes a critical evaluation of whether poison pills are as powerful as most observers, apparently including Coates, appear to believe.

This author believes that shark repellent amendments had the effect of causing virtually all bids to be for any and all shares, and causing planned cash-out mergers to be at the same price. Not only did this comply with most shark repellents' requirements, it also eliminated the ability of target management to claim that a bid was coercive and unfair, and thus should be defeated. As institutional investors have come to dominate share ownership in the United States, their opposition has made it infeasible for managers to secure shareholder approval for shark repellents in many corporations. As in the case of dual class voting, this has led to adoption of such charter amendments by some companies before they make their initial public offering of stock. By the 1980s this led many states to adopt "fair price" requirement antitakeover statutes, which mimicked the shark repellents, but did not require shareholder approval. These statutes were either opt-out (mandatory unless the board took action to reject their application) or opt-in, which required the board's action to make them applicable. These statutes are described more fully in Chapter Seven, *infra*.

D. PROTECTING THE BOARD FROM PROXY FIGHTS

Delaware General Corporation Law §§ 109, 141, 223, 228, 242; Model Business Corporation Act §§ 7.27, 8.03, 8.06, 8.08, 8.10, 10.20–10.21.

NOTE ON CONDEC CORPORATION V. LUNKENHEIMER CO.

230 A.2d 769 (Del.Ch. 1967).

Condec Corporation had been rebuffed by Lunkenheimer's officers in seeking to negotiate a merger with Lunkenheimer, and undertook an initial tender offer that obtained approximately 5% of Lunkenheimer's common stock, followed by a second tender offer that, if successful, would give it majority ownership of Lunkenheimer. But before it could close its second tender offer, Lunkenheimer management negotiated a share exchange with a "white knight,", U.S. Industries, in which Lunkenheimer issued 75,000 shares of its common stock in exchange for preferred stock of U.S. Industries, which had the effect of diluting the interest of Condec to less than majority ownership. The purpose of this issuance was to facilitate an asset sale to U.S. Industries, which required shareholder approval, which Condec could have blocked. Condec then sued to cancel the issuance of these shares, and prevailed. The Chancery Court held that, without a business purpose for the issuance of the new common shares, Lunkenheimer's board had violated its fiduciary duties to this shareholder to deny it control. Citing Cheff v. Mathes, the court noted that Lunkenheimer's board had not engaged in any serious investigation of Condec, and had no reason to believe it represented a threat to the company or its shareholders. Absent such proof, Lunkenheimer could not show a business purpose to justify its actions. The court concluded that "[t]his rather is a case of a stockholder with a contractual right to assert voting control being deprived of such control by what is virtually a corporate legerdemain. Manipulation of this type is not permissible." 230 A.2d at 777.

Blasius Industries, Inc. v. Atlas Corporation
564 A.2d 651 (Del.Ch. 1988).

■ ALLEN, CHANCELLOR.

Two cases pitting the directors of Atlas Corporation against that company's largest (9.1%) shareholder, Blasius Industries, have been consolidated and tried together. Together, these cases ultimately require the court to determine who is entitled to sit on Atlas' board of directors. Each, however, presents discrete and important legal issues.

The first of the cases was filed on December 30, 1987. As amended, it challenges the validity of board action taken at a telephone meeting of December 31, 1987 that added two new members to Atlas' seven member board. That action was taken as an immediate response to the delivery to Atlas by Blasius the previous day of a form of stockholder consent that, if joined in by holders of a majority of Atlas' stock, would have increased the board of Atlas from seven to fifteen members and would have elected eight new members nominated by Blasius.

As I find the facts of this first case, they present the question whether a board acts consistently with its fiduciary duty when it acts, in good faith and with appropriate care, for the primary purpose of preventing or impeding an unaffiliated majority of shareholders from expanding the board and electing a new majority. For the reasons that follow, I conclude that, even though defendants here acted on their view of the corporation's interest and not selfishly, their December 31 action constituted an offense to the relationship between corporate directors and shareholders that has traditionally been protected in courts of equity. As a consequence, I conclude that the board action taken on December 31 was invalid and must be voided. * * *

The facts set forth below represent findings based upon a preponderance of the admissible evidence, as I evaluate it.

I.

[Blasius was formed by two former commercial bankers, Michael Lubin and Warren Delano, apparently for the purpose of engaging in financially motivated takeovers, using junk bond financing. Blasius had raised $60 million through a junk bond offering, and its public filings disclosed that it lacked the funds to service this debt from its own operations. In July, 1987, Blasius began to accumulate shares in Atlas, and on October 29, 1987 it filed a Schedule 13D that disclosed that Blasius and its affiliates owned 9.1% of Atlas. Blasius disclosed that it intended to encourage management to consider a restructuring or another transaction to enhance shareholder value. Blasius also disclosed that it was exploring the feasibility of obtaining control of Atlas, either through a tender offer or representation on the Atlas board.

Atlas was run by a new CEO, Weaver, who was in the process of restructuring its operations to focus on its gold mining business. It had just announced closure of its uranium mining operations, and Weaver thought that the present restructuring should be given a chance to work before further restructurings were considered. On October 30, he wrote in his diary:

> 13D by Delano & Lubin came in today. Had long conversation w/MAH and Mark Golden [of Goldman, Sachs] on issue. All agree we must dilute these people down by the acquisition of another Co. W/stock, or merger or something else.

At a meeting between representatives of both sides on December 2, 1987, Blasius' principals suggested that Atlas engage in a leveraged restructuring that involved asset sales and distribution of cash and corporate debentures to shareholders. Following the meeting, the Atlas representatives agreed that such a restructuring was infeasible. Following the meeting Mr. Lubin of Blasius put his proposal in a letter sent to Atlas. Mr. Weaver and Atlas management reacted negatively, although they sent the proposal to Goldman Sachs, their investment bankers, for evaluation. Atlas management felt that this would amount to a substantial liquidation of Atlas at a time when its prospects were bright.]

* * *

The Delivery of Blasius' Consent Statement.

On December 30, 1987, Blasius caused Cede & Co. (the registered owner of its Atlas stock) to deliver to Atlas a signed written consent (1) adopting a precatory resolution recommending that the board develop and implement a restructuring proposal, (2) amending the Atlas bylaws to, among other things, expand the size of the board from seven to fifteen members—the maximum number under Atlas' charter, and (3) electing eight named persons to fill the new directorships. Blasius also filed suit that day in this court seeking a declaration that certain bylaws adopted by the board on September 1, 1987 acted as an unlawful restraint on the shareholders' right, created by Section 228 of our corporation statute, to act through consent without undergoing a meeting.

The reaction was immediate. Mr. Weaver conferred with Mr. Masinter, the Company's outside counsel and a director, who viewed the consent as an attempt to take control of the Company. They decided to call an emergency meeting of the board, even though a regularly scheduled meeting was to occur only one week hence, on January 6, 1988. The point of the emergency meeting was to act on their conclusion (or to seek to have the board act on their conclusion) "that we should add at least one and probably two directors to the board. . . ." A quorum of directors, however, could not be arranged for a telephone meeting that day. A telephone meeting was held the next day. At that meeting, the board voted to amend the bylaws to increase the size of the board from seven to nine and appointed John M. Devaney and Harry J. Winters, Jr. to fill those newly created positions. Atlas' Certificate of Incorporation creates staggered terms for directors; the terms to which Messrs. Devaney and Winters were appointed would expire in 1988 and 1990, respectively.

The Motivation of the Incumbent Board In Expanding the Board and Appointing New Members.

In increasing the size of Atlas' board by two and filling the newly created positions, the members of the board realized that they were thereby precluding the holders of a majority of the Company's shares from placing a majority of new directors on the board through Blasius' consent solicitation, should they want to do so. Indeed the evidence establishes that that was the principal motivation in so acting.

The conclusion that, in creating two new board positions on December 31 and electing Messrs. Devaney and Winters to fill those positions the board was principally motivated to prevent or delay the shareholders from possibly placing a majority of new members on the board, is critical to my analysis of the central issue posed by the first filed of the two pending cases. If the board in fact was not so motivated, but rather had taken action completely independently of the consent solicitation, which merely had an incidental impact upon the possible effectuation of any action authorized by the shareholders, it is very unlikely that such action would be subject to judicial nullification. The board, as a general matter, is under no fiduciary obligation to suspend its active management of the firm while the consent solicitation process goes forward.

* * *

II.

Plaintiff attacks the December 31 board action as a selfishly motivated effort to protect the incumbent board from a perceived threat to its control of Atlas. Their conduct is said to constitute a violation of the principle, applied in such cases as Schnell v. Chris Craft Industries, Del. Supr., 285 A.2d 437 (1971), that directors hold legal powers subjected to a supervening duty to exercise such powers in good faith pursuit of what they reasonably believe to be in the corporation's interest. The December 31 action is also said to have been taken in a grossly negligent manner, since it was designed to preclude the recapitalization from being pursued, and the board had no basis at that time to make a prudent determination about the wisdom of that proposal, nor was there any emergency that required it to act in any respect regarding that proposal before putting itself in a position to do so advisedly.

* * *

III.

* * *

While I am satisfied that the evidence is powerful, indeed compelling, that the board was chiefly motivated on December 31 to forestall or preclude the possibility that a majority of shareholders might place on the Atlas board eight new members sympathetic to the Blasius proposal, it is less clear with respect to the more subtle motivational question: whether the existing members of the board did so because they held a good faith belief that such shareholder action would be self-injurious and shareholders needed to be protected from their own judgment.

On balance, I cannot conclude that the board was acting out of a self-interested motive in any important respect on December 31. I conclude rather that the board saw the "threat" of the Blasius recapitalization proposal as posing vital policy differences between itself and Blasius. It acted, I conclude, in a good faith effort to protect its incumbency, not selfishly, but in order to thwart implementation of the recapitalization that it feared, reasonably, would cause great injury to the Company.

The real question the case presents, to my mind, is whether, in these circumstances, the board, even if it is acting with subjective good faith (which will typically, if not always, be a contestable or debatable judicial conclusion), may validly act for the principal purpose of preventing the shareholders from electing a majority of new directors. The question thus posed is not one of intentional wrong (or even negligence), but one of authority as between the fiduciary and the beneficiary (not simply legal authority, i.e., as between the fiduciary and the world at large).

IV.

It is established in our law that a board may take certain steps—such as the purchase by the corporation of its own stock—that have the effect of defeating a threatened change in corporate control, when those steps are taken advisedly, in good faith pursuit of a corporate interest, and are reasonable in relation to a threat to legitimate corporate interests posed by the proposed change in control. Does this rule—that the reasonable exercise of good faith and due care generally validates, in equity, the exercise of legal authority even if the act has an entrenchment effect—apply to action designed for the primary purpose of interfering with the effectiveness of a stockholder vote? Our authorities, as well as sound principles, suggest that the central importance of the franchise to the scheme of corporate governance, requires that, in this setting, that rule not be applied and that closer scrutiny be accorded to such transaction.

1. *Why the deferential business judgment rule does not apply to board acts taken for the primary purpose of interfering with a stockholder's vote, even if taken advisedly and in good faith.*

A.   *The question of legitimacy.*

The shareholder franchise is the ideological underpinning upon which the legitimacy of directorial power rests. Generally, shareholders have only two protections against perceived inadequate business performance. They may sell their stock (which, if done in sufficient numbers, may so affect security prices as to create an incentive for altered managerial performance), or they may vote to replace incumbent board members.

It has, for a long time, been conventional to dismiss the stockholder vote as a vestige or ritual of little practical importance. It may be that we are now witnessing the emergence of new institutional voices and arrangements that will make the stockholder vote a less predictable affair than it has been. Be that as it may, however, whether the vote is seen functionally as an unimportant formalism, or as an important tool of discipline, it is clear that it is critical to the theory that legitimates the exercise of power by some (directors and officers) over vast aggregations of property that they do not own. Thus, when viewed from a broad, institutional perspective, it can be seen that matters involving the integrity of the shareholder voting process involve considerations not present in any other context in which directors exercise delegated power.

B.   *Questions of this type raise issues of the allocation of authority as between the board and the shareholders.*

The distinctive nature of the shareholder franchise context also appears when the matter is viewed from a less generalized, doctrinal point of view. From this point of view, as well, it appears that the ordinary considerations to which the business judgment rule originally responded are simply not present in the shareholder voting context.[2] That is, a decision by the board to act for the primary purpose of preventing the effectiveness of a shareholder vote inevitably involves the question who, as between the principal and the agent, has authority with respect to a matter of internal corporate governance. That, of course, is true in a very specific way in this case which deals with the question who should constitute the board of directors of the corporation, but it will be true in every instance in which an incumbent board seeks to thwart a shareholder majority. A board's decision to act to prevent the shareholders from creating a majority of new board positions and filling them does not involve the exercise of the corporation's power over its property, or with respect to its rights or obligations; rather, it involves allocation, between shareholders as a class and the board, of effective power with respect to governance of the corporation. This need not be the case with respect to other forms of corporate action that may have an entrenchment effect—such as the stock buybacks present in Unocal, Cheff or Kors v. Carey. Action designed principally to interfere with the effectiveness of a vote inevitably involves a conflict between the board and a shareholder majority. Judicial review of such action involves a determination of the legal and equitable obligations of an agent towards his principal. This is not, in my opinion, a question that a court may leave to the agent finally to decide so long as he does so honestly and competently; that is, it may not be left to the agent's business judgment.

---

[2] Delaware courts have long exercised a most sensitive and protective regard for the free and effective exercise of voting rights. This concern suffuses our law, manifesting itself in various settings. For example, the perceived importance of the franchise explains the cases that hold that a director's fiduciary duty requires disclosure to shareholders asked to authorize a transaction of all material information in the corporation's possession, even if the transaction is not a self-dealing one. See, e.g., Smith v. Van Gorkom, Del. Supr., 488 A.2d 858 (1985); In re Anderson Clayton Shareholders' Litigation, Del.Ch., 519 A.2d 669, 675 (1986).

A similar concern, for credible corporate democracy, underlies those cases that strike down board action that sets or moves an annual meeting date upon a finding that such action was intended to thwart a shareholder group from effectively mounting an election campaign. See, e.g., Schnell v. Chris Craft, *supra*; Lerman v. Diagnostic Data, Inc., Del.Ch., 421 A.2d 906 (1980); Aprahamian v. HBO, Del.Ch., 531 A.2d 1204 (1987).

The cases invalidating stock issued for the primary purpose of diluting the voting power of a control block also reflect the law's concern that a credible form of corporate democracy be maintained. See Canada Southern Oils, Ltd. v. Manabi Exploration Co., Inc., Del.Ch., 33 Del.Ch. 537, 96 A.2d 810 (1953); Condec Corporation v. Lunkenheimer Company, Del.Ch., 43 Del.Ch. 353, 230 A.2d 769 (1967); Phillips v. Insituform of North America, Inc., Del.Ch., C.A. No. 9173, Allen, C. (August 27, 1987).

Similarly, a concern for corporate democracy is reflected (1) in our statutory requirement of annual meetings (8 Del. C. § 211), and in the cases that aggressively and summarily enforce that right. See, e.g., Coaxial Communications, Inc. v. CNA Financial Corp., Del. Supr., 367 A.2d 994 (1976); Speiser v. Baker, Del.Ch., 525 A.2d 1001 (1987), and (2) in our consent statute (8 Del. C. § 228) and the interpretation it has been accorded. See Datapoint Corp. v. Plaza Securities Co., Del. Supr., 496 A.2d 1031 (1985) (order); Allen v. Prime Computer, Inc., Del. Supr., 538 A.2d 1113 (1988); Frantz Manufacturing Company v. EAC Industries, Del. Supr., 501 A.2d 401 (1985).

2. *What rule does apply: per se invalidity of corporate acts intended primarily to thwart effective exercise of the franchise or is there an intermediate standard?*

Plaintiff argues for a rule of per se invalidity once a plaintiff has established that a board has acted for the primary purpose of thwarting the exercise of a shareholder vote. Our opinions in Canada Southern Oils, Ltd. v. Manabi Exploration Co., Del.Ch., 33 Del.Ch. 537, 96 A.2d 810 (1953) and Condec Corporation v. Lunkenheimer Company, Del.Ch., 43 Del.Ch. 353, 230 A.2d 769 (1967) could be read as support for such a rule of per se invalidity. Condec is informative.

There, plaintiff had recently closed a tender offer for 51% of defendants' stock. It had announced no intention to do a follow-up merger. The incumbent board had earlier refused plaintiffs' offer to merge and, in response to its tender offer, sought alternative deals. It found and negotiated a proposed sale of all of defendants' assets for stock in the buyer, to be followed up by an exchange offer to the seller's shareholders. The stock of the buyer was publicly traded in the New York Stock Exchange, so that the deal, in effect, offered cash to the target's shareholders. As a condition precedent to the sale of assets, an exchange of authorized but unissued shares of the seller (constituting about 15% of the total issued and outstanding shares after issuance) was to occur. Such issuance would, of course, negate the effective veto that plaintiffs' 51% stockholding would give it over a transaction that would require shareholder approval. Plaintiff sued to invalidate the stock issuance.

The court concluded, as a factual matter, that: "... the primary purpose of the issuance of such shares was to prevent control of Lunkenheimer from passing to Condec...." 230 A.2d at 775. The court then implied that not even a good faith dispute over corporate policy could justify a board in acting for the primary purpose of reducing the voting power of a control shareholder:

> Nonetheless, I am persuaded on the basis of the evidence adduced at trial that the transaction here attacked unlike the situation involving the purchase of stock with corporate funds was clearly unwarranted because it unjustifiably strikes at the very heart of corporate representation by causing a stockholder with an equitable right to a majority of corporate stock to have his right to a proportionate voice and influence in corporate affairs to be diminished by the simple act of an exchange of stock which brought no money into the Lunkenheimer treasury, was not connected with a stock option plan or other proper corporate purpose, and which was obviously designed for the primary purpose of reducing Condec's stockholdings in Lunkenheimer below a majority.

A per se rule that would strike down, in equity, any board action taken for the primary purpose of interfering with the effectiveness of a corporate vote would have the advantage of relative clarity and predictability.[4] It also has the advantage of most vigorously enforcing the concept of corporate democracy. The disadvantage it brings along is, of course, the disadvantage a per se rule always has: it may sweep too broadly.

In two recent cases dealing with shareholder votes, this court struck down board acts done for the primary purpose of impeding the exercise of stockholder voting power. In doing so, a per se rule was not applied. Rather, it was said that, in such a case, the board bears the heavy burden of demonstrating a compelling justification for such action.

In Aprahamian v. HBO & Company, Del.Ch., 531 A.2d 1204 (1987), the incumbent board had moved the date of the annual meeting on the eve of that meeting when it learned that a dissident stockholder group had or appeared to have in hand proxies representing a majority of the outstanding shares. The court restrained that action and compelled the meeting to occur as noticed, even though the board stated that it had good business reasons to move the meeting date forward, and that that action was recommended by a special committee. The court concluded as follows:

> The corporate election process, if it is to have any validity, must be conducted with scrupulous fairness and without any advantage being conferred or denied to any candidate or slate of candidates. In the interests of corporate democracy, those in charge of the election machinery of a corporation must be held to the highest standards of providing for and conducting corporate elections. The business judgment rule therefore does not confer any presumption of propriety on the acts of directors in postponing the annual meeting. Quite to the contrary. When the election machinery appears, at least facially, to have been manipulated those in charge of the election have the burden of persuasion to justify their actions.

Aprahamian, 531 A.2d at 1206–07.

* * *

In my view, our inability to foresee now all of the future settings in which a board might, in good faith, paternalistically seek to thwart a shareholder vote, counsels against the adoption of a per se rule invalidating, in equity, every board action taken for the sole or primary purpose of thwarting a shareholder vote, even though I recognize the transcending significance of the franchise to the claims to legitimacy of

---

[4]   While it must be admitted that any rule that requires for its invocation the finding of a subjective mental state (i.e., a primary purpose) necessarily will lead to controversy concerning whether it applies or not, nevertheless, once it is determined to apply, this per se rule would be clearer than the alternative discussed below.

our scheme of corporate governance. It may be that some set of facts would justify such extreme action. This, however, is not such a case.

3. *Defendants have demonstrated no sufficient justification for the action of December 31 which was intended to prevent an unaffiliated majority of shareholders from effectively exercising their right to elect eight new directors.*

The board was not faced with a coercive action taken by a powerful shareholder against the interests of a distinct shareholder constituency (such as a public minority). It was presented with a consent solicitation by a 9% shareholder. Moreover, here it had time (and understood that it had time) to inform the shareholders of its views on the merits of the proposal subject to stockholder vote. The only justification that can, in such a situation, be offered for the action taken is that the board knows better than do the shareholders what is in the corporation's best interest. While that premise is no doubt true for any number of matters, it is irrelevant (except insofar as the shareholders wish to be guided by the board's recommendation) when the question is who should comprise the board of directors. The theory of our corporation law confers power upon directors as the agents of the shareholders; it does not create Platonic masters. It may be that the Blasius restructuring proposal was or is unrealistic and would lead to injury to the corporation and its shareholders if pursued. Having heard the evidence, I am inclined to think it was not a sound proposal. The board certainly viewed it that way, and that view, held in good faith, entitled the board to take certain steps to evade the risk it perceived. It could, for example, expend corporate funds to inform shareholders and seek to bring them to a similar point of view. See, e.g. Hall v. Trans-Lux Daylight Picture Screen Corporation, Del.Ch., 20 Del.Ch. 78, 171 A. 226, 227 (1934); Hibbert v. Hollywood Park, Inc., Del. Supr., 457 A.2d 339 (1982). But there is a vast difference between expending corporate funds to inform the electorate and exercising power for the primary purpose of foreclosing effective shareholder action. A majority of the shareholders, who were not dominated in any respect, could view the matter differently than did the board. If they do, or did, they are entitled to employ the mechanisms provided by the corporation law and the Atlas certificate of incorporation to advance that view. They are also entitled, in my opinion, to restrain their agents, the board, from acting for the principal purpose of thwarting that action.

I therefore conclude that, even finding the action taken was taken in good faith, it constituted an unintended violation of the duty of loyalty that the board owed to the shareholders. I note parenthetically that the concept of an unintended breach of the duty of loyalty is unusual but not novel. See Lerman v. Diagnostic Data, *supra*; AC Acquisitions Corp. v. Anderson, Clayton & Co., Del.Ch., 519 A.2d 103 (1986). That action will, therefore, be set aside by order of this court.

NOTE ON THE AFTERMATH

On November 2, 1988 Blasius terminated its proxy solicitation against Atlas and agreed to enter into a ten-year standstill agreement along with dismissal of all pending litigation between the parties. The terms of the agreement were that Blasius would not participate in any proxy or consent solicitation of Atlas' shareholders. In consideration of these moves by Blasius, Atlas agreed to reimburse Blasius $1.6 million in expenses related to its consent and proxy solicitations.

QUESTIONS

1. On October 29, 1987 Blasius had filed a Schedule 13D disclosing its ownership of 9.1% of Atlas. On December 30, Blasius filed its written consent for shareholder action, authorized by section 228 of the Delaware General Corporation Law. Assuming that it was filed solely on behalf of Blasius as owner of 9.1% of Atlas' stock, what was the legal effect of that filing? See Del. Gen. Corp. Law § 228. What practical effect would it have had on the board of Atlas and on Mr. Weaver?

2. What is the source of the board's statutory power to amend bylaws to enlarge its own size? Are there any statutory limits on that power? See Del. Gen. Corp. L. §§ 109(a) and 141(b).

3. Why doesn't Blasius simply amend its consent to amend the bylaws to increase the board's size beyond 15?

4. Does the business judgment rule apply to the board's action here? What is the court's explanation for its holding on this issue?

5. Are there statutory limits on the board's power to interfere with shareholder voting?

6. What is the burden on directors who interfere with shareholder voting? How could they meet that burden? Could a board ever argue that it simply knows better than the shareholders as a justification?

PROBLEM

The following hypothetical appears in footnote 5 of the Blasius opinion:

"Imagine the facts of Condec changed very slightly and coming up in today's world of corporate control transactions. Assume an acquiring company buys 25% of the target's stock in a small number of privately negotiated transactions. It then commences a public tender offer for 26% of the company stock at a cash price that the board, in good faith, believes is inadequate. Moreover, the acquiring corporation announces that it may or may not do a second-step merger, but if it does one, the consideration will be junk bonds that will have a value, when issued, in the opinion of its own investment banker, of no more than the cash being offered in the tender offer. In the face of such an offer, the board may have a duty to seek to protect the company's shareholders from the coercive effects of this inadequate offer. Assume, for purposes of the hypothetical, that neither newly amended Section 203, nor any defensive device available to the target specifically, offers protection. Assume that the target's board turns to the market for corporate control to attempt to locate a more fairly priced alternative that would be available to all shareholders. And assume that just as the tender offer is closing, the board locates an all cash deal for all shares at a price materially higher than that offered by the acquiring corporation. Would the board of the target corporation be justified in issuing sufficient shares to the second acquiring corporation to dilute the 51% stockholder down so that it no longer had a practical veto over the merger or sale of assets that the target board had arranged for the benefit of all shares? It is not necessary to now hazard an opinion on that abstraction."

What do you think the outcome would be if such a case arose?

NOTE ON UNOCAL REVIEW V. BLASIUS REVIEW

The overlap between the Blasius doctrine and the Unocal doctrine, which appear to have different burdens of proof for boards charged with overreactions to threats of loss of control, was noted by Vice Chancellor Strine in Chesapeake Corporation v. Shore, 771 A.2d 293 (Del.Ch. 2000), where the board adopted a supermajority voting requirement in the bylaws in anticipation of a proxy fight as part of a hostile bid. He stated:

> [I]n Stroud v. Grace, the Delaware Supreme Court held that Unocal must be applied to any defensive measure touching upon issues of control, regardless of whether that measure also implicates voting rights. In so ruling, the Court noted that "board action interfering with the exercise of the franchise often arises during a hostile contest for control where an acquiror launches both a proxy fight and a tender offer." When a case involves defensive measures of such a nature, the trial court is not to ignore the teaching of Blasius but must "recognize the special import of protecting the shareholders' franchise within Unocal's requirement that any defensive measure be proportionate and 'reasonable in relation to the threat posed.'" Therefore, a "board's unilateral decision to adopt a defensive measure touching upon issues of control that purposely disenfranchises its shareholders is strongly suspect under Unocal, and cannot be sustained without a compelling justification."

* * *

In reality, invocation of the Blasius standard of review usually signals that the court will invalidate the board action under examination. Failure to invoke Blasius, conversely, typically indicates that the board action survived (or will survive) review under Unocal.

Given this interrelationship and the continued vitality of Schnell v. Chris-Craft, one might reasonably question to what extent the Blasius "compelling justification" standard of review is necessary as a lens independent of or to be used within the Unocal frame. If Unocal is applied by the court with a gimlet eye out for inequitably motivated electoral manipulations or for subjectively well-intentioned board action that has preclusive or coercive effects, the need for an additional standard of review is substantially lessened. Stated differently, it may be optimal simply for Delaware courts to infuse our Unocal analyses with the spirit animating Blasius and not hesitate to use our remedial powers where an inequitable distortion of corporate democracy has occurred.

Nevertheless, Vice Chancellor Strine concluded that the existing law required him first to examine the bylaw under Unocal, because it was a defensive measure. He wrote:

> To the extent that I further conclude that the Supermajority Bylaw was adopted for the primary purpose of interfering with or impeding the stockholder franchise, the Bylaw cannot survive a Unocal review unless it is supported by a compelling justification.[6]

> To apply this approach in a reasoned manner, I will first examine the Supermajority Bylaw employing purely the Unocal standard. After examining the defendant's justifications for the Bylaw and whether the Bylaw is a proportionate response under Unocal, I will then determine whether the compelling justification standard of Blasius is implicated.

A similar conclusion was reached by Vice Chancellor Lamb in Aquila, Inc. v. Quanta Services, Inc., 805 A.2d 196 (Del. Ch. 2002). Aquila had entered into an agreement with Quanta to purchase stock with a limitation that it could not purchase more than 49.9% of Quanta's stock on a fully diluted basis, and Quanta agreed not to adopt a rights plan that would dilute Aquila's interest below that level. At a time when Aquila owned 38.5% and announced that it intended to buy enough stock to control Quanta (49.9% of the fully diluted shares is more than a majority of the outstanding shares), Quanta resisted, and amended its rights plan to reduce the triggering amount to 39%. When Aquila announced its intent to conduct a proxy fight for control of the board, Quanta created a trust for employee benefits, and placed eight million shares in the trust, which would be voted by the trustees in accordance with the instructions of the employee-beneficiaries. Employees are thought to be reliable voters against a change in control, and the court

---

[6]   Stroud, 606 A.2d at 92 n.3.

concluded that this would dilute the voting power of Aquila by 10%. In considering whether to apply Unocal or Blasius, Vice Chancellor Lamb began with his conclusion, that the creation of the trust did not make it impossible for Aquila to win a proxy contest, and thus applied Unocal. He noted that this reduced Aquila's voting power from 38% to 34%, but that Aquila still had a 2 to 1 advantage over management, assuming that all trust shares were voted in its favor. While declining to issue a preliminary injunction, he noted that if management won a proxy contest that was challenged by Aquila, the ultimate legality of the trust shares could be decided on the merits at that time, and the voting of those shares set aside if necessary.

The courts have discussed issues of shareholder coercion or preclusion in other contexts. In Stroud v. Grace, 606 A.2d 75, 91 (Del. 1992), the Delaware Supreme Court approved a lower court statement of the rule that "where boards of directors deliberately employed various legal strategies either to frustrate or completely disenfranchise a shareholder vote . . . [t]here can be no dispute that such conduct violates Delaware law."

In Williams v. Geier, 671 A.2d 1368, 1382–83 (Del. 1996), noted in Part 2.A of this chapter (following Unocal), the Delaware Supreme Court further explained that "[w]rongful coercion may exist where the board or some other party takes actions which have the effect of causing the stockholders to vote in favor of the proposed transaction for some reason other than the merits of that transaction."

In Datapoint Corp. v. Plaza Securities Co., 496 A.2d 1031 (Del. 1985), the Delaware Supreme Court struck down a bylaw imposing an advance notice requirement on shareholder consents, and delaying the effective date of action approved by such consents. The court found that the bylaw conflicted with the provisions of § 228 giving shareholders a statutory right to act through consents, and that the delays were both arbitrary and unreasonable, since they were designed to frustrate shareholder action by giving the board time to oppose a consent solicitation.

In Prime Computer, Inc. v. Allen, 1988 WL 5277 (Del.Ch.1988), Chancellor Allen extended this doctrine, relying on Datapoint, and struck down a bylaw adopted by the board regulating the procedures for filing of shareholder consents. Noting that the regulations adopted in the bylaws seemed reasonable on their face, the court nevertheless struck them down, on the basis that Section 228, creating a stockholder right to act by written consent unless limited in the certificate of incorporation, created an absolute shareholder right the board could not limit. The opinion stated:

> "The board may propose and recommend an amendment of the charter to that effect, but it may not, consistent with the particular grant of Section 228, arrogate to itself through its power to amend the corporation's by-laws, the right to substantially delay implementation of action taken pursuant to that section." 1988 WL 5277 at *6.

There are statements in a number of decisions that if a rights plan inhibits a proxy contest, it would be held invalid. In Moran v. Household

Int'l, Inc., 500 A.2d 1346, 1355 (Del. Ch. 1985), sustaining a "flip-over" plan, the court rejected plaintiff's argument that the particular plan would restrict shareholders' rights to conduct a proxy contest. The negative implication of this is that a plan that restricted the shareholders' rights would be invalid.

In Sutton Holding Corp. v. DeSoto, Fed. Sec. L. Rep. (CCH) ¶ 96,012 1991 WL 80223, Chancellor Allen examined a "change of control" provision added to corporate pension plans that provided that the company could not terminate its pension plans for a period of five years after a change of control, despite the fact that the plans were seriously overfunded, and the fact that the incumbent board was planning on terminating these plans for the benefit of existing shareholders. While declining to rule on the validity of these amendments because of federal law issues, Chancellor Allen was highly critical of the amendments, stating that "[p]rovisions in corporate instruments that are intended principally to restrain or coerce the free exercise of the stockholder franchise are deeply suspect." 1991 WL 80223 at *1. Note that the pension plan's provisions did not facially affect shareholder voting rights; they simply provided a new contract term in an agreement between the company and its employees. Further, he noted that the dominant motivation was protection of directors, not plan beneficiaries:

> "Provisions of this sort—like so-called poison pill stock rights plans—are designed to deter a change in control not to create useful rights in the event they are triggered." *Id.* at 4.

The transfer of the Blasius approach into Unocal situations became clearer in Unitrin, Inc. v. American General Corp., 651 A.2d 1361, 1378 (Del. 1995). The Delaware Supreme Court stated, after reviewing its own decisions, that "[i]n the modern takeover lexicon, it is now clear that since Unocal, this Court has consistently recognized that defensive measures which are either preclusive or coercive are included within the common law definition of draconian. . . ." 651 A.2d at 1386–87.

In MM Companies, Inc. v. Liquid Audio, Inc., 813 A.2d 1118 (Del. 2003), the Delaware Supreme Court faced board action that did not preclude a meaningful shareholder vote, but limited the potential consequences of that vote under certain contingencies. MM had sought to obtain control of Liquid Audio, and had made several purchase offers that had been rejected by the Liquid Audio board. In response, the Liquid Audio board had entered into a merger agreement with another corporation, which would not close before the annual meeting. Thereafter, MM announced its intention to nominate two candidates for the two vacancies on Liquid Audio's staggered five member board at the next annual meeting. Thereafter, the Liquid Audio board, concerned that the merger might be frustrated, amended the bylaws to increase the board to seven, and named two persons to fill the newly created vacancies, positions that would not expire at the next annual meeting. The board admitted that its purpose was to limit the potential effect of an MM victory at the annual meeting, expressing concern that two incumbents might resign if relations on the board became too acrimonious, giving MM a majority of the board, while if only one resigned, the board might be deadlocked. The Chancery Court concluded that this action was taken for the primary purpose of diminish the influence of any directors elected by MM. The Chancery Court dismissed MM's suit, concluding that Blasius did not apply because the board's action did not impact the shareholder vote on election of directors in any way, and rejected a Unocal claim, on the basis that the board expansion was not coercive or preclusive.

The Delaware Supreme Court reversed, finding simply that the primary purpose of the board's actions was "to interfere with or impede the effective exercise of the shareholder franchise in a contested election for directors," which shifted the burden to the board to show a "compelling justification" for its actions. At another point, the court noted that the board's action was "for the primary purpose of diminishing the influence of MM's two nominees on a five-member Board by eliminating either the possibility of deadlock on the board or of MM controlling the board, if one or two Director Defendants resigned from the board." Under those circumstances, the Supreme Court reversed and remanded.

Mercier v. Inter-Tel, Incorporated, 929 A.2d 786 (Del. Ch. 2007) illustrates that Blasius is most concerned with director accountability and proxy fights for control of board seats. Vice Chancellor Strine summarized his opinion as follows:

> In this decision based on a preliminary injunction record, I conclude that well-motivated, independent directors may reschedule an imminent special meeting at which the stockholders are to consider an all cash, all shares offer from a third-party acquiror when the directors: (1) believe that the merger is in the best interests of the stockholders; (2) know that if the meeting proceeds the stockholders will vote down the merger; (3) reasonably fear that in the wake of the merger's rejection, the acquiror will walk away from the deal and the corporation's stock price will plummet; (4) want more time to communicate with and provide information to the stockholders before the stockholders vote on the merger and risk the irrevocable loss of the pending offer; and (5) reschedule the meeting within a reasonable time period and do not preclude or coerce the stockholders from freely deciding to reject the merger.

929 A.2d at 787–788.

NOTE ON FEDERAL LAW CONCERNING DEFENSES TO PROXY FIGHTS

The prospect of a proxy fight is one that many incumbent directors dread and try to avoid. Similarly, CEOs try to avoid being surprised at shareholders' meetings by motions made from the floor, or even questions that could put management in an unfavorable light. One solution has been for boards to adopt bylaws that require advance notice of requests to place matters on the agenda for shareholders' meetings. Many of these are drawn from the precedent of the SEC's proxy rules with respect to shareholder proposals to be included in management's proxy materials. Rule 14a–8(e) provides that "The proposal must be received at the company's principal executive offices not less than 120 calendar days before the date of the company's proxy statement released to shareholders in connection with the previous year's annual meeting. However, if the company did not hold an annual meeting the previous year, or if the date of this year's annual meeting has been changed by more than 30 days from the date of the previous year's meeting, then the deadline is a reasonable time before the company begins to print and send its proxy materials." Accordingly, many corporations have adopted, usually through board action, bylaws with similar requirements for placing any matter on the agenda. It may be possible, however, to go too far with bylaw restrictions, as a matter of federal securities law. A bylaw that frustrated shareholders' exercise of their franchise under the SEC's proxy rules was held invalid as a matter of federal law in SEC v. Transamerica Corp., 163 F.2d 511 (3d Cir. 1947), *infra* in Chapter Seven, Part 4.A.

Judicial interpretation of these bylaws in Delaware has been hostile to attempts to block shareholder proposals. In Jana Master Fund, Ltd. v. CNET Networks, Inc., 2008 Del. Ch. 35, affirmed, 947 A.2d 1120 (Del. 2008), CNET's advance notice bylaw, Article II, § 3, provided as follows:

> Any stockholder of the Corporation that has been the beneficial owner of at least $1,000 of securities entitled to vote at an annual meeting for at least one year *may seek to transact other corporate business* at the annual meeting, provided that such business is set forth in a written notice and mailed by certified mail to the Secretary of the Corporation and received no later than 120 calendar days in advance of the date of the Corporation's proxy statement released to security-holders in connection with the previous year's annual meeting of security holders (or, if no annual meeting was held in the previous year or the date of the annual meeting has been changed by more than 30 calendar days from the date contemplated at the time of the previous year's proxy statement, a reasonable time before the solicitation is made). *Notwithstanding the foregoing, such notice must also comply with any applicable federal securities laws establishing the circumstances under which the Corporation is required to include the proposal in its proxy statement or form of proxy.* [Emphasis added.]

JANA sought to solicit proxies to replace two incumbent directors, expand the board from eight to thirteen and nominate five candidates to fill the new directorships, which would give it a majority on the board. JANA wrote CNET notifying it of JANA's intent to solicit proxies for these purposes, and requested inspection of a shareholder list under section 220 of the Del. GCL. CNET refused, arguing that JANA failed to state a proper purpose because its request was not timely under the advance notice bylaw. Chancellor Chandler held that the bylaw was not applicable to JANA's proposal, which was to solicit its own proxies, because the bylaw only applied to requests to have a shareholder's proposals included in the company's proxy under Rule 14a–8 of the Exchange Act. He summarized his holding:

The language of the Notice Bylaw leads to only one reasonable conclusion: the bylaw applies solely to proposals and nominations that are intended to be included in the company's proxy materials pursuant to Rule 14a–8. One may parse the bylaw as follows: (1) notice of CNET's annual meeting will be provided to stockholders sometime between ten and sixty days before the meeting is held; (2) any stockholder who has owned $1,000 of stock for at least a year before the meeting may seek to transact other corporate business at the meeting; (3) to do so, that stockholder must send the CNET secretary notice of what business he/she plans to conduct a certain number of days before CNET needs to send out its proxy materials; and, finally, (4) in addition, such notice must also comply with the federal securities laws governing shareholder proposals a corporation must include in its own proxy materials. There are three related reasons I conclude this bylaw can be read only to apply to proposals under Rule 14a–8. First, the notion that a stockholder "may seek to transact other corporate business" does not make sense outside the context of Rule 14a–8. Second, it is reasonable to conclude this bylaw applies only to proposals shareholders want included on management's proxy materials because the bylaw sets the deadline for notice specifically in advance of the release of management's proxy form. Third, and most importantly, the explicit language of the final sentence makes clear that the scope of the bylaw is limited to proposals and nominations a shareholder wishes to have included on management's form of proxy.

A similar result was reached by Vice Chancellor Noble in Levitt Corp. v. Office Depot, Inc., 2008 Del. Ch. LEXIS 47 one month after the JANA decision. Here Levitt sought to nominate two candidates for election to Office Depot's board. Levitt filed its own proxy statement soliciting proxies, but did not give notice under Office Depot's advance notice bylaw. Office Depot took the position that Levitt's nominations could not properly be brought before the meeting, and Levitt brought suit and won. The bylaw read as follows:

Section 14. Stockholder Proposals. At an annual meeting of the stockholders, only such business shall be conducted as shall have been properly brought before the meeting. To be properly brought before an annual meeting, business must be (i) specified in the notice of the meeting (or any supplement thereto) given by or at the direction of the Board of Directors, (ii) otherwise properly brought before the meeting by or at the direction of the Board of Directors or (iii) otherwise properly brought before the meeting by a stockholder of the corporation who was a stockholder of record at the time of giving of notice provided for in this Section, who is entitled to vote at the meeting and who complied with the notice procedures set forth in this Section. For business to be properly brought before an annual meeting by a stockholder, the stockholder must have given timely notice thereof in writing to the Secretary. . . .

To be timely, a stockholder's notice shall be received at the company's principal office . . . , not less than 120 calendar days before the date of Company's proxy statement released to shareholders in connection with the previous year's annual meeting. . . .

Such stockholder's notice shall set forth as to each matter the stockholder proposes to bring before the annual meeting (i) a brief description of the business desired to be brought before the meeting and the reasons for conducting such business at the meeting and any material interest in such business of such stockholder and the beneficial owner, if any, on whose behalf the proposal is made; and (ii) as to the stockholder giving the notice and the beneficial owner, if any, on whose behalf the proposal is made (A) the name and address of such stockholder . . . , (B) the class and number of shares of the corporation which are owned of record and beneficially . . . , and (iii) in the event that such business includes a proposal to amend either the Articles of Incorporation or the Bylaws of the corporation, the language of the proposed amendment. . . .

Nothing in these Bylaws shall be deemed to affect any rights of the stockholders to request inclusion of proposals in the corporation's proxy statement pursuant to Rule 14a–8 under the Exchange Act.

Vice Chancellor Noble held that the election of directors was covered by the term "business" in the first sentence of the bylaw, despite the absence of a specific reference to nominations and elections of directors. Second, he held that nomination of directors was covered by the bylaw, as the nomination is an essential part of the election process. But he then held that notice had been given by Home Depot that satisfied these requirements as the election of directors was mentioned as a subject for action in Office Depot's own notice of the meeting.

ISS guidelines advise shareholders to vote against proposed advance notice bylaws.

QUESTIONS

1. What changes would you make to Office Depot's bylaws to make them more restrictive?

2. Who has authority to adopt such a bylaw? See MBCA §§ 10.20 to 10.21; Del. GCL § 109.

3. What is the effect of the last sentence of Del. GCL § 109(a)? In Nomad Acquisition Corp. v. Damon Corp., Fed.Sec.L.Rep. ¶ 94,040 (Del.Ch. 1988), the Delaware Chancery Court denied a preliminary injunction against a board-adopted bylaw that required 60 days advance notice before stockholders could submit a nomination of a candidate for the board. See also Kidsco, Inc. v. Dinsmore, 674 A.2d 483, 490 (1995), aff'd,

670 A.2d 1338 (Del. 1995) (holding that a bylaw adopted by the board requiring 60 days' notice of special meetings was reasonable). But see Datapoint Corp. v. Plaza Securities Co., 496 A.2d 1031 (Del. Supr. 1985) (invalidating a bylaw that required 60 days advance notice and delayed the effective date of stockholder action taken by written consent for another 60 days, on the basis that it imposed an unreasonable delay on the effectiveness of stockholder action).

4. Does common practice determine the meaning of § 109(a)? In Mentor Graphics Corp. v. Quickturn Design Systems, Inc., 728 A.2d 25, affirmed on other grounds, Quickturn Design Systems, Inc. v. Shapiro, 721 A.2d 1281 (Del. 1998), Quickturn's bylaws provided that if any special meeting is requested by shareholders, the corporation would fix the record date for, and determine the time and place of, that special meeting, which must take place not less than 90 days nor more than 100 days after the receipt and determination of the validity of the shareholders' request. The board justified its adoption of this bylaw in part on the basis that a bidder's proposal might stampede the shareholders into making a decision without adequate time to become adequately informed. The Chancery Court rejected the plaintiffs' arguments that most proxy contests are determined in 30 to 35 days, and that sophisticated financial institutions, which generally determine the outcome of these contests, do not require three times that long to make a decision. The board was entitled to consider the needs of non-institutional investors, the court held. The court relied in part on the expert testimony of Professor Bernard Black, who testified that a 1998 study by the Investor Responsibility Research Corporation revealed that of 1922 large publicly traded companies, 880 (46%) have some form of advance notice by-law. Of those by-laws, the most common notice period (adopted by 335 companies) is 50 to 70 days, and the second most common notice period (adopted by 223 companies) is 75 to 100 days.

NOTE ON FILLING VACANCIES ON THE BOARD

Moon v. Moon Motor Car Co., 151 A. 298, 302 (Del.Ch. 1930), referred to the "inherent right" of shareholders to fill new positions on the board of directors. In Steinkraus v. GIH Corp., 1991 WL 3922 (Del.Ch. 1991), the court denied a motion to dismiss a complaint challenging a bylaw raising the required vote for the election of directors, on the ground that the court needed to determine whether the bylaw was designed to preclude an effective vote at a stockholders' meeting. But Del. G.C.L. § 223 authorizes the board to fill both vacancies and newly created directorships, unless otherwise provided in either the certificate of incorporation or bylaws. In DiEleuterio v. Cavaliers of Delaware, Inc., Del.Ch., 1987 WL 6338 (Del. Ch. 1987), a plaintiff challenged board action denying stockholders' claims that the stockholders had validly filled newly created directors' positions. The corporation's bylaws provided that the remaining board members should designate a "successor director" whenever an office of director became vacant. Chancellor Allen read the bylaw as signifying a limitation on board power—that it could only fill vacancies, rather than newly created directorships, and that it could only fill them until the next meeting of the shareholders. The decision did not address the question of whether a more broadly worded bylaw would run afoul of the final sentence of § 109(a).

MBCA § 8.10(a) grants concurrent power to both shareholders and the remaining directors to fill vacancies, unless otherwise provided in the articles of incorporation. Because directors of public corporations can act more rapidly than shareholders, the default rule is that directors will fill vacancies. The same provision defines vacancies to include newly created positions.

NOTE ON HOLLINGER INTERNATIONAL, INC. V. BLACK AND BYLAW AMENDMENTS LIMITING BOARD POWER

In Hollinger International, Inc. v. Black, 844 A.2d 1022 (Del.Ch. 2004), the Delaware courts confronted a controlling shareholder at odds with a majority of the board, who unilaterally amended the bylaws through use of his super-voting shares. Corporate investigations had disclosed that Lord Conrad Black had been paid large sums for his personal covenants not to compete with the buyer when Hollinger International sold subsidiaries, thus diverting part of the sale proceeds from International to Black. At the same time, the board determined that it should explore the possibility of the sale of all or part of the company, in part because of Black's dire cash situation. Black, in the meantime, sought to frustrate that effort by selling his holding company, Hollinger, Inc. ("Inc.") which, through super-voting shares, had 72.8% of the voting power but only 30% of the equity of International. Various agreements were reached between the board and Black, including his commitment to repay funds that the company concluded were improperly diverted, and to support the company in its efforts to explore sales of part or all of its assets to benefit all shareholders. The board repeatedly discovered that Black was violating these covenants, and, in order to prevent a sale of the holding company, considered, among other things, adoption of a poison pill that would apply to any buyer of the holding company. The board formed a Corporate Review Committee ("CRC"), which was comprised of all directors other than Black, Mrs. Black, and a Black ally, Colson. The CRC was given broad authority to act for the company and to adopt such measures as a shareholder rights plan.

Fearing this, Black caused Inc. to file a written consent with International amending the bylaws, to set an 80% quorum requirement for board meetings, and unanimous consent for certain "Special Board Matters," which covered changes in the size of the board, filling vacancies, approving a merger or sale of assets in excess of $1 million, and amending or repealing any bylaw of the company. Because Black and his allies held 3 of the 11 board seats, this would have given them a veto over major transactions, if only by their absence. Vice Chancellor Strine's opinion made it perfectly clear that

Black had behaved very badly, and had breached his duties to International. With that as a preface, he then addressed the validity of the bylaw amendments.

"*Were The Bylaw Amendments Properly Adopted?*

"I turn now to International's challenge to the Bylaw Amendments. As discussed in part previously, the Bylaw Amendments prevent the International board from acting on any matter of significance except by unanimous vote; set the board's quorum requirement at 80%; require that seven-days' notice be given for special meetings; and provide that the stockholders, and not the directors, shall fill board vacancies.

"International argues quite plausibly that the Bylaw Amendments were designed to ensure that Black, and thereafter the Barclays (who had contracted with Black to buy Hollinger, Inc.), can veto any action at the International board level that they oppose. Black admitted that the Bylaw Amendments were designed to protect against the adoption of the Rights Plan and would give him (and other non-independent directors allied to him) the ability to prevent the International independent directors—who constitute the board's majority—from pursuing strategic options he opposes. Quite obviously, the Bylaw Amendments also deliver on Black's contractual obligation to the Barclays to take measures to thwart International from engaging in any significant transactions, including asset sales or the signing of a merger agreement.

"International argues that the Bylaw Amendments constitute an attempt by Black to cement the injury he caused to International's Strategic Process through his prior violations of his fiduciary and contractual duties. In essence, the Bylaw Amendments permit Black to proceed with the Barclay Transaction even though that Transaction was the product of improper and inequitable conduct. Because of the inequitable motivations behind the Bylaw Amendments, International argues that they must be declared ineffective. As to one particular aspect of the Bylaw Amendments—the abolition of the CRC and the termination of its authority—International also argues that the Bylaw Amendments are not simply inequitable, but violative of the DGCL as well.

"By contrast to International, the defendants contend that the Bylaw Amendments simply are a proper attempt by Inc. as a majority stockholder to prevent itself from being wrongly excluded from exercising the power that legitimately flows from voting control. It is the International independent directors, they argue, and not Inc., who are acting inequitably. By attempting to exclude Black, Mrs. Black, and Colson from participating in the Strategic Process and from preventing Inc. from acting to impede the adoption of the Rights Plan, the independent directors, the defendants claim, have overstepped their bounds. The defendants therefore contend that the Bylaw Amendments are a legitimate response to the independent directors' overreaching. More mundanely, the defendants argue that all of the Bylaw Amendments are consistent with the DGCL and International's charter.

"Before opining as to which side is, in my view, correct, it is useful to highlight the distinction these claims raise. It is a venerable and useful one in corporate law. In general, there are two types of corporate law claims. The first is a legal claim, grounded in the argument that corporate action is improper because it violates a statute, the certificate of incorporation, a bylaw or other governing instrument, such as a contract. The second is an equitable claim, founded on the premise that the directors or officers have breached an equitable duty that they owe to the corporation and its stockholders. Schnell v. Chris-Craft Industries, Inc. is the classic recent statement of the principle that 'inequitable action does not become permissible simply because it is legally possible.'[7]

"In addressing the Bylaw Amendments, and the later challenge to the Rights Plan, I am mindful of the distinction between these types of claims. The DGCL is intentionally designed to provide directors and stockholders with flexible authority, permitting great discretion for private ordering and adaptation. That capacious grant of power is policed in large part by the common law of equity, in the form of fiduciary duty principles. The judiciary deploys its equitable powers cautiously to avoid intruding on the legitimate scope of action the DGCL leaves to directors and officers acting in good faith. The business judgment rule embodies that commitment to proper judicial restraint. At the same time, Delaware's public policy interest in vindicating the legitimate expectations stockholders have of their corporate fiduciaries requires its courts to act when statutory flexibility is exploited for inequitable ends.

"The Bylaw Amendments Are Not Inconsistent With The DGCL

"With those principles in mind, I now determine whether the Bylaw Amendments are effective. I begin by rejecting International's claim that the aspect of the Bylaw Amendments that abolishes the CRC is statutorily invalid. International bases that argument on § 141(c)(2), which states in pertinent part that:

> "Any such committee, to the extent provided in the resolution of the board of directors, or in the bylaws of the corporation, shall have and may exercise all the powers and authority of the board of directors in the management of the business and affairs of the corporation. . . .

"International contends that § 141(c)(2) empowers only directors to eliminate a committee established by a board resolution and not stockholders acting through a bylaw.

"I agree with the defendants that this argument is not convincing. Stockholders are invested by § 109 with a statutory right to adopt bylaws. By its plain terms, § 109 provides stockholders with a broad right to adopt bylaws 'relating to the business of the corporation, the conduct of its affairs, and its rights or powers or the rights or powers of its stockholders, directors,

---

[7]   Schnell v. Chris-Craft Indus., Inc., 285 A.2d 437, 439 (Del. 1971).

officers or employees.' This grant of authority is subject to the limitation that the bylaws may not conflict with law or the certificate of incorporation.

"Traditionally, the bylaws have been the corporate instrument used to set forth the rules by which the corporate board conducts its business.[8] To this end, the DGCL is replete with specific provisions authorizing the bylaws to establish the procedures through which board and committee action is taken.[9] While there has been much scholarly debate about the extent to which bylaws can—consistent with the general grant of managerial authority to the board in § 141(a)—limit the scope of managerial freedom a board has, e.g., to adopt a rights plan, there is a general consensus that bylaws that regulate the process by which the board acts are statutorily authorized.[10] This includes the extent to, and manner in, which the board shall act through committees.[11] Indeed, before the recent Bylaw Amendments, the International Bylaws heavily regulated the corporation's committee procedures.

"In Frantz Manufacturing Co. v. EAC Industries,[12] the Delaware Supreme Court made clear that bylaws could impose severe requirements on the conduct of a board without running afoul of the DGCL. In Frantz, a majority stockholder implemented bylaw amendments when it feared that the incumbent board would divest it of its voting power. The amendments

---

[8]   See Gow v. Consolidated Coppermines Corp., 19 Del.Ch. 172, 165 A. 136, 140 (Del.Ch. 1933) ("As the charter is an instrument in which the broad and general aspects of the corporate entity's existence and nature are defined, so the by-laws are generally regarded as the proper place for the self-imposed rules and regulations deemed expedient for its convenient functioning to be laid down."); see also 1 R. Franklin Balotti & Jesse A. Finkelstein, The Delaware Law of Corporations & Business Organizations § 1.10, at 1–12 (2002 Supp.) (quoting id.); 18A Am. Jur. 2d Corporations § 311 (2003) ("Bylaws are the laws adopted by the corporation for the regulation of its actions and the rights and duties of its members.").

[9]   E.g., 8 Del. C. § 141(b) (allowing bylaws that set the number of directors on a board); id. (allowing bylaws that set the number of directors required for a quorum, with a statutory floor of 1/3 the total number of directors); id. (permitting bylaws that set the vote requirements for board action, with a statutory floor of a majority of directors present at meeting where quorum is met); id. § 141(f) (authorizing bylaws that preclude board action without a meeting).

[10]   For example, Professor Hamermesh's well-regarded and well-known article about stockholder-adopted bylaws argues that bylaws cannot be used to impede the managerial authority of the board to use a shareholder rights plan. But it also recognizes that a core function of the bylaws is to address the process by which the board makes decisions. Lawrence A. Hamermesh, Corporate Democracy and Stockholder-Adopted By-Laws: Taking Back the Street?, 73 Tul. L. Rev. 409, 484–85 (1998) (discussing bylaws affecting board governance, and noting that "the stockholders have considerable authority to adopt by-laws limiting the way in which the board of directors conducts its business"). Other distinguished scholars also believe that stockholders have broad statutory power to pervasively regulate board processes in the bylaws, albeit subject to the constraints of equity. See generally John C. Coates IV & Bradley C. Faris, Second-Generation Shareholder Bylaws: Post-Quickturn Alternatives, 56 Bus. Law. 1323 (2001); John C. Coffee, Jr., The Bylaw Battlefield: Can Institutions Change the Outcome of Corporate Control Contests?, 51 U. Miami L. Rev. 605 (1997); Jeffrey N. Gordon, "Just Say Never?" Poison Pills, Deadhand Pills, and Shareholder-Adopted Bylaws: An Essay for Warren Buffett, 19 Cardozo L. Rev. 511 (1997).

[11]   E.g., 8 Del. C. § 141(c)(2) (authorizing the bylaws, within certain limits, to set forth the ceiling of powers a board committee may have); id. (permitting bylaws that allow committee members unanimously to appoint a replacement member of a board committee, should a current member of that committee be absent or disqualified); id. § 141(f) (allowing the bylaws permit committee action without a meeting); id. § 141(i) (permitting the bylaws to restrict board committees from having telephonic meetings).

[12]   501 A.2d 401 (Del. 1985).

required, among other things, that there be unanimous attendance and board approval for any board action, and unanimous ratification of any committee action. The Supreme Court found that the bylaws were consistent with the terms of the DGCL. In so ruling, the Court noted that the 'bylaws of a corporation are presumed to be valid, and the courts will construe the bylaws in a manner consistent with the law rather than strike down the bylaws.'

"Here, International argues that the Bylaw Amendments run afoul of § 141(c)(2) because that provision does not, in its view, explicitly authorize a bylaw to eliminate a board committee created by board resolution. By its own terms, however, § 141(c)(2) permits a board committee to exercise the power of the board only to the extent 'provided in the resolution of the board . . . or in the bylaws of the corporation.' As the defendants note, the statute therefore expressly contemplates that the bylaws may restrict the powers that a board committee may exercise. This is unremarkable, given that bylaws are generally thought of as having a hierarchical status greater than board resolutions, and that a board cannot override a bylaw requirement by merely adopting a resolution.[13] Further, in Frantz, the Delaware Supreme Court ruled that bylaws requiring that the full board decide matters by unanimous vote are permissible.

"Moreover, I find International's argument that the failure of § 141(c)(2) to use magic words like 'unless otherwise provided in the bylaws' renders board-created committees invulnerable from elimination through a bylaw amendment without merit. The words of § 141(c)(2) plainly subordinate board resolutions creating and empowering committees to overriding bylaw provisions, especially when read in concert, as they must be, with the capacious authority over a board's processes that § 109 and other provisions of § 141 plainly grant.

"For these reasons, I agree with the defendants that the provision in the Bylaw Amendments eliminating the CRC does not contravene § 141(c)(2).[14] The question therefore becomes whether that and the other Bylaw Amendments are impermissible because they were adopted for an inequitable purpose.

"*The Bylaw Amendments Are Inequitable*

"In Frantz, the Supreme Court also made clear that the rule of Schnell—that inequitable action does not become permissible simply because it is legally possible—applies to bylaw amendments. In Frantz, the Supreme Court, citing Schnell, reviewed bylaw amendments undertaken by the majority stockholder to ensure that they were not inconsistent with any rule

---

[13] Cf. 18A Am. Jur. 2d Corporations § 311 (2003) ("A resolution is not a bylaw. It is an informal enactment of a temporary nature providing for the disposition of certain administrative business of the corporation. In contrast, bylaws are the laws adopted by the corporation for the regulation of its actions and the rights and duties of its members.").

[14] For similar reasons, I reject International's argument that that provision in the Bylaw Amendments impermissibly interferes with the board's authority under § 141(a) to manage the business and affairs of the corporation. Sections 109 and 141, taken in totality, and read in light of Frantz, make clear that bylaws may pervasively and strictly regulate the process by which boards act, subject to the constraints of equity.

of common law and were reasonable in application. In the circumstances of that case, the Supreme Court found the very restrictive bylaws at issue proper because the majority stockholder—which had committed no acts of wrongdoing—was acting to protect itself from being diluted.

"In this case, the Bylaw Amendments were clearly adopted for an inequitable purpose and have an inequitable effect. In November 2003, Black was confronted with a very difficult set of circumstances. One option for him was to play it tough. He could have caused Inc. to file a written consent removing the entire board (using the total and personal dominion he clearly exercises over Inc.). If he had played it tough and did not act quickly or boldly enough to remove the board, Black could have been stripped of all his offices, been confronted with a board-adopted shareholder rights plan, a strong board reference to the SEC, and other events that he wished to avoid— including an immediate lawsuit against Inc. Instead of this approach, Black undertook to cut the best deal he could and made binding contractual obligations to International."

E. POISON PILLS

Delaware Gen. Corp. Law, §§ 151, 157; Model Bus. Corp. Act §§ 6.02, 6.24.

Poison pills, also known as "shareholder rights plans" or "share purchase rights plans," originated with language drawn from antidilution and antidestruction provisions protecting the holders of convertible securities and warrants to purchase stock of a company. In each case the right to acquire stock of the issuing company on the terms set out in the convertibles or warrants was subject to (i) dilution in value if new shares were issued at prices below the exercise price in the right, whether through a stock dividend or cheap sales, and (ii) destruction if the common stock of the company disappeared through a merger in which the issuing company was not the surviving corporation. Parkinson v. West End Street Railway Company, 173 Mass. 446; 53 N.E. 891 (1899). Over time sophisticated drafters developed language designed to protect these rights, by having them (i) adjust the number of shares that could be acquired for the exercise price in the case of dilution and (ii) flip over into rights to purchase stock of any surviving corporation in a merger to which the issuing corporation was a party. Elaborate price formulas were developed to help preserve the benefit of the bargain originally represented by the right to acquire the target's common stock.

When Brown-Forman Distillers Corporation made a hostile bid for Lenox, Inc., Lenox's advisers realized that the Brown family prized its 62% control of Brown-Forman, and designed a plan to destroy that control should Brown-Forman succeed in its takeover of Lenox. A new class of convertible preferred stock was issued as a dividend to all Lenox common stockholders. One preferred share was issued for each outstanding share of common stock. The terms of the preferred, issued under the Lenox board's authority to set the terms of "blank preferred," provided that each share of preferred stock was convertible into 40 shares of common stock. In the event of a merger of Lenox with a party that had gained control of Lenox, the preferred was convertible into common stock of the surviving and acquiring corporation. The conversion price for the preferred was set to assure that the holders of preferred received value at least equal to that offered in the front end cash tender offer. But more importantly, the plan was designed to assure that Lenox shareholders received common stock in the surviving corporation, thus diluting the Brown family's control over Brown-Forman.

This represented the first stage in the development of poison pills— the so-called "flip-over" pill. Crown Zellerbach Corporation adopted a flip-over plan. Rather than issue preferred to common stockholders, Crown Zellerbach issued each common shareholder one common stock purchase right for each share of common stock owned. These rights were exercisable at $100 per common share at a time when the stock was trading for approximately $30. They only became exercisable when someone became the owner of 20% of Crown Zellerbach's stock, or made a tender offer for 30% or more of its stock. They had a ten year life. Because the rights were so far "out of the money," they had no current value on issue, and thus had no impact on the balance sheet.* The interesting feature was the so-called "flip-over" right. The rights became exercisable for common stock upon the occurrence of several events: (1) a self-dealing transaction between the bidder and Crown, such as a merger of the bidder into Crown or the bidder's sale of assets to Crown for Crown stock, or (2) a second stage merger with a successful bidder. In such transactions the rights became exercisable for the bidder's stock, at a 50% discount from its market price.

The typical right was "stapled" to the common stock of the company, in that it could not be transferred separately from the common stock, and indeed, was represented by the outstanding common stock certificates. These rights also were not exercisable when held by a bidder, thus assuring that the remaining minority shareholders received treatment more favorable than the bidder, and could thus dilute the value of the bidder's shareholders. Typically rights could be redeemed at a nominal price by the target's board prior to the acquisition of a significant block of stock by a potential bidder, or prior to the announcement of a tender offer for such a block. This redemption power gave the target's board leverage to negotiate with a potential bidder, since the target's board could make a takeover feasible by redeeming the rights.

---

* This is because the rights are "out of the money," in the sense that exercise is highly unlikely, and thus does not dilute earnings per share. Further, accounting guidelines do not require the redemption price for the rights, which is typically nominal, to be treated as an obligation of the company, presumably for the same reason.

The weakness of the flip-over plan was demonstrated when Sir James Goldsmith acquired 51% of Crown Zellerbach's stock, which was an amount that terminated the board's power to redeem the rights. Goldsmith, on the other hand, could not undertake a second stage merger without suffering enormous dilution of his investment through the exercise of the flip-over rights. After a standoff, the parties settled their differences when Crown Zellerbach repurchased Goldsmith's shares in exchange for a major part of Crown's assets. But the lesson was obvious; a flip-over rights plan may prevent a second stage merger, but it will not necessarily prevent a change of control. And it prevented the board from seeking an alternative transaction with a more acceptable bidder.

This incident was followed by the development of the flip-in rights plan, which now has both a flip-in feature with antidilution protection, and a flip-over feature to protect the value of the rights from destruction.

The Illusory Protections of the Poison Pill

William J. Carney and Leonard A. Silverstein.
79 Notre Dame Law Review 101 (2003).

I.   THE OPERATION OF A RIGHTS PLAN

Rights are issued as pro rata distributions to all common stockholders.[11] The right is typically the right to purchase one unit of a new series of preferred stock.[12] The preferred stock unit has rights that are essentially equivalent to those of the common, with minor distinctions.[13] These rights are exercisable at the projected "long term value" of the common stock—the price the stock is predicted to reach at the end of the ten year life of the rights—a price typically three to five times higher than the current market price of the common stock.[14] To reach these valuations, financial advisers to the adopting company's board are required to make heroic assumptions about growth rates for

---

[11]   The date of the declaration of the dividend of rights is generally called the "Record Date" or the "Rights Dividend Declaration Date."

[12]   While there are no legal barriers to using whole shares of preferred, many companies lack sufficient authorized but unissued shares to accomplish this, and thus use fractions of a share.

[13]   Each unit has the same dividend and liquidation rights as the common, with the theoretical difference that the preferred's rights to payment are "prior" to those of the common, to satisfy what are thought to be legal requirements of a priority of some kind.

[14]   See, e.g., Wachtell, Lipton, Rosen & Katz, *The Share Purchase Rights Plan* (1996), *reprinted in* Ronald J. Gilson & Bernard S. Black, THE LAW AND FINANCE OF CORPORATE ACQUISITIONS: 1999 SUPPLEMENT 10, 15 and Martin Lipton & Erica H Steinberger, 1 TAKEOVERS & FREEZEOUTS § 6.03[4][b][I], at 6–61 (Release 27, 1999). A recent study of 341 rights plans adopted in 1998 showed median exercise prices were 5.1 times the price of the common stock at the time of the announcement, but only 3.5 times the high stock price for the 12 months preceding adoption of the rights plan, suggesting that declining stock prices may be a primary motivating factor in the adoption of rights plans. Houlihan Lokey Howard & Zukin, *Stockholder Rights Plan Study* 4 (1999).

company profits—typically in excess of 17% per year compounded for the ten year life of the rights plan.[15]

These rights are initially "stapled" to the common stock, in the sense that they can only be transferred with the common stock, and are not immediately exercisable on issue.[16] The rights separate from the common stock certificates and rights certificates are issued and become transferable apart from the common stock on a "Distribution Date." This occurs when a bidder appears, either by making a tender offer for a significant block of target shares, typically 30%,[17] or by becoming an "Acquiring Person" by acquiring a somewhat smaller block, typically 15% on the "Acquisition Date".[18] This makes it more difficult for a bidder to make a tender offer for a package that includes both the common stock and the rights because those who hold rights certificates are no longer necessarily identical with the shareholders. Prior to the Acquisition Date, the rights are redeemable for a nominal amount.[19]

The board's power to redeem the rights for a nominal amount generally terminates on the Acquisition Date.[20] This prevents a bidder that has taken a substantial position from waging a proxy fight to replace the board with new members, who will redeem the rights using its newly acquired shares to win the contest.[21]

More importantly, at the Acquisition Date, the rights are no longer exercisable to acquire a preferred stock unit at an unrealistic price—it was never contemplated that the preferred stock rights would be exercised on their original terms.[22] In the event the bidder acquires a

---

[15] The implied annual growth rate for earnings required to achieve these valuations was 17.7%. *Id.*

[16] By the terms of the rights agreement, the rights are initially represented by the common stock certificates, which will contain a notation to this effect.

[17] In some plans the rights separate ten days after the date of first announcement that the bidder either acquires the triggering amount of shares or announces a tender offer that would result in such ownership. Wachtell, Lipton, Rosen & Katz, *supra* note 14 at 15.

[18] A survey of rights plans adopted in 1998 found thresholds ranging from 10% to 35%, with a median of 15% and a mean of 16%. Houlihan Lokey Howard & Zukin, *supra* note 14 at 2. In 1999 the triggers may have been somewhat lower. More than 75% of the firms adopting or amending rights plans in 1999 set the trigger at or below 15%, with two-thirds of all adopting firms selecting the 15% level. Pat McGurn, *Guest Features-Poison Pills: The Storm of 1999 Trickles into 2000*, INVESTOR RELATIONS BUSINESS, Mar. 20, 2000, in LEXIS/NEWS/ALLNWS. The ISS Study shows that approximately 95 out of 115 plans used a 15% threshold, while approximately ten set the threshold at 10%. ISS Study, *supra* note 1.

[19] McGurn, supra note 18, at 16.

[20] *Id.*

[21] It does not prevent a bidder who has not yet reached the triggering amount from waging such a proxy fight, however, as AT & T did in its fight for control of NCR, and as Farley Industries did in its successful attempt to take over West Point-Pepperell, a fabric manufacturer. This threat was the inspiration for the "dead hand" pill, that attempted to protect the tenure of incumbent directors who were not otherwise protected by provisions for a staggered board, removal only for cause, and prohibitions against board-packing.

[22] The Internal Revenue Service has concluded that the probability of exercise of these rights is so remote that the distribution of the rights as a dividend does not constitute the distribution of stock or property to shareholders, and thus has no tax consequences—

specified substantial block and becomes an "Acquiring Person," the rights "flip in" and become exercisable for the target's common stock (the "flip-in") at a discount, typically 50% of current market value.[23] The exercise price for the preferred becomes the exercise price for multiple shares of common stock. Thus, if the exercise price was $100 per unit of preferred, the holder of a right now has the right to purchase common stock with a market value (pre-Acquisition Date) of $200 for $100.[24] The key to the operation of this plan is discrimination against the bidder—rights are void in the bidder's hands.

These rights have an important anti-destruction provision—a merger of the target into the bidder does not destroy the rights—they "flip over" to become exercisable in the bidder's common stock, on the same bargain basis as the flip-in rights—a 50% discount, using the same exercise price. Thus the dilution of the bidder's shareholders is identical, whether the flip-in or flip-over rights are triggered.[25]

II.   THE IMPACT OF A RIGHTS PLAN

A.   Introductory Problems

We now examine how a rights plan would operate if triggered. We begin with a simple observation: a rights plan can only dilute the investment that a bidder has already made when it crosses the threshold that triggers the rights. If the threshold is 15%, that is the most that can be taken from a bidder through dilution, hardly enough, by itself, to deter a determined bidder prepared to pay a premium for a target it perceives to be undervalued. Because most rights plans only provide a 50%

---

shareholders do not realize any taxable income on the receipt of rights. Rev. Rul. 90–11, 1990–1 C.B. 10.

[23] Thus the holder of a right would obtain the right to purchase $200 worth of target common stock at an exercise of price of $100. See Wachtell, Lipton, Rosen & Katz, *supra* note 14 at 15 and 1 Lipton & Steinberger, *supra* note 14 at § 6.03[4][b][I], at 6–62.

[24] Because companies may lack sufficient authorized but unissued shares of common stock to honor the rights, some plans now provide for a flip-in to be exercisable in "common stock equivalents," which are generally preferred share units with terms comparable to common stock. The number of preferred units is increased, so the exercise obtains for the rights holder a number of units equal to the number of shares of common stock that two times the exercise price could acquire. Because "blank check" preferred shares can be divided by the board into as many units as the board determines, and because these preferred units are the economic equivalent of the common stock, there is no limit to the number of shares that can be issued on exercise of the rights. See Wachtell, Lipton, Rosen & Katz, supra note 14 at 37 (Section 11(a) of the Rights Plan). Another solution provided by many rights plans is to allow the board to exchange the rights for one share of common stock. This avoids forcing shareholders to pay cash to exercise the rights. The difficulty, as we will show, is that the smaller number of dilutive shares issued reduces the dilution of the bidder's investment. See Table 5, *infra*. Finally, many rights plans provide that in the event the issuer lacks sufficient shares to honor all the rights, it will be obligated to pay rights holders "damages"—the difference between the value of what they receive on exercise and the value of what they were entitled to. To avoid insolvency issues, these obligations are generally conditioned on availability of sufficient cash, and create a continuing obligation to pay cash as it becomes legally available for payment.

[25] See text *infra* at Part II.B.7. Both the flip-in and flip-over rights have antidilution protection for rights holders of the type commonly found in convertible securities and options.

discount from market price, they will not appropriate all of the bidder's initial investment.

One of the difficulties in examining the operation of rights plans is that none have operated. In the 1980s Sir James Goldsmith acquired a sufficient amount of the stock of Crown Zellerbach Corporation to make its flip-over rights non-redeemable, but did not engage in a self-dealing event, such as a takeout merger, that allowed exercise of the flip-over rights.[26] No flip-in plan has ever been deliberately triggered,[27] although the authors experienced a close call in one case, and there have been a few other apparently inadvertent triggering events.[28] Several uncertainties present themselves in assessing the impact of a rights plan. If the rights plan flips in, will rights holders exercise immediately or will they wait until immediately before expiration, as rational holders of conventional options will do? While shares should be valued on a fully diluted basis in efficient markets, uncertainty about the target's receipt of cash and its investment or disposition by the target could influence the market value of its stock after the flip-in, and thus the cost of acquisition. We discuss this issue in sections II.B.2 and II.B.6, *infra*.

Because of the lack of operational experience, several other questions cannot be answered definitively. What will a target do with proceeds received from the exercise of the rights? If rights are exercised, the target would receive cash representing a multiple of the aggregate market value of its current equity, and would be unlikely to have any massive positive net present value projects in which to invest. In essence, it will probably hold cash or equivalents. If the proceeds are simply held by the target, the bidder can recapture them upon obtaining 100% control. If they are distributed to other shareholders in a discriminatory manner, the bidder's dilution losses are increased. We explore this in

---

[26] See Carney [Mergers and Acquisitions] *supra* note 4 at 264. The earliest rights plans lacked a flip-in feature; they only operated if the bidder engaged in a merger or other business combination with the target.

[27] 1 Arthur Fleischer, Jr. and Alexander R. Sussman, TAKEOVER DEFENSE, § 5.02[A], 5–18 to –19 (6th ed. 2002).

[28] In our case, the investor that crossed the triggering threshold also failed to file a timely Schedule 13D, so there was no public announcement of the acquisition of the amount that would have constituted it an "Acquiring Person," which allowed a settlement. Among the issuers that experienced inadvertent triggering events are Pediatrix Medical Group, Michel Chandler, *Shareholder Nearly Triggers a Poison Pill at Ailing Pediatrix*, MIAMI HERALD, Sept. 21, 1999, C3; Newcor, Inc., News Digest, RUBBER & PLASTICS NEWS, July 24, 2000, p. 4; *Worldtex, Inc., Business Briefs*, THE CHARLOTTE OBSERVER, Mar.29, 2000, LEXIS: News: Allnews; Illini Bank, Craig Woker, *Illinois Bank Sweeps Legal Doubleheader*, THE AMERICAN BANKER, Mar. 3, 2000, 5; Rawlings Sporting Goods Co. Inc., Al Stamborski, *Rawlings and 2 Investors Avoid Triggering Poison Pill*, ST. LOUIS POST DISPATCH, May 7, 1999, C11; BJ Services, David Ivanovich, *BJ Services Swallows Poison Pill; Takeover Defense Set Off by Mistake*, THE HOUSTON CHRONICLE, Jan. 7, 1994, Business Section, 1. Harold Simmons did trigger separation of a flip-in, flip-over plan of NL Industries in the 1980s, by acquiring 20% of its shares, but the flip-in rights did not become exercisable until occurrence of a business combination or the bidder's increase in its holdings by more than 1%. Amalgamated Sugar Co. v. NL Industries, 644 F.Supp. 1229 (S.D.N.Y. 1986). Newell Cos. announced that it would swallow a poison pill of Wm. E. Wright Co., but there is no indication whether it was a flip-in pill. *Newell to Swallow "Poison Pill,"* CHICAGO TRIBUNE, Oct. 21, 1985, Business Section, 3.

Part II.B.6, *infra*. Similarly, what if rights are not exercised immediately, but are only exercised after the bidder has increased its ownership beyond the minimum amount required to trigger the rights? The obvious answer is that this means the bidder has a larger investment subject to dilution, and thus larger losses. This is also explored in Part II.B.6.

B.   Calculating Bidder Dilution

We begin our discussion of bidder dilution with a caution: it is only half the picture. Too often analysis stops with an observation that a hostile bidder's initial investment will be massively diluted by crossing the threshold that permits exercise of the flip-in rights. While this is true, it gives an incomplete picture of the costs imposed by a rights plan on a determined bidder; it is a static rather than a dynamic analysis. As we noted earlier, the typical rights plan's flip-in rights are triggered by a 15% acquisition. If a bidder's initial investment is totally destroyed by the exercise of the rights, the rights plan has added only 15% to the bidder's costs of a total acquisition. Dilution is never 100% because the bidder remains the owner of some diminished percentage of the outstanding shares, so the bidder's actual losses (added costs) will be somewhat less.[29]

We begin our analysis by examining the operation of a typical preferred stock rights plan, with flip-in rights triggered at the 15% level, with the rights exercisable at a 50% discount from market price. We assume that rights have been issued at an exercise price four times the current (pre-bid) market price of the common stock. We further assume immediate exercise of the rights, and receipt of the proceeds by the target. We will then show that triggering flip-in rights at the minimum ownership level is a dominant strategy, because triggering with the bidder owning larger amounts always puts more of the bidder's investment at risk—at least until unrealistically high levels of ownership are attained. Table 1 below sets out the assumptions in our examples:

TABLE 1. ASSUMPTIONS FOR A TYPICAL PREFERRED STOCK RIGHTS PLAN

1.	Target shares outstanding:	1,000,000
2.	Pre-bid market price per share:	$10.00
3.	Bidder's per share cost for the first 15%:	$15.00[30]
4.	Expected takeover bid price per share:	$15.00
5.	Exercise price for preferred stock rights:	$40.00

---

[29] It is impossible for a rights plan to destroy the bidder's entire investment, because whatever the percentage, the bidder retains some shares in the target.

[30] This is a simplifying assumption; it is likely that the bidder's average cost per share for the first 15% will be less than $15 per share. The differences in results are modest, however. See Part II.B.4, *infra*.

6. Assumed market value per share of target shares
   for calculating common stock acquisition price: $15.00

7. Flip-in trigger: 15%

8. Flip-in discount: 50%

9. Shares issuable per right if the market price is $15
   (*$80/15*):   5.3333333

1. The Operation of a Flip-In Rights Plan

We now assume that a bidder acquires the minimum amount of shares necessary to trigger the rights, so that shares now trade on a fully diluted basis. Because the bidder receives no rights and suffers dilution, its percentage ownership is severely diluted, from 15% to 2.7%. But, unlike prior examples, we assume that the bidder is determined, and then proceeds to acquire the remaining public shares at the takeover premium of 50% over the pre-bid value of the target.

Table 2 shows the bidder's costs of a complete acquisition using these assumptions:

TABLE 2. BIDDER'S COST OF ACQUISITION USING A MINIMUM PURCHASE WITH A PREFERRED STOCK RIGHTS PLAN

Bidder's initial acquisition of 150,000 shares @ $15.00		$2,250,000
Rights flip in for 5.3333333333 shares for 850,000 rights—		
Shares Outstanding:		
New shares	4,533,333	
Original shares	1,000,000	
Total shares	5,533,333	
Proceeds of exercise: (*850,000 × $40*):	$34,000,000	
Market's estimate of value of target:	$49,000,000	
Value per fully diluted share		
(*$49,000,000/5,533,333*):	$8,855,421	
Value of bidder's 150,000 shares:	$1,328,313	
Bidder's dilution losses:	$921,688	
Bidder's cost for remaining shares		
(*5,383,333 × $8,855,422*) =		47,671,688
Total Cost to Bidder:		$49,921,688

If we assume that the proceeds of exercise of the rights have been retained intact by the target, once the bidder has gained control it can capture the $34,000,000 proceeds, leaving a net cost of $15,921,688. The dilution loss, $921,688, represents 41% of the bidder's initial investment.[31] Put another and more dynamic way, it represents 9.2% of the target's pre-bid value, or 6.1% of the bidder's original estimate of the cost of an acquisition, absent the rights plan. Premiums of this general magnitude are supported by studies of the premiums added to the cost of acquisitions by the presence of rights plans.[32]

The expected cost of a rights plan to a bidder is the bidder's cost per share times the number of shares held by the bidder, minus the post-issue (fully diluted) market value of the target's shares held by the bidder, which is a function of the market value of the entire company divided by the post-issue number of target shares. This can be expressed as equation (1):

where L = bidder's loss through dilution; c = bidder's average pre-trigger cost per share; m = pre-trigger market price; a = bidder's share ownership at the time flip-in rights are triggered; x = shares outstanding before dilutive issuance; d = number of shares issued in dilutive distribution; p = proceeds from exercise of rights $(x\text{-}a)e$; and e = exercise price of rights.

Equation (1) expresses the obvious truth that the bidder's loss can be no more than the bidder's investment in the target (ma) at the time the rights become exercisable, ameliorated by the new value received upon exercise of the rights (p), and limited by the fact that the bidder will retain some percentage ownership in the firm absent issuance of an infinite number of new shares at a zero exercise price.

---

[31] If the target immediately dividended the proceeds before the bidder completed the acquisition, the bidder would receive a small portion (2.71%) of the $34,000,000 dividend. This would amount to $921,400, virtually eliminating the dilution of its investment (but not its ownership percentage) previously suffered. This is explored *infra* in Part II.B.6.

[32] According to a study of premiums obtained between 1992 and 1996, the presence of a rights plan increased premiums by almost 8% of firm value, as reported in Georgeson & Company Inc.'s study of premiums obtained by companies with and without pills for the period 1992–1996. Georgeson & Co., *Mergers & Acquisitions: Poison Pills and Shareholder Value, 1992–1996*, at 1 http://www.georgeson.com/pdf/M&Apoisonpill.pdf. (visited 6/11/03). An earlier study found bid improvements of 14% for targets with pills that were subsequently taken over. Office of the Chief Economist, Securities and Exchange Commission, *The Effects of Poison Pills on the Wealth of Target Shareholders*, 41 (1986). This study examines early versions of rights plans in a small sample, given the date of the study. A Morgan Stanley study of deals between 1988 and 1995 reports gains to firms with pills of approximately 16%. Mark S. Porter, *Poison Pills Add Premium to Deal Pricing*, 10 No. 31 INVESTMENT DEALERS' DIGEST 2 (Aug. 4, 1997); John C. Coates IV, *Empirical Evidence on Structural Takeover Defenses: Where Do We Stand?*, 54 U. MIAMI L. REV. 783, 794, text at n. 44 (2000). Coates notes an update that produced similar results. *Id.* At n. 45, citing Kenneth A. Bertsch, *Poison Pills*, Investor Responsibility Research Center, Corporate Governance Series 1998 Background Report E at 21 (Jun. 25, 1998). Comment & Schwert, *supra* note 1, at 30–31, also find premium increases in this range. These percentage gains are higher than the dilution inflicted by our model. This may be a result of the issuance of more shares than our model suggests. A magazine reported a Morgan Stanley study of acquisitions since 1997 showed a median premium for firms with pills of 35.9% vs. 31.9% for firms without pills. *Daily Briefing: The Bids Sure Are Getting Hostile*, BUSINESS WEEK ONLINE, Jan. 4, 2002, LEXIS. Table 3 demonstrates how increasing the number of shares issued can increase bidder dilution.

Another variation on the rights plan is less popular, because it in effect puts a reservation price on the company's stock at which the board admits that an offer is adequate. These plans, called "back-end" or "poison put" plans, give common shareholders the right to force the company to repurchase their shares at a stated price upon the occurrence of a triggering event of the kind described above. In effect, they protect the common stockholders of the target from a takeout at a price that is less than a price the board has determined is adequate. Obviously if a bidder is willing to pay this price for all shares of the company, the plan will not deter a bid. On the other hand, the plan may obligate the company to pay out a large amount to its shareholders. Payment of such an amount could, in theory, render the company insolvent, thus making the distribution illegal, or even push it into bankruptcy. In order to guard against such events, most poison put plans provide that if the company lacks sufficient funds to make the full payments without insolvency, it shall make such payments from time to time as cash becomes available. In some cases shareholders who elect to exercise their rights and put their shares to the company may receive promissory notes bearing market interest rates, with payments due in a relatively short time, but subject to postponement in the event of insolvency.

Because of the opposition of some activist institutional investors, some plans have been modified to weaken the board's hand. Some pills have been made "chewable," in the sense that they give shareholders some control over the continuation of the effectiveness of the rights plan. Some, for example, give shareholders the right to revoke the rights plan in the face of a bona fide takeover offer. Others may provide for automatic nullification if a bid meets certain criteria, such as a fully financed cash tender offer left open for at least 60 days, that is accompanied by a fairness opinion from a recognized investment bank, and carry a premium of at least 65% over the stock's average closing price for the past 90 days and over the highest closing price for the past 52 weeks (Southwest Airlines). In other cases, boards commit to have the pill reviewed by a special committee of independent directors every few years.

Rev. Rul. 90–11
1990–1 C.B. 10.

Adoption of poison pill plans. The adoption of a "poison pill" plan by a corporation does not cause any taxpayer to realize gross income.

ISSUE

What are the federal income tax consequences, if any, of a corporation's adoption of a plan as described below, commonly referred to as a "poison pill" plan, which provides the corporation's shareholders with the right to purchase additional shares of stock upon the occurrence of certain events?

FACTS

X is a publicly held domestic corporation. X's board of directors adopted a plan (the "Plan") that provides the common shareholders of X with "poison pill" rights (the "Rights"). The adoption of the Plan constituted the distribution of a dividend under state law. The principal purpose of the adoption of the Plan was to establish a mechanism by which the corporation could, in the future, provide shareholders with rights to purchase stock at substantially less than fair market value as a means of responding to unsolicited offers to acquire X.

* * *

Until the issuance of the Rights certificates, as described below, the Rights are not exercisable or separately tradable, nor are they represented by any certificate other than the common stock certificate itself. If no triggering event occurs, the Rights expire a years [sic—ed.] after their creation.

* * *

At the time X's board of directors adopted the Plan, the likelihood that the Rights would, at any time, be exercised was both remote and speculative.

HOLDING

The adoption of the Plan by X's board of directors does not constitute the distribution of stock or property by X to its shareholders, an exchange of property or stock (either taxable or nontaxable), or any other event giving rise to the realization of gross income by any taxpayer. This revenue ruling does not address the federal income tax consequences of any redemption of Rights, or of any transaction involving Rights subsequent to a triggering event.

Moran v. Household International, Inc.

500 A.2d 1346 (Del. 1985).

■ McNEILLY, JUSTICE:

This case presents to the Court for review the most recent defensive mechanism in the arsenal of corporate takeover weaponry—the Preferred Share Purchase Rights Plan ("Rights Plan" or "Plan"). The validity of this mechanism has attracted national attention. Amici curiae briefs have been filed in support of appellants by the Security and Exchange Commission ("SEC")[1] and the Investment Company Institute.

---

[1]   The SEC split 3–2 on whether to intervene in this case. The two dissenting Commissioners have publicly disagreed with the other three as to the merits of the Rights Plan. 17 Securities Regulation & Law Report 400; The Wall Street Journal, March 20, 1985, at 6.

An amicus curiae brief has been filed in support of appellees ("Household") by the United Food and Commercial Workers International Union.

In a detailed opinion, the Court of Chancery upheld the Rights Plan as a legitimate exercise of business judgment by Household. Moran v. Household International, Inc., Del.Ch., 490 A.2d 1059 (1985). We agree, and therefore, affirm the judgment below.

I

The facts giving rise to this case have been carefully delineated in the Court of Chancery's opinion. *Id.* at 1064–69. A review of the basic facts is necessary for a complete understanding of the issues.

On August 14, 1984, the Board of Directors of Household International, Inc. adopted the Rights Plan by a fourteen to two vote.[2] The intricacies of the Rights Plan are contained in a 48-page document entitled "Rights Agreement." Basically, the Plan provides that Household common stockholders are entitled to the issuance of one Right per common share under certain triggering conditions. There are two triggering events that can activate the Rights. The first is the announcement of a tender offer for 30 percent of Household's shares ("30% trigger") and the second is the acquisition of 20 percent of the Household's shares by any single entity or group ("20% trigger").

If an announcement of a tender offer for 30 percent of Household's shares is made, the Rights are issued and are immediately exercisable to purchase 1/100 share of new preferred stock for $100 and are redeemable by the Board for $.50 per Right. If 20 percent of Household's shares are acquired by anyone, the Rights are issued and become non-redeemable and are exercisable to purchase 1/100 of a share of preferred. If a Right is not exercised for preferred, and thereafter, a merger or consolidation occurs, the Rights holder can exercise each Right to purchase $200 of the common stock of the tender offeror for $100. This "flip-over" provision of the Rights Plan is at the heart of this controversy.

* * *

Household did not adopt its Rights Plan during a battle with a corporate raider, but as a preventive mechanism to ward off future advances. The Vice-Chancellor found that as early as February 1984, Household's management became concerned about the company's vulnerability as a takeover target and began considering amending its charter to render a takeover more difficult. After considering the matter, Household decided not to pursue a fair price amendment.

---

[2]   Household's Board has ten outside directors and six who are members of management. Messrs. Moran (appellant) and Whitehead voted against the Plan. The record reflects that Whitehead voted against the Plan not on its substance but because he thought it was novel and would bring unwanted publicity to Household.

In the meantime, appellant Moran, one of Household's own Directors and also Chairman of the Dyson-Kissner-Moran Corporation, ("D-K-M"), which is the largest single stockholder of Household, began discussions concerning a possible leveraged buy-out of Household by D-K-M. D-K-M's financial studies showed that Household's stock was significantly undervalued in relation to the company's break-up value. It is uncontradicted that Moran's suggestion of a leveraged buy-out never progressed beyond the discussion stage.

Concerned about Household's vulnerability to a raider in light of the current takeover climate, Household secured the services of Wachtell, Lipton, Rosen and Katz ("Wachtell, Lipton") and Goldman, Sachs & Co. ("Goldman, Sachs") to formulate a takeover policy for recommendation to the Household Board at its August 14 meeting. After a July 31 meeting with a Household Board member and a pre-meeting distribution of material on the potential takeover problem and the proposed Rights Plan, the Board met on August 14, 1984.

Representatives of Wachtell, Lipton and Goldman, Sachs attended the August 14 meeting. The minutes reflect that Mr. Lipton explained to the Board that his recommendation of the Plan was based on his understanding that the Board was concerned about the increasing frequency of "bust-up"[3] takeovers, the increasing takeover activity in the financial service industry, such as Leucadia's attempt to take over Arco, and the possible adverse effect this type of activity could have on employees and others concerned with and vital to the continuing successful operation of Household even in the absence of any actual bust-up takeover attempt. Against this factual background, the Plan was approved.

Thereafter, Moran and the company of which he is Chairman, D-K-M, filed this suit. On the eve of trial, Gretl Golter, the holder of 500 shares of Household, was permitted to intervene as an additional plaintiff. The trial was held, and the Court of Chancery ruled in favor of Household. Appellants now appeal from that ruling to this Court.

II

The primary issue here is the applicability of the business judgment rule as the standard by which the adoption of the Rights Plan should be reviewed. Much of this issue has been decided by our recent decision in Unocal Corp. v. Mesa Petroleum Co., Del. Supr., 493 A.2d 946 (1985). In Unocal, we applied the business judgment rule to analyze Unocal's discriminatory self-tender. We explained:

> When a board addresses a pending takeover bid it has an obligation to determine whether the offer is in the best interests of the corporation and its shareholders. In that respect a board's

---

[3] "Bust-up" takeover generally refers to a situation in which one seeks to finance an acquisition by selling off pieces of the acquired company.

duty is no different from any other responsibility it shoulders, and its decisions should be no less entitled to the respect they otherwise would be accorded in the realm of business judgment.

Id. at 954 (citation and footnote omitted).

Other jurisdictions have also applied the business judgment rule to actions by which target companies have sought to forestall takeover activity they considered undesirable. * * *

This case is distinguishable from the ones cited, since here we have a defensive mechanism adopted to ward off possible future advances and not a mechanism adopted in reaction to a specific threat. This distinguishing factor does not result in the Directors losing the protection of the business judgment rule. To the contrary, pre-planning for the contingency of a hostile takeover might reduce the risk that, under the pressure of a takeover bid, management will fail to exercise reasonable judgment. Therefore, in reviewing a pre-planned defensive mechanism it seems even more appropriate to apply the business judgment rule. See Warner Communications v. Murdoch, D. Del., 581 F.Supp. 1482, 1491 (1984).

Of course, the business judgment rule can only sustain corporate decision making or transactions that are within the power or authority of the Board. Therefore, before the business judgment rule can be applied it must be determined whether the Directors were authorized to adopt the Rights Plan.

III

Appellants vehemently contend that the Board of Directors was unauthorized to adopt the Rights Plan. First, appellants contend that no provision of the Delaware General Corporation Law authorizes the issuance of such Rights. Secondly, appellant, along with the SEC, contend that the Board is unauthorized to usurp stockholders' rights to receive hostile tender offers. Third, appellants and the SEC also contend that the Board is unauthorized to fundamentally restrict stockholders' rights to conduct a proxy contest. We address each of these contentions in turn.

A.

While appellants contend that no provision of the Delaware General Corporation Law authorizes the Rights Plan, Household contends that the Rights Plan was issued pursuant to 8 Del. C. §§ 151 (g) and 157. It explains that the Rights are authorized by § 157[7] and the issue of

---

[7] The power to issue rights to purchase shares is conferred by 8 Del. C. § 157 which provides in relevant part:

Subject to any provisions in the certificate of incorporation, every corporation may create and issue, whether or not in connection with the issue and sale of any shares of stock or other securities of the corporation, rights or options entitling the holders thereof to purchase from the corporation any shares of its capital stock of any class or

preferred stock underlying the Rights is authorized by § 151.[8] Appellants respond by making several attacks upon the authority to issue the Rights pursuant to § 157.

Appellants begin by contending that § 157 cannot authorize the Rights Plan since § 157 has never served the purpose of authorizing a takeover defense. Appellants contend that § 157 is a corporate financing statute, and that nothing in its legislative history suggests a purpose that has anything to do with corporate control or a takeover defense. Appellants are unable to demonstrate that the legislature, in its adoption of § 157, meant to limit the applicability of § 157 to only the issuance of Rights for the purposes of corporate financing. Without such affirmative evidence, we decline to impose such a limitation upon the section that the legislature has not. Compare Providence & Worchester Co. v. Baker, Del. Supr., 378 A.2d 121, 124 (1977) (refusal to read a bar to protective voting provisions into 8 Del. C. § 212(a)).

As we noted in Unocal:

> [O]ur corporate law is not static. It must grow and develop in response to, indeed in anticipation of, evolving concepts and needs. Merely because the General Corporation Law is silent as to a specific matter does not mean that it is prohibited.

493 A.2d at 957. See also Cheff v. Mathes, Del. Supr., 199 A.2d 548 (1964).

Secondly, appellants contend that § 157 does not authorize the issuance of sham rights such as the Rights Plan. They contend that the Rights were designed never to be exercised, and that the Plan has no economic value. In addition, they contend the preferred stock made subject to the Rights is also illusory, citing Telvest, Inc. v. Olson, Del.Ch., C.A. No. 5798, Brown, V.C. (March 8, 1979).

Appellants' sham contention fails in both regards. As to the Rights, they can and will be exercised upon the happening of a triggering mechanism, as we have observed during the current struggle of Sir James Goldsmith to take control of Crown Zellerbach. See Wall Street

---

classes, such rights or options to be evidenced by or in such instrument or instruments as shall be approved by the board of directors.

[8] 8 Del. C. § 151(g) provides in relevant part:

When any corporation desires to issue any shares of stock of any class or of any series of any class of which the voting powers, designations, preferences and relative, participating, optional or other rights, if any, or the qualifications, limitations or restrictions thereof, if any, shall not have been set forth in the certificate of incorporation or in any amendment thereto but shall be provided for in a resolution or resolutions adopted by the board of directors pursuant to authority expressly vested in it by the provisions of the certificate of incorporation or any amendment thereto, a certificate setting forth a copy of such resolution or resolutions and the number of shares of stock of such class or series shall be executed, acknowledged, filed, recorded, and shall become effective, in accordance with § 103 of this title.

Journal, July 26, 1985, at 3, 12.* As to the preferred shares, we agree with the Court of Chancery that they are distinguishable from sham securities invalidated in Telvest, *supra*. The Household preferred, issuable upon the happening of a triggering event, have superior dividend and liquidation rights.**

Third, appellants contend that § 157 authorizes the issuance of Rights "entitling holders thereof to purchase from the corporation any shares of its capital stock of any class . . . " (emphasis added). Therefore, their contention continues, the plain language of the statute does not authorize Household to issue rights to purchase another's capital stock upon a merger or consolidation.

Household contends, inter alia, that the Rights Plan is analogous to "anti-dilution" provisions which are customary features of a wide variety of corporate securities. While appellants seem to concede that "anti-destruction" provisions are valid under Delaware corporate law, they seek to distinguish the Rights Plan as not being incidental, as are most "anti-destruction" provisions, to a corporation's statutory power to finance itself. We find no merit to such a distinction. We have already rejected appellants' similar contention that § 157 could only be used for financing purposes. We also reject that distinction here.

"Anti-destruction" clauses generally ensure holders of certain securities of the protection of their right of conversion in the event of a merger by giving them the right to convert their securities into whatever securities are to replace the stock of their company. The fact that the rights here have as their purpose the prevention of coercive two-tier tender offers does not invalidate them.

* * *

Having concluded that sufficient authority for the Rights Plan exists in 8 Del. C. § 157, we note the inherent powers of the Board conferred by 8 Del. C. § 141(a), concerning the management of the corporation's "business and affairs" (emphasis added), also provides the Board additional authority upon which to enact the Rights Plan. Unocal, 493 A.2d at 953.[11]

---

* At the time of adoption of the rights plan, the Household common stock was trading in the range of $30–33. Because each 1/100 had the same dividend and liquidation rights as the common, it was highly unlikely that any shareholder would ever exercise rights to purchase the preferred stock. Rights in Crown Zellerbach preferred were not exercised after Sir James Goldsmith's acquisition of its common stock. Ed.

** Each 1/100 of a share of preferred stock had the same dividend and liquidation rights as the common stock, except (to the extent this is possible), they were prior and superior to the rights of the common stock. Ed.

[11] 8 Del. C. § 141(a) provides:

(a) The business and affairs of every corporation organized under this chapter shall be managed by or under the direction of a board of directors, except as may be otherwise provided in this chapter or in its certificate of incorporation. If any such provision is made in the certificate of incorporation, the powers and duties conferred or imposed upon the board of directors by this chapter shall be exercised or performed to such

B.

Appellants contend that the Board is unauthorized to usurp stockholders' rights to receive tender offers by changing Household's fundamental structure. We conclude that the Rights Plan does not prevent stockholders from receiving tender offers, and that the change of Household's structure was less than that which results from the implementation of other defensive mechanisms upheld by various courts.

Appellants' contention that stockholders will lose their right to receive and accept tender offers seems to be premised upon an understanding of the Rights Plan which is illustrated by the SEC amicus brief which states:

> "The Chancery Court's decision seriously understates the impact of this plan. In fact, as we discuss below, the Rights Plan will deter not only two-tier offers, but virtually all hostile tender offers."

The fallacy of that contention is apparent when we look at the recent takeover of Crown Zellerbach, which has a similar Rights Plan, by Sir James Goldsmith. Wall Street Journal, July 26, 1985, at 3, 12. The evidence at trial also evidenced many methods around the Plan ranging from tendering with a condition that the Board redeem the Rights, tendering with a high minimum condition of shares and Rights, tendering and soliciting consents to remove the Board and redeem the Rights, to acquiring 50% of the shares and causing Household to self-tender for the Rights. One could also form a group of up to 19.9% and solicit proxies for consents to remove the Board and redeem the Rights. These are but a few of the methods by which Household can still be acquired by a hostile tender offer.

In addition, the Rights Plan is not absolute. When the Household Board of Directors is faced with a tender offer and a request to redeem the Rights, they will not be able to arbitrarily reject the offer. They will be held to the same fiduciary standards any other board of directors would be held to in originally approving the Rights Plan. See Unocal, 493 A.2d at 954–55, 958.

* * *

There is little change in the governance structure as a result of the adoption of the Rights Plan. The Board does not now have unfettered discretion in refusing to redeem the Rights. The Board has no more discretion in refusing to redeem the Rights than it does in enacting any defensive mechanism.

The contention that the Rights Plan alters the structure more than do other defensive mechanisms because it is so effective as to make the corporation completely safe from hostile tender offers is likewise without

---

extent and by such person or persons as shall be provided in the certificate of incorporation.

merit. As explained above, there are numerous methods to successfully launch a hostile tender offer.

C.

Appellants' third contention is that the Board was unauthorized to fundamentally restrict stockholders' rights to conduct a proxy contest. Appellants contend that the "20% trigger" effectively prevents any stockholder from first acquiring 20% or more shares before conducting a proxy contest and further, it prevents stockholders from banding together into a group to solicit proxies if, collectively, they own 20% or more of the stock.[12] In addition, at trial, appellants contended that read literally, the Rights Agreement triggers the Rights upon the mere acquisition of the right to vote 20% or more of the shares through a proxy solicitation, and thereby precludes any proxy contest from being waged.[13]

Appellants seem to have conceded this last contention in light of Household's response that the receipt of a proxy does not make the recipient the "beneficial owner" of the shares involved which would trigger the Rights. In essence, the Rights Agreement provides that the Rights are triggered when someone becomes the "beneficial owner" of 20% or more of Household stock. Although a literal reading of the Rights Agreement definition of "beneficial owner" would seem to include those shares which one has the right to vote, it has long been recognized that the relationship between grantor and recipient of a proxy is one of agency, and the agency is revocable by the grantor at any time. Henn, Corporations § 196, at 518. Therefore, the holder of a proxy is not the "beneficial owner" of the stock. As a result, the mere acquisition of the right to vote 20% of the shares does not trigger the Rights.

The issue, then, is whether the restriction upon individuals or groups from first acquiring 20% of shares before waging a proxy contest fundamentally restricts stockholders' right to conduct a proxy contest. * * *

We conclude that there was sufficient evidence at trial to support the Vice-Chancellor's finding that the effect upon proxy contests will be minimal. Evidence at trial established that many proxy contests are won with an insurgent ownership of less than 20%, and that very large holdings are no guarantee of success. There was also testimony that the key variable in proxy contest success is the merit of an insurgent's issues, not the size of his holdings.

---

[12] Appellants explain that the acquisition of 20% of the shares trigger the Rights, making them non-redeemable, and thereby would prevent even a future friendly offer for the ten-year life of the Rights.

[13] The SEC still contends that the mere acquisition of the right to vote 20% of the shares through a proxy solicitation triggers the rights. We do not interpret the Rights Agreement in that manner.

IV

Having concluded that the adoption of the Rights Plan was within the authority of the Directors, we now look to whether the Directors have met their burden under the business judgment rule.

The business judgment rule is a "presumption that in making a business decision the directors of a corporation acted on an informed basis, in good faith and in the honest belief that the action taken was in the best interests of the company." Aronson v. Lewis, Del. Supr., 473 A.2d 805, 812 (1984) (citations omitted). Notwithstanding, in Unocal we held that when the business judgment rule applies to adoption of a defensive mechanism, the initial burden will lie with the directors. The "directors must show that they had reasonable grounds for believing that a danger to corporate policy and effectiveness existed. . . . [T]hey satisfy that burden 'by showing good faith and reasonable investigation. . . .'" Unocal, 493 A.2d at 955 (citing Cheff v. Mathes, 199 A.2d at 554–55). In addition, the directors must show that the defensive mechanism was "reasonable in relation to the threat posed." Unocal, 493 A.2d at 955. Moreover, that proof is materially enhanced, as we noted in Unocal, where, as here, a majority of the board favoring the proposal consisted of outside independent directors who have acted in accordance with the foregoing standards. Unocal, 493 A.2d at 955; Aronson, 473 A.2d at 815. Then, the burden shifts back to the plaintiffs who have the ultimate burden of persuasion to show a breach of the directors' fiduciary duties. Unocal, 493 A.2d at 958.

There are no allegations here of any bad faith on the part of the Directors' action in the adoption of the Rights Plan. There is no allegation that the Directors' action was taken for entrenchment purposes. Household has adequately demonstrated, as explained above, that the adoption of the Rights Plan was in reaction to what it perceived to be the threat in the market place of coercive two-tier tender offers. Appellants do contend, however, that the Board did not exercise informed business judgment in its adoption of the Plan.

Appellants contend that the Household Board was uninformed since they were inter alia, told the Plan would not inhibit a proxy contest, were not told the plan would preclude all hostile acquisitions of Household, and were told that Delaware counsel opined that the plan was within the business judgment of the Board.

As to the first two contentions, as we explained above, the Rights Plan will not have a severe impact upon proxy contests and it will not preclude all hostile acquisitions of Household. Therefore, the Directors were not misinformed or uninformed on these facts.

Appellants contend that Delaware counsel did not express an opinion on the flip-over provision of the Rights, rather only that the Rights would constitute validly issued and outstanding rights to subscribe to the preferred stock of the company.

To determine whether a business judgment reached by a board of directors was an informed one, we determine whether the directors were grossly negligent. Smith v. Van Gorkom, Del. Supr., 488 A.2d 858, 873 (1985). Upon a review of this record, we conclude the Directors were not grossly negligent. The information supplied to the Board on August 14 provided the essentials of the Plan. The Directors were given beforehand a notebook which included a three-page summary of the Plan along with the articles on the current takeover environment. The extended discussion between the Board and representatives of Wachtell, Lipton and Goldman, Sachs before approval of the Plan reflected a full and candid evaluation of the Plan. Moran's expression of his views at the meeting served to place before the Board a knowledgeable critique of the Plan. The factual happenings here are clearly distinguishable from the actions of the directors of Trans Union Corporation who displayed gross negligence in approving a cash-out merger. *Id.*

In addition, to meet their burden, the Directors must show that the defensive mechanism was "reasonable in relation to the threat posed". The record reflects a concern on the part of the Directors over the increasing frequency in the financial services industry of "boot-strap" and "bust-up" takeovers. The Directors were also concerned that such takeovers may take the form of two-tier offers.[14] In addition, on August 14, the Household Board was aware of Moran's overture on behalf of D-K-M. In sum, the Directors reasonably believed Household was vulnerable to coercive acquisition techniques and adopted a reasonable defensive mechanism to protect itself.

V

In conclusion, the Household Directors receive the benefit of the business judgment rule in their adoption of the Rights Plan.

The Directors adopted the Plan pursuant to statutory authority in 8 Del. C. §§ 141, 151, 157. We reject appellants' contentions that the Rights Plan strips stockholders of their rights to receive tender offers and that the Rights Plan fundamentally restricts proxy contests.

The Directors adopted the Plan in the good faith belief that it was necessary to protect Household from coercive acquisition techniques. The Board was informed as to the details of the Plan. In addition, Household has demonstrated that the Plan is reasonable in relation to the threat posed. Appellants, on the other hand, have failed to convince us that the Directors breached any fiduciary duty in their adoption of the Rights Plan.

While we conclude for present purposes that the Household Directors are protected by the business judgment rule, that does not end

---

[14] We have discussed the coercive nature of two-tier tender offers in Unocal, 493 A.2d at 956, n.12. We explained in Unocal that a discriminatory self-tender was reasonably related to the threat of two-tier tender offers and possible greenmail.

the matter. The ultimate response to an actual takeover bid must be judged by the Directors' actions at that time, and nothing we say here relieves them of their basic fundamental duties to the corporation and its stockholders. Unocal, 493 A. 2d at 954–55, 958; Smith v. Van Gorkom, 488 A. 2d at 872–73; Aronson, 473 A.2d at 812–13; Pogostin v. Rice, Del. Supr., 480 A.2d 619, 627 (1984). Their use of the Plan will be evaluated when and if the issue arises.

Affirmed.

QUESTIONS

1. Does the court apply the business judgment test or the Unocal test? Why? Do you agree with the court's analysis?

2. Was there statutory authority to issue flip-over rights?

3. Did issuance of the rights usurp the right of stockholders to receive tender offers?

4. Does issuance of the rights restrict stockholders' rights to conduct a proxy contest?

5. If each 1/100 of a share of preferred has the same dividend and liquidation rights as the common stock, how can the court distinguish these shares from the "sham preferred" invalidated in Telvest v. Olson? In the Chancery Court's opinion, 490 A.2d 1059 (1985), Vice Chancellor Walsh described the preferred in Household as follows: "Its dividend right is tied to the dividend for the common at the rate of 100 times the dividend declared on common stock. Its liquidation preference is similarly linked to payment received by common shareholders." 490 A.2d at 1066. Does the fact that each share of preferred has greater dividend and liquidation rights than the common matter, if the actual units (1/100) have rights identical to the common?

6. Vice Chancellor Walsh distinguished the Household Preferred from the OSI preferred in the following terms:

    "Despite their present contingent status, the preferred are hardly sham securities. The rights are separately tradeable, and the preferred issuable, only in the event of a triggering event and at such time their combined economic significance will be obvious— they serve to protect shareholders from the coercion of a partial tender offer. Even when issued, however, the preferred will not affect existing voting rights or impose a supermajority approval on prospective mergers. Their dividend and liquidation preferences are independently established in relation to Household's common stock. They also survive a merger at a stated exchange rate and thus they may be viewed as having an antidestructive effect, contractually secured in the Rights Plan. It cannot be said that the rights are so lacking in economic substance as to be void as a matter of law."

What economic rights do the rights have prior to distribution? What rights will be associated with the preferred prior to the flip-in?

7. If the rights were exercisable for a fraction of a preferred share at $100 at a time when the common stock was trading between $30 and $33, how likely is it that the preferred will ever issue?

8. If the exercise price for the preferred fractions is set at the "long-term value" of the common—its expected value in ten years, and if the rights expire at the end of ten years, just as they might be "in the money," how can they ever have value?

9. If it is expected that the rights will never be exercised for the preferred shares, how can they have economic significance?

10. If the only significance of the rights is their ability to deter takeovers and takeouts, how do the preferred shares differ from those issued by OSI?

11. Do these rights truly discourage proxy fights? Consider the following commentary:

    "When dissident shareholder groups try to convince other shareholders to vote for them, the Rights Plan throws up several obstacles. For example, in most Rights Plans, all shares held by a 'beneficial owner' are counted toward the maximum number of shares that can be held without crossing the threshold level. A shareholder group is considered to be the beneficial owner of any stock that it has the right to vote, either directly or indirectly, except pursuant to revocable proxies given in response to public solicitations that the SEC has reviewed. This beneficial ownership definition precludes dissident shareholders from entering into agreements with other shareholders concerning the reimbursement of their proxy contest expenses or about the slate of candidates they intend to nominate for directors." (footnotes omitted.) Randall S. Thomas, Judicial Review of Defensive Tactics in Proxy Contests: When is Using a Rights Plan Right?, 46 Vand. L. Rev. 503, 513 (1993).

12. Can you draft a definition of "beneficial ownership" that avoids this problem, and permits proxy fights?

NOTE

Airgas, Inc. v. Air Products, and Chemicals, Inc., 8 A.3d 1182 (Del. 2010), affirmed the discretion of a board to refuse to redeem a rights plan in the face of rising bids from a hostile bidder that ultimately reached a 61% premium over the pre-bid market price. The board concluded in good faith that its long-term plan for Airgas was more valuable than the bid. The evidence of good faith here was extraordinary. Air Products ran a successful proxy battle to install three of its nominees on the board, and ultimately those nominees, after hearing the views of three financial advisors to the board, agreed that the bid was inadequate. As one commentary noted, companies should keep in place a current and credible long-term plan in order to enhance the probability of successfully defending against such a bid.

Selectica, Inc. v. Versata Enterprises, Inc., 2010 Del. Ch. LEXIS 39, affirmed 2010 Del. LEXIS 506, involved the use of a poison pill not to prevent a takeover (although it would have that effect if left in place) but to prevent an "ownership change" within the meaning of section 382 of the Internal Revenue Code, dealing with net operating loss ("NOL") carryforwards. Selectica had operated at a loss since it became a public company in 2000, and had, according to one opinion, approximately $165 million NOLs, which could be carried forward as an offset against future taxable income for up to twenty years. The Treasury has always been concerned that companies might attempt to "traffic" in NOLs, and use them to reduce taxes for unrelated businesses. Section 382 of the IRC imposes limitations on their use after an "ownership change," which occurs when more than 50% of a firm's stock ownership changes over a three-year period. Since many companies' shares are widely held and trade regularly, this rule is limited to those who have held, during the relevant three-year period, 5% or more of the company's stock. Steel Partners, a private equity fund, had held 14.9% of Selectica's stock, and a competitor and potential buyer, Versata, held approximately 6.1%. A 2006 study showed that prior changes in ownership had cost Selectica $24.6 million in forfeited NOLs. By November of 2008 cumulative acquisitions by 5% shareholders had reached 40%, putting Selectica close to another "ownership change" that would forfeit more NOLs. By February 2009 at least half a dozen prospects had offered letters of intent, and by April Selectica had entered into exclusive negotiations with a potential buyer.

During this period Versata had been engaged in litigation with Selectica and offered to settle by purchasing Selectica for prices the Selectica board rejected. At the same time Steel Partners was urging a sale that would realize the value of Selectica's NOLs. Selectica had adopted a standard poison pill, which would be triggered at the 15% ownership level. The board was advised that its NOLs were a significant asset that was at risk if present or future 5% shareholders acquired another 10% of its stock. Thereafter the board amended its poison pill to decrease the triggering ownership amount to 5%, while grandfathering existing 5% shareholders and permitting them to purchase modest increments. Trilogy, Inc., the parent of Versata, purchased additional shares to reach 6.7% ownership, and thus triggered the rights plan. The rights plan allowed Selectica's board to declare Trilogy an "exempt person" during the ten days following the trigger, upon its determination that Trilogy would not jeopardize the NOLs. When Trilogy refused to sign a stand-still agreement, the board let the rights be triggered. The rights plan allowed the board to satisfy the rights by exchanging each right for one new share of common stock (excluding Trilogy), which it did, diluting Trilogy to 3.3% ownership. At the same time the board adopted a new 5% pill (the "Reloaded NOL Pill"). Selectica sought a declaratory judgment that its actions were valid and proper.

Trilogy and Versata challenged the board's adoption of a 5% pill as unrelated to a threat to Selectica, largely on the ground that the NOLs were of uncertain value, since no one could know whether Selectica would have any earnings, much less a large amount that could be offset by the NOLs. Because several of the directors were holding office temporarily, the Chancery Court held that the board did not meet the requirements for "material enhancement" of deference under Unocal. But the court held that a threat to the NOLs met the test for a threat to a corporate objective, which was affirmed by the Delaware Supreme Court. Both courts noted the growing number of 5% triggers in pills designed to protect NOLs.

Turning to the reasonableness of the response to the perceived threat, the court noted that a typical pill with a 15% trigger is not regarded as preclusive or coercive, noting that Moran v. Household International held that pills do not affect the right of stockholders to receive tender offers or restrict proxy contests. The Supreme Court rejected Trilogy's argument that restricting ownership to 4.9% made a proxy contest impossible, because holding a large block was essential to credibility in a proxy fight. It stated that "A defensive measure is preclusive where it 'makes a bidder's ability to wage a successful proxy contest and gain control either mathematically impossible or realistically unattainable." The court noted evidence that challengers with ownership in that range had succeeded in gaining board seats in a number of proxy contests in micro-cap companies such as Selectica. The court set a high standard for preclusion: "either the mathematical impossibility or realistic unattainability of a proxy contest. . . ." The Chancery Court found that the board had evaluated the potential consequences of adoption, including discouragement of institutional investors, prevention of 5% shareholders selling their shares as a single block, and discouragement of takeovers, and satisfied its Unocal obligations. These rulings applied to both the amendment of the original pill and the adoption of the subsequent Reloaded NOL Pill. The Supreme Court held that exchanging one share for each right was a more modest response than issuing purchase rights for more shares, in that it diluted Trilogy by a smaller amount (from 6.7% to 3.3%, or slightly more than 50%).

Recall that the author's co-authored article, "The Illusory Protections of the Poison Pill," at the beginning of this Part 2.E of this Chapter, using the example of a rights plan with a 15% trigger, showed that a bidder would lose approximately 41% of its initial investment if the hypothetical pill were triggered. If this is extended to pills at the 5% level, this would amount to approximately 2% of the total value of the target. This explains why Versata was willing to swallow the pill and suffer its dilution. It is small wonder that the Selectica board chose to reload its plan by adopting a new rights plan. There are a number of ways to tweak a poison pill to get maximum power out of it, but if the bidder has only bought 5% of the target's stock, that's the only investment subject to loss. If a company's stock is undervalued by more than 5%, adoption of a pill won't assure a fair price for shareholders in a hostile acquisition.

The co-authors of the "Illusory Protections" article have developed the a stronger poison-pill defense, called the "Reload Poison Pill."(c) In this version of the pill, if a determined bidder triggers the rights plan and accepts the dilution caused by the issuance of new shares, and then begins to acquire more shares of the target, the rights automatically "reload" and are activated every time the bidder (or any new bidder) reaches the triggering ownership level. With this plan, there is no end to the dilution that can be inflicted on a hostile bidder. Under one version of this plan, the board of directors can end the carnage at any time by redeeming the rights if a bidder is willing to make an offer that the board determines benefits all stockholders.

eBay Domestic Holdings, Inc. v. Newmark, 2010 Del. Ch. LEXIS 187, rejected a claim that protecting the corporate culture of craiglist.inc was a sufficient justification for adopting a rights plan in a closely-held corporation with only three shareholders. eBay had purchased 28% of craigslist in 2004 from a third party pursuant to a shareholders agreement with the other shareholders, Jim Buckmaster ("Jim") and Craig Newmark ("Craig") and craigslist itself. In exchange for certain veto powers of charter amendments and other major changes, eBay agreed to join Craig and Jim in a stockholders' agreement that granted each a right of first refusal to purchase eBay shares should one of them want to sell. The agreement acknowledged that eBay had a right to establish a competing online classifieds site, but if it did so, eBay relinquished its veto powers and the right of first refusal was extinguished. Conflicts quickly developed between the shareholders, largely over Jim and Craig's lack of concern for maximizing profits, and their belief that craigslist should be operated primarily as a community service. Craigslist, for example, does not sell advertising space on its website, or advertise or market its services. Its revenue consists solely of fees for online job postings in certain cities and apartment listings in New York City. In contrast, eBay operates with a more conventional profit-maximizing model. As part of the agreement with eBay, craigslist reincorporated in Delaware with a three-person board and cumulative voting rights, giving eBay one seat on the board. As conflicts began over the craigslist business model, eBay first acquired a German site offering classified ads on automobiles, and ultimately launched its own competing site, Kijiji, in 2007, with the result of releasing eBay from the rights of first refusal.

When eBay showed no interest in selling its shares to craigslist or Jim and Craig, planning began to allay concerns that eBay would retain the shares, with the access to competitive information it had. The focus was on diluting eBay's interest sufficiently to deny it access to a board seat. The result was amending the charter to implement a staggered board to exclude eBay from electing a director and adoption of a rights plan. Applying Unocal, Chancellor Chandler found that eBay did not represent a takeover threat, and that there was no proper purpose for its adoption. The Chancellor rejected craigslist's argument that it was designed to protect its corporate culture (operating as a public service at a low profit), because that was not a legally protectible culture. The opinion reviewed this issue in light of Chancellor Allen's lower court opinion in Paramount Communications, Inc.

v. Time Incorporated, 571 A.2d 1140 (Del. 1990), infra, Chapter Eight, Part 1.B:

> More importantly, Time did not hold that corporate culture, standing alone, is worthy of protection as an end in itself. Promoting, protecting, or pursuing non-stockholder considerations must lead at some point to value for stockholders. When director decisions are reviewed under the business judgment rule, this Court will not question rational judgments about how promoting non-stockholder interests—be it through making a charitable contribution, paying employees higher salaries and benefits, or more general norms like promoting a particular corporate culture—ultimately promote stockholder value. * * *

> Ultimately, defendants failed to prove that craigslist possesses a palpable, distinctive, and advantageous culture that sufficiently promotes stockholder value to support the indefinite implementation of a poison pill. Jim and Craig did not make any serious attempt to prove that the craigslist culture, which rejects any attempt to further monetize its services, translates into increased profitability for stockholders. I am sure that part of the reason craigslist is so popular is because it offers a free service that is also extremely useful. It may be that offering free classifieds is an essential component of a successful online classifieds venture. After all, by offering free classifieds, craigslist is able to attract such a large community of users that real estate brokers in New York City gladly pay fees to list apartment rentals in order to access the vast community of craigslist users. Likewise, employers in select cities happily pay fees to advertise job openings to craigslist users. Neither of these fee-generating activities would have been possible if craigslist did not provide brokers and employers access to a sufficiently large market of consumers, and brokers and employers may not have reached that market without craigslist's free classifieds.

> Giving away services to attract business is a sales tactic, however, not a corporate culture. Jim, Craig, and the defense witnesses advisedly described craigslist's business using the language of "culture" because that was what carried the day in Time. To the extent business measures like loss-leading products, money-back coupons, or putting products on sale are cultural artifacts, they reflect the American capitalist culture, not something unique to craigslist. Having heard the evidence and judged witness credibility at trial, I find that there is nothing about craigslist's corporate culture that Time or Unocal protects. The existence of a distinctive craigslist "culture" was not proven at trial. It is a fiction, invoked almost talismanically for purposes of this trial in order to find deference under Time's dicta.

In Leonard Loventhal Account v. Hilton Hotels Corp., 780 A.2d 245 (Del. 2001), the plaintiff challenged Hilton's adoption of a rights plan on grounds it claimed were not raised in Moran. The Chancery Court held that they were largely covered by Moran, and thus precluded by the doctrine of *stare decisis*. The Delaware Supreme Court agreed. One count relied on language in the Hilton rights agreement, not present in Household's agreement, that each holder of a right, by accepting the same, consents and agrees with Hilton and the other rights holders, to certain terms. The plaintiff argued that this meant the rights agreement was a multi-party agreement that required the consent of the shareholders. But the Supreme Court rejected this argument, holding that Moran held that the board could unilaterally adopt a rights agreement. Plaintiff argued that the rights agreement imposed impermissible transfer restrictions on shares—that could not be imposed without the consent of the shareholders. Again, the court noted that Moran held that the rights agreement did not affect the trading of Household shares, and thus ruled against that claim. Nor does the rights plan's placing of a legend on shares impermissibly alter Hilton's common stock without a shareholder vote, because the legend merely gives notice of the actions Moran permitted a board to undertake.

Other courts have examined whether rights plans that exclude bidders represent an unlawful discrimination. See, e.g., The Amalgamated Sugar Co. v. NL Industries, Inc., 644 F.Supp. 1229 (S.D.N.Y. 1986) (applying New Jersey law); West Point-Pepperell, Inc. v. Farley, Inc., 711 F.Supp. 1088 (N.D.Ga. 1988) (applying Georgia law); Minstar Acquiring Corp. v. AMF Inc., 621 F.Supp. 1252 (S.D.N.Y. 1985) (applying New Jersey law to a "poison put" rights plan). See also Asarco Inc. v. Court, 611 F.Supp. 468 (D.N.J. 1985) (voiding discriminatory voting plan under New Jersey law). In each case the legislature reacted by passing legislation to validate these plans.

Legislatures have responded to the questions raised by rights plans in a variety of ways. In every case where a rights plan was invalidated by a court as in excess of statutory authority, the statute was later amended to authorize such discriminatory features. Even states that did not experience such rulings took steps to amend their statutes. Section 151(a) of the Delaware Act was amended by adding the language beginning with "Any of the voting powers, designations, preferences . . . may be made dependent upon facts ascertainable outside the certificate of incorporation. . . ."

NOTE ON THE APPLICATION OF UNOCAL TO REDEMPTION OF RIGHTS

Recall that in Moran Justice McNeilly wrote that when the Household Board is faced with a bid and a request to redeem the rights, "they will not be able to arbitrarily reject the offer. They will be held to the same fiduciary standards any other board of directors would be held to in originally approving the Rights Plan." In City Capital Associates v. Interco, Inc., 551 A.2d 787 (Del.Ch. 1988), after a series of bids by a hostile bidder, management had responded with a restructuring proposal that it believed was worth at least $76, in the face of a $74 cash bid for all shares. Conceding the good faith of management in its belief that its plan was superior and that the Interco bid was "inadequate," the Chancery Court noted that the value of the management plan was inherently debatable, and that it was clear there were no threats of the Unocal type—this was not a two-tier bid. The Chancery Court held that in the absence of coercion, the shareholders, not management, were entitled to the final judgment about which proposal was more valuable, and that management's decision not to redeem the rights was not justified under Unocal standards. For a similar reaction under Nevada law, see Hilton Hotels Corp. v. ITT Corp., 978 F.Supp. 1342 (D. Nev. 1997).

The reaction of the Delaware Supreme Court to the Interco holding, in Paramount Communications, Inc. v. Time, Inc., 571 A.2d 1140 (Del. 1990), *infra*, Chapter Eight, Part 1, was negative: "Plaintiffs' position represents a fundamental misconception of our standard of review under Unocal principally because it would involve the court in substituting its judgment for what is a 'better' deal for that of a corporation's board of directors. To the extent that the Court of Chancery has recently done so in certain of its opinions, we hereby reject such approach as not in keeping with a proper Unocal analysis. See, e.g., Interco, 551 A.2d 787, and its progeny. . . ."

Later cases have suggested that boards may "just say no" to hostile bids on the basis of inadequacy of price (the "Nancy Reagan defense"). This line of cases begins with Paramount Communications, Inc. v. Time, Inc., 571 A.2d 1140, 1153 (1990), *infra*, Chapter Eight, Part 1, that inadequate value is a "legally cognizable threat" under Unocal. In Unitrin, Inc. v. American General Corp., 651 A.2d 1361, 1384 (Del. 1995), noted *infra*, part 2.F of this chapter, the court sustained a defensive stock repurchase where "the Board determined that Unitrin's stock was undervalued by the market at current levels. . . ."

Chancellor Chandler reaffirmed the power of a board to "just say no" in Air Products and Chemicals, Inc. v. Airgas, Inc., 16 A.3d 48 (Del. Ch. 2011). He began his opinion with a denial of the "just say no" language, reaffirming traditional Delaware standards of review of takeover defenses:

> This case poses the following fundamental question: Can a board of directors, acting in good faith and with a reasonable factual basis for its decision, when faced with a structurally non-coercive, all-cash, fully financed tender offer directed to the stockholders of the corporation, keep a poison pill in place so as to prevent the stockholders from making their own decision about whether they want to tender their shares—even after the incumbent board has lost one election contest, a full year has gone by since the offer was first made public, and the stockholders are fully informed as to the target board's views on the inadequacy of the offer? If so, does that effectively mean that a board can "just say never" to a hostile tender offer?
>
> The answer to the latter question is "no." A board cannot "*just* say no" to a tender offer. Under Delaware law, it must first pass through two prongs of exacting judicial scrutiny by a judge who will evaluate the actions taken by, and the motives of, the board. Only

a board of directors found to be acting in good faith, after reasonable investigation and reliance on the advice of outside advisors, which articulates and convinces the Court that a hostile tender offer poses a legitimate threat to the corporate enterprise, may address that perceived threat by blocking the tender offer and forcing the bidder to elect a board majority that supports its bid.

Addressing the apparent conflict between stockholders willing to accept a bid and a board that still regarded the bid as inadequate, the Chancellor wrote:

> For the reasons much more fully described in the remainder of this Opinion, I conclude that, as Delaware law currently stands, the answer must be that the power to defeat an inadequate hostile tender offer ultimately lies with the board of directors. As such, I find that the Airgas board has met its burden under Unocal to articulate a legally cognizable threat (the allegedly inadequate price of Air Products' offer, coupled with the fact that a majority of Airgas's stockholders would likely tender into that inadequate offer) and has taken defensive measures that fall within a range of reasonable responses proportionate to that threat. I thus rule in favor of defendants.

In an oblique reference to previous Chancery Court opinions such as Interco, Chancellor Chandler wrote:

> Although I have a hard time believing that inadequate price alone (according to the target's board) in the context of a non-discriminatory, all-cash, all-shares, fully financed offer poses any "threat"—particularly given the wealth of information available to Airgas's stockholders at this point in time—under existing Delaware law, it apparently does. Inadequate price has become a form of "substantive coercion" as that concept has been developed by the Delaware Supreme Court in its takeover jurisprudence. That is, the idea that Airgas's stockholders will disbelieve the board's views on value (or in the case of merger arbitrageurs who may have short-term profit goals in mind, they may simply ignore the board's recommendations), and so they may mistakenly tender into an inadequately priced offer. Substantive coercion has been clearly recognized by our Supreme Court as a valid threat.

Thus, convinced that the board's view that the company was worth at least $78 per share in a sale, and that the current $70 bid was inadequate, was held in good faith, the court dismissed the suit against the directors of Airgas.

These decisions, which seemed to some to give boards autonomy to leave poison pills in place and "just say no" have led to shareholder responses. These developments are described in the following excerpt from John C. Coffee, The Bylaw Battlefield: Can Institutions Change the Outcome of Corporate Control Contests?, 51 U. Miami L. Rev. 605, 611–613 (1997):

"Following Wallace Computer Services, Inc.'s successful takeover defense in 1995 against the tender offer made for it by Moore Corporation (which defense was successful, notwithstanding the fact that nearly 75% of the Wallace shares were tendered to Moore, Guy Wyser-Pratte, a well-known takeover arbitrager who controlled a 2.3% stake in Wallace Computer, commenced a proxy solicitation for a bylaw amendment that would have required the Wallace Computer board in the future to redeem its poison pill if the company received a 'fair' takeover proposal, which was defined as a fully financed cash bid at 25% or more above the then market price of the stock. The proxy solicitation was diligently pursued and, for a time, seemed to be winning, but on the eve of the vote a crucial block switched sides and left the insurgents with only 36% of the votes actually cast. Nonetheless, a 36% vote in favor of a mandatory bylaw amendment may well be a record outcome for insurgents.

"The final and latest development involves a judicial decision that runs precisely counter to the SEC's reading of bylaw amendments. On May 1, 1996, a non-binding resolution sponsored by the Teamsters General Fund calling for a shareholder vote prior to the adoption of any poison pill was supported by 65% of the votes cast at the Fleming Companies, Inc. annual shareholder meeting. Nonetheless, less than two months later, Fleming's board adopted a new 10–year shareholder rights plan.

"In response, the Teamsters General Fund drafted a mandatory bylaw amendment that purportedly nullified the new pill and required an after-the-fact shareholder vote to approve any future poison pill. When Fleming declined to include the proposed bylaw amendment in its proxy materials, the Teamsters sued—and won."

Shareholder bylaw proposals raise questions about the allocation of power between shareholders and directors that have not been explored much in American corporate law. In addition to the Coffee article, see Macey, *supra* for a discussion of this issue. Delaware General Corporation Law § 141(a) provides that "The business and affairs of every corporation . . . shall be managed by or under the direction of a board of directors, except as may be otherwise provided in this chapter or in the certificate of incorporation." Amendment of the certificate of incorporation requires consent of the board of directors as well as the shareholders, under Del. G.C.L. § 242(b). Can a bylaw adopted by the shareholders, which is authorized under § 109(a), restrict the discretion of the board with respect to decisions concerning redemption of rights plans, or even their adoption? Macey, *supra*, argues that it can. Macey reads the exception in § 141(a) for "otherwise provided in this chapter" to extend to shareholder-adopted bylaws under § 109, and argues that § 109(b) expressly authorizes shareholder restrictions on board powers, because the bylaws may contain "any provision, not inconsistent with law . . . relating to the rights or powers of its stockholders, directors, officers or employees." Macey does not discuss other provisions of the Delaware act that allow restrictions on directors' powers. For example § 350, dealing with statutory close corporations, provides that a written agreement among stockholders holding a majority of the shares of the corporation that restricts or interferes with the discretion or powers of the board shall not be invalid on the ground that it relates to the conduct of the business and affairs of the corporation. Is the negative implication that outside of close corporations, no such restrictions are permitted? For a view contrary to Macey's, see Lawrence A. Hamermesh, Corporate Democracy and Stockholder-Adopted By-Laws: Taking Back the Street?, 73 Tulane L. Rev. 409 (1998).

The Fleming case is set out below. Note that Oklahoma has copied the Delaware General Corporation Law. The following are the cross references to the Delaware and Oklahoma statutes cited in the opinion:

Oklahoma	Delaware
1013	109
1038	157

International Brotherhood of Teamsters General Fund v. Fleming Companies, Inc.

975 P.2d 907 (Okla. 1999).

■ SIMMS, J:

The United States Court of Appeals, Tenth Circuit, John C. Porfilio, Presiding Judge, pursuant to 20 O.S. 1991, § 1601, certified to the Oklahoma Supreme Court the following question of law:

> Does Oklahoma law [A] restrict the authority to create and implement shareholder rights plans exclusively to the board of directors, or [B] may shareholders propose resolutions requiring that shareholder rights plans be submitted to the shareholders for vote at the succeeding annual meeting?

We answer the first part of the question in the negative and the second part affirmatively. We hold under Oklahoma law there is no exclusive authority granted boards of directors to create and implement shareholder rights plans, where shareholder objection is brought and passed through official channels of corporate governance. We find no Oklahoma law which gives exclusive authority to a corporation's board of directors for the formulation of shareholder rights plans and no authority which precludes shareholders from proposing resolutions or bylaw amendments regarding shareholder rights plans. We hold shareholders may propose bylaws which restrict board implementation of shareholder rights plans, assuming the certificate of incorporation does not provide otherwise.

* * *

Teamsters were critical of Fleming's rights plan, seeing it as a means of entrenching the current Fleming board of directors in the event

Fleming became the target of a takeover. In 1996, the Teamsters organized and introduced a non-binding resolution for the annual shareholders meeting. The 1996 resolution called on the Fleming board to redeem the existing rights plan. The then current rights plan had been in effect since 1986 and was scheduled for renewal. The Teamsters proposal was met with apparent hostility from Fleming's board and the rights plan remained intact, despite a majority shareholder vote in agreement with the Teamsters' resolution to redeem it.

The following year, 1997, Teamsters mounted a more organized effort to change the continued implementation of the rights plan. Teamsters prepared a proxy statement for inclusion in the proxy materials for the 1997 annual shareholder's meeting. With the proxy effort, the Teamsters proposed an amendment to the company's bylaws which would require any rights plan implemented by the board of directors to be put to the shareholders for a majority vote. The proposal was essentially a ratification procedure wherein the shareholders would force the board to formulate a rights plan both the board and shareholders could agree on or do away with such a plan altogether.

Fleming refused to include the resolution in its 1997 proxy statement, declaring the proposal was not a subject for shareholder action under Oklahoma law. Teamsters then brought an action in the Federal District Court for the Western District of Oklahoma. The district court ruled in favor of the Teamsters, the court finding that "shareholders, through the devise of bylaws, have a right of review." Fleming appealed to the 10th Circuit Court of Appeals, which submitted the certified question to this Court.

Fleming sought to postpone any shareholder vote on the 1997 proxy issue until after the resolution of this case. But the U.S. District Court and later the 10th Circuit denied Fleming's motion to suspend the injunction. Fleming was then forced to allow its shareholders to vote on the Teamsters' proxy. The Teamsters' resolution passed with approximately 60% of the voted shares.

Fleming's position is that 18 O.S. 1991 § 1038 gives the board of directors authority to create and issue shareholder rights plans, subject only to limits which might exist in the corporation's certificate of incorporation; and that shareholders cannot through bylaws restrict the board's powers to implement a rights plan. The Teamsters' position is that 18 O.S. 1991 § 1013 gives shareholders of a publicly traded corporation, such as Fleming, the authority to adopt bylaws addressing a broad range of topics from a corporation's business, corporate affairs, and rights and powers of shareholders and directors.[6] It is this apparent conflict which brings this federal certified question to this Court.

---

[6]   18 O.S. 1991 § 1013(A) & (B):

This is a case of first impression in Oklahoma and there is little guidance from other states. Oklahoma and Delaware have substantially similar corporation acts, especially with regard to Title 18, §§ 1013 & 1038 which are of primary concern here. 8 Del. C. § 109(a) & (b); 8 Del. C. § 157. However, a review of Delaware decisions revealed no comparable case from that state.

The 10th Circuit's question is ultimately one of corporate governance and what degree of control shareholders can exact upon the corporations in which they own stock.

In the scheme of corporate governance the role of shareholders has been purposefully indirect. Shareholders' direct authority is limited. This is true for obvious reasons. Large corporations with perhaps thousands of stockholders could not function if the daily running of the corporation was subject to the approval of so many relatively attenuated people. However, the authority given a board of directors under the Oklahoma General Corporation Act, 18 O.S. 1991 § 1027, is not without shareholder oversight, 18 O.S. 1991 § 1013(B).

Fleming's argument relies on this passage, 18 O.S. 1991 § 1038 (emphasis added):

> Subject to any provisions in the certificate of incorporation, every corporation may create and issue . . . rights or options entitling the holders thereof to purchase from the corporation any shares of its capital stock of any class or classes, such rights or options to be evidenced by or in such instrument or instruments as shall be approved by the board of directors.

In making its argument, Fleming asserts that the word "corporation" is synonymous with "board of directors" as the term is used in 18 § 1038. Therefore, according to Fleming, "every corporation may create and issue . . . rights and options[.]", can actually be read to say "[every corporation's] board of directors] may create and issue . . . rights and options[.]" However, in light of the fact that both terms, "corporation" and "board of

---

Bylaws

A. The original or other bylaws of a corporation may be adopted, amended or repealed by the incorporators, by the initial directors if they were named in the certificate of incorporation, or, before a corporation has received any payment for any of its stock, by its board of directors. After a corporation has received any payment for any of its stock, the power to adopt, amend or repeal bylaws shall be in the shareholders entitled to vote, or, in the case of a nonstock corporation, in its members entitled to vote; provided, however, any corporation, in its certificate of incorporation, may confer the power to adopt, amend or repeal bylaws upon the directors or, in the case of a nonstock corporation, upon its governing body by whatever name designated. The fact that such power has been so conferred upon the directors or governing body, as the case may be, shall not divest the shareholders or members of the power, nor limit their power to adopt, amend or repeal bylaws.

B. The bylaws may contain any provision, not inconsistent with law or with the certificate of incorporation, relating to the business of the corporation, the conduct of its affairs, and its rights or powers or the rights or powers of its shareholders, directors, officers or employees.

directors", are used distinctly throughout the General Corporation Act and within the text of 18 § 1038 itself, this assertion is flawed. Further, the Former Business Corporation Act, 18 § 1.2(1) and (23), defines "corporation" and "director" differently. The statutes indicate our legislature has an understanding of the distinct definitions it assigns to these terms, and we find it unlikely the legislature would interchange them as Fleming contends.

While this Court would agree with Fleming that a corporation may create and issue rights and options within the grant of authority given it in 18 § 1038, it does not automatically translate that the board of directors of that corporation has in itself the same breadth of authority.

* * *

We find nothing in the Oklahoma General Corporation Act, 18 O.S. 1991 § 1001 et seq., or existing case law which indicates the shareholder rights plan is somehow exempt from shareholder adopted bylaws. Fleming argues that only the certificate of incorporation can limit the board's authority to implement such a plan, relying on § 1038. While this Court might agree that a certificate of incorporation, which somehow precludes bylaw amendments directed at shareholder rights plans, could preclude the Teamsters from seeking the bylaw changes which are proposed in this case, neither party has indicated Fleming's certificate speaks in any way to the board's authority or shareholder constraints regarding shareholder rights plans. We find no authority to support the contention that a certificate of incorporation which is silent with regard to shareholder rights plans precludes shareholder enacted bylaws regarding the implementation of rights plans.

A number of states have taken affirmative steps to ensure their domestic corporations, and in many instances the board of directors itself, are able to implement shareholder rights plans to protect the company from takeover. The legislation is typically called a shareholders rights plan endorsement statute. However, the Oklahoma legislature has not passed such legislation. There are at least twenty-four states with these share rights plan endorsement statutes.[7]

* * *

---

[7]   John H. Matheson & Brent A. Olson, Shareholder Rights and Legislative Wrongs: Toward Balanced Takeover Legislation, 59 Geo. Wash. L. Rev. 1425, 1554–58 (August 1991).

Examples of states with shareholder rights plan endorsement statutes are as follows:

Colorado, Co. St. § 7–106–208; Georgia, Ga. St. § 14–2–624; Hawaii, Hi. St. § 415–20; Idaho, Id. St. §§ 30–1610, 30–1706; Illinois, Il. St. Ch. 805 § 516.05(f); Indiana, In. St. 23–1–35–1(f), 23–1–26–5; Iowa, Ia. St. § 490.624A; Kentucky, Ky. St. § 271B.12–210(5), Massachusetts, Ma. St. 156B§ 32A; Michigan, Mi. St. Ch. 450 § 1342a; Nevada, Nv. St. 78.378; New Jersey, NJ. St. 14A:7–7(1) & (3); New York, McKinney's Bus. Corp. Law Ch. 4, Art. 5, § 505(2)(a)(i) & (ii); North Carolina, NC. St. § 55–6–24(a) & (b); Ohio, Oh. St. § 1701.16; Oregon, Or. St. § 60.157(1) & (2); Pennsylvania, Pa. St. 15 Pa.C.S.A. § 1525, § 2513; Rhode Island, Ri. St. § 7–5.2–7; South Dakota, SD.St. § 47–33–5; Tennessee, Tn. St. § 48–16–205; Utah, Ut. St. § 16–1 10a–624; Virginia, Va. St. § 13.1—646; Wyoming, Wy.St. § 17–16–624; Wisconsin, Wi. St. 180.0624.

These examples illustrate how a board of directors can operate with relative autonomy when a rights plan endorsement statute applies. This does not suggest the absence of a share rights plan endorsement statute in Oklahoma precludes the implementation of such a takeover defense. We merely find that without the authority granted in such an endorsement statute, the board may well be subject to the general procedures of corporate governance, including the enactment of bylaws which limit the board's authority to implement shareholder rights plans.

This Court understands much of the reasoning behind the enactment of rights plan endorsement statutes and why so many state legislatures are inclined to facilitate this takeover protection for their domestic corporations. In addition, we understand Fleming's desire to have a rights plan available for quick, and more effective, implementation. However, if, as in this case, the certificate of incorporation does not offer directors this broad authority to protect against mergers and takeover, corporations must look to Oklahoma's legislature, not this Court, which is more properly vested with the means to offer boards such authority.

In answering this certified question, we do not suggest all shareholder rights plans are required to submit to shareholder approval, ratification or review; this is not the question presented to us. Instead, we find shareholders may, through the proper channels of corporate governance, restrict the board of directors authority to implement shareholder rights plans.

———————

QUESTIONS

1. Where does the court find a source of authority for a shareholder-enacted bylaw that limits the power of the board?

2. How does the Fleming court reconcile the board's statutory authority to adopt rights plans and specify their terms with shareholder power to limit the board's powers?

3. What significance does the court attach to the absence of a shareholder rights plan endorsement statute in Oklahoma? Would the presence of a statute such as the Idaho statute quoted by the court have an impact on the allocation of power between shareholders and directors?

———————

NOTE ON INVACARE CORPORATION V. HEALTHDYNE TECHNOLOGIES, INC.

968 F.Supp. 1578 (N.D. Ga. 1997).

Healthdyne had adopted a "dead hand" poison pill, which provided that its poison pill could only be redeemed or amended by a majority directors who were members of the Board prior to the adoption of the rights plan, (the "continuing directors") or who were subsequently elected to the Board with the recommendation and approval of the other continuing directors. The effect of the continuing directors provision was that a shareholder vote to replace the incumbent directors with a bidder's slate of directors who were willing to redeem the rights, would mean that the new Board of Directors could not redeem the rights plan because they would not be "continuing directors." The Georgia version of section 624 of the Model Business Corporation Act in effect at that time was a "share rights plan endorsement statute" of the kind cited in the Fleming case, adopted in response to a ruling under the prior statute that a rights plan was invalid because of its unequal treatment of shareholders. O.C.G.A. § 14–2–624(c), in its authorization of the creation options on shares, provided in part:

> "Nothing contained in Section 14–2–601 of this Part shall be deemed to limit the board of directors' authority to determine, in its sole discretion, the terms and conditions of the rights, options, or warrants issuable pursuant to this Code section. Such terms and conditions need not be set forth in the articles of incorporation."

When Invacare made a hostile bid for Healthdyne, it sought to propose a shareholder-adopted bylaw that would have provided:

> "the incumbent Board of Directors will be in violation of the Bylaws if such Board, including any requisite group of continuing directors, falls to immediately take all necessary action (prior to consideration of the election of directors at the Annual Meeting) to amend any shareholder rights plan of the Company to remove all such limitations."

The court held that the grant of authority in section 624(c), quoted above, precluded shareholders from limiting the authority of the board in this area, relying on the grant of power to the board "in its sole discretion." It also noted Georgia had provided that "a bylaw limiting the authority of the board of directors . . . may only be adopted, amended or repealed by the shareholders." O.C.G.A. § 14–2–1020 (a deviation from the Model Act). Because the court found that the proposed bylaw was contrary to the grant of power to the board "in its sole discretion" with respect to options, it invalidated the bylaw. The Court also relied on Georgia's version of Model Act § 7.32, dealing with shareholder agreements, which requires unanimous shareholder consent to limit shareholder power to restrict the powers of the board. Note that this provision was derived from N.Y. Bus. Corp. Law § 620; see also North Carolina, N.C. Gen. Stat. § 55–73, and in South Carolina, S.C. Code § 12–16.22. Professor Latty, the drafter of the original version of this provision for North Carolina, characterized it as a safe harbor for shareholder agreements, writing: "Conversely, the provision does not limit validation of agreements to those that meet the language of this statutory provision. So, unless the court goes out of its way to read in a negative implication the court might still validate, at least as against certain parties, a side agreement that has *not* been signed by all, or that is *not* in writing, etc., as the circumstances of the case may appear to the court to require." Elvin R. Latty, The Close Corporation and the New North Carolina Business Corporation Act, 34 N.C. L. Rev. 432, 438 (1956). What effect should this explanation have on the uses of this section in limiting shareholder powers?

We now turn to Delaware law on dead hand and "slow hand" poison pills. Keep in mind the Fleming court's interpretation of language identical to the provisions of Delaware law as you read these cases.

Carmody v. Toll Brothers, Inc.

723 A.2d 1180 (Del.Ch. 1998).

■ JACOBS, VICE CHANCELLOR.

At issue on this Rule 12(b)(6) motion to dismiss is whether a most recent innovation in corporate antitakeover measures—the so-called "dead hand" poison pill rights plan—is subject to legal challenge on the basis that it violates the Delaware General Corporation Law and/or the fiduciary duties of the board of directors who adopted the plan. As explained more fully below, a "dead hand" rights plan is one that cannot be redeemed except by the incumbent directors who adopted the plan or their designated successors. As discussed below, the Court finds that the "dead hand" feature of the rights plan as described in the complaint (the "Rights Plan") is subject to legal challenge on both statutory and fiduciary grounds, and that because the complaint states legally cognizable claims for relief, the pending motion to dismiss must be denied.

I.   FACTS

A.   *Background Leading to Adoption of the Plan*

The firm whose rights plan is being challenged is Toll Brothers (sometimes referred to as "the company"), a Pennsylvania-based Delaware corporation that designs, builds, and markets single family luxury homes in thirteen states and five regions in the United States. The company was founded in 1967 by brothers Bruce and Robert Toll, who are its Chief Executive and Chief Operating Officers, respectively, and who own approximately 37.5% of Toll Brothers' common stock. The company's board of directors has nine members, four of whom (including Bruce and Robert Toll) are senior executive officers. The remaining five members of the board are "outside" independent directors.

* * *

B.   *The Rights Plan*

* * *

The Rights Plan was adopted on June 12, 1997, at which point Toll Brothers' stock was trading at approximately $18 per share—near the low end of its established price range of $16 3/8 to $25 3/16 per share. After considering the industry economic and financial environment and other factors, the Toll Brothers board concluded that other companies engaged in its lines of business might perceive the company as a potential target for an acquisition. The Rights Plan was adopted with that problem in mind, but not in response to any specific takeover proposal or threat. The company announced that it had done that to protect its stockholders from "coercive or unfair tactics to gain control of the Company" by placing the stockholders in a position of having to accept or reject an unsolicited offer without adequate time.

1.   *The Rights Plan's "Flip In" and "Flip Over" Features*

* * *

The complaint alleges that the purpose and effect of the company's Rights Plan, as with most poison pills, is to make any hostile acquisition of Toll Brothers prohibitively expensive, and thereby to deter such acquisitions unless the target company's board first approves the acquisition proposal. The target board's "leverage" derives from another critical feature found in most rights plans: the directors' power to redeem the Rights at any time before they expire, on such conditions as the directors "in their sole discretion" may establish. To this extent there is little to distinguish the company's Rights Plan from the "standard model." What is distinctive about the Rights Plan is that it authorizes only a specific, defined category of directors—the "Continuing Directors"—to redeem the Rights. The dispute over the legality of this "Continuing Director" or "dead hand" feature of the Rights Plan is what drives this lawsuit.

2.   *The "Dead Hand" Feature of the Rights Plan*

In substance, the "dead hand" provision operates to prevent any directors of Toll Brothers, except those who were in office as of the date of the Rights Plan's adoption (June 12, 1997) or their designated successors, from redeeming the Rights until they expire on June 12, 2007. * * *

According to the complaint, this "dead hand" provision has a twofold practical effect. First, it makes an unsolicited offer for the company more unlikely by eliminating a proxy contest as a useful way for a hostile acquiror to gain control, because even if the acquiror wins the contest, its newly-elected director representatives could not redeem the Rights. Second, the "dead hand" provision disenfranchises, in a proxy contest, all shareholders that wish the company to be managed by a board empowered to redeem the Rights, by depriving those shareholders of any practical choice except to vote for the incumbent directors. Given these effects, the plaintiff claims that the only purpose that the "dead hand" provision could serve is to discourage future acquisition activity by making any proxy contest to replace incumbent board members an exercise in futility.

II. OVERVIEW OF THE PROBLEM AND THE PARTIES' CONTENTIONS

* * *

A. *Overview*

The critical issue on this motion is whether a "dead hand" provision in a "poison pill" rights plan is subject to legal challenge on the basis that it is invalid as ultra vires, or as a breach of fiduciary duty, or both. Although that issue has been the subject of scholarly comment,[9] it has yet to be decided under Delaware law, and to date it has been addressed by only two courts applying the law of other jurisdictions.[10]

Some history may elucidate the issue by locating its relevance within the dynamic of state corporate takeover jurisprudence. Since the 1980s, that body of law, largely judge-made, has been racing to keep abreast of the ever-evolving and novel tactical and strategic developments so characteristic of this important area of economic endeavor that is swiftly becoming a permanent part of our national (and international) economic landscape.

For our purposes, the relevant history begins in the early 1980s with the advent of the "poison pill" as an antitakeover measure. That innovation generated litigation focused upon the issue of whether any poison pill rights plan could validly be adopted under state corporation

---

[9] See, e.g., Shawn C. Lese, Note, Preventing Control From the Grave: A Proposal for Judicial Treatment of Dead Hand Provisions in Poison Pills, 96 Col. L. Rev. 2175 (1996) (cited herein as "Lese"); Jeffrey N. Gordon, "Just Say Never" Poison Pills, Dead hand Pills and Shareholder Adopted By-Laws: An Essay for Warren Buffett, 19 Cardozo L. Rev. 511 (1997) (cited herein as "Gordon"); Daniel A. Neff, The Impact of State Statutes and Continuing Director Rights Plans, 51 U. Miami L. Rev. 663 (1997) (cited herein as "Neff"); and Meredith M. Brown and William D. Regner, 2 Shareholder Rights Plans: Recent Toxopharmological Developments, Insights (Aspen, Law & Business, Oct., 1997) (cited herein as "Brown and Regner").

[10] The jurisdictions that have directly addressed the legality of the dead hand poison pill are New York see Bank of New York Co., Inc. v. Irving Bank Corp., et al., N.Y. Sup. Ct., 139 Misc. 2d 665, 528 N.Y.S.2d 482 (1988), and the United States District Court for the Northern District of Georgia, see Invacare Corp. v. Healthdyne Technologies, Inc., N.D. Ga., 968 F.Supp. 1578 (1997) (applying Georgia law). In Delaware, the issue arose in Davis Acquisition, Inc. v. NWA, Inc., 1989 WL 40845 (Del.Ch.1989), Allen, C. (Apr. 25, 1989), but was not decided because the preliminary injunction motion was resolved on other grounds. In Sutton Holding Corp. v. DeSoto, Inc., Del. Ch., C.A. No. 12051, Allen, C, 1991 WL 80223 (May 13, 1991), the validity of a "continuing director" provision was presented indirectly (but again was not decided) in the context of an amendment to a pension plan prohibiting its termination or a reduction of benefits in the event of a "change of control." That term was defined as a new, substantial shareholder becoming the beneficial owner of 35% or more of the corporation's voting stock without the prior approval of two thirds of the board and a majority of the "continuing directors."

law. The seminal case, Moran v. Household International, Inc.,[11] answered that question in the affirmative.

* * *

It being settled that a corporate board could permissibly adopt a poison pill, the next litigated question became: under what circumstances would the directors' fiduciary duties require the board to redeem the rights in the face of a hostile takeover proposal?[12] That issue was litigated, in Delaware and elsewhere, during the second half of the 1980s. The lesson taught by that experience was that courts were extremely reluctant to order the redemption of poison pills on fiduciary grounds. The reason was the prudent deployment of the pill proved to be largely beneficial to shareholder interests: it often resulted in a bidding contest that culminated in an acquisition on terms superior to the initial hostile offer.

Once it became clear that the prospects were unlikely for obtaining judicial relief mandating a redemption of the poison pill, a different response to the pill was needed. That response, which echoed the Supreme Court's suggestion in Moran, was the foreseeable next step in the evolution of takeover strategy: a tender offer coupled with a solicitation for shareholder proxies to remove and replace the incumbent board with the acquiror's nominees who, upon assuming office, would redeem the pill.[13] Because that strategy, if unopposed, would enable hostile offerors to effect an "end run" around the poison pill, it again was predictable and only a matter of time that target company boards would develop counter-strategies. With one exception—the "dead hand" pill—these counter-strategies proved "successful" only in cases where the purpose was to delay the process to enable the board to develop alternatives to the hostile offer. The counterstrategies were largely unsuccessful, however, where the goal was to stop the proxy contest (and as a consequence, the hostile offer) altogether.

For example, in cases where the target board's response was either to (i) amend the by-laws to delay a shareholders meeting to elect directors, or (ii) delay an annual meeting to a later date permitted under the bylaws, so that the board and management would be able to explore alternatives to the hostile offer (but not entrench themselves), those responses were upheld.[14] On the other hand, where the target board's response to a proxy contest (coupled with a hostile offer) was (i) to move

---

[11]   Del. Ch., 490 A.2d 1059, 1072, aff'd, Del Supr., 500 A.2d 1346 (1985) ("Moran").

[12]   Brown & Regner, n.9, *supra*.

[13]   See Unitrin, Inc. v. American General Corp., Del. Supr., 651 A.2d 1361, 1379 (1995); Kidsco, Inc. v. Dinsmore, Del.Ch., 674 A.2d 483, 490 (1995), aff'd, 670 A.2d 1338 (1995).

[14]   See, e.g., Stahl v. Apple Bancorp, Inc., Del.Ch., 579 A.2d 1115 (1990) (upholding postponement of annual meeting to a later date permitted by bylaws to enable target board to explore alternatives to hostile offer); Kidsco, Inc. v. Dinsmore, n.15, *supra*, (upholding amendment of bylaws to give target board an additional 25 days before calling a shareholder-initiated special meeting, to enable shareholders to vote on a pending merger proposal, and, if the proposal were defeated, to enable the board to explore other alternatives).

the shareholders meeting to a later date to enable the incumbent board to solicit revocations of proxies to defeat the apparently victorious dissident group, or (ii) to expand the size of the board, and then fill the newly created positions so the incumbents would retain control of the board irrespective of the outcome of the proxy contest, those responses were declared invalid.[15]

This litigation experience taught that a target board, facing a proxy contest joined with a hostile tender offer, could, in good faith, employ non-preclusive defensive measures to give the board time to explore transactional alternatives. The target board could not, however, erect defenses that would either preclude a proxy contest altogether or improperly bend the rules to favor the board's continued incumbency.

In this environment, the only defensive measure that promised to be a "show stopper" (i.e., had the potential to deter a proxy contest altogether) was a poison pill with a "dead hand" feature. The reason is that if only the incumbent directors or their designated successors could redeem the pill, it would make little sense for shareholders or the hostile bidder to wage a proxy contest to replace the incumbent board. Doing that would eliminate from the scene the only group of persons having the power to give the hostile bidder and target company shareholders what they desired: control of the target company (in the case of the hostile bidder) and the opportunity to obtain an attractive price for their shares (in the case of the target company stockholders). It is against that backdrop that the legal issues presented here, which concern the validity of the "dead hand" feature, attain significance.

* * *

III. ANALYSIS

* * *

Having considered and rejected the threshold defenses, the Court turns to the crux of this case—the validity under Delaware law of the "dead hand" feature of the Toll Brothers Rights Plan.

---

[15] See, Aprahamian v. HBO & Co., Del.Ch., 531 A.2d 1204 (1987) (shareholders' meeting moved to later date for the purpose of defeating the apparent victors in proxy contest. Held: invalid); Blasius Indus. v. Atlas Corp., Del.Ch., 564 A.2d 651 (1988) (in response to an announced proxy contest, target board amended bylaws to create two new board positions, then filled those positions to retain board control, irrespective of outcome of proxy contest. Held: invalid).

Another statutorily permissible defensive device—the "staggered" or classified board—was useful, but still of limited effectiveness. Because only one third of a classified board would stand for election each year, a classified board would delay—but not prevent—a hostile acquiror from obtaining control of the board, since a determined acquiror could wage a proxy contest and obtain control of two thirds of the target board over a two year period, as opposed to seizing control in a single election.

B.   *The Validity of the "Dead Hand" Provision*

* * *

2.   *The Statutory Invalidity Claims*

Having carefully considered the arguments and authorities marshaled by both sides, the Court concludes that the complaint states legally sufficient claims that the "dead hand" provision of the Toll Brothers Rights Plan violates 8 Del. C. §§ 141(a) and (d). There are three reasons.

First, it cannot be disputed that the Rights Plan confers the power to redeem the pill only upon some, but not all, of the directors. But under § 141(d), the power to create voting power distinctions among directors exists only where there is a classified board, and where those voting power distinctions are expressed in the certificate of incorporation. Section 141(d) pertinently provides:

> . . . The certificate of incorporation may confer upon holders of any class or series of stock the right to elect 1 or more directors who shall serve for such term, and have such voting powers as shall be stated in the certificate of incorporation. The terms of office and voting powers of the directors elected in the manner so provided in the certificate of incorporation may be greater than or less than those of any other director or class of directors. . . . (emphasis added)

The plain, unambiguous meaning of the quoted language is that if one category or group of directors is given distinctive voting rights not shared by the other directors, those distinctive voting rights must be set forth in the certificate of incorporation. In the case of Toll Brothers (the complaint alleges), they are not.

Second, § 141(d) mandates that the "right to elect 1 or more directors who shall . . . have such [greater] voting powers" is reserved to the stockholders, not to the directors or a subset thereof. Absent express language in the charter, nothing in Delaware law suggests that some directors of a public corporation may be created less equal than other directors, and certainly not by unilateral board action.[33] Vesting the pill redemption power exclusively in the Continuing Directors transgresses the statutorily protected shareholder right to elect the directors who would be so empowered. For that reason, and because it is claimed that the Rights Plan's allocation of voting power to redeem the Rights is nowhere found in the Toll Brothers certificate of incorporation, the complaint states a claim that the "dead hand" feature of the Rights Plan is ultra vires, and hence, statutorily invalid under Delaware law.

Third, the complaint states a claim that the "dead hand" provision would impermissibly interfere with the directors' statutory power to

---

[33]   Gordon, 19 Cardozo L. Rev. at 537.

manage the business and affairs of the corporation. That power is conferred by 8 Del. C. § 141(a), which mandates:

> The business and affairs of every corporation organized under this chapter shall be managed by or under the direction of a board of directors, *except as may be otherwise provided in this chapter or in its certificate of incorporation.* . . . (emphasis added)

The "dead hand" poison pill is intended to thwart hostile bids by vesting shareholders with preclusive rights that cannot be redeemed except by the Continuing Directors. Thus, the one action that could make it practically possible to redeem the pill—replacing the entire board—could make that pill redemption legally impossible to achieve. The "dead hand" provision would jeopardize a newly-elected future board's ability to achieve a business combination by depriving that board of the power to redeem the pill without obtaining the consent of the "Continuing Directors," who (it may be assumed) would constitute a minority of the board. In this manner, it is claimed, the "dead hand" provision would interfere with the board's power to protect fully the corporation's (and its shareholders') interests in a transaction that is one of the most fundamental and important in the life of a business enterprise.

* * *

The defendants offer two arguments in response. First, they contend that the Rights Plan does not facially preclude or interfere with proxy contests as a means to gain control, or coerce shareholders to vote for or against any particular director slate. The second argument is that the "dead hand" provision is tantamount to a delegation to a special committee, consisting of the Continuing Directors, of the power to redeem the pill.

Neither contention has merit. The first is basically an argument that the Rights Plan does not violate any fiduciary duty of the board. That is unresponsive to the statutory invalidity claim. The second argument rests upon an analogy that has no basis in fact. In adopting the Rights Plan, the board did not, nor did it purport to, create a special committee having the exclusive power to redeem the pill. The analogy also ignores fundamental structural differences between the creation of a special board committee and the operation of the "dead hand" provision of the Rights Plan. The creation of a special committee would not impose long term structural power-related distinctions between different groups of directors of the same board. The board that creates a special committee may abolish it at any time, as could any successor board. On the other hand, the Toll Brothers "dead hand" provision, if legally valid, would embed structural power-related distinctions between groups of directors that no successor board could abolish until after the Rights expire in 2007.

For these reasons, the statutory invalidity claims survive the motion to dismiss.[34]

3.   *The Fiduciary Duty Invalidity Claims*

Because the plaintiff's statutory invalidity claims have been found legally cognizable, the analysis arguably could end at this point. But the plaintiff also alleges that the board's adoption of the "dead hand" feature violated its fiduciary duty of loyalty. For the sake of completeness, that claim is addressed as well.

The duty of loyalty claim, to reiterate, has two prongs. The first is that the "dead hand" provision purposefully interferes with the shareholder voting franchise without any compelling justification, and is therefore unlawful under Blasius. The second is that the "dead hand" provision is a "disproportionate" defensive measure, because it either precludes or materially abridges the shareholders' rights to receive tender offers and to wage a proxy contest to replace the board. Under Unocal/Unitrin, in such circumstances the board's approval of the "dead hand" provision would not enjoy the presumption of validity conferred by the business judgment review standard, and therefore would be found to constitute a breach of fiduciary duty.

I conclude, for the reasons next discussed, that both fiduciary duty claims are cognizable under Delaware law.

a)   *The Blasius Fiduciary Duty Claim*

The validity of antitakeover measures is normally evaluated under the Unocal/Unitrin standard. But where the defensive measures purposefully disenfranchise shareholders, the board will be required to satisfy the more exacting Blasius standard, which our Supreme Court has articulated as follows:[35]

> A board's unilateral decision to adopt a defensive measure touching "upon issues of control" that purposefully

---

[34]   The defendants rely upon Invacare Corp. v. Healthdyne Technologies, Inc., 968 F.Supp. 1578 (N.D.Ga. 1997). That case is distinguishable and inapposite. In Invacare, the United States District Court for the Northern District of Georgia, applying Georgia law, upheld a "continuing director" provision of a target company's rights plan. It was argued that the continuing director provision was invalid because it imposed significant limitations upon the board's powers that should have been, but were not, included in the articles of incorporation or the bylaws, as Georgia's corporation statute required. The court rejected that argument. Distinguishing Bank of New York, the court held that the Georgia Business Corporation Code had no statutory requirement mandating that limitations on the directors' power be expressed in the certificate of incorporation. That court noted that the Georgia statute gave the board "sole discretion" to determine the terms and conditions of a rights plan, and that the Official Comment stated that the board's discretion is limited only by its fiduciary obligations to the corporation. The court also found that the Georgia Fair Price statutory provision, which required unanimous approval by the "continuing directors" or recommendation by at least two thirds of the "continuing directors" and approval by a specified percentage of shareholder votes, supported the conclusion that "Georgia corporate law embraces the concept of continuing directors as part of a defense against hostile takeovers." 968 F.Supp. at 1580. The relevant Delaware corporate statutory scheme, like New York's, differs materially from that of Georgia.

[35]   Stroud v. Grace, Del. Supr., 606 A.2d 75, 92 n.3 (1992).

disenfranchises its shareholders is strongly suspect under Unocal, and cannot be sustained without a "compelling justification."

The complaint alleges that the "dead hand" provision purposefully disenfranchises the company's shareholders without any compelling justification. The disenfranchisement would occur because even in an election contest fought over the issue of the hostile bid, the shareholders will be powerless to elect a board that is both willing and able to accept the bid, and they "may be forced to vote for [incumbent] directors whose policies they reject because only those directors have the power to change them."[36]

A claim that the directors have unilaterally "created a structure in which shareholder voting is either impotent or self defeating"[37] is necessarily a claim of purposeful disenfranchisement. Given the Supreme Court's rationale for upholding the validity of the poison pill in Moran, and the primacy of the shareholder vote in our scheme of corporate jurisprudence, any contrary view is difficult to justify. In Moran, the Supreme Court upheld the adoption of a poison pill, in part because its effect upon a proxy contest would be "minimal,"[38] but also because if the board refused to redeem the plan, the shareholders could exercise their prerogative to remove and replace the board. In Unocal the Supreme Court reiterated that view that the safety valve which justifies a board being allowed to resist a hostile offer a majority of shareholders might prefer, is that the shareholders always have their ultimate recourse to the ballot box.[39] Those observations reflect the fundamental value that the shareholder vote has primacy in our system of corporate governance because it is the "ideological underpinning upon which the legitimacy of directorial power rests."[40] * * *

The defendants contend that the complaint fails to allege a valid stockholder disenfranchisement claim, because the Rights Plan does not on its face limit a dissident's ability to propose a slate or the shareholders' ability to cast a vote. The defendants also urge that even if the Plan might arguably have that effect, it could occur only in a very specific and unlikely context, namely, where (i) the hostile bidder makes a fair offer that it is willing to keep open for more than one year, (ii) the current

---

[36] Gordon, 19 Cardozo L. REV. at 540.

[37] *Id.*

[38] Moran, 500 A.2d at 1355.

[39] Unocal, 493 A.2d at 959 ("If the shareholders are displeased with the action of their elected representatives, the powers of corporate democracy are at their disposal to turn the board out.").

[40] Blasius, 564 A.2d at 659; see also, Unitrin, 651 A.2d at 1378 ("This Court has been and remains assiduous in its concern about defensive actions designed to thwart the essence of corporate democracy by disenfranchising stockholders."); and Paramount Communications, Inc. v. QVC Network, Inc., Del. Supr., 637 A.2d 34, 42 (1994) ("Because of the overriding importance of voting rights, this Court and the Court of Chancery have consistently acted to protect stockholders from unwarranted interference with such rights.").

board refuses to redeem the Rights, and (iii) the offeror wages two successful proxy fights and is committed to wage a third.

This argument, in my opinion, begs the issue and is specious. It begs the issue because the complaint does not claim that the Rights Plan facially restricts the shareholders' voting rights. What the complaint alleges is that the "dead hand" provision will either preclude a hostile bidder from waging a proxy contest altogether, or, if there should be a contest, it will coerce those shareholders who desire the hostile offer to succeed to vote for those directors who oppose it—the incumbent (and "Continuing") directors. Besides missing the point, the argument is also specious, because the hypothetical case the defendants argue must exist for any disenfranchisement to occur, rests upon the unlikely assumption that the hostile bidder will keep its offer open for more than one year. Given the market risks inherent in financed hostile bids for public corporations, it is unrealistic to assume that many bidders would be willing to do that.

For these reasons, the plaintiff's Blasius-based breach of fiduciary duty claim is cognizable under Delaware law.

b)   *The* Unocal/*Unitrin Fiduciary Duty Claim*

The final issue is whether the complaint states a legally cognizable claim that the inclusion of the "dead hand" provision in the Rights Plan was an unreasonable defensive measure within the meaning of Unocal. I conclude that it does.

* * *

The complaint at issue here is far from conclusory. Under Unitrin, a defensive measure is disproportionate (i.e., unreasonable) if it is either coercive or preclusive. The complaint alleges that the "dead hand" provision "disenfranchises shareholders by forcing them to vote for incumbent directors or their designees if shareholders want to be represented by a board entitled to exercise its full statutory prerogatives." That is sufficient to claim that the "dead hand" provision is coercive. The complaint also alleges that that provision "makes an offer for the Company much more unlikely since it eliminates use of a proxy contest as a possible means to gain control . . . [because] . . . any directors elected in such a contest would still be unable to vote to redeem the pill;" and the provision "renders future contests for corporate control of Toll Brothers prohibitively expensive and effectively impossible." A defensive measure is preclusive if it makes a bidder's ability to wage a successful proxy contest and gain control either "mathematically impossible" or "realistically unattainable."[51] These allegations are sufficient to state a claim that the "dead hand" provision makes a proxy contest "realistically unattainable," and therefore, disproportionate and unreasonable under Unocal.

---

[51]   Unitrin, 651 A.2d at 1388–89; see also, Gordon, 19 Cardozo L. Rev. at 541.

IV. CONCLUSION

The Court concludes that for the reasons discussed above, the complaint states claims under Delaware law upon which relief can be granted.[52] Accordingly, the defendants' motion to dismiss is denied. IT IS SO ORDERED.

————————

QUESTIONS

1. What statutes does the court rely on to find that the "dead hand" provision is invalid?

2. Why does the court refuse to treat the "dead hand" provision as simply a delegation by the board to a special committee, authorized by section 141(c)?

3. Why does the court conclude that the "dead hand" provision interferes with the board's power to manage the business and affairs of the corporation under section 141(a)? Note that in Blasius the court held that certain defensive actions in the face of a bidder were not part of the board's power to manage. What is the distinction between the two cases?

4. How does the court distinguish this limitation from the normal limits a board imposes on itself when it commits the corporation to a contract?

5. Does the court hold that this complaint states a claim for relief under Blasius? What is the nature of that claim?

6. Does the court hold that this complaint states a claim for relief under Unocal? What is the nature of that claim? Why does the court apply a Unocal test rather than a business judgment test? Does the following language from Unitrin, Inc. v. American General Corp., 651 A.2d 1361, 1374 (Del. 1995) explain this?

   "The business judgment rule has traditionally operated to shield directors from personal liability arising out of completed actions involving operational issues. When the business judgment rule is applied to defend directors against personal liability, as in a derivative suit, the plaintiff has the initial burden of proof and the ultimate burden of persuasion. In such cases, the business judgment rule shields directors from personal liability if, upon review, the court concludes the directors' decision can be attributed to any rational business purpose.

————————

[52] For the sake of clarity, it must be emphasized that the "dead hand" provision at issue here is of unlimited duration; that is, it remains effective during the entire life of the poison pill. There are also "dead hand" provisions of limited duration (e.g., six months), which are sometimes referred to as "diluted" or "deferred redemption" provisions. Some commentators have urged that such limited duration "dead hand" provisions stand on a different footing and should be upheld; others have argued the contrary. See Lese, 96 Col. L. Rev at 2210; and Gordon, 19 Cardozo L. Rev. at 542. In any event, this case does not involve the validity of a "dead hand" provision of limited duration, and nothing in this Opinion should be read as expressing a view or pronouncement on that subject.

"Conversely, in transactional justification cases involving the adoption of defenses to takeovers, the director's actions invariably implicate issues affecting stockholder rights. In transactional justification cases, the directors' decision is reviewed judicially and the burden of going forward is placed on the directors. If the directors' actions withstand Unocal's reasonableness and proportionality review, the traditional business judgment rule is applied to shield the directors' defensive decision rather than the directors themselves."

Quickturn Design Systems, Inc. v. Shapiro

721 A.2d 1281 (Del. 1998).

■ HOLLAND, JUSTICE:

This is an expedited appeal from a final judgment entered by the Court of Chancery. The dispute arises out of an ongoing effort by Mentor Graphics Corporation ("Mentor"), a hostile bidder, to acquire Quickturn Design Systems, Inc. ("Quickturn"), the target company. The plaintiffs-appellees are Mentor[1] and an unaffiliated stockholder of Quickturn. The named defendants-appellants are Quickturn and its directors.

In response to Mentor's tender offer and proxy contest to replace the Quickturn board of directors, as part of Mentor's effort to acquire Quickturn, the Quickturn board enacted two defensive measures. First, it amended the Quickturn shareholder rights plan ("Rights Plan") by adopting a "no hand" feature of limited duration (the "Delayed Redemption Provision" or "DRP") Second, the Quickturn board amended the corporation's by-laws to delay the holding of any special stockholders meeting requested by stockholders for 90 to 100 days after the validity of the request is determined (the "Amendment" or "By-Law Amendment").

Mentor filed actions for declaratory and injunctive relief in the Court of Chancery challenging the legality of both defensive responses by Quickturn's board. The Court of Chancery conducted a trial on the merits. It determined that the By-Law Amendment is valid. It also concluded, however, that the DRP is invalid on fiduciary duty grounds.

In this appeal, Quickturn argues that the Court of Chancery erred in finding that Quickturn's directors breached their fiduciary duty by adopting the Delayed Redemption Provision. We have concluded that, as a matter of Delaware law, the Delayed Redemption Provision was invalid. Therefore, on that alternative basis, the judgment of the Court of Chancery is affirmed.

---

[1]   Mentor and MGZ Corp., a wholly owned Mentor subsidiary specially created as a vehicle to acquire Quickturn, are referred to collectively as Mentor. Unless otherwise indicated, Mentor and Howard Shapiro, the shareholder plaintiff in Court of Chancery Civil Action No. 16588, are referred to collectively as "Mentor."

STATEMENT OF FACTS

The Parties

Mentor (the hostile bidder) is an Oregon corporation, headquartered in Wilsonville, Oregon, whose shares are publicly traded on the NASDAQ national market system. Mentor manufactures, markets, and supports electronic design automation ("EDA") software and hardware. * * *

Quickturn [is a Delaware corporation that] invented, and was the first company to successfully market, logic emulation technology, which is used to verify the design of complex silicon chips and electronics systems. Quickturn is currently the market leader in the emulation business, controlling an estimated 60% of the worldwide emulation market and an even higher percentage of the United States market. Quickturn maintains the largest intellectual property portfolio in the industry, which includes approximately twenty-nine logic emulation patents issued in the United States, and numerous other patents Issued in foreign jurisdictions. * * *

Quickturn's board of directors consists of eight members, all but one of whom are outside, independent directors. All have distinguished careers and significant technological experience. Collectively, the board has more than 30 years of experience in the EDA industry and owns one million shares (about 5%) of Quickturn's common stock.

Since 1989, Quickturn has historically been a growth company, having experienced increases in earnings and revenues during the past seven years. Those favorable trends were reflected in Quickturn's stock prices, which reached a high of $15.75 during the first quarter of 1998, and generally traded in the $15.875 to $21.25 range during the year preceding Mentor's hostile bid.

Since the spring of 1998, Quickturn's earnings, revenue growth, and stock price levels have declined, largely because of the downturn in the semiconductor industry and more specifically in the Asian semiconductor market. Historically, 30%–35% of Quickturn's annual sales (approximately $35 million) had come from Asia, but in 1998, Quickturn's Asian sales declined dramatically with the downturn of the Asian market.[5] Management has projected that the negative impact of the Asian market upon Quickturn's sales should begin reversing itself sometime between the second half of 1998 and early 1999.

Quickturn-Mentor Patent Litigation

Since 1996, Mentor and Quickturn have been engaged in patent litigation that has resulted in Mentor being barred from competing in the United States emulation market. Because its products have been

---

[5] By the summer of 1998, Quickturn's stock price had declined to $6 per share. On August 11, 1998, the closing price was $8.00. It was in this trough period that Mentor, which had designs upon Quickturn since the fall of 1997, saw an opportunity to acquire Quickturn for an advantageous price.

adjudicated to infringe upon Quickturn's patents, Mentor currently stands enjoined from selling, manufacturing, or marketing its emulation products in the United States. Thus, Mentor is excluded from an unquestionably significant market for emulation products.

* * *

Mentor's Interest in Acquiring Quickturn

Mentor began exploring the possibility of acquiring Quickturn. If Mentor owned Quickturn, it would also own the patents, and would be in a position to "unenforce" them by seeking to vacate Quickturn's injunctive orders against Mentor in the patent litigation. * * *

Mentor Tender Offer and Proxy Contest

On August 12, 1998, Mentor announced an unsolicited cash tender offer for all outstanding common shares of Quickturn at $12.125 per share, a price representing an approximate 50% premium over Quickturn's immediate pre-offer price, and a 20% discount from Quickturn's February 1998 stock price levels. Mentor's tender offer, once consummated, would be followed by a second step merger in which Quickturn's nontendering stockholders would receive, in cash, the same $12.125 per share tender offer price.

Mentor also announced its intent to solicit proxies to replace the board at a special meeting. Relying upon Quickturn's then-applicable by-law provision governing the call of special stockholders meetings, Mentor began soliciting agent designations from Quickturn stockholders to satisfy the by-law's stock ownership requirements to call such a meeting.

Quickturn Board Meetings

* * *

Under the Williams Act, Quickturn was required to inform its shareholders of its response to Mentor's offer no later than ten business days after the offer was commenced. During that ten day period, the Quickturn board met three times, on August 13, 17, and 21, 1998. During each of those meetings, it considered Mentor's offer and ultimately decided how to respond.

* * *

The Quickturn board held its third and final meeting in response to Mentor's offer on August 21, 1998. Again, the directors received extensive materials and a further detailed analysis performed by H & Q [Hambrecht & Quist, investment bankers]. The focal point of that analysis was a chart entitled "Summary of Implied Valuation." That chart compared Mentor's tender offer price to the Quickturn valuation ranges generated by H & Q's application of five different methodologies. The chart showed that Quickturn's value under all but one of those methodologies was higher than Mentor's $12.125 tender offer price.

Quickturn's Board Rejects Mentor's Offer as Inadequate

After hearing the presentations, the Quickturn board concluded that Mentor's offer was inadequate, and decided to recommend that Quickturn shareholders reject Mentor's offer. The directors based their decision upon: (a) H & Q's report; (b) the fact that Quickturn was experiencing a temporary trough in its business, which was reflected in its stock price; (c) the company's leadership in technology and patents and resulting market share; (d) the likely growth in Quickturn's markets (most notably, the Asian market) and the strength of Quickturn's new products (specifically, its Mercury product); (e) the potential value of the patent litigation with Mentor; and (f) the problems for Quickturn's customers, employees, and technology if the two companies were combined as the result of a hostile takeover.

Quickturn's Defensive Measures

At the August 21 board meeting, the Quickturn board adopted defensive measures in response to Mentor's hostile takeover bid. First, the board amended Article II, § 2.3 of Quickturn's by-laws, which permitted stockholders holding 10% or more of Quickturn's stock to call a special stockholders meeting. The By-Law Amendment provides that if any such special meeting is requested by shareholders, the corporation (Quickturn) would fix the record date for, and determine the time and place of, that special meeting, which must take place not less than 90 days nor more than 100 days after the receipt and determination of the validity of the shareholders' request. [The Chancery Court upheld this bylaw as a reasonable response under Unocal, and Mentor did not appeal this decision.]

Second, the board amended Quickturn's shareholder Rights Plan by eliminating its "dead hand" feature and replacing it with the Deferred Redemption Provision, under which no newly elected board could redeem the Rights Plan for six months after taking office, if the purpose or effect of the redemption would be to facilitate a transaction with an "Interested Person" (one who proposed, nominated or financially supported the election of the new directors to the board). Mentor would be an Interested Person.

The effect of the By-Law Amendment would be to delay a shareholder-called special meeting for at least three months. The effect of the DRP would be to delay the ability of a newly-elected, Mentor-nominated board to redeem the Rights Plan or "poison pill" for six months, in any transaction with an Interested Person. Thus, the combined effect of the two defensive measures would be to delay any acquisition of Quickturn by Mentor for at least nine months.

* * *

DELAYED REDEMPTION PROVISION VIOLATES
FUNDAMENTAL DELAWARE LAW

In this appeal, Mentor argues that the judgment of the Court of Chancery should be affirmed because the Delayed Redemption Provision is invalid as a matter of Delaware law. According to Mentor, the Delayed Redemption Provision, like the "dead hand" feature in the Rights Plan that was held to be invalid in Toll Brothers will impermissibly deprive any newly elected board of both its statutory authority to manage the corporation under 8 Del. C § 141(a) and its concomitant fiduciary duty pursuant to that statutory mandate. We agree.

Our analysis of the Delayed Redemption Provision in the Quickturn Rights Plan is guided by the prior precedents of this Court with regard to a board of directors authority to adopt a Rights Plan or "poison pill." In Moran, this Court held that the "inherent powers of the Board conferred by 8 Del. C. § 141(a) concerning the management of the corporation's 'business and affairs' provides the Board additional authority upon which to enact the Rights Plan." Consequently, this Court upheld the adoption of the Rights Plan in Moran as a legitimate exercise of business judgment by the board of directors. In doing so, however, this Court also held "the rights plan is not absolute".

> When the Household Board of Directors is faced with a tender offer and a request to redeem the Rights [Plan], they will not be able to arbitrarily reject the offer. They will be held to the same fiduciary standards any other board of directors would be held to in deciding to adopt a defensive mechanism, the same standards as they were held to in originally approving the Rights Plan.[33]

In Moran, this Court held that the "ultimate response to an actual takeover bid must be judged by the Directors' actions at the time and nothing we say relieves them of their fundamental duties to the corporation and its shareholders." Consequently, we concluded that the use of the Rights Plan would be evaluated when and if the issue arises.

One of the most basic tenets of Delaware corporate law is that the board of directors has the ultimate responsibility for managing the business and affairs of a corporation. Section 141(a) requires that any limitation on the board's authority be set out in the certificate of incorporation. The Quickturn certificate of incorporation contains no provision purporting to limit the authority of the board in any way. The Delayed Redemption Provision, however, would prevent a newly elected board of directors from completely discharging its fundamental management duties to the corporation and its stockholders for six months. While the Delayed Redemption Provision limits the board of

---

[33] [Moran v. Household International, Inc., Del. Supr., 500 A.2d 1346, 1354 (1985)]; See also Unocal Corp. v. Mesa Petroleum Co., 493 A.2d at 954–55, 958.

directors' authority in only one respect, the suspension of the Rights Plan, it nonetheless restricts the board's power in an area of fundamental importance to the shareholders—negotiating a possible sale of the corporation. Therefore, we hold that the Delayed Redemption Provision is invalid under Section 141(a), which confers upon any newly elected board of directors full power to manage and direct the business and affairs of a Delaware corporation.

In discharging the statutory mandate of Section 141(a), the directors have a fiduciary duty to the corporation and its shareholders. This unremitting obligation extends equally to board conduct in a contest for corporate control. The Delayed Redemption Provision prevents a newly elected board of directors from completely discharging its fiduciary duties to protect fully the interests of Quickturn and its stockholders.

This Court has recently observed that "although the fiduciary duty of a Delaware director is unremitting, the exact course of conduct that must be charted to properly discharge that responsibility will change in the specific context of the action the director is taking with regard to either the corporation or its shareholders."[42] This Court has held "to the extent that a contract, or a provision thereof, purports to require a board to act or not act in such a fashion as to limit the exercise of fiduciary duties, it is invalid and unenforceable."[43] The Delayed Redemption Provision "tends to limit in a substantial way the freedom of [newly elected] directors' decisions on matters of management policy."[44] Therefore, "it violates the duty of each [newly elected] director to exercise his own best judgment on matters coming before the board."[45]

In this case, the Quickturn board was confronted by a determined bidder that sought to acquire the company at a price the Quickturn board concluded was inadequate. Such situations are common in corporate takeover efforts. In Revlon, this Court held that no defensive measure can be sustained when it represents a breach of the directors' fiduciary duty. A fortiori, no defensive measure can be sustained which would require a new board of directors to breach its fiduciary duty. In that regard, we note Mentor has properly acknowledged that in the event its slate of directors are elected, those newly elected directors will be required to discharge their unremitting fiduciary duty to manage the corporation for the benefit of Quickturn and its stockholders.

---

[42] Malone v. Brincat, Del. Supr., 722 A.2d 5 (1998).

[43] See Paramount Communications, Inc. v. QVC Network, Inc., 637 A.2d at 51 (emphasis added). See, e.g. Mills Acquisition Co. v. MacMillan, Inc., 559 A.2d at 1281 (holding that a "board of directors . . . may not avoid its active and direct duty of oversight in a matter as significant as the sale of corporate control"); Grimes v. Donald, Del.Ch., C.A. No. 13358, slip op. at 17, Allen, C., 1995 WL 54441 (Jan. 11, 1995, revised Jan. 19, 1995), aff'd, aff'd, Del.Supr., 673 A.2d 1207 ("the board may not either formally or effectively abdicate its statutory power and its fiduciary duty to manage or direct the management of the business and affairs of this corporation").

[44] Abercrombie v. Davies, Del Ch., 35 Del.Ch. 599, 123 A.2d 893, 899 (1956), rev'd on other grounds, Del. Supr., 36 Del.Ch. 371, 130 A.2d 338 (1957).

[45] Id.

Conclusion

The Delayed Redemption Provision would prevent a new Quickturn board of directors from managing the corporation by redeeming the Rights Plan to facilitate a transaction that would serve the stockholders' best interests, even under circumstances where the board would be required to do so because of its fiduciary duty to the Quickturn stockholders. Because the Delayed Redemption Provision impermissibly circumscribes the board's statutory power under Section 141(a) and the directors' ability to fulfill their concomitant fiduciary duties, we hold that the Delayed Redemption Provision is invalid. On that alternative basis, the judgment of the Court of Chancery is affirmed.

After this decision Quickturn ultimately agreed to be acquired by a white knight, Cadence Design Systems Inc. in exchange for Cadence stock, worth $23 per Quickturn share, 14 months after completion of the merger. Mentor, assuming it still owned its Cadence stock, thus earned $11 per share on its Quickturn investment, according to the Chancery Court. Nevertheless, Mentor applied to the Chancery Court for attorneys' fees, on the basis that it had created a benefit for Quickturn's shareholders by challenging its rights plan. The Chancery Court denied the application, on the theory that bidders for corporate control, unlike other shareholders, need no further incentives from fee awards to encourage them to challenge management actions. Further, Mentor had waited too long—the proceeds of the beneficial sale had been disbursed to all the shareholders. To allow Mentor to recover after disbursement would mean that the buyer, Cadence, and its shareholders would bear an additional cost. Mentor Graphics Corp. v. Quickturn Design Systems Inc., 789 A.2d 1216 (2001).

QUESTIONS

1. The court concluded that any limits on the board's power must be set out in the certificate of incorporation, as provided in section 141(a). How can you reconcile this with the language of section 109(b), which provides that "[t]he bylaws may contain any provision, not inconsistent with law or with the certificate of incorporation, relating to the business of the corporation, the conduct of its affairs, and its rights or powers or the *rights or powers of its stockholders, directors*, officers or employees?"

2. If Mentor's proxy fight were successful and its slate were elected as the sole directors of Quickturn, how difficult would it be for such directors to carry out their fiduciary duties to the Quickturn public shareholders if the Deferred Redemption Provision remained in place? What if Mentor announced in advance that its directors would vote in favor of a merger of Quickturn and Mentor, and would redeem the rights?

3. How would you expect a court in a Model Business Corporation Act jurisdiction to decide a similar case? See MBCA §§ 7.32 and 8.01.

At one point over 3,000 companies had adopted rights plans. But opposition from ISS and institutional investors persuaded many companies to either end their plans or not renew them when they expired. Only 999 public companies had rights plans in place as of March 31, 2010.

Critics of rights plans come from two sources. One is Risk Metrics (formerly ISS), which gives corporations negative marks for having a rights plan triggered at less than 20% (the vast majority have 15% triggers), and gives positive credit for plans that allow exemption from the pill for bidders making fully funded offers for all shares at a "fair" price ("qualified offer" or "chewable" pills), and for plans that require independent directors to review the pill periodically ("Tide" provisions). As of 2010 Risk Metrics disapproved of any rights plans with a duration of over twelve months unless they are approved by shareholders. Second, activist shareholders seeking to make a quick profit on a sale at any premium seem to be behind some campaigns. Neither group seems much impressed by the evidence that shareholders do better when the board has the leverage and negotiating power obtained with a rights plan. Another advisory firm, Glass Lewis, advertises that its recommendations are more favorable to management. A recent study of poison pill adoptions found that they enhanced takeover premiums but did not reduce completion rates after major Delaware decisions approving of their use. Randall A. Heron and Erik Lee, The Effect of Poison Pill Adoptions and Court Rulings on Firm Entrenchment, 35 Journal of Finance 286 (2015).

NOTE ON LOAN PROVISIONS TO ACCELERATE DEBT AFTER A CHANGE OF CONTROL

Some loan agreements provide that in the event of a change of control of the debtor, the loan repayment obligation is accelerated so the entire amount becomes due and payable immediately. These terms may be the result of arm's length bargaining, and the result of negative covenants precluding mergers and similar transactions without the consent of the lender. Lenders may be concerned that additional debt may be undertaken by the surviving corporation, or that the combined businesses may be more risky than those of the original borrower. On the other hand, these provisions may be suggested by the borrower as a takeover defense. In these cases it is more likely that a change of control may be more broadly defined, to include, for example, not simply a change in ownership of a majority of the debtor's shares, but also a change in a majority of the debtor's directors without the approval of the existing "continuing directors." The resemblance to a Dead Hand provision is obvious. Determining whether the purposes of such clauses is legitimate protection of the lender's interest or a takeover defense may be more subtle and fact intensive than in the case of Dead Hand provisions.

In San Antonio Fire & Police Pension Fund v. Amylin Pharmaceuticals, Inc., 983 A.2d 304, 307 (Del. Ch.), aff'd 981 A.2d 1173 (Del. 2009) Vice Chancellor Lamb stated that when directors are asked to approve board candidates to avoid acceleration they cannot arbitrarily refuse to do so. And in Kallick v. SandRidge Energy, Inc., 2013 Del. Ch. LEXIS 63, Chancellor Strine suggested that all such provisions might be subject to challenge. In this case a large shareholder proposed to amend bylaws to eliminate a staggered board and elect a new slate of directors. The board solicited the revocation of consents, stating that these actions would constitute a change of control that triggered acceleration of $4 billion in debt. A shareholder suit requested that the board be enjoined from soliciting consent revocations until it approved the insurgent slate. Chancellor Strine granted the preliminary injunction, and stated that a board "that acts in good faith must seek to protect the stockholders' ability to make an uncoerced choice of directors." He also stated that a board "may only fail to approve a dissident slate if the board determines that passing control to the slate would constitute a breach of the duty of loyalty, in particular, because the proposed slate poses a danger that the company would not honor its legal duty to repay its creditors."

NOTE ON STAGGERED BOARD PROVISIONS

While a rights plan is a powerful defense against a takeover, the board of directors normally retains the power to redeem the rights at any time prior to the triggering of their exercisability. Normally they can be redeemed at a nominal price, perhaps one cent per right, so redemption has no impact on the target company's finances. This redemption power is necessary to provide the board with the bargaining power to approve business combinations of which the board approves. But this creates the risk that the incumbent directors might find themselves replaced, either through a proxy fight to remove them, to replace them at annual meetings, or to enlarge the board and to elect representatives of a bidder to the board. This technique has been used several times. When Farley industries made a hostile bid for West Point Pepperell (see Grace Bros. v. Farley Industries, 264 Ga. 817, 450 S.E.2d 814 (1994), *infra*, Chapter Nine, Part 5), West Point had adopted a rights plan. But Farley's cash tender offer, at an attractive premium over the market, was conditioned on West Point's redemption of its rights plan or a declaration of its invalidity. Further, Farley solicited proxies from the West Point shareholders to allow Farley to gain control of the board and cause the new directors to vote to redeem the rights. AT & T used the same technique to gain control of NCR Corporation. Other similar acquisitions involved IBM's acquisition of Lotus Development Corp. in 1995; Ingersoll-Rand's bid for Clark Equipment Co. in 1995; and Tyson Foods Inc.'s 1994 bid for WLR Foods Inc. As of 2005, 52.7% of 5,000 companies surveyed had staggered boards.[15] A Conference Board report states that in 2002 60% of public companies had staggered boards, while by 2011 the number was less than half, and less than one-third of S&P 500 companies retained staggered boards.*

As a result of the specter of proxy fights to remove directors, many companies have taken steps to assure this will not happen. First, some statutes provide that if a board is classified (multi-year terms with only some terms expiring each year), directors can only be removed for cause, unless the articles of incorporation provide otherwise. See, e.g., Del. Code, tit. 8, § 141(k); Off. Code Ga. Ann. § 14–2–808(d). The Model Business Corp. Act provides that directors may be removed with or without cause unless the articles of incorporation provide they may only be removed for cause. Model Bus. Corp. Act § 8.08(a). Frequently charter amendments providing for such protection are locked in by requirements that they can only be amended by a supermajority vote. Activist institutional investors also opposed these provisions. There were six such proposals in 1999, of which three came to a vote, and eleven proposals in 2000, with shareholders voting on seven. In 2000 the average proposal received the support of 54.6% of the shares voted.[17] ISS recommends that shareholder vote against amendments to stagger a board.

Classified boards also provide protection for incumbents, since it would take two annual meetings for a bidder to gain control of a board with three classes of directors. An important supplement to these provisions is the adoption of charter and bylaw provisions that preclude a bidder from beginning a proxy fight to enlarge the board of directors and fill the vacancies with directors willing to redeem rights and take other steps to facilitate a hostile bid. For a discussion of the power of this defense, see Lucian Arye Bebchuk, John C. Coates IV & Guhan Subramanian, The Powerful Antitakeover Force of Staggered Boards: Theory, Evidence, and Policy, 54 Stan. L. Rev. 887 (2002).

Once a bidder has launched a bid and a proxy solicitation to replace the board at a forthcoming meeting, what can an incumbent board do to defeat the solicitation? In Hilton Hotels Corp. v. ITT Corp., 978 F.Supp. 1342 (D. Nev. 1997) (applying Nevada law, guided by Delaware principles) ITT, the target, proposed a spin-off of most of its assets into a new corporation that would have a staggered board and a requirement for an 80% vote to remove directors without cause. In addition to holding that there was no Unocal "threat," the court held that the spin-off would absolutely preclude the shareholders from electing a new board majority at the forthcoming annual meeting, which also offended the Unocal proportionality standard.

---

[15] Reena Aggarwal & Rohan Williamson, Did New Regulations Target the Relevant Corporate Governance Attributes?, working paper (2006) at http://papers.ssrn.com/sol3/papers.cfm?abstract_id=859264&high=%20Did%20Regulations%20Target%20the%20Relevant%20Corporate%20Reena%20Aggarwal (last visited 3/10/07).

* https://www.conference-board.org/retrievefile.cfm?filename=TCB-DN-V3N24-11.pdf&type=subsite (last visited 6/4/2016).

[17] Favole, supra note ** at 15.

Airgas, Inc. v. Air Products, and Chemicals, Inc., 8 A.3d 1182 (Del. 2010), ruled on the novel question of what constitutes a "term" for a director on a staggered board. The Airgas board was staggered into three classes, with one class elected at each annual meeting. At the 2010 annual meeting in September, the hostile bidder, Air Products, nominated three candidates to fill the three vacancies on the board, and they were elected by the shareholders. At the same time, Air Products proposed a bylaw amendment moving the next annual meeting to January 2011—four months later, which was approved by holders of 45% of the shares entitled to vote. Airgas sued to invalidate the bylaw, as in conflict with a bylaw provision that requires a 67% vote to alter the staggered board provision. The Chancery Court sustained the bylaw, on the basis that Airgas's charter provides simply that directors' terms expire at the annual meeting held in the third year after their election. Thus, the fact that incumbent directors' terms were shortened by eight months did not violate either the charter or the existing bylaw requirements.

The Delaware Supreme Court took this as a question of contract interpretation, and held that the charter language was ambiguous, and looked to extrinsic evidence. Justice Ridgely noted a division in standard language used to implement a staggered board:

Many corporations provide in their charters that each class of directors serves until the "annual meeting of stockholders to be held in the third year following the year of their election." There are variations on this language, providing (for example) that each class of directors serves until the "third succeeding annual meeting following the year of their election" (collectively, the "Annual Meeting Term Alternative"). On the other hand, some corporations, such as the firm involved in Essential Enterprises v. Automatic Steel Products, Inc.,[11] provide in their charters that each class serves for a "term of three years.

Justice Ridgely then looked to the common understanding of the Airgas version of such language:

Here, we find the industry practice and understanding of similar charter language to be persuasive. Of the eighty-nine Fortune 500 Delaware corporations that have staggered boards, fifty-eight corporations use the Annual Meeting Term Alternative. More important, forty-six of those fifty-eight Delaware corporations, or 79%, expressly represent in their proxy statements that their staggered-board directors serve three year terms. Indeed, Air Products itself uses the Annual Meeting Term Alternative in its charter, and represents in its proxy statement that: "Our Board is divided into three classes for purposes of election, with *three-year terms of office* ending in successive years."

---

[11]   39 Del. Ch. 93 (1960)—Ed.

He then found that model forms and commentary were consistent with this understanding of the annual meeting approach, and thus reversed the Chancery Court.

QUESTIONS

1. Who can adopt provisions requiring a staggered board? See MBCA § 8.06; Del. GCL § 141.

2. What effect do provisions requiring staggered boards have on removal of directors? See MBCA § 8.08; Del. GCL § 141.

3. Can the board unilaterally limit the power of shareholders to enlarge the board, or must it seek shareholder consent to such a change? See MBCA § 8.03; Delaware G.C.L. § 109 provides that shareholders have the power to amend bylaws, but this power may also be granted to the board of directors, which it is in virtually all publicly held corporations. The final sentence of § 109(a) provides: "The fact that such power has been so conferred upon the directors or governing body, as the case may be, shall not divest the stockholders or members of the power, nor limit their power to adopt, amend or repeal by-laws." What does this mean for board power to limit the size of the board?

4. If a board is expanded in size, who has the power to fill the newly created directorships? See MBCA § 8.10; Del. GCL § 223.

F. STOCK REPURCHASES

Corporations repurchase their shares for a variety of reasons. In some cases repurchasing shares from holders of less than a "round lot" (100 shares) may simply be a device to save a company the cost of mailings and proxy solicitations for very small shareholders. In others, it is an alternative to a dividend distribution. Where a company has no positive net present value prospects—that is—no projects expected to return more than the company's cost of capital, share repurchases are a way of disposing of excess cash. Share repurchases can also be used to signal the market that management expects better performance in the future, and believes that the stock is currently undervalued. As in Cheff v. Mathes, noted *supra*, Part 2.A of this chapter, repurchases can be used to persuade a potential hostile bidder to abandon its takeover efforts, if the shares are repurchased from the bidder at an attractive price, often above the current market price. These repurchases are called "greenmail." The incidence of greenmail has declined in the 1990s, most likely due to an effective tax rate of 84% imposed on greenmail payments by Internal Revenue Code § 5881, adopted in 1987. Prior to this time there was a vigorous debate about whether greenmail could ever benefit target company shareholders. See Macey and McChesney, A Theoretical

Analysis of Corporate Greenmail, 95 Yale L.J. 13 (1985) and Gordon and Kornhauser, Takeover Defense Tactics: A Comment on Two Models, 96 Yale L. J. 295 (1986). For a holding that payment of greenmail is a violation of directors' duties when the purpose is entrenchment, and that the greenmailer may have aided and abetted the violation, see Heckmann v. Ahmanson, 214 Cal.Rptr. 177 (Cal. App. 1985).

AC Acquisitions Corp. v. Anderson, Clayton & Co.

519 A.2d 103 (Del.Ch. 1986).

■ ALLEN, CHANCELLOR.

This case involves a contest for control of Anderson, Clayton & Co., a Delaware corporation ("Anderson, Clayton" or the "Company"). Plaintiffs, Bear, Stearns & Co., Inc., Gruss Petroleum Corp. and Gruss Partners ("BS/G") are shareholders of Anderson, Clayton who, through a newly formed corporation—AC Acquisitions Corp.—are currently making a tender offer for any and all shares of Anderson, Clayton at $56 per share cash. That offer, which may close no earlier than midnight tonight, is subject to several important conditions as detailed below. BS/G has announced an intention, if it succeeds through its tender offer in acquiring 51% of the Company's stock, to do a follow-up merger at $56 per share cash.

BS/G publicly announced its tender offer on August 21, 1986, having failed to bring defendants to the bargaining table despite attempts over several months. On the following day, Anderson, Clayton announced the commencement of a self-tender offer for approximately 65% of its outstanding stock at $60 per share cash. The Company also announced that, in connection with the closing of the self-tender offer, the Company would sell stock to a newly-formed Employee Stock Ownership Plan ("ESOP") amounting to 25% of all issued and outstanding stock following such sale. This alternative transaction (the "Company Transaction") itself is a continuation in another form of a recapitalization of the Company that had been approved by the Company's Board in February, 1986.

* * * Pending before the Court at this time is plaintiffs' motion for an order preliminarily enjoining the Company from (1) buying any shares of the Company's stock pursuant to its pending self-tender offer, (2) selling any of the Company's stock to the newly-established ESOP and (3) taking any steps to finance the self-tender offer or (4) attempting to apply or enforce a "fair price" provision contained in Article 11 of the Company's restated certificate of incorporation to any BS/G second-step merger at $56 per share.

In summary, plaintiffs contend that this relief is justified because the Company Transaction is an economically coercive transaction that deprives shareholders of the option presented by the BS/G offer, which provides demonstrably greater current value than is offered in the Company Transaction; and that in structuring the Company Transaction and in its timing the Board has breached its fiduciary duties of care and loyalty to the shareholders because the Company Transaction is designed and effective to deprive shareholders of effective choice, to entrench the existing Board and protect it from the discipline of the market for corporate control.

* * *

[Anderson, Clayton was faced with the prospect that four aging stockholders, owning 30% of its shares, would need to sell some of their stock for estate planning purposes. Accordingly, the AC board retained First Boston & Co. to explore alternatives. A management buyout foundered, and First Boston was asked to explore the sale of the company. Plaintiffs alleged that First Boston's efforts in this respect were weak, since neither it nor another obvious candidate were contacted. Instead of a sale or liquidation of the company, First Boston recommended a recapitalization, involving a merger and a shareholder vote, that would result in a partial liquidation, involving payment of substantial amounts of cash to shareholders and the issuance of large amounts of debt by the recapitalized company. First Boston estimated the value of this transaction at between $43 and $47 per share. When the recapitalization transaction was approved by the AC board and recommended to the shareholders, BS/G offered $54 per share all cash. The AC board never entered into meaningful negotiations with BS/G. Instead, it revised the transaction in the form of a share repurchase at $60 per share, coupled with the sale of a substantial portion of stock to the company's ESOP. The results were essentially the same as the previous recapitalization, but would not require a shareholder vote. First Boston was able to raise its estimate of the value of the Company Transaction to a range of $52.34 to $57.34, depending on the value of the remaining common stock (the "stub shares.")]

III.

* * *

Ordinarily when a court is required to review the propriety of a corporate transaction challenged as constituting a breach of duty or is asked to enjoin a proposed transaction on that ground, it will, in effect, decline to evaluate the merits or wisdom of the transaction once it is shown that the decision to accomplish the transaction was made by directors with no financial interest in the transaction adverse to the corporation and that in reaching the decision the directors followed an appropriately deliberative process. See Aronson v. Lewis, Del. Supr., 473 A.2d 805 (1984); Kaplan v. Centex Corp., Del.Ch., 284 A.2d 119 (1971); Smith v. Van Gorkom, Del. Supr., 488 A.2d 858 (1985).[9] This deference—

---

[9]   In saying that, in such circumstances, courts will generally in effect decline to review the merits of the transaction, I recognize that some cases acknowledge a possibility—perhaps

the business judgment rule—is, of course, simply a recognition of the allocation of responsibility made by section 141(a) of the General Corporation Law and of the limited institutional competence of courts to assess business decisions.

* * *

Because the effect of the proper invocation of the business judgment rule is so powerful and the standard of entire fairness so exacting, the determination of the appropriate standard of judicial review frequently is determinative of the outcome of derivative litigation. Perhaps for that reason, the Delaware Supreme Court recognized in Unocal Corp. v. Mesa Petroleum Co., Del. Supr., 493 A.2d 946 (1985) that where a board takes action designed to defeat a threatened change in control of the company, a more flexible, intermediate form of judicial review is appropriate. In such a setting the "omnipresent specter that a board may be acting primarily in its own interests," 493 A.2d at 954 (emphasis added), justifies the utilization of a standard that has two elements. First, there must be shown some basis for the Board to have concluded that a proper corporate purpose was served by implementation of the defensive measure and, second, that measure must be found reasonable in relation to the threat posed by the change in control that instigates the action. See Unocal, 493 A.2d at 955. . . .

* * *

It is this standard of review applicable to corporate steps designed to defeat a threat to corporate control that I believe is applicable to the pending case. While this proposed stock repurchase derives from an earlier proposed recapitalization that itself may be said to have been defensive only in a general, preemptive way, there are elements of the present Company Transaction that are crucial to this case and that do not derive from the abandoned recapitalization. These elements are unmistakably reactive to the threat to corporate control posed by the BS/G $56 cash offer. Specifically, the timing of the self-tender offer and the decision to tender for 65.5% of the outstanding stock at $60 per share (rather than, as just one example, distributing the available $480,000,000 through an offer for 69% of the Company's 12,207,644 shares at $57) are elements of the transaction that go to the heart of plaintiff's complaint about coercion and that were obviously fixed in reaction to the timing and price of the BS/G offer.

I turn then to the two legs of the Unocal test.

---

more theoretical than real—that a decision by disinterested directors following a deliberative process may still be the basis for liability if such decision cannot be "attributed to any rational business purpose," Sinclair Oil Corp. v. Levien, Del. Supr., 280 A.2d 717, 720 (1971), or is "egregious" Aronson v. Lewis, *supra* at 805.

A.

The first inquiry concerns the likelihood that defendants will be able to demonstrate a "reasonable ground for believing that a danger to corporate policy or effectiveness" exists by reason of the BS/G offer. Unocal, 493 A.2d at 955. Stated in these precise terms, the Company Transaction may seem not to satisfy this aspect of the Unocal test. There is no evidence that the BS/G offer—which is non-coercive and at a concededly fair price—threatens injury to shareholders or to the enterprise. However, I take this aspect of the test to be simply a particularization of the more general requirement that a corporate purpose, not one personal to the directors, must be served by the stock repurchase. As so understood, it seems clear that a self-tender in these circumstances meets this element of the appropriate test.

Unlike most of our cases treating defensive techniques, the Board does not seek to justify the Company Transaction as necessary to fend off an offer that is inherently unfair. Rather, Defendants account for their creation of the Company Transaction as the creation of an option to shareholders to permit them to have the benefits of a large, tax-advantaged cash distribution together with a continuing participation in a newly-structured, highly-leveraged Anderson, Clayton. The Board recognizes that the BS/G offer—being for all shares and offering cash consideration that the Board's expert advisor could not call unfair—is one that a rational shareholder might prefer. However, the Board asserts—and it seems to me to be unquestionably correct in this that a rational shareholder might prefer the Company Transaction. One's choice, if given an opportunity to effectively chose, might be dictated by any number of factors most of which (such as liquidity preference, degree of aversion to risk, alternative investment opportunities and even desire or disinterest in seeing the continuation of a distinctive Anderson, Clayton identity) are distinctive functions of each individual decision-maker. Recognizing this, the Board contends that "the decision in this fundamentally economic contest lies properly with the shareholders" and that the Board "has preserved the ability of the stockholders to choose between these two options." *Id.*

The creation of such an alternative, with no other justification, serves a valid corporate purpose (certainly so where, as here, that option is made available to all shareholders on the same terms). That valid corporate purpose satisfies the first leg of the Unocal test.

B.

The fatal defect with the Company Transaction, however, becomes apparent when one attempts to apply the second leg of the Unocal test and asks whether the defensive step is "reasonable in relation to the threat posed." The BS/G offer poses a "threat" of any kind (other than a threat to the incumbency of the Board) only in a special sense and on the assumption that a majority of the Company's shareholders might prefer an alternative to the BS/G offer. On this assumption, it is reasonable to create an option that would permit shareholders to keep an equity interest in the firm, but, in my opinion, it is not reasonable in relation to such a "threat" to structure such an option so as to preclude as a practical matter shareholders from accepting the BS/G offer. As explained below, I am satisfied that the Company Transaction, if it proceeds in its current time frame, will have that effect.

If all that defendants have done is to create an option for shareholders, then it can hardly be thought to have breached a duty. Should that option be, on its merits, so attractive to shareholders as to command their majority approval, that fact alone, while disappointing to BS/G, can hardly be thought to render the Board's action wrongful. But plaintiffs join issue on defendants' most fundamental assertion that the Board has acted to create an option and to "preserve the ability of the stockholders to choose." Plaintiffs contend to the contrary that the Company Transaction was deliberately structured so that no rational shareholder can risk tendering into the BS/G offer. Plaintiffs say this for two related reasons: (1) Stockholders tendering into the BS/G offer have no assurance that BS/G will take down their stock at $56 a share since that offer is subject to conditions including a minimum number of shares tendered and abandonment of the Company Transaction; and (2) Tendering shareholders would thereby preclude themselves from participating in the "fat" front-end of the Company Transaction and risk having the value of all their shares fall very dramatically. In such circumstances, plaintiffs say, to characterize the Board's action as an attempt to preserve the ability of shareholders to choose is a charade. They claim the Company Transaction is coercive in fact and in the circumstances presented, improperly so in law.

May the Company Transaction be said to be coercive in the sense that no rational profit-maximizing shareholder can reasonably be expected to reject it? If it is concluded that the Company Transaction is coercive in this sense, one must ask why it is so and if, in these particular circumstances, this coercive aspect precludes a determination that the action is reasonable in light of the "threat" posed by the BS/G offer.

I conclude as a factual matter for purposes of this motion that no rational shareholder could afford not to tender into the Company's self-tender offer at least if that transaction is viewed in isolation. The record is uncontradicted that the value of the Company's stock following the effectuation of the Company Transaction will be materially less than $60 per share. The various experts differ only on how much less. Shearson, Lehman opines that the Company's stock will likely trade in a range of $22–$31 per share after consummation of the Company Transaction. First Boston is more hopeful, informally projecting a range of $37–52. What is clear under either view, however, is that a current shareholder who elects not to tender into the self-tender is very likely, upon consummation of the Company Transaction, to experience a substantial loss in market value of his holdings. The only way, within the confines of the Company Transaction, that a shareholder can protect himself from such an immediate financial loss, is to tender into the self-tender so that he receives his pro rata share of the cash distribution that will, in part, cause the expected fall in the market price of the Company's stock.[11]

I conclude that an Anderson, Clayton stockholder, acting with economic rationality, has no effective choice as between the contending offers as presently constituted. Even if a shareholder would prefer to sell all of his or her holdings at $56 per share in the BS/G offer, he or she may not risk tendering into that proposal and thereby risk being frozen out of the front end of the Company Transaction, should the BS/G offer not close.[12]

Thus, I conclude that if the Board's purpose was both to create an option to BS/G's any-and-all cash tender offer and to "preserve the ability of the shareholders to choose between those options" it has, as a practical matter, failed in the latter part of its mission.

The creation of an option of the kind represented by the Company Transaction need not have the collateral effect of foreclosing possible acceptance of the BS/G option by those shareholders who might prefer that alternative. The problem and its solution is one of timing. It would, in my opinion, be manifestly reasonable in relation to the limited "threat" posed by the BS/G any-and-all cash offer, for the Company to announce an alternative form of transaction (perhaps even a "front-end loaded" transaction of the kind the self-tender doubtlessly is)[13] to be available promptly should a majority not tender into the BS/G offer. An alternative timed in such a way would be a defensive step, in that it would make the change in control threatened by the BS/G offer less likely; it would afford to shareholders an alternative that, due to the non-coercive nature of the BS/G offer, would be readily available to shareholders if a majority of the shareholders in fact prefers it; and it would leave unimpaired the ability of shareholders effectively to elect the BS/G option if a majority of shareholders in fact prefers that option. A board need not be passive, Unocal, 493 A.2d at 954, even in the face of an any-and-all cash offer at

---

[11] As a matter of fairly rudimentary economics it can readily be seen that a self-tender, being for less than all shares, can always be made at a price higher than the highest rational price that can be offered for all of the enterprises stock. See Bradley and Rosenzweig, Defensive Stock Repurchases, 99 Harv. L. Rev. 1378 (May, 1986).

[12] BS/G could, by making its tender offer subject to no conditions, cure the coercive aspect of the Company Transaction, but it has no legal duty to extend an unconditional offer whereas the Board does have a legal duty to its shareholders to exercise its judgment to promote the stockholders' interests. Thus, in assessing the legal consequences in these circumstances of the conclusion that the Company Transaction has a coercive impact, I do not consider it relevant that plaintiffs, were they willing to do so, could counter that coercive effect by assuming additional risk.

[13] That is the $60 cash consideration offered is of greater current value than the stock with which a non-tendering shareholder will be left following consummation of the Company Transaction.

a fair price with an announced follow up merger offering the same consideration. But in that special case, a defensive step that includes a coercive self-tender timed to effectively preclude a rational shareholder from accepting the any-and-all offer cannot, in my opinion, be deemed to be reasonable in relation to any minimal threat posed to stockholders by such offer.

What then is the legal consequence of a conclusion that the Company Transaction is a defensive step that is not reasonable in relation to the threat posed? The first consequence is that the Board's action does not qualify for the protections afforded by the business judgment rule. In the light of that fact, the obvious entrenchment effect of the Company Transaction and the conclusion that that transaction cannot be justified as reasonable in the circumstances, I conclude that it is likely to be found to constitute a breach of a duty of loyalty, albeit a possibly unintended one. (I need not and do not express any opinion on the question of subjective intent.) Where director action is not protected by the business judgment rule, mere good faith will not preclude a finding of a breach of the duty of loyalty. Rather, in most such instances (which happen to be self-dealing transactions), the transaction can only be sustained if it is objectively or intrinsically fair; an honest belief that the transaction was entirely fair will not alone be sufficient.

QUESTIONS

1. Were there strategic reasons for abandoning a recapitalization plan in favor of a self-tender offer? If so, what were they?

2. Note that the AC board had previously adopted a recapitalization plan to create shareholder value. Here, as in Paramount Communications, Inc. v. Time, Inc., 571 A.2d 1140 (Del. 1990), *infra*, Chapter Eight, Part 1, this decision was made without the pressure of a pending tender offer. Was this original decision protected by the business judgment rule?

3. How is this case distinguishable from Unocal, *supra* part 2.A of this chapter?

4. How could the board have made the Company Transaction non-coercive? Would this have provided shareholders a meaningful choice?

In re Unitrin, Inc. Shareholders Litigation
651 A.2d 1361 (Del.1995).

■ HOLLAND, J.

This is an appeal from the Court of Chancery's entry of a preliminary injunction on October 13, 1994, upon plaintiffs' motions in two actions: American General Corporation's ("American General") suit against

Unitrin, Inc. ("Unitrin") and its directors; and a parallel class action brought by Unitrin stockholders. An interlocutory appeal was certified by the Court of Chancery on October 24, 1994. This Court accepted the appeal on October 27, 1994.

American General, which had publicly announced a proposal to merge with Unitrin for $2.6 billion at $50–3/8 per share, and certain Unitrin shareholder plaintiffs, filed suit in the Court of Chancery, *inter alia,* to enjoin Unitrin from repurchasing up to 10 million shares of its own stock (the "Repurchase Program").[2] On August 26, 1994, the Court of Chancery temporarily restrained Unitrin from making any further repurchases. After expedited discovery, briefing and argument, the Court of Chancery preliminarily enjoined Unitrin from making further repurchases on the ground that the Repurchase Program was a disproportionate response to the threat posed by American General's inadequate all cash for all shares offer, under the standard of this Court's holding in Unocal Corp. v. Mesa Petroleum Co., Del. Supr., 493 A.2d 946 (1985) ("Unocal").

* * *

This Court has concluded that the Court of Chancery erred in applying the proportionality review Unocal requires by focusing upon whether the Repurchase Program was an 'unnecessary' defensive response. See Paramount Communications, Inc. v. QVC Network, Inc., 637 A.2d at 45–46. The Court of Chancery should have directed its enhanced scrutiny: first, upon whether the Repurchase Program the Unitrin Board implemented was draconian, by being either preclusive or coercive and; second, if it was not draconian, upon whether it was within a range of reasonable responses to the threat American General's Offer posed. * * *

The Parties

* * *

The record reflects that the [five out of seven] non-employee directors each receive a fixed annual fee of $30,000. They receive no other significant financial benefit from serving as directors. At the offering price proposed by American General, the value of Unitrin's non-employee directors' stock exceeded $450 million.

* * *

American General's Offer

* * *

On July 12, 1994, American General sent a letter to Vie [a member of Unitrin's executive committee] proposing a consensual merger transaction in which it would "purchase all of Unitrin's 51.8 million outstanding shares of common stock for $50–3/8 per share, in cash" (the "Offer"). The Offer was conditioned on the development of a merger agreement and regulatory approval. The Offer price represented a 30% premium over the market price of Unitrin's shares. In the Offer, American General stated that it "would consider offering a higher price" if "Unitrin could demonstrate additional value." American General also offered to consider tax-free "alternatives to an all cash transaction."

Unitrin's Rejection

Upon receiving the American General Offer, the Unitrin Board's Executive Committee (Singleton, Vie, and Jerome) engaged legal counsel and scheduled a telephonic Board meeting for July 18. At the July 18 special meeting, the Board reviewed the terms of the Offer. The Board was advised that the existing charter and bylaw provisions might not effectively deter all types of takeover strategies. It was suggested that the Board consider adopting a shareholder rights plan and an advance notice provision for shareholder proposals.

The Unitrin Board met next on July 25, 1994 in Los Angeles for seven hours. [3]All directors attended the meeting. The principal purpose of the meeting was to discuss American General's Offer.

Vie reviewed Unitrin's financial condition and its ongoing business strategies. The Board also received a presentation from its investment advisor, Morgan Stanley & Co. ("Morgan Stanley"), regarding the financial adequacy of American General's proposal. Morgan Stanley expressed its opinion that the Offer was financially inadequate. [4]Legal counsel expressed concern that the combination of Unitrin and American General would raise antitrust complications due to the resultant decrease in competition in the home service insurance markets.

The Unitrin Board unanimously concluded that the American General merger proposal was not in the best interests of Unitrin's shareholders and voted to reject the Offer. [5]The Board then received advice from its legal and financial advisors about a number of possible defensive measures it might adopt, including a shareholder rights plan ("poison pill") [6]and an advance notice bylaw provision for shareholder proposals. Because the Board apparently thought that American General intended to keep its Offer private, the Board did not implement any defensive measures at that time.

American General's Publicity

Unitrin's Initial Responses

On August 2, 1994, American General issued a press release announcing its Offer to Unitrin's Board to purchase all of Unitrin's stock for $50–3/8 per share. The press release also noted that the Board had rejected American General's Offer. After that public announcement, the trading volume and market price of Unitrin's stock increased.

At its regularly scheduled meeting on August 3, the Unitrin Board discussed the effects of American General's press release. The Board noted that the market reaction to the announcement suggested that speculative traders or arbitrageurs were acquiring Unitrin stock. The Board determined that American General's public announcement constituted a hostile act designed to coerce the sale of Unitrin at an inadequate price. The Board unanimously approved the poison pill and the proposed advance notice bylaw that it had considered previously.

Beginning on August 2 and continuing through August 12, 1994, Unitrin issued a series of press releases to inform its shareholders and the public market: first, that the Unitrin Board believed Unitrin's stock was worth more than the $50–3/8 American General offered; second, that the Board felt that the price of American General's Offer did not reflect Unitrin's long term business prospects as an independent company; third, that "the true value of Unitrin [was] not reflected in the [then] current market price of its common stock," and that because of its strong financial position, Unitrin was well positioned "to pursue strategic and financial opportunities;" fourth, that the Board believed a merger with American General would have anticompetitive effects and might violate antitrust laws and various state regulatory statutes; and fifth, that the Board had adopted a shareholder rights plan (poison pill) to guard against undesirable takeover efforts.

Unitrin's Repurchase Program

The Unitrin Board met again on August 11, 1994. The minutes of that meeting indicate that its principal purpose was to consider the Repurchase Program. At the Board's request, Morgan Stanley had prepared written materials to distribute to each of the directors. Morgan Stanley gave a presentation in which alternative means of implementing the Repurchase Program were explained. Morgan Stanley recommended that the Board implement an open market stock repurchase. The Board voted to authorize the Repurchase Program for up to ten million shares of its outstanding stock.

On August 12, Unitrin publicly announced the Repurchase Program. The Unitrin Board expressed its belief that "Unitrin's stock is undervalued in the market and that the expanded program will tend to increase the value of the shares that remain outstanding." The announcement also stated that the director stockholders were not participating in the Repurchase Program, and that the repurchases "will increase the percentage ownership of those stockholders who choose not to sell."

Unitrin's August 12 press release also stated that the directors owned 23% of Unitrin's stock, that the Repurchase Program would cause that percentage to increase, and that Unitrin's certificate of incorporation included a supermajority voting provision.

* * *

Unocal is Proper Review Standard

* * *

The Court of Chancery held that all of the Unitrin Board's defensive actions merited judicial scrutiny according to Unocal. [9]The record supports the Court of Chancery's determination that the Board perceived American General's Offer as a threat and adopted the Repurchase Program, along with the poison pill and advance notice bylaw, as defensive measures in response to that threat. Therefore, the Court of Chancery properly concluded the facts before it required an application of Unocal and its progeny.

American General Threat

Reasonableness Burden Sustained

* * *

The Unitrin Board identified two dangers it perceived the American General Offer posed: inadequate price and antitrust complications. The Court of Chancery characterized the Board's concern that American General's proposed transaction could never be consummated because it may violate antitrust laws and state insurance regulations as a "makeweight excuse" for the defensive measure. It determined, however, that the Board reasonably believed that the American General Offer was inadequate and also reasonably concluded that the Offer was a threat to Unitrin's uninformed stockholders.

* * *

Proportionality Burden

Chancery Approves Poison Pill

* * *

With regard to the second aspect or proportionality test of the initial Unocal burden, the Court of Chancery analyzed each stage of the Unitrin Board's defensive responses separately. Although the Court of Chancery characterized Unitrin's antitrust concerns as "makeweight," it acknowledged that the directors of a Delaware corporation have the prerogative to determine that the market undervalues its stock and to protect its stockholders from offers that do not reflect the long term value of the corporation under its present management plan. The Court of Chancery concluded that Unitrin's Board believed in good faith that the American General Offer was inadequate and properly employed a poison pill as a proportionate defensive response to protect its stockholders from a "low ball" bid. [No appeal was taken from this ruling.]

* * *

Proportionality Burden

Chancery Enjoins Repurchase Program

The Court of Chancery did not view either its conclusion that American General's Offer constituted a threat, or its conclusion that the poison pill was a reasonable response to that threat, as requiring it, *a fortiori,* to conclude that the Repurchase Program was also an appropriate response. The Court of Chancery then made two factual findings: first, the Repurchase Program went beyond what was "necessary" to protect the Unitrin stockholders from a "low ball" negotiating strategy; and second, it was designed to keep the decision to combine with American General within the control of the members of the Unitrin Board, as stockholders, under virtually all circumstances. Consequently, the Court of Chancery held that the Unitrin Board failed to demonstrate that the Repurchase Program met the second aspect or proportionality requirement of the initial burden Unocal ascribes to a board of directors.

The Court of Chancery framed the ultimate question before it as follows:

> This case comes down to one final question: Is placing the decision to sell the company in the hands of stockholders who are also directors a disproportionate response to a low price offer to buy all the shares of the company for cash?

The Court of Chancery then answered that question:

> I conclude that because the only threat to the corporation is the inadequacy of an opening bid made directly to the board, and the board has already taken actions that will protect the stockholders from mistakenly falling for a low ball negotiating strategy, a repurchase program that intentionally provides members of the board with a veto of any merger proposal is not reasonably related to the threat posed by American General's negotiable all shares, all cash offer.

In explaining its conclusion, the Court of Chancery reasoned that:

> I have no doubt that a hostile acquiror can make an offer high enough to entice at least some of the directors that own stock to break ranks and sell their shares. Yet, these directors undoubtedly place a value, probably a substantial one, on their management of Unitrin, and will, at least subconsciously, reject an offer that does not compensate them for that value. . . . The prestige and perquisites that accompany managing Unitrin as a member of its Board of directors, even for the non-officer directors that do not draw a salary, may cause these stockholder directors to reject an excellent offer unless it includes this value in its "price parameter."

The Court of Chancery concluded that, although the Unitrin Board had properly perceived American General's inadequate Offer as a threat and had properly responded to that threat by adopting a "poison pill," the additional defensive response of adopting the Repurchase Program was unnecessary and disproportionate to the threat the Offer posed. Accordingly, it concluded that the plaintiffs had "established with reasonable probability that the [Unitrin Board] violated its duties under Unocal [by authorizing the Repurchase Program]" because the Board had not sustained its burden of demonstrating that the Repurchase Program was a proportionate response to American General's Offer. Therefore, the Court of Chancery held that the plaintiffs proved a likelihood of success on that issue and granted the motion to preliminarily enjoin the Repurchase Program.

Proxy Contest

Supermajority Vote

Repurchase Program

Before the Repurchase Program began, Unitrin's directors collectively held approximately 23% of Unitrin's outstanding shares. Unitrin's certificate of incorporation already included a "shark-repellent" provision barring any business combination with a more-than-15% stockholder unless approved by a majority of continuing directors or by a 75% stockholder vote ("Supermajority Vote"). Unitrin's shareholder directors announced publicly that they would not participate in the Repurchase Program and that this would result in a percentage increase of ownership for them, as well as for any other shareholder who did not participate.

The Court of Chancery found that by not participating in the Repurchase Program, the Board "expected to create a 28% voting block to support the Board's decision to reject [a future] offer by American General." From this underlying factual finding, the Court of Chancery concluded that American General might be "chilled" in its pursuit of Unitrin:

> Increasing the board members' percentage of stock ownership, combined with the supermajority merger provision, does more than protect uninformed stockholders from an inadequate offer, it chills any unsolicited acquiror from making an offer.

* * *

Takeover Strategy

Tender Offer/Proxy Contest

* * *

The Court of Chancery concluded that Unitrin's adoption of a poison pill was a proportionate response to the threat its Board reasonably perceived from American General's Offer. Nonetheless, the Court of Chancery enjoined the additional defense of the Repurchase Program as disproportionate and "unnecessary."

The record reflects that the Court of Chancery's decision to enjoin the Repurchase Program is attributable to a continuing misunderstanding, i.e., that in conjunction with the longstanding Supermajority Vote provision in the Unitrin charter, the Repurchase Program would operate to provide the director shareholders with a "veto" to preclude a successful proxy contest by American General. [26]The origins of that misunderstanding are three premises that are each without record support. Two of those premises are objective misconceptions and the other is subjective.

* * *

The subjective premise was the Court of Chancery's sua sponte determination that Unitrin's outside directors, who are also substantial stockholders, would not vote like other stockholders in a proxy contest, i.e., in their own best economic interests. At American General's Offer price, the outside directors held Unitrin shares worth more than $450 million. Consequently, Unitrin argues the stockholder directors had the same interest as other Unitrin stockholders generally, when voting in a proxy contest, to wit: the maximization of the value of their investments.

In rejecting Unitrin's argument, the Court of Chancery stated that the stockholder directors would be 'subconsciously' motivated in a proxy contest to vote against otherwise excellent offers which did not include a 'price parameter' to compensate them for the loss of the 'prestige and perquisites' of membership on Unitrin's Board. The Court of Chancery's subjective determination that the stockholder directors of Unitrin would reject an 'excellent offer,' unless it compensated them for giving up the 'prestige and perquisites' of directorship, appears to be subjective and without record support. It cannot be presumed.

It must be the subject of proof that the Unitrin directors' objective in the Repurchase Program was to forego the opportunity to sell their stock at a premium. In particular, it cannot be presumed that the prestige and perquisites of holding a director's office or a motive to strengthen collective power prevails over a stockholder-director's economic interest. Even the shareholder-plaintiffs in this case agree with the legal proposition Unitrin advocates on appeal: stockholders are presumed to act in their own best economic interests when they vote in a proxy contest.

Without Repurchase Program
Actual Voting Power Exceeds 25%

The first objective premise relied upon by the Court of Chancery, unsupported by the record, is that the shareholder directors needed to implement the Repurchase Program to attain voting power in a proxy contest equal to 25%. The Court of Chancery properly calculated that if the Repurchase Program was completed, Unitrin's shareholder directors would increase their absolute voting power to 25%. It then calculated the odds of American General marshaling enough votes to defeat the Board and its supporters.

The Court of Chancery and all parties agree that proxy contests do not generate 100% shareholder participation. The shareholder plaintiffs argue that 80–85% may be a usual turnout. Therefore, *without* the Repurchase Program, the director shareholders' absolute voting power of 23% would already constitute *actual voting power greater than 25%* in a proxy contest with normal shareholder participation below 100%. *See* Berlin v. Emerald Partners, Del. Supr., 552 A.2d 482 (1989).

Supermajority Vote

No Realistic Deterrent

The second objective premise relied upon by the Court of Chancery, unsupported by the record, is that American General's ability to succeed in a proxy contest depended on the Repurchase Program being enjoined because of the Supermajority Vote provision in Unitrin's charter. Without the approval of a target's board, the danger of activating a poison pill renders it irrational for bidders to pursue stock acquisitions above the triggering level. Instead, "bidders intent on working around a poison pill must launch and win proxy contests to elect new directors who are willing to redeem the target's poison pill." Joseph A. Grundfest, *Just Vote No: A Minimalist Strategy for Dealing with Barbarians Inside the Gates,* 45 Stan. L. Rev. 857, 859 (1993).

As American General acknowledges, a less than 15% stockholder bidder need not proceed with acquiring shares to the extent that it would ever implicate the Supermajority Vote provision. In fact, it would be illogical for American General or any other bidder to acquire more than 15% of Unitrin's stock because that would not only trigger the poison pill, but also the constraints of 8 *Del. C.* § 203. If American General were to initiate a proxy contest *before* acquiring 15% of Unitrin's stock, it would need to amass only 45.1% of the votes assuming a 90% voter turnout. If it commenced a tender offer at an attractive price contemporaneously with its proxy contest, it could seek to acquire 50.1% of the outstanding voting stock.

The record reflects that institutional investors own 42% of Unitrin's shares. Twenty institutions own 33% of Unitrin's shares. It is generally accepted that proxy contests have re-emerged with renewed significance as a method of acquiring corporate control because "the growth in institutional investment has reduced the dispersion of share ownership." Lucian A. Bebchuk & Marcel Kahan, *A Framework for Analyzing Legal Policy Towards Proxy Contests,* 78 Cal. L. Rev. 1071, 1134 (1990).[31] "Institutions are more likely than other shareholders to vote at all, more likely to vote against manager proposals, and more likely to vote for proposals by other shareholders." Bernard S. Black, *The Value of Institutional Investor Monitoring: The Empirical Evidence,* 39 UCLA L. Rev. 895, 925 (1992). *See also* John Pound, *Shareholder Activism and Share Values: The Causes and Consequences of Countersolicitations Against Management Antitakeover Proposals,* 32 J.L. & Econ. 357, 368 (1989).

With Supermajority Vote

After Repurchase Program

Proxy Contest Appears Viable

The assumptions and conclusions American General sets forth in this appeal for a different purpose are particularly probative with regard to the effect of the institutional holdings in Unitrin's stock. American General's two predicate assumptions are a 90% stockholder turnout in a proxy contest and a bidder with 14.9% holdings, i.e., the maximum the bidder could own to avoid triggering the poison pill and the Supermajority Vote provision. American General also calculated the votes available to the Board or the bidder with and without the Repurchase Program:

> Assuming no Repurchase [Program], the [shareholder directors] would hold 23%, the percentage collectively held by the [directors] and the bidder would be 37.9%, and the percentage of additional votes available to either side would be 52.1%.

> Assuming the Repurchase [Program] is fully consummated, the [shareholder directors] would hold 28%, the percentage collectively held by the bidder and the [directors] would be 42.9%, and the percentage of additional votes available to either side would be 47.1%.

American General then applied these assumptions to reach conclusions regarding the votes needed for the 14.9% stockholder bidder to prevail: first, in an election of directors; and second, in the subsequent vote on a merger. With regard to the election of directors, American General made the following calculations:

> Assume 90% stockholder turnout. To elect directors, a plurality must be obtained; assuming no abstentions and only two competing slates, one must obtain the votes of 45.1% of the shares.

> The percentage of additional votes the bidder needs to win is: 45.1% − 14.9% (maximum the bidder could own and avoid the poison pill, § 203 and supermajority) = **30.2%.**

A merger requires approval of a majority of outstanding shares, 8 *Del. C.* § 251, not just a plurality. In that regard, American General made the following calculations:

Assume 90% stockholder turnout. To approve a merger, one must obtain the favorable vote of 50.1% of the shares.

The percentage of additional votes the bidder needs to win is 50.1% − 14.9% = **35.2%.**

Consequently, to prevail in a proxy contest with a 90% turnout, the percentage of additional shareholder votes a 14.9% shareholder bidder needs to prevail is 30.2% for directors and 35.2% in a subsequent merger. The record reflects that institutional investors held 42% of Unitrin's stock and 20 institutions held 33% of the stock. Thus, American General's own assumptions and calculations in the record support the Unitrin Board's argument that "it is hard to imagine a company more readily susceptible to a proxy contest concerning a pure issue of dollars."[33]

The conclusion of the Court of Chancery that the Repurchase Program would make a proxy contest for Unitrin a "theoretical" possibility that American General could not realistically pursue may be erroneous and appears to be inconsistent with its own earlier determination that the "repurchase program strengthens the position of the Board of Directors to defend against a hostile bidder, but will not deprive the public stockholders of the 'power to influence corporate direction through the ballot.' " Even a complete implementation of the Repurchase Program, in combination with the pre-existing Supermajority Vote provision, would not appear to have a preclusive effect upon American General's ability successfully to marshall enough shareholder votes to win a proxy contest. A proper understanding of the record reflects that American General or any other 14.9% shareholder bidder could apparently win a proxy contest with a 90% turnout.

The key variable in a proxy contest would be the merit of American General's issues, not the size of its stockholdings. Moran v. Household Int'l, Inc., Del. Supr., 500 A.2d 1346, 1355 (1985). If American General presented an attractive price as the cornerstone of a proxy contest, it could prevail, irrespective of whether the shareholder directors' absolute voting power was 23% or 28%. In that regard, the following passage from the Court of Chancery's Opinion is poignant:

> "Harold Hook, the Chairman of American General, admitted in his deposition that the repurchase program is not a "show stopper" because the directors that own stock will act in their own best interest if the price is high enough. (Hook Dep. at 86–87). Fayez Sarofim, one of the Unitrin directors that holds a substantial number of shares, testified that 'everything has a price parameter.' "

---

[33] That institutions held a high percentage of Unitrin's stock is not as significant as the fact that the relatively concentrated percentage of stockholdings would facilitate a bidder's ability to communicate the merits of its position.

Consequently, a proxy contest apparently remained a viable alternative for American General to pursue notwithstanding Unitrin's poison pill, Supermajority Vote provision, and a fully implemented Repurchase Program.

* * *

Range of Reasonableness

Proper Proportionality Burden

* * *

The Court of Chancery applied an incorrect legal standard when it ruled that the Unitrin decision to authorize the Repurchase Program was disproportionate because it was "unnecessary." The Court of Chancery stated:

> Given that the Board had already implemented the poison pill and the advance notice provision, the repurchase program was unnecessary to protect Unitrin from an inadequate bid.

In *QVC,* this Court recently elaborated upon the judicial function in applying enhanced scrutiny, citing Unocal as authority, albeit in the context of a sale of control and the target board's consideration of one of several reasonable alternatives. That teaching is nevertheless applicable here:

> a court applying enhanced judicial scrutiny should be deciding whether the directors made *a reasonable* decision, not *a perfect* decision. If a board selected one of several reasonable alternatives, a court should not second guess that choice even though it might have decided otherwise or subsequent events may have cast doubt on the board's determination. Thus, courts will not substitute their business judgment for that of the directors, but will determine if the directors' decision was, on balance, within a range of reasonableness. *See* Unocal, 493 A.2d at 955–56; Macmillan, 559 A.2d at 1288; Nixon, 626 A.2d at 1378.

Paramount Communications, Inc. v. QVC Network, Inc., Del. Supr., 637 A.2d 34, 45–46 (1994) (emphasis in original). The Court of Chancery did not determine whether the Unitrin Board's decision to implement the Repurchase Program fell within a "range of reasonableness."

The record reflects that the Unitrin Board's adoption of the Repurchase Program was an apparent recognition on its part that all shareholders are not alike. This Court has stated that distinctions among types of shareholders are neither inappropriate nor irrelevant for a board of directors to make, *e.g.,* distinctions between long-term shareholders and short-term profit-takers, such as arbitrageurs, and their stockholding objectives. *Id.* In Unocal itself, we expressly acknowledged that "a board may reasonably consider the basic stockholder interests at stake, including those of short term speculators, whose actions may have fueled the coercive aspect of the offer at the expense of the long term investor." Unocal, 493 A.2d at 955–56. *See also* Ivanhoe Partners v. Newmont Mining Corp., Del. Supr., 535 A.2d 1334, 1341–42 (1987).

The Court of Chancery's determination that the Unitrin Board's adoption of the Repurchase Program was unnecessary constituted a substitution of its business judgment for that of the Board, contrary to this Court's "range of reasonableness" holding in Paramount Communications, Inc. v. QVC Network, Inc., 637 A.2d at 45–46. Its decision to enjoin the Repurchase Program as an "unnecessary" *addition* to other complementary defensive mechanisms is also inconsistent with a similar analysis in Shamrock Holdings, Inc. v. Polaroid Corp., Del. Ch., 559 A.2d 278 (1989). In Shamrock, the Court of Chancery refused to enjoin any one of a series of transactions which included a repurchase plan. With respect to a repurchase program, the Court of Chancery held that a self-tender offer and buy-back plan constituted a reasonable proportionate response to the perceived threat to Polaroid shareholders by offering "some immediate value to those holders interested in cash while increasing the equity interest held by the remaining stockholders." Although Shamrock dealt with an offer that did not reflect the very profitable litigation embodied in the Kodak patent case settlement and therefore implicated a potentially more serious threat than that involved here, Shamrock is nevertheless applicable considering American General's negotiable "low-ball" bid.

Draconian Defenses

Coercive or Preclusive

Range of Reasonableness

* * *

An examination of the cases applying Unocal reveals a direct correlation between findings of proportionality or disproportionality and the judicial determination of whether a defensive response was draconian because it was either coercive or preclusive in character. In *Time,* for example, this Court concluded that the Time board's defensive response was reasonable and proportionate since it was not aimed at 'cramming down' on its shareholders a management-sponsored alternative, *i.e.,* was not coercive, and because it did not preclude Paramount from making an offer for the combined Time-Warner company, *i.e.,* was not preclusive.

This Court also applied Unocal's proportionality test to the board's adoption of a "poison pill" shareholders' rights plan in Moran v. Household Int'l, Inc., Del. Supr., 500 A.2d 1346 (1985). After acknowledging that the adoption of the rights plan was within the directors' statutory authority, this Court determined that the implementation of the rights plan was a proportionate response to the theoretical threat of a hostile takeover, in part, because it did not "strip" the stockholders of their right to receive tender offers *and* did not fundamentally restrict proxy contests, *i.e.*, was not preclusive. *Id.* at 1357.

More than a century before Unocal was decided, Justice Holmes observed that the common law must be developed through its application and "cannot be dealt with as if it contained only the axioms and corollaries of a book of mathematics." Oliver Wendell Holmes, Jr., *The Common Law* 1 (1881). As common law applications of Unocal's proportionality standard have evolved, at least two characteristics of draconian defensive measures taken by a board of directors in responding to a threat have been brought into focus through enhanced judicial scrutiny. In the modern takeover lexicon, it is now clear that since Unocal, this Court has consistently recognized that defensive measures which are either preclusive or coercive are included within the common law definition of draconian.

If a defensive measure is not draconian, however, because it is not either coercive or preclusive, the Unocal proportionality test requires the focus of enhanced judicial scrutiny to shift to "the range of reasonableness." Paramount Communications, Inc. v. QVC Network, Inc., Del. Supr., 637 A.2d 34, 45–46 (1994). Proper and proportionate defensive responses are intended and permitted to thwart perceived threats. When a corporation is not for sale, the board of directors is the defender of the metaphorical medieval corporate bastion and the protector of the corporation's shareholders. The fact that a defensive action must not be coercive or preclusive does not prevent a board from responding defensively before a bidder is at the corporate bastion's gate.

The *ratio decidendi* for the "range of reasonableness" standard is a need of the board of directors for latitude in discharging its fiduciary duties to the corporation and its shareholders when defending against perceived threats. The concomitant requirement is for judicial restraint. Consequently, if the board of directors' defensive response is not draconian (preclusive or coercive) and is within a "range of reasonableness," a court must not substitute its judgment for the board's.

This Case

Repurchase Program

Proportionate With Poison Pill

In this case, the initial focus of enhanced judicial scrutiny for proportionality requires a determination regarding the defensive responses by the Unitrin Board to American General's offer. We begin, therefore, by ascertaining whether the Repurchase Program, as an addition to the poison pill, was draconian by being either coercive or preclusive.

A limited nondiscriminatory self-tender, like some other defensive measures, may thwart a current hostile bid, but is not inherently coercive. Moreover, it does not necessarily preclude future bids or proxy contests by stockholders who decline to participate in the repurchase. *Cf.* AC Acquisitions Corp. v. Anderson, Clayton & Co., Del. Ch., 519 A.2d 103 (1986) (enjoining a coercive self-tender and restructuring plan). A selective repurchase of shares in a public corporation on the market, such as Unitrin's Repurchase Program, generally does not discriminate because all shareholders can voluntarily realize the same benefit by selling. *See* Larry E. Ribstein, *Takeover Defenses and the Corporate Contract,* 78 Geo. L.J. 71, 129–31 (1989). *See also* Michael Bradley & Michael Rosenzweig, *Defensive Stock Repurchases,* 99 Harv. L. Rev. 1377 (1986). Here, there is no showing on this record that the Repurchase Program was coercive.

We have already determined that the record in this case appears to reflect that a proxy contest remained a viable (if more problematic) alternative for American General even if the Repurchase Program were to be completed in its entirety. Nevertheless, the Court of Chancery must determine whether Unitrin's Repurchase Program would only inhibit American General's ability to wage a proxy fight and institute a merger or whether it was, in fact, preclusive [39]because American General's success would either be mathematically impossible or realistically unattainable. If the Court of Chancery concludes that the Unitrin Repurchase Program was not draconian because it was not preclusive, one question will remain to be answered in its proportionality review: whether the Repurchase Program was within a range of reasonableness?

* * *

Conclusion

We hold that the Court of Chancery correctly determined that the Unocal standard of enhanced judicial scrutiny applied to the defensive actions of the Unitrin defendants in establishing the poison pill and implementing the Repurchase Program. The Court of Chancery's finding, that the Repurchase Program was a disproportionate defensive response, was based on faulty factual predicates, unsupported by the record. This error was exacerbated by its application of an erroneous legal standard of "necessity" to the Repurchase Program as a defensive response.

The interlocutory judgment of the Court of Chancery, in favor of American General, is REVERSED. This matter is REMANDED for further proceedings in accordance with this opinion.

QUESTIONS

1. Is the repurchase program coercive, or likely to be coercive in the same way that Anderson Clayton's repurchase offer was?

2.   Why doesn't the court discuss economic coercion in this case?

3.   Does the court's conclusion about how these directors would vote their shares suggest whether they should be treated as independent directors under the Unocal test? There are studies that indicate that even inside directors' behavior depends strongly on the extent of stock ownership in their companies. Walkling and Long have found significant differences in the wealth effects of takeovers on managers who resist and accede to bids.[38] Executives who did not contest tender offers stood to gain 8.2 times their annual salary from a successful offer, while those who contested stood to gain only 1.9 times their annual salary.[39] For arguments that courts should employ stock ownership levels in determining the amount of deference to be given to directors in takeover defense settings, see Carney, Controlling Management Opportunism in the Market For Corporate Control: An Agency Cost Model, 1988 Wis. L. Rev. 385.

NOTE

Some rights plans contain "grandfather" provisions for existing shareholders that already exceed the trigger point in the plan. When the directors of Barnes & Noble responded to an 18% accumulation of its shares by billionaire Ron Burkle's Yucaipa Corporation, who was agitating for changes in its business model, they adopted a rights plan that would be triggered at the 20% ownership level. The founder and chairman of Barnes & Noble, Leonard Riggio, controlled more than 30% of Barnes & Noble's common stock. Riggio's holdings were grandfathered under the rights plan, provided he did not acquire additional shares. Burkle had had conversations with another investment firm, Aletheia, that had followed Burkle's investment lead in the past, and as a result acquired a significant holding in Barnes & Noble, so their combined holdings reached 37%. Burkle threatened a proxy fight for the three directorships open at the next annual meeting, and after trying to assure Barnes & Noble's board that he would not increase his holdings, requested that the trigger on the rights plan be raised to 37%, which was approximately the total holdings of Riggio, the rest of the board, and Barnes & Noble's stockholding employees. When this was refused and Yucaipa brought suite challenging the rights plan, it argued in part that the low threshold precluded a proxy fight for board seats. Vice Chancellor Strine rejected that claim (and Yucaipa witnesses admitted that it did not preclude victory for Yucaipa), assuming a 91% turnout in a proxy contest and a vigorous and persuasive campaign by Yucaipa, which started with virtual

---

[38] Walkling & Long, Strategic Issues in Cash Tender Offers: Predicting Bid Premiums, Probability of Success, and Target Management's Response, 4, No. 2 Midland Corp. Fin. J. 57, 63–64 (1986). See also Walkling & Long, Agency Theory, Managerial Welfare, and Takeover Bid Resistance, 5, No. 1 Rand. J. Econ. 54 (1984).

[39] Walkling & Long, Strategic Issues, *supra*, at 63–64.

assurance of support from an equal number of shares. Yucaipa American Alliance Fund II, L.P. v. Riggio, 2010 Del. Ch. LEXIS 172 (2010).

Does Unitrin suggest that a court will take seriously a board's concerns about undervalued stock and investor ignorance? Consider the later reaction of Vice Chancellor Strine in Chesapeake Corporation v. Shore, 771 A.2d 293 (Del.Ch. 2000), where Shorewood's board, having made a hostile bid for Chesapeake, was faced with a counter-bid from Chesapeake for control of Shorewood. The Shorewood board recognized that Chesapeake was takeover proof under Virginia law, and that it might wage a fight for control of the Shorewood board. The Shorewood board had adopted a supermajority voting rule for shareholder amendments to the bylaws on the basis that a bid was inadequate and circumstances created a threat of shareholder confusion, that shareholders and the market would not fully appreciate developments at Chesapeake:

"According to the defendants' deposition and trial testimony, they were concerned as early as the November board meetings that the market would not understand: (1) the value of Shorewood's investment in a plant in China; (2) the efficiencies that Shorewood would achieve due to certain investments and plant closures; (3) the synergies associated with Shorewood's acquisition of Queens Group and two smaller companies; and (4) Shorewood's attempt to position itself to take advantage of an international trend towards use of a smaller group of packaging suppliers by manufacturers.

"In any event, regardless of when the confusion threat was identified, that threat hardly emerges as a particularly dangerous one. The defendants admit that the company had disclosed all material information regarding the business factors they felt the stockholders could not understand.

"Indeed, the factors identified by the Shorewood directors as not being adequately reflected in the company's market price are all discussed in industry analyst reports from respected investment banks like Lehman Brothers and Goldman Sachs. These reports set one-year price targets for Shorewood's stock which exceeded Chesapeake's $16.50 a share offer by as much as $7.50 a share.

"Undermining the risk of confusion is Marc Shore's and Liebman's belief that Shorewood management has strong credibility with the investment community. In that regard, Shore testified at his deposition that Shorewood could have beaten off Chesapeake's $16.50 per share offer, because the company would have been able to convince its stockholders that Shorewood was worth more than that. For his part, director O'Donnell said that Shorewood can communicate anything to its stockholders, given enough time.

"The most the Shorewood directors are able to credibly say is that stockholders will never understand the relevant information as deeply as the directors do or that the stockholders might choose to blind themselves to it in favor of a short-term return. Some of the directors, e.g., Andrew Shore, also attributed the possibility for confusion to 'securities laws' that supposedly inhibit the directors from being as optimistic publicly as they are privately.

"In sum, the evidence is insubstantial that would support any conclusion that, as of the end of November 1999, there was a real risk that the Shorewood stockholders would not be able to grasp the information necessary to make an informed judgment about whether to sell their stock or to execute a consent on behalf of Chesapeake. Given the fact that at that time over 80% of Shorewood's shares were held by management and institutional holders, the board's own ability to undertake more vigorous communication efforts, and the fact that reputable analysts were already tracking the stock, the risk of confusion was at best quite a weak one.

"Although no one will ever point to the Shorewood board's actions as a model of how to analyze an acquisition bid, I am persuaded that the board had sufficient, good faith reasons to conclude that both the $16.50 and $17.25 a share offers were inadequate from a price perspective. Both of these offers trailed Shorewood's one-year high and, according to information provided to the board by O'Donnell and unrebutted by Chesapeake, lagged the price at which comparable transactions had been effected in the specialty packaging industry. The price offered also trailed the values placed on the company's stock by independent analysts.

"On the other hand, the defendants have not convinced me that the threat posed by Chesapeake's all-shares, all-cash Tender Offer was a particularly dangerous one.[40] The defendants must concede that there was nothing structurally coercive about Chesapeake's bid—for example, it was not in any sense a front-end loaded, two-tiered tender offer. At the time of the $17.25 Tender Offer, Shorewood also had in place a poison pill and had eliminated Chesapeake's ability to call a special stockholders' meeting. Thus Chesapeake was forced to present its Tender Offer indirectly, through the more deliberative consent solicitation process. Even after a successful consent solicitation, the Tender Offer could not go forward until a new Shorewood board was seated and redeemed the pill after proper deliberations.

"In addition, Chesapeake had indicated that its Offer was negotiable and that it might be willing to pay more if Shorewood's negotiators could persuade Chesapeake that Shorewood had greater value. Chesapeake had also offered to discuss the structure of the transaction and its openness to engaging in another form of transaction (e.g., a stock deal) that might have more favorable tax advantages to Shorewood stockholders. Therefore, the Shorewood board had the option of taking Chesapeake up on these representations and influencing the level of its bid through negotiations.

"I reach a different conclusion about whether the Shorewood board legitimately identified the second threat it relies upon: the risk of stockholder confusion. Though the defendants claim that this issue first came to the fore

---

[40] *Interco*, 551 A.2d at 798 *(mere price inadequacy of an all-cash, all-shares offer presented a modest threat);* In re Unitrin Inc. Shareholders Litig., 1994 WL 698483 (Del.Ch.), C.A. Nos. 13656, 13699, Chandler, V.C. (Oct. 13, 1994, rev. Oct. 14, 1994) (all-cash, all-shares offer that was inadequate but negotiable posed a "mild" threat), rev'd on other grounds, *651 A.2d 1361.*

in November, there is no persuasive evidence that this is so. Rather, this threat appears to have emerged out of Shorewood's 'A Team' of advisors in December. The evidence that the board actually—in its very brief November meetings—concentrated on whether stockholders would be unable to sort out the relevant issues after effective disclosures from management is not convincing.

"The board has not come close to demonstrating that it identified this threat at any time 'after a reasonable investigation' and 'in good faith.' The board seemed to have slighted, if not totally disregarded, key issues such as the facts that:

" * institutional investors and management holders comprised over 80% of the Shorewood electorate;

" * Shorewood was followed by analysts from several major brokerage houses that were regularly briefed by Shorewood management on the company's strategy and initiatives;

" * Shorewood had disclosed information about all of the strategic issues that supposedly were not understood by the market;

" * analysts had factored these issues into their reports on Shorewood's value;

" * Shorewood's board had the opportunity to address the confusion issue through more complete and consistent disclosures to its stockholders; and

" * Shorewood's management believed it had strong credibility on Wall Street and felt that it could communicate effectively about key corporate issues if given the time and resources.

"Nor did the board conduct any sort of informal survey of its largest stockholders or the analyst community to see if they were befuddled by the Chesapeake Tender Offer. This would not have been difficult, given the fact that several analysts follow Shorewood and given the concentrated institutional investor holdings in Shorewood."

———————

G. WHITE KNIGHTS, CONFIDENTIALITY AND STANDSTILL AGREEMENTS

Prospective sellers frequently insist that prospective buyers sign a confidentiality agreement of the kind set out in Appendix D before gaining access to proprietary information about the seller. These agreements generally require the prospective buyer to treat all non-public information received in the course of inspecting the seller as confidential, and, if negotiations break down, to return all documents received or copied to the seller. These agreements may recite that the information is the property of the target, and may not be used in any way by the bidder except to evaluate the proposed transaction. These agreements will frequently include a clause requiring all outside consultants used by the bidder—attorneys, brokers and accountants—to agree to the same terms before receiving any of this information. When a letter of intent, term sheet or preliminary agreement is signed, it will frequently contain these provisions, in contemplation of the bidder's due diligence.

While these agreements may prevent disclosure of confidential information, they do not, by themselves, preclude the bidder from using it for its own purposes. For example, the bidder might trade on this inside information. Since it was obtained at arm's length during negotiations, until 2000, it was likely that the bidder would owe no fiduciary duties to the target, and thus would not be subject to Rule 10b–5 liabilities. See Frigitemp Corp. v. Financial Dynamics Fund, Inc., 524 F.2d 275 (2d Cir. 1975), cited with approval in Chiarella v. United States, 445 U.S. 222 (1980). Securities Exchange Act Rule 10b5–2 changed these rules in 2000 by providing that a "duty of trust or confidence" exists whenever a person agrees to maintain information in confidence. But even aside from insider trading, the prospective bidder may use the information to formulate an uninvited bid, or to hire away key employees of the target. To protect against employee raiding, confidentiality agreements may contain a "no poach" clause that precludes hiring target employees for a period.

Targets sometimes wish to preclude any unsolicited tender offers that might take advantage of this confidential information. In many cases, the target may be unable to release this information to its own shareholders, because to do so would damage the company. A bidder's release of the same information in a tender offer would cause the same harm. One example involved discussions between General Portland, Inc. and LaFarge Coppee, S.A. over a possible investment or acquisition by LaFarge. LaFarge entered into a confidentiality agreement that it would use non-public information furnished by General Portland only to evaluate a transaction with General Portland. LaFarge agreed that it would not purchase any General Portland securities while in possession of the confidential information. Ultimately LaFarge made an unsolicited bid to purchase to General Portland's board of directors, apparently as a prelude to a tender offer. General Portland obtained an injunction against any tender offers by LaFarge, on the basis that LaFarge's Williams Act filings would be required to disclose the confidential information. Here the confidential information involved detailed operating cost information on a plant by plant basis that would allow competitors to underbid General Portland. The trial court found that General Portland's board had acted in the best interests of its shareholders in negotiating the agreement with LaFarge. General Portland Inc. v. LaFarge Coppee, S.A., 1981 WL 1408 (N.D. Tex. 1981) described in Bialkin, "The Use of Standstill Agreements in Corporate Transactions," in 8th ANN. INST. ON SEC. REG. 33, 34–39 (1982).

Requiring the bidder not to purchase additional shares or begin a tender offer without target approval (a "standstill agreement") solves this problem for target firms. Standstill agreements can also serve to assure an orderly auction. Where a company decides to use an investment banker to seek prospective bidders, it may wish to assure that all bids are received at the same time, and that no bidder jumps the gun by beginning a tender offer designed to close before the bid deadline, thus precluding the company from shopping as thoroughly as it wishes, and being able to negotiate terms of the acquisition. Under these circumstances access to non-public information about the company is the carrot used to secure bidder agreement to the terms of the auction process.

In Martin Marietta Materials, Inc. v. Vulcan Materials Company, 2012 Del. Ch. LEXIS 93, affirmed 45 A.3d 148 (Del. 2012), Chancellor Strine interpreted a confidentiality agreement that did not contain an express standstill agreement to bar an uninvited tender offer by one of the parties. In the court's words:

> Under the NDA, "[e]ach party . . . shall use the other party's Evaluation Material solely for the purpose of evaluating a Transaction." A "Transaction" is defined as "a possible business combination transaction [ ] between [Martin Marietta] and [Vulcan] or one of their respective subsidiaries." * * * The definition of Transaction was modified by Martin Marietta from a "possible transaction . . . which could take the form of a purchase, sale or exchanges of businesses or assets, involving [Martin Marietta] and [Vulcan]." Martin Marietta therefore replaced the looser term "involving" and inserted a tighter term "between" that is more easily read than "involving" to require joint agreement of the two companies themselves.
>
> Martin Marietta also broadened the requirement to keep confidential the fact that the parties were discussing a transaction. Not satisfied with language that precluded the revelation of the fact that "discussions are taking place concerning a Transaction," Martin Marietta added language preventing the disclosure of the fact that discussions have [been] taking place. In other words, Martin Marietta sought to protection from disclosure that discussions had occurred in the past, thus preventing any disclosure in the event that discussions terminated without any agreed-upon Transaction. Martin Marietta also suggested that the parties' agreement to enter into the NDA itself be kept confidential.

When discussions ended without an agreement, Martin Marietta began a hostile tender offer, and sued for declaratory relief that the disclosures made about these negotiations made in its tender offer materials did not violate the NDA. Vulcan counterclaimed for an injunction on the basis of the breach of the NDA's terms, and prevailed. Martin argued that its disclosure obligations under the federal securities laws trumped the NDA. Chancellor Strine rejected this argument, because the disclosure obligations were only triggered by Martin's decision to make a tender offer. Vulcan argued that the NDA only contemplated use of the confidential material for a business combination transaction "between" the parties, and excluded a tender offer by one of the parties to the shareholders of the other. While finding the language somewhat ambiguous, Chancellor Strine was persuaded by the amendments Martin had insisted upon, that the contemplated transaction was a voluntary combination "between" the corporations, which would have required the consent of Vulcan. Under those circumstances, Martin's disclosures were in breach of the agreement, and Martin was enjoined from proceeding with its tender offer.

Finally, where a company wishes to remain independent, selling a significant block of stock to a "white knight"—a party that does not wish to obtain control—may serve this purpose well, although with today's poison pills and staggered boards, this is less attractive than it once was. Nevertheless, where a company is subject to supermajority voting requirements for mergers with interested stockholders, either through charter provisions or state antitakeover laws, selling a significant block to a white squire that will then have a veto power over a merger may be attractive. The difficulty for company management is assuring that the white knight stays that way—supportive of management and independence—and does not later seek control. The standstill agreement can serve this purpose.

The confidentiality agreement can also be used to prevent a bidder from "poaching" key employees after due diligence has revealed their value. See Appendix D, section 11.

Ivanhoe Partners v. Newmont Mining Corporation
535 A.2d 1334 (Del. 1987).

■ MOORE, JUSTICE.

We accepted this expedited interlocutory appeal from a decision of the Court of Chancery, denying a preliminary injunction to plaintiffs, in order to address certain defensive maneuvers taken in a battle for the control of Newmont Mining Corporation ("Newmont"), one of the largest gold producers in North America. In an attempt to block a hostile tender offer by Ivanhoe Partners and Ivanhoe Acquisition Corporation (collectively "Ivanhoe"),[1] Newmont declared a $33 per share dividend to all its stockholders, which helped its largest shareholder, Consolidated

---

[1]   Ivanhoe Partners is a Texas general partnership. Ivanhoe Acquisition Corporation is a Delaware corporation specifically formed to make a tender offer for Newmont. Both entities have been formed and are controlled by T. Boone Pickens, Jr.

Gold Fields PLC ("Gold Fields")[2], to engage in a "street sweep" of Newmont stock, thereby increasing Gold Field's ownership of Newmont from 26% to 49.7%.[3] The "street sweep" and its related transactions, including the dividend, and the extension of and amendments to a previously existing standstill agreement with Newmont, if proper, will effectively defeat Ivanhoe's bid.

* * *

Ivanhoe sought to enjoin the foregoing maneuvers as inequitable entrenchment devices violative of Newmont's and Gold Fields' fiduciary duties to Newmont shareholders under Delaware law. The Court of Chancery granted a temporary restraining order enjoining the consummation of Gold Fields' street sweep pending determination of Ivanhoe's motion for a preliminary injunction.[4]

However, after a subsequent hearing, the court vacated the temporary restraining order and denied Ivanhoe's motion for a preliminary injunction, ruling that any breach of fiduciary duty which may have existed prior to the temporary restraining order had been rectified by a subsequent amendment to the standstill agreement between Newmont and Gold Fields. We therefore consider the propriety of all these transactions under the fiduciary obligations established in Unocal Corp. v. Mesa Petroleum Co., Del. Supr., 493 A.2d 946 (1985), and Revlon, Inc. v. MacAndrews & Forbes Holdings Inc., Del. Supr., 506 A.2d 173 (1986).[5]

The Vice Chancellor found, and the record supports his conclusions, that the decisions of Newmont's board to facilitate the street sweep by issuance of the dividend, and to consummate a new standstill agreement, were taken in good faith after reasonable investigation in response to threats by both Gold Fields and Ivanhoe to Newmont's corporate policy and effectiveness. Under the circumstances, Newmont had both the power and the duty to oppose Ivanhoe's tender offer. The record also

---

[2]   Gold Fields is a multinational producer of gold, with interests and operations in South Africa, Australia, and the United States. Gold Fields' principal holding company, Consolidated Gold Fields PLC, is a United Kingdom corporation. Consolidated Gold Fields, PLC's subsidiaries, Gold Fields American Corporation, and The Special Purpose, Inc., are both Delaware corporations. Gold Fields executed the street sweep through its subsidiaries, Gold Fields American Corporation and The Special Purpose, Inc. These corporations will be referred to collectively as "Gold Fields."

[3]   "Street sweep" refers to the rapid acquisition of securities on the open market during and shortly after the pendency of a tender offer for the same class of securities. The shares are ordinarily purchased at a premium from arbitrageurs.

[4]   In response to Newmont's opposition to Ivanhoe's takeover bid, numerous class action lawsuits were filed on behalf of Newmont stockholders, against Newmont, its directors and Gold Fields. Those class actions were consolidated in the Court of Chancery and in this Court. For the purpose of this decision the interests of Ivanhoe and the class plaintiffs are essentially identical.

[5]   This appeal was heard on an expedited basis in light of the pending Ivanhoe offer and the Newmont-Gold Fields transactions. We accepted the appeal on Friday, October 16, 1987, received the plaintiffs' opening briefs on October 23, the defendants' answering briefs on October 30, the plaintiffs' reply briefs on November 2, and heard argument on Wednesday, November 4.

sustains the conclusion that these defensive measures were reasonable in relation to the threats posed, and that the board acted to meet them in the proper exercise of its sound business judgment. Further, the Revlon obligation to conduct a sale of the corporation did not arise under the circumstances here. Newmont was not for sale. Thus, there was no duty of its directors to maximize "the company's value at a sale for the stockholders' benefit." Accordingly, there being no entrenchment, the defensive measures adopted by Newmont are protected by the business judgment rule. We, therefore, affirm.

I.

* * *

In 1981 Gold Fields began vigorously acquiring Newmont stock.[6] Newmont immediately sued to enjoin Gold Fields' acquisition of a significant or controlling interest. Ultimately, Newmont agreed to allow Gold Fields to purchase up to a one-third interest in the company, but in return Newmont demanded that Gold Fields sign a standstill agreement. That accord, which in 1983 was amended and extended for ten years, limited Gold Fields' interest in Newmont to 33 1/3%, restricted Gold Fields' representation on the board to one third the total number of directors, required Gold Fields and Newmont to support the other's director nominees, and gave Newmont a right of first refusal in the event Gold Fields decided to sell its interest. Of particular significance is that the standstill agreement also provided that Gold Fields could terminate the arrangement at its option upon acquisition by a third party of 9.9% or more of Newmont's outstanding shares. Gold Fields maintained a 26% interest from 1981 until recently, when Ivanhoe's purchase of 9.95%, triggered Gold Fields' option to terminate the contract.

On August 13, 1987 Ivanhoe announced that it had acquired 8.7% of Newmont. Significantly, Ivanhoe soon took the deliberate step to increase its Newmont holdings to 9.95%, which thereby freed Gold Fields to terminate the standstill agreement. This was done intentionally with the hope that Gold Fields then would ally itself with Mr. Pickens and his Ivanhoe affiliates, either to take over Newmont and to divide it among themselves, or to reach some other mutually advantageous arrangement. This Ivanhoe tactic prompted a series of strategic maneuvers and responses by each of the three parties. In anticipation of a battle with Ivanhoe, Newmont began implementing traditional defensive measures.[7] However, in doing so Newmont found itself in the peculiar position of having simultaneously to fear and to court Gold Fields. Although

---

[6]   Before acquiring more than a 50% interest in Newmont, Gold Fields would have had to obtain shareholder approval, clearance in the United States under the Hart-Scott-Rodino Antitrust Improvements Act of 1976, and the approval of the London Stock Exchange. Aside from these legal barriers Gold Fields had a fundamental corporate policy of limiting its ownership to minority interests in foreign (non-U.K.) corporations.

[7]   On August 18, 1987 the Newmont board approved "golden parachutes" which called for substantial severance payments to twenty-five key management employees.

Newmont and Gold Fields had enjoyed a compatible business association for some time, Gold Fields now was freed of its prior constraints. It had the option to acquire control of Newmont. In order to maintain a balance in their relationship, Newmont exempted Gold Fields from these defensive measures. Nonetheless, the Vice Chancellor found that Gold Fields' was rationally perceived as a threat to Newmont's continued independence. Specifically, throughout its relationship with Newmont, Gold Fields had demonstrated that it had its own independent objectives which were not necessarily congruent with Newmont's.

* * *

On August 31 Ivanhoe sent Newmont a letter requesting a meeting to discuss the acquisition by Ivanhoe of all of the remaining Newmont common stock.[8] By separate letter, Ivanhoe solicited Gold Fields to discuss "a broad range of alternatives" concerning the disposition of their Newmont stock. On September 8, when these letters proved fruitless, Ivanhoe commenced a hostile tender offer for 42% of Newmont at $95 per share. Among other things the tender offer was contingent upon Ivanhoe's obtaining financing, the source of which was not disclosed.[9]

Furthermore, the Offer to Purchase disclosed that Ivanhoe would seek to acquire all remaining shares in a second step transaction at $95 per share cash which, likewise, was subject to obtaining financing. The offer stated that no specific second step transaction had been devised, and that there was no firm commitment to do so.

The Newmont directors had to quickly address numerous problems.[10] Based in part upon a presentation by its independent financial adviser, Goldman, Sachs and Company ("Goldman Sachs"), the board determined that the $95 offer was inadequate. When Ivanhoe attempted to remove the current board by shareholder consent, the directors amended the bylaws to delay the effect of any consent solicitation for twenty days. The board also undertook two major tasks to defend against the perceived Ivanhoe and Gold Fields threats. First, in an effort to protect Newmont's independence, the board began exploring alternatives with Gold Fields to discourage it from terminating the standstill agreement. Second, the board proposed an aggressive business and capital program (the "Gold Plan") which included the disclosure of

---

[8] In Wall Street parlance this is known as a "bear hug" letter which is commonly understood to mean a proposal by a hostile bidder to acquire all of the target's outstanding stock in a privately negotiated transaction.

[9] Ivanhoe now claims to have commitments for financing of up to 1.25 billion dollars.

[10] Newmont's board consisted of nine members: three management directors; two outside directors affiliated with Gold Fields; and four independent directors. Throughout the board's consideration and adoption of the various defensive mechanisms described here, the two Gold Fields' directors recused themselves. Thus all relevant actions taken by the remaining directors bore the imprimatur of a board majority consisting of four independent directors.

liberal estimates of reserves and a corresponding increase in the gold production estimates by 50%.[11]

Ivanhoe then raised its tender offer price to $105 on September 16. Two days later the Newmont Board met to consider the revised offer and found that it, too, was inadequate. The Board's decision was made after a second presentation by Goldman Sachs which included revised figures based on the Gold Plan.[12] At the same meeting Newmont's management offered a "restructuring" proposal designed to deal with the threats posed by Gold Fields and Ivanhoe. This proposal consisted of the declaration of a large dividend to be financed by the sale of Newmont's non-gold assets, and the signing of a new standstill agreement with Gold Fields to insure Newmont's independence. The purpose of the dividend was to reduce liquidity, thus making Newmont a less attractive target, to distribute the value of its non-gold assets to all of the shareholders (including Ivanhoe), and to facilitate Gold Fields' street sweep. Significantly, the proposed standstill agreement would limit Gold Fields' control of Newmont, thereby assuring the latter's continued independence.

Although Gold Fields had considered breaking the standstill agreement and going into the open market to purchase control of Newmont, Ivanhoe Partners, 533 A.2d at 596, the prospect of accomplishing a similar yet more restricted objective with only a small capital investment was very attractive.[13] Thus, the dividend became the linchpin for negotiating the new standstill agreement.

By September 20, 1987 Newmont and Gold Fields had reached an accord. This new agreement allowed Gold Fields to purchase up to 49.9% of Newmont stock, but effectively limited its representation on the Newmont board to 40% of the total directors. Additionally, Gold Fields was required to support the board's slate of nominees for the remaining board positions, and was prohibited from transferring its interest to any third party who refused to be bound by the standstill.

Once executed, the new agreement was delivered to Newmont in escrow conditioned upon the declaration of a $33 dividend.[14] On September 21 and 22, Gold Fields, consistent with the terms of the accord, and facilitated by the dividend, "swept the street", purchasing

---

[11] The Gold Plan called for the acceleration of exploration and production activities. Although Ivanhoe strenuously disputes the trial court's findings, there is support for a conclusion that even though the Gold Plan was timed to defeat the Ivanhoe offer, the adoption of the Gold Plan and the resulting higher Newmont stock valuation, were not mere "puffery".

[12] The valuation by Goldman Sachs is a much disputed issue in this case. We find it significant that in its final analysis, Goldman Sachs opined that at a price of $105 per share Ivanhoe would still acquire the two Newmont gold subsidiaries at an 8.7% discount.

[13] Throughout this period Gold Fields' investment banker, The First Boston Corporation, urged Gold Fields to break the standstill agreement and independently sweep the street, gain control of Newmont, and declare a dividend.

[14] The $33 figure represents the liquidation value of the non-gold assets. Ivanhoe Partners, 533 A.2d at 597.

approximately 15.8 million Newmont shares at an average price of $98 per share and increasing their interest to 49.7%.

* * *

II.

* * *

A.   *The Ivanhoe Threat*

This Court has recognized the coercive nature of two-tier partial tender offers. Unocal, 493 A.2d at 956. Here, not only did the Ivanhoe offer fit perfectly the mold of such a coercive device, but after reasonable investigation the offer was found by the Newmont board to be inadequate. The Vice Chancellor held that this finding of inadequacy was justified, and his conclusion is fully supported by the record. Furthermore, Newmont and Gold Fields specifically recognized that Mr. Pickens, who controls Ivanhoe, had been involved in several attempts to acquire and break-up other corporations, resulting in the payment of "greenmail" or severe restructuring of the target companies. The series of Ivanhoe maneuvers, including the secret acquisition of shares, the "bear hug" letter, the coercive partial tender offer and inadequate bid were all viewed by the defendants as classic elements of Mr. Pickens' typical modus operandi. Thus, the Newmont board could properly conclude that the Ivanhoe tender offer was not in the shareholders' best interests or those of their company.

B.   *The Gold Fields Threat*

Gold Fields did not make a public bid for Newmont, and in more recent years there appears to have been a congenial relationship between the two companies. From the outset Gold Fields publicly expressed its support for the Newmont management. A Gold Fields press release stated:

> Consolidated Gold Fields has had a long, close and valued relationship with Newmont. Although Ivanhoe Partners' actions give Gold Fields the right to terminate the standstill agreement, we do not intend to exercise that right at this time, and we have no wish to seek control of Newmont. We strongly support Newmont management and believe it to be in our interest as the largest shareholder, and in the interest of all Newmont shareholders, that management be allowed to continue to direct Newmont's affairs. . . .

Throughout the weeks of harried activity Gold Fields continued to publicly support Newmont's management. Despite this, Newmont contends that it was threatened by the stark possibility that Gold Fields would cancel the 1983 standstill agreement and acquire control of the company, thus leaving the remaining shareholders without protection on the "back end". The record is replete with examples of the reality of this threat. A clear danger was posed by Ivanhoe's deliberate acquisition of

9.95% of Newmont shares, designed to free Gold Fields from the agreement, thereby permitting Ivanhoe and Gold Fields to ally themselves against Newmont. But even without Ivanhoe, Gold Fields now could wrest control away from the public shareholders. In addition, as the Newmont board was aware, Gold Fields had the necessary financial backing to unilaterally "sweep the street" and obtain control of Newmont. Finally, the threat which Gold Fields posed was real. The Gold Fields board had in fact paused to weigh its options. Throughout these maneuvers it had considered in earnest the possibility of either independently purchasing control of Newmont or selling its interest to Ivanhoe.

C. *The Response*

Ivanhoe argues that, even if it and Gold Fields did pose a threat to Newmont's corporate policy and effectiveness, the Newmont directors failed to satisfy the second part of their Unocal burden—that their response be reasonable in relation to the threat posed. In examining that contention, Unocal requires us to carefully assess the reasonableness of the defensive measures employed and the results achieved. Because Newmont's actions here are so inextricably related, the principles of Unocal require that they be scrutinized collectively as a unitary response to the perceived threats.

It is significant that throughout the consideration and adoption of these proposals, the Gold Fields directors recused themselves from participation in the Newmont board meetings, leaving an alliance of four independent and three management directors. Thus, with the independent directors in the majority, proof that the board acted in good faith and upon reasonable investigation is materially enhanced.

Turning to the $33 dividend, it served two significant purposes in defending against Ivanhoe's inadequate and coercive tender offer. First, the dividend distributed the heretofore undervalued non-gold assets to all of Newmont's shareholders. In doing so Newmont effectively eliminated the means by which Ivanhoe might have acquired Newmont's gold assets at a substantial discount to the detriment of the other stockholders. Second, the dividend provided the financial impetus needed to persuade Gold Fields to engage in the street sweep. Although Gold Fields had the requisite financing to implement such action independently of the dividend, its board was reluctant to invest the $1.6 billion dollars needed to obtain a majority interest in Newmont.

The resulting standstill agreement also was a reasonable response to the Gold Fields threat. To forestall Gold Fields entry into the open market to purchase a controlling interest to the detriment of Newmont's public shareholders, Newmont obtained the new standstill agreement which restricted Gold Fields' ability to purchase and exercise control of the corporation. Thus, Newmont exchanged the $33 dividend for a revised standstill agreement, which not only limited Gold Fields' ownership to 49.9%, but, significantly, restricted its board membership to 40%. This guaranteed Newmont's continued independence under a board consisting of 40% Gold Fields directors, 40% independent directors and 20% management nominated directors. Further, the 49.9% limit on Gold Fields' stock ownership protected Newmont's public shareholders from being squeezed out by an unbridled majority shareholder.

The final element of the tripartite defensive measure employed against Ivanhoe was the so-called "street sweep". Ivanhoe contends that Newmont and Gold Fields breached their fiduciary duties to the shareholders who sold their stock in that maneuver. * * * Under Unocal we must determine whether the use of the street sweep, aided by Newmont, was a reasonable response to the Ivanhoe threat. Viewed in isolation the measure was a Gold Fields defense to protect its own interest in Newmont. However, for the purpose of evaluating the fiduciary duties of Newmont, we view the street sweep as part of Newmont's own comprehensive defensive strategy.

* * *

We, therefore, are satisfied that under all the circumstances Newmont's actions in facilitating the street sweep were reasonable. The measure was an essential part of Newmont's defensive plan, which enabled Newmont to maintain its independent status for the benefit of its other stockholders.

* * *

III.

Ivanhoe claims that the Newmont directors breached the duties imposed upon them in Revlon by refusing to entertain Ivanhoe's bid. Ivanhoe argues that under Revlon the board was charged with securing the highest available price for the company. However, the facts presented here do not implicate this Revlon principle.

Revlon involved the lock-up of a corporation amidst a bidding war for the company between a hostile party and a friendly bidder. The lock-up was effected after the board of directors had authorized management to "sell" the corporation. This Court held that when "the break-up of [a] company [is] inevitable . . . [the] duty of the board . . . [changes] from the preservation of [the company] as a corporate entity to the maximization of the company's value at a sale for the stockholders' benefit." Under such circumstances the directors became auctioneers "charged with getting the best price for the stockholders at a sale of the company." *Id.* This involves duties of loyalty and care. The former embodies not only an affirmative duty to protect the interests of the corporation, but also an obligation to refrain from conduct which would injure the corporation and its stockholders or deprive them of profit or advantage. In short, directors must eschew any conflict between duty and self-interest. They cannot succumb to influences which convert an otherwise valid business decision into a faithless act. On the other hand, the duty of care requires a director, when making a business decision, to proceed with a "critical eye" by acting in an informed and deliberate manner respecting the corporate merits of an issue before the board.

Revlon applies here only if it was apparent that the sale of Newmont was "inevitable". The record, however, does not support such a finding for two reasons.

First, Newmont was never for sale. During the short period in which these events occurred, the Newmont board held fast to its decision to keep the company independent. Ivanhoe Partners, 533 A.2d at 603. Ultimately, this goal was achieved by the standstill agreement and related defensive measures.

Second, there was neither a bidding contest, nor a sale. The only bidder for Newmont was Ivanhoe. Gold Fields was not a bidder, but wished only to protect its already substantial interest in the company. It did so through the street sweep. Thus, the Newmont board did not "sell" the company to Gold Fields. The latter's purchases were from private sellers. While Gold Fields now owns 49.7% of the stock, its representation on the board is only 40% because of the restrictions of the standstill agreement. These facts do not strip the Newmont board of the presumptions of independence and good faith under the business judgment rule. Even though Newmont's declaration of the dividend facilitated the street sweep, it did not constitute a "sale" of the company by Newmont.

On this record we are satisfied that the fiduciary obligations imposed by Revlon to sell a company to the highest bidder are not applicable here. We, therefore, find no merit in plaintiffs' contentions.

IV.

In conclusion, Newmont's directors had both the duty and responsibility to oppose the threats presented by Ivanhoe and Gold Fields. Further, the actions taken were reasonable in relation to the threats posed. The comprehensive defensive scheme consisting of the dividend, standstill agreement, and street sweep accomplished the two essential objectives of thwarting the inadequate coercive Ivanhoe offer, and of insuring the continued interest of the public shareholders in the independent control and prosperity of Newmont. Under the circumstances, the board's actions taken by a majority of independent directors, are entitled to the protection of the business judgment rule. Thus, unless the appellants demonstrate that the directors were solely or primarily motivated by entrenchment concerns, or another breach of a duty of loyalty or care, "this Court will not substitute its judgment for that of the board." The record does not support an entrenchment claim respecting the Newmont board's actions, and Ivanhoe failed to present evidence of any other breach of fiduciary duty. While the Vice Chancellor initially found two entrenching effects of the September 20 standstill agreement, which were cured by the September 27 amendment, we do not agree that the September 20 standstill breached any fiduciary duty. The agreement ensured an independent board. The transfer restriction perpetuated the independent nature of the board and did not entrench Newmont management. The voting provision only required Gold Fields to cast its votes for the nominees of the entire independent board. Thus the September 20 standstill agreement was not a breach of the Newmont directors' duty of loyalty. This record clearly indicates that Ivanhoe has failed to meet its burden of proof. Accordingly, the judgment of the Court of Chancery, denying Ivanhoe's motion for a preliminary injunction, is AFFIRMED.

QUESTIONS

1. How real was the coercive threat of Ivanhoe, if its securities filings announced an intent to complete a takeout at the same price as the front-end tender offer?

2. What business purpose does Newmont offer for resisting all changes of control?

3. How could a dividend be challenged as an entrenchment device?

4. In Revlon, Inc. v. MacAndrews & Forbes Holdings, Inc. 506 A.2d 173 (Del. 1985), discussed *infra* in Chapter Eight, Part 1, the court held that once the break-up or sale of a firm becomes inevitable, the directors become "auctioneers," with a duty to maximize the value shareholders will receive. In Paramount Communications Inc. v. QVC Network, Inc., 637 A.2d 34, 43 (Del. 1994), *infra* Chapter Eight, Part 1, the court defined a "sale" that triggered Revlon duties as a transaction in which "the proposed sale of control would provide the new controlling shareholder with the power to alter that vision." 637 A.2d at 43. The court stated: "Once control has shifted, the current Paramount stockholders will have no leverage in the future to demand another control premium." Has that situation occurred here? How could a court reconcile the result here with the opposite result in QVC?

H. DISCLOSURE OBLIGATIONS

Takeover defenses that have the effect of entrenching management in power can have substantial effects on the value of a company's stock. They may also influence investors' opinions about the loyalty of corporate management. For these reasons the Securities and Exchange Commission has been concerned with making certain that adequate disclosures are made to investors respecting these matters. For example, when a company is offering stock to the public in a registered offering, it will be necessary to describe the securities in compliance with Regulation S-K, Item 202. Item 202(a)(5) provides as follows:

"(5) Describe briefly or cross reference to a description in another part of the document, any provision of the registrant's charter or by-laws that would have an effect of delaying, deferring or preventing a change in control of the registrant and that would operate only with respect to an extraordinary corporate transaction involving the registrant (or any of its subsidiaries), such as a merger, reorganization, tender offer, sale or transfer of substantially all of its assets, or liquidation. Provisions and arrangements required by law or imposed by governmental or judicial authority need not be described or discussed pursuant to this paragraph (a)(5). Provisions or arrangements adopted by the registrant to effect, or further, compliance with laws or governmental or judicial mandate are not subject to the immediately preceding sentence where such compliance did not require the specific provisions or arrangements adopted."

Similarly, if a proxy statement proposes some amendment of the rights or terms of a class of securities for a shareholder vote, disclosure of this same information is required under Schedule 14A, Item 12(b), 17 C.F.R. § 240.14a–101. Item 19 of Schedule 14A also provides:

"If action is to be taken with respect to any amendment of the registrant's charter, bylaws or other documents as to which information is not required above, state briefly the reasons for and the general effect of such amendments.

1.   *Instructions.* Where the matter to be acted upon is the classification of directors, state whether vacancies which occur during the year may be filled by the board of directors to serve only until the next annual meeting or may be so filled for the remainder of the full term.

2.   Attention is directed to the discussion of disclosure regarding anti-takeover and similar proposals in Release No. 34–15230 (October 13, 1978)."

Disclosure in Proxy and Information Statements: Anti-Takeover or Similar Proposals

Securities Exchange Act of 1934 Release No. 15230 (October 13, 1978).

The Advisory Committee on Corporate Disclosure in its report urged the Commission staff to review closely proxy materials containing anti-takeover proposals in order to ensure that there is adequate discussion of their disadvantages as well as advantages. In February of 1978, the Commission responded with an indication that the suggestion would be implemented administratively and would be the subject of specific instructions to the staff of the Division of Corporate Finance.

The Division is now making these instructions available to the public in the form of a statement of its views in order to assist registrants in preparing proxy or information statements which may contain such proposals for the upcoming proxy season. It should be noted, however, that these instructions have neither been reviewed nor approved by the Commission and therefore only reflect the views of the staff of the Division of Corporation Finance. The Division stresses, moreover, that these instructions are merely for the guidance of the staff and are subject to revision without formal notice. The Division also notes that the facts and circumstances underlying particular proxy or information statements or other filings must be given great weight and that the importance and effect of these instructions will vary as the context requires.

I.   *Background*

The increased use of tender offers to obtain corporate control has prompted many companies to consider defensive techniques to fend off hostile offers. In the past, these defensive measures have typically focused on actions taken on the eve of a tender offer or during a tender offer contest.[19] The primary purpose of such measures has been to deter

---

[19]   These measures include, but are not limited to the following:

(a) repurchase its own securities, to make it less likely for the tender offeror to obtain control of the company;

(b) induce friendly third parties to make open market purchases of the target company's securities;

(c) announce dividend increases, or stock splits;

(d) issue additional shares or classes of stock;

(e) take steps to create an incompatibility between the target company and the tender offeror, for example, in inducing possible anti-trust violations should the tender offer be successful;

(f) arrange a defensive merger;

(g) enter into restrictive loan agreements, with default to occur should the tender offer succeed;

(h) institute litigation, challenging either directly or collaterally the conduct or effect of the tender offer;

(i) arrange for cross or circular ownership of voting stock by parent and subsidiary corporations;

(j) make the dismissal of directors expensive, by entering into costly employment contracts;

(k) negotiate contracts—for example, labor, rent, loans or leases—which provide for acceleration, increase, or renegotiation of payment in the event of a change in management;

(l) acquire other companies or accelerating the payment of outstanding debt for the purpose of spending access cash, thereby making the balance sheet of the target company less attractive to a potential offeror;

(m) judicial action seeking a temporary or permanent injunction against the bidder alleging antitrust violations, inadequate disclosure and other securities laws violations; and

(n) triggering the application of state anti-takeover statutes.

unfriendly takeovers by relying, for the most part, on the single most effective weapon in the arsenal of the subject company-delay.[20] Recently, companies which view themselves as potential subject companies have given increased attention to other defensive measures, such as internal controls in the company's charter or bylaws. As with the delay techniques, the primary purpose of the defensive charter provisions is to deter unfriendly takeovers. Rather than using delay as the means to accomplish this purpose, these measures are designed to make the subject company unattractive as a potential target long before any specific tender offer is announced. By making a tender offer impracticable or by increasing the bidder's costs and likelihood of failure should an offer be made, these provisions are intended to cause a potential bidder to look elsewhere, rather than commence a tender offer for such a company.

Typically, a corporation proposing to adopt amendments to its charter or bylaws is required by state corporation law to submit the proposal to a shareholder vote.[21] In such cases, corporations subject to, inter alia, Section 12 of the Securities Exchange Act of 1934 ["Exchange Act"] (15 U.S.C. 78a et seq., as amended by Pub. L. No. 94–29 (June 4, 1975)) are required to furnish either proxy materials or information statements to shareholders, pursuant to Regulation 14A (17 CFR 240.14a–1 to 240.14a–103) or Regulation 14c (17 CFR 240.14c–1 to 240.14c–101), respectively. Over the years, the Division has reviewed many proxy and information statements containing anti-takeover measures and has gained a great deal of experience in identifying issues, formulating comments and dealing with registrants and their counsel.

Since at least since 1969, the Division has taken the position that when management sponsors anti-takeover proposals and other devices to insulate management from removal, the issuer's proxy material or information statements should disclose in a prominent place that the over-all effect of the proposal is to render more difficult the accomplishment of mergers or the assumption of control by a principal stockholder, and thus to make difficult the removal of management. Moreover, the Report recommended that the Commission staff should intensively review proxy materials containing anti-takeover proposals with a view to requiring more adequate and uniform disclosure of the advantages and disadvantages of the management's proposals.

In view of this recommendation and the increased attention given to defensive measures, the Division wishes to advise registrants that the

---

[20] Since time is of the essence to a bidder in tender offers, delay permits the subject company to prepare and consolidate an effective defense and to frustrate the bidder's efforts.

[21] A table listing a number of anti-takeover provisions, including novel measures, is appended to this release as Attachment A. This table is not intended to be an exclusive listing of all such measures. Proxy materials or information statements may contain variations of the provisions listed or other proposals which may be or operate as defensive charter provisions but which may not be included in the table. * * *

treatment of anti-takeover proposals in proxy materials or information statements will generally be reviewed for compliance with the position stated below. It is hoped that this advance notice will facilitate the preparation of proxy materials or information statements for the upcoming proxy season.

II. *Position of Division of Corporation Finance With Respect to Disclosure in Proxy or Information Statements Containing Anti-Takeover Proposals*

The Division's review of proxy and information statements containing anti-takeover measures will continue to focus on three areas: the placement of the disclosure in the statement; the disclosure of anti-takeover proposals generally; and the disclosure of specific types of provisions being proposed.

A. *Placement of Disclosure*

If a proxy or information statement contains an anti-takeover proposal, it should be included in a list of all proposals in the proxy soliciting material or disclosed in the information statement. The listing should be placed in the notice or forepart of the materials. If more than one anti-takeover proposal is included, they should not be separated by unrelated proposals in the listing made in the notice of materials.

The disclosure concerning an anti-takeover proposal should be set forth in a prominent place in the proxy or information statement. All of the information which is related to the proposal should set forth in one place in the materials. If disclosure in more than one place cannot be avoided, cross-references are suggested. If the statement contains more than one anti-takeover proposal, the disclosure of each should generally not be separated by unrelated information or other proposals in the statement.

B. *Content of Disclosure*

1. *General Issues*

Despite significant variations in the form and operation of anti-takeover proposals, there are several areas in which certain basic disclosures are generally applicable. These include:

a. *The reason(s) for the proposal and the bases of such reason(s).*

The proxy or information should clearly indicate why management is proposing to amend the corporation's charter or by-laws. The term "bases" for the reasons means an explanation of the factors and/or principles supporting or serving as a foundation for the reason stated.

If the proposal is the result of management's knowledge of any specific effort to accumulate the issuer's securities or to obtain control of the issuer by means of a merger, tender offer, solicitation in opposition to management or otherwise, a description of any such effort should be included. If the measure is not the result of any specific effort, disclosure should be made to that effect and a statement included as to why, in the absence of such efforts, the measure is being proposed at this time.

Disclosure should also be made as to whether the corporation's charter or by-laws presently contain other provisions having an anti-takeover effect, whether the instant proposal is part of a plan by management to adopt a series of such amendments, and whether management presently intends to propose other anti-takeover measures in future proxy solicitations. If similar measures have been adopted, are being proposed or considered, the inter-relationship of the proposals/provisions should be discussed. A chart or table which would list charter or by-law provisions that have already been adopted which can be used as defensive provisions may also be appropriate. This chart, among other things, may include disclosure concerning a class of authorized, but unissued, common or preferred securities with respect to which the board of directors retains the power to determine voting rights. Additionally, an indication should be made whether or not cumulative voting is provided under the corporation's charter or by-laws or pursuant to state law.

b.   *The over-all effects of the proposal, if adopted.*

The impact of the proposed amendments upon management's tenure and upon any proposal to alter the structure of the corporation should be disclosed. If appropriate, such disclosure should include statements that the over-all effects of the proposal, if adopted, may (would) be to render more difficult or to discourage a merger, tender offer or proxy contest, the assumption of control by a holder of a larger block of the corporation's securities and the removal of incumbent management. A statement that the proposal could make the accomplishment of a given transaction more difficult even if it is favorable to the interests of shareholders may be warranted. Thus, the disclosure should focus on the effects of making the removal of management more difficult even if such removal would be beneficial to shareholders generally, and the effect of limiting shareholder participation in certain transactions such as mergers or tender offers whether or not such transactions are favored by incumbent management.

c.   *The advantages and disadvantages of the proposal.*

Although this item may overlap disclosure of the effects of the transaction, information should be included concerning and advantages and disadvantages of the proposal both to incumbent management and to shareholders generally. For example, if one of the effects of the proposal would be to render the accomplishment of a tender offer more difficult, the disclosure could include statements to the effect that such a provision may be beneficial to management in a hostile tender offer and may have an adverse impact on shareholders who may want to participate in such a tender offer. The favorable aspects of the proposal, to either management or shareholders, should also be disclosed.

d.   *Disclosure of how the proposal will operate.*

Because of the complicated nature of many of these proposals, it may be beneficial to shareholders to include an explanation of the operation of the proposal, if adopted. In the past, examples of the operation of staggered boards have been disclosed. Accordingly, an explanation of the operation of the proposal(s) should also be included in the proxy or information statement. Such an explanation is intended to assist shareholders in their understanding of what they are being asked to vote in favor of.

e.   *Whether the proposal was the subject of a vote of the issuer's board of directors and, if so, the results of such vote.*

Additionally, consideration should also be given to identifying any dissenting directors and stating the reasons given for any such dissent if available.

f.   *Limitations on the adoption of such proposals.*

Disclosure should be included as to whether the rules or practices or any stock exchange on which the issuer's securities are listed reserve the right to refuse to list or to de-list any stock which has unusual voting provisions that tender or nullify or restrict its voting.

g.   *Comparison of anti-takeover measure with comparable provision under state corporation law.*

If the charter or by-law amendment pertains to a matter that is specifically addressed under state corporation law, a comparison of the provision of such state corporation statute with those of the instant proposal should be furnished. For example, if the defensive charter amendment concerns the vote necessary to approve an extraordinary corporate transaction such as a merger, the provision of the proposal, such as the minimum percentage required, should be compared with that under the state statute.

2.   *Issues Involving Some Specific Anti-Takeover Proposals*

Because of the varied nature of anti-takeover proposals, disclosure specifically applicable to the type of proposal should also be made. Where applicable, the disclosure should include the following:

a.   *Supermajority[22] Voting Provisions*

One of the specific effects should be indicated to be that management may obtain a veto power over mergers regardless of whether the transaction is desired by or beneficial to a majority of the shareholders

---

[22] Supermajority means any percentage requirement that exceeds the comparable requirement under applicable state law. If the requirement under state law is 66 2/3% to approve a merger, a supermajority provision would be any percentage in excess of the state requirement—such as 80%.

and thereby assists management in retaining their present positions. Another specific effect would be to give the holders of minority of the total shares outstanding and entitled to vote a veto power over a merger which management and/or a majority of the shareholders may believe is desirable and beneficial. In these types of proposals, disclosure should be included of the aggregate percentage of outstanding voting securities beneficially owned by management, the board of directors and principal shareholders of the corporation (including any persons or groups of persons who have filed a Schedule 13D with the Commission). If a supermajority is not needed to repeal such a provision and/or a supermajority is not needed to adopt the provision, disclosure of the reasons should be made.

b.   *Classification of Directors to Serve for Staggered Terms*

Unlike certain internal corporate defense measures, staggered board provisions affect every election of directors and are not triggered by the occurrence of a particular event such as a hostile merger. Thus, such systems of electing directors make it more difficult for shareholders to change the majority of directors even when the only reason for the change may be the performance of the present directors. The fact that the provision, if adopted, would be applicable to every election of directors, rather than only an election occurring after a change in control of the issuer, should be disclosed. The number of annual meetings necessary to change the majority of the directors under the staggered system should be contrasted to the number of annual meetings necessary for change under the present system. If a purpose of the proposed amendment is to limit the voting power of a particular block of common stock or to frustrate accumulations of such blocks, appropriate disclosure should be made. If one of the reasons for the proposal is to ensure the continuity of the Board of Directors and/or management, it is suggested that management be asked to disclose whether there have been any problems with respect to such continuity in the past and, if so, to furnish a description of them.

c.   *Authorization of Certain Classes of Common or Preferred Stock*

In certain circumstances, the authorization of classes of preferred or common stock with either unspecified voting rights or rights providing for the approval of extraordinary corporate transactions may be used to create voting impediments or to frustrate persons seeking to effect a merger or to otherwise gain control of the issuer. If used for such a purpose, disclosure should be included as to whether the securities could be privately placed and, if such placement is contemplated by the issuer, whether the purchasers have any affiliation with the issuer or any agreement or understanding as to the manner in which the securities are to be voted.

In certain instances, a proposal to increase the amount authorized of a class of voting securities may have an anti-takeover effect. If used for such a purpose, the considerations discussed above would be applicable. Moreover, such additional shares could be used to dilute the stock ownership of persons seeking to obtain control of the issuer. If the purpose for the increase in the authorization is stated to be the elimination of later delays associated with a stockholder vote on specific issuances, reference should be made to any stock exchange requirements calling for a stockholder vote on issuances of additional shares. Additionally, the number of shares unissued and not reserved for issuance should be stated.

Attachment A. Table Relating to Internal Corporate Controls or Anti-Takeover Measure Disclosed in Proxy or Information Statement

Defensive corporate charter amendments/provisions may include, but are not limited, to:

(1)   Classification of directors or staggering of boards

(2)   Provisions to abolish cumulative voting

(3)   Provisions establishing supermajority approval requirements (for example, requiring an 80% favorable vote) for certain corporate transactions including, but not limited to, any proposed merger or sale of assets

(4)   Provisions requiring a supermajority vote to cancel a supermajority provision as described in category 3 above, but not to adopt one

(5)   Provisions requiring a supermajority vote to amend the corporate charter in any relevant respect

(6)   Provisions which reduce the supermajority required for a merger to a lesser majority unless the other party to the transaction is a "related corporation" (such as one owning more than 5% of any class of voting securities of the issuer) in which case a merger would require supermajority approval of the common stock as a class in addition to approval by the holders of the voting power to all securities of the issuer entitled to vote

(7)   The creation of a class of equity securities either common or preferred to be placed privately; the favorable vote of which is necessary to approve any tender offer, merger, sale or exchange of assets or other extraordinary corporate transaction

(8)   Provisions which prevent the removal of directors without cause or by a supermajority vote

(9)   Provisions prohibiting the removal from office for any reason of a director elected for a term longer than one year,

notwithstanding any change in control due to tender offers, mergers or other transactions

(10) Provisions prohibiting the calling of special shareholder meetings altogether or allowing them to be called only upon the request of a holder or holders of a supermajority of the shares outstanding

(11) Provisions establishing the maximum permissible number of directors

(12) Provisions providing for the election of stand-by successor directors at the same time as the regular directors, who will fill a position upon the death or resignation of a regular director

(13) Reincorporation of the issuer in a state with an anti-takeover statute

(14) Creation of an Employee Stock Ownership Plan which, because of its size, percentage of total outstanding securities of the issuer which it may own, voting or other provisions, may be used in defense in a contested takeover attempt

(15) Provisions requiring the consideration for any merger following a tender offer to be no less than the highest consideration offered pursuant to the tender offer

(16) Shareholder approval of long term "sweetheart" employment contracts with executive officers of the issuer which cannot be abrogated or rescinded.

ODS Technologies, L.P. v. Marshall

832 A.2d 1254 (Del.Ch. 2003).

■ CHANDLER, CHANCELLOR.

Plaintiff ODS Technology, L.P. d/b/a TVG Network ("TVG") filed this action on September 5, 2003. TVG seeks to enjoin Youbet.com, Inc. ("Youbet") from proceeding with its annual meeting of shareholders (the "Annual Meeting") pending the correction of alleged breaches of the duty of disclosure in connection with the Proxy Statement filed by Youbet in advance of the Annual Meeting. This Court expedited the proceedings and on September 24, 2003, heard TVG's motion for a preliminary injunction.

I. BACKGROUND

Plaintiff TVG, a shareholder of Youbet, is a Delaware limited partnership that develops interactive gambling systems for horse racing and owns intellectual property rights related to such systems.

Defendant Youbet is a Delaware corporation that provides services which enable individuals to gamble on horse racing events over the internet. The remaining defendants are members of Youbet's board of directors (the "Board"). Defendant Charles Champion has served as Youbet's CEO since September 2000 and Chairman of Youbet's board since August 5, 2003. Defendant David Marshall is co-founder of Youbet and current Vice Chairman of Youbet's board. Defendant Guy Chipparoni has been a director of Youbet since 1998; Defendant Gary Adelson since April 2002; Defendant James Edgar since June 2002; and Defendant Joseph Barletta since December 2002.

On May 18, 2001, TVG and Youbet entered into a License and Content Agreement (the "License Agreement") pursuant to which TVG granted Youbet non-exclusive licenses to certain of TVG's patent rights and simulcast audio and video content. According to a Youbet press release issued on May 21, 2001, the License Agreement was "integral to [Youbet] gaining broad market penetration and growth."

In partial consideration for providing these licenses and intellectual property rights to Youbet, TVG received two warrants. The parties also signed a related Warrant Issuance Agreement. The Initial Warrant, exercised on June 13, 2002, entitled TVG to purchase 3,884,650 shares of Youbet common stock. The Additional Warrant entitled TVG to purchase a number of shares of Youbet common stock which, when aggregated with the 3,884,650 shares issued under the Initial Warrant, would result in TVG owning 51% of Youbet's common stock on a fully diluted basis. The aggregate exercise price exceeds $41 million. TVG has not exercised the Additional Warrant, and it expires on May 18, 2004.

The Warrant Issuance Agreement includes a clause that requires Youbet "to use its best efforts" to enable TVG to designate a number of directors to Youbet's board of directors based on TVG's ownership of Youbet common stock according to a specified formula set forth in the agreement (the "Board Representation Clause"). Under the formula, if TVG owns more than 49.9% of Youbet's outstanding common stock, TVG is entitled to designate three-fifths of the Board members. Additionally, the Additional Warrant contains a provision which states that Youbet "will not, by amendment to its Certificate of Incorporation or through any reorganization, recapitalization, conveyance or transfer of assets, consolidation, merger, dissolution, issuance or sales of securities or other agreement or voluntary act, avoid or seek to avoid the observance or performance of any of the terms to be observed or performed hereunder by [Youbet], or take any act which is inconsistent with the rights granted to [TVG] in this Warrant or otherwise conflicts with the provisions hereof" (the "No Impairment Clause").

In the early part of 2002, Youbet began to consider the possibility that TVG would exercise the Additional Warrant. The Monitor Group, a consulting firm, was employed to assist Youbet in developing its strategy to address TVG and the Additional Warrant. On June 7, 2003, Youbet management, including its CEO Mr. Champion, and the Monitor Group, met to consider the implications of the Additional Warrant. A summary of this meeting, entitled "Summary from June 7th Offsite on Additional Warrant," indicates that among the things considered to "discourage TVG from exercising [the] warrant" were "Stagger Board of Directors" and "Super majority without shareholder vote." On June 15, 2003, a document produced by Monitor entitled "Gemstar / TVG Warrant Workshop: Background Material" was distributed by Youbet's general counsel to Messrs. Champion and Barletta, among others. This document provides detailed information about TVG, the Additional Warrant, the Board Representation Clause, and the No Impairment Clause and was prepared in advance of a meeting held on June 17, 2003 regarding the Additional Warrant. A substantially similar document was provided to Marshall on June 19, 2003. A third document relating to the Additional Warrant was also prepared by Youbet and/or Monitor, but the record is unclear when, if ever, management or the Board received this document.

On July 31, 2003, the Board met to consider, among other things, a proposal to change Youbet's bylaws. The minutes of the meeting state that Youbet's general counsel reviewed the proposed changes to the bylaws and that a discussion by the Board followed. "Specifically the Board discussed amending the Corporations [sic] Certificate of Incorporation and By-laws to provide for the classification of the Board into three classes of 3 directors, with 3 year staggered terms of office ["Staggered Board Provision"]; and to provide that future amendments to the Certificate of Incorporation and By-laws must be approved by an affirmative vote of at least 66 2/3% of the votes of the outstanding shares of the Company's Common Stock ["Supermajority Provision"]" [collectively the "Amendments"]. Deposition testimony indicates that in its deliberations on these issues the Board considered TVG. Specifically, the Board considered the interaction between the Amendments and the Warrant Issuance Agreement and the Additional Warrant, including the Board Representation Clause and the No Impairment Clause,[12] and whether the Amendments would violate the Additional Warrant or the Warrant Issuance Agreement. The Board considered whether the Amendments would decrease the likelihood that TVG would exercise the Additional Warrant.[14] In addition, it appears that near the end of the meeting, Monitor provided the Board a detailed description of the "pros and cons" for Youbet shareholders if TVG exercised the Additional Warrant. The Board unanimously adopted a resolution approving the

---

[12] In his deposition testimony Marshall stated "the Board clearly understood TVG had a warrant in the company and that there could be implications from staggering the board, and therefore, relating to the change of the bylaws to two-thirds vote."

[14] Marshall stated in deposition testimony that "the discussion was that having a staggered board could make [TVG] less inclined . . . to exercise the warrant."

Amendments, scheduled the Annual Meeting for September 26, 2003, and set the record date for the Annual Meeting as August 4, 2003.

On August 13, 2003, Youbet filed its Preliminary Proxy Statement with the Securities and Exchange Commission ("SEC").[16] Youbet's Definitive Proxy Statement was filed with the SEC and distributed to shareholders on August 25, 2003. Distributed with the Proxy Statement was Youbet's most recently filed Annual Report, Form 10-KSB. Youbet's Form 10-KSB incorporates by reference as exhibits the License Agreement and the Warrant Issuance Agreement.

The Proxy Statement states that the Staggered Board Provision is "designed to assure continuity and stability." The section of the Proxy Statement related to the Staggered Board Provision also states:

> The proposed classified board amendment will extend the time required to effect a change in control of the Board of Directors through the election of directors and may discourage hostile takeover bids for the Company. . . . If the Company implements a classified Board of Directors, even if a takeover bidder were to acquire a majority of the voting power of the Company's outstanding Common Stock, it will take at least two annual meetings to effectuate a change in control of the Board of Directors because only a minority of the directors will be elected at each meeting. . . . This provision of the Certificate will not be subject to amendment by vote of less than 66 2/3% of the voting power of all outstanding stock of the Company entitled to vote present, in person or represented by proxy on such an amendment at a stockholders' meeting duly called for such purpose. This could discourage certain takeover attempts, perhaps including some takeovers that stockholders may feel would be in their best interests. . . . The classified board proposal will tend to perpetuate present management.

The section of the Proxy Statement related to the Supermajority Provision similarly states that it is designed to promote continuity and stability, and that "if this proposed amendment . . . is approved, it may discourage hostile takeover bids for the Company, perhaps including some takeovers that majority of stockholders may feel would be in their best interests." The two sections relating to the proposed Amendments do not discuss TVG.

The Proxy Statement discloses, in sections unrelated to the Amendments, items related to TVG. Specifically, the Proxy Statement discloses that TVG is the beneficial owner of 51% of Youbet's outstanding common stock due to the Additional Warrant, that the Additional

---

[16] Youbet filed its Preliminary Proxy Statement, providing notice to stockholders of the proposed Amendments, after the record date set by the Board. Champion testified that one of the reasons for selecting an early record date was to prevent TVG from exercising the Additional Warrant and obtaining the votes necessary to defeat the Amendments.

Warrant is "currently exercisable," and that the "aggregate exercise price" is $41,082,442 based on the defined exercise price of $2.50 per share of common stock. In another section, the Proxy Statement discusses the License Agreement between TVG and Youbet, and that the License Agreement required Youbet to issue TVG the Initial and Additional Warrants. Also, as noted above, Youbet's Form 10-KSB was distributed with the Proxy Statement. The Form 10-KSB discloses additional information relating to the Warrant Issuance Agreement and the License Agreement, and incorporates both agreements by reference as exhibits. The Proxy Statement and the Form 10-KSB do not discuss the Board Representation Clause, the No Impairment Clause, or the Cross-Default Provision.

II. ANALYSIS

The plaintiff alleges that the Proxy Statement is materially misleading and defendants have breached their fiduciary duty to disclose fully and fairly to stockholders all material information in seeking stockholder approval of the Amendments. Plaintiff seeks to enjoin the September 26, 2003, Annual Meeting pending the issuance of corrective disclosures. The core disclosure claims all concern information about TVG as it relates to the Amendments, but are separated into three more specific allegations. First, plaintiff contends that because the Proxy Statement does not disclose that the Board considered TVG, the Additional Warrant, the Warrant Issuance Agreement, and whether the Amendments might affect TVG's rights, it is materially misleading. Plaintiff insists that the Amendments were a defensive measure aimed at TVG and such information is material. Second, plaintiff argues the Proxy Statement fails to disclose the consequences of frustrating TVG's rights under the Additional Warrant. And, finally, plaintiff contends that the Proxy Statement fails to accurately describe the nature of TVG's rights under the Warrant Issuance Agreement, the Additional Warrant, or the License Agreement, especially since the Board Representation Clause, the No Impairment Clause, and the Cross-Default Provision are not discussed in the Proxy Statement.

The standard on a motion for preliminary injunction is well-settled. In order to prevail, the plaintiff must establish: (1) a reasonable likelihood of success on the merits of at least one claim; (2) that irreparable harm will be suffered by the plaintiff if the injunction is denied; and (3) that the harm that the plaintiff will suffer if the injunction is not granted outweighs the harm that the defendant will suffer if the injunction is granted.

A. Reasonable Likelihood of Success

The basic legal standard used to determine the plaintiff's likelihood of success on the merits is familiar: the defendant directors have the duty to disclose in a non-misleading manner all material facts bearing on the decision of the Youbet stockholders' to approve the Amendments.[23] The test for materiality is as follows:

> An omitted fact is material if there is a substantial likelihood that a reasonable shareholder would consider it important in deciding how to vote. . . . It does not require proof of a substantial likelihood that disclosure of the omitted fact would have caused a reasonable investor to change his vote. What the standard does contemplate is a showing of a substantial likelihood that, under all the circumstances, the omitted fact would have assumed actual significance in the deliberations of the reasonable shareholder. Put another way, there must be a substantial likelihood that the disclosure of the omitted fact would have been viewed by the reasonable investor as having significantly altered the "total mix" of information made available.[24]

Under this standard, the issue becomes whether information considered by the Board regarding the interrelationship between the Amendments and TVG's rights under the Additional Warrant, the Warrant Issuance Agreement, and the License Agreement "would have assumed actual significance in the deliberations of the reasonable shareholder."[25]

The factual record established during discovery demonstrates that TVG's warrant to acquire a 51% stake in Youbet was thoroughly analyzed by senior management and some directors, with the assistance of hired consultants, in the weeks preceding the July 31st Board meeting. Whole documents are devoted to this subject. Before the Board meeting, Youbet evaluated the option of adopting a staggered board and a supermajority provision as defensive measures aimed at frustrating TVG's ability to obtain control of the Company—the exact measures ultimately adopted at the July 31st Board meeting. At the meeting itself, the interaction between TVG's various rights under the Warrant Issuance Agreement and the Additional Warrant and the Amendments was discussed, as well as whether the Amendments would affect TVG's actual exercise of the Additional Warrant. Additionally, the advantages and disadvantages to shareholders of TVG's exercise of the Additional Warrant were presented to the Board. Given the entirety of the factual record, it is hard to escape the conclusion that the Amendments were specifically designed as defensive measures aimed directly at TVG.[26]

---

[23] See, e.g., Malone v. Brincat, 722 A.2d 5, 10 (Del. 1998); Skeen v. Jo-Ann Stores, Inc., 750 A.2d 1170, 1174 (Del. 2000); McMullin v. Beran, 765 A.2d 910, 925 (Del. 2000).

[24] Arnold v. Society for Sav. Bancorp., 650 A.2d 1270, 1277 (Del. 1994) (quoting TSC Indus. v. Northway, Inc., 426 U.S. 438, 449, 48 L. Ed. 2d 757, 96 S. Ct. 2126 (1976)).

[25] Id.

[26] This conclusion is buttressed by the Make Whole Clause and the setting of the record date preceding the Preliminary Proxy Statement. Given the existence of the Make Whole Clause, it is unlikely that there are other potential acquirors of Youbet. Even if a potential acquiror purchased 51% of Youbet's stock on the open market, TVG's warrant would still allow it to acquire a 51% stake. Additionally, the fact that Youbet was concerned about TVG exercising

The Proxy Statement, however, fails to accurately depict the purposes or effects of the Amendments—purposes and effects the Board itself found relevant in its deliberations.[27] A reasonable shareholder, when reading the Proxy Statement and Form 10-KSB, is given the impression that the Amendments are merely routine measures adopted on a "clear day" and designed to ensure "continuity and stability," and that little, if any, consideration was given to TVG when adopting the Amendments. This impression is false and misleading.

Delaware law requires a full and fair explanation of the rationale for a proposal that directors are recommending stockholders to approve. The Board is required to disclose its motivations candidly, a proposition that "hardly needs citation of authority." Delaware does not stand alone on this point, however. The Securities and Exchange Commission has for some time recognized that full disclosure of the purposes and effects of defensive measures is of actual significance to shareholders.[31] Ultimately, the Board should have disclosed that the Amendments were adopted with TVG in mind and provided shareholders with the necessary information about TVG's rights in order for shareholders to make an informed decision about how to cast their votes.

Defendants' disclosures actually cross the line from omitting material information to become affirmatively misleading. Reading the Proxy Statement's generic justifications for adoption of the Amendments, in my opinion, would leave a reasonable shareholder with the impression that TVG was not a factor—the opposite of the truth. In other words, by stating that the Amendments would discourage hostile takeover bids generally, without mentioning TVG specifically, the Proxy Statement creates the negative inference that the Board was unaware that TVG might be discouraged from attempting to acquire control of the company. The Board's generic, partial disclosure of the purposes of adopting the Amendments is materially misleading absent mentioning TVG.

Defendants have argued strenuously that the disclosures sought by the plaintiff would require "speculation." There is nothing speculative, however, about requiring the Board to disclose its true rationale for recommending the Amendments. Defendants are correct that Delaware authority cautions against requiring disclosures of speculative information in order to shield shareholders from misleading or unreliable information, but it is not speculative to require the Board to disclose

---

the warrant in advance of the Annual Meeting suggests that the Amendments were targeted at TVG. See supra note 16.

[27] The fact that the Board considered this information material is perhaps the strongest evidence that this information is material to a shareholder

[31] SEC Release No. 34–15230, 1978 WL 186739, at *2–3 (Oct. 13, 1978) (requiring disclosure of the reason for amendments and "an explanation of the factors and/or principles supporting or serving as the foundation for the reason stated"). See also Highland Capital, 1990 WL 3973, at *3 (citing Release); S.E.C. v. Dorchester Gas Corp., 1984 WL 2369, at 2 & n.1 (D.D.C. Jan. 9, 1984) (citing Release and "emphasizing the need for adequate and accurate disclosure with respect to anti-takeover and other defensive measures").

known risks accompanied by adoption of the Amendments.[33] One does not need to speculate to disclose that the Board actually considered whether the Amendments would discourage TVG from exercising the Additional Warrant or might violate the Warrant Issuance Agreement.[34]

The Defendants make much of the fact that the License Agreement and Warrant Issuance Agreement are referenced as exhibits to the Form 10-KSB and cites Wolf v. Assaf[35] and Orman v. Cullman[36] for the proposition that disclosures made within a Form 10-K distributed with a proxy statement provide adequate notice to shareholders. These cases are of no assistance to the Defendants. The disclosures in the Form 10-KSB are largely duplicative of the disclosures in the Proxy Statement. Moreover, in both Wolf and Orman the material information was in the Form 10-Ks, but here the License Agreement and Warrant Issuance Agreement are only incorporated by reference and are actually attached to an unrelated distribution to shareholders made two years earlier. Additionally, although those agreements are disclosed in the Form 10-KSB, the portions of those agreements relevant to a reasonable shareholder are neither highlighted nor mentioned directly in connection with the Amendments. The failure to disclose the Board's consideration of these agreements as they relate to the Amendments is not "cured by reason that it could be uncovered by an energetic shareholder reading an SEC filing."[37] Furthermore, even if a shareholder read through the entirety of the License Agreement and the Warrant Issuance Agreement, it is incredible to suggest that a reasonable shareholder would identify the Board Representation Clause or Cross-Default Clause as significant to the Amendments when the Proxy Statement itself mentions neither TVG generally nor these provisions specifically when discussing those same Amendments. To conclude otherwise would create a "super" shareholder standard and create almost limitless opportunities for deception of the "reasonable" shareholder. TVG has firmly established a

---

[33] The term "speculation" conjures up the idea that the Board would be engaging in mere conjecture or guesswork if it was required to disclose the advantages and disadvantages of frustrating TVG's ability to acquire control of the Company. But the documentary record indicates that these risks were well know by senior management and the Board. Regardless, in contexts such as this where the disclosure of the effects of the Amendments is material to shareholder deliberations, some disclosure of "soft information" may be required. R.S.M., Inc. v. Alliance Capital Mgmt. Holdings, L.P., 790 A.2d 478, 502 n.39 (Del.Ch. 2001); Zirn [v. VLI], 681 A.2d [1050] at 1059 [(Del. 1996)].

[34] Requiring the Board to disclose that it considered whether the Amendments would infringe on TVG's contractual rights does not require self-flagellation. Youbet's contention is that, in fact, the Board concluded that the Amendments would not violate TVG's rights. The Board was under a duty to disclose whether the prospect of litigation was relevant to the decision to adopt the Amendments. See In re TWA, Inc. Shareholders Litig., 1988 WL 111271, at *12 (Del.Ch. Oct. 21, 1988) (directors do not have to adopt the plaintiff's legal conclusions, but must disclose their own conclusions when relevant to the decision made).

[35] 1998 WL 326662 (Del.Ch. 1998).

[36] 794 A.2d 5 (Del.Ch. 2002).

[37] Trans World Airlines, 1988 WL 111271 at *10.

reasonable likelihood of success on the merits of its claim for a breach of the fiduciary duty of disclosure.

* * *

III. CONCLUSION

For the reasons stated, I grant plaintiff's motion for a preliminary injunction. * * *

———

The Aftermath

TVG is also known as Gemstar-TV Guide International. In later SEC filings it disclosed that shortly after filing this complaint on September 5, 2003, it filed a demand for arbitration with the American Arbitration Association. During the process of preparation for an arbitration hearing TVG delivered a letter to Youbet exercising its right under the Warrant Issuance Agreement (the "Initial Agreement") to designate one TVG director. In February 2004 the parties reached a settlement, which provided for a reduction in the purchase price under the Additional Warrant Agreement, and a promise by Youbet that if TVG notified Youbet by April 1, 2004 that it did not intend to exercise the Additional Warrant that Youbet would issue one million shares to TVG and pay it $725,000 for its legal expenses. On March 31, 2004, TVG notified Youbet that it did not intend to exercise the Additional Warrant, and the additional one million shares were issued. This left TVG with slightly over 5 million Youbet shares, amounting to 16.9% of Youbet's common stock outstanding.

———

QUESTIONS

1. What parts of Release 15230 would you argue were violated if you represented the plaintiff?

2. The SEC's disclosure regulations permit incorporation by reference of previously filed disclosure documents, including exhibits such as the agreements at issue here. Why isn't this enough to satisfy the court? What does it say about the court's expectations about readers of the proxy statement?

3. As of September, 2010 approximately 56% of Youbet's stock was owned by mutual funds and other financial institutions. This is perhaps slightly lower than average for companies listed on NASDAQ. If Institutional Shareholders (ISS) were to issue a negative recommendation on voting for these proposals, what would their chances of success be? Do you think that making an argument such as this might have influenced the court?

———

PROBLEM

You represent a corporation which has hired outside counsel for the particular task of advising on takeover defenses. Among the recommendations was that the board recommend to the shareholders that they amend the corporate charter to provide for a staggered board. Further, the outside counsel have recommended that the board adopt a shareholder rights plan that would not require shareholder approval. Counsel has made several presentations to the board about this matter, and has presented a draft of the proposed rights plan, but has suggested that the board not decide whether to adopt a rights plan until after the shareholders' meeting. Proxy advisers to the board are concerned that if multiple takeover defenses are presented to the shareholders at one time, there may be an adverse reaction among institutional investors.

What disclosures about the proposed rights plan, if any, should be made in the proxy materials?

I.   THE MERGER TAX AND CORPORATE REACTIONS

When a merger of public companies is announced, shareholder class actions challenging the decision of the seller's board arise as night follows day. The author was on a board that approved a sale of the company, and outside counsel advised the directors that he had seen as few as two and as many as twenty separate suits follow the announcement. In the author's case the deal obtained an 89% premium over the pre-announcement bid, suggesting that claims of inadequate compliance with Revlon duties were quite weak. Frequently the plaintiffs' attorneys will settle for cosmetic changes in the disclosures proposed in the board's public disclosures. These disclosures obtain no substantive improvement in the deal price, which was the essence of the complaint. In many cases the defendants simply move to oppose the grant of a preliminary injunction and for dismissal. At this point the predictable response is negotiations over settlement, which involve cosmetic and sometimes immaterial changes in the proxy statement, and agreement on the award of fees to the plaintiffs' attorneys. In recent years the Delaware Chancery Court has challenged many of these settlements as providing little or no substantial benefit for the shareholders, and has reduced the amount of the fee award.* More recently, it has denied approval to such settlements altogether.

With this attitude facing them, many plaintiffs' attorneys began to bring suit against Delaware corporate defendants in other jurisdictions, in the hope that this might provide friendlier treatment of attorneys' fees in disclosure-only cases. (Often these cases begin with claims of Revlon

---

*   Phillip R. Sumpter, *Adjusting Attorneys' Fee Awards: The Delaware Court of Chancery's Answer to Incentivizing Meritorious Disclosure-Only Settlements*, 15 U. PA. BUS. L. 669 (2013).

violations, but when it becomes obvious these are weak claims, evolve into settlements based on agreed-upon supplemental disclosures. Chancellor Leo Strine has written on the subject, noting that corporations incorporate in Delaware in order to select its law as the governing law, regardless of where suits are brought, under the Internal Affairs Doctrine.*

Delaware corporations have responded to the proliferation of jurisdictions in which they might be sued by adopting by-laws that state that venue over all such suits lies exclusively in Delaware, a position of which Chancellor Strine approved, arguing that Delaware judges were the most authoritative source of Delaware law.

---

* Leo Strine, Jr., Putting Stockholders First, Not the First-Filed Complaint, 69 BUS. LAW. 1 (2013).

CHAPTER SEVEN

STATE TAKEOVER LAWS

In this chapter we examine the legislative response of the states to hostile takeover bids. We have previously examined the defensive measures available to target companies to protect shareholders from coercive or inadequate bids, and the more general provisions of state appraisal statutes to protection of minority interests in mergers. The student should ask, while reading this chapter, what market failures might justify further legislation to regulate takeovers, or perhaps what market failures have fostered the adoption of these statutes. The other way to examine this area, especially with the later takeover statutes, is to ask whether management, as an interest group, was likely to have been responsible for lobbying for antitakeover laws that were either "opt-out," so management had to take no action to obtain protection, or opt-in through board action where previously shareholder approval might have been required for a change in the articles of incorporation. These laws may have been passed to accommodate local target management teams when they found themselves unable to secure shareholder approval of shark repellent amendments or unable to avoid shareholder disapproval of defenses such as poison pills.

1. FIRST GENERATION DISCLOSURE AND "FAIRNESS" STATUTES

The following case involves a typical "first generation" state takeover statute. Beginning in 1968, 37 states adopted such statutes in the following 13 years. Roberta Romano, Law as a Product: Some Pieces of the Incorporation Puzzle, 1 Journal of Law, Economics and Organization 225, 234 (1985).

Edgar v. MITE Corp.
102 S.Ct. 2629, 73 L.Ed.2d 269 (1982).

■ JUSTICE WHITE delivered an opinion, Parts I, II, and V-B of which are the opinion of the Court.*

The issue in this case is whether the Illinois Business Take-Over Act, Ill. Rev. Stat., ch. 121½, para. 137.51 et seq. (1979), is unconstitutional under the Supremacy and Commerce Clauses of the Federal Constitution.

---

* The Chief Justice joins the opinion in its entirety; Justice Blackmun joins Parts I, II, III, and IV; Justice Powell joins Parts I and V-B; and Justice Stevens and Justice O'Connor join Parts I, II, and V.

I

Appellee MITE Corp. and its wholly owned subsidiary, MITE Holdings, Inc., are corporations organized under the laws of Delaware with their principal executive offices in Connecticut. Appellant James Edgar is the Secretary of State of Illinois and is charged with the administration and enforcement of the Illinois Act. Under the Illinois Act any takeover offer for the shares of a target company must be registered with the Secretary of State. A target company is defined as a corporation or other issuer of securities of which shareholders located in Illinois own 10% of the class of equity securities subject to the offer, or for which any two of the following three conditions are met: the corporation has its principal executive office in Illinois, is organized under the laws of Illinois, or has at least 10% of its stated capital and paid-in surplus represented within the State. An offer becomes registered 20 days after a registration statement is filed with the Secretary unless the Secretary calls a hearing. The Secretary may call a hearing at any time during the 20-day waiting period to adjudicate the substantive fairness of the offer if he believes it is necessary to protect the shareholders of the target company, and a hearing must be held if requested by a majority of a target company's outside directors or by Illinois shareholders who own 10% of the class of securities subject to the offer. If the Secretary does hold a hearing, he is directed by the statute to deny registration to a tender offer if he finds that it "fails to provide full and fair disclosure to the offerees of all material information concerning the take-over offer, or that the take-over offer is inequitable or would work or tend to work a fraud or deceit upon the offerees. . . ."

On January 19, 1979, MITE initiated a cash tender offer for all outstanding shares of Chicago Rivet & Machine Co., a publicly held Illinois corporation, by filing a Schedule 14D-1 with the Securities and Exchange Commission in order to comply with the Williams Act. The Schedule 14D-1 indicated that MITE was willing to pay $28 per share for any and all outstanding shares of Chicago Rivet, a premium of approximately $4 over the then-prevailing market price. MITE did not comply with the Illinois Act, however, and commenced this litigation on the same day by filing an action in the United States District Court for the Northern District of Illinois. The complaint asked for a declaratory judgment that the Illinois Act was pre-empted by the Williams Act and violated the Commerce Clause. In addition, MITE sought a temporary restraining order and preliminary and permanent injunctions prohibiting the Illinois Secretary of State from enforcing the Illinois Act.

* * * On . . . February 2 the District Court issued a preliminary injunction prohibiting the Secretary of State from enforcing the Illinois Act against MITE's tender offer for Chicago Rivet.

* * *

The United States Court of Appeals for the Seventh Circuit affirmed sub nom. MITE Corp. v. Dixon, 633 F.2d 486 (1980). It agreed with the District Court that several provisions of the Illinois Act are pre-empted by the Williams Act and that the Illinois Act unduly burdens interstate commerce in violation of the Commerce Clause. We noted probable jurisdiction, 451 U.S. 968 (1981), and now affirm.

* * *

III

We first address the holding that the Illinois Take-Over Act is unconstitutional under the Supremacy Clause. We note at the outset that in passing the Williams Act, which is an amendment to the Securities Exchange Act of 1934, Congress did not also amend § 28(a) of the 1934 Act, 15 U.S.C. § 78bb(a).[1] In pertinent part, § 28(a) provides as follows:

> "Nothing in this title shall affect the jurisdiction of the securities commission (or any agency or officer performing like functions) of any State over any security or any person insofar as it does not conflict with the provisions of this title or the rules and regulations thereunder." 48 Stat. 903.

Thus Congress did not explicitly prohibit States from regulating takeovers; it left the determination whether the Illinois statute conflicts with the Williams Act to the courts. Of course, a state statute is void to the extent that it actually conflicts with a valid federal statute; and

> "[a] conflict will be found 'where compliance with both federal and state regulations is a physical impossibility . . . ,' Florida Lime & Avocado Growers, Inc. v. Paul, 373 U.S. 132, 142–143 (1963), or where the state 'law stands as an obstacle to the accomplishment and execution of the full purposes and objectives of Congress.' "

Our inquiry is further narrowed in this case since there is no contention that it would be impossible to comply with both the provisions of the Williams Act and the more burdensome requirements of the Illinois law. The issue thus is . . . whether the Illinois Act frustrates the objectives of the Williams Act in some substantial way.

The Williams Act, passed in 1968, was the congressional response to the increased use of cash tender offers in corporate acquisitions, a device that had "removed a substantial number of corporate control contests from the reach of existing disclosure requirements of the federal securities laws." The Williams Act filled this regulatory gap. The Act imposes several requirements. First, it requires that upon the

---

[1]   There is no evidence in the legislative history that Congress was aware of state takeover laws when it enacted the Williams Act. When the Williams Act was enacted in 1968, only Virginia had a takeover statute. The Virginia statute, Va. Code § 13.1–528 (1978), became effective March 5, 1968; the Williams Act was enacted several months later on July 19, 1968. Takeover statutes are now in effect in 37 States. Sargent, On the Validity of State Takeover Regulation: State Responses to MITE and Kidwell, 42 Ohio St. L. J. 689, 690, n. 7 (1981).

commencement of the tender offer, the offeror file with the SEC, publish or send to the shareholders of the target company, and furnish to the target company detailed information about the offer. * * * Second, stockholders who tender their shares may withdraw them during the first 7 days of a tender offer and if the offeror has not yet purchased their shares, at any time after 60 days from the commencement of the offer. Third, all shares tendered must be purchased for the same price; if an offering price is increased, those who have already tendered receive the benefit of the increase.

There is no question that in imposing these requirements, Congress intended to protect investors. But it is also crystal clear that a major aspect of the effort to protect the investor was to avoid favoring either management or the takeover bidder. * * * As the legislation evolved, therefore, Congress disclaimed any "intention to provide a weapon for management to discourage takeover bids," and expressly embraced a policy of neutrality. As Senator Williams explained: "We have taken extreme care to avoid tipping the scales either in favor of management or in favor of the person making the takeover bids." This policy of "evenhandedness," represented a conviction that neither side in the contest should be extended additional advantages vis-a-vis the investor, who if furnished with adequate information would be in a position to make his own informed choice. We, therefore, agree with the Court of Appeals that Congress sought to protect the investor not only by furnishing him with the necessary information but also by withholding from management or the bidder any undue advantage that could frustrate the exercise of an informed choice. * * *

IV

The Court of Appeals identified three provisions of the Illinois Act that upset the careful balance struck by Congress and which therefore stand as obstacles to the accomplishment and execution of the full purposes and objectives of Congress. We agree with the Court of Appeals in all essential respects.

A

The Illinois Act requires a tender offeror to notify the Secretary of State and the target company of its intent to make a tender offer and the material terms of the offer 20 business days before the offer becomes effective. During that time, the offeror may not communicate its offer to the shareholders. Meanwhile, the target company is free to disseminate information to its shareholders concerning the impending offer. The contrast with the Williams Act is apparent. Under that Act, there is no precommencement notification requirement; the critical date is the date a tender offer is "first published or sent or given to security holders." 15 U.S.C. § 78n(d)(1). See also 17 CFR § 240.14d–2 (1981).

We agree with the Court of Appeals that by providing the target company with additional time within which to take steps to combat the offer, the precommencement notification provisions furnish incumbent management with a powerful tool to combat tender offers, perhaps to the detriment of the stockholders who will not have an offer before them during this period. These consequences are precisely what Congress determined should be avoided, and for this reason, the precommencement notification provision frustrates the objectives of the Williams Act.

* * *

B

For similar reasons, we agree with the Court of Appeals that the hearing provisions of the Illinois Act frustrate the congressional purpose by introducing extended delay into the tender offer process. The Illinois Act allows the Secretary of State to call a hearing with respect to any tender offer subject to the Act, and the offer may not proceed until the hearing is completed. The Secretary may call a hearing at any time prior to the commencement of the offer, and there is no deadline for the completion of the hearing. Although the Secretary is to render a decision within 15 days after the conclusion of the hearing, that period may be extended without limitation. Not only does the Secretary of State have the power to delay a tender offer indefinitely, but incumbent management may also use the hearing provisions of the Illinois Act to delay a tender offer. The Secretary is required to call a hearing if requested to do so by, among other persons, those who are located in Illinois "as determined by post office address as shown on the records of the target company and who hold of record or beneficially, or both, at least 10% of the outstanding shares of any class of equity securities which is the subject of the take-over offer." Since incumbent management in many cases will control, either directly or indirectly, 10% of the *target company's shares, this provision allows management to delay the commencement of an offer by insisting on a hearing. As the Court of Appeals observed, these provisions potentially afford management a "powerful weapon to stymie indefinitely a takeover." In enacting the Williams Act, Congress itself "recognized that delay can seriously impede a tender offer" and sought to avoid it.

* * *

As we have said, Congress anticipated that investors and the takeover offeror would be free to go forward without unreasonable delay. The potential for delay provided by the hearing provisions upset the balance struck by Congress by favoring management at the expense of stockholders. We therefore agree with the Court of Appeals that these hearing provisions conflict with the Williams Act.

C

The Court of Appeals also concluded that the Illinois Act is pre-empted by the Williams Act insofar as it allows the Secretary of State of

Illinois to pass on the substantive fairness of a tender offer. Under para. 137.57.E of the Illinois law, the Secretary is required to deny registration of a takeover offer if he finds that the offer "fails to provide full and fair disclosure to the offerees . . . or that the take-over offer is inequitable . . ." (emphasis added). The Court of Appeals understood the Williams Act and its legislative history to indicate that Congress intended for investors to be free to make their own decisions. We agree. Both the House and Senate Reports observed that the Act was "designed to make the relevant facts known so that shareholders have a fair opportunity to make their decision." Thus, as the Court of Appeals said, "[the] state thus offers investor protection at the expense of investor autonomy—an approach quite in conflict with that adopted by Congress."

V

The Commerce Clause provides that "Congress shall have Power . . . [to] regulate Commerce . . . among the several States." U.S. Const., Art. I, § 8, cl. 3. "[At] least since Cooley v. Board of Wardens, 12 How. 299 (1852), it has been clear that 'the Commerce Clause . . . even without implementing legislation by Congress is a limitation upon the power of the States.'" Not every exercise of state power with some impact on interstate commerce is invalid. A state statute must be upheld if it "regulates evenhandedly to effectuate a legitimate local public interest, and its effects on interstate commerce are only incidental . . . unless the burden imposed on such commerce is clearly excessive in relation to the putative local benefits." Pike v. Bruce Church, Inc., 397 U.S. 137, 142 (1970), citing Huron Cement Co. v. Detroit, 362 U.S. 440, 443 (1960). The Commerce Clause, however, permits only incidental regulation of interstate commerce by the States; direct regulation is prohibited. The Illinois Act violates these principles for two reasons. First, it directly regulates and prevents, unless its terms are satisfied, interstate tender offers which in turn would generate interstate transactions. Second, the burden the Act imposes on interstate commerce is excessive in light of the local interests the Act purports to further.

A

States have traditionally regulated intrastate securities transactions,[16] and this Court has upheld the authority of States to enact "blue-sky" laws against Commerce Clause challenges on several occasions. Hall v. Geiger-Jones Co., 242 U.S. 539 (1917); Caldwell v. Sioux Falls Stock Yards Co., 242 U.S. 559 (1917); Merrick v. N. W. Halsey & Co., 242 U.S. 568 (1917). The Court's rationale for upholding blue-sky laws was that they only regulated transactions occurring within the regulating States. * * * Congress has also recognized the validity of such laws governing intrastate securities transactions in § 28(a) of the

---

[16] For example, the Illinois blue-sky law, Ill. Rev. Stat., ch. 121 ½, para. 137.1 et seq. (1979 and Supp. 1980), provides that securities subject to the law must be registered "prior to sale in this State. . . ." para. 137.5.

Securities Exchange Act, a provision "designed to save state blue-sky laws from pre-emption."

The Illinois Act differs substantially from state blue-sky laws in that it directly regulates transactions which take place across state lines, even if wholly outside the State of Illinois. A tender offer for securities of a publicly held corporation is ordinarily communicated by the use of the mails or other means of interstate commerce to shareholders across the country and abroad. Securities are tendered and transactions closed by similar means. Thus, in this case, MITE Corp., the tender offeror, is a Delaware corporation with principal offices in Connecticut. Chicago Rivet is a publicly held Illinois corporation with shareholders scattered around the country, 27% of whom live in Illinois. MITE's offer to Chicago Rivet's shareholders, including those in Illinois, necessarily employed interstate facilities in communicating its offer, which, if accepted, would result in transactions occurring across state lines. These transactions would themselves be interstate commerce. Yet the Illinois law, unless complied with, sought to prevent MITE from making its offer and concluding interstate transactions not only with Chicago Rivet's stockholders living in Illinois, but also with those living in other States and having no connection with Illinois. * * *

It is therefore apparent that the Illinois statute is a direct restraint on interstate commerce and that it has a sweeping extraterritorial effect. Furthermore, if Illinois may impose such regulations, so may other States; and interstate commerce in securities transactions generated by tender offers would be thoroughly stifled. In Shaffer v. Farmers' Grain Co., *supra*, [268 U.S. 189] at 199, the Court held that "a state statute which by its necessary operation directly interferes with or burdens [interstate] commerce is a prohibited regulation and invalid, regardless of the purpose with which it was enacted." The Commerce Clause also precludes the application of a state statute to commerce that takes place wholly outside of the State's borders, whether or not the commerce has effects within the State. * * *

Because the Illinois Act purports to regulate directly and to interdict interstate commerce, including commerce wholly outside the State, it must be held invalid as were the laws at issue in Shaffer v. Farmers Grain Co. and Southern Pacific.

B

The Illinois Act is also unconstitutional under the test of Pike v. Bruce Church, Inc., 397 U.S., at 142, for even when a state statute regulates interstate commerce indirectly, the burden imposed on that commerce must not be excessive in relation to the local interests served by the statute. The most obvious burden the Illinois Act imposes on interstate commerce arises from the statute's previously described nationwide reach which purports to give Illinois the power to determine whether a tender offer may proceed anywhere.

* * *

Appellant also contends that Illinois has an interest in regulating the internal affairs of a corporation incorporated under its laws. The internal affairs doctrine is a conflict of laws principle which recognizes that only one State should have the authority to regulate a corporation's internal affairs—matters peculiar to the relationships among or between the corporation and its current officers, directors, and shareholders—because otherwise a corporation could be faced with conflicting demands. See Restatement (Second) of Conflict of Laws § 302, Comment b, pp. 307–308 (1971). That doctrine is of little use to the State in this context. Tender offers contemplate transfers of stock by stockholders to a third party and do not themselves implicate the internal affairs of the target company. Furthermore, the proposed justification is somewhat incredible since the Illinois Act applies to tender offers for any corporation for which 10% of the outstanding shares are held by Illinois residents. The Act thus applies to corporations that are not incorporated in Illinois and have their principal place of business in other States. Illinois has no interest in regulating the internal affairs of foreign corporations.

We conclude with the Court of Appeals that the Illinois Act imposes a substantial burden on interstate commerce which outweighs its putative local benefits. It is accordingly invalid under the Commerce Clause.

The judgment of the Court of Appeals is

Affirmed.

QUESTIONS

1. Why do timing differences for disclosure between Illinois and federal regulation create a conflict that requires preemption, in the view of Justices White and Blackmun and Chief Justice Burger?

2. Why do requirements in the Illinois Act concerning a hearing by the Illinois Securities Commissioner on compliance with Illinois law create a conflict with federal regulation in Justice White's opinion?

3. Until 1996 section 18 of the Securities Act of 1933 read as follows: "Nothing in this title shall affect the jurisdiction of the securities commission (or any agency or office performing like functions) of any State or Territory of the United States, or the District of Columbia, over any security or any person." Various states had adopted securities laws that gave local regulators the authority to prohibit offerings that they did not believe were "fair, just and equitable" to local investors. These statutes were never treated as preempted by the Securities Act of 1933, which is purely a disclosure statute. Why does Justice White's opinion find a conflict with the Williams Act, in view of similar language in section 28(a) of the Securities Exchange Act?

4. Under the same statutes as described in question 4, why does Justice White's opinion find that the Illinois statute is a burden on commerce in a way that state blue sky laws are not?

5. Mr. Justice White's opinion stated that there was no contention that it would be impossible to comply with the terms of both the Illinois law and the Williams Act. He also stated in footnote 11 (not included in this edited version) that SEC Rule 14d–2(b), defining the beginning of a tender offer and requiring withdrawal within five days if the offer does not actually begin, became effective after the tender offer in Edgar v. Mite began. Recall that Justice White's opinion on the Supremacy Clause (Parts III and IV) was joined only by Chief Justice Burger and Justice Blackmun. Would the presence of Rule 14d–2(b) at the time of Mite's tender offer have been likely to cause other justices to join in this part of the opinion? What do you believe the SEC's purpose was in adopting this rule?

6. If the Williams Act already requires adequate disclosure of takeover bids, both of a prospective bidder's intent to make such a bid in Schedule 13D and of the terms of the bid, and the bidder's future plans and proposals in Schedule 14D-1, what further benefits could be provided for target shareholders by statutes such as the Illinois act?

7. Why does Justice White's opinion point out in Part V.B. that the Illinois statute did not regulate self-tender offers by a target?

8. The "internal affairs" doctrine of choice of law recognizes that only one jurisdiction should be allowed to regulate relations within a corporation. (See Rev. Model Bus. Corp. Act § 15.05(c)), which codifies this rule in many jurisdictions.) Why does the majority (White, Burger, Powell, Stevens and O'Connor) reject this as a justification for the Illinois act's interference with interstate commerce in Part V.B?

---

2. SECOND GENERATION STATUTES, THE WILLIAMS ACT AND THE COMMERCE CLAUSE

The decision in Edgar v. MITE Corp. led to declarations that a number of other first-generation statutes were also invalid, and to legislative repeal of many of the others. It was clear that these statutes were dead letters after 1982. A "second generation" of state takeover statutes followed quickly. These statutes abandoned the securities regulation model in favor of a corporate law model, applicable only to locally incorporated firms. The earliest form of the so-called "second generation" statutes to be widely adopted was the so-called "fair price" statute, which required mergers with "interested shareholders" (bidders that had acquired a significant stock position but had not received prior approval of the target's board) to secure high shareholder votes to approve mergers between bidder and target. This type of statute was adopted by 23 states in eight years, and by 27 states by 1999. While it could also be adopted through a charter amendment, the advantage of the statute, from the perspective of corporate management, was that it was optional, either because corporations could opt out of its coverage or opt into its coverage through action of the board of directors, without the shareholder approval required for charter amendments. Romano has described the role of corporate management in lobbying for the Connecticut version of this statute.* For a discussion of the rate of adoption of these statutes and their sponsorship by corporate management, see William J. Carney, The Production of Corporate Law, 71 So. Cal. L. Rev. 715 (1998).

Two forms of second generation takeover statutes could be seen as substitutes for each other, although many states chose to adopt both. In the "control share" statutes, considered in this part, a bidder was stripped of voting rights upon reaching certain ownership thresholds, unless voting power was restored by the remaining shareholders. It is considered in the following case. It was adopted by 25 states in eight years, and 15 of these states adopted such a statute in the three years after the Supreme Court's decision in CTS Corp. v. Dynamics Corporation of America, below. By1999 27 states had adopted such laws. In "business combination" statutes, the alternative form, considered in the next section of this chapter, mergers between bidder and target were forbidden for a period of time, usually three years from the bidder's acquisition of a significant ownership position, with certain exceptions. These statutes were adopted by 23 states in 12 years, and in 19 states in the first four years. By 1999 33 states had adopted such statutes. If these two statutes are taken together, one or both of them were adopted by 34 states in eight years. Few adoptions occurred after 1991, largely because a recession in the United States and the collapse of the junk bond market that provided financing for some hostile takeovers eliminated the major sources of financing for hostile takeovers. With a small resurgence in hostile takeovers, two more states added such statutes in 1997.

CTS Corp. v. Dynamics Corporation of America

481 U.S. 69, 107 S.Ct. 1637, 95 L.Ed.2d 67 (1987).

■ JUSTICE POWELL delivered the opinion of the Court.

These cases present the questions whether the Control Share Acquisitions Chapter of the Indiana Business Corporation Law, Ind. Code § 23–1–42–1 et seq. (Supp. 1986), is pre-empted by the Williams Act, or violates the Commerce Clause of the Federal Constitution.

---

*   Roberta Romano, The Political Economy of Takeover Statutes, 73 Virginia Law Review 111, 122–26 (1987).

I

A

* * * Beginning on August 1, 1987, the Act will apply to any corporation incorporated in Indiana, unless the corporation amends its articles of incorporation or bylaws to opt out of the Act. Before that date, any Indiana corporation can opt into the Act by resolution of its board of directors. The Act applies only to "issuing public corporations." The term "corporation" includes only businesses incorporated in Indiana. An "issuing public corporation" is defined as:

"a corporation that has:

"(1) one hundred (100) or more shareholders;

"(2) its principal place of business, its principal office, or substantial assets within Indiana; and

"(3) either:

"(A) more than ten percent (10%) of its shareholders resident in Indiana;

"(B) more than ten percent (10%) of its shares owned by Indiana residents; or

"(C) ten thousand (10,000) shareholders resident in Indiana." § 23–1–42–4(a).

The Act focuses on the acquisition of "control shares" in an issuing public corporation. Under the Act, an entity acquires "control shares" whenever it acquires shares that, but for the operation of the Act, would bring its voting power in the corporation to or above any of three thresholds: 20%, 33 1/3%, or 50%. An entity that acquires control shares does not necessarily acquire voting rights. Rather, it gains those rights only "to the extent granted by resolution approved by the shareholders of the issuing public corporation." Section 23–1–42–9(b) requires a majority vote of all disinterested[1] shareholders holding each class of stock for

---

[1] "Interested shares" are shares with respect to which the acquiror, an officer, or an inside director of the corporation "may exercise or direct the exercise of the voting power of the corporation in the election of directors." § 23–1–42–3. If the record date passes before the acquiror purchases shares pursuant to the tender offer, the purchased shares will not be "interested shares" within the meaning of the Act; although the acquiror may own the shares on the date of the meeting, it will not "exercise . . . the voting power" of the shares.

As a practical matter, the record date usually will pass before shares change hands. Under Securities and Exchange Commission (SEC) regulations, the shares cannot be purchased until 20 business days after the offer commences. 17 CFR § 240.14e–1(a) (1986). If the acquiror seeks an early resolution of the issue—as most acquirors will—the meeting required by the Act must be held no more than 50 calendar days after the offer commences, about three weeks after the earliest date on which the shares could be purchased. See § 23–1–42–7. The Act requires management to give notice of the meeting "as promptly as reasonably practicable . . . to all shareholders of record as of the record date set for the meeting." § 23–1–42–8(a). It seems likely that management of the target corporation would violate this obligation if it delayed setting the record date and sending notice until after 20 business days had passed. Thus, we assume that the record date usually will be set before the date on which federal law first permits purchase of the shares.

passage of such a resolution. The practical effect of this requirement is to condition acquisition of control of a corporation on approval of a majority of the pre-existing disinterested shareholders.

The shareholders decide whether to confer rights on the control shares at the next regularly scheduled meeting of the shareholders, or at a specially scheduled meeting. The acquiror can require management of the corporation to hold such a special meeting within 50 days if it files an "acquiring person statement,"[4] requests the meeting, and agrees to pay the expenses of the meeting. If the shareholders do not vote to restore voting rights to the shares, the corporation may redeem the control shares from the acquiror at fair market value, but it is not required to do so. Similarly, if the acquiror does not file an acquiring person statement with the corporation, the corporation may, if its bylaws or articles of incorporation so provide, redeem the shares at any time after 60 days after the acquiror's last acquisition.

B

On March 10, 1986, appellee Dynamics Corporation of America (Dynamics) owned 9.6% of the common stock of appellant CTS Corporation, an Indiana corporation. On that day, six days after the Act went into effect, Dynamics announced a tender offer for another million shares in CTS; purchase of those shares would have brought Dynamics' ownership interest in CTS to 27.5%. * * * On March 27, the board of directors of CTS, an Indiana corporation, elected to be governed by the provisions of the Act.

Four days later, on March 31, Dynamics moved for leave to amend its complaint to allege that the Act is pre-empted by the Williams Act, and violates the Commerce Clause, Art. I, § 8, cl. 3. Dynamics sought a temporary restraining order, a preliminary injunction, and declaratory relief against CTS' use of the Act. On April 9, the District Court ruled that the Williams Act pre-empts the Indiana Act and granted Dynamics' motion for declaratory relief. * * * A week later, on April 17, the District Court issued an opinion accepting Dynamics' claim that the Act violates the Commerce Clause. * * *

* * * On April 23—23 days after Dynamics first contested application of the Act in the District Court—the Court of Appeals issued an order affirming the judgment of the District Court. * * *

II

The first question in these cases is whether the Williams Act pre-empts the Indiana Act. As we have stated frequently, absent an explicit indication by Congress of an intent to pre-empt state law, a state statute is pre-empted only

---

[4] An "acquiring person statement" is an information statement describing, inter alia, the identity of the acquiring person and the terms and extent of the proposed acquisition. See § 23–1–42–6.

" 'where compliance with both federal and state regulations is a physical impossibility . . . ,' or where the state 'law stands as an obstacle to the accomplishment and execution of the full purposes and objectives of Congress. . . .' " Ray v. Atlantic Richfield Co., 435 U.S. 151, 158 (1978).

Because it is entirely possible for entities to comply with both the Williams Act and the Indiana Act, the state statute can be pre-empted only if it frustrates the purposes of the federal law.

A

* * * The Williams ... requires the offeror to file a statement disclosing information about the offer, including: the offeror's background and identity; the source and amount of the funds to be used in making the purchase; the purpose of the purchase, including any plans to liquidate the company or make major changes in its corporate structure; and the extent of the offeror's holdings in the target company.

Second, the Williams Act, and the regulations that accompany it, establish procedural rules to govern tender offers. For example, stockholders who tender their shares may withdraw them while the offer remains open, and, if the offeror has not purchased their shares, any time after 60 days from commencement of the offer. The offer must remain open for at least 20 business days. If more shares are tendered than the offeror sought to purchase, purchases must be made on a pro rata basis from each tendering shareholder. Finally, the offeror must pay the same price for all purchases; if the offering price is increased before the end of the offer, those who already have tendered must receive the benefit of the increased price.

B

The Indiana Act differs in major respects from the Illinois statute that the Court considered in Edgar v. MITE Corp., 457 U.S. 624 (1982). After reviewing the legislative history of the Williams Act, Justice White, joined by Chief Justice Burger and Justice Blackmun (the plurality), concluded that the Williams Act struck a careful balance between the interests of offerors and target companies, and that any state statute that "upset" this balance was pre-empted.

The plurality then identified three offending features of the Illinois statute. * * * Justice White's opinion first noted that the Illinois statute provided for a 20-day precommencement period. During this time, management could disseminate its views on the upcoming offer to shareholders, but offerors could not publish their offers. The plurality found that this provision gave management "a powerful tool to combat tender offers." This contrasted dramatically with the Williams Act; Congress had deleted express precommencement notice provisions from the Williams Act. According to the plurality, Congress had determined that the potentially adverse consequences of such a provision on shareholders should be avoided. Thus, the plurality concluded that the Illinois provision "frustrate[d] the objectives of the Williams Act." The second criticized feature of the Illinois statute was a provision for a hearing on a tender offer that, because it set no deadline, allowed management "to stymie indefinitely a takeover." The plurality noted that " 'delay can seriously impede a tender offer,' " and that "Congress anticipated that investors and the takeover offeror would be free to go forward without unreasonable delay." Accordingly, the plurality concluded that this provision conflicted with the Williams Act. The third troublesome feature of the Illinois statute was its requirement that the fairness of tender offers would be reviewed by the Illinois Secretary of State. Noting that "Congress intended for investors to be free to make their own decisions," the plurality concluded that " '[t]he state thus offers investor protection at the expense of investor autonomy—an approach quite in conflict with that adopted by Congress.' "

C

As the plurality opinion in MITE did not represent the views of a majority of the Court,[5] we are not bound by its reasoning. We need not question that reasoning, however, because we believe the Indiana Act passes muster even under the broad interpretation of the Williams Act articulated by Justice White in MITE. As is apparent from our summary of its reasoning, the overriding concern of the MITE plurality was that the Illinois statute considered in that case operated to favor management against offerors, to the detriment of shareholders. By contrast, the statute now before the Court protects the independent shareholder against the contending parties. Thus, the Act furthers a basic purpose of the Williams Act, " 'plac[ing] investors on an equal footing with the takeover bidder' ".

The Indiana Act operates on the assumption, implicit in the Williams Act, that independent shareholders faced with tender offers often are at a disadvantage. By allowing such shareholders to vote as a group, the Act protects them from the coercive aspects of some tender offers. If, for example, shareholders believe that a successful tender offer will be followed by a purchase of nontendering shares at a depressed price, individual shareholders may tender their shares—even if they doubt the tender offer is in the corporation's best interest—to protect themselves from being forced to sell their shares at a depressed price. * * * In such a situation under the Indiana Act, the shareholders as a group, acting in the corporation's best interest, could reject the offer, although individual shareholders might be inclined to accept it. The

---

[5]   Justice White's opinion on the pre-emption issue, 457 U.S., at 630–640, was joined only by Chief Justice Burger and by Justice Blackmun. Two Justices disagreed with Justice White's conclusion. See id., at 646–647 (POWELL, J., concurring in part); id., at 655 (STEVENS, J., concurring in part and concurring in judgment). Four Justices did not address the question. See id., at 655 (O'CONNOR, J., concurring in part); id., at 664 (MARSHALL, J., with whom BRENNAN, J., joined, dissenting); id., at 667 (REHNQUIST, J., dissenting).

desire of the Indiana Legislature to protect shareholders of Indiana corporations from this type of coercive offer does not conflict with the Williams Act. Rather, it furthers the federal policy of investor protection.

In implementing its goal, the Indiana Act avoids the problems the plurality discussed in MITE. Unlike the MITE statute, the Indiana Act does not give either management or the offeror an advantage in communicating with the shareholders about the impending offer. The Act also does not impose an indefinite delay on tender offers. Nothing in the Act prohibits an offeror from consummating an offer on the 20th business day, the earliest day permitted under applicable federal regulations, see 17 CFR § 240.14e–1(a) (1986). Nor does the Act allow the state government to interpose its views of fairness between willing buyers and sellers of shares of the target company. Rather, the Act allows shareholders to evaluate the fairness of the offer collectively.

D

The Court of Appeals based its finding of pre-emption on its view that the practical effect of the Indiana Act is to delay consummation of tender offers until 50 days after the commencement of the offer. As did the Court of Appeals, Dynamics reasons that no rational offeror will purchase shares until it gains assurance that those shares will carry voting rights. Because it is possible that voting rights will not be conferred until a shareholder meeting 50 days after commencement of the offer, Dynamics concludes that the Act imposes a 50-day delay. This, it argues, conflicts with the shorter 20-business-day period established by the SEC as the minimum period for which a tender offer may be held open. We find the alleged conflict illusory.

The Act does not impose an absolute 50-day delay on tender offers, nor does it preclude an offeror from purchasing shares as soon as federal law permits. If the offeror fears an adverse shareholder vote under the Act, it can make a conditional tender offer, offering to accept shares on the condition that the shares receive voting rights within a certain period of time. The Williams Act permits tender offers to be conditioned on the offeror's subsequently obtaining regulatory approval. There is no reason to doubt that this type of conditional tender offer would be legitimate as well.[9]

Even assuming that the Indiana Act imposes some additional delay, nothing in MITE suggested that any delay imposed by state regulation, however short, would create a conflict with the Williams Act. The

---

[9] Dynamics argues that conditional tender offers are not an adequate alternative because they leave management in place for three extra weeks, with "free rein to take other defensive steps that will diminish the value of tendered shares." Brief for Appellee 37. We reject this contention. In the unlikely event that management were to take actions designed to diminish the value of the corporation's shares, it may incur liability under state law. But this problem does not control our pre-emption analysis. Neither the Act nor any other federal statute can assure that shareholders do not suffer from the mismanagement of corporate officers and directors. Cf. Cort v. Ash, 422 U.S. 66, 84 (1975).

plurality argued only that the offeror should "be free to go forward without unreasonable delay." 457 U.S., at 639 (emphasis added). In that case, the Court was confronted with the potential for indefinite delay and presented with no persuasive reason why some deadline could not be established. By contrast, the Indiana Act provides that full voting rights will be vested—if this eventually is to occur—within 50 days after commencement of the offer. This period is within the 60-day period Congress established for reinstitution of withdrawal rights in 15 U. S. C. § 78n(d)(5). We cannot say that a delay within that congressionally determined period is unreasonable.

Finally, we note that the Williams Act would pre-empt a variety of state corporate laws of hitherto unquestioned validity if it were construed to pre-empt any state statute that may limit or delay the free exercise of power after a successful tender offer. State corporate laws commonly permit corporations to stagger the terms of their directors. By staggering the terms of directors, and thus having annual elections for only one class of directors each year, corporations may delay the time when a successful offeror gains control of the board of directors. Similarly, state corporation laws commonly provide for cumulative voting. By enabling minority shareholders to assure themselves of representation in each class of directors, cumulative voting provisions can delay further the ability of offerors to gain untrammeled authority over the affairs of the target corporation.

In our view, the possibility that the Indiana Act will delay some tender offers is insufficient to require a conclusion that the Williams Act pre-empts the Act. The longstanding prevalence of state regulation in this area suggests that, if Congress had intended to pre-empt all state laws that delay the acquisition of voting control following a tender offer, it would have said so explicitly. The regulatory conditions that the Act places on tender offers are consistent with the text and the purposes of the Williams Act. Accordingly, we hold that the Williams Act does not pre-empt the Indiana Act.

III

As an alternative basis for its decision, the Court of Appeals held that the Act violates the Commerce Clause of the Federal Constitution. We now address this holding. On its face, the Commerce Clause is nothing more than a grant to Congress of the power "to regulate Commerce . . . among the several States . . . ," Art. I, § 8, cl. 3. But it has been settled for more than a century that the Clause prohibits States from taking certain actions respecting interstate commerce even absent congressional action. See, e. g., Cooley v. Board of Wardens, 12 How. 299 (1852). The Court's interpretation of "these great silences of the Constitution," has not always been easy to follow. Rather, as the volume and complexity of commerce and regulation have grown in this country, the Court has articulated a variety of tests in an attempt to describe the difference between those regulations that the Commerce Clause permits and those regulations that it prohibits.

A

The principal objects of dormant Commerce Clause scrutiny are statutes that discriminate against interstate commerce. The Indiana Act is not such a statute. It has the same effects on tender offers whether or not the offeror is a domiciliary or resident of Indiana. Thus, it "visits its effects equally upon both interstate and local business," Lewis v. BT Investment Managers, Inc., *supra*, at 36.

* * * Because nothing in the Indiana Act imposes a greater burden on out-of-state offerors than it does on similarly situated Indiana offerors, we reject the contention that the Act discriminates against interstate commerce.

B

This Court's recent Commerce Clause cases also have invalidated statutes that may adversely affect interstate commerce by subjecting activities to inconsistent regulations. * * * The Indiana Act poses no such problem. So long as each State regulates voting rights only in the corporations it has created, each corporation will be subject to the law of only one State. No principle of corporation law and practice is more firmly established than a State's authority to regulate domestic corporations, including the authority to define the voting rights of shareholders. See Restatement (Second) of Conflict of Laws § 304 (1971) (concluding that the law of the incorporating State generally should "determine the right of a shareholder to participate in the administration of the affairs of the corporation"). Accordingly, we conclude that the Indiana Act does not create an impermissible risk of inconsistent regulation by different States.

C

The Court of Appeals did not find the Act unconstitutional for either of these threshold reasons. Rather, its decision rested on its view of the Act's potential to hinder tender offers. We think the Court of Appeals failed to appreciate the significance for Commerce Clause analysis of the fact that state regulation of corporate governance is regulation of entities whose very existence and attributes are a product of state law. As Chief Justice Marshall explained:

> "A corporation is an artificial being, invisible, intangible, and existing only in contemplation of law. Being the mere creature of law, it possesses only those properties which the charter of its creation confers upon it, either expressly, or as incidental to its very existence. These are such as are supposed best calculated to effect the object for which it was created." Trustees of Dartmouth College v. Woodward, 4 Wheat. 518, 636 (1819).

Every State in this country has enacted laws regulating corporate governance. By prohibiting certain transactions, and regulating others, such laws necessarily affect certain aspects of interstate commerce. This necessarily is true with respect to corporations with shareholders in States other than the State of incorporation. Large corporations that are listed on national exchanges, or even regional exchanges, will have shareholders in many States and shares that are traded frequently. The markets that facilitate this national and international participation in ownership of corporations are essential for providing capital not only for new enterprises but also for established companies that need to expand their businesses. This beneficial free market system depends at its core upon the fact that a corporation—except in the rarest situations—is organized under, and governed by, the law of a single jurisdiction, traditionally the corporate law of the State of its incorporation.

These regulatory laws may affect directly a variety of corporate transactions. Mergers are a typical example. In view of the substantial effect that a merger may have on the shareholders' interests in a corporation, many States require supermajority votes to approve mergers. See, e. g., 2 MBCA § 73 (requiring approval of a merger by a majority of all shares, rather than simply a majority of votes cast); MBCA § 11.03 (same). By requiring a greater vote for mergers than is required for other transactions, these laws make it more difficult for corporations to merge. State laws also may provide for "dissenters' rights" under which minority shareholders who disagree with corporate decisions to take particular actions are entitled to sell their shares to the corporation at fair market value. By requiring the corporation to purchase the shares of dissenting shareholders, these laws may inhibit a corporation from engaging in the specified transactions.

It thus is an accepted part of the business landscape in this country for States to create corporations, to prescribe their powers, and to define the rights that are acquired by purchasing their shares. A State has an interest in promoting stable relationships among parties involved in the corporations it charters, as well as in ensuring that investors in such corporations have an effective voice in corporate affairs.

There can be no doubt that the Act reflects these concerns. The primary purpose of the Act is to protect the shareholders of Indiana corporations. It does this by affording shareholders, when a takeover offer is made, an opportunity to decide collectively whether the resulting change in voting control of the corporation, as they perceive it, would be desirable. A change of management may have important effects on the shareholders' interests; it is well within the State's role as overseer of corporate governance to offer this opportunity. The autonomy provided by allowing shareholders collectively to determine whether the takeover is advantageous to their interests may be especially beneficial where a hostile tender offer may coerce shareholders into tendering their shares.

* * *

Dynamics argues in any event that the State has "'no legitimate interest in protecting the nonresident shareholders.'" Dynamics relies heavily on the statement by the MITE Court that "insofar as the . . . law burdens out-of-state transactions, there is nothing to be weighed in the balance to sustain the law." But that comment was made in reference to an Illinois law that applied as well to out-of-state corporations as to in-state corporations. We agree that Indiana has no interest in protecting nonresident shareholders of nonresident corporations. But this Act applies only to corporations incorporated in Indiana. We reject the contention that Indiana has no interest in providing for the shareholders of its corporations the voting autonomy granted by the Act. Indiana has a substantial interest in preventing the corporate form from becoming a shield for unfair business dealing. Moreover, unlike the Illinois statute invalidated in MITE, the Indiana Act applies only to corporations that have a substantial number of shareholders in Indiana. See Ind. Code § 23–1–42–4(a)(3) (Supp. 1986). Thus, every application of the Indiana Act will affect a substantial number of Indiana residents, whom Indiana indisputably has an interest in protecting.

D

Dynamics' argument that the Act is unconstitutional ultimately rests on its contention that the Act will limit the number of successful tender offers. There is little evidence that this will occur. But even if true, this result would not substantially affect our Commerce Clause analysis. * * * We have rejected the "notion that the Commerce Clause protects the particular structure or methods of operation in a . . . market." Exxon Corp. v. Governor of Maryland, 437 U.S., at 127. The very commodity that is traded in the securities market is one whose characteristics are defined by state law. Similarly, the very commodity that is traded in the "market for corporate control"—the corporation—is one that owes its existence and attributes to state law. Indiana need not define these commodities as other States do; it need only provide that residents and nonresidents have equal access to them. This Indiana has done. Accordingly, even if the Act should decrease the number of successful tender offers for Indiana corporations, this would not offend the Commerce Clause.[11]

IV

On its face, the Indiana Control Share Acquisitions Chapter evenhandedly determines the voting rights of shares of Indiana corporations. The Act does not conflict with the provisions or purposes of

---

[11] CTS also contends that the Act does not violate the Commerce Clause—regardless of any burdens it may impose on interstate commerce—because a corporation's decision to be covered by the Act is purely "private" activity beyond the reach of the Commerce Clause. Because we reverse the judgment of the Court of Appeals on other grounds, we have no occasion to consider this argument.

the Williams Act. To the limited extent that the Act affects interstate commerce, this is justified by the State's interests in defining the attributes of shares in its corporations and in protecting shareholders. Congress has never questioned the need for state regulation of these matters. Nor do we think such regulation offends the Constitution. Accordingly, we reverse the judgment of the Court of Appeals.

It is so ordered.

QUESTIONS

1. Justice Powell's majority opinion concludes that the Indiana Act, unlike the Illinois Act in MITE, does not conflict with the Williams Act because the voting provisions provide protection for target shareholders against an unfair or coercive bid, by allowing them to vote on it in advance. How does this differ from the fairness review by the Illinois Securities Commissioner that the MITE plurality found in conflict with the even-handed approach of the Williams Act?

2. What is the significance of the fact that Justice Powell, writing for the majority, took care to distinguish the Illinois statute's conflicts with the Williams Act, when he did not join in the preemption portion of Justice White's MITE opinion? It is also worth noting that Justice White, author of the MITE plurality opinion, along with Justice Blackmun, dissented from Justice Powell's opinion on preemption grounds. They were joined in their dissent by Justice Stevens, who had not joined Justice White on preemption grounds in MITE.

3. Note that if the shareholders do not vote to restore voting rights to the control shares, the corporation may redeem the control shares from the acquiror at fair market value, but it is not required to do so. If a bidder has paid a control premium to acquire shares in a tender offer, only to lose the votes attached to them, is the fair market value of non-voting common stock likely to be as high as the price the bidder paid? Is this a financial penalty for conducting a tender offer?

4. Justice Powell's opinion also states that, unlike the Illinois Act, the Indiana Act protects independent shareholders against the contending parties. How does it protect against entrenched management?

5. What is the collective action problem that Justice Powell believes faces target shareholders, and how does he believe the Indiana statute solves that problem? Is this a complete catalog of the collective action problems facing shareholders in a takeover bid? If not, is it the only relevant one? Why?

6. Justice Powell's majority opinion also concludes that the Indiana Act does not conflict with the Williams Act by imposing a 50-day waiting period between the start of a tender offer and any possible vote. Why not? Is his analysis weakened by the withdrawal rights mandated for the entire period of a tender offer by Exchange Act Rule 14d–7?

7. Dynamics' argument that the Indiana statute discriminates against out-of-state entities was rejected by the court. What was the nature of that argument? Suppose Dynamics had been able to prove that most corporations subject to the coverage of the act had Indiana headquarters with top management resident in Indiana, and that most shares in these companies were owned by non-residents. Would the fact that local managers were capable of providing political support for benefits gained at the expense of non-resident shareholders be likely to change the majority's opinion? What expense would you argue is imposed on shareholders by this statute?

8. If the purpose of the Indiana act is to protect Indiana shareholders, why is one of the conditions to the application of the act that the corporation have its principal place of business, its principal office, or substantial assets in Indiana?

9. If the majority believes that the purpose of the Indiana statute is to protect shareholders, how would its opinion be affected by event studies showing declines in stock prices upon enactment of such laws?[*] Would evidence that such statutes were generally promoted by corporate managers, and sometimes (when time was available) opposed by investors be relevant?[**]

10. Assess the impact of the Indiana statute for a corporation that has already adopted the usual array of takeover defenses—a charter amendment requiring a supermajority vote for a takeout merger, a provision requiring advance notice of shareholder proposals, a staggered board of directors that requires cause for removal that is at the maximum size permissible without a charter amendment, and a poison pill (without a dead hand provision). How much of a barrier does the Indiana statute add to a successful takeover?

PROBLEM

Assume that your client has acquired majority control of a Delaware corporation headquartered in Delaware, that has over 50% in value of its assets located in California, more than 50% of its payroll paid in California, over 50% of its gross sales in California and over half of its shares held by California residents. Under these circumstances, California Corporation

---

[*] Roberta Romano, THE GENIUS OF AMERICAN LAW, 62 (1993), reported three event studies that found negative stock price responses to the adoption of Indiana's statute: Jonathan Karpoff and Paul Malatesta, The Wealth Effects of Second-Generation State Takeover Legislation, 25 J. Fin. Econ. 291 (1989); William S. Pugh and John S. Jahera, State Antitakeover Legislation and Shareholder Wealth, 13 J. Fin. Res. 221 (1990) (finding negative reactions on introduction date but insignificant movement at other significant legislative dates); and J. Gregory Sidak & Susan E. Woodward, Corporate Takeovers, the Commerce Clause, and the Efficient Anonymity of Shareholders, 84 Nw. U. L. Rev. 1092 (1990),

[**] Roberta Romano, The Political Economy of Takeover Statutes, 73 Va. L. Rev. 111 (1987); Henry N. Butler, Corporate-Specific Anti-Takeover Statutes and the Market for Corporate Charters. (Symposium: the Risks and Rewards of Regulating Corporate Takeovers) 1988 Wis. L. Rev. 365; William J. Carney, The Production of Corporate Law, 71 So. Cal. L. Rev. 715 (1998).

Code § 2115 applies. Among the terms of California law made applicable to such "pseudo-foreign corporations" are the provisions of Cal. Corp. Code § 1001(d) which requires a 90% shareholder vote to approve a sale of substantially all assets to a controlling corporation; § 1201(a), which requires approval by holders of each class of preferred shares in a merger, regardless of their contract rights. Do these provisions conflict with Delaware law? See Del. G.C.L. § 251(c). If there is a conflict, which law controls? Is the California provision constitutionally valid after CTS? For an earlier view, see Western Air Lines, Inc. v. Sobieski, 191 Cal.App.2d 399, 12 Cal.Rptr. 719 (1961). For a post-CTS view, see National City Lines, Inc. v. LLC Corporation, Fed. Sec. L. Rep. (CCH) ¶ 98,374 (W.D. Mo.1981), reversed on other grounds, 687 F.2d 1122 (8th Cir.1982).

Voting rules in mergers become confusing when one of the entities is based in California but incorporated elsewhere. California, unlike virtually all other states, does not strictly follow the Internal Affairs Doctrine of choice of law, which dictates that the law of the state of incorporation will govern relationships among the officers, directors, shareholders and the corporation. This rule is codified in MBCA § 15.05(c). The difficulties for transactional lawyers began with Western Air Lines, Inc. v. Sobieski, 191 Cal. App.2d 399, 12 Cal. Rptr. 719 (1961). Western, a Delaware corporation (subsequently acquired by Delta Air Lines), had 30% of its shares held by California residents and its operational center in California. Western's board proposed to eliminate cumulative voting after an insurgent group sought board seats, and prepared to solicit proxies from its shareholders to approve the amendment to its certificate of incorporation. Sobieski, the Corporations Commissioner of California, asserted that elimination of cumulative voting constituted an exchange of a new class of shares for the outstanding shares, which subjected the transaction to the California Securities Act, which gave the Commissioner authority to determine whether an exchange was "fair, just or equitable." He determined that it was not fair and denied a permit for the transaction. On appeal his position was sustained by the California Court of Appeals. Western argued that this amendment and the vote to obtain its approval were part of the internal affairs of the corporation, and thus subject only to Delaware law. The court conceded that California had no jurisdiction over the internal affairs of a Delaware corporation, but that it had jurisdiction over a sale or exchange of stock in California. The Commissioner and the court characterized Western as "pseudo-foreign corporation," because of its significant contacts with the state.

California has codified this doctrine, expanding it from its basis under the California Securities Act, to cover "pseudo-foreign corporations" under various provisions of California law, including mergers and asset sales. Cal. Corp. Code § 2115, with an exclusion for corporations with shares traded on the New York or American stock exchanges or on the NASDAQ National Market. Pseudo-foreign corporations are defined as those that conduct half their business in California as measured by a formula weighing property, payroll and sales located in California, and more than 50% of its shares are held in California. The California courts have consistently upheld the validity of these provisions against challenges under the full faith and credit clause, the commerce clause and the equal protection clause, generally finding that what was mandatory under California law was a permitted option under the law of the state of incorporation.

Delaware courts recently have taken a different view of this conflict. Examen, Inc. was a privately owned Delaware corporation headquartered in California that apparently met the "pseudo-foreign corporation" standards of California law. Examen entered into a merger agreement with Reed Elsevier, Inc., which Examen's board approved on Feb. 15, 2005 that expired on April 15, 2005. Examen had a class of preferred stock outstanding that had no separate class voting rights in its certificate of incorporation, meaning that all shares would vote as a single group under Del. GCL § 251(c). VantagePoint Venture Partners 1996, owns 83% of the preferred stock, convertible into 1.6 million common shares, in addition to the 8.6 million common shares already outstanding. On March 3, 2006, Examen filed suit in the Delaware Chancery Court seeking a declaratory judgment that its merger vote is subject only to Delaware law, and that California law does not govern. In response, on March 8 VantagePoint sued in the California courts seeking discovery to establish that Examen is subject to Cal. Corp. Code § 2115, and that if it is, that separate class voting is required, which would give VantagePoint a veto power over the merger. Following the lead of the California decisions, VantagePoint argued that there was no irreconcilable conflict between the two laws, and that California law, just like the rules of stock exchanges, simply gave stockholders an additional layer of protection that is not inconsistent with Delaware law. The Chancery Court noted that VantagePoint's argument was weakened by the language of § 2115(b), which provided that the listed provisions of California law "shall apply to a foreign corporation as defined in subdivision (a) (*to the exclusion of the law of the jurisdiction in which it is incorporated*). . . ." (Emphasis supplied.) VantagePoint responded that Delaware law permits separate class voting; it simply doesn't mandate it. The Chancery Court rejected this argument, noting that application of California law would be "in derogation of the rights of Examen's other stockholders," so that the court could not enforce both Delaware and California law. The Chancery Court treated this as a question of choice of law, and applied the internal affairs doctrine of choice of law of Delaware to hold that the law of Delaware, and not that of California, applies to a Delaware corporation.

On expedited appeal, the Delaware Supreme Court affirmed. Citing *dicta* in a case involving the validity of takeover defenses under the Commerce Clause, CTS Corp. v. Dynamics Corp. of America, 481 U.S. 69 (1987) [see page 510, *infra*], in which Justice Powell noted that the court had struck down statutes that imposed inconsistent regulations on activities. But it was not content to affirm simply on the choice of law grounds. The court noted that California's attempt to supplant the law of the state of incorporation for a pseudo-foreign corporation might apply in one year when the criteria were met, but not apply in a subsequent year, leaving a corporation uncertain about the governing law. The court held that under the Due Process Clause "directors and officers of corporations 'have a significant right to know what law will apply to their actions' and 'stockholders . . . have a right to know by what standards of accountability they may hold those managing the corporation's business and affairs," and that the internal affairs doctrine is mandated by constitutional principles. The opinion went on, gratuitously, to suggest that the California courts would likely agree with this analysis in light of cases such as CTS. VantagePoint Venture Partners 1996 v. Examen, Inc., 871 A.2d 1108 (2005).

---

3. THIRD GENERATION STATUTES, THE WILLIAMS ACT AND THE COMMERCE CLAUSE

Read Del. Gen. Corp. Law § 203.

Amanda Acquisition Corporation v. Universal Foods Corporation

877 F.2d 496 (7th Cir.1989).

■ EASTERBROOK, CIRCUIT JUDGE.

States have enacted three generations of takeover statutes in the last 20 years. Illinois enacted a first-generation statute, which forbade acquisitions of any firm with substantial assets in Illinois unless a public official approved. * * *

Indiana enacted a second-generation statute, applicable only to firms incorporated there and eliminating governmental veto power. Indiana's law provides that the acquiring firm's shares lose their voting power unless the target's directors approve the acquisition or the shareholders not affiliated with either bidder or management authorize restoration of votes. * * *

Wisconsin has a third-generation takeover statute. Enacted after CTS, it postpones the kinds of transactions that often follow tender offers (and often are the reason for making the offers in the first place). Unless the target's board agrees to the transaction in advance, the bidder must wait three years after buying the shares to merge with the target or acquire more than 5% of its assets. We must decide whether this is consistent with the Williams Act and Commerce Clause.

I

Amanda Acquisition Corporation is a shell with a single purpose: to acquire Universal Foods Corporation, a diversified firm incorporated in Wisconsin and traded on the New York Stock Exchange. Universal is covered by Wisconsin's anti-takeover law. Amanda is a subsidiary of High Voltage Engineering Corp., a small electronics firm in Massachusetts. Most of High Voltage's equity capital comes from Berisford Capital PLC, a British venture capital firm, and Hyde Park Partners L.P., a partnership affiliated with the principals of Berisford.

Chase Manhattan Bank has promised to lend Amanda 50% of the cost of the acquisition, secured by the stock of Universal.

In mid-November 1988 Universal's stock was trading for about $25 per share. On December 1 Amanda commenced a tender offer at $30.50, to be effective if at least 75% of the stock should be tendered.[1] This all-cash, all-shares offer has been increased by stages to $38.00.[2] Amanda's financing is contingent on a prompt merger with Universal if the offer succeeds, so the offer is conditional on a judicial declaration that the law is invalid. (It is also conditional on Universal's redemption of poison pill stock. For reasons that we discuss below, it is unnecessary to discuss the subject in detail.)

No firm incorporated in Wisconsin and having its headquarters, substantial operations, or 10% of its shares or shareholders there may "engage in a business combination with an interested stockholder . . . for 3 years after the interested stockholder's stock acquisition date unless the board of directors of the [Wisconsin] corporation has approved, before the interested stockholder's stock acquisition date, that business combination or the purchase of stock". An "interested stockholder" is one owning 10% of the voting stock, directly or through associates (anyone acting in concert with it). A "business combination" is a merger with the bidder or any of its affiliates, sale of more than 5% of the assets to bidder or affiliate, liquidation of the target, or a transaction by which the target guarantees the bidder's or affiliates debts or passes tax benefits to the bidder or affiliate. The law, in other words, provides for almost hermetic separation of bidder and target for three years after the bidder obtains 10% of the stock—unless the target's board consented before then. No matter how popular the offer, the ban applies: obtaining 85% (even 100%) of the stock held by non-management shareholders won't allow the bidder to engage in a business combination, as it would under Delaware law. Wisconsin firms cannot opt out of the law, as may corporations subject to almost all other state takeover statutes. In Wisconsin it is management's approval in advance, or wait three years. Even when the time is up, the bidder needs the approval of a majority of the remaining investors, without any provision disqualifying shares still held by the managers who resisted the transaction. The district court found that this statute "effectively eliminates hostile leveraged buyouts". As a practical matter, Wisconsin prohibits any offer contingent on a merger between bidder and target, a condition attached to about 90% of contemporary tender offers.

---

[1]   Wisconsin has, in addition to § 180.726, a statute modeled on Indiana's, providing that an acquiring firm's shares lose their votes, which may be restored under specified circumstances. Wis. Stat. § 180.25(9). That law accounts for the 75% condition, but it is not pertinent to the questions we resolve.

[2]   Universal contends that an increase after the district court's opinion makes the case moot, or at least requires a remand. It does not. The parties remain locked in combat. Price has no effect on the operation of the Wisconsin law, and as that is the sole issue we shall decide there is no need to remand for further proceedings.

Amanda filed this suit seeking a declaration that this law is preempted by the Williams Act and inconsistent with the Commerce Clause. It added a pendent claim that the directors' refusal to redeem the poison-pill rights violates their fiduciary duties to Universal's shareholders. The district court declined to issue a preliminary injunction. * * *

II

* * *

A

If our views of the wisdom of state law mattered, Wisconsin's takeover statute would not survive. Like our colleagues who decided MITE and CTS, we believe that antitakeover legislation injures shareholders. Managers frequently realize gains for investors via voluntary combinations (mergers). If gains are to be had, but managers balk, tender offers are investors' way to go over managers' heads. If managers are not maximizing the firm's value—perhaps because they have missed the possibility of a synergistic combination, perhaps because they are clinging to divisions that could be better run in other hands, perhaps because they are just not the best persons for the job—a bidder that believes it can realize more of the firm's value will make investors a higher offer. Investors tender; the bidder gets control and changes things. The prospect of monitoring by would-be bidders, and an occasional bid at a premium, induces managers to run corporations more efficiently and replaces them if they will not.

* * *

B

Skepticism about the wisdom of a state's law does not lead to the conclusion that the law is beyond the state's power, however. We have not been elected custodians of investors' wealth. States need not treat investors' welfare as their summum bonum. Perhaps they choose to protect managers' welfare instead, or believe that the current economic literature reaches an incorrect conclusion and that despite appearances takeovers injure investors in the long run. Unless a federal statute or the Constitution bars the way, Wisconsin's choice must be respected.

Amanda relies on the Williams Act of 1968, incorporated into §§ 13(d), (e) and 14(d)–(f) of the Securities Exchange Act of 1934, 15 U.S.C. §§ 78m(d), (e), 78n(d)–(f). The Williams Act regulates the conduct of tender offers. Amanda believes that Congress created an entitlement for investors to receive the benefit of tender offers, and that because Wisconsin's law makes tender offers unattractive to many potential bidders, it is preempted.

Preemption has not won easy acceptance among the Justices for several reasons. First there is § 28(a) of the '34 Act, 15 U.S.C. § 78bb(a), which provides that "nothing in this chapter shall affect the jurisdiction of the securities commission . . . of any State over any security or any person insofar as it does not conflict with the provisions of this chapter or the rules and regulations thereunder." Although some of the SEC's regulations (particularly the one defining the commencement of an offer) conflict with some state takeover laws, the SEC has not drafted regulations concerning mergers with controlling shareholders, and the Act itself does not address the subject. States have used the leeway afforded by § 28(a) to carry out "merit regulation" of securities—"blue sky" laws that allow securities commissioners to forbid sales altogether, in contrast with the federal regimen emphasizing disclosure.* So § 28(a) allows states to stop some transactions federal law would permit, in pursuit of an approach at odds with a system emphasizing disclosure and investors' choice. Then there is the traditional reluctance of federal courts to infer preemption of "state law in areas traditionally regulated by the States". States have regulated corporate affairs, including mergers and sales of assets, since before the beginning of the nation.

* * *

The Williams Act regulates the process of tender offers: timing, disclosure, proration if tenders exceed what the bidder is willing to buy, best-price rules. It slows things down, allowing investors to evaluate the offer and management's response. Best-price, proration, and short-tender rules ensure that investors who decide at the end of the offer get the same treatment as those who decide immediately, reducing pressure to leap before looking. After complying with the disclosure and delay requirements, the bidder is free to take the shares. MITE held invalid a state law that increased the delay and, by authorizing a regulator to nix the offer, created a distinct possibility that the bidder would be unable to buy the stock (and the holders to sell it) despite compliance with federal law. Illinois tried to regulate the process of tender offers, contradicting in some respects the federal rules. Indiana, by contrast, allowed the tender offer to take its course as the Williams Act specified but "sterilized" the acquired shares until the remaining investors restored their voting rights. Congress said nothing about the voting power of shares acquired in tender offers. Indiana's law reduced the benefits the bidder anticipated from the acquisition but left the process alone. So the Court, although accepting Justice White's views for the purpose of

---

*   In 1996 Congress adopted the National Securities Markets Improvement Act, preempting much of state regulation of securities offerings, by amending section 18 of the Securities Act of 1933 to provide that no state shall require registration of any "covered security" (or any security that will be a covered security after the offering) and that no state shall prohibit the use of any offering document prepared on behalf of the issuer of any covered security, and that no state shall prohibit or condition the offer or sale of any security based on the merits of the offering or the issuer. A "covered security" is defined as (1) one authorized for listing on the New York Stock Exchange or National Market System of NASDAQ or any exchange or system with comparable listing standards, (2) any security sold to a "qualified purchaser" as defined by SEC rule, or (3) sold pursuant to exemptions from registration under Federal law. There was no comparable amendment of § 28(a) of the Securities Exchange Act. Ed.

argument, held that Indiana's rules do not conflict with the federal norms.

* * *

Any bidder complying with federal law is free to acquire shares of Wisconsin firms on schedule. Delay in completing a second-stage merger may make the target less attractive, and thus depress the price offered or even lead to an absence of bids; it does not, however, alter any of the procedures governed by federal regulation. Indeed Wisconsin's law does not depend in any way on how the acquiring firm came by its stock: open-market purchases, private acquisitions of blocs, and acquisitions via tender offers are treated identically. Wisconsin's law is no different in effect from one saying that for the three years after a person acquires 10% of a firm's stock, a unanimous vote is required to merge. Corporate law once had a generally-applicable unanimity rule in major transactions,[2] a rule discarded because giving every investor the power to block every reorganization stopped many desirable changes. (Many investors could use their "hold-up" power to try to engross a larger portion of the gains, creating a complex bargaining problem that often could not be solved.) Wisconsin's more restrained version of unanimity also may block beneficial transactions, but not by tinkering with any of the procedures established in federal law.

Only if the Williams Act gives investors a right to be the beneficiary of offers could Wisconsin's law run afoul of the federal rule. No such entitlement can be mined out of the Williams Act, however. Schreiber v. Burlington Northern, Inc., 472 U.S. 1, 86 L. Ed. 2d 1, 105 S. Ct. 2458 (1985), holds that the cancellation of a pending offer because of machinations between bidder and target does not deprive investors of their due under the Williams Act. The Court treated § 14(e) as a disclosure law, so that investors could make informed decisions; it follows that events leading bidders to cease their quest do not conflict with the Williams Act any more than a state law leading a firm not to issue new securities could conflict with the Securities Act of 1933. * * *

C

* * *

When state law discriminates against interstate commerce expressly—for example, when Wisconsin closes its border to butter from Minnesota—the negative Commerce Clause steps in. The law before us is not of this type: it is neutral between inter-state and intra-state commerce. Amanda therefore presses on us the broader, all-weather, be-reasonable vision of the Constitution. Wisconsin has passed a law that unreasonably injures investors, most of whom live outside of Wisconsin,

---

[2]   See William J. Carney, Fundamental Corporate Changes, Minority Shareholders, and Business Purposes, 1980 Am. Bar Found. Res. J. 69, 77–97; Bayless Manning, The Shareholder's Appraisal Remedy: An Essay for Frank Coker, 72 Yale L. J. 223, 226–30 (1962), for two descriptions of the rule, both at common law and in the early state corporate codes.

and therefore it has to be unconstitutional, as Amanda sees things. Although Pike v. Bruce Church, Inc., 397 U.S. 137, 25 L. Ed. 2d 174, 90 S. Ct. 844 (1970), sometimes is understood to authorize such general-purpose balancing, a closer examination of the cases may support the conclusion that the Court has looked for discrimination rather than for baleful effects. At all events, although MITE employed the balancing process described in Pike to deal with a statute that regulated all firms having "contacts" with the state, CTS did not even cite that case when dealing with a statute regulating only the affairs of a firm incorporated in the state, and Justice Scalia's concurring opinion questioned its application. The Court took a decidedly confined view of the judicial role: "We are not inclined 'to second-guess the empirical judgments of lawmakers concerning the utility of legislation,' Kassel v. Consolidated Freightways Corp., 450 U.S. [662] at 679 [101 S. Ct. 1309, 67 L. Ed. 2d 580] (BRENNAN, J., concurring in judgment)." Although the scholars whose writings we cited in Part II.A conclude that laws such as Wisconsin's injure investors, Wisconsin is entitled to give a different answer to this empirical question—or to decide that investors' interests should be sacrificed to protect managers' interests or promote the stability of corporate arrangements.

* * *

Wisconsin, like Indiana, is indifferent to the domicile of the bidder. A putative bidder located in Wisconsin enjoys no privilege over a firm located in New York. So too with investors: all are treated identically, regardless of residence. Doubtless most bidders (and investors) are located outside Wisconsin, but unless the law discriminates according to residence this alone does not matter. * * *

Wisconsin could exceed its powers by subjecting firms to inconsistent regulation. Because § 180.726 applies only to a subset of firms incorporated in Wisconsin, however, there is no possibility of inconsistent regulation. Here, too, the Wisconsin law is materially identical to Indiana's. CTS, 481 U.S. at 88–89. This leaves only the argument that Wisconsin's law hinders the flow of interstate trade "too much". CTS dispatched this concern by declaring it inapplicable to laws that apply only to the internal affairs of firms incorporated in the regulating state. 481 U.S. at 89–94. States may regulate corporate transactions as they choose without having to demonstrate under an unfocused balancing test that the benefits are "enough" to justify the consequences.[10]

* * *

---

[10] The First Circuit considered in Hyde Park Partners the possibility that CTS had declared balancing of inter-and intra-state effects under Pike unnecessary when the state regulates a firm's internal affairs. 839 F.2d at 844–47. To be on the safe side, that court weighed effects of the Massachusetts law and found that most of its provisions were too inconsequential to be unconstitutional. Wisconsin's law is made of sterner stuff, and we can't avoid the issue so easily.

Affirmed.

NOTE ON BUSINESS COMBINATION STATUTES

Three district judges have found Delaware's business combination statute withstands both Commerce Clause and Williams Act preemption challenges. BNS Inc. v. Koppers Co., 683 F.Supp. 458 (D. Del.1988) sustained the statute against the Williams Act preemption challenge on the basis that the pro-management effects were incidental to protecting shareholders from coercive offers. Holding that the statute would be sustained "so long as it does not prevent an appreciable number of hostile bidders from navigating the statutory exceptions," the court reviewed conflicting expert opinions on whether the 85% threshold would prohibit all bids, and declined to rule the statute invalid in the absence of facts, rather than unsubstantiated opinions, refuting Delaware's position that the statute would not deter bids. The court applied a four-part test to determine whether the statute provided such a "meaningful opportunity":

> "First, does the statute protect independent shareholders from coercion? Second, does the statute give either management or the offeror an advantage in communicating with stockholders? This question may be reformulated to fit the circumstances of the present case by phrasing it as whether the statute gives either management or the offeror an advantage in consummating or defeating an offer. Third, does the statute impose an indefinite or unreasonable delay on offers? And fourth, does the statute allow the state government to interpose its views of fairness between willing buyers and sellers?"

683 F.Supp. at 469. In RP Acquisition Corp. v. Staley Continental, Inc., 686 F.Supp. 476 (D. Del.1988), plaintiffs accepted the court's invitation to present facts concerning the deterrent effect of the statute, offering an empirical study by Gregg Jarrell, former Chief Economist of the SEC, studying 29 hostile takeovers. Jarrell stated that historically in hostile bids 16% of the stock is in management hands or held by unresponsive shareholders ("dead shares"). Jarrell found that management in Fortune 500 companies held an average of 9.45% of all shares, while in smaller companies the figures run between 11% and 21.2%. Because the Delaware statute excluded management shares in making the 85% calculation, the court was not impressed. Jarrell defined hostile tender offers as those bids that never culminate in a merger agreement. He found that 16 of 29 bids, or 55%, reached the 85% shareholding level. The court ruled that these figures undercut the plaintiff's position, and demonstrated that hostile offers would have a "meaningful opportunity for success" under the Delaware statute. 686 F.Supp. at 482–83. A recent study of hostile takeover cases in Delaware found that no hostile bidder since 1990 has been able to reach the 85% tender offer required to avoid the statute, and suggests that this evidence might call into question the earlier rulings, that were based on much smaller studies.

Guhan Subramanian, Steven Herscovici and Brian Barbetta, Is Delaware's Antitakeover Statute Unconstitutional? Evidence from 1988–2008 65 Bus. Law. 685 (2010).

Other cases upholding these statutes include City Capital Associates Limited Partnership v. Interco, Inc., 696 F.Supp. 1551 (D. Del.1988), aff'd on other grounds, 860 F.2d 60 (3d Cir.1988); Vernitron Corp. v. Kollmorgen Corp., No. 89 Civ. 241 (S.D. N.Y) (JES) (2/9/89), reported in 21, No. 8 Sec. Reg. & L. Rep. (BNA) 315 (Feb. 24, 1989) and West Point-Pepperell, Inc. v. Farley, Inc., 711 F.Supp. 1096 (N.D. Ga.1989).

Extraterritoriality Effects

In Tyson Foods Inc. v. McReynolds, 865 F.2d 99 (6th Cir.1989), Tennessee's Business Combination Act, Control Share Acquisition Act, and Investor Protection Act were all held unconstitutional as applied to a target Delaware corporation covered by their terms. Tennessee's Authorized Corporation Protection Act allowed foreign corporations to opt in to Tennessee's Business Combination Act and its Control Share Acquisition Act. Foreign corporations qualify if they have "substantial assets" in Tennessee and are either incorporated in or have their principal offices in Tennessee. While conceding that states have a legitimate state interest in protecting shareholders of resident corporations, the Sixth Circuit noted that these statutes "protect incumbent management and not the shareholders." Further, in allowing foreign corporations to opt in, they directly regulate commerce, rather than merely having a permitted incidental effect. Here the burden imposed on interstate commerce was excessive, compared to the protection granted resident shareholders. Regulating a national tender offer to protect local interests violates the Commerce Clause. "Under the Commerce Clause, one state simply cannot regulate the commercial activity of the citizens of the other forty-nine states." Further, the court noted the risk of inconsistent regulation, since several states could impose their own requirements on tender offers and subsequent corporate action.

Professor Roberta Romano, in her book, THE GENIUS OF AMERICAN CORPORATE LAW, at 58–59 (1993), explains the passage of state takeover statutes as follows:

> "Like most pork-barrel legislation such as public works ('rivers and harbors') bills, takeover statutes are almost always unanimously approved. The likely explanation for such legislative unanimity is that the benefits and beneficiaries (real or supposed) of such legislation are highly concentrated—many, if not most, of the target company's managers and workers reside within the state— while the costs are borne largely by a loosely organized, geographically dispersed group, shareholders."

In short, most of the beneficiaries are local residents capable of providing political support for local politicians, while shareholders are dispersed across the nation, unable to organize to oppose the legislation, and unable to provide or deny political support to local legislators. Similarly, most potential bidders are non-residents with little local influence. Empirical studies generally show investor losses upon the passage of such statutes. Would proof of such a pattern provide evidence of discrimination against interstate commerce?

---

4. THE PROXY RULES AND FEDERAL PREEMPTION OF STATE TAKEOVER STATUTES

Securities Exchange Act, §§ 14(a) and (e); Rules 14a–3, 14a–8.

A. THE PREEMPTION DOCTRINE AND THE PROXY REGULATIONS; THE PURPOSES OF FEDERAL REGULATION

Securities and Exchange Commission v. Transamerica Corporation

163 F.2d 511 (3d Cir.1947).

■ Opinion by BIGGS:

There are two appeals at bar. One is that of Transamerica Corporation (No. 9240), the other is the appeal of the Securities and Exchange Commission (No. 9259). Both are from an order of the United States District Court for the district of Delaware entered September 9, 1946. What this order was and what it effected is discussed hereinafter. It seems appropriate to deal with both appeals in one opinion.

* * *

On January 2, 1946, Gilbert, the owner of record of seventeen shares of Transamerica's stock, wrote the management, submitting four proposals which he desired to present for action by shareholders at the next annual stockholders' meeting to be held on April 25, 1946. The first, second and fourth of these proposals were as follows:

(1) To have independent public auditors of the books of Transamerica elected by the stockholders, beginning with the annual meeting of 1947, a representative of the auditing firm last chosen to attend the annual meeting each year.

(2) To amend By-law 47 in order to eliminate therefrom the requirement that notice of any proposed alteration or amendment of the by-laws be contained in the notice of meeting.

(4) [sic] To require an account or a report of the proceedings at the annual meeting to be sent to all stockholders.

It appears that proposal (1) was in the form of a by-law amendment; Gilbert, the Commission and the corporation all so regarding it. Gilbert identified the second proposal also as a by-law amendment. The fourth proposal was designated by Gilbert as "a straight resolution." The Commission demanded of Transamerica that it accede to Gilbert's proposals. The corporation refused the Commission's demands.

The Commission therefore filed a complaint in the court below to enjoin Transamerica and its officers, inter alia, from making use of any proxy solicited by it for use at the annual meeting, from making use of the mails or any instrumentality of interstate commerce to solicit proxies or from making use of any soliciting material without complying with the Commission's demands, and for other relief which need not be detailed here.

* * * No substantial question of fact being in dispute, the learned trial judge disposed of the case on the Commission's motion for summary judgment under Rule 56, 28 U.S.C.A. following section 723c. * * * As to proposal (2), the court concluded that Transamerica's management was not compelled to give notice in the notice of meeting of a stockholder's proposal to change By-Law 47 and hence the management was entitled to rule, notice not being given, the proposal out of order. * * *

We think it will be of assistance in understanding what is involved if we deal first with the respective major contentions of each of the parties; then treat with the specific proposals involved, some of the contentions of the parties in respect to them and the applicable rulings of the court below. Respecting the major contentions of the parties, it will be observed that the decision in the case at bar must turn in some part on the interpretation to be placed on that portion of Proxy Rule X–14A–7* which provides that if a qualified security holder has given the management reasonable notice that he intends to present for action at a meeting of security holders "a proposal which is a proper subject for action by security holders" the management shall set forth the proposal and provide means by which the security holders can vote on the proposal as provided in Proxy Rule X–14A–2.

* * *

As to (2) the proposal to amend By-Law 47 in order to eliminate the requirement that notice be given in the notice of any meeting of any proposed alteration or amendment of the by-laws, the court below decided in favor of Transamerica and against the Commission. As the learned District Judge pointed out, as Transamerica has contended and as has been stated herein, By-law 47 provides that the by-laws may be altered or amended by an affirmative vote of a majority of the stock issued and outstanding and entitled to vote at any regular or special meeting of stockholders if notice of the proposed alteration or amendment is contained in the notice of the meeting. The court below took the view that because notice was not given by management, management was entitled to rule out of order any proposal to amend this By-law. * * *

---

*   This is the predecessor of current Rule 14a–8, 17 C.F.R. 240.14a–8. Ed.

That the law of Delaware will permit stockholders of a Delaware corporation to act validly on a stockholder's proposal to amend by-laws is clear beyond any doubt. Section 12 of the General Corporation Law of Delaware provides that "The original by-laws of a corporation may be adopted by the incorporators. Thereafter, the power to make, alter or repeal by-laws shall be in the stockholders, but any corporation may, in the certificate of incorporation, confer that power upon the directors." Transamerica's charter imposes no impediment for Article X of the charter provides: "In furtherance and not in limitation of the powers conferred by statute, the board of directors is expressly authorized: (a) To make and alter the by-laws of this corporation without any action on the part of the stockholders; but the by-laws made by the directors and the power so conferred may be altered or repealed by the stockholders." In short if it were not for the block interposed by the notice provisions of By-Law 47, it would be clear that Gilbert's second proposal would be a proper subject for stockholder action.

* * *

The conclusions reached by the court below in respect to Gilbert's proposals (2) and (4) may be supported only by applying the notice provision of By-law 47 in all its strictness. Admittedly, so long as the notice provision of By-Law 47 remains in effect unless management sees fit to include notice of a by-law amendment proposed by a stockholder in the notice of meeting the proposed amendment can never come before the stockholders' meeting with complete correctness. The same would be true even if one per centum of the stockholders backed the proposed amendment. But Transamerica's position is overnice and is untenable. In our opinion Gilbert's proposals are proper subjects for stockholder action within the purview of Proxy Rule X–14A–7 since all are subjects in respect to which stockholders have the right to act under the General Corporation Law of Delaware.

* * * If this minor provision may be employed as Transamerica seeks to employ it, it will serve to circumvent the intent of Congress in enacting the Securities Exchange Act of 1934. It was the intent of Congress to require fair opportunity for the operation of corporate suffrage. The control of great corporations by a very few persons was the abuse at which Congress struck in enacting Section 14(a). We entertain no doubt that Proxy Rule X–14A–7 represents a proper exercise of the authority conferred by Congress on the Commission under Section 14(a). This seems to us to end the matter. The power conferred upon the Commission by Congress cannot be frustrated by a corporate by-law.

QUESTIONS

1. What effect would the proxy rules, particularly Rule 14a–8, have on director-adopted bylaws that required lengthy notices to the corporation before shareholders could present proposals at shareholders meetings? Rule 14a–8(a)(3) requires a shareholder's proposal to be submitted to the corporation not less than 120 days before the date of the corporation's previous year's proxy statement. Would a 180 day notice requirement conflict with Rule 14a–8? How does Justice White's conclusion that the Illinois takeover statute created opportunities for delay beyond those contemplated by Congress in the Williams Act apply here?

2. One can assume that one purpose for the lengthy advance notice requirement in Rule 14a–8 is to allow the SEC to hold a hearing upon complaint of a rejected shareholder, so the SEC can order a corporation to include a shareholder's proposal in its proxy materials. If the shareholder did not propose to include its proposal in management's proxy materials, would a 120 day advance notice requirement run afoul of the general purpose of the proxy rules and section 14(a), which is to provide full disclosure to shareholders?

3. Recall the debate over whether the Williams Act preempted the Illinois and Indiana takeover statutes. Did TransAmerica's bylaw make it impossible to comply with the provisions of the proxy rules? Does it conflict with the Congressional policy of requiring a "fair opportunity for the operation of corporate suffrage"?

4. What do these cases suggest about the validity of "dead hand" poison pills under Federal law?

PROBLEMS

Problem 1.

Miss. Code Ann. § 79–25–3 (1998) provides definitions for a "fair price" statute. The remainder of the statute requires an 80% shareholder vote to approve a merger with an "Interested Shareholder" (an owner of 20% or more of a corporation's shares), unless the merger is previously approved by the "Continuing Directors" or meets certain "fair price" requirements. Does the definition of "beneficial owner" set out below create a conflict between the SEC's proxy rules, which encourage proxy solicitations, and the provisions of the Mississippi statute? (Similar provisions exist in other jurisdictions. See, e.g., Off. Code of Georgia § 14–2–1110(4).)

Definitions. In Sections 79–25–3 to 79–25–9, the following terms have the meanings ascribed herein:

* * *

(d) "Beneficial owner," when used with respect to any voting stock, means a person: (i) That, individually or with any of its affiliates or associates, beneficially owns voting stock, directly or indirectly; or (ii) That, individually or with any of its affiliates or associates, has: (A) The right to acquire voting stock (whether such right is exercisable immediately or only after the passage of time), pursuant to any agreement, arrangement or understanding, or upon the exercise of conversion rights, exchange rights, warrants or options, or otherwise; or (B) The right to vote voting stock pursuant to any agreement, arrangement or understanding; or (iii) That has any agreement, arrangement or understanding for the purpose of acquiring, holding, voting, exercising investment power over, or disposing of voting stock with any other person that beneficially owns, or whose affiliates or associates beneficially own, directly or indirectly, such shares of voting stock.

Problem 2.

Georgia's Business Combination statute, Off. Code Ga. Ann. § 14–2–1110 (4) provides the following definition of "beneficial owner" of shares:

"(4) 'Beneficial owner' means a person shall be considered to be the beneficial owner of any equity securities:

"(A) Which such person or any of such person's affiliates or associates owns, directly or indirectly;

"(B) Which such person or any of such person's affiliates or associates, directly or indirectly, has:

"(i) The right to acquire, whether such right is exercisable immediately or only after the passage of time, pursuant to any agreement, arrangement, or understanding or upon the exercise of conversion rights, exchange rights, warrants or options, or otherwise; or

"(ii) The right to vote pursuant to any agreement, arrangement, or understanding; or

"(C) Which are owned, directly or indirectly, by any other person with which such person or any of such person's affiliates or associates has any agreement, arrangement, or understanding for the purpose of acquiring, holding, voting, or disposing of equity securities."

This definition applies to Georgia's version of the Business Combination statute (which prohibits mergers for five years, unless (1) the target board approves the merger before the bidder becomes beneficial owner of 10% or more of the voting power of the corporation; (2) the bidder gains beneficial ownership of at least 90% of the target's shares in the transaction in which it became a beneficial owner of 10% or more (excluding management shares) or (3) obtained the affirmative vote of holders of at least 90% of the remaining shares (excluding management shares).

1. Does this statute preclude a proxy fight that would remove and replace the current directors, in order to obtain redemption of outstanding rights in a poison pill plan?

2. Does this statute conflict with the SEC proxy rules, permitting shareholder proposals at shareholders' meetings? See SEC v. Transamerica Corp., *supra*, at the beginning of Part 4.A of this chapter.

3. Suppose a corporation adopts a rights plan that contained a similar definition of beneficial ownership? Is it valid or in conflict with federal law?

B. DISGORGEMENT STATUTES

In 1990 Pennsylvania enacted a statute that combined several features. It contained a "control shares" provision like Indiana's. 15 Pa. Consol. Stat. Ann. §§ 2561–2567. But the Pennsylvania statute is triggered by the acquisition of specified voting rights, including those acquired by a proxy solicitation. Thus far no courts have ruled upon the validity of these provisions. Pennsylvania's 1990 legislation, 15 Pa. Consol. Stat. Ann. §§ 2571–2576, described below, contains a unique set of provisions requiring disgorgement of profits by bidders under certain circumstances.

Note, How Do Pennsylvania Directors Spell Relief? Act 36

Jeffrey L. Silberman.
17 Del. J. Corp. L. 115, 138—140 (1991).

"B. Disgorgement of Profits Subchapter

"The provision of Act 36 which disgorges the profits of certain controlling shareholders following attempts to acquire control[145] is a new animal in the forest of antitakeover statutes. The Pennsylvania legislature has apparently borrowed a provision from section 16 of the Securities and Exchange Act, which punishes those who engage in insider trading by allowing the issuing company to recover any profits that the insider has realized as a result of his unlawful conduct.[146]

"Subchapter H begins with a general policy statement: 'The purpose of this subchapter is to protect certain registered corporations and legitimate interests of various groups related to such corporations from certain manipulative and coercive transactions.'[147] More specifically, Subchapter H is designed to (1) prevent payment of greenmail,[148] (2) ensure that persons who put corporations 'in play' do not take actions which benefit themselves at the expense of the corporation or its

---

[145] 15 Pa. Cons. Stat. Ann. §§ 2571–2574 (Purdon 1990) [hereinafter Subchapter H].

[146] See 15 U.S.C. § 78p(b) (1988) (providing that persons with certain knowledge, or insiders, who benefit from insider trading, must disgorge the profits which result from the use of this information).

[147] 15 Pa. Cons. Stat. Ann. § 2572(a) (Purdon 1990).

[148] *Id.* § 2572(a)(1).

community,[149] and (3) discourage speculators from putting Pennsylvania corporations 'in play.'[150] The legislature justifies its enactment of Subchapter H by stating that it recognizes its right to protect the corporations its laws create.[151] This is a direct reference to CTS's endorsement of the internal affairs doctrine.[152] Apparently, the legislature is reading CTS to broadly endorse the state's right to regulate its corporations, and reasonably so. Its express purpose is not, however, to curtail either proxy solicitations by the corporation[153] or proxy contests concerning matters other than those related to putting corporations in play.[154] These policy statements are instead intended to express the legislature's desire to suppress only the hostile takeover, not to completely eliminate the proxy as a tool for shareholder participation in corporate affairs. This creates a problem, however, in that the statute not only deters the 'corporate raider,' but it also deters 'every-day' stockholders who may have legitimate concerns about the effectiveness of a corporation's management.

"The general rule of the disgorgement provision states that any profit[155] realized by a person who is or was a 'controlling person'[156] from the sale of any equity security[157] of the target corporation within eighteen months after the person becomes a controlling person will belong to the corporation.[158] A controlling person is defined very broadly to include a person or group who has acquired, offered to acquire, or publicly disclosed the intent to acquire over twenty percent of the total voting rights entitled to be cast in an election of directors.[159] Equity securities acquired

---

[149]   *Id.* § 2572(a)(3). Also, Subchapter H is designed to promote stable relationships among all parties associated with the corporation, presumably including suppliers and communities. *Id.* § 2572(a)(2).

[150]   *Id.* § 2572(a)(4).

[151]   *Id.* § 2572(a).

[152]   See *supra* note 81 and accompanying text.

[153]   15 Pa. Cons. Stat. Ann. § 2572(b)(2) (Purdon 1990). Once again, the corporation is exempted by the statute, and, once again, we must ask the question whether a director who is in fact acting independently is deemed to be acting as the corporation. In all of these corporation-exempting provisions, this question becomes relevant when evaluating whether the statute favors management in violation of the Williams Act's mandate of neutrality. See *infra* notes 192–93 and accompanying text.

[154]   15 Pa. Cons. Stat. Ann. § 2572(b)(1) (Purdon 1990). Specifically, the legislature is not attempting to curtail proxy contests regarding cumulative voting provisions, environmental issues, or business transactions in foreign countries. *Id.*

[155]   "Profit" is defined by the statute as the positive value of the difference between consideration received by the sale of the security and the consideration paid for acquiring the security. *Id.* § 2573 (defining "profit").

[156]   *Id.* § 2573 (defining "controlling person or group").

[157]   "Equity security," as used in the statute, refers to all shares, stock, or similar security. *Id.* (defining "equity security").

[158]   *Id.* § 2575(1).

[159]   *Id.* § 2573(1)(i). A controlling person may also be a person or group who has publicly disclosed that it seeks to acquire control of the corporation through any means. *Id.* § 2573(1)(ii). Finally, a controlling person may be two or more persons acting in concert, not necessarily pursuant to an agreement, for the purpose of selling, buying, or voting equity securities of the corporation. *Id.* § 2573(2).

within two years prior to or eighteen months after the acquiror becomes a controlling person are subject to this disgorgement provision.[160] Again, it must be pointed out that a controlling person need not buy or acquire shares of stock to trigger the disgorgement provision. All that is required is an acquisition of voting rights. Thus, the solicitation of proxies may trigger Subchapter H.

"Reading the statute literally, any shareholder who merely mentions a desire, whether seriously or not, to acquire twenty percent of the voting rights would be subject to disgorgement.[161] Taking into consideration the broad definition of who may be a controlling person, what activities will trigger the statute, and the type of 'punishment' it mandates, it is not difficult to see why Act 36 has drawn so much negative reaction."

Ohio has adopted a similar disgorgement statute, although its coverage of proxies is less clear. Ohio Rev. Code Ann. § 1707.043. Stephen M. Bainbridge, in Redirecting State Takeover Laws at Proxy Contests, 1992 Wis. L. Rev. 1071, 1094–95, describes some exemptions from the definition of control shares in the Pennsylvania statute:

"As adopted, the statute exempts all management proxy solicitations.[100] It also provides a safe harbor for insurgent solicitations satisfying two conditions: (1) the solicitation is made in accordance with applicable federal proxy rules; and (2) the proxies given do not empower the holder to vote the covered shares on any matter except those described in the proxy statement and in accordance with the instructions of the giver of the proxy.[101] The first condition is problematic because it opens the door for application of the disgorgement remedy not only to fraudulent proxy solicitations, but also to those that fail to comply with some technical aspect of the federal proxy rules.[102] The second condition is equally problematic. Proxies normally grant the holder discretionary authority to vote on procedural and other unanticipated matters that arise during a shareholders meeting.[103] The second condition precludes

---

[160] *Id.* § 2574(2).

[161] See *id.* § 2573 (defining controlling person in extremely broad, ambiguous terms). This broad interpretation is, in part, due to the definition of "publicly disclosed or caused to be disclosed." This term includes, but is not limited to:

[A]ny disclosure . . . that becomes public made by a person:

(1) with the intent or expectation that such disclosure become public; or

(2) to another where the disclosing person knows, or reasonable [sic] should have known, that the receiving person was not under an obligation to refrain from making such disclosure, directly or indirectly, to the public and such receiving person does make such disclosure, directly or indirectly, to the public. *Id.* § 2562.

[100] 15 PA. CONS. STAT. ANN. § 2572(b)(2) (Purdon 1991).

[101] *Id.* § 2574(b)(3).

[102] ROSENBAUM & PARKER, [THE PENNSYLVANIA TAKEOVER ACT OF 1990: SUMMARY AND ANALYSIS (1990)] *supra* note 95, at 14

[103] Under SEC Rule 14a–4(c)(1), a proxy may grant discretionary authority to vote on matters which the solicitor of the proxy did not know were to come before the meeting. The Rule

insurgents (but not management) from seeking that normal discretionary authority.

* * *

"Why was the statute cut back at all? Perhaps the legislature never truly intended to affect proxy contests not involving control. A possible motive more relevant to this Article, however, is legislative concern over Exchange Act section 14(a)'s possible application to the issues at hand. Indeed, SEC Chairman Richard C. Breeden told the Pennsylvania legislature that the bill 'could do substantial damage to the shareholders' well-established federal right to use the proxy machinery to replace the board of directors.'[106] The threat of SEC efforts to preempt the Pennsylvania statute was quite clear."

QUESTIONS

1. Do the provisions of the Pennsylvania statute that trigger the disgorgement rules upon receipt of sufficient proxies offend section 14(a) of the Williams Act sufficiently to be preempted by it?

2. Silberman, *supra*, argues that section 14(a) is a disclosure statute, and that nothing in Pennsylvania's disgorgement provisions precludes disclosure by potential bidders waging a proxy contest. Does this address the shareholder access rules promulgated by the SEC in Rule 14a–8?

3. What effect would you expect the adoption of such a statute to have on the value of firms incorporated in Pennsylvania?

4. Does the Pennsylvania statute allow a meaningful opportunity for success in a proxy fight for control of the board, in order to secure redemption of a poison pill?

The Genius of American Corporate Law

Roberta Romano.
68–69 (1993).

"Pennsylvania's disgorgement statute provides, paradoxically, a good example of the beneficent effect of state competition. Event studies of Pennsylvania firms have identified large significant negative abnormal returns at the time the legislation was enacted.[25] Institutional

---

requires, however, that the proxy statement or proxy card expressly state that such discretionary authority is being granted. 17 C.F.R. § 240.14a–4(c)(1)(1990).

[106] ROSENBAUM & PARKER, *supra* note 95, at 21 (emphasis deleted).

[25] For example, Szewczyk and Tsetsekos, "State Intervention in the Market for Corporate Control." For a review of several studies of this statute, which all report similar results, see M.

investors threatened to sell their shares in firms covered by the statute, and a majority of corporations opted out of the statute.[26] Of publicly traded firms with a Pennsylvania domicile whose choices were identified, as detailed in table 4–2, 127 firms opted out of all or part of the statute, while 72 firms did not. The proportion opting out is higher among larger firms (which are firms more likely to have a higher proportion of institutional investors): 32 firms listed on the New York Stock Exchange opted out and 11 did not. In fact, exchange-listed firms that opted out have a higher proportion of institutional owners than those that did not.[28] These data indicate that when a particular corporation's investors express concern about the impact of a particular corporation statute on their firm, managers will be responsive to their concerns. Researchers have further found that firms experience positive abnormal returns on opting out of the statute.[29]"

C. DIRECTORS' DUTIES AND LIABILITIES

Too often this book focuses on Delaware law to the exclusion of other states, which is in part a function of Delaware's dominance as the state of incorporation of publicly traded companies, and also its highly developed jurisprudence in this area. Michal Barzuza has recently surveyed the other states, and concluded while judicial standards of review of directors' actions vary considerably, states with strong antitakeover statutes, poison pill endorsement statutes and other constituency statutes, consistently judge target directors' actions under the relaxed business judgment standard, rather than the heightened scrutiny of cases such as Unocal, Blasius, and Revlon (to be treated in Chapter Eight, Part 1). Michal Barzuza, The State of State Antitakeover Law, 95 Va. L. Rev. 1973 (2009). What follows is an example of a director protection statute.

Mass. Ann. Laws ch. 156B, § 50A (1999).

§ 50A. *Terms of Office of Directors; Election of Successors; Exemption of Corporation From Section; Removal of Directors; Definitions.*

(a) Except as provided in paragraph (b) of this section and notwithstanding anything to the contrary in this chapter or in the articles of organization or by-laws of any registered corporation, the

---

Wayne Marr, "Survey of Empirical Studies: Pennsylvania Act 36," *Financial Analysts Journal*, vl. 48 (1992), p. 52.

[26] See Leslie Wayne, "Many Companies in Pennsylvania Reject State's Takeover Protection," *New York Times* (July 20, 1990), p. 1. Firms were permitted to opt out of the statute by board approval (by amending corporate bylaws) within ninety days of the effective date.

[28] Szewczyk and Tsetsekos, "State Intervention in the Market for Corporate Control," p. 18.

[29] Ibid.; Marr, "Survey of Empirical Studies: Pennsylvania's Act 36." The full sample of firms opting out of all provisions experience significant positive abnormal returns, but the abnormal return for the subset of firms that only partially opt out is insignificant.

directors of a registered corporation shall be classified, with respect to the time for which they severally hold office, into three classes, as nearly equal in number as possible; the term of office of those of the first class ("Class I Directors") to continue until the first annual meeting following the date such registered corporation becomes subject to this paragraph (a) and until their successors are duly elected and qualified; the term of office of those of the second class ("Class II Directors") to continue until the second annual meeting following the date such registered corporation becomes subject to this paragraph (a) and until their successors are duly elected and qualified; and the term of office of those of the third class ("Class III Directors") to continue until the third annual meeting following the date such registered corporation becomes subject to this paragraph (a) and until their successors are duly elected and qualified. At each annual meeting of a registered corporation subject to this section, the successors to the class of directors whose term expires at that meeting shall be elected to hold office for a term continuing until the annual meeting held in the third year following the year of their election and until their successors are duly elected and qualified. On or prior to the date on which a registered corporation first convenes an annual meeting following the time at which such registered corporation becomes subject to paragraph (a), the board of directors of such registered corporation shall adopt a vote designating, from among its members, directors to serve as Class I Directors, Class II Directors and Class III Directors. Notwithstanding this paragraph (a), the articles of organization may confer upon holders of any class or series of preference or preferred stock the right to elect one or more directors who shall serve for such term, and have such voting powers, as shall be stated in the articles of organization; provided, however, that no such provision of the articles of organization which confers upon such holders any such right and which is filed with the state secretary after the effective date of this paragraph (a) shall become effective unless prior to its adoption it was approved by a vote of a majority in number of the directors of such registered corporation.

(b)(i) The provisions of this section shall apply to every registered corporation (whether or not notice of an annual meeting of such registered corporation has been given on or prior to the effective date of this section), unless the board of directors of such registered corporation, or the stockholders of such registered corporation by a vote of two-thirds of each class of stock outstanding at a meeting duly called for the purpose of such vote which meeting occurs after January 1, 1992, shall adopt a vote providing that such corporation elects to be exempt from the provisions of paragraph (a) of this section. Upon adoption of any such vote, the provisions of paragraph (a) of this section shall, unless otherwise provided in such vote, become immediately ineffective with respect to such registered corporation and the provisions of section 50 of this chapter shall become immediately effective with respect to such registered corporation as soon as the provisions of paragraph (a) of this section are no longer effective.

(ii) In the event that any registered corporation shall so elect by vote of the board of directors to be exempt pursuant to clause (i) of this paragraph (b) such registered corporation may at any time thereafter adopt a vote of its board of directors electing to be subject to the provisions of paragraph (a) of this section. In the event that any registered corporation shall so elect by vote of 2/3 of the shareholders adopted after January 1, 1992 to be exempt pursuant to clause (i) of this paragraph (b) such registered corporation may at any time thereafter adopt a vote of 2/3 of the shareholders electing to be subject to the provisions of paragraph (a) of this section. Upon adoption of any such vote, the provisions of this section shall, unless otherwise provided in such vote, immediately become effective.

(c) Notwithstanding anything to the contrary in this chapter or in the articles of organization or by-laws of any registered corporation, in the case of directors of a registered corporation who are classified with respect to the time for which they severally hold office pursuant to paragraph (a) of this section, stockholders may effect, by the affirmative vote of a majority of the shares outstanding and entitled to vote in the election of directors, the removal of any director or directors or the entire board of directors only for cause.

(d) Notwithstanding anything to the contrary in this chapter or in the articles of organization or by-laws of any registered corporation, in the case of directors of a registered corporation who are classified with respect to the time for which they severally hold office pursuant to paragraph (a) of this section, (i) vacancies and newly created directorships, whether resulting from an increase in the size of the board of directors, from the death, resignation, disqualification or removal of a director or otherwise, shall be filled solely by the affirmative vote of a majority of the remaining directors then in office, even though less than a quorum of the board of directors, (ii) any director elected in accordance with clause (i) of this paragraph (d) shall hold office for the remainder of the full term of the class of directors in which the vacancy occurred or the new directorship was created and until such director's successor shall have been elected and qualified, (iii) no decrease in the number of directors constituting the board of directors shall shorten the term of any incumbent director, and (iv) the number of directors of a registered corporation subject to paragraph (a) of this section shall be fixed only by vote of its board of directors.

(e) As used in this section, the following words shall have the following meanings:—

(1) "Annual meeting", any annual meeting of stockholders and any special meeting of stockholders in lieu of an annual meeting provided for by law, the articles of organization, by-laws or otherwise.

(2) "Cause", with respect to the removal of any director of a registered corporation, only (i) conviction of a felony, (ii) declaration of unsound mind by order of court, (iii) gross dereliction of duty, (iv) commission of an action involving moral turpitude, or (v) commission of an action which constitutes intentional misconduct or a knowing violation of law if such action in either event results both in an improper substantial personal benefit and a material injury to the registered corporation.

(3) "Registered corporation", any corporation to which the provisions of paragraph (a) of section three of this chapter apply, and which has a class of voting stock registered under the Securities Exchange Act of 1934, as amended; provided, that if a corporation is subject to paragraph (a) of this section at the time it ceases to have any class of voting stock so registered, such corporation shall nonetheless be deemed to be a registered corporation for a period of twelve months following the date it ceased to have such stock registered.

(f)   Nothing in this section shall be deemed to amend, modify or otherwise effect the validity of any provision of the articles of organization or by-laws of any corporation during any period that it elects not to be subject to paragraph (a) of this section, whether or not currently in effect, providing for the division of directors into classes as contemplated by section fifty of this chapter. No provision of the articles of organization or by-laws of any registered corporation that is subject to paragraph (a) of this section, whether or not currently in effect, shall render inapplicable any provision of this section or require the board of directors of such corporation to adopt any vote pursuant to paragraph (b) of this section. No vote adopted by a board of directors electing not to be subject to paragraph (a) of this section shall render invalid, or prevent adoption of, any amendment to such corporation's articles of organization as contemplated by section fifty of this chapter.

This statute was reportedly passed in 1990 in response to the bid of BTR plc, an English holding company, for Norton Company, a Massachusetts corporation. Stephen M. Bainbridge, Redirecting State Takeover Laws at Proxy Contests, 1992 Wis. L. Rev. 1071, 1090–91. A similar statute was rejected by the Georgia General Assembly in 1997 during Invacare's bid for Healthdyne Technologies, Inc. For a discussion of this statute, see Bainbridge, *supra* at 1127–28.

QUESTIONS

1.   Is a statute such as this likely to thwart a takeover bid? Notice that it doesn't prevent the bidder from buying a majority of the shares of the target, and voting in its own board candidates over the next two years.

See Ronald J. Gilson, The Case Against Shark Repellent Amendments: Structural Limitations on the Enabling Concept, 34 Stan. L. Rev. 775, 793–96 (1982).

2. Does this statute discriminate against proxy solicitations by potential bidders in a manner inconsistent with the proxy regulations?

3. Does this statute have any shareholder protection features, or is it designed purely to protect management from a proxy fight for control of the board?

4. Is a statute like this the functional equivalent of a "slow hand" poison pill, of the kind described in Chapter Six, Part 2.E?

5. Does this statute provide hostile bidders with a meaningful opportunity for success in completing a takeover of a corporation?

D. "OTHER CONSTITUENCY" STATUTES

Thirty-one states have adopted so-called "other constituency" statutes that permit target boards to consider the interests of groups other than shareholders in the face of a hostile bid. Typically they authorize boards to take into account the interests of employees, creditors, customers, suppliers and the communities in which the corporations operate. Some statutes simply permit these considerations to be employed by all directors; others authorize corporations to amend their charters to provide such authority to directors. These statutes are discussed in Eric W. Orts, Beyond Shareholders: Interpreting Corporate Constituency Statutes, 61 Geo. Wash. L. Rev. 14 (1992); John H. Matheson & Brent A. Olson, Shareholder Rights and Legislative Wrongs: Toward Balanced Takeover Legislation, 59 Geo. Wash. L. Rev. 1425 (1991) and Lawrence E. Mitchell, A Theoretical and Practical Framework for Enforcing Corporate Constituency Statutes, 70 Tex. L. Rev. 579 (1992). For a generally negative view of constituency considerations, see William J. Carney, Does Defining Constituencies Matter?, 59 U. Cinn. L. Rev. 385 (1990). The drafters of the Model Business Corporation Act determined not to include such a provision in the Model Act. Committee on Corporate Law, Other Constituencies Statutes: Potential for Confusion, 45 Bus. Law. 2253 (1990).

QUESTION

1. Delaware has not adopted an "other constituencies" statute. Recall the discussion of the board's ability to consider other constituencies in Unocal v. Mesa Petroleum Co., in Chapter Six, Part 2.A, and the limits imposed on that ability in Revlon, Inc. v. MacAndrews & Forbes Holdings, Inc., *infra*, Chapter Eight, Part 1. What authority would a charter amendment give a board to consider other constituencies at the

expense of shareholders? What would you estimate the likelihood that shareholders would adopt such an amendment? Oddly enough, such provisions stemmed largely from charter amendments, perhaps originating with the amendment of Control Data Corporation's charter in 1978.

NOTE

In Herald Co. v. Seawell, 472 F.2d 1081, 1094–95 (10th Cir.1972), the court rejected a derivative action challenging the use of corporate funds for stock repurchases designed to enable the employees ultimately to control the target corporation through a stock trust, a predecessor of an ESOP. In justifying management's right to use corporate funds to benefit employees, particularly against a bid from an outsider for control of a local newspaper, the Denver Post, the court stated:

"Basic in many of the rules of law pertaining to the relationship between officers and directors of a corporation and the corporate stockholders is the motive of profit for the corporation. A corporation publishing a newspaper such as the Denver Post certainly has other obligations besides the making of profit. It has an obligation to the public, that is, the thousands of people who buy the paper, read it, and rely upon its contents. Such a newspaper is endowed with an important public interest. It must adhere to the ethics of the great profession of journalism. The readers are entitled to a high quality of accurate news coverage of local, state, national, and international events. The newspaper management has an obligation to assume leadership, when needed, for the betterment of the area served by the newspaper. Because of these relations with the public, a corporation publishing a great newspaper such as the Denver Post is, in effect, a quasi-public institution.

"Such a newspaper corporation, not unlike some other corporations, also has an obligation to those people who make its daily publication possible. A great number of the employees are either members of a profession or highly skilled and specialized in their crafts. Many of them have dedicated their lives to this one endeavor. The appellants' sincere interest in their employees also refutes the allegation of illegal design. The Post's concern for their employees is exemplified in all the employee benefits provided. For instance, the employees are given, inter alia, hospitalization insurance, medical insurance, and retirement pensions. Indeed, approximately 11% of the Post's total expenses go for these employee benefits. With the implementation of the Employees Stock Trust, employees also will be allowed eventually to own the Post. Since, prior to institution of legal proceedings in 1968, the Post Employees Stock Trust was following an almost identical course as had occurred in the Milwaukee plan, it can generally be said that within 35 years Post employees should own 85 to 90% of the paper.

"The facts show appellants' motive for implementing the Employees Stock Trust was to benefit the public, the corporation and the employees. Any contrary finding under the law and the evidence is clearly erroneous.

Indeed, appellants' conduct was quite in harmony with that encouraged under Colorado law."

In AMP Incorporated v. Allied Signal Inc., 1998 WL 778348 (E.D. Pa.1998), the district court rejected a challenge to a board's amendment of its poison pill that would make it nonredeemable upon any change of control that involved a majority of a bidder's nominees. The court noted Pennsylvania's other constituencies statute, 15 Pa. Cons. Stat. Ann. § 1715(c), after granting permission to consider the interests of employees, suppliers, customers and creditors, specifically provided that the fiduciary duties of the board to not require it "to act as the board of directors, a committee of the board or an individual director solely because of the effect such action might have on an acquisition or potential or proposed acquisition of control of the corporation or the consideration that might be offered or paid to shareholders in such an acquisition." The court concluded: "Thus, in amending the poison pill and fixing it as non-amendable and non-redeemable, AMP did not act beyond the scope of its statutory authority."

CHAPTER EIGHT

GETTING THE BEST DEAL: THE BOARD'S INFORMATIONAL DUTIES

Revised Model Business Corporation Act §§ 8.30 & 8.31; Del. GCL § 141(e).

1. THE CONDUCT OF THE SELLING EFFORT

A. SALES

If the power of a board of directors to negotiate a contract of merger or sale of assets that binds the corporation remains subject to its fiduciary duties, what must a board do to satisfy that obligation? The answer to this question is also the key to what a buyer can demand and expect to enforce in an acquisition agreement. The answer from the Delaware courts has evolved dramatically over time.

NOTE ON SMITH V. VAN GORKOM

488 A.2d 858 (Del. 1985).

Trans Union Corporation was a publicly traded rail car leasing company. It generated large cash flows, but because of a combination of depreciation deductions and investment tax credits, apparently had little or no taxable income at the time in question.* As a result, it was unable to utilize the increasing investment tax credits (ITCs) that were available. Throughout the 1970s Trans Union had been acquiring small companies in order to make use of its tax losses and deductions. The 1980 revised five year plan submitted by management to the board in July of that year recognized this problem. The plan projected continued growth in Trans Union's cash flows, so that it would do no more than "break even" for tax purposes, meaning past loss carryforwards could not be utilized. The plan mentioned four alternative uses of this cash: (1) stock repurchases; (2) dividend increases; (3) a major acquisition program and (4) combinations of the above. Making a major acquisition that would generate $150 million a year of taxable income, enabling Trans Union to take full advantage of its tax situation, was considered, but this was estimated to cost more than $750 million, or more than the current value of Trans Union's assets. Because Trans Union's debt-equity ratio was more than 60%, it was unlikely that a public company would be interested in purchasing it. Among other things, at

---

* Typically this is a temporary condition, as accelerated depreciation deductions decline in size and income continues. It only persists in expanding businesses, where firms continue to buy new capital assets in increasing amounts.—Ed.

the price that Trans Union would desire, the interest payments would probably reduce the earnings per share of a public corporation, and Jerome Van Gorkom, Trans Union's President, concluded that a private company would be more likely to purchase Trans Union. Van Gorkom asked Carl Petersen, Trans Union's controller, to calculate whether it would be reasonable for a prospective purchaser to acquire Trans Union in a leveraged buyout. Mr. Peterson assumed that such a purchaser would contribute $200 million in equity and would borrow $490 million at 14% (this was an era of high inflation), which would be repaid from Trans Union's cash flows, which had recently been projected by The Boston Consulting Group in a study of Trans Union.

On August 27, 1980 and again on Sept. 5 Jerome Van Gorkom, CEO, who was nearing retirement age, met with senior management to discuss the ITC problem. Romans, the Chief Financial Officer (CFO) presented preliminary calculations on a possible leveraged buyout (LBO) at $50, which he indicated would be easy, and at $60, which he indicated would be difficult. Van Gorkom indicated that he would be willing to sell at $55 per share. (The stock was trading at around $38 at the time. It had traded at prices between $24.25 and $39.50 for the five years from 1975 through 1979.) Thereafter, Van Gorkom told the company's controller to prepare a set of pro forma calculations on the feasibility of an LBO at $55.

On September 13 Van Gorkom met with his friend Jay Pritzker, a well known Chicago financier, and proposed a sale of Trans Union to Pritzker at $55 per share. Two days later Pritzker advised Van Gorkom that he was interested in a purchase at that price. "By September 18, after two more meetings that included two Trans Union officers and an outside consultant, Van Gorkom knew that Pritzker was ready to propose a cash merger at $55 per share if Pritzker could also have the option to buy one million shares of Trans Union Treasury stock at $38 per share. . . . Pritzker also insisted that the Trans Union Board act on his proposal within three days, i.e., by Sunday, September 21 and instructed his attorney to draft the merger documents*.]

On September 19, without consulting Trans Union's legal department, Van Gorkom engaged outside counsel as merger specialists. He called for meetings of senior management and the board of directors for the next day, but only those officers who had met with Pritzker knew the subject of the meetings. Trans Union's regular investment bankers, Salomon Brothers, were not invited to the meeting which lasted two hours. The merger agreement was not initially presented to the board, and was not read by the directors prior to or during the meeting. It arrived too late to be studied. Van Gorkom explained the agreement to the board in about 20 minutes. At the time of the September 20, 1980 meeting the Board was acutely aware of Trans Union and its prospects. The problems created by accumulated investment tax credits and accelerated depreciation were discussed repeatedly at Board meetings, and all of the directors understood the

---

*   Jay Pritzker's brother Robert disputes this account, and insists that Van Gorkom set the deadlines. Symposium: Theory Informs Business Practice: Roundtable Discussion: Corporate Governance, 77 Chi.-Kent. L. Rev. 235, 237 (2001).—Ed.

problem thoroughly. Moreover, at the July, 1980 Board meeting the directors had reviewed Trans Union's newly prepared five-year forecast, and at the August, 1980 meeting Van Gorkom presented the results of a comprehensive study of Trans Union made by The Boston Consulting Group. This study was prepared over an 18 month period and consisted of a detailed analysis of all Trans Union subsidiaries, including competitiveness, profitability, cash throw-off, cash consumption, technical competence and future prospects for contribution to Trans Union's combined net income. Pritzker agreed to give the board 90 days to accept any better offers, but it could not solicit such offers or furnish non-public information to other bidders. The board discussed the terms, and accepted the offer, subject to two changes: (1) that Trans Union reserved the right to accept any better offer received during the 90 days and (2) Trans Union could share its non-public information with other potential bidders.

On September 22, Trans Union issued a press release announcing the signing of a definitive merger agreement. After the October 8 board meeting, another press release was issued announcing the 90 day market test, and that Pritzker had exercised his option to purchase 1 million shares at $38. Trans Union's press release also announced that Trans Union was now permitted actively to seek other offers and had retained Salomon Brothers for that purpose; and that if a more favorable offer were not received before February 1, 1981, Trans Union's shareholders would thereafter meet to vote on the Pritzker proposal. During the market test period, Trans Union received only two serious offers, one of which was contingent on obtaining financing, and the other of which fell through when the prospective buyer insisted that Trans Union rescind its agreement with Pritkzer to give it more time. On January 26, the board voted to proceed with the Pritzker merger.

The Chancery court applied the business judgment rule to the transaction, and held that the board's conduct was not reckless or improvident, but informed. The dissenting opinion in the Supreme Court noted that the outside directors on the Trans Union board were a distinguished group of Chicago area executives who had been well aware of Trans Union's problems, and had reviewed the new five year plan, as well as a study by an outside consulting group, the Boston Consulting Group.

The Supreme Court held that "[u]nder the business judgment rule there is no protection for directors who have made 'an unintelligent or unadvised judgment.'" The duty to exercise an informed business judgment "is in the nature of a duty of care . . ." The Supreme Court concluded that the Board of Directors did not reach an informed business judgment on September 20, 1980 in voting to "sell" the Company for $55 per share pursuant to the Pritzker cash-out merger proposal. The court's reasons were that the "directors (1) did not adequately inform themselves as to Van Gorkom's role in forcing the "sale" of the Company and in establishing the per share purchase price; (2) were uninformed as to the intrinsic value of the Company; and (3) given these circumstances, at a minimum, were grossly negligent in approving the "sale" of the Company upon two hours' consideration, without prior notice, and without the exigency of a crisis or emergency."

The defendants rely on the following factors to sustain the Trial Court's finding that the Board's decision was an informed one: (1) the magnitude of the premium or spread between the $55 Pritzker offering price and Trans Union's current market price of $38 per share; (2) the amendment of the Agreement as submitted on September 20 to permit the Board to accept any better offer during the "market test" period; (3) the collective experience and expertise of the Board's "inside" and "outside" directors; and (4) their reliance on Brennan's legal advice that the directors might be sued if they rejected the Pritzker proposal. The court rejected all of these justifications.

As for the adequacy of the price, the court emphasized the lack of information about "intrinsic" or "true" value, and stated that 'using market price as a basis for concluding that the premium adequately reflected the true value of the Company was a clearly faulty, indeed fallacious, premise. . . ." The fact that the board had previously reviewed the five year forecast and the Boston Consulting Group's report was rejected as evidence to support the board's valuation, on the basis that no one referred to these studies at the board meeting.

The 90 day time period for a market test was rejected by the court, on the basis that the agreement provided that Trans Union could not actively seek buyers, despite the subsequent press release by Trans Union that it was now permitted to seek buyers actively, and had retained an investment bank for that purpose. The court rejected this argument because there was no evidence presented that an active search had been engaged in, or that the original agreement had been amended to permit this. The court concluded that the board was grossly negligent in approving the transaction.

After the reversal the defendants settled the litigation for $23 million. $10 million came from the directors' and officers' liability policy, while the Pritzkers paid the remaining $13 million. In the words of Robert Pritzker, one of the directors, Allen Wallis was an academic, and "[f]or him to pay $1.3 million which he didn't have would have bankrupted him. It just didn't seem quite appropriate. One of the directors had passed away and his widow was the one who was supposed to come up with the $1.3 million. It just didn't seem fair. As a matter of fact, I think it was $13-and-a-half million, as I recall now. So we felt that we were the beneficiaries of the whole event. The directors didn't do anything wrong, why should they bear the responsibility? They had nothing to gain and everything to lose. Our feeling was that morally we owed it to them. So, our deal was we would pay 90 percent of that $1.35 million for each one, and they would pay 10 percent to charity. We felt they ought to have something, but not so gross a number. And, incidentally, Van Gorkom paid three or four of their charity contributions. He was about as high class as you could be." Symposium: Theory Informs Business Practice: Roundtable Discussion: Corporate Governance, 77 Chi.-Kent. L. Rev. 235, 238 (2001).

What does it take to be fully informed? One answer is to take more time, to ask more questions of management, and to obtain more financial data from management. One example that is frequently cited by the courts involved a recess of a meeting for a period of a week while additional information was compiled and distributed to the board. Treadway v. Care Corp., 638 F.2d 357 (2d Cir. 1980). Some decisions after Trans Union suggest that more deliberation alone is not enough; that valuation performed in a vacuum, even by an expert, may not be sufficient for a board to fulfill its duty to be fully informed. For example, in Hanson Trust PLC v. ML SCM Acquisition, Inc., 781 F.2d 264 (2d Cir. 1986), the court of appeals reversed the trial court's denial of a preliminary injunction to stop a successful bidder's exercise of an option to purchase SCM's crown jewel assets, two divisions that constituted 50% of its earnings. The SCM board had received a fairness opinion from its investment bankers that the option prices were fair. The court declined to hold that the board could rely on this opinion of experts, stating that "The proper exercise of due care by a director in informing himself of material information and in overseeing the outside advice on which he might appropriately rely is, of necessity, a precondition to performing his ultimate duty. . . ." 781 F.2d at 276. Because the board had not followed all of the procedures followed in Treadway, *supra*, the court held its decision was not protected by the business judgment rule.

The Trans Union decision was widely criticized, with one author calling it "one of the worst decisions in the history of corporate law." Daniel R. Fischel, The Business Judgment Rule and the Trans Union Case, 40 Bus. Law. 1437, 1455 (1985). This author describes investment bankers' fairness opinions as intended to provide liability cover for directors under the "reliance upon experts" language of Del. C.G.L. § 141(e) and MBCA § 8.30(d), (e) and (f). Carney, Fairness Opinions: How Fair Are They and Why We Should Do Nothing About It, 70 Wash. U. L. Q. 523 (1992).

The Trans Union decision was reaffirmed in Cede & Co. v. Technicolor, Inc., 634 A.2d 345 (Del. 1993), without acknowledgment of the controversy surrounding the earlier decision. Kamerman, the CEO of Technicolor, had negotiated the sale of Technicolor to MacAndrews & Forbes Group, headed by Ronald Perelman. Unlike Trans Union, Kamerman had negotiated price with Perelman, who had increased his offer. Further, Kamerman (and later the board) had the assistance of Goldman Sachs, which advised about the fairness of the final price and presented a 78-page "board book." Nevertheless, the board was not advised of these developments until a special meeting was called to approve the sale. The Chancery court "presumed that the board decision was not adequately informed to earn the protection of the business judgment rule, and was affirmed by the Supreme Court, which adopted "the Chancellor's presumed findings of the directors' failure to reach an informed decision. . . ." 634 A.2d at 370.

In later cases the Delaware Supreme Court has approved of deals where an agreed price was to be subsequently tested by the market. Lear Corporation was a premier parts supplier to the automobile industry that suffered when consumer preferences changed to smaller more fuel efficient vehicles. Lear engaged Lear hired J.P. Morgan to advise it. In 2006, after Carl Icahn acquired stock in the market at $16–17 per share, Lear engaged in a sale of new shares to him at $23, giving him 24% of the outstanding shares. Icahn's purchases led the market to anticipate an acquisition, and the market price rose to $30. In 2007 Icahn proposed to Rossiter, Lear's CEO, that a going private transaction would be good for Lear. The Lear board formed a special committee, and Rossiter negotiated with Icahn. Icahn initially offered $35, and after negotiations raised his bid to $36.

Icahn indicated that if the board wanted to conduct an auction he would pull his bid, but he would allow shopping once a deal was signed. The board, reviewing the fact that the stock had risen from $15 and withdrawal of the bid could cause the stock to decline, allowing Icahn to return at a lower price. Icahn's terms were a 45 day "go-shop" period when Lear could solicit bids. This would be followed by a "window shop" period when Lear could consider superior proposals, but could not solicit them. If the board accepted a superior bid, Lear would pay Icahn a termination fee. In In re Lear Corporation Shareholder Litigation, 926 A.2d 94 (Del. Ch. 2007), the court rejected a shareholder suit that the board had not performed its duty, noting that no other bidders expressed serious interest in Lear. The court held that the termination fees were not so high as to preclude competing bids.

Revlon, Inc. v. MacAndrews & Forbes Holdings, Inc.

506 A.2d 173 (Del. 1986).

■ MOORE, JUSTICE:

In this battle for corporate control of Revlon, Inc. (Revlon), the Court of Chancery enjoined certain transactions designed to thwart the efforts of Pantry Pride, Inc. (Pantry Pride) to acquire Revlon. The defendants are Revlon, its board of directors, and Forstmann Little & Co. and the latter's affiliated limited partnership (collectively, Forstmann). The injunction barred consummation of an option granted Forstmann to purchase certain Revlon assets (the lock-up option), a promise by Revlon to deal exclusively with Forstmann in the face of a takeover (the no-shop provision), and the payment of a $25 million cancellation fee to Forstmann if the transaction was aborted. The Court of Chancery found that the Revlon directors had breached their duty of care by entering into the foregoing transactions and effectively ending an active auction for the company. The trial court ruled that such arrangements are not illegal per se under Delaware law, but that their use under the circumstances here was impermissible. We agree. See MacAndrews & Forbes Holdings, Inc. v. Revlon, Inc., Del. Ch., 501 A.2d 1239 (1985). Thus, we granted this expedited interlocutory appeal to consider for the first time the validity of such defensive measures in the face of an active bidding contest for corporate control. Additionally, we address for the first time the extent to which a corporation may consider the impact of a takeover threat on constituencies other than shareholders. See Unocal Corp. v. Mesa Petroleum Co., Del. Supr., 493 A.2d 946, 955 (1985).

In our view, lock-ups and related agreements are permitted under Delaware law where their adoption is untainted by director interest or other breaches of fiduciary duty. The actions taken by the Revlon directors, however, did not meet this standard. Moreover, while concern for various corporate constituencies is proper when addressing a takeover threat, that principle is limited by the requirement that there be some rationally related benefit accruing to the stockholders. We find no such benefit here.

Thus, under all the circumstances we must agree with the Court of Chancery that the enjoined Revlon defensive measures were inconsistent with the directors' duties to the stockholders. Accordingly, we affirm.

I.

The somewhat complex maneuvers of the parties necessitate a rather detailed examination of the facts. The prelude to this controversy began in June 1985, when Ronald O. Perelman, chairman of the board and chief executive officer of Pantry Pride, met with his counterpart at Revlon, Michel C. Bergerac, to discuss a friendly acquisition of Revlon by Pantry Pride. Perelman suggested a price in the range of $40–50 per share, but the meeting ended with Bergerac dismissing those figures as considerably below Revlon's intrinsic value. All subsequent Pantry Pride overtures were rebuffed, perhaps in part based on Mr. Bergerac's strong personal antipathy to Mr. Perelman.

Thus, on August 14, Pantry Pride's board authorized Perelman to acquire Revlon, either through negotiation in the $42–$43 per share range, or by making a hostile tender offer at $45. Perelman then met with Bergerac and outlined Pantry Pride's alternate approaches. Bergerac remained adamantly opposed to such schemes and conditioned any further discussions of the matter on Pantry Pride executing a standstill agreement prohibiting it from acquiring Revlon without the latter's prior approval.

On August 19, the Revlon board met specially to consider the impending threat of a hostile bid by Pantry Pride.[3] At the meeting, Lazard Freres, Revlon's investment banker, advised the directors that $45 per share was a grossly inadequate price for the company. Felix Rohatyn and William Loomis of Lazard Freres explained to the board that Pantry Pride's financial strategy for acquiring Revlon would be through "junk bond" financing followed by a break-up of Revlon and the disposition of its assets. With proper timing, according to the experts, such transactions could produce a return to Pantry Pride of $60 to $70 per share, while a sale of the company as a whole would be in the "mid

---

[3] There were 14 directors on the Revlon board. Six of them held senior management positions with the company, and two others held significant blocks of its stock. Four of the remaining six directors were associated at some point with entities that had various business relationships with Revlon. On the basis of this limited record, however, we cannot conclude that this board is entitled to certain presumptions that generally attach to the decisions of a board whose majority consists of truly outside independent directors.

50" dollar range. Martin Lipton, special counsel for Revlon, recommended two defensive measures: first, that the company repurchase up to 5 million of its nearly 30 million outstanding shares; and second, that it adopt a Note Purchase Rights Plan. Under this plan, each Revlon shareholder would receive as a dividend one Note Purchase Right (the Rights) for each share of common stock, with the Rights entitling the holder to exchange one common share for a $65 principal Revlon note at 12% interest with a one-year maturity. The Rights would become effective whenever anyone acquired beneficial ownership of 20% or more of Revlon's shares, unless the purchaser acquired all the company's stock for cash at $65 or more per share. In addition, the Rights would not be available to the acquiror, and prior to the 20% triggering event the Revlon board could redeem the rights for 10 cents each. Both proposals were unanimously adopted.

Pantry Pride made its first hostile move on August 23 with a cash tender offer for any and all shares of Revlon at $47.50 per common share and $26.67 per preferred share, subject to (1) Pantry Pride's obtaining financing for the purchase, and (2) the Rights being redeemed, rescinded or voided.

The Revlon board met again on August 26. The directors advised the stockholders to reject the offer. Further defensive measures also were planned. On August 29, Revlon commenced its own offer for up to 10 million shares, exchanging for each share of common stock tendered one Senior Subordinated Note (the Notes) of $47.50 principal at 11.75% interest, due 1995, and one-tenth of a share of $9.00 Cumulative Convertible Exchangeable Preferred Stock valued at $100 per share. Lazard Freres opined that the notes would trade at their face value on a fully distributed basis.[4] Revlon stockholders tendered 87 percent of the outstanding shares (approximately 33 million), and the company accepted the full 10 million shares on a pro rata basis. The new Notes contained covenants which limited Revlon's ability to incur additional debt, sell assets, or pay dividends unless otherwise approved by the "independent" (non-management) members of the board.

At this point, both the Rights and the Note covenants stymied Pantry Pride's attempted takeover. The next move came on September 16, when Pantry Pride announced a new tender offer at $42 per share, conditioned upon receiving at least 90% of the outstanding stock. Pantry Pride also indicated that it would consider buying less than 90%, and at an increased price, if Revlon removed the impeding Rights. While this offer was lower on its face than the earlier $47.50 proposal, Revlon's

---

[4] Like bonds, the Notes actually were issued in denominations of $1,000 and integral multiples thereof. A separate certificate was issued in a total principal amount equal to the remaining sum to which a stockholder was entitled. Likewise, in the esoteric parlance of bond dealers, a Note trading at par ($1,000) would be quoted on the market at 100.

investment banker, Lazard Freres, described the two bids as essentially equal in view of the completed exchange offer.

The Revlon board held a regularly scheduled meeting on September 24. The directors rejected the latest Pantry Pride offer and authorized management to negotiate with other parties interested in acquiring Revlon. Pantry Pride remained determined in its efforts and continued to make cash bids for the company, offering $50 per share on September 27, and raising its bid to $53 on October 1, and then to $56.25 on October 7.

In the meantime, Revlon's negotiations with Forstmann and the investment group Adler & Shaykin had produced results. The Revlon directors met on October 3 to consider Pantry Pride's $53 bid and to examine possible alternatives to the offer. Both Forstmann and Adler & Shaykin made certain proposals to the board. As a result, the directors unanimously agreed to a leveraged buyout by Forstmann. The terms of this accord were as follows: each stockholder would get $56 cash per share; management would purchase stock in the new company by the exercise of their Revlon "golden parachutes";[5] Forstmann would assume Revlon's $475 million debt incurred by the issuance of the Notes; and Revlon would redeem the Rights and waive the Notes covenants for Forstmann or in connection with any other offer superior to Forstmann's. The board did not actually remove the covenants at the October 3 meeting, because Forstmann then lacked a firm commitment on its financing, but accepted the Forstmann capital structure, and indicated that the outside directors would waive the covenants in due course. Part of Forstmann's plan was to sell Revlon's Norcliff Thayer and Reheis divisions to American Home Products for $335 million. Before the merger, Revlon was to sell its cosmetics and fragrance division to Adler & Shaykin for $905 million. These transactions would facilitate the purchase by Forstmann or any other acquiror of Revlon.

When the merger, and thus the waiver of the Notes covenants, was announced, the market value of these securities began to fall. The Notes, which originally traded near par, around 100, dropped to 87.50 by October 8. One director later reported (at the October 12 meeting) a "deluge" of telephone calls from irate noteholders, and on October 10 the Wall Street Journal reported threats of litigation by these creditors.

Pantry Pride countered with a new proposal on October 7, raising its $53 offer to $56.25, subject to nullification of the Rights, a waiver of the Notes covenants, and the election of three Pantry Pride directors to the Revlon board. On October 9, representatives of Pantry Pride, Forstmann and Revlon conferred in an attempt to negotiate the fate of Revlon, but could not reach agreement. At this meeting Pantry Pride announced that

---

[5]   In the takeover context "golden parachutes" generally are understood to be termination agreements providing substantial bonuses and other benefits for managers and certain directors upon a change in control of a company.

it would engage in fractional bidding and top any Forstmann offer by a slightly higher one. It is also significant that Forstmann, to Pantry Pride's exclusion, had been made privy to certain Revlon financial data. Thus, the parties were not negotiating on equal terms.

Again privately armed with Revlon data, Forstmann met on October 11 with Revlon's special counsel and investment banker. On October 12, Forstmann made a new $57.25 per share offer, based on several conditions.[6] The principal demand was a lock-up option to purchase Revlon's Vision Care and National Health Laboratories divisions for $525 million, some $100–$175 million below the value ascribed to them by Lazard Freres, if another acquiror got 40% of Revlon's shares. Revlon also was required to accept a no-shop provision. The Rights and Notes covenants had to be removed as in the October 3 agreement. There would be a $25 million cancellation fee to be placed in escrow, and released to Forstmann if the new agreement terminated or if another acquiror got more than 19.9% of Revlon's stock. Finally, there would be no participation by Revlon management in the merger. In return, Forstmann agreed to support the par value of the Notes, which had faltered in the market, by an exchange of new notes. Forstmann also demanded immediate acceptance of its offer, or it would be withdrawn. The board unanimously approved Forstmann's proposal because: (1) it was for a higher price than the Pantry Pride bid, (2) it protected the noteholders, and (3) Forstmann's financing was firmly in place.[7] The board further agreed to redeem the rights and waive the covenants on the preferred stock in response to any offer above $57 cash per share. The covenants were waived, contingent upon receipt of an investment banking opinion that the Notes would trade near par value once the offer was consummated.

Pantry Pride, which had initially sought injunctive relief from the Rights plan on August 22, filed an amended complaint on October 14 challenging the lock-up, the cancellation fee, and the exercise of the Rights and the Notes covenants. Pantry Pride also sought a temporary restraining order to prevent Revlon from placing any assets in escrow or transferring them to Forstmann. Moreover, on October 22, Pantry Pride again raised its bid, with a cash offer of $58 per share conditioned upon

---

[6]   Forstmann's $57.25 offer ostensibly is worth $1 more than Pantry Pride's $56.25 bid. However, the Pantry Pride offer was immediate, while the Forstmann proposal must be discounted for the time value of money because of the delay in approving the merger and consummating the transaction. The exact difference between the two bids was an unsettled point of contention even at oral argument.

[7]   Actually, at this time about $400 million of Forstmann's funding was still subject to two investment banks using their "best efforts" to organize a syndicate to provide the balance. Pantry Pride's entire financing was not firmly committed at this point either, although Pantry Pride represented in an October 11 letter to Lazard Freres that its investment banker, Drexel Burnham Lambert, was highly confident of its ability to raise the balance of $350 million. Drexel Burnham had a firm commitment for this sum by October 18.

nullification of the Rights, waiver of the covenants, and an injunction of the Forstmann lock-up.

On October 15, the Court of Chancery prohibited the further transfer of assets, and eight days later enjoined the lock-up, no-shop, and cancellation fee provisions of the agreement. The trial court concluded that the Revlon directors had breached their duty of loyalty by making concessions to Forstmann, out of concern for their liability to the noteholders, rather than maximizing the sale price of the company for the stockholders' benefit. MacAndrews & Forbes Holdings, Inc. v. Revlon, Inc., 501 A.2d at 1249–50.

II.

To obtain a preliminary injunction, a plaintiff must demonstrate both a reasonable probability of success on the merits and some irreparable harm which will occur absent the injunction. Additionally, the Court shall balance the conveniences of and possible injuries to the parties.

A.

We turn first to Pantry Pride's probability of success on the merits. The ultimate responsibility for managing the business and affairs of a corporation falls on its board of directors. 8 Del.C. § 141(a). In discharging this function the directors owe fiduciary duties of care and loyalty to the corporation and its shareholders. These principles apply with equal force when a board approves a corporate merger pursuant to 8 Del.C. § 251(b); Smith v. Van Gorkom, Del. Supr., 488 A.2d 858, 873 (1985); and of course they are the bedrock of our law regarding corporate takeover issues. While the business judgment rule may be applicable to the actions of corporate directors responding to takeover threats, the principles upon which it is founded—care, loyalty and independence must first be satisfied.

If the business judgment rule applies, there is a "presumption that in making a business decision the directors of a corporation acted on an informed basis, in good faith and in the honest belief that the action taken was in the best interests of the company." Aronson v. Lewis, 473 A.2d at 812. However, when a board implements anti-takeover measures there arises "the omnipresent specter that a board may be acting primarily in its own interests, rather than those of the corporation and its shareholders . . . " Unocal Corp. v. Mesa Petroleum Co., 493 A.2d at 954. This potential for conflict places upon the directors the burden of proving that they had reasonable grounds for believing there was a danger to corporate policy and effectiveness, a burden satisfied by a showing of good faith and reasonable investigation. In addition, the directors must analyze the nature of the takeover and its effect on the corporation in order to ensure balance—that the responsive action taken is reasonable in relation to the threat posed. *Id.*

* * *

D.

However, when Pantry Pride increased its offer to $50 per share, and then to $53, it became apparent to all that the break-up of the company was inevitable. The Revlon board's authorization permitting management to negotiate a merger or buyout with a third party was a recognition that the company was for sale. The duty of the board had thus changed from the preservation of Revlon as a corporate entity to the maximization of the company's value at a sale for the stockholders' benefit. This significantly altered the board's responsibilities under the Unocal standards. It no longer faced threats to corporate policy and effectiveness, or to the stockholders' interests, from a grossly inadequate bid. The whole question of defensive measures became moot. The directors' role changed from defenders of the corporate bastion to auctioneers charged with getting the best price for the stockholders at a sale of the company.

III.

This brings us to the lock-up with Forstmann and its emphasis on shoring up the sagging market value of the Notes in the face of threatened litigation by their holders. Such a focus was inconsistent with the changed concept of the directors' responsibilities at this stage of the developments. The impending waiver of the Notes covenants had caused the value of the Notes to fall, and the board was aware of the noteholders' ire as well as their subsequent threats of suit. The directors thus made support of the Notes an integral part of the company's dealings with Forstmann, even though their primary responsibility at this stage was to the equity owners.

The original threat posed by Pantry Pride—the break-up of the company—had become a reality which even the directors embraced. Selective dealing to fend off a hostile but determined bidder was no longer a proper objective. Instead, obtaining the highest price for the benefit of the stockholders should have been the central theme guiding director action. Thus, the Revlon board could not make the requisite showing of good faith by preferring the noteholders and ignoring its duty of loyalty to the shareholders. The rights of the former already were fixed by contract. The noteholders required no further protection, and when the Revlon board entered into an auction-ending lock-up agreement with Forstmann on the basis of impermissible considerations at the expense of the shareholders, the directors breached their primary duty of loyalty.

The Revlon board argued that it acted in good faith in protecting the noteholders because Unocal permits consideration of other corporate constituencies. Although such considerations may be permissible, there are fundamental limitations upon that prerogative. A board may have regard for various constituencies in discharging its responsibilities, provided there are rationally related benefits accruing to the stockholders. Unocal, 493 A.2d at 955. However, such concern for non-stockholder interests is inappropriate when an auction among active bidders is in progress, and the object no longer is to protect or maintain the corporate enterprise but to sell it to the highest bidder.

* * *

A lock-up is not per se illegal under Delaware law. Its use has been approved in an earlier case. Thompson v. Enstar Corp., Del. Ch., 509 A.2d 578 (1984). Such options can entice other bidders to enter a contest for control of the corporation, creating an auction for the company and maximizing shareholder profit. Current economic conditions in the takeover market are such that a "white knight" like Forstmann might only enter the bidding for the target company if it receives some form of compensation to cover the risks and costs involved. However, while those lock-ups which draw bidders into the battle benefit shareholders, similar measures which end an active auction and foreclose further bidding operate to the shareholders' detriment.

Recently, the United States Court of Appeals for the Second Circuit invalidated a lock-up on fiduciary duty grounds similar to those here. Hanson Trust PLC, et al. v. ML SCM Acquisition Inc., et al., 781 F.2d 264 (2nd Cir. 1986). Citing Thompson v. Enstar Corp., *supra*, with approval, the court stated:

> In this regard, we are especially mindful that some lock-up options may be beneficial to the shareholders, such as those that induce a bidder to compete for control of a corporation, while others may be harmful, such as those that effectively preclude bidders from competing with the optionee bidder. 781 F.2d at 274.

In Hanson Trust, the bidder, Hanson, sought control of SCM by a hostile cash tender offer. SCM management joined with Merrill Lynch to propose a leveraged buy-out of the company at a higher price, and Hanson in turn increased its offer. Then, despite very little improvement in its subsequent bid, the management group sought a lock-up option to purchase SCM's two main assets at a substantial discount. The SCM directors granted the lock-up without adequate information as to the size of the discount or the effect the transaction would have on the company. Their action effectively ended a competitive bidding situation. The Hanson Court invalidated the lock-up because the directors failed to fully inform themselves about the value of a transaction in which management had a strong self-interest. "In short, the Board appears to have failed to ensure that negotiations for alternative bids were conducted by those whose only loyalty was to the shareholders." *Id.* at 277.

The Forstmann option had a similar destructive effect on the auction process. Forstmann had already been drawn into the contest on a preferred basis, so the result of the lock-up was not to foster bidding, but to destroy it. The board's stated reasons for approving the transaction were: (1) better financing, (2) noteholder protection, and (3) higher price. As the Court of Chancery found, and we agree, any distinctions between the rival bidders' methods of financing the proposal were nominal at best, and such a consideration has little or no significance in a cash offer for any and all shares. The principal object, contrary to the board's duty of care, appears to have been protection of the noteholders over the shareholders' interests.

While Forstmann's $57.25 offer was objectively higher than Pantry Pride's $56.25 bid, the margin of superiority is less when the Forstmann price is adjusted for the time value of money.* In reality, the Revlon board ended the auction in return for very little actual improvement in the final bid. The principal benefit went to the directors, who avoided personal liability to a class of creditors to whom the board owed no further duty under the circumstances. Thus, when a board ends an intense bidding contest on an insubstantial basis, and where a significant by-product of that action is to protect the directors against a perceived threat of personal liability for consequences stemming from the adoption of previous defensive measures, the action cannot withstand the enhanced scrutiny which Unocal requires of director conduct. See Unocal, 493 A.2d at 954–55.

In addition to the lock-up option, the Court of Chancery enjoined the no-shop provision as part of the attempt to foreclose further bidding by Pantry Pride. MacAndrews & Forbes Holdings, Inc. v. Revlon, Inc., 501 A.2d at 1251. The no-shop provision, like the lock-up option, while not per se illegal, is impermissible under the Unocal standards when a board's primary duty becomes that of an auctioneer responsible for selling the company to the highest bidder. The agreement to negotiate only with Forstmann ended rather than intensified the board's involvement in the bidding contest.

It is ironic that the parties even considered a no-shop agreement when Revlon had dealt preferentially, and almost exclusively, with Forstmann throughout the contest. After the directors authorized management to negotiate with other parties, Forstmann was given every negotiating advantage that Pantry Pride had been denied: cooperation from management, access to financial data, and the exclusive opportunity to present merger proposals directly to the board of directors. Favoritism for a white knight to the total exclusion of a hostile bidder might be justifiable when the latter's offer adversely affects shareholder interests, but when bidders make relatively similar offers, or dissolution of the company becomes inevitable, the directors cannot fulfill their enhanced Unocal duties by playing favorites with the contending factions. Market forces must be allowed to operate freely to bring the

---

* If we assume a three-month delay to close the Forstmann merger, Forstmann's $57.25, discounted at 10% per annum, has a present value of $55.85.—Ed.

target's shareholders the best price available for their equity.[16] Thus, as the trial court ruled, the shareholders' interests necessitated that the board remain free to negotiate in the fulfillment of that duty.

The court below similarly enjoined the payment of the cancellation fee, pending a resolution of the merits, because the fee was part of the overall plan to thwart Pantry Pride's efforts. We find no abuse of discretion in that ruling.

* * *

V.

In conclusion, the Revlon board was confronted with a situation not uncommon in the current wave of corporate takeovers. A hostile and determined bidder sought the company at a price the board was convinced was inadequate. The initial defensive tactics worked to the benefit of the shareholders, and thus the board was able to sustain its Unocal burdens in justifying those measures. However, in granting an asset option lock-up to Forstmann, we must conclude that under all the circumstances the directors allowed considerations other than the maximization of shareholder profit to affect their judgment, and followed a course that ended the auction for Revlon, absent court intervention, to the ultimate detriment of its shareholders. No such defensive measure can be sustained when it represents a breach of the directors' fundamental duty of care. See Smith v. Van Gorkom, Del. Supr., 488 A.2d 858, 874 (1985). In that context the board's action is not entitled to the deference accorded it by the business judgment rule. The measures were properly enjoined. The decision of the Court of Chancery, therefore, is affirmed.

The hostile takeover of cosmetics giant Revlon was a shot across the bow to those skeptics who ignored the awesome power of junk bond financing. Ronald Perelman, through the use of his Fort Lauderdale-based supermarket chain Pantry Pride and the raw financial power of Michael Millken's Drexel, Burnham Lambert, gave a telling lesson that in the financial world, David could slay Goliath. Pantry Pride had a net worth of $145 million after it had been discharged from bankruptcy in 1981. Conversely, when Perelman initially approached the CEO of Revlon, Michael Bergerac, to discuss a merger possibility, Revlon had a net worth over $1 billion. The relationship between Perelman and Bergerac, as the court pointed out, was not friendly. The cultured Bergerac, considered one of the elite players on Wall Street, was neither

---

[16] By this we do not embrace the "passivity" thesis rejected in Unocal. See 493 A.2d at 954–55, nn. 8–10. The directors' role remains an active one, changed only in the respect that they are charged with the duty of selling the company at the highest price attainable for the stockholders' benefit.

impressed with Perelman's aggressive ways, nor his Jewish heritage. To Bergerac, dealing with Perelman was beneath him.

In the end, Perelman won the battle but perhaps lost the war. The Delaware court's decision, undoing the anti-takeover actions of Revlon, were key to Perelman's eventual $3 billion leveraged buyout of the company. However, once in control, Revlon turned out to be much harder to manage for Perelman as compared to taking it over. Perelman took the company public in 1996, with the stock nearing $60 by mid-1998. However, by the fall of 2003, Revlon stock had dropped significantly, to $3-a-share.

QUESTIONS

1. Is this a duty of loyalty case or a duty of care case?

2. When are lock-up options permissible after this decision? Can a lock-up option be granted in advance of any search for a competing offer when an attractive bid is received?

3. What caused the directors' role to shift from defenders of the corporate bastion to auctioneers?

4. Why does the court reject protection of the noteholders as a valid purpose for the board? What rights to noteholders have that may distinguish them from stockholders?

5. When would considering the interests of corporate constituencies other than shareholders (e.g., employees, creditors, suppliers, customers or local communities) provide benefits that are rationally related to shareholder interests?

6. Could benefitting constituencies also benefit shareholders in the context of an auction?

NOTE

Duties to be informed about a transaction begin at the stage of selecting advisors for the board. In a number of cases investment banks have suffered conflicts of interest by seeking to participate in assisting buyers obtain funds to finance the transaction, thus motivating the advisers to assure completion of a deal, even if remaining independent or some other course might maximize shareholder value. See, e.g., In re Rural Metro Corp. Stockholders Litigation, 88 A.3d 54, affirmed *sub. nom.* RBC Capital Markets, LLC v. Jervis, 2015 Del. LEXIS 629 (Del. 2015); In re Del Monte Foods Co. Shareholders Litigation, 25 A.3d 813 (Del. Ch. 2011). As a result, counsel for boards of prospective sellers are now preparing conflict questionnaires for investment banks seeking to serve as advisers.

PROBLEMS

Problem 1.

Your client is the largest franchisee of a fast food company that has been experiencing difficulties. Earnings are flat, and the stock has declined about 75% from its high price of several years ago. The franchisor's 33% stockholder and company founder is the CEO and dominant force in the company. The franchisor's outside directors are disturbed about the way things are going, and several of them have expressed this concern to your client's CEO. Your client believes that it could do a better job of running the franchisor than the current management team, and would like to get a look at the franchisor's records to determine how bad things really are, and what can be done to fix them. Your client is willing to purchase part or all of the franchisor, provided it ends up in control and able to implement a turn-around strategy. Because your client is not yet ready to make a bid, and does not have its financing lined up, it does not want to trigger the franchisor's board's Revlon duties. Your client recognizes that to obtain access to confidential records of the franchisor it will have to enter into an agreement to hold that information confidential. At the same time, it must give the franchisor's board some reason to grant it access to these records. As the franchisee's lawyer, what would you say in a letter to the franchisor's board proposing such access?

If you represented the franchisor, can you advise the franchisor's board whether it can commit to such an agreement, assuming that Delaware law is likely to be applied?

Problem 2.

Your client has engaged in an auction which has come down to two final bidders, which have been given three weeks to engage in additional due diligence and formulate final bids. One bidder suggests that the payments scheduled for target company officers under certain golden parachutes be converted into stock in the successful bidder. This would reduce this bidder's cash costs by $30 million, thus enabling it to increase its bid. Can you inform the other bidder of this proposal? Must you inform the other bidder? What if the proposing bidder insists on confidentiality for the terms of its offer?

The following case involves the use of a leveraged Employee Stock Ownership Plan ("ESOP") as the vehicle for purchasing a controlling interest in a company. Leveraged ESOPs borrow most of the funds employed for the stock purchase from banks that, until 1996, were permitted to exclude one-half of the interest received from taxable income. Given competition among banks, this meant that these tax savings were passed along to the borrower in the form of a lower interest rate than any other buyer could obtain, due to the tax subsidy. The creating corporation entered into a commitment to fund the ESOP annually to allow it to service the loan, and guarantees the loan to the bank. This allowed a newly created ESOP to purchase a very large percentage of a company's shares immediately after its creation.

Barkan v. Amsted Industries, Incorporated

567 A.2d 1279 (Del., 1989).

■ WALSH, JUSTICE:

This is an appeal from a Court of Chancery decision that approved the settlement of several class action lawsuits. The litigation arose out of a management-sponsored leveraged buyout ("MBO") of all of the common stock of Amsted Industries, Inc. ("Amsted") by members of Amsted's management and a newly formed employee stock ownership plan ("ESOP"). * * * Leonard Barkan ("Barkan"), appeals from the settlement order, charging that the Chancellor's decision constituted an abuse of discretion.

Barkan asserts three separate grounds for challenging the Chancellor's approval of the settlement. First, he argues that the Chancellor neglected to recognize that Amsted's directors had breached their fiduciary duties of loyalty and due care. Specifically, Barkan argues that the directors failed to implement procedures designed to maximize Amsted's sale price once its sale became inevitable, as required by Revlon, Inc. v. MacAndrews & Forbes Holdings, Inc., Del. Supr., 506 A.2d 173 (1986). According to Barkan, the Chancellor applied an impermissibly strict standard in determining the likelihood of this claim's success. * * *

The record contains evidence that the MBO was essentially fair to shareholders and that Amsted's directors did not seek to thwart higher bids. Under our standard of review, we cannot say that the Chancellor abused his discretion in approving the settlement. * * * Accordingly, we affirm the Chancellor's decision in all respects.

I

The facts giving rise to this litigation are essentially uncontroverted, but their complexities merit some discussion. In early 1985, Charles Hurwitz ("Hurwitz") began acquiring a significant number of shares of Amsted common stock through an entity known as Associates. Although Hurwitz claimed that the shares were being purchased for investment purposes only, he was widely recognized as a sophisticated investor in the market for corporate control. Accordingly, Amsted's board of directors retained Goldman, Sachs & Co. in May, 1985, to counsel them concerning possible responses to Hurwitz's overture. Goldman Sachs advised the board that Hurwitz had earned a reputation for attempting to acquire control of a corporation at a price below its real value or, alternatively, to extract "greenmail." The investment bankers suggested an array of possible defenses to the challenge posed by Hurwitz. These included a stock purchase rights plan [a "poison pill"], a stock repurchase by the corporation, a friendly acquisition by a third party, a management-sponsored leveraged buyout, and a management-sponsored leveraged buyout involving an ESOP.

* * *

With the rights plan in place, Amsted began to consider the possibility of undertaking a leveraged buyout involving an ESOP. Because such a transaction offered significant tax advantages, it was felt that it would provide shareholders with the highest possible price for their shares. On September 26, 1985, the Amsted board authorized the establishment of an ESOP, although no definite proposal for undertaking an MBO was discussed at that time. On October 22, 1985, however, the Amsted board established a Special Committee of its members to investigate the merits of any transaction involving a change of corporate control. The Special Committee was composed of directors who were neither officers of Amsted nor beneficiaries of the ESOP. Although the Special Committee was given the power to evaluate the fairness of any acquisition proposal made by a third party, the Committee was instructed not to engage in an active search for alternatives to an MBO.

Several days later, on October 29, 1985, the Amsted board terminated certain pension plans covering substantially all Amsted employees who were not subject to collective bargaining agreements. The board's goal was to make the excess assets in the plans (estimated by Goldman Sachs to be worth approximately $75 million) available to finance an MBO. On November 4, 1985, an MBO proposal was finally presented to the Amsted board by the ESOP trustees and members of Amsted senior management (the "MBO Group"). Under the proposal, the MBO Group would purchase all of Amsted's outstanding stock for $37 per share of cash and $27 per share in principal amount of a new issue of subordinated discount debentures, valued at $11 per share.

The next day, the first of the suits involved in this litigation was filed. Three similar suits were filed in the course of the following week. It was the plaintiffs in these four suits who eventually reached the settlement with Amsted that is the subject of this appeal. At about the same time, the MBO proposal hit a roadblock. Citibank, which had informally agreed to assemble financing for the deal, concluded that the proposed transaction was too highly leveraged and withdrew its support. On November 13, 1985, First National Bank of Chicago ("First National") agreed to take Citibank's place. However, First National proposed that $3 per share of cash in the original proposal be replaced with preferred stock having a face value of $4 and a market value of $3. The total value of this package of consideration remained $48 per share.

Through the rest of November, December, and much of January, Goldman Sachs and the MBO Group worked to arrange financing for the transaction proposed by First National. By late January, however, the MBO Group decided that the value of the consideration offered would have to be reduced. Decreased earnings in the first quarter of fiscal year 1986 (which ended December 31, 1985) led the MBO Group to doubt Amsted's ability to perform at the level previously anticipated. Accordingly, when the MBO Group finally went to Amsted's board with a proposal on January 29, 1986, they offered a $45 per share package, with $31 per share in cash, $4 per share in preferred stock valued at $3 per share, and $27 in principal amount of subordinated discount debentures valued at $11 per share.

The Special Committee met that day to consider the proposal. Salomon Brothers, the Special Committee's investment advisors, opined that a price of $45 was "high in the range of fairness." The Special Committee, however, directed Salomon Brothers to seek an increase in the cash component of the package. The MBO Group quickly agreed to offer an additional $1.25 in cash, making the total consideration worth $46.25 per share. The Special Committee approved the increased offer and recommended it to the full board, which also gave its blessing to the MBO. The board also voted to redeem the common stock purchase rights plan in order to make the transaction possible. An Exchange Offer followed shortly thereafter on February 5, 1986.

At this point, the long-quiescent Hurwitz approached Goldman Sachs and voiced his dissatisfaction with the adequacy of the offer. After some negotiation, Hurwitz agreed to tender his shares if the cash component of the transaction were increased again, by $.75 per share to $33 per share. Goldman Sachs agreed to recommend such an increase if the plaintiffs in the four lawsuits filed in November, 1985 could be persuaded to reach a settlement. The plaintiffs had not yet conducted any discovery nor amended their complaints to reflect the developments that had occurred since November. Nevertheless, on February 10, 1986, the plaintiffs agreed to a full settlement, conditioned upon their being permitted to conduct "confirmatory discovery" at a later date. On February 19, 1986, the Exchange Offer was amended to reflect the increased cash consideration. The Offer closed on March 5, 1986, with 89% of the outstanding stock having been tendered. The MBO itself was closed on June 2, 1986.

On March 12, 1986, Barkan commenced his action challenging the Exchange Offer. On July 3, 1986, the original plaintiffs and the defendants filed a Stipulation and Agreement of Compromise and Settlement (the "Settlement Agreement") with the Court of chancery. The Settlement Agreement was approved by the Chancellor, who determined that although difficult questions were raised by the course of events leading to the settlement, the settlement was fundamentally fair.

* * *

IV

* * *

Barkan also challenges the correctness of the Chancellor's evaluation of the merits of his breach of duty claims. He asserts that the directors of Amsted committed egregious breaches of their duties and that the Chancellor overlooked clear evidence of impropriety in finding that the process that led to the MBO and the Settlement Agreement was fair to shareholders. In short, Barkan would have us rule that his claims would not be "difficult to prove." We find, however, that there is ample evidence in the record to support the Chancellor's evaluation of Barkan's breach of duty claims.

There is some dispute among the parties as to the meaning of Revlon, as well as its relevance to the outcome of this case. We believe that the general principles announced in Revlon, in Unocal Corp. v. Mesa Petroleum Co., Del. Supr., 493 A.2d 946 (1985), and in Moran v. Household International, Inc., Del. Supr., 500 A.2d 1346 (1985) govern this case and every case in which a fundamental change of corporate control occurs or is contemplated. However, the basic teaching of these precedents is simply that the directors must act in accordance with their fundamental duties of care and loyalty. Unocal, 493 A.2d at 954–55; Revlon, 506 A.2d at 180. It is true that a court evaluating the propriety of a change of control or a takeover defense must be mindful of "the omnipresent specter that a board may be acting primarily in its own interests, rather than those of the corporation and its shareholders." Unocal, 493 A.2d at 954. Nevertheless, there is no single blueprint that a board must follow to fulfill its duties. A stereotypical approach to the sale and acquisition of corporate control is not to be expected in the face of the evolving techniques and financing devices employed in today's corporate environment. Mills Acquisition Co. v. MacMillan, Inc., Del. Supr., 559 A.2d 1261, 1286–88 (1988). Rather, a board's actions must be evaluated in light of relevant circumstances to determine if they were undertaken with due diligence and in good faith. If no breach of duty is found, the board's actions are entitled to the protections of the business judgment rule.

This Court has found that certain fact patterns demand certain responses from the directors. Notably, in Revlon we held that when several suitors are actively bidding for control of a corporation, the directors may not use defensive tactics that destroy the auction process. Revlon, 506 A.2d at 182–85. When it becomes clear that the auction will result in a change of corporate control, the board must act in a neutral manner to encourage the highest possible price for shareholders. Id. However, Revlon does not demand that every change in the control of a Delaware corporation be preceded by a heated bidding contest. Revlon is merely one of an unbroken line of cases that seek to prevent the conflicts of interest that arise in the field of mergers and acquisitions by demanding that directors act with scrupulous concern for fairness to shareholders. When multiple bidders are competing for control, this concern for fairness forbids directors from using defensive mechanisms to thwart an auction or to favor one bidder over another. *Id.* When the board is considering a single offer and has no reliable grounds upon which to judge its adequacy, this concern for fairness demands a canvas of the market to determine if higher bids may be elicited. In re Fort Howard Corp. Shareholders Litig., Del. Ch., C.A. No. 991 (Aug. 8, 1988). When, however, the directors possess a body of reliable evidence with which to evaluate the fairness of a transaction, they may approve that transaction without conducting an active survey of the market. As the Chancellor recognized, the circumstances in which this passive approach is acceptable are limited. "A decent respect for reality forces one to admit that . . . advice [of an investment banker] is frequently a pale substitute for the dependable information that a canvas of the relevant market can provide." In re Amsted Indus. Litig., letter op. at 19–20. The need for adequate information is central to the enlightened evaluation of a transaction that a board must make. Nevertheless, there is no single method that a board must employ to acquire such information. Here, the Chancellor found that the advice of the Special Committee's investment bankers, when coupled with the special circumstances surrounding the negotiation and consummation of the MBO, supported a finding that Amsted's directors had acted in good faith to arrange the best possible transaction for shareholders. Our own review of the record leads us to rule that the Chancellor's finding was well within the scope of his discretion.

Several factors provide the basis for the Chancellor's finding. First, the investment community had been aware that Amsted was a likely target for a takeover or an MBO from the moment that Hurwitz announced his sizeable interest in the corporation. In the parlance of the market, Hurwitz's actions put Amsted "in play." Yet in the ten months that passed between Hurwitz's appearance on the scene and the closing of the Exchange Offer, not one bidder emerged to make an offer for control of Amsted. Of course, Amsted was shielded by its stock purchase rights plan during much of this period. Nevertheless, the spate of takeover litigation that has confronted Delaware courts in recent years readily demonstrates that such "poison pills" do not prevent rival bidders from expressing their interest in acquiring a corporation. * * * [W]hen it is widely known that some change of control is in the offing and no rival bids are forthcoming over an extended period of time, that fact is supportive of the board's decision to proceed.

More important, the Amsted board had valid reasons for believing that no rival bidder would be able to surpass the price offered by the MBO Group. Including an ESOP in the transaction allowed the MBO Group to receive significant tax advantages that could be reflected in the price offered to shareholders. Even so, the MBO Group had some difficulty arranging financing for its proposal because lenders felt that the performance of the corporation might be dampened by cyclical downturns. In fact, such an event occurred in late 1985, as Amsted's earnings for the first quarter of fiscal year 1986 suffered a significant decline. Thus, when in late January, 1986, Salomon Brothers opined that $45 per share was a very fair price, the Board had good reason not only to accept Salomon Brothers opinion, but also to believe that no alternative deal could give shareholders a better price. As the MBO Group increased its offer to $46.25 and then to $47 per share, the evidence supporting the fairness of the deal increased still further. Thus, we believe that when the Exchange Offer was made, the directors could conclude in good faith that they had approved the best possible deal for shareholders.

We certainly do not condone in all instances the imposition of the sort of "no-shop" restriction that bound Amsted's Special Committee. Where a board has no reasonable basis upon which to judge the adequacy of a contemplated transaction, a no-shop restriction gives rise to the inference that the board seeks to forestall competing bids. Even here, a judicious market survey might have been desirable, since it would have made it clear beyond question that the board was acting to protect the shareholder's interests. Thus, while numerous factors—timing, publicity, tax advantages, and Amsted's declining performance—point to the directors' good faith belief that the shareholders were getting the best price, we decline to fashion an iron-clad rule for determining when a market test is not required. The evidence that will support a finding of good faith in the absence of some sort of market test is by nature circumstantial; therefore, its evaluation by a court must be open-textured. However, the crucial element supporting a finding of good faith is knowledge. It must be clear that the board had sufficient knowledge of relevant markets to form the basis for its belief that it acted in the best interests of the shareholders. The situations in which a completely passive approach to acquiring such knowledge is appropriate are limited. The Chancellor found this to be such a situation, however, and we believe his finding to be within the scope of his discretion.

* * *

VI

We conclude that the Chancellor did not abuse his discretion in approving a full settlement found of the lawsuits challenging the MBO. The Chancellor correctly found that none of the plaintiffs' allegations had a high probability of success on the merits and that an adequate consideration had been paid for their release. These findings are supported by ample evidence on the record. Accordingly, the Order of the Court of Chancery is affirmed.

QUESTIONS

1. How can the court justify the Board's instructions to the Special Committee not to seek alternatives to an MBO?

2. How could the Amsted board be certain the price was the best obtainable?

3. Assuming that the poison pill is an effective defense against a hostile takeover bid, how can the court be comfortable that there was no bidder interest in Amsted?

4. Which is more reliable in this case, the reactions of prospective lenders or the advice of the board's financial advisers?

5. Note that the November 4 MBO proposal included $27 per share in principal amount of a new issue of subordinated discount debentures, valued at $11 per share. Why is there such a difference between face value and projected market value? Does this provide the Amsted Board with any information about value?

6. Why is a no-shop permissible here when there has been no shopping for alternative bids? Did this no-shop have the effect of drawing a bidder into making a bid?

7. Note that the Amsted Board terminated certain pension plans to make excess assets in the plans available to finance an MBO. Where pension plans provide promises of fixed payments to retired employees ("defined benefit" plans), the investments may appreciate at such a rate that the assets in the plan are more than sufficient to make the promised payments, and thus are "overfunded." In this case an employer may sometimes reduce its future contributions to the plan, or it may terminate the plan by purchasing pre-paid annuities for employees that protect their vested claims, thus freeing up the cash for other uses by the employer. What does such a termination right say about board duties to employees versus shareholders?

NOTE

Many of the decisions invalidating board action approving a sale in the absence of adequate shopping have involved management-led leveraged buyouts, where a conflict of interest was present and the board appeared to favor management in the bidding. Mills Acquisition Co. v. MacMillan, Inc., 559 A.2d 1261 (Del. Supr. 1989); Revlon, *supra*; Hanson Trust PLC v. ML SCM Acquisition, Inc., 781 F.2d 264 (2d Cir. 1986), Edelman v. Freuhauf Corp., 798 F.2d 882 (6th Cir. 1986) and Black & Decker Corp. v. American Standard, Inc., 682 F.Supp. 772, Fed. Sec. L. Rep. (CCH) ¶ 93,685 (D.Del. 1988).

Barkan is just one example of a case that allowed a board to diverge from a strict "auction" model of putting a company up for sale. In In re Fort Howard Corporation Shareholders Litigation, 1988 WL 83147 (Del. Ch.

1988) the management team became concerned about Fort Howard's low stock price after the market crash of October 1987, and feared that a takeover bid at a low price might succeed. Having first consulted with investment bankers about the feasability of an MBO, the CEO approached the board about their interest in such a transaction. He informed the board that management was not yet in a position to make a proposal, and that if the board's willingness to entertain an offer was announced too early, a lower-value hostile bid might succeed before management could make an offer. The board agreed, after satisfying itself that a post-contract market test would be sufficient. After vigorous negotiating, the Board's financial adviser informed the board that management and its investment banker could not finance a bid higher than the one presently offered, and the board approved the MBO. A press release announced the deal, and that the company was available for offers from other parties. Eight other bidders inquired, and received the same information that management's investment banker had. No other bids were forthcoming. Chancellor Allen was bothered by the favoritism shown management, but concluded that the market test was a real one, and that there were no barriers to a higher bid, in the form of lock-up options on the company's stock or a prohibitively high break-up fee. The court ruled that the board could favor one bidder over others, if it believed this would further shareholder interests. In response to the argument that Revlon required an auction, Chancellor Allen wrote, "that is not my understanding of Revlon," and that the Revlon decision was based on the board's lack of good faith in favoring one bidder over another.

In re Holly Farms Corporation Shareholders Litigation, [1988–89 Decisions] FED. SEC. L. REP. (CCH) ¶ 94,181 (Del. Ch. 1988) involved a board's acceptance of a white knight's offer without ever letting a hostile bidder know an auction was under way. Tyson Foods' representative had met with Holly's CEO to express interest in an acquisition, but had been told by Holly's CEO that the board had instructed him that Holly wished to remain independent. When Tyson made a written offer to Holly's CEO, the Holly board instructed its financial adviser, Morgan Stanley, to explore alternatives, one of which included ConAgra, which had previously indicated interest in an acquisition of Holly. Subsequently, Tyson began a cash tender offer at $52 per share, which Morgan Stanley opined was inadequate. On November 11, 1988, Holly's CEO wrote Tyson that the Holly board would meet on November 16 to consider all its alternatives, but that no decision had yet been made on whether to sell the company. Tyson increased its offer to $54. The board met and approved a leveraged recapitalization and an acquisition by ConAgra with an estimated value of $54, which it concluded was in the best interest of its shareholders. Thereafter, Tyson claimed it was willing to offer $57. In enjoining the merger, the court noted that the Holly board negotiated vigorously with ConAgra, but never made a serious effort to negotiate with Tyson, and never told Tyson it had determined to sell Holly.

In In re Netsmart Technologies, Inc. Shareholders Litigation, 924 A.2d 171 (Del. Ch. 2007), Vice Chancellor Strine reviewed the actions of a board and special committee in selling a microcap company, with a market capitalization of less than $100 million. While the company was the dominant player in a niche medical information market, it received little attention from analysts and its stock price languished. While looking for strategic alliances the company's financial adviser had mentioned the possibility that it could be purchased to numerous larger industry participants over the previous five years. It was only when a private equity firm expressed some interest in an acquisition that management and the board began actively to consider a sale. With the financial adviser, management recommended that the search be limited to private equity buyers, bypassing operating firms in the medical field. Two reasons were given: putting the company up for auction in a public way could harm its relationships with customers and its stock value if no buyers were found, and sharing information with potential competitors could be harmful. Further, private equity buyers had been outbidding strategic buyers in the recent past. The financial advisers identified seven private equity firms, some of whom had made medical acquisitions recently, and targeted them for an auction. Vice Chancellor Strine rejected claims that the special committee had acted in bad faith, although the record was less than clear on how diligently the committee had participated in the auction process. But he held that the auction process was fatally flawed by the exclusion of a canvas of any strategic buyers. Vice Chancellor Strine wrote:

> In a targeted canvass, confidentiality issues could have been responsibly addressed, and there is no record basis to believe that strategic acquirers (which have their own confidentiality concerns) were more likely to leak than private equity firms. And, of course, Conway and William Blair claim to have tossed out Netsmart's name to strategic players through the years, when Netsmart was more, not less vulnerable, in terms of retaining and acquiring customers. And, like the canvass of private equity buyers, there was no need to fish with a seine net for strategic buyers. The Special Committee could have used a fly rod in that market, too.

Vice Chancellor Strine rejected the defendants' claim that they had retained a fiduciary out to deal with any buyers who might show up on their own, although they relinquished the right to actively shop the company during the "window shopping" period. He concluded that the company was so small that many prospects might never notice the announcement of its deal, and might not be aware of its attractions. Nevertheless, he declined to enjoin the purchase altogether, because there might not be any better offers, and only enjoined the shareholder vote until the deficiencies he found in the proxy disclosures were remedied.

In re Novell, Inc. Shareholders Litigation, 2013 Del. Ch. LEXIS 1 involved the question of whether directors were protected from liability under exculpatory language adopted pursuant to section 102(b)(7) of the Delaware code. Vice Chancellor Noble denied a motion to dismiss the complaint, holding that charges of favoring one bidder stated a claim of bad faith, not covered by exculpatory clauses. In this case the board began with a thorough search for candidates through its investment banker after receiving an unsolicited acquisition proposal. As part of this process, the board authorized one bidder, Attachmate, to partner with two of Novel's principal shareholders, to assist in financing its bid. After nine proposals were received by the bid deadline, the board determined to pursue discussions with five of them, including Attachmate, and made presentations to all of them. Several months later the board requested "best and final offers" from Attachmate and "Party C." While the bids were close, Party C's bid was a few cents higher. Despite this, the board granted Attachmate exclusive negotiating rights. During this period the board received a letter of intent from a third party to buy much of its patent portfolio for a significant cash payment, which would allow any buyer to increase its offer. The board informed Attachmate of this, but not Party C. At a later date, Attachmate raised its bid to $5.25 per share, while Party C offered $5.75. Party C was never offered the opportunity to work with Novell's largest shareholders.

Absent some reasonable explanation, the Novell Defendants and their financial advisor treated Party C in a way that was both adverse and materially different from the way they treated Attachmate. Party C could not team with any other interested bidder and, more importantly, was not informed of the Patent Sale which would have provided a substantial amount of cash at closing. The availability of additional funds might have allowed (or incentivized) Party C to increase its offer. Because its offer was roughly comparable to the price Attachmate was offering, it is reasonably conceivable that Party C would have increased its bid to an amount higher than that of Attachmate.

An independent and disinterested board, however, is not absolutely required to treat all bidders equally. The Board could have dealt with bidders differently if the shareholders' interests justified such a course. From the factual sources (primarily, the Amended Complaint) available to the Court on this motion to dismiss, those reasons—if they existed—cannot be ascertained. Perhaps the Attachmate offer was more credible. Perhaps Attachmate had no more due diligence needs. Perhaps Attachmate had its funding for the transaction arranged, while Party C was still searching for financing. Perhaps Novell had been for sale too long and there was concern that the process would become "stale" or that, if Party C were allowed an opportunity to evaluate the benefits of the Patent Sale, Attachmate would lose interest in a possible transaction.

The Amended Complaint, when considered under the applicable standard, states a reasonably conceivable claim that the Novell Defendants treated a serious bidder in a materially different way and that approach might have deprived shareholders of the best offer reasonably attainable. It might not take much evidence from the Novell Defendants to put that disparate treatment in a different context and to show that Plaintiffs' claim lacks merit. The Novell Defendants, however, do not have the opportunity to "prove their case" on a motion to dismiss.

The Amended Complaint, thus, states a claim for a breach of fiduciary duty. The question becomes one of whether the Novell Defendants acted in bad faith or merely breached the duty of care. In the absence of bad faith, their actions would be exculpated by the Section 102(b)(7) provision in Novell's charter. If their conduct is adequately alleged to have been in bad faith, the exculpation provision will not shield them at this point.

A fiduciary's conduct was in bad faith if the fiduciary acted with a purpose other than advancing shareholder interests (i.e., the best interests of the corporation), intentionally violated relevant positive law, intentionally failed to respond to a known duty or exhibited a conscious disregard of a known duty. If the allegations involve a fiduciary's duty to act, the effort required to satisfy that duty is minimal. In that context, the question is whether the fiduciary "utterly failed to attempt to obtain the best sale price." Here, the Amended Complaint demonstrates that the Board, through the prolonged sales process, far exceeded that threshold.

A plaintiff has the burden to overcome the presumption that a fiduciary acts in good faith. One way to accomplish that objective would be for the plaintiff to demonstrate that the fiduciary's actions were "so far beyond the bounds of reasonable judgment that it seems essentially inexplicable on any ground other than bad faith." This formulation of the bad faith standard best captures the focus of the Plaintiffs' challenge. Why the Novell Defendants did not tell Party C about the proceeds of the Patent Sale has no apparent answer in the record before the Court. That conduct, coupled with the fact that Novell kept Attachmate fully informed, is enough for pleading stage purposes to support an inference that the Board's actions were in bad faith. As indicated, there may be a plausible explanation for their conduct, but the Court does not have access to those facts. Because it is reasonably conceivable that the Plaintiffs may be able to demonstrate that the Novell Defendants' conduct was in bad faith, the exculpation of the Section 102(b)(7) charter provision is not available. Accordingly, this claim may not be dismissed at this time.

In contrast, Vice Chancellor Noble dismissed a complaint alleging bad faith discrimination against a prospective buyer in In re BJ's Wholesale Club, Inc., 2013 WL 453941 (Del. Ch.). BJ's board became aware of the interest of private equity firm Leonard Green & Partners, L.P. ("LGP") when it filed a Schedule 13D with the SEC, disclosing its 9.5% ownership and its interest in a buyout of BJ's. The board created an independent special committee and ultimately employed Morgan Stanley as its financial advisor. It issued a press release announcing it had decided to explore strategic alternatives.

Party A, apparently either Costco or Sam's Club, the only two direct competitors, expressed its interest to Morgan Stanley. Morgan Stanley was "dismissive" of Party A's expression of interest, because it had no previous acquisition experience. The special committee determined that it would not be comfortable sharing confidential information with Party A. Subsequently Party A offered to acquire BJ's at a price of $55–$60 per share, subject to certain conditions. The special committee determined that it would not be appropriate to pursue the Party A offer. Apparently Party A did not pursue the matter further. The special committee did share a confidential offering memorandum with twenty-three private equity firms. At this point Party B, a private equity firm, proposed a hybrid transaction that involved a recapitalization, which Party B valued at $60–$72 per share, which was rejected as well. In the final round of bidding, only LGP submitted an offer. After negotiations with the special committee, this offer was raised from $50 to $51.25, which represented a 38% premium over BJ's market price before the LGP announcement. In determining that bad faith was not sufficiently alleged, Vice Chancellor Noble wrote:

> Morgan Stanley's dismissive disposition toward Party A and Sen's characterization of Party A's interest, as told to her by a banker at Morgan Stanley, does not support a reasonable inference that the Board acted in bad faith. First, why the Court should attribute Morgan Stanley's attitude toward Party A to Sen, the Special Committee or the Board is not adequately pleaded in the Complaint. Even assuming that Sen believed and communicated to the Board that Party A's interest was "something to shrug off," her statement is not necessarily indicative of bad faith. Nor does it reasonably show the Board's disposition toward Party A as a possible acquirer. Something of a negative attitude toward a competitor is not unusual. Second, and more importantly, the Defendant Directors had no reason not to rely upon Morgan Stanley's advice that strategic buyers, including Party A, would not likely be interested or that their interest would not likely lead to a serious offer. Thus, even if the Board had adopted an indifferent attitude toward Party A, that attitude would not have been unreasonable given the fact that Party A, according to Morgan Stanley, had no history of acquiring domestic companies. At the very least, any judgment that the Board did make that Party A was not a serious bidder was not "so far beyond the bounds of reasonable judgment that it seems essentially inexplicable on any ground other than bad faith."

> Similarly, the Board's decision not to share confidential information with Party A does not raise an inference of bad faith. Because Party A was one of only two direct channel competitors to BJ's, the Board could reasonably have had concerns about sharing confidential business information with a competitor, especially where, as here, the seriousness of Party A's interest was in doubt. That decision, therefore, was also not "so far beyond the bounds of reasonable judgment that it seems essentially inexplicable on any ground other than bad faith."

The court granted the motion to dismiss.

C&J Energy Services, Inc. v. City of Miami General Employees' and Sanitation Employees' Retirement Trust

107 A.3d 1049 (Del. 2014).

■ STRINE, CHIEF JUSTICE:

I.   INTRODUCTION

This is an appeal from the Court of Chancery's imposition of an unusual preliminary injunction. City of Miami General Employees' and Sanitation Employees' Retirement Trust ("the plaintiffs") brought a class action on behalf of itself and other stockholders in C & J Energy Services, Inc. ("C & J") to enjoin a merger between C & J and a division of its competitor, Nabors Industries Ltd. ("Nabors"). The proposed transaction is itself unusual in that C & J, a U.S. corporation, will acquire a subsidiary of Nabors, which is domiciled in Bermuda, but Nabors will retain a majority of the equity in the surviving company. To obtain more favorable tax rates, the surviving entity, C & J Energy Services, Ltd. ("New C & J"), will be based in Bermuda, and thus subject to lower corporate tax rates than C & J currently pays.

To temper Nabors' majority voting control of the surviving company, C & J negotiated for certain protections, including a bye-law[2] guaranteeing that all stockholders would share *pro rata* in any future sale of New C & J, which can only be repealed by a unanimous stockholder vote. C & J also bargained for a "fiduciary out" if a superior proposal was to emerge during a lengthy passive market check, an unusual request for the buyer in a change of control transaction. And during that market check, a potential competing bidder faced only modest deal protection barriers.

Although the Court of Chancery found that the C & J board harbored no conflict of interest and was fully informed about its own company's value, the court determined there was a "plausible" violation of the board's Revlon duties because the board did not affirmatively shop the company either before or after signing. On that basis, the Court of Chancery enjoined the stockholder vote for 30 days, despite finding no reason to believe that C & J stockholders—who must vote to approve the transaction—would not have a fair opportunity to evaluate the deal for themselves on its economic merits.

* * *

We assume for the sake of analysis that Revlon was invoked by the pending transaction because Nabors will acquire a majority of New C &

---

[2]   Under Bermuda law, by-laws are spelled "bye-laws."

J's voting shares. But we nonetheless conclude that the Court of Chancery's injunction cannot stand. A preliminary injunction must be supported by a finding by the Court of Chancery that the plaintiffs have demonstrated a reasonable probability of success on the merits. The Court of Chancery made no such finding here, and the analysis that it conducted rested on the erroneous proposition that a company selling itself in a change of control transaction is required to shop itself to fulfill its duty to seek the highest immediate value. But Revlon and its progeny do not set out a specific route that a board must follow when fulfilling its fiduciary duties, and an independent board is entitled to use its business judgment to decide to enter into a strategic transaction that promises great benefit, even when it creates certain risks.[7] When a board exercises its judgment in good faith, tests the transaction through a viable passive market check, and gives its stockholders a fully informed, uncoerced opportunity to vote to accept the deal, we cannot conclude that the board likely violated its Revlon duties. It is too often forgotten that Revlon, and later cases like QVC, primarily involved board resistance to a competing bid after the board had agreed to a change of control, which threatened to impede the emergence of another higher-priced deal. No hint of such a defensive, entrenching motive emerges from this record.

* * *

II. FACTS

* * *

B. The Key Players in the Deal Dynamic

C & J, a Delaware corporation founded in 1997, is an oilfield services provider. The company went public in 2011 and currently has a market capitalization of over $730 million. C & J's board has seven directors, five of whom are independent. The only management directors are C & J's founder, chairman, and CEO, Comstock, and its CFO, Randy McMullen. Nabors, which has a total market capitalization of over $3 billion, is a Bermuda exempt company that also provides oilfield services. As noted, Nabors' CEO and chairman is Anthony Petrello. Nabors has two primary divisions: a completions and productions services division ("Nabors CPS") and a drilling and rig services division. None of C & J's board members had any prior affiliation with Nabors before beginning discussions about the transaction challenged in this litigation.

C. Citi's Trauber Introduces Nabors' Petrello
and C & J's Comstock

In 2013, C & J's board began to explore strategic acquisitions to grow its business, and authorized Comstock to lead the search. By the end of

---

[7]   See, e.g., Lyondell Chemical Co. v. Ryan, 970 A.2d 235, 243 (Del.2009); Paramount Communications Inc. v. QVC Network Inc., 637 A.2d 34, 44 (Del.1994) ("Delaware law recognizes that there is 'no single blueprint' that directors must follow."); In re Fort Howard Corp. S'holders Litig., 1988 WL 83147 (Del. Ch. Aug. 8, 1988) (a pre-signing auction is not required where directors allowed for an effective post-signing market check).

the year, Comstock had identified at least three potential "strategic partners" and made an offer for one company, but no discussions advanced beyond the initial stages.

In January 2014, Stephen Trauber, Vice Chairman and Global Head of Energy Investment Banking at Citi, approached Comstock with an unsolicited pitch book, suggesting Nabors CPS as a target. Nabors was at that point considering different options for Nabors CPS, including selling it or taking it public. * * * [Director] Ma further explained that the board did not consider engaging other bankers because Comstock "wanted to keep it confidential and not let [the deal] leak to other banks in the industry," and the other directors agreed that the deal was "a highly confidential situation" and that "any leak could meaningfully change the economics of the transaction."

* * *

D.   Negotiating the Deal

Consistent with the plaintiffs' depiction of Trauber as a banker for the deal, the transaction process began with a January 2014 meeting between Comstock and McMullen, on behalf of C & J, and Petrello, on behalf of Nabors, with Trauber in an as-yet-undefined role. After that meeting, Comstock believed that a transaction was worth pursuing: he perceived that Nabors CPS was underutilized by Nabors because the company was focused on its other division, and he thought that Nabors CPS would be a "good fit . . . operationally, culturally, and strategically."

Discussions between Comstock and Petrello continued over the next several months. On March 5, C & J's senior management met with Petrello and other Nabors executives to analyze the transaction, including the possibility of structuring the deal so that the surviving company would be domiciled outside of the U.S. and thus pay tax at lower rates, through what is now widely called a "corporate inversion." Because Nabors is a Bermuda-based company, C & J could avoid paying U.S. corporate taxes by merging into Nabors and re-domiciling in Bermuda. The tax benefits from structuring the transaction in this way are substantial—Citi estimated the savings as worth $200 million in net present value.

Both parties agreed that Comstock and C & J's management team would manage the combined entity. But for the re-domiciling to be effective for tax purposes, Nabors would need to own a majority of the new company. On April 3, 2014, Comstock convened a special board meeting to discuss the potential deal. Comstock had previously discussed acquiring Nabors CPS with some of the directors, but the April 3 meeting appears from the record to be the first time he received formal approval to negotiate. C & J's board conveyed excitement about the substantial tax benefits that re-domiciling in Bermuda would provide, in addition to the other deal synergies, but also expressed worry about losing control because Nabors would own a majority of the stock in the surviving entity.

Director Ma testified in her deposition that the board was aware of the importance of a change of control because legal counsel had explained during a board call "what the Revlon rules were."

After discussing the tradeoffs between losing control and tax savings, C & J's directors unanimously approved a non-binding offer of $2.6 billion, which Comstock delivered in a letter to Petrello dated April 4.

E.   Pricing the Deal

Petrello rejected the April 4 offer, asserting that Nabors CPS was worth a minimum of $3.2 billion. The parties continued to negotiate over price while Comstock and his team conducted due diligence on Nabors CPS. The plaintiffs contend that these negotiations were tainted by Comstock's self-interest, because Petrello made overtures assuring Comstock that he would receive a lucrative compensation package if the deal was completed.

After Petrello rejected Comstock's offer, Comstock emailed the other directors on April 14 to inform them of his intention to raise C & J's offer to $2.75 billion to keep the deal alive. He explained that he believed "[t]he upside potential here is like no other M&A deal we have come across." But he acknowledged concerns from board members about "the slippery slope up on pricing," and the need to "be very vigilant" in proving "the possibility of . . . results in due diligence." The other board members agreed to raise the offer. Accordingly, Comstock sent a second letter to Petrello on April 16, offering $2.75 billion, which represented a multiple of 6.9 over 2014 EBITDA.

On April 22, Nabors released its first quarter results for 2014, which were lower than Nabors expected and worse than Comstock or C & J's board had anticipated. Comstock expressed concern that Nabors CPS was unlikely to generate its forecasted EBITDA for 2014, which would threaten the proposed valuation for the deal. At the same time, Comstock questioned the credibility of Nabors' financial results, although he stated in his deposition that he was reacting to what turned out to be an error in Nabors' proprietary accounting system.

Notwithstanding these negative developments for Nabors, Petrello rejected the $2.75 billion offer on April 23, arguing that the proposal did not reflect the full intrinsic value of Nabors CPS, or the value of the synergies the combination would create. According to Nabors Red Lion Ltd.'s Form S-4 filing with the SEC, C & J's board members discussed Petrello's demands, but there is no evidence of these discussions in the record before us. Comstock responded to Petrello in a letter dated April 25, noting his fear that Nabors CPS would be unable to achieve the level of EBITDA projected earlier in the month. But rather than reduce the valuation he was using as a basis for price negotiations, Comstock agreed to use more favorable forward-looking projections into 2015 and "stretch" the multiple from 6 to 6.5. The April 25 letter set a maximum value for Nabors CPS at $2.9 billion.

Because there is no evidence that this new offer was approved by the board in advance, there is at least some support for the plaintiffs' contention that Comstock at times proceeded on an "ask for forgiveness, rather than permission" basis. But as the defendants hasten to point out, the board gave Comstock broad authority to negotiate, and he kept them apprised of major developments, even if he did not seek approval at every stage of the process.

To wit, on April 29, C & J's board met for its regularly scheduled meeting. According to the minutes, Comstock presented an update on the negotiations with Nabors, including Petrello's response to the April 23 offer. That evening, after the board meeting, Comstock and Petrello agreed to a deal based on a valuation of $2.925 billion for Nabors CPS during a telephone conversation. The plaintiffs accurately contend that Petrello used this conversation to assure Comstock that he and his fellow C & J managers would receive aggressive employment agreements. But the record also reflects that Comstock did not follow up on these overtures to discuss specifics during the negotiation process.

The plaintiffs allege that the valuation adjustments made following the announcement of Nabors CPS' decline in performance demonstrate that the C & J stockholders got a bad deal. But there is also a colorable basis to believe that Comstock was playing the negotiation game skillfully when he reacted to the downward movement in Nabors CPS' performance as he did.[43] The record contains evidence that Comstock attempted to protect C & J stockholders using strategic negotiating tactics; for example, Comstock made clear throughout the process that he was willing to cease negotiations if terms protecting C & J's stockholders were not reflected in the final deal. He also revealed in internal emails with McMullen and other C & J directors that he thought focusing on Nabors CPS' declining performance would be an effective negotiating strategy to keep the price low, and that the deal was worthwhile because of the value he and his management team could bring to the combined entity. In other words, the record can be reasonably read to suggest that Comstock believed in good faith that he should not pile onto Nabors' woes, but rather use the evidence of Nabors CPS' declining performance to keep the price negotiations at a positive value for C & J while ensuring that, in the end, the company secured an asset

---

[43] Although the plaintiffs attempt to cast many of Comstock's statements in an ominous light, at least a plausible reading of the record suggests that Comstock was aggressively negotiating to create value for C & J's stockholders, and that his belief that the deal would be valuable to them was sincere. Comstock could have been using his communications as a "cover" for his true self-interest in pursuing a deal, but many of his emails and text messages—in which he discusses his often negative perceptions of Nabors; Nabors' banker, Goldman; his own bankers, Citi and Tudor; Petrello; and others—read as authentically salty, sent by a sophisticated businessman and the founder of the company, who believed he had found a deal that would grow "his" company and benefit all stockholders.

whose acquisition he believed would generate valuable benefits for C & J's stockholders. We also note that Comstock ultimately lowered C & J's offer to $2.86 billion days before closing because C & J's "diligence only proved" some of Nabors CPS' projected EBITDA.

Moreover, we note that Comstock continually shared the details of the valuation changes and negotiations with the C & J board, which was majority-independent, and which had the final say in approving the deal before it went to a stockholder vote. Although it authorized Comstock to continue negotiations on its behalf in the April 3 meeting, C & J's board remained engaged in the process. By way of example, the board met seven times between April 3 and June 24. The truncated record contains several emails from Comstock to the other directors during that time, keeping them apprised of relevant findings from his diligence, including the declining state of Nabors CPS' business. Ma confirmed in her affidavit and deposition that the board broadly authorized Comstock to negotiate a deal and he "brief[ed] us all along the way." During the negotiating process, Trauber remarked in an email to Comstock that in his "26 years" of doing "hundreds" of deals, he had "never seen a CEO have to provide their board so much data day-to-day and have to constantly answer emails from the board." Even if the board was not aware of every "blow by blow," the record suggests that the board was informed about the transaction they would eventually vote to approve, especially the final terms of the deal.

The board also considered whether to actively shop C & J to potential buyers. Ma testified at her deposition that the board asked Citi whether "other strategic bidders" would be interested in C & J, and the board "considered potential strategic bidders for C & J as part of our ability and certainty in closing the Nabors transaction." She noted that Citi assessed the probability of engagement from other potential buyers as "low."

F.   The Final Deal Terms

After these extensive negotiations, Comstock and Petrello agreed to a valuation for Nabors CPS of $2.86 billion, which was premised on a forecast of Nabors CPS' 2015 EBITDA of $445 million and an implied multiple of 6.4. This price was lower than Petrello's initial ask of $3.2 billion, but higher than C & J's initial offer of $2.6.

To consummate the transaction, Nabors would create a new subsidiary, Red Lion, into which it would transfer its CPS business. C & J would then merge with Red Lion. C & J's former stockholders would own 47% of the combined entity, and their shares would be converted into Red Lion common stock on a 1:1 basis in a tax-free transaction. Nabors would own the remaining 53%, and receive approximately $938 million in cash. The entity would then be renamed C & J Energy Services, Ltd., and be listed under C & J's current ticker, CJES, on the New York Stock Exchange. Because New C & J would be a Bermuda corporation, the rights of its stockholders would be governed by Bermuda law, rather than Delaware law.

To ensure that C & J's stockholders would retain some control over New C & J, C & J's board also insisted on several corporate governance protections. Under the merger agreement, C & J stockholders would have the power to designate four board members, including Comstock as the chairman of the board. Comstock would become CEO and McMullen would become President and CFO. To ensure that C & J retained a controlling interest in the entity, C & J also negotiated the following requirements:

(i) For a period of five years, a two-thirds vote of the stockholders of the combined entity will be required to amend the bye-laws (unless approved by Comstock and at least three directors not nominated by Nabors); sell the company; issue stock; or repurchase more than 15% of the outstanding shares of the company in a given year;

(ii) *In the event of a sale of the company or major assets, all stockholders will receive consideration of the same type and of the same amount calculated on a per share basis. This bye-law provision cannot be amended without a unanimous stockholder vote;*

(iii) From the closing date until the earlier of the five year anniversary of the effective date or the date that Nabors owns less than 15% of the combined entity's shares (the "standstill" period), Nabors will be prohibited (without a two-thirds board vote) from acquiring additional shares beyond its ownership stake as of closing; soliciting or encouraging any proposal for a business combination; soliciting or becoming a participant in the solicitation of any proxy related to any vote, or agreeing to vote with any person undertaking a "solicitation"; participating in a "group" with respect to securities of the combined entity; granting proxies to any third party (other than as recommended by the board) or entering into any understanding or agreement with respect to the voting of equity securities of the combined entity; seeking additional representation on, or proposing any changes to the size of, the board of directors;

(iv) Board members will be nominated by a three-member nominating committee, two of whom will be current C & J directors. The board will be classified with current C & J directors in each class;

(v) Without a two-thirds vote of the combined entity's board, and during the standstill period, Nabors can only sell its stock to a person or group that is not subject to SEC Rule 13d, *i.e.,* the transferee cannot (i) hold the securities with the "purpose, or with the effect of, changing or influencing the control" or (ii) own more than 20% of the combined entity. *If Nabors chooses to sell more than 10% of the outstanding shares to a person or group, the combined entity will have a right of first refusal. Nabors will be prohibited from selling its stock to certain competitors. If any other company wishes to buy a controlling stake in the combined entity, they will be required to make an offer for the whole company;* and

(vi) If Nabors violates any of the standstill provisions of the merger agreement, the violation will provide a basis to terminate the employment of certain members of the post-merger management team who are currently affiliated with Nabors.

C & J also bargained for a no-solicitation clause with a "fiduciary out" to allow C & J to negotiate with third parties under certain circumstances; a "fiduciary out" allowing C & J to terminate the deal in favor of a superior proposal; and a modest $65 million termination fee (2.27% of the deal value). And although Comstock signed a voting support agreement committing his shares to vote for the merger, he would be released from that agreement if the C & J board changed its recommendation in favor of the deal or otherwise exercised its "fiduciary out."

C & J's board considered the formal terms of the transaction at a special board meeting on June 24. Citi and Tudor both presented valuation analyses and fairness opinions to the board. Both financial advisors found that the transaction would be fair to stockholders, and that it would add value to C & J's stock.

Following discussions, the board unanimously approved the transaction, subject to the approval of C & J stockholders, with the intention to close before the end of 2014. The deal was publicly announced the following day, on June 25. The stock market reacted positively to the news: shares of both companies' stock rose, and analyst coverage largely viewed the transaction as favorable to C & J's stockholders.

* * *

III. ANALYSIS
* * *

B. *The Plaintiffs Have Not Demonstrated A Reasonable Probability Of Success On The Merits*

1. *The Court of Chancery's Ruling Rested on an Erroneous Understanding of What* Revlon *Requires of a Board of Directors*

Not only did the Court of Chancery fail to apply the appropriate standard of review, its ruling rested on an erroneous understanding of what Revlon requires. Revlon involved a decision by a board of directors to chill the emergence of a higher offer from a bidder because the board's CEO disliked the new bidder, after the target board had agreed to sell the company for cash. Revlon made clear that when a board engages in a change of control transaction, it must not take actions inconsistent with achieving the highest immediate value reasonably attainable.

But Revlon does not require a board to set aside its own view of what is best for the corporation's stockholders and run an auction whenever the board approves a change of control transaction. As this Court has made clear, "there is no single blueprint that a board must follow to fulfill its duties,"[84] and a court applying Revlon's enhanced scrutiny must decide "whether the directors made a *reasonable* decision, not a *perfect* decision."

In a series of decisions in the wake of Revlon, Chancellor Allen correctly read its holding as permitting a board to pursue the transaction it reasonably views as most valuable to stockholders, so long as the transaction is subject to an effective market check under circumstances in which any bidder interested in paying more has a reasonable opportunity to do so. Such a market check does not have to involve an active solicitation, so long as interested bidders have a fair opportunity to present a higher-value alternative, and the board has the flexibility to eschew the original transaction and accept the higher-value deal. The ability of the stockholders themselves to freely accept or reject the board's preferred course of action is also of great importance in this context.

Here, the Court of Chancery seems to have believed that Revlon required C & J's board to conduct a pre-signing active solicitation process in order to satisfy its contextual fiduciary duties. It did so despite finding that C & J's board had no improper motive to sign a deal with Nabors and that the board was well-informed as to C & J's value, and despite the fact that Comstock, one of C & J's largest stockholders, had a strong motive to maximize the value of his shares, and had no reason to do a deal just to secure his (unthreatened) management future. Not only that, but the employer of one of C & J's directors, Ma, was a private equity firm that owned 10% of C & J stock and was therefore unlikely to support a transaction that would compromise the value of its large equity position.

The Court of Chancery imposed a pre-signing solicitation requirement because of its perception that C & J's board did not have "an impeccable knowledge of the value of the company that it is selling." In so ruling, the Court of Chancery seemed to imply that Revlon required "impeccable knowledge," and that there was only one reasonable way to comply, *i.e.,* requiring a company to actively shop itself, which ignores

---

[84] Barkan v. Amsted Industries, Inc., 567 A.2d 1279, 1286 (Del.1989); see also Unitrin, Inc. v. American General Corp., 651 A.2d 1361, 1374 (Del.1995) ("[E]nhanced judicial scrutiny mandated . . . is not intended to lead to a structured, mechanistic, mathematical exercise . . . [it is] a flexible paradigm that jurists can apply to the myriad of 'fact scenarios' that confront corporate boards.").

the Court of Chancery's own well-reasoned precedent and that of this Court, including our recent decision in Lyondell. And the court's perception that the board was not adequately informed was in tension with its other findings, grounded in the record, that C & J's directors were well-informed as to Nabors CPS' value.

Nor does the record indicate that C & J's board was unaware of the implications of structuring the deal so that Nabors would have majority voting control over the surviving entity. As the undisputed facts demonstrate, the C & J board was aware that Nabors would own a majority of the voting stock of New C & J, and indeed that such a shift in control was required to effect the tax-motivated re-domiciling that the board believed would be beneficial to C & J's stockholders. The board took steps to mitigate the effects of that change in control, including by providing that a two-thirds vote will be required to amend the corporate bye-laws, sell the company, or issue stock for a period of five years; and preventing Nabors from acquiring additional shares or selling its shares for the five year standstill period. Most important, the board negotiated for a bye-law providing that all stockholders will receive *pro rata* consideration in any sale of the company or its assets, a bye-law that cannot be repealed without unanimous stockholder approval.

* * *

It is also important to note that there were no material barriers that would have prevented a rival bidder from making a superior offer. As discussed, the C & J board negotiated for a broad "fiduciary out" that enabled the board to terminate the transaction with Nabors if a more favorable deal emerged. This was an unusual protection for a buyer of assets to secure, because sellers (for logical reasons) rarely give buyers such an out. Consistent with his fiduciary duties as a C & J director, Comstock's voting support agreement would fall away upon a decision by the C & J board to exercise its out, leaving him free to vote in favor of a higher priced deal. Therefore, if a competing bidder emerged, it faced only the barrier of a $65 million termination fee. Further, the transaction was announced on July 25, and was not expected to be consummated until near the end of 2014, a period of time more than sufficient for a serious bidder to express interest and to formulate a binding offer for the C & J board to accept.

In prior cases like In re Fort Howard Corporation Shareholders Litigation, this sort of passive market check was deemed sufficient to satisfy Revlon. But as the years go by, people seem to forget that Revlon was largely about a board's resistance to a particular bidder and its subsequent attempts to prevent market forces from surfacing the highest bid. QVC was of a similar ilk. But in this case, there was no barrier to the emergence of another bidder and more than adequate time for such a bidder to emerge. The Court of Chancery was right to be "skeptical that another buyer would emerge." As important, the majority of C & J's board is independent, and there is no apparent reason why the board would not be receptive to a transaction that was better for stockholders than the Nabors deal.

It is also contextually relevant that C & J's stockholders will have the chance to vote on whether to accept the benefits and risks that come with the transaction, or to reject the deal and have C & J continue to be run on a stand-alone basis. Although the C & J board had to satisfy itself that the transaction was the best course of action for stockholders, the board could also take into account that its stockholders would have a fair chance to evaluate the board's decision for themselves. As the Court of Chancery noted, "[t]he shareholders are adequately informed."

Given these factors, we conclude that the Court of Chancery failed to apply the correct legal analysis when it imposed the injunction. Because the Court of Chancery could not find that the plaintiffs had met their burden while misapplying Revlon and reading it to require an active market check in all circumstances, it certainly could not have found a reasonable probability of success when applying Revlon faithfully.

* * *

For all these reasons, the order of the Court of Chancery is hereby REVERSED. The mandate shall issue immediately.

———————

QUESTIONS

1. Recall that Revlon stated that when a change of control becomes inevitable, "The directors' role changed from defenders of the corporate bastion to auctioneers. . . ." Does this opinion change the implications of that statement?

2. How does the board's business judgment allow it to select a single buyer, satisfied that this is the best possible deal for the shareholders?

3. What is EBITDA? Why is it discussed more than net profits?

4. On April 3, 2014, the C & J board gave Comstock approval to negotiate with Nabors. The board approved an offer of $2.6 billion at that meeting. Later the board members, apparently individually but not as a board, agreed to raise the offer, which Comstock did, to $2.75 billion. On April 25 Comstock raised the offer to $2.9 billion, apparently without advance approval by the board. On April 29 the C & J board met and discussed the negotiations. Thereafter Comstock raised the offer to $2.925 billion and ultimately lowered it to $2.86 billion when due diligence did not prove Nabors' expected EBITDA. How does the court deal with the issue of whether the board was properly informed and properly approved Comstock's offers?

5. Since C & J had not explored the possibility of a sale of control with any other prospective buyers, why does the court accept the imposition of a "no-solicitation" clause with a fiduciary out to terminate the deal in the

case of a superior proposal? Doesn't Revlon require some search for buyers?

_____

NOTE

In re Volcano Corp. Stockholder Litigation, 2016 Del. Ch. LEXIS 99, involved a Revlon challenge to a sale of the company. The sale was accomplished in accordance with section 251(h) of the Delaware GCL, adopted in 2016. Pursuant to a merger agreement, a cash tender offer for any and all shares was followed by a short form merger for the same consideration. The court rejected Revlon scrutiny, and imposed business judgment level scrutiny and deference. The tender offer to fully informed stockholders obtained 89% of the shares, and was followed by a short form merger. The court held that given acceptance by a majority of fully informed shareholdes, the business judgment rule should apply.

_____

In re Dollar Thrifty Shareholder Litigation
2010 Del. Ch. LEXIS 192.

■ STRINE, VICE CHANCELLOR.

I.   Introduction

The plaintiffs seek a preliminary injunction preventing the consummation of a merger under a merger agreement under which Hertz Global Holdings, Inc. will buy all the shares of its smaller rental car industry rival Dollar Thrifty Automotive Group, Inc. for $32.80 per share in cash (including a $200 million special dividend that will only be paid in the event of the merger) and 0.6366 shares of Hertz stock for each share of Dollar Thrifty stock (the "Merger," and the "Merger Agreement" respectively). The Merger consideration was worth $41 per share as of signing. The plaintiffs criticize the Dollar Thrifty board (the "Board") for failing to conduct a pre-signing auction and for signing up a Merger Agreement that yielded only a modest premium over the closing price of Dollar Thrifty's stock on the last trading day before the Merger Agreement was signed. Even worse, the plaintiffs say, the Merger Agreement included a termination fee and matching rights that the plaintiffs believe have a quelling effect on any topping bidder. The plaintiffs say this even though another large industry player, Avis Budget Group, Inc., has come forward with a bid that nominally tops the Hertz bid, by offering a combination of cash and stock equal to $46.50 per share. In formulating that bid, Avis was able to receive confidential, non-public information from Dollar Thrifty and has had many months to put together its financing and other terms. At this point, the Dollar Thrifty Board has already determined that Avis's bid would be superior to

Hertz's if it could be assured that Avis would actually close. But Avis, unlike Hertz, has refused to promise to pay *any* reverse termination fee in the event that antitrust approval for an Avis-Dollar Thrifty merger cannot be attained and has also not matched the level of divestitures Hertz is willing to make to achieve antitrust approval.

A vote is scheduled on September 16, 2010 for the Dollar Thrifty stockholders to decide whether to accept the Hertz deal. At this point, the only thing apparently standing between Avis and a deal with Dollar Thrifty is its willingness to address Dollar Thrifty's concern over closing certainty by offering to pay a reverse termination fee that compensates Dollar Thrifty for the risk of non-consummation. The deal protections in the Merger Agreement have not prevented Avis from presenting a competing bid, and the termination fee represents a very small percentage cost to Avis of its topping bid. Indeed, the termination fee does not constitute a material impediment for any topping bidder who wishes to make a materially superior offer to Hertz's, it at best deters fractional topping. In that sense, the deal protections actually encourage an interloper to dig deep and to put on the table a clearly better offer rather than to emerge with pennies more.

On the record before me, I must deny the plaintiffs' motion. Despite the plaintiffs' skillful advocacy, the record after factual discovery does not support their claim that the Dollar Thrifty Board likely breached its fiduciary duty to take reasonable steps to maximize the value Dollar Thrifty stockholders would receive. Rather, the record reveals that the Dollar Thrifty Board, and its CEO Scott Thompson, has managed Dollar Thrifty successfully through a financial crisis that saw the company on the brink of insolvency and improved its performance to the point where the company was profitable and receiving plaudits from the stock market. The Board did so by economizing on costs and engaging in profitable arbitrage in handling the company's rental car fleet. Throughout the last several years, while managing the company, the Board has been open to selling the company if a deal favorable to the stockholders could be achieved. To that end, the Board engaged in lengthy discussions with both Hertz and Avis in the last several years. Each of Hertz and Avis ultimately walked away, in circumstances when they could have bought the company at a bargain price.

By the end of 2009 when Hertz again approached Dollar Thrifty, Dollar Thrifty's performance had stabilized and its stock price had risen sharply, from under $1 per share in March 2009, up to $26.97 on December 22, 2009. Despite having misgivings about again discussing a sale with an industry rival that had failed to come through before, the Board took a deep breath, exhaled, and determined that it had to listen to Hertz. After achieving assurances from Hertz that it would offer a price in the mid-thirties, a substantial premium to the prevailing market price and as important to the Board, a good price in terms of the company's fundamental earnings potential, the Board decided to engage in negotiations with Hertz, while simultaneously focusing on managing the business. The Board expressly considered whether to reach out to Avis and other possible buyers. But the Board concluded that Avis was not well positioned financially to make a bid given its own leverage position and the state of the credit markets and due to the somewhat greater antitrust risk the Board's advisors believed a deal with Avis presented. The Board also took into account the strong possibility that Hertz would go away if the company went into auction mode, a possibility buttressed by Hertz's demonstrated willingness to take a pass on Dollar Thrifty at lower price levels and its demand for exclusivity. Equally important, the Board was worried that a failed public auction could damage the company, including by distracting and creating anxiety among company employees, who had been through difficulty in recent years involving downsizing and increased expectations for personal productivity.

The Board therefore decided to engage solely with Hertz but reserving for itself the opportunity in any merger agreement to consider a post-signing topping bid. After months of difficult negotiations during which Dollar Thrifty shut down talks in order to extract better terms, Hertz and Dollar Thrifty had narrowed their differences. Near the end of this process, Avis's CEO made an awkward and oblique overture to Thompson, asking him to go to dinner through a banker. The Avis CEO never said what he wanted, and gave off signals that made it possible that he wanted to talk about employing Thompson at Avis. This feeble inquiry came at a very sensitive time in the final stages of the Hertz negotiations.

Using Hertz's desire to announce a deal before its own tepid earnings release and Dollar Thrifty's expected strong earnings release as leverage, Dollar Thrifty got Hertz to improve its offer to $41 per share, comprised mostly of cash but also of Hertz stock. Critically, Dollar Thrifty also got Hertz to agree to divest assets generating up to $335 million in revenue if necessary to achieve antitrust approval, and to pay a reverse termination fee of $44.6 million if antitrust approval was not achieved. In exchange, Dollar Thrifty agreed that it would pay an identical termination fee but only if it signed up a higher valued deal within a year.

By the time these terms were reached, Dollar Thrifty's stock price had continued to increase, and the $41 per share constituted a relatively modest 5.5% premium to market. But it represented a price near the top range of the discounted cash flow valuations presented to the Board. Moreover, the Dollar Thrifty Board, while pleased that the company's position had improved, realized that the company did not have a strong long-term growth story and thought that it would be useful to lock in a price when the company was being fully valued. Most importantly, the Board also considered that signing up a deal with Hertz would provide

Avis with a strong incentive to either put up or shut up, because the Dollar Thrifty stockholders would likely approve the sale to Hertz if Avis did not act and Avis risked, by not acting, forever losing the chance to buy one of the last remaining smaller players in the rental car space.

In concluding that this approach to value maximization was reasonable, I give credit to the record that shows that the entire Dollar Thrifty Board had no conflict of interest that gave them a motive to do other than the right thing. The record reveals no preference on the part of the Board for Hertz over Avis or any other acquirer. The CEO, Thompson, has a huge incentive not to sell at a suboptimal price because he has a large chunk of actual common stock and has no apparent desire to work for an industry competitor. When directors who are well motivated, have displayed no entrenchment motivation over several years, and who diligently involve themselves in the deal process choose a course of action, this court should be reluctant to second-guess their actions as unreasonable.

Based on the circumstances the Board confronted, I cannot find that its course of action was unreasonable. To wish to sell in sight of the top of the market and to not be driven solely by the market premium is a reasonable determination to make when a company's stock has run up sharply during the period of negotiations and when the company's internal estimates of its own earnings potential suggest the deal price is highly favorable. To do so in a manner that provides, as the Board has done, a fair opportunity for a topping bid and that actually creates a powerful incentive for another industry rival to finally act with definitiveness rather than coyness, cannot also be deemed unreasonable. In fact, on this record, it appears that the Board's determination to sign up a deal with Hertz is what actually kicked Avis into mature action. Avis did not even own a share of Dollar Thrifty before the Hertz Merger Agreement was signed and, consistent with the Board's concerns about Avis's financial capacity and ability to secure regulatory approval, took three months to secure financing to make a bid, and has yet to offer a reverse termination fee to deal with antitrust risk.

By its actions, the Board gave the stockholders the chance to take a floor price that was very attractive in light of the Board's estimate of the company's fundamental value, left them uncoerced to turn down the deal if they preferred to remain independent because the termination fee is only payable if a higher value deal is accepted, and left the door open to a higher bidder. Although I have no doubt that other reasonable approaches could have been taken, the approach the Dollar Thrifty Board took here emerges, on this record, as a reasonable one and that is what is necessary to satisfy its duties.

At this stage, this court has no basis to intervene. The plaintiffs do not seriously challenge the Dollar Thrifty Board's refusal to accept a topping bid from Avis that does not include a reverse termination fee or some other adequate closing assurance. Value is not value if it is not ultimately paid. Avis is free to make an economic move and to have its bid accepted without unreasonable impediment by the Hertz Merger Agreement. The Dollar Thrifty stockholders are free to accept or reject the Hertz deal on their own. In other words, the free play of economic forces and the reward-risk calculus of the Dollar Thrifty stockholders should determine the outcome without the injection of the uncertainty of an injunction against board action that seems to have had the effect of ginning up competition for Dollar Thrifty between two highly-motivated industry rivals.

* * *

III. Legal Analysis

* * *

B.   The Merits

* * *

6.   Plaintiffs Have Not Demonstrated A Likelihood Of Success On The Merits

For all these reasons, I find that the plaintiffs have not demonstrated a reasonable probability of success on the merits of their Revlon claim. At bottom, the record depicts a well-motivated and diligent board that responded with openness, rather than resistance, to an expression of interest by a party that had twice before failed to consummate a merger. It had reason to be dubious about Hertz, but it was willing to take a chance, so long as it did not disrupt the company's operations. Rather than rolling over for Hertz, the Board bargained hard, shut down the process a few times, and moved Hertz up from its initial expression of interest at $30 to $41 per share. The Board also extracted real closing certainty, through antitrust divestiture provisions and a reverse termination fee, while leaving room for a likely player like Avis to actually realize that if it didn't move this time, it would never be able to again. By doing what it did, the Board set a floor under the market price of Dollar Thrifty stock, at a level that was very high in comparison to the averages over the prior year and very high in relation to the company's DCF value, left its stockholders with the choice of turning down the deal at relatively low cost, and the chance to reap more from a bidder like Avis who might top.

Although other reasonable approaches might have existed, including one that involved contacting Avis pre-signing and trying to stimulate a pre-signing auction, the question is whether the approach the Board took was unreasonable. On this record, the Board has demonstrated that its approach was a reasonable one, that was the product of considerable deliberation.

Indeed, although I tend toward the Fort Howard view of directors' ability to predict the future[227] as compared to the Omnicare omniscience view,[228] the objective evidence seems to indicate that the Board's strategy worked and made Avis step forward. In that regard, Avis's seriousness about making a viable bid any earlier has to be discounted by its lack of owning one share, its failure to make anything other than a tepid dinner invitation, and the fact that it took it three months to actually get lender approval to make a bid.

C.   The Risks Of An Injunction Outweigh The Benefits To The Shareholders

Finally, on this record, it would be difficult to justify the entry of an injunction even if the plaintiffs' have satisfied, as they must, their merits burden. From all appearances, the risks of an injunction seem to be greater than the benefit, when judged from the standpoint of the Dollar Thrifty stockholders. Although an injunction would not release Hertz at this point, it would introduce a period of uncertainty and delay. Rather than exerting leverage on Avis to actually reach terms with the Board on a better deal, it would leave Dollar Thrifty in a period of limbo in which both Hertz and Avis would have the chance to dicker, while Dollar Thrifty's employees find it hard to concentrate on the job at hand, wondering what the fate of their employer and their jobs will be. On this record, the only thing preventing Avis from being deemed the superior bidder is its failure to offer any form of reverse termination fee whatsoever. The termination fee and matching rights the plaintiffs obsess over are not inhibiting competition, and I am not persuaded that the uncertain effect of a preliminary injunction would produce any benefit to the Dollar Thrifty stockholders, whereas I do fear that an injunction would pose genuine risk to them. If Dollar Thrifty terminates the Merger Agreement to sign up with Avis, it will have to pay Hertz $44.6 million plus up to $5 million in expenses. If Avis does not close because it does not attain antitrust approval, Dollar Thrifty would be out upwards of $44.6 million, receive no compensation from Avis under its proposal, have lost the Hertz deal, suffered the productivity-reducing effects on its work force of a lengthy sales process, and come out at the end with no deal. That scenario poses real risks to Dollar Thrifty's stockholders that the Board is entitled to consider. In other words, the balance of harms tilts against an injunction, especially because the

---

[227] In re Fort Howard Corp. S'holder Litig., 1988 Del. Ch. LEXIS 110, 1988 WL 83147, at *14 (Del. Ch. Aug. 8, 1988) ("Revlon explicitly recognized that a disinterested board may enter into lock-up agreements [and by implication other deal protection devices] if the effect was to promote, not to impede, shareholder interests. (That can only mean if the *intended* effect is such, for the validity of the agreement itself cannot be made to turn upon how accurately the board did foresee the future).") (emphasis in original).

[228] Omnicare, 818 A.2d [914] at 933 [infra, Part 2.D of this chapter] ("The latitude a board will have in either maintaining or using the defensive devices it has adopted to protect the merger it approved will vary according to the degree of benefit or detriment to the stockholders' interests that is presented by the value or terms of the subsequent competing transaction.").

Dollar Thrifty stockholders are free to turn down the Hertz deal for themselves if they are confident that either the company will thrive on its own or that Avis will actually come through with a higher binding deal, secure antitrust approval, and pay the promised consideration.

In recent days, Avis issued a press release indicating its willingness to increase its offer if the Dollar Thrifty stockholders turn down the Hertz deal, but still refusing to offer up any reverse termination fee. The plaintiffs sent this to me for consideration. The press release confirms, rather than undercuts, my belief that an injunction would be imprudent. Rather than justify its refusal to offer a reverse termination fee on economic grounds, Avis says it would be unfair for it to have to offer up a reverse termination fee when it is willing to do a deal in which it gets no termination fee if Dollar Thrifty signs with it and then does another deal with someone else at a higher price. More like a child arguing with a parent about the comparative treatment of his sibling than a determined buyer, Avis says that "fairness" demands that it be treated equally with Hertz. Economic seriousness might suggest a focus on addressing the Dollar Thrifty Board's apparently legitimate concern about closing certainty and not ignoring the reality that Hertz expended resources in the merger negotiation process and bound itself firmly and publicly to a deal several months before Avis even made a financed bid, taking business risks Avis had the chance in prior years to take and never would. Notably, Avis has chosen not to litigate for itself and to subject itself to discovery.

This sort of negotiating dynamic—which is what the Avis letter is—is one best not intruded upon by a judge, when an independent board and the Dollar Thrifty stockholder base are well positioned to address Avis's overtures for themselves. In so stating, it is notable that the current dynamic is obviously exerting pressure on Avis to increase its bid and, at some point, one would think that economics, rather than concerns about symmetrical treatment with Dollar Thrifty's first merger partner, would impel Avis, if it is serious, to address the Board's demand for a reverse termination fee. Avis is, of course, the master of its own bid, though, and the plaintiffs have presented no rational basis for me to conclude that it is unreasonable for the Board to demand a reverse termination fee from Avis.

IV. Conclusion

For all these reasons, the plaintiffs' motion for a preliminary injunction is denied.

NOTE

In re Family Dollar Stores, Inc., 2014 Del. Ch. LEXIS 263, involved similar circumstances. There were three important chain stores in the small box, budget store category: Family Dollar Stores, Inc. ("Family"), with more than 8,100 stores, Dollar Tree, Inc. ("Tree"), with 4,900 stores, and Dollar General, Inc. ("General"), with more than 11,300 stores in 40 states. Initially, Family and General had some preliminary conversations about a combination, which did not indicate great interest by General's management. Thereafter, coinciding with the firing of the president due to disappointing results, Family's board created an advisory committee to consider strategic options. On advice of investment bankers, the advisory committee concluded that only Tree and General would consider a strategic acquisition. Thereafter Tree's investment banker indicate that Tree's CEO would be contacting Family's CEO about a business combination. Because of the risk that General might not be interested in acquiring Family, leaving only Tree as a prospective bidder, the Family board decided to negotiate solely with Tree

When Tree made a formal offer, the board met and heard a presentation about the antitrust risks of combining with either Tree or General, advising that a combination with Tree was low risk, and might involve minimal divestment of Tree stores, while a combination with General carried a very high risk of divestment of a large number of stores or denial by the Federal Trade Commission (FTC). The board turned down Tree's initial offer as inadequate, indicating it would consider a more adequate offer. Thereafter, General's CEO contacted Family's CEO to indicate continuing interest in an acquisition. As instructed by his board, Family's CEO told the General executive that he desired for his antitrust counsel to meet with General's counsel to discuss antitrust problems. The General CEO deferred that request and indicate that General would refine its proposal and return.

Thereafter, Tree raised its bid, and Family informed it that this bid was also inadequate, but that the board would discuss a bid a few dollars higher. Family's CEO met again with General's CEO, who asked if Family was considering combining with Tree, because General did not think such a combination would be feasible. Because of a non-disclosure agreement, Family's CEO did not disclose the discussions with Tree. Family's board feared that if General knew about these discussions, it might attempt to destroy them by making a hostile bid for control of Tree, leaving Family with no prospective buyers. Thereafter, Family and Tree agreed to a merger, at $74.50 per share, including stock for 25% of the purchase price of the shares and the balance in cash. Family's investment bankers informed the board. After the merger was announced, General offered $78.50 in cash, with a promise to agree with the FTC to divest the same proportion of its stores as Tree's commitment to 500 stores represented. After several more rounds, General increased its commitment to divest as many as 1,500 stores, and raised its bid to $80 cash. Tree responded that it was willing to live with a "come hell or high water" commitment, that it would divest however many stores were required to obtain FTC approval. Family's lawyers gave General's bid a 40% chance of success with the FTC.

Family and Tree proceeded to pursue FTC approval and filed proxy materials for shareholder approval, while General filed proxy materials to oppose the approval. The court noted the "fiduciary out" provision in the merger agreement that allowed Family to negotiate with General or others if the determined that a superior proposal—one reasonably likely to be completed on the terms proposed, is received. The court held that the board was reasonable in its belief that General was unlikely to complete its bid on the terms proposed, give its unwillingness to increase the number of stores to be divested beyond 1,500, and dismissed General's motion for a preliminary injunction.

Note that the board was allowed to reject an $80 bid in favor of a $74.50 bid. In holding that this was reasonable, the court is, in effect, holding that the "expected value" of the Tree bid was higher than the expected value of the General bid. This can be quantified, assuming the advice the board received from its antitrust counsel put a 100% chance of approval on the Tree bid and only a 40% chance on the General bid, as follows:

Bid	x	Probability	=	Expected Value
$74.50		1.00		$74.50
$80		0.4		$32.00

In contrast, In re Answers Corp. Shareholders Litigation, 2012 WL 1253072 (Del. Ch.), involved a charge that directors engaged in bad faith in rushing through a sale before higher earnings would be revealed that might raise the market price above the bidder's agreed price, and thus jeopardize the transaction. Answers was controlled by a private equity firm, Redpoint, that owned about 30% of the outstanding shares—too many to liquidate through market sales in a very thin market for the stock. Redpoint (which had two representatives on the board) informed the board that it wished to liquidate through a corporate sale, and that if management did not proceed with expedition, it would be removed and replaced. Redpoint's board members began contacting potential buyers. They were contacted by the representative of another private equity firm, that controlled AFCV, which expressed interest in acquiring Answers. Just after Answers and AFCV entered into a confidentiality agreement, one major Answers shareholder sold several hundred thousand shares into the market in two days, driving Answers' share price from about $8 to $4.58 in a single week.

At this point negotiations began with AFCV offering $7.50 to $8.25 per share. In late October 2010, Answers informed AFCV that its earnings would improve in the last quarter of 2010, and that improvements would continue through 2011. None of this information was made public. When AFCV raised its offer to $10.25, Answers agreed to it, without any no-talk or termination fee provision, other than reimbursement of AFCV's expenses if Answers agreed to a superior transaction. AFCV pressed for a quick two-week market check by Answers over the Christmas and New Years holiday period, but Answers was advised by its financial advisor that such a check was too short, especially over the holidays. Nevertheless Answers proceeded with such a check, which did not turn up any buyer interest. Answers' stock price began rising in late January, 2011, and the Answers management persuaded AFCV to raise its bid to $10.50, which Answers' advisor concluded was fair. Proxy materials for an April shareholders meeting were sent out on February 7. On April 8 the board received an offer of $13.50 from another party, which the board rejected three days later on the basis that financing was uncertain. That bid was subsequently raised to $14, but the court refused to enjoin the shareholders' meeting on the theory that the offer was widely known to the market. The shareholders approved the AFCV transaction on April 14.

A shareholder class action alleging breach of fiduciary duties by the board, including breaches of the duty of loyalty, followed. Vice Chancellor Noble denied a motion to dismiss, despite the presence of exculpatory charter language invoking the protections of Del. G.C.L. § 102(b)(7). The opinion characterized the charges as follows:

> The Complaint adequately alleges that all of the members of the Board breached their duty of loyalty. The Complaint alleges, in a non-conclusory manner, that Rosenschein, Beasley, and Dyal were financially interested in the Merger, and that the remainder of the Board consciously failed to seek the highest value reasonably available for Answers' shareholders. Rosenschein allegedly knew that he would lose his job as Answers' President and CEO if he did not sell the Company, and thus, it was in Rosenschein's self-interest to have Answers engage in a change of control transaction.

> Furthermore, the Complaint alleges that Beasley and Dyal sought a sale of the Company in order to achieve liquidity for Redpoint. Liquidity has been recognized as a benefit that may lead directors to breach their fiduciary duties." Although "all of . . . [Answers'] shareholders received cash in the Merger, *liquidity* was a benefit unique to . . . [Redpoint]." According to the Complaint, "[Redpoint's] interest in a prompt liquidation event conflicted with those of common shareholders who, unlike Redpoint, could sell their shares into the market. . . ." Moreover, the Complaint asserts that Beasley and Dyal's desire to gain liquidity for Redpoint caused them to manipulate the sales process. Thus, the Complaint alleges sufficient facts to suggest that Beasley and Dyal were interested in the Merger.

> As for the rest of the Board members, the Complaint adequately alleges that they acted in bad faith. As stated above, once a board has initiated a sales process, it has a duty to seek the highest value reasonably available for the company's shareholders *regardless of where that value comes from.* A board acts in bad faith, if it consciously disregards that duty. Sternlicht, Segall, Tebbe, and Kramer allegedly knew that Rosenschein, Beasley, and Dyal wanted to end the sales process quickly so that the Board would enter into the Merger Agreement before the market price for Answers' stock rose above AFCV's offer price. Nevertheless, they agreed to expedite the sales process. In other words, the Complaint alleges that Sternlicht, Segall, Tebbe, and Kramer agreed to manipulate the sales process to enable the Board to enter quickly into the Merger Agreement before Answers' public shareholders

appreciated the Company's favorable prospects. That is a well-pled allegation that those Board members consciously disregarded their duty to seek the highest value reasonably available for Answers' shareholders. Thus, the Complaint adequately pleads that the Board breached its duty of loyalty by conducting a flawed sales process.

In Chen v. Howard-Anderson, 87 A.3d 648 (Del. Ch. 2014), the court held that the exculpatory authorization in Del. G.C.L. § 102(b)(7) only protected directors, and did not protect a CEO from liability, whether acting in his director or officer capacity. The court stated "([a]lthough legislatively possible, there currently is no statutory provision authorizing comparable exculpation of corporate officers."). Because the plaintiffs have assembled evidence sufficient to support claims against Howard-Anderson and Seeley in their capacity as officers, the Exculpatory Provision does not protect them." 87 A.3d at 686.

NOTE ON ENFORCEMENT OF STANDSTILL AGREEMENTS

What happens if a target conducts a level-playing field auction and requires any participating bidder to reach agreement on ancillary terms, such as the form of a management contract with a manager of the enterprise, if only one bidder reaches such agreement, and its bid is accepted? If each bidder has signed a standstill agreement prohibiting bids outside the auction for 18 months following completion of the auction, what risk does a disappointed bidder take by making a public bid that tops the auction winner's bid? In one case, it forced the winner to raise its own bid to secure approval of the equity holders in a Real Estate Investment Trust (REIT). Thereafter, the winner sued the topping bidder for damages on the basis that it had tortiously interfered with its own contractual relations with the target, and caused the equity holders to reject its first bid. In Ventas, Inc. v. HCP, Inc., 647 F.3d 291 (6th Cir. 2011), the court noted that under governing Kentucky law, the action required a showing of malice or some significant wrongful conduct. The court found support for wrongful conduct in the misleading statements HCP made publicly at the time of its topping bid, that its bid was identical to the Ventas bid except for HCP's higher price, when HCP had failed to reach agreement with the REIT's manager, a requirement of the auction. Although HCP eventually withdrew its bid, the unitholders, by then mostly arbitrageurs, had little incentive to accept Ventas' original bid. The court affirmed the trial court's judgment on the basis that HCP engaged in fraudulent conduct with the intention of inflicting harm on Ventas.

In structured auction situations the prospective seller often includes a provision in the standstill agreement that prohibits the bidder from making an offer without an express invitation from the seller's board, and precludes the bidder from publicly or privately asking the board to waive these restrictions. This is often referred to as the "Don't Ask, Don't Waive" provision. The purpose is to force all bidders to make their final and best bids in the auction process, knowing that there will be no second chance if a bidder has remorse after losing. The difficulty is that the concept of a formal end to the auction process is at odds with the Delaware courts' view that the target board's fiduciary duties don't end until the deal is closed.

Then-Chancellor (now Chief Justice) Strine expressed, in *obiter dicta*, the view that under certain circumstances these clauses are enforceable. In In re Topps Co. Shareholders Litigation, 926 A.2d 58, 91 (Del. Ch. 2007), he wrote:

> Standstills serve legitimate purposes. When a corporation is running a sale process, it is responsible, if not mandated, for the board to ensure that confidential information is not misused by bidders and advisors whose interests are not aligned with the corporation, to establish rules of the game that promote an orderly auction, and to give the corporation leverage to extract concessions from the parties who seek to make a bid.

In that case he found that the provision had been used for wrongful purposes, and enjoined a stockholder vote until the board waived the standstill. Several other cases contain expressions of doubt about the use of these provisions in the particular circumstances.

Commentators have suggested some guidelines for the use of these provisions in view of the misgivings expressed in remarks from the bench in recent cases: " . . . for directors to utilize these agreements consistently with their fiduciary duties, they must at least: (1) be fully informed and determine that utilizing the provisions constitutes the best way to maximize stockholder value, (2) inform stockholders of the provisions' purposes and effects, and (3) allow the winner to enforce the provisions, or, if not, waive the 'don't ask' clauses for the losing bidders." Peter J. Walsh et al., " 'Don't Ask, Don't Waive' Standstill Provisions: Impermissible Limitations on Director Fiduciary Obligations or Legitimate Value-Maximizing Tool?", Business Law Today, Jan. 23, 2013, at http://apps.americanbar.org/buslaw/blt/content/2013/01/delawareinsider.shtml.

B. DELEGATING THE BOARD'S DUTIES

Directors of public companies are often dispersed across the country, and sometimes even across other nations. While modern communications have made meeting telephonically relatively easy, and documents can be disseminated in advance of meetings through the internet, frequent board meetings are still difficult. The author is on a board that at one time had directors living from Munich to the Bay area, which created difficulties in selecting a time for a meeting. Many directors have demanding full-time jobs that make it difficult for them to give the detailed attention necessary to counsel during a period of dynamic change, such as acquisition negotiations. It is often difficult to find a director able and willing to lead the negotiation process, other than the Chief Executive Officer of the company. The following case is complicated by the fact that management also wants to engage in a management buyout ("MBO") of the company.

Jim Brown v. Brett Brewer, et al.

2010 U.S. Dist. LEXIS 60863 (C.D. Cal.).

■ GEORGE H. KING, UNITED STATES DISTRICT JUDGE.

This shareholder class action arises out of News Corporation's ("News Corp.") 2005 acquisition of Intermix Media, Inc. ("Intermix"), formerly known as eUniverse Inc., a company which owned, among other internet businesses, the social networking website MySpace. Plaintiff Jim Brown ("Plaintiff"), individually and on behalf of all members of the certified class of former Intermix shareholders, claims that Defendants . . . , the eight Intermix directors at the time of the company's sale, breached their fiduciary duties under state law and violated Section 14(a) of the Securities and Exchange Act of 1934 and SEC Rule 14a–9. * * * This matter is before us on the Parties' Cross-Motions for Summary Judgment. We have considered the papers filed and all of the admissible evidence, and deem this matter appropriate for resolution without oral argument. As the Parties are familiar with the facts in this case, we will repeat them only as necessary. Accordingly, we rule as follows.

* * *

II.   Count IV: Breach of Fiduciary Duty Claim

A.   *Delaware Law on Corporate Fiduciary Duties Generally*

Delaware law governs Plaintiff's state law claim of breach of fiduciary duty. Under Delaware law, all directors and officers of a corporation owe their shareholders fiduciary duties of loyalty and care.

1.   Duty of Care

"Director liability for breaching the duty of care 'is predicated upon concepts of gross negligence.' The Delaware General Corporation Law permits a corporation to include a provision in its charter "eliminating or limiting the personal liability of a director to the corporation or its stockholders for monetary damages for breach of fiduciary duty as a director." DEL. CODE ANN. tit. 8, § 102(b)(7). While such an exculpatory provision may eliminate any liability for breaches of the duty of care, it "shall not eliminate or limit the liability of a director: (i) For any breach of the director's duty of loyalty to the corporation or its stockholders; (ii) for acts or omissions not in good faith or which involve intentional misconduct or a knowing violation of law; . . . or (iv) for any transaction from which the director derived an improper personal benefit." Intermix's charter exculpates Defendants from any duty of care claims. Accordingly,

Defendants assert this provision as their fifth affirmative defense: "The breach of fiduciary duty claim is barred, in whole or in part, by the exculpatory provision contained in Intermix's Certificate of Incorporation." In light of this provision, we conclude that the director Defendants cannot be liable for any purported breach of fiduciary duty based solely on their duty of care. Plaintiff does not argue otherwise.

* * *

2. Duty of Loyalty

To hold a director liable for breach of the duty of loyalty, the plaintiff must establish that "a majority of the Director Defendants either [1] stood on both sides of the merger or were dominated and controlled by someone who did; or [2] failed to act in good faith, i.e., where a fiduciary intentionally fails to act in the face of a known duty to act, demonstrating a conscious disregard for his duties. Lyondell Chem. Co. v. Ryan, 970 A.2d 235, 239–40 (Del. 2009) ("Lyondell") ("Because the trial court determined that the board was independent and was not motivated by self-interest or ill will, the sole issue is whether the directors are entitled to summary judgment on the claim that they breached their duty of loyalty by failing to act in good faith.").

* * *

With respect to the second basis for demonstrating breach of the duty of loyalty, Delaware courts have noted that "the requirement to act in good faith is a subsidiary element, i.e., a condition, of the fundamental duty of loyalty." Stone v. Ritter, 911 A.2d 362, 369–70 (Del. 2006). ("[T]he fiduciary duty of loyalty is not limited to cases involving a financial or other cognizable fiduciary conflict of interest. It also encompasses cases where the fiduciary fails to act in good faith.").

* * *

The Delaware Supreme Court has explained what constitutes bad faith by way of a spectrum of directorial conduct. "At one end of the spectrum, [there is] a category of acts involving non-exculpable, so-called 'subjective bad faith,' that is, fiduciary conduct motivated by an actual intent to do harm." The second category of conduct, which is at the opposite end of the spectrum, involves lack of due care—that is, fiduciary action taken solely by reason of gross negligence and without any malevolent intent." Disney, 906 A.2d at 64. The court observed that "grossly negligent conduct, without more, does not and cannot constitute a breach of the fiduciary duty to act in good faith." The third category identified by the Delaware Supreme Court is the one at issue in this case: "intentional dereliction of duty or a conscious disregard for one's responsibilities." "Such misconduct, according to the Court, is 'properly treated as a non-exculpable, non-indemnifiable violation of the fiduciary duty to act in good faith.' "

* * *

B. Scope of Plaintiff's Claim of Breach of the Duty of Loyalty

* * *

1.   Bad Faith in Revlon Auction Context

The obligation to act in good faith, which is a necessary component of satisfying the duty of loyalty, requires directors to act for the purpose of advancing corporate well-being. Therefore, any "intentional dereliction of duty, a conscious disregard for one's responsibilities[,]" constitutes bad faith, or the failure to act in good faith. Disney, 906 A.2d at 66; Stone, 911 A.2d at 370 ("Where directors fail to act in the face of a known duty to act, thereby demonstrating a conscious disregard for their responsibilities, they breach their duty of loyalty by failing to discharge that fiduciary obligation in good faith."). In this case, Plaintiff and the shareholder class which he represents argue Defendants consciously disregarded their responsibilities in selling Intermix to News Corp. for $12 per share, when, so they contend, a likely topping bid from Viacom was imminent.

* * *

Having considered all of the admissible evidence before us and viewing it in the light most favorable to Plaintiff as we must under Rule 56, we conclude that there are genuine, triable issues of material fact sufficient to defeat Defendants' Motion for Summary Judgment on this Revlon claim. These issues fall into three categories: (1) whether Intermix CEO Rosenblatt impermissibly tilted the playing field in favor of News Corp.; (2) whether the remaining board members consciously disregarded their duties; and (3) whether the purported risk of a direct bid for MySpace, which would have frozen the MySpace Option, precludes a finding that Defendants consciously disregard their duties.

a.   Rosenblatt

Plaintiff proffers evidence tending to show that during the crucial week leading up to the July 18, 2005 merger, [Defendant] Rosenblatt evaded Viacom's advances, even though Viacom's representatives were communicating that a competing bid was imminent. Plaintiff raises at least two interrelated triable issues: (1) whether Rosenblatt was self-interested in the merger transaction; and (2) whether he impermissibly steered the auction in News Corp.'s favor.

As to Rosenblatt's purported self-interest, there is evidence of Rosenblatt's motivation for the alleged bidder favoritism, namely his anticipation of future employment with News Corp. In one particularly revealing email sent on July 15, Rosenblatt excitedly endorses News Corp.'s Ross Levinsohn's vision: "So, we create the Fox Internet group, all our units (myspace, alena, grab) fall under it, plus all new acquisitions, and you are CEO Fox Internet and I am Fox Internet grand Puba!!!!" Rosenblatt continues: "I would like to discuss my specific role and structure whenever you are ready. It is no rush unless Peter and

Rupert want me to sign an employment agreement by Sunday [July 17, 2005]. . . ." In an earlier email in that same chain, Rosenblatt wrote: "[I] am burning some real equity with every major media company by getting [the deal] done. . . . u [sic] have no idea the pain I will suffer on Monday. U [sic] better have a good job for me cause I ain't [sic] gonna work in this town again. . . ." On July 13, Rosenblatt wrote: "tell Thom Murdoch and I cut the deal in 30 mins [sic] and I got 100% of what we wanted. Deal closing by Monday." This evidence at least raises the inference that Rosenblatt had a strong interest in seeing a merger transaction with News Corp. completed and had made up his mind that Intermix would be sold to News Corp. as of July 13.

Moreover, Plaintiff points to several key pieces of documentary evidence and witness testimony which tend to support his contention that (1) Rosenblatt, in representing the Intermix board through the Transaction Committee ("TC"), (2) [Defendant] Sheehan, who also sat on the TC, and (3) their agents, deliberately dodged, if not frustrated, an arguably imminent bid from Viacom.

First, on July 6, Montgomery responded to an email announcing "Viacom coming in hard" by telling Rosenblatt: "You need to dance with [Viacom] . . . slow them down. I know you can do it."

Second, TWP, specifically Robert Kitts ("Kitts"), was aware that Epstein was trying to reach them to talk about a potential Viacom bid. Epstein noted on July 16 that Kitts never called him back as promised. ("We exchanged subsequent emails and he indicated he would call me, but he never did.")).

Third, on July 15, [Defendant] Mosher wrote Rosenblatt following one of Rosenblatt's updates to the full board, saying "Viacom sounds like a pipedream."

Fourth, on July 15, Judy McGrath of MTV wrote Rosenblatt to inform him that Viacom was "coming with a bid early next week." She added: "We really want to be with you on this, and hope to get in the ring for it. . . ." Rosenblatt replied evasively, failing to correct her mistaken impression that the auction would still be ongoing after Monday: "I am on a call but thanks so much for the email. . . . I will call you back soon. . . ." Rosenblatt could not recall precisely whether he had returned her call: "I may have tried. I think, actually, I do think I tried and I couldn't get a hold of her."

Fifth, Viacom's CEO Thomas Freston ("Freston"), who reiterated Viacom's interest in purchasing Intermix to Rosenblatt, has testified that he was only told that the process with the competing bidder was "moving quickly." He testified that he could not "recall if [Rosenblatt] said that they were going to do a deal by Sunday." When asked whether Rosenblatt had communicated that a deal would be completed by Sunday, he stated that he did not believe so. Kitts of TWP also confirmed that he failed to give Viacom any hard deadline by which to submit a bid.

Sixth, Chris DeWolfe, MySpace's CEO, to document his difficulties in staying in the auction process: "Chris, quick concerns. . . . Intermix management did not show up on Friday as promised during our time there. . . . Intermix legal cancels their time with our legal today at the last minute. . . . Heard you guys got called off the ad sales call abruptly. . . . In short, I have had a team of 20+ people here working for 72 hours straight on a significant bid, is there anything I need to know?"

Seventh, on July 17, Van Toffler of MTV also emailed Rosenblatt directly to complain politely about the perceived run-around: "They are in the office working round [*sic*] the clock so we can put forth a number to you this week. They mentioned a couple of calls were cancelled at the end of the day Friday, and seemed a bit concerned. Is there anything I can do to help the process for both of us as this is clearly on the fast track?" Again, Rosenblatt replied in such a way that a reasonable jury could infer an intent to evade an arguably imminent competing bid: "We like you and your guys a ton also. Chris called back or will your GC today. Have a great weekend[.]"

Eighth, on July 17, Kitts of TWP, pursuant to the Intermix board's instructions, informed Viacom that it would be "in their best interest" to make a bid that evening. Kitts admitted that he did not give Viacom a hard and fast deadline, but that he "relied upon the message [he] delivered as code that [Epstein] should get a bid in this evening." Furthermore, Kitts admitted in the deposition that he had been instructed to ask for a bid on a timetable that he knew was infeasible. Kitts testified that he was aware of an upcoming Viacom board meeting, "at which [a potential bid] was going to be discussed." The Viacom board was not scheduled to meet until the evening of Tuesday July 19, 2005.

On the other hand, Defendants present the following evidence of events leading up to the July 18th merger, which they argue demonstrates the board members' good faith. News Corp. initially signaled that it would be willing to purchase Intermix in the $8–10 price range. During the Tuesday July 12, 2005 meeting between Rosenblatt, Rupert Murdoch, and Peter Chernin, News Corp. indicated that it would pay $12 per share, as long as the MySpace Option was exercised and a merger agreement was executed by no later than Sundaym July 17, 2005. At the 2:00 p.m. meeting on July 15, the Intermix board of directors rejected News Corp.'s proposal to enter into exclusive negotiations as premature. At the 8:00 p.m. meeting on July 15, the Intermix board rejected the non-binding term sheet including a variety of deal protections as "too strong a deterrent to other potential bidders." At the 8:00 p.m. meeting on July 16, TWP advised the board that it would be reasonable to approve a merger with News Corp. rather than waiting for Viacom to present an offer. At the 7:30 p.m. TC meeting on July 17, the committee directed TWP to contact Viacom and/or its representative, Morgan Stanley, to ascertain whether Viacom would be making an offer the next morning. At the 10:00 p.m. Intermix board meeting on July 17, TWP advised that Viacom was not prepared to make any offer until its board met on Tuesday July 19 and approved a bid. At the 3:45 a.m. board meeting on July 18, both Montgomery and TWP presented their valuation analyses, explaining that $12 per share was a fair price for Intermix, and the Board voted to approve the merger. On July 18, Intermix entered into a merger agreement with News Corp.'s Fox Interactive Media. Defendants contend, and the record reflects, that throughout hiis process the board met repeatedly, authorized ongoing discussions with both competing bidders, and consulted legal and financial advisers.

Viewing the evidence as a whole and in the light most favorable to Plaintiff, we conclude that there are at least triable issues of fact as to whether Rosenblatt acted in good faith, whether he impermissibly skewed the auction in favor of News Corp. for a purpose other than maximizing shareholder value, knowing that a Viacom bid was likely and imminent, and whether this arguably disparate treatment of Viacom and News Corp. had any effect on Viacom's appreciation of the arguable need to make an offer by the evening of July 17, 2005.

b.   The Other Directors

I.   Sheehan

In addition to Rosenblatt, there are also triable issues of fact as to whether Sheehan consciously disregarded his fiduciary duties. On Friday July 15, Stuart Epstein ("Epstein"), the Morgan Stanley investment banker representing Viacom, tried to reach Sheehan but was unsuccessful. Sheehan instructed his secretary as follows: "Do not tell [Epstein] anything about what I am doing or where I am[.]" In reply to his email, Sheehan's secretary informed him that she told Epstein that he was "unavailable." A reasonable jury could conclude that this email chain evinces Sheehan's intent to avoid Viacom's representatives.

ii.   The Other Six Directors

In Gesoff v. IIC Industries, Inc., 902 A.2d 1130 (Del. Ch. 2006), the court stated that bad faith may be found where directors have "acted with conscious disregard *or made decisions with knowledge that they lacked material information.*" Few Delaware cases attempt to define precisely what conduct reaches the level of actionable bad faith, but there is at least agreement that "adopting a 'we don't care about the risks' attitude concerning a material corporate decision" constitutes bad faith. In re Walt Disney Co. Derivative Litig., 825 A.2d 275, 289 (Del. Ch. 2003) (finding bad faith claim properly alleged where factual allegations, if true, implied that "the defendant directors *knew* that they were making material decisions without adequate information and without adequate deliberation, and that they simply did not care if the decisions caused the corporation and its stockholders to suffer injury or loss") (emphasis in original).

Having reviewed the record in full, we conclude that there is sufficient admissible evidence to create a triable question of fact as to whether the rest of the board, as in Macmillan, "plac[ed] the entire process in the hands of" Rosenblatt and to a lesser extent Sheehan and thereby "materially contributed to the [allegedly] unprincipled conduct of those upon whom it looked with a blind eye." 559 A.2d at 1281.

On February 9, 2005, the Intermix board of directors formed a Transaction Committee comprised of [Defendants] Rosenblatt, Sheehan, and Quandt. From that point until July 18, 2005 when the merger was announced, it is undisputed that the Board received most of its information about the negotiations from its self-interested CEO, Rosenblatt. Indeed, it is undisputed that Rosenblatt was the only board member who had some first-hand information as to the circumstances of Viacom's efforts to put in a bid. Crucially, one of the board members testified that Rosenblatt had led him to believe "[t]hat Viacom was less urgent about the deal and hadn't taken the time or done the same level of work as Fox Network" and that Viacom was a "pipedream." This phrase is admittedly not indicative of *conscious* wrongdoing. However, there is a triable question as to whether the other board members consciously abdicated their responsibilities as corporate fiduciaries in allegedly swallowing Rosenblatt's version of events and utterly failing to assess the situation for themselves.

More generally, a reasonable fact-finder could conclude that the other board members acted in bad faith by making "decisions with knowledge that they lacked material information." With respect to their knowledge of the relative likelihood of a Viacom bid, [Defendant] Mosher stated that he could not recall if he or any other board member had "asked any questions regarding Viacom or its status." Additionally, he could not recall whether he had "any knowledge of whether anyone from management was providing equal information to Viacom and Fox News Corp about the time line" for submitting a bid for Intermix.

With respect to their knowledge of bidder favoritism, though Mosher testified that he could not recall the board ever instructing Rosenblatt to favor one bidder over another, he also could not definitively represent that the board had *not* so instructed Rosenblatt. Other board members besides Rosenblatt have also testified that they were unaware that any due diligence meetings with Viacom had been cancelled. Furthermore, [Defendant] Brewer testified that he was simply unaware that Viacom was conducting due diligence over the July 16–17, 2005 weekend.

With respect to their knowledge of the fairness of the merger price, Rosenblatt did not inform Brewer that he was requesting $12 per share from News Corp. until the day of the "handshake deal" with Rupert Murdoch; it is unclear when the rest of the board learned this information. He also did not explain how that requested price was derived. Brewer testified that the board did not ask, and Mosher could not recall whether any board member sought an explanation. Moreover, Brewer testified that the board as a whole never conducted any independent analysis to determine what "an appropriate price per share" would be. Additionally, Mosher confirmed that the board had not "directed the management team to go get the specific valuation work done prior to the acquisition." Finally, Brewer has testified that he could not even recall whether any of the directors had asked "any questions about [Montgomery and TWP's] fairness presentations." Though Brewer's failure to recall what everyone had specifically asked back in 2005 would be understandable, a reasonable jury might draw a negative inference from his representation that he could not recall any discussion as to the investment banks' analyses.

Construing all of the above testimony in the light most favorable to Plaintiff as we must on Defendants' motion for summary judgment, we conclude that it is at least triable as to whether the remaining six board members consciously disregarded their duties and acted in bad faith. There is evidence in the record suggesting that no one on the board asked any questions about the requested per share price, the treatment of the competing bidders, the fairness valuations, or the relative likelihood of a Viacom bid. A reasonable jury could infer that this evidence demonstrates the other six directors consciously abdicated their roles as corporate fiduciaries required by law to do their utmost to maximize shareholder wealth. Of course, we remain mindful that even gross negligence, premised on "simple inattention or failure to be informed of all facts material to the decision[,]" violates only the duty of care and is not actionable as bad faith. Disney, 906 A.2d at 66. Nevertheless, we think a reasonable jury could find that the other six directors exceeded the bounds of negligent conduct, willfully proceeded to their decisions knowing they lacked material information, Gesoff, 902 A.2d at 1165, and thereby consciously disregarded their fiduciary duties. Disney, 906 A.2d at 66 ("Cases have arisen where corporate directors have no conflicting self-interest in a decision, yet engage in misconduct that is more culpable than simple inattention or failure to be informed of all facts material to the decision. To protect the interests of the corporation and its shareholders, fiduciary conduct of this kind, which does not involve disloyalty (as traditionally defined) but is qualitatively more culpable than gross negligence, should be proscribed.").

* * *

V. Conclusion

Plaintiff's Motion for Summary Judgment is DENIED. Defendants' Motion for Summary Judgment is hereby GRANTED in part and DENIED in part as set forth in this Order. Within thirty (30) days hereof, counsel SHALL file a joint status report setting forth their views regarding further mediation in light of these rulings.

IT IS SO ORDERED.

_____

QUESTIONS

1. Given the potential that a CEO may have an interest in continuing employment if the corporation is sold, what justification could be given for allowing a CEO to be on a special transaction committee, much less lead the negotiations?

2. If you are an independent director living and working at a location remote from the corporate headquarters and/or the location of negotiations, how could you serve on a special transaction committee?

3. How could independent directors not serving on a special monitor the behavior of the CEO and any other insiders serving on a committee to assure total loyalty?

4. What role could counsel play to protect the board from any disloyalty or lack of diligence on the part of the CEO?

5. How should counsel advise the CEO at the start of any such process?

6. Should one assume that incumbent management is always interested in preserving their positions, and that their actions in negotiations should always be regarded with suspicion?

_____

In re Pennaco Energy, Inc. Shareholders Litigation
787 A.2d 691 (Del. Ch. 2001).

■ STRINE, VICE CHANCELLOR.

Shareholder plaintiffs seek a preliminary injunction against the February 5, 2001 closing of a tender offer by an acquisition subsidiary of Marathon Oil ("Marathon") for all the shares of Pennaco Energy, Inc. ("Pennaco").

[Pennaco was a small public company formed in early 1998 to explore for and produce natural "methane" gas from coal beds in the Powder River Basin in Wyoming. Early in its existence its officers, Rady and Warren, had explored the possibility of a joint venture to finance exploitation with twenty or more larger oil companies, which had been fully informed about Pennaco's properties and their potential.] On October 23, 1998, Pennaco consummated such a partnership with CMS Oil & Gas Co ("CMS"). The partnership involved the sale to CMS of a 50% working interest in nearly 500,000 acres in an "Area of Mutual Interest" ("AMI") in the Powder River Basin. The sale price yielded Pennaco a hefty profit on its costs to purchase the acreage, thereby allowing the company to develop its other acreage in the Powder River Basin at a productive clip. The partnership also gave Pennaco access to CMS's pipeline infrastructure, which facilitated extraction from the AMI properties.

Pennaco Receives Feelers About A Sale

Pennaco's ability to identify and acquire the production rights on attractive energy-producing properties was soon noticed by other industry players. Thus, in the first half of 2000, the company received feelers about whether it was willing to be acquired. Rather than resisting any overtures, Rady and his management team were willing to provide information and discuss an acquisition with any reputable company in the industry. Rady also made it a practice to inform the board about these inquiries.

* * *

[Thereafter, in July of 2000, the board approved amending the employment agreements of Rady and Warren, increasing their severance compensation in the event of a change of control.]

What The Pennaco Board Did Not Do

Although Pennaco was not prohibited by its confidentiality agreement with Marathon from exploring if other parties were interested in purchasing the company, neither Pennaco's board nor its management did anything to canvass the market. Nor did Pennaco retain an investment banker for this purpose. Instead, the directors focused solely on Marathon.

Management, however, did begin to identify investment bankers for possible retention in connection with Marathon's interest or an alternative transaction that might arise. Among the firms that management contacted were Lehman Brothers, Credit Suisse First Boston ("CSFB"), and Bear Stearns.

* * *

Marathon Makes Its First Bid

After three weeks of due diligence involving regular communications with Pennaco executives, Marathon made its first specific offer. On December 7, 2000, Cazalot offered to purchase all of Pennaco's shares at $17 per share.

The Pennaco board met the next day and decided that the offer was inadequate. After considering the advisability of pursuing a sale in view of the potential gains and risks associated with continuing to operate Pennaco as a stand-alone, the board decided, however, to continue discussions with Marathon because a sale at the right price could be the company's best strategy. The board authorized Rady to reject the $17 offer and to seek a price "north of $20 a share." Management was also authorized to retain outside counsel and a financial advisor.

* * *

On December 9, 2000, Rady told Cazalot that his offer was insufficient and tried to convince Cazalot to raise his bid. In support of that effort, Warren sent a key Marathon executive an e-mail the next day containing arguments justifying a higher value for Pennaco (the "Warren E-Mail").

The Warren E-Mail first tried to convince Marathon that Pennaco's oil reserves were more extensive than were indicated by Pennaco's most recent reserve report, which was the internal June 30 Reserve Report. Without burdening the reader with an explanation of the nuances involved, it is critical to note that gas companies like Pennaco are valued principally on their ability to produce natural gas. Thus, purchasers such as Marathon will look to the so-called "reserves" of a target company as an important part of their pricing decisions. For purposes of this opinion, it is sufficient for the reader to understand that the market places the highest value on "proven" reserves, less value on "probable" reserves, even less value on "possible" reserves, and the lowest value on unevaluated land whose reserve potential is not known.

As of June 30, 2000, Pennaco's proven oil reserves were estimated at 195 billion cubic feet of natural gas, and its combined probable/possible reserves were possibly as high as 875 billion cubic feet of natural gas, for a total of 1.070 trillion cubic feet. Pennaco also owned 273,000 acres that had not been evaluated.

In his E-Mail, Warren attempted to convince Marathon that Pennaco's reserve numbers as of that time exceeded the publicly disclosed June 30, 2000 estimates. In particular, Warren stated:

> We would expect our year-end proved to exceed the 195 Bcf mid-year number. . . .

> We are in the process of engineering . . . additional probable reserves and would fully expect our total proved, probable and possible reserves to then exceed 1.5 Tcf based on our current acreage position. . . .

At the same time as he was trying to convince Marathon that Pennaco's reserves were higher than on June 30, 2000, Warren also tried to convince Marathon that Pennaco was worth more than $20 a share based on the June 30 Reserve Report. To that end, Warren presented a net asset valuation (the "Warren NAV") using the June 30 Reserve Report. That valuation placed a value of $200 an acre on Pennaco's unevaluated acreage, a per acre figure that Warren identified as "conservative." The Warren NAV produced a per share valuation range of $21.23 to $24.93 a share.

Pennaco And Marathon Agree In Principle To A Deal At $19 A Share

On December 14, 2000, Cazalot increased Marathon's offer to $19 a share. Rady took this offer to his board the same day. The board instructed Rady to see if there was "any more room above the $19 a share."

At the same meeting, the board authorized the retention of Lehman Brothers as the company's investment banker.[11] The Lehman team was to be led by Gregory Pipkin, an extremely well-qualified investment banker who leads Lehman's energy practice. Pipkin also happened to be a personal friend of Rady's and Warren's. Lehman was to receive a fee for issuing its fairness opinion, as well as a percentage of transaction value. The percentage Lehman was to receive was lower for the $19 deal with Marathon than it would have been for a higher value transaction with another party. Nonetheless, the lower percentage provided Lehman with $3 million for a deal at the $19 level then on the table.

The next day, Rady contacted Cazalot and tried to get Marathon to go to $20 a share, or at least to $19.50. Cazalot refused, stating that $19 was Marathon's "absolute, final best, top offer" and that they could "not go even a penny above $19 a share." Rady then relented and agreed to recommend that price to his board.

Pennaco held a board meeting that day. Lehman was authorized to begin work on a fairness opinion as a prelude to any formal board action on the $19 price. The board also discussed with outside counsel its fiduciary duties and issues relating to the opportunities for a post-agreement "market check."

Lehman Issues Its Fairness Opinion And An Agreement With Marathon Is Finalized

On December 22, 2000, the Pennaco board met to hear an oral presentation from Lehman regarding its fairness opinion. Lehman's presentation to the board displayed several different ways of valuing Pennaco's equity, including trading price, comparable companies, comparable acquisitions, and NAV ["Net Asset Value"] calculations.

* * *

At the end of its presentation, Lehman issued its oral opinion that $19 a share was a fair price. The Pennaco board then voted to formally approve a sale at that price as fair and in the best interest of Pennaco's stockholders.

Pennaco Negotiates For Minimal Deal Protections So As To Ensure That There Will Be A Post-Agreement Market Check

As of December 22, 2000, Pennaco had done nothing to see whether other buyers might exist. But Pennaco did negotiate for itself a relatively non-restrictive no-shop clause in the merger agreement. That clause permitted Pennaco to talk and provide information to any party that could reasonably be expected to make a superior offer that could be consummated without undue delay.

Furthermore, Pennaco had resisted Marathon's request for a termination fee equal to 5% of the value placed on Pennaco's equity in

---

[11]   Vinson & Elkins was also retained as outside counsel.

the transaction, and had settled on a termination fee at the more traditional level of 3%.[12] The merger agreement was otherwise devoid of impediments to a higher bid.

As another assurance that a post-agreement market check would exist, Pennaco obtained an agreement that Marathon would not commence its tender offer until the second week of January, 2001. This breathing room was designed to give potential bidders time to examine the transaction, get over any holiday reveries, and make a competing bid.

At the close of business December 22, 2000, Pennaco announced the transaction by press release. Pipkin of Lehman Brothers got edgy at the time of the release and made phone calls to a list of industry players who he believed might be inclined to make a topping bid. Pipkin did so without Pennaco's knowledge and in arguable violation of the no-shop clause.

* * *

The plaintiffs contend that the Pennaco directors' decision to focus exclusively on Marathon and not to seek out other bidders was not a reasonable one. This failure, plaintiffs assert, cannot be cured by a post-market check occurring in the midst of holiday distractions—especially a market check hampered by the termination fee.

Furthermore, the plaintiffs argue that the Pennaco board was a cozy one dominated by defendants Rady and Warren, who had interests adverse to those of the other Pennaco stockholders. According to the plaintiffs, Rady and Warren intentionally dressed the company up for sale while stocking their own larders with options and enhanced severance packages. These emoluments gave Rady and Warren an incentive to lock in a deal that could be closed at less than the best price, because it was to their unique benefit to secure a solid price that would accelerate their options and guarantee them immediate severance benefits over five times more lucrative than their total compensation for the year 2000. If they pushed Marathon too hard for a good price, they could endanger their lucrative severance packages. Better for Rady and Warren, plaintiffs suggest, to lock in a good deal and their severance, than to risk their severance by seeking the best deal available. In addition, the plaintiffs also insinuate that the substantial increase in severance to Rady and Warren materially reduced the consideration a potential acquiror would pay for Pennaco's shares.

* * *

For several reasons, I conclude that the plaintiffs do not have a reasonable probability of ultimate success on their so-called Revlon

---

[12] The termination fee was a slightly smaller percentage of the value of the combined equity and debt of Pennaco as measured by the transaction price. While Delaware cases have tended to use equity value as the benchmark for measuring a termination fee, no case has squarely addressed which benchmark is appropriate. Each benchmark has analytical arguments in its favor.

claim. While one would not commend the Pennaco board's actions as a business school model of value maximization, the process the directors used to sell the company cannot be characterized as unreasonable.

The board's actions must be evaluated in the context of Pennaco's market posture. Even the plaintiffs concede that Pennaco was a source of industry interest. The company was followed by reputable analysts. The company communicated with the market in a bullish manner, and freely communicated with interested parties. The company had done an extensive search for a joint venture partner in 1998, which brought it to the attention of twenty to thirty industry players. Not only that, the company had reincorporated in Delaware to facilitate its participation in the mergers and acquisitions market.

As important, the Pennaco board's knowledge of the company has not been seriously challenged. The board is comprised of members with relevant expertise and experience in the energy business, and who had grown a start-up energy business impressively in a short period of time. There is no basis to believe that the board itself did not have a sound basis to evaluate the price at which a sale of the company would be advantageous.

In these circumstances, the court cannot say that it was unreasonable for the Pennaco board to deal with Marathon on an exclusive basis. Marathon was a major industry player with great financial clout. As all of the investment banks seeking Pennaco's business pointed out, there is no risk-free approach to selling a company, and dealing with one bidder at a time has its own advantages. Thus, the mere fact that the Pennaco board decided to focus on negotiating a favorable price with Marathon and not to seek out other bidders is not one that alone supports a breach of fiduciary duty claim.[13]

Nor does the record support the inference that the Pennaco board's negotiating strategy was unreasonable and perfunctory. To the contrary, the record suggests that Rady and Warren bargained hard to get a favorable price. They succeeded in obtaining a $2 per share increase in Marathon's initial offer, but were unable to get any offer over $19. Given what Rady knew about the company and the information contained in the pitch books from Lehman and CSFB, his decision to recommend that price to his board subject to a formal fairness opinion from Lehman is not a seriously litigable quibble.

---

[13] Barkan v. Amsted Industries, Inc., Del. Supr., 567 A.2d 1279, 1287 (1989) (when "directors possess a body of reliable information with which to evaluate the fairness of a transaction, they may approve [a] transaction without conducting an active survey of the market"). Cf. McMillan v. Intercargo Corp. ("Intercargo II"), 2000 Del. Ch. LEXIS 70, *36, Del. Ch., C.A No. 16963, 2000 WL 516265, at *9, Strine, V.C. (Apr. 20, 2000) ("Whether it is wiser for a disinterested board to take a public approach to selling a company versus a more discreet approach relying upon target marketing by an investment bank is the sort of business strategy question Delaware courts ordinarily do not answer.").

Likewise, the court is unpersuaded by the plaintiffs' argument that the Pennaco board should have obtained an updated reserve report to justify a higher price. To conclude that the board's decision not to do so and instead to bargain based on the June 30 Reserve Report was unreasonable would involve second-guessing of the kind QVC proscribes.

The plaintiffs, of course, place heavy weight on the timing of Lehman's involvement and the fact that it entered the fray after the shooting had stopped. That chronological fact is true, but depends for its legal force on the assertion that a board must use an outside advisor to negotiate price and cannot do so itself on an informed basis. While there is case law that might be read as suggesting that a board's knowledge of the value of its own business is not sufficient,[14] the more traditional view is that an informed board is, of course, free to manage a corporation in all its aspects.[15] It is unlikely the court will later conclude that it was unreasonable for Pennaco's board to conclude price negotiations, subject to confirmation from Lehman that the tentatively-fixed $19 price was fair.

On the other hand, there is little doubt that the validity of the Pennaco board's decision to proceed in the manner it did would be subject to great skepticism had the board acceded to demands to lock up the transaction from later market competition. That is, if the merger agreement with Marathon contained onerous deal protection measures that presented a formidable barrier to the emergence of a superior offer, the Pennaco board's failure to canvass the market earlier might tilt its actions toward the unreasonable.

But it appears that the Pennaco board was careful to balance its single buyer negotiation strategy by ensuring that an effective post-agreement market check would occur. The merger agreement's provisions leave Marathon exposed to competition from rival bidders, with only the modest and reasonable advantages of a 3% termination fee and matching rights. The plaintiffs' attack on the termination fee's level is make-weight and at odds with precedent upholding the validity of fees at this level.[16]

The board also retained significant flexibility to deal with any later-emerging bidder and ensured that the market would have a healthy

---

[14]   See Smith v. Van Gorkom, Del. Supr., 488 A.2d 858 (1985).

[15]   See, e.g., In re Formica Corp. Shareholders Litig., 1989 Del. Ch. LEXIS 27, *37–38, Del. Ch., Cons. C.A. No. 10598, Jacobs, V.C. (Mar. 22, 1989) (holding that directors were capable of assessing the fairness of a transaction based on their own knowledge); Chesapeake Corp. v. Shore, 2000 Del. Ch. LEXIS 20, *103, Del. Ch., C.A. No. 17626, 2000 WL 193119, at *31, Strine, V.C. (2000) (board possessed sufficient knowledge to determine that an offer was inadequate).

[16]   Intercargo II, 2000 Del. Ch. LEXIS 70, *39, 2000 WL 516265, at *10 ("it is difficult to see how a 3.5% termination fee would have deterred a rival bidder who wished to pay materially more . . ."); see also Matador Capital Management Corp. v. BRC Holdings, Inc., Del. Ch., 729 A.2d 280, 291–92 n.15 (1998) (stating that fees in this range are generally considered reasonable); Goodwin v. Live Entertainment, Inc., 1999 Del. Ch. LEXIS 5, Del. Ch., C.A. No. 15765, 1999 WL 64265, at *23, Strine, V.C. (Jan. 25, 1999) (same).

period of time to digest the proposed transaction. As such, no substantial barriers to the emergence of a higher bid existed. Indeed, the fact that no higher bid has come forth in these circumstances is itself "evidence that the directors, in fact, obtained the highest and best transaction reasonably available."[17]

Finally, it is worth noting that the board had information that suggested that the Marathon offer was highly attractive from a financial point of view. Putting aside the formal valuation techniques that support this inference, the price's relationship to Pennaco's prior trading history buttresses this conclusion. Although Pennaco was a company that enjoyed favorable market treatment from the get-go, the Marathon offer exceeded the company's all-time trading high by nearly 10% and presented a healthy premium to all relevant benchmarks.

For all these reasons, I conclude that the plaintiffs are not likely to succeed on their Revlon claim.

NOTE

Section 5.02 of the Merger Agreement between Marathon and Pennaco signed on December 22 contained the following language:

Section 5.02. No Solicitation.

(a) From the date hereof, the Company shall not (whether directly or indirectly through advisors, agents, representatives or other intermediaries), and the Company shall use its reasonable best efforts to cause its officers, directors, advisors, representatives and other agents (collectively, its "Representatives") not to, directly or indirectly, (i) continue any discussions or negotiations, if any, with any parties, other than Parent and Sub, conducted heretofore with respect to any Company Takeover Proposal (as hereinafter defined) or which could reasonably be expected to lead to a Company Takeover Proposal, (ii) solicit, initiate or knowingly encourage any inquiries relating to, or the submission of, any Company Takeover Proposal, (iii) participate in any discussions or negotiations regarding any Company Takeover Proposal, or, in connection with any Company Takeover Proposal, furnish to any person any information or data with respect to or access to the properties of the Company, or take any other action to facilitate the making of any proposal that constitutes or may reasonably be expected to lead to any Company Takeover Proposal or (iv) enter into any agreement with respect to any Company Takeover Proposal. Notwithstanding the foregoing, the Company or the Company Board shall be permitted to furnish information with respect to the Company and participate in discussions or negotiations regarding an unsolicited bona fide Company Takeover Proposal if, and only to the extent that, a majority of the entire Company Board determines in good faith that such Company

---

[17] Matador, 729 A.2d at 293.

Takeover Proposal could reasonably be expected to result in a Superior Company Proposal, in which case the Company will not disclose any information to such person without entering into a customary confidentiality agreement containing confidentiality provisions substantially identical to those contained in the Confidentiality Agreement (as hereinafter defined); provided, however, that such confidentiality agreement shall not prohibit the presentation of a Company Takeover Proposal to Parent. The Company shall promptly (but in no case later than 48 hours after actual receipt by an officer of the Company) provide Parent with a copy of any written Company Takeover Proposal received and a written statement with respect to any non-written Company Takeover Proposal received, which statement shall include the material terms thereof (but may omit the identity of the person making the Company Takeover Proposal). The Company shall keep Parent informed on a reasonably current basis of any material developments with respect to any discussions regarding any Company Takeover Proposal.

(b)   Nothing contained in Section 5.02(a) shall prohibit the Company or the Company Board from (i) taking and disclosing to the Company's stockholders a position contemplated by Rule 14e–2(a) promulgated under the Exchange Act (or any similar communications) in connection with the making or amendment of a tender offer or exchange offer or (ii) making any disclosure to the Company's stockholders required by applicable Law, provided that the Company Board shall not recommend that the stockholders of the Company tender their shares of Company Common Stock in connection with any such tender or exchange offer unless the Company Board, by majority vote of the entire Company Board, shall have determined in good faith, based upon (among other things) the advice of its independent financial advisors and outside counsel, that the relevant Company Takeover Proposal constitutes a Superior Company Proposal.

(c)   For purposes of this Agreement:

"Company Takeover Proposal" means any inquiry, proposal or offer (other than by Parent, Sub or any of their affiliates) for (i) a merger, consolidation, share exchange, dissolution, recapitalization, liquidation or other business combination involving the Company, (ii) the acquisition by any person in any manner, directly or indirectly, of a number of shares of any class of equity securities of the Company equal to or greater than 15% of the number of such shares outstanding before such acquisition or (iii) the acquisition by any person in any manner, directly or indirectly, of assets that generate or constitute a substantial part of the net revenues, net income or assets of the Company, in each case other than the Transactions.

"Superior Company Proposal" means any bona fide written Company Takeover Proposal made by a third party (other than by Parent, Sub or any of their affiliates) to acquire directly or indirectly (i) all the equity securities or (ii) the assets of the Company substantially as an entirety, which the Company Board determines in good faith (based on, among other things, the advice of its independent financial advisors and outside counsel), taking into account all legal, financial, regulatory and other aspects of the proposal and the person making such proposal, (x) would, if consummated, be more favorable, from a financial point of view, to the holders of Company Common Stock than the Transactions and (y) is reasonably likely to be consummated without undue delay.

QUESTIONS

1. Can you distinguish the information the Pennaco directors had from that of the directors in Smith v. Van Gorkom? How does Vice Chancellor Strine make this distinction?

2. The court held that the "no-shop" clause in the Marathon-Pennaco agreement satisfied the board's Revlon duties while the provision in Smith v. Van Gorkom did not? What are the differences?

3. What benefit did the company get out of the amended termination payment agreements with its officers?

C. MERGERS OF EQUALS

Paramount Communications, Inc. v. Time Incorporated

571 A.2d 1140 (Del. 1990).

■ HORSEY, JUSTICE:

Paramount Communications, Inc. ("Paramount") and two other groups of plaintiffs ("Shareholder Plaintiffs"), shareholders of Time Incorporated ("Time"), a Delaware corporation, separately filed suits in the Delaware Court of Chancery seeking a preliminary injunction to halt Time's tender offer for 51% of Warner Communication, Inc.'s ("Warner") outstanding shares at $70 cash per share. The court below consolidated the cases and, following the development of an extensive record, after discovery and an evidentiary hearing, denied plaintiffs' motion. In a 50-page unreported opinion and order entered July 14, 1989, the Chancellor refused to enjoin Time's consummation of its tender offer, concluding that the plaintiffs were unlikely to prevail on the merits.

* * *

I.

[Two facts are critical for understanding the Time-Paramount dispute. First, the Time board was dominated by outside directors with distinguished credentials in other enterprises. Only four of twelve Time board members were "insiders" whose principal activities depended on continued employment at Time. One outside director, Henry R. Luce III (son of Time's founder), had a large amount of his personal and Luce Foundation wealth invested in Time stock.

Second, since 1983 Time management and its board had spent considerable time studying the profitability of vertically integrating into the production of cable programming and related entertainment ventures. By 1987, after considering mergers with or acquisitions of many entertainment and communications firms, Time's management concluded that Warner communications represented the best fit with Time. In so deciding, management considered and rejected the possibility of combining with Paramount Communications. Time's board approved negotiations with Warner only on condition that Time controlled the board of the resulting corporation, and thereby preserved a management culture committed to Time's journalistic integrity. This commitment had meant that the Editor of Time Magazine did not report to top officers of the company who might be more concerned about profits than quality journalism, but rather reported to a committee of the board of directors itself.

Time management had initiated joint venture discussions with Warner in 1987, but they failed because of tax and other problems. But Warner soon reemerged as the focus of Time management's strategic thinking. By July 1988 Time's management proposed new negotiations with Warner. This second round of talks, surmounting difficult negotiations over issues such as board control and management succession, led to a merger agreement in March 1989. The agreement provided that senior management would be shared between J. Richard Munro, Time's CEO, and Stephen Ross, Warner's powerful CEO, for a period of five years until Ross' expected retirement. Thereafter, the agreement provided that a Time executive would be the successor as CEO of the combined company. Time also entered into a "no-shop" agreement, promising that it would neither solicit nor encourage any takeover attempts, an unusual provision for a buyer. Further, Time paid some major banks a "dry-up" fee, to refrain from financing bids for Time, a highly unusual tactic. As part of the agreement with Warner, Time concluded a lock-up exchange agreement, under which each company would receive between 9 and 11 percent of the shares of the other.

In some respects the merger appeared to be an acquisition of Time by Warner. Time management had recognized that in order to impose its corporate governance requirements about management succession and preservation of the "Time Culture," it would have to pay a premium for the Warner shares. Warner shareholders would control 61 percent of the common stock of the new Time-Warner company and 50 percent of the board. In several critical respects, however, Time's existing board would retain control of the new entity. A Time executive would be the sole chief executive officer (after five years of sharing the position with a Warner executive). The "Time culture," a major concern of the Time board, was preserved by ensuring that the senior editor of Time magazine would retain editorial independence from management by reporting to a special committee of the board.

The structure of the original merger, a stock-for-stock exchange, required Time shareholder approval, and a vote was set for June 1989. All this careful planning was interrupted by Paramount's surprise cash bid of $175 per share for Time stock.* Before consulting with his own board, Time's CEO, J. Richard Munro, sent an aggressively worded letter to Paramount's CEO, Martin Davis, which attacked Davis' personal integrity and called Paramount's offer "smoke and mirrors."

When the bid was announced, Time stock rose $44 to $170 per share, and ultimately reached $182.75 per share. Paramount indicated that its bid was fully negotiable, although it conditioned it on cancellation of the Time-Warner merger, Time's relinquishment of various defensive measures it had in place, and on receiving certain regulatory approvals (standard conditions in any hostile bid). Over the next eight days, Time's board met three times to consider the Paramount bid. Time's board never considered the Paramount bid seriously, in the stated belief that it had a binding commitment to Warner, and that a combination with Warner represented greater potential for Time. The board also concluded that Paramount's initial offer was inadequate, despite advice from its investment bankers before Paramount's bid that the stock of the merged Time-Warner would initially trade at about $150, and possibly as high as $175.

Nevertheless, Time's board feared that shareholders would not share its view of likely future values and took steps to protect the Time-Warner combination. By restructuring the deal as a cash bid for 51% of Warner shares at $70 per Warner share followed by a takeout merger for cash and securities valued at $70 (a 56 percent premium over Warner's stock price before the merger announcement), a vote by Time shareholders could be avoided. The cash bid had the advantage of accelerating the combination, since no proxy statement or waiting period for shareholder notice was needed. The acquisition thus could close within 20 business days, well before Paramount could secure regulatory approvals for its bid. To finance the bid Time would incur new debt of at least $10 billion, which would effectively wipe out all current earnings of the combined entities after interest payments. It also wiped out one of the principal

---

*   Paramount's offer was subject to a number of conditions, the most pertinent of which were the following:

1. termination of the Time-Warner merger agreement (or the agreement being left subject to a vote in which Paramount controlled 51% of the vote);

2. termination or invalidation of the Share Exchange Agreement under circumstances in which there would be no liability to Time;

3. Paramount to be satisfied in its sole discretion that all material approvals, consents and franchise transfers relating to Time's programming and cable television business had been obtained on terms satisfactory to Paramount;

4. removal of a number of Time-created or Time-controlled impediments to closing of the offer (e.g., redemption of a "poison pill" preferred rights purchase plan) or effectuation of a second-stage merger (e.g., supermajority voting requirements of 8 Del. c. § 203 and supermajority voting provisions of Time's certificate of incorporation) and

5. financing and majority acceptance of the offer.—Ed.

benefits of the original merger agreement—the lack of debt inherent in the stock merger structure, and the freedom to finance new projects that came with it. After Time's decision Paramount raised its offer to $200 per share, which was rejected three days later by the Time Board.

Paramount sued to enjoin Time's purchase of Warner shares, but the Delaware Chancery Court denied a preliminary injunction. The Delaware Supreme Court affirmed the denial in July 1989, although its written opinion was not issued until February 1990. Time thus was able to complete its share purchase without further interference from Paramount and without a shareholder vote.

There were many reasons to second-guess the decision made by Time's board. Most prominently Time-Warner's stock has fared indifferently since the purchase of Warner shares. Time shares traded between $105 and $122 during March, 1989, after news of the merger agreement with Warner but before the announcement of the Paramount bid. The price stood at $126 when Paramount made its bid. In May 1991, Time-Warner traded at around $119.

There was other contemporaneous evidence that Time was paying an excessively high price for Warner shares. Time offered a 12 percent premium for Warner in the initial merger proposal. Warner's investment bankers described this offer as "one hell of a deal" for Warner. Yet Time ultimately paid a 56 percent premium in the subsequent cash bid. Time's advisors conceded that the market would not value the combined Time-Warner as highly as Paramount's cash bid upon completion, but instead insisted that these markets were inefficient in failing to recognize the synergies present in the merger.

The steady escalation of the future prices predicted by Time's own investment bankers hardly seemed sufficient to justify the Time board's belief that Time shareholders ultimately would realize gains greater than those offered by the Paramount bid. When confronted with the Paramount bid, Time's adviser, Wasserstein Perella, estimated that in the short term Time-Warner stock would probably trade at around $150, but it might also trade as high as $160–$175. In its written presentation to the board, Wasserstein, Perella estimated a 1990 trading range of $106–$188. Later, at trial, additional experts for Time predicted a range of Time-Warner stock prices for the next three years from $208–$402, described by the Chancery Court as "a range that a Texan might feel at home on."]

* * *

II

The Shareholder Plaintiffs first assert a Revlon claim. They contend that the March 4 Time-Warner agreement effectively put Time up for sale, triggering Revlon duties, requiring Time's board to enhance short-term shareholder value and to treat all other interested acquirors on an equal basis. The Shareholder Plaintiffs base this argument on two facts: (i) the ultimate Time-Warner exchange ratio of .465 favoring Warner, resulting in Warner shareholders' receipt of 62% of the combined company; and (ii) the subjective intent of Time's directors as evidenced in their statements that the market might perceive the Time-Warner merger as putting Time up "for sale" and their adoption of various defensive measures.

The Shareholder Plaintiffs further contend that Time's directors, in structuring the original merger transaction to be "takeover-proof," triggered Revlon duties by foreclosing their shareholders from any prospect of obtaining a control premium. In short, plaintiffs argue that Time's board's decision to merge with Warner imposed a fiduciary duty to maximize immediate share value and not erect unreasonable barriers to further bids. Therefore, they argue, the Chancellor erred in finding: that Paramount's bid for Time did not place Time "for sale"; that Time's transaction with Warner did not result in any transfer of control; and that the combined Time-Warner was not so large as to preclude the possibility of the stockholders of Time-Warner receiving a future control premium.

* * *

The Court of Chancery posed the pivotal question presented by this case to be: Under what circumstances must a board of directors abandon an in-place plan of corporate development in order to provide its shareholders with the option to elect and realize an immediate control premium? As applied to this case, the question becomes: Did Time's Board, having developed a strategic plan of global expansion to be launched through a business combination with Warner, come under a fiduciary duty to jettison its plan and put the corporation's future in the hands of its shareholders?

While we affirm the result reached by the Chancellor, we think it unwise to place undue emphasis upon long-term versus short-term corporate strategy. Two key predicates underpin our analysis. First, Delaware law imposes on a board of directors the duty to manage the business and affairs on the corporation. 8 Del. C. § 141(a). This broad mandate includes a conferred authority to set a corporate course of action, including time frame, designed to enhance corporate profitability. Thus, the question of "long-term" versus "short-term" values is largely irrelevant because directors, generally, are obliged to chart a course for a corporation which is in its best interest without regard to a fixed investment horizon. Second, absent a limited set of circumstances as defined under Revlon, a board of directors, while always required to act in an informed manner, is not under any per se duty to maximize shareholder value in the short term, even in the context of a takeover. In our view, the pivotal question presented by this case is: "Did Time, by entering into the proposed merger with Warner, put itself up for sale?" A resolution of that issue through application of Revlon has a significant hearing upon the resolution of the derivative Unocal issue.

A.

We first take up plaintiffs' principal Revlon argument, summarized above. In rejecting this argument, the Chancellor found that original Time-Warner merger agreement not to constitute a "change of control" and concluded that the transaction did not trigger Revlon duties. The Chancellor's conclusion is premised on a finding that "[b]efore the merger agreement was signed, control of the corporation existed in a fluid aggregation of unaffiliated shareholders representing a voting majority—in other words, in the market." The Chancellor's findings of fact are supported by the record and his conclusion is correct as a matter of law. However, we premise our rejection of plaintiffs' Revlon claim on different grounds, namely, the absence of any substantial evidence to conclude that Time's board, in negotiating with Warner, made the dissolution or breakup of the corporate entity inevitable, as was the case in Revlon.

Under Delaware law there are, generally speaking and without excluding other possibilities, two circumstances which may implicate Revlon duties. The first, and clearer one, is when a corporation initiates an active bidding process seeking to sell itself or to effect a business reorganization involving a clear break-up of the company. See, e.g., Mills Acquisition Co. v. MacMillan, Inc., Del. Supr., 559 A.2d 1261 (1988). However, Revlon duties may also be triggered where, in response to a bidder's offer, a target abandons its long-term strategy and seeks an alternative transaction also involving the breakup of the company. Thus, in Revlon, when the board responded to Pantry Pride's offer by contemplating a "bust-up" sale of assets in a leveraged acquisition, we imposed upon the board a duty to maximize immediate shareholder value and an obligation to auction the company fairly. If, however, the board's reaction to a hostile tender offer is found to constitute only a defensive response and not an abandonment of the corporation's continued existence, Revlon duties are not triggered, though Unocal duties attach.

The plaintiffs insist that even though the original Time-Warner agreement may not have worked "an objective change of control," the transaction made a "sale" of Time inevitable. Plaintiffs rely on the subjective intent of Time's board of directors and principally upon certain board members' expressions of concern that the Warner transaction might be viewed as effectively putting Time up for sale. Plaintiffs argue that the use of a lock-up agreement, a no-shop clause, and so-called "dry-up" agreements prevented shareholders from obtaining a control premium in the immediate future and thus violated Revlon.

We agree with the Chancellor that such evidence is entirely insufficient to invoke Revlon duties; and we decline to extend Revlon's application to corporate transactions simply because they might be construed as putting a corporation either "in play" or "up for sale." The adoption of structural safety devices alone does not trigger Revlon. Rather, as the Chancellor stated, such devices are properly subject to a Unocal analysis.

Finally, we do not find in Time's recasting of its merger agreement with Warner from a share exchange to a share purchase a basis to conclude that Time had either abandoned its strategic plan or made a sale of Time inevitable. The Chancellor found that although the merged Time-Warner company would be large (with a value approaching approximately $30 billion), recent takeover cases have proven that acquisition of the combined company might nonetheless be possible. The legal consequence is that Unocal alone applies to determine whether the business judgment rule attaches to the revised agreement. Plaintiffs' analogy to MacMillan thus collapses and plaintiffs' reliance on MacMillan is misplaced.

B.

We turn now to plaintiffs' Unocal claim. We begin by noting, as did the Chancellor, that our decision does not require us to pass on the wisdom of the board's decision to enter into the original Time-Warner agreement. That is not a court's task. Our task is simply to review the record to determine whether there is sufficient evidence to support the Chancellor's conclusion that the initial Time-Warner agreement was the product of a proper exercise of business judgment. MacMillan, 559 A.2d at 1288.

We have purposely detailed the evidence of the Time board's deliberative approach, beginning in 1983–84, to expand itself. Time's decision in 1988 to combine with Warner was made only after what could be fairly characterized as an exhaustive appraisal of Time's future as a corporation. After concluding in 1983–84 that the corporation must expand to survive, and beyond journalism into entertainment, the board combed the field of available entertainment companies. By 1987 Time had focused upon Warner; by late July 1988 Time's board was convinced that Warner would provide the best "fit" for Time to achieve its strategic objectives. The record attests to the zealousness of Time's executives, fully supported by their directors, in seeing to the preservation of Time's "culture," i.e., its perceived editorial integrity in journalism. We find ample evidence in the record to support the Chancellor's conclusion that the Time board's decision to expand the business of the company through its March 3 merger with Warner was entitled to the protection of the business judgment rule.

The Chancellor reached a different conclusion in addressing the Time-Warner transaction as revised three months later. He found that the revised agreement was defense-motivated and designed to avoid the potentially disruptive effect that Paramount's offer would have had on consummation of the proposed merger were it put to a shareholder vote.

Thus, the court declined to apply the traditional business judgment rule to the revised transaction and instead analyzed the Time board's June 16 decision under Unocal. The court ruled that Unocal applied to all director actions taken, following receipt of Paramount's hostile tender offer, that were reasonably determined to be defensive. Clearly that was a correct ruling and no party disputes that ruling.

In Unocal, we held that before the business judgment rule is applied to a board's adoption of a defense measure, the burden will lie with the board to prove (a) reasonable grounds for believing that a danger to corporate policy and effectiveness existed; and (b) that the defensive measures adopted was reasonable in relation to the threat posed. Unocal, 493 A.2d 946. Directors satisfy the first part of the Unocal test by demonstrating good faith and reasonable investigation. We have repeatedly stated that the refusal to entertain an offer may comport with a valid exercise of a board's business judgment. See, e.g., MacMillan, 559 A.2d at 1285 n.35; Van Gorkom, 488 A.2d at 881; Pogostin v. Rice, Del. Supr., 480 A.2d 619, 627 (1984).

Unocal involved a two-tier, highly coercive tender offer. In such a case, the threat is obvious: shareholders may be compelled to tender to avoid being treated adversely in the second stage of the transaction. In subsequent cases the Court of Chancery has suggested that an all-cash, all-shares offer, falling within a range of values that a shareholder might reasonably prefer, cannot constitute a legally recognized "threat" to shareholder interests sufficient to withstand a Unocal analysis. AC Acquisitions Corp. v. Anderson, Clayton (Co., Del. Ch., 519 A.2d 103 (1986)); see Grand Metropolitan, PLC v. Pillsbury Co., Del. Ch., C.A. No. 10319, Duffy, J. (Dec. 16, 1988); City Capital Associates v. Interco, Inc., Del. Ch., 551 A.2d 787 (1988). In those cases, the Court of Chancery determined that whatever danger existed related only to the shareholders and only to price and not to the corporation.

From those decisions by our Court of Chancery, Paramount and the individual plaintiffs extrapolate a rule of law that an all-cash, all-shares offer with values reasonably in the range of acceptable price cannot pose any objective threat to a corporation or its shareholders. Thus, Paramount would have us hold that only if the value of Paramount's offer were determined to be clearly inferior to the value created by management's plan to merge with Warner could the offer be viewed—objectively—as a threat.

Implicit in the plaintiffs' argument is the view that a hostile tender offer can pose only two types of threats: the threat of coercion that results from a two-tier offer promising unequal treatment for nontendering shareholders; and the threat of inadequate value from an all-shares, all-cash offer at a price below what a target board in good faith deems to be the present value of its shares. See, e.g., Interco, 551 A.2d at 797; see also BNS, Inc. v. Koppers, D. Del., 683 F.Supp. 458 (1988). Since Paramount's offer was all-cash, the only conceivable "threat," plaintiffs argue, was inadequate value. We disapprove of such a narrow and rigid construction of Unocal, for the reasons which follow.

Plaintiffs' position represents a fundamental misconception of our standard of review under Unocal principally because it would involve the court in substituting its judgment for what is a "better" deal for that of a corporation's board of directors. To the extent that the Court of Chancery has recently done so in certain of its opinions, we hereby reject such approach as not in keeping with a proper Unocal analysis. See, e.g., Interco, 551 A.2d 787, and its progeny; but see TW Services, Inc. v. SWT Acquisition Corp., Del. Ch., C.A. No. 10427, Allen, C. (March 2, 1989).

The usefulness of Unocal as an analytical tool is precisely its flexibility in the face of a variety of fact scenarios. Unocal is not intended as an abstract standard; neither is it a structured and mechanistic procedure of appraisal. Thus, we have said that directors may consider, when evaluating the threat posed by a takeover bid, the "inadequacy of the price offered, nature and timing of the offer, questions of illegality, the impact on 'constituencies' other than shareholders, the risk of nonconsummation and the quality of securities being offered in the exchange." 493 A.2d at 955. The open-ended analysis mandated by Unocal is not intended to lead to a simple mathematical exercise: that is, of comparing the discounted value of Time-Warner's expected trading price at some future date with Paramount's offer and determining which is the higher. Indeed, in our view, precepts underlying the business judgment rule mitigate against a court's engaging in the process of attempting to appraise and evaluate the relative merits of a long-term versus a short-term investment goal for shareholders. To engage in such an exercise is a distortion of the Unocal process and, in particular, the application of the second part of Unocal's test, discussed below.

In this case, the Time board reasonably determined that inadequate value was not the only legally cognizable threat that Paramount's all-cash, all-shares offer could present. Time's board concluded that Paramount's eleventh hour offer posed other threats. One concern was that Time shareholders might elect to tender into Paramount's cash offer in ignorance or a mistaken belief of the strategic benefit which a business combination with Warner might produce. Moreover, Time viewed the conditions attached to Paramount's offer as introducing a degree of uncertainty that skewed a comparative analysis. Further, the timing of Paramount's offer to follow issuance of Time's proxy notice was viewed as arguably designed to upset, if not confuse, the Time stockholders' vote. Given this record evidence, we cannot conclude that the Time board's decision of June 6 that Paramount's offer posed a threat to corporate policy and effectiveness was lacking in good faith or dominated by motives of either entrenchment or self-interest.

Paramount also contends that the Time board had not duly investigated Paramount's offer. Therefore, Paramount argues, Time was unable to make an informed decision that the offer posed a threat to Time's corporate policy. Although the Chancellor did not address this issue directly, his findings of fact do detail Time's exploration of the available entertainment companies, including Paramount, before determining that Warner provided the best strategic "fit." In addition, the court found that Time's board rejected Paramount's offer because Paramount did not serve Time's objectives or meet Time's needs. Thus, the record does, in our judgment, demonstrate that Time's board was adequately informed of the potential benefits of a transaction with Paramount. We agree with the Chancellor that the Time board's lengthy pre-June investigation of potential merger candidates, including Paramount, mooted any obligation on Time's part to halt its merger process with Warner to reconsider Paramount. Time's board was under no obligation to negotiate with Paramount. Unocal, 493 A.2d at 954–55; see also MacMillan, 559 A.2d at 1285 n.35. Time's failure to negotiate cannot be fairly found to have been uninformed. The evidence supporting this finding is materially enhanced by the fact that twelve of Time's sixteen board members were outside independent directors.

We turn to the second part of the Unocal analysis. The obvious requisite to determining the reasonableness of a defensive action is a clear identification of the nature of the threat. As the Chancellor correctly noted, this "requires an evaluation of the importance of the corporate objective threatened; alternative methods of protecting that objective; impacts of the 'defensive' action, and other relevant factors." It is not until both parts of the Unocal inquiry have been satisfied that the business judgment rule attaches to defensive actions of a board of directors. Unocal, 493 A.2d at 954. As applied to the facts of this case, the question is whether the record evidence supports the Court of Chancery's conclusion that the restructuring of the Time-Warner transaction, including the adoption of several preclusive defensive measures, was a reasonable response in relation to a perceived threat.

Paramount argues that, assuming its tender offer posed a threat, Time's response was unreasonable in precluding Time's shareholders from accepting the tender offer or receiving a control premium in the immediately foreseeable future. Once again, the contention stems, we believe, from a fundamental misunderstanding of where the power of corporate governance lies. Delaware law confers the management of the corporate enterprise to the stockholders' duly elected board representatives. 8 Del. C. § 141(a). The fiduciary duty to manage a corporate enterprise includes the selection of a time frame for achievement of corporate goals. That duty may not be delegated to the stockholders. Van Gorkom, 488 A.2d at 873. Directors are not obliged to abandon a deliberately conceived corporate plan for a short-term shareholder profit unless there is clearly no basis to sustain the corporate strategy. See, e.g., Revlon, 506 A.2d 173.

Although the Chancellor blurred somewhat the discrete analyses required under Unocal, he did conclude that Time's board reasonably perceived Paramount's offer to be a significant threat to the planned Time-Warner merger and that Time's response was not "overly broad." We have found that even in light of a valid threat, management actions that are coercive in nature or force upon shareholders a management-sponsored alternative to a hostile offer may be struck down as unreasonable and nonproportionate responses. MacMillan, 559 A.2d 1261; AC Acquisitions Corp., 519 A.2d 103.

Here, on the record facts, the Chancellor found that Time's responsive action to Paramount's tender offer was not aimed at "cramming down" on its shareholders a management-sponsored alternative, but rather had as its goal the carrying forward of a pre-existing transaction in an altered form. Thus, the response was reasonably related to the threat. The Chancellor noted that the revised agreement and its accompanying safety devices did not preclude Paramount from making an offer for the combined Time-Warner company or from changing the conditions of its offer so as not to make the offer dependent upon the nullification of the Time-Warner agreement. Thus, the response was proportionate. We affirm the Chancellor's rulings as clearly supported by the record. Finally, we note that although Time was required, as a result of Paramount's hostile offer, to incur a heavy debt to finance its acquisition of Warner, that fact alone does not render the board's decision unreasonable so long as the directors could reasonably perceive the debt load not to be so injurious to the corporation as to jeopardize its well being.

C.

Conclusion

Applying the test for grant or denial of preliminary injunctive relief, we find plaintiffs failed to establish a reasonable likelihood of ultimate success on the merits. Therefore, we affirm.

———————

QUESTIONS

1. Is the court applying a Unocal standard here? Why doesn't the court apply a Revlon standard here?

2. Is there any evidence of management entrenchment purposes?

3. Is there any evidence that management dominated the board deliberations?

4. Was the board's refusal to consider the Paramount cash bid exercise of an informed business judgment?

5. Why does the court decide the Board's response to Paramount was reasonable in proportion to the threat to the Time-Warner combination?

6. Does this mean a board can "just say no" to a hostile bid? Can it create an alternative business plan once a bidder appears, and then defend that plan?

———————

After the Delaware Supreme Court decision, Time went ahead and purchased Warner Communications for a then record in the media industry, $14.1 billion. Time's shareholders, however, were not nearly as pleased. Although Time's stock split four for one within seven years after the merger, the company missed out on the 90's bull market entirely, mainly because of the debt-laden acquisition of Warner. Time shareholders received an annualized compounded return of 3.8% through 1996 compared to the 10.5% return on the S & P 500. As for Paramount, the predator became the prey. In 1994 Viacom, Inc., bought the company for $9.6 billion.

———————

NOTE ON THE APPLICATION OF TIME-PARAMOUNT

While the Chancery Court's opinion in this and prior decisions about the importance of market values to board decisions was criticized, the Chancery Court's discussion on this issue may remain important. Chancellor Allen wrote:

> The legal analysis that follows treats the distinction that the Time board implicitly drew between current share value maximization and long-term share value maximization. For some, this is a false distinction. "The lawyers may talk about a premium for control. But to a true believer of efficient markets, there cannot be a premium for control."[1] Therefore, before turning to the legal analysis that does employ that distinction, I pause to address in some brief way the notion that the distinction between any long-term and short-term stock value, at least where there is a large, active, informed market for the shares of the company, is an error; that the nature of such markets is precisely to discount to a current value the future financial prospects of the firm; and that markets

———————

[1] The statement is Professor Martin Shubik's, the Seymour H. Knox Professor of Mathematical Institutional Economics at Yale. Professor Shubik apparently is not a true believer in efficient markets. He goes on to suggest:

> If, in contradistinction to the adherents of the single, efficient market, we suggest that there are several more or less imperfect markets involving the market for a few shares, the market for control, the market for going-business assets, and the market for assets in liquidation, then we have a structure for interpreting what is going on in terms of arbitrage among these different markets.

Shubik, "Corporate Control, Efficient Markets, and the Public Good," Knights, Raiders & Targets: The Impact of the Hostile Takeover, (Coffee, Lowenstein and Rose-Ackerman eds. 1988).

with their numberless participants seeking information and making judgments do this correctly (at least in the limited sense that no one without inside information can regularly do it better).[2]

This view may be correct. It may be that in a well-developed stock market, there is no discount for long-term profit maximizing behavior except that reflected in the discount for the time value of money. It may be the case that when the market valued the stock of Time at about $125 per share following the announcement of the merger, an observer blessed with perfect foresight would have concurred in that value now of the future stream of all returns foreseen into eternity. Perhaps wise social policy and sound business decisions ought to be premised upon the assumptions that underlie that view. But just as the Constitution does not enshrine Mr. Herbert Spencer's social statics, neither does the common law of directors' duties elevate the theory of a single, efficient capital market to the dignity of a sacred text.

Directors may operate on the theory that the stock market valuation is "wrong" in some sense, without breaching faith with shareholders. No one, after all, has access to more information concerning the corporation's present and future condition. It is far from irrational and certainly not suspect for directors to believe that a likely immediate market valuation of the Time-Warner merger will undervalue the stock. The record in this case refers to instances in which directors did function on a theory that they understood better than the public market for the firm's shares what the value of their firm was, and were shown by events to be correct:

The Walt Disney Company case is an example of an entertainment company that rejected a $72.50 hostile offer in June 1984 and is now trading at the equivalent of $380 per 1984 share. Another example of an entertainment company that achieved better results by remaining independent and growing than by cashing in when it was undervalued in the market is Warner itself. In early 1984, Warner was the subject of unsolicited interest on the part of Rupert Murdoch. At that time Warner was selling for $10 to $12 a share, adjusted for a subsequent two-for-one split. Today, of course—five and a half years later—Warner is the subject of a $70 per share merger agreement with Time and was selling at $45 (or about four times its early 1984 price) before its merger with Time was announced.

It is somewhat ironic that the market was valuing Time at about $125 a share after the merger announcement, while Chancellor Allen defended the board's right to conclude that was too low. Post-merger the stock traded between $100–$115, suggesting the market had far more insight on the value of the merger than the Time board or its advisers.

---

[2] See, e.g., Gordon & Kornhauser, "Efficient Markets, Costly Information and Securities Research." 60 N. Y. U. L. Rev. 761 (1985).

The Delaware Supreme Court has extended the reasoning of the Revlon case to the sale of a controlling interest in a corporation. Paramount Communications Inc. v. QVC Network Inc., 637 A.2d 34, 43 (Del. 1994). An agreement between Paramount and Viacom Corporation originally called for a merger of Paramount into Viacom. The dominant shareholder of Viacom, Sumner Redstone, owned 85.2% of Viacom's voting Class A stock and 69.2% of its nonvoting Class B stock. The Paramount board had approved a merger with Viacom, coupled with a cash tender offer for a majority of Paramount's shares, in which the remaining Paramount shareholders would receive stock in Viacom. Paramount shareholders would have received a minority equity position in the surviving corporation, which would have been controlled by Redstone. The Supreme Court determined that this was a sale of control, because "[i]rrespective of the present Paramount Board's vision of a long-term strategic alliance with Viacom, the proposed sale of control would provide the new controlling shareholder with the power to alter that vision." 637 A.2d at 43. The court stated: "Once control has shifted, the current Paramount stockholders will have no leverage in the future to demand another control premium. As a result, the Paramount stockholders are entitled to receive, and should receive, a control premium and/or protective devices of significant value. There being no such protective provisions in the Viacom-Paramount transaction, the Paramount directors had an obligation to take the maximum advantage of the current opportunity to realize for the stockholders the best value reasonably available." *Id.* Because of this, the Paramount Board was not permitted to treat the merger as a merger of equals, but was required to treat it as a sale. As a result, it could not treat the competing QVC bid as a threat to a long-term corporate strategy of achieving a strategic combination. For a case allowing target management to sell up to a 49% interest to a "white knight" to fend off an uninvited bidder, see Ivanhoe Partners v. Newmont Mining Corporation, 535 A.2d 1334 (Del. 1987), *infra*, Chapter 4, Part 1.G. The QVC court distinguished Ivanhoe because of the contractual limits placed on the power of the 49% shareholder to control the policies of the corporation, and to acquire additional stock (a standstill agreement). Would such arrangements preserve the power of the corporation to obtain a control premium for its public shareholders?

Since the Time-Paramount decision, the Delaware Chancery Court has held that a Revlon type of auction was not required where a management group controlling 48% of a company's shares proposed a management buyout of the public shareholders. Freedman v. Restaurant Associates, Inc., [1990–91 Decisions] Fed. Sec. L. Rep. (CCH) ¶ 95,617 (Del. Ch. 1990). The Chancery Court held that Revlon did not impose a duty to shop, and that the only obligation was to make an informed judgment and to act reasonably in attempting to get the best deal for the shareholders. The case is distinguishable from Revlon and its progeny by management's announcement that its shares were not for sale, its refusal to deal with a prospective competing buyer, and the use of its majority votes on the board to reject a higher offer. The Chancery court did state that these actions were subject to review as conflict of interest transactions.

This narrow view of the reach of Revlon was reaffirmed in Herd v. Major Realty Corp., [1990–91 Decisions] Fed. Sec. L. Rep. (CCH) ¶ 95,772 (Del. Ch. 1990), where a board approved a merger after rejecting competing bids from two other bidders, without shopping for the highest price. The merger allowed the public shareholders to remain shareholders in the surviving enterprise, or to accept cash for their shares. Most shareholders remained shareholders in the surviving corporation, and indeed held a large majority of its outstanding shares.

One author has suggested that whether Revlon duties are triggered in mergers may depend on how the transaction is characterized by management. Paramount always characterized the transaction as a sale of Paramount, while Time was always characterized as a strategic alliance, designed to preserve Time's corporate culture and strategies. Yet even this article concedes that it will be difficult to characterize a transaction as a strategic alliance if a new majority shareholder emerges as a result of the combination. Anthony J. Dennis, "Is It All in the Packaging? Mergers & Acquisitions in the Wake of Paramount/QVC," BUSINESS LAW TODAY 7, 10 (July/August 1994).

Recall that tax-free "A" reorganizations, normally thought of as stock-for-stock transactions," remain tax-free for stock recipients if there is a sufficient continuity of interest of target shareholders in the combined enterprise (Chapter Three, Part 2.A.ii). Normally, this is thought of as involving something close to investing approximately half of the target's value in stock of the surviving corporation. This means that offers can be structured to offer target shareholders choices between stock in the acquiring corporation and cash. These cases naturally raise questions of where the divide lies between Revlon and Business Judgment Rule standards.

In re Lukens, Inc. Shareholders Litigation, 757 A.2d 720 (Del. Ch. 1999) involved a proposed stock-for-stock merger in which Lukens shareholders could elect to receive up to 62% of the proposed merger consideration in cash rather than stock of the acquirer, Bethlehem Steel Corporation. Vice Chancellor Lamb assumed that such a transaction implicated Revlon duties, without explaining why. He then held that the board had fulfilled its Revlon duties in the transaction.

In re Smurfit-Stone Container Corp. Shareholder Litigation, 2011 Del. Ch. LEXIS 79, involved a bid that offered 50% cash and 50% stock, resulting in Smurfit-Stone stockholders owning approximately 45% of the bidder, Rock-Tenn Company. This was not an election by each shareholder, but a fixed formula. After reviewing the Lukens case, Vice Chancellor Parsons held that Revlon applied:

> Thus far, this Court has not been instructed otherwise, and, while the stock portion of the Merger Consideration is larger than the portion in Lukens, I am persuaded that Vice Chancellor Lamb's reasoning applies here, as well. Defendants attempt to distinguish Lukens on its facts, arguing that "they offer no support to plaintiffs' position." I disagree. While the factual scenarios are not identical, there are some material similarities. Most important of these is

that the Court in Lukens was wary of the fact that a majority of holders of Lukens common stock potentially could have elected to cash out their positions entirely, subject to the 62% total cash consideration limit. In this case, Defendants emphasize that no Smurfit-Stone stockholder involuntarily or voluntarily can be cashed out completely and, after consummation of the Proposed Transaction, the stockholders will own slightly less than half of Rock-Tenn. While the facts of this case and Lukens differ slightly in that regard, Defendants lose sight of the fact that while no Smurfit-Stone stockholder will be cashed out 100%, 100% of its stockholders who elect to participate in the merger will see approximately 50% of their Smurfit-Stone investment cashed out. As such, like Vice Chancellor Lamb's concern that potentially there was no "tomorrow" for a substantial majority of Lukens stockholders, the concern here is that there is no "tomorrow" for approximately 50% of each stockholder's investment in Smurfit-Stone. That each stockholder may retain a portion of her investment after the merger is insufficient to distinguish the reasoning of Lukens, which concerns the need for the Court to scrutinize under Revlon a transaction that constitutes an end-game for all or a substantial part of a stockholder's investment in a Delaware corporation.

Distinguishing QVC, Vice Chancellor Parsons wrote:

> But, the fact that control of Rock-Tenn after consummation will remain in a large pool of unaffiliated stockholders, while important, neither addresses nor affords protection to the portion of the stockholders' investment that will be converted into cash and thereby be deprived of its long-run potential.

> Based on the foregoing, therefore, I conclude that Plaintiffs are likely to succeed on their argument that the approximately 50% cash and 50% stock consideration here triggers Revlon.

Query: If the Smurfit-Stone shareholders can reinvest their cash portion in Rock-Tenn shares through the market, how are they forced out of the long-term potential of Smurfit and Rock-Tenn?

In In re Santa Fe Pac. Corp., 1995 Del. Ch. LEXIS 70 (Del. Ch.) Santa Fe was involved in a merger into Burlington Northern, Inc. in which the Santa Fe shareholders would receive 33% cash and 67% stock in Burlington Northern. Vice Chancellor Jacobs held that Revlon did not apply, since Burlington Northern was a widely held corporation with no controlling shareholder.

Straddling the line, in Chen v. Howard-Anderson, 87 A.3d 648 (Del. Ch. 2014) the court held that where the cash and stock components in a merger are relatively equal, the standard of review is ordinarily enhanced scrutiny unless the merger has been approved by a fully informed, non-coerced stockholder vote, but nevertheless applied enhanced scrutiny because evidence suggested that disclosure deficiencies (cured before the vote) undermined the vote.

PROBLEMS

Problem 1.

Your corporate client is a multi-divisional corporation operating in several distinct businesses—home furniture sales through a well-known nationwide chain of stores, manufacture of a nationally known brand of raincoats, shoe manufacture, and a variety of smaller businesses. The company has little debt, and has surplus cash at the present time. Its takeover defenses are in place, including a flip-in, flip-over poison pill that is triggered by the acquisition of 20% or more of its common stock by any single person or entity. Like virtually all rights plans, these rights are redeemable by the board for a period after a tender offer is announced, at a nominal price.

Suddenly the client is confronted with a hostile bid at $70 per share, a substantial premium over the pre-bid market, for all of its shares, for cash. The bidder announces that the shareholders who do not tender will be cashed out in a second stage merger at the same price as the cash tender offer. The only condition to completion of the tender offer is redemption of the poison pill rights by the company's board. The bidder has disclosed that its financing is firm, and that much of the indebtedness incurred to finance the bid will ultimately be secured by the company's assets. In short, this is a highly leveraged acquisition. The bidder has also disclosed that it will be necessary to sell off some of the company's divisions in order to pay off part of the debt if the acquisition is successful.

Your client has consulted its investment banker, who has opined that the bid is within the range of fairness, but at the low end of the range, and is thus "inadequate." The investment banker advises that the company could emulate the bidder's strategy, and create more value for its shareholders. Thus, the company could declare a dividend to its shareholders of its surplus cash, and an additional dividend of short-term notes, payable within two years, and a final dividend of some long-term notes. The total package of cash and notes would have a value of $64 per share, according to the investment bankers. The common stock would then have a market value of $8 to $10 per share, meaning that the recapitalization transaction would have a total value of $72 to $74 per share. It would be necessary for the company to sell off some of its divisions in order to pay off the short-term debt, probably the same divisions the hostile bidder would sell—the so-called "crown jewels"— the furniture chain and the raincoat manufacturer. No shareholder vote would be required to complete the recapitalization, and any shareholder vote that might be required on any subsequent asset sale will come too late to allow shareholders to accept the bid.

The hostile bidder, who is also a shareholder in the company, raises its bid to $74 cash and brings a derivative action against the board of directors in the Delaware courts to compel the board to redeem the rights. The bidder argues that the target's management is a competing management team seeking control of the target, and that an auction is under way, which requires imposition of the Revlon rule of neutrality. The bidder further argues that the rights plan has served its purpose once it has bought enough time for the target's board to formulate a response to the bid. The bidder argues that once management has formulated a plan, it should allow shareholders to choose between its plan and the cash tender offer.

The target's board is composed of a majority of outside, independent directors, who constituted themselves a special committee for purposes of the decisions to recapitalize. Your senior partner has asked you to outline the arguments to be made under Delaware law that management can leave the rights plan in place, and refuse to redeem the rights.

This problem is drawn from City Capital Associates Ltd. v. Interco, Inc., 551 A.2d 787 (Del. Ch. 1988). Would the Chancery Court have reached the same decision after Time-Paramount?

Problem 2.

Your client is a former conglomerate corporation. During the 1970s it was controlled by a deal-maker who bought and sold a variety of businesses through the corporation. After his retirement in the 1980s, the new management moved away from conglomerate status. At present the corporation owns one active business: a lawn equipment manufacturer. It has previously sold off a sporting goods division to another company, in exchange for stock in the other company. The other company's stock is widely traded and listed on the New York Stock Exchange. Your client has attempted to sell its lawn equipment business, but has been unable to find any takers in over a year of searching, at least at its asking price.

Your client's CEO is a dynamic executive who has previously taken control of several companies and reformed their operations and made them highly profitable. He now believes he has found another such opportunity. A billionaire owns several businesses that have languished, and is interested in engaging in a merger with your client. The billionaire owns the vast majority of the shares of his two companies, and if a merger occurs, he will own a controlling interest in your client, which would be the surviving corporation. The CEO believes this is a unique opportunity: that these two corporations have some assets that have not been fully exploited, and he believes he and his management team have the talents to exploit them. You have mentioned the Revlon case to him, and he is adamant that he does not want to "shop" his company.

Advise the board of directors on their obligations.

Problem 3.

Your company is considering an offer to merge with another company of roughly the same size. The other company is offering a stock for stock merger, using its stock at a ratio that gives your shareholders a premium over the current market value of their stock. Further, the other company has offered to assure you that the market value of its stock to be received by your shareholders will not fall below a certain floor price by the time the merger is consummated. The positions on the board of the surviving company will be split equally between the two companies' current directors, and the CEO of the other company has offered to share the CEO position with your company's CEO. The only condition to the merger is that the shareholders of the other company must wind up with at least 50.1% of the stock in the surviving corporation, because the other company has certain agreements that prohibit a change of control. The other company has one 30% shareholder and a 25% shareholder. These two shareholders have not always agreed with each other in the past.

Can your company enter into a binding merger agreement without shopping? Can it sign a no-shop agreement?

Problem 4.

Your client is a computer software company that has experienced some marketing setbacks, and as a result was in financial difficulty. Like many computer software companies, a majority of its stock is held by employees (although it is a '34 Act reporting company). A few months ago, it appeared that the company would not be able to renew its lines of credit with its banks. As a result, the board determined to seek an equity partner—someone who would purchase a significant minority stock interest in the company, and lend the company additional funds to replace its bank financing. For this purpose it hired a well-known investment banking firm. This search failed, and the board approved a search for a merger partner. Every prospect approached by the investment bankers was required to sign a confidentiality agreement and a stand-still agreement, by which it agreed it would not make any offers to buy the company or its shares except through negotiations with the board. The stand-still agreement had a five year life, and is still in effect. After a search, the board entered into negotiations with another software company. These negotiations resulted in a letter of intent for a proposed merger. As a result of the merger, the client's shareholders would have received a significant interest in the merged company, but the merged company would have had a dominant (40%) shareholder, the present parent of the other software company. Because the other software company changed its position during the course of the negotiations, no definitive agreement was signed.

The letter of intent contained an exclusivity period, during which your client could only negotiate with the other software company. As soon as the exclusivity period expired, your client located a wealthy individual investor capable of fulfilling its original goal: of taking a minority equity interest in the company, while furnishing senior financing. Accordingly, an agreement was reached by which the investor would purchase preferred stock carrying one third of the voting rights in the company, as well as options to purchase one third of the company's common stock at increasing prices over the next five years. As the options are exercised, the voting rights disappear from the preferred under this arrangement. The investor entered into a stand-still agreement, agreeing not to purchase more than 50% of the company's stock for the next five years. At the same time, banks agreed to renew lines of credit, in view of this infusion of new capital.

The client has sent out proxy statements to its shareholders for a proposed special meeting to authorize the new preferred stock. As soon as the mailing is complete, the software company that originally negotiated with the client writes to the client's CEO and its entire board of directors, offering to purchase all of the client's stock for cash, at a price about 15% above the market.

Advise the board on their obligations. Review *Binks v. DSL.net, Inc.*, 2010 Del. Ch. LEXIS 98.

----

2. THE EFFECT OF THE NEVER-ENDING DUTY ON DEAL STRUCTURE

The Buyer's Risks of Losing the Target

Bidders face at least four problems in negotiating with a prospective seller. First, the bidder expects to expend resources investigating the target and negotiating with it. If no deal is struck, in virtually all cases these expenses will be borne by the bidder. Second, revelation of the negotiations and of the terms offered by the bidder conveys valuable information to other prospective bidders, who can "free ride" on the first bidder's efforts. Third, the bidder has no way of knowing whether its best bid is the highest bid that could be found for the target if it were aggressively shopped, and thus cannot quantify the risk that its efforts will be wasted. Finally, bidders are aware of the "winner's curse" in auction theory—that the "winner" at an auction is by definition the one willing to pay more than the consensus market valuation of the asset, and may well have paid too much. Getting involved in an active auction, then, by incurring research costs others may not have to incur, is not an attractive proposition for prospective bidders.

Bidders' expenses cover a variety of areas. First, there are search costs, to identify possible acquisition targets. This sometimes takes the form of investment banker's fees. In other cases it takes the more direct form of a finder's fee, often paid to a business broker. The most famous formula for these fees is the so-called Lehman formula, in which the bidder pays the finder 5% on the first $1 million of purchase price, 4% on the second million, 3% on the third, 2% on the 4th, and 1% on the entire balance of the purchase price. A study by Cambridge Associates, reported in the Nov. 16, 1987 issue of PENSIONS & INVESTMENT AGE, p. 4, reported that the average investment banking fee paid in an acquisition by an industrial corporation was $1.8 million. A subsequent study for the Federal Reserve Bank of Atlanta by economists William Curt Hunter and Mary Beth Walker reported a range of fees from $100,000 to $20 million. The average transaction had a price of $831 million and a $5 million fee to investment bankers, or less than 1% of the transaction price. In terms of the gain to shareholders of both combining companies, measured by changes in stock prices, they represented 6.6% of the total gains. Hunter & Walker, An Empirical Examination of Investment Banking Merger Fee

Contracts, 56 SO. ECON. J. 1117 (1990). No studies have reported on investment bankers' fees in failed negotiations, but Hunter and Walker report that contingent fee contracts are the dominant form of fee arrangement.

Many leveraged buyout transactions have generated large fees. Morgan Stanley & Co. was reported to have earned fees of $80 million, or 2.4% of the value of the transaction, in the $3.3 billion LBO of Burlington Industries. The Remaking of Morgan Stanley, 21 Institutional Investor 89 (Nov. 1987). Morgan Stanley was also reported to have earned fees of $54 million, or over 1.25% of the value of the $4.2 billion transaction involving Owens-Illinois Corporation. *Id.* at 91. Total fees of approximately $125–$130 million for a leveraged recapitalization or "public LBO" were challenged unsuccessfully in British Printing & Communication Corp. v. Harcourt, Brace, Jovanovich, Inc., 664 F.Supp. 1519, 1527 (S.D.N.Y.1987). These fees included an investment banker's fee of $46 million for arranging a $1.9 billion loan, or a fee of over 2% of the value of the loan. In its merger with NYNEX, Bell Atlantic agreed to pay Merrill Lynch advisory fees of $30 million, of which $1.5 million was a fixed obligation and the remainder payable upon completion of the transaction.

Where the purchase is to be financed with funds to be acquired by the bidder, additional costs will be incurred. Loan commitment fees may have to be paid before the bidder can make a credible offer to a reluctant target, and where the bidder expects to seek funds from public capital markets, some initial steps toward a public offering may need to be taken. One case reported anticipated expenses of $17 million in connection with raising $1 billion in debt financing. West Point-Pepperell, Inc. v. J. P. Stevens & Co., Inc., Del. Super. Nos. 9634, 9763 (Apr. 8, 1988). Staff and executive time will be consumed by the investigation and negotiation process. In some cases outside experts must be retained in order to evaluate the target—in the form of estimates of mineral reserves, environmental audits to determine potential liabilities, and the like. Accountants may be retained to advise on the structure of the acquisition in order to maximize tax advantages, and counsel will perform an important (and frequently costly) role in carrying out parts of the due diligence activities discussed in Chapter 5.

The magnitude of these expenditures formed the basis for a debate among Professors Frank Easterbrook and Daniel Fischel, on one side, and Ronald Gilson and Lucien Bebchuk, on the other. Easterbrook and Fischel took the position that a first bidder's pre-acquisition expenses were substantial, and that increasing the risk that the bid would be topped by another bidder who was enabled to free ride on the first bidder's efforts would deter a significant number of first bids, and leave target shareholders worse off. Easterbrook & Fischel, The Proper Role of a Target's Management in Responding to a Tender Offer, 94 HARV. L.

Rev. 1161 (1981); Auctions and Sunk Costs in Tender Offers, 35 STAN. L. REV. 1 (1982). Gilson and Bebchuk, in contrast, argued that while defensive tactics used to preserve target independence decrease shareholder value, their use to create auctions increases shareholder value. Gilson, Seeking Competitive Bids Versus Pure Passivity in Tender Offer Defense, 35 STAN. L. R. REV. 51 (1982); Bebchuk, The Case for Facilitating Competing Tender Offers, 95 HARV. L. REV. 1028 (1982); and The Case for Facilitating Competing Tender Offers: A Reply and Extension, 35 STAN. L. REV. 23 (1982). All parties seemed to agree that a free rider problem exists, and that revelation of information at an early stage would be costly to first bidders. The disagreements centered around the magnitude of the first bidder's expenses, and whether the bidder would be likely to win often enough that the marginal effect on the number of first bids would be insignificant. No convincing empirical evidence was offered by any of the combatants.

For our purposes, it is only important that these costs exist, and that bidders would prefer a regime of exclusive dealing with a target, in order to minimize both the risk of being topped by another bidder, and the risk of loss of the expenses of investigation and negotiation.

A. LETTERS OF INTENT

United Acquisition Corp. v. Banque Paribas

631 F.Supp. 797 (S.D.N.Y.1985).

■ WALKER, DISTRICT JUDGE.

Introduction

Plaintiff United Acquisition Corp. ("UAC") seeks the aid of this court to enforce what it claims to be a binding contract to purchase all of the stock of United Refining, Inc. ("URI") from the defendants, Banque Paribas ("Paribas"), Banque Paribas Suisse, S.A. ("Paribas Swiss") and the Royal Bank of Canada ("Royal Bank"). Specifically, plaintiff seeks an order enjoining defendant from selling any stock of URI or its URI's subsidiaries to any third parties. * * *

Facts

URI is a holding company which owns all of the issued stock of its operating company, United Refining Company ("URC") with headquarters in Warren, Pennsylvania. * * *

[Paribas, Paribas Swiss and Royal Bank had become the sole owners of URI through foreclosure in August of 1985. The banks appointed their own nominees to the URI board. Michel Jacquet, Executive Vice President and General manager of the New York branch of Paribas, hired Joe A. Ris to manage URI on a temporary basis. Ris was appointed president and CEO of URI's operating subsidiaries.

It was understood that URI was for sale, and Ris was approached by John Catsimatidis, with whom he had worked on a bankruptcy reorganization, who had indicated that he and his associate, Michael Sherman, were available as investors. On November 15, 1985, Catsimatidis wrote a letter on the stationary of his company, UAC, addressed to Paribas, offering to purchase the common stock of URI for $2.5 million. It stated in part:

> "UAC and the Banks shall immediately direct their respective attorneys to commence preparation of a mutually satisfactory form of Agreement, which shall, among other things, (i) provide for payment of the price in cash at closing against transfer to UAC of good title to the stock free of any liens, encumbrances, and security interests; (ii) require a closing not later than November 27, 1985 or a later date in the sole discretion of UAC; and (iii) [sic] warranties and conditions which are customary in transactions of this kind."

According to Catsimatidis, neither the timing of the agreement or the closing nor the necessity to wire funds were discussed. When asked whether the discussion was strictly on price, Catsimatidis testified: "Cash deal, cash American money on the table, exchange of stock, usual representations and warranties." Catsimatidis was then asked whether there was any discussion about what the usual representations and warranties would include. He responded "I am sure it is whatever the SEC requires."

The banks did not accept the offer. At a meeting with Jacquet on December 4, Catsimatidis offered $2.5 million in cash plus $2 million on confirmation of a reorganization plan for the URC companies, to which Jacquet did not respond at the meeting. Subsequently Catsimatidis testified that they had not discussed the time of the agreement or closing, but stated that he understood that it was a "cash deal" with the "usual representations and warranties." Catsimatidis was then asked whether there was any discussion about what the usual representations and warranties would include. He responded "I am sure it is whatever the SEC requires." He followed this up with a letter to Jacquet "amending" his November 15 letter to reflect the terms offered that day. The November 15 letter had required "preparation of a mutually satisfactory form of agreement."

Later on December 4, Jacquet told Ris the offer was not acceptable, but that a $4 million offer would be more likely to get approval. The following morning, December 5, Ris told Catsimatidis that if he arrived with $4 million, it was his. Later that morning they met with Jacquet, who, according to Catsimatidis, said, "Look, John, the deal. You need $4 million all cash and you got a deal." Catsimatidis countered with an offer of $3 million cash and the balance over four months, which Jacquet did not accept, but asked for bank references. As the meeting ended,

Catsimatidis said he would try to come up with all cash "whether we do it three and one or four all cash." Catsimatidis then visited his bank and arranged for $4 million, and called his $4 million all cash offer to Ris, who relayed it to Jacquet. Catsimatidis then called Jacquet to confirm his offer, and Jacquet asked him to wire the funds, but Catsimatidis said at 4:00 p.m. it was too late to wire funds. Catsimatidis then instructed his attorney to prepare a written agreement. The attorney prepared a 19-page agreement, including twenty paragraphs of representations and warranties, some of which had not previously been discussed, which was delivered to Paribas that same evening.

On the morning of December 6 Catsimatidis was told that Jacquet had cleared the deal with the Paribas Suisse, and to be in Jacquet's office at 10:00 to complete the deal. They waited until 11:45, when a secretary explained they were having trouble with the Royal Bank, and that they should return to their offices to await a call. In the meantime, the creditors' committee in the bankruptcy reorganization had made a $4 million all cash offer. Jacquet testified that he had been waiting for the wire funds to arrive from Catsimatidis. Catsimatidis came prepared to write a personal check, but that he could have wired the funds within five minutes if requested. By the time the Royal Bank telephoned its approval of the Catsimatidis transaction, Jacquet told them Catsimatidis had not wired the funds as instructed, and that the creditors committee had made a better offer. Once he had received this offer, Jacquet telephoned Catsimatidis to tell him there was no deal.]

[O]n December 9, 1985, UAC instituted the instant action and moved for a temporary restraining order to prevent the delivery of URI shares to the Creditors Committee. In its complaint, UAC alleges that the "negotiations with Ris and other representatives of the defendants . . . culminated on December 5, 1985, in an agreement whereby the defendants agreed to sell and UAC agreed to buy all of the URI stock for $4,000,000 in cash" and that the defendants breached that oral agreement.

This court denied plaintiff's motion for a temporary restraining order and directed that prompt discovery take place. On December 13, 1985 the court held a trial on both the preliminary and permanent injunctions. At trial the court received in evidence the depositions of Catsimatidis, Jacquet, Aiello, Sherman, Ris and Dionisi, the affidavits of the parties, and documentary exhibits.

* * *

For the reasons that follow, this court holds that the plaintiff has failed to make a showing going to the merits necessary to sustain an order for either a preliminary or permanent injunction. The plaintiff has not successfully demonstrated that the parties intended to be contractually bound by anything other than the final written agreement. Moreover, even if, contrary to the clear weight of the evidence at the hearing, the conduct of the parties on December 5, 1985 had resulted in an oral agreement to sell the URI stock, that agreement is unenforceable under N.Y. U.C.C. Law 8–319 for lack of either a writing or an admission by a party against whom enforcement is sought.

A.   The Existence of a Contract

The Second Circuit has held that under New York law "there are still situations where the absence of a signed, formal agreement is fatal to an argument that a contract exists." Reprosystem, B.V. v. SCM Corp., 727 F.2d 257 (2d Cir.1984). The alternative New York rules on this subject were summarized in V'Soske v. Barwick, 404 F.2d 495 (2d Cir.1968), cert. denied, 394 U.S. 921, 89 S.Ct. 1197, 22 L.Ed.2d 454 (1969) and quoted in Reprosystem:

> First, if the parties intend not to be bound until they have executed a formal document embodying their agreement, they will not be bound until then; and second, the mere fact that the parties contemplate memorializing their agreement in a formal document does not prevent their informed agreement from taking effect prior to that event. These rules, placing emphasis on intention rather than form, are sensible and reasonable.

727 F.2d at 261. Thus, the intention of the parties is paramount and "when a party gives forthright, reasonable signals that it means to be bound only by a written agreement, courts should not frustrate that intent." R.G. Group, Inc. v. Horn & Hardart Co., 751 F.2d 69, 75 (1984) (finding that parties had intended to be bound only by written contract, notwithstanding statement by defendant franchisors' representative over telephone to would-be franchisee that the parties had reached a "handshake agreement.") In Reprosystem, B.V., *supra*, the intent of the parties to have a signed written contract controlled even where extensive negotiations had been completed, no problems remained and final drafts had been prepared.

In R.G. Group, *supra*, the Second Circuit outlined four factors that "courts have looked to in deciding whether the parties' words and deeds within a given bargaining context, show an intent to be bound only by a written agreement." 751 F.2d at 75. While no single factor is decisive, each provides significant guidance. The four factors are: (1) whether a party has explicitly stated "that it reserves the right to be bound only when a written agreement is signed." (2) "whether one party has partially performed, and that performance has been accepted by the party disclaiming the contract"; (3) "whether there is literally nothing left to negotiate or settle so that all that remained to be done was to sign what had already been fully agreed to"; and (4) "whether the agreement concerns those complex and substantial business matters where requirements that contracts be in writing are the norm rather than the exception." *Id*. at 75, 76.

In the present case, the evidence on each of these factors supports the defendant's position. To begin with, Catsimatidis' own actions following what he claims was a binding agreement on December 5, 1985 demonstrate that he did not intend to be bound by anything other than a written agreement. After learning from Ris that there was a "deal" at $4 million cash, he instructed his attorney on December 5 to prepare a written agreement which was drafted that evening. That evening, when he was informed about difficulties in the negotiations concerning representations and warranties running in his favor, he did not instruct his attorney to stop negotiating the additional terms since they already had a contract. Instead, Catsimatidis instructed his attorney to "straighten it out." Indeed he had continuously expressed a need for a written contract from the onset of the negotiations. In his letter dated November 15, 1985, confirming his offer of $2,500,000 for the URI stock, Catsimatidis states that the parties shall "direct their respective attorneys to commence preparation of a mutually satisfactory form of Agreement . . . " On December 4, 1985, Catsimatidis personally drafted, signed and sent another letter confirming his new offer and expressly incorporating the terms of the November 15, 1985 letter, except as amended, including the term requiring a written agreement. There is no language in the draft agreement prepared by Catsimatidis' attorneys to indicate that it was drafted pursuant to an oral agreement or that there was any intent other than that the writing be the definitive agreement. Indeed the draft expressly states that: "This Agreement has been duly executed and delivered by the Seller and each of the Banks and constitutes the legal, valid and binding obligation of each such party, enforceable in accordance with its terms."

There is no partial performance upon which plaintiff relies. Catsimatidis states that he was prepared to perform on Friday, December 6 and he did, in fact, offer a certified check to Paribas officials on Monday, December 9. These officials, however, never accepted the check. Only when a party accepts performance does it signal that the parties understand that a contract is in effect. R.G. Group, *supra*, 751 F.2d at 76.

The oral agreement on December 5 as to the price of the deal left much to negotiate. Plaintiff proposed a Stock Purchase Agreement with numerous representations and warranties that had not been the subject of any discussions during the previous negotiations between the parties. These provisions were not merely formalistic clauses in a written agreement; they involved substantial matters to be negotiated or settled.

Some of the representations and warranties that UAC insisted upon were: (1) that the audited financial statements of URI for fiscal years ended August 31, 1984 and the unaudited financial statements of URI for the fiscal year ended August 31, 1985 and for the month ended September 30, 1985 are complete and correct and have been prepared in accordance with generally accepted accounting principles consistently applied; (2) that since September 30, 1985 neither URI nor its subsidiaries had issued any securities, borrowed or incurred liabilities other than current liabilities, mortgaged any property, sold any trademarks, patents, trade secrets, etc., made any changes in employee compensation, suffered any casualty that was not fully covered by insurance; (3) that URI or its subsidiaries had good and valid title to each of the properties and assets reflected on the balance sheet as of September 30, 1985; (4) that URI has filed all federal and state tax returns required to be filed for all tax years prior to August 31, 1985; (5) that neither URI nor any subsidiary is a party to any agreement adversely affecting to any material extent the business, properties or assets, operations or conditions of URI or any such subsidiary; (6) that neither URI nor any subsidiary has any employment contracts in force or is obligated to participate in or contribute to any multi-employer retirement plan; (7) that URI is not a party to any contract or commitment involving more than $25,000 or having a term of more than one year except as set forth in a Disclosure Statement dated March 6, 1985; (8) that URI and its subsidiaries are in compliance with federal and state and local laws, ordinances and governmental regulations; and (9) that URI is in compliance with ERISA.

From these requested provisions, it is clear that UAC was concerned not only over whether URI had good title to the assets referred to on its balance sheets but also whether URI had incurred any substantial liabilities or encumbrances. UAC had good reason to include such warranty provisions. URI's latest financial statements were unaudited, it was involved in bankruptcy proceedings, and it had only recently been purchased by the defendants. The provisions, however, would thrust a potentially substantial liability upon the banks. Whether the risk of this liability was to be borne by UAC or the defendants was not only subject to negotiations after the December 5, 1985 agreement on the price term, but was actually being negotiated that evening by the attorneys. Further negotiations were held over the banks' insistence on an indemnification.

The fourth factor in R.G. Group, *supra* is whether the agreement concerns those complex and substantial business matters where requirements that contracts be in writing are the norm rather than the exception. The sale of all of the stock and transfer of control of a business normally requires a writing precisely because numerous representations and warranties usually have to be negotiated to allocate the risk of losses between the buyer and seller. Catsimatidis recognized this in his November 15 letter. The drafting of the Stock Purchase Agreement by Catsimatidis' attorney was consistent with this norm. Moreover, evidence of this practice is found from the fact that both parties acted in a manner fully consistent with a requirement of a writing up until the time that it was apparent that there would be no deal. As mentioned above, Catsimatidis insisted in his original offer of November 15, 1985 and again on December 4, 1985 that the parties should direct their respective attorneys to prepare a mutually satisfactory form of Agreement and, following the December 5, 1985 oral agreement as to the price of the stock, Catsimatidis instructed his attorney to draft a written agreement. Jacquet testified that one condition of the contract was that there be a written agreement. Consistent with Jacquet's testimony is the fact that before negotiations began with Catsimatidis, Jacquet has reached an oral agreement as to price with another potential buyer of URI stock, Guinan. When Guinan walked away from the deal prior to a writing, there was not a hint that Jacquet could have enforced the agreement. Finally, a further indication that writings are usual in stock purchases is that, as will be discussed *infra*, such transactions are governed by the Statute of Frauds, N.Y. U.C.C. 8–319, which as a general matter requires a writing for a sale of securities.

Plaintiff's argument that defendants' conditions of sale other than the price, namely, approval by the Royal Bank and wiring of the funds to Paribas were a "sham" and, in any event, were fulfilled by the Royal Bank's acceptance of the price term on December 6 and by Catsimatidis' willingness to tender payment coupled with defendants' failure to designate an account for wiring the funds begs the core question. That question is: did the parties intend to be bound by an oral agreement or by the execution of a written agreement? This court finds it was the latter.

This court finds the evidence to be clear, indeed overwhelming, that the "deal" reached orally on December 5 was only as to the price of the transaction for the sale of the company and that both parties fully expected there to be executed a written agreement embodying not only that term, but also the outcome of subsequent negotiations as to the representations and warranties sought by the buyer and the release and indemnification sought by the seller. Such an agreement was first contemplated in the plaintiff's letter of November 15, 1985, was manifested in the draft Stock Purchase Agreement that plaintiff requested his attorneys to prepare on December 5 after the price term had been agreed upon and was the subject of negotiations that evening. In sum, contrary to plaintiff's contention, the parties failed to form an oral contract on December 5, 1985.

Accordingly, this Court holds that plaintiff has failed to sustain its burden of showing either a likelihood of success on the merits or sufficiently serious questions going to the merits to make them fair ground for litigation.

* * *

Conclusion

Since the evidence clearly shows that the parties did not intend to be contractually bound until the execution of a written agreement to purchase URI stock and that there was no admission by a party against whom enforcement is sought, or its agent, of the existence of an oral contract such as would satisfy N.Y. U.C.C. § 8–319(d), the court holds that plaintiff, while making out a case for irreparable harm, has failed to establish the requisites going to the merits for the preliminary injunction requested. The preliminary and permanent injunction having been consolidated for trial pursuant to Rule 65 (a) (2), the court denies the motion for a preliminary injunction and enters judgment for the defendants on the permanent injunction.

So Ordered.

QUESTIONS

1.   What did Catsimatidas intend in his letter of Nov. 15 when he stated that UAC and the banks should immediately direct their respective attorneys to prepare an agreement which would contain "warranties and conditions which are customary in transactions of this kind"?

      What did Catsimatidas mean when he testified that "I am sure it is whatever the SEC requires"?

2.   If Catsimatidas had omitted reference to the usual and customary warranties and conditions in his Nov. 15 letter, and merely stated that the attorneys should prepare a "mutually satisfactory form of Agreement, which shall . . . provide for transfer to UAC of good title to the stock . . . " would the result have been different?

3.   Note that Dykhouse, Catsimatidas' attorney, prepared the form of acquisition agreement on December 5, containing twenty paragraphs of representations and warranties. Are these merely boilerplate or are they the starting point for negotiations? Which of these do you think the buyer is likely to consider negotiable? Given the banks' relatively recent acquisition of control of URI, would this affect their willingness to give any or all of these representations and warranties? In this regard, examine §§ 4.1(a) and 4.1(k) of the "Agreement and Plan of Merger" (hereinafter "Merger Agreement") in Appendix C.

      "(1) that the audited financial statements of URI for fiscal years ended August 31, 1984 and the unaudited financial statements of URI for the fiscal year ended August 31, 1985 and for the month ended September 30, 1985 are complete and correct and have been prepared in accordance with generally accepted accounting principles consistently applied;"

      See Merger Agreement, § 4.1(f).

      "(2) that since September 30, 1985 neither URI nor its subsidiaries had issued any securities, borrowed or incurred liabilities other than current liabilities, mortgaged any property, sold any trademarks, patents, trade secrets, etc., made any changes in employee compensation, suffered any casualty that was not fully covered by insurance;"

See Merger Agreement, § 4.1(c), (h)(ii)(C), and (j).

"(3) that URI or its subsidiaries had good and valid title to each of the properties and assets reflected on the balance sheet as of September 30, 1985;"

See Merger Agreement, § 4.1(m).

"(4) that URI has filed all federal and state tax returns required to be filed for all tax years prior to August 31, 1985;"

See Merger Agreement, § 4.1(o).

"(5) that neither URI nor any subsidiary is a party to any agreement adversely affecting to any material extent the business, properties or assets, operations or conditions of URI or any such subsidiary;"

See Merger Agreement, § 4.1(l).

"(6) that neither URI nor any subsidiary has any employment contracts in force or is obligated to participate in or contribute to any multi-employer retirement plan;"

See Merger Agreement, §§ 4.1(j)(iv).

"(7) that URI is not a party to any contract or commitment involving more than $25,000 or having a term of more than one year except as set forth in a Disclosure Statement dated March 6, 1985;"

See Merger Agreement, § 4.1(l).

"(8) that URI and its subsidiaries are in compliance with federal and state and local laws, ordinances and governmental regulations; and"

See Merger Agreement, § 4.1(e), (f), (j)(ii), (k).

"(9) that URI is in compliance with ERISA."

See Merger Agreement, § 4.1(j)(ii).

4. Did Catsimatidas expect his lawyer to produce lengthy representations and warranties and negotiate over them at length? Is there any disparity of views between lawyer and client over the need to negotiate an elaborate agreement?

5. If Catsimatidas was willing to deliver $4 million cash so quickly on the morning after his lawyer had delivered the purchase agreement to the banks' attorneys, what does this indicate about his view of the importance of the representations and warranties? Are they either unimportant, or the entire basis for a quick closing?

6. Was there any other way Dykhouse could have protected his client while producing a binding agreement? Would it have been enough to preface the document as representing a memorialization of an oral agreement previously reached?

NOTE

John A. Catsimatidis is a billionaire businessman and radio talk show host. He is the owner, president, chairman, and CEO of Gristedes Foods, the largest grocery chain in Manhattan, and the Red Apple Group, a real estate and aviation company with about $700 million to $800 million in holdings in New York, Florida, and the U.S. Virgin Islands. Catsimatidis also owns the Hellenic Times, a Greek-American newspaper based in Manhattan. He is also the chairman and CEO of the Red Apple Group subsidiary United Refining Company. He currently hosts a talk-radio show on WNYM. He ran for mayor of New York in 2013 in the Republican primary.

Turner Broadcasting System, Inc. v. McDavid
693 S.E.2d 873 (Ga. App. 2010).

[This dispute involved negotiations between Turner and McDavid for the sale of the Atlanta Hawks NBA team and the Atlanta Thrashers NHL team to McDavid.]

On April 30, 2003, the parties executed a "Letter of Intent," outlining the proposed sale terms and establishing a 45-day exclusive negotiating period. On June 14, 2003, the Letter of Intent expired with no agreement, but the parties continued to negotiate. When McDavid inquired about extending the Letter of Intent, Turner's principal negotiator told him, "Don't worry about it. We're very, very close to a deal. You're our guy."

* * *

On July 30, 2003, the parties engaged in a conference call. During the conference call, McDavid's advisors stated that McDavid would agree to Turner's proposed resolution of the [pending] tax issue on the condition that it would resolve all the issues and finalize the deal. Turner's CEO, Phil Kent, agreed and announced, "we have a deal."

The parties subsequently exchanged multiple drafts of the purchase agreement and its exhibits. During the legal drafting process, the parties' counsel identified additional "open issues" for the written agreements.

"On or about August 1, 2003, Turner drafted an internal memo to its employees and planned for a press conference to publicly announce the deal with McDavid. In August 2003, Turner consulted with McDavid and his advisor on team management decisions, including the hiring of a general manager and head coach for the Hawks. Turner also obtained McDavid's approval before hiring a trainer, assistants, and scouts.

On or about August 16, 2003, as the drafting process continued, Turner's executive and principal negotiator, James McCaffrey, approached McDavid about a simplified restructure for the transaction, assuring him that the restructure would "not change the deal," that the "deal was done," and that "they were ready to close on the deal that [they] made on July 30th." McDavid agreed to the simplified restructure, and the attorneys circulated revised draft agreements that reflected the restructured terms.

On August 19, 2003, the corporate board of directors of Time Warner, Turner's parent company, approved the sale of the assets to McDavid based upon the restructured terms. However, two of the board members, Ted Turner and Steve Case, opposed the deal, concerned that the assets had been undervalued and had resulted in a "fire sale."

On the day after the Turner board of directors meeting, Ted Turner's son-in-law, Rutherford Seydel, and the son of a member of the Hawks board of directors, Michael Gearon, Jr., approached Turner about purchasing the assets on behalf of their corporation, Atlanta Spirit, LLC. While Turner continued to exchange drafts of the purchase agreement with appellees, it also began negotiations with Atlanta Spirit.

On or about September 12, 2003, McDavid and Turner verbally reached a final agreement on each of the alleged open items for the written agreement and Turner's principal negotiator announced, "[t]he deal is done. Let's get documents we can sign and we'll meet in Atlanta for a press conference and a closing [early next week]." But later that same day, Turner's principal negotiator and its in-house counsel signed an agreement for the sale of the assets to Atlanta Spirit.

On September 15, 2003, as McDavid was preparing to travel to Atlanta for the closing and a press conference to announce the sale, he received a phone call informing him that Turner was "going in another direction" and had sold the assets to Atlanta Spirit. McDavid and his advisors, who had spent months finalizing the McDavid deal, were "stunned," "shocked," "disappointed," and felt "completely broadsided."

McDavid filed suit against Turner, alleging claims of breach of an oral contract to sell the assets, promissory estoppel, fraud, and breach of a confidentiality agreement. Turner denied the existence of any binding agreement, arguing that the parties had not executed a final written purchase agreement and had continued to negotiate the material terms of the transaction. Following an eight-week trial, the jury returned a verdict in favor of McDavid on the breach of oral contract claim and awarded $281 million in damages.

* * *

As an initial matter, Georgia law recognizes that oral contracts falling outside the purview of the Statute of Frauds[4] may be binding and enforceable.

> In determining whether there was a mutual assent, courts apply an objective theory of intent whereby one party's intention is deemed to be that meaning a reasonable man in the position of the other contracting party would ascribe to the first party's manifestations of assent, or that meaning which the other contracting party knew the first party ascribed to his manifestations of assent. Further, in cases such as this one, the circumstances surrounding the making of the contract, such as correspondence and discussions, are relevant in deciding if there was a mutual assent to an agreement. Where such extrinsic evidence exists and is disputed, the question of whether a party has assented to the contract is generally a matter for the jury.

(Citations and punctuation omitted.) McKenna, 286 Ga. App. [828] at 832 (1) [(2007)]. In this case, the determination of whether an oral contract existed, notwithstanding the parties' failure to sign a written agreement, was a question of fact for the jury to decide. See McKenna, 286 Ga. App. at 832–833 (1).

(a) *Parties' Intent to be Bound.*

(i) *The Parties' Expressions and Conduct.* The parties' objective manifestations of their mutual assent and intent to be bound to the McDavid acquisition deal included testimony that Turner's CEO formally announced, "we have a deal" during the parties' July 30th conference call. On or about August 16, 2003, Turner's principal negotiator, further confirmed the existence of an agreement during discussions pertaining to the deal restructure by stating that the "deal was done," and that "they were ready to close on the deal that [they] made on July 30th." And yet again, on or about September 12, 2003, during the course of another conference call to confirm the parties' final agreement on the terms to be incorporated into the written agreements, Turner's principle negotiator announced, "[t]he deal is done. Let's get documents we can sign and we'll meet in Atlanta for a press conference and a closing [early next week]."

In addition, Turner engaged in conduct from which the jury could conclude that an agreement had been reached. On or about August 1, 2003, Turner drafted an internal memo to its employees and planned for a press conference to publicly announce the deal with McDavid.[5] Furthermore, in August 2003, Turner consulted with McDavid and his advisor on team management decisions, including the hiring of a general manager and head coach for the Hawks. Turner also obtained McDavid's approval before hiring a trainer, assistants, and scouts.[6] There was

---

[4]   See OCGA § 13–5–30 (providing that agreements relating to certain subject matters must be in writing and signed by the party to be obligated). The parties do not contend that the oral agreement at issue was subject to the Statute of Frauds requirements.

testimony that according to industry standards, a buyer typically would not be given such formal input on team decisions until after the parties were committed and had formed an agreement. This evidence authorized the jury to conclude that both parties intended to be bound to the McDavid acquisition deal.

* * *

(iii) *Contemplation of Written Instrument.* It is undisputed that the parties intended to sign written documents that memorialized the terms of their oral agreement. McDavid and his advisors testified that in accordance with the customary deal-making process, the parties first had to reach an oral agreement upon the material terms, and then the lawyers were expected to prepare the written documents that memorialized the parties' agreed upon terms.[9] The evidence further established that the parties' respective lawyers exchanged multiple draft agreements purportedly attempting to ensure that the documents reflected the agreed upon terms.[10] And, while the draft agreements contained a merger clause providing that the written agreement would "supersede all prior agreements, understandings and negotiations, both written and *oral*," (emphasis supplied) such language could be construed as acknowledging the possibility of an oral agreement, particularly under these circumstances in which the merger clause did not become effective.

McDavid's witnesses further testified that all of the material issues for the written agreements had been resolved by mid-September, when they were planning to travel to Atlanta to formally sign the documents and publicly announce the deal. The evidence thus authorized a finding that the only reason for the failure to execute the written agreements was Turner's refusal to proceed with McDavid's deal and its decision to consummate a deal with Atlanta Spirit instead.

While circumstances indicating that the parties intended to prepare a subsequent writing is strong evidence that they did not intend to be bound by a preliminary agreement, contrary evidence bearing upon the parties' intent to be bound and reflecting the existence of a binding oral agreement presents a question of fact for the jury's determination. Moreover, "[a]lthough the parties contemplated the future execution of a written [ ] agreement, the jury was authorized to find that a binding oral

---

[9]   According to McDavid's counsel for the transaction, "[t]he principals had a deal. It was up to the lawyers to make sure that it was reflected accurately in the documents[.] . . . [W]hen there's a deal, there's a deal. . . . There's a point beyond which you don't have the right to say, . . . [']I'm walking, or, I have changed my mind.['] And we felt, without any doubt, that we were past that point."

[10]   Both parties expressed frustration with the manner in which the lawyers were handling the drafting process. In a June 13, 2003 email exchange with Turner's CEO regarding the television rights, Turner's principal negotiator had indicated, "[n]one of this is open. All details left, nothing that would impact economics by a penny. Perhaps too muc[h] lawyering on BOTH sides[.] . . . [S]eems like both camps of lawyers don't like each other, maybe causing them to be . . . overly aggressive[.]"

agreement was in effect, and the failure to sign the written instrument did not affect the validity of the oral agreement."

QUESTION

1. Would the parties have met the standards required in New York according to R.G. Group, Inc. v. Horn & Hardart, Co., 751 F.2d 69, discussed in United Acquisition Corp. v. Banque Paribas, *supra*?

DRAFTING A LETTER OF INTENT OR TERM SHEET

Precontractual Liability and Preliminary Agreements: Fair Dealing and Failed Negotiations

E. Allan Farnsworth.
87 Colum. L. Rev. 217, 288–89 (1987).

Letters of Intent in Mergers and Acquisitions.—During negotiations for a corporate acquisition or merger, the parties often sign a letter of intent. The letter, usually prepared by counsel to the purchaser, indicates the nature of the contemplated transaction and summarizes its basic terms, including terms of payment and the principal conditions to the closing. These may include, for example, approvals by government agencies and consents by third parties, raising of financing by the purchaser, and achievement of stated net earnings by the target. The letter will often recite that a "formal agreement" is contemplated or that the letter is "subject to" such an agreement, and it may go on to provide that it is "not legally binding" or that it creates "no rights or duties in favor of either party."

The use of letters of intent is by no means universal, for though it may be to the purchaser's advantage to tempt the target with a simplified version of the deal, the risk that other potential purchasers will appear on the scene may encourage the purchaser to accelerate the negotiations in the hope of reaching ultimate agreement sooner. But the greater the complexity of the transaction and the delay before its expected consummation, the more likely the use of a letter of intent.

Much time and effort over the past two decades has gone into litigating whether such letters are binding. Experienced practitioners recommend the inclusion of a provision clearly stating that the letter is non-binding, and such negations of liability have been held to be effective.[296] But the drafter must take care to avoid language that is inconsistent or less than clear. Thus a provision that a letter was "subject to agreement on a formal contract" did not prevent the letter from being binding where the letter spoke of "this offer" being "accepted" and where it "by its terms, formality and the extraordinary care in its execution, indicate[d] that the signatories intended to bind themselves to an enforceable contract"[297] and a provision that if the parties failed to make a final agreement "they shall be under no further obligation to one another" was held not to make a letter non-binding to the extent that they had undertaken to "make every reasonable effort to agree upon and have prepared" such a contract.[298] Furthermore, most of the letters of intent involved in litigation have been silent as to their binding character, and courts have split on whether the parties are bound by the terms in such letters,[299] confirming the recommendation that the parties be explicit if a non-binding agreement is wanted.

If the parties are bound by the terms of the letter, it is what is called in this Article an agreement with open terms. The parties are bound by the agreed terms and are under an implied obligation to negotiate open terms. But the agreement may be binding in a more limited sense. The letter may provide, or at least suggest, that the parties undertake to continue negotiating. Including such language in a binding agreement with open terms adds nothing, since absent such language a court will imply an obligation to negotiate the open terms. If the agreement with open terms is not binding, however, a question arises whether the language amounts to an enforceable agreement to negotiate. On this courts have also split.

New York law has added one more factor to those set forth in R.G. Group, Inc. v. Horn & Hardart Co., 751 F.2d 69 (2d Cir.1984). In Teachers Insurance & Annuity Association v. Tribune Co., 670 F.Supp. 491, 499 (S.D.N.Y.1987), the court added whether the intent to be bound was revealed by the language of the agreement. The court also stated that "[t]here is a strong presumption against finding binding obligation in

---

[296] Pepsico, Inc. v. W.R. Grace & Co., 307 F.Supp. 713, 715 (S.D.N.Y.1969) ("neither of us will be under any legal obligation . . . unless and until such an agreement is executed and delivered.")

[297] Field v. Golden Triangle Broadcasting, Inc., 451 Pa. 410, 416–17, 305 A.2d 689, 693 (1973), cert. denied, 414 U.S. 1158 (1974).

[298] Itek Corp. v. Chicago Aerial Indus., 248 A.2d 625, 627 (Del.1968); cf. American Cyanamid Co. v. Elizabeth Arden Sales Corp., 331 F.Supp. 597, 602 (S.D.N.Y.1971) (letter conditioned on approval by purchaser's board of directors and providing that "neither party shall have any obligation" if there was no approval might at least be an irrevocable offer).

[299] Cases holding such agreements are, or at least may be, binding include V'Soske v. Barwick, 404 F.2d 495 (2d Cir.1968), cert. denied 394 U.S. 921 (1969); Mid-Continent Tel. Corp. v. Home Tel. Co., 319 F.Supp. 1176 (N.D.Miss.1970); Pennzoil Co. v. Getty Oil Co., No. 7425 (Civ.) (Del. Ch. Feb. 6, 1984) (LEXIS, States library, Del. file); and Borg-Warner Corp. v. Anchor Coupling Co., 16 Ill.2d 234, 156 N.E.2d 513 (1958). A leading case to the contrary is Reprosystem, B.V. v. SCM Corp., 727 F.2d 257 (2d Cir.), cert. denied, 469 U.S. 828 (1984).

agreements which include open terms, call for future approvals and expressly anticipate future preparation and execution of contract documents." *Id.* This was approved in Arcadian Phosphates, Inc. v. Arcadian Corp., 884 F.2d 69, 72–73 (2d Cir.1989).

Letters of intent also frequently contain what Farnsworth characterizes as a stop-gap agreement, which governs some aspect of the relationship during negotiations. Thus, a letter of intent may also contain a confidentiality agreement, binding the prospective buyer to treat certain information obtained from the prospective seller as confidential, both during negotiations, and thereafter, should negotiations fail. Importantly, many such letters also contain a "stand-still" agreement, barring the prospective buyer from acquiring shares in the target for a specific period, and a "no-poach" provision, barring the prospect from hiring away target employees for a period.

Farnsworth stated that "[i]t is, to be sure, a simple matter for parties who do not wish to be bound by a preliminary agreement to say so, and courts have generally honored such provisions for 'gentlemen's agreement' Language like 'not binding until final agreement is executed' will suffice, and is sometimes used in letters of intent in connection with mergers and acquisitions. Farnsworth, Precontractual Liability and Preliminary Agreements: Fair Dealing and Failed Negotiations, 87 Colum. L. Rev. 217, 257 (1987). If this is so, why would parties fail to include such language if they do not intend to be bound? A possible answer from an experienced practitioner appears in Freund, ANATOMY OF A MERGER, 62 (1975). It represents a view widely held by sophisticated practitioners at the time:

"The agreement in principle usually contains a provision making the transaction subject to the execution of a definitive contract between the parties, containing terms, conditions, representations, and covenants appropriate to an acquisition of the type involved. This makes it clear that what has been signed is purely a letter of intent, with no legally binding effect. Some purchasers' lawyers insist on gilding the lily at this point, by the inclusion of language proclaiming that the document only expresses intention, has no binding effect, should not be construed as any sort of obligation on the part of the parties, and so forth. I find that most purchasers would just as soon not include all that excess verbiage. The feeling seems to be that the principals of the seller, who are usually less sophisticated in such matters, will somehow feel more bound without the caveats, even though they realize as an intellectual matter that the agreement in principle is not definitive."

Given the uncertainties about a letter of intent, when would a lawyer advise a client interested in buying a company to use one? One commentator described it as follows:

" . . . in most cases, a letter of intent is an invention of the devil and should be avoided at all costs. That is true from the point of view of the seller, as well as from the point of view of the buyer.

"One reason for this is the case law, which creates uncertainty because it is all over the place. The case law illustrates that in many cases the crucial factor is not what the letter of intent says, but what the parties demonstrate in their course of conduct."

Volk, *The Letter of Intent*, 16th ANN. INST. SEC. REG. 143, 145 (Friedman et al. eds, 1985).

Those who regard the letter of intent as useful argue that when negotiations are likely to be complex and lengthy, a letter of intent may refresh recollections of the parties, and may prevent one side from renegotiating terms previously accepted. The proponents also point out that most business executives take the moral obligation of a letter of intent quite seriously and are less likely to back out of a transaction during lengthy negotiations. Does a lawyer's advice that a letter of intent may not be binding undercut the moral foundations for this attitude? In Itek Corp. v. Chicago Aerial Industries, Inc., 248 A.2d 625, 629 (Del.1968), the Delaware Supreme Court found an obligation to negotiate in good faith arising from a letter of intent requiring the parties to "make every reasonable effort to agree upon and have prepared as quickly as possible" a definitive agreement.

In other cases, courts have held that letters of intent constituted binding contracts, notwithstanding language that they were "subject to execution of a definitive agreement." American Cyanamid Co. v. Elizabeth Arden Sales Corp., 331 F.Supp. 597 (S.D.N.Y.1971) and Mid-Continent Tel. Corp. v. Home Tel. Co., 319 F.Supp. 1176 (N.D.Miss.1970).

In many cases letters of intent continue to be treated as nonbinding statements of intention that only memorialize the basic terms on which agreement has already been reached. See, e.g., Dunhill Securities Corp. v. Microthermal Applications, Inc., 308 F.Supp. 195 (S.D.N.Y.1969).

Where parties had entered into a non-binding term sheet for a license agreement if their negotiations for a merger failed, Vice Chancellor Parsons held that the prospective licensor acted in bad faith in demanding dramatically higher license fees after the merger failed. PharmAthene, Inc. v. SIGA Techs., Inc., 2011 Del. Ch. LEXIS 136. After terminating merger negotiations because of the increased value of its lead drug and turning to the license agreement, SIGA took the position that the entire letter of intent was now nonbinding, a position rejected by the court. In a subsequent appeal, the court awarded PharmAthene expectation damages based on the expected future revenue stream from SIGA's lead drug, and this was affirmed by the Delaware Supreme Court. PharmAthene, Inc. v. SIGA Techs., Inc., 2015 Del. LEXIS 678.

California Natural, Inc. v. Nestle Holdings, Inc.

631 F.Supp. 465 (D.N.J.1986).

■ BROTMAN, DISTRICT JUDGE.

[California Natural, Inc. ("CNI") is a food processing firm that engaged in extended negotiations with Nestle Holdings, Inc. and Nestle Enterprises, Inc. ("Nestle" between August, 1983 and January, 1984 in which it was contemplated that Nestle was to acquire CNI. On January 25, 1984, Nestle informed CNI that it had decided against such action. CNI then filed this lawsuit alleging breach of contract, promissory estoppel, and fraud. This ruling is on the cross motions for summary judgment.

The complaint alleged that an oral agreement was reached on Oct. 19, 1983, with both parties agreeing there would be a written asset acquisition agreement and completion of an audit of CNI. CNI representatives claimed that the matters left to be decided were mere "formalities," while Nestle witnesses claimed there would be no definitive acquisition agreement until an asset purchase agreement was executed. Thereafter CNI negotiated to sell to Cummins Diesel Engines, Inc. up to November 21. More negotiations with Nestle also occurred, until a letter of intent was signed on November 29.]

The Letter of Intent itself is another major point of contention between the parties. CNI asserts that the Letter contains the "material terms of the acquisition agreement" which it argues was already concluded. By contrast, Nestle contends that this Letter of Intent may not be used as any evidence of a binding oral agreement. Defendants rely on [P] 11 of the Letter of Intent, which states that

> this letter constitutes only a Letter of Intent and a statement of our present intentions regarding the transactions set forth above, and neither constitutes nor should be construed as evidence of any form of offer or binding contract (emphasis added)

This section of the Letter also provides that the "consummation of the transactions" proposed in the Letter would be "expressly subject" to the execution of an asset purchase agreement and a number of other conditions including approval by Nestle's Board of Directors and an accounting review of CNI. Finally, Nestle argues, this Letter contains several examples of "material" items requiring future negotiation. Nestle asserts that the Letter represents strong evidence that the parties lacked any binding agreement by November 29, 1983.

After the parties signed the Letter of Intent, CNI's Board of Directors met [on December 8, 1983] to discuss the "ongoing negotiations to sell the [CNI] assets" to Nestle. At that meeting the Board "ratified, approved and affirmed" the Letter of Intent and "authorized and directed CNI's officers to" negotiate the sale of the assets of CNI to Nestle. *Id.* There is no mention of any CNI-Nestle oral agreement in the Board minutes.

During December, Nestle's lawyers drafted the asset purchase agreement called for in the Letter of Intent. They sent a draft to CNI on January 5, 1984. Plaintiff has complained about the amount of time that elapsed before it received this draft. Cullen wrote a letter in the interim to Carpenter expressing CNI's concern about this delay and his uncertainty over Nestle's "intentions." The parties debated the content of this agreement during January. According to Nestle, some issues concerning the agreement were never resolved. CNI asserts, however, that nothing on its part prevented the deal or the asset purchase agreement from being completed.

On January 25, 1984, Carpenter called Cullen to inform him that Nestle had decided not to go forward with the CNI acquisition. * * *

III. *Analysis*

A. *Breach of Contract Claim*

1. *Existence of Oral Agreement*

[The court concluded that contradictory affidavits precluded the entry of summary judgment for either party.]

2. *Application of the Statute of Frauds*

Assuming arguendo that the parties did enter into an oral agreement, the court must still make the legal determination of whether the statute of frauds restricts the enforceability of the agreement. The New Jersey statute of frauds provides in relevant part that

> a contract for the sale of personal property is not enforceable by way of action or defense beyond five thousand dollars in amount or value of remedy unless there is some writing which indicates that a contract for sale has been made between the parties at a defined or stated price, reasonably identifies the subject matter, and is signed by the party against whom enforcement is sought by his authorized agent.

N.J.S.A. 12A:1–206 (emphasis added). * * *

Based on an analysis of the memoranda submitted by CNI, the court holds as a matter of law that CNI has not satisfied the statute of frauds through a writing. CNI contends, however, that it has satisfied the statute of frauds due to the doctrine of promissory estoppel.[4]

---

[4] One exception to the signature requirement is when there is a transaction between merchants and the party seeking to enforce the contract must have sent a "writing in confirmation of the contract" to which there was no objection from the opposing party within 10 days of the party's receipt of the writing. N.J.S.A. 12A:2–201(2); Trilco Terminal v. Prebilt

3.   Satisfaction of Statute of Frauds
Through Promissory Estoppel

A party can avoid the application of the statute of frauds and enforce an otherwise unenforceable oral agreement through the doctrine of promissory estoppel. A prima facie case of promissory estoppel requires:

(1)   a clear and definite promise by the promisor;

(2)   the promise must be made with the expectation that the promisee will rely thereon;

(3)   the promisee must in fact reasonably rely on the promise; and

(4)   detriment of a definite and substantial nature must be incurred in reliance on the promise.

The Malaker Corp. v. First Jersey National Bank, 163 N.J. Super. 463, 479, 395 A.2d 222 (App.Div.1978).

This is another area in which Nestle has presented strong evidence to support its argument that CNI failed to create a genuine issue of material fact. For example, its evidence of a lengthy and complex negotiating process creates great doubt that it ever made a "clear and definite promise" to purchase CNI. The exchange of draft Letters of Intent also strongly supports the view that any reliance by CNI on a Nestle promise was not "reasonable." Despite such evidence, however, a factual issue remains on all elements of the promissory estoppel defense.

CNI has presented sufficient evidence to avoid summary judgment on the estoppel issue. First, its deposition testimony creates a factual issue as to whether there was a "clear and definite" promise made by Biggar to Cullen on October 19, 1983. This same testimony creates a factual issue on Nestle's alleged expectations of CNI's reasonable reliance on that promise. CNI claims that it relied on Nestle's promise by terminating or not pursuing discussions with other potential purchasers of CNI. Finally, CNI contends through deposition testimony that it lost "credibility" and "customers" due to Nestle's refusal to complete the acquisition agreement. This creates a factual issue of a real detriment to CNI stemming from its reliance.

In seeking summary judgment on the promissory estoppel issue, Nestle relies in large part on the decision in Chromalloy American Corp. v. Universal Housing Systems of America, Inc., 495 F.Supp. 544 (S.D.N.Y.1980), aff'd mem., 697 F.2d 289 (2d Cir.1982). In that case the district court held that as a result of "written disclaimers of contractual liability which were made, any reliance on the existence of an ... agreement [based on a prior oral promise] was unreasonable." 495

Corporation, *supra* 167 N.J. Super. at 451. There was no exchange of the Biggar memorandum in this case. [Biggar, President of Nestle, had dictated a memorandum that CNI claimed was evidence of an agreement, but it had apparently not been transcribed prior to the litigation, nor signed or delivered by Nestle to CNI.—Ed.]

F.Supp. at 551. Consequently, the court rejected the attempted use of the promissory estoppel doctrine by the party seeking to enforce the agreement. That case is distinguishable from the one at bar, however, because the court relied on "undisputed facts" indicating "conclusive evidence of an intent to be bound only by a formal writing." *Id.* at 550 (emphasis added). As noted several times, CNI and Nestle are in dispute about whether there was such intent in this case. Courts that have rejected the promissory estoppel defense have usually based that decision on full fact findings. See, e.g., Transport Management Co. v. American Radiator and Standard Sanitary Corp., 326 F.2d 62 (3d Cir.1963). Until all factual issues are resolved in the case at bar, the court cannot rule as a matter of law that CNI's reliance was unreasonable.

For all the above reasons, the court will deny the motions for summary judgment relating to the breach of contract claim. The existence of an oral agreement remains an open factual issue. As a result of the statute of frauds, however, this alleged agreement is unenforceable beyond $5000 unless plaintiff prevails in demonstrating all the elements of the doctrine of promissory estoppel. The court holds as a matter of law, however, that the statute of frauds applies and that CNI has not satisfied it through a sufficient writing.

* * *

III. *Conclusion*

Based on the submissions and arguments of the parties, the court has made the following decisions. First, the court will deny the cross-motions for summary judgment on plaintiff's breach of contract and promissory estoppel claims. Any oral agreement which may have been reached will not be enforceable beyond $5000 unless plaintiff proves the applicability of the doctrine of promissory estoppel. Second, the court will deny the cross-motions for summary judgment on plaintiff's fraudulent misrepresentation claim. Third, the court will deny the cross-motions for summary judgment on the punitive damages claim.

The court will enter an appropriate order.

QUESTIONS

1. How much clearer could Nestle have made the letter of intent to negate any inference of formation of a contract?

2. How does the plaintiff avoid the clear language of the letter of intent for purposes of summary judgment?

3. If the language in the letter of intent negating any evidence of any form of binding offer or contract and making it expressly subject to conditions about an asset purchase agreement and an audit of CNI preclude its use as proof of the existence of a binding contract for purposes of the statute

of frauds, why doesn't it permit a finding of summary judgment for Nestle on CNI's breach of contract claim?

4. Is Nestle's position better or worse because of the execution of the letter of intent?

5. What is the effect of the letter of intent on CNI's promissory estoppel argument?

6. Why does the Court not apply the Chromalloy decision to reject CNI's promissory estoppel claim?

B. THE EFFECT OF NO-SHOP CLAUSES

The impact of cases such as Transunion and Revlon is that boards feel an obligation to keep listening to new prospective buyers even after they have signed a definitive agreement. These cases taught that a board has a continuing duty to inform its shareholders if a better offer comes along after the board has approved a definitive agreement. Obviously, advising shareholders that a better deal is around the corner will assure a negative vote on the deal being presented to them. This means that a definitive agreement is little more than a "put option" for targets—they can sell at the agreed price if it suits them, or take the higher price a later bidder offers. We now examine how buyers can address the problems this doctrine creates for them.

ACE Limited v. Capital re Corporation

747 A.2d 95 (Del. Ch. 1999).

■ STRINE, VICE CHANCELLOR.

Plaintiff ACE Limited ("ACE") has filed a motion requesting a temporary restraining order against defendant Capital re Corporation ("Capital re"). ACE requests that I issue an order that restrains Capital re from taking any action to terminate the June 10, 1999 Agreement and Plan of Merger between and among ACE, Capital re, and Cap re Acquisition Corporation (the "Merger Agreement"). Capital re's board of directors wishes to terminate the Merger Agreement and accept an all cash, all shares bid that it believes is financially superior to the Merger Agreement. ACE contends that Capital re cannot, under the Merger Agreement's no-talk and termination provisions, validly terminate the Merger Agreement.

Because Capital re's argument that termination is permitted by the Merger Agreement is the more plausible one; because ACE's contrary construction, if correct, suggests that the Merger Agreement's no-talk provision is likely invalid; and because the risk of harm to Capital re stockholders outweighs the need to protect ACE from irreparable injury, I deny ACE's motion.

I.   Factual Background

A.   ACE and Capital re Enter Into A Merger Agreement

Capital re, a Delaware corporation, is a specialty reinsurance corporation in the business of municipal and non-municipal guaranty reinsurance, mortgage guaranty reinsurance, title reinsurance, and trade credit reinsurance. ACE is a Cayman Islands holding company that, through subsidiaries, engages in the insurance and reinsurance industries internationally.

According to ACE, Capital re was in a capital crunch earlier this year. Although Capital re does not admit that this was the reason, it says that for more than a year it has been exploring a possible business combination or capital infusion. During this exploration, Capital re engaged ACE in discussions about strategic options. As a result of those discussions, ACE provided Capital re with a cash infusion of $75 million in February 1999 in exchange for newly issued Capital re shares, which ultimately amounted to 12.3% of the company's outstanding common shares.

This infusion was apparently insufficient to calm the markets because in March of 1999 Moody's Investors Service, Inc. downgraded Capital re's financial rating from AAA to AA2. ACE contends that a further downgrading would have seriously affected Capital re's earnings and that Capital re therefore contacted ACE in May of 1999 to discuss solutions, including a possible business combination with ACE.

Negotiations following this contact bore fruit in the form of the binding Merger Agreement between ACE and Capital re, which was publicly announced on June 11, 1999. The terms of the Merger Agreement provide for Capital re stockholders to receive .6 of a share of ACE stock for each share of Capital re they hold. On June 10, 1999, the value of .6 of a share of ACE was over $17.00.

B.   The Merger Agreement's "No-Talk" And "Fiduciary Out" Provisions

At the time the Capital re board executed the Merger Agreement, it knew that ACE, which owns 12.3% of Capital re's stock, had stockholder voting agreements with stockholders holding another 33.5% of Capital re's shares. According to ACE, "representatives of Capital re significantly participated in the negotiation of, and in obtaining, the shareholder agreements" and Capital re encouraged the 33.5% holders to sign the agreements. These agreements obligated the 33.5% holders to support the merger if the Capital re board of directors did not terminate the Merger Agreement in accordance with its provisions. Put simply, ACE would control nearly 46% of the vote going into the merger vote and therefore needed very few of the remaining votes to prevail. Thus the Capital re board knew when it executed the Merger Agreement that unless it terminated the Merger Agreement, ACE would have, as a virtual certainty, the votes to consummate the merger even if a materially more valuable transaction became available.

Although ACE and Capital re both agree that the merger, if effectuated, will not result in a "change of control" of Capital re within the meaning of the Delaware Supreme Court's opinion in Paramount Communications. v. QVC, the merger is obviously a transaction of great significance for Capital re's stockholders and for ACE. The parties therefore bargained over the circumstances in which the Capital re board could consider another party's acquisition or merger proposal and/or terminate the Merger Agreement.

For its part, ACE says it wanted the "strongest, legally binding commitment from Capital re, consistent with the Capital re board's fiduciary duties." This was natural given the investment ACE had made in Capital re and the significant resources and organizational energy necessary to consummate the merger. Most of all, ACE viewed the merger as a unique strategic opportunity enabling it to expand into a specialized reinsurance market that is, in ACE's view, quite difficult to enter from scratch.

On the other hand, the Capital re board knew that the "fiduciary out" in the Merger Agreement was crucial if it was to protect its stockholders' rights. Because ACE had contracts in hand guaranteeing it success in a merger vote unless the Capital re terminated the Merger Agreement, the board's decision whether to terminate was determinative. Capital re suggests that the stockholder agreements with the 33.5% holders were tied to this termination provision purposely, so that if there was a proposal that the Capital re board deemed "superior," the 33.5% holders would also be free to consider it. Because the merger would be consummated even if circumstances had greatly changed and even if a much more valuable offer was available unless the board could validly terminate the agreement, Capital re claims that the board was careful to negotiate sufficient flexibility for itself to terminate the Merger Agreement if necessary to protect the Capital re stockholders.

The negotiations on this issue resulted in two important sections of the contract. The first, § 6.3 (the "no-talk"), generally operates to prohibit Capital re and "its officers, directors, agents, representatives, advisors or other intermediaries" from "soliciting, initiating, encouraging, . . . or taking any action knowingly to facilitate the submission of any inquiries, proposals, or offers . . . from any person." Of most importance on this motion, § 6.3 also restricts Capital re from participating in discussions or negotiations with or even providing information to a third party in connection with an "unsolicited bona fide Transaction Proposal," unless the following conditions are met:

- Capital re's board concludes "in good faith . . . based on the advice of its outside financial advisors, that such

Transaction Proposal is reasonably likely to be or to result in a Superior Proposal";

- Capital re's board concludes "in good faith . . . based on the written advice of its outside legal counsel, that participating in such negotiations or discussions or furnishing such information is required in order to prevent the Board of Directors of the Company from breaching its fiduciary duties to its stockholders under the [Delaware General Corporation Law]";

- The competing offeror enters into a confidentiality agreement no less favorable to Capital re than its confidentiality agreement with ACE, a copy of which must be provided to ACE; and

- The company's directors provide ACE with contemporaneous notice of their intent to negotiate or furnish information with the competing offeror.[7]

Section 6.3 is therefore the logical gateway through which the Capital re Board must pass in order to position themselves to terminate the Merger Agreement under § 8.3.[8] Section 8.3 of the Merger Agreement, in turn, enables the Capital re board to terminate the Merger Agreement only if, among other things:

- Capital re "is not in material breach of any of the terms of [the] Agreement";

- the Capital re board "authorizes [Capital re] . . . to enter into a binding written agreement concerning a transaction that constitutes a Superior Proposal and [Capital re] notifies [ACE] in writing that it intends to enter into such an agreement, attaching the most current version of such agreement to such notice";

- ACE "does not make, prior to five business days after receipt of [Capital re's] written notification . . . an offer that the [Capital re] Board . . . determines, in good faith after consultation with its financial advisors, is at least as favorable, as the Superior Proposal, taking into account the long term prospects and interests of [Capital re] and its stockholders";

- Capital re, prior to such termination, pays ACE a $25 million termination fee.[9]

---

7   Merger Agreement, § 6.3.

8   That a third party would consummate a superior proposal under § 8.3, without negotiations with or material information from Capital re strikes me as highly implausible.

9   Merger Agreement, §§ 8.3, 8.5.

C. ACE's Stock Takes A Beating

Since the merger was announced on June 11, 1999, ACE has seen the price of its stock fall significantly. As a result, the value of the consideration the marketplace deemed Capital re stockholders to be receiving in the merger dropped precipitously to less than $10 a share on October 6, 1999.[10]

It was under these less than auspicious economic circumstances that the merger headed for an October 7, 1996 vote.

D. XL Capital Limited Makes An Unsolicited Higher Bid And Capital re Decides To Terminate The Merger Agreement

On October 6, 1999—a day before the stockholder vote on the merger—Capital re's board of directors received an offer from XL Capital Ltd., a Bermuda-based insurer, to purchase 100% of the company's stock for $12.50 a share, Based on the price of ACE's stock that day, the market considered the merger significantly less valuable for Capital re stockholders than the XL Capital Offer.

In the face of this offer, the Capital re board immediately convened an emergency meeting. At that meeting, the board received written advice from their outside counsel, Michael J. Silver of Hogan & Hartson, that entering into discussions with XL Capital was "consistent with" their fiduciary duties. The written advice did not say that the board was "required to" discuss the XL Capital offer in order to fulfill their fiduciary duties. But Silver gave oral advice at the meeting that was stronger and that reflected the general tenor of advice he had earlier given in a lengthy May 1999 memorandum explaining to the board its fiduciary obligations in the context of entering the Merger Agreement with ACE. The minutes of the meeting state:

> Mr. Silver stated that the ACT transaction was originally viewed by the Board as a strategic merger not involving a sale of control; accordingly, the Board was not required to accept a cash offer even if its current value was nominally higher than the value of the ACE shares received in the merger. However, he noted that the Merger Agreement specifically contemplated consideration of certain competing offers and that it was appropriate, if the Board considered the XL offer to be reasonably likely to result in a Superior Proposal, for the Board to conclude that consideration of the XL offer is required in order to satisfy its fiduciary obligations to stockholders.

In an affidavit, Silver explains that his hastily prepared (given the exigencies) and more equivocal letter opinion reflected his judgment that whether the board was required to explore the XL Capital offer hinged on its business judgment that the XL Capital offer was likely to yield a higher and attainable value than the merger. Until this judgment was

---

[10] The Merger Agreement has an upper "collar" but no lower one.

made, he could not opine that such exploration was required. By his letter opinion, Silver claims, he was opining that if the board made such a judgment, then a decision by the board that discussions with XL Capital were required was an appropriate one under Delaware law.

After considering Silver's advice, the board determined that the value of the XL Capital Offer was so substantially superior to the merger that it was duty-bound to enter discussions with XL Capital. As a result of those discussions, XL Capital raised its bid to $13.00 on October 10, 1999. That same day, the Capital re board met and received presentations from its investment banker, Goldman Sachs, and its legal advisors. The Capital re board concluded that the XL Capital offer was more advantageous to Capital re than the merger. As a result, Capital re sent written notice to ACE that it considered the $13.00 offer a "superior proposal" within the meaning in the Merger Agreement and that it intended to terminate the Merger Agreement pursuant to § 8.3 unless ACE increased the merger consideration within five business days.

ACE claims that in the spirit of compromise and despite what it regarded as a clear breach of contract by Capital re, it offered on October 14 to increase the merger consideration so that Capital re stockholders would receive a combination of ACE stock and cash with a value at least equal to $13.00 a share and in some instances yielding a value somewhat higher. ACE apparently formalized that bid on October 18, 1999.

That same day, XL Capital increased its all cash, all shares bid to $14.00. This resulted in Capital re sending another termination notice to ACE, giving ACE five days to match XL Capital's offer. The deadline for ACE to match that offer expires today, October 25, 1999.

Rather than match the latest XL Capital offer, ACE filed this action on October 21, 1999 seeking to enjoin Capital re from terminating the Merger Agreement. Argument on this motion was held earlier today.

II. The Contentions Of The Parties

ACE argues that Capital re has violated the plain language of the Merger Agreement. Its major claim is that Capital re was forbidden to engage in discussions with XL Capital unless it received written legal advice from outside counsel opining that the board's fiduciary duties mandated such discussions. Because the board did not receive such advice, its decision to enter negotiations with XL Capital and to start a bidding war between ACE and XL Capital is, in ACE's view, a clear breach of contract.

ACE further contends that the only appropriate remedy for this breach is an injunction against termination of the Merger Agreement. Because its contracts with the 33.5% holders are binding only so long as the Capital re board does not terminate the Merger Agreement in accordance with § 8.3, ACE fears that it will never be able, as a practical matter, to bind the 33.5% holders to their contract, even if I later find that Capital re breached § 6.3 of the Merger Agreement and therefore had no right to terminate under § 8.3.

* * *

Capital re, of course, takes a quite different view. It argues that § 6.3 of the Merger Agreement leaves the determination of whether the board must enter discussions with another offeror to the board's own good faith judgment. Although the board is required to consider the written advice of outside counsel in that process, the board must ultimately make its own decision. According to Capital re, its board did just that because the economic disparity between the value of the merger and the XL Capital offer was so great that the board could not, in good conscience, fail to consider it. In so determining, the board was conscious that if it did not consider the XL Capital offer, it could never go on to consider whether to terminate the Merger Agreement in accordance with § 8.3. Without such a termination, the board knew that ACE would have the voting power to consummate the merger even if the merger was no longer in the best interests of Capital re's other stockholders. Moreover, Capital re asserts, the totality of the legal advice given to the board by Silver supported a good-faith determination that consideration of the XL Capital offer was required.

* * *

IV. Legal Analysis

A. ACE's Merits Showing Weighs Against Issuance Of The TRO

In analyzing the merits, it is useful to break down the analysis into two parts. First, I will discuss what is in my view the probable better interpretation of the contract. Second, I will discuss the implications of reading the contract the way ACE contends it should be read.

Although perhaps not so clear as to preclude another interpretation, § 6.3 of the Agreement is on its face better read as leaving the ultimate "good faith" judgment about whether the board's fiduciary duties requited it to enter discussions with XL Capital to the board itself. Though the board must "base" its judgment on the "written advice" of outside counsel, the language of the contract does not preclude the board from concluding, even if its outside counsel equivocates (as lawyers sometimes tend to do) that such negotiations are fiduciarily mandated.

Here, the Capital re board had good economic reason to believe that consummation of the merger in the face of the XL Capital offer was adverse to the interests of the Capital re stockholders. The board knew that if it did not explore the XL Capital offer, the Capital re stockholders—including the 33.5% holders—would be forced into the merger even though the merger's value had plummeted since June 10, 1999 and even though the XL Capital offer was more valuable. Given these circumstances, it seems likely that in the end a fact-finder will conclude that the board had a good faith basis for determining that it must talk with XL Capital and not simply let the Capital re stockholders ride the merger barrel over the financial falls. Furthermore, even if the contract is read as ACE wishes, Silver's written legal advice, when taken as a totality, coupled with his oral advice, and viewed in light of the necessarily hurried deliberative process undertaken by the Capital re board on October 6, 1999, might well be found to be a sufficient basis for a good faith decision by the board,

But ACE, of course, contends that it specifically bargained for the language requiring the Capital re board to "base" its judgment on the "written advice" of outside counsel so as to lock up the merger as tightly as legally permissible. At this stage, it would be presumptuous to contend that the contact is not susceptible of this reading. Moreover, although Silver's affidavit plausibly explains his rather equivocal October 6 written advice, the inference ACE advocates—that Silver did not have a sufficient good faith belief that the discussions with XL Capital were legally mandated to issue a written opinion to that effect—is one that might ultimately be proven correct.

Therefore, it is important that I consider that ACE's interpretation of the contracts and the facts may be the best one and determine whether the TRO should issue in that light. Looked at even in that way, however, ACE is not in any better position to obtain a TRO, for reasons I now explain.

In an article soon to be published in the Cardozo Law Review, Professor Paul Regan has carefully considered the contract, agency, and trust law principles that provide guidance to determine when a court might decline to enforce a contract between one party and another.[23] As Professor Regan points out, there are many circumstances in which the high priority our society places on the enforcement of contracts between private parties gives way to even more important concerns.

One of the circumstances in which this is so is when the trustee or agent of certain parties enters into a contract that contains provisions that exceed the trustee's or agent's authority. In such a circumstance, the law looks to a number of factors to determine whether the other party to the contract can enforce its contractual rights, including whether the other party had reason to know that the trustee or agent was making promises beyond her legal authority, whether the contract is executory or consummated, whether the trustee's or agent's ultra vires promise implicates public policy concerns of great importance, and the extent to which the other party has properly relied upon the contract.[24] Generally, where the other party had reason to know that the trustee or agent was on thin ice, where the trustee's or agent's breach has seriously negative consequences for her ward, and where the contract is as yet still

---

[23] Paul R. Regan, Great Expectations? A Contract Law Analysis For Preclusive Corporate LockUps, 21 Cardozo Law Rev.1 (Oct. 1999) (forthcoming).

[24] See generally. *Id.*

unperformed, the law will not enforce the contract but may award reliance damages to the other party if that party is sufficiently non-culpable for the trustee's or agent's breach.[25]

Indeed, Restatement (Second) of Contracts § 193 explicitly provides that a "promise by a fiduciary to violate his fiduciary duty or a promise that tends to induce such a violation is unenforceable on public policy grounds." The comments to that section indicate that "directors and other officials of a corporation act in a fiduciary capacity and are subject to the rule in this Section." It is therefore perhaps unsurprising that the Delaware law of mergers and acquisitions has given primacy to the interests of stockholders in being free to maximize the value from their ownership of their stock without improper compulsion from executory contracts entered into by boards—that is from contracts that essentially disable the board and the stockholders from doing anything other than accepting the contract even if another much more valuable opportunity comes along.

But our case law does not do much to articulate an explicit rationale for this emphasis on the rights of the target stockholders over the contract rights of the suitor. The Delaware Supreme Court's opinion in Paramount v. QVC comes closest in that respect. That case emphasizes that a suitor seeking to "lock up" a change-of-control transaction with another corporation is deemed to know the legal environment in which it is operating. Such a suitor cannot importune a target board into entering into a deal that effectively prevents the emergence of a more valuable transaction or that disables the target board from exercising its fiduciary responsibilities. If it does, it obtains nothing.

For example, in response to Viacom's argument that it had vested contract rights in the no-shop provision in the Viacom-Paramount Merger Agreement, the Supreme Court stated:

> The No-Shop Provision could not validly define or limit the fiduciary duties of the Paramount directors. To the extent that a contract, or a provision thereof, purports to require a board to act or not to act in such a fashion as to limit the exercise of fiduciary duties, it is invalid and unenforceable. Despite the arguments of Paramount and Viacom to the contrary, the Paramount directors could not contract away their fiduciary obligations. Since the No-Shop Provision was invalid, Viacom never had any vested contract rights in the provision.[28]

As to another invalid feature of the contract, the Court explained why this result was, in its view, an equitable one:

---

[25] *Id.*

[28] [Paramount Comms. v.] QVC [Network, Del. Supr.], 637 A.2d 34, 51 (1993) (citation omitted).

Viacom, a sophisticated party with experienced legal and financial advisors, knew of (and in fact demanded) the unreasonable features of the Stock Option Agreement. It cannot be now heard to argue that it obtain vested contract rights by negotiating and obtaining contractual provisions from a board acting in violation of its fiduciary duties. . . . Likewise, we reject Viacom's arguments and hold that its fate must rise or fall, and in this instance fall, with the determination that the actions of the Paramount Board were invalid.

In his article, Professor Regan persuasively articulates how QVC can be explained in view of the major factors traditionally applied in contract, agency, and trust law to determine whether to enforce a contract that contains provisions that are fiduciarily improper or that result from a fiduciary breach. He recommends that courts consider four factors when examining whether an acquiror's or merger partner's contract rights should give way to the need to protect the target company's stockholders from a fiduciary breach, Although Professor Regan concentrates on the application of this analysis in the specific context of a corporate change of control where so-called Revlon duties are implicated, the logical force of his analysis is appropriately brought to bear in this context, which although not so clearly as a change of control transaction an "ownership" rather than an "enterprise" issue, certainly implicates many of the same policy concerns.[30] As a literal matter, a stock-for-stock merger in which stockholders are required to exchange their existing property for another form of property would seem to be an "ownership" issue.

The factors Professor Regan identifies are: "(1) whether the acquiror knew, or should have known, of the target board's breach of fiduciary duty; (2) whether the . . . transaction remains pending or is already consummated at the time judicial intervention is sought, (3) whether the board's violation of fiduciary duty relates to policy concerns that are especially significant; and (4) whether the acquiror's reliance interest under the challenged agreement merits protection in the event the court were to declare the agreement unenforceable." The first three of these factors commend themselves to me as a sensible framework for weighing the equities in this context, and their application supports my conclusion that ACE is unlikely to prevail on the merits even if ACE is correct about what the Merger Agreement means.[32]

---

[30] *Id.* at 91–98 (discussing the difference between enterprise issues (e.g., what product to manufacture) and more fundamental ownership issues affecting stockholder property rights).

[32] Professor Regan's fourth factor does not bear one way or the other on whether the TRO should be granted. That factor only goes to whether ACE should, upon a final determination that Capital re breached § 6.3, at least receive reliance damages. Because ACE demanded § 6.3 and knew of its possible, if not likely, invalidity, this would cut against ACE's claim. In any event, the Merger Agreement already provides ACE with a $25 million payment in the event of termination. Thus the only question in the end will be whether the court should go further and award additional damages.

First, consideration of whether ACE should have known that § 6.3 was so restrictive that the Capital re board could not properly agree to it necessarily requires an examination of its actual operative effect. If § 6.3 of the Merger Agreement in fact required the Capital re board to eschew even discussing another offer unless it received an opinion of counsel stating that such discussions were required, and if ACE demanded such a provision, it is likely that § 6.3 will ultimately be found invalid. It is one thing for a board of directors to agree not to play footsie with other potential bidders or to stir up an auction. That type of restriction is perfectly understandable, if not necessary, if good faith business transactions are to be encouraged. It is quite another thing for a board of directors to contractually agree that it will not consider another offer in a context where its refusal to do so guarantees that the original transaction will be consummated, however more valuable than the original transaction and however less valuable the original transaction has become since the Merger Agreement was signed, unless a lawyer is willing to sign an opinion indicating that in the less than precise context of a Merger Agreement not implicating Revlon but potentially precluding other transactions in a manner that raises one's eyebrows in view of Unocal,[33] his client board is "required" to consider that offer.[34]

In one sense, such a provision seems innocuous. I mean, can't the board find someone willing to give the opinion? What is wrong with a contract that simply limits a board from discussing another offer unless the board's lawyers are prepared to opine that such discussions are required?

But in another sense, the provision is much more pernicious in that it involves an abdication by the board of its duty to determine what its own fiduciary obligations require at precisely that time in the life of the company in which the board's own judgment is most important.[35] In the typical case, one must remember, the target board is defending the original deal in the face of an arguably more valuable transaction. In that context, does it make sense for the board to be able to hide behind their lawyers?

---

[33] Unocal Corp. v. Mesa Petroleum Co., Del. Supr., 493 A.2d 946 (1985).

[34] It may well be a different matter for a board to agree to put a Merger Agreement to a vote if there are no other provisions tied to the agreement that operate to preclude the stockholders from freely voting down the merger and accepting another deal or opting for no deal at all. In this regard, see the recent amendment to 8 Del. C. § 251 enabling a board to agree to put a merger to a vote even where its recommendation about the merger has changed.

[35] Cf 8 Del. C. 141(a) (unless statute or corporation's certificate of incorporation provides otherwise, corporation's business and affairs must be managed by or under the direction of the board of directors); see also Jackson v. Turnbull, Del. Ch., C.A. No. 13042, 1994 WL 174668, at *5, Berger, V.C. (Feb. 8, 1994) (finding that board of directors impermissibly delegated to a third party their statutory responsibility to determine the appropriate consideration in a merger transaction), aff'd, Del. Supr., 653 A.2d 306 (1994); Field v. Carlisle Corp., Del. Ch., 31 Del. Ch. 227, 68 A.2d 817, 820 (1949) (board of directors may not delegate, except as may be explicitly authorized by statute, the duty to determine the value of the property acquired as consideration for the issuance of stock).

More fundamentally, one would think that there would be limited circumstances in which a board could prudently place itself in the position of not being able to entertain and consider a superior proposal to a transaction dependent on a stockholder vote.[36] The circumstances in this case would not seem to be of that nature, because the board's inability to consider another offer in effect precludes the stockholders (including the 33.5% holders) from accepting another offer. For the superior proposal "out" in §§ 6.3 and 8.3 of the Merger Agreement to mean anything, the board must be free to explore such a proposal in good faith. A ban on considering such a proposal, even one with an exception where legal counsel opines in writing that such consideration is "required," comes close to self-disablement by the board. Our case law takes a rather dim view of restrictions that tend to produce such a result.[37]

Indeed, ACE admits that it pushed Capital re to the outer limits of propriety, but it claims to have stopped short of pushing Capital re beyond that limit, But as I read ACE's view of what § 6.3 means in the context of this Merger Agreement, ACE comes close to saying that § 6.3 provides no "out" at all. According to ACE, it is now clear, per QVC, that a board need not obtain the highest value reasonably available unless it decides to engage in a change of control transaction. The ACE-Capital re merger is not a change of control. Therefore, this syllogism goes, there is no circumstance in which the Capital re board must consider another higher offer to fulfill its fiduciary duties. Thus Capital re could not get its outside counsel to issue such an opinion, and the board's contrary judgment of its duties could not have been in good faith. QVC, Q.E.D.

There at least two problems with such logic. As an initial matter, this interpretation renders § 6.3 meaningless, a result that as a matter of contract construction is disfavored and lends support to my conclusion that Capital re's construction is the better one.

As a matter of corporate law, QVC does not say that directors have no fiduciary duties when they are not in "Revlon-land." QVC simply defines when a board enters Revlon-land and is required to seek the highest available value. But QVC does not say that a board can, without exercising due care, enter into a non-change of control transaction affecting stockholder ownership rights and embed in that agreement provisions that guarantee that the transaction will occur and that

---

[36] One legitimate circumstance may be where a board has actively canvassed the market, negotiated with various bidders in a competitive environment, and believes that the necessity to close a transaction requires that the sales contest end. But where a board has not explored the marketplace with confidence and is negotiating a deal that requires stockholder approval and would result in a change in stockholder ownership interests, a board's decision to preclude itself—and therefore the stockholders—from entertaining other offers is less justifiable.

[37] See, e.g., *QVC*, 637 A.2d at 51; cf. Quickturn Graphics Design Systems v. Shapiro, Del. Supr., 721 A.2d 1281 at 1287 (1998) (poison pill that could not be redeemed by new board of directors was invalid because it improperly divested the board of their statutory authority and duty to manage the affairs of the corporation).

therefore absolutely preclude stockholders from receiving another offer that even the board deems more favorable to them. Put somewhat differently, QVC does not say that a board can, in all circumstances, continue to support a Merger Agreement not involving a change of control when: (1) the board negotiated a Merger Agreement that was tied to voting agreements ensuring consummation if the board does not terminate the agreement; (2) the board no longer believes that the merger is a good transaction for the stockholders; and (3) the board believes that another available transaction is more favorable to the stockholders. The fact that the board has no Revlon duties does not mean that it can contractually bind itself to sit idly by and allow an unfavorable and preclusive transaction to occur that its own actions have brought about. The logic of QVC itself casts doubt on the validity of such of contract.

In this necessarily hurried posture, it is impossible to examine in depth the appropriate doctrinal prism through which to evaluate the no-talk in the Merger Agreement. In the wake of QVC, parties have tended to embed provisions[42] in stock-for-stock mergers that are intentionally designed to prevent another bidder, through a tender offer or rival stock-for-stock bid, from preventing the consummation of a transaction.[43] When corporate boards assent to provisions in Merger Agreements that have the primary purpose of acting as a defensive barrier to other transactions not sought out by the board, some of the policy concerns that animate the Unocal standard of review might be implicated. In this case, for example, if § 6.3 is read as precluding board consideration of alternative offers—no matter how much more favorable—in this non-change of control context, the board's approval of the Merger Agreement is as formidable a barrier to another offer as a non-redeemable poison pill. Absent an escape clause, the Merger Agreement guarantees the success of the merger vote and precludes any other alternative, no matter how much more lucrative to the Capital re stockholders and no matter whether the Capital re board itself prefers the other alternative.[44] As a practical matter, it might therefore be possible to construct a plausible argument that a no-escape Merger Agreement that locks up the necessary votes constitutes an unreasonable preclusive and coercive defensive obstacle within the meaning of Unocal.[45]

But Unocal to one side, one can state with much more doctrinal certainty that the Capital re board was still required to exercise its

---

[42]   Such as no-shops, cross-stock options, and termination fees.

[43]   Corporate boards may also seek out a stock-for-stock transaction precisely for the purpose of fending off possible cash offers. That is, the entire transaction may have a defensive motive.

[44]   That is, it could be said that there is in the board's view no "threat" against which legitimate defensive barriers are needed.

[45]   Unocal Corp. v. Mesa Petroleum, 493 A.2d 946 (1985); Unitrin, Inc. v. American General Corp., Del. Supr., 651 A.2d 1361, 1387–88 (1995) (a defensive measure that is preclusive and coercive in relating to a threat is invalid).

bedrock duties of care and loyalty when it entered the Merger Agreement.[46] If the board mistakenly entered into a merger agreement believing erroneously that it had negotiated an effective out giving it the ability to consider more favorable offers, its mistake might well be found to be a breach of its duty of care. In this context where the board is making a critical decision affecting stockholder ownership and voting rights, it is especially important that it negotiate with care and retain sufficient flexibility to ensure that the stockholders are not unfairly coerced into accepting a less than optimal exchange for their shares. As Chancellor Chandler recently noted, "No-talk provisions . . . are troubling precisely because they prevent a board from meeting its duty to make an informed judgment with respect to even considering whether to negotiate with a third party."[47]

Examined under either doctrinal rubric, § 6.3 as construed by ACE is of quite dubious validity. As a sophisticated party who bargained for, nay demanded § 6.3 of the Merger Agreement, ACE was on notice of its possible invalidity. This factor therefore cuts against its claim that its contract rights should take precedence over the interests of the Capital re stockholders who could be harmed by enforcement of § 6.3.[48] For all these reasons, the first factor identified by Professor Regan as relevant to determining whether § 6.3 would be enforceable weighs heavily against ACE and undercuts the probability that it could enforce the provision against Capital re.

The second factor—timing—also weighs against ACE. The merger has not closed, the eggs have not been "scrambled," and the court would not be in the position of unscrambling them. Put another way, the transaction has not gotten to the point where ACE's investment and settled expectations in the deal are so substantial that it is unfair for ACE's contract rights to give way to the interests of Capital re's stockholders. In this sense, this factor operates not unlike the distinction Delaware law makes between the relief available to a stockholder plaintiff who proves that a transaction is tainted by breaches of fiduciary duty by the board.[49] If the stockholder makes his claim before the transaction is consummated, the court may enjoin the transaction.[50] If the plaintiff waits until the transaction is consummated to assert his

---

[46] Phelps Dodge Corp. v. Cyprus Amax Minerals Co., Del. Ch., C.A. No. 17398, tr. at 99–100, 1999 WL 1054255, Chandler, C. (Sept. 27, 1999) (ruling at preliminary injunction hearing that although target's board of directors had no duty to negotiate in a transaction not involving a change of control or sale of the company, "even the decision not to negotiate . . . must be an informed one" and that the board "should not have completely foreclosed the opportunity" to negotiate with a third party through a no-talk provision and that such foreclosure may constitute a breach of a board's duty of care).

[47] *Id.* at 99.

[48] QVC, 637 A.2d at 51; Great Expectations, 21 Cardozo L. Rev. at 76–81.

[49] Great Expectations, *21 Cardozo L. Rev, at 79–81* (pointing out this analogy and citing to Arnold v. Society for Savings Bancorp, Inc., Del. Supr., 678 A.2d 533 *(1996)* as well explaining the logic for this distinction).

[50] *Id.*

claim, the equities usually weigh against undoing the transaction, and the plaintiff is left to the remedy of damages (if available).[51]

The third factor—the importance of the public policy interest at stake—also cuts against enforcement of § 6.3, if read as ACE claims it should be. Delaware law invests a substantial amount of authority in corporate boards to manage the affairs of corporations. But this investment of authority is dependent on the corresponding responsibility of corporate boards to exercise this authority in a careful and loyal manner. These fiduciary responsibilities are of special importance in situations where a board is entering into a transaction as significant as a merger affecting stockholder ownership rights. For that (sometimes unspoken) reason, our law has subordinated the contract rights of third party suitors to stockholders' interests in not being improperly subjected to a fundamental corporate transaction as a result of a fiduciary breach by their board.[52]

For all these reasons, I conclude that ACE is unlikely to be able to convince a court on final hearing that Capital re breached a valid contractual provision by entering into discussions with XL Capital.

* * *

V. Conclusion

For all the foregoing reasons, ACE's motion for a TRO is denied. IT IS SO ORDERED.

QUESTIONS

1. Why didn't Capital re's attorney, Silver, advise the board that participating in discussions or negotiations with XL Capital was required in order to prevent the board from breaching its fiduciary duties to the shareholders? What advice did the attorney give? Why? Was he correct?

2. Could the Capital re board have complied with its fiduciary duties by ignoring the XL Capital bid and declining to negotiate with XL Capital?

3. Would the court have reached a different result if Ace hadn't obtained voting commitments from holders of 33.5% of Capital re's stock?

---

[51] *Id.*

[52] In this regard, one additional reason why the law might also give precedence to stockholders' interests over those of acquirors is that the acquiror has the (at least theoretical) opportunity—through a tender offer or election contest—to deal directly with the "principals"—i.e., the stockholders—rather than the "agents"—i.e., the board. If an acquiror wishes to reduce the risk that the agent will exceed its authority, it has options for direct dealing (subject to reasonable defensive measures by the target board). Where a sophisticated acquiror chooses to deal with the directors-agents only and to enter an agreement that arguably precludes the stockholders-principals from any meaningful choice in the matter, the would-be acquiror's expectation rights in its contract are less compelling than the need to protect the stockholder-principals from improper action by the directors-agents.

4. If ACE's interpretation of the merger agreement is correct, could there ever be circumstances that would mandate discussions with third parties in a "merger of equals"?

5. Why does the court discuss Paramount v. QVC in the context of a merger of equals?

6. Why does the court discuss Unocal in the context of a merger agreement?

7. What distinction does the court draw between "ownership" and "enterprise" issues? What does this mean for board duties in the context of a "merger of equals"?

8. Why is it "pernicious" for a board to rely on advice of counsel about the extent of its fiduciary duties?

9. Would a board be better able to enter into a "no-talk" provision if it had first conducted a canvas of the market? Had Time, Inc. done so before reaching agreement with Warner? How much discussion and negotiation occurred between Time and Paramount?

10. In a "merger of equals" not involving voting agreements by major shareholders, would you feel comfortable with the "no-talk" provision in this case? If not, what revisions would you feel required to make?

In re IXC Communications, Inc. Shareholders Litigation

1999 WL 1009174 (Del. Ch. 1999).

■ STEELE, V.C.

One of the plaintiff shareholders of IXC Communications, Inc., in these two consolidated actions seeks to preliminarily enjoin: (1) the October 29, 1999 vote of the IXC shareholders on a proposed merger with Cincinnati Bell, Inc. ("CBI"); and, (2) the enforcement of certain terms of the Merger Agreement.

Should the Court of Chancery intervene and enjoin a shareholder vote on a merger agreement submitted for their approval when that vote will be part of a democratic governance process: (1) in which shareholders are adequately informed; and, (2) in which shareholders will be free to exercise their judgment based upon their individual assessment of their own economic interests? No.

Where the plaintiffs fail to show that the IXC shareholders are either inadequately informed or are misinformed about either the terms of the merger or the process by which it came about and the vote will be a valid and independent exercise of the shareholders' franchise, without any specific preordained result which precludes them from rationally determining the fate of the proposed merger the Court of Chancery has no basis to intervene to frustrate the exercise of the shareholder franchise in law or equity. Plaintiffs do not present clear factual support for their contentions that the IXC directors' breached their fiduciary duties and thereby tainted the merger process. Plaintiffs, therefore, are not likely to succeed on the merits at trial. Therefore, I can not grant the extraordinary measure of injunctive relief. Plaintiffs' request for a preliminary injunction is denied.

Background

IXC is a telecommunications company which owns fiber-optic digital communications networks. In the latter half of 1998 IXC's earnings growth failed to meet expectations, causing an erosion in the company's stock price and concern within the IXC board about the company's management. The IXC board focused its efforts on reevaluating IXC's business strategy and began considering the potential for strategic alternatives. On February 5, 1999 IXC publicly announced that it had retained Morgan Stanley Dean Witter in order to consider possible merger or sale options. This announcement was to send a message to the "universe" of players in the telecommunications market that IXC was interested in potential partners or acquirors, as the case might be, and to notify the financial world that IXC was serious about making dramatic changes to improve its financial condition. However, IXC made it clear it did not want Morgan Stanley making "outbound" solicitations which would make it appear that the company must be sold. Recognizing that the February 5 announcement came on the heels of negative financial reportings, IXC wanted to send a message that parties with enough interest could approach them for possible strategic partnering, but IXC did not want to appear to be desperate to sell.

In the ensuing months, IXC had various contacts with interested parties, some expressing interest enough to actually negotiate terms with IXC and leading IXC to perform due diligence review. The list of companies with whom IXC communicated in some capacity about a joint transaction reads like a who's who of telecommunications players: AT&T, MCI WorldCom, Teleglobe, Bell Atlantic, Cable & Wireless, Bell South, IDT, RSL, GTS, and Qwest.

IXC negotiated with PSINET, the first serious suitor, during February and March, 1999. These negotiations reached a level of mutual due diligence review and a skeletal merger agreement. However, the parties never finalized the transaction and while it is not totally clear, PSINET apparently lost interest in merging with IXC. Like many of the facts in this case, the details surrounding the end of a PSINET-IXC deal are in dispute. Whatever the case, IXC decided not to pursue PSINET but continued to field inquiries from other companies.

Through the spring of 1999 inquiries from other companies also produced varying degrees of engagement between IXC and potential "partners." Some led to presentations to the IXC board and more rounds of discussions about a potential strategic transaction. . . .

* * *

In late May, Oak Hill Partners and CBI met with IXC's largest shareholder General Electric Pension Trust ("GEPT") [which owned 26.5% of IXC's outstanding common stock] to discuss the possibility of a merger between CBI and IXC. IXC director Richard Irwin took part, negotiating material terms with CBI, keeping the board abreast of the details. The parties entered into standstill and confidentiality agreements shortly thereafter. Through June and into early July, IXC and CBI performed mutual due diligence. In mid-July the parties began to fix the terms of a merger. From July 18–20 all of the relevant parties met to hammer out the final Merger Agreement, which they approved on July 20. The relevant terms of the Agreement are:

1.   The shareholders of IXC receive 2.0976 shares of CBI for every IXC share, with CBI as the surviving entity.

2.   A mutual "no-solicitation" (or "no-talk") provision preventing the parties from entertaining other potential deals. The provision also contained a fiduciary out, permitting the board of IXC to ultimately oppose the merger, should it see fit. This provision was later amended, to permit either side to consider "superior proposals."

3.   A $105 million termination fee and a cross-option agreement (which would be triggered with the termination fee) permitting CBI to purchase 19.9% of IXC's shares of common stock for $52.25 per share, with a profit cap of $26.25 million.

4.   CBI and GEPT made a side deal through which GEPT agreed to support the merger on condition that CBI purchase one-half of its IXC holdings for $50 per share. This deal consisted of two agreements: the GEPT Stock Purchase Agreement and the GEPT Stockholder Agreement. The Stock Purchase Agreement effectuated the CBI purchase of 50% of GEPT's IXC shares and the Stockholder Agreement bound GEPT to support the merger. Apparently GEPT conditioned its support for the Stockholder Agreement on CBI's agreeing to the Stock Purchase Agreement. CBI conditioned its support for the Merger Agreement on GEPT's signing the Stockholder Agreement. The entire Merger Agreement rested upon this side transaction.

* * *

Discussion
* * *

Reasonable Likelihood of Success on the Merits

1.   Fiduciary Duty Claims

Under Delaware law a breach of fiduciary duty analysis in the context of a merger begins with the rebuttable presumption that a company's board of directors has acted with care, loyalty, and in "good faith." Unless this presumption is sufficiently rebutted, by showing either (1) the board did not fulfill its duties by acting to inform itself fully; or, (2) the board's actions were driven by some interest other than those of the shareholders, then this Court must defer to the discretion of the board and acknowledge that the board's decisions are entitled to the benefit of the business judgment rule. If either failure to act with care or misplaced loyalty are shown, then heightened judicial scrutiny attaches and the burden shifts to the board to show that its actions were entirely fair to the shareholders.

* * *

After having evaluated the facts and arguments offered by both sides and the merit of the claims underlying the motion here I do not find that the plaintiffs have met the standard required for such extraordinary relief. The plaintiffs have not demonstrated sufficiently that the actions of the IXC board in seeking out a strategic partner or in fashioning the CBI merger were either uninformed or disloyal such that heightened scrutiny applies. Therefore, I feel obligated to defer to the board's substantive business judgment and allow the shareholders to pass ultimate judgment on their actions at the October 29 vote.

A. Duty of Care—Failure of the Board to Inform Itself Adequately

I find, based upon the record before me, that the plaintiffs fail to demonstrate that IXC board inadequately informed itself about and inadequately evaluated numerous potential suitors over the course of its search for a strategic partner.

* * *

The plaintiffs contend that the now defunct no-talk provisions in the Merger Agreement, highlight a pattern of "willful blindness." The no-talk provisions emerged late in the process. IXC and CBI later retracted the provision, permitting the Board to hear any proposals it sees fit and continued the Board's receptivity to a fiduciary out concept without shopping the company under perceived adverse circumstances. No superior offers were received and therefore none were turned away. Further, the assertion that the board "willfully blinded" itself by approving the now defunct "no-talk" provision in the Merger Agreement is unpersuasive, particularly considering how late in the process this provision came. Provisions such as these are common in merger agreements and do not imply some automatic breach of fiduciary duty. Even so, IXC and CBI since retracted the provision, permitting the Board to hear any proposals it sees fit.

I am comfortable concluding that the IXC board met its duty of care by informing itself over the nearly six months lasting from the February 5 public announcement to the late July approval of the IXC-CBI merger, where the record reflects no incoming interest from May 1999 and a fiduciary out provision in the merger agreement which would have allowed the board to entertain any proposal superior to CBI's.

* * *

The request for a preliminary injunction is denied.

QUESTIONS

1. How did the no-talk provision in this case differ from that in the preceding cases?

2. If a board can only escape the no-talk provision to consider a "superior proposal," does this give it the ability to furnish information to a potential bidder before it has made a "superior proposal"? If not, how meaningful is this escape clause likely to be?

3. If a "superior proposal" is made to a board subject to a strict "no talk" agreement, what are the board's duties toward its shareholders before a merger vote?

4. Are there factual distinctions between this case and the preceding "no-talk" opinions that cause Vice Chancellor Steele to reach a different result?

NOTE

"M&A lawyers spent the first part of the year [2000] trying to reconcile the somewhat inconsistent Delaware cases of late last year, Phelps Dodge/Cyprus Amax, ACE/Cap re and In re ICX Communications. These decisions dealt with the question of how completely one can protect a friendly deal against competing bids through the use of 'no shop' and 'no talk' provisions.

"At least two trends in the use of these deal protection devices have developed in reaction to these cases. Both have made it a bit easier for hostile bidders to break up an existing stock-for-stock deal. The first trend is that M&A practitioners have significantly cut back on the use of 'no talk' provisions that bar a target company in a pending deal from having discussions with a competing bidder. Second, M&A lawyers are requiring that targets retain greater flexibility under the merger agreement to opt for a superior competing bid, even where the original deal is a stock merger that does not trigger 'Revlon duties.' This flexibility is being provided either by requiring a meaningful 'fiduciary out,' so that the target can terminate the original deal in favor of the competing bid, or by assuring that the target's shareholders have the ability to vote down the original deal if a better one comes along. The latter requires that the first bidder not be allowed to 'lock up' too many target shares so as to prevent a meaningful vote."

Paul T. Schnell, M&A Highlights for the First Six Months of 2000—Sartorial and Otherwise, 4 No. 3, THE M&A LAWYER 2, 3 (June 2000).

NOTE

Here is the no-shop provision governing BellSouth in its merger agreement with AT&T Corporation in the Spring of 2006. The reader may wish to compare it with the parallel provision of Section 5.2 of Appendix C.

6.2 *Acquisition Proposals*

(a) *No Solicitation or Negotiation*. The Company agrees that neither it nor any of its Subsidiaries nor any of its or its Subsidiaries' officers and directors shall, and that it shall use its reasonable best efforts to instruct and cause its and its Subsidiaries' directors, officers, employees, investment bankers, attorneys, accountants and other advisors or representatives (such directors, officers, employees, investment bankers, attorneys, accountants and other advisors or representatives, collectively, "Representatives") not to, directly or indirectly:

(i) initiate, solicit, or knowingly facilitate or encourage, any inquiries or the making of any proposal or offer that constitutes or could reasonably be likely to lead to an Acquisition Proposal (as defined below); or

(ii) engage in, continue or otherwise participate in any discussions or negotiations regarding, or provide any non-public information or data to any Person who has made, or proposes to make, or otherwise knowingly facilitate, or encourage an Acquisition Proposal.

Notwithstanding anything in this Agreement to the contrary, prior to the time, but not after, this Agreement is approved by the Company's shareholders pursuant to the Company Requisite Vote, the Company may (A) provide information in response to a request therefor by a Person who has made a bona fide written Acquisition Proposal that was not initiated, solicited, facilitated or encouraged, in violation of this Section 6.2 or by the Company's Representatives, prior to the time such Acquisition Proposal was first made after the date hereof, if the Company receives from the Person so requesting such information an executed confidentiality agreement on terms substantially similar to those contained in the Non-Disclosure Agreement, dated as of February 16, 2006, (the "Confidentiality Agreement"), by and between Parent and the Company together with a customary standstill agreement on terms no more favorable to such Person than the standstill applicable to Parent except that the term of such standstill agreement may be shorter than the time of the standstill applicable to Parent (but not less than 9 months) and other provisions of the standstill may be more favorable to such Person (to the extent customary) in which case the term and other provisions of the standstill applicable to Parent shall, for so long as this Agreement is in effect, automatically be reduced to be as favorable to Parent as such other standstill agreement is to such Person or made more favorable to Parent; or (B) engage in discussions or negotiations with any Person who has made a bona fide written Acquisition Proposal that was not initiated, solicited, facilitated or encouraged, in violation of this Section 6.2 or by the Company's representatives, prior to the time such Acquisition Proposal was first made after the date hereof, if, in each case referred to in clause (A) or (B) above, the Board of Directors of the Company determines in good faith (after consultation with its financial advisers and legal counsel) that such action is necessary in order for the directors of the Company to comply with their fiduciary duties under applicable Law; and in the case referred to in clause (B) above, if the Board of Directors of the Company, has determined in good faith based on all the information then available and after consultation with its financial advisers and legal counsel that such Acquisition Proposal either constitutes a Superior Proposal or is reasonably likely to result in a Superior Proposal.

(b) *Definitions*. For purposes of this Agreement:

"*Acquisition Proposal*" means (i) any proposal or offer with respect to a merger, joint venture, partnership, consolidation, dissolution, liquidation, tender offer, recapitalization, reorganization, share exchange, business combination, acquisition, distribution or similar transaction outside the ordinary course of business involving the Company or any direct or indirect interest in Cingular or any of the Company's Significant Subsidiaries; provided that in no event shall any transaction involving the Company or any of the Company's Significant Subsidiaries that is expressly permitted by Sections 6.1(a)(ix) or (xiii) and which proposal could not reasonably be expected to result in a Superior Proposal be deemed to constitute an "Acquisition Proposal", or (ii) any proposal or offer to acquire in any manner, directly or indirectly, 15% or more of the Company Shares or 15% or more of the consolidated assets (including, without limitation, equity interests in Subsidiaries of the Company); provided that in no event shall a proposal or offer made by or on behalf of Parent or any of its Subsidiaries, be deemed to constitute an "Acquisition Proposal."

"*Superior Proposal*" means a bona fide Acquisition Proposal involving assets of the Company or its Subsidiaries representing at least 50% of the fair market value of the consolidated assets of the Company (including its interest in Cingular and YP.com) or at least 50% of the outstanding Company Shares and otherwise for the purpose of this definition substituting 50% for each reference to 15% in the definition of "Acquisition Proposal", that was not initiated, solicited, facilitated or encouraged, in violation of this Section 6.2 or by the Company's Representatives prior to the time such Acquisition Proposal was first made after the date hereof, that the Board of Directors of the Company determines in good faith (after consultation with its financial advisers and legal counsel) is reasonably likely to be consummated in accordance with its terms, taking into account all legal, financial and regulatory aspects of the proposal and the Person making the proposal, and if consummated, would result in a transaction more favorable to the Company's shareholders from a financial point of view than the transaction contemplated by this Agreement (after taking into account any revisions to the terms of the transaction contemplated by this Agreement agreed to by Parent pursuant to Section 6.2(c)).

(c) *Company Recommendation*. (i) The Board of Directors of the Company, and each committee thereof, shall not:

(x)   except as expressly permitted by this Section 6.2, withhold or withdraw, or qualify or modify in a manner reasonably likely to be understood to be adverse to Parent (or publicly resolve to withhold or withdraw or so publicly qualify or modify), the Company Recommendation or approve or recommend to the Company's shareholders any Acquisition Proposal; or

(y)   cause or permit the Company to enter into any letter of intent, memorandum of understanding, agreement in principle, acquisition agreement, merger agreement or other agreement (other than a confidentiality agreement referred to in Section 6.2(a) entered into in the circumstances referred to in Section 6.2(a)) for any Acquisition Proposal.

(ii)   Notwithstanding anything to the contrary set forth in this Agreement, prior to the time, but not after, this Agreement is approved by the Company's shareholders by the Company Requisite Vote, the Company's Board of Directors shall be permitted (A) to withhold or withdraw, or qualify or modify in a manner reasonably likely to be understood to be adverse to Parent, the Company Recommendation (a "Company Recommendation Change") if but only if (i) the Company has received a Superior Proposal, (ii) the Board of Directors of the Company determines in good faith (after consultation with its financial advisers and outside legal counsel), that, as a result of such Superior Proposal, a Company Recommendation Change is necessary in order for the directors of the Company to comply with their fiduciary duties under applicable Law, (iii) three business days have elapsed following delivery by the Company to Parent of written notice advising Parent that the Board of Directors of the Company intends to so make a Company Recommendation Change, specifying the material terms and conditions of the Superior Proposal and identifying the Person making the Superior Proposal, (iv) the Company has given Parent the opportunity to propose to the Company revisions to the terms of the transactions contemplated by this Agreement (notwithstanding section 12.10 of the Limited Liability Company Agreement of Cingular, dated as of October 2, 2000, as amended), and the Company and its Representatives shall have, if requested by Parent, negotiated in good faith with Parent and its Representatives regarding any revisions to the terms of the transactions contemplated by this Agreement proposed by Parent and the Board of Directors of the Company shall continue to believe in good faith, as a result of such Acquisition Proposal, that a Company Recommendation Change is necessary in order for the directors of the Company to comply with their fiduciary duties under applicable Law and in light of any revisions to the terms of the transaction contemplated by this Agreement to which Parent shall have agreed and (v) the Company shall have complied with its obligations set forth in Section 6.2 of this Agreement in all material respects or (B) to approve, or recommend to the shareholders of the Company, any Superior Proposal made after the date of this Agreement (any such action, a "Company Superior Proposal Action") if the Board of Directors of the Company determines in good faith (after consultation with its financial advisers and legal counsel) that such action is necessary in order for the directors of the Company to comply with their fiduciary duties under applicable Law, provided that the Company's Board of Directors may not take a Company Superior Proposal Action unless all of the conditions in clause (A) above have been satisfied (substituting the term "Company Superior Proposal Action" for the term "Company Recommendation Change" in clauses (A)(ii) and (iii)) and the Acquisition Proposal continues to be a Superior Proposal in light of any revisions to the terms of the transaction contemplated by this Agreement to which Parent shall have agreed.

(d) *Parent Recommendation*. The Board of Directors of Parent, and each committee thereof, shall not, except as expressly permitted by this Section 6.2, withhold or withdraw, or qualify or modify in a manner reasonably likely to be understood to be adverse to the Company (or publicly resolve to withhold or withdraw or so publicly qualify or modify), the Parent Recommendation or approve or recommend to the Parent's stockholders any Acquisition Proposal. Notwithstanding anything to the contrary set forth in this Agreement, prior to the time, but not after, the issuance of Parent Common Stock required to be issued in the Merger is approved by Parent's stockholders by the Parent Requisite Vote, Parent's Board of Directors shall be permitted (A) to withhold or withdraw, or qualify or modify in a manner reasonably likely to be understood to be adverse to the Company, the Parent Recommendation (a "*Parent Recommendation Change*") if and only if (i) Parent has received a Superior Proposal, (ii) the Board of Directors of Parent determines in good faith, after receiving the advice of its financial advisers and of outside legal counsel, that, as a result of such Superior Proposal, a Parent Recommendation Change is necessary in order for the directors of Parent to comply with their fiduciary duties under applicable Law, (iii) three business days have elapsed following delivery by Parent to the Company of written notice advising the Company that the Board of Directors of Parent has resolved to so make a Parent Recommendation Change, specifying the material terms and conditions of the Superior Proposal and identifying the Person making the Superior Proposal, (iv) Parent has given the Company the opportunity to propose to Parent revisions to the terms of the transactions contemplated by this Agreement, and Parent and its Representatives shall have, if requested by the Company, negotiated in good faith with the Company and its Representatives regarding any revisions to the terms of the transactions contemplated by this Agreement proposed by the Company, and the Board of Directors of Parent shall continue to believe in good faith, as a result of such Acquisition Proposal, that a Parent Recommendation Change is necessary in order for the directors of Parent to comply with their fiduciary duties under applicable Law in light of any revisions to the terms of the transaction contemplated by this Agreement to which the Company shall have agreed or (B) to approve, or recommend to the shareholders of Parent, any Superior Proposal made after the date of this Agreement (any such action, a "*Parent Superior Proposal Action*") if the Board of Directors of Parent determines in good faith (after consultation with its financial advisers and legal counsel) that such action is necessary in order for the directors of Parent to comply with their fiduciary duties under applicable Law, *provided* that Parent's Board of Directors may not take a Parent Superior Proposal Action unless all of the conditions in clause (A) above have been satisfied (substituting the term "Parent Superior Proposal Action" for the term "Parent Recommendation Change" in clauses (A)(ii) and (iii)) and the Acquisition Proposal continues to be a Superior Proposal in light of any revisions to the terms of the transaction contemplated by this Agreement to which the Company shall have agreed. Solely for purposes of Sections 6.2(d), 6.2(g) and 8.3(a) to the extent applicable to an Acquisition Proposal made to Parent all references to "Acquisition Proposal" and "Superior Proposal" shall be read as if all references to "the Company" in those terms as defined in Section 6.2(b) were references instead to "Parent," as if all references to "Company Shares" were references to "Parent Common Stock," as if all references to "Parent" were references to "the Company," as if the reference in the definition of "Acquisition Proposal" to "SectionWS 6.1(a)(ix) or (xiii)" was instead a reference to "Section 6.1(b)(viii)," and as if the reference in the definition of "Superior Proposal" to "Section 6.2(c)" was instead a reference to "Section 6.2(d)."

(e)   *Certain Permitted Disclosure*. Nothing contained in this Section 6.2 shall be deemed to prohibit the Company from complying with its disclosure obligations under U.S. federal or state Law, including under Sections 14d–9 and 14e–2 of the Exchange Act; *provided*, *however*, that if such disclosure has the substantive effect of withholding; or withdrawing; or qualifying or modifying in a manner reasonably likely to be understood to be adverse to Parent, the Company Recommendation, Parent shall have the right to terminate this Agreement as set forth in Section 8.4(a). Nothing contained in this Section 6.2 shall be deemed to prohibit Parent from complying with its disclosure obligations under U.S. federal or state Law, including under Sections 14d–9 and 14e–2 of the Exchange Act; *provided*, *however*, that if such disclosure has the substantive effect of withholding; or withdrawing; or qualifying or modifying in a manner reasonably likely to be understood to be adverse to the Company the Parent Recommendation, the Company shall have the right to terminate this Agreement as set forth in Section 8.3(a).

(f)   *Existing Discussions*. The Company agrees that it will immediately cease and cause to be terminated any existing activities, discussions or negotiations with any Persons conducted heretofore with respect to any Acquisition Proposal. The Company agrees that it will take the necessary steps to promptly inform the individuals or entities referred to in the first sentence hereof of the obligations undertaken in this Section 6.2. The Company also agrees that it will promptly request each Person that has heretofore executed a confidentiality agreement in connection with its consideration of acquiring it or any of its Subsidiaries to return or destroy all confidential information heretofore furnished to such Person by or on behalf of it or any of its Subsidiaries.

(g) *Notice*. Each of the Company and Parent (the "Receiving Party") agrees that it will promptly (and, in any event, within 24 hours) notify the other if any inquiries, proposals or offers with respect to an Acquisition Proposal with respect to it or its Subsidiaries are received by it from any Person, any non-public information is requested from the Receiving Party who has made, or proposes to make, an Acquisition Proposal with respect to it or its Subsidiaries, or any discussions or negotiation with the Receiving Party are sought to be initiated or continued by a Person who has made, or proposes to make, an Acquisition Proposal with respect to it or its Subsidiaries, indicating, in connection with such notice, the name of such Person and the material terms and conditions of any such Acquisition Proposal (including, if applicable, copies of any written requests, proposals or offers, including proposed agreements) and thereafter shall keep the other informed, on a current basis, of the status and terms of any such Acquisition Proposal (including any amendments thereto that are of, or are related to, any material term) and the status of any such discussions or negotiations, including any change in the Receiving Party's intentions as previously notified. The Receiving Party agrees that it will deliver to Parent or the Company, as the case may be, a new notice with respect to each Acquisition Proposal with respect to it or its Subsidiaries that has been materially revised or modified and, prior to taking any Company Superior Proposal Action or Parent Superior Proposal Action, as the case may be, or any Company Recommendation Change or Parent Recommendation Change, as the case may be, with respect to any such materially revised or modified Acquisition Proposal, a new three-business-day period shall commence, for purposes of Section 6.2(c) or 6.2(d), as the case may be, from the time Parent or the Company, as the case may be, receives such notice. The Company also agrees to provide any information to Parent that it is providing to another Person pursuant to this Section 6.2 as soon as practicable after it provides such information to such other Person if the Company has not previously furnished such information to Parent.

In re Lear Corporation Shareholder Litigation

926 A.2d 94 (Del. Ch. 2007).

■ STRINE, VICE CHANCELLOR.

I. Introduction

[Lear Corporation is one of the leading automotive parts suppliers in the world, although its business is concentrated with U.S. manufacturers, and to a large extent consists of supplying parts for light trucks and SUVs. As sales of these vehicles have declined with the rise in gas prices, so have Lear's sales suffered. At the same time, large amounts of Lear's debt were maturing. There were rumors of possible bankruptcy. By 2005 Lear was engaged in a restructuring to keep itself solvent. In 2005 Lear's board hired J. P. Morgan Securities, Inc. ("JP Morgan" to provide advisory services on a restructuring, which included divesting underperforming business units and restructuring of its debt, which continued into 2006.]

In early 2006, [Carl] Icahn took a large, public position in Lear stock, with initial purchases at $16–17 per share. Given Icahn's history of prodding issuers toward value-maximizing measures, this news bolstered Lear's flagging stock price, causing it to rise to $21 per share in July, 2006. . . . Later in 2006, Icahn deepened his investment in Lear, by purchasing $200 million of its stock—raising his holdings to 24%—through a secondary offering in which the company sold him stock at $23. The funds raised in that private placement were used by Lear to reduce its debt and help with its ongoing restructuring.

Icahn's purchase led the stock market to believe that a sale of the company had become likely, leading the stock to trade higher, reaching $30 within a few days of his purchase, and trading in that range during the remainder of 2006. Icahn's investment also combined with another reality: Lear's board had eliminated the corporation's poison pill in 2004, and promised not to reinstate it except in very limited circumstances.

In early 2007, Icahn suggested to Lear's CEO [Rossiter] that a going private transaction might be in Lear's best interest. After a week of discussions, Lear's CEO told the rest of the board. The board formed a Special Committee, which authorized the CEO to negotiate merger terms with Icahn.

[During those negotiations, Icahn only moved modestly from his initial offering price of $35 per share, going to $36 per share after Rossiter rejected his initial offer and went to the Special Committee for instructions. Several directors thought the price should be between $36 and $38. When Rossiter informed Icahn that the Special Committee had rejected his bid, Icahn countered at $35.25. Rossiter rejected that bid immediately based on the Special Committee's suggested range, and later in the same telephone call Icahn offered $36, which he said was his highest and best price. Rossiter took that bid to the Special Committee.

With advice from JP Morgan, the Special Committee took into account the gloomy projections for both the industry and Lear, and recommended the bid to the full board. Icahn indicated that if the board desired to conduct a pre-signing auction, it was free to do that, but he would pull his offer. But Icahn made it clear that he would allow the company to freely shop his bid after signing, during a so-called go-shop period, but only so long as he received a termination fee of approximately 3%. In view of the fact that Icahn's bid was twice the stock's price before he began to purchase Lear stock, the board feared that if they rejected his bid and started an auction, the stock would fall back down, and he would come in later at a lower price. Over the next few days while detailed merger negotiations took place, the board authorized JP Morgan to engage in a quick search for other buyers. No serious expressions of interest appeared. At the end of the process JP Morgan gave its opinion that $36 was fair, and the board approved the transaction, with its "go shop" and "window shop" provisions, and a termination fee.]

The board did the deal on those terms. After signing, the board's financial advisors aggressively shopped Lear to both financial and strategic buyers. None made a topping bid during the go shop period. Since that time, Lear has been free to entertain an unsolicited superior bid. None has been made.

Stockholders plaintiffs have moved to enjoin the upcoming merger vote, arguing that the Lear board breached its Revlon duties and has failed to disclose material facts necessary for the stockholders to cast an informed vote.

In this decision, I largely reject the plaintiffs' claims. Although the Lear Special Committee made an infelicitous decision to permit the CEO to negotiate the merger terms outside the presence of Special Committee supervision, there is no evidence that that decision adversely affected the overall reasonableness of the board's efforts to secure the highest possible value. The board retained for itself broad leeway to shop the company after signing, and negotiated deal protection measures that did not present an unreasonable barrier to any second-arriving bidder. Moreover, the board obtained Icahn's agreement to vote his equity position for any bid superior to his own that was embraced by the board, thus signaling Icahn's own willingness to be a seller at the right price. Given the circumstances faced by Lear, the decision of the board to lock in the potential for its stockholders to receive $36 per share with the right for the board to hunt for more emerges as reasonable. The board's post-signing market check was a reasonable one that provided adequate assurance that no bidder willing to materially top Icahn existed. Thus, I conclude that it is unlikely that the plaintiffs would, after trial, succeed on their claims relating to the sale process.

* * *

II. Factual Background

* * *

C. The Merger Terms

1. The Merger Agreement

The Merger Agreement grants Icahn two primary deal protections for allowing its offer to be used as a stalking horse: a termination fee payable if Lear accepted a superior proposal from another bidder and matching rights in the event that a superior proposal is presented. In exchange, the Lear board secured an ability to actively solicit interest from third parties for 45 days (the so-called "go-shop" period), a fiduciary out that permitted the board to accept an unsolicited superior third-party bid after the go-shop period ended, a reverse termination fee payable if AREP [American Real Estate Partners, LP, Icahn's acquisition vehicle] breached the Merger Agreement, and a voting agreement that required Icahn, AREP, and their affiliates to vote their shares in favor of any superior proposal that AREP did not match.

The termination fee that AREP would be entitled to depended on the nature and timing of Lear's termination of the Merger Agreement. Both parties had a right to terminate the Merger Agreement if that Agreement was not approved by Lear's stockholders, but if no superior transaction was completed within a year of the negative stockholder vote, no termination fee was due. If, however, a superior proposal was accepted by Lear such that the company "substantially concurrently" terminated the Merger Agreement and entered into an alternate acquisition agreement, AREP was entitled to a termination fee contingent on the timing of termination. Likewise, AREP could claim a break-up fee if the Lear board withdrew its support (or failed to reconfirm its support when requested to do so) for the AREP offer.

In the event that AREP was entitled to a termination fee, the amount of that fee depended on the timing of the termination of the Merger Agreement. If the Agreement was terminated during the go-shop period, Lear was required to pay to AREP a fee of $73.5 million plus up to $6 million in reasonable and documented expenses. At most, this amounted to a payment of $79.5 million, which is 2.79% of the equity value of the transaction or 1.9% of the total $4.1 billion enterprise value of the deal. In the alternative, if the merger was called off after the go-shop period ended, AREP was entitled to a higher fee of $85,225 million as well as up to $15 million in expense reimbursements. This payment of roughly $100 million amounted to 3.52% of the equity, or 2.4% of the enterprise, valuation of Lear. Viewed in light of the 79.8 million Lear shares outstanding on a fully diluted basis at the time of the merger, the $79.5 million break-up fee due upon termination during the go-shop period translated into a willingness to pay a little less than a dollar more than Icahn's $36 bid. The $100 million fee equated to a bid increase of roughly $1.25 per share.

In addition to these termination fees, AREP was protected by a contractual right to match certain superior bids that Lear received. If Lear fielded a superior proposal, the Merger Agreement forced Lear to notify AREP of the proposal's terms and afforded AREP ten days to determine whether it would increase its offer to match the superior terms. If the superior proposal was in excess of $37 per share, AREP only had a single chance to match, but if it did not cross that threshold, Lear was obligated to allow AREP three days to match each successive bid. In the event that AREP decided not a match a superior proposal, it was obligated to vote its bloc of shares in favor of that transaction under the voting agreement it executed in combination with the Merger Agreement. The combination of match rights with the voting agreement signaled the willingness of Icahn to be either a buyer or seller in a transaction involving Lear.

In exchange for the protections that Icahn and AREP received, the Merger Agreement permitted the Lear board to pursue other buyers for 45 days and then to passively consider unsolicited bids until the merger closed. But, once that 45-day window closed, a second phase, which might be called a "no-shop" or "window-shop" period, began during which the Lear board retained the right to accept an unsolicited superior proposal.

Lear was also protected in the event that AREP breached the Merger Agreement's terms by a reverse termination fee of $250 million. That fee would be triggered if AREP failed to satisfy the closing conditions in the Merger Agreement, was unable to secure financing for the $4.1 billion transaction, or otherwise breached the Agreement. But AREP's liability to Lear was limited to its right to receive this fee.

* * *

III. Legal Analysis

* * *

B.   The Plaintiffs' Revlon Claims

* * *

Although I do not, as will soon be seen, view this negotiation process as a disaster warranting the issuance of an injunction, it is far from ideal and unnecessarily raises concerns about the integrity and skill of those trying to represent Lear's public investors. In reflecting on why this approach was taken, I consider it less than coincidental that Rossiter did not tell the board about Icahn's interest in making a going private proposal until seven days after it was expressed. Although a week seems a short period of time, it is not in this deal context. In seven days, a newly formed Special Committee's advisors can help the Committee do a lot of thinking about how to go about things and what the Committee should seek to achieve; that includes thinking about the Committee's price and deal term objectives, and the most effective way to reach them.

The Lear Special Committee was deprived of important deliberative and tactical time, and, as a result, it quickly decided on an approach to the process not dissimilar to those taken on most issues that come before corporate boards that do not involve conflicts of interest. That is, the directors allowed the actual work to be done by management and signed off on it after the fact. But the work that Rossiter was doing was not like most work. It involved the sale of the company in circumstances in which Rossiter (and his top subordinates) had economic interests that were not shared by Lear's public stockholders.*

Acknowledging all that, though, I am not persuaded that the Special Committee's less-than-ideal approach to the price negotiations with Icahn makes it likely that the plaintiffs, after a trial, will be able to demonstrate a Revlon breach. To fairly determine whether the defendants breached their Revlon obligations, I must consider the entirety of their actions in attempting to secure the highest price reasonably available to the corporation. Reasonableness, not perfection, measured in business terms relevant to value creation, rather than by what creates the most sterile smell, is the metric.[19]

When that metric is applied, I find that the plaintiffs have not demonstrated a reasonable probability of success on their Revlon claim. The overall approach to obtaining the best price taken by the Special Committee appears, for reasons I now explain, to have been reasonable.

First, as many institutional investors and corporate law professors have advocated that all public corporations should do, Lear had gotten rid of its poison pill in 2004. Although it is true that the Lear board had reserved the right to reinstate a pill upon a vote of the stockholders or of a majority of the board's independent directors, it was hardly in a position to do that lightly, given the potential for such action to upset institutional investors and the influential proxy advisory firm, ISS.** At the very least, Lear's public elimination of its pill signaled a willingness to ponder the merits of unsolicited offers. That factor is one that the Lear board was entitled to take into account in designing its approach to value maximization.

Relatedly, Icahn's investment moves in 2006 also stirred the pot, as the plaintiffs admit. Indeed, they go so far as to acknowledge that Lear

---

* Shortly before Icahn expressed an interest in an acquisition, Rossiter asked the board to change his employment arrangements to allow him to cash in his retirement benefits, which were unfunded and had a nominal value of $10 million if he retired at that time. But if Lear filed for bankruptcy, he became an unsecured creditor, with little chance of receiving the benefits. Rossiter also had severance payments of $15.1 million in the event of a change of control.—Ed.

[19] E.g., QVC, 637 A.2d at 45 ("[C]ourt[s] applying enhanced judicial scrutiny should be deciding whether the directors made a reasonable decision, not a perfect decision. If a board selected one of several reasonable alternatives, a court should not second-guess that choice even though it might have decided otherwise or subsequent events may have cast doubt on the board's determination.").

** ISS is "Institutional Shareholder Services," which provides voting advice to institutional investors, and promulgates an extensive set of corporate governance standards.—Ed.

could be perceived as having been on sale from April 2006 onward. As the plaintiffs also admit, Icahn has over the years displayed a willingness to buy when that is to his advantage and to sell when that is to his advantage. The M&A markets know this. Icahn's entry as a player in the Lear drama would have drawn attention from buyers with a potential interest in investing in the automobile sector.

In considering whether to sign up a deal with Icahn at $36 or insist on a full pre-signing auction, these factors were relevant. No one had asked Lear to the dance other than Icahn as of that point, even though it was perfectly obvious that Lear was open to invitations. Although a formal auction was the clearest way to signal a desire for bids, it also presented the risk of losing Icahn's $36 bid. If Icahn was going to be put into an auction, he could reasonably argue that he would pull his bid and see what others thought of Lear before making his move. If the response to the auction was under whelming, he might then pick up the company at a lower price.

The Lear board's concern about this possibility was, in my view, reasonable, given the lack of, with one exception, even a soft overture from a potential buyer other than Icahn in 2006. That exception was a call that Rossiter had gotten from Cerberus when Lear's market price was still well below $20 per share. But that exception is interesting in itself. Once Icahn's second investment became public and his deepened position was announced in October 2006, Cerberus never made a move. Likewise, when Cerberus was contacted during the pre-signing market check and as part of the go-shop process, it never signaled a hunger for Lear or a price at which it would be willing to do a deal.

Also relevant to the question of whether an auction was advisable was the lack of ardor that other major Lear stockholders had for the opportunity to buy equity in the secondary offering along with Icahn. That Lear is worth $60 per share, an idea whose implications I will discuss, they passed on the chance to buy additional stock at $23 per share in October 2006. Given this history, I cannot conclude that it was unreasonable for the Lear board not to demand a full auction before signing its Merger Agreement with Icahn. There were important risks counseling against such an insistence, especially if the board could to some extent have it both ways by locking in a floor of $36 per share while securing a chance to prospect for more.

Second, I likewise find that the plaintiffs have not demonstrated a likelihood of success on their argument that the Lear board acted unreasonably in agreeing to the deal protections in the Merger Agreement rather than holding out for even greater flexibility to look for a higher bid after signing with Icahn. In so finding, I give relatively little weight to the two-tiered nature of the termination fee. The go-shop period was truncated and left a bidder hard-pressed to do adequate due diligence, present a topping bid with a full-blown draft merger agreement, have the Lear board make the required decision to declare the new bid a superior offer, wait Icahn's ten-day period to match, and then have the Lear board accept that bid, terminate its agreement with Icahn, and "substantially concurrently" enter into a merger agreement with it. All of these events had to occur within the go-shop period for the bidder to benefit from the lower termination fee. This was not a provision that gave a lower break fee to a bidder who entered the process in some genuine way during the go-shop period—for example, by signing up a confidentiality stipulation and completing some of the key steps toward the achievement of a definitive merger agreement at a superior price. Rather, it was a provision that essentially required the bidder to get the whole shebang done within the 45-day window. It is conceivable, I suppose, that this could occur if a ravenous bidder had simply been waiting for an explicit invitation to swallow up Lear. But if that sort of Kobayashi-like buyer existed, it might have reasonably been expected to emerge before the Merger Agreement with Icahn was signed based on Lear's lack of a rights plan and the publicity given to Icahn's prior investments in the company.

That said, I do not find convincing the plaintiffs' argument that the combination of the fuller termination fee that would be payable for a bid meeting the required conditions after the go-shop period with Icahn's contractual match right were bid-chilling. The termination fee in that scenario amounts to 3.5% of equity value and 2.4% of enterprise value. For purposes of considering the preclusive effect of a termination fee on a rival bidder, it is arguably more important to look at the enterprise value metric because, as is the case with Lear, most acquisitions require the buyer to pay for the company's equity and refinance all of its debt. But regardless of whether that is the case, the percentage of either measure the termination fee represents here is hardly of the magnitude that should deter a serious rival bid. The plaintiffs' claim to the contrary is based on the median of termination fees identified in a presentation made by JPMorgan in two-tiered post-signing processes of 1.8% of equity value during the go-shop period and 2.9% thereafter. The plaintiffs also state that Icahn should have gotten a lower fee because he would profit from a topping bid through his equity stake. These factors are not ones that I believe would, after trial, convince me that the board's decision to accede to Icahn's demand for a 3.5% fee (2.8% during the go-shop) was unreasonable. Icahn was tying up $1.4 billion in capital to make a bid for a corporation in a troubled industry, was agreeing to allow the target to shop the company freely for 45 days and to continue to work freely with Lear concerning any emerging bidders during that process, and was agreeing to vote his shares for any superior bid accepted by the Lear board.

Likewise, match rights are hardly novel and have been upheld by this court when coupled with termination fees despite the additional obstacle they are present.[20] And, in this case, the match right was actually a limited one that encouraged bidders to top Icahn in a material way. As described, a bidder whose initial topping move was over $37 could limit Icahn to only one chance to match. Therefore, a bidder who was truly willing to make a materially greater bid than Icahn had it within its means to short-circuit the match right process. Given all those factors, and the undisputed reality that second bidders have been able to succeed in the face of a termination fee/matching right combination of this potency,[21] I am skeptical that a trial record would convince me that the Lear board acted unreasonably in assenting to the termination fee and match right provisions in the Merger Agreement.

* * *

Finally, the plaintiffs have attempted to persuade me that the Lear board has likely breached its Revlon duties because the it had hoped that Icahn would offer more than $36 per share, that some Lear stockholders think that $36 per share is too low, and because the plaintiffs have presented a valuation expert opining that the value of Lear was in the high-$30s to mid-$40s range. This is not an appraisal proceeding, and I have no intention to issue my own opinion as to Lear's value.

But what I have done is reviewed the record on valuation carefully. Lear is one of the nation's largest corporations. Before Icahn emerged, the stock market had abundant information about Lear and its future prospects. It valued Lear at much less than $36 per share—around $17 per share in March and April 2006. After Icahn emerged, the stock market perceived that Lear had greater value based on Icahn's interest and the likelihood of a change of control transaction involving a purchase of all of the firm's equity, not just daily trades in minority shares.

Although the $36 price may have been below what the Lear board hoped to achieve, they had a reasonable basis to accept it. The valuation information in the record, when fairly read, does not incline me toward a finding that the Lear board was unreasonable in accepting the Icahn bid. Although the plaintiffs' valuation expert originally opined that a fair range would be in the "high-$30s" to "mid-$40s," his DCF analysis suggests a range below the merger price, once that DCF analysis is properly adjusted to correct for errors in computing the discount rate he himself admits were either in error or inconsistent. When corrected to use an appropriate discount rate and to consider current industry circumstances, the plaintiff's own expert's DCF value for Lear based on its Long Range Plan with Current Industry Outlook ranges from $27.13 to $35.75. Moreover, to the extent that plaintiffs' expert relies upon the

---

[20] *E.g.,* In re Toys 'R' Us, Inc. S'holder Litig., 877 A.2d 975, 980 (Del. Ch. 2005) (finding that inclusion of a termination fee and the presence of matching rights in a merger agreement did not act as a serious barrier to any bidder willing to pay materially more for the target entity).

[21] Defendants have cited 15 transactions within the past three years in which intervening bids were made despite termination fees of 3% or more and contractual match rights in the merger agreements.

$45.19 median of his DCF models, that reliance appears questionable as those models produce a range between $9.81 and $107.54 per share.

At this stage, the more important point is this. The Lear board had sufficient evidence to conclude that it was better to accept $36 if a topping bid did not emerge than to risk having Lear's stock price return to the level that existed before the market drew the conclusion that Lear would be sold because Icahn had bought such a substantial stake. Putting aside the market check, the $36 per share price appears as a reasonable one on this record, when traditional measures of valuation, such as the DCF, are considered. More important, however, is that the $36 price has been and is still being subjected to a real world market check, which is unimpeded by bid-deterring factors.

If, as the plaintiffs say, their expert is correct that Lear is worth materially more than $36 per share and that some major stockholders believe that Lear is worth $60 per share, a major chance to make huge profits is being missed by those stockholders and by the market for corporate control in general. While it may be that that is the case, I cannot premise an injunction on the Lear board's refusal to act on an improbability of that kind. Stockholders who have a different view on value may freely communicate with others, subject to their compliance with the securities laws, about their different views on value. Stockholders may vote no and seek appraisal. But the plaintiffs are in no position ask me to refuse the Lear electorate the chance to freely determine whether a guaranteed $36 per share right now is preferable to the risks of continued ownership of Lear stock.

VI. Conclusion

For the foregoing reasons, the plaintiffs' motion for a preliminary injunction is largely denied, with the exception that a preliminary injunction will issue preventing the merger vote until supplemental disclosure of the kind required by the decision is issued.* The defendants shall provide the court on June 18 their proposal as to the form of that disclosure, and the timing of its provision to stockholders. So long as the court is satisfied about substance and timing, the merger vote may be able to proceed as currently scheduled. The plaintiffs and defendants shall collaborate on an implementing order, which shall be presented on June 18 as well.

––––––––––––

QUESTIONS

1.   Note there are three stages to termination fees: (1) a period during which Lear can terminated without payment of a termination fee; (2) a period when the fee of 2.79% of the cost of Lear's equity; and (3) a fee of

––––––––––––
   *   Additional disclosures about Rossiter's retirement and severance arrangements were required.—Ed.

approximately $3.52% of Lear's equity. What was the purpose of the three-tier fee arrangement?

2.   What were the conditions that would obligate Icahn to pay a reverse termination fee of $250 million, or approximately 6% of the $4.1 million purchase price?

3.   Why would Lear enter into a reverse termination fee of $250 million when its losses, assuming the stock would return to its pre-Icahn price, would be approximately half of the $4.1 billion purchase price?

NOTE

During the growth of Management Buyouts financed by private equity firms some sellers have been insisting on (and getting) "go-shop" provisions that permit the seller to actively shop the company after signing a definitive agreement. Commentators suggest that this phenomenon has developed because a strong sellers' market has existed in the period 2005–07, with the availability of cheap financing because of low interest rates, the huge growth in private equity funds seeking acquisitions accompanied by growth in "strategic acquisitions" by other operating companies, as opposed to "financial acquisitions" by private equity funds. Stephen J. Glover & Jonathan P. Goodman, Go-Shops: Are They Here to Stay?, 11 No. 6 The M&A Lawyer 1 (June 2007).

The authors describe the go-shop periods as being from 20 to 50 days, and suggest that the length of the shopping period should probably depend on how extensively the company was shopped before entering into a definitive agreement. In some cases the go-shop period is followed by a fiduciary out period, during which the company can consider unsolicited bids, which would include bids from those contacted during the go-shop period. These agreements are sometimes accompanied by a reduced termination fee if the target accepts a superior bid during the go-shop period, in the range of 40% to 60% of the full termination fee payable after that time. Maytag Corporation entered into such an agreement with Ripplewood Capital. Guhan Subramanian found that "(1) go-shops yield more search in aggregate (pre- and post-signing) than the traditional no-shop route; (2) "pure" go-shop deals, in which there is no pre-signing canvass of the marketplace, yield a higher bidder 17 percent of the time; and (3) target shareholders receive approximately 5 percent higher returns through the pure go-shop process relative to the no-shop route." He did caution that these findings did not hold for management buyouts. Subramanian, Go-Shops vs No-Shops in Private Equity Deals: Evidence and Implications, 63 Bus. Law. 729 (2008).

Standstill agreements have been used to control the conduct of auctions, to assure that bidders know they have only one chance to bid, and thus to encourage them to make their best offers the first time. To assure compliance, these agreements often prohibit the bidder from publicly or privately asking the target's board to waive the standstill. These are known as "don't ask, don't waive" provisions. These provisions have been challenged in court on the basis that they negate the board's continuing obligation to be informed about superior bids, although it should be noted that they do not prevent non-signing bidders from bidding. In In re Topps Co. Shareholder Litigation, 926 A.2d 58, 91, n. 28 (Del. Ch. 2007) then Vice-Chancellor Strine observed that a board conducting a good faith auction could use such a provision, although he enjoined its use in the particular case.

C. BONDING PERFORMANCE

The previous cases illustrate a dilemma for both buyers and sellers. For sellers, it suggests that the end of a negotiating process may be just the beginning of an auction. If the board has a duty to keep seeking out better offers, and to terminate merger agreements at any time a better offer appears, what incentives do buyers have to negotiate with a prospective seller, when their efforts may simply be the opening move in an auction? Why invest resources in negotiating a deal, performing the necessary due diligence, securing financing and utilizing professionals for advice, if the deal may evaporate at any time?

Buyers have sought several kinds of protection against disappointment that can result from the sellers' fiduciary duties to continue to seek a higher price during the period between execution of a merger agreement and the closing. Since specific performance will not be available, they have turned to various forms of liquidated damages provisions, although typically that terminology has not been used. There are three basic forms. The first is a termination fee, or break-up fee, payable when the seller terminates the agreement, typically because a better offer has come along. The second is a topping fee, which provides that the frustrated bidder will receive a share of the seller's gains from accepting a higher subsequent bid. Usually these are set as a percentage of the difference between the higher bid and the seller's bid.

Lock-up options can serve similar functions, but they can also serve other functions. The phrase "lock-up option" is sometimes used to describe two rather different forms of options. The first is an option on authorized but unissued shares of the target corporation, while the second is an option on particular assets of the target, often called a "crown jewel option," because it frequently involves those parts of the target the first bidder regards as the target's most attractive assets.

What of lock-up options with second bidders, so-called white knights? Typically white knights are given this appellation because they are seen as management's saviors from a hostile first bidder. This implies that they save management from the only thing likely to concern managers—unemployment—by giving target management some assurance of continued employment after the white knight completes an acquisition. But this is not always true, as second bidders may be solicited by independent directors to increase competition and raise the ultimate sales price.

Crown jewel options typically are only exercisable if the first bidder is defeated. If they were exercisable prior to completion of an acquisition, the first bidder might choose to acquire only the most desirable parts of a company, leaving a crippled target in the hands of the shareholders. Crown jewel options typically are granted at some discount from what the target board believes is the fair market value of the optioned assets, in order to create a reward for the first bidder in the event it is ultimately defeated. The great difficulty faced by the target's board in granting such options is demonstrating that an informed business judgment was exercised in pricing the assets to be optioned. Typically these assets have not been shopped for sale prior to this time, so no market check is available. Boards are forced to rely on the sometimes suspect valuations furnished either by management or by investment bankers, often produced hastily.

A third form of break-up fee is the "topping fee," which is a payment set on the basis of the profits to the target from the disappointed buyer's initiation of an auction for the target. These fees are usually set as a percentage of the premium received by the target over the disappointed buyer's last bid. In effect, the first bidder is treated as having created this value by initiating an auction, and the target agrees to share any premiums with the first bidder. This is less frequently employed, perhaps because the potential payout is so large that courts would be likely to strike it down.

Samjens Partners I v. Burlington Industries, Inc.

663 F.Supp. 614 (S.D.N.Y.1987).

■ SHIRLEY WOHL KRAM, J.

* * *

This case is presently before the Court upon plaintiffs' [Samjens] motion, pursuant to Rule 65 of the Federal Rules of Civil Procedure, for a preliminary injunction prohibiting the defendants from: 1) implementing the merger agreement [between Burlington, a Delaware corporation, on the one hand, and Morgan Stanley Group, Inc. and its subsidiaries, BI/MS Holdings, Inc. and BII Acquisition Corp.] or accepting shares tendered pursuant to Morgan's tender offer until defendants have either terminated the break-up fee and expense reimbursement provision of the merger agreement or granted other competitive bidders the same terms as offered to Morgan; 2) pursuing Burlington's May 14, 1987 self-tender offer; 3) accepting for payment or paying for any shares tendered into the self-tender offer; and 4) pursuing the merger agreement or the Morgan tender offer until they have filed corrective disclosures.

FACTS

The following constitutes the Court's findings of fact. Beginning in February 1987, various affiliates of the plaintiffs commenced purchasing Burlington shares in the open market. On April 7, 1987, defendant Frank Greenberg, Burlington's president, heard a report on television that a group led by Asher Edelman and Dominion Textile, principals of Samjens, had acquired a stake in Burlington. The same report was published the next day in the newspaper U.S.A. Today. On April 14, 1987, Samjens filed its Schedule 13D, indicating that it had obtained a 7.6 percent stake in Burlington.

Immediately upon hearing that Edelman had acquired a stake in Burlington, Greenberg began to interview investment banking firms to serve as advisors. The search lasted for approximately one week, and culminated in the retention of First Boston Corporation ("FB") and Kidder, Peabody ("KP") to advise Burlington "with respect to a takeover defense. . . ." * * *

In response to the takeover rumor, various groups approached Burlington to inquire about a possible deal. On April 21, 1987, Robert Greenhill of Morgan sent a letter to Greenberg requesting a meeting to discuss the possibility of a deal between Morgan and Burlington. The letter stated, "We would have no interest except in proceeding on a basis agreed upon by your management."

Three days later, Edelman sent the first of a series of letters to Greenberg. It stated that Samjens had acquired a 7.6 percent share of Burlington and offered to purchase Burlington in a negotiated transaction at $60 per share. Edelman threatened a hostile tender offer if Burlington refused a negotiated transaction.

On April 29, 1987, representatives of Burlington's management met with Morgan for the first time. Representing Morgan were Donald Brenner, Alan Goldberg, and Robert Greenhill. In preparation for the meeting, Goldberg obtained a "canned" document from Morgan's files that Morgan used when negotiating merger agreements and edited it for use at the meeting with Burlington. The document listed the general issues that arise in mergers and did not represent a draft agreement or offer. The document, titled "Agenda", contained a number of "talking points". Included among them were:

— MS interested in purchasing Vermont with management.[2]

— MS would pursue the transaction only if senior management supported the deal.

— Management would be given 10% of the company equity at closing and allocated an additional 10% upon achieving an agreed to set of performance measures.

---

[2] Vermont was Morgan's code name for Burlington.

— From an operating point of view after the deal this company will be run 100% by the current management team.

— In addition since equity is non-liquidated investment for a time period we would expect senior management's compensation to be significantly adjusted upward. In Container Corp. there was an adjustment factor of 50% and in Mary Kay it was 125%.

— In addition MS is committed to lucrative incentive plans for senior management.

The other points included a description of the proposed financing and a proposed price of $65 per share.

Various topics were discussed at the meeting. Morgan told Burlington that it would decide the future of Burlington's senior management after a merger closed. The evidence indicates that this is, in fact, Morgan's policy in all of its mergers. Morgan also told Burlington that it had closed only one merger in which the company's management did not participate in the ownership. Finally, Morgan told Burlington that it expected that management would participate in the ownership of the new company. The bulk of the meeting, however, was spent discussing Morgan's proposed financing. The meeting ended inconclusively, and the parties held a number of subsequent meetings.

* * *

[The court described a process that began with a $67 tender offer on May 6, 1987 by Samjens for all of Burlington's common stock, which management rejected as inadequate, followed by Burlington's self-tender offer for 25% of its own stock at $80 per share. Samjens responded by increasing its bid to $72.]

On May 20, 1987, Morgan and Burlington agreed to a merger agreement under which Morgan agreed to make a tender offer for all Burlington shares at $76 per share. Pursuant to the merger agreement, Burlington agreed to condition its self-tender offer on Morgan's failure to complete its tender offer. Plaintiffs challenge three aspects of the agreement: 1) Section 6.3(b) which requires the Board to opt out of the North Carolina Shareholder Protection Act; 2) Section 6.5 which prohibits the Board from soliciting other bids unless advised by counsel that its fiduciary duty requires it to do so (the "no-shop clause"); and 3) Section 8.3 which agrees to pay Morgan approximately $25 million if its tender offer fails (the "break-up fee") and to pay in addition up to $25 million in expenses.

The merger agreement was considered and approved by the Board at an all-day meeting on May 19 and another meeting on May 20, 1987. The following description of these meetings is based on the uncontradicted deposition testimony of various persons who were at the meetings. The May 19 meeting began with a briefing by independent counsel as to the Board's fiduciary duty. The investment bankers then informed the Board that they had discussed possible bids for Burlington with approximately 25 parties. Included among them were Citicorp, Kohlberg, Kravitz and Roberts, and Morgan. Although the former two parties had shown interest in bidding for Burlington, only Morgan had made a firm bid. The Board asked questions about Morgan's proposed price, its reputation, and its financing. It also pressed the bankers as to the likelihood of other offers, and was told that while there was interest, there were no other guaranteed offers. The Board was told that even if the other parties were to make bids, they would need time. In the early afternoon, the Board decided to begin negotiations with Morgan. It designated Joseph Barr, the senior independent director, to conduct the negotiations.

The deposition testimony of the persons at the negotiations unanimously indicates that negotiations with Morgan over the next two days covered four main topics: the fees, the no-shop clause, the price of the bid, and the financing. The Board rejected payment of a $7 million "hello fee" to Morgan just for entering into the agreement, and Morgan dropped the request. The Board also asked the bankers whether the break-up fee was standard practice and whether it and the other fees were too high. FB and KP did a survey of break-up fees in approximately 20 recent leveraged buyouts, and found that the one percent fee in the Morgan proposal was average. The Board was informed that Morgan was firm in its request for the fees, as they represented compensation for the risk that Morgan was taking in tying up its capital. The Board was unhappy with the original form of the no-shop clause, and insisted on inserting a condition that they could accept other bids if their fiduciary duty required it. Barr's testimony indicates that he understood this condition to mean that, if the Board received a higher bid than Morgan's, it could accept it. Finally, the Board negotiated a higher share price than Morgan had originally offered and satisfied itself that Morgan's financing was secure.

Two other topics received careful attention from the Board. First, the members inquired vigorously as to whether management had been guaranteed equity participation in the merged company, and were assured by management and Morgan representatives that there had been discussions but no agreement. Second, the Board considered whether to contact Samjens and inform it of the bid. FB and KP informed the Board, however, that Samjens had been contacted and did not plan to bid higher. The Board was informed of the May 19 letter from Edelman requesting that he be told of any prospective agreement or any higher bid, but did not understand the letter as a firm offer to raise Samjens' bid. The May 19 letter, it should be noted, does not state that Samjens was ready, willing, and able to raise its offer. The letter only requested a chance to "shop" any other bid. Board members indicated other reasons they were unwilling to contact Edelman: 1) Burlington had already offered Edelman a chance to receive information but he had not agreed to sign a confidentiality agreement; 2) Samjens had not terminated its tender offer as requested; 3) they suspected that Edelman used insider information in launching the tender offer; and 4) they did not want to risk antagonizing Morgan and losing its offer by allowing Edelman to review Morgan's bid and bid against it if he wished, as Edelman had requested.

* * *

PRELIMINARY INJUNCTION

[The court held that Samjens had failed to prove irreparable injury, and then turned to whether Samjens had established the likelihood of success on the merits.]

* * *

2.   *The Merger Agreement*

Plaintiffs claim that the Board violated its duty to Burlington shareholders by failing to conduct a required auction for Burlington and by considering the Morgan merger agreement in a hasty, perfunctory, and biased manner. Plaintiffs claim that in approving the break-up fees, expense arrangements, and the no-shop provisions, the Board breached its fiduciary duty to the shareholders.[8]

* * *

In coordinating the bidding process, the board can institute strategies, such as granting a "lock-up" agreement, a break-up fee, or a no-shop agreement to a "white knight", but only if their strategies enhance the bidding. [Revlon, 506 A.2d] at 183, 184. Such arrangements may also be legitimately necessary to convince a "white knight" to enter the bidding by providing some form of compensation for the risks it is undertaking. *Id.* Arrangements which effectively end the auction, however, are generally detrimental to shareholders' interests and not protected by the business judgment rule. *Id.* at 181, 183.

The board is under a further duty, when conducting the auction, to deal fairly with the bidders. It cannot deal selectively to fend off a hostile bidder.

* * *

d.   *The Approval of the Morgan Stanley Merger Agreement*

On May 19, the Board was informed that approximately 25 entities had expressed interest in Burlington. Only Morgan, however, was willing to make a bid. When the Board decided to enter into negotiations with Morgan, it was clear that Burlington would be sold, the auction began, and the Board was no longer defending the company, but attempting to

---

[8]   The parties agree that since Burlington is incorporated in the state of Delaware, Delaware law applies. See Zion v. Kurtz, 50 N.Y.2d 92, 100 (1980).

get the best bid for it. The evidence indicates the Board fulfilled its duty to do so.

* * *

The merger agreement is not so onerous as to end the auction or exclude other bidders. The breakup fee and related expenses total approximately 2 percent of the value of the company, leaving other parties free to bid. There is also no auction-ending lock-up agreement. In fact, the merger did not end the auction: in response to the merger, Samjens increased its bid to $77, and Morgan has responded with a bid of $78. Thus, the merger agreement has increased the value to the shareholders by $6 per share, and Samjens has hinted that it might make a higher bid.

The evidence also indicates that the Board reached all of its decisions after thorough consultation with its financial and legal advisors. Its decisions were based on reasonable and thorough investigations, and its conclusions were justifiable and in good faith. The Board did not rush. Its investment bankers solicited bids over an eight day period. When the Board was assured that Morgan's bid was the best, it pursued its negotiations with Morgan over a two-day period. The Board fulfilled its duty of care in the takeover contest, and its decision is entitled to the protection of the business judgment rule. In short, if the procedure the Board followed and the merger agreement it approved were not protected by the business judgment rule, the Court doubts that any merger agreements would ever be allowed in the context of takeover contests. This case indicates that this would be detrimental to shareholders. The merger agreement approved in this case has resulted, so far, in an increase of $6 per share in the Price that will be paid to shareholders.

Plaintiffs' version of how the auction should have been conducted is unrealistic and ignores a number of important factors. First, the Board was operating under time pressure caused by Samjens. The Samjens offer was to expire on June 3. Thus, when the Board met on May 19, it had only two weeks to find an alternative to an inadequate bid. Morgan was the only party ready to make a bid, all other parties needed additional time. Second, although Morgan might have been Burlington's white knight, it was not Burlington's patron saint. Morgan was involved in negotiations with Burlington because it saw an opportunity to make money. Thus, it wanted a response to its bid quickly, it wanted compensation for the risk it was undertaking in tying up its capital, and it did not want to serve as a "stalking horse" and have its bid shopped around. In light of this, however, the Board spent two days negotiating the merger agreement, and bargained vigorously with Morgan.

e. *Dealings with Edelman*

Plaintiffs claim that the Board was biased, and should have contacted Edelman before accepting the bid from Morgan. The reasons the Board did not contact Edelman were stated earlier. Even if the Board was incorrect in understanding that Samjens did not plan to make another offer, the failure to contact him was still justified. Management had offered to provide Edelman with the same information it had given other interested parties, but Edelman refused to sign a confidentiality agreement. Edelman wanted to be informed of other bids before he bid, but the Board justifiably thought it would be unwise to do so. The Board did not deal selectively with Edelman. Instead, he dealt selectively with the Board, according to his own rules. Nor did the Board freeze Edelman out of the auction. The merger agreement the Board signed did not end the auction, it provided a starting point for further bidding. Edelman was free to—and did—raise his bid after it was signed. If the Board was unfair with Edelman, it was only because it forced him to dig deeper into his pockets to the benefit of Burlington shareholders.

Samjens also complains that the Board has not offered it a break-up fee and therefore has treated it unfairly. It complains that if it purchases Burlington, it must pay a $50 million penalty due to the expense and break-up fee provisions. Samjens forgets, however, that it has purchased approximately 13 percent of Burlington shares in the pretender offer market at an average price of $50 per share. Thus, Samjens enters the bidding process with a nearly $80 million advantage over other prospective bidders who must pay at least $78 per share for all outstanding shares. Denying Samjens a break-up fee thus helps to even the playing field.

* * *

CONCLUSION

The Court has found that the plaintiffs are not threatened with irreparable injury and are not likely to succeed on the merits of their claims. The motion for a preliminary injunction is thus denied.

———————

QUESTIONS

1. When did Burlington's board shift from a Unocal mode to a Revlon mode?

2. Why didn't the court treat the board as having a conflict of interest with respect to Morgan?

3. Why doesn't the court hold that Burlington dealt with Morgan to the exclusion of Samjens, in violation of Revlon?

4. Would it be prudent or permissible for a board to give a break-up fee as well as a no-shop clause?

5. Did Samjens make a tactical error in making its last bid of $77 after Burlington had entered into the agreement with Morgan?

———————

Brazen v. Bell Atlantic Corporation

695 A.2d 43 (Del.1997).

■ VEASEY, CHIEF JUSTICE:

In this appeal, the issues facing the Court surround the question of whether a two-tiered $550 million termination fee in a merger agreement is a valid liquidated damages provision or whether the termination fee was an invalid penalty and tended improperly to coerce stockholders into voting for the merger.

Although there are judgmental aspects involved in the traditional liquidated damages analysis applicable here, we do not apply the business judgment rule as such. We hold that the termination fee should be analyzed as a liquidated damages provision because the merger agreement specifically so provided. Under the appropriate test for liquidated damages, the provisions at issue here were reasonable in the context of this case. We further find that the fee was not a penalty and was not coercive. Accordingly, we affirm the judgment of the Court of Chancery, but upon an analysis that differs somewhat from the rationale of that Court.

Facts

In 1995, defendant below-appellee, Bell Atlantic Corporation, and NYNEX Corporation entered into merger negotiations. In January 1996, NYNEX circulated an initial draft merger agreement that included a termination fee provision. Both parties to the agreement determined that the merger should be a stock-for-stock transaction and be treated as a merger of equals. Thus, to the extent possible, the provisions of the merger agreement, including the termination fee, were to be reciprocal.

Representatives of Bell Atlantic and NYNEX agreed that a two-tiered $550 million termination fee was reasonable for compensating either party for damages incurred if the merger did not take place because of certain enumerated events. The termination fee was divided into two parts. First, either party would be required to pay $200 million if there were both a competing acquisition offer for that party and either (a) a failure to obtain stockholder approval, or (b) a termination of the agreement. Second, if a competing transaction were consummated within eighteen months of termination of the merger agreement, the consummating party would be required to pay an additional $350 million to its disappointed merger partner.

In the negotiations where such a fee was discussed, the parties took into account the losses each would have suffered as a result of having focused attention solely on the merger to the exclusion of other significant opportunities for mergers and acquisitions in the telecommunications industry. The parties concluded that, with the recent passage of the national Telecommunications Act of 1996, the entire competitive landscape had been transformed for the regional Bell operating companies, creating a flurry of business combinations. The parties further concluded that the prospect of missing out on alternative transactions due to the pendency of the merger was very real. The "lost opportunity" cost issue loomed large. The negotiators also considered as factors in determining the size of the termination fee (a) the size of termination fees in other merger agreements found reasonable by Delaware courts, and (b) the lengthy period during which the parties would be subject to restrictive covenants under the merger agreement while regulatory approvals were sought.

Bell Atlantic and NYNEX decided that $550 million, which represented about 2% of Bell Atlantic's approximately $28 billion market capitalization, would serve as a "reasonable proxy" for the opportunity cost and other losses associated with the termination of the merger. In addition, senior management advised Bell Atlantic's board of directors that the termination fee was at a level consistent with percentages approved by Delaware courts in earlier transactions, and that the likelihood of a higher offer emerging for either Bell Atlantic or NYNEX was very low.

* * *

In addition, section 9.2(e) of the merger agreement states,

> NYNEX and Bell Atlantic agree that the agreements contained in Sections 9.2(b) and (c) above are an integral part of the transactions contemplated by this Agreement and constitute liquidated damages and not a penalty. If one Party fails to promptly pay to the other any fee due under such Sections 9.2(b) and (c), the defaulting Party shall pay the costs and expenses (including legal fees and expenses) in connection with any action, including the filing of any lawsuit or other legal action, taken to collect payment, together with interest on the amount of any unpaid fee at the publicly announced prime rate of Citibank, N.A. from the date such fee was required to be paid.

Finally, section 9.2(a), also pertinent to this appeal, states,

> In the event of termination of this Agreement as provided in Section 9.1 hereof, and subject to the provisions of Section 10.1 hereof, this Agreement shall forthwith become void and there shall be no liability on the part of any of the Parties except (i) as set forth in this Section 9.2 . . . and (ii) nothing herein shall relieve any Party from liability for any willful breach hereof.

Plaintiff below-appellant, Lionel L. Brazen, a Bell Atlantic stockholder, filed a class action against Bell Atlantic and its directors for declaratory and injunctive relief. Plaintiff alleged that the termination fee was not a valid liquidated damages clause because it failed to reflect an estimate of actual expenses incurred in preparation for the merger. Plaintiffs alleged that the $550 million payment was "an unconscionably high termination or 'lockup' fee," employed "to restrict and impair the exercise of the fiduciary duty of the Bell Atlantic board and coerce the shareholders to vote to approve the proposed merger. . . ."

The parties filed cross-motions for summary judgment. Bell Atlantic sought a declaration that the decision to include and structure the termination fee was a valid exercise of business judgment. The Court of Chancery denied the relief sought by plaintiff after concluding that the termination fee structure and terms were protected by the business judgment rule and that plaintiff failed to rebut its presumptions.

Scope And Standard of Review

On appeal, this Court reviews de novo both as to the facts and the law a Court of Chancery decision on a motion for summary judgment.

* * *

Termination Fee as Liquidated Damages

The Court of Chancery determined that the proper method for analyzing the termination fee in this merger agreement was to employ the business judgment rule rather than the test accepted by Delaware courts for analyzing the validity of liquidated damages provisions. In arriving at this determination, the Court of Chancery concluded that a liquidated damages analysis was not appropriate in this case because, notwithstanding section 9.2(e) of the merger agreement, which states that the $550 million fee constitutes liquidated damages,

> the event which triggers payment of the fees is not a breach but a termination. Liquidated damages, by definition, are damages paid in the event of a breach. . . . In addition, the Merger Agreement clearly provides that nothing in the Agreement (including the payment of termination fees) "shall relieve any Party from liability for any willful breach hereof." Accordingly, the Boards' decision to include these termination fees, which are triggered by a termination of the Merger Agreement and payment of which will not hinder either party's ability to recover damages from a breach, is protected by the business judgment rule and the fees will not be struck down unless plaintiff demonstrates that their inclusion was the result of disloyal or grossly negligent acts.

Plaintiff argued below and argues again here that the proper analysis for determining the validity of the termination fee in section 9.2(c) of the merger agreement is to analyze it as a liquidated damages clause employing a test different from the business judgment rule. We agree.

The express language in section 9.2(e) of the agreement unambiguously states that the termination fee provisions "constitute liquidated damages and not a penalty."[9] The Court of Chancery correctly found that liquidated damages, by definition, are damages paid in the event of a breach of a contract. While a breach of the merger agreement is not the only event that would trigger payment of the termination fee, the express language of section 9.2(c) states that a party's breach of section 7.2 (which provides that the parties are required to take all action necessary to convene a stockholders' meeting and use all commercially reasonable efforts to secure proxies to be voted in favor of the merger), coupled with other events, may trigger a party's obligation to pay the termination fee.

Thus, we find no compelling justification for treating the termination fee in this agreement as anything but a liquidated damages provision, in light of the express intent of the parties to have it so treated.[11]

Analyzing the Validity of Liquidated Damages

In Lee Builders v. Wells, a case involving a liquidated damages provision equal to 5% of the purchase price in a contract for the sale of land, the Court of Chancery articulated the following two-prong test for analyzing the validity of the amount of liquidated damages: "Where the damages are uncertain and the amount agreed upon is reasonable, such an agreement will not be disturbed."[12]

Plaintiff argues that the termination fee, if properly analyzed as liquidated damages, fails the Lee Builders test because both portions of the fee are punitive rather than compensatory, having nothing to do with actual damages but instead being designed to punish Bell Atlantic stockholders and the subsequent third-party acquirer if Bell Atlantic were ultimately to agree to merge with another entity. We find, however, that the termination fee safely passes both prongs of the Lee Builders test.

To be a valid liquidated damages provision under the first prong of the test, the damages that would result from a breach of the merger agreement must be uncertain or incapable of accurate calculation.

---

[9]   At oral argument in this Court, counsel for Bell Atlantic explained that the liquidated damages language was "boilerplate" terminology for termination fees in merger transactions such as this one. So be it, but in our view, the drafters of corporate documents bear the responsibility for the selection of appropriate and clear language. See Kaiser v. Matheson, Del. Supr., 681 A.2d 392, 398–99 (1996). Accordingly, the parties to this merger cannot disown their own language.

[11]   Such treatment is not without precedent. In Kysor Indus. Corp. v. Margaux, Inc., Del. Super., 674 A.2d 889 (1996), the contractual language analyzed by the court stated, "In the event that Margaux breaches its undertakings, . . . Margaux shall promptly . . . (b) pay as liquidated damages to Kysor a termination fee equal to Three Hundred Thousand Dollars ($300,000)." *Id.* at 892–93. The Superior Court analyzed the termination fee, not as a termination fee, but as liquidated damages. Because the analytical approach employed by the Superior Court in Kysor would give force and effect to both sections 9.2(c) and 9.2(e) of the merger agreement now before this Court, analyzing the termination fee under the liquidated damages rubric is the better approach.

[12]   Lee Builders v. Wells, Del. Ch., 34 Del. Ch. 307, 103 A.2d 918, 919 (1954); accord Wilmington Housing Authority v. Pan Builders, Inc., D. Del., 665 F.Supp. 351, 354 (1987); RESTATEMENT (SECOND) OF CONTRACTS § 356 (1981).

Plaintiff does not attack the fee on this ground. Given the volatility and uncertainty in the telecommunications industry due to enactment of the Telecommunications Act of 1996 and the fast pace of technological change, one is led ineluctably to the conclusion that advance calculation of actual damages in this case approaches near impossibility.

Plaintiff contends, however, that the $550 million fee violates the second prong of the Lee Builders test, i.e., that it is not a reasonable forecast of actual damages, but rather a penalty intended to punish the stockholders of Bell Atlantic for not approving the merger. Plaintiff's attack is without force.

Two factors are relevant to a determination of whether the amount fixed as liquidated damages is reasonable. The first factor is the anticipated loss by either party should the merger not occur. The second factor is the difficulty of calculating that loss: the greater the difficulty, the easier it is to show that the amount fixed was reasonable. In fact, where the level of uncertainty surrounding a given transaction is high, "experience has shown that . . . the award of a court or jury is no more likely to be exact compensation than is the advance estimate of the parties themselves."[14] Thus, to fail the second prong of Lee Builders, the amount at issue must be unconscionable or not rationally related to any measure of damages a party might conceivably sustain.

Here, in the face of significant uncertainty, Bell Atlantic and NYNEX negotiated a fee amount and a fee structure that take into account the following: (a) the lost opportunity costs associated with a contract to deal exclusively with each other; (b) the expenses incurred during the course of negotiating the transaction; (c) the likelihood of a higher bid emerging for the acquisition of either party; and (d) the size of termination fees in other merger transactions. The parties then settled on the $550 million fee as reasonable given these factors. Moreover, the $550 million fee represents 2% of Bell Atlantic's market capitalization of $28 billion. This percentage falls well within the range of termination fees upheld as reasonable by the courts of this State.[17] We hold that it is within a range of reasonableness and is not a penalty.

This is not strictly a business judgment rule case. If it were, the Court would not be applying a reasonableness test. The business judgment rule is a presumption that directors are acting independently, in good faith and with due care in making a business decision. It applies when that decision is questioned and the analysis is primarily a process

---

[14] 5 ARTHUR L. CORBIN, CORBIN ON CONTRACTS § 1060, at 348 (1964).

[17] See, e.g., Kysor, 674 A.2d at 897 (where the Superior Court held that a termination fee of 2.8% of Kysor's offer was reasonable); Roberts v. General Instrument Corp., Del. Ch., C.A. No. 11639, slip op. at 21, Allen, C. (Aug. 13, 1990) (breakup fee of 2% described as "limited"); Lewis v. Leaseway Transp. Corp., Del. Ch., C.A. No. 8720, slip op. at 6, Chandler, V.C. (May 16, 1990) (dismissing challenge to a transaction which included a breakup fee and related expenses of approximately 3% of transaction value); Braunschweiger v. American Home Shield Corp., Del. Ch., C.A. No. 10755, slip op. at 19–20, Allen, C. (Oct. 26, 1989) (2.3% breakup fee found not to be onerous).

inquiry. Courts give deference to directors' decisions reached by a proper process, and do not apply an objective reasonableness test in such a case to examine the wisdom of the decision itself.

Since we are applying the liquidated damages rubric, and not the business judgment rule, it is appropriate to apply a reasonableness test, which in some respects is analogous to some of the heightened scrutiny processes employed by our courts in certain other contexts. Even then, courts will not substitute their business judgment for that of the directors, but will examine the decision to assure that it is, "on balance, within a range of reasonableness."[20] Is the liquidated damages provision here within the range of reasonableness? We believe that it is, given the undisputed record showing the size of the transaction, the analysis of the parties concerning lost opportunity costs, other expenses and the arms-length negotiations.

Plaintiff further argues that the termination fee provision was coercive. Plaintiff contends that (a) the stockholders never had an option to consider the merger agreement without the fee, and (b) regardless of what the stockholders thought of the merits of the transaction, the stockholders knew that if they voted against the transaction, they might well be imposing a $550 million penalty on their company. Plaintiff contends that the termination fee was so enormous that it "influenced" the vote. Finally, plaintiff argues that the fee provision was meant to be coercive because the drafters deliberately crafted the termination fees to make them applicable when Bell Atlantic's stockholders decline to approve the transaction as opposed to a termination resulting from causes other than the non-approval of the Bell Atlantic stockholders. We find plaintiff's arguments unpersuasive.

First, the Court of Chancery properly found that the termination fee was not egregiously large. Second, the mere fact that the stockholders knew that voting to disapprove the merger may result in activation of the termination fee does not by itself constitute stockholder coercion. Third, we find no authority to support plaintiff's proposition that a fee is coercive because it can be triggered upon stockholder disapproval of the merger agreement, but not upon the occurrence of other events resulting in termination of the agreement.

---

[20] [Paramount Communications, Inc. v.] QVC [Network, Inc.], 637 A.2d [34,] at 45 [(Del.1994)]. It is to be noted that, in QVC, the termination fee of $100 million, which was 1.2% of the original merger agreement, was upheld by the Vice Chancellor because it "represents a fair liquidated amount to cover Viacom's expenses should the Paramount-Viacom merger not be consummated." QVC Network, Inc. v. Paramount Communications, Inc., Del. Ch., 635 A.2d 1245, 1271 (1993), aff'd on other grounds, Paramount Communications, Inc. v. QVC Network, Inc., Del. Supr., 637 A.2d at 50 n.22 and accompanying text (termination fee considered in context with other measures in that case was problematic, but termination fee, standing alone, was not considered by Supreme Court since there was no cross-appeal to present the issue). See also In re J.P. Stevens & Co., Inc. Litigation, Del. Ch., 542 A.2d 770, 783 (1988), interlocutory appeal refused, (Del. Supr., 540 A.2d 1088 1988) (reasonable termination fee negotiated in good faith upheld as conventional and not product of disloyal action).

In Williams v. Geier, this Court enunciated the test for stockholder coercion. Wrongful coercion that nullifies a stockholder vote may exist "where the board or some other party takes actions which have the effect of causing the stockholders to vote in favor of the proposed transaction for some reason other than the merits of that transaction."[21] But we also stated in Williams v. Geier that "in the final analysis ... the determination of whether a particular stockholder vote has been robbed of its effectiveness by impermissible coercion depends on the facts of the case."

In this case, the proxy materials sent to stockholders described very clearly the terms of the termination fee. Since the termination fee was a valid, enforceable part of the merger agreement, disclosure of the fee provision to stockholders was proper and necessary. Plaintiff has not produced any evidence to show that the stockholders were forced into voting for the merger for reasons other than the merits of the transaction. To the contrary, it appears that the reciprocal termination fee provisions, drafted to protect both Bell Atlantic and NYNEX in the event the merger was not consummated, were an integral part of the merits of the transaction. Thus, we agree with the finding of the Court of Chancery that, although the termination fee provision may have influenced the stockholder vote, there were "no structurally or situationally coercive factors" that made an otherwise valid fee provision impermissibly coercive in this setting.

Conclusion

Because we find that actual damages in this case do not lend themselves to reasonably exact calculation, and because we further find that the $550 million termination fee was a reasonable forecast of damages and that the fee was neither coercive nor unconscionable, we hold that the fee is a valid liquidated damages provision in this merger agreement.

In light of the foregoing, we affirm, albeit on somewhat different grounds, the judgment of the Court of Chancery.

NOTE

The following is taken from the NYNEX—Bell Atlantic merger agreement.

"SECTION 9.1—Termination. This Agreement may be terminated at any time before the Effective Time, in each case as authorized by the respective Board of Directors of NYNEX or Bell Atlantic:

"(a) By mutual written consent of each of NYNEX and Bell Atlantic;

---

[21] Williams v. Geier, Del. Supr., 671 A.2d 1368, 1382–83 (1996) (citations omitted).

"(b) By either NYNEX or Bell Atlantic if the Merger shall not have been consummated on or before April 21, 1997 (the 'Termination Date'); provided, however, that the right to terminate this Agreement under this Section 9.1(b) shall not be available to any Party whose failure to fulfill any obligation under this Agreement has been the cause of, or resulted in, the failure of the Effective Time to occur on or before the Termination Date; and provided, further, that if on the Termination Date the conditions to the Closing set forth in Sections 8.1(c) or (d) shall not have been fulfilled, but all other conditions to the Closing shall be fulfilled or shall be capable of being fulfilled, then the Termination Date shall be extended to September 30, 1997. The Parties agree that any amendment of this Agreement to extend the Termination Date beyond September 30, 1997 shall be made without any amendment to or renegotiation of any other material provisions of this Agreement;

"(c) By either NYNEX or Bell Atlantic if a court of competent jurisdiction or governmental, regulatory or administrative agency or commission shall have issued an order, decree or ruling or taken any other action (which order, decree or ruling the Parties shall use their commercially reasonable efforts to lift), in each case permanently restraining, enjoining or otherwise prohibiting the transactions contemplated by this Agreement, and such order, decree, ruling or other action shall have become final and nonappealable;

"(d) By either NYNEX or Bell Atlantic if the other shall have breached, or failed to comply with, in any material respect any of its obligations under this Agreement or any representation or warranty made by such other Party shall have been incorrect in any material respect when made or shall have since ceased to be true and correct in any material respect, and such breach, failure or misrepresentation is not cured within 30 days after notice thereof and such breaches, failures or misrepresentations, individually or in the aggregate and without regard to materiality qualifiers contained therein, results or would reasonably be expected to result in a Material Adverse Effect on NYNEX or Bell Atlantic, with or without including its ownership of NYNEX and its Subsidiaries after the Merger;

"(e) By either NYNEX or Bell Atlantic upon the occurrence of (i) a Material Adverse Effect or an event which could reasonably be expected to result in a Material Adverse Effect on Bell Atlantic (either with or without including its ownership of NYNEX and its Subsidiaries after the Merger), Bell Atlantic North, Bell Atlantic South, NYNEX, New England Telephone and Telegraph Company or New York Telephone Company under Section 8.1(d) hereof arising from an action by a state or federal governmental body, agency or official which has become final and nonappealable, or (ii) any other Material Adverse Effect, or an event which could reasonably be expected to result in a Material Adverse Effect on the other (which in the case of Bell Atlantic shall not include its ownership of NYNEX and its Subsidiaries after the Merger), or, after the Effective Time, Bell Atlantic, including its ownership of NYNEX and its Subsidiaries;

"(f) By either NYNEX or Bell Atlantic if the Board of Directors of the other or any committee of the Board of Directors of the other (i) shall withdraw or modify in any adverse manner its approval or recommendation of this Agreement or the Merger or, in the case of the Board of Directors or any committee of the Board of Directors of Bell Atlantic, the Certificate Amendment or the issuance of Bell Atlantic Common Stock pursuant to the Merger Agreement, (ii) shall fail to reaffirm such approval or recommendation upon such Party's request, (iii) shall approve or recommend any acquisition of the other or a material portion of its assets or any tender offer for shares of its capital stock, in each case, other than by a Party or an affiliate thereof, or (iv) shall resolve to take any of the actions specified in clause (i) above;

"(g) By either NYNEX or Bell Atlantic if any of the required approvals of the stockholders of NYNEX or of Bell Atlantic shall fail to have been obtained at a duly held stockholders meeting of either of such companies, including any adjournments thereof; or

"(h) By either NYNEX or Bell Atlantic, prior to the approval of this Agreement by the stockholders of such Party, upon five days' prior notice to the other, if, as a result of an Acquisition Proposal (as defined in Section 6.3 hereof) received by such Party from a person other than a Party to this Agreement or any of its affiliates, the Board of Directors of such Party determines in good faith that their fiduciary obligations under applicable law require that such Acquisition Proposal be accepted; provided, however, that (i) the Board of Directors of such Party shall have concluded in good faith, after considering applicable provisions of state law and after giving effect to all concessions which may be offered by the other Party pursuant to clause (ii) below, on the basis of oral or written advice of outside counsel, that such action is necessary for the Board of Directors to act in a manner consistent with its fiduciary duties under applicable law and (ii) prior to any such termination, such Party shall, and shall cause its respective financial and legal advisors to, negotiate with the other Party to this Agreement to make such adjustments in the terms and conditions of this Agreement as would enable such Party to proceed with the transactions contemplated hereby;

"provided, however, that no termination shall be effective pursuant to Sections 9.1(f), (g) or (h) under circumstances in which an Initial NYNEX Termination Fee or an Initial Bell Atlantic Termination Fee is payable by the terminating Party under Section 9.2(b) or (c), as the case may be, unless concurrently with such termination, such termination fee is paid in full by the terminating Party in accordance with the provisions of Sections 9.2(b) or (c), as the case may be.

"SECTION 9.2—Effect of Termination. (a) In the event of termination of this Agreement as provided in Section 9.1 hereof, and subject to the provisions of Section 10.1 hereof, this Agreement shall forthwith become void and there shall be no liability on the part of any of the Parties, except (i) as set forth in this Section 9.2 and in Sections 4.10, 4.16, 5.10, 5.16 and 10.3 hereof, and (ii) nothing herein shall relieve any Party from liability for any willful breach hereof.

"(b) If (i) this Agreement (A) is terminated by Bell Atlantic pursuant to Section 9.1(f) hereof or by NYNEX or Bell Atlantic pursuant to Section 9.1(g) hereof because of the failure to obtain the required approval from the NYNEX stockholders or by NYNEX pursuant to Section 9.1(h) hereof, or (B) is terminated as a result of NYNEX's material breach of Section 7.2 hereof which is not cured within 30 days after notice thereof to NYNEX, and (ii) at the time of such termination or prior to the meeting of NYNEX's stockholders there shall have been an Acquisition Proposal (as defined in Section 6.3 hereof) involving NYNEX or any of its Significant Subsidiaries (whether or not such offer shall have been rejected or shall have been withdrawn prior to the time of such termination or of the meeting), NYNEX shall pay to Bell Atlantic a termination fee of $200 million (the 'Initial NYNEX Termination Fee'). In addition, if, within one and one-half years of any such termination described in clause (i) of the immediately preceding sentence that gave rise to the obligation to pay the Initial NYNEX Termination Fee, NYNEX, or the Significant Subsidiary of NYNEX which was the subject of such Acquisition Proposal (the 'NYNEX Target Party'), becomes a subsidiary (as defined below) of the person which made (or the affiliate of which made) an Acquisition Proposal described in clause (ii) of the immediately preceding sentence or of any Offering Person (as defined below) or accepts a written offer to consummate or consummates an Acquisition Proposal with such person or any Offering Person, then, upon the signing of a definitive agreement relating to any such Acquisition Proposal, or, if no such agreement is signed then at the closing (and as a condition to the closing) of such NYNEX Target Party becoming such a subsidiary or of any such Acquisition Proposal, NYNEX shall pay to Bell Atlantic an additional termination fee equal to $350 million.

"(c) If (i) this Agreement (A) is terminated by NYNEX pursuant to Sections 9.1(f) hereof or NYNEX or Bell Atlantic pursuant to Section 9.1(g) hereof because of the failure to obtain the required approval from the Bell Atlantic stockholders or by Bell Atlantic pursuant to Section 9.1(h) hereof, or (B) is terminated as a result of Bell Atlantic's material breach of Section 7.2 hereof which is not cured within 30 days after notice thereof to Bell Atlantic, and (ii) at the time of such termination or prior to the meeting of Bell Atlantic's stockholders there shall have been an Acquisition Proposal (as defined in Section 6.3 hereof) involving Bell Atlantic or any of its Significant Subsidiaries (whether or not such offer shall have been rejected or shall have been withdrawn prior to the time of such termination or of the meeting), Bell Atlantic shall pay to NYNEX a termination fee of $200 million (the 'Initial Bell Atlantic Termination Fee'). In addition, if, within one and one-half years of any such termination described in clause (i) of the immediately preceding sentence that gave rise to the obligation to pay the Initial Bell Atlantic Termination Fee, Bell Atlantic, or the Significant Subsidiary of Bell Atlantic which was the subject of such Acquisition Proposal (the 'Bell Atlantic Target Party'), becomes a subsidiary of the person which made (or the affiliate of which made) an Acquisition Proposal described in clause (ii) of the immediately preceding sentence or of any Offering Person or accepts a written offer to consummate or consummates an Acquisition Proposal with such person or any Offering Person, then, upon the signing of a definitive agreement relating to any such Acquisition Proposal, or, if no such agreement is signed then at the closing (and as a condition to the closing) of such Bell Atlantic Target Party becoming such a subsidiary or of any such Acquisition Proposal, Bell Atlantic shall pay to NYNEX an additional termination fee equal to $350 million.

"(d) Each termination fee payable under Sections 9.2(b) and (c) above shall be payable in cash. For purposes of this Section 9.2, an 'Offering Person' shall be any offeror who makes an Acquisition Proposal to NYNEX, the NYNEX Target Party or their respective Representatives, or Bell Atlantic, the Bell Atlantic Target Party or their respective Representatives, as the case may be, before or within one hundred twenty days after any termination described in Section 9.2(b)(i) or 9.2(c)(i) and 'subsidiary' shall mean with respect to any person, any corporation or other legal entity of which such person owns, directly or indirectly, more than 50% of the stock or other equity interests the holders of which are generally entitled to vote for the election of the board of directors or other governing body of such corporation or other legal entity.

"(e) NYNEX and Bell Atlantic agree that the agreements contained in Sections 9.2(b) and (c) above are an integral part of the transactions contemplated by this Agreement and constitute liquidated damages and not a penalty. If one Party fails to promptly pay to the other any fee due under such Sections 9.2(b) and (c), the defaulting Party shall pay the costs and expenses (including legal fees and expenses) in connection with any action, including the filing of any lawsuit or other legal action, taken to collect payment, together with interest on the amount of any unpaid fee at the publicly announced prime rate of Citibank, N.A. from the date such fee was required to be paid."

QUESTIONS

1. Why should the fact that a provision is a liquidated damages provision take it out of the Business Judgment Rule type of review?

2. If the uncertainty of actual damages is a feature allowing greater deference to decisions about liquidated damages, and if mergers always involve opportunity costs, how can a court ever impose limits on break-up fees?

3. Why isn't the challenge to the coerciveness of the termination fee on shareholders' decisions on how to vote subjected to the Blasius test?

4. What does the court mean when it says that while the size of the fee may have influenced the stockholder vote, there were no "structurally or situationally coercive factors"? Can you think of other cases where the court has condemned such factors?

5. If a merger requires shareholder approval, how can a board of directors bind the corporation to a termination fee even if the shareholders reject the merger proposal?

6. Could Bell Atlantic have avoided this type of reasonableness review by characterizing this fee as a termination fee rather than as liquidated damages? (Note it did reserve the right to sue for willful breach.)

7. How could there be a breach of the merger agreement that was not willful?

8. How can a board bind a corporation to an agreement that requires shareholder approval?

9. If you represented a plaintiff, how would you prove a termination fee had a coercive effect on a shareholder vote?

10. Will a break-up fee be treated differently than a lock-up option by the courts?

11. How can a lock-up option or a break-up fee be granted in advance of any search for a competing offer when an attractive merger bid is received?

NOTE ON LOCK-UP OPTIONS AND BREAK-UP FEES

For discussions of lock-ups and related devices, see Herzel & Shepro, Negotiated Acquisitions: The Impact of Competition in the United States, 44 Bus. Law. 301 (1989); Bainbridge, Exclusive Merger Agreements and Lock-Ups in Negotiated Corporate Acquisitions, 75 Minn. L. Rev. 239 (1990); Ayres, Analyzing Stock Lock-Ups: Do Target Treasury Sales Foreclose or Facilitate Takeover Auctions?, 90 Colum. L. Rev. 682 (1990) and Fraidin &

Hanson, Toward Unlocking Lockups, 103 Yale L. J. 1739 (1994). Professor Bainbridge takes the position that lock-ups are properly evaluated as conflict of interest transactions. Herzel & Shepro point out that delays in completion of acquisitions have added to the risks and uncertainty of acquisitions by increasing competition for targets. Recall that Easterbrook & Fischel have argued that management should remain passive in the face of bids, in order to increase the probability that a first bidder will be successful, thus encouraging first bids. Easterbrook & Fischel, The Proper Role of a Target's Management in Responding to a Tender Offer, 94 HARV. L. Rev. 1161 (1981). Does a lock-up to a first bidder achieve this goal? Ayres argues that not all lockups will foreclose other bidders, and in some cases a bidder receiving a lock-up option will profit more by allowing another bidder to acquire the firm. Ayres would draw the line on permissible lock-ups where the recipient's expected gains from losing the auction are equal to its gains from winning. Fraidin & Hanson take a similar position, except they argue that the likelihood of lock-up options that more than compensate bidders for their risk of loss ("supracompensatory lockups") is so low that courts should enforce all lock-ups. The difficulty posed by these authors is how one could measure gains from winning an auction, as the court noted in Brazen. Perhaps that explains why there are few if any instances of second bidders buying out first bidders, although there have been a few cases where two competing buyers have agreed to split the target's businesses between them.

An empirical study covering lock-up options from 1988–1995 finds that while lock-up options inhibit bidder competition, the overall target returns are higher and bidder returns are lower where lock-ups are employed. This evidence is inconsistent with target management use of lock-ups to benefit themselves at shareholder expense, and more consistent with management's use of lock-ups to enhance bargaining power. Timothy R. Burch, Locking Out Rival Bidders: The Use of Lockup Options in Corporate Mergers, 60 J. Fin. Econ. 103 (2001).

Numerous decisions have held that lock-up options are not improper per se. Buffalo Forge v. Ogden Corp., 717 F.2d 757, 758–59 (2d Cir.1983); Hastings-Murtagh v. Texas Air Corp., 649 F.Supp. 479, 484 (S.D.Fla.1986); Thompson v. Enstar Corp., 509 A.2d 578 (Del.Ch.1984); Warner Communications, Inc. v. Murdoch, 581 F.Supp. 1482, 1491 (D.Del.1984), and Revlon, *supra*. Fraidin and Hanson report that Delaware courts have enjoined all lock-ups that are challenged by a nonrecipient bidder who has made a higher bid contingent upon invalidation of the lockup, and have enforced all lockups where no such competing bid exists. 103 Yale L.J. at 1765–66.

Matador Capital Management Corporation v. BRC Holdings, Inc., 729 A.2d 280 (Del. Ch. 1998), approved a termination fee of approximately 5% of the deal value. Termination fees are used in other settings as well. In re 995 Fifth Avenue Associates, L.P., 96 B.R. 24 (Bankr. S.D.N.Y. 1989) held that payment of a break-up fee following a sale of a debtor's property at auction for $16 million was not unreasonable. The Delaware Chancery Court approved a topping fee of 20% of the gains over the bidder's top price in West

Point-Pepperell, Inc. v. J.P. Stevens & Co., 540 A.2d 1089 (Del.Supr.1988). A topping fee of 25% of the excess over the bidder's last bid was approved in CRTF Corp. v. Federated Department Stores, 683 F.Supp. 422, 436, 440–41 (S.D.N.Y.1988). See also Gray v. Zondervan Corp., 712 F.Supp. 1275 (W.D.Mich.1988), approving a lock-up option, topping fee and termination fee that caused a bidder to increase its bid from $12.50 to $13.50, when a competing bidder had offered only a $.25 increase.

Lock-up options can also substitute for a break-up fee. Thus, when American Hospital gave Hospital Corporation an option to purchase 35% of its shares, it was the same as a 35% topping fee. When Baxter Tavenal made a much higher cash bid and it became apparent that the proposed merger of American Hospital and Hospital Corporation could not obtain shareholder approval, Hospital Corporation's option rights were settled for $200 million. Wall Street Journal, June 16, 1985, p. 2; Lock-Ups Designed to Promote Completion of Acquisition, National L. J., Aug. 19, 1985, at p. 15. A lock-up on 24.9% of the target's stock was reported in Keyser v. Commonwealth Nat'l Fin. Corp., 644 F.Supp. 1130, 1137 (M.D.Pa.1986), and of 16.6% in Yanow v. Scientific Leasing, Inc., Fed. Sec. L. Rep. ¶ 93,660 (Del. Ch., 1988).

A target's freedom to set the lock-up option is constrained in some cases by New York Stock Exchange Rule 312.00, which prohibits issuance of stock or options on stock in excess of 20% of previously outstanding shares without shareholder approval.

A recent study of 2,067 acquisitions found that the grant of a lock-up option deterred second bidders but also found that "target shareholders are not systematically harmed by their use. In fact, the average and median returns to target shareholders are significantly higher in merger deals with lockup options. This holds even after controlling for merger-specific characteristics such as deal completion, a hostile deal attitude, litigation associated with the merger, institutional ownership, the target's market-to-book, size, free cash flow and profit, shareholder anticipation of a lockup option, and a measure of the likelihood the target would have multiple interested bidders." Timothy R. Burch, "Locking Out Rival Bidders: The Use of Lockup Options in Corporate Mergers," 60 J. Fin. Econ. 103, 106 (2001). The author concludes that while lock-up options may be used by target management to favor one bidder over another at shareholder expense, in general the grant of a lock-up option provides target management with additional bargaining power to extract a higher price from the first bidder. Query: How do these findings square with the holdings in Revlon on crown jewel options? Can you distinguish crown jewel options from stock lock-ups triggered by losing out to a higher bid?

During the collapse of the debt markets in 2007 sellers became much more wary about the ability of buyers to finance their acquisitions and close deals. As a result, two phenomena occurred. First, sellers wanted to preserve their rights to specific performance, and were successful in many cases. Second, buyers either omitted an out for a failure to get financing altogether, or if they did retain an out, it was subject to strict contract specifications. Similarly, buyers sometimes were willing to omit antitrust approval as a condition to performance, or perhaps specify the limits on assets they were obligated to sell in order to obtain approval. These were called "come Hell or high water" provisions. Where there was a financing out, sellers insisted on reverse termination or break fees. Because these fees were not being paid by sellers subject to Revlon duties and constraints, they were often higher than sellers' termination fees. Mars, Inc., agreed to a $1 billion reverse termination fee in its $23 billion acquisition of Wm. Wrigley Jr. Co., or 4.3% of the deal and Pfizer agreed to pay Wyeth $4.5 billion, or 6.6% of its purchase price of $68 billion, more than double the termination fee Wyeth agreed to pay Pfizer. David Marcus, No Uncertain Terms, The Deal Magazine, Dec. 11, 2009, at http://www.thedeal.com/newsweekly/2009/12/no_uncertain_terms (last visited 1/4/10).

A study of 127 announced transactions in 2014 involving U.S. publicly traded target companies in which there was a disclosed termination fee revealed the following fees as a percentage of transaction value:

Transaction Termination Fee Annual Summary

Year	2010	2011	2012	2013	2014
Mean	3.5%	3.3%	3.5%	3.5%	3.3%
Median	3.3%	3%	3.5%	3.4%	3.4%

Houlihan Lokey Howard & Zukin, 2014 Transaction Termination Fee Study (2015)

NOTE ON PARAMOUNT COMMUNICATIONS, INC. V. QVC NETWORK, INC.

This case involves a challenge to a lock-up option (equivalent to a topping fee) as well as the board's protection under the Time-Paramount "merger of equals" doctrine.

In Paramount Communications, Inc. v. QVC Network, Inc., 637 A.2d 34 (Del.1994), the Paramount board agreed to a stock for stock merger with Viacom Corporation, while rejecting offers from QVC of a combination of QVC stock and cash that the court held were clearly more valuable. The court applied Revlon duties, holding that the proposed Paramount-Viacom transaction was not a "merger of equals" within the meaning of Paramount Communications, Inc. v. Time, Inc., 571 A.2d 1140 (Del.1989), *supra*, Part 1.C of this chapter. In holding that the Paramount board had breached its fiduciary duties, the court first described the protective devices contained in the Paramount-Viacom merger agreement:

"First, under the No-Shop Provision, the Paramount Board agreed that Paramount would not solicit, encourage, discuss, negotiate, or endorse any competing transaction unless: (a) a third party "makes an unsolicited written, bona fide proposal, which is not subject to any material contingencies relating to financing"; and (b) the Paramount Board determines that discussions or negotiations with the third party are necessary for the Paramount Board to comply with its fiduciary duties.

"Second, under the Termination Fee provision, Viacom would receive a $100 million termination fee if: (a) Paramount terminated the Original Merger Agreement because of a competing transaction; (b) Paramount's stockholders did not approve the merger; or (c) the Paramount Board recommended a competing transaction.

"The third and most significant deterrent device was the Stock Option Agreement, which granted to Viacom an option to purchase approximately 19.9 percent (23,699,000 shares) of Paramount's outstanding common stock at $69.14 per share if any of the triggering events for the Termination Fee occurred. In addition to the customary terms that are normally associated with a stock option, the Stock Option Agreement contained two provisions that were both unusual and highly beneficial to Viacom: (a) Viacom was permitted to pay for the shares with a senior subordinated note of questionable marketability instead of cash, thereby avoiding the need to raise the $1.6 billion purchase price (the 'Note Feature'); and (b) Viacom could elect to require Paramount to pay Viacom in cash a sum equal to the difference between the purchase price and the market price of Paramount's stock (the 'Put Feature'). Because the Stock Option Agreement was not 'capped' to limit its maximum dollar value, it had the potential to reach (and in this case did reach) unreasonable levels.

"Those defensive measures, coupled with the sale of control and subsequent disparate treatment of competing bidders, implicated the judicial scrutiny of Unocal, Revlon, Macmillan, and their progeny. We conclude that the Paramount directors' process was not reasonable, and the result achieved for the stockholders was not reasonable under the circumstances.

"When entering into the Original Merger Agreement, and thereafter, the Paramount Board clearly gave insufficient attention to the potential consequences of the defensive measures demanded by Viacom. The Stock Option Agreement had a number of unusual and potentially 'draconian' provisions, including the Note Feature and the Put Feature. Furthermore, the Termination Fee, whether or not unreasonable by itself, clearly made Paramount less attractive to other bidders, when coupled with the Stock Option Agreement. Finally, the No-Shop Provision inhibited the Paramount Board's ability to negotiate with other potential bidders, particularly QVC which had already expressed an interest in Paramount."

QUESTIONS

1. How did the "no-shop" provision prevent the Paramount board from considering a higher bid from QVC? What were the conditions to such permission? Were they preclusive or coercive?

2. If Paramount entered into an agreement with QVC at a better price, what would prevent Viacom from engaging in short-term borrowing to

exercise its option on Paramount stock, which it would then be able to sell at the higher price bid by QVC? How does this differ from being able to settle the value of the options (the difference between the exercise price and the successful QVC bid) for cash?

3.   The court refers to the combination of "the Note Feature and the Put Feature [and] the Termination Fee, whether or not unreasonable by itself" as clearly making Paramount less attractive to other bidders. . . ." Compare this with Unitrin, where a combination of defenses was judged individually. Does it matter that the court rejects the Time-Paramount doctrine here, thus moving the case to the Revlon mode of review?

PROBLEM

You represent a private investment banking firm that holds a 20% stake in a small publicly held outdoor furniture manufacturer. The Manufacturer is debt free, and holds a dominant position in its market because it makes a superior quality product. Because it is a "high end" manufacturer, it is relatively immune from recessions, because buyers of this type of furniture are less affected by economic downturns than the general population. Consequently, even in today's market, this company represents a prospect for a relatively leveraged acquisition.

The company's stock has not done particularly well, although sales and earnings have grown steadily over the past five years. Your client believes that earnings will continue to grow, and that the company represents a better value than the market has recognized. Consequently, your client wishes to propose a leveraged buyout. The company's stock is currently trading at $8.00. The CEO of your client has indicated that at $12.00 the client will be a buyer, but at $15 it will be a seller of its stock, so putting it in play with the offer is not entirely unattractive.

Your client will invest substantial funds in legal fees proposing and negotiating the acquisition, and in obtaining a loan commitment from a financial institution for the balance of the funds for the acquisition (since your client already owns 20% of the equity, this will be enough equity to allow debt financing for the entire purchase price). Because of this investment, your client wants to make its original proposal, of a buyout of all other shareholders at $12 through a cash merger, in the form of a draft letter of intent that provides for a break-up fee of 2% of the purchase price in the event that the company is sold to another, or, in the alternative, 10% of any sale price in excess of $8.00, whichever is greater. The letter of intent will contain customary language, setting out the parties' intent to engage in a cash merger at $12, and that the company's board of directors will use its best efforts to secure shareholder approval, subject to its fiduciary duties.

The company has not been looking for a buyer, and the board has done no shopping. In order to put pressure on the board to accept the letter of intent, your client asks you to prepare a brief memorandum arguing why the board should sign the letter as drawn.

1. What arguments can you provide?

2. Can you assure the board that it will not be in breach of its fiduciary duties if it signs such a letter of intent?

3. Can you argue, using the reasoning of Ayres and Fraidin & Hanson, that this arrangement won't be a deal killer if another bidder values the company at a slightly higher price?

———————

Read Del. G.C.L. § 146 (formerly § 251(c)) and § 203.

Omnicare, Inc. v. NCS Healthcare, Inc.

818 A.2d 914 (Del., 2003).

■ HOLLAND, JUSTICE, for the majority:

[This proceeding was brought by Omnicare to invalidate a merger agreement between NCS and Genesis on fiduciary duty grounds. Omnicare also challenges Voting Agreements between Genesis and Jon H. Outcalt and Kevin B. Shaw, two major NCS stockholders, who collectively own over 65% of the voting power of NCS stock. The Voting Agreements irrevocably commit these stockholders to vote for the merger.

NCS Healthcare is a Delaware corporation engaged in providing pharmacy services to long-term care institutions, including nursing facilities. At the time of the events that resulted in this litigation, NCS had 18,461,599 shares of Class A common stock and 5,255,210 shares of Class B common stock outstanding. The only difference was that the Class A shares had one vote per share, while the Class B shares had ten votes. Upon transfer of a B share, it automatically converted into a Class A share.]

The defendant Jon H. Outcalt is Chairman of the NCS board of directors. Outcalt owns 202,063 shares of NCS Class A common stock and 3,476,086 shares of Class B common stock. The defendant Kevin B. Shaw is President, CEO and a director of NCS. At the time the merger agreement at issue in this dispute was executed with Genesis, Shaw owned 28,905 shares of NCS Class A common stock and 1,141,134 shares of Class B common stock.

The NCS board has two other members, defendants Boake A. Sells and Richard L. Osborne. Sells is a graduate of the Harvard Business School. He was Chairman and CEO at Revco Drugstores in Cleveland, Ohio from 1987 to 1992, when he was replaced by new owners. Sells currently sits on the boards of both public and private companies. Osborne is a full-time professor at the Weatherhead School of Management at Case Western Reserve University. He has been at the university for over thirty years. Osborne currently sits on at least seven corporate boards other than NCS.

* * *

Beginning in late 1999, changes in the timing and level of reimbursements by government and third-party providers adversely affected market conditions in the health care industry. As a result, NCS began to experience greater difficulty in collecting accounts receivables, which led to a precipitous decline in the market value of its stock. NCS common shares that traded above $20 in January 1999 were worth as little as $5 at the end of that year. By early 2001, NCS was in default on approximately $350 million in debt, including $206 million in senior bank debt and $102 million of its 5 3/4 Convertible Subordinated Debentures (the "Notes"). After these defaults, NCS common stock traded in a range of $0.09 to $0.50 per share until days before the announcement of the transaction at issue in this case.

NCS began to explore strategic alternatives that might address the problems it was confronting. As part of this effort, in February 2000, NCS retained UBS Warburg, L.L.C. to identify potential acquirers and possible equity investors. UBS Warburg contacted over fifty different entities to solicit their interest in a variety of transactions with NCS. UBS Warburg had marginal success in its efforts. By October 2000, NCS had only received one non-binding indication of interest valued at $190 million, substantially less than the face value of NCS's senior debt. This proposal was reduced by 20% after the offeror conducted its due diligence review.

NCS Financial Deterioration

In December 2000, NCS terminated its relationship with UBS Warburg and retained Brown, Gibbons, Lang & Company as its exclusive financial advisor. During this period, NCS's financial condition continued to deteriorate. In April 2001, NCS received a formal notice of default and acceleration from the trustee for holders of the Notes. As NCS's financial condition worsened, the Noteholders formed a committee to represent their financial interests (the "Ad Hoc Committee"). At about that time, NCS began discussions with various investor groups regarding a restructuring in a "pre-packaged" bankruptcy. NCS did not receive any proposal that it believed provided adequate consideration for its stakeholders. At that time, full recovery for NCS's creditors was a remote prospect, and any recovery for NCS stockholders seemed impossible.

Omnicare's Initial Negotiations

In the summer of 2001, NCS invited Omnicare, Inc. to begin discussions with Brown Gibbons regarding a possible transaction. On July 20, Joel Gemunder, Omnicare's President and CEO, sent Shaw a written proposal to acquire NCS in a bankruptcy sale under Section 363 of the Bankruptcy Code. This proposal was for $225 million subject to satisfactory completion of due diligence. NCS asked Omnicare to execute a confidentiality agreement so that more detailed discussions could take place.[3]

In August 2001, Omnicare increased its bid to $270 million, but still proposed to structure the deal as an asset sale in bankruptcy. Even at $270 million, Omnicare's proposal was substantially lower than the face value of NCS's outstanding debt. It would have provided only a small recovery for Omnicare's Noteholders and no recovery for its stockholders. In October 2001, NCS sent Glen Pollack of Brown Gibbons to meet with Omnicare's financial advisor, Merrill Lynch, to discuss Omnicare's interest in NCS. Omnicare responded that it was not interested in any transaction other than an asset sale in bankruptcy.

There was no further contact between Omnicare and NCS between November 2001 and January 2002. Instead, Omnicare began secret discussions with Judy K. Mencher, a representative of the Ad Hoc Committee. In these discussions, Omnicare continued to pursue a transaction structured as a sale of assets in bankruptcy. In February 2002, the Ad Hoc Committee notified the NCS board that Omnicare had proposed an asset sale in bankruptcy for $313,750,000[, which was still less than the face value of NCS's debt and provided nothing for its stockholders].

NCS Independent Board Committee

In January 2002, Genesis was contacted by members of the Ad Hoc Committee concerning a possible transaction with NCS. Genesis executed NCS's standard confidentiality agreement and began a due diligence review. Genesis had recently emerged from bankruptcy because, like NCS, it was suffering from dwindling government reimbursements.

Genesis previously lost a bidding war to Omnicare in a different transaction. This led to bitter feelings between the principals of both companies. More importantly, this bitter experience for Genesis led to its insistence on exclusivity agreements and lock-ups in any potential transaction with NCS.

[In March 2002 the NCS board formed a special committee, consisting of Sells and Osborne. The Independent Committee met for the first time on May 14, 2002, and agreed with the suggestion of a Brown Gibbons representative, Pollack, that NCS seek a "stalking horse merger partner" to obtain the highest possible value. Later in May 2002 representatives of Brown Gibbons and Sells met with representatives of Genesis. Genesis made it clear that if it were to engage in negotiations with NCS, it would not do so as a "stalking horse" that would later be

---

[3]   Discovery had revealed that, at the same time, Omnicare was attempting to lure away NCS's customers through what it characterized as the "NCS Blitz." The "NCS Blitz" was an effort by Omnicare to target NCS's customers. Omnicare has engaged in an "NCS Blitz" a number of times, most recently while NCS and Omnicare were in discussions in July and August 2001.

outbid. Thus Genesis "wanted a degree of certainty that to the extent [it] was willing to pursue a negotiated merger agreement . . . , [it] would be able to consummate the transaction [it] negotiated and executed." Genesis then offered full payment of the NCS senior debt, full assumption of trade credit obligations, an exchange offer for the NCS Notes for a combination of cash and Genesis common stock equal to the par value of the NCS Notes (but without payment of accrued interest), and $20 million for the NCS common stock. After further negotiations, Genesis added another $4 million worth of Genesis common stock for the NCS stockholders, for a total of $24 million.

At this time, June 26, Genesis demanded that NCS enter into an exclusivity arrangement with Genesis. On July 2 the Independent Committee met and decided to propose that it would grant an exclusivity agreement only in exchange for improved terms, which included repayment of the Notes in cash and Genesis stock. At its July 3 meeting the Independent Committee was told that Genesis wanted a complete lockup that would preclude a higher bid from Omnicare, which had previously waited until the last minute to outbid Genesis in another acquisition.]

After NCS executed the exclusivity agreement, Genesis provided NCS with a draft merger agreement, a draft Noteholders' support agreement, and draft voting agreements for Outcalt and Shaw, who together held a majority of the voting power of the NCS common stock. [The merger agreement between Genesis and NCS contained a provision authorized by Section 251(c) (now § 146) of Delaware's corporation law. It required that the Genesis agreement be placed before the corporation's stockholders for a vote, even if the NCS board of directors no longer recommended it. At the insistence of Genesis, the NCS board also agreed to omit any effective fiduciary clause from the merger agreement.] Genesis and NCS negotiated the terms of the merger agreement over the next three weeks. During those negotiations, the Independent Committee and the Ad Hoc Committee persuaded Genesis to improve the terms of its merger.

The parties were still negotiating by July 19, and the exclusivity period was automatically extended to July 26. At that point, NCS and Genesis were close to executing a merger agreement and related voting agreements. Genesis proposed a short extension of the exclusivity agreement so a deal could be finalized. On the morning of July 26, 2002, the Independent Committee authorized an extension of the exclusivity period through July 31.

Omnicare Proposes Negotiations

By late July 2002, Omnicare came to believe that NCS was negotiating a transaction, possibly with Genesis or another of Omnicare's competitors, that would potentially present a competitive threat to Omnicare. Omnicare also came to believe, in light of a run-up in the price of NCS common stock, that whatever transaction NCS was negotiating probably included a payment for its stock. Thus, the Omnicare board of directors met on the morning of July 26 and, on the recommendation of its management, authorized a proposal to acquire NCS that did not involve a sale of assets in bankruptcy.

On the afternoon of July 26, 2002, Omnicare faxed to NCS a letter outlining a proposed acquisition. The letter suggested a transaction in which Omnicare would retire NCS's senior and subordinated debt at par plus accrued interest, and pay the NCS stockholders $3 cash for their shares. Omnicare's proposal, however, was expressly conditioned on negotiating a merger agreement, obtaining certain third party consents, and completing its due diligence. [Mencher, a member of the Ad Hoc Committee of Noteholders, told an Omnicare representative that it was unlikely to succeed with its due diligence condition, but Omnicare refused to drop this condition at the time. Omnicare sent messages to NCS requesting negotiations, but the exclusivity agreement prevented NCS officials from returning those calls. The Independent Committee met and decided that discussions with Omnicare created an unacceptable risk that Genesis would terminate negotiations. Nevertheless, the Independent Committee resolved to negotiate with Genesis for improved terms.]

Genesis Merger Agreement and Voting Agreements

Genesis responded to the NCS request to improve its offer as a result of the Omnicare fax the next day. On July 27, Genesis proposed substantially improved terms. First, it proposed to retire the Notes in accordance with the terms of the indenture, thus eliminating the need for Noteholders to consent to the transaction. This change involved paying all accrued interest plus a small redemption premium. Second, Genesis increased the exchange ratio for NCS common stock to one-tenth of a Genesis common share for each NCS common share, an 80% increase. Third, it agreed to lower the proposed termination fee in the merger agreement from $10 million to $6 million. In return for these concessions, Genesis stipulated that the transaction had to be approved by midnight the next day, July 28, or else Genesis would terminate discussions and withdraw its offer.

The Independent Committee and the NCS board both scheduled meetings for July 28. The committee met first. Although that meeting lasted less than an hour, the Court of Chancery determined the minutes reflect that the directors were fully informed of all material facts relating to the proposed transaction. After concluding that Genesis was sincere in establishing the midnight deadline, the committee voted unanimously to recommend the transaction to the full board.

The full board met thereafter. After receiving similar reports and advice from its legal and financial advisors, the board concluded that "balancing the potential loss of the Genesis deal against the uncertainty of Omnicare's letter, results in the conclusion that the only reasonable alternative for the Board of Directors is to approve the Genesis transaction." The board first voted to authorize the voting agreements with Outcalt and Shaw, for purposes of Section 203 of the Delaware General Corporation Law ("DGCL"). The board was advised by its legal counsel that "under the terms of the merger agreement and because NCS shareholders representing in excess of 50% of the outstanding voting power would be *required* by Genesis to enter into stockholder voting agreements contemporaneously with the signing of the merger agreement, and would agree to vote their shares in favor of the merger agreement, shareholder approval of the merger would be assured even if the NCS Board were to withdraw or change its recommendation. *These facts would prevent NCS from engaging in any alternative or superior transaction in the future.*" (emphasis added).

After listening to a *summary* of the merger terms, the board then resolved that the merger agreement and the transactions contemplated thereby were advisable and fair and in the best interests of all the NCS stakeholders. The NCS board further resolved to recommend the transactions to the stockholders for their approval and adoption. A definitive merger agreement between NCS and Genesis and the stockholder voting agreements were executed later that day. The Court of Chancery held that it was not a *per se* breach of fiduciary duty that the NCS board never read the NCS/Genesis merger agreement word for word.[4]

[Hours after the NCS/Genesis transaction documents were executed, on August 1, Omnicare announced that it would launch a cash tender offer for NCS shares at $3.50 per share, subject to completion of due diligence. Because the NCS board was unable to determine that this was a "superior proposal," it felt constrained not to negotiate with Omnicare. It sought, and apparently did not receive, permission from Genesis to negotiate with Omnicare. On October 6, Omnicare eliminated its due diligence condition and irrevocably committed to purchase NCS shares at $3.50 cash. On October 21, NCS' financial advisor withdrew its fairness opinion about the Genesis merger, and the NCS board withdrew its recommendation of the merger to its shareholders.

In a filing with the Securities Exchange Commission the NCS board explained that while it had withdrawn its endorsement of the Genesis merger, the success of that merger had already been predetermined by the commitment to hold a shareholders' meeting (the Section 251(c) commitment) and the proxies delivered by Outcalt and Shaw to Genesis allowing it to vote to approve the merger.]

---

[4]   See, e.g., Smith v. Van Gorkom, 488 A.2d 858, 883, n. 25 (Del. 1985).

LEGAL ANALYSIS

Business Judgment or Enhanced Scrutiny

The prior decisions of this Court have identified the circumstances where board action must be subjected to enhanced judicial scrutiny before the presumptive protection of the business judgment rule can be invoked. One of those circumstances was described in Unocal: when a board adopts defensive measures in response to a hostile takeover proposal that the board reasonably determines is a threat to corporate policy and effectiveness. In Moran v. Household, we explained why a Unocal analysis also was applied to the adoption of a stockholder's rights plan, even in the absence of an immediate threat. Other circumstances requiring enhanced judicial scrutiny give rise to what are known as Revlon duties, such as when the board enters into a merger transaction that will cause a change in corporate control, initiates an active bidding process seeking to sell the corporation, or makes a break up of the corporate entity inevitable.[17]

Merger Decision Review Standard

* * *

The Court of Chancery concluded that, because the stock-for-stock merger between Genesis and NCS did not result in a change of control, the NCS directors' duties under Revlon were not triggered by the decision to merge with Genesis.* The Court of Chancery also recognized, however, that Revlon duties are imposed "when a corporation initiates an active bidding process seeking to sell itself." The Court of Chancery then concluded, alternatively, that Revlon duties had not been triggered because NCS did not start an active bidding process, and the NCS board "abandoned" its efforts to sell the company when it entered into an exclusivity agreement with Genesis.

After concluding that the Revlon standard of enhanced judicial review was completely inapplicable, the Court of Chancery then held that it would examine the decision of the NCS board of directors to approve the Genesis merger pursuant to the business judgment rule standard. After completing its business judgment rule review, the Court of Chancery held that the NCS board of directors had not breached their duty of care by entering into the exclusivity and merger agreements with Genesis. The Court of Chancery also held, however, that "even applying the more exacting Revlon standard, the directors acted in conformity with their fiduciary duties in seeking to achieve the highest and best transaction that was reasonably available to [the stockholders]."

---

[17] Paramount Communications Inc. v. QVC Network Inc., 637 A.2d at 47; Revlon, Inc. v. MacAndrews & Forbes Holdings, Inc., 506 A.2d 173, 182 (Del. 1986).

* The Vice Chancellor noted that in this case NCS public shareholders would exit a company where Outcalt and Shaw held control through ownership of their Class B shares, to a situation where Genesis had no controlling shareholder or group.—Ed.

* * *

The Court of Chancery's decision to review the NCS board's decision to merge with Genesis under the business judgment rule rather than the enhanced scrutiny standard of Revlon is not outcome determinative for the purposes of deciding this appeal. We have assumed arguendo that the business judgment rule applied to the decision by the NCS board to merge with Genesis.[23] We have also assumed arguendo that the NCS board exercised due care when it: abandoned the Independent Committee's recommendation to pursue a stalking horse strategy, without even trying to implement it; executed an exclusivity agreement with Genesis; acceded to Genesis' twenty-four hour ultimatum for making a final merger decision; and executed a merger agreement that was summarized but never completely read by the NCS board of directors.[24]

Deal Protection Devices Require Enhanced Scrutiny

The dispositive issues in this appeal involve the defensive devices that protected the Genesis merger agreement. The Delaware corporation statute provides that the board's management decision to enter into and recommend a merger transaction can become final only when ownership action is taken by a vote of the stockholders. Thus, the Delaware corporation law expressly provides for a balance of power between boards and stockholders which makes merger transactions a shared enterprise and ownership decision. Consequently, a board of directors' decision to adopt defensive devices to protect a merger agreement may implicate the stockholders' right to effectively vote contrary to the initial recommendation of the board in favor of the transaction.[25]

It is well established that conflicts of interest arise when a board of directors acts to prevent stockholders from effectively exercising their right to vote contrary to the will of the board. The "omnipresent specter" of such conflict may be present whenever a board adopts defensive devices to protect a merger agreement. The stockholders' ability to effectively reject a merger agreement is likely to bear an inversely proportionate relationship to the structural and economic devices that the board has approved to protect the transaction.

In Paramount v. Time, the original merger agreement between Time and Warner did not constitute a "change of control." The plaintiffs in Paramount v. Time argued that, although the original Time and Warner merger agreement did not involve a change of control, the use of a lock-up, no-shop clause, and "dry-up" provisions violated the Time board's Revlon duties. This Court held that "[t]he adoption of structural safety

---

[23] Paramount Communications, Inc. v. Time Inc., 571 A.2d 1140, 1152 (Del. 1989).

[24] But see Smith v. Van Gorkom, 488 A.2d 858 (Del. 1985).

[25] See MM Companies v. Liquid Audio, Inc., 813 A.2d 1118, 1120 (Del. 2003).

devices alone does not trigger Revlon. Rather, as the Chancellor stated, *such devices are properly subject to a* Unocal *analysis*."

In footnote 15 of Paramount v. Time, we stated that legality of the structural safety devices adopted to protect the original merger agreement between Time and Warner were not a central issue on appeal. That is because the issue on appeal involved the "Time's board [decision] to recast its consolidation with Warner into an outright cash and securities acquisition of Warner by Time." Nevertheless, we determined that there was substantial evidence on the record to support the conclusions reached by the Chancellor in applying a Unocal analysis to each of the structural devices contained in the original merger agreement between Time and Warner.

There are inherent conflicts between a board's interest in protecting a merger transaction it has approved, the stockholders' statutory right to make the final decision to either approve or not approve a merger, and the board's continuing responsibility to effectively exercise its fiduciary duties at all times after the merger agreement is executed. These competing considerations require a threshold determination that board-approved defensive devices protecting a merger transaction are within the limitations of its statutory authority and consistent with the directors' fiduciary duties. Accordingly, in Paramount v. Time, we held that the business judgment rule applied to the Time board's original decision to merge with Warner. We further held, however, that defensive devices adopted by the board to protect the original merger transaction must withstand enhanced judicial scrutiny under the Unocal standard of review, even when that merger transaction does not result in a change of control.[34]

Enhanced Scrutiny Generally

* * *

A board's decision to protect its decision to enter a merger agreement with defensive devices against uninvited competing transactions that may emerge is analogous to a board's decision to protect against dangers to corporate policy and effectiveness when it adopts defensive measures in a hostile takeover contest. In applying Unocal's enhanced judicial scrutiny in assessing a challenge to defensive actions taken by a target corporation's board of directors in a takeover context, this Court held that the board "does not have unbridled discretion to defeat perceived threats by any draconian means available."[46] Similarly, just as a board's statutory power with regard to a merger decision is not absolute, a board does not have unbridled discretion to defeat any perceived threat to a merger by protecting it with any draconian means available.

---

[34]   [571 A.2d] at 1151–55; Unocal Corp. v. Mesa Petroleum Co., 493 A.2d 946 (Del. 1985); see In re Santa Fe Pacific Corp. Shareholder Litigation, 669 A.2d 59 (Del. 1995).

[46]   Unocal Corp. v. Mesa Petroleum Co., 493 A.2d at 955.

Since Unocal, "this Court has consistently recognized that defensive measures which are either preclusive or coercive are included within the common law definition of draconian."[47] In applying enhanced judicial scrutiny to defensive actions under Unocal, a court must "evaluate the board's overall response, including the justification for each contested defensive measure, and the results achieved thereby." If a "board's defensive actions are inextricably related, the principles of Unocal require that such actions be scrutinized collectively as a unitary response to the perceived threat."

Therefore, in applying enhanced judicial scrutiny to defensive devices designed to protect a merger agreement, a court must first determine that those measures are not preclusive or coercive *before* its focus shifts to the "range of reasonableness" in making a proportionality determination. If the trial court determines that the defensive devices protecting a merger are not preclusive or coercive, the proportionality paradigm of Unocal is applicable. The board must demonstrate that it has reasonable grounds for believing that a danger to the corporation and its stockholders exists if the merger transaction is not consummated. That burden is satisfied "by showing good faith and reasonable investigation." Such proof is materially enhanced if it is approved by a board comprised of a majority of outside directors or by an independent committee.

When the focus of judicial scrutiny shifts to the range of reasonableness, Unocal requires that any defensive devices must be proportionate to the perceived threat to the corporation and its stockholders if the merger transaction is not consummated. Defensive devices taken to protect a merger agreement executed by a board of directors are intended to give that agreement an advantage over any subsequent transactions that materialize before the merger is approved by the stockholders and consummated. This is analogous to the favored treatment that a board of directors may properly give to encourage an initial bidder when it discharges its fiduciary duties under Revlon.

* * *

The latitude a board will have in either maintaining or using the defensive devices it has adopted to protect the merger it approved will vary according to the degree of benefit or detriment to the stockholders' interests that is presented by the value or terms of the subsequent competing transaction.

* * *

Deal Protection Devices

Defensive devices, as that term is used in this opinion, is a synonym for what are frequently referred to as "deal protection devices." Both terms are used interchangeably to describe any measure or combination

---

[47] Unitrin, Inc. v. Am. Gen. Corp., 651 A.2d at 1387.

of measures that are intended to protect the consummation of a merger transaction. Defensive devices can be economic, structural, or both.

Deal protection devices need not all be in the merger agreement itself. In this case, for example, the Section 251(c) provision in the merger agreement was combined with the separate voting agreements to provide a structural defense for the Genesis merger agreement against any subsequent superior transaction. Genesis made the NCS board's defense of its transaction absolute by insisting on the omission of any effective fiduciary out clause in the NCS merger agreement.

Genesis argues that stockholder voting agreements cannot be construed as deal protection devices taken by a board of directors because stockholders are entitled to vote in their own interest. Genesis cites Williams v. Geier and Stroud v. Grace for the proposition that voting agreements are not subject to the Unocal standard of review. Neither of those cases, however, holds that the operative effect of a voting agreement must be disregarded *per se* when a Unocal analysis is applied to a comprehensive and combined merger defense plan.

In this case, the stockholder voting agreements were inextricably intertwined with the defensive aspects of the Genesis merger agreement. In fact, the voting agreements with Shaw and Outcalt were the linchpin of Genesis' proposed tripartite defense. Therefore, Genesis made the execution of those voting agreements a non-negotiable condition precedent to its execution of the merger agreement. In the case before us, the Court of Chancery held that the acts which locked-up the Genesis transaction were the Section 251(c) provision and "the execution of the *voting agreement* by Outcalt and Shaw."

With the assurance that Outcalt and Shaw would irrevocably agree to exercise their majority voting power in favor of its transaction, Genesis insisted that the merger agreement reflect the other two aspects of its concerted defense, i. e., the inclusion of a Section 251(c) provision and the omission of any effective fiduciary out clause. Those dual aspects of the merger agreement would not have provided Genesis with a complete defense in the absence of the voting agreements with Shaw and Outcalt.

These Deal Protection Devices Unenforceable

In this case, the Court of Chancery correctly held that the NCS directors' decision to adopt defensive devices to *completely* "lock up" the Genesis merger mandated "special scrutiny" under the two-part test set forth in Unocal. That conclusion is consistent with our holding in Paramount v. Time that "safety devices" adopted to protect a transaction that did not result in a change of control are subject to enhanced judicial scrutiny under a Unocal analysis. The record does not, however, support the Court of Chancery's conclusion that the defensive devices adopted by the NCS board to protect the Genesis merger were reasonable and proportionate to the threat that NCS perceived from the potential loss of the Genesis transaction.

Pursuant to the judicial scrutiny required under Unocal's two-stage analysis, the NCS directors must first demonstrate "that they had reasonable grounds for believing that a danger to corporate policy and effectiveness existed. . . ." To satisfy that burden, the NCS directors are required to show they acted in good faith after conducting a reasonable investigation. The threat identified by the NCS board was the possibility of losing the Genesis offer and being left with no comparable alternative transaction.

The second stage of the Unocal test requires the NCS directors to demonstrate that their defensive response was "reasonable in relation to the threat posed." This inquiry involves a two-step analysis. The NCS directors must first establish that the merger deal protection devices adopted in response to the threat were not "coercive" or "preclusive," and then demonstrate that their response was within a "range of reasonable responses" to the threat perceived. In Unitrin, we stated:

- A response is "coercive" if it is aimed at forcing upon stockholders a management-sponsored alternative to a hostile offer.

- A response is "preclusive" if it deprives stockholders of the right to receive all tender offers or precludes a bidder from seeking control by fundamentally restricting proxy contests or otherwise.

* * *

This Court enunciated the standard for determining stockholder coercion in the case of Williams v. Geier. A stockholder vote may be nullified by wrongful coercion "where the board or some other party takes actions which have the effect of causing the stockholders to vote in favor of the proposed transaction for some reason other than the merits of that transaction." In Brazen v. Bell Atlantic Corporation, we applied that test for stockholder coercion and held "that although the termination fee provision may have influenced the stockholder vote, there were 'no structurally or situationally coercive factors' that made an otherwise valid fee provision impermissibly coercive" under the facts presented.

In Brazen, we concluded "the determination of whether a particular stockholder vote has been robbed of its effectiveness by impermissible coercion depends on the facts of the case." In this case, the Court of Chancery did not expressly address the issue of "coercion" in its Unocal analysis. It did find as a fact, however, that NCS's public stockholders (who owned 80% of NCS and overwhelmingly supported Omnicare's offer) will be forced to accept the Genesis merger because of the structural defenses approved by the NCS board. Consequently, the record reflects that any stockholder vote would have been robbed of its effectiveness by the impermissible coercion that predetermined the outcome of the merger without regard to the merits of the Genesis transaction at the time the vote was scheduled to be taken. Deal protection devices that result in such coercion cannot withstand Unocal's enhanced judicial scrutiny standard of review because they are not within the range of reasonableness.

Although the minority stockholders were not forced to vote for the Genesis merger, they were required to accept it because it was *a fait accompli*. The record reflects that the defensive devices employed by the NCS board are preclusive and coercive in the sense that they accomplished *a fait accompli*. In this case, despite the fact that the NCS board has withdrawn its recommendation for the Genesis transaction and recommended its rejection by the stockholders, the deal protection devices approved by the NCS board operated in concert to have a preclusive and coercive effect. Those tripartite defensive measures—the Section 251(c) provision, the voting agreements, and the absence of an effective fiduciary out clause—made it "mathematically impossible" and "realistically unattainable" for the Omnicare transaction or any other proposal to succeed, no matter how superior the proposal.[72]

The deal protection devices adopted by the NCS board were designed to coerce the consummation of the Genesis merger and preclude the consideration of any superior transaction. The NCS directors' defensive devices are not within a reasonable range of responses to the perceived threat of losing the Genesis offer because they are preclusive and coercive. Accordingly, we hold that those deal protection devices are unenforceable.

Effective Fiduciary out Required

The defensive measures that protected the merger transaction are unenforceable not only because they are preclusive and coercive but, alternatively, they are unenforceable because they are invalid as they operate in this case. Given the specifically enforceable irrevocable voting agreements, the provision in the merger agreement requiring the board to submit the transaction for a stockholder vote and the omission of a fiduciary out clause in the merger agreement completely prevented the board from discharging its fiduciary responsibilities to the minority stockholders when Omnicare presented its superior transaction. "To the extent that a [merger] contract, or a provision thereof, purports to require a board to act or not act in such a fashion as to limit the exercise of fiduciary duties, it is invalid and unenforceable."[74]

In QVC, this Court recognized that "[w]hen a majority of a corporation's voting shares are acquired by a single person or entity, or

---

[72] See Unitrin, Inc. v. Am. Gen. Corp., 651 A.2d at 1388–89; see also Carmody v. Toll Bros., Inc., 723 A.2d 1180, 1195 (Del. Ch. 1998) (citations omitted).

[74] Paramount Communications Inc. v. QVC Network Inc., 637 A.2d 34, 51 (Del. 1993) (citation omitted). *Restatement (Second) of Contracts* § 193 explicitly provides that a "promise by a fiduciary to violate his fiduciary duty *or a promise that tends to induce such a violation is unenforceable on grounds of public policy.*" The comments to that section indicate that "[d]irectors and other officials of a corporation act in a fiduciary capacity and are subject to the rule stated in this Section." Restatement (Second) of Contracts § 193 (1981) (emphasis added).

by *a cohesive group acting together* [as in this case], there is a significant diminution in the voting power of those who thereby become minority stockholders." Therefore, we acknowledged that "[i]n the absence of devices protecting the minority stockholders, stockholder votes are likely to become mere formalities," where a cohesive group acting together to exercise majority voting powers have already decided the outcome. Consequently, we concluded that since the minority stockholders lost the power to influence corporate direction through the ballot, "minority stockholders must rely for protection solely on the fiduciary duties owed to them by the directors."

Under the circumstances presented in this case, where a cohesive group of stockholders with majority voting power was irrevocably committed to the merger transaction, "[e]ffective representation of the financial interests of the minority shareholders imposed upon the [NCS board] an affirmative responsibility to protect those minority shareholders' interests."[79] The NCS board could not abdicate its fiduciary duties to the minority by leaving it to the stockholders alone to approve or disapprove the merger agreement because two stockholders had already combined to establish a majority of the voting power that made the outcome of the stockholder vote a foregone conclusion.

The Court of Chancery noted that Section 251(c) of the Delaware General Corporation Law now permits boards to agree to submit a merger agreement for a stockholder vote, even if the Board later withdraws its support for that agreement and recommends that the stockholders reject it.[80] The Court of Chancery also noted that stockholder voting agreements are permitted by Delaware law. In refusing to certify this interlocutory appeal, the Court of Chancery stated "it is simply nonsensical to say that a board of directors abdicates its duties to manage the 'business and affairs' of a corporation under Section 141(a) of the DGCL by agreeing to the inclusion in a merger agreement of a term authorized by § 251(c) of the same statute."

Taking action that is otherwise legally possible, however, does not *ipso facto* comport with the fiduciary responsibilities of directors in all circumstances. The synopsis to the amendments that resulted in the enactment of Section 251(c) in the Delaware corporation law statute specifically provides: "the amendments are not intended to address the question of whether such a submission requirement is appropriate in any particular set of factual circumstances." Section 251 provisions, like the no-shop provision examined in QVC, are "presumptively valid in the

---

[79]   McMullin v. Beran, 765 A.2d 910, 920 (Del. 2000).

[80]   Section 251(c) was amended in 1998 to allow for the inclusion in a merger agreement of a term requiring that the agreement be put to a vote of stockholders whether or not their directors continue to recommend the transaction. Before this amendment, Section 251 was interpreted as precluding a stockholder vote if the board of directors, after approving the merger agreement but before the stockholder vote, decided no longer to recommend it. *See* Smith v. Van Gorkom, 488 A.2d 858, 887–88 (Del. 1985). [This was moved to § 146 in 2003.—Ed.]

abstract." Such provisions in a merger agreement may not, however, "validly define or limit the directors' fiduciary duties under Delaware law or prevent the [NCS] directors from carrying out their fiduciary duties under Delaware law."

Genesis admits that when the NCS board agreed to its merger conditions, the NCS board was seeking to assure that the NCS creditors were paid in full and that the NCS stockholders received the highest value available for their stock. In fact, Genesis defends its "bulletproof" merger agreement on that basis. We hold that the NCS board did not have authority to accede to the Genesis demand for an absolute "lock-up."

The directors of a Delaware corporation have a continuing obligation to discharge their fiduciary responsibilities, as future circumstances develop, after a merger agreement is announced. Genesis anticipated the likelihood of a superior offer after its merger agreement was announced and demanded defensive measures from the NCS board that *completely* protected its transaction. Instead of agreeing to the absolute defense of the Genesis merger from a superior offer, however, the NCS board was required to negotiate a fiduciary out clause to protect the NCS stockholders if the Genesis transaction became an inferior offer. By acceding to Genesis' ultimatum for complete protection *in futuro*, the NCS board disabled itself from exercising its own fiduciary obligations at a time when the board's own judgment is most important, i.e, receipt of a subsequent superior offer.

Any board has authority to give the proponent of a recommended merger agreement reasonable structural and economic defenses, incentives, and fair compensation if the transaction is not completed. To the extent that defensive measures are economic and reasonable, they may become an increased cost to the proponent of any subsequent transaction. Just as defensive measures cannot be draconian, however, they cannot limit or circumscribe the directors' fiduciary duties. Notwithstanding the corporation's insolvent condition, the NCS board had no authority to execute a merger agreement that subsequently prevented it from effectively discharging its ongoing fiduciary responsibilities.

* * *

The NCS board was required to contract for an effective fiduciary out clause to exercise its continuing fiduciary responsibilities to the minority stockholders.[88] The issues in this appeal do not involve the general validity of either stockholder voting agreements or the authority of directors to insert a Section 251(c) provision in a merger agreement. In

---

[88] See Paramount Communications Inc. v. QVC Network Inc., 637 A.2d at 42–43. Merger agreements involve an ownership decision and, therefore, cannot become final without stockholder approval. Other contracts do not require a fiduciary out clause because they involve business judgments that are within the exclusive province of the board of directors' power to manage the affairs of the corporation. See Grimes v. Donald, 673 A.2d 1207, 1214–15 (Del. 1996).

this case, the NCS board combined those two otherwise valid actions and caused them to operate in concert as an absolute lock up, in the absence of an effective fiduciary out clause in the Genesis merger agreement.

In the context of this preclusive and coercive lock up case, the protection of Genesis' contractual expectations must yield to the supervening responsibility of the directors to discharge their fiduciary duties on a continuing basis. The merger agreement and voting agreements, as they were combined to operate in concert in this case, are inconsistent with the NCS directors' fiduciary duties. To that extent, we hold that they are invalid and unenforceable.

Conclusion

With respect to the Fiduciary Duty Decision, the order of the Court of Chancery dated November 22, 2002, denying plaintiffs' application for a preliminary injunction is reversed. With respect to the Voting Agreements Decision, the order of the Court of Chancery dated October 29, 2002 is reversed to the extent that decision permits the implementation of the Voting Agreements contrary to this Court's ruling on the Fiduciary Duty claims.

* * *

■ VEASEY, CHIEF JUSTICE, with whom STEELE, JUSTICE, joins dissenting:

* * *

The process by which this merger agreement came about involved a joint decision by the controlling stockholders and the board of directors to secure what appeared to be the only value-enhancing transaction available for a company on the brink of bankruptcy. The Majority adopts a new rule of law that imposes a prohibition on the NCS board's ability to act in concert with controlling stockholders to lock up this merger. The Majority reaches this conclusion by analyzing the challenged deal protection measures as isolated board actions. The Majority concludes that the board owed a duty to the NCS minority stockholders to refrain from acceding to the Genesis demand for an irrevocable lock-up notwithstanding the compelling circumstances confronting the board and the board's disinterested, informed, good faith exercise of its business judgment.

Because we believe this Court must respect the reasoned judgment of the board of directors and give effect to the wishes of the controlling stockholders, we respectfully disagree with the Majority's reasoning that results in a holding that the confluence of board and stockholder action constitutes a breach of fiduciary duty. The essential fact that must always be remembered is that this agreement and the voting commitments of Outcalt and Shaw concluded a lengthy search and intense negotiation process in the context of insolvency and creditor pressure where no other viable bid had emerged. Accordingly, we endorse the Vice Chancellor's well-reasoned analysis that the NCS board's action before the hostile bid emerged was within the bounds of its fiduciary duties under these facts.

We share with the Majority and the independent NCS board of directors the motivation to serve carefully and in good faith the best interests of the corporate enterprise and, thereby, the stockholders of NCS. It is now known, of course, after the case is over, that the stockholders of NCS will receive substantially more by tendering their shares into the topping bid of Omnicare than they would have received in the Genesis merger, as a result of the post-agreement Omnicare bid and the injunctive relief ordered by the Majority of this Court. Our jurisprudence cannot, however, be seen as turning on such ex post felicitous results. Rather, the NCS board's good faith decision must be subject to a real-time review of the board action before the NCS-Genesis merger agreement was entered into.

An Analysis of the Process Leading to the Lock-up Reflects a Quintessential, Disinterested and Informed Board Decision Reached in Good Faith

The Majority has adopted the Vice Chancellor's findings and has assumed arguendo that the NCS board fulfilled its duties of care, loyalty, and good faith by entering into the Genesis merger agreement. Indeed, this conclusion is indisputable on this record. The problem is that the Majority has removed from their proper context the contractual merger protection provisions. The lock-ups here cannot be reviewed in a vacuum. A court should review the entire bidding process to determine whether the independent board's actions permitted the directors to inform themselves of their available options and whether they acted in good faith.[92]

Going into negotiations with Genesis, the NCS directors knew that, up until that time, NCS had found only one potential bidder, Omnicare. Omnicare had refused to buy NCS except at a fire sale price through an asset sale in bankruptcy. Omnicare's best proposal at that stage would not have paid off all creditors and would have provided nothing for stockholders. The Noteholders, represented by the Ad Hoc Committee, were willing to oblige Omnicare and force NCS into bankruptcy if Omnicare would pay in full the NCS debt. Through the NCS board's efforts, Genesis expressed interest that became increasingly attractive. Negotiations with Genesis led to an offer paying creditors off and conferring on NCS stockholders $24 million—an amount infinitely superior to the prior Omnicare proposals.

But there was, understandably, a sine qua non. In exchange for offering the NCS stockholders a return on their equity and creditor payment, Genesis demanded certainty that the merger would close. If the

---

[92] See, e. g., Malpiede v. Townson, 780 A.2d 1075, 1089 (Del. 2001) (concluding that the board made an informed decision to refrain from returning to a rival bidder to solicit another offer because the board conducted a "lengthy sale process" that spanned one year).

NCS board would not have acceded to the Section 251(c) provision, if Outcalt and Shaw had not agreed to the voting agreements and if NCS had insisted on a fiduciary out, there would have been no Genesis deal! Thus, the only value-enhancing transaction available would have disappeared. NCS knew that Omnicare had spoiled a Genesis acquisition in the past, and it is not disputed by the Majority that the NCS directors made a reasoned decision to accept as real the Genesis threat to walk away.[94]

When Omnicare submitted its conditional eleventh-hour bid, the NCS board had to weigh the economic terms of the proposal against the uncertainty of completing a deal with Omnicare. Importantly, because Omnicare's bid was conditioned on its satisfactorily completing its due diligence review of NCS, the NCS board saw this as a crippling condition, as did the Ad Hoc Committee. As a matter of business judgment, the risk of negotiating with Omnicare and losing Genesis at that point outweighed the possible benefits. The lock-up was indisputably a sine qua non to any deal with Genesis.

A lock-up permits a target board and a bidder to "exchange certainties." Certainty itself has value. The acquirer may pay a higher price for the target if the acquirer is assured consummation of the transaction. The target company also benefits from the certainty of completing a transaction with a bidder because losing an acquirer creates the perception that a target is damaged goods, thus reducing its value.

* * *

While the present case does not involve an attempt to hold on to only one interested bidder, the NCS board was equally concerned about "exchanging certainties" with Genesis. If the creditors decided to force NCS into bankruptcy, which could have happened at any time as NCS was unable to service its obligations, the stockholders would have received nothing. The NCS board also did not know if the NCS business prospects would have declined again, leaving NCS less attractive to other bidders, including Omnicare, which could have changed its mind and again insisted on an asset sale in bankruptcy.

Situations will arise where business realities demand a lock-up so that wealth-enhancing transactions may go forward. Accordingly, any bright-line rule prohibiting lock-ups could, in circumstances such as these, chill otherwise permissible conduct.

---

[94] In Citron v. Fairchild Camera & Instrument Corp., we noted that "whether the constraints are self-imposed or attributable to bargaining tactics of an adversary seeking a final resolution of a belabored process must be considered" in analyzing the target's decision to accept an ultimatum from a bidder. 569 A.2d 53, 67 (Del. 1989). Based on Genesis's prior dealings with Omnicare, NCS had good reason to take the Genesis ultimatum seriously.

Our Jurisprudence Does Not Compel This Court to Invalidate the Joint Action of the Board and the Controlling Stockholders

The Majority invalidates the NCS board's action by announcing a new rule that represents an extension of our jurisprudence. That new rule can be narrowly stated as follows: A merger agreement entered into after a market search, before any prospect of a topping bid has emerged, which locks up stockholder approval and does not contain a "fiduciary out" provision, is per se invalid when a later significant topping bid emerges. As we have noted, this bright-line, per se rule would apply regardless of (1) the circumstances leading up to the agreement and (2) the fact that stockholders who control voting power had irrevocably committed themselves, *as stockholders*, to vote for the merger. Narrowly stated, this new rule is a judicially-created "third rail" that now becomes one of the given "rules of the game," to be taken into account by the negotiators and drafters of merger agreements. In our view, this new rule is an unwise extension of existing precedent.

Although it is debatable whether Unocal applies—and we believe that the better rule in this situation is that the business judgment rule should apply[102]—we will, nevertheless, assume *arguendo*—as the Vice Chancellor did—that Unocal applies. Therefore, under Unocal the NCS directors had the burden of going forward with the evidence to show that there was a threat to corporate policy and effectiveness and that their actions were reasonable in response to that threat. The Vice Chancellor correctly found that they reasonably perceived the threat that NCS did not have a viable offer from Omnicare—or anyone else—to pay off its creditors, cure its insolvency and provide some payment to stockholders. The NCS board's actions—as the Vice Chancellor correctly held—were reasonable in relation to the threat because the Genesis deal was the "only game in town," the NCS directors got the best deal they could from Genesis and-but-for the emergence of Genesis on the scene—there would have been no viable deal.

* * *

In our view, the Majority misapplies the Unitrin concept of "coercive and preclusive" measures to preempt a proper proportionality balancing. Thus, the Majority asserts that "in applying *enhanced judicial scrutiny*

---

[102] The basis for the Unocal doctrine is the "omnipresent specter" of the board's self-interest to entrench itself in office. Unocal Corp. v. Mesa Petroleum Co., 493 A.2d 946, 954 (Del. 1985). NCS was not plagued with a specter of self-interest. Unlike the Unocal situation, a hostile offer did not arise here until *after* the market search and the locked-up deal with Genesis. The Unocal doctrine applies to unilateral board actions that are defensive and reactive in nature. Thus, a Unocal analysis was necessary in Paramount Communications v. Time Inc. because Time and Warner restructured their original transaction from a merger to an acquisition *in response* to the Paramount bid. 571 A.2d 1140, 1148 (Del. 1989). In Time, the original Time-Warner stock-for-stock merger, which this Court held was entitled to the presumption of the business judgment rule, was jettisoned by the parties in the face of Paramount's topping bid. *Id.* at 1152. The merger was replaced with a new transaction which was an all cash tender offer by Time to acquire 51 of the Warner stock. It was the revised agreement, not the original merger agreement, that was found to be "defense-motivated" and subject to Unocal. *Id.*

to *defensive devices* designed to protect a merger agreement, . . . a court must . . . determine that those measures are not preclusive or coercive. . . ." Here, the deal protection measures were not adopted unilaterally by the board to fend off an existing hostile offer that threatened the corporate policy and effectiveness of NCS.[105] They were adopted because Genesis—the "only game in town"—would not save NCS, its creditors and its stockholders without these provisions.

* * *

The very measures the Majority cites as "coercive" were approved by Shaw and Outcalt through the lens of their independent assessment of the merits of the transaction. The proper inquiry in this case is whether the NCS board had taken actions that "have the effect of causing the stockholders to vote in favor of the proposed transaction for some reason other than the merits of that transaction."[109] Like the termination fee upheld as a valid liquidated damages clause against a claim of coercion in Brazen v. Bell Atlantic Corp., the deal protection measures at issue here were "an integral part of the merits of the transaction" as the NCS board struggled to secure—and did secure—the only deal available.

Outcalt and Shaw were fully informed stockholders. As the NCS controlling stockholders, they made an informed choice to commit their voting power to the merger. The minority stockholders were deemed to know that when controlling stockholders have 65% of the vote they can approve a merger without the need for the minority votes. Moreover, to the extent a minority stockholder may have felt "coerced" to vote for the merger, which was already a *fait accompli*, it was a meaningless coercion—or no coercion at all—because the controlling votes, those of Outcalt and Shaw, were already "cast." Although the fact that the controlling votes were committed to the merger "precluded" an overriding vote against the merger by the Class A stockholders, the pejorative "preclusive" label applicable in a Unitrin fact situation has no application here. Therefore, there was no meaningful minority stockholder voting decision to coerce.

In applying Unocal scrutiny, we believe the Majority incorrectly preempted the proportionality inquiry. In our view, the proportionality inquiry must account for the reality that the contractual measures

---

[105] The Majority states that our decisions in Williams v. Geier and Stroud v. Grace do not hold that "the operative effect of a voting agreement must be disregarded *per se* when a Unocal analysis is applied to a comprehensive and combined merger defense plan." *Majority Opinion* at 46. In Stroud v. Grace, however, we noted that "The record clearly indicates, and [plaintiff] . . . concedes, that over 50 of the outstanding shares of . . . [the corporation] are under the direct control of [the defendants]. . . . These directors controlled the corporation in fact and law. *This obviates any threat contemplated by* Unocal. . . ." 606 A.2d 75, 83 (Del. 1992) (emphasis supplied). According to Stroud, then, Shaw's and Outcalt's decision to enter into the voting agreements should not be subject to a Unocal analysis because they controlled the corporation "in fact and law." *Id.* Far from a breach of duty, the joint action of the stockholders and directors here represents "the highest and best form of corporate democracy." Williams v. Geier, 671 A.2d 1368, 1381 (Del. 1996).

[109] Geier, 671 A.2d at 1382–83 (citations omitted).

protecting this merger agreement were necessary to obtain the Genesis deal. The Majority has not demonstrated that the director action was a disproportionate response to the threat posed. Indeed, it is clear to us that the board action to negotiate the best deal reasonably available with the only viable merger partner (Genesis) who could satisfy the creditors and benefit the stockholders, was reasonable in relation to the threat, by any practical yardstick.

An Absolute Lock-up is Not a Per Se Violation of Fiduciary Duty

We respectfully disagree with the Majority's conclusion that the NCS board breached its fiduciary duties to the Class A stockholders by failing to negotiate a "fiduciary out" in the Genesis merger agreement. What is the practical import of a "fiduciary out?" It is a contractual provision, articulated in a manner to be negotiated, that would permit the board of the corporation being acquired to exit without breaching the merger agreement in the event of a superior offer.

In this case, Genesis made it abundantly clear early on that it was willing to negotiate a deal with NCS but only on the condition that it would not be a "stalking horse." Thus, it wanted to be certain that a third party could not use its deal with NCS as a floor against which to begin a bidding war. As a result of this negotiating position, a "fiduciary out" was not acceptable to Genesis. The Majority Opinion holds that such a negotiating position, if implemented in the agreement, is invalid per se where there is an absolute lock-up. We know of no authority in our jurisprudence supporting this new rule, and we believe it is unwise and unwarranted. * * *

■ STEELE, JUSTICE, dissenting:

* * *

In my opinion, Delaware law mandates deference under the business judgment rule to a board of directors' decision that is free from self interest, made with due care and in good faith.

* * *

Importantly, Smith v. Van Gorkom, correctly casts the focus on any court review of board action challenged for alleged breach of the fiduciary duty of care "only upon the basis of the information then reasonably available to the directors and relevant to their decision. . . ." Though criticized particularly for the imposition of personal liability on directors for a breach of the duty of care, Van Gorkom still stands for the importance of recognizing the limited circumstances for court intervention and the importance of focusing on the timing of the decision attacked.

* * *

In the factual context of this case, the NCS board had thoroughly canvassed the market in an attempt to find an acquirer, save the company, repay creditors and provide some financial benefit to stockholders. They did so in the face of silence, tepid interest to outright hostility from Omnicare. The only *bona fide*, credible merger partner NCS could find during an exhaustive process was Genesis, a company that had experienced less than desirable relations with Omnicare in the past. Small wonder NCS' only viable merger partner made demands *and concessions* to acquire contract terms that enhanced assurance that the merger would close. The NCS board agreed to lock up the merger with contractual protection provisions in order to avoid the prospect of Genesis walking away from the deal leaving NCS in the woefully undesirable position of negotiating with a company that had worked for months against NCS' interests by negotiating with NCS' creditors. Those negotiations suggested no regard for NCS' stockholders' interests, and held out only the hope of structuring a purchase of NCS in a bankruptcy environment.

The contract terms that NCS' board agreed to included no insidious, camouflaged side deals for the directors or the majority stockholders nor transparent provisions for entrenchment or control premiums. At the time the NCS board and the majority stockholders agreed to a voting lockup, the terms were the best reasonably available for all the stockholders, balanced against a genuine risk of no deal at all. The cost benefit analysis entered into by an independent committee of the board, approved by the full board and independently agreed to by the majority stockholders cannot be second guessed by courts with no business expertise that would qualify them to substitute their judgment for that of a careful, selfless board or for majority stockholders who had the most significant economic stake in the outcome.

We should not encourage proscriptive rules that invalidate or render unenforceable precommitment strategies negotiated between two parties to a contract who will presumably, in the absence of conflicted interest, bargain intensely over every meaningful provision of a contract after a careful cost benefit analysis. Where could this plain common sense approach be more wisely invoked than where a board, free of conflict, fully informed, supported by the equally conflict-free holders of the largest economic interest in the transaction, reaches the conclusion that a voting lockup strategy is the best course to obtain the most benefit for all stockholders?

* * *

Delaware corporate citizens now face the prospect that in *every* circumstance, boards must obtain the highest price, even if that requires breaching a contract entered into at a time when no one could have reasonably foreseen a truly "Superior Proposal." The majority's proscriptive rule limits the scope of a board's cost benefit analysis by taking the bargaining chip of foregoing a fiduciary out "off the table" in all circumstances. For that new principle to arise from the context of this case, when Omnicare, after striving to buy NCS on the cheap by buying off its creditors, slinked back into the fray, reversed its historic antagonistic strategy and offered a conditional "Superior Proposal" seems entirely counterintuitive.

* * *

I believe that the absence of a suggestion of self-interest or lack of care compels a court to defer to what is a business judgment that a court is not qualified to second guess. However, I recognize that another judge might prefer to view the reasonableness of the board's action through the Unocal prism before deferring. Some flexible, readily discernable standard of review must be applied no matter what it may be called. Here, one deferring or one applying Unocal scrutiny would reach the same conclusion. When a board agrees rationally, in good faith, without conflict and with reasonable care to include provisions in a contract to preserve a deal in the absence of a better one, their business judgment should not be second-guessed in order to invalidate or declare unenforceable an otherwise valid merger agreement. The fact that majority stockholders free of conflicts have a choice and every incentive to get the best available deal and then make a rational judgment to do so as well neither unfairly impinges upon minority shareholder choice or the concept of a shareholder "democracy" nor has it any independent significance bearing on the reasonableness of the board's separate and distinct exercise of judgment.

* * *

Therefore, I respectfully dissent.

QUESTIONS

1. Why does Justice Holland treat deal protection devices in the same way as defensive measures against hostile bids?

2. Justice Holland says that once it is determined that a defensive measure is not coercive or preclusive, the court must then determine whether the defensive measure is proportional to the threat. Is this a change from prior Delaware law? Can you discern any standards for a proportionality test from this opinion?

3. What is the "section 251(c) provision" that Justice Holland describes as an aspect of the defense against competing bids?

4. Justice Holland finds that NCS's public shareholders, who own 80% of its stock, would be precluded from accepting the Omnicare bid because of the "structural defenses approved by the board." Suppose that NCS had not been subject to section 203, and that Genesis had simply obtained irrevocable proxies from Shaw and Outcalt to vote their shares in favor of the merger, and a section 251(c) commitment in the merger agreement to allow a shareholder vote on the merger? Would the grant

of a commitment to proceed to a stockholder vote alone, the result of which would have been foreordained, have constituted a breach of Unocal duties?

5. Does this opinion mean that a prospective buyer cannot obtain a commitment from controlling shareholders either (1) to vote for a merger or (2) sell their shares at the tender offer price?

6. Review Delaware GCL § 203. Why would the company's signature on the voting agreements be important to Genesis?

7. If a corporation had opted out of § 203 and a buyer had obtained the proxies of controlling shareholders to vote for the merger and a § 251(c) commitment to proceed to a stockholder vote, would it be a breach of fiduciary duty for a board to not provide a fiduciary out? What would have happened under these circumstances if the board concluded its fiduciary duties required it to recommend the Omnicare offer?

8. After this decision, is there any way that a buyer can obtain assurance that the bargain it strikes will be honored by a prospective selling corporation?

9. If a board cannot commit to finality in accepting an offer, how can it control future auctions to assure that best bids are made when the board announces that this is the final chance to bid?

10. If the board has failed to meet Unocal standards, why doesn't the Supreme Court remand this case to the Chancery Court for consideration of the entire fairness of the board's actions?

The Aftermath

Omnicare prevailed in a bidding contest that ensued after this decision, and acquired NCS. The increase in price over the Genesis bid was $99 million, or approximately $3.90 per share. On remand, plaintiff's attorneys applied for attorneys' fees of $13.5 million. The Vice Chancellor found that approximately half of the increased price, or $48 million, or $1.90 per share, was represented by the difference between Genesis' price in the merger agreement and the Omnicare offer pending at the time of the litigation, while the balance, $51 million, or $2.00 per share, was attributable to the subsequent bidding contest. The court awarded attorneys' fees of $10 million, which it described as slightly in excess of 15% of the benefit achieved from the added $48 million, and 5% of the next $51 million added by the auction.

NOTE ON THE EFFECT OF OMNICARE ON SUBSEQUENT DEAL PROTECTION DEVICES

Practitioners have responded to the restrictions imposed by the Omnicare decision in a variety of ways. Here is one report:

"We reviewed an unscientific sampling of mergers announced after Omnicare that included lock-up arrangements with controlling (or near-controlling) shareholders of the target company. The typical approach has been to include a meaningful fiduciary out (that is, no 'force-the-vote' provision, with target board able to terminate the merger agreement to accept a superior deal), while reducing the incentive of the large shareholder to seek an alternative bid by having the shareholder agree to forego upside in the event of a topping deal. For example:

1. In Riverwood Holding's stock merger with Graphic Packaging (signed March 233, 2003), the controlling shareholder of Graphic Packaging agreed to give up 75% of its profit from a topping bid up to $20 million and 50% of its profit on the next $20 million.

2. In the acquisition of Lillian Vernon by an affiliate of Ripplewood Holdings and Zelnick Media (signed April 15, 2003), a 41% shareholder of Lillian Vernon agreed to give up 50% of its profit from a topping bid."

William D. Regner, Looking at Lock-ups: Orman and Omnicare, 8 No. 6 THE M & A LAWYER 20, 22 (Nov./Dec. 2004).

Query: Suppose a buyer insisted on a "topping fee" from a control shareholder that was 110% of any premium that shareholder received from a second bid. Would the control shareholder's "no" vote on a second merger proposal be subject to legal challenge? Would this constitute illegal vote-buying? See Schreiber v. Carney, Chapter 4, Part 1.B.

Recent private equity deals have employed a modified or "limited" force-the-vote provision, that provides some exceptions to the meeting requirement, such as a board's good faith determination that an alternative proposal is indeed a "superior proposal," after making a determination based on advice of counsel that its fiduciary duties require it to terminate the transaction, and require advance notice to the first buyer so it can exercise any right to match such a bid that it may have. Some agreements have also prohibited shareholders who have signed agreements with the first buyer not to vote in favor of any other transaction for a period of time.

In re Openlane, Inc. Shareholders Litigation, 2011 WL 4599662 (Del. Ch. 2011), Vice Chancellor Noble refused to grant injunctive relief where no fiduciary out clause was included in the merger agreement and the target was obligated to seek shareholder approval within 24 hours of execution of the merger agreement. If no such consent was received, either side could terminate the agreement without penalty. While the directors and officers held 68% of the voting stock, 75% shareholder approval was required. Under these conditions, the court held that the no-shop clause was meaningless because of the short time within which shareholder approval was required.

In re BioClinica, Inc. Shareholder Litigation, 2013 WL 673736 (Del. Ch.), involved a shareholder claim that merger protective devices precluded competing offers, in violation of the Omnicare holding. Vice Chancellor Glascock denied a motion for expedited proceedings to enjoin the merger, holding that the complaint did not state a colorable claim for relief. BioClinica's board had engaged in an eight month search for buyers, in which approximately fifteen candidates had signed a nondisclosure and standstill agreement. This standstill agreement provided:

> "Nothing contained in this Section 7 shall restrict the Receiving Party from making a cash tender offer for all of the outstanding capital stock of the Company after such time as both (i) a third party has commenced, within the meaning of Rule 14d–2 of the Exchange Act, a cash tender offer for the Company at a lower price per share than the price per share offered by the Receiving Party in its tender offer and (ii) the Company has recommended to its stockholders that they accept such third party's tender offer."

After entering into an agreement to be acquired by JLL Partners in a cash tender offer and merger, BioClinica was sued on the basis that its combination of devices—standstills, a no-shop clause, a top-up feature, matching rights and a poison pill—precluded other offers. Plaintiffs argued that while the standstill agreements permitted tender offers, the poison pill would preclude such bids. The poison pill contained standard terms, such that the announcement of commencement of a tender offer would trigger the rights of shareholders to purchase. But the court noted that this only gave shareholders the right to purchase preferred share units at a price that was preclusively high, and that the rights did not convert to the right to purchase common stock at a bargain price until an "Acquisition Date," when a bidder acquired 20% or more of Bioclinica's shares. Because Bioclinica's board had the right to redeem the pill at any time before the Acquisition Date, the court held the protections were not preclusive. The opinion explained this as follows:

> "The effect of the pill on a bidder would be as follows. If the bidder announced a tender offer, conditioned on redemption of the pill, BioClinica would distribute the Rights Certificates. The common shareholders would then have the right to purchase the over-priced Preferred Stock. No rational shareholder would exercise that right. If the bidder's hostile tender offer were higher than the JLL tender offer, the stockholders would withdraw their tendered shares from the JLL tender offer. The Merger Agreement contains a fiduciary-out clause which would allow the BioClinica board to deal with superior offers. JLL has contracted for the right to increase its offer and match the price offered by the hostile bidder. Therefore, the auction would continue, ensuring the stockholders received the highest price available to them. If, for

some reason, the BioClinica board refused to redeem the pill, even when faced with a superior offer, the BioClinica stockholders and the hostile bidder would be free to petition this Court for relief. Therefore, as in [In re] Orchid [Cellmark Inc. S'holder Litig., 2011 Del. Ch. LEXIS 75], 'a sophisticated buyer could navigate these shoals if it wanted to make a serious bid.' I find that the Plaintiffs have not pled a colorable claim that these deal-protection devices, when combined, impermissibly lock up the Merger Agreement."

In re Comverge, Inc. Shareholders Litigation, 2014 WL 6686570 (Del. Ch.), involved a sale by directors under the duress of the threat of a default on debt that would preclude new financing to raise working capital, and exclusive dealing with the entity that held the debt. Among other claims in the complaint was one that the directors gave deal protections that would preclude other bids. The directors were protected under an exculpatory clause authorized under Del. G.C.L. § 102(b)(7), and the court dismissed all of the claims about the sale process because of it. It did not dismiss the claim based on deal protection provisions. These included a bridge loan to Comverge that was convertible into Comverge common stock at $1.40 per share when the acquisition price was $1.75 per share. In a $48 million dollar deal, Comverge had a 30-day "go-shop" period, which could be extended by 10 days if Comverge had received and was negotiating a potentially superior proposal. During this period, Comverge would be obligated to pay a termination fee of $1.206 million and up to $1.5 million in the bidder's expenses. After the go-shop period, the termination fee would rise to $1.93 million. The board's potential liability was to be tested under the exception in § 102(b)(7)(ii) for acts not in good faith. The court stated:

"I turn, therefore, to the go-shop period and the termination fee. A go-shop of 30 days with the possibility of a 10-day extension, like the one agreed to here, is within the range of typical go-shop periods. I note also that the case law places more emphasis on the length of a post-signing go-shop if there was not an effective market check before signing. Comverge actively had engaged in a search for strategic transactions for some 18 months before the Merger Agreement. During that time, the Board and its financial advisors canvassed the market and entered confidentiality agreements with numerous strategic and financial buyers. These facts suggest that the Board and the Committee had sufficient time to ascertain whether any interested parties were waiting in the wings. Considered in isolation, therefore, it seems inconceivable to me that the length of the go-shop period here would be found unreasonable.

"The trouble for the Comverge Defendants is that a post-signing market check of the length they used or longer is useless if the termination or break-up fee structure is preclusive in nature. The Merger Agreement provided for a two-tier termination fee: Comverge would pay HIG $1.206 million if the Company entered into a superior transaction during the go-shop period, and $1.93 million after the go-shop expired. Additionally, Comverge agreed to reimburse HIG for expenses up to $1.5 million under either scenario. If the lower of the termination fees were used, the total payable to HIG would be

5.55% of the deal's equity value and 5.2% of its enterprise value; using the higher of the fees, those percentages would be 7% and 6.6%, respectively. At the motion to dismiss stage, drawing all reasonable inferences in favor of Plaintiffs, I cannot rule out the possibility that the higher end of those figures might apply. Even assuming the lesser 5.55% metric is used, however, that percentage tests the limits of what this Court has found to be within a reasonable range for termination fees. This is true even for a micro-cap acquisition like this one (approximately $48 million),—situations in which the case law tends to provide somewhat greater latitude in this regard.

"The more difficult question is whether I should include the Convertible Notes in the termination fee analysis. As noted above, the Convertible Notes were executed in conjunction with the Merger Agreement, and were the vehicle by which HIG provided Comverge with $12 million in bridge financing. Plaintiffs argue that, in practical terms, the Notes' conversion privilege could result in a $3 million payment to HIG if Comverge entered into a superior transaction, and therefore should be added to the termination fee and the expense reimbursement. In that case, the total "termination" payment easily could be at least $5.7 million during the go-shop period and $6.43 million afterward, amounting, respectively, to 11.6% or 13.1% of the equity value of the transaction. Under the Note Purchase Agreement, the Convertible Notes may be converted into 8,571,428 shares of Comverge common stock at a conversion price of $1.40 per share. Plaintiffs' argument is that, if a topping bidder were to emerge, they would have to offer at least $1.76 per share to beat HIG's offer. If HIG elected to convert the Notes into equity and then tender into the superior offer, it would net 36 cents per share. In that hypothetical case, the topping bidder would have to pay $3.085 million more to acquire Comverge than the roughly $48 million price HIG had negotiated, and that extra amount would go into HIG's pocket. Plaintiffs contend that amount should be taken into account along with the termination fees as part of the cost to the topping bidder of simply getting into the game. That would make the total "termination payment" soar to as much as 13% of equity value of the transaction or more.

"Defendants have not cited any case under Delaware law where a break-up fee at that level has been found within a range of reasonableness; rather, they argue that it would be a mistake to consider the conversion feature of the Notes alongside the termination fees. In addition, Defendants assert that, in any event, the Company so badly needed liquidity that the Convertible Notes cannot be seen as anything other than reasonable under the circumstances. It is difficult to evaluate Defendants' first argument on the preliminary record before me. At the motion to dismiss stage, the relevant inquiry is whether it is reasonably conceivable that the Convertible Notes could have functioned, in effect, as part of an unreasonably high termination fee, not whether the Notes conclusively did so in this case.

"The provision regarding the conversion privilege in the Note Purchase Agreement governing the Convertible Notes is complicated and incorporates several sections of the Merger Agreement. Based on my preliminary reading of that provision and the relevant sections of the Merger Agreement and the

Forbearance Agreement, I cannot rule out the possibility that the Convertible Notes would exacerbate the effect of the termination fee, as Plaintiffs suggest it would. Although it is unclear whether Plaintiffs ultimately will prevail on this particular point after a more complete development of the facts and the applicable legal principles, drawing all inferences in favor of Plaintiffs, it is reasonably conceivable at this stage that the Convertible Notes theoretically could have worked in tandem with the termination fees effectively to prevent a topping bid.

"This conclusion is buttressed by the fact that, as the relevant events were unfolding, Comverge's largest stockholder, Raging Capital, expressed its understanding of the interplay between the Merger Agreement and the Convertible Notes by stating that, "[W]e view this bridge loan as essentially a second break-up fee designed to have a chilling effect on the ability of a third-party to submit a competing bid." This Court previously has observed that: "The preclusive aspect of any termination fee is properly measured by the effect it would have on the desire of any potential bidder to make a topping bid." When making such a determination under the enhanced scrutiny of Revlon, the proper inquiry "examines whether the board granting the deal protections had a reasonable basis to accede to the other side's demand for them in negotiations." In conducting that examination, cases like Louisiana Municipal Police Employees Retirement System v. Crawford instruct that the Court should consider all of the facts and circumstances relevant to the board's decision. Specifically, this Court must:

> "consider a number of factors, including without limitation: the overall size of the termination fee, as well as its percentage value; the benefit to shareholders, including a premium (if any) that directors seek to protect; the absolute size of the transaction, as well as the relative size of the partners to the merger; the degree to which a counterparty found such protections to be crucial to the deal, bearing in mind differences in bargaining power; and the preclusive or coercive power of *all* deal protections included in a transaction, taken as a whole.

"Having conducted such an examination, I conclude that it is reasonably conceivable that the Director Defendants acted unreasonably in agreeing to the potentially preclusive termination fees and the Convertible Notes. In reaching that conclusion, I consider it reasonable to infer at this point that the Convertible Notes may have been viewed by potential bidders as additional termination fees, which effectively would bring the total termination payments to over $6 million, resulting in a termination fee of 13% of the equity value of the transaction. These potential findings of unreasonable deal protection measures are cause for legitimate concern, particularly in the context of a deal with a *negative* premium to market. This circumstance distinguishes this case from many in which this Court has not questioned the reasonableness of similar deal protection devices."

3.   THE RISKS OF SELLING AT TOO HIGH A PRICE

Until now we have been concerned with getting the best price possible for shareholders. The following materials suggest that seller's boards of directors and selling shareholders may need to be concerned that they do not extract too high a price, at least when the funds for the purchase are borrowed, and secured by the assets of the target corporation—in short, a leveraged buyout ("LBO"). Leveraged buyouts first developed in the 1980s with the discovery of the usefulness of junk bond financing. After a decline in such financings during the 1990s, they have made a full recovery after 2001, with the development of "private equity" funds—large pools of capital raised from institutional investors seeking higher returns than the overall market offered, especially during the early years of the new century. By 2007 one commentator explained the proliferation of leveraged buyouts by these funds as a function of a combination of a relatively low overall stock market valuation and the relatively low cost of debt financing, even using junk bonds. Higher levels of corporate debt can lead to higher levels of default. Typically in a leveraged buyout transaction at least some classes of lenders obtain a security interest in all of the assets of the debtor corporation, which increases the risk for unsecured creditors. The following materials examine the extent to which pre-existing creditors of the debtor corporation are protected either by contract or legal doctrines, or both. After a collapse of leveraged financings in 2008–2010 they began to return, albeit with more modest leverage, in 2010.

NOTE ON CONTRACTUAL AND STATUTORY CREDITOR PROTECTION

Corporate statutes governing mergers generally provide that creditors of constituent corporations become creditors of the surviving corporation by operation of law. See, e.g., Rev. Model Bus. Corp. Act § 11.07(a)(4) and Del. Gen. Corp. L. § 259(a). But these provisions may not be enough to satisfy all creditors. A merged company can possess very different credit risks than some of the constituent corporations, and a leveraged buyout transaction can radically change the debt-equity ratio of the acquired company, and thus increase the risk of default. Because interest rates on existing debt will not automatically change to reflect this new element of risk, creditors can suffer serious economic losses from leveraged acquisitions in particular. The RJR Nabisco leveraged buyout imposed huge losses on bondholders. For the legal aftermath, holding that no duties to bondholders were violated by this transaction, see Metropolitan Life Ins. Co. v. RJR Nabisco, Inc., 716 F.Supp. 1504 (S.D.N.Y. 1989).

Long-term creditors find that scale economies permit the writing of elaborate covenants to bind the debtor corporation against engaging in actions that would jeopardize the creditor's security. Banks may insist on these terms in loan agreements, and underwriters may insist on such terms in debenture indentures for debt to the publicly offered by the corporation.

Smith & Warner, On Financial Contracting: An Analysis of Bond Covenants
7 J. Fin. Econ. 117, 126–27, 128 (1979).

"Some indenture agreements contain a flat prohibition on mergers. Others permit the acquisition of other firms provided that certain conditions are met. For example, *Commentaries** suggests restrictions in which the merger is permitted only if the net tangible assets of the firm, calculated on a post-merger basis, meet a certain dollar minimum, or are at least a certain fraction of long-term debt. The merger can also be made contingent on there being no default on any indenture provision after the transaction is completed.

"The acquisition and consolidation of the firm into another can be permitted subject to certain requirements. For example, the corporation into which the company is merged must assume all of the obligations in the initial indenture. Article 800 of the American Bar Foundation *Model Debenture Indenture Provisions* also requires that there be no act of default after completion of the consolidation, and that the company certify that fact through the delivery to the trustee of an officer's certificate and an opinion of counsel."

"Lenders and underwriters can insist on similar protection in the event of sales of assets by a corporation. Indebtedness may be secured by mortgages on property, so that a sale of the property requires a satisfaction of the indebtedness before the mortgage can be released. But much debt is unsecured. This has become especially true during the 1980's when financial restructurings led to much more highly leveraged capital structures, in which only the most senior indebtedness might be secured, while all junior tiers looked only to the company's cash flows for their repayment.

"The transfer of the assets of the obligor substantially as an entirety can be restricted by standard boilerplate. The contract can also require that the firm not 'otherwise than in the ordinary course of business, sell lease, transfer or otherwise dispose of any substantial part of its properties and assets, including ... any manufacturing plant or substantially all properties and assets constituting the business of a division, branch, or other unit operation.[20] Another restriction is to permit asset disposition only up to a fixed dollar amount, or only so long as (1) the proceeds from the sale are applied to the purchase of new fixed

---

* American Bar Foundation, COMMENTARIES ON MODEL DEBENTURE INDENTURE PROVISIONS (1971). This is the "bible" for drafters of corporate debt instruments, along with later "simplified" indentures promulgated by the ABA that contain fewer protective covenants for creditors.—Ed.

[20] *Commentaries* (p. 427, sample covenant 2).

assets, or (2) some fraction of the proceeds is used to retire the firm's debt.[21]"

The fact that such covenants can be written does not mean that they are always used, however. Each covenant reduces the debtor's flexibility, and debtors may in some cases be willing to incur higher interest costs to compensate creditors for relinquishing some of these protections. Smith and Warner sampled 87 indentures, and found that 39.1% contained restrictions on merger activities, while 35.6% contained restrictions on disposition of assets. *Id.* at 122–23. In the aftermath of the RJR Nabisco leveraged buyout, investors insisted on new protections against LBOs, and required either repayment of the bonds or a resetting of the interest rate to reflect the new risks. But these protections did not persist; apparently investors preferred higher returns to the greater protection they received, at the cost of flexibility for debtors. See Steven L. Schwarcz, Rethinking a Corporation's Obligations to Creditors, 17 Cardozo L. Rev. 647 (1996).

Trade creditors generally do not enter into such elaborate contracts with their customers. Because the amounts of the credit extension tend to be smaller, economies of scale do not apply to the writing of costly contracts. Further, these creditors generally extend credit on a short-term basis, and can refuse to extend additional credit if they become nervous about prospects of repayment. Frequently the nervousness of such creditors is the cause of a Chapter 11 filing, since it enables the debtor to obtain new credit, because administrative expenses of running the debtor during the reorganization proceedings receive a higher priority. Trade creditors also are able to "free ride" on the indenture protections provided in issues of unsecured debt, which will prohibit or limit some risky activities.

In all cases trade creditors as well as others receive some basic protection from general laws.

---

[21] Such provisions typically apply to the retirement of the firm's funded (i.e., long-term) debt. The covenants in a particular bond issue requires that *all* the firm's debt be retired on a prorated basis. To require only that the particular bond issue containing the covenant be retired might well violate the firm's other debt agreements.

Read Uniform Fraudulent Transfer Act, §§ 4–7; Rev. Model Bus. Corp. Act §§ 6.40 and 8.33; Del. Gen. Corp. L. §§ 160, 170 and 174.

Wieboldt Stores, Inc. v. Schottenstein

94 Bankr. 488 (N.D. Ill. 1988).

■ JAMES F. HOLDERMAN, DISTRICT JUDGE.

Wieboldt Stores, Inc. ("Wieboldt") filed this action on September 18, 1987 under the federal bankruptcy laws, 11 U.S.C. §§ 101 et seq., the state fraudulent conveyance laws, Ill. Rev. Stat. ch. 59, section 4, and the Illinois Business Corporation Act, Ill. Rev. Stat. ch. 32, para. 1.01 et seq. Pending before the court are numerous motions to dismiss this action under Rules 9(b), 12(b)(2), 12(b)(6) and 19 of the Federal Rules of Civil Procedure.

I.   INTRODUCTION

Wieboldt's complaint against the defendants concerns the events and transactions surrounding a leveraged buyout ("LBO") of Wieboldt by WSI Acquisition Corporation ("WSI"). WSI, a corporation formed solely for the purpose of acquiring Wieboldt, borrowed funds from third-party lenders and delivered the proceeds to the shareholders in return for their shares. Wieboldt thereafter pledged certain of its assets to the LBO lenders to secure repayment of the loan.

The LBO reduced the assets available to Wieboldt's creditors. Wieboldt contends that, after the buyout was complete, Wieboldt's debt had increased by millions of dollars, and the proceeds made available by the LBO lenders were paid out to Wieboldt's then existing shareholders and did not accrue to the benefit of the corporation. Wieboldt's alleged insolvency after the LBO left Wieboldt with insufficient unencumbered assets to sustain its business and ensure payment to its unsecured creditors. Wieboldt therefore commenced this action on behalf of itself and its unsecured creditors, seeking to avoid the transactions constituting the LBO on the grounds that they are fraudulent under federal and state fraudulent conveyance laws.

II.   FACTS

A.   PARTIES

1.   *Wieboldt*

William A. Wieboldt began operating Wieboldt in Chicago as a dry goods store in 1883. * * * In 1982 Wieboldt's business was operated out of twelve stores and one distribution center in the Chicago metropolitan area. At that time, Wieboldt employed approximately 4,000 persons and had annual sales of approximately $190 million. Its stock was publicly traded on the New York Stock Exchange.

During the 1970's, demographic changes in Wieboldt's markets, increased competition from discount operations, and poor management caused Wieboldt's business to decline. Wieboldt showed no profit after 1979 and was able to continue its operations only by periodically selling its assets to generate working capital. These assets included its store in Evanston, Illinois and some undeveloped land.

2.   *Defendants*

Wieboldt brings this action against 119 defendants. These defendants can be grouped into three non-exclusive categories: (1) controlling shareholders, officers and directors; (2) other shareholders of Wieboldt's common stock who owned and tendered more than 1,000 shares in response to the tender offer ("Schedule A shareholders"); and (3) entities which loaned money to fund the tender offer.

a.   *Controlling Shareholders, Officers and Directors*

The individuals and entities who controlled Wieboldt in 1982 became controlling shareholders as a direct or indirect result of a 1982 takeover effort. At some time prior to or during 1982, Julius and Edmond Trump . . . purchased 30 percent of Wieboldt's outstanding shares by launching a takeover. After the takeover, the Trump brothers conveyed approximately one-half of these shares to Jerome Schottenstein and, directly or indirectly, to certain persons and entities affiliated with Mr. Schottenstein (collectively referred to as the "Schottenstein interests"). As a result of these transactions, the Schottenstein interests and the Trump brothers (through its agent, MBT Corporation) (collectively referred to as the "Trump interests") each owned approximately 15 percent of Wieboldt's then outstanding shares and became Wieboldt's controlling shareholders.[3]

* * *

c.   *The LBO Lenders and Related Entities*

On November 20, 1985 WSI commenced a tender offer for all outstanding shares of Wieboldt's common stock, for all of Wieboldt's outstanding shares of preferred stock, and for all outstanding options to purchase Wieboldt's stock. The tender offer was financed through three related financial transactions between Wieboldt and certain lenders and affiliated parties. These three transactions effected the LBO of Wieboldt.

* * *

B.   THE TENDER OFFER AND RELATED TRANSACTIONS

By January, 1985 Wieboldt's financial health had declined to the point at which the company was no longer able to meet its obligations as they came due. On January 23, 1985 WSI sent a letter to Mr. Schottenstein in which WSI proposed a possible tender offer for Wieboldt common stock at $13.50 per share. The following day, Mr. Schottenstein informed Wieboldt's Board of Directors of the WSI proposal and the

---

[3] The Trump brothers, MBT Corporation, Mr. Schottenstein and the Schottenstein affiliates are collectively referred to in this opinion as "controlling shareholders."

Board agreed to cooperate with WSI in evaluating the financial and operating records of the company. WSI proceeded to seek financing from several lenders, including Household Commercial Financial Services ("HCFS").

During 1985 it became apparent to Wieboldt's Board that WSI would accomplish its tender offer by means of an LBO through which WSI would pledge substantially all of Wieboldt's assets, including the company's fee and leasehold real estate assets, as collateral. Many of these real estate assets already served as collateral for $35 million in secured loan obligations from Continental Illinois National Bank ("CINB") and other bank creditors. Wieboldt was at least partially in default on these obligations at the time of the LBO.

In order to free these assets for use as collateral in obtaining tender offer financing, WSI intended to sell the One North State Street property and pay off the CINB loan obligations. In furtherance of these efforts, WSI entered into a joint venture with Bennett & Kahnweiler Associates ("BKA"), a real estate broker. WSI and BKA intended to sell the One North State Street property to a partnership for $30,000,000. The partnership would then mortgage the property to a funding source. Accordingly, BKA applied for and BAMIRCO [BA Mortgage and International Realty Corporation] accepted a first mortgage term loan on the property.

The sale of the One North State Street property did not generate sufficient funds to pay off the CINB loan obligations. Consequently, WSI sought additional funds from GECC [General Electric Credit Corporation] through the sale of Wieboldt's customer charge card accounts. GECC agreed to enter into an accounts purchase agreement after WSI acquired Wieboldt through the tender offer. One term of the accounts purchase agreement required Wieboldt to pledge all of its accounts receivable to GECC as additional security for Wieboldt's obligations under the agreement.

Thus, by October, 1985 HCFS, BAMIRCO, and GECC had each agreed to fund WSI's tender offer, and each knew of the other's loan or credit commitments.[7] These lenders were aware that WSI intended to use the proceeds of the financing commitments to (1) purchase tendered shares of Wieboldt stock; (2) pay surrender prices for Wieboldt stock options; or (3) eliminate CINB loan obligations.

The Board of Directors was fully aware of the progress of WSI's negotiations. The Board understood that WSI intended to finance the tender offer by pledging a substantial portion of Wieboldt's assets to its lenders, and that WSI did not intend to use any of its own funds or the funds of its shareholders to finance the acquisition. Moreover, although

---

    [7]   HCFS committed an amount sufficient to fund the offer; BAMIRCO committed $28 million; and GECC extended WSI a line of credit which was not to exceed $35 million.

the Board initially believed that the tender offer would produce $10 million in working capital for the company, the members knew that the proceeds from the LBO lenders would not result in this additional working capital.

Nevertheless, in October, 1985 the Board directed Mr. Darrow and Wieboldt's lawyers to work with WSI to effect the acquisition. During these negotiations, the Board learned that HCFS would provide financing for the tender offer only if Wieboldt would provide a statement from a nationally recognized accounting firm stating that Wieboldt was solvent and a going concern prior to the planned acquisition and would be solvent and a going concern after the acquisition. Mr. Darrow informed WSI that Wieboldt would only continue cooperating in the LBO if HCFS agreed not to require this solvency certificate. HCFS acceded to Wieboldt's demand and no solvency certificate was ever provided to HCFS on Wieboldt's behalf.

On November 18, 1985 Wieboldt's Board of Directors voted to approve WSI's tender offer, and on November 20, 1985 WSI announced its offer to purchase Wieboldt stock for $13.50 per share. By December 20, 1985 the tender offer was complete and WSI had acquired ownership of Wieboldt through its purchase of 99 percent of Wieboldt's stock at a total price of $38,462,164.00. All of the funds WSI used to purchase the tendered shares were provided by HCFS and were secured by the assets which BAMIRCO and GECC loan proceeds had freed from CINB obligations. After the LBO,

> 1. Wieboldt's One North State Street property was conveyed to ONSSLP [One North State Street Limited Partnership] as beneficiary of a land trust established with Boulevard Bank as trustee;
>
> 2. Substantially all of Wieboldt's remaining real estate holdings were subject to first or second mortgages to secure the HCFS loans; and
>
> 3. Wieboldt's customer credit card accounts were conveyed to GECC and Wieboldt's accounts receivable were pledged to GECC as security under the GECC accounts purchase agreement.

In addition, Wieboldt became liable to HCFS on an amended note in the amount of approximately $32.5 million. Wieboldt did not receive any amount of working capital as a direct result of the LBO.

On September 24, 1986 certain of Wieboldt's creditors commenced an involuntary liquidation proceeding against Wieboldt under Chapter 7 of the United States Bankruptcy Code ("the Code"). On the same day, Wieboldt filed a voluntary reorganization proceeding pursuant to Chapter 11 of the Code. Wieboldt's Chapter 11 proceeding is entitled In re Wieboldt Stores, Inc., 68 Bankr. 578 (N.D.N.Y. 1986), and is pending on the docket of Bankruptcy Judge Susan Pierson DeWitt of the United States Bankruptcy Court for the Northern District of Illinois.

C.   THE COMPLAINT

[The complaints alleged that WSI's tender offer and the resulting LBO was a fraudulent conveyance, both under Illinois state law and the federal bankruptcy code. Count I alleged that insiders and controlling shareholders in Wieboldt tendered their shares with actual intent to hinder, delay or defraud Wieboldt's unsecured creditors. Other counts alleged that the tender offer to other Wieboldt shareholders was a fraudulent conveyance because the resulting LBO rendered Wieboldt insolvent, or with insufficient capital to continue the business in which it was engaged. Some of the counts also alleged that Wieboldt did not receive fair consideration for the property conveyed, and was insolvent at the time of the conveyances. This decision is on defendants' motion to dismiss.]

* * *

III. DISCUSSION

* * *

1.   *Applicability of Fraudulent Conveyance Law*

Both the federal Bankruptcy Code and Illinois law protect creditors from transfers of property that are intended to impair a creditor's ability to enforce its rights to payment or that deplete a debtor's assets at a time when its financial condition is precarious. Modern fraudulent conveyance law derives from the English Statute of Elizabeth enacted in 1570, the substance of which has been either enacted in American statutes prohibiting such transactions or has been incorporated into American law as a part of the English common law heritage. See Sherwin, "Creditors' Rights Against Participants in a Leveraged Buyout," 72 Minn. L. Rev. 449, 465–66 (1988).

The controlling shareholders, insider shareholders, and some of the Schedule A shareholders argue that fraudulent conveyance laws do not apply to leveraged buyouts. These defendants argue (1) that applying fraudulent conveyance laws to public tender offers effectively allows creditors to insure themselves against subsequent mismanagement of the company; (2) that applying fraudulent conveyance laws to LBO transactions and thereby rendering them void severely restricts the usefulness of LBOs and results in great unfairness; and (3) that fraudulent conveyance laws were never intended to be used to prohibit or restrict public tender offers.

Although some support exists for defendants' arguments,[13] this court cannot hold at this stage in this litigation that the LBO in question

---

[13] See, e.g., Baird & Jackson, "Fraudulent Conveyance Law and Its Proper Domain," 38 Vand. L. Rev. 829 (1985).

here is entirely exempt from fraudulent conveyance laws. Neither Section 548 of the Code nor the Illinois statute exempt such transactions from their statutory coverage. Section 548 invalidates fraudulent "transfers" of a debtor's property. Section 1101(4) defines such a transfer very broadly to include "every mode, direct or indirect, absolute or conditional, voluntary or involuntary, of disposing of or parting with property or with an interest in property, including retention of title as a security interest." 11 U.S.C. § 1101(4). Likewise, the Illinois statute applies to gifts, grants, conveyances, assignments and transfers. Ill. Rev. Stat. ch. 59, section 4. The language of these statutes in no way limits their application so as to exclude LBOs.

In addition, those courts which have addressed this issue have concluded that LBOs in some circumstances may constitute a fraudulent conveyance.

The court is aware that permitting debtors to avoid all LBO transfers through the fraudulent conveyance laws could have the effect of insuring against a corporation's subsequent insolvency and failure. In light of the case law and the broad statutory language, however, this court sees no reason to hold as a general rule that LBOs are exempt from the fraudulent conveyance laws. As the court stated in Anderson, "if this holding is too broad in the light of the present marketplace, it is the legislature, not the courts, that must narrow the statute."

2. *The Structure of the Transaction*

Although the court finds that the fraudulent conveyance laws generally are applicable to LBO transactions, a debtor cannot use these laws to avoid any and all LBO transfers. In this case, certain defendants argue that they are entitled to dismissal because the LBO transfers at issue do not fall within the parameters of the laws. These defendants argue that they are protected by the literal language of Section 548 of the Code and the "good faith transferee for value" rule in Section 550.[15] They contend, initially, that they did not receive Wieboldt property during the tender offer and, secondarily, that, even if they received Wieboldt property, they tendered their shares in good faith, for value, and without

---

[15] While Section 548 defines the nature of the transactions that are avoidable by the debtor, Section 550 places limits on Section 548 by defining the kind of transferee from whom a debtor may recover transferred property. Section 550(a) permits a trustee to recover fraudulently transferred property from

    1. the initial transferee;

    2. the entity for whose benefit such transfer was made; or

    3. an immediate or mediate transferee of such initial transferee (a "subsequent transferee").

11 U.S.C. § 550(a). Section 550(b) states that a trustee may not recover from

    1. a subsequent transferee who takes the property for value, in good faith, and without knowledge of the voidability of the transfer; or

    2. an immediate or mediate good faith transferee of such a transferee.

11 U.S.C. § 550(b).

the requisite knowledge and therefore cannot be held liable under Section 550.

The merit of this assertion turns on the court's interpretation of the tender offer and LBO transactions. Defendants contend that the tender offer and LBO were composed of a series of interrelated but independent transactions. They assert, for example, that the transfer of property from HCFS to WSI and ultimately to the shareholders constituted one series of several transactions while the pledge of Wieboldt assets to HCFS to secure the financing constituted a second series of transactions. Under this view, defendants did not receive the debtor's property during the tender offer but rather received WSI's property in exchange for their shares.

Wieboldt, on the other hand, urges the court to "collapse" the interrelated transactions into one aggregate transaction which had the overall effect of conveying Wieboldt property to the tendering shareholders and LBO lenders. This approach requires the court to find that the persons and entities receiving the conveyance were direct transferees who received "an interest of the debtor in property" during the tender offer/buyout, and that WSI and any other parties to the transactions were "mere conduits" of Wieboldt's property. If the court finds that all the transfers constituted one transaction, then defendants received property from Wieboldt and Wieboldt has stated a claim against them.

Few courts have considered whether complicated LBO transfers should be evaluated separately or collapsed into one integrated transaction. However, two United States Courts of Appeals opinions provide some illumination on this issue. See Kupetz v. Wolf, 845 F.2d 842 (9th Cir. 1988); United States v. Tabor Court Realty, 803 F.2d 1288 (3rd Cir. 1986), cert. denied McClellan Realty Co. v. United States, 483 U.S. 1005, 107 S. Ct. 3229, 97 L. Ed. 2d 735 (1987).

In Kupetz, the debtor corporation (Wolf & Vine) was owned in equal shares by an individual, Morris Wolf, and the Marmon Group. When Mr. Wolf retired, Marmon decided to sell the company and concluded that David Adashek was a suitable buyer. Mr. Adashek subsequently obtained control of the company through a series of transactions which constituted an LBO. Thereafter, Wolf & Vine could not service the additional debt that resulted from the buyout. The company eventually filed for bankruptcy under Chapter 11 of the Code.

* * *

The Ninth Circuit affirmed the district court's decision and declined to strike down the LBO on fraudulent conveyance grounds. The court concluded that the trustee could not avoid the transfer to the shareholders because (1) they did not sell their shares in order to defraud Wolf & Vine's creditors; (2) they did not know that Mr. Adashek intended to leverage the company's assets to finance the purchase of shares; and

(3) the LBO had the indicia of a straight sale of shares and was not Wolf & Vine's attempt to redeem its own shares. * * *

[In United States v. Tabor Court Realty, *supra*, the court held that the LBO lender was liable for the fraudulent conveyance, finding that all three parties—the lender, the debtor, and the purchaser, participated in the loan negotiations, and that the transactions thus should be integrated.] * * *

Neither of these cases involved transactions which were identical to the WSI-Wieboldt buyout. However, the Kupetz and Tabor Court opinions are nonetheless significant because the courts in both cases expressed the view that an LBO transfer—in whatever form—was a fraudulent conveyance if the circumstances of the transfer were not "above board." Kupetz, 845 F.2d at 847. Thus, even though the court in Kupetz declined to hold the selling shareholders liable, there was no showing in Kupetz that the shareholders intended to defraud Wolf & Vine's creditors nor even knew that the purchaser intended to finance the takeover by leveraging the company's assets. On the other hand, the court in Tabor Court found the LBO lender liable because it participated in the negotiations surrounding the LBO transactions and knew that the proceeds of its loan to Great American would deplete the debtor's assets to the point at which it was functionally insolvent under the fraudulent conveyance and bankruptcy laws. These cases indicate that a court should focus not on the formal structure of the transaction but rather on the knowledge or intent of the parties involved in the transaction.

Applying this principle to defendants' assertions, it is clear that, at least as regards the liability of the controlling shareholders, the LBO lenders, and the insider shareholders, the LBO transfers must be collapsed into one transaction. The complaint alleges clearly that these participants in the LBO negotiations attempted to structure the LBO with the requisite knowledge and contemplation that the full transaction, tender offer and LBO, be completed.[20] The Board and the insider shareholders knew that WSI intended to finance its acquisition of Wieboldt through an LBO . . . and not with any of its own funds. . . . They knew that Wieboldt was insolvent before the LBO and that the LBO would result in further encumbrance of Wieboldt's already encumbered assets. * * * Attorneys for Schottenstein Stores apprised the Board of the fraudulent conveyance laws and suggested that they structure the LBO so as to avoid liability. * * * Nonetheless, these shareholders recommended that Wieboldt accept the tender offer and themselves tendered their shares to WSI. * * *

---

[20] Although many of the allegations in the complaint refer to the state of mind and activities of the Board of Directors, these allegations may fairly be imputed to the controlling shareholders. The controlling shareholders nominated a majority of the directors to their positions on the Board. In addition, many of the individuals who served on the Board were "insiders" to Schottenstein Stores, Inc. or MBT Corporation.

Wieboldt's complaint also alleges sufficient facts to implicate the LBO lenders in the scheme. HCFS, BAMIRCO and GECC were well aware of each other's loan or credit commitments to WSI and knew that WSI intended to use the proceeds of their financing commitments to purchase Wieboldt shares or options and to release certain Wieboldt assets from prior encumbrances. * * * Representatives of the lenders received the same information concerning the fraudulent conveyance laws as did the Board of Directors.[21] * * * These LBO lenders agreed with WSI and the Board of Directors to structure the LBO so as to avoid fraudulent conveyance liability. * * *

The court, however, is not willing to "collapse" the transaction in order to find that the Schedule A shareholders also received the debtor's property in the transfer. While Wieboldt directs specific allegations of fraud against the controlling and insider shareholders and LBO lenders, Wieboldt does not allege that the Schedule A shareholders were aware that WSI's acquisition encumbered virtually all of Wieboldt's assets. Nor is there an allegation that these shareholders were aware that the consideration they received for their tendered shares was Wieboldt property. In fact, the complaint does not suggest that the Schedule A shareholders had any part in the LBO except as innocent pawns in the scheme. They were aware only that WSI made a public tender offer for shares of Wieboldt stock. (Complaint para. 98). Viewing the transactions from the perspective of the Schedule A shareholders and considering their knowledge and intent, therefore, the asset transfers to the LBO lenders were indeed independent of the tender offer to the Schedule A shareholders.

This conclusion is in accord with the purpose of the fraudulent conveyance laws. The drafters of the Code, while attempting to protect parties harmed by fraudulent conveyances, also intended to shield innocent recipients of fraudulently conveyed property from liability. Thus, although Subsection (a) of Section 550 permits a trustee to avoid a transfer to an initial transferee or its subsequent transferee, Subsection (b) of that Section limits recovery from a subsequent transferee by providing that a trustee may not recover fraudulently conveyed property from a subsequent transferee who takes the property in good faith, for value, and without knowledge that the original transfer was voidable. Subsection (b) applies, however, only to subsequent transferees.

Similarly, the LBO lenders and the controlling and insider shareholders of Wieboldt are direct transferees of Wieboldt property. Although WSI participated in effecting the transactions, Wieboldt's complaint alleges that WSI was a corporation formed solely for the purpose of acquiring Wieboldt stock. The court can reasonably infer from

---

[21] Because of the close association between BAMIRCO and the other State Street defendants, the court can impute BAMIRCO's knowledge to the other defendants for the purpose of this motion to dismiss.

the complaint, therefore, that WSI served mainly as a conduit for the exchange of assets and loan proceeds between LBO lenders and Wieboldt and for the exchange of loan proceeds and shares of stock between the LBO lenders and the insider and controlling shareholders. On the other hand, the Schedule A shareholders are not direct transferees of Wieboldt property. From their perspective, WSI was the direct transferee of Wieboldt property and the shareholders were merely indirect transferees because WSI was an independent entity in the transaction.

In sum, the formal structure of the transaction alone cannot shield the LBO lenders or the controlling and insider shareholders from Wieboldt's fraudulent conveyance claims. These parties were aware that the consideration they received for their financing commitments or in exchange for their shares consisted of Wieboldt assets and not the assets of WSI or any other financial intermediary. The Schedule A shareholders, on the other hand, apparently unaware of the financing transactions, participated only to the extent that they exchanged their shares for funds from WSI. Therefore, based on the allegations in the complaint, the court concludes that:

1.   the motions to dismiss filed by the LBO lenders, insider shareholders, and controlling shareholders are denied at this point because these parties received Wieboldt property through a series of integrated LBO transactions; and

2.   the Schedule A shareholders' motions to dismiss are granted because these defendants did not receive Wieboldt property through the separate exchange of shares for cash.

3.   The Elements of a Fraudulent Conveyance

As discussed above, the transfers to and between the debtor and the LBO lenders, controlling shareholders, and insider shareholders are subject to the provisions in Section 548(a) of the Code and Section 4 of the Illinois statute. The court now must determine whether Wieboldt's complaint states sufficient facts to allege the elements of these causes of action.

a.   Section 548(a)(1)

In order to state a claim for relief under Section 548(a)(1) of the Code, a debtor or trustee must allege (1) that the transfer was made within one year before the debtor filed a petition in bankruptcy, and (2) that the transfer was made with the actual intent to hinder, delay or defraud the debtor's creditors. 11 U.S.C. § 548(a)(1). Although defendants do not dispute that the LBO transfers occurred within a year of the date on which Wieboldt filed for bankruptcy, they vigorously assert that Wieboldt has failed to properly allege "intent to defraud" as required by Section 548(a)(1).

"Actual intent" in the context of fraudulent transfers of property is rarely susceptible to proof and "must be gleaned from inferences drawn from a course of conduct." A general scheme or plan to strip the debtor of its assets without regard to the needs of its creditors can support a finding of actual intent. In addition, certain "badges of fraud" can form the basis for a finding of actual intent to hinder, delay or defraud. 4 Collier on Bankruptcy para. 548.02[5] (15th ed. 1987).[24]

Counts I and III of Wieboldt's complaint state a claim under Section 548(a)(1). Count I, which Wieboldt brings against the controlling and insider shareholders, states that these defendants exchanged their shares with the actual intent to hinder, delay or defraud Wieboldt's unsecured creditors. (Complaint, para. 109). Count III states that the State Street defendants received Wieboldt's interest in One North State Street property with the actual intent to defraud Wieboldt's unsecured creditors. (Complaint para. 118). The complaint also states generally that the LBO Lenders and the controlling and insider shareholders structured the LBO transfers in such a way as to attempt to evade fraudulent conveyance liability. (Complaint paras. 80–83). These allegations are a sufficient assertion of actual fraud. Defendants' motions to dismiss Counts I and III are therefore denied.

b.   *Section 548(a)(2)*

Unlike Section 548(a)(1), which requires a plaintiff to allege "actual fraud," Section 548(a)(2) requires a plaintiff to allege only constructive fraud. A plaintiff states a claim under Section 548(a)(2) by alleging that the debtor (1) transferred property within a year of filing a petition in bankruptcy; (2) received less than the reasonably equivalent value for the property transferred; and (3) either (a) was insolvent or became insolvent as a result of the transfer, (b) retained unreasonably small capital after the transfer, or (c) made the transfer with the intent to incur debts beyond its ability to pay. 11 U.S.C. § 548(a)(2).

Defendants argue that Wieboldt's allegation of insolvency is insufficient as a matter of law to satisfy the insolvency requirement in Section 548(a)(2)(B)(i). Section 101(31)(A) of the Code defines "insolvency" as a condition which occurs when the sum of an entity's debts exceeds the sum of its property "at a fair valuation." 11 U.S.C. § 101(31)(A). Wieboldt's complaint alleges that the corporation was insolvent in November, 1985 "in that the fair saleable value of its assets was exceeded by its liabilities when the illiquidity of those assets is taken into account." (Complaint, paras. 112, 121).

Wieboldt's allegations satisfy the "insolvency" requirement of Section 548(a)(2)(B)(i). Defendants' attempt to distinguish Wieboldt's phrase "fair saleable value" from Section 101(31)(A)'s "fair valuation" is,

---

[24] For example, when a debtor conceals a fact or makes false pretenses, reserves rights in the property which is transferred, or creates a closely held corporation to receive the transfer, or when the value of the transfer is unconscionably greater than the consideration received for it, the transaction is said to bear the "badge of fraud." 4 Collier on Bankruptcy para. 548.02[4](15th ed. 1987).

as Wieboldt suggests, "hypertechnical." "Fair valuation" is near enough in meaning to "fair value of saleable assets" to defeat defendants' motion to dismiss. In addition, Wieboldt did not destroy its claim of insolvency by characterizing its assets as "illiquid" at the time of the transfer. In determining "fair valuation," a court must consider the property's intrinsic value, selling value, and the earning power of the property. Black's Law Dictionary, 538 (5th Ed. 1979). Assets may be reduced by the value of the assets that cannot be readily liquidated. Briden v. Foley, 776 F.2d 379, 382 (1st Cir. 1985). The complaint meets the financial condition test of Section 548(a)(2)(B)(i).

Finally, defendants claim that Wieboldt cannot state a claim under Section 548(a)(2) because it received "reasonably equivalent value" in the transfer to the shareholders and the conveyance of the One North State Street property. Wieboldt granted a security interest in substantially all of its real estate assets to HCFS and received from the shareholders in return 99 percent of its outstanding shares of stock.[25] * * * This stock was virtually worthless to Wieboldt. Wieboldt received less than a reasonably equivalent value in exchange for an encumbrance on virtually all of its non-inventory assets, and therefore has stated a claim against the controlling and insider shareholders.

Likewise, the court need not dismiss Wieboldt's Section 548(a)(2) claim against the State Street defendants on the grounds that Wieboldt received reasonably equivalent value in exchange for its One North State Street property. The effect and intention of the parties to the One North State Street conveyance was to generate funds to purchase outstanding shares of Wieboldt stock. Although Wieboldt sold the property to ONSSLP for $30 million,[26] and used the proceeds to pay off part of the $35 million it owed CINB, Wieboldt did not receive a benefit from this transfer. * * *. Defendants knew that the conveyance would neither increase Wieboldt's assets nor result in a net reduction of its liabilities. In fact, all parties to the conveyance were aware that the newly unencumbered assets would be immediately remortgaged to HCFS to finance the acquisition. * * * According to the complaint, therefore, Wieboldt received less than reasonably equivalent value for the conveyance of the One North State Street property and has stated a claim against the State Street defendants under Section 548(a)(2).

---

[25] Defendants argue that WSI (and not Wieboldt) received the outstanding shares of Wieboldt stock. However, a court analyzing an allegedly fraudulent transfer must direct its attention to "what the Debtor surrendered and what the Debtor received, irrespective of what any third party may have gained or lost." In re Ohio Corrugating Co., 70 Bankr. 920, 927 (Bkrtcy. N.D. Ohio 1987). As discussed in Section C.2. of this opinion, the court considers the tender offer and buyout transfers as one transaction for the purposes of this motion.

[26] In reality, Wieboldt conveyed the property to ONSSLP as beneficiary of a land trust with Boulevard Bank as trustee. * * *

In sum, Counts II and IV of Wieboldt's complaint state a claim under Section 548(a)(2). Defendants' motions to dismiss these counts are denied.

c.   *Illinois Fraudulent Conveyance Law*

Under Section 544(b) of the Code, a trustee may avoid transfers that are avoidable under state law if there is at least one creditor at the time who has standing under state law to challenge the transfer. 11 U.S.C. § 544(b). Wieboldt utilizes this section to pursue a claim under the Illinois fraudulent conveyance statute, Ill. Rev. Stat. ch. 59, § 4.

The Illinois fraudulent conveyance statute is similar to Section 548 of the Code. The statute provides that:

> Every gift, grant, conveyance, assignment or transfer of, or charge upon any estate, real or personal, . . . made with the intent to disturb, delay, hinder or defraud creditors or other person, . . . shall be void as against the creditors, purchasers and other persons.

Ill. Rev. Stat. ch. 59, § 4 (1976). Illinois courts divide fraudulent conveyances into two categories: fraud in law and fraud in fact. Tcherepnin v. Franz, 475 F.Supp. 92, 96 (N.D. Ill. 1979). In fraud in fact cases, a court must find a specific intent to defraud creditors; in fraud in law cases, fraud is presumed from the circumstances. *Id.*

Count VIII of Wieboldt's complaint purports to state a claim against the insider and controlling shareholders, Schedule A shareholders, and State Street defendants for fraud in law. Fraud in law occurs when a debtor makes a voluntary transfer without consideration, and the transfer impairs the rights of creditors. Tcherepnin v. Franz, 457 F.Supp. 832, 836 (N.D. Ill. 1978). To state a claim for fraud in law, a plaintiff must allege: (1) a voluntary gift; (2) an existing or contemplated indebtedness against the debtor; and (3) the failure of the debtor to retain sufficient property to pay the indebtedness. Wieboldt's complaint alleges that the LBO transfers were fraudulent because "Wieboldt did not receive fair consideration for the property it conveyed and was insolvent at the time of the conveyance because it was then unable to meet its obligations as they became due." * * *

Wieboldt's complaint clearly alleges the elements of fraud in law. Although Wieboldt's complaint does not specifically allege that it made a "voluntary gift," a transfer for grossly inadequate consideration is deemed to be a "voluntary gift" under Illinois law. As previously discussed, Wieboldt did not receive a benefit from these transfers. * * * Second, Wieboldt clearly was obligated to a number of entities at the time of the transfers and in fact had defaulted on its obligations to CINB. (Complaint paras. 43, 55). Finally, Wieboldt alleges that the LBO transfers rendered it insolvent. * * * An insolvent corporation does not have sufficient assets to repay its obligations. The complaint therefore satisfies the elements of fraud in law under Section 4.

* * *

5.   Illinois Business Corporation Act

In Count XI, Wieboldt attempts to state a claim under Sections 8.65(a)(1) and 9.10(c)(1) of the Illinois Business Corporations Act of 1983 ("IBCA"), Ill. Rev. Stat. ch. 32, paras. 8.65(a)(1) and 9.10(c)(1). Section 9.10(c)(1) prohibits a board of directors from authorizing a distribution to shareholders that would have the effect of rendering the corporation insolvent.* Section 8.65(a)(1) provides that directors who assent to a distribution prohibited by Section 9.10 are jointly and severally liable to the corporation for the amount of the distribution.** Defendants assert that Wieboldt fails to state a claim against the directors for an illegal distribution to shareholders because (1) the directors did not assent to such distribution within the meaning of Section 8.65, and (2) Wieboldt did not make a distribution to shareholders within the meaning of Sections 8.65 and 9.10.

As an initial matter, Wieboldt has fairly alleged that the directors assented to the alleged distribution. The minutes from the November 18, 1985 Special Meeting of Wieboldt's Board of Directors indicate that the Board unanimously adopted a resolution on that date approving the WSI tender offer and merger and recommending it to the shareholders. * * * This vote constituted the directors' voluntary assent to the group of transactions which allegedly resulted in a pledge of Wieboldt assets in exchange for Wieboldt shares.

The directors' primary contention is that the exchange between HCFS and the shareholders was not an improper distribution. Both Wieboldt and the directors contend that legislative history controls the meaning of the term "distribution" as it is used in Section 9.10. Wieboldt maintains that the court must "collapse" this transaction and find that the Board made an illegal distribution because the effect of the payment of cash from HCFS to the shareholders was to transfer Wieboldt assets to Wieboldt shareholders. Wieboldt maintains that the Illinois statute encompasses such an indirect transfer. The directors assert that the Illinois statute does not contemplate a transfer whereby no corporate assets pass directly from the corporation to its shareholders.

Neither Section 9.10 nor any other section of the IBCA defines the term "distribution" as it is used in the Act. However, the Revised Model Business Corporations Act ("MBCA"), from which the IBCA derives, defines "distribution" very broadly. Section 1.40(6) provides that the term "distribution" encompasses:

---

*   This language appears to be comparable to that in Model Bus. Corp. Act § 6.40(c).—Ed.

**   This language is comparable to that in Model Bus. Corp. Act § 7.33.—Ed.

a direct or indirect transfer of money or other property (except [a corporation's] own shares) or incurrence of indebtedness by a corporation to or for the benefit of its shareholders in respect to any of its shares. A distribution may be in the form of a declaration or payment of a dividend; a purchase, redemption, or other acquisition of shares; a distribution of indebtedness; or otherwise.

Model Business Corporations Act Annotated, 1.40(6) at 73 (3d. ed. vol. 1). The Official Comment to Section 1.40(6) indicates that the definition is "intended to include any . . . transaction in which the substance is clearly the same as a typical dividend or share repurchase, no matter how structured or labeled." *Id.* at 77.

Although the Illinois Legislature did not incorporate the MBCA's definition of "distribution" into the IBCA, the Legislature's failure to adopt this definition does not indicate an intention to restrict the section to a narrow category of direct transfers. The predecessor to the IBCA, the Business Corporations Act of 1933, contained three provisions which regulated the directors' power to distribute corporate assets to shareholders. By enacting 9.10 for the express purpose of superseding the prior act, the Illinois Legislature adopted a more general description of prohibited corporate distributions. In the absence of contrary authority, it appears likely that the Illinois Legislature contemplated a broad range of transfers, including indirect transfers such as the exchange of cash and shares between HCFS and the shareholders. The directors' motions to dismiss Count XI therefore are denied.

* * *

QUESTIONS

1. Did the lenders give value in exchange for their security interests? If so, why are they held liable for a fraudulent conveyance?

2. What is the difference between the insiders and the controlling shareholder, on the one hand, and the Class A shareholders, on the other?

3. What is the difference between the Class A shareholders, who were named as defendants, and the remaining public shareholders, who were not sued? Why weren't these shareholders sued?

4. As a prospective LBO buyer, how can you structure a transaction to avoid "integration?"

5. Why hadn't any creditors obtained contractual protection against LBOs? Could they have done so economically? If one creditor has such protection, what is the effect upon other creditors?

6.   Would the directors have been better protected from liability if they had sought an expert's "solvency" opinion that the post-LBO Wieboldt's would have adequate capital for its business? See In re Munford, below.

For an interesting discussion of fraudulent conveyance law in the context of leveraged buyouts, see Douglas Baird and Thomas Jackson, "Fraudulent Conveyance Law and Its Proper Domain", 38 Van. L. Rev. 829 (1985). See also Sherwin, Creditors' Rights Against Participants in a Leveraged Buyout, 72 Minn. 449 (1988) and Richard Kummert, State Statutory Restrictions on Financial Distributions by Corporations to Shareholders: Part I, 55 Wash. L. Rev. 359 (1980) and . . . Part II, 59 Wash. L. Rev. 185 (1984).

Matter of Munford, Inc., d.b.a. Majik Market, Debtor

97 F.3d 456 (11th Cir. 1996).

■ HATCHETT, CHIEF JUDGE:

In this corporate leveraged-buy-out merger case, we affirm the district court's ruling that Georgia's stock distribution and repurchase statutes apply.

FACTS

In May 1988, the Panfida Group offered to purchase Munford, Inc., a public company on the New York Stock Exchange, through a leverage buy out (LBO) structured as a reverse triangle merger for $18 per share. Under the terms of the proposed merger agreement, the Panfida Group agreed to create Alabama Acquisition Corporation (AAC) and a subsidiary, Alabama Merger Corporation (AMC), and through AAC or AMC deposit the funds necessary to purchase Munford, Inc.'s outstanding stock with Citizens & Southern Trust Company. As evidence of its commitment to purchase Munford, Inc., the Panfida Group bought 291,100 of Munford, Inc.'s stock. In June 1988, the Panfida Group also told Munford, Inc.'s board of directors that it, upon the sale of Munford, Inc., intended to put additional capital into Munford, Inc. but would only invest as much as Citibank required to finance the proposed merger.

After consulting its lawyers and financial experts at Shearson Lehman Brothers (Shearson), the board of directors accepted the Panfida Group's offer pending shareholder approval of the purchase agreement. Prior to the directors seeking shareholder approval, the Panfida Group learned that Munford, Inc. had potential environmental liability. Consequently, the Panfida Group reduced the purchase price from $18.50 a share to $17 a share. On October 18, 1988, the shareholders approved the merger plan. On November 29, 1988, the sale of Munford, Inc. to the

Panfida Group closed. Pursuant to the purchase agreement, the LBO transaction converted each share of common stock into the right to receive the merger price of $17 per share and extinguished the shareholders' ownership in Munford, Inc. On January 2, 1990, thirteen months after the merger, Munford, Inc. filed for Chapter 11 proceedings in bankruptcy court.

PROCEDURAL HISTORY

On June 17, 1991, Munford, Inc. brought an adversary proceeding in bankruptcy court in the Northern District of Georgia on behalf of itself and unsecured creditors pursuant to 11 U.S.C. §§ 544(b) and 1107(a) (1988), seeking to avoid transfers of property, disallow claims and recover damages against former shareholders, officers, directors, and Shearson. In Count III of its complaint, Munford, Inc. asserted that the directors violated legal restrictions under Georgia's distribution and share repurchase statutes in approving the LBO merger. Specifically, Munford, Inc. asserts that the LBO transaction constituted a distribution of corporate assets that rendered Munford, Inc. insolvent. The directors moved for summary judgment contending that the Georgia distribution and repurchase statutes did not apply to LBO mergers. On August 10, 1994, the district court, adopting the bankruptcy court's report and recommendation in part, denied the directors' motion for summary judgment on Munford, Inc.'s stock repurchase and distribution claim, ruling that Georgia's stock distributions and repurchase restrictions applied to LBO transactions. The district court also found that a genuine issue of material fact existed as to whether the LBO merger rendered Munford, Inc. insolvent in violation of Georgia law. On August 26, 1994, the district court amended its order and entered final judgment pursuant to Federal Rules of Civil Procedure 54(b) to permit this appeal. Fed.R.Civ.P. 54(b).

CONTENTIONS

The directors contend that the district court erred in concluding that the LBO merger constituted a distribution of assets within the meaning of Georgia's distribution and repurchase statutes. They contend that these statutes do not apply to an arm's-length sale of a company to a third party through an LBO merger. In the alternative, the directors contend that they should not face personal liability for alleged violations of Georgia's distribution and repurchase statutes because they approved the LBO merger in good faith with the advice of legal counsel.

Munford, Inc. contends that the district court properly denied the directors' motion for summary judgment on this claim.

ISSUE

The sole issue on appeal is whether the district court erred in ruling that Georgia's stock distribution and repurchase statutes apply to a leverage acquisition of a corporation.

DISCUSSION

We review the denial of summary judgment de novo applying the same legal standard that controlled the district court in rendering its decision. Brown v. Crawford, 906 F.2d 667, 669 (11th Cir.1990), cert. denied, 500 U.S. 933, 111 S. Ct. 2056, 114 L. Ed. 2d 461 (1991).

Georgia's capital surplus distribution statute provides, in pertinent part:

> (a) The board of directors of a corporation may from time to time distribute to shareholders out of capital surplus of the corporation a portion of its assets in cash or property subject to the following [provision]:
>
> > (1) No such distribution shall be made at a time when the corporation is insolvent or when such distribution would render the corporation insolvent[.]

O.C.G.A. § 14–2–91 (1988). Similarly, Georgia's stock repurchasing statute prohibits directors of a corporation from repurchasing the corporation's shares when such purchase would render the corporation insolvent. O.C.G.A. § 14–2–92(e) (1982). Under both statutes, directors who vote for or assent to a corporate distribution or stock repurchase in violation of these statutes are jointly and severally liable for the amount distributed or paid to the extent the payments violated the restrictions. O.C.G.A. § 14–2–154(a)(1), (2) (1982).

The directors appeal the district court's denial of summary judgment contending that Georgia's distribution and share repurchase statutes do not apply to LBO mergers. The directors argue that Georgia's distribution and repurchase statutes only apply in circumstances where the directors take assets of the corporation and either distribute them to shareholders or use them to repurchase shares. In both cases, the directors assert, control of the company does not change hands and the directors determine the source of the assets used. The directors note that in this case the Panfida Group owned Munford, Inc. at the completion of the LBO merger and thereafter ran the company. The directors therefore argue that only Georgia's merger statutes apply to this transaction.

The district court denied the directors' motion for summary judgment adopting the reasoning of the bankruptcy court. The bankruptcy court, in analyzing the LBO merger, considered the substance of the transaction and equated the LBO merger to a stock distribution or repurchase, disregarding the fact that Munford, Inc. had new owners and stockholders as a result of the merger at the time the shareholders received the LBO payments. The bankruptcy court specifically found that: (1) the directors "approved or assented to the underlying merger agreement which structured and required payment to the shareholders"; (2) the merger agreement contemplated the Panfida Group's pledging of "virtually all of Munford[, Inc.]'s assets as collateral" for the loan that funded the LBO payments made to the shareholders; and (3) the directors knew or should have known "the source, purpose, or use of" Munford, Inc.'s assets prior to or at the time the directors approved the merger plan. Based on these findings, the bankruptcy court concluded that a reasonable jury could conclude that the merger rendered Munford, Inc. insolvent in violation of Georgia's distribution and stock repurchase statutes.

In reaching its conclusion, the bankruptcy court rejected a Fourth Circuit case that refused to apply Virginia's corporate distribution statute to recapture payments made to shareholders pursuant to an LBO merger. See C-T of Virginia, Inc. v. Barrett, 958 F.2d 606 (4th Cir.1992).

In C-T of Virginia, the Fourth Circuit held that the LBO merger did not constitute a distribution within the meaning of Virginia's share repurchase and distribution statutes reasoning that Virginia's distribution statute

> [was] not intended to obstruct an arm's-length acquisition of an enterprise by new owners who have their own plans for commercial success. The reason for this distinction is simple: a corporate acquisition, structured as a merger, is simply a different animal from a distribution.

C-T of Virginia, 958 F.2d at 611. The court in C-T of Virginia further reasoned that because such distribution statutes derive from the regulation of corporate dividends courts should limit their restriction to situations in which shareholders after receiving the transfer from the corporation retain their status as owners of the corporation.

The bankruptcy court, in this case, rejected this line of reasoning, reasoning that the legislature enacted the distribution and share repurchase statutes of the Georgia Code to protect creditors "by prohibiting transfers at a time when a corporation is insolvent or would be rendered insolvent." Such intent, the bankruptcy court noted, "furthers the longstanding principle that creditors are to be paid before shareholders." We agree with the district court and the reasoning of the bankruptcy court and decline to join the Fourth Circuit in holding that "[a] corporate acquisition, structured as a merger, is simply a different animal from a distribution." C-T of Virginia, Inc., 958 F.2d at 611.

We note that the LBO transaction in this case did not merge two separate operating companies into one combined entity. Instead, the LBO transaction represented a "paper merger" of Munford, Inc. and AMC, a shell corporation with very little assets of its own. To hold that Georgia's distribution and repurchase statutes did not apply to LBO mergers such as this, while nothing in these statutes precludes such a result, would frustrate the restrictions imposed upon directors who authorize a corporation to distribute its assets or to repurchase shares from stockholders when such transactions would render the corporation insolvent. We therefore affirm the district court's ruling that Georgia's restrictions on distribution and stock repurchase apply to LBO.

In the alternative, the directors argue that their approval of the LBO merger should not subject them to liability under the distribution and repurchase statutes because they approved the merger in good faith and with the advice of legal counsel. Because we are not aware of any Georgia courts that recognize good faith or reasonable reliance on legal counsel's advice as an affirmative defense to liability under Georgia's distribution and repurchase statutes, we reject this argument.

CONCLUSION

For the reasons stated above, we affirm the district court's denial of the directors' motion for summary judgment on Munford, Inc.'s stock distribution and repurchase claim.

Affirmed.

QUESTIONS

1. Georgia adopted the current version of the Model Business Corporation Act effective in 1989. Would MBCA § 6.40(d) have changed the outcome in this case?

2. The Court of Appeals characterized the LBO transaction as merely a "paper merger" that did not escape the regulation of the distribution statutes. O.C.G.A. § 14–2–103, as it became effective in 1989, after the Munford transaction, provides "Each provision of this chapter shall have independent legal significance." The notes to this section state an intent to adopt the rule of construction of Delaware, under such cases as Hariton v. Arco Electronics, *supra*, Chapter 4, Part 4.A. Would the presence of this statute make a difference in future cases?

3. In C-T of Virginia, Inc. v. Barrett, 958 F.2d 606 (4th Cir. 1992), cited in Munford, the Court of Appeals noted that at the time of the cash payment, the recipients were "former shareholders" rather than shareholders of the corporation, because their shares had been canceled in the merger. Is this a persuasive distinction? Is it more persuasive because the merger created new shareholders—those in the merging corporation, whose shares survived the merger?

4. Should it make a difference if an LBO is undertaken by outside third parties or by management?

5. Should it matter that the merger provisions of the statute provide no creditor protection against highly leveraged mergers?

6. If directors have decided to sell the company, and a proposed LBO offers the highest price for the company, how can directors satisfy their Revlon duties without running a risk of liability under distribution provisions?

7. Assuming that the directors resign at the effective time of the merger, what causes the subsequent insolvency, the decision to borrow against the corporation's assets or the manner in which the corporation is financed and operated subsequent to the merger?

8. Should an infusion of new working capital by the buyers make a difference in directors' liability if the company still becomes insolvent? What about an infusion of new and better management?

CHAPTER NINE

CONFLICTS AMONG SHAREHOLDERS

1. MAJORITY SHAREHOLDERS' SALE DECISIONS

NOTE ON EMERSON RADIO CORP. V. INTERNATIONAL JENSEN, INC.

In Emerson Radio Corp. v. International Jensen, Inc., 1996 WL 483086, the Delaware Chancery Court sustained board actions that partially discriminated against Emerson Radio Corp. in an auction. Jensen's board determined to sell the company, and employed investment bankers to find buyers. Ultimately only one serious buyer appeared: Recoton Corporation. The transaction was complicated by the fact that Recoton did not want to purchase the entire business, preferring to buy only Jensen's brand name businesses in loudspeakers and related audio products. Robert Shaw, CEO of Jensen and owner of 37% of its stock, solved this problem by agreeing to buy the business Recoton did not want, Jensen's Original Equipment Manufacturing ("OEM") business, with part of the purchase price being Shaw's waiver of golden parachute payments worth $4.8 million. Recoton agreed to a merger valued at $8.90 per share, with part in cash and part in Recoton stock.

After this agreement was announced Emerson and its adviser, Bankers Trust, entered the picture. Emerson had not previously been contacted because it had recently emerged from bankruptcy reorganization and had suffered losses for recent accounting periods. From mid-January until May 1, the Jensen board negotiated with Emerson and attempted to obtain assurances that it would be able to finance a bid. On May 1, the William Blair Leveraged Capital Fund, L.P. ("Blair"), which owned 26% of Jensen's stock, in an attempt to move the auction process to a close, gave Recoton an option to purchase its shares for $8.90, and agreed to vote in favor of a Recoton transaction. Shaw had previously agreed to accept $8.90 for his stock, while Recoton would offer a higher price to the public shareholders, presumably because Shaw's purchase of the OEM involved some additional benefit not being received by the public stockholders. Thereafter, Emerson offered a series of "two-tier" bids, as did Recoton, all of which contemplated higher payments to the public shareholders than to Shaw and Blair. The Jensen board was advised by counsel that it could not accept a discriminatory offer unless Shaw and Blair agreed to it, and that Blair could not, because it was bound to Recoton by its May 1 agreement. As a result, the Jensen Board ultimately accepted Recoton's offer of $11 per share for the public shareholders and $8.90 for Shaw and Blair, which was the highest bid at the announced deadline. Two days after the close of the auction, Emerson raised its bid to the public shareholders to $12 per share, with $8.90 for Shaw and Blair.

The Chancery Court declined to apply the entire fairness rule, because it found Jensen's board had acted independently, without undue influence from Shaw. The court rejected all of Emerson's claims that it was discriminated against unlawfully, in the following terms:

"Emerson complains that it was treated in a discriminatory manner. Emerson did receive disparate treatment, but it was for valid reasons, and that treatment did not impede Emerson from making its best bid(s). Although Emerson was not allowed to conduct due diligence until March of this year, that was because it did not sign a confidentiality agreement until March 4, 1996. For six weeks thereafter, Emerson was permitted to conduct due diligence, which was completed by April 26, 1996.

"The Committee also required Emerson to furnish evidence of its ability to finance its proposals, but the Committee had valid reasons for concern on that score. Emerson had recently emerged from bankruptcy and had reported a loss of $7.7 million for the last quarter, and a loss of $13.4 million for the past fiscal year. Negotiating with Emerson could put at risk the fully financed transaction that Jensen had already contracted for with Recoton. The Special Committee was, therefore, entitled to assurance that any competing offer would be 'for real', i.e., financeable. Upon receiving the necessary financing documentation and Global's commitment to participate, the Committee was willing to—and did—deal with Emerson. Thus, any disparate treatment of Emerson was for the benefit of Jensen's shareholders, and had no adverse impact upon Emerson's ability to compete in the auction. MacMillan, 559 A.2d at 1288."

Query: Would the result be the same after the Omnicare decision?

Hollinger Inc. v. Hollinger International, Inc.

844 A.2d 1022 (Del. Ch. 2004).

■ STRINE, VICE CHANCELLOR.

[This case considered the validity of certain shareholder-adopted bylaws designed to hobble a board of directors that had turned hostile to its controlling shareholder, Lord Conrad Black.

Hollinger International, Inc. ("International") was a holding company for a chain of newspapers, most notably the Daily Telegraph of London, the Chicago Sun-Times and several community papers in the Chicago area and The Jerusalem Post in Israel. International was controlled by Black through his control (65%) of Ravelston Corp., which in turn controlled (78%) Hollinger Inc. ("Inc."), which owned 30 %of the equity in International but 73% of its voting power. Black became the subject of a board investigation for his behavior, described briefly below, and later found himself in financial straits that caused him to attempt to sell his controlling interest in International by selling Hollinger, Inc.]

Rather, in this case, defendant Conrad M. Black, the ultimate controlling stockholder of Hollinger International, Inc. ("International"), a Delaware public company, has repeatedly behaved in a manner inconsistent with the duty of loyalty he owed the company. Black faced potentially serious accusations of self-dealing on his own behalf, and on behalf of an intermediate holding company he dominates and controls, at the expense of International. He sued for peace realizing that International's independent directors might strip him of all his corporate offices and refer certain matters to the Securities and Exchange Commission before Black could take steps to remove them (and knowing that he faced serious personal repercussions if he took that aggressive step). The indignity Black faced was galling to him, as the International board was largely filled with outside directors Black had hand-selected and with whom he had a personal relationship.

To calm the roiled waters, Black made a formal contract, the "Restructuring Proposal," involving many key features. They included his agreement to resign as Chief Executive Officer and to repay certain funds without any admission of wrongdoing. Critically, Black also agreed to stay on as Chairman and devote his principal time and energy to leading a "Strategic Process" involving the development of a value-maximizing transaction for International, such as the sale of the company or some of its assets. Black told the International directors that this Process would be for the "equal and ratable" benefit of all of International's stockholders, and that he would refrain from consummating transactions at the level of the intermediate holding company he dominated, except under strict conditions.

But, Black immediately violated his newly undertaken obligations by diverting to himself a valuable opportunity presented to International—the possible sale of one of its flagship newspapers, the Daily Telegraph, or the company as a whole to the Barclays, English brothers who own newspapers, hotels and other businesses. Black accomplished this diversion in a cunning and calculated way, fully detailed in this opinion. During the course of his dealings, Black misrepresented facts to the International board, used confidential company information for his own purposes without permission, and made threats, as he would put it, of "multifaceted dimensions" towards International's independent directors.

As the culmination of his misconduct, Black unveiled a transaction involving the sale of the holding company through which Black wields voting control of International to the Barclays. The "Barclays Transaction," if consummated, would prevent International from realizing the benefits of the Strategic Process Black had contractually promised to lead with fidelity and energetic commitment. Effectively, the

Barclays Transaction would end the Strategic Process before the bidding even began. The Barclays Transaction was also one that Black had, by contractual promise in the Restructuring Proposal, agreed not to effect.

When the International board took measures to stop the Barclays Transaction by considering a shareholder rights plan, Black caused the holding company he controlled to file a written consent enacting "Bylaw Amendments" requiring unanimous action by the International board for any significant decision, abolishing a committee that had been created to consider how International should respond to the Barclays Transaction, and thereby effectively permitting himself to disable International's independent directors from obstructing the completion of Black's injurious course of conduct. Believing the Bylaw Amendments to be unlawful and inequitable, the International independent directors, through a committee previously authorized to take such action, adopted a shareholder rights plan (the "Rights Plan") to prevent Black from consummating the Barclays Transaction, contingent on a judicial declaration that their decision was permissible. International then brought this suit seeking 1) a preliminary injunction against the Barclays Transaction and further breaches of the Restructuring Proposal; 2) a declaration that the Bylaw Amendments were ineffective because they were, among other things, adopted for an inequitable purpose; and 3) a determination that the Rights Plan was properly adopted.

* * *

Black Causes Inc. To File A Written Consent Giving Him Personal Veto Power Over The Strategic Process

The same day that he wanted the Barclays to convince Lazard [International's financial adviser in running an auction] to pull a Benedict Arnold, Black caused Inc. to file a written consent profoundly affecting the operation of the International board. That consent amended the bylaws of International to provide:

- Written notice of any meeting of the International board must be given at least seven days before the meeting.

- Any notice of a special meeting of the Board must include a statement of all business to be conducted at the meeting.

- Committees must provide directors at least 24-hours written notice of the committee meetings.

- Committees, other than the Special Committee, must provide a report of the substance of all actions taken at their meetings to the full Board within five days thereof.

- The presence of at least 80% of the directors is required to have a quorum at a meeting of the Board for the transaction of most business [which allowed Black and his allies to block a quorum].

- A quorum of all of the directors holding office is required for the board to take action on certain "Special Board Matters," including, among other things, changing the number of directors or filling any vacancy on the board; approving a merger or a sale of all or substantially all of the assets of the company; approving a sale of assets having a value of more than $1 million; and amending or repealing any bylaw of the company.

- Unanimous assent of all directors is required for the approval of any Special Board Matter.

- The audit and Special Committees will remain in place, with all of the powers and authority given to those committees in the original board resolutions that created them, while all other committees of the Board are dissolved. The effect of this particular provision was to abolish the CRC and strip the Special Committee of any added authority it was given in the January 20th board resolution.

- New committees may be established only be a unanimous vote of the board at a meeting at which all directors are present.

It is plain that these "Bylaw Amendments" fundamentally altered the power that the International independent directors possessed at the time the Restructuring Proposal was signed. At that time, Black, Mrs. Black, and Colson were only three of the eleven directors. While Inc. had the right as a stockholder to vote as it wished on transactions resulting from the Strategic Process, the independent board majority had the practical authority to shape the options, using the managerial authority vested in them by § 141 of the Delaware General Corporation Law ("DGCL").

After the Bylaw Amendments, Black could unilaterally block any material sale of assets, disable the board from adopting a shareholder rights plan, and prevent the signing of a merger agreement. That is, Inc. had taken steps to give Black, as a director, the power to honor his promise to the Barclays to prevent transactions like these until the Barclays Transaction was consummated.

[Vice Chancellor Strine found that Black had violated his fiduciary duties to the corporation. Essentially Black had seized a corporate opportunity to sell the Telegraph to the Barclays for himself and Inc., by attempting to block the board from selling it.]

* * *

Legal Analysis

Overview Of The Legal Issues Presented

The parties have filed multiple claims for which expedited consideration has been sought.

For its part, International seeks final relief on two counts of its complaint. These counts challenge the validity of the Bylaw Amendments. In one respect, International alleges that the Bylaw Amendments are per se unlawful. To wit, International argues that the aspect of the Bylaw Amendments that abolishes the CRC and strips it of the authority invested in it by the board resolution creating that committee is inconsistent with 8 Del. C. § 141(c)(2) and invalid. As to the remainder of the Bylaw Amendments, International concedes that they do not violate any statutory prohibition on the topics that may be addressed in a Delaware corporation's bylaws. Instead, International says that the Bylaw Amendments must be declared ineffective because they were adopted in bad faith for an inequitable purpose.

* * *

Were The Bylaw Amendments Properly Adopted?

I turn now to International's challenge to the Bylaw Amendments. As discussed in part previously, the Bylaw Amendments prevent the International board from acting on any matter of significance except by unanimous vote; set the board's quorum requirement at 80%; require that seven-days' notice be given for special meetings; and provide that the stockholders, and not the directors, shall fill board vacancies.

International argues quite plausibly that the Bylaw Amendments were designed to ensure that Black, and thereafter the Barclays, can veto any action at the International board level that they oppose. Black admitted that the Bylaw Amendments were designed to protect against the adoption of the Rights Plan and would give him (and other non-independent directors allied to him) the ability to prevent the International independent directors—who constitute the board's majority—from pursuing strategic options he opposes. Quite obviously, the Bylaw Amendments also deliver on Black's contractual obligation to the Barclays to take measures to thwart International from engaging in any significant transactions, including asset sales or the signing of a merger agreement.

International argues that the Bylaw Amendments constitute an attempt by Black to cement the injury he caused to International's Strategic Process through his prior violations of his fiduciary and contractual duties. In essence, the Bylaw Amendments permit Black to proceed with the Barclay Transaction even though that Transaction was the product of improper and inequitable conduct. Because of the inequitable motivations behind the Bylaw Amendments, International argues that they must be declared ineffective. As to one particular aspect of the Bylaw Amendments—the abolition of the CRC and the termination of its authority—International also argues that the Bylaw Amendments are not simply inequitable, but violative of the DGCL as well.

By contrast to International, the defendants contend that the Bylaw Amendments simply are a proper attempt by Inc. as a majority stockholder to prevent itself from being wrongly excluded from exercising the power that legitimately flows from voting control. It is the International independent directors, they argue, and not Inc., who are acting inequitably. By attempting to exclude Black, Mrs. Black, and Colson from participating in the Strategic Process and from preventing Inc. from acting to impede the adoption of the Rights Plan, the independent directors, the defendants claim, have overstepped their bounds. The defendants therefore contend that the Bylaw Amendments are a legitimate response to the independent directors' overreaching. More mundanely, the defendants argue that all of the Bylaw Amendments are consistent with the DGCL and International's charter.

Before opining as to which side is, in my view, correct, it is useful to highlight the distinction these claims raise. It is a venerable and useful one in corporate law. In general, there are two types of corporate law claims. The first is a legal claim, grounded in the argument that corporate action is improper because it violates a statute, the certificate of incorporation, a bylaw or other governing instrument, such as a contract. The second is an equitable claim, founded on the premise that the directors or officers have breached an equitable duty that they owe to the corporation and its stockholders. Schnell v. Chris-Craft Industries, Inc. is the classic recent statement of the principle that "inequitable action does not become permissible simply because it is legally possible.[124]

> In addressing the Bylaw Amendments, and the later challenge to the Rights Plan, I am mindful of the distinction between these types of claims. The DGCL is intentionally designed to provide directors and stockholders with flexible authority, permitting great discretion for private ordering and adaptation. That capacious grant of power is policed in large part by the common law of equity, in the form of fiduciary duty principles. The judiciary deploys its equitable powers cautiously to avoid intruding on the legitimate scope of action the DGCL leaves to directors and officers acting in good faith. The business judgment rule embodies that commitment to proper judicial restraint. At the same time, Delaware's public policy interest in vindicating the legitimate expectations stockholders have of their corporate fiduciaries requires its courts to act when statutory flexibility is exploited for inequitable ends.

---

[124] Schnell v. Chris-Craft Indus., Inc., 285 A.2d 437, 439 (Del. 1971).

The Bylaw Amendments Are Not Inconsistent With The DGCL

With those principles in mind, I now determine whether the Bylaw Amendments are effective. I begin by rejecting International's claim that the aspect of the Bylaw Amendments that abolishes the CRC is statutorily invalid. International bases that argument on § 141(c)(2), which states in pertinent part that:

> Any such committee, to the extent provided in the resolution of the board of directors, or in the bylaws of the corporation, shall have and may exercise all the powers and authority of the board of directors in the management of the business and affairs of the corporation. . . .

International contends that § 141(c)(2) empowers only directors to eliminate a committee established by a board resolution and not stockholders acting through a bylaw.

I agree with the defendants that this argument is not convincing. Stockholders are invested by § 109 with a statutory right to adopt bylaws. By its plain terms, § 109 provides stockholders with a broad right to adopt bylaws "relating to the business of the corporation, the conduct of its affairs, and its rights or powers or the rights or powers of its stockholders, directors, officers or employees." This grant of authority is subject to the limitation that the bylaws may not conflict with law or the certificate of incorporation.

Traditionally, the bylaws have been the corporate instrument used to set forth the rules by which the corporate board conducts its business. To this end, the DGCL is replete with specific provisions authorizing the bylaws to establish the procedures through which board and committee action is taken. While there has been much scholarly debate about the extent to which bylaws can—consistent with the general grant of managerial authority to the board in § 141(a)—consistent with the *general* grant of managerial authority to the board in § 141(a)—limit the scope of managerial freedom a board has, e.g., to adopt a rights plan, there is a general consensus that bylaws that regulate the process by which the board acts are statutorily authorized. This includes the extent to, and manner in, which the board shall act through committees. Indeed, before the recent Bylaw Amendments, the International Bylaws heavily regulated the corporation's committee procedures.

In Frantz Manufacturing Co. v. EAC Industries,[132] the Delaware Supreme Court made clear that bylaws could impose severe requirements on the conduct of a board without running afoul of the DGCL. In Frantz, a majority stockholder implemented bylaw amendments when it feared that the incumbent board would divest it of its voting power. The amendments required, among other things, that there be unanimous attendance and board approval for any board action,

---

[132] 501 A.2d 401 (Del. 1985).

and unanimous ratification of any committee action. The Supreme Court found that the bylaws were consistent with the terms of the DGCL. In so ruling, the Court noted that the "bylaws of a corporation are presumed to be valid, and the courts will construe the bylaws in a manner consistent with the law rather than strike down the bylaws."

Here, International argues that the Bylaw Amendments run afoul of § 141(c)(2) because that provision does not, in its view, explicitly authorize a bylaw to eliminate a board committee created by board resolution. By its own terms, however, § 141(c)(2) permits a board committee to exercise the power of the board only to the extent "provided in the resolution of the board . . . or in the bylaws of the corporation." As the defendants note, the statute therefore expressly contemplates that the bylaws may restrict the powers that a board committee may exercise. This is unremarkable, given that bylaws are generally thought of as having a hierarchical status greater than board resolutions, and that a board cannot override a bylaw requirement by merely adopting a resolution. Further, in Frantz, the Delaware Supreme Court ruled that bylaws requiring that the full board decide matters by unanimous vote are permissible.

Moreover, I find International's argument that the failure of § 141(c)(2) to use magic words like "unless otherwise provided in the bylaws" renders board-created committees invulnerable from elimination through a bylaw amendment without merit. The words of § 141(c)(2) plainly subordinate board resolutions creating and empowering committees to overriding bylaw provisions, especially when read in concert, as they must be, with the capacious authority over a board's processes that § 109 and other provisions of § 141 plainly grant.

For these reasons, I agree with the defendants that the provision in the Bylaw Amendments eliminating the CRC does not contravene[136] The question therefore becomes whether that and the other Bylaw Amendments are impermissible because they were adopted for an inequitable purpose.

The Bylaw Amendments Are Inequitable

In Frantz, the Supreme Court also made clear that the rule of Schnell—that inequitable action does not become permissible simply because it is legally possible—applies to bylaw amendments. In Frantz, the Supreme Court, citing Schnell, reviewed bylaw amendments undertaken by the majority stockholder to ensure that they were not inconsistent with any rule of common law and were reasonable in application. In the circumstances of that case, the Supreme Court found

---

[136] For similar reasons, I reject International's argument that that provision in the Bylaw Amendments impermissibly interferes with the board's authority under § 141(a) to manage the business and affairs of the corporation. Sections 109 and 141, taken in totality, and read in light of Frantz, make clear that bylaws may pervasively and strictly regulate the process by which boards act, subject to the constraints of equity.

the very restrictive bylaws at issue proper because the majority stockholder—which had committed no acts of wrongdoing—was acting to protect itself from being diluted.

In this case, the Bylaw Amendments were clearly adopted for an inequitable purpose and have an inequitable effect. In November 2003, Black was confronted with a very difficult set of circumstances. One option for him was to play it tough. He could have caused Inc. to file a written consent removing the entire board (using the total and personal dominion he clearly exercises over Inc.). If he had played it tough and did not act quickly or boldly enough to remove the board, Black could have been stripped of all his offices, been confronted with a board-adopted shareholder rights plan, a strong board reference to the SEC, and other events that he wished to avoid—including an immediate lawsuit against Inc. Instead of this approach, Black undertook to cut the best deal he could and made binding contractual obligations to International.

Those obligations have been discussed at fulsome length already, but they clearly included a duty of energetic fidelity to the Strategic Process, a Process that was to be controlled by the entire board. In the Restructuring Proposal, changes had been made to the board to strengthen its independent majority. Black understood that it was that independent board that would ultimately oversee his co-leadership of the Strategic Process with Paris.

* * *

Summary of the Merits Rulings

It is useful to summarize my merit conclusions. First, International has shown a reasonable probability of success on the merits of its claims that Black violated the Restructuring Proposal and his fiduciary duties. Indeed, those findings are not entirely probabilistic because I make final and necessary findings to that same effect in ruling on the Bylaw Amendments and the Rights Plan. Second, the Bylaw Amendments are ineffective because they were undertaken for inequitable purposes and were the culmination of a pattern of wrongful conduct. Finally, for the reasons indicated, the CRC's adoption of the Rights Plan was a proper exercise of statutory authority that was consistent with the CRC's fiduciary duty to protect the corporation.

International Is Entitled To An Injunction Against The Barclays Transaction

* * *

Conclusion

For all the foregoing reasons, 1) the Bylaw Amendments are declared ineffective and judgment will be entered to that effect; 2) the Rights Plan was permissibly adopted and a declaration to that effect is proper; and 3) International is entitled to a preliminary injunction against the Barclays Transaction and further breaches of the Restructuring Proposal. An implementing order shall be submitted by the plaintiffs, upon approval as to form.

_____

QUESTIONS

1. If Black held 73% of the voting power, why did he need to limit the board's power to engage in fundamental transactions? Couldn't he just vote against any sale of the company as a shareholder?

2. Absent Black's history of wrongdoing, would another shareholder be able to adopt bylaw amendments such as these without encountering legal problems?

3. If leaving business matters exclusively to the board is required by section 141(a) (see Quickturn Design Systems, Inc. v. Shapiro, supra Chapter Six, Part 2.E), could one argue that these bylaws, which give a controlling shareholder a veto power over board action on any matter, offend that provision?

_____

The Aftermath

After this decision the International board determined to sell The Daily Telegraph to the Barclays for $1.21 billion after an auction was conducted by Lazard Freres. Black sued to enjoin the sale, on the ground that it was a sale of substantially all the assets, requiring a shareholder vote. See Note on Hollinger, Inc. v. Hollinger International, Inc. 858 A.2d 342 (Del. Ch. 2004) in Chapter Four, Part 4. Vice Chancellor Strine held that it was not a sale of substantially all the assets of International, and thus did not require a shareholder vote. The auction managed to raise bids by 40%, and one investor noted that the Barclay's offer to Black for Inc.'s 32% stake in International valued the entire company at $1.38 billion, while this sale produced nearly that much for a fraction of it. The International board indicated that it would consider a post-sale dividend, which one investor estimated in the range of $10 per share. Subsequently Lord Black was indicted in U.S. District Court in Illinois for violation of a 28-word addendum to 18 U.S.C. § 1346 (the federal mail fraud and wire fraud statute), added by Congress in 1988, which states: "For the purposes of this chapter, the term, *scheme or artifice to defraud* includes a scheme or artifice to deprive another of the intangible right of honest services. Black was convicted under this statute in 2007 of honest services fraud, in addition to obstruction of justice. He was given a six-and-a-half-year sentence. On June 24, 2010 the Supreme Court ruled unanimously in the cases of Black and Jeffrey Skilling, former Enron executive, that the law against "honest services" fraud is too vague to constitute a crime unless a bribe or kickback was involved.

_____

NOTE ON BOARD DUTIES IN THE PRESENCE OF MAJORITY SHAREHOLDERS' DECISIONS TO SELL OR RETAIN THEIR SHARES

What happens to a board's Revlon duties in the context of a controlling shareholder that either decides not to sell once an active auction has been initiated, or decides to conduct its own auction? Mendel v. Carroll, 651 A.2d 297 (Del. Ch.1994) involved a proposed cashout merger by a family group, the Carroll family, which owned between 48% and 52% of the outstanding shares of Katy Industries, Inc. at the time this dispute arose. The Carroll family had signed various agreements designed to preserve their joint control, and had made it clear that they were not interested in selling their shares. Over a period of time they engaged in negotiations with the board, through an independent committee, about a transaction that would buy out the public stockholders, ultimately at a proposed price of $25.75 per share, which the independent committee's investment bankers advised was fair. A merger agreement was signed and a shareholders' meeting scheduled to approve the merger. Before the meeting could be held prospective buyers offered $27.80 per share. As a result, the independent committee advised the board that it could no longer continue its recommendation that a buyout at $25.75 was fair. The Carroll family exercised its right to terminate the merger agreement. The bidder, as part of its offer demanded an option on 20% of the outstanding shares of the company at the proposed acquisition price, in order to assure a possibility of shareholder approval of the merger over the opposition of the Carroll family. Because of its doubts about the legality of such an option, the board declined to give it, and a shareholder suit to force the board to grant the option ensued.

Plaintiffs took the position that the board's initial approval of a cash merger with the Carroll family interests placed Katy's board in a Revlon situation, with a duty to maximize shareholder values on a current basis. The court rejected the Revlon analysis, concluding that even when family ownership dropped slightly below 50%, it still "had the effective power, acting in concert, to control the outcome of any stockholder election." Under these circumstances, the Carroll family already had a control block, which would trade at a premium. Thus, the Carroll family members "were not buying corporate control. With either 48% or 52% of the outstanding stock, they already had it." Under these circumstances, the board's duty was to protect the rights of the public shareholders in a takeout merger, but this did not create Revlon duties. "But while that obligation may authorize the board to take extraordinary steps to protect the minority from plain overreaching, it does not authorize the board to deploy corporate power against the majority stockholders, in the absence of a threatened serious breach of fiduciary duty by the controlling stock." Because the Carroll family consistently opposed any sale of its shares, control of the company was never up for sale.

One recent Delaware decision examined the question of board duties where the controlling shareholder made its own decision to sell the company, and conducted its own selling process. In McMullin v. Beran, 765 A.2d 910 (Del. 2000), the Delaware Supreme Court reversed the Chancery Court's dismissal of a minority shareholders' complaint where the 80% shareholder, Atlantic Richfield Company ("ARCO"), conducted the process of seeking buyers and negotiating the sale of ARCO Chemical Company ("Chemical"). ARCO apparently needed cash to complete another acquisition, and, after being approached by Lyondell Petrochemical Company ("Lyondell"), employed its financial advisor, Smith Barney, to contact a number of buyers and gauge their interest in purchasing Chemical. After a period of negotiations ARCO and Lyondell reached agreement on a purchase price, and on a tender offer followed by a cash-out merger at the same price. The Chemical board met once to approve the transaction. According to the complaint, it heard a report from Smith Barney about the sale process, and the fairness opinion of its own financial adviser, Merrill Lynch, that the price was fair from a financial point of view. The tender offer obtained 99% of Chemical's stock, and a cash-out merger followed.

The complaint, aside from alleging ARCO's control of the Chemical board, alleged that the Chemical board had failed to meet its Revlon duties to become informed that the merger price was the best price that could reasonably be obtained for the public shareholders. The Supreme Court stated the board's duties under the circumstances as follows:

> The questions presented in this case require an examination of the Chemical Board's statutory duty and fiduciary responsibilities to minority shareholders in the specific context of evaluating a proposal for a sale of the entire corporation to a third party at the behest of the majority shareholder. When a board is presented with the majority shareholder's proposal to sell the entire corporation to a third party, the ultimate focus on value maximization is the same as if the board itself had decided to sell the corporation to a third party.[1] When the entire sale to a third-party is proposed, negotiated and timed by a majority shareholder, however, the board cannot realistically seek any alternative because the majority shareholder has the right to vote its shares in favor of the third-party transaction it proposed for the board's consideration.[2] Nevertheless, in such situations, the directors are obliged to make an informed and deliberate judgment, in good faith, about whether the sale to a third party that is being proposed by the majority shareholder will result in a maximization of value for the minority shareholders.[3]
>
> In this case, because the minority shareholders of Chemical were powerless to out-vote ARCO, they had only one decision to make: whether to accept the tender offer from Lyondell or to seek an appraisal value of their shares in the ensuing merger. Given ARCO's majority shareholder 80% voting power, under the circumstances of this case, the Chemical Directors did not have the

---

[1]   [Citing Mendel v. Carroll, 651 A.2d at 305.]—Ed.

[2]   Bershad v. Curtiss-Wright Corp., Del. Supr, 535 A.2d 840, 845 (1987).

[3]   8 Del. C. § 251; see Paramount v. QVC Network, Inc., Del. Supr., 637 A.2d 34 (1994); Sealy Mattress Co.of New Jersey v. Sealy, Inc., Del. Ch., 532 A.2d 1324, 1338 (1987).

ability to act on an informed basis to secure the best value reasonably available for all shareholders in any alternative to the third-party transaction with Lyondell that ARCO had negotiated.[4] The Chemical Directors did, however, have the duty to act on an informed basis to independently ascertain how the merger consideration being offered in the third party transaction with Lyondell compared to Chemical's value as a going concern.

As noted, a board of directors has a duty under 8 Del. C. § 251(b) to act in an informed and deliberate manner in determining whether to approve an agreement of merger before submitting the proposal to the stockholders. In the absence of a majority shareholder, we have held that directors "may not abdicate that duty by leaving to the shareholders alone the decision to approve or disapprove the agreement."[5] A fortiori, when the proposal to merge with a third party is negotiated by the majority shareholder, the board cannot abdicate that duty by leaving it to the shareholders alone to approve or disprove the merger agreement[6] because the majority shareholder's voting power makes the outcome a preordained conclusion. To paraphrase the Court of Chancery in a similar context and applying its holding to this case:

> Once having assumed the position of directors of [Chemical], a corporation that had stockholders other than [ARCO], [the directors] become fiduciaries for the minority shareholders, with a concomitant affirmative duty to protect the interests of the minority, as well as the majority, stockholders. Thus, the [Chemical] Board, in carrying out its affirmative duty to protect the interests of the minority, could not abdicate its obligation to make an informed decision on the fairness of the merger by simply deferring to the judgment of the controlling shareholder. . . .[7]

The court noted that the opinion of Merrill Lynch was merely that the price was "fair," not that it was the best price obtainable, and that thus the complaint alleged a failure of the board to be fully informed. Further, the duty of the board to the minority shareholders was to inform them if the acquisition price might be exceeded by the appraised value of their shares in an appraisal proceeding.

Query: How is a subsidiary board, which is unable to conduct a credible auction as an alternative to the parent's sale process, to determine if the price is the best obtainable? Recall that in Barkan v. Amsted Industries, Inc., 567 A.2d 1279 (Del. 1989), in Part 1 of Chapter Eight, *supra*, the court stated: " . . . advice [of an investment banker] is frequently a pale substitute for the

---

    4   See Paramount Communications v. QVC Network, Inc., Del. Supr., 637 A.2d 34 (1994).

    5   See Paramount Communications, Inc. v. Time, Inc., Del. Supr., 571 A.2d 1140, 1142–1143 n.4 (1989) (quoting Smith v. Van Gorkom, Del. Supr., 488 A.2d 858, 873 (1985)). See generally Aronson v. Lewis, Del. Supr., 473 A.2d 805, 811–13 (1984). See also Pogostin v. Rice, Del. Supr., 480 A.2d 619 (1984).

    6   Sealy Mattress Co. of New Jersey v. Sealy, Inc., Del. Ch., 532 A.2d 1324, 1338 (1987).

    7   *Id.*

dependable information that a canvas of the relevant market can provide." Second, how can a board accurately predict the results of an appraisal proceeding, when Delaware courts are capable of awarding dissenting shareholders nearly four times the market value of shares before the transaction, in at least one case? See Rapid-American Corp. v. Harris, 603 A.2d 796, *infra*, Part 3.D of this chapter.

Orman v. Cullman

2004 WL 2348395 (Del.Ch. 2004).

■ CHANDLER, CHANCELLOR.

This case is about a merger transaction in which one tobacco company, Swedish Match AB, purchased an equity stake in another tobacco company, General Cigar Holdings, Inc. Members of the Cullman family are the controlling shareholders of General Cigar. Swedish Match did not purchase control of General Cigar, as it wanted the Cullmans to continue managing the company after the merger.

Although Swedish Match paid a significant premium above the market price for the public shares in General Cigar, plaintiff Joseph Orman sued the General Cigar board of directors for breach of their fiduciary duties in negotiating the merger terms. In earlier stages of this lawsuit, the Court has dismissed certain claims and has permitted others to go forward. After an extended period of discovery, defendants have renewed their motion for summary judgment on the remaining breach of fiduciary duty claim. Defendants contend that a fully informed vote of a majority of the public shareholders in favor of the merger operates to extinguish plaintiff's claim. This contention raises the following question: Were the General Cigar public shareholders impermissibly coerced to vote for the merger because of a lock-up provision required by Swedish Match as part of the transaction?

The answer to this question, in my opinion, is no. The undisputed facts demonstrate that the lock-up did not coerce the public shareholders to approve the merger for reasons unrelated to its merits. Public shareholders of General Cigar retained full authority to veto the transaction, the board had negotiated an effective fiduciary out, and any interested third party was free to purchase the publicly owned shares of General Cigar. For these and other reasons set forth later in this Opinion, I will enter summary judgment in favor of defendants and against the plaintiff.

I. BACKGROUND

General Cigar Holdings, Inc. was founded in 1906 by the Cullman family. General Cigar became a public company through an IPO in February 1997 at an IPO price of $18.00 per share. The prospectus issued in connection with the IPO informed potential investors that certain members of the Cullman and Ernst families (the "Cullmans") would "have substantial control over the Company and may have the power . . . to approve any action requiring stockholder approval, including . . . approving mergers." The Cullmans' control over General Cigar was by virtue of their exclusive power over the Company's Class B common stock, which is entitled to ten votes per share. Following the IPO, the Company's stock traded as high as $33.25 per share. Throughout 1998 and 1999, however, the stock traded as low as $5.50 per share.

At the end of April 1999, General Cigar sold part of its business to Swedish Match AB. Later that year, Swedish Match contacted the Company to discuss "acquiring a significant stake" in General Cigar's business. In November 1999, the Company's board authorized management to pursue discussions with Swedish Match. On December 2, 1999, Edgar Cullman Sr., General Cigar's chairman, informed the board that he and Edgar Cullman Jr., the Company's CEO, were meeting with a representative of Swedish Match in London to discuss an acquisition. At the early December meeting in London, Swedish Match expressed a high level of interest in making an equity investment in General Cigar. Swedish Match also indicated that "they wanted Edgar M. Cullman, Sr. and Edgar M. Cullman, Jr. to maintain management responsibility and day-to-day control of General Cigar." Swedish Match's interest, and desire to have the Cullmans remain in control of General Cigar, was reaffirmed at meetings in New York from December 19–21, 1999.[11] At these meetings, General Cigar made their management available in order to permit Swedish Match to begin their due diligence process.

Given the continuing interest of Swedish Match, General Cigar's board created a special committee to advise and make recommendations to the full board concerning any transaction with Swedish Match. The special committee consisted of Dan Lufkin, Thomas Israel, and Francis Vincent, Jr. The chairman of the special committee, Lufkin, believed it was the committee's responsibility to ensure that the public shareholders were "fairly represented." Although the special committee was charged with advising the board regarding any transaction with Swedish Match, it was not authorized to solicit offers by third parties. The special committee also did not negotiate directly with Swedish Match. Instead, the negotiations were conducted primarily by Peter J. Solomon Company Limited, an investment company owned by a member of the Company's board, Peter Solomon. The special committee retained Wachtell, Lipton, Rosen & Katz ("Wachtell") to serve as legal counsel to the committee. The special committee also retained Deutsche Bank Securities Inc.

---

[11] Dan Lufkin, a member of the General Cigar board, testified that Swedish Match had "no interest in buying this company without the Cullmans." Deposition of Dan W. Lufkin ("Lufkin Dep.") at 75. The Cullmans also indicated their desire to retain the majority of their equity in the Company and to continue controlling day-to-day operations.

("Deutsche Bank") to render a fairness opinion on any proposals made by Swedish Match.

During the negotiations that led to the merger, Swedish Match required that the Cullmans enter into a stockholders' voting agreement. "Under that agreement, the Cullmans agreed not to sell their shares, and to vote their shares against any alternative acquisition proposal for a specified period following any termination of the merger between Swedish Match and General Cigar." According to Swedish Match's CFO:

> A central purpose of the voting agreement was to protect Swedish Match against the risk that the Cullmans or General Cigar would "shop" Swedish Match's offer to other potential bidders. Because the Cullmans held a controlling interest in General Cigar, the voting agreement would prevent an alternative bidder from acquiring control of General Cigar during the specified period if the merger did not go forward. This protection was particularly important to Swedish Match because the merger agreement did not contain a termination fee or expense reimbursement provision.

Swedish Match originally asked that the Cullmans agree to a restricted period of three years. This was rejected. The restricted period was later negotiated down to one year.

Drafts of the merger agreement and the voting agreement were sent to the Cullmans and the special committee on January 18, 2000. These drafts reflected a potential transaction structure in which the Cullmans would sell approximately one third of their equity interest to Swedish Match at a price of $15.00 per share followed by a merger into a Swedish Match subsidiary in which public shareholders would also receive $15.00 per share. The voting agreement circulated on January 18 contained a requirement that the Cullmans not sell their shares, and to vote their shares against any alternative acquisition proposal, for one year following any termination of the merger agreement between Swedish Match and General Cigar. Following the merger, General Cigar would be owned 64% by Swedish Match and 36% by the Cullmans. The Cullmans, specifically Edgar Cullman Sr. and Edgar Cullman Jr., however, would remain in control of the Company.[31]

The special committee met on January 19, 2000. Wachtell and Deutsche Bank attended the meeting. At this meeting, Lufkin informed the full committee that Swedish Match agreed to increase the price paid to the public shareholders to $15.25 per share. In exchange for this slightly higher offer, Swedish Match required the Cullmans to increase the restricted period under the voting agreement from twelve to eighteen months. Deutsche Bank made a presentation at the meeting and opined

---

[31] Proxy Statement at 23–24. This Court has already determined that the transaction did not involve a sale of control. Orman v. Cullman, 794 A.2d 5, 42 n. 1441 (Del. Ch. 2002).

that from a financial point of view the offer price of $15.25 per share was fair to the public shareholders. After Deutsche Bank's presentation, discussion ensued, and the special committee voted unanimously to recommend that the full board approve the merger. After the special committee's meeting, the full board met, approved the merger, and the relevant documents were signed by all parties on the evening of January 19, 2000. A public announcement was made the following day.

As noted earlier, the voting agreement between the Cullmans and Swedish Match required that the Cullmans vote their Class B shares, constituting a majority of the voting power of the Company, in favor of the merger and against any alternative acquisition of the Company for eighteen months after termination of the merger agreement. The voting agreement, however, reveals that the Cullmans were bound only in their capacities as shareholders and that nothing in the voting agreement limits or affects their actions as officers or directors of General Cigar. Moreover, the merger agreement permitted General Cigar's board to entertain unsolicited acquisition proposals from potential acquirers if the board, upon recommendation by the special committee, concluded that such a proposal was *bona fide* and would be more favorable to the public shareholders than the proposed merger with Swedish Match. The agreement also permitted the board to withdraw its recommendation of the merger with Swedish Match if the board concluded, upon consultation with outside counsel, that its fiduciary duties so required.

On April 10, 2000, almost three months after the public announcement of the Swedish Match transaction, General Cigar filed the proxy statement relating to the shareholder vote on the proposed merger. As expected, the proxy statement attached the merger agreement, the voting agreement, and contained the background relating to the proposed merger. The proxy statement also revealed (1) that the merger could not occur without the approval of the merger by the Class A shareholders and (2) that the Cullmans agreed to vote their shares of Class A common stock held by them pro rata in accordance with the vote of the Class A public shareholders. In other words, the merger could not proceed without approval by a "majority of the minority." The shareholder meeting was held on May 8, 2000. The public shareholders, *i.e.*, a majority of the minority, overwhelmingly approved the merger.[45]

II. ANALYSIS

* * *

C. *Plaintiff's Arguments*

Although plaintiff has stated that the only issue is whether the shareholder vote was tainted by improper coercion, he (somewhat

---

[45] Affidavit of Joseph Aird, Ex. F (submitted in connection with defendants' original summary judgment motion, D.I. No. 36). The public shareholders approved the transaction by a vote of 10,009,994 shares in favor to 24,686 against, with 9,353 abstaining. *Id.*

predictably) has raised two arguments ancillary to that issue that must be addressed. I will discuss these two ancillary arguments first, and then turn my attention to the coercion issue.

1. The Special Committee

Plaintiff argues that the special committee provided no protection to the Company's public shareholders because (1) the special committee members "had personal motivations . . . unlike the motivation of the average stockholder" and (2) the committee had a "lackadaisical attitude." Both of these points are not well taken.

* * *

2. The Voting Agreement

Apart from the coercion issue, plaintiff also argues that members of the Cullman and Ernst families on General Cigar's board breached their fiduciary duties "by entering into the voting agreement."[57] Plaintiff's argument, which rests on a misapplication of Paramount Communications, Inc. v. QVC Network, Inc. and Omnicare, Inc. v. NCS Healthcare Inc., is without merit.

In Paramount, the Supreme Court noted that "to the extent that a contract, or a provision thereof, purports to require a board to act in such a fashion as to limit the exercise of fiduciary duties, it is invalid and unenforceable." In Omnicare, the Supreme Court made a similar observation. I do not question the general validity of these statements, but they have no application here because in both cases the challenged action was the directors' entering into a contract in their capacity *as directors*. The Cullmans entered into the voting agreement *as shareholders*. Nothing in the voting agreement prevented the Cullmans from exercising their duties *as officers and directors*. For example, the Cullmans could have voted, as directors, to withdraw their recommendation that the public shareholders approve the merger. This factual distinction from Paramount and Omnicare is meaningful.

In Bershad v. Curtiss-Wright Corporation,[62] the Supreme Court held that "a majority stockholder is under no duty to sell its holdings in a corporation, even if it is a majority shareholder, merely because the sale would profit the minority." This principle of Delaware law was more recently recognized in Peter Schoenfeld Asset Management, LLC v. Shaw,[64] where this Court observed:

> A majority shareholder has discretion as to when to sell his stock and to whom, a discretion that comes from the majority shareholder's rights *qua* shareholder. This is true even when a

---

[57] AB at 10. Edgar Cullman, Sr., Edgar Cullman, Jr., John L. Ernst, and Susan R. Cullman were on the General Cigar board and entered into the voting agreement.

[62] 535 A.2d 840 (Del. 1987).

[64] 2003 Del. Ch. LEXIS 79 (Del. Ch. July 10, 2003), *aff'd*, 840 A.2d 642, 2003 Del. LEXIS 624 (Del. Dec. 17, 2003).

proposed transaction would result in the minority sharing in a control premium.

Nothing in Paramount or Omnicare displaces this longstanding principle. In fact, Omnicare found that "the stockholders with majority voting power ... had an *absolute right* to sell or exchange their shares with a third party at any price."[66]

Plaintiffs challenge both to the voting and merger agreement's deal protection mechanisms are more properly analyzed *vis-a-vis* the board's decision to recommend that the Company's public shareholders approve the merger and whether the shareholders' ensuing vote was improperly coerced. This is the task to which I now turn.

3.   The Deal Protection Mechanisms

Although the parties have framed the Court's inquiry as relating only to the issue whether the deal protection mechanisms "coerced" the shareholder vote, plaintiff suggests that Omnicare requires a more taxing process of judicial review. Whether the deal protection devices were "coercive" now appears to be but one part of a larger analytical framework.

In Omnicare, the board of directors of NCS Healthcare, Inc. approved a merger with Genesis Health Ventures, Inc. The deal was "protected" with a three-part defense that included: (1) the inclusion of a Section 251(c) provision in the merger agreement;[67] (2) the absence of any effective fiduciary out clause; and (3) a voting agreement between two shareholders and Genesis which ensured that a majority of shareholders voted in favor of the transaction. After the merger was approved by the board another suitor, Omnicare, Inc., forwarded a superior proposal. The NCS board then reversed course, recommending that the NCS shareholders vote against the Genesis merger. The NCS board's change of heart had no practical effect, however, because the three deal protection mechanisms, working in tandem, "guaranteed ... that the transaction proposed by Genesis would obtain NCS stockholder's approval." "Because of the structural defenses approved by the NCS board," the Genesis merger was "a *fait accompli*."

A bare majority of the Supreme Court found that the tripartite deal protection mechanism was invalid. The majority concluded that deal protection devices, even when those devices protect a proposed merger that does not result in a change of control, require enhanced scrutiny. Specifically, the Omnicare majority applied the two-stage analysis of Unocal Corp. v. Mesa Petroleum Co. n71 The first stage of the Unocal analysis requires a board to demonstrate "that they have reasonable

---

[66]   818 A.2d at 938 (emphasis added). *Omnicare* did not address the "general validity" of stockholder voting agreements. *Id.* at 939.

[67]   Such a provision requires that a merger agreement be placed before a corporation's stockholders for a vote, even if the corporation's board of directors no longer recommends it. 8 Del. C. § 251(c).

grounds for believing that a danger to corporate policy and effectiveness existed" without such measures. The second stage of Unocal proceeds in two steps: the board must establish that the deal protection devices are (1) not coercive or preclusive and (2) within a range of reasonable responses to the danger to corporate policy and effectiveness. The analysis is disjunctive—if the deal protection devices are coercive or preclusive they are not within a range of reasonable responses, but those devices may be outside the range of reasonable responses even if not coercive or preclusive.

In Omnicare, the majority found that the NCS board's reasonable grounds for believing there was a danger to corporate policy and effectiveness were "the possibility of losing the Genesis offer and being left with no comparable alternative transaction." Nevertheless, the majority held that the deal protection devices were coercive and preclusive because they accomplished a *fait accompli, i.e.,* they "made it 'mathematically impossible' and 'realistically unattainable' for . . . any other proposal to succeed, no matter how superior the proposal." The Unocal inquiry ended there. But the Omnicare majority held "alternatively" that the NCS board was required to negotiate a fiduciary out clause into the merger agreement because the voting agreement and the Section 251(c) provision, in the absence of a fiduciary out clause, resulted in an absolute lock-up of the Genesis transaction. The Court reasoned that even though a majority of shareholders (via the voting agreement) had agreed to support the merger, the NCS board was nonetheless continually obligated to "exercise its continuing fiduciary responsibilities to the minority stockholders."

Applying the first stage of the Unocal analysis is simple in this case. During the negotiations that led to the merger, Swedish Match "required" some form of deal protection. If the special committee and full board had not approved the inclusion of the deal protection devices, they risked losing the Swedish Match transaction and being left with no comparable alternative transaction. As in Omnicare itself, this is reasonable grounds for believing that a danger to corporate policy and effectiveness existed.

Applying the second stage of the Unocal analysis is also straightforward. Williams v. Geier provides the standard for determining if deal protection measures are coercive.[81] The measures are improper if they "have the effect of causing the stockholders to vote in favor of the proposed transaction for some reason other than the merits of that transaction." An example of such impermissible coercion was found in Lacos Land Company v. Arden Group, Inc.[83] In Lacos Land., Arden's principal shareholder and CEO made "an explicit threat . . . that unless

---

[81] Plaintiff does not argue that the deal protection measures were "preclusive" under Unocal; only "coercion" is at issue.

[83]   517 A.2d 271 (Del. Ch. 1986).

[certain] proposed amendments were approved, he would use his power (and not simply his power *qua* shareholder) to block transactions that may be in the best interests of [Arden]." The threat to block transactions in the best interest of Arden was unrelated to the merits of the proposed amendments under consideration by the shareholders and constituted impermissible coercion. The basic teaching of Lacos Land, as discussed in Williams, is that fiduciaries cannot threaten stockholders so as to cause the vote to turn on factors extrinsic to the merits of the transaction.

Now, compare Lacos Land with Brazen v. Bell Atlantic Corporation. In Brazen, Bell Atlantic and NYNEX Corporation negotiated a merger agreement with a $550 million termination fee provision that could be triggered if Bell Atlantic's shareholders voted not to approve merger. The Supreme Court found that the termination fee was "an integral part of the merits of the transaction." The Court further stated "although the termination fee provision may have influenced the stockholder vote, there were no structurally or situationally coercive factors that made an otherwise valid fee provision impermissibly coercive in this setting."

Here, like Brazen, the deal would not have occurred without the inclusion of deal protection mechanisms, *i.e.*, the deal protection mechanisms were "an integral part of the merits of the transaction." But the circumstances here are distinguishable from Lacos Land because General Cigar's public shareholders were not encouraged to vote in favor of the Swedish Match transaction for reasons unrelated to the transaction's merits. Instead, the "lock-up" negotiated in this case, is similar to the termination fee found permissible by the Supreme Court in Brazen.[91] That is, nothing in this record suggests that the lock-up had the effect of causing General Cigar's stockholders to vote in favor of the proposed transaction for some reason other than the merits of that transaction. Furthermore, unlike the situation in Omnicare, the deal protection mechanisms at issue in this case were not tantamount to "*a fait accompli.*" The public shareholders were free to reject the proposed deal, even though, permissibly, their vote may have been influenced by the existence of the deal protection measures.[92] Because General Cigar's public shareholders retained the power to reject the proposed transaction with Swedish Match, the fiduciary out negotiated by General Cigar's

---

[91] Plaintiff also appears to argue that the board breached its fiduciary duty by failing to negotiate for a break-up fee in lieu of the voting agreement lock-up. First, voting agreements, of course, are perfectly legal. And nothing in the record indicated that Swedish Match would have agreed to a different provision, such as a break-up fee. Second, there is no preference in the law for one form of deal protection device over another. And third, how would a board determine, in advance, that one particular form of defensive device, would be the "least coercive" of any array of devices? Ultimately, this argument, in my opinion, leads nowhere.

[92] Plaintiff never addresses the deeper question of how it is fair to say that a minority was coerced by a voting and ownership structure that was fully disclosed to the minority before they bought into a corporation whose capital structure was so organized. In fact, the coercion of which plaintiff complains is more properly understood as the coercion resulting from the fact that the Cullmans owned a controlling interest. Surely it cannot be the case that whenever a controlling stockholder can vote against a sale the out voted minority can assert a coercion claim.

board was a meaningful and effective one—it gave the General Cigar board power to recommend that the shareholders veto the Swedish Match deal. That is to say, had the board determined that it needed to recommend that General Cigar's shareholders reject the transaction, the shareholders were fully empowered to act upon that recommendation because the public shareholders (those not "locked-up" in the voting agreement) retained the power to reject the proposed merger.[93] For these reasons, I conclude as a matter of law that the deal protection mechanisms present here were not impermissibly coercive.[94]

The last step of the Unocal analysis is a determination of whether the deal protection devices were within a range of reasonable responses to the danger to corporate policy and effectiveness. As mentioned, the danger in this case was the risk of losing the Swedish Match transaction and being left with no comparable alternative transaction. In fact, without the deal protection mechanisms "there would have been no merger." General Cigar's shareholders could have lost the significant premium that Swedish Match's offer carried, no small concern given the uncertain future of the tobacco business. In addition, "the latitude a board will have in either maintaining or using the defensive devices it has adopted to protect the merger it approved will vary according to the degree of benefit or detriment to the stockholders' interests that is presented by the value or terms of the subsequent competing transaction."[98] Notably, there was no competing bid for General Cigar; no alternative transaction was available to its shareholders. General Cigar's board should therefore be afforded the maximum latitude regarding its decision to recommend the Swedish Match merger.

In sum, the argument that Omnicare applies in the circumstances here is misplaced. The General Cigar board retained a fiduciary out, allowing it to consider superior proposals and recommend against the Swedish Match deal. Importantly, a majority of the nonaffiliated public shareholders could have rejected the deal on its merits. Unlike Omnicare, nothing in the merger or stockholder agreements made it "mathematically certain" that the transaction would be approved. If the shareholders believed $15.25 per share (a 75% premium over the market

---

[93] Moreover, there was nothing in either the merger agreement or the voting agreement to prevent a third party from making a tender offer for the publicly-held shares that Swedish Match sought to acquire.

[94] The relevant question "is not whether a [proposal] is coercive, but whether it is actionably coercive." Weiss v. Samsonite Corp., 741 A.2d 366, 372 (Del. Ch.), aff'd, 746 A.2d 277 (Del. 1999) (TABLE). "For the word [coercion] to have much meaning for purposes of legal analysis, it is necessary in each case that a normative judgment be attached to the concept ('inappropriately coercive' or 'wrongfully coercive,' etc.)." Lacos Land, 517 A.2d at 277. The line between "coercion" and "actionable coercion" is whether the vote to approve turned on factors extrinsic to the merits of the transaction.

[98] Omnicare, 818 A.2d at 933. I pass over the practical difficulty implied by this balancing test: how can a board know, at the time of adopting defensive devices, the terms of a transaction that emerges at a later time? As formulated, the test would appear to result in judicial invalidation of negotiated contractual provisions based on the advantages of hindsight.

price) did not reflect General Cigar's intrinsic value (and the market also misunderstood that value), they could have said, "no thanks, I would rather make an investment bet on the long term prospects of this company." These shareholders were fully informed about the offer. They knew that no other offer or potential buyer had appeared, although nothing prevented it. They knew that no termination fee would be paid if they rejected the proposal. It is true, as plaintiffs repeatedly point out, that the Cullman vote against any future, hypothetical deal was "locked-up" for 18 months. It was this deal or nothing, at least for that period of time.[99] Again, however, no other suitor was waiting in the wings. And, assuming a shareholder believed that General Cigar's long term intrinsic value was greater than $15.25 per share, was an 18 month delay a meaningful "cost" that could be said realistically to "coerce" the shareholders' vote? The Cullman lock-up hardly seems unreasonable, given the absence of other deal protection devices in this particular transaction and given the buyer's understandable concern about transaction costs and market uncertainties. Unless being in a voting minority automatically means that the shareholder is coerced (because the minority shareholder's investment views or hopes have been precluded by a majority), plaintiff's concept of coercion is far more expansive than Omnicare or any other decisional authority brought to my attention. As a matter of law, therefore, the approval of the Swedish Match proposal by a fully informed majority of the minority public shareholders was not impermissibly coerced. As a result of that ratifying vote, plaintiff's remaining fiduciary duty claim is extinguished.

III. CONCLUSION

The vote of General Cigar's shareholders to approve the transaction with Swedish Match was fully informed and not actionably coerced. Given that there are no allegations of gift or waste, the fully informed, ratifying vote of the General Cigar shareholders disposes of plaintiff's fiduciary duty claims. Summary judgement is entered in favor of defendants and against the plaintiff.

_____

QUESTIONS

1. In Omnicare the controlling shareholders entered into an agreement to vote their Class B (10 vote) shares for a merger. In this case the controlling shareholders entered into an agreement to vote their Class B (10 vote) shares for a merger. How does the Chancellor distinguish theOmnicare decision?

_____

[99] A third party could nonetheless have made a tender offer for the public shares. In addition, the Cullman's could have waited out the 18 month delay, or the Cullmans could have breached and put Swedish Match in the position of proving its non-speculative damages from a breach of the no-sale clause.

2. In both cases the merger agreements committed the target board to a shareholder vote under Del. GCL § 251(c) (now § 146). Given the voting commitments of the controlling shareholders in both cases, how is this case distinguishable?

3. If General Cigar had been subject to the antitakeover provisions of Del. GCL § 203, could the controlling shareholder have entered into the voting agreement with Swedish Match without prior board approval? Would this have had any effect on the outcome?

4. What effect did the agreement that the merger would not go through unless approved by holders of a majority of the shares held by the public have on the outcome?

5. What effect did the "fiduciary out" have on the outcome?

NOTE ON IN RE LNR PROPERTY CORP. SHAREHOLDERS LITIGATION

In In re LNR Property Corp. Shareholders Litigation, 896 A.2d 169 (Del. Ch. 2005), Miller, who owned 31% of the voting stock and 77.35% of the voting power through super-voting shares, negotiated the sale of the company to a buyer. As part of the sale, Miller and several executives agreed to invest a substantial portion of the sale proceeds ($150 million of his $586 million proceeds) in the buyer's stock, in exchange for a 20% interest in the buyer. Aside from a $4 million change of control premium received by Miller, it appeared that all shareholders would receive the same price for their shares in the cash merger. Plaintiffs' complaint alleged that Miller had a disabling conflict of interest that was not cured by appointment of a special committee that had no power to seek a higher offer, and that relied for its valuation advice on the investment bank that assisted Miller in negotiating the sale. Miller moved to dismiss, on the theory that his interest was identical to that of all other shareholders in getting the best price for his shares, so there was no conflict of interest, and the business judgment rule would protect the decision. Vice Chancellor Lamb denied the motion to dismiss, writing:

"There is authority for the proposition that the mere fact that a controller has or may be acquiring some interest in the buyer does not automatically trigger entire fairness review. For example, in Orman v. Cullman, the court found that a controller who sold a portion of his interest to a third party while maintaining a controlling stake in the resulting corporation was sufficiently unconflicted so as to permit business judgment rule review of the transaction, where there was both an active special board committee with full bargaining power that actually negotiated the final terms of the transaction, and the merger agreement contained a majority of the minority vote condition.

"Here, Miller allegedly negotiated the merger transaction with Cerberus while also agreeing to acquire a substantial (20.4%) stake in the resulting company. Looking at only the bare bones of the complaint, the court cannot reasonably conclude from the facts alleged that Miller's interests were aligned with those of the stockholders. Instead, the well pleaded allegations in the complaint, if true, could support a reasonable inference that Miller was sufficiently conflicted at the time he negotiated the sale that he would rationally agree to a lower sale price in order to secure a greater profit from his investment in Riley Property. If this is shown to be the case, the transaction will be subject to entire fairness review.

"Of course, the defendants may be able to show at the summary judgment stage that Miller, as they argue, negotiated this transaction as a seller, not a buyer, and that the board and the Special Committee were entitled to repose confidence in his unconflicted motivation to obtain the maximum price for all LNR stockholders. In that case, the court may well be able to conclude that the measures taken by the board and the Special Committee to protect the interests of the minority were adequate in the circumstances to invoke the business judgment standard of review. Nonetheless, those facts and circumstances do not appear in the well pleaded allegations of the complaint."

---

2. SALES OF CONTROL

Abraham v. Emerson Radio Corp.
901 A.2d 751 (Del. Ch. 2006).

■ STRINE, VICE CHANCELLOR.

In this opinion, I address a claim against a sporting goods company's controlling stockholder that sold its control bloc for a premium to a strategic buyer that also operated in that same market space. According to the conclusory allegations of the complaint, the buyer somehow misused its control of the acquired subsidiary to usurp its assets for the buyer's benefit and to the unfair detriment of the subsidiary's other stockholders. The plaintiff alleges that the controller should have suspected that the buyer had improper designs for the subsidiary simply because the buyer announced its intention to capitalize on the synergies between the buyer's operating assets and those of the subsidiary. In fact, the plaintiff refuses to stop short of advocating that a selling controller should be deemed, as a matter of law, to be on notice that any buyer who is also a competitor likely has improper motives.

The former controller and its major stockholder and CEO have moved to dismiss the claims against them. Although I reject their argument that the complaint should be dismissed on demand excusal grounds, I agree with their argument that the complaint fails to state a claim. Even assuming for the sake of argument that a controlling stockholder can be held liable for negligently selling control to a buyer with improper motives (as opposed to when it knows it is selling to a looter or an otherwise dishonest and predatory buyer), the plaintiff has failed to state a claim. The complaint is devoid of facts supporting a rational inference that the controller should have suspected that the buyer, another listed public company, had plans to extract illegal rents from the subsidiary. At most, the complaint pleads facts suggesting that the controller knew that it was selling to a strategic buyer who would attempt to capitalize on possible synergies between itself and its new non-wholly owned subsidiary. That mundane prospect provides no rational basis for a seller to conclude that the buyer intends to embark on a course of illegal usurpation of the subsidiary's assets for its own unfair benefit. As a result, even assuming a negligence-based theory of liability exists under our law in these circumstances, the complaint is not viable. Under Delaware law, a controller remains free to sell its stock for a premium not shared with the other stockholders except in very narrow circumstances. The complaint here fails to plead facts supporting the existence of such circumstances. Therefore, it is dismissed.

I.   The Complaint's Recitation of Facts

The following recitation of facts is drawn from the plaintiff's complaint.

The plaintiff is a long-term owner of thousands of shares of nominal defendant Sport Supply Group, Inc.

Sport Supply was founded in 1972 by defendant Michael J. Blumenfeld, who served for several decades as the company's chief executive officer. It went public in 1991 and obtained a listing on the NASDAQ. In 1996, defendant Emerson Radio Corp. obtained a controlling interest in Sport Supply, and Blumenfeld stepped down as CEO. He was replaced by defendant Geoffrey P. Jurick, who was Emerson's CEO and controlling stockholder. Through open market purchases, Emerson increased its ownership of Sport Supply into a majority position by 2002, and by 2005, it owned 53.2% of the shares.

As of the period relevant to the case, Sport Supply had become the nation's largest direct marketer of sporting goods to bulk buyers, such as schools, universities, youth leagues, military bases, and amateur sport teams. Sport Supply's franchise is built on direct catalog and internet sales, having established a successful business-to-business marketing operation through an internet site that has won industry awards.

Despite its market niche, Sport Supply, rather than enjoying profits, suffered losses in the early part of this century. Therefore, in 2003, Sport Supply undertook a strategy to increase sales, reduce expenses, and return to profitability. In early 2004, as part of that strategy, Sport Supply voluntarily delisted its stock, thereby reducing the administrative and regulatory costs attendant to the status of a listed company, but also eliminating many of the integrity-assuring and informational benefits resulting from the regulatory regime for public companies. Following delisting, Sport Supply shares traded on quotes in the pink sheets. Nonetheless, Sport Supply's board and managers portrayed the move as a net gain for all stockholders, as the benefit from the increased marginal profitability resulting from lower regulatory costs was thought to exceed the value of the lost regulatory protections.

The strategy to increase Sport Supply's profitability began to show results in late 2004, when the company reported its first profit in years. The price of the company's shares increased from the $1–2 range to $3 per share very late in the year. The plaintiff alleges that even at this higher price, Sport Supply shares suffered from the discounts usually imposed by the market on the shares of companies with thin floats, trading on the pink sheets, and with a majority stockholder. Nonetheless, by mid-2005, Sport Supply continued to improve its performance, remaining profitable and seeing its share price increase to $3.65 per share.

Then, on July 5, 2005, the event that largely inspires this complaint occurred. Emerson announced that it had sold its majority stake, some 4.75 million shares, for $32 million, or $6.74 per share. The premium to the prior day's closing price of Sport Supply stock was 86%.

The buyer was defendant Collegiate Pacific, Inc. Collegiate Pacific participates in the same industry as Sport Supply, and it just so happened that Sport Supply's founder and long-time CEO, defendant Blumenfeld, was Collegiate's CEO and largest stockholder. According to the complaint, which is cursory on this point, Collegiate "engages in the manufacture, marketing, and distribution of sporting goods and equipment and soft goods, as well as physical education, recreational, and leisure products to the institutional market in the United States." Without detail, the complaint also indicates that Collegiate is a "competitor [of Sport Supply] with interests in many similar lines of business." The shares of Collegiate are listed on the American Stock Exchange.

In the sales agreement with Collegiate, Emerson agreed that all the Sport Supply directors would resign and be replaced by directors selected by Collegiate. Collegiate used its new voting power to designate its chief operating officer and director, defendant Arthur J. Coerver, and its vice president of marketing and director, defendant Harvey Rothenberg, as directors of Sport Supply. The complaint does not allege who the other directors, if any, of Sport Supply were after July 2005, and alleges that Coerver and Rothenberg either constituted the entire board or at least a majority of it.

According to the complaint, Emerson was aware that Collegiate's interest in Sport Supply did not involve simply its desire to own a majority of Sport Supply's stock. Rather, Collegiate believed there to be value in Sport Supply's assets, which, used under Collegiate's management, could generate value. To this point, the complaint quotes from a July 5, 2005 Collegiate press release (the "July Press Release"):

> Adam Blumenfeld, President of Collegiate Pacific, commented further: *"This transaction places a multitude of valuable assets under Collegiate Pacific's managerial umbrella.* Among them:
>
> * * *
>
> — *Proprietary Customer Lists and Trade Names * * **
>
> — *Robust and Scalable SAP IT Platform.*
>
> — *Industry-Best Internet Platform powered by SAP—processed more than 75,000 web orders in FY05.*
>
> * * *

Without specifying what Collegiate or Emerson had done wrong, the complaint portrays Collegiate's announcement as an expression of intent to execute a plan in which it would usurp the value of Sport Supply's assets for itself, without paying for them. In other words, the complaint alleges that Collegiate paid Emerson for a majority bloc of stock, but secured more than that. What it supposedly secured was the right to plunder Sport Supply's assets, not in a good faith effort to secure synergistic gains for both Collegiate and Sport Supply, but simply to divert the value of Sport Supply for Collegiate's exclusive benefit. The complaint contains no recitation of facts illustrating what vital organs of Sport Supply that Collegiate intended to extract for itself, or how Collegiate planned to perform the procedure.

The July Press Release also contained optimistic projections for Collegiate's performance for the rest of the year and 2006. According to the complaint, Collegiate knew or recklessly disregarded that these results were not achievable, because its costs for acquiring Emerson's stake in Sport Supply and other targets were running higher than it had originally estimated, and because Collegiate's outstanding notes were due to be treated as converted into common shares as of the end of September 2005. The higher costs and the need to treat the notes as converted allegedly foreshadowed lower per share earnings, which would, when recognized by the market, result in downward pressure on Collegiate's share price.

On September 8, 2005, Collegiate announced that it had entered into a merger agreement with Sport Supply. The agreement provided for Collegiate to acquire the remainder of the Sport Supply's shares at an exchange rate of 0.56 of a Collegiate share for each Sport Supply minority share. At the then-market price, this would have provided the minority with value equal to the $6.74 per share received by Emerson. But the merger agreement contained no collar.

On November 14, 2005, Collegiate announced that increased acquisition costs and the "as converted" treatment of its notes had reduced its earnings expectations. In the same announcement, Collegiate stated that " '[a] number of joint initiatives [with Sport Supply] have been put in place since July 1, 2005, and we look forward to fully realizing their economic benefits, which we expect to occur later in fiscal 2006 and more dramatically in fiscal 2007.' " The market reacted negatively to the lowered estimates, and Collegiate's shares dropped in price from $10.83 per share on November 11, 2005 to $9.25 per share on November 17, 2005.

The decline in Collegiate's stock price cratered the merger. A large institutional holder negotiated a sale of 1.66 million Sport Supply shares to Collegiate for $5.50 per share in cash. Then, on November 22, 2005, Collegiate announced that the merger agreement had been terminated because the deal was unlikely to close in a timely manner under the " 'previously contemplated terms. . . .' "

At the termination of the merger agreement, the story told by the complaint becomes even more conclusory and devoid of factual specificity, with the complaint simply stating:

> Despite the failure to close the merger, Collegiate continued apace to employ Sport Supply's assets to enhance Collegiate's business, all without proper payment to Sport Supply, or its shareholders. That Collegiate's actions have resulted in a diminution of the value of Sport Supply is shown by the fact that Collegiate was willing to pay $6.74 per share in cash for Sport Supply shares in July 2005; $6.74 worth of volatile stock in September 2005; and then $5.50 in cash in November 2005. Sport Supply shares last traded on December 12, 2005 at $4.85 per share, almost 30% lower than the price received by Emerson.

II. The Counts In The Complaint

The complaint attempts to state two viable counts. The first is pled as a direct, class claim against Emerson and Jurick. It seeks recompense for the allegedly improper sale by Emerson of its control position in Sport Supply to Collegiate. Recognizing that Emerson had a presumptive right to sell its majority stake for a premium, the plaintiff pleads that Emerson (and Jurick, as its alleged controller and as Sport Supply's then Chairman and CEO) allegedly knew that Collegiate, upon acquiring control of Sport Supply, would "set out to transfer Sport Supply's valuable assets to the use and benefit of Collegiate's shareholders to the detriment of Sport Supply's shareholders." Therefore, the complaint seeks an order "equitably re-distribut[ing]" the premium Emerson received from Collegiate to Sport Supply's public shareholders.

The second count is pled as a derivative claim on behalf of Sport Supply against Collegiate, and defendants Coerver and Rothenberg. That claim is closely related to the first count against Emerson and Jurick. Essentially, the second count contends that Collegiate was not entitled, by virtue of becoming Sport Supply's majority stockholder, to "the unfettered use and enjoyment of Sport Supply's assets and technologies without fair compensation, arrived at on terms that would be the same as if the parties bargained at arm's length and in good faith." * * *

III. The Pending Motion To Dismiss Brought By Emerson And Jurick

What gives rise to this opinion is the motion by defendants Emerson and Jurick to dismiss Count I of the complaint, which is the Count pled against them. * * *

B. Does The Complaint State A Claim Upon Which Relief Can Be Granted?

Because demand is excused, I now concentrate on Emerson's other major argument, which is that the complaint fails to plead facts that state a claim upon which relief can be granted. * * *

The essence of Emerson's argument that the complaint fails to state a claim is simple: under Delaware law, Emerson was free, as a general matter, to sell its majority bloc in Sport Supply for a premium that was not shared with the other Sport Supply stockholders.[21] Emerson concedes that there are exceptions to the general rule. In particular, it concedes that there is precedent suggesting that a controlling stockholder who sells to a looter may be held liable for breach of fiduciary duty if the looter later injures the corporation and the former controller either (i) knew the buyer was a looter, or (ii) was aware of circumstances that would "alert a reasonably prudent person to a risk that his buyer [was] dishonest or in some material respect not truthful." In the latter circumstance, that precedent suggests that "a duty devolves upon the seller to make such inquiry as a reasonably prudent person would make, and generally to exercise care so that others who will be affected by his actions should not be injured by [the] wrongful conduct." Unlike the plaintiff, however, Emerson argues that, even if this precedent accurately recites the law, the complaint fails to state a claim.

Before explaining why I agree with Emerson, I must add a prefatory caution. Although Emerson has not raised the issue, I am dubious that our common law of corporations should recognize a duty of care-based claim against a controlling stockholder for failing to (in a court's judgment) examine the bona fides of a buyer, at least when the corporate charter contains an exculpatory provision authorized by 8 Del. C. § 102(b)(7). After all, the premise for contending that the controlling stockholder owes fiduciary duties in its capacity as a stockholder is that the controller exerts its will over the enterprise in the manner of the board itself. When the board itself is exempt from liability for violations of the duty of care, by what logic does the judiciary extend liability to a

---

[21] For an excellent article accurately describing this area of Delaware corporation law, *see* Ronald J. Gilson & Jeffrey N. Gordon, *Controlling Controlling Shareholders*, 152 U. Pa. L. Rev. 785, 794 (2003) (citing Harris v. Carter, 582 A.2d 222, 234 (Del. Ch. 1990) and In re Sea-Land Corp. S'holders Litig., 1987 WL 11283, at *5 (Del.Ch. May 22, 1987)).

controller exercising its ordinarily unfettered right to sell its shares? I need not answer that question here, but do note that the unthinking acceptance that a greater class of claims ought to be open against persons who are ordinarily not subject to claims for breach of fiduciary duty at all—stockholders—than against corporate directors is inadequate to justify recognizing care-based claims against sellers of control positions. Lest the point be misunderstood, drawing the line at care would do nothing to immunize a selling stockholder who sells to a known looter or predator, or otherwise proceeds with a sale conscious that the buyer's plans for the corporation are improper.[24] But it would impose upon the suing stockholders the duty to show that the controller acted with scienter and did not simply fail in the due diligence process.[25]

Here, however, I need not confront that more interesting question. By its own terms, the complaint simply fails to plead circumstances suggesting that Emerson knew, suspected, or should have suspected that Collegiate was either a looter or was dishonest and had improper plans for Sport Supply. It is, of course, true that the complaint is long on conclusory statements that Collegiate somehow misappropriated the assets of Sport Supply after acquiring control. By contrast with Harris, where the plaintiff pled specific facts creating an inference that the seller should have been suspicious of the buyer's honesty, the plaintiff relies upon cutting and pasting press releases by Collegiate. Even as cut and paste, they do not create any inference that Emerson should have been suspicious that Collegiate would engage in improper behavior as Sport Supply's new controller. Rather, they are the typical statements of a strategic buyer who owns assets that can work together synergistically with the new target. Nothing in the quoted language suggests that Collegiate intended to usurp the assets of Sport Supply for its exclusive use, and no rational seller in Emerson's position would assume that was the unspoken intention of a strategic buyer that was itself a listed public company.

* * *

Contrary to the plaintiff's assertions, nothing in that release should have put Emerson on notice that Collegiate had an improper plan to harm the minority stockholders of Sport Supply by draining off the company's assets for Collegiate's exclusive benefit. Rather, the press release simply suggested that Collegiate, like a typical strategic buyer,

---

[24] Remember, also, that the purchaser who becomes the new controller would, of course, be subject to liability for its own fiduciary misconduct.

[25] Professors Gilson and Gordon express this limit on the right to sell at a premium nicely, and as existing when it is "apparent [to the controller] that the purchaser is likely to extract illegal levels of private benefits from operating the controlled corporation." Gilson & Gordon at 796. As I read their work, the term "apparent" means that the seller saw that the buyer was a likely looter and proceeded in the face of that knowledge.

would attempt to capitalize on the synergistic benefits that could flow to both entities from an affiliation.[28]

Likewise, the complaint is devoid of anything but the most conclusory of allegations that defendant Jurick sold his corporate office or that Emerson received a payment for assets of Sport Supply, rather than just its stock. It is perfectly routine for a selling controller to cause its appointees to resign, permitting the new controller to use its newly-acquired voting power to control the board. After all, one buys control for a reason.

The complaint pleads no facts that suggest that Emerson received payments from Collegiate on notice that Collegiate was actually seeking to pay for the right to steal Sport Supply's assets. There are simply conclusory allegations that Emerson "knew" that Collegiate would "set out to use to transfer Sport Supply's valuable assets to the use and benefit of Collegiate's shareholders to the detriment of Sport Supply's shareholders." How Emerson would have known that is not made at all plain. The plaintiff does not plead facts suggesting that Emerson knew or should have suspected that it was being paid, not for the rights properly belonging to a controlling stockholder, but for the power to plunder Sport Supply.

* * *

Of course, the complaint goes on at some length regarding the failure of Collegiate to consummate a merger with Sport Supply at a price identical to that paid to Emerson for its control position. But the failure of Collegiate to consummate a merger does nothing to buttress the plaintiff's effort to state a claim against Emerson. Indeed, the complaint pleads that even after Collegiate's merger proposal went away, the stock price of Sport Supply remained higher than it was before Emerson sold its position—some $4.85 per share—and that the operating results of the company have improved. Moreover, the reality that Collegiate pursued a merger option does not help the plaintiff create an inference that it had plans to steal Sport Supply's assets out the back door, much less one that Emerson should have known about or suspected existed. Whatever the plaintiff thinks of Collegiate's failed stock-for-stock merger proposal, that proposal hardly suggests that Collegiate meant to keep Sport Supply as a mere public shell, from which all the internal value would be extracted for Collegiate. Nor does the fact that Collegiate bought a large bloc of Sport Supply stock from a large institutional holder for $5.50 per share support such an inference.

---

[28] As Gilson and Gordon point out, there is nothing intrinsically wrong with a parent and non-wholly owned subsidiary operating in a synergistic manner, because such synergies can benefit the subsidiary's minority stockholders. Gilson & Gordon at 795. If specific synergistic interactions are alleged to be unfair, our law, of course, permits those interactions to be challenged by an appropriately pled complaint. *Id.* The mere allegation that a parent and subsidiary were engaged in joint activity, without more, does not state a claim.

No doubt the plaintiff would have enjoyed selling out at the price obtained by Emerson, but the plaintiff did not take the non-diversifiable risk necessary to secure a control premium. But the complaint, as pled, suggests that the plaintiff is better off now as a result of operating improvements at Sport Supply that have increased its profitability and stock price. Put simply, pure control premium envy is not a cognizable claim for a minority stockholder under Delaware law.[33]

The circumstances when a controller is subject to liability for selling its shares are not capacious and are exceptions to the general rule that controllers are free, as is any other stockholder, to alienate their shares, provided they comply with any transfer provisions in the relevant corporate instruments and in statutory law. The general rule's utility would be gutted by permitting a plaintiff to state a claim simply by alleging that a controller sold its control position to another solvent, public company in the same industry that announced its intention to capitalize on the synergies between itself and its new controlled subsidiary and that thereafter acted on those intentions in a manner that the plaintiff, in a wholly conclusory and unspecific manner, alleges were unfair to the subsidiary. To hold that such circumstances give rise to a claim opening the door to discovery puts a toll on that which our law says is a basic right of every stockholder, even those who own control: to sell. At the very least, a plaintiff seeking to state a claim must plead facts that indicate that the controller knew there was a risk that the buyer was a looter or otherwise intended to extract illegal rents from the subsidiary, at the expense of the subsidiary's remaining stockholders. The plaintiff here has not done that, and therefore even assuming that a controller can be held liable for mere carelessness in this context, the complaint against defendants Emerson and Jurick must be dismissed.

IV. Conclusion

For the foregoing reasons, the complaint fails to state a claim upon which relief can be granted against defendants Emerson and Jurick. Therefore, the count in the complaint, Count I, directed against them is DISMISSED. IT IS SO ORDERED.

---

[33] *See* Hollinger Int'l, Inc. v. Black, 844 A.2d 1022, 1087 (Del. Ch. 2004) ("As a typical matter, the replacement of a subsidiary's controlling corporate stockholder through a transaction at the parent level should pose no cognizable threat to the subsidiary. The parent has a legitimate right to sell itself absent breaching some recognized duty to the subsidiary. There is utility to respecting this general freedom, which is a natural expectation of the owner of a controlling position and this freedom should be expected by the subsidiary's minority stockholders who have no common or statutory right to tag-along in a transfer of control at the parent level.") (citing Gilson & Gordon at 793–96), *aff'd*, 872 A.2d 559 (Del. 2005); *see also* Mendel v. Carroll, 651 A.2d 297, 306–07 (Del. Ch. 1994) (opining that a board of directors would breach its fiduciary duties if it issued a dilutive option for the sole purpose of diluting an existing controlling stockholder and enabling the corporation to be sold in a transaction in which the controller's control premium was then shared with the other, former, minority stockholders; in other words, finding that corporate boards could not expropriate the controller's property (its control position and its premium-generating potential) solely for the purpose of redistributing the expropriated value to the minority).

NOTE

Not surprisingly, the general legal doctrine in this area has been that ownership of shares is ownership of private property, and that the owners are free to sell it for the best price they can obtain. But in 1932 Berle and Means, in their famous book, THE MODERN CORPORATION AND PRIVATE PROPERTY, at 244, took the position that "control" was a corporate asset, and that any premium paid for a control block in excess of the market price belonged to the corporation and to all its shareholders. While this doctrine has never been accepted by the courts, it maintained considerable currency with academic commentators through the 1960s, perhaps until Henry Manne's pathbreaking article, "Mergers and the Market for Corporate Control," was published in 1965 (see Chapter Two). Some other commentators of the Berle & Means period suggested that whenever a premium was paid for control, it must mean that the buyer was going to obtain corporate benefits to the exclusion of the other shareholders, and thus the sellers should account to the other shareholders for the amount of the premium. Andrews, The Stockholder's Right to Equal Opportunity in the Sale of Shares, 78 Harv. L. Rev. 505 (1965). For a later survey that suggests this area has languished since the 1960s, see Robert W. Hamilton, Private Sale of Control Transactions: Where We Stand Today, 36 Case Western Res. L. Rev. 248 (1985).

The Abraham opinion mentions two grounds for holding control shareholders liable when selling control at a premium. One involves sales to looters. In these cases the corporations are typically financial corporations, which are relatively easy to loot, often highly leveraged, so that it takes a relatively small equity investment to obtain control over large amounts of liquid assets. Often sellers are held to be on notice of the buyer's intent to loot by obtaining a price that seems unrealistically high for the mere equity in the corporation. See, e.g., DeBaun v. First Western Bank & Trust Co., 120 Cal. Rptr. 354 (Cal. Ct. App. 1975) and Gerdes v. Reynolds, 28 N.Y.S.2d 622 (N.Y. Sup. 1941) (sale of controlling interest in an investment trust).

The other ground, mentioned only in passing in the Abraham decision, involves the "sale of corporate office." Directors are fiduciaries, and may not profit personally by selling their office to another. Essex Universal Corporation v. Yates, 305 F.2d 572 (2d Cir. 1962), involved such a charge where the buyer of 28.3% of the stock of a publicly traded corporation obtained a contract commitment that the existing board members would resign seriatim and appoint the buyer's candidates. The legal question raised was whether the buyer had purchased enough shares so that it would be able to elect its own candidates to the board at the next annual meeting, or whether part of the control premium paid was for corporate office. Chief Judge Lumbard wrote:

"The easy and immediate transfer of corporate control to new interests is ordinarily beneficial to the economy and it seems inevitable that such transactions would be discouraged if the purchaser of a majority stock interest were required to wait some period before his purchase of control could become effective. Conversely it would greatly hamper the efforts of any existing majority group to dispose of its interest if it could not assure the purchaser of immediate control over corporation operations. I can see no reason why a purchaser of majority control should not ordinarily be permitted to make his control effective from the moment of the transfer of stock.

"Thus if Essex had been contracting to purchase a majority of the stock of Republic, it would have been entirely proper for the contract to contain the provision for immediate replacement of directors. Although in the case at bar only 28.3 per cent of the stock was involved, it is commonly known that a person or group owning so large a percentage of the voting stock of a corporation which, like Republic, has at least the 1,500 shareholders normally requisite to listing on the New York Stock Exchange, is almost certain to have share control as a practical matter. If Essex was contracting to acquire what in reality would be equivalent to ownership of a majority of stock, i.e., if it would as a practical certainty have been guaranteed of the stock voting power to choose a majority of the directors of Republic in due course, there is no reason why the contract should not similarly be legal. Whether Essex was thus to acquire the equivalent of majority stock control would, if the issue is properly raised by the defendants, be a factual issue to be determined by the district court on remand.

"Because 28.3 per cent of the voting stock of a publicly owned corporation is usually tantamount to majority control, I would place the burden of proof on this issue on Yates as the party attacking the legality of the transaction."

The remaining important case in this area, Perlman v. Feldman, 219 F.2d 173 (2d Cir.) cert. denied, 349 U.S. 952 (1955), involved a large shareholder who was also a CEO and director of the company, who rejected a merger proposal that would have benefitted all shareholders equally, and then caused the sale of a controlling block, including his shares, at a premium over the market. The opinion does not mention the merger opportunity, which could have been viewed as a corporate opportunity seized by the director and officer who was also a controlling shareholder, but rather cites applicable Indiana state law about the duties of directors to conclude that Perlman, as controlling shareholder, was also subject to a fiduciary duty, and was required to share the premium with all shareholders. The majority opinion has doctrinal holes in it that were vigorously criticized by the dissenting judge, and while the opinion is often used in corporate law casebooks, it is little followed. Vice Chancellor Strine, for example, takes no note of it, in focusing on the duties of directors in Abraham.

In re Zhongpin Inc. Stockholders Litig., 2014 Del. Ch. LEXIS 252, held that a company's founder, Chairman and CEO was a controlling stockholder with only 17% ownership. While he had not controlled the directors' decision concerning his going-private bid, he was indispensable to the company, which precluded negotiating with other bidders without his consent and left the committee with no leverage to negotiate a higher price.

QUESTIONS

1. If you represent a corporate board where a large but not majority shareholder is negotiating to sell its shares to a third party, how would you advise the board about its duties?

2. Does the board have any duty to assure that a future controlling shareholder will not act in a manner unfair to minority shareholders, perhaps by engaging in a takeout merger at an unfairly low price? What could a board do under these circumstances to prevent such actions?

3. If the buyer wishes to assure itself of control under circumstances similar to those in the Essex case, how can resigning directors assure themselves that they are not participating in the sale of corporate offices?

4. If the board is concerned that the buyer is in financial straits, and may loot the company after taking control and replacing the current directors, what duties does the board (independent of the selling shareholder) have to the corporation and the remaining shareholders? See Unocal v. Mesa Petroleum Co., *supra* in Chapter Six, Part 2.A.

5. Given Manne's explanation of the gains from transfers of control in Chapter Two, part 4, does this discussion of control premia have much power in today's corporate setting?

6. Assume that banks have been selling for 1½ times book value and a particular bank is purchased for 4 times book value. What should a court conclude about the control premium?

---

3. MINORITY SHAREHOLDERS' APPRAISAL RIGHTS

A. PROCEDURAL REQUIREMENTS

Delaware General Corporation Law, § 262(d)–(k); Model Business Corporation Act §§ 13.20–13.26, 13.30.

Magner v. One Securities Corporation

574 S.E.2d 555 (Ga. App. 2002), certiorari denied, (Ga. 2003).[*]

■ ELLINGTON, JUDGE.

Richard E. Magner and the Magner Family, LLC appeal from the superior court order granting summary judgment to One Securities

---

[*]   Note that Georgia is a Model Act jurisdiction, and that the last four numbers of each section of Georgia law correspond to the Model Act numbering system. Georgia adopted the

Corporation ("OSC") and Benefit Plan Services, Inc. ("BPS") in this declaratory judgment action. Appellees OSC and BPS sought a declaration establishing whether Magner or the LLC preserved any right of dissent to mergers which cashed out Magner's minority shareholder interest in the corporations. In the event the court concluded such dissenters' rights existed, OSC and BPS asked for a judicial appraisal of the value of that interest. Magner and the LLC counterclaimed, challenging the validity of the mergers and seeking rescission. OSC and BPS moved for summary judgment on whether Magner or the LLC had dissenters' rights. * * * The court entered summary judgment in favor of the corporations on both motions, concluding the mergers were valid and that neither Magner nor the LLC had dissenters' rights. Finding no reversible error, we affirm.

* * *

OSC and BPS are private, closely held Subchapter S corporations that designed, sold, and administered employee compensation and benefit plans. Barbara and Ronald Balser owned two-thirds of the corporations; Magner owned one-third. The boards of both corporations were comprised of the Balsers, O. C. Russell, and Stephen Berman. On March 22, 1999, the corporations held a joint board of directors meeting. * * * At this meeting, the directors approved a plan to merge OSC and BPS into Giotto, Inc. and Giotto Administrative Services, Inc., respectively, shell corporations created for this purpose a year before. The purpose of the mergers, which the directors had been discussing for several months before the meeting, was to cash out Magner's interest in the corporations. The directors agreed to pay Magner the "fair value" of his stock, an amount that had been determined by an independent appraiser. The directors determined that OSC and BPS would be the corporate entities surviving the mergers and the Balsers would remain as the sole shareholders of the merged corporations. The directors set the record date for shareholders entitled to vote on the mergers as March 25, 1999. Finally, the directors authorized the senior management of both corporations to work with legal counsel to effect the mergers.

On March 26, 1999, the boards notified Magner in writing that a special shareholders' meeting of both corporations would be held on April 6, 1999, to vote on the merger plans. The notices set the record date, named the merging and surviving corporations, and advised Magner of his dissenters' rights. A plan of merger was attached to the notices. The attached plan of merger, however, contained a typographical error listing the fair value of all of Magner's stock as the price per share. Consequently, on April 3, 1999, the boards sent Magner a corrected notice and rescheduled the meeting for April 15, 1999.

Model Act in the 1980s, and its statute does not reflect all of the provisions of the current version of the Model Act.—Ed.

On April 9, 1999, Magner wrote the corporations instructing them to cancel his shares in OSC and BPS and to reissue them to the LLC effective April 14. Although Magner asserted he did this "for estate planning and asset protection purposes," it appears everyone understood that transferring Magner's stock into a limited liability company could destroy the corporations' Subchapter S status and result in increased tax liability. Through counsel, the corporations wrote Magner and asked him not to make the transfer, informing him of the tax consequences of that act. The corporations assert that Magner, through his attorney, agreed to postpone the decision to cancel his shares and to reissue the stock to the LLC. Magner, however, claims the corporations simply failed to honor his request to make the transfer. In any event, the corporations sought legal and tax advice and determined an argument existed for preserving Subchapter S status if the direction of the mergers was reversed, allowing the Giotto shell corporations to be the surviving entities. Consequently, on April 15, 1999, the board reissued its notice of meeting to Magner, stating that the shell entities would survive the merger, and rescheduled the meeting to April 26, 1999. The notice, like all previous notices, was attached to a plan of merger.

On April 26, 1999, OSC and BPS held a special meeting of shareholders. The Balsers, representing the majority of the shareholders, approved and adopted the merger agreements between the corporations and the shell entities as proposed. Magner, who attended the meeting through counsel, did not vote on either merger. During the meeting, the Balsers' stock was retired and Magner's stock was converted into the right to receive cash in the amount previously established as the stock's fair value. The mergers became effective on April 27, 1999, when the Certificates of Merger and Name Change were filed with the Secretary of State.

On May 4, OSC and BPS notified Magner of his dissenters' rights, offered him the established fair value of his stock, and directed him to demand payment and tender his shares to the corporations by June 7, 1999, if he intended to perfect his dissenters' rights. Instead, on May 12, Magner demanded that his stock in both corporations be recorded as having been transferred to the LLC as of April 14, 1999. The corporations complied with Magner's request, reissuing the stock of OSC and BPS to the Magner Family, LLC, as of April 14, 1999. On June 7, both Magner and the LLC delivered to the corporations documents entitled "Dissenter's Demand for Payment" and tendered the LLC's stock certificates. On June 11, OSC and BPS informed Magner and the LLC that because Magner cancelled his shares, he forfeited his dissenters' rights. Moreover, because the LLC was not a shareholder of record in either corporation on March 25, 1999, it was not entitled to dissent. Again, the corporations offered to pay Magner the appraised fair value of his interest. Magner rejected the offer and, instead, demanded over $16 million for his combined interest in both corporations. On September 3,

1999, the corporations filed the instant declaratory judgment action, or, in the alternative, sought a judicial appraisal pursuant to O.C.G.A. § 14–2–1330.

* * *

2. Magner contends he and the LLC properly perfected dissenters' rights and are, therefore, entitled to a judicial appraisal. We disagree.

O.C.G.A. § 14–2–1302 (a) provides that a "record shareholder of the corporation is entitled to dissent from, and obtain payment of the fair value of his shares in the event of" certain enumerated events, including the "consummation of a plan of merger." O.C.G.A. § 14–2–1301 (a)(1). The procedure for perfecting dissenters' rights is "extremely technical and must be . . . followed within the time [limits] provided; otherwise the shareholder risks losing such appraisal rights." Kaplan's Nadler Ga. Corporation Law (2001 ed.), § 12–20.

To perfect these rights following the merger, Magner, as the record shareholder, was required to "demand payment and deposit his certificates in accordance with the terms of the [dissenters'] notice" he was sent. O.C.G.A. § 14–2–1323(a). See also O.C.G.A. § 14–2–1301 (4) (a dissenter is a shareholder who exercises his rights in accordance with O.C.G.A. §§ 14–2–1320 through 14–2–1327). If Magner failed to do as instructed in the dissenters' notice, the Code states he "is not entitled to payment for his shares under [the dissenters' rights] article." O.C.G.A. § 14–2–1323(c).

Magner did not tender his stock certificates and demand payment as required by the Code. Instead, he cancelled his certificates and had new certificates issued to another legal entity. By this act, Magner placed his certificates beyond his power to tender to the corporation. Consequently, Magner gave up his right to dissent, a right which attached to the possession of those particular stock certificates.

The LLC has no dissenters' rights because it was not a record shareholder on the record date, March 25, 1999. A "record shareholder" is defined in the Code, in relevant part, as "the person in whose name [the] shares are registered in the records of a corporation." § 14–2–1301 (7). Moreover, a record shareholder, as that term is used in the dissenters' rights provisions, contemplates a shareholder who also held shares on the "record date" for purposes of a particular corporate transaction or event. See O.C.G.A. §§ 14–2–707; 14–2–1302; 14–2–1320 through 14–2–1323. For example, O.C.G.A. § 14–2–707 allows the directors to fix a record date so that the corporation may determine, with some degree of certainty, the shareholders entitled to notice, to make demands, to vote, and to take any other action. The commentary to O.C.G.A. § 14–2–1323 explains that the record date "is the cut-off date for determining who has dissenters' rights under this article" and "the demand for payment . . . is the definitive statement by the dissenter." In cases like the instant one, the Code contemplates a demand for payment being made by one who previously received notice of the corporate action and properly expressed an intent to dissent prior to the shareholders' vote. See O.C.G.A. §§ 14–2–1321; 14–2–1322. As the commentary to O.C.G.A. § 14–2–1323 explains, the demand is "confirmation of the 'intention' expressed earlier."

In this case, the LLC was not a record shareholder in either OSC or BPS on the record date set by the corporation. As such, it was not entitled to participate in the event at issue: the mergers. It had no right to dissent and obtain payment for its shares under the dissenters' rights statutes. For these reasons, the trial court properly granted summary judgment in favor of OSC and BPS.

QUESTION

1. Does the treatment of the LLC and Magner as separate stockholders elevate form over substance? If Magner is the only member of Magner Family LLC, is he a "beneficial owner" for whom a "record shareholder" could dissent MBCA § 13.03?

NOTE

Model Act § 13.03(a) provides that a record shareholder may assert appraisal rights on behalf of a beneficial owner, and subsection (b) provides that a beneficial owner may assert his or her appraisal rights only if the record shareholder consents in writing to this action, and the consent is delivered to the corporation in a timely fashion. In contrast, Del. G.C.L. § 262(a) defines "stockholder" as "a holder of record of stock in a stock corporation. . . ." Thus beneficial owners cannot demand appraisal in their own name, but must proceed through their nominee record owner. See Salt Dome Oil Corp. v. Schenck, 41 A.2d 583 (Del.Ch. 1945) and Enstar Corp. v. Senouf, 535 A.2d 1351 (Del. 1987).

B. THE ENTERPRISE TO BE VALUED

Cede & Co. v. Technicolor, Inc.

684 A.2d 289 (Del.1996).

■ HOLLAND, JUSTICE:

[Technicolor was acquired by MacAndrews & Forbes Holdings, Inc., of which Ronald Perelman was the dominant figure. Perelman negotiated with Technicolor management, headed by its CEO, Kamerman, for a $23 cash tender offer followed by a $23 cash merger. The appeal addressed the question of whether the firm to be appraised was "Kamerman's Technicolor" or "Perelman's Technicolor."]

Facts

* * *

Technicolor engaged in a number of distinct businesses through separate operating units. Technicolor's Professional Services Group was its main source of revenue and profit. The Videocassette Duplicating Division operated one of the largest duplicating facilities in the world. The Consumer Services Group operated film processing laboratories ("Consumer Photo Processing Division" or "CPPD"), which provided film processing services to other photofinishers. CPPD also operated the Standard Manufacturing Company ("Standard"), which manufactured film splicers and associated equipment. The Government Services Group ("Government Services") provided photographic and non-photographic support and management services under contract to governmental agencies. Technicolor's Gold Key Entertainment Division ("Gold Key"), licensed motion pictures and other programs for television exhibition. The Audio Visual Division ("Audio Visual") distributed film and video equipment.

Morton Kamerman ("Kamerman"), Technicolor's Chief Executive Officer and Board Chairman, concluded that Technicolor's principal business, theatrical film processing, did not offer sufficient long-term growth for Technicolor. Kamerman proposed that Technicolor enter the field of rapid processing of consumer film by establishing a network of stores across the country offering one-hour development of film. The business, named One Hour Photo ("OHP"), would require Technicolor to open approximately 1,000 stores over five years and to invest about $150 million.

In May 1981, Technicolor's Board of Directors approved Kamerman's plan. The following month, Technicolor announced its ambitious venture with considerable fanfare. On the date of its OHP announcement, Technicolor's stock had risen to a high of $22.13.

In the months that followed, Technicolor fell behind on its schedule for OHP store openings. The few stores that did open reported operating losses. At the same time, Technicolor's other major divisions were experiencing mixed, if not disappointing, results.

As of August 1982, Technicolor had opened only twenty-one of a planned fifty OHP retail stores. Its Board was anticipating a $5.2 million operating loss for OHP in fiscal 1983. On August 25, 1982, the Technicolor Board "authorized the company's officers to seek a buyer for Gold Key." During 1982, Technicolor also decided to terminate the Audio Visual Division. Nevertheless, Kamerman remained committed to OHP. In Technicolor's Annual Report, issued September 7, 1982, Kamerman stated, "We remain optimistic that the One Hour Photo business represents a significant growth opportunity for the Company."

Technicolor's September 1982 financial statements, for the fiscal year ending June 1982, reported an eighty percent decline of consolidated net income—from $17.073 million in fiscal 1981 to $3.445 million in 1982. Profits had declined in Technicolor's core business, film processing. Technicolor's management also attributed the decline in profits to write-offs for losses in its Gold Key and Audio Visual divisions, which had already been targeted for sale. By September 1982, Technicolor's stock had reached a new low of $8.37 after falling by the end of June to $10.37 a share.

* * *

[A period of direct negotiations between Perelman and Kamerman followed.] On October 27, Kamerman and Perelman reached an agreement by telephone. Perelman initially offered $22.50 per share for Technicolor's stock. Kamerman countered with a figure of $23 per share. He also stated that he would recommend its acceptance to the Technicolor Board. Perelman agreed to the $23 per share price.

The Technicolor Board convened on October 29, 1982 to consider MAF's proposal. All nine directors of Technicolor attended the meeting. Kamerman outlined the history of his negotiations with Perelman. Kamerman explained the basic structure of the transaction: a tender offer by MAF at $23 per share for all the outstanding shares of common stock of Technicolor; and a second-step merger with the remaining outstanding shares converted into $23 per share, with Technicolor becoming a wholly owned subsidiary of MAF. Kamerman recommended that MAF's $23 per share offer be accepted in view of the present market value of Technicolor's shares. Kamerman stated that accepting $23 a share was "advisable rather than shooting dice" on the prospects of Technicolor's OHP venture.

On October 29, 1982, the Technicolor Board agreed to the acquisition proposal by MAF. The Technicolor Board: approved the Agreement and Plan of Merger with MAF; recommended to the stockholders of Technicolor the acceptance of the offer of $23 per share; and recommended the repeal of the supermajority provision in Technicolor's Certificate of Incorporation. Technicolor filed forms 14D-9 and 13D with the Securities and Exchange Commission which reflected those Board actions and recommendations.

In November 1982, MAF commenced an all-cash tender offer of $23 per share to the shareholders of Technicolor. When the tender offer closed on November 30, 1982, MAF had gained control of Technicolor. By December 3, 1982, MAF had acquired 3,754,181 shares, or 82.19%, of Technicolor's shares. Thereafter, MAF and Technicolor were consolidated for tax and financial reporting purposes.

The Court of Chancery made a factual finding that, "upon acquiring control" of Technicolor, Perelman and his associates "began to dismember what they saw as a badly conceived melange of businesses." Perelman testified: "Presumably we made the evaluation of the business of Technicolor before we made the purchase, not after." That evaluation assumed the retention of the Professional and Government Services Groups and the disposition of OHP, CPPD, Gold Key and Audio Visual.

Consequently, immediately after becoming Technicolor's controlling shareholder, MAF "started looking for buyers for several of the [Technicolor] divisions." Bear Stearns & Co. was also retained by MAF in December 1982 to assist it in disposing of Technicolor assets. A target date of June 30, 1983 was set for liquidating all of Technicolor's excess assets. As of December 31, 1982, MAF was projecting that $54 million would be realized from asset sales.

In December 1982, the Board of Technicolor notified its stockholders of a special shareholders meeting on January 24, 1983. At the meeting, the Technicolor shareholders voted to repeal the supermajority amendment and in favor of the proposed merger. MAF and Technicolor completed the merger.

Valuation of Technicolor Perelman Plan or Kamerman Plan

The merger was accomplished on January 24, 1983. The parties agree that the appraised value of Technicolor must be fixed as of that date. See Alabama By-Products Corp. v. Neal, Del. Supr., 588 A.2d 255, 256–57 (1991). There is a fundamental disagreement between the litigants, however, concerning the nature of the enterprise to be appraised.

Cinerama argues that the Court of Chancery should have valued Technicolor as it existed on the date of the merger and, in particular, with due regard for the strategies that had been conceived and implemented following the merger agreement by MAF's controlling shareholder, Ronald O. Perelman ("Perelman Plan"). Technicolor argues that the Court of Chancery properly considered Technicolor without regard to the Perelman Plan and only as it existed on or before October 29, 1982, with the then extant strategies that had been conceived and implemented by Technicolor's Chairman, Morton Kamerman ("Kamerman Plan"). * * *

The economic experts for both parties used a form of discounted cash flow methodology to value Technicolor. * * * The fundamental nature of the disagreement between the parties about the Perelman Plan and the Kamerman Plan, however, resulted in different factual assumptions by their respective experts.

Question of Law Perelman Plan or Kamerman Plan

The Court of Chancery recognized that the parties' disagreement about valuing Technicolor based upon either the Perelman Plan or the Kamerman Plan presented a question of law with regard to the proper interpretation of the appraisal statute. See 8 Del. C. § 262(h). According to the Court of Chancery, that legal issue is whether in valuing Technicolor as of January 24, 1983, the court should assume the business plan for Technicolor that MAF is said by [Cinerama] to have had in place at that time [Perelman Plan], or whether a proper valuation is premised upon ignoring such changes as Mr. Perelman had in mind because to the extent they create value they are "elements of value arising from the accomplishment or expectation of the merger." 8 Del. C. § 262(h).

* * *

Court of Chancery's Holding Majority Acquiror Principle Proximate Cause Exception

The Court of Chancery acknowledged that, based upon the quoted language from Weinberger, Cinerama's legal argument appeared to be persuasive. The Court of Chancery concluded, however, "that reading [of Weinberger] is too difficult to square with the plain words of the statute to permit the conclusion that that is what was intended." The Court of Chancery then stated "in order to understand the quoted passage [from Weinberger] when read together with the statutory language, I assume an unexpressed phrase to the effect 'unless, but for the merger, such elements of future value would not exist.' " According to the Court of Chancery, the language in Weinberger would read: "But elements of future value, including the nature of the enterprise, which are known or susceptible of proof as of the date of the merger and not the product of speculation, may be considered [unless, but for the merger, such elements of future value would not exist]." Weinberger v. UOP, Inc., Del. Supr., 457 A.2d 701, 713 (1983).

In explaining the "but for" caveat that it had superimposed upon this Court's holding in Weinberger, the Court of Chancery reasoned that, as a matter of policy, the valuation process in a statutory appraisal proceeding should be the same irrespective of whether a merger is accomplished in one or two steps:

> Delaware law traditionally and today accords to a dissenting shareholder "his proportionate interest in a going concern" and that going concern is the corporation in question, with its asset deployment, business plan and management unaffected by the plans or strategies of the acquiror. When value is created substituting new management or by redeploying assets "in connection with the accomplishment or expectation" of a merger, that value is not, in my opinion, a part of the "going concern" in which a dissenting shareholder has a legal (or equitable) right to participate.

If one accepts this principle, the question arises how is it to be applied in a two-step arms'-length acquisition transaction. In such a transaction there will be a period following close [to] the first-step tender offer in which the [majority] acquiror may, as a practical matter, be in a position to influence or change the nature of the corporate business, or to freeze controversial programs until they are reviewed following the second-step merger.

Accordingly, the Court of Chancery concluded that "future value that would not exist but for the merger . . . even if it is capable of being proven on the date of the merger," is irrelevant in a Delaware statutory appraisal proceeding. (Emphasis added.) Consequently, the Court of Chancery held "that value added to [Technicolor] by the implementation or the expectation of the implementation of Mr. Perelman's new business plan for [Technicolor] is not value to which, in an appraisal action, [Cinerama] is entitled to a pro rata share, but is value that is excluded from consideration by the statutory exclusion for value arising from the merger or its expectation."

Legal scholars have written extensively with regard to the economic desirability of including or excluding certain valuation elements in an appraisal proceeding,[5] especially with regard to cash-out two-step mergers. See, e.g., John C. Coffee, Jr., Transfers of Control and the Quest for Efficiency: Can Delaware Law Encourage Efficient Transactions While Chilling Inefficient Ones? 21 DEL. J. CORP. L. 359 (1996); Robert B. Thompson Exit, Liquidity, and Majority Rule: Appraisal's Role in Corporate Law, 84 GEO. L.J. 1 (1993).[6] The Court of Chancery's construction of "fair value" followed logically from its concept of what was economically desirable and efficient. However, the majority acquiror principle and correlative proximate cause exception for two-step mergers, upon which the Court of Chancery premised its holding, are inconsistent with this Court's interpretation of the appraisal statute in Weinberger.

All Relevant Factors Only Speculation Excluded

* * *

The seminal decision by this Court regarding an appraisal proceeding is Weinberger v. UOP, Inc., Del. Supr., 457 A.2d 701 (1983). In Weinberger, this Court broadened the process for determining the "fair value" of the company's outstanding shares by including all generally accepted techniques of valuation used in the financial community. Weinberger v. UOP, Inc., 457 A.2d at 712–13; see Technicolor I, 542 A.2d at 1186–87. The result of that expansion was the holding in Weinberger that "the standard 'Delaware block' or weighted average method of valuation, formerly employed in appraisal and other

---

[5] See, e.g., Frank H. Easterbrook & Daniel R. Fischel, The Economic Structure of Corporate Law (Harvard Univ. Press 1991); Benjamin Hermalin & Alan Schwartz, Buyouts in Large Companies, 25 J. Legal Stud. 351 (1996); Lynn A. Stout, Are Takeover Premiums Really Premiums? Market Price, Fair Value, and Corporate Law, 99 Yale L.J. 1235 (1990); Angie Woo, Note, Appraisal Rights in Mergers of Publicly-Held Delaware Corporations: Something Old, Something New, Something Borrowed, and Something B.L.U.E., 68 S. Cal. L. Rev. 719 (1995).

[6] See also Bate C. Toms, III, Compensating Shareholders Frozen Out in Two-Step Mergers, 78 Colum. L. Rev. 548 (1978).

stock valuation cases, shall no longer exclusively control such proceedings." Weinberger v. UOP, Inc., 457 A.2d at 712–13.

The Delaware appraisal statute provides that the Court of Chancery:

> shall appraise the shares, determining their fair value exclusive of any element of value arising from the accomplishment or expectation of the merger or consolidation, together with a fair rate of interest, if any, to be paid upon the amount determined to be the fair value. In determining such fair value, the Court shall take into account all relevant factors.

8 Del. C. § 262(h). In Weinberger, this Court construed the appraisal statute. That construction required this Court to reconcile the dual mandates of Section 262(h) which direct the Court of Chancery to: determine "fair" value based upon "all relevant factors;" but, to exclude "any element of value arising from the accomplishment or expectation of the merger." In making that reconciliation, the ratio decidendi of this Court was, as follows:

> *Only the speculative elements of value that may arise from the "accomplishment or expectation" of the merger are excluded. We take this to be a very narrow exception to the appraisal process,* designed to eliminate use of pro forma data and projections of a speculative variety relating to the completion of a merger. But elements of future value, including the nature of the enterprise, which are known or susceptible of proof as of the date of the merger and not the product of speculation, may be considered. When the trial court deems it appropriate, fair value also includes any damages, resulting from the taking, which the stockholders sustain as a class. If that was not the case, then the obligation to consider "all relevant factors" in the valuation process would be eroded. We are supported in this view not only by [Tri-Continental Corp. v. Battye, Del. Supr., 31 Del. Ch. 523, 74 A.2d 71, 72 (1950)], but also by the evolutionary amendments to section 262.

Weinberger v. UOP, Inc., 457 A.2d at 713 (emphasis added). * * *

After examining the evolution of the statutory text in Section 262(h), this Court concluded "there is a legislative intent to fully compensate shareholders for whatever their loss may be, subject only to the narrow limitation that one can not take speculative effects of the merger into account." *Id.* at 714 (emphasis added). * * *

Perelman Plan Susceptible of Proof/Non-Speculative

The underlying assumption in an appraisal valuation is that the dissenting shareholders would be willing to maintain their investment position had the merger not occurred. Cavalier Oil Corp. v. Harnett, Del. Supr., 564 A.2d 1137, 1145 (1989). Accordingly, the Court of Chancery's task in an appraisal proceeding is to value what has been taken from the shareholder, i.e., the proportionate interest in the going concern. *Id.* at 1144 (citing Tri-Continental Corp. v. Battye, Del. Supr., 31 Del. Ch. 523, 74 A.2d 71, 72 (1950)). To that end, this Court has held that the corporation must be valued as an operating entity. *Id.* We conclude that the Court of Chancery did not adhere to this principle.

The Court of Chancery determined that Perelman "had a fixed view of how [Technicolor's] assets would be sold before the merger and had begun to implement it" prior to January 24, 1983. Consequently, the Court of Chancery found that the Perelman Plan for Technicolor was the operative reality on the date of the merger. Nevertheless, the Court of Chancery held that Cinerama was not entitled to an appraisal of Technicolor as it was actually functioning on the date of the merger pursuant to the Perelman Plan.

The Court of Chancery reached that holding by applying its majority acquiror principle and correlative proximate cause exception. The Court of Chancery excluded any value that was admittedly part of Technicolor as a going concern on the date of the merger, if that value was created by substituting new management or redeploying assets during the transient period between the first and second steps of this two-step merger, i.e., Perelman's Plan. The Court of Chancery reasoned that valuing Technicolor as a going concern, under the Perelman Plan, on the date of the merger, would be tantamount to awarding Cinerama a proportionate share of a control premium, which the Court of Chancery deemed to be both economically undesirable and contrary to this Court's holding in Bell v. Kirby Lumber Corp., Del. Supr., 413 A.2d 137, 140–42 (1980). Thus, the Court of Chancery concluded "that value [added by a majority acquiror] is not . . . a part of the 'going concern' in which a dissenting shareholder has a legal (or equitable) right to participate."

* * *

In a two-step merger, to the extent that value has been added following a change in majority control before cash-out, it is still value attributable to the going concern, i.e., the extant "nature of the enterprise," on the date of the merger. See Rapid-American Corp. v. Harris, 603 A.2d at 805. The dissenting shareholder's proportionate interest is determined only after the company has been valued as an operating entity on the date of the merger. Cavalier Oil Corp. v. Harnett, 564 A.2d at 1144; cf. Walter W.B. v. Elizabeth P.B., Del. Supr., 462 A.2d 414, 415 (1983). Consequently, value added to the going concern by the "majority acquiror," during the transient period of a two-step merger, accrues to the benefit of all shareholders and must be included in the appraisal process on the date of the merger. See Rapid-American Corp. v. Harris, 603 A.2d 796; Cavalier Oil Corp. v. Harnett, 564 A.2d 1137; cf. Walter W.B. v. Elizabeth P.B., 462 A.2d at 415.

In this case, the question in the appraisal action was the fair value of Technicolor stock on the date of the merger, January 24, 1983, as

Technicolor was operating pursuant to the Perelman Plan. The Court of Chancery erred, as a matter of law, by determining the fair value of Technicolor on the date of the merger "but for" the Perelman Plan; or, in other words, by valuing Technicolor as it was operating on October 29, 1982, pursuant to the Kamerman Plan. By failing to accord Cinerama the full proportionate value of its shares in the going concern on the date of the merger, the Court of Chancery imposed a penalty upon Cinerama for lack of control. Cavalier Oil Corp. v. Harnett, 564 A.2d at 1145; accord Rapid-American Corp. v. Harris, 603 A.2d at 805–07; Bell v. Kirby Lumber Corp., 413 A.2d at 140–42.

* * *

Conclusion

The judgment of the Court of Chancery in the appraisal action is reversed.

_____

QUESTIONS

1. Why does the court not treat Perelman's plan as not an "element of value arising from the accomplishment or expectation of the merger or consolidation"? Would Perelman have implemented a business plan for Technicolor if he did not believe MacAndrews & Forbes Holdings, Inc. could complete the merger?

2. If you represent a bidder planning a two-step takeover, how can you minimize the impact of the bidder's plans to increase the value of the target on the appraisal value of the firm? In considering your answer, review a bidding firm's disclosure obligations under Securities Exchange Act Schedule 13D-1, Item 4, which is treated in Chapter Eleven, Part 3.C.

3. Does this rule reduce the incentives of bidders to take over troubled firms? Why?

_____

NOTE

In a 1990 opinion in the appraisal case, Cede & Co. and Cinerama, Inc. v. Technicolor, Inc., 1990 WL 161084, Chancellor Allen described the outcome as follows:

> "Ronald Perelman's leveraged acquisition of Technicolor in the two-step transaction agreed upon on October 29, 1982, by the Technicolor board must rank as one of the most successful change of corporate control transactions in a decade that was to become first crowded and later littered with such transactions. MAF's $23 cash price represented a large (more than 100%) premium over the September 1982 market prices of Technicolor's stock. The $105

million stock acquisition cost was funded almost entirely with bank credit and other borrowings. Upon acquiring control of the company Mr. Perelman and his associates, Bruce Slovin and Robert Carlton began to dismember what they saw as a badly conceived melange of businesses. Within one year these entrepreneurs had sold several of those businesses for approximately $55.7 million in cash ($11 per share) and paid about half of the bank debt used to acquire the company. Remarkably, the sale of these businesses did not significantly alter Technicolor's positive cash flow. The remaining businesses (including importantly Technicolor's traditional business of theatrical film processing and a new business of producing videocassette under contract with copyright owners) were apparently thereafter managed with skill and good luck. As modified during the course of MAF's ownership, Technicolor was later sold in an arm's length transaction to Carlton, PLC in 1988 for some $738 million in cash. In the annals of the effective uses of leverage, the account of MAF's original minimal cash contribution to the acquisition of Technicolor certainly deserves a place."

This opinion is just one of many in this case, which ultimately has become the Delaware version Jarndyce v. Jarndyce in Dickens' BLEAK HOUSE, which, coincidentally, involved a court of chancery, albeit in a different jurisdiction and with corruption never evident in the Delaware courts involved in corporate law. Without detailing the entire procedural history of the case, it has been remanded to the Chancery Court by the Supreme Court on five occasions. The last (as of this writing) decision was reached by Chancellor Chandler (who replaced Chancellor Allen when he left the bench for a law teaching post) on December 31, 2003, 2003 Del Ch. LEXIS 146. Recall that the merger called for cash payments of $23.00 per share. Chancellor Allen valued the shares at $21.60. After a nine day new trial Chancellor Chandler valued them at $23.22. Cinerama owned 201,200 shares. The net gain from the twenty year appraisal process over the merger consideration was thus $44,264. Chancellor Chandler summarized the problem as follows:

"Although 8 Del. C. § 262 requires this Court to determine 'the fair value' of a share of Technicolor on January 24, 1983, it is one of the conceits of our law that we purport to declare something as elusive as *the* fair value of an entity on a given date, especially a date more than two decades ago. Experience in the adversarial battle of the experts' appraisal process under Delaware law teaches one lesson very clearly: valuation decisions are impossible to make with anything approaching complete confidence. Valuing an entity is a difficult intellectual exercise, especially when business and financial experts are available to organize data in support of wildly divergent valuations for the same entity. For a judge who is not an expert in corporate finance, one can do little more than try to detect gross distortions in the experts' opinions. This effort should, therefore, not be understood, as a matter of intellectual honesty, as resulting in *the* fair value of a corporation on a given date. The value of a corporation is not a point on a line, but a range of reasonable values, and the judge's task is to assign one particular value within this range as the most reasonable value in light of all of the relevant evidence and based on considerations of fairness."

2003 Del. Ch. LEXIS 146, at *5–*6.

C. VALUATION METHODS

i.   COURTS AS NON-EXPERTS IN VALUATION

We begin with a question involving an arm's length merger. Assuming that each party has its own self-interest in mind, and that neither directors nor shareholders of either company have any conflicting interests, what reason is there to believe that the agreed consideration in the merger is not full consideration for the interests given up by shareholders? The answer to this question is largely path-dependent. At first courts issued injunctions to stop unconsented mergers, on the theory that it took unanimous consent to change the terms of the contract (the articles of incorporation). This gave way to recognition that a single stubborn minority shareholder could hold out and block a valuable transaction. So courts began enjoining mergers only until the majority provided a bond to protect the economic interest of the minority. This is a move from a property rule to a liability rule, by judicial creation. This was followed in early 20th century by adoption of appraisal statutes. This codified the liability rule—the property of a minority shareholder could be "taken," but only for fair compensation. Bayless Manning famously described this as giving the majority to overrule a minority. Manning, The Shareholder's Appraisal Remedy: An Essay for Frank Coker, 72 Yale L.J. 223 (1962). These statutes required the corporation to pay "fair value" to a shareholder that objected to a merger. See Carney, Fundamental Corporate Changes, Minority Shareholders and Business Purposes, 1980 Am. Bar Found. Res. J. 69. In recent years the focus of the appraisal remedy has been on interested shareholder transactions under Model Business Corporation Act § 13.02.

The issue of valuation has long troubled courts, where judges are trained in law but not in financial economics. Reliance on experts was necessary for judges to become informed. Where markets were weak (not engaged in frequent trades of homogenous assets, experts are forced to rely on various methods. In real estate, where no two homes are generally alike, appraisers rely on several methods, to overcome the concern that any one is misleading. Comparable sales represent one method, but this is flawed because no two homes that are sold in the same time frame are perfectly alike. Appraisers often overcome this by hypothetically adjusting the size or other characteristics of one home to make it more comparable to another—a speculative enterprise at best. Another method used is reproduction cost, using currently known building costs. But if homes are not new, they are subject to either wear and tear or some degree of obsolescence, as tastes and technologies change. Estimating the amount of this depreciation in value is at best an informed guess. As a result, appraisers typically use at least these two methods and weight them to come up with an appraisal.

Courts once did (and still do in some cases) use approximately the same method. In one well-known case, Piemonte v. New Boston Garden Corp., 387 N.E.2d 1145 (Mass. 1979), the court was required to appraise a corporation that owned both the famous sports arena, the Boston Garden, plus the Boston Bruins Hockey team. There were only sporadic transfers of shares in the company, leaving market value as highly questionable. Ultimately, the court used three estimates of value and weighted them as follows:

	Value		Weight		Result
Market Value:	$26.50	x	10%	=	$2.65
Earnings Value:	$52.60	x	40%	=	$21.04
Net Asset Value:	$103.16	x	50%	=	$51.58
	Total Value Per Share:				$75.27

An observer might ask why an informed arm's length buyer would pay $103.15 that could only produce earnings worth about half that amount. This author has never seen a discussion of the contradictions inherent in such a relationship.

A well-known Delaware case presents an extreme example of the problems inherent in this approach. Francis I. duPont & Co. v. Universal City Studios, Inc., 312 A.2d 344 (1973). This was a conflict of interest case, where a parent owning 92% of the stock of Universal Pictures merged it into a new wholly owned subsidiary, Universal City. The studios had amortized the value of these films to zero in many cases, thus understating their fair market value going forward. Accordingly, both earnings and asset value were understated. The court excluded market value entirely in its calculation, on the basis that the market was thin.

The earnings of Universal were on an upward track prior to the merger, more than doubling in the previous five years. Apparently this was an era when television began to demand old films from studio libraries. This accounted for the earnings growth, which plaintiffs argued would continue. The custom of the courts was to use a five-year average of earnings to eliminate random movements. Earnings per share were as follows:

1961 $3.32
1962 $4.96
1963 $6.22
1964 $6.32
1965 $8.02

The five-year average was $5.77. The court rejected future projections of earnings on the basis of uncertainty:

> I do not agree with the shareholders that the "pre-1965 earnings had become an anachronism" at the time of merger. I view Universal's situation at that time as one of change in the nature of its market, not in the fundamental nature of its business. It was undoubtedly clear at the time of merger that the new television market had contributed substantially to Universal's earnings and would continue to do so for at least the short term. It was also evident that television presented a relatively permanent new market. But I do not think it realistic to say that that market was of such a revolutionary character as to assure for time without end either a trend of increasing earnings or a comparatively high level of earnings. The fact is that, with or without the television market, Universal's earning experience over the long term remains subject to the variables in its managerial and artistic talent, the ability and ingenuity of competitors and the uncertainties of public tastes in entertainment.

The court rejected expert testimony about valuing earnings, concluding, apparently that existing law trumped market realities:

> The stockholders argue that averaging past earnings is proper only when the earnings history has been erratic. In support of that proposition, Mr. Stanley Nabi, managing partner of a NYSE brokerage house and an investment and financial analyst, testified that the accepted practice among security analysts is to capitalize present earnings, and to give the trend of earnings important consideration in the selection of the multiplier. The stockholders argue that Universal's earnings history was not erratic but, in fact, had a steady and rapid growth. They contend that the Appraiser therefore should have used the current (1965) earnings as the figure to be capitalized.
>
> This argument is not persuasive even if Mr. Nabi's testimony as to the accepted practice among security analysts for capitalizing earnings is conceded to be correct. Whatever that practice may currently be, the policy of Delaware law is that averaging earnings over the five years immediately preceding the merger should be the rule and not the exception. In short, a choice among alternative techniques for capitalizing earnings has been

made and no persuasive conceptual reason has been shown to change that choice now.

That practice ended with Weinberger v. UOP, 457 A.2d 701 (Del. 1983), a breach of fiduciary duty case where the complaint alleged, among other things, that the price paid to minority public shareholders in a cash-out merger was "unfair." In providing valuation guidance to the Chancery Court on remand, the court stated:

"In this breach of fiduciary duty case, the Chancellor perceived that the approach to valuation was the same as that in an appraisal proceeding. Consistent with precedent, he rejected plaintiff's method of proof and accepted defendants' evidence of value as being in accord with practice under prior case law. This means that the so-called 'Delaware block' or weighted average method was employed wherein the elements of value, i.e., assets, market price, earnings, etc., were assigned a particular weight and the resulting amounts added to determine the value per share. This procedure has been in use for decades. However, to the extent it excludes other generally accepted techniques used in the financial community and the courts, it is now clearly outmoded. It is time we recognize this in appraisal and other stock valuation proceedings and bring our law current on the subject.

"While the Chancellor rejected plaintiff's discounted cash flow method of valuing UOP's stock, as not corresponding with 'either logic or the existing law', it is significant that this was essentially the focus, i.e., earnings potential of UOP, of Messrs. Arledge and Chitiea in their evaluation of the merger [for UOP]. Accordingly, the standard 'Delaware block' or weighted average method of valuation, formerly employed in appraisal and other stock valuation cases, shall no longer exclusively control such proceedings. We believe that a more liberal approach must include proof of value by any techniques or methods which are generally considered acceptable in the financial community and otherwise admissible in court, subject only to our interpretation of § 262(h), *infra*. This will obviate the very structured and mechanistic procedure that has heretofore governed such matters. Fair price obviously requires consideration of all relevant factors involving the value of a company. This has long been the law of Delaware as stated in Tri-Continental Corp., 74 A.2d at 72:

"The basic concept of value under the appraisal statute is that the stockholder is entitled to be paid for that which has been taken from him, viz., his proportionate interest in a going concern. By value of the stockholder's proportionate interest in the corporate enterprise is meant the true or intrinsic value of his stock which has been taken by the merger. In determining what figure represents this true or intrinsic value, the appraiser and the courts must take into consideration all factors and elements which reasonably might enter into the fixing of value. Thus, market value, asset value, dividends, earning prospects, the nature of the enterprise and any other facts which were known or which could be ascertained as of the date of merger and which throw any light on *future prospects* of the merged corporation are not only pertinent to an inquiry as to the value of the dissenting stockholders' interest, but *must be considered* by the agency fixing the value. (Emphasis added.)

"This is not only in accord with the realities of present day affairs, but it is thoroughly consonant with the purpose and intent of our statutory law. Under 8 Del. C. § 262(h), the Court of Chancery:

"shall appraise the shares, determining their *fair* value exclusive of any element of value arising from the accomplishment or expectation of the merger, together with a fair rate of interest, if any, to be paid upon the amount determined to be the *fair* value. In determining such *fair* value, the Court shall take into account *all relevant factors* ... (Emphasis added)

"It is significant that section 262 now mandates the determination of 'fair' value based upon 'all relevant factors'. Only the speculative elements of value that may arise from the 'accomplishment or expectation' of the merger are excluded. We take this to be a very narrow exception to the appraisal process, designed to eliminate use of *pro forma* data and projections of a speculative variety relating to the completion of a merger. But elements of future value, including the nature of the enterprise, which are known or susceptible of proof as of the date of the merger and not the product of speculation, may be considered. When the trial court deems it appropriate, fair value also includes any damages, resulting from the taking, which the stockholders sustain as a class. If that was not the case, then the obligation to consider 'all relevant factors' in the valuation process would be eroded. We are supported in this view not only by Tri-Continental Corp., 74 A.2d at 72, but also by the evolutionary amendments to section 262."

This leaves the question of what are these modern methods of valuation. The court mentioned the future prospects of the corporation as relevant, without stating what modern finance does: that only the future expected profits of a corporation are relevant to valuation of its stock. Historic earnings may inform us about expectations to some extent, but they are relevant largely to the question of the volatility of the earnings of the corporation, and its impact on the discount rate to be used.

ii.   EXPERT VALUATION OF STOCKS

Simply put, the modern valuation process is one of taking expected future earnings and discounting the entire stream of these earnings to present value. Behind this is the conclusion that this is what investors value: the stream of earnings available to the firm *after* they purchase their shares. These earnings are made available to the shareholders in the form of dividends and other distributions, or in reinvestment in the firm (retained earnings) on their behalf, which should grow the future earnings stream available for distribution. When we discuss "expected" future earnings, this is obviously an educated guess, based on past earnings trends, assessments of future competition, and the strength of the company's market position. Newspapers are filled with stories of companies that have missed their estimates on projected revenues and profits, illustrating the difficulties in this area. Management's public projections are often for a quarter, and never more than a year. The perils of projecting growth over longer periods of time. Frequently experts will use the existing rate of growth in earnings as the expected growth rate for a limited period—almost never longer than five years. This method assumes that whatever a company is doing to make earnings grow will be limited in the future by competition, or perhaps by saturation of the market. Thereafter, experts will use the earnings of that last year of growth for the indefinite future. It's not perfect, but it's the best experts have been able to accomplish. Picking stocks that will beat the market is hard, even for professionals. Most mutual funds don't beat broad market averages, after deductions for expenses. As a result, more and more investors are turning to so-called "index funds," which mimic broad market averages, and with a buy and hold strategy incur much lower expenses.

The other difficult part of the process, at least for purposes of its brief treatment in this book, is the choice of a discount rate. The discount rate is the rate of return that investors will demand on a particular investment, and is obviously related to the riskiness of the investment and the expected volatility of its returns. Finding a risk-free rate is relatively easy: what is the current yield on U.S. Treasury securities, which are absolutely safe? We can observe that returns on other classes of investments carry higher rates, which investors demand for accepting risk. Thus, even high-grade corporate bonds carry higher interest rates than Treasuries, and common stocks carry even higher returns as a class. The stock market as a whole carries an expected (and historic) rate of return above the risk-free rate, which is called the "equity premium"—the amount investors demand to hold a diversified portfolio of stocks, rather than treasuries.

Not all stocks are equally risky. Some have much higher variance in their earnings and stock prices than others. This variance is caused by two types of factors. The first is what will probably occur to most readers first—bad news for a company: the market doesn't like its new line of autos, its new programming for a tv network, a bad choice of fashions for a retailer, etc. If you only hold one stock, this kind of bad news can be pretty disastrous, because individual stocks can drop a long way in value in a short time when there's this kind of bad news. From early January of 2004 to July of 2006, Ford Motor Company's stock fell by 60% in value, for example. During that same period the Standard & Poor's 500 stock index rose by nearly 20%. The lesson: some companies and their stocks can be hit hard by bad news. While Ford is a component of the S & P 500, its poor performance was offset by the good performance of many more companies. For example, Anadarko Petroleum Corp. rose about 80% during the same period.

The lesson is an obvious one—don't put all your eggs in one basket—diversify! One study showed that the average volatility of a single stock was 49.24% annually, while the average volatility of a 500 stock portfolio was 19.27%, or less than 40% of the one-stock portfolio.* You can reduce your risk by 60%, and with the right selection of stocks, receive the same expected return as on the one-stock portfolio! It sounds like an irresistible idea, doesn't it? And it is. Rational investors don't hold one-stock portfolios, but hold many more stocks (you can get most of this diversification with as few as 30 stocks). That last 19% of volatility isn't related to the performance of individual stocks so much as it's related to overall market conditions in the economy. That's the second risk that influences what rate of return investors demand on stocks, and thus pricing.

So how do rational investors pick stocks? Aside from diversifying, they decide how much risk they can bear in order to get higher returns. Diversification means individual circumstances for companies don't matter. The only thing left is how a portfolio of stocks reacts to changes in the overall economy. This is the measure of a stock's movement in relation to overall market averages, such as the S & P 500. It is a stock's beta. A beta of one means that the stock's price is expected to move in tandem with the market's average (all other things being equal). Stocks with a beta of one will be priced by investors so they are expected to yield the same return as the overall market, which is (1) the risk-free rate plus (2) the equity premium, which is simply observed in the market. Some stocks are less volatile than the market, such as utility stocks. As of February 29, 2016, American Electric Power had a beta of 0.225, for example. (You can look up many betas on Yahoo! Finance by going to "key statistics" for an individual stock.) That means its price is expected to

---

* Meir Statman, How Many Stocks Make a Diversified Portfolio?, 22 J. Financial & Quantitative Analysis, 353 (1987).

move only about one-third as much as a market average. As a result, investors will demand a lower rate of return on it—(1) the risk-free rate plus (2) 0.225 x equity premium. Similarly, a high beta stock, such as General Motors, calls for a higher return: (1) the risk-free rate plus (2) 1.655 x equity premium.

One more thing. We can construct a portfolio with a certain level of risk by selecting a pool of stocks where none of them have the beta we want. It's only important that the average beta meets our target. We can also get there by mixing in risk-free Treasuries if we're seeking a lower beta, or by borrowing (which increases our risk) to achieve higher betas. Because of this ability, one finance text contained the aphorism, "seen one stock, seen them all."

A further caution: there are some problems with the Capital Asset Pricing Model ("CAPM"). Eugene Fama and Richard French have found that firm size (market capitalization) matters, and that investors require an additional premium on top of the calculated rate for small-cap stocks. Presumably this reflects the greater risk found in these stocks beyond simple volatility, captured in beta. These companies may, for example, lack the market power of larger firms, or perhaps the management depth. In any event, when discounting earnings for small cap stocks investors require a small-cap premium to be incorporated in the discount rate. Fama and French, Size and Book-to-Market Factors in Earnings and Returns, 50 Journal of Corporate Finance 131 (1995).

With this we have traveled with amazing speed and superficiality through modern portfolio theory and the CAPM, which describes the theory underlying valuation in the next cases. Before continuing, we should note one famous dissenter from these theories, Warren Buffett, the legendary head of Berkshire Hathaway, which has outperformed the market and all other investment managers over a very long period. Berkshire Hathaway's investments grew at a rate of 23% compounded annually from 1964–1988, while general markets grew at about a 10% rate, according to his letter to stockholders in 1988. Buffett ignores the function of stock volatility in assessing risk. Caring about cyclical stock volatility over a business cycle assumes that investors are traders, and may sell at the bottom of a market and buy at its peak. Buffett's view is much longer term. He selects companies for their good management and strong competitive position in their markets, with the intention of holding these investments much longer than one market cycle. While a number of good companies meet these criteria, Buffett looked for those few companies that he and his colleagues viewed as not properly (efficiently) priced. This derived from the teachings of a legendary professor at Columbia Business School, Benjamin Graham. It is generally known as "value" investing.

In re Appraisal of Ancestry.com, Inc.

2015 Del. Ch. LEXIS 21; 2015 WL 399726.

■ GLASSCOCK, VICE CHANCELLOR.

I am tasked with determining the "fair value" of shares of a publicly-traded company, in this case shares formerly held by the Petitioners, who were cashed out in the purchase of Ancestry, Inc. ("Ancestry" or the "Company") by a private equity investor, Permira Advisors, LLC ("Permira"). The sale was at a 40% premium to the market price untainted by the auction process, which process itself involved a market canvas and uncovered a motivated buyer. The price paid stockholders who tendered in the sale was $32. The Petitioners' valuation expert proved something of a moving target; he argued that the fair value of a share of Ancestry stock at the time of the merger was as high as $47, but at least $42.81. The Respondent's expert opined that fair value was $30.63, despite the fact that the buyer, a non-strategic investor with actual money at risk, was willing to pay more.

* * *

I.   BACKGROUND FACTS

[Ancestry is the pioneer in online family genealogy, having digitized and indexed huge numbers of historical records. It has over two million subscribers. For a while through clever promotions, the revenues and profits grew rapidly. It had its initial public offering in November, 2009, at $13.50 per share. By early 2011, the stock traded at over $40 per share. Competition has developed, however. The Church of Jesus Christ of the Latter Day Saints has maintained the world's largest collection of ancestral data, which it began digitizing, and FamilySearch.org began providing free access to these records.

There was evidence that Ancestry had saturated the market for genealogical records, and that the number of families that are interested in such records was limited. By early 2012 Ancestry stock traded in the low $20s, and the company began to consider strategic alternatives, including a search for buyers. Qatalyst Partners, a financial advisor, was retained to do the search, and reached out to a number of potential bidders, both potential strategic and financial buyers. Ultimately seven potential bidders submitted non-binding preliminary indications of interest, with bids ranging from $30 to $38. The four highest bidders were invited to engage in full due diligence. The due diligence activity was discouraging—monthly subscribers were declining.]

* * *

2.   Management Projections

Ancestry did not prepare management projections in the ordinary course of business; the projections prepared in connection with the sales process were "the first time that [Ancestry had] ever done long-term projections." In fact, "[u]p until that point [May 2012,] [Ancestry] had frankly never done anything out past [ ] one year."

Hochhauser [Ancestry's CFO and COO] worked with Curtis Tripoli, head of Ancestry's financial planning and analysis ("FP & A") group, and his team, as well as Sullivan, in preparing the Company's projections. The goal was to "come up with a set of optimistic projections that we could stand in front of a room and walk through and present, but that we know are going to be very optimistic." The motivation to be optimistic derived in part from the belief that potential bidders were "going to cut back or discount what we say, so we want to give ourselves some room or some cushion."

a.   The May Projections

In early May, a set of projections was developed that addressed the key metrics of Ancestry's business—GSAs, churn, and SAC (the "Initial May Projections"). According to Sullivan [Ancestry's CEO] "the view was that these were forecasts that were going to be used by people that were going to . . . potentially bid to buy the company. And so we determined that we wanted those to certainly be optimistic, even aggressive."

Hochhauser presented these projections to the Company's directors at a May 15 board meeting. Hochhauser noted in a May 14 email to the board enclosing materials for the meeting that he had adjusted the projections to account for NBC's recent cancellation of Who Do You Think You Are?. After reviewing these projections, "the board's push-back was that you guys really need to turn—you know, be a touch more aggressive here and accelerate your growth."

Hochhauser took the board's "feedback [to] try to make [the projections] more aggressive" and in fact "made them slightly more aggressive." In these new projections (the "May Sales Projections," and collectively with the Initial May Projections, the "May Projections"), management "turned the dials—GSA, SAC, churn—as much as [they] could while maintaining . . . credibility." Specifically, "to go much beyond what [management] did, you would have to assume some new business, creation of new business." These updated projections were presented to and approved by the board, and provided to interested parties during the sales process.

b.   The October Projections

After receiving the May Sales Projections, some bidders commented that the assumptions were optimistic and aggressive. That fall, partly in response to bidder feedback, management developed a new set of projections (the "October Projections"). Qatalyst had also been "pretty clear . . . that they likely couldn't render a fairness opinion based upon those May numbers." As Hochhauser put it, "[i]f we're selling the company, the board would need to have the best set of numbers they could possibly have to make an important decision."

To develop the October Projections, Hochhauser, working with Curtis, and others in Ancestry's FP & A group, along with Sullivan, underwent the "[s]ame process mechanically" as they had for the May Projections. In August, however, the budget process had begun, and the Company "had actualized or closed the months leading up through September." Accordingly, "2012 was sort of a tighter set of numbers."

The updated numbers, in addition to the incorporation of bidder feedback, led to projections that were more conservative than the May Sales Projections previously approved by the board and provided to bidders. As Hochhauser noted, in this set of projections, management— "shooting for the bull's eye of numbers"—was "not trying to be optimistic or pessimistic. We're trying to be right down the middle." Sullivan relayed that the "philosophy" behind these projections was "accuracy."

On October 11, the October Projections were finalized. These Projections included two scenarios—Scenario A and Scenario B (the "Scenarios")—which were not weighted; instead, they were meant to act as outer "goalposts" of a range, with the goal being "to just look between the two of them." At trial, management opined that these were the best estimates of the Company's future performance. Notably, however, at the time the Scenarios were being created, management was also contemplating equity rollovers into the new company.

* * *

[The merger was announced on October 22. In the following two months, no topping bid emerged, despite a fiduciary out in the agreement. On December 27, 2012, 99% of voting shareholders approved the merger, which closed the following day.]

* * *

C. The Appraisal Remedy

Ancestry received written demands for appraisal dated December 6, 2012 from Cede & Co., nominee for The Depository Trust Company ("DTC") and record holder of the 160,000 shares over which Petitioners Merlin Partners LP ("Merlin") and The Ancora Merger Arbitrage Fund, LP ("Ancora" and, together with Merlin, the "Merlin Petitioners") assert beneficial ownership. Ancestry received a written appraisal demand dated December 18, 2012 from Cede & Co., as record owner of the 1,255,000 shares for which Merion Capital, L.P. ("Merion") asserts beneficial ownership.

D. Experts' Valuations

The experts of both the Petitioners and Respondent relied exclusively on a discounted cash flow ("DCF") analysis to value Ancestry as of the Merger Date, as opposed to comparable companies and comparable transactions analyses, recognizing that the latter would be irrelevant or unhelpful here, given Ancestry's unique business and the concomitant difficulty of finding comparable companies or transactions.

The Petitioners' expert, William S. Wisialowski, initially opined that Ancestry was valued at $42.97; after making certain corrections to his analysis, he adjusted this valuation to $43.65, then to $43.05. At his deposition, however, Wisialowski testified that, "[b]ased on the information that was given to [him]," he would not provide a fairness opinion at a price below $47 per share. Finally, at trial, Wisialowski opined that the value of Ancestry was "at least" $42.81 per share; $42.81 is more than 30% higher than the merger price, resulting in a discrepancy of approximately $500 million between the two values.

The Respondent's expert, Gregg A. Jarrell, arrived at a value of $30.63 per share. In arriving at $30.63, Jarrell testified that "the $32 is within that range from a discounted cash flow analysis. And that provides a great deal of comfort to me that the discounted cash flow analysis has validity, is economically meaningful." Wisialowski's analysis, by comparison, resulted in a "big discrepancy" between the value of the Company and the merger price. As Jarrell testified:

> [I]f that were me that was faced up with that big discrepancy, I would have to try to find out a way to reconcile those two numbers, or why would these smart, professional, profit-oriented professional private equity investors leave that much money on the table? Why wouldn't someone pay $33 for this company if, in fact, it were validly worth [$]42 to [$]47 as a stand-alone company? You know, that's a huge valuation gap and that's a lot of implied profit that's been left on the table. And that, to my mind, would create a lot of discomfort regarding my DCF valuation.

* * *

1. Valuation Background

By way of brief background, and to provide context before recounting the experts' respective calculations and assumptions,

> [t]he basic premise underlying the DCF methodology is that the value of a company is equal to the value of its projected future cash flows, discounted at the opportunity cost of capital. Put simply, the DCF method involves three basic components: (i) cash flow projections; (ii) a terminal value; and (iii) a discount rate.

The method "involves several discrete steps":

> First, one estimates the values of future cash flows for a discrete period, based, where possible, on contemporaneous management projections. Then, the value of the entity attributable to cash flows expected after the end of the discrete period must be estimated to produce a so-called terminal value, preferably using a perpetual growth model. Finally, the value of the cash flows for the discrete period and the terminal value

must be discounted back using the capital asset pricing model
or "CAPM."

In this case, the experts disagreed on each of these components-the
projections to use for future cash flows, the terminal value, and the
discount rate-and the components that make up each of those, in addition
to the role of stock-based compensation. I describe the discrepancies in
the inputs of Wisialowski and Jarrell, and their respective rationales,
below.

2. Projections

Wisialowski developed a set of "blended" management projections,
which weighted the Initial May Projections and October Scenario B
equally. Wisialowski testified that his arrival at this weighting did not
involve much precision. He did not attempt to determine the probability
of either projection occurring; instead, he testified at trial that he "was
tempering-[he] was mixing the projections to say maybe they were half
right on this growth rate and half right on this growth rate and put those
together." He explained: "What I try to do is come up with what I felt was
a minimum defensible conservative valuation of the company."

Jarrell, on the other hand, relied exclusively on the October
Projections, weighting both October Scenarios equally. He opined that
the October Projections were more reliable because they incorporated
bidder feedback, the realities of the auction process, and other
information that management had learned since May; they were also
closer to Wall Street estimates.

3. Terminal Value

Calculating terminal value involves four key components: perpetuity
growth rate, the EBIT margin, the "plowback" ratio, and the projected
tax rate.

As for perpetuity growth rate, Wisialowski adopted 3.0%, which he
characterized as the most conservative assumption in his entire model.
Jarrell agreed that this was "on the low side," and adopted a 4.5% growth
rate. This difference did not garner much discussion at trial,
comparatively speaking, as both choices could be seen as conservative for
their respective sides. That is, had Wisialowski adopted a higher growth
rate, his valuation could have been more favorable to the Petitioners; had
Jarrell adopted a lower growth rate, his valuation could have been more
favorable to the Respondent.

The remaining three components generated a more vigorous dispute.

First, Jarrell and Wisialowski disagreed as to whether it was
necessary to normalize EBIT margins during the perpetuity period-
Jarrell believed it necessary; Wisialowski did not. Normalization of EBIT
margins is based on the idea that the EBIT projection for the last year of
the projections period may not be appropriate to apply in perpetuity; as
Jarrell explained at trial:

The perpetuity period, in theory, is a period where you're in long-run competitive equilibrium. In long-run competitive equilibrium, there's a tendency for margins to be lower than they are in the forecast period because competition in the long run is more fierce than it is in the short run. Any barriers to entry that Ancestry has in the short run, owing to whatever advantages that they've generated, tend to erode in the long run rather than get better, and that reflects itself as competition for price, and the margin goes down.

Thus, rather than apply the projected margin for the final year of the projections period in perpetuity, Jarrell averaged the projected margins and used that figure, which had been "normalized to a sustainable level," in calculating terminal value. He averaged the projected EBIT margins for 2013 through 2016 (as projected in Scenarios A and B), resulting in a normalized EBIT margin of 26.1% for Scenario A and 27.3% for Scenario B, as compared to the historical actual EBIT margin of 18.2% for the years 2004–2012, and the actual EBIT margin of 26.3% for the year 2012.

The Petitioners criticized Jarrell's approach on two grounds, first asserting that normalization "was unnecessary given the pessimistic outlook already adopted by the Scenarios." Second, they contend, even if one were to normalize, "normalized profit margins should reflect the *midpoint* of the company's business cycle," because "[a]s the company reaches a steady state, the cost structure evolves and becomes stable." Because Ancestry had been growing, "the average margins used by Jarrell would not reflect a mid-point of its business cycle," and "Jarrell conducted no analysis to determine whether his EBIT margin assumption during the perpetuity period *was* the midpoint of Ancestry's business cycle."

While criticizing Jarrell's approach, the Petitioners offered little in the way of substantive support of Wisialowski's approach, other than to characterize it as "appropriate[ ]," "given Ancestry's consistent trend of increasing margins." Wisialowski used 38.8% in his terminal period calculation, which is his EBITDA margin projection for 2016, and is higher than any margin Ancestry ever achieved. Wisialowski arrived at 38.8% by blending the projected EBITDA margins from the last projected year of each of the Initial May Projections and October's Scenario B. Jarrell noted that, had Wisialowski normalized his EBITDA margins, his figure would have been 37.3%. The effect of this discrepancy is to drive the terminal value, and thus the DCF, of the respective experts further apart; *i.e.*, the Petitioners' expert's valuation comes out higher, and the Respondent's expert's valuation comes out lower.

Second, the experts arrived at different plowback ratios, which is the percentage of net operating profit after tax that is reinvested in capital expenditures. The idea is that "[i]n order to adequately support a perpetual growth rate in excess of expected inflation (*i.e.*, positive real growth), a firm will need to reinvest in capital expenditures at a sustainable rate that is above that of projected depreciation." Jarrell's plowback ratio was 12% of his terminal period cash flows, which he arrived at by considering plowback for Scenarios A and B (12.1% and 11.5%, respectively), and the historical plowback, which was 11.9%. In light of his 4.5% perpetuity growth rate, with 2% expected inflation, this 12% plowback ratio implied a return on investment of 22.8% going forward-"a very pro increases-value assumption." By comparison, Wisialowski used a 4.8% plowback ratio and criticized Jarrell's higher figure. Jarrell noted, however, that because of Wisialowski's 3% perpetuity growth rate, again assuming 2% expected inflation, Wisialowski's projected return on investment comes out to 22.6%; in other words, the assumptions used by each expert result, essentially, in a wash.

Finally, as to projected tax rate, Jarrell used 38%, while Wisialowski used 35%. "This difference has a material effect on the valuation-if Jarrell had used a 35% tax rate, it would raise his valuation by $0.97; if Wisialowski used a 38% tax rate, [ ] it would lower his valuation by $1.17." Jarrell's marginal tax rate figure is based on historical actual effective tax rates, which the Petitioners criticized as improper and not representative of the Company's future. Jarrell defended his figure by suggesting that, although an average tax rate may be lower than a marginal rate, one cannot rely, in perpetuity, on whatever variables resulted in a lower tax rate in a given year. He found it more reasonable to remain consistent with the Company's long-term historical average tax rate. Wisialowski arrived at 35% by using 34%-a figure presented by PricewaterhouseCoopers in a presentation to Permira as to the likely tax rate "for the foreseeable future," but not explicitly a tax rate in perpetuity-and adding 1%, to "[be] conservative."

4. Discount Rate

Wisialowski calculated a discount rate of 10.96%, while Jarrell calculated 11.71%. This resulted in a $4.27 per share difference in their valuations. The discrepancy turns largely on the experts' respective "beta"-that is, discount for risk based on the stock's movement as compared to the market-calculations; Wisialowski calculated beta of 1.107, later updated to 1.095, while Jarrell calculated 1.30.

Key inputs in beta calculations include the market proxy, the observation period, and the sample period. The experts used different inputs on all accounts, at least in their initial reports; they ultimately agreed on the most appropriate sample period, while remaining in disagreement over the market proxy and observation period.

First, the experts used different market proxies in their regression analyses. Wisialowski "selected the beta resulting from the regression of ACOM [Ancestry stock] against the NASDAQ Composite for all data since its IPO on a weekly basis." Wisialowski opted to use NASDAQ as the market proxy because he believed it to contain a number of companies similar to Ancestry. He then applied this beta to an *S & P 500-based* equity risk premium, though his report identified that a NASDAQ-derived beta should be multiplied by a NASDAQ equity risk premium. Jarrell used the S & P 500 as his market proxy for the regression analysis. In post-trial briefing, the Petitioners asserted that they "[do] not take issue with regressing Ancestry's weekly beta against the S & P 500 if a weekly observation period is used, which results in a beta of 1.137."

Second, Wisialowski and Jarrell used different observation periods, which can be daily, weekly, or monthly. Wisialowski used a weekly observation period, while Jarrell used a monthly period. Wisialowski characterized this as the "biggest difference" in their respective calculations. Wisialowski testified that many valuations use monthly data, but that, for Ancestry, this resulted in only 30 data points, whereas using 36 to 60 is recommended; thus, he used weekly data to generate more points. Jarrell testified that daily or weekly trading prices can include statistical "noise" that affects the accuracy of the beta calculation, but noted that, "all else equal, the more observations, the better in terms of statistical precision." He used a monthly period, which he described as "sort of the standard of the services," having found "noise" when he conducted further calculations.

Third, while Wisialowski observed the period from the IPO through the date of the merger in his initial report, Jarrell excluded the period in which the auction process had become public. In his rebuttal report and at trial, Wisialowski conceded that Jarrell's approach was sound. However, Wisialowski testified that when he adjusted the time period to use Jarrell's approach, his beta decreased, thus driving a further gap between the experts' calculations.

5.   Stock-Based Compensation

Wisialowski, in his initial DCF analysis, did not take into account Ancestry's practice of providing stock-based compensation ("SBC") to its employees. Jarrell, by contrast, contends that a failure to account for SBC expenses within a DCF model may result in overvaluation. Scenarios A and B of the October Projections did not include projections for SBC, however; he instead used a figure—3.2% of revenues-taken from the May Projections.

In his rebuttal report, Wisialowski "built a model to estimate the number of options granted each year and the future stock price of Ancestry in order to measure the cash flow required to eliminate any dilution from future option grants and their exercise." For his model, he maintained his 50/50 weighting of the May Projections with Scenario B, but, as noted, because the October Projections did not include SBC projections, Wisialowski chose 1%, which he said was based on "total personnel expense and SBC of 23.5% for Scenario B, which is slightly higher than the combined figure for the [May Projections]." Ultimately, he calculated a difference in share value of approximately $0.50. Wisialowski explained that he decided

> not to include any impact for SBC in my DCF analysis because adding the future stock trading price adds yet another level of assumptions which are difficult to prove. That being said, I strongly believe that my estimates are conservative and Jarrell's are just plain wrong. I continue to believe that non-inclusion of SBC expense in FCF for purposes of a DCF-based valuation is the proper treatment and the treatment recognized by this Court.

* * *

III. APPRAISAL ANALYSIS

A.   *The Appraisal Standard*

Characterized as, at one time, a liquidity option and, more recently, as a check on opportunism, the appraisal statute allows dissenting stockholders to receive judicially-determined fair value of their stock. After determining that appraisal petitioners have standing, as I have done here, the Court shall determine the fair value of the shares exclusive of any element of value arising from the accomplishment or expectation of the merger or consolidation, together with interest, if any, to be paid upon the amount determined to be the fair value. In determining such fair value, the Court shall take into account all relevant factors.

"Appraisal is, by design, a flexible process." Section 262 "vests the Chancellor and Vice Chancellors with significant discretion to consider 'all relevant factors' and determine the going concern value of the underlying company." Our Supreme Court has declined to "graft common law gloss on the statute," in light of the General Assembly's determination that this Court's consideration of "all relevant factors" is fair, albeit imperfect. Thus, and in the absence of "inflexible rules governing appraisal," "it is within the Court of Chancery's discretion to select one of the parties' valuation models as its general framework, or fashion its own, to determine fair value in the appraisal proceeding."

Although the Supreme Court "has defined 'fair value' as the value to a stockholder of the firm as a going concern, as opposed to the firm's value in the context of an acquisition or other transaction," this Court has relied on the merger price as an indicia of fair value, "so long as the process leading to the transaction is a reliable indicator of value and merger-specific value is excluded." In fact, this Court has held, where the transaction giving rise to the appraisal resulted from an arm's-length process between two independent parties, and [ ] no structural impediments existed that might materially distort "the crucible of objective market reality," a reviewing court should give substantial evidentiary weight to the merger price as an indicator of fair value.

B. Ancestry's Fair Value

In an appraisal action, as pointed out above, "[b]oth parties bear the burden of establishing fair value by a preponderance of the evidence," which effectively means that neither party has the burden, and the burden instead falls on this Court. Upon consideration of the sales process, the experts' opinions, and my own DCF analysis, conducted in light of certain concerns with both experts' analyses, I find that Ancestry's value as of the Merger Date is $32. To explain that conclusion, I turn first to the evidence of valuation reflected in the market price.

1.   The Sales Process

The sales process was reasonable, wide-ranging and produced a motivated buyer. It has been approved of, as free from the taint of breaches of fiduciary duty, by this Court. In a bench ruling denying motion for a preliminary injunction, then-Chancellor Strine noted that: "The process looked like they segmented the market carefully, logical people were [brought] in, a competent banker who appears at every turn to have done sensible things, ran it." The Court characterized that process as one "that had a lot of vibrancy and integrity":

* * *

Of course, a conclusion that a sale was conducted by directors who complied with their duties of loyalty is not dispositive of the question of whether that sale generated fair value. But the process here, described in full earlier in this Memorandum Opinion, appears to me to represent an auction of the Company that is unlikely to have left significant stockholder value unaccounted for. On the other hand, as is typical in a non-strategic acquisition, I find no synergies that are likely to have pushed the purchase price above fair value. The Defendant's expert, although arguing that fair value is somewhat below the sales price, concedes as much.

It is within that context of the auction process, which generated a sale price of $32 per share, that I turn first to a significant issue in Ancestry's valuation-its projections-before turning to the evidence of value by way of the experts' opinions.

2.   Company Projections

Both sets of projections that formed the basis of discounted cash flow analyses and provided the underpinnings of the experts' respective valuations are imperfect. Ancestry's management made no business projections in the regular course of business; its first set of long-term projections, the Initial May Projections, were made aggressive to bolster a potential sale of the company and revised after encouragement by the board to be even more aggressive, resulting in the May Sales Projections. Notably, one particular assumption underlying these projections-that churn would decrease over time-was directly called into question by potential bidders during their due diligence processes.

The October Scenarios are also questionable. They were made in light of an understanding that the May Projections could not support a fairness opinion for the proposed transaction and at a time when management was contemplating large rollovers of their own positions in Ancestry stock. I note that at the same time management was creating the October Scenarios, the CEO was doing private projection "hacks," anticipating joyfully a possible growth rate for his rollover interest substantially greater than those management projections. Nonetheless, I find the Scenarios more reliable than the May Projections. Testimony indicated that the October Scenarios were management's best estimates as of the time of the merger. They included hard numbers, rather than projections, for several additional months of data compared to the May Projections. The Scenarios also took into account feedback from the Company's financial advisor, relayed from bidders, that the May Projections were too optimistic.

It is within this context that I turn to the experts' analyses. The Petitioners' expert, Wisialowski, contended that the May Sales Projections were so unsupportably rosy that potential investors lost confidence in management; thus, he focused instead on the Initial May Projections. The Initial May Projections were not approved by the board and were not presented to bidders. Notably, the Initial May Projections that the Wisialowski champions were only marginally more conservative than the May Sales Projections he rejects. Notwithstanding his support for the Initial May Projections, I conclude that Wisialowski believed that a DCF based on the Initial May Projections alone (which, again, he contended to be the more conservative of the May Projections) would itself be unsupportably high. Ultimately, he used a blended projection from the Initial May Projections and the better case October Scenario, which Scenario he contended was tainted and unsupportably low, yet still incorporated into his valuation. It is unclear how "blending" two unsupportable sets of projections gives a number on which this Court can rely.

The Respondent's expert, Jarrell, relied solely on the October Projections, because management represented them as the best prediction as of the date of the merger. Again, I note that those projections were (1) not developed in the ordinary course of business, (2) done in light of the information that the banker would be unable to provide a fairness opinion based on management's May Projections, and (3) done at a time when management knew that it would be rolling over its own equity in the company rather than being cashed out. Therefore, a DCF based on these projections leaves room for doubt. That said, this Court has recognized that management is, as a general proposition, in the best position to know the business and, therefore, prepare projections; "in a number of cases Delaware Courts have relied on projections that were prepared by management outside of the ordinary course of business and with the possibility of litigation." As described below, therefore, and despite the factors that make the October Projections problematic, I find that an equal weighting of the Scenarios is a better platform on which to base a DCF analysis than a blend of the Initial May Projections and the best case October Scenario, as employed by Wisialowski.

3. DCF Analysis

While I will not burden this Memorandum Opinion by reciting the qualifications of the competing experts here, I note that both are respected in their field, and well qualified to offer valuation opinions. That said, I find each respective approach less than fully persuasive. It is clear to me that the Petitioners' expert tailored his DCF analysis by blending together what he described as the "unbelievable" best case October Scenario with the Initial May Projections simply in order to come up with a number that was "defensible"-that is, higher than the merger price, but not astronomically so as would have been the case if he used the more "reliable" projection alone. The Respondent's expert candidly suggested that, if he had reached a valuation that departed from the merger price by as much as the Petitioners' expert, he "would have to tried to find out a way to reconcile those two numbers," in other words, he would have tailored his analysis to fit the merger price. Neither of these approaches gives great confidence in the DCF analysis of either expert, since both appear to be result-oriented riffs on the market price. Ultimately, I am faced with an appraisal action where an open auction process has set a market price, where both parties' experts agree that there are no comparable companies to use for purposes of valuation, and where management did not create projections in the normal course of business, thus giving reason to question management projections, which were done in light of the transaction and in the context of obtaining a fairness opinion. As Wisialowski repeatedly testified, he saw it as his job to "torture the numbers until they confess[ed]." I note that (beyond any moral concerns) it is well-known that the problem with relying on torture is the possibility of *false* confession. Accordingly, my own analysis of the value of Ancestry follows.

While the concept of a DCF valuation-that value is derived from the sum of future revenue discounted to present value-is quite simple, the calculation itself is complex. The following discussion is laden with formulas through which the discount rate and terminal value are arrived at. I freely admit that the formulas did not spring form the mind of this judge, softened as it has been by a liberal arts education. * * * Although I will address, with specificity, the experts' contentions and my findings with respect thereto, I find that, as a general matter, Jarrell was more credible and his analysis is more likely to result in a fair value of Ancestry. I diverge with him on two significant points: first, his beta calculation, and specifically, his use of a monthly observation period; and second, his use of a 4.5% growth rate coupled with a 12% plowback ratio.

I will discuss my findings as they specifically relate to the evidence offered by the two experts, but I am largely adopting the methodology advanced by Jarrell. Employing that methodology, my valuation of Ancestry as of the Merger Date, based solely on a DCF analysis, is $31.79.

* * *

As an initial matter, the parties dispute whether a two-stage or three-stage discounted cash flow method is most appropriate. This issue turns largely on the projections upon which I rely, and, as discussed below, I rely on the October Projections in my analysis. Accordingly, I agree here with Jarrell that a three-stage model is unnecessary.

a. Projections

Driving the bulk of the substantial valuation differential between the analyses performed by Jarrell and Wisialowski is the key input: management projections. Jarrell relies on the October Scenarios, despite evidence suggesting that they were produced in light of the need to justify the sales price. Wisialowski, on the other hand, created his own projections, by blending the Initial May Forecast with the best case October Scenario, presumably because relying solely on the Initial May Forecast-which Wisialowski touts as the most reliable-would produce a valuation so high as to be likely rejected out-of-hand. The evidence suggests that the May projections were created to drive a high sales price; like the October Scenarios, they were not created in the ordinary course of business.

This Court has expressed skepticism in past cases as to management-prepared projections when those projections are not made in the ordinary course, and are instead made in contemplation of the sale of the company. But management is uniquely situated in its knowledge of the Company, and while management projections are imperfect, hindsight-driven post hoc "projections" are more so; notably, both experts here rely on (different) management projections. Thus, and for the reasons set out above, I find it most appropriate here to rely upon the October Scenarios, as Jarrell did. These projections represented management's best view of the Company, and as discussed above, I do not find the May Projections to be reliable. Therefore, I will rely exclusively on the October Projections, weighing Scenarios A and B at 50% each because management declined to present either Scenario as more likely.

b. Terminal Value

The experts disagreed as to the appropriate perpetuity growth rate, but Jarrell pointed out that, in light of their respective plowback ratios, the differences were not particularly significant. That is, with Jarrell's perpetuity growth rate and plowback ratio, the rate of return on investment would be 22.8%, while Wisialowski's figures would generate a 22.6% return on investment. Ultimately, in light of this Court's prior methodology, where it has assumed zero plowback, and Jarrell's forthright statement that Wisialowski's lower plowback rate was reasonable in relation to his lower growth rate, I am adopting Wisialowski's figures, a 3% growth rate and 4.8% plowback, here.

The more significant of their disputes concerns the normalization of EBIT margins. Jarrell found it important to normalize, while Wisialowski did not; the Petitioners argue that normalization was not necessary given the pessimistic view of the Scenarios Jarrell used. Because I find the October Projections to be management's best view of the Company going forward, not necessarily a pessimistic one, normalization is appropriate. I find Jarrell's averaging of the 2013 through 2016 EBIT margin projections, which figure was then used as his future projection, appropriate. This results in a normalized EBIT margin of 26.1% for Scenario A and 27.3% for Scenario B.

Finally, the experts disagreed over the appropriate tax rate. Although I sympathize with the Petitioners' contention that few (if any) companies pay their marginal tax rates in perpetuity, it strikes me as overly speculative to apply the current tax rate in perpetuity. I agree with this Court's approach in Henke v. Trilithic Inc. to use the marginal tax rate "[b]ecause of the transitory nature of tax deductions and credits."

Because I find weighted average cost of capital ("WACC") to be 10.71%, as discussed below, and I am otherwise adopting Jarrell's methodology here, including his calculation of NOPAT* that includes a working capital adjustment, also discussed below, the terminal value is calculated using the perpetuity growth model as follows:

Thus, the Terminal Value for Scenario A is $1,538.51 million; for Scenario B it is $1,692.86 million. As discounted to the present value as of the Merger Date, the Terminal Value is $1,077.57 million for Scenario A and $1,185.68 million for Scenario B.

c.   Discount Rate

I cannot adopt either expert's discount rate in full. In calculating beta, Wisialowski used NASDAQ as the market proxy; I find that the S & P 500 is a more suitable market proxy in light of its broader sampling of the market. Wisialowski also initially used an inappropriate measurement period, running through the Merger Date, which failed to account for increases in stock price once the auction process became public. I find that Jarrell, on the other hand, should have used weekly data, rather than monthly, to generate a larger sample size, notwithstanding his assertion that *daily* inputs involved statistical "noise." Jarrell's monthly data generated 30 data points, to which he attributes a 99% confidence level. However, the valuation literature suggests using at least 36 data points, with some sources suggesting at

---

*   "NOPAT" is net operating profit after taxes.—Ed.

least 60 and Jarrell did not adequately explain why, specifically, a weekly input would be inappropriate here.

Using a weekly observation period, S & P 500 as the market proxy, and an observation period from the Company's IPO through June 5, 2012, just before news of the auction broke, I find beta to be 1.137.

* * *

Jarrell assumed 5% debt in Ancestry's capital structure; Wisialowski did not include any. The Petitioners contend that had Wisialowski included 5% debt, his valuation would have increased by $0.38, and thus, they do not object to my use of Jarrell's capital structure assumption. Under Jarrell's assumptions, the cost of debt is 3.81%. He also applied a 38% tax rate, which, as discussed above, I find to be appropriate.

Both experts calculated the discount rate using the WACC methodology, which I therefore adopt. WACC is calculated as follows:

WACC = [KD x WD x (1—t)] + (KE x WE)

Where: KD = Cost of debt capital = 3.81%

WD = Average weight of debt in capital structure = 5%

t = Effective tax rate for the company = 38%

KE = Cost of equity capital = 11.15%, as calculated below

WE = Average weight of equity capital in capital structure = 95%

To calculate the cost of equity capital, both experts used the Capital Asset Pricing Model ("CAPM"), which is calculated as follows:

$KE = RF + (ï$ x $RERP) + RESP$

Where:

RF = Risk-free rate = 2.47%

$ï$ = Beta = 1.137

$RERP$ = Equity risk premium = 6.11%

$RESP$ = Equity size premium = 1.73%

KE = 11.15%

Thus, $WACC$ = [.0381 x .05 x (1–.38)] + (.1115 x .95) = .1071, or 10.71%

* * *

f.   My Valuation Results

Ancestry's calculated equity value is the sum of its enterprise value plus net cash. Its enterprise value is the sum of the present value of free cash flows during the projection period, the present value of the NOL tax benefit, and the present value of the terminal value based on constant growth.

Using a DCF analysis, for Scenario A, I calculated $30.33 as the price per share. For Scenario B, I calculated $33.24 as the price per share.* Weighted equally, the value derived from discounted cash flow is $31.79. The actual market price as determined by the sale is $32. These are the two competing valuations that the statutory "all relevant factors" directive charges me to take into account. The question becomes, should I rely on the DCF to reach fair value, using what appears to be a relatively untainted market-derived valuation as a check, or should my analysis be the reverse? Because the inputs here, the October Scenarios (as well as the alternative May Projections) are problematic for the reasons addressed at length above, and because the sales process here was robust, I find fair value in these circumstances best represented by the market price. The DCF valuation I have described is close to the market, and gives me comfort that no undetected factor skewed the sales process. I note that my DCF value-while higher than Jarrell's-is still below that paid by the actual acquirer without apparent synergies; it would be hubristic indeed to advance my estimate of value over that of an entity for which investment represents a real-not merely an academic-risk, by insisting that such entity paid too much.

V.   CONCLUSION

For the foregoing reasons, I find that the merger price of $32 is the best indicator of Ancestry's fair value as of the Merger Date. The Petitioners are entitled to interest at the legal rate. The parties should confer and submit an appropriate form of order consistent with this Opinion.

QUESTIONS

1.   What are the incentives of each expert in a case such as this?

2.   How did these experts' incentives influence the projected future revenues used by each expert?

3.   Why does the court not give great credence to either experts' discounted cash flow valuations?

4.   Assume that the proxy materials for the merger fairly disclosed the details of the efforts of the Ancestry board and management to shop the company broadly, and to fight for the highest possible price. Where the price was 40% above the unaffected market price, why would sophisticated investors spend money on legal fees and experts to challenge the price? Consider that this decision was reached on October 14, 2014, about 22 months after the merger closed. Delaware General Corporation Law § 262(i) requires payment of the fair value of the shares after determination of fair value. Section 262(h) provides that interest accrues from the effective date of the merger at 5% over the

----

*   Management's October projections contained two scenarios.—Ed.

Federal Reserve discount rate in effect over the period before payment. When the discount rate was 0.75% during the relevant period, and the interest rate payable on two-year Treasury bills was between approximately 0.25% and 0.5%, does a legal interest rate on appraisal of 5.75% explain why some appraisal cases might be brought?

5. Why did the experts not rely on valuations of comparable companies or comparable transactions, as a real estate appraiser might have done?

6. The court discusses two valuation periods for predicting cash flows—one based on current projections and the other, the "terminal value," using a "perpetual growth model." Why is there a difference?

7. Does it surprise you that neither expert's valuation corresponded exactly with the ultimate merger price? Are there inherent flaws in the valuation exercise described in the case?

8. The court notes that an earlier hearing on an injunction action found that neither directors nor officers had any serious conflicts of interest, and that the search for buyers was conducted competently by the financial adviser and in good faith. Given the fact that this is an appraisal proceeding, why does it treat the fiduciary duties of directors and advisers so extensively?

NOTE

In Huff Fund Investment Partnership v. Ckx, Inc., 2015 Del. LEXIS 77, the Delaware Supreme Court affirmed without opinion a similar ruling on value by the Chancery Court.

In calculating the cost of capital the court added an "equity size" premium of 1.73%. This has become an accepted adjustment by both courts and experts. Apparently this represents an additional return demanded by investors for the risks of investing in smaller companies, which may include less efficient stock pricing because fewer analysts follow a stock, less liquidity when an investors wishes to buy or sell a block of the stock, and perhaps the fact that smaller cap companies may not have the degree of market dominance and power possessed by some large cap companies. The investment bank Morgan Stanley acquired a consulting company to obtain is proprietary "Barra Beta," which includes the following factors: volatility, momentum, size, size nonlinearity, trading activity, growth, earnings yield, value, earnings variability, leverage, currency sensitivity, dividend yield, and a non-estimation universe indicator. Because the weight of each factor is not revealed, it does not meet the evidentiary standard of wide acceptance, and has been treated as inadmissible by the Delaware Chancery Court.[*]

In recent years the Delaware courts have become more skeptical of shareholder suits that were settled for cosmetic changes in disclosure documents, with no monetary benefit for shareholders, and have declined to

---

[*] Global GT LP v. Golden Telecom, Inc., 993 A.2d 497, 520 (Del. Ch.), affirmed, 11 A.3d 214 (2011).

approve the size of the attorneys' fees included in the settlement. As that developed, attorneys have turned to appraisal actions on behalf of large shareholders, for the reasons suggested above and, in the past, because of the "wild card" nature of some appraisal awards (see the Rapid-American case that follows). In an era of low interest rates, another reason developed. Delaware General Corporation Law § 262(h) provides that the company shall pay interest on an award from the date of the merger to the date of the judgment at a rate 5% over the Federal Reserve discount rate. As of March 2016 the interest rate on short-term Treasury Bills was zero. The interest rate on high grade commercial paper of 90 days duration was under 1%, according to the Federal Reserve Board.* The 5% premium over the discount rate was a guaranteed profit for speculators able to borrow cheaply in this era. Note the name of one of the petitioners above: Ancora Merger Arbitrage Fund. A number of funds developed to engage in this kind of appraisal arbitrage. In 2016 the Governor of Delaware signed an act amending Delaware GCL § 262(h) allowing corporations to pay the merger consideration at any time while the appraisal case is pending, thus limiting the interest award to the difference between the appraisal award and the consideration already received. In a case such as Ancestry, it would eliminate the interest payment entirely. The act also amended section 262(g) to eliminate the right to appraisal if sought by less than 1% of the shares entitled to appraisal, or the amount sought is less than $1 million, except in parent-subsidiary mergers, where appraisal rights would continue without these limits.

D. MINORITY DISCOUNTS, CONTROL PREMIA AND LEVERAGE

In Cavalier Oil Corp. v. Harnett, 564 A.2d 1137 (Del. 1989), the Delaware Supreme Court rejected the notion of a minority discount for shares owned by a person holding a small portion of the company's shares. It explained this in the following terms:

"Cavalier's final claim of error is directed to the Vice Chancellor's refusal to apply a minority discount in valuing Harnett's EMSI stock. Cavalier contends that Harnett's 'de minimis' (1.5%) interest in EMSI is one of the 'relevant factors' which must be considered under Weinberger's expanded valuation standard. In rejecting a minority or marketability discount, the Vice Chancellor concluded that the objective of a section 262 appraisal is 'to value the *corporation* itself, as distinguished from a specific fraction of its shares as they may exist in the hands of a particular shareholder' [emphasis in original]. We believe this to be a valid distinction.

"A proceeding under Delaware's appraisal statute, 8 Del. C. § 262, requires that the Court of Chancery determine the 'fair value' of the

---

* http://www.federalreserve.gov/releases/cp/ (last visited Mar. 4, 2016).

dissenting stockholders' shares. The fairness concept has been said to implicate two considerations: fair dealing and fair price. Weinberger v. UOP, Inc., 457 A.2d at 711. Since the fairness of the merger process is not in dispute, the Court of Chancery's task here was to value what has been taken from the shareholder: 'viz. his proportionate interest in a going concern.' Tri-Continental Corp. v. Battye, Del. Supr., 31 Del.Ch. 523, 74 A.2d 71, 72 (1950). To this end the company must be first valued as an operating entity by application of traditional value factors, weighted as required, but without regard to post-merger events or other possible business combinations. See Bell v. Kirby Lumber Corp., Del. Supr., 413 A.2d 137 (1980). The dissenting shareholder's proportionate interest is determined only after the company as an entity has been valued. In that determination the Court of Chancery is not required to apply further weighting factors at the shareholder level, such as discounts to minority shares for asserted lack of marketability.

* * *

"The application of a discount to a minority shareholder is contrary to the requirement that the company be viewed as a 'going concern.' Cavalier's argument, that the only way Harnett would have received value for his 1.5% stock interest was to sell his stock, subject to market treatment of its minority status, misperceives the nature of the appraisal remedy. Where there is no objective market data available, the appraisal process is not intended to reconstruct a pro forma sale but to assume that the shareholder was willing to maintain his investment position, however slight, had the merger not occurred. Discounting individual share holdings injects into the appraisal process speculation on the various factors which may dictate the marketability of minority shareholdings. More important, to fail to accord to a minority shareholder the full proportionate value of his shares imposes a penalty for lack of control, and unfairly enriches the majority shareholders who may reap a windfall from the appraisal process by cashing out a dissenting shareholder, a clearly undesirable result." 564 A.2d at 1144–45.

The cases in other jurisdictions are mixed on the application of a minority discount. For cases approving such a discount, see Moore v. New Ammest, Inc., 630 P.2d 167 (Kans. App. 1984); Perlman v. Permonite Mfg. Co. 568 F.Supp. 222 (N.D. Ind. 1983), aff'd, 734 F.2d 1283 (7th Cir. 1984) (applying Indiana law); Independence Tube Corp. v. Levine, 535 N.E.2d 927 (Ill. App. 1988); Atlantic States Construction, Inc. v. Beavers, 314 S.E.2d 245 (Ga. App. 1984); Shear v. Gabovitch, 685 N.E.2d 1168 (Mass. App. 1997); and McCann Ranch, Inc. v. Quigley-McCann, 915 P.2d 239 (Mont. 1996). Contra: Woodward v. Quigley, 133 N.W.2d 38 (Ia. 1965); In re Valuation of Common Stock of McLoon Oil Co., 565 A.2d 997 (Me. 1989); MT Properties, Inc. v. CMC Real Estate Corp., 481 N.W.2d 383 (Minn. App. 1992); Charland v. Country View Golf Club, Inc., 588

A.2d 609 (R.I. 1991); Hunter v. Mitek Industries, 721 F.Supp. 1102 (E.D. Mo. 1989) (applying Missouri law). Cases rejecting a minority discount include Swope v. Siegel-Robert, Inc., 243 F.3d 486 (8th Cir. 2001) (applying Missouri law); Brown v. Arp & Hammond Hardware Co., 141 P.3d 673 (Wyo. 2006) holding that Wyoming's version of the 1984 Model Act did not define fair value, and thus did not authorize a minority discount. In many of these cases the decision seems to turn upon the statutory language: does the statute require compensation for a pro rata share of the entire corporation, or is the shareholder only entitled to be compensated for that which was taken from her? See, e.g., English v. Artromick International, Inc., 2000 WL 1125637 (Ohio App. 10 Dist.) (applying a minority discount where statute required appraisal of "fair cash value" of shares, and distinguishing it from "fair value.")

Delaware's attempts to value the entire firm and to give a dissenting shareholder her pro rata share of the value of the entire firm are a clear rejection of the concept of a minority discount. The Revised Model Business Corporation presently takes a similar approach. Revisions to M.B.C.A. § 13.01(4) now define "fair value" for appraisal purposes as follows:

> "(4) 'Fair value' means the value of the corporation's shares determined:
>
> (i)   immediately before the effectuation of the corporate action to which the shareholder objects;
>
> (ii) using customary and current valuation concepts and techniques generally employed for similar businesses in the context of the transaction requiring appraisal; and
>
> (iii) without discounting for lack of marketability or minority status except, if appropriate, for amendments to the articles of incorporation pursuant to section 13.02(a)(5)."

This language has been adopted by sixteen states that follow the Model Act approach. One court has used this approach, citing the Model Act, even where this language was not adopted by the state. Blitch v. Peoples Bank, 540 S.E.2d 667 (Ga. App. 2000). See, e.g., Advanced Communication Design, Inc. v. Follett, 615 N.W.2d 285 (Minn. 2000). The decision seemed to confuse marketability discounts with minority discounts, holding that "a result that allows majority shareholders to reap a windfall by buying out dissenting or oppressed shareholders at a discount that encourages corporate squeeze-outs is contrary to the statutory purpose to provide a remedy to minority shareholders. . . ."

Other courts have differed with both the Model Act drafters and Delaware on the question of a marketability (as opposed to a minority) discount in closely held corporations. In English v. Artromick International, Inc., 2000 WL 1125637 (Ohio App. 10 Dist.), the court applied both minority and marketability discounts. The opinion noted that the valuation process permitted evidence of any factor that a reasonable person would take into consideration in determining value, and that a minority interest was such a factor. As for a marketability discount, the court distinguished the Ohio statute, which required payment of "fair cash value" from cases applying a "fair value" standard, and declined "to find that marketability discounts are either against public policy or are not relevant to valuing minority interest in freeze-out mergers." See also Balsamides v. Protameen Chemicals, Inc., 734 A.2d 721 (N.J. 1999), where the court ordered that the oppressed minority shareholder had the right to buy out the shares of the oppressing majority. Here the court applied a marketability discount, holding that because of the illiquid nature of the corporation's shares, their value was reduced, and a marketability discount should be applied to avoid unfairly burdening the oppressed shareholder making the purchase.

QUESTIONS

1. Note that until about 1999 the Revised Model Business Corporation Act, § 13.01(3), provided that " 'fair value' with respect to a dissenter's shares, means the value of the shares immediately before the effectuation of the corporate action. . . ." Does this suggest a minority discount? But see current M.B.C.A. § 13.01(4)(iii). See also Blitch v. Peoples Bank, 540 S.E.2d 667 (Ga. App. 2000), cert. applied for (holding that minority discounts are not appropriate under the new Model Act language, and applying it to the former Model Act language).

2. Note also that Del. Gen. Corp. L. § 262(a) gives a dissenting shareholder the right "to an appraisal by the Court of Chancery of the fair value of his shares of stock. . . ." Does this suggest a minority discount?

3. Does the type of transaction involved matter in determining value? For example, M.B.C.A. § 13.01(3) formerly provided that value shall be determined as of a date immediately before the effectuation of the corporate action, "excluding any appreciation or depreciation in anticipation of the corporate action, unless exclusion would be inequitable." In adopting this language in 1977, the ABA Committee on Corporate Laws explained that this was intended to give courts the authority to award a higher value in freeze-out mergers. American Bar Association, Section of Corporation, Banking and Business Law, Committee on Corporate Laws, Changes in the Model Business Corporation Act Affecting Dissenters' Rights, 32 Bus. Lawyer 1855, 1864, 1874 (1977). What reasons might exist to justify a distinction between freeze-out mergers and other mergers? This language has been eliminated in recent revisions, which now place this definition in § 13.01(4). In the comment to this section, the drafters state that it is intended to allow flexibility of methodology in valuation, "but excluding any element of value attributable to the unique synergies of the actual

purchaser of the corporation or its assets." Does this signal any change in the law of those states adopting the new version?

4. In Tri-Continental Corp. v. Battye, 74 A.2d 71, 72 (1950), the court read the similar language of the predecessor to Del. GCL § 262(a) to mean that "The basic concept of value under the appraisal statute is that the stockholder is entitled to be paid for that which has been taken from him, viz., his proportionate interest in a going concern." Is this consistent with the statutory language?

5. If all small lots of shares traded in market transactions carry a minority discount, did Hartnett pay a pro rata share of the value of the entire corporation when he purchased his EMSI stock?

6. If Hartnett purchased at a price reflecting a minority discount, what is the "fair value of his shares of stock"?

7. If an investor pays a control premium for shares, does payment of a proportionate share of firm value to minority shareholders deprive the minority shareholder of the benefit of its bargain? Does it make a difference whether the transaction is an arm's length merger with a third party or a take-out merger?

8. Recall that Del. Gen. Corp. L. § 262(b) denies appraisal to shareholders of certain widely-traded companies if they receive shares of stock in either the surviving corporation (which would by definition be widely traded) or in another such company in a merger. This denial is justified in part on the basis that the unhappy shareholder can sell her shares into the market if displeased with the transaction. Manning, The Shareholder's Appraisal Remedy: An Essay for Frank Coker, 72 Yale L.J. 223 (1962). Is this treatment consistent with the approach in Cavalier Oil Corp. v. Hartnett?

Rapid-American Corporation v. Harris

603 A.2d 796 (Del. 1992).

■ MOORE, JUSTICE.

This consolidated appeal challenges the results of a statutory appraisal of Rapid-American Corporation ("Rapid") which awarded certain dissenting shareholders $51.00 per share. * * *

Appellees and cross-appellants ("Harris"), owned 58,400 shares of Rapid before the merger. Harris brought a statutory appraisal action pursuant to 8 Del. C. § 262, contesting the merger consideration. The merger price included cash and securities worth approximately $28.00 per share. After a trial in the Court of Chancery, the court awarded Harris $51.00 per share plus simple interest.

Rapid now challenges the trial court's decision to award Harris $51.00 per share. It claims that the results of the appraisal are unrealistic because the $51.00 award represents a 200% premium over Rapid's unaffected market price at the time of the merger. Rapid maintains that the trial court's error was the result of its decision to adopt Harris' valuation technique. Rapid claims that Harris' appraisal methodology violated Delaware law.

Harris further claims that the trial court erred when it failed to include a "control premium" in its valuation of Rapid. Harris argues that the inclusion of a "control premium" was necessary to compensate Rapid's shareholders for their 100% ownership in three operating subsidiaries. * * *

After carefully examining the record, we affirm the trial court's decision to adopt Harris' valuation technique. Harris' methodology does not contravene Delaware law. * * *

Finally, we reverse the denial of a "control premium" to Harris. We find that the trial court had an affirmative duty to consider the nature of the enterprise as an element of its valuation. Rapid, as a parent company owning a 100% interest in three valuable subsidiaries, was entitled to an adjustment of its inherent value as a going concern to reflect the economic reality of its structure at the corporate level. The valuation technique the trial court applied artificially discounted Rapid's ownership interest in its subsidiaries and deprived all of Rapid's shareholders of fair value.

* * *

I.

The underlying facts of this case are not in serious dispute. Rapid was a publicly-held conglomerate receiving 99% of its net sales and most of its operating profits from three wholly-owned subsidiaries. These subsidiaries included the McCrory Corporation ("McCrory"), Schenley Industries, Inc. ("Schenley"), and McGregor-Duniger, Inc. ("McGregor"). Rapid and each subsidiary had a full and distinct set of executives and operating officers. All of the subsidiaries maintained independent financial reports and records.

* * *

A.

The merger transaction leading to the appraisal began in 1974. At that time, Riklis, Rapid's CEO and Chairman, began to purchase Rapid's shares in the open market through his interests in Kenton and AFC. Rapid also contemporaneously began to repurchase large blocks of its own shares. The repurchase program ultimately increased Riklis' control of Rapid's outstanding shares.

On April 11, 1980, Rapid announced that it had agreed to merge with Kenton into a newly reformed Rapid-American corporation. On the eve of the merger, Kenton and AFC controlled 46.5% of Rapid's outstanding stock. After the merger was effectuated on January 31, 1981, Rapid's shareholders received a compensation package worth approximately $28. The compensation included $45 principal in a newly-issued 10% sinking fund subordinated debenture, $3 in cash and an additional $.25. This nominal cash fee represented settlement consideration for certain pending derivative suits.

Rapid employed an independent Transaction Review Committee ("TRC") to evaluate the merger price. The TRC retained Bear Stearns & Co. to provide financial advice. The TRC also employed Standard Research Consultants ("SRC") to determine, among other things, the fairness of the proposed transaction to Rapid's shareholders. Arthur H. Rosenbloom, SRC's head consultant and expert witness at trial, led the investigation. The examination continued for approximately six months. SRC ultimately concluded that the $28.00 compensation package was fair to Rapid's shareholders.

SRC's valuation technique considered Rapid on a consolidated basis. It evaluated Rapid based on an analysis of earnings and dividends. SRC calculated price/earnings ratios for each subsidiary and adjusted its figures to include certain dividend ratios. It figured each subsidiaries' contribution to the parent's operating income for a set period of time to calculate Rapid's ultimate value. SRC then tested its figures against various established financial ratios of similarly situated corporations.

Harris retained Willamette Management Associates, Inc. ("WMA") to evaluate the merger consideration. In contrast to SRC's technique, WMA separately evaluated each of Rapid's subsidiaries. * * *

* * * The court also faulted SRC for its decision not to treat Rapid on a debt-free basis. Finally, the court explicitly rejected SRC's valuation, and held that it violated Delaware law. The court found that SRC's valuation technique "determined the value of [Harris'] shares as freely trading minority shareholders instead of considering Harris' proportionate (1.5%) [sic] interest in Rapid as a going concern. . . ."

The court adopted a modified version of WMA's valuation technique in a highly detailed, forty-three page opinion. It then ruled that Rapid's fair value at the time of the merger was $51.00 per share. The trial court also awarded Harris 12.75% simple interest.

B.

The Court of Chancery adopted WMA's comparative analysis. It examined each of Rapid's subsidiaries as a separate entity. It then compared the subsidiaries to a group of comparable publicly-traded companies.

* * *

The Vice Chancellor rejected WMA's inclusion of a "control premium" in its final evaluation of each Rapid subsidiary. It found that the addition of a "control premium" violated Delaware law. The court reasoned that the "control premium" contravened the proscription against weighing factors affecting valuation "at the shareholder level."

* * *

III.

We now consider the merits of Harris' cross-appeal. The trial court determined the publicly traded equity ("PTE") value of Rapid's shares after adopting WMA's "segmented" comparative valuation technique. The court, however, refused to add a "control premium" to the PTE for each of Rapid's operating subsidiaries. The court, citing Cavalier, reasoned that adding a "control premium" violated 8 Del. C. § 262 because it contravened the general proscription against weighing any additional factors affecting valuation "at the shareholder level."

Harris claims that the trial court's decision to exclude a "control premium" constituted legal error. He argues that the court should have considered and valued Rapid's 100% interest in its subsidiaries. Harris maintained that WMA's valuation technique only compared its subsidiaries' PTE's with the individual shares of similar corporations trading in the market. He notes that the market price of these comparable corporations are discounted and do not reflect a control premium. Harris concludes that the trial court effectively treated Rapid as a minority shareholder in its wholly-owned subsidiaries. Harris contends that the trial court gave the new, privately-held Rapid, a windfall at his expense.

Rapid claims that the trial court did not commit error. Rapid, citing to Cavalier and Bell, argues that the addition of a control premium violates Delaware law because it takes into account Rapid's liquidation value. In sum, Rapid assumes that it could not realize a "control premium" unless it was sold to a third party. Rapid also argues that Harris only owned 1.2% of its outstanding shares and factually was not entitled to realize a "control premium."

* * *

B.

This Court, in accordance with the statutory mandate, has consistently held that a dissenting stockholder in an appraisal action is only entitled to "that which has been taken from him [or, in other words] his proportionate interest in a going concern." Two distinct but related concepts emerge from the statutory scheme. First, a court cannot assign value to any "speculative" events arising out of the merger or consolidation. Second, the court must value the dissenter's proportionate interest in the corporation as a "going concern" taking into account all other "relevant factors" affecting value. In accordance with this principle, a court cannot adjust its valuation to reflect a shareholder's individual interest in the enterprise. As Cavalier succinctly states:

The dissenting shareholder's proportionate interest is determined only after the company as an entity has been valued. In that determination the [trial court] is not required to apply further weighing factors at the shareholder level, such as discounts to minority shares for asserted lack of marketability.

Rapid, in apparent agreement with the trial court, seizes upon Cavalier, and argues that the phrase "such as" similarly prohibits a court from adding "a control premium" at the shareholder level. Rapid indicates that adding a control premium at the shareholder level violates this Court's decision in Bell. It reasons that a control premium typically only "arises out" of the merger and is not part of Rapid's going-concern value.

We disagree with the trial court's characterization of the "control premium" in this case as an impermissible shareholder level adjustment. Its reliance on Cavalier and Bell is misplaced. The "control premium" Harris urged the trial court to adopt represented a valid adjustment to its valuation model which "applied a [bonus] at the company level against all assets. . . ."

C.

***

Tri-Continental recognized that a court had the authority to discount the value of the enterprise at the corporate level. The company appraised in Tri-Continental was a leveraged closed-end mutual fund. The court understood that the shares of a leveraged closed-end mutual fund ordinarily trade at a discount of its underlying assets. The court concluded.

The full value of the corporate assets to the corporation is not the same as the value of those assets to the common stockholder because of the factor of discount. To fail to recognize this conclusion . . . is to fail to face the economic facts and to commit error.

Cavalier also recognized the importance of assigning a realistic market value to the appraised corporation. Cavalier claimed that the Tri-Continental decision authorized shareholder level discounts to devalue the shares of the minority dissenters. The Court rejected that argument. It correctly interpreted Tri-Continental as standing for the proposition that an appraisal valuation must include consideration of the unique nature of the enterprise. It drew the important distinction between assigning value at the corporate level and the shareholder level. *Id.* Cavalier authorized corporate level discounting as a means of establishing the intrinsic value of the enterprise. The court, however, rejected shareholder level discounting. It found that an appraisal explicitly considering the minority discount at the shareholder level both injects speculative elements into the calculation, and more importantly:

> Fails to accord to a minority shareholder the full proportionate value of his shares [which] imposes a penalty for lack of control, and unfairly enriches the majority shareholders who may reap a windfall from the appraisal process by cashing out a dissenting shareholder, a clearly undesirable result.

Rapid misses the fundamental point that Harris was not claiming a "control premium" at the shareholder level. Harris urged the trial court to add a premium at the parent level to compensate all of Rapid's shareholders for its 100% ownership position in the three subsidiaries. WMA's valuation technique arrived at comparable values using the market price of similar shares. These shares presumptively traded at a price that discounted the "control premium."

The trial court's decision to reject the addition of a control premium within the WMA valuation model placed too much emphasis on market value. * * *

Rapid was a parent company with a 100% ownership interest in three valuable subsidiaries. The trial court's decision to exclude the control premium at the corporate level practically discounted Rapid's entire inherent value. The exclusion of a "control premium" artificially and unrealistically treated Rapid as a minority shareholder. Contrary to Rapid's arguments, Delaware law compels the inclusion of a control premium under the unique facts of this case.[2] Rapid's 100% ownership interest in its subsidiaries was clearly a "relevant" valuation factor and the trial court's rejection of the "control premium" implicitly placed a disproportionate emphasis on pure market value.

We also reject Rapid's implicit claim that the inclusion of a "control premium" violates our decision in Bell. Rapid seems to contend that a "control premium" is only payable when the corporation is liquidated. It concludes that the addition of a "control premium" incorrectly inflates Rapid's worth to an acquisition value instead of pricing its inherent value as a going concern.

We reject Rapid's arguments because Bell is easily distinguishable on its facts. Unlike Bell, the WMA valuation technique did not assume that an acquiror would liquidate Rapid. WMA's valuation technique added the "control premium" to reflect market realities. Rapid may have had a different value as a going concern if the court had considered that it enjoyed a 100% interest in its three major subsidiaries.

---

[2] We are fully aware of the Court of Chancery's decision in Cede & Co. v. Technicolor, Inc., Del. Ch., Civ. A. No. 7129, Allen, C. (Oct. 19, 1990), which explicitly rejected the inclusion of a "control premium" in a calculation of the intrinsic value of dissenting shares. *Id.* at 50–52 & n.41. We note that Cede is factually distinguishable and did not consider a corporate level "control premium." We now express no view on the particular merits of the trial court's holding in Cede, a case in which an appeal is now pending before this Court.

We recognize that the term "control premium" may be misleading here. The past decade has proven that an acquiror is often willing to pay a "control premium" in return for a majority interest in a corporation. Nonetheless, the WMA valuation technique utilized the control premium as a means of making its valuation more realistic. Under the circumstances presented here, the trial court was under a duty to assess the value of Rapid's full ownership in its subsidiaries.

Harris also argues that the control premium increases Rapid's fair value to $73.28 per diluted share, and urges us to adopt that sum on appeal. The trial court explicitly rejected the control premium without analysis. It now must reconsider that action. There is no basis for us to adopt Harris' claimed valuation.

Accordingly, we reverse the Court of Chancery and remand. The court must consider the "control premium," together with all other traditional valuation elements, and determine what, if any, additional value is to be ascribed to Harris' stock above the $51.00 per share initial finding.

NOTE

On remand, then Vice Chancellor Chandler added $22.29 as a control premium to the $51 valuation he had previously determined.

QUESTIONS

1. Why did both appraisers value the subsidiaries rather than Rapid as a whole?

2. What did the Chancery Court mean when it criticized the SRC report as valuing Harris' shares "as freely trading minority shareholders"?

3. What rationale supports WMA's addition of a control premium to the values it found for Rapid-American's subsidiaries? If Rapid had liquidated the subsidiaries and become the direct owner of their assets and businesses, does this mean the control premium would disappear?

4. If a control premium means that a controlling block of shares is worth more per share than a minority block, how can a 100% ownership carry a control premium?

5. Tri-Continental Corp. v. Battye, 74 A.2d 71 (Del. 1950), involved a discount of the asset value of a closed-end mutual fund. Closed-end mutual funds are organized like business corporations, in that they issue shares that are subsequently traded in markets, in contrast to open-end funds, which continuously redeem and reissue shares. Closed-end funds' shares typically trade at prices that deviate from their "net asset value," which is their pro rata share of the investments owned by

the funds. Where the investments are publicly traded securities, determining net asset value is a simple task; one performed daily by open-end funds. These deviations from net asset value for closed-end companies' shares generally are discounts from net asset value. Thus the value of a closed-end fund's assets in its hands is less than the value of the same assets in the market, and the Tri-Continental court recognized that this factor should be taken into account in an appraisal proceeding. How does this relate to a discussion of whether a shareholder in Rapid-American should be accorded a control premium?

6.   What does the court mean when it says that Harris was not claiming a control premium at the shareholder level?

7.   Bell v. Kirby Lumber Corp., 413 A.2d 137 (Del. 1980) involved a company where use of liquidation values was rejected by the Delaware Supreme Court, on the theory that the firm was to be valued as a going concern, with the expectation that it would consider, despite the fact that its liquidation value, according to asset appraisals, was over $600, while its value based on its income was approximately $150. Note that WMA's valuation added a control premium, but the court stated that this didn't involve a liquidation valuation, because WMA didn't assume that an acquiror was going to liquidate Rapid-American. From the perspective of the present shareholders of Rapid-American, isn't a sale of their entire interest to a new buyer equivalent to a liquidation?

Appraising the Non-Existent: The Delaware Courts' Struggle with Control Premiums

William J. Carney and Mark Heimendinger.
152 U. Penn. L. Rev. 845 (2003).

Appraisal proceedings have hardly been the Delaware courts' finest moments. For decades these courts eschewed evidence based on widely accepted finance methodology, holding rather that determinations of value were questions of law and not fact.[18] It was not until 1983 that the Delaware Supreme Court permitted introduction of evidence obtained through modern valuation methods.[19] While the current methodology is generally market-based, the courts nevertheless continue to speak about value in ways that show a deep misunderstanding of valuation methodology, and distrust of market values.[20] Indeed, the Delaware

---

[18] See, *e.g.* Francis I. duPont & Co. v. Universal City Studios, 312 A.2d 344, 348–49 (Del.Ch.1973), aff'd, 334 A.2d 216 (Del.1975). For a criticism of the former "Delaware Block" methodology, *see* David Cohen, Comment: Valuation in the Context of Share Appraisal, 34 Emory L.J. 117 (1985).

[19] Weinberger v. UOP, Inc., Del. Supr., 457 A.2d 701 (1983).

[20] While the market value of a company's stock does not necessarily accurately estimate such company's future cash flows, The Efficient Capital Markets Hypothesis ("ECMH") demonstrates that a certain deference needs to be given to market value. See RICHARD A. BREALEY & STEWART C. MYERS, Principles of Corporate Finance 368–374 (6th ed. 2000)

Supreme Court has stated that "the 'market price of shares may not be representative of true value.' "[21] In Smith v. Van Gorkom, the Supreme Court criticized a board that relied on a 46% premium over the market because it was uninformed about "intrinsic value."[22] More recently the Supreme Court rejected an appraised valuation that was 200% above the pre-transaction market value, on the basis that the "trial court's decision to reject the addition of a control premium . . . placed too much emphasis on market value."[23] The court criticized the Chancery Court's valuation as *too low*, because it failed to add a control premium to the market price of comparable companies to reach the asserted value of the whole firm, rather than the "discounted" market price of a small block of shares in the trading market. The pre-announcement market price was $17.25;[24] the consideration paid in the cash-out merger was worth approximately $28;[25] the appraised value initially determined by the Chancery Court was $51;[26] and the final value awarded after remand, including the control premium, was $73.29.[27] If a shareholder purchased shares immediately before the announcement, the gain was 325%. This bizarre result has received relatively little attention, except to the extent that it has become an accepted part of Delaware law.[28] While the Delaware courts appear to believe they are using the science of financial economics in their valuation efforts, their misunderstandings have led to windfalls for dissenting shareholders.

* * *

A.   Common Sense About Control Premiums

We argue here that the received economic wisdom of courts may contain some fundamental misconceptions about value. The misunderstanding involved is an appealing one in part because control premiums are observed. It also has a certain intuitive quality that seems to confirm its truthfulness. Whenever control of a company is transferred, it is easy to observe that the transfer occurs at a price above the previous

---

(setting forth a caution to management to pay attention to market values in a chapter entitled "The Six Lessons of Market Efficiency"). We caution courts to head this advice.

[21] Paramount Communications, Inc. v. Time Inc., Del. Supr., 571 A.2d 1140, 1150 n.12 (1989). While we do not argue that this statement is false, the statement fails to suggest any of the reasons for this shortcoming, such as the existence of material non-public information. *But see* Part IV(B); Daniel R. Fischel, Symposium: Management and Control of the Modern Business Corporation: Corporate Control Transactions: Market Evidence in Corporate Law, 69 U. Chi. L. Rev. 941 (2002) (arguing in favor of giving often conclusive weight on market evidence when valuing corporations).

[22] 488 A.2d 858 (Del.1985). This misguided search for the Holy Grail of intrinsic value began with Tri-Continental Corp. v. Battye, 74 A.2d 71, 72 (Del. 1950).

[23] Rapid-American Corp. v. Harris, 603 A.2d 796, 806 (Del. 1992).

[24] Harris v. Rapid American Corp., 1992 Del. Ch. LEXIS 75, *7.

[25] Harris v. Rapid American Corp., 1990 Del. Ch. LEXIS 166, *3.

[26] *Id*. at *52.

[27] 1992 Del. Ch. LEXIS 75 at *13.

[28] *But see* Richard A. Booth, Minority Discounts and Control Premiums in Appraisal Proceedings, 57 Bus. Law.127 (2001).

market value of the shares, assuming the market did not anticipate the transfer. A rich empirical literature demonstrates that these premiums exist, and they can be large. Michael Jensen estimated shareholder gains from mergers and acquisitions at $400 billion between 1977 and 1986, while Joseph Grundfest found total shareholder gains of $167 billion between 1981 and 1986, and a third study found premiums of $118.4 billion in the same period.[66] From this it is easy to see how one could conclude that such premiums inhere in all companies, and should be considered when valuing any particular company. The intuitive appeal stems from the desire to protect minorities from overreaching by majorities, and the apparent belief that whenever any shareholders receive something different in kind (shares rather than cash), there has been some element of overreaching or unfairness. We argue that absent an actual transfer of control, control premiums represent probabilities of a control transfer at a premium. Where the probability is close to zero, so is the premium.

Our reasons for suggesting this is a misunderstanding are relatively simple: control premiums only occur in transactions involving a transfer of control where there are thought to be gains from trade. These premiums are observed only because of a perception by the purchaser that the transaction offers some opportunity to create new value, not previously existing within the target firm.[67] Even if all values, both present and potential, are valued in the market price for the firm's shares, one would not expect to find a discernable control premium in a widely held firm that is well managed and appears to offer little probability of a transfer of control. Any small probability of a control transaction will already be reflected in the market price, because all shareholders expect to have an equal opportunity to share in such a premium, should it appear, absent a dominant shareholder.

---

[66] Michael Jensen, The Takeover Controversy: Analysis and Guidance, 4 Midland Corp. Fin. J. 6 (1986); Joseph Grundfest & Bernard Black, Stock Market Profits from Takeover Activity Between 1981 and 1986: $167 Billion is a Lot of Money, Securities and Exchange Commission News Release, Sept. 28, 1987; Gregg A. Jarrell, James A. Brickely and Jeffry M. Netter, The Market for Corporate Control: The Empirical Evidence Since 1980, 2, No. 1 J. Econ. Persp. 49 (1988); further evidence of such premiums is offered in Lawrence A. Hamermesh, Premiums in stock for stock mergers and some consequences in the Law of Director Fiduciary Duties, in this symposium. 152 U. Pa. L. Rev. ___ (forthcoming, 2003).

[67] They are offered in public tender offers in order to overcome free rider problems. *See* Sanford J. Grossman & Oliver D. Hart, *Takeover Bids, the Free-Rider Problem, and the Theory of the Corporation*, 11 BELL J. ECON. 42, 42–43 (1980). In the case of a negotiated purchase of control from a single shareholder or a group, the premium is offered both to account for the private benefits control shareholders receive and to provide a price that at least meets their reservation price, but may well be higher because of the uncertainties of negotiating under conditions of bilateral monopoly. In Cooper v. Pabst Brewing Co., 1993 Del. Ch. LEXIS 91, *23, Vice Chancellor Hartnett rejected the blended value of a takeover bid as the measure of the target's value on the date of the merger, stating that it "is often an unreliable guide to the true market value because it may reflect a control premium and other factors connected with the acquiror's intentions but unrelated to the value of the firm as a going concern."

B. Stories of Separate Markets

We turn now to the academic discussion of the market for corporate control and the arguments that have flowed from it about control premiums. We argue that control premiums are reflected in all stock prices, as explained at the beginning of section A.

The phrase "market for corporate control" was introduced in 1965 by Manne's classic article.[68] Manne introduced the concept of a market for corporate control without claiming that it was somehow separate from the market for small lots of shares. He simply claimed that as management quality and effort declined, so did expected earnings, so that stock prices would decline relative to well-managed companies. This lower stock price would both facilitate and provide the impetus for takeovers, costly as they might be. As he pointed out "the potential return from the successful take-over and revitalization of a poorly run company can be enormous."[69] While other explanations of gains have since been offered, Manne's explanation remains a central one. It integrates control transactions with trading transactions in an important way. A takeover bid introduces important new information about the value of a firm—that someone, other than current management, believes it can produce greater cash flows for investors from the existing assets.[70] In the parlance of efficient market analysis, this is "news." The fact that a takeover bid is a low-probability event for many firms explains why even prices of badly managed firms do not rise to reflect the full value of a potential control premium; they reflect only its expected value under conditions of uncertainty.[71] Many firms are well-managed and consequently offer few potential gains in a takeover. In such a case both the probability of and expected gains from a takeover bid may be trivial. But in both cases, efficient markets should set prices to reflect the particular situation of each firm.

Not all scholars accept this view. One explanation of a lack of acceptance has been offered by Martin Shubik: "These assumptions [of efficient capital markets] are set up to rule out, by assumption, the possibility that the market for a few shares of the stock of a corporation and the market for control of a corporation may be fundamentally

---

[68] Henry G. Manne, Mergers and the Market for Corporate Control, 73 J. Pol. Econ. 110 (1965). For a review of the impact of this and other articles of Manne's on thinking about takeover premiums, *see* William J. Carney, The Legacy of "The Market for Corporate Control" and the Origins of the Theory of the Firm, 50 Case Wes. Res. L. Rev. 215 (1999).

[69] Manne, *supra* note 68, at 113.

[70] The market price of the target's stock reflects the anticipated takeover bid in advance of its announcement. Michael Bradley, Interfirm Tender Offers and the Market for Corporate Control, 41 J. Bus. 345, 361–64 (1980).

[71] *Id.*

different markets."[72] Shubik elaborates his challenge to the law of one price:

> "The lawyers may talk about a premium for control. But to a true believer of efficient markets, there cannot be a premium for control. If, in contradistinction to the adherents of the single, efficient market, we suggest that there are several more or less imperfect markets involving the market for a few shares, the market for control, the market for going-business assets, and the market for assets in liquidation, then we have a structure for interpreting what is going on in terms of arbitrage among these markets."[73]

Shubik's argument uses the term "market" loosely.[74] Stigler has described markets as a situation where prices of homogeneous goods are identical.[75] Discrete markets exist when different prices appear, which are generally not arbitraged away because of transaction costs, transportation costs, or cultural differences that inhibit complete arbitrage.[76] Significantly different prices are not observed for the same stock at the same time, except perhaps in the irrelevant sense of different reservation prices.[77] A takeover bid appears in the same market in which trading occurs, and the news of the bid instantaneously moves the market price to a new level, approximating traders' estimations of the bid's prospect for success, discounting for the time value of money and the probability of oversubscription and prorating.[78] Thus there is no

---

[72]   Martin Shubik, Corporate Control, Efficient Markets, and the Public Good, in Knights, Raiders & Targets: The Impact of the Hostile Takeover 31, 32–33 (John C. Coffee, Jr., Louis Lowenstein and Susan Rose-Ackerman, eds. 1988)

[73]   Shubik, *supra* note 72, at 33. *See also* Lynn A. Stout, Are Takeover Premiums Really Premiums? Market Price, Fair Value, and Corporate Law, 99 Yale L.J. 1235 (1990). Shubik's language was quoted by Chancellor Allen in Paramount Communications, Inc. v. Time Incorporated, 1989 Del. Ch. LEXIS 77, *55. n. 13; Fed. Sec. L. Rep. (CCH) ¶ 94,514. We believe Shubik is mistaken when he claims that true believers in efficient capital markets hold that there cannot be a control premium. *See* Manne, *supra* note 68. Shubik argues that when hostile takeovers occur, conditions approximating zero transaction costs in perfectly competitive markets no longer exist. Shubik, *supra* note 72, at 35–36. Of course he is right, but this only goes to the probability and size of a control premium. Because not all bad managers are removed by takeovers because of these costs does not necessarily mean there are separate markets.

[74]   One cannot be too critical of various uses of the term "market," however. Two distinguished economists have written: "The term . . . market as commonly used is so turgid of meaning that we can not hope to explain every entity to which the name is attached in common or even technical literature." Armen Alchian and Harold Demsetz, Production, Information Costs, and Economic Organization, 62 Am. Econ. Rev. 777, 785 (1973).

[75]   George Stigler, THE THEORY OF PRICE 85 (3d ed. 1966).

[76]   Shubik correctly argues that the pool of purchasers of the assets of a firm may be different (thinner) than the pool of purchasers of its shares. In some cases, if there is only one prospective asset purchaser, conditions of bilateral monopoly exist, making prediction of control premiums impossible. But this does not address the probability of a transaction in control.

[77]   In that sense, investors are price-takers, not price searchers. Auctions exist to deal with the problem of heterogeneous goods, to allow efficient price-searching. The New York Stock Exchange is a "continuous auction market" to search for prices intertemporally, as "news" continuously alters reservation prices of both buyers and sellers.

[78]   This is not to say that markets operate with perfect efficiency in eliciting bids, anticipating the probability of bids, or the probable outcome of a bidder's interest. *See* Guhan

evidence of the simultaneous existence of market prices for control and for minority interests. This demonstrates that the law of one price prevails at any one time, and that prices changes only when the probability of an event such as a change of control changes.[79]

Another version of the separate market story is offered without any attempt at a theory: it simply asserts that all publicly traded shares reflect an implicit minority discount.[80] Responding to an assertion without a theory is impossible, and probably not worthwhile. It is, unfortunately, the currently operative assumption of the Delaware courts.

While economists have developed sophisticated models demonstrating how arbitrage occurs between markets[81] none of that is necessary in this context, because only one market exists for the shares of each company.

NOTE ON JUDICIAL REACTIONS TO THE RAPID-AMERICAN DECISION

The Delaware courts have limited the Rapid-American decision to the specific method of appraisal used in that case—a sum of the parts analysis of separate subsidiaries on a comparative basis with similar companies. In Berger v. Pubco Corp., 906 A.2d 132 (Del. Ch. 2009), Chancellor Chandler rejected using that methodology in a case using discounted cash flow valuations, writing:

> First, as to the control premium issue, I conclude that the addition of a control premium in this case is not appropriate. Both appraisers used the discounted cash flow and book value methodologies. Under Delaware law, it is appropriate to add a control premium when appraisers use a comparable public company methodology. This has been the teaching of cases following the Delaware Supreme Court's decision in Rapid-American Corp. v. Harris. Since the comparable public company methodology was not a methodology used by either appraiser in

---

Subramanian, The Drivers of Market Efficiency in Revlon Transactions, J. Corp. L. (forthcoming 2003).

[79] Coates provides an expanded description of arbitrage under these conditions, pointing out that the presence of a controlling shareholder in the target means that market prices will also reflect the risk that a bidder will acquire control directly from the controlling shareholder and the probability that the new controlling shareholder will deal more or less fairly with the public minority shareholders. John C. Coates IV, "Fair Value" As An Avoidable Rule of Corporate Law: Minority Discounts in Conflict Transactions, 147 U. Pa. L. Rev. 1251, 1265, n. 46 (1999) (citing Lucian Ayre Bebchuk, Efficient and Inefficient Sales of Corporate Control, 109 Q. J. Econ. 957, 961–64 (1994)).

[80] Shannon P. Pratt, et al., VALUING A BUSINESS 304–05 (3d ed. 1996). *See also* Coates, *supra* note 79, at 1265.

[81] Shubik, *supra* note 72, at 36, citing Kenneth Arrow and G. Debreu, Existence of an Equilibrium for a Competitive Economy, 22 Econometrica 215 (1954).

this case, I decline to extend the rule of Rapid-American in these circumstances. Even the Court in Rapid-American held that the inclusion of a control premium was required "under the unique facts" of that case, which was based on comparable values using the market price of similar shares of stock. Cases decided in the Court of Chancery since Rapid-American have clearly held that the addition of a control premium to a discounted cash flow valuation, as here, is not appropriate. Authoritative commentators have likewise observed that it is improper and illogical to add a control premium to a discounted cash flow valuation. Accordingly, the value of Pubco's shares should not be increased by a control premium because no such premium was implicit in any valuation methodology used by the appraisers.

E. THE EXCLUSIVITY OF APPRAISAL

Model Business Corporation Act § 13.02(d).

Grace Bros. v. Farley Industries, Inc.

264 Ga. 817, 450 S.E.2d 814 (Ga. 1994).

■ THOMPSON, JUSTICE.

William Farley, and entities associated with him, made a tender offer of $58 per share for all of the outstanding common stock of West Point Pepperell ("WPP").[82] The offer was approved by WPP's board of directors and ninety-five percent of WPP's stock was tendered to Farley.

The tender offer negotiations led to a merger agreement in which West Point Acquisition Corporation and WPP agreed to use their best efforts to merge West Point Tender Corporation and WPP. The agreement provided that the remaining shareholders of WPP (holding 5% of the outstanding common stock) would be paid the tender offer price of $58 per share when the merger was complete.

Approximately two years later, Farley announced that the merger could not be completed because of various financial setbacks and the parties formally terminated the merger agreement. Farley's financial troubles continued and a reorganization plan was contemplated. At that point, Joseph L. Lanier, Jr.,[83] Grace Brothers, Ltd.,[84] and Kidder

---

[82] Farley used a number of companies, including Farley Industries, Inc., West Point Tender Corporation and West Point Acquisition Corporation (now called Valley Fashions Corporation), to purchase WPP. They are referred to collectively, as "Farley."

[83] At the time of the tender offer, Lanier was president and CEO of WPP. He owned approximately 22,000 shares of WPP stock. He did not tender his shares pursuant to the Farley tender offer.

[84] Grace Brothers, Ltd., did not own any WPP stock at the time of the tender offer. It began acquiring WPP stock after it was announced that the merger would not be completed.

Peabody & Co., Inc.,[85] brought suit against Farley, WPP and officers and directors of WPP. In their complaint, as amended, plaintiffs asserted multiple claims directly (i.e., individually) and derivatively. They sought specific performance, or, alternatively, damages for breach of the merger agreement. They also sought damages for interference with the merger agreement, breach of fiduciary duty, unjust enrichment, corporate waste and violations of the Fair Price Requirements act.

While the litigation was pending, Farley announced plans to complete the merger and force the cash-out of the minority shareholders at $46 per share. Plaintiffs tried to enjoin the merger, alleging Farley failed to comply with procedural requirements and that the proxy statement contained material misstatements. The court refused to grant injunctive relief.

Defendants moved to dismiss on the ground that plaintiffs lacked standing to assert their claims, and for summary judgment. The court granted defendants' motions and entered final judgment in their favor. Plaintiffs brought this appeal and sought a stay of the merger pending appeal. The trial court refused to grant a stay. This court likewise refused to stay the merger pending appeal.

In December, 1993, the merger was completed and WPP became West Point Stevens. Pursuant to the merger, minority shareholders are to receive $46 per share. Kidder Peabody & Co., Inc., and Grace Brothers, Ltd., accepted the $46 per share merger price and tendered their WPP stock. Lanier dissented from the merger and pursued the statutory appraisal process. See OCGA § 14–2–1301, et seq.

1.   Plaintiffs' assertion that they can maintain their claims derivatively must fail. The law is well settled that a former shareholder in a merged corporation has no standing to maintain a shareholder's derivative action. After all, the "commenced or maintained" language in the shareholders' derivative statute, OCGA § 14–2–741, requires a continuation of shareholder status throughout litigation, and that status comes to an end with a corporate merger.

2.   Plaintiffs assert they have standing to bring their claims against defendants directly. In Thomas v. Dickson, 250 Ga. 772, 774 (301 S.E.2d 49) (1983), this court recognized the general rule that "a shareholder seeking to recover misappropriated corporate funds may only bring a derivative suit." Nevertheless, we permitted the minority shareholder of a close corporation to bring a direct action against the majority shareholders for misappropriation of corporate funds because exceptional circumstances were present. In so doing, we assumed, without deciding, that the misappropriation of corporate funds was primarily of a derivative nature and not a "direct injury." Thus, we

---

[85]   Kidder Peabody & Co., Inc. owned 4,347 shares of WPP when it was announced that the merger would not take place. Thereafter, it purchased more than 120,000 additional shares of WPP stock.

reserved the question of whether a direct action was available to a shareholder who suffers a "direct injury."

In Phoenix Airline Svcs. v. Metro Airlines, 260 Ga. 584 (397 S.E.2d 699) (1990), we observed that, under Delaware law,[86] a shareholder can maintain a direct action if he alleges a "special injury," i.e., an injury which is separate and distinct from that suffered by other shareholders, or a wrong involving a contractual right of a shareholder which exists independently of any right of the corporation. *Id.* at 586. This standard was applied by the Court of Appeals in Holland v. Holland Heating & Air C., 208 Ga. App. 794, 797 (432 S.E.2d 238) (1993), and is generally recognized as the test that distinguishes derivative from direct claims. We adopt this test and hold that, outside the context of a close corporation, a shareholder must be injured in a way which is different from the other shareholders or independently of the corporation to have standing to assert a direct action.

One of plaintiffs' claims—that defendants breached their fiduciary duty to minority shareholders by failing to seek consummation of the original merger agreement—meets this test. That claim asserts an injury separate and distinct from any injury to the corporation or the majority shareholders because only the minority shareholders stood to receive $58 per share upon consummation of the merger agreement.[8]

> Where, as here, it is sufficiently alleged that the effect of the controlling stockholders self-serving manipulation of corporate affairs causes a singular economic injury to minority interests alone, the minority have stated a cause of action for "special" injury. . . .

Plaintiffs' other claims are founded upon injuries which are no different from that suffered by the corporation or the other shareholders. It follows that the remainder of plaintiffs' direct claims cannot be sustained because they are, in the final analysis, derivative claims.

Plaintiffs erroneously assert that they are entitled to bring direct claims for breach of the merger agreement because they are third-party beneficiaries of the agreement. Section 9.08 of the agreement expressly states that "nothing in this Agreement, express or implied, is intended to confer upon any other person any rights or remedies of any nature whatsoever under or by reason of this Agreement. . . ." Thus, a plain reading of the merger agreement demonstrates that the parties did not intend to confer third-party beneficiary status on anyone.

3. The statutory appraisal remedy is exclusive. OCGA § 14–2–1302 (b); Comment, Note to 1989 Amendment. The only exceptions to the

---

[86] See Phoenix Airline Svcs. v. Metro Airlines, 194 Ga. App. 120, 123 (390 S.E.2d 219) (1989).

[8] Plaintiffs cannot maintain this direct claim, however, because the statutory appraisal remedy is exclusive where the shareholder's objection is essentially a complaint about price. See Division 3.

exclusivity of appraisal are the failure "to comply with procedural requirements . . . of the articles of incorporation or bylaws of the corporation or the vote required to obtain approval of the corporate action was obtained by fraudulent and deceptive means . . . "[11] *Id.*

Because plaintiffs do not come within the exceptions to the dissenters' rights statute, they must pursue their statutory remedies; they cannot collaterally attack the merger. *Id.* "If [plaintiffs] are allowed to maintain their present action, the viability of [the dissenter's rights statute] will be destroyed. Future dissenting shareholders would be able to circumvent the risks of [pursuing the statutory appraisal process] by simply maintaining a separate legal action."

Plaintiffs argue that their direct claim for breach of fiduciary duty cannot be raised in a shareholders' appraisal proceeding and that, therefore, they should be able to pursue that claim independently. In this connection, they assert that their claim is unrelated to the "fair value" of their shares. We cannot accept this assertion. The essence of plaintiffs' claim is they would have been paid more money per share if defendants had not breached their fiduciary duty to seek consummation of the merger agreement. This boils down to nothing more than a complaint about stock price.

Again, our statutory appraisal remedy is exclusive. It permits a dissenting shareholder to be paid the fair value of his shares and preempts any other remedy where the claim is essentially one regarding the price the shareholder is to receive for his shares. OCGA § 14–2–1302 (b); Comment, Note to 1989 Amendment. As courts in other jurisdictions with dissenters' rights statutes have observed: "[A] 'remedy beyond the statutory procedure is not available where the shareholder's objection is essentially a complaint regarding the price which he received for his shares.'"

This is not to say that dissenting shareholders have absolutely no remedy for alleged wrongdoing committed before the merger. On the contrary, shareholders who object to a merger are entitled to receive the fair value of their shares prior to the effectuation of the merger. OCGA § 14–2–1301 (5). And any facts which shed light on the value of the dissenting shareholders' interests are to be considered in arriving at "fair value."

* * *

Judgment affirmed. All the Justices concur.

---

[11] We observe that with regard to the "fraud" exception, the Comment, Note to 1989 Amendment, *supra*, states that "only 'actual fraud,' involving traditional notions of deception, permits collateral attack on the corporate action." Thus, a claim that "a fiduciary has acted unfairly" cannot be used "to litigate valuation issues that are appropriately disposed of in appraisal proceedings." Comment, Note to 1989 Amendment, *supra*.

QUESTIONS

1. Does the narrow definition of "fraud" in Georgia allow fiduciaries to breach duties to minority shareholders, subject only to the appraisal remedy?

2. Why do minority shareholders seem to prefer equitable actions to appraisal proceedings?

3. How can a minority shareholder assert a claim in appraisal that takes into account damages suffered as a result of direct claims, such as a breach of the original merger agreement, to which the shareholder claims to be a third party beneficiary?

4. How can a shareholder in a Georgia corporation structure a demand for payment that takes account of any wrongdoing alleged? If a shareholder is dissatisfied with the amount offered by the corporation for his or her shares, the shareholder must estimate the fair value of the shares and demand payment of that amount, plus interest, under Revised Model Business Corporation Act § 13.28. Recall that once a merger is consummated, the shareholder is no longer a shareholder, and no longer has standing to demand access to corporate records, and is only entitled to receive financial statements from the corporation. See Revised Model Business Corporation Act § 13.25(a).

Some cases in jurisdictions that have adopted the Model Business Corporation Act have followed the Georgia approach. Fleming v. International Pizza Supply Corp., 676 N.E.2d 1051 (Ind.1997) held that appraisal was exclusive under a version of § 13.02(b) that did not contain the exception for fraud and illegality, intended to legislatively reverse a contrary decision under the prior statute, Gabhart v. Gabhart, 267 Ind. 370, 370 N.E.2d 345 (1977). To the same effect, see Stringer v. Car Data Systems, Inc., 314 Or. 576, 841 P.2d 1183 (1992). See also Sound Infiniti, Inc. v. Snyder, 2008 WL 2486563, (Wash. App.), holding that complaints about prior breaches of fiduciary duty could be incorporated in an appraisal proceeding. See also Szaloczi v. John R. Behrmann Revocable Trust, 90 P.3d 835 (Colo. 2004) and Bingham Consolidation Co. v. Groesbeck, 105 P.3d 365 (Ut. App. 2004). In IRA ex rel. Oppenheimer v. Brenner Companies, Inc., 107 N.C.App. 16, 419 S.E.2d 354, disc. rev. denied, 332 N.C. 666, 424 S.E.2d 401 (1992), the court held that statutory appraisal under the Model Act's provision was exclusive unless the plaintiff could show the traditional elements of fraud, which include false representation or concealment of a material fact. This holding was followed in Werner Profit Sharing Plan v. Alexander, 502 S.E.2d 897 (N.C.App.1998). But in Strasenburgh v. Straubmuller, 284 N.J.Super. 168, 664 A.2d 497 (1995), interpreting a similar statute, the court distinguished between plaintiffs' derivative claims, which were covered by the appraisal remedy, and direct claims of separate harm to the minority shareholders, which it held were not precluded by the appraisal statute. Williams v. Stanford, 977 So.2d 722 (Fla. App. 2008) applied the current version of the Model Act's exclusivity language ("fraud or material misrepresentation") to find that prior fraudulent acts, plus a self-dealing sale by the majority stockholder at an allegedly low price, excused appraisal's exclusivity, citing Weinberger v. UOP as support. Szaloczi v. John R. Behrmann Revocable Trust, 90 P.3d 835 (Colo. 2004) held that a dissenting shareholder could not also bring a separate action for damages for breach of fiduciary duty in connection with the same merger, although a plaintiff could seek equitable relief. Another case, applying the Model Business Corporation Act, relied in part on the Grace decision to hold that damage claims for breach of fiduciary duty were includible in an appraisal valuation. Bingham Consolidation Co. v. Groesbeck, 2004 Ut. App. 434, 105 P.3d 365 (Utah App. 2004). For a more extensive treatment of this subject see Robert B. Thompson, Exit, Liquidity, and Majority Rule: Appraisal's Role in Corporate Law, 84 Geo. L.J. 1, 44 (1995).

F.   APPRAISAL EXCEPTIONS AND FORM OVER SUBSTANCE

Louisiana Mun. Police Employees'
Retirement System v. Crawford

918 A.2D 1172 (Del. Ch. 2007).

■ CHANDLER, CHANCELLOR.

[Caremark was concerned that it was an intermediary between pharmaceutical companies and health plans, and that this could cause it to be eliminated as a cost-cutting move. Caremark had discussions with two companies about business combinations—Express Scripts, another intermediary, where negotiations terminated after a disappointing earnings report by Express Scripts—and CVS. The Caremark-CVS combination was always envisioned as a stock-for-stock "merger of equals" where neither side would be seen as the acquiror, and both companies would have equal board representation. When an agreement was reached, it was agreed that Caremark stockholders would own about 45% of the combined company, in a stock-for-stock merger. The agreement contained a "force the vote" provision similar to that in the Omnicare case, a no-shop provision and a "last look" provision that gave either party a right of first refusal if a better offer were received. Each party committed to a termination fee of $675 million if either board changed its recommendation of the merger and the company merged with another suitor within twelve months.

This agreement, approved by both boards on November 1, 2006, was disrupted by Express Script's higher bid for Caremark on December 15. The bid was 15% higher than the closing price of Caremark stock at the time, or over $3 billion more than the value of the CVS deal. Thereafter Ryan, CEO of CVS, called Crawford, CEO of Caremark, and proposed that Caremark declare a special dividend at the time of the merger, to enhance the merger consideration for Caremark shareholders. The dividend would be declared before the merger, but would be payable only if the Caremark shareholders approved the merger.

Express Scripts sued to enjoin the merger on various grounds, but the most innovative one involved the claim that the Caremark proxy statement failed to inform its shareholders that they had appraisal rights under Del. GCL § 262. This section provides that appraisal is not available for shareholders of a public company who receive shares in another public company.]

VI. APPRAISAL RIGHTS

Plaintiffs contend the $6 special cash dividend triggers appraisal rights under 8 Del. C. § 262. Defendants respond that the special dividend has been approved and will be payable by Caremark and, thus, has independent legal significance preventing it from being recognized as merger consideration. Thus, according to defendants, dissenting Caremark shareholders will have no appraisal rights after the CVS/Caremark merger.

Section 262 of the DGCL grants appraisal rights to stockholders who are required, by the terms of the merger, to accept any consideration other than shares of stock in the surviving company, shares of stock listed on a national securities exchange, or cash received as payment for fractional shares. The $6 "special dividend," although issued by the Caremark board, is fundamentally cash consideration paid to Caremark shareholders on behalf of CVS.

Defendants are unsuccessful in their efforts to cloak this cash payment as a "special dividend." CVS and Caremark filed a joint proxy in which they informed shareholders of the merger terms and recommended merger approval. This proxy statement lists details of the special cash dividend:

> CVS separately granted a waiver to Caremark from the restrictions set forth in Section 6.01(b) of the merger agreement to permit Caremark to pay a one-time, special cash dividend to holders of record of Caremark common stock (on a record date to be set by the Caremark board of directors) in the amount of $2.00 per share of Caremark common stock held by each such holder on such record date, which dividend shall, under the terms of the CVS waiver, be declared prior to the Caremark special meeting, but *shall only become payable upon or after the effective time of the merger, and such payment shall be conditioned upon occurrence of the effective time of the merger.*

Thus, defendants specifically condition payment of the $6 cash "special dividend" on shareholder approval of the merger agreement. Additionally, the payment becomes due upon or even *after* the effective time of the merger. These facts belie the claim that the special dividend has legal significance independent of the merger. CVS, by terms of the CVS/Caremark merger agreement, controls the value of the dividend. Defendants even warn in their public disclosures that the special cash dividend might be treated as merger consideration for tax purposes. In this case, the label "special dividend" is simply cash consideration dressed up in a none-too-convincing disguise. When merger consideration includes partial cash and stock payments, shareholders are entitled to appraisal rights. So long as payment of the special dividend remains conditioned upon shareholder approval of the merger, Caremark shareholders should not be denied their appraisal rights simply because their directors are willing to collude with a favored bidder to "launder" a cash payment. As Caremark failed to inform shareholders of their appraisal rights, the meeting must be enjoined for at least the statutorily required notice period of twenty days.

* * *

VIII.   CONCLUSION

Based on the foregoing reasons, this Court enjoins any vote of Caremark shareholders with respect to the CVS/Caremark merger for at least twenty days after defendants properly disclose to shareholders (a) their right to seek appraisal and (b) the structure of fees paid to Caremark's bankers. At this stage, however, no broader injunction is necessary. The balance of the equities weighs in favor of permitting informed shareholders to speak directly to their fiduciaries without further intervention by this Court.

No party should infer from the fact that I am denying plaintiffs an injunction that existence of appraisal rights and the disclosure of all material information to informed, disinterested shareholders somehow excuses violations of fiduciary duties under Delaware law. This Opinion addresses only a preliminary injunction, an extraordinary remedy granted to parties in order to preserve rights that would otherwise be extinguished over the course of litigation. * * *

QUESTIONS

1. The court characterizes Caremark's cash dividend to its own shareholders as "fundamentally paid to Caremark shareholders on behalf of CVS." What reasoning underlies this conclusion?

2. Recall the discussion of "independent legal significance" following Hariton v. Arco Electronics, Inc. in Chapter Four, Part 4.A, at pages 135–138. Recall that while Keller v. Wilson held that unpaid preferred

dividends were vested property rights that could not be divested by a charter amendment, Federal United Corp. v. Havender held that a merger was an act of independent legal significance, and that preferred share rights could be altered in that way. What effect does this decision have on your confidence that those decisions will be followed in the future?

---

4. FAIRNESS TESTS: WEINBERGER AND ITS PROGENY

A. TRIGGERS OF THE DUTY

Read Del. Gen. Corp. L. § 144 and Rev. Model Bus. Corp. Act §§ 8.60–8.63.

Weinberger v. UOP, Inc.

457 A.2d 701 (Del.1983).

■ MOORE, JUSTICE:

This post-trial appeal was reheard en banc from a decision of the Court of Chancery. It was brought by the class action plaintiff below, a former shareholder of UOP, Inc., who challenged the elimination of UOP's minority shareholders by a cash-out merger between UOP and its majority owner, The Signal Companies, Inc. Originally, the defendants in this action were Signal, UOP, certain officers and directors of those companies, and UOP's investment banker, Lehman Brothers Kuhn Loeb, Inc. The present Chancellor held that the terms of the merger were fair to the plaintiff and the other minority shareholders of UOP. Accordingly, he entered judgment in favor of the defendants.

Numerous points were raised by the parties, but we address only the following questions presented by the trial court's opinion:

1) The plaintiff's duty to plead sufficient facts demonstrating the unfairness of the challenged merger;

2) The burden of proof upon the parties where the merger has been approved by the purportedly informed vote of a majority of the minority shareholders;

3) The fairness of the merger in terms of adequacy of the defendants' disclosures to the minority shareholders;

4) The fairness of the merger in terms of adequacy of the price paid for the minority shares and the remedy appropriate to that issue; and

5) The continued force and effect of Singer v. Magnavox Co., Del. Supr., 380 A.2d 969, 980 (1977), and its progeny.

In ruling for the defendants, the Chancellor re-stated his earlier conclusion that the plaintiff in a suit challenging a cash-out merger must allege specific acts of fraud, misrepresentation, or other items of misconduct to demonstrate the unfairness of the merger terms to the minority. We approve this rule and affirm it.

The Chancellor also held that even though the ultimate burden of proof is on the majority shareholder to show by a preponderance of the evidence that the transaction is fair, it is first the burden of the plaintiff attacking the merger to demonstrate some basis for invoking the fairness obligation. We agree with that principle. However, where corporate action has been approved by an informed vote of a majority of the minority shareholders, we conclude that the burden entirely shifts to the plaintiff to show that the transaction was unfair to the minority. But in all this, the burden clearly remains on those relying on the vote to show that they completely disclosed all material facts relevant to the transaction.

Here, the record does not support a conclusion that the minority stockholder vote was an informed one. Material information, necessary to acquaint those shareholders with the bargaining positions of Signal and UOP, was withheld under circumstances amounting to a breach of fiduciary duty. We therefore conclude that this merger does not meet the test of fairness, at least as we address that concept, and no burden thus shifted to the plaintiff by reason of the minority shareholder vote. Accordingly, we reverse and remand for further proceedings consistent herewith.

In considering the nature of the remedy available under our law to minority shareholders in a cash-out merger, we believe that it is, and hereafter should be, an appraisal under 8 Del. C. § 262 as hereinafter construed. * * *

Our treatment of these matters has necessarily led us to a reconsideration of the business purpose rule announced in the trilogy of Singer v. Magnavox Co., *supra*; Tanzer v. International General Industries, Inc., Del. Supr., 379 A.2d 1121 (1977); and Roland International Corp. v. Najjar, Del. Supr., 407 A.2d 1032 (1979). For the reasons hereafter set forth we consider that the business purpose requirement of these cases is no longer the law of Delaware.

I.

The facts found by the trial court, pertinent to the issues before us, are supported by the record, and we draw from them as set out in the Chancellor's opinion.

[Signal was a diversified company traded on the New York Stock Exchange, which had sold a major division in 1974. Thereafter Signal bargained with the UOP board, which ultimately approved a cash tender offer for a majority of UOP's shares at $21, at a time when UOP's stock had been trading on the New York Stock Exchange at $14. Signal proceeded to elect six of UOP's thirteen board members, and when UOP's

President stepped down, he was replaced by James Crawford, a long-time Signal employee. Crawford was also made a director. By 1977 Signal determined to consider acquiring the minority interests in UOP.]

The trial court found that at the instigation of certain Signal management personnel, including William W. Walkup, its board chairman, and Forrest N. Shumway, its president, a feasibility study was made concerning the possible acquisition of the balance of UOP's outstanding shares. This study was performed by two Signal officers, Charles S. Arledge, vice president (director of planning), and Andrew J. Chitiea, senior vice president (chief financial officer). Messrs. Walkup, Shumway, Arledge and Chitiea were all directors of UOP in addition to their membership on the Signal board.

Arledge and Chitiea concluded that it would be a good investment for Signal to acquire the remaining 49.5% of UOP shares at any price up to $24 each. Their report was discussed between Walkup and Shumway who, along with Arledge, Chitiea and Brewster L. Arms, internal counsel for Signal, constituted Signal's senior management. In particular, they talked about the proper price to be paid if the acquisition was pursued, purportedly keeping in mind that as UOP's majority shareholder, Signal owed a fiduciary responsibility to both its own stockholders as well as to UOP's minority. It was ultimately agreed that a meeting of Signal's Executive Committee would be called to propose that Signal acquire the remaining outstanding stock of UOP through a cash-out merger in the range of $20 to $21 per share.

The Executive Committee meeting was set for February 28, 1978. As a courtesy, UOP's president, Crawford, was invited to attend, although he was not a member of Signal's executive committee. On his arrival, and prior to the meeting, Crawford was asked to meet privately with Walkup and Shumway. He was then told of Signal's plan to acquire full ownership of UOP and was asked for his reaction to the proposed price range of $20 to $21 per share. Crawford said he thought such a price would be "generous", and that it was certainly one which should be submitted to UOP's minority shareholders for their ultimate consideration. He stated, however, that Signal's 100% ownership could cause internal problems at UOP. He believed that employees would have to be given some assurance of their future place in a fully-owned Signal subsidiary. Otherwise, he feared the departure of essential personnel. Also, many of UOP's key employees had stock option incentive programs which would be wiped out by a merger. Crawford therefore urged that some adjustment would have to be made, such as providing a comparable incentive in Signal's shares, if after the merger he was to maintain his quality of personnel and efficiency at UOP.

Thus, Crawford voiced no objection to the $20 to $21 price range, nor did he suggest that Signal should consider paying more than $21 per share for the minority interests. Later, at the Executive Committee meeting the same factors were discussed, with Crawford repeating the position he earlier took with Walkup and Shumway. Also considered was the 1975 tender offer and the fact that it had been greatly oversubscribed at $21 per share. For many reasons, Signal's management concluded that the acquisition of UOP's minority shares provided the solution to a number of its business problems.

Thus, it was the consensus that a price of $20 to $21 per share would be fair to both Signal and the minority shareholders of UOP. Signal's executive committee authorized its management "to negotiate" with UOP "for a cash acquisition of the minority ownership in UOP, Inc., with the intention of presenting a proposal to [Signal's] board of directors . . . on March 6, 1978". Immediately after this February 28, 1978 meeting, Signal issued a press release stating:

> The Signal Companies, Inc. and UOP, Inc. are conducting negotiations for the acquisition for cash by Signal of the 49.5 per cent of UOP which it does not presently own, announced Forrest N. Shumway, president and chief executive officer of Signal, and James V. Crawford, UOP president.
>
> Price and other terms of the proposed transaction have not yet been finalized and would be subject to approval of the boards of directors of Signal and UOP, scheduled to meet early next week, the stockholders of UOP and certain federal agencies.

The announcement also referred to the fact that the closing price of UOP's common stock on that day was $14.50 per share.

Two days later, on March 2, 1978, Signal issued a second press release stating that its management would recommend a price in the range of $20 to $21 per share for UOP's 49.5% minority interest. This announcement referred to Signal's earlier statement that "negotiations" were being conducted for the acquisition of the minority shares.

Between Tuesday, February 28, 1978 and Monday, March 6, 1978, a total of four business days, Crawford spoke by telephone with all of UOP's non-Signal, i.e., outside, directors. Also during that period, Crawford retained Lehman Brothers to render a fairness opinion as to the price offered the minority for its stock. He gave two reasons for this choice. First, the time schedule between the announcement and the board meetings was short (by then only three business days) and since Lehman Brothers had been acting as UOP's investment banker for many years, Crawford felt that it would be in the best position to respond on such brief notice. Second, James W. Glanville, a long-time director of UOP and a partner in Lehman Brothers, had acted as a financial advisor to UOP for many years. Crawford believed that Glanville's familiarity with UOP, as a member of its board, would also be of assistance in enabling Lehman Brothers to render a fairness opinion within the existing time constraints.

Crawford telephoned Glanville, who gave his assurance that Lehman Brothers had no conflicts that would prevent it from accepting the task. Glanville's immediate personal reaction was that a price of $20 to $21 would certainly be fair, since it represented almost a 50% premium over UOP's market price. Glanville sought a $250,000 fee for Lehman Brothers' services, but Crawford thought this too much. After further discussions Glanville finally agreed that Lehman Brothers would render its fairness opinion for $150,000.

During this period Crawford also had several telephone contacts with Signal officials. In only one of them, however, was the price of the shares discussed. In a conversation with Walkup, Crawford advised that as a result of his communications with UOP's non-Signal directors, it was his feeling that the price would have to be the top of the proposed range, or $21 per share, if the approval of UOP's outside directors was to be obtained. But again, he did not seek any price higher than $21.

Glanville assembled a three-man Lehman Brothers team to do the work on the fairness opinion. These persons examined relevant documents and information concerning UOP, including its annual reports and its Securities and Exchange Commission filings from 1973 through 1976, as well as its audited financial statements for 1977, its interim reports to shareholders, and its recent and historical market prices and trading volumes. In addition, on Friday, March 3, 1978, two members of the Lehman Brothers team flew to UOP's headquarters in Des Plaines, Illinois, to perform a "due diligence" visit, during the course of which they interviewed Crawford as well as UOP's general counsel, its chief financial officer, and other key executives and personnel.

As a result, the Lehman Brothers team concluded that "the price of either $20 or $21 would be a fair price for the remaining shares of UOP". They telephoned this impression to Glanville, who was spending the weekend in Vermont.

On Monday morning, March 6, 1978, Glanville and the senior member of the Lehman Brothers team flew to Des Plaines to attend the scheduled UOP directors meeting. Glanville looked over the assembled information during the flight. The two had with them the draft of a "fairness opinion letter" in which the price had been left blank. Either during or immediately prior to the directors' meeting, the two-page "fairness opinion letter" was typed in final form and the price of $21 per share was inserted.

On March 6, 1978, both the Signal and UOP boards were convened to consider the proposed merger. Telephone communications were maintained between the two meetings. Walkup, Signal's board chairman, and also a UOP director, attended UOP's meeting with Crawford in order to present Signal's position and answer any questions that UOP's non-Signal directors might have. Arledge and Chitiea, along with Signal's other designees on UOP's board, participated by conference telephone.

All of UOP's outside directors attended the meeting either in person or by conference telephone.

First, Signal's board unanimously adopted a resolution authorizing Signal to propose to UOP a cash merger of $21 per share as outlined in a certain merger agreement and other supporting documents. This proposal required that the merger be approved by a majority of UOP's outstanding minority shares voting at the stockholders meeting at which the merger would be considered, and that the minority shares voting in favor of the merger, when coupled with Signal's 50.5% interest would have to comprise at least two-thirds of all UOP shares. Otherwise the proposed merger would be deemed disapproved.

UOP's board then considered the proposal. Copies of the agreement were delivered to the directors in attendance, and other copies had been forwarded earlier to the directors participating by telephone. They also had before them UOP financial data for 1974–1977, UOP's most recent financial statements, market price information, and budget projections for 1978. In addition they had Lehman Brothers' hurriedly prepared fairness opinion letter finding the price of $21 to be fair. Glanville, the Lehman Brothers partner, and UOP director, commented on the information that had gone into preparation of the letter.

Signal also suggests that the Arledge-Chitiea feasibility study, indicating that a price of up to $24 per share would be a "good investment" for Signal, was discussed at the UOP directors' meeting. The Chancellor made no such finding, and our independent review of the record, detailed *infra*, satisfies us by a preponderance of the evidence that there was no discussion of this document at UOP's board meeting. Furthermore, it is clear beyond peradventure that nothing in that report was ever disclosed to UOP's minority shareholders prior to their approval of the merger.

After consideration of Signal's proposal, Walkup and Crawford left the meeting to permit a free and uninhibited exchange between UOP's non-Signal directors. Upon their return a resolution to accept Signal's offer was then proposed and adopted. While Signal's men on UOP's board participated in various aspects of the meeting, they abstained from voting. However, the minutes show that each of them "if voting would have voted yes".

On March 7, 1978, UOP sent a letter to its shareholders advising them of the action taken by UOP's board with respect to Signal's offer. This document pointed out, among other things, that on February 28, 1978 "both companies had announced negotiations were being conducted".

Despite the swift board action of the two companies, the merger was not submitted to UOP's shareholders until their annual meeting on May 26, 1978. In the notice of that meeting and proxy statement sent to shareholders in May, UOP's management and board urged that the merger be approved. The proxy statement also advised:

> The price was determined after discussions between James V. Crawford, a director of Signal and Chief Executive Officer of UOP, and officers of Signal which took place during meetings on February 28, 1978, and in the course of several subsequent telephone conversations. (Emphasis added.)

In the original draft of the proxy statement the word "negotiations" had been used rather than "discussions". However, when the Securities and Exchange Commission sought details of the "negotiations" as part of its review of these materials, the term was deleted and the word "discussions" was substituted. The proxy statement indicated that the vote of UOP's board in approving the merger had been unanimous. It also advised the shareholders that Lehman Brothers had given its opinion that the merger price of $21 per share was fair to UOP's minority. However, it did not disclose the hurried method by which this conclusion was reached.

As of the record date for UOP's annual meeting, there were 11,488,302 shares of UOP common stock outstanding, 5,688,302 of which were owned by the minority. At the meeting only 56%, or 3,208,652, of the minority shares were voted. Of these, 2,953,812, or 51.9% of the total minority, voted for the merger, and 254,840 voted against it. When Signal's stock was added to the minority shares voting in favor, a total of 76.2% of UOP's outstanding shares approved the merger while only 2.2% opposed it.

By its terms the merger became effective on May 26, 1978, and each share of UOP's stock held by the minority was automatically converted into a right to receive $21 cash.

II.

A.

A primary issue mandating reversal is the preparation by two UOP directors, Arledge and Chitiea, of their feasibility study for the exclusive use and benefit of Signal. This document was of obvious significance to both Signal and UOP. Using UOP data, it described the advantages to Signal of ousting the minority at a price range of $21—$24 per share. Mr. Arledge, one of the authors, outlined the benefits to Signal:[6]

Purpose of the Merger

　　1)　Provides an outstanding investment opportunity for Signal—(Better than any recent acquisition we have seen.)

　　2)　Increases Signal's earnings.

---

[6]　The parentheses indicate certain handwritten comments of Mr. Arledge.

3)   Facilitates the flow of resources between Signal and its subsidiaries—(Big factors—works both ways.)

4)   Provides cost savings potential for Signal and UOP.

5)   Improves the percentage of Signal's "operating earnings" as opposed to "holding company earnings".

6)   Simplifies the understanding of Signal.

7)   Facilitates technological exchange among Signal's subsidiaries.

8)   Eliminates potential conflicts of interest.

Having written those words, solely for the use of Signal, it is clear from the record that neither Arledge nor Chitiea shared this report with their fellow directors of UOP. We are satisfied that no one else did either. This conduct hardly meets the fiduciary standards applicable to such a transaction. While Mr. Walkup, Signal's chairman of the board and a UOP director, attended the March 6, 1978, UOP board meeting and testified at trial that he had discussed the Arledge-Chitiea report with the UOP directors at this meeting, the record does not support this assertion. Perhaps it is the result of some confusion on Mr. Walkup's part. In any event Mr. Shumway, Signal's president, testified that he made sure the Signal outside directors had this report prior to the March 6, 1978, Signal board meeting, but he did not testify that the Arledge-Chitiea report was also sent to UOP's outside directors.

* * *

Actually, it appears that a three-page summary of figures was given to all UOP directors. Its first page is identical to one page of the Arledge-Chitiea report, but this dealt with nothing more than a justification of the $21 price. Significantly, the contents of this three-page summary are what the minutes reflect Mr. Walkup told the UOP board. However, nothing contained in either the minutes or this three-page summary reflects Signal's study regarding the $24 price.

The Arledge-Chitiea report speaks for itself in supporting the Chancellor's finding that a price of up to $24 was a "good investment" for Signal. It shows that a return on the investment at $21 would be 15.7% versus 15.5% at $24 per share. This was a difference of only two-tenths of one percent, while it meant over $17,000,000 to the minority. Under such circumstances, paying UOP's minority shareholders $24 would have had relatively little long-term effect on Signal, and the Chancellor's findings concerning the benefit to Signal, even at a price of $24, were obviously correct. Levitt v. Bouvier, Del. Supr., 287 A.2d 671, 673 (1972).

Certainly, this was a matter of material significance to UOP and its shareholders. Since the study was prepared by two UOP directors, using UOP information for the exclusive benefit of Signal, and nothing whatever was done to disclose it to the outside UOP directors or the minority shareholders, a question of breach of fiduciary duty arises. This problem occurs because there were common Signal-UOP directors participating, at least to some extent, in the UOP board's decision-making processes without full disclosure of the conflicts they faced.[7]

B.

In assessing this situation, the Court of Chancery was required to:

> examine what information defendants had and to measure it against what they gave to the minority stockholders, in a context in which "complete candor" is required. In other words, the limited function of the Court was to determine whether defendants had disclosed all information in their possession germane to the transaction in issue. And by "germane" we mean, for present purposes, information such as a reasonable shareholder would consider important in deciding whether to sell or retain stock. . . . Completeness, not adequacy, is both the norm and the mandate under present circumstances.

Lynch v. Vickers Energy Corp., Del. Supr., 383 A.2d 278, 281 (1977) (Lynch I). This is merely stating in another way the long-existing principle of Delaware law that these Signal designated directors on UOP's board still owed UOP and its shareholders an uncompromising duty of loyalty. The classic language of Guth v. Loft, Inc., Del. Supr., 5 A.2d 503, 510 (1939), requires no embellishment:

> A public policy, existing through the years, and derived from a profound knowledge of human characteristics and motives, has established a rule that demands of a corporate officer or director, peremptorily and inexorably, the most scrupulous observance of his duty, not only affirmatively to protect the interests of the corporation committed to his charge, but also to refrain from doing anything that would work injury to the corporation, or to deprive it of profit or advantage which his skill and ability might properly bring to it, or to enable it to make in the reasonable and lawful exercise of its powers. The rule that requires an undivided and unselfish loyalty to the corporation demands that there shall be no conflict between duty and self-interest.

---

[7] Although perfection is not possible, or expected, the result here could have been entirely different if UOP had appointed an independent negotiating committee of its outside directors to deal with Signal at arm's length. See, e.g., Harriman v. E.I. du Pont De Nemours & Co., 411 F.Supp. 133 (D. Del.1975). Since fairness in this context can be equated to conduct by a theoretical, wholly independent, board of directors acting upon the matter before them, it is unfortunate that this course apparently was neither considered nor pursued. Johnston v. Greene, Del. Supr., 121 A.2d 919, 925 (1956). Particularly in a parent-subsidiary context, a showing that the action taken was as though each of the contending parties had in fact exerted its bargaining power against the other at arm's length is strong evidence that the transaction meets the test of fairness. Getty Oil Co. v. Skelly Oil Co., Del. Supr., 267 A.2d 883, 886 (1970); Puma v. Marriott, Del. Ch., 283 A.2d 693, 696 (1971).

Given the absence of any attempt to structure this transaction on an arm's length basis, Signal cannot escape the effects of the conflicts it faced, particularly when its designees on UOP's board did not totally abstain from participation in the matter. There is no "safe harbor" for such divided loyalties in Delaware. When directors of a Delaware corporation are on both sides of a transaction, they are required to demonstrate their utmost good faith and the most scrupulous inherent fairness of the bargain. The requirement of fairness is unflinching in its demand that where one stands on both sides of a transaction, he has the burden of establishing its entire fairness, sufficient to pass the test of careful scrutiny by the courts.

There is no dilution of this obligation where one holds dual or multiple directorships, as in a parent-subsidiary context. Levien v. Sinclair Oil Corp., Del. Ch., 261 A.2d 911, 915 (1969). Thus, individuals who act in a dual capacity as directors of two corporations, one of whom is parent and the other subsidiary, owe the same duty of good management to both corporations, and in the absence of an independent negotiating structure (see note 7, *supra*), or the directors' total abstention from any participation in the matter, this duty is to be exercised in light of what is best for both companies. The record demonstrates that Signal has not met this obligation.

C.

The concept of fairness has two basic aspects: fair dealing and fair price. The former embraces questions of when the transaction was timed, how it was initiated, structured, negotiated, disclosed to the directors, and how the approvals of the directors and the stockholders were obtained. The latter aspect of fairness relates to the economic and financial considerations of the proposed merger, including all relevant factors: assets, market value, earnings, future prospects, and any other elements that affect the intrinsic or inherent value of a company's stock. However, the test for fairness is not a bifurcated one as between fair dealing and price. All aspects of the issue must be examined as a whole since the question is one of entire fairness. However, in a non-fraudulent transaction we recognize that price may be the preponderant consideration outweighing other features of the merger. Here, we address the two basic aspects of fairness separately because we find reversible error as to both.

D.

Part of fair dealing is the obvious duty of candor required by Lynch I, *supra*. Moreover, one possessing superior knowledge may not mislead any stockholder by use of corporate information to which the latter is not privy. Delaware has long imposed this duty even upon persons who are not corporate officers or directors, but who nonetheless are privy to matters of interest or significance to their company. Brophy v. Cities Service Co., Del. Ch., 70 A.2d 5, 7 (1949). With the well-established

Delaware law on the subject, and the Court of Chancery's findings of fact here, it is inevitable that the obvious conflicts posed by Arledge and Chitiea's preparation of their "feasibility study", derived from UOP information, for the sole use and benefit of Signal, cannot pass muster.

The Arledge-Chitiea report is but one aspect of the element of fair dealing. How did this merger evolve? It is clear that it was entirely initiated by Signal. The serious time constraints under which the principals acted were all set by Signal. It had not found a suitable outlet for its excess cash and considered UOP a desirable investment, particularly since it was now in a position to acquire the whole company for itself. For whatever reasons, and they were only Signal's, the entire transaction was presented to and approved by UOP's board within four business days. Standing alone, this is not necessarily indicative of any lack of fairness by a majority shareholder. It was what occurred, or more properly, what did not occur, during this brief period that makes the time constraints imposed by Signal relevant to the issue of fairness.

The structure of the transaction, again, was Signal's doing. So far as negotiations were concerned, it is clear that they were modest at best. Crawford, Signal's man at UOP, never really talked price with Signal, except to accede to its management's statements on the subject, and to convey to Signal the UOP outside directors' view that as between the $20–$21 range under consideration, it would have to be $21. The latter is not a surprising outcome, but hardly arm's length negotiations. Only the protection of benefits for UOP's key employees and the issue of Lehman Brothers' fee approached any concept of bargaining.

As we have noted, the matter of disclosure to the UOP directors was wholly flawed by the conflicts of interest raised by the Arledge-Chitiea report. All of those conflicts were resolved by Signal in its own favor without divulging any aspect of them to UOP.

This cannot but undermine a conclusion that this merger meets any reasonable test of fairness. The outside UOP directors lacked one material piece of information generated by two of their colleagues, but shared only with Signal. True, the UOP board had the Lehman Brothers' fairness opinion, but that firm has been blamed by the plaintiff for the hurried task it performed, when more properly the responsibility for this lies with Signal. There was no disclosure of the circumstances surrounding the rather cursory preparation of the Lehman Brothers' fairness opinion. Instead, the impression was given UOP's minority that a careful study had been made, when in fact speed was the hallmark, and Mr. Glanville, Lehman's partner in charge of the matter, and also a UOP director, having spent the weekend in Vermont, brought a draft of the "fairness opinion letter" to the UOP directors' meeting on March 6, 1978 with the price left blank. We can only conclude from the record that the rush imposed on Lehman Brothers by Signal's timetable contributed to the difficulties under which this investment banking firm attempted to perform its responsibilities. Yet, none of this was disclosed to UOP's minority.

Finally, the minority stockholders were denied the critical information that Signal considered a price of $24 to be a good investment. Since this would have meant over $17,000,000 more to the minority, we cannot conclude that the shareholder vote was an informed one. Under the circumstances, an approval by a majority of the minority was meaningless. Lynch I, 383 A.2d at 279, 281; Cahall v. Lofland, Del. Ch., 114 A. 224 (1921).

Given these particulars and the Delaware law on the subject, the record does not establish that this transaction satisfies any reasonable concept of fair dealing, and the Chancellor's findings in that regard must be reversed.

* * *

The plaintiff has not sought an appraisal, but rescissory damages of the type contemplated by Lynch v. Vickers Energy Corp., Del. Supr., 429 A.2d 497, 505–06 (1981) (Lynch II). In view of the approach to valuation that we announce today, we see no basis in our law for Lynch II's exclusive monetary formula for relief. On remand the plaintiff will be permitted to test the fairness of the $21 price by the standards we herein establish, in conformity with the principle applicable to an appraisal—that fair value be determined by taking "into account all relevant factors" [see 8 Del. C. § 262(h), *supra*]. * * * While a plaintiff's monetary remedy ordinarily should be confined to the more liberalized appraisal proceeding herein established, we do not intend any limitation on the historic powers of the Chancellor to grant such other relief as the facts of a particular case may dictate. The appraisal remedy we approve may not be adequate in certain cases, particularly where fraud, misrepresentation, self-dealing, deliberate waste of corporate assets, or gross and palpable overreaching are involved. Under such circumstances, the Chancellor's powers are complete to fashion any form of equitable and monetary relief as may be appropriate, including rescissory damages. Since it is apparent that this long completed transaction is too involved to undo, and in view of the Chancellor's discretion, the award, if any, should be in the form of monetary damages based upon entire fairness standards, i.e., fair dealing and fair price. Obviously, there are other litigants, like the plaintiff, who abjured an appraisal and whose rights to challenge the element of fair value must be preserved. Accordingly, the quasi-appraisal remedy we grant the plaintiff here will apply only to: (1) this case; (2) any case now pending on appeal to this Court; (3) any case now pending in the Court of Chancery which has not yet been appealed but which may be eligible for direct appeal to this Court; (4) any case challenging a cash-out merger, the effective date of which is on or before February 1, 1983; and (5) any proposed merger to be presented at a shareholders' meeting, the notification of which is mailed to the stockholders on or before February 23, 1983. Thereafter, the provisions of 8 Del. C. § 262, as herein construed, respecting the scope of an appraisal and the means for perfecting the same, shall govern the financial remedy available to minority shareholders in a cash-out merger. Thus, we return to the well established principles of Stauffer v. Standard Brands, Inc., Del. Supr.,41 Del. Ch. 7, 187 A.2d 78 (1962) and David J. Greene & Co. v. Schenley Industries, Inc., Del. Ch., 281 A.2d 30 (1971), mandating a stockholder's recourse to the basic remedy of an appraisal.

III.

Finally, we address the matter of business purpose. The defendants contend that the purpose of this merger was not a proper subject of inquiry by the trial court. The plaintiff says that no valid purpose existed—the entire transaction was a mere subterfuge designed to eliminate the minority. The Chancellor ruled otherwise, but in so doing he clearly circumscribed the thrust and effect of Singer. Weinberger v. UOP, 426 A.2d at 1342–43, 1348–50. This has led to the thoroughly sound observation that the business purpose test "may be . . . virtually interpreted out of existence, as it was in Weinberger".[19]

The requirement of a business purpose is new to our law of mergers and was a departure from prior case law . . .

In view of the fairness test which has long been applicable to parent-subsidiary mergers, the expanded appraisal remedy now available to shareholders, and the broad discretion of the Chancellor to fashion such relief as the facts of a given case may dictate, we do not believe that any additional meaningful protection is afforded minority shareholders by the business purpose requirement of the trilogy of Singer, Tanzer, Najjar, and their progeny. Accordingly, such requirement shall no longer be of any force or effect.

The judgment of the Court of Chancery, finding both the circumstances of the merger and the price paid the minority shareholders to be fair, is reversed. The matter is remanded for further proceedings consistent herewith. Upon remand the plaintiff's post-trial motion to enlarge the class should be granted.

Reversed and Remanded.

QUESTIONS

1. Why does the court not discuss this case under section 144 of the Delaware Act? What aspects of a transaction in which a dominant

---

[19] Weiss, The Law of Take Out Mergers: A Historical Perspective, 56 N.Y.U. L. Rev. 624, 671, n. 300 (1981).

shareholder deals with a subsidiary would not be fully protected by the provisions of this section?

2. Who has the initial burden of proof on the fairness of a takeout merger under Weinberger?

3. Can the majority stockholder avoid bearing the burden of proof on fairness? How?

4. What aspects of the transaction does the Court suggest may fail to meet the standard of fair dealing?

5. How could Signal have prepared its study of the price it was willing to pay for UOP without disclosing it under Weinberger? Assume that a study identical to that of Arledge and Chitiea had been prepared by Signal employees who had no connection with UOP, and was presented to the Signal board. If any UOP directors sat on the Signal board, would they be obligated to disclose this to the other UOP directors?

6. In part II.B. of its opinion, the Delaware Supreme Court states that the Chancery Court was required to "examine what information defendants had and to measure it against what they gave to the minority stockholders, in a context in which 'complete candor' is required." Does this mean that majority shareholders must always disclose their "reservation price," that is, the highest price they would be willing to pay, to the minority?

7. Note that the court states that where directors serve on the boards of both parent and subsidiary and participate in the decisions, their fiduciary duty to both companies "is to be exercised in light of what is best for both companies." How would you advise any such directors to behave in light of this standard?

8. Why does the court emphasize that the Signal study showed that acquisition of the remaining UOP shares would be a good deal for Signal at any price up to $24? Does this mean any price under $24 was unfair?

9. Assuming no real changes occurred in UOP from the date prior to the original tender offer in 1974, and that stock market prices remained generally stable, was $21 a good deal for the UOP minority shareholders? Why or why not?

10. How would you advise a board to structure its processes to take out minority shareholders in a subsidiary corporation after Weinberger?

11. Are all minority shareholders complaints in takeout mergers likely to boil down to money? If so, after Weinberger, how many times would you predict that equitable challenges would be likely to succeed in these cases?

12. If fairness has two aspects, fair dealing and fair price, can a majority shareholder sustain the validity of a cash-out merger if the price is fair but the procedures are not?

PROBLEM

Assume a similar takeout merger in a corporation organized under the provisions of Revised Model Business Corporation Act cited below.

1. See RMBCA §§ 8.60(4), 8.61 and 8.62. How would the outcome in the preceding case be influenced by these provisions?

2. Would it matter which persons were assigned the role of producing the information produced by Arledge and Chitiea?

3. If disclosure is required, precisely what would be required to be disclosed?

B. USE OF SPECIAL COMMITTEES

NOTE ON THE LIMITS OF SPECIAL COMMITTEES

See Revised Model Business Corporation Act § 8.25(e) and Delaware General Corporation Law § 141(c)(1).

The Weinberger opinion spoke of the use of special committees of the board to solve the problems of conflicts of interest. Both Delaware law and the Model Business Corporation Act, cited above, authorize committees generally to exercise the full power of the board, but then limit that power by prohibiting a committee from acting on fundamental corporate changes that require shareholder approval, such as mergers, sales of all assets, and other forms of reorganization that would be involved in a parent-subsidiary merger. If the board of directors ultimately must take action to approve such transactions, how does the use of a special committee solve the problems that arose in Weinberger?

The Delaware Supreme Court answered this question in Krasner v. Moffett, 826 A.2d 277 (2003). Two related companies in the Freeport-McMoran group were proposing to merge, and each board appointed a special committee to negotiate the merger. This suit was brought by shareholders of Freeport-McMoran Sulphur, Inc. ("FSC"), who claimed that the exchange ratio was unfair, and that review was subject to the entire fairness standard of Weinberger because of the conflicts of interest of five of the seven directors. The Chancery Court dismissed the complaint, on the grounds that no challenge had been raised with respect to the two directors who served as the special committee. The Supreme Court reversed, stating:

> Because the plaintiffs have sufficiently alleged facts to suggest that the MEC transaction was "not approved by a majority consisting of disinterested directors," the plaintiffs are entitled at the pleading stage to the inferences that may lead to the conclusion that the business judgment rule would not apply to the FSC board's decision to approve the MEC merger and to recommend it to the

FSC stockholders. The defendants argue that by using the special committee process the directors have cleansed the conflicts of interest in the transaction and are entitled to the presumptions of the business judgment rule at the pleading stage.

We do not, however, reach that issue because the FSC directors, not the plaintiffs, bear the burden of proving that the MEC merger was approved by a committee of disinterested directors, acting independently, with real bargaining power to negotiate the terms of the merger. The defendants cannot satisfy this burden at the pleading stage of this action.

826 A.2d at 284–85.

NOTE ON ROSENBLATT V. GETTY

Rosenblatt v. Getty, 493 A.2d 929 (Del. 1985) involved a 1977 take-out transaction that successfully withstood a Weinberger type of review. Getty Oil owned, directly and indirectly, about 80% of the stock of Skelly Oil Company, and, under pressure from a minority shareholder in Skelly, proposed a merger to exchange Getty stock for Skelly stock. Realizing the high likelihood of a challenge to any such merger, the Getty board prepared to structure the transaction to withstand a later challenge. Thus, Getty determined to use the "Delaware Block" method in the valuation of both companies. As a preliminary matter, both boards agreed to use the same petroleum engineering firm, DeGolyer & McNaughton ("D & M") to evaluate their respective reserves. Each board selected a committee of independent directors to negotiate the merger. Getty entered the negotiations determined to comply with Delaware law, while the Skelly board entered the negotiations determined to get the best price it could for its shareholders. Because Skelly's reserves were less than Getty's, Skelly's goal was to de-emphasize the value of reserves and emphasize the value of current earnings, because Skelly's recent profits were at record levels. With respect to valuing assets other than reserves, Getty had applied a conservative and consistent technique to valuation, while Skelly chose the method that produce the highest value for each asset, without regard to consistency. This led to disputes and hard feelings between the parties. While they both agreed with D & M's reserve estimates, they disagreed about how to value the reserves, and ultimately agreed to let D & M value their respective reserves on a binding basis.

Even this agreement did not resolve their disputes about the respective values of the companies. Wide differences remained in their estimates of earnings values, asset values, and even market values, and the weights each side attached to these items varied. Impasse was reached at one point, until Getty relented and offered a higher exchange ratio for the Skelly stock.

In response to a Weinberger challenge to the fairness of the process, the Delaware Supreme Court noted that two Skelly directors resigned because of their involvement in representing Getty in the transaction, noted the vigor with which the Skelly representatives negotiated, and then dealt with an accusation that Getty denied Skelly critical information about a projection of declining earnings at Getty. While there was a dispute about whether these projections were in fact revealed to the Skelly representatives, the court distinguished this case from Weinberger in the following terms:

"Second, the Arledge-Chitiea report, used secretly by and exclusively for Signal, was prepared by two Signal directors, who were also UOP directors, using UOP information obtained solely in their capacities as UOP directors. Here, the decreased earnings projection was prepared by a member of Getty's management for Getty's use as part of its annual reporting function. Moreover, there is not the slightest indication that its disclosure could have materially affected the exchange ratio negotiations. Third, the merger in Weinberger was expressly conditioned on approval of a majority of UOP's minority shareholders; here, there was no such condition.

"While it has been suggested that Weinberger stands for the proposition that a majority shareholder must under all circumstances disclose its top bid to the minority, that clearly is a misconception of what we said there.[8] The sole basis for our conclusions in Weinberger regarding the non-disclosure of the Arledge-Chitiea report was because Signal appointed directors on UOP's board, who thus stood on both sides of the transaction, violated their undiminished duty of loyalty to UOP. It had nothing to do with Signal's duty, as the majority stockholder, to the other shareholders of UOP.[9]"

Kahn v. Lynch Communication Systems, Inc.

638 A.2d 1110 (Del.1994).

■ HOLLAND, JUSTICE:

This is an appeal by the plaintiff-appellant, Alan R. Kahn ("Kahn"), from a final judgment of the Court of Chancery which was entered after a trial. The action, instituted by Kahn in 1986, originally sought to enjoin the acquisition of the defendant-appellee, Lynch Communication Systems, Inc. ("Lynch"), by the defendant-appellee, Alcatel U.S.A. Corporation ("Alcatel"), pursuant to a tender offer and cash-out merger. * * *

* * * Kahn alleged that Alcatel was a controlling shareholder of Lynch and breached its fiduciary duties to Lynch and its shareholders. According to Kahn, Alcatel dictated the terms of the merger; made false, misleading, and inadequate disclosures; and paid an unfair price.

---

[8] See Herzel and Colling, Establishing Procedural Fairness in Squeeze-Out Mergers After Weinberger v. UOP, 39 Business Law. 1525, 1532 (1984); Herzel and Colling, Squeeze-Out Mergers in Delaware—The Delaware Supreme Court Decision in Weinberger v. UOP, 7 Corp. L. Rev. 195, 207 (1984).

[9] See Payson and Inskip, Weinberger v. UOP, Inc.: Its Practical Significance In The Planning and Defense of Cash-Out Mergers, 8 Del. J Corp. L. 83, 89 (1983).

The Court of Chancery concluded that Alcatel was, in fact, a controlling shareholder that owed fiduciary duties to Lynch and its shareholders. It also concluded that Alcatel had not breached those fiduciary duties. Accordingly, the Court of Chancery entered judgment in favor of the defendants.

Kahn has raised three contentions in this appeal. Kahn's first contention is that the Court of Chancery erred by finding that "the tender offer and merger were negotiated by an independent committee," and then placing the burden of persuasion on the plaintiff, Kahn. Kahn asserts the uncontradicted testimony in the record demonstrated that the committee could not and did not bargain at arm's length with Alcatel. * * *

This Court has concluded that the record supports the Court of Chancery's finding that Alcatel was a controlling shareholder. However, the record does not support the conclusion that the burden of persuasion shifted to Kahn. Therefore, the burden of proving the entire fairness of the merger transaction remained on Alcatel, the controlling shareholder. Accordingly, the judgment of the Court of Chancery is reversed. The matter is remanded for further proceedings in accordance with this opinion.

Facts

* * *

In 1981, Alcatel acquired 30.6 percent of Lynch's common stock pursuant to a stock purchase agreement. As part of that agreement, Lynch amended its certificate of incorporation to require an 80 percent affirmative vote of its shareholders for approval of any business combination. In addition, Alcatel obtained proportional representation on the Lynch board of directors and the right to purchase 40 percent of any equity securities offered by Lynch to third parties. The agreement also precluded Alcatel from holding more than 45 percent of Lynch's stock prior to October 1, 1986. By the time of the merger which is contested in this action, Alcatel owned 43.3 percent of Lynch's outstanding stock; designated five of the eleven members of Lynch's board of directors; two of three members of the executive committee; and two of four members of the compensation committee.

In the spring of 1986, Lynch determined that in order to remain competitive in the rapidly changing telecommunications field, it would need to obtain fiber optics technology to complement its existing digital electronic capabilities. Lynch's management identified a target company, Telco Systems, Inc. ("Telco"), which possessed both fiber optics and other valuable technological assets. The record reflects that Telco expressed interest in being acquired by Lynch. Because of the supermajority voting provision, which Alcatel had negotiated when it first purchased its shares, in order to proceed with the Telco combination Lynch needed Alcatel's consent. [Alcatel refused to consent to the acquisition, and instead proposed a merger of Lynch with Celwave, an indirect subsidiary of Alcatel's parent, CGE. After negotiations about the exchange ratio in which an independent committee of Lynch directors was advised by its own investment advisers, Thomson McKinnon Securities, Inc. and Kidder, Peabody & Co., Inc., the independent committee unanimously opposed the Celwave merger.]

* * *

Alcatel responded to the Independent Committee's action on November 4, 1986, by withdrawing the Celwave proposal. Alcatel made a simultaneous offer to acquire the entire equity interest in Lynch, constituting the approximately 57 percent of Lynch shares not owned by Alcatel. The offering price was $14 cash per share.

On November 7, 1986, the Lynch board of directors revised the mandate of the Independent Committee. It authorized Kertz, Wineman, and Beringer to negotiate the cash merger offer with Alcatel. At a meeting held that same day, the Independent Committee determined that the $14 per share offer was inadequate. The Independent Committee's own legal counsel, Skadden, Arps, Slate, Meagher & Flom ("Skadden Arps"), suggested that the Independent Committee should review alternatives to a cash-out merger with Alcatel, including a "white knight" third party acquiror, a repurchase of Alcatel's shares, or the adoption of a shareholder rights plan.

On November 12, 1986, Beringer, as chairman of the Independent Committee, contacted Michiel C. McCarty ("McCarty") of Dillon Read, Alcatel's representative in the negotiations, with a counteroffer at a price of $17 per share. McCarty responded on behalf of Alcatel with an offer of $15 per share. When Beringer informed McCarty of the Independent Committee's view that $15 was also insufficient, Alcatel raised its offer to $15.25 per share. The Independent Committee also rejected this offer. Alcatel then made its final offer of $15.50 per share.

At the November 24, 1986 meeting of the Independent Committee, Beringer advised its other two members that Alcatel was "ready to proceed with an unfriendly tender at a lower price" if the $15.50 per share price was not recommended by the Independent Committee and approved by the Lynch board of directors. Beringer also told the other members of the Independent Committee that the alternatives to a cash-out merger had been investigated but were impracticable.[3] After meeting with its financial and legal advisors, the Independent Committee voted unanimously to recommend that the Lynch board of directors approve Alcatel's $15.50 cash per share price for a merger with Alcatel. The Lynch

---

[3]   The minutes reflect that Beringer told the Committee the "white knight" alternative "appeared impractical with the 80% approval requirement"; the repurchase of Alcatel's shares would produce a "highly leveraged company with a lower book value" and was an alternative "not in the least encouraged by Alcatel"; and a shareholder rights plan was not viable because of the increased debt it would entail.

board met later that day. With Alcatel's nominees abstaining, it approved the merger.

Alcatel Dominated Lynch Controlling Shareholder Status

This Court has held that "a shareholder owes a fiduciary duty only if it owns a majority interest in or exercises control over the business affairs of the corporation." Ivanhoe Partners v. Newmont Mining Corp., Del. Supr., 535 A.2d 1334, 1344 (1987) (emphasis added). With regard to the exercise of control, this Court has stated:

> [A] shareholder who owns less than 50% of a corporation's outstanding stocks does not, without more, become a controlling shareholder of that corporation, with a concomitant fiduciary status. For a dominating relationship to exist in the absence of controlling stock ownership, a plaintiff must allege domination by a minority shareholder though actual control of corporation conduct.

Citron v. Fairchild Camera & Instrument Corp., Del. Supr., 569 A.2d 53, 70 (1989) (quotations and citation omitted).

Alcatel held a 43.3 percent minority share of stock in Lynch. Therefore, the threshold question to be answered by the Court of Chancery was whether, despite its minority ownership, Alcatel exercised control over Lynch's business affairs. Based upon the testimony and the minutes of the August 1, 1986 Lynch board meeting, the Court of Chancery concluded that Alcatel did exercise control over Lynch's business decisions.

* * * The record supports the Court of Chancery's factual finding that Alcatel dominated Lynch.

At the August 1 meeting, Alcatel opposed the renewal of compensation contracts for Lynch's top five managers. According to Dertinger, Christian Fayard ("Fayard"), an Alcatel director, told the board members, "you must listen to us. We are 43 percent owner. You have to do what we tell you." The minutes confirm Dertinger's testimony. They recite that Fayard declared, "you are pushing us very much to take control of the company. Our opinion is not taken into consideration."

Although Beringer and Kertz, two of the independent directors, favored renewal of the contracts, according to the minutes, the third independent director, Wineman, admonished the board as follows:

> Mr. Wineman pointed out that the vote on the contracts is a "watershed vote" and the motion, due to Alcatel's "strong feelings," might not carry if taken now. Mr. Wineman clarified that "you [management] might win the battle and lose the war." With Alcatel's opinion so clear, Mr. Wineman questioned "if management wants the contracts renewed under these circumstances." He recommended that management "think twice." Mr. Wineman declared: "I want to keep the

management. I can't think of a better management." Mr. Kertz agreed, again advising consideration of the "critical" period the company is entering.

The minutes reflect that the management directors left the room after this statement. The remaining board members then voted not to renew the contracts.

At the same meeting, Alcatel vetoed Lynch's acquisition of the target company, which, according to the minutes, Beringer considered "an immediate fit" for Lynch. Dertinger agreed with Beringer, stating that the "target company is extremely important as they have the products that Lynch needs now." Nonetheless, Alcatel prevailed. The minutes reflect that Fayard advised the board: "Alcatel, with its 44% equity position, would not approve such an acquisition as . . . it does not wish to be diluted from being the main shareholder in Lynch."

The record supports the Court of Chancery's underlying factual finding that "the non-Alcatel [independent] directors deferred to Alcatel because of its position as a significant stockholder and not because they decided in the exercise of their own business judgment that Alcatel's position was correct." The record also supports the subsequent factual finding that, notwithstanding its 43.3 percent minority shareholder interest, Alcatel did exercise actual control over Lynch by dominating its corporate affairs. The Court of Chancery's legal conclusion that Alcatel owed the fiduciary duties of a controlling shareholder to the other Lynch shareholders followed syllogistically as a logical result of its cogent analysis of the record.

Entire Fairness Requirement Dominating Interested Shareholder

A controlling or dominating shareholder standing on both sides of a transaction, as in a parent-subsidiary context, bears the burden of proving its entire fairness. Weinberger v. UOP, Inc., Del. Supr., 457 A.2d 701, 710 (1983) * * *

* * * The policy rationale for the exclusive application of the entire fairness standard to interested merger transactions has been stated as follows:

> Parent subsidiary mergers, unlike stock options, are proposed by a party that controls, and will continue to control, the corporation, whether or not the minority stockholders vote to approve or reject the transaction. The controlling stockholder relationship has the potential to influence, however subtly, the vote of [ratifying] minority stockholders in a manner that is not likely to occur in a transaction with a noncontrolling party.

> Even where no coercion is intended, shareholders voting on a parent subsidiary merger might perceive that their disapproval could risk retaliation of some kind by the

controlling stockholder. For example, the controlling stockholder might decide to stop dividend payments or to effect a subsequent cash out merger at a less favorable price, for which the remedy would be time consuming and costly litigation. At the very least, the potential for that perception, and its possible impact upon a shareholder vote, could never be fully eliminated. Consequently, in a merger between the corporation and its controlling stockholder—even one negotiated by disinterested, independent directors—no court could be certain whether the transaction terms fully approximate what truly independent parties would have achieved in an arm's length negotiation. Given that uncertainty, a court might well conclude that even minority shareholders who have ratified a . . . merger need procedural protections beyond those afforded by full disclosure of all material facts. One way to provide such protections would be to adhere to the more stringent entire fairness standard of judicial review.

Citron v. E.I. Du Pont de Nemours & Co., 584 A.2d 490 at 502.

Once again, this Court holds that the exclusive standard of judicial review in examining the propriety of an interested cash-out merger transaction by a controlling or dominating shareholder is entire fairness. Weinberger v. UOP, Inc., 457 A.2d 701 at 710–11. The initial burden of establishing entire fairness rests upon the party who stands on both sides of the transaction. *Id.* However, an approval of the transaction by an independent committee of directors or an informed majority of minority shareholders shifts the burden of proof on the issue of fairness from the controlling or dominating shareholder to the challenging shareholder-plaintiff. See Rosenblatt v. Getty Oil Co., 493 A.2d 929 at 937–38. Nevertheless, even when an interested cash-out merger transaction receives the informed approval of a majority of minority stockholders or an independent committee of disinterested directors, an entire fairness analysis is the only proper standard of judicial review. See *id.*

Independent Committees Interested Merger Transactions

It is a now well-established principle of Delaware corporate law that in an interested merger, the controlling or dominating shareholder proponent of the transaction bears the burden of proving its entire fairness. Weinberger v. UOP, Inc., Del. Supr., 457 A.2d 701, 710–11 (1983). It is equally well-established in such contexts that any shifting of the burden of proof on the issue of entire fairness must be predicated upon this Court's decisions in Rosenblatt v. Getty Oil Co., Del. Supr., 493 A.2d 929 (1985) and Weinberger v. UOP, Inc., Del. Supr., 457 A.2d 701 (1983). In Weinberger, this Court noted that "particularly in a parent-subsidiary context, a showing that the action taken was as though each of the contending parties had in fact exerted its bargaining power against the other at arm's length is strong evidence that the transaction meets the test of fairness." 457 A.2d 701 at 709–10 n. 7 (emphasis added). Accord Rosenblatt v. Getty Oil Co., 493 A.2d 929 at 937–38 & n. 7. In Rosenblatt, this Court pointed out that "[an] independent bargaining structure, while not conclusive, is strong evidence of the fairness" of a merger transaction. Rosenblatt v. Getty Oil Co., 493 A.2d 929 at 938 n. 7.

The same policy rationale which requires judicial review of interested cash-out mergers exclusively for entire fairness also mandates careful judicial scrutiny of a special committee's real bargaining power before shifting the burden of proof on the issue of entire fairness. A recent decision from the Court of Chancery articulated a two-part test for determining whether burden shifting is appropriate in an interested merger transaction. Rabkin v. Olin Corp., Del. Ch., C.A. No. 7547, 1990, aff'd, Del. Supr., 586 A.2d 1202 (1990). In Olin, the Court of Chancery stated:

> The mere existence of an independent special committee . . . does not itself shift the burden. At least two factors are required. First, the majority shareholder must not dictate the terms of the merger. Rosenblatt v. Getty Oil Co., Del. Ch., 493 A.2d 929, 937 (1985). Second, the special committee must have real bargaining power that it can exercise with the majority shareholder on an arms length basis.

16 Del. J. Corp. L. 851 at 861–62. This Court expressed its agreement with that statement by affirming the Court of Chancery decision in Olin on appeal.

Lynch's Independent Committee

In the case sub judice, the Court of Chancery observed that although "Alcatel did exercise control over Lynch with respect to the decisions made at the August 1, 1986 board meeting, it does not necessarily follow that Alcatel also controlled the terms of the merger and its approval." This observation is theoretically accurate, as this opinion has already stated. Weinberger v. UOP, Inc., 457 A.2d 701 at 709–10 n. 7. However, the performance of the Independent Committee merits careful judicial scrutiny to determine whether Alcatel's demonstrated pattern of domination was effectively neutralized so that "each of the contending parties had in fact exerted its bargaining power against the other at arm's length." Id. The fact that the same independent directors had submitted to Alcatel's demands on August 1, 1986 was part of the basis for the Court of Chancery's finding of Alcatel's domination of Lynch. Therefore, the Independent Committee's ability to bargain at arm's length with Alcatel was suspect from the outset.

The Independent Committee's original assignment was to examine the merger with Celwave which had been proposed by Alcatel. The record reflects that the Independent Committee effectively discharged that assignment and, in fact, recommended that the Lynch board reject the merger on Alcatel's terms. Alcatel's response to the Independent Committee's adverse recommendation was not the pursuit of further negotiations regarding its Celwave proposal, but rather its response was an offer to buy Lynch. That offer was consistent with Alcatel's August 1, 1986 expressions of an intention to dominate Lynch, since an acquisition would effectively eliminate once and for all Lynch's remaining vestiges of independence.

The Independent Committee's second assignment was to consider Alcatel's proposal to purchase Lynch. The Independent Committee proceeded on that task with full knowledge of Alcatel's demonstrated pattern of domination. The Independent Committee was also obviously aware of Alcatel's refusal to negotiate with it on the Celwave matter.

Burden of Proof Shifted Court of Chancery's Finding

The Court of Chancery began its factual analysis by noting that Kahn had "attempted to shatter" the image of the Independent Committee's actions as having "appropriately simulated" an arm's length, third-party transaction. The Court of Chancery found that "to some extent, [Kahn's attempt] was successful." The Court of Chancery gave credence to the testimony of Kertz, one of the members of the Independent Committee, to the effect that he did not believe that $15.50 was a fair price but that he voted in favor of the merger because he felt there was no alternative.

The Court of Chancery also found that Kertz understood Alcatel's position to be that it was ready to proceed with an unfriendly tender offer at a lower price if Lynch did not accept the $15.50 offer, and that Kertz perceived this to be a threat by Alcatel. The Court of Chancery concluded that Kertz ultimately decided that, "although $15.50 was not fair, a tender offer and merger at that price would be better for Lynch's stockholders than an unfriendly tender offer at a significantly lower price." The Court of Chancery determined that "Kertz failed either to satisfy himself that the offered price was fair or oppose the merger."

In addition to Kertz, the other members of the Independent Committee were Beringer, its chairman, and Wineman. Wineman did not testify at trial. Beringer was called by Alcatel to testify at trial. Beringer testified that at the time of the Committee's vote to recommend the $15.50 offer to the Lynch board, he thought "that under the circumstances, a price of $15.50 was fair and should be accepted" (emphasis added).

Kahn contends that these "circumstances" included those referenced in the minutes for the November 24, 1986 Independent Committee meeting: "Mr. Beringer added that Alcatel is 'ready to proceed with an unfriendly tender at a lower price' if the $15.50 per share price is not recommended to, and approved by, the Company's Board of Directors." In his testimony at trial, Beringer verified, albeit reluctantly, the accuracy of the foregoing statement in the minutes: "[Alcatel] let us know that they were giving serious consideration to making an unfriendly tender" (emphasis added).

* * *

The Power to Say No, The Parties' Contentions, Arm's Length Bargaining

The Court of Chancery properly noted that limitations on the alternatives to Alcatel's offer did not mean that the Independent Committee should have agreed to a price that was unfair:

> The power to say no is a significant power. It is the duty of directors serving on [an independent] committee to approve only a transaction that is in the best interests of the public shareholders, to say no to any transaction that is not fair to those shareholders and is not the best transaction available. It is not sufficient for such directors to achieve the best price that a fiduciary will pay if that price is not a fair price.

(Quoting In re First Boston, Inc. Shareholders Litig., Del. Ch., C.A. 10338 (Consolidated), Allen, C., 1990 WL 78836, slip op. at 15–16 (June 7, 1990)).

* * *

Alcatel's Entire Fairness Burden Did Not Shift to Kahn

A condition precedent to finding that the burden of proving entire fairness has shifted in an interested merger transaction is a careful judicial analysis of the factual circumstances of each case. Particular consideration must be given to evidence of whether the special committee was truly independent, fully informed, and had the freedom to negotiate at arm's length. Weinberger v. UOP, Inc., Del. Supr., 457 A.2d 701, 709–10 n. 7 (1983). See also American Gen. Corp. v. Texas Air Corp., Del. Ch., C.A. Nos. 8390, 8406, 8650 & 8805, Hartnett, V.C., 1987 WL 6337, slip op. at 11 (Feb. 5, 1987), reprinted in 13 Del. J. Corp. L. 173, 181 (1988). "Although perfection is not possible," unless the controlling or dominating shareholder can demonstrate that it has not only formed an independent committee but also replicated a process "as though each of the contending parties had in fact exerted its bargaining power at arm's length," the burden of proving entire fairness will not shift. Weinberger v. UOP, Inc., 457 A.2d 701 at 709–10 n. 7. See also Rosenblatt v. Getty Oil Co., Del. Supr., 493 A.2d 929, 937–38 (1985).

* * *

The Court of Chancery's determination that the Independent Committee "appropriately simulated a third-party transaction, where negotiations are conducted at arm's-length and there is no compulsion to reach an agreement," is not supported by the record. Under the circumstances present in the case sub judice, the Court of Chancery erred in shifting the burden of proof with regard to entire fairness to the contesting Lynch shareholder-plaintiff, Kahn. The record reflects that the ability of the Committee effectively to negotiate at arm's length was compromised by Alcatel's threats to proceed with a hostile tender offer if the $15.50 price was not approved by the Committee and the Lynch board. The fact that the Independent Committee rejected three initial offers, which were well below the Independent Committee's estimated valuation for Lynch and were not combined with an explicit threat that Alcatel was "ready to proceed" with a hostile bid, cannot alter the conclusion that any semblance of arm's length bargaining ended when the Independent Committee surrendered to the ultimatum that accompanied Alcatel's final offer. See Rabkin v. Philip A. Hunt Chem. Corp., Del. Supr., 498 A.2d 1099, 1106 (1985).

Conclusion

Accordingly, the judgment of the Court of Chancery is reversed. This matter is remanded for further proceedings consistent herewith, including a redetermination of the entire fairness of the cash-out merger to Kahn and the other Lynch minority shareholders with the burden of proof remaining on Alcatel, the dominant and interested shareholder.

QUESTIONS

1. Does the Lynch opinion explain why fairness of price is examined as well as fairness of procedure? What does the court mean when it says that "the exclusive standard of judicial review in examining the propriety of an interested cash-out merger by a controlling or dominating shareholder is entire fairness."?

2. If the independent committee exercised its business judgment in good faith that $15.50 was better than the lower tender offer price Alcatel threatened, why didn't this satisfy the standard of section 144 of the Delaware Act?

3. Does the court offer a reason for ignoring the safe harbors from judicial challenge created by section 144?

4. The court stated that the fact that Lynch had no alternatives to a merger at $15.50 didn't mean the special committee should approve the transaction, even when Alcatel threatened a tender offer at a lower price. How would rejecting the merger offer have helped Lynch shareholders? Is this a business judgment?

5. If Alcatel's veto power over other transactions is the reason why the court concludes the special committee didn't act independently, how can a controlling shareholder ever show such independence?

6. Is this dispute over anything other than price? If not, why aren't the plaintiffs left with their right to seek appraisal? Compare the Rabkin court's interpretation of Weinberger with the language in Weinberger about the exclusivity of the appraisal remedy.

7. Did the Skelly independent committee have any options other than merging with Getty and Mission in Rosenblatt v. Getty, *supra*? Did Skelly get its asking price? If not, how do you explain the different results? If you represented a plaintiff minority shareholder in a situation similar to that in Rosenblatt v. Getty after the decision in Kahn v. Lynch, could you examine the independent directors in a manner designed to bring the case within the rule of Kahn v. Lynch? What would you want to demonstrate?

8. With an 80% shareholder vote required for a merger with Alcatel, is there reason to argue that Alcatel lacked coercive power over the shareholders? If this is true, what is the rationale behind a fairness inquiry?

9. How does the analysis of control here compare with that in Ivanhoe Partners v. Newmont Mining Corporation in Chapter Six, part 2.G? Is there a reason for differential treatment?

Kahn v. M & F Worldwide Corp.

88 A.3d 635 (Del. 2014).

■ HOLLAND, JUSTICE:

This is an appeal from a final judgment entered by the Court of Chancery in a proceeding that arises from a 2011 acquisition by MacAndrews & Forbes Holdings, Inc. ("M & F" or "MacAndrews & Forbes")—a 43% stockholder in M & F Worldwide Corp. ("MFW")—of the remaining common stock of MFW (the "Merger"). From the outset, M & F's proposal to take MFW private was made contingent upon two stockholder-protective procedural conditions. First, M & F required the Merger to be negotiated and approved by a special committee of independent MFW directors (the "Special Committee"). Second, M & F required that the Merger be approved by a majority of stockholders unaffiliated with M & F. The Merger closed in December 2011, after it was approved by a vote of 65.4% of MFW's minority stockholders.

The Appellants initially sought to enjoin the transaction. They withdrew their request for injunctive relief after taking expedited discovery, including several depositions. The Appellants then sought post-closing relief against M & F, Ronald O. Perelman, and MFW's directors (including the members of the Special Committee) for breach of fiduciary duty. Again, the Appellants were provided with extensive discovery. The Defendants then moved for summary judgment, which the Court of Chancery granted.

Court of Chancery Decision

The Court of Chancery found that the case presented a "novel question of law," specifically, "what standard of review should apply to a going private merger conditioned upfront by the controlling stockholder on approval by both a properly empowered, independent committee and an informed, uncoerced majority-of-the-minority vote." The Court of Chancery held that business judgment review, rather than entire fairness, should be applied to a very limited category of controller mergers. That category consisted of mergers where the controller voluntarily relinquishes its control—such that the negotiation and approval process replicate those that characterize a third-party merger.

The Court of Chancery held that, rather than entire fairness, the business judgment standard of review should apply "if, but only if: (i) the controller conditions the transaction on the approval of both a Special Committee and a majority of the minority stockholders; (ii) the Special Committee is independent; (iii) the Special Committee is empowered to freely select its own advisors and to say no definitively; (iv) the Special Committee acts with care; (v) the minority vote is informed; and (vi) there is no coercion of the minority."

The Court of Chancery found that those prerequisites were satisfied and that the Appellants had failed to raise any genuine issue of material fact indicating the contrary. The court then reviewed the Merger under the business judgment standard and granted summary judgment for the Defendants.

Appellants' Arguments

The Appellants raise two main arguments on this appeal. First, they contend that the Court of Chancery erred in concluding that no material disputed facts existed regarding the conditions precedent to business judgment review. The Appellants submit that the record contains evidence showing that the Special Committee was not disinterested and independent, was not fully empowered, and was not effective. The Appellants also contend, as a legal matter, that the majority-of-the-minority provision did not afford MFW stockholders protection sufficient to displace entire fairness review.

Second, the Appellants submit that the Court of Chancery erred, as a matter of law, in holding that the business judgment standard applies to controller freeze-out mergers where the controller's proposal is conditioned on both Special Committee approval and a favorable majority-of-the-minority vote. Even if both procedural protections are adopted, the Appellants argue, entire fairness should be retained as the applicable standard of review.

Defendants' Arguments

The Defendants argue that the judicial standard of review should be the business judgment rule, because the Merger was conditioned *ab initio* on two procedural protections that together operated to replicate an arm's-length merger: the employment of an active, unconflicted negotiating agent free to turn down the transaction; and a requirement that any transaction negotiated by that agent be approved by a majority of the disinterested stockholders. The Defendants argue that using and establishing pretrial that both protective conditions were extant renders a going private transaction analogous to that of a third-party arm's-length merger under Section 251 of the Delaware General Corporation Law. That is, the Defendants submit that a Special Committee approval in a going private transaction is a proxy for board approval in a third-party transaction, and that the approval of the unaffiliated, noncontrolling stockholders replicates the approval of all the (potentially) adversely affected stockholders.

FACTS

MFW and M & F

MFW is a holding company incorporated in Delaware. Before the Merger that is the subject of this dispute, MFW was 43.4% owned by MacAndrews & Forbes, which in turn is entirely owned by Ronald O. Perelman. MFW had four business segments. Three were owned through a holding company, Harland Clarke Holding Corporation ("HCHC"). They were the Harland Clarke Corporation ("Harland"), which printed bank checks; Harland Clarke Financial Solutions, which provided technology products and services to financial services companies; and Scantron Corporation, which manufactured scanning equipment used for educational and other purposes. The fourth segment, which was not part of HCHC, was Mafco Worldwide Corporation, a manufacturer of licorice flavorings.

The MFW board had thirteen members. They were: Ronald Perelman, Barry Schwartz, William Bevins, Bruce Slovin, Charles Dawson, Stephen Taub, John Keane, Theo Folz, Philip Beekman, Martha Byorum, Viet Dinh, Paul Meister, and Carl Webb. Perelman, Schwartz, and Bevins were officers of both MFW and MacAndrews & Forbes. Perelman was the Chairman of MFW and the Chairman and CEO of MacAndrews & Forbes; Schwartz was the President and CEO of MFW and the Vice Chairman and Chief Administrative Officer of MacAndrews & Forbes; and Bevins was a Vice President at MacAndrews & Forbes.

The Taking MFW Private Proposal

In May 2011, Perelman began to explore the possibility of taking MFW private. At that time, MFW's stock price traded in the $20 to $24 per share range. MacAndrews & Forbes engaged a bank, Moelis & Company, to advise it. After preparing valuations based on projections that had been supplied to lenders by MFW in April and May 2011, Moelis valued MFW at between $10 and $32 a share.

On June 10, 2011, MFW's shares closed on the New York Stock Exchange at $16.96. The next business day, June 13, 2011, Schwartz sent a letter proposal ("Proposal") to the MFW board to buy the remaining MFW shares for $24 in cash. The Proposal stated, in relevant part:

The proposed transaction would be subject to the approval of the Board of Directors of the Company [i.e., MFW] and the negotiation and execution of mutually acceptable definitive transaction documents. It is our expectation that the Board of Directors will appoint a special committee of independent directors to consider our proposal and make a recommendation to the Board of Directors. *We will not move forward with the transaction unless it is approved by such a special committee. In addition, the transaction will be subject to a non-waivable condition requiring the approval of a majority of the shares of the Company not owned by M & F or its affiliates.* . . .

. . . In considering this proposal, you should know that in our capacity as a stockholder of the Company we are interested only in acquiring the shares of the Company not already owned by us and that in such capacity we have no interest in selling any of the shares owned by us in the Company nor would we expect, in our capacity as a stockholder, to vote in favor of any alternative sale, merger or similar transaction involving the Company. If the special committee does not recommend or the public stockholders of the Company do not approve the proposed transaction, such determination would not adversely affect our future relationship with the Company and we would intend to remain as a long-term stockholder.

In connection with this proposal, we have engaged Moelis & Company as our financial advisor and Skadden, Arps, Slate, Meagher & Flom LLP as our legal advisor, and we encourage the special committee to retain its own legal and financial advisors to assist it in its review.

MacAndrews & Forbes filed this letter with the U.S. Securities and Exchange Commission ("SEC") and issued a press release disclosing substantially the same information.

The Special Committee Is Formed

The MFW board met the following day to consider the Proposal. At the meeting, Schwartz presented the offer on behalf of MacAndrews & Forbes. Subsequently, Schwartz and Bevins, as the two directors present who were also directors of MacAndrews & Forbes, recused themselves from the meeting, as did Dawson, the CEO of HCHC, who had previously expressed support for the proposed offer.

The independent directors then invited counsel from Willkie Farr & Gallagher—a law firm that had recently represented a Special Committee of MFW's independent directors in a potential acquisition of a subsidiary of MacAndrews & Forbes—to join the meeting. The independent directors decided to form the Special Committee, and resolved further that:

[T]he Special Committee is empowered to: (i) make such investigation of the Proposal as the Special Committee deems appropriate; (ii) evaluate the terms of the Proposal; (iii) negotiate with Holdings [i.e., MacAndrews & Forbes] and its representatives any element of the Proposal; (iv) negotiate the terms of any definitive agreement with respect to the Proposal (it being understood that the execution thereof shall be subject to the approval of the Board); (v) report to the Board its recommendations and conclusions with respect to the Proposal, including a determination and *recommendation as to whether the Proposal is fair and in the best interests of the stockholders of the Company other than Holdings* and its affiliates and should be approved by the Board; and (vi) determine to elect not to pursue the Proposal. . . .

. . . [T]he Board shall not approve the Proposal without a prior favorable recommendation of the Special Committee. . . .

. . . [T]he Special Committee [is] empowered to retain and employ legal counsel, a financial advisor, and such other agents as the Special Committee shall deem necessary or desirable in connection with these matters. . . .

The Special Committee consisted of Byorum, Dinh, Meister (the chair), Slovin, and Webb. The following day, Slovin recused himself because, although the MFW board had determined that he qualified as an independent director under the rules of the New York Stock Exchange, he had "some current relationships that could raise questions about his independence for purposes of serving on the Special Committee."

ANALYSIS

What Should Be the Review Standard?

Where a transaction involving self-dealing by a controlling stockholder is challenged, the applicable standard of judicial review is "entire fairness," with the defendants having the burden of persuasion. In other words, the defendants bear the ultimate burden of proving that the transaction with the controlling stockholder was entirely fair to the minority stockholders. In Kahn v. Lynch Communication Systems, Inc., however, this Court held that in "entire fairness" cases, the defendants may shift the burden of persuasion to the plaintiff if either (1) they show that the transaction was approved by a well-functioning committee of independent directors; or (2) they show that the transaction was approved by an informed vote of a majority of the minority stockholders.

This appeal presents a question of first impression: what should be the standard of review for a merger between a controlling stockholder and its subsidiary, where the merger is conditioned *ab initio* upon the approval of both an independent, adequately-empowered Special

Committee that fulfills its duty of care, and the uncoerced, informed vote of a majority of the minority stockholders. The question has never been put directly to this Court.

Almost two decades ago, in Kahn v. Lynch, we held that the approval by *either* a Special Committee or the majority of the noncontrolling stockholders of a merger with a buying controlling stockholder would shift the burden of proof under the entire fairness standard from the defendant to the plaintiff. Lynch did not involve a merger conditioned by the controlling stockholder on both procedural protections. The Appellants submit, nonetheless, that statements in Lynch and its progeny could be (and were) read to suggest that even if both procedural protections were used, the standard of review would remain entire fairness. However, in Lynch and the other cases that Appellants cited, Southern Peru and Kahn v. Tremont, the controller did not give up its voting power by agreeing to a non-waivable majority-of-the-minority condition. That is the vital distinction between those cases and this one. The question is what the legal consequence of that distinction should be in these circumstances.

The Court of Chancery held that the consequence should be that the business judgment standard of review will govern going private mergers with a controlling stockholder that are conditioned *ab initio* upon (1) the approval of an independent and fully-empowered Special Committee that fulfills its duty of care and (2) the uncoerced, informed vote of the majority of the minority stockholders.

The Court of Chancery rested its holding upon the premise that the common law equitable rule that best protects minority investors is one that encourages controlling stockholders to accord the minority both procedural protections. A transactional structure subject to both conditions differs fundamentally from a merger having only one of those protections, in that:

> By giving controlling stockholders the opportunity to have a going private transaction reviewed under the business judgment rule, a strong incentive is created to give minority stockholders much broader access to the transactional structure that is most likely to effectively protect their interests. . . . That structure, it is important to note, is critically different than a structure that uses only one of the procedural protections. The "or" structure does not replicate the protections of a third-party merger under the DGCL approval process, because it only requires that one, and not both, of the statutory requirements of director and stockholder approval be accomplished by impartial decisionmakers. The "both" structure, by contrast, replicates the arm's-length merger steps of the DGCL by "requir[ing] two independent approvals, which it is fair to say serve independent integrity-enforcing functions."

Before the Court of Chancery, the Appellants acknowledged that "this transactional structure is the optimal one for minority shareholders." Before us, however, they argue that neither procedural protection is adequate to protect minority stockholders, because "possible ineptitude and timidity of directors" may undermine the special committee protection, and because majority-of-the-minority votes may be unduly influenced by arbitrageurs that have an institutional bias to approve virtually any transaction that offers a market premium, however insubstantial it may be. Therefore, the Appellants claim, these protections, even when combined, are not sufficient to justify "abandon[ing]" the entire fairness standard of review.

With regard to the Special Committee procedural protection, the Appellants' assertions regarding the MFW directors' inability to discharge their duties are not supported either by the record or by well-established principles of Delaware law. As the Court of Chancery correctly observed:

> Although it is possible that there are independent directors who have little regard for their duties or for being perceived by their company's stockholders (and the larger network of institutional investors) as being effective at protecting public stockholders, the court thinks they are likely to be exceptional, and certainly our Supreme Court's jurisprudence does not embrace such a skeptical view.

Regarding the majority-of-the-minority vote procedural protection, as the Court of Chancery noted, "plaintiffs themselves do not argue that minority stockholders will vote against a going private transaction because of fear of retribution." Instead, as the Court of Chancery summarized, the Appellants' argued as follows:

> [Plaintiffs] just believe that most investors like a premium and will tend to vote for a deal that delivers one and that many long-term investors will sell out when they can obtain most of the premium without waiting for the ultimate vote. But that argument is not one that suggests that the voting decision is not voluntary, it is simply an editorial about the motives of investors and does not contradict the premise that a majority-of-the-minority condition gives minority investors a free and voluntary opportunity to decide what is fair for themselves.

Business Judgment Review Standard Adopted

We hold that business judgment is the standard of review that should govern mergers between a controlling stockholder and its corporate subsidiary, where the merger is conditioned *ab initio* upon both the approval of an independent, adequately-empowered Special Committee that fulfills its duty of care; and the uncoerced, informed vote of a majority of the minority stockholders. We so conclude for several reasons.

First, entire fairness is the highest standard of review in corporate law. It is applied in the controller merger context as a substitute for the dual statutory protections of disinterested board and stockholder approval, because both protections are potentially undermined by the influence of the controller. However, as this case establishes, that undermining influence does not exist in every controlled merger setting, regardless of the circumstances. The simultaneous deployment of the procedural protections employed here create a countervailing, offsetting influence of equal—if not greater—force. That is, where the controller irrevocably and publicly disables itself from using its control to dictate the outcome of the negotiations and the shareholder vote, the controlled merger then acquires the shareholder-protective characteristics of third-party, arm's-length mergers, which are reviewed under the business judgment standard.

Second, the dual procedural protection merger structure optimally protects the minority stockholders in controller buyouts. As the Court of Chancery explained:

> [W]hen these two protections are established up-front, a potent tool to extract good value for the minority is established. From inception, the controlling stockholder knows that it cannot bypass the special committee's ability to say no. And, the controlling stockholder knows it cannot dangle a majority-of-the-minority vote before the special committee late in the process as a deal-closer rather than having to make a price move.

Third, and as the Court of Chancery reasoned, applying the business judgment standard to the dual protection merger structure:

> . . . is consistent with the central tradition of Delaware law, which defers to the informed decisions of impartial directors, especially when those decisions have been approved by the disinterested stockholders on full information and without coercion. Not only that, the adoption of this rule will be of benefit to minority stockholders because it will provide a strong incentive for controlling stockholders to accord minority investors the transactional structure that respected scholars believe will provide them the best protection, a structure where stockholders get the benefits of independent, empowered negotiating agents *to bargain for the best price and say no* if the agents believe the deal is not advisable for any proper reason, plus the critical ability to determine for themselves whether to accept any deal that their negotiating agents recommend to them. A transactional structure with both these protections is fundamentally different from one with only one protection.

Fourth, the underlying purposes of the dual protection merger structure utilized here and the entire fairness standard of review both converge and are fulfilled at the same critical point: *price*. Following Weinberger v. UOP, Inc., this Court has consistently held that, although entire fairness review comprises the dual components of fair dealing and fair price, in a non-fraudulent transaction "price may be the preponderant consideration outweighing other features of the merger." The dual protection merger structure requires two price-related pretrial determinations: first, that a fair price was achieved by an empowered, independent committee that acted with care; and, second, that a fully-informed, uncoerced majority of the minority stockholders voted in favor of the price that was recommended by the independent committee.

The New Standard Summarized

To summarize our holding, in controller buyouts, the business judgment standard of review will be applied if and only if: (i) the controller conditions the procession of the transaction on the approval of both a Special Committee and a majority of the minority stockholders; (ii) the Special Committee is independent; (iii) the Special Committee is empowered to freely select its own advisors and to say no definitively; (iv) the Special Committee meets its duty of care in negotiating a fair price; (v) the vote of the minority is informed; and (vi) there is no coercion of the minority.

* * *

This approach is consistent with Weinberger, Lynch and their progeny. A controller that employs and/or establishes only one of these dual procedural protections would continue to receive burden-shifting within the entire fairness standard of review framework. Stated differently, unless both procedural protections for the minority stockholders are established prior to trial, the ultimate judicial scrutiny of controller buyouts will continue to be the entire fairness standard of review.

Having articulated the circumstances that will enable a controlled merger to be reviewed under the business judgment standard, we next address whether those circumstances have been established as a matter of undisputed fact and law in this case.

Dual Protection Inquiry

* * *

We begin by reviewing the record relating to the independence, mandate, and process of the Special Committee. In Kahn v. Tremont Corp., this Court held that "[t]o obtain the benefit of burden shifting, the controlling stockholder must do more than establish a perfunctory special committee of outside directors."

Rather, the special committee must "function in a manner which indicates that the controlling stockholder did not dictate the terms of the transaction and that the committee exercised real bargaining power 'at an arms-length.'" As we have previously noted, deciding whether an independent committee was effective in negotiating a price is a process so fact-intensive and inextricably intertwined with the merits of an entire fairness review (fair dealing and fair price) that a pretrial determination of burden shifting is often impossible. Here, however, the Defendants have successfully established a record of independent committee effectiveness and process that warranted a grant of summary judgment entitling them to a burden shift prior to trial.

We next analyze the efficacy of the majority-of-the-minority vote, and we conclude that it was fully informed and not coerced. That is, the Defendants also established a pretrial majority-of-the-minority vote record that constitutes an independent and alternative basis for shifting the burden of persuasion to the Plaintiffs.

The Special Committee Was Independent

The Appellants do not challenge the independence of the Special Committee's Chairman, Meister. They claim, however, that the three other Special Committee members—Webb, Dinh, and Byorum—were beholden to Perelman because of their prior business and/or social dealings with Perelman or Perelman-related entities.

The Appellants first challenge the independence of Webb. They urged that Webb and Perelman shared a "longstanding and lucrative business partnership" between 1983 and 2002 which included acquisitions of thrifts and financial institutions, and which led to a 2002 asset sale to Citibank in which Webb made "a significant amount of money." The Court of Chancery concluded, however, that the fact of Webb having engaged in business dealings with Perelman nine years earlier did not raise a triable fact issue regarding his ability to evaluate the Merger impartially.[21] We agree.

Second, the Appellants argued that there were triable issues of fact regarding Dinh's independence. The Appellants demonstrated that between 2009 and 2011, Dinh's law firm, Bancroft PLLC, advised M & F and Scientific Games (in which M & F owned a 37.6% stake), during which time the Bancroft firm earned $200,000 in fees. The record reflects that Bancroft's limited prior engagements, which were inactive by the time the Merger proposal was announced, were fully disclosed to the Special Committee soon after it was formed. The Court of Chancery found that the Appellants failed to proffer any evidence to show that compensation received by Dinh's law firm was material to Dinh, in the sense that it would have influenced his decisionmaking with respect to the M & F proposal. The only evidence of record, the Court of Chancery concluded, was that these fees were "de minimis" and that the Appellants

---

[21]   Beam ex rel. Martha Stewart Living Omnimedia, Inc. v. Stewart, 845 A.2d 1040, 1051 (Del. 2004) ("Allegations that [the controller] and the other directors . . . developed business relationships before joining the board . . . are insufficient, without more, to rebut the presumption of independence.").

had offered no contrary evidence that would create a genuine issue of material fact.

The Court of Chancery also found that the relationship between Dinh, a Georgetown University Law Center professor, and M & F's Barry Schwartz, who sits on the Georgetown Board of Visitors, did not create a triable issue of fact as to Dinh's independence. No record evidence suggested that Schwartz could exert influence on Dinh's position at Georgetown based on his recommendation regarding the Merger. Indeed, Dinh had earned tenure as a professor at Georgetown before he ever knew Schwartz.

* * *

Third, the Appellants urge that issues of material fact permeate Byorum's independence and, specifically, that Byorum "had a business relationship with Perelman from 1991 to 1996 through her executive position at Citibank." The Court of Chancery concluded, however, the Appellants presented no evidence of the nature of Byorum's interactions with Perelman while she was at Citibank. Nor was there evidence that after 1996 Byorum had an ongoing economic relationship with Perelman that was material to her in any way. Byorum testified that any interactions she had with Perelman while she was at Citibank resulted from her role as a senior executive, because Perelman was a client of the bank at the time. Byorum also testified that she had no business relationship with Perelman between 1996 and 2007, when she joined the MFW Board.

* * *

To evaluate the parties' competing positions on the issue of director independence, the Court of Chancery applied well-established Delaware legal principles. To show that a director is not independent, a plaintiff must demonstrate that the director is "beholden" to the controlling party "or so under [the controller's] influence that [the director's] discretion would be sterilized." Bare allegations that directors are friendly with, travel in the same social circles as, or have past business relationships with the proponent of a transaction or the person they are investigating are not enough to rebut the presumption of independence.

A plaintiff seeking to show that a director was not independent must satisfy a materiality standard. The court must conclude that the director in question had ties to the person whose proposal or actions he or she is evaluating that are sufficiently substantial that he or she could not objectively discharge his or her fiduciary duties. Consistent with that predicate materiality requirement, the existence of some financial ties between the interested party and the director, without more, is not disqualifying. The inquiry must be whether, applying a subjective standard, those ties were material, in the sense that the alleged ties could have affected the impartiality of the individual director.

The Appellants assert that the materiality of any economic relationships the Special Committee members may have had with Mr. Perelman "should not be decided on summary judgment." But Delaware courts have often decided director independence as a matter of law at the summary judgment stage. In this case, the Court of Chancery noted, that despite receiving extensive discovery, the Appellants did "nothing . . . to compare the actual circumstances of the [challenged directors] to the ties [they] contend affect their impartiality" and "fail[ed] to proffer any real evidence of their economic circumstances."

* * *

The record supports the Court of Chancery's holding that none of the Appellants' claims relating to Webb, Dinh or Byorum raised a triable issue of material fact concerning their individual independence or the Special Committee's collective independence.

The Special Committee Was Empowered

It is undisputed that the Special Committee was empowered to hire its own legal and financial advisors, and it retained Willkie Farr & Gallagher LLP as its legal advisor. After interviewing four potential financial advisors, the Special Committee engaged Evercore Partners ("Evercore"). The qualifications and independence of Evercore and Willkie Farr & Gallagher LLP are not contested.

Among the powers given the Special Committee in the board resolution was the authority to "report to the Board its recommendations and conclusions with respect to the [Merger], including a determination and recommendation as to whether the Proposal is fair and in the best interests of the stockholders. . . ." The Court of Chancery also found that it was "undisputed that the [S]pecial [C]ommittee was empowered not simply to 'evaluate' the offer, like some special committees with weak mandates, but to negotiate with [M & F] over the terms of its offer to buy out the noncontrolling stockholders. This negotiating power was accompanied by the clear authority to say no definitively to [M & F]" and to "make that decision stick." MacAndrews & Forbes promised that it would not proceed with any going private proposal that did not have the support of the Special Committee. Therefore, the Court of Chancery concluded, "the MFW committee did not have to fear that if it bargained too hard, MacAndrews & Forbes could bypass the committee and make a tender offer directly to the minority stockholders."

The Court of Chancery acknowledged that even though the Special Committee had the authority to negotiate and "say no," it did not have the authority, as a practical matter, to sell MFW to other buyers. MacAndrews & Forbes stated in its announcement that it was not interested in selling its 43% stake. Moreover, under Delaware law, MacAndrews & Forbes had no duty to sell its block, which was large enough, again as a practical matter, to preclude any other buyer from succeeding unless MacAndrews & Forbes decided to become a seller.

Absent such a decision, it was unlikely that any potentially interested party would incur the costs and risks of exploring a purchase of MFW.

Nevertheless, the Court of Chancery found, "this did not mean that the MFW Special Committee did not have the leeway to get advice from its financial advisor about the strategic options available to MFW, including the potential interest that other buyers might have *if MacAndrews & Forbes was willing to sell.*" The undisputed record shows that the Special Committee, with the help of its financial advisor, did consider whether there were other buyers who might be interested in purchasing MFW, and whether there were other strategic options, such as asset divestitures, that might generate more value for minority stockholders than a sale of their stock to MacAndrews & Forbes.

The Special Committee Exercised Due Care

The Special Committee insisted from the outset that MacAndrews (including any "dual" employees who worked for both MFW and MacAndrews) be screened off from the Special Committee's process, to ensure that the process replicated arm's-length negotiations with a third party. In order to carefully evaluate M & F's offer, the Special Committee held a total of eight meetings during the summer of 2011.

From the outset of their work, the Special Committee and Evercore had projections that had been prepared by MFW's business segments in April and May 2011. Early in the process, Evercore and the Special Committee asked MFW management to produce new projections that reflected management's most up-to-date, and presumably most accurate, thinking. Consistent with the Special Committee's determination to conduct its analysis free of any MacAndrews influence, MacAndrews— including "dual" MFW/MacAndrews executives who normally vetted MFW projections—were excluded from the process of preparing the updated financial projections. Mafco, the licorice business, advised Evercore that all of its projections would remain the same. Harland Clarke updated its projections. On July 22, 2011, Evercore received new projections from HCHC, which incorporated the updated projections from Harland Clarke. Evercore then constructed a valuation model based upon all of these updated projections.

The updated projections, which formed the basis for Evercore's valuation analyses, reflected MFW's deteriorating results, especially in Harland's check-printing business. Those projections forecast EBITDA for MFW of $491 million in 2015, as opposed to $535 million under the original projections.

On August 10, Evercore produced a range of valuations for MFW, based on the updated projections, of $15 to $45 per share. Evercore valued MFW using a variety of accepted methods, including a discounted cash flow ("DCF") model. Those valuations generated a range of fair value of $22 to $38 per share, and a premiums paid analysis resulted in a value range of $22 to $45. MacAndrews & Forbes's $24 offer fell within the range of values produced by each of Evercore's valuation techniques.

Although the $24 Proposal fell within the range of Evercore's fair values, the Special Committee directed Evercore to conduct additional analyses and explore strategic alternatives that might generate more value for MFW's stockholders than might a sale to MacAndrews. The Special Committee also investigated the possibility of other buyers, e.g., private equity buyers, that might be interested in purchasing MFW. In addition, the Special Committee considered whether other strategic options, such as asset divestitures, could achieve superior value for MFW's stockholders. Mr. Meister testified, "The Committee made it very clear to Evercore that we were interested in any and all possible avenues of increasing value to the stockholders, including meaningful expressions of interest for meaningful pieces of the business."

The Appellants insist that the Special Committee had "no right to solicit alternative bids, conduct any sort of market check, or even consider alternative transactions." But the Special Committee did just that, even though MacAndrews' stated unwillingness to sell its MFW stake meant that the Special Committee did not have the practical ability to market MFW to other buyers. The Court of Chancery properly concluded that despite the Special Committee's inability to solicit alternative bids, it could seek Evercore's advice about strategic alternatives, including values that might be available if MacAndrews was willing to sell.

Although the MFW Special Committee considered options besides the M & F Proposal, the Committee's analysis of those alternatives proved they were unlikely to achieve added value for MFW's stockholders. The Court of Chancery summarized the performance of the Special Committee as follows:

> [t]he special committee did consider, with the help of its financial advisor, whether there were other buyers who might be interested in purchasing MFW, and whether there were other strategic options, such as asset divestitures, that might generate more value for minority stockholders than a sale of their stock to MacAndrews & Forbes.

On August 18, 2011, the Special Committee rejected the $24 a share Proposal, and countered at $30 per share. The Special Committee characterized the $30 counteroffer as a negotiating position. The Special Committee recognized that $30 per share was a very aggressive counteroffer and, not surprisingly, was prepared to accept less.

On September 9, 2011, MacAndrews & Forbes rejected the $30 per share counteroffer. Its representative, Barry Schwartz, told the Special Committee Chair, Paul Meister, that the $24 per share Proposal was now far less favorable to MacAndrews & Forbes—but more attractive to the minority—than when it was first made, because of continued declines in

MFW's businesses. Nonetheless, MacAndrews & Forbes would stand behind its $24 offer. Meister responded that he would not recommend the $24 per share Proposal to the Special Committee. Later, after having discussions with Perelman, Schwartz conveyed MacAndrews's "best and final" offer of $25 a share.

At a Special Committee meeting the next day, Evercore opined that the $25 per share price was fair based on generally accepted valuation methodologies, including DCF and comparable companies analyses. At its eighth and final meeting on September 10, 2011, the Special Committee, although empowered to say "no," instead unanimously approved and agreed to recommend the Merger at a price of $25 per share.

Influencing the Special Committee's assessment and acceptance of M & F's $25 a share price were developments in both MFW's business and the broader United States economy during the summer of 2011. For example, during the negotiation process, the Special Committee learned of the underperformance of MFW's Global Scholar business unit. The Committee also considered macroeconomic events, including the downgrade of the United States' bond credit rating, and the ongoing turmoil in the financial markets, all of which created financing uncertainties.

In scrutinizing the Special Committee's execution of its broad mandate, the Court of Chancery determined there was no "evidence indicating that the independent members of the special committee did not meet their duty of care. . . ." To the contrary, the Court of Chancery found, the Special Committee "met frequently and was presented with a rich body of financial information relevant to whether and at what price a going private transaction was advisable." The Court of Chancery ruled that "the plaintiffs d[id] not make any attempt to show that the MFW Special Committee failed to meet its duty of care. . . ." Based on the undisputed record, the Court of Chancery held that, "there is no triable issue of fact regarding whether the [S]pecial [C]ommittee fulfilled its duty of care." In the context of a controlling stockholder merger, a pretrial determination that the price was negotiated by an empowered independent committee that acted with care would shift the burden of persuasion to the plaintiffs under the entire fairness standard of review.

Majority of Minority Stockholder Vote

We now consider the second procedural protection invoked by M & F—the majority-of-the-minority stockholder vote.[38] Consistent with the second condition imposed by M & F at the outset, the Merger was then

---

[38] The MFW board discussed the Special Committee's recommendation to accept the $25 a share offer. The three directors affiliated with MacAndrews & Forbes, Perelman, Schwartz, and Bevins, and the CEOs of HCHC and Mafco, Dawson and Taub, recused themselves from the discussions. The remaining eight directors voted unanimously to recommend the $25 a share offer to the stockholders

put before MFW's stockholders for a vote. On November 18, 2011, the stockholders were provided with a proxy statement, which contained the history of the Special Committee's work and recommended that they vote in favor of the transaction at a price of $25 per share.

The proxy statement disclosed, among other things, that the Special Committee had countered M & F's initial $24 per share offer at $30 per share, but only was able to achieve a final offer of $25 per share. The proxy statement disclosed that the MFW business divisions had discussed with Evercore whether the initial projections Evercore received reflected management's latest thinking. It also disclosed that the updated projections were lower. The proxy statement also included the five separate price ranges for the value of MFW's stock that Evercore had generated with its different valuation analyses.

Knowing the proxy statement's disclosures of the background of the Special Committee's work, of Evercore's valuation ranges, and of the analyses supporting Evercore's fairness opinion, MFW's stockholders—representing more than 65% of the minority shares—approved the Merger. In the controlling stockholder merger context, it is settled Delaware law that an uncoerced, informed majority-of-the-minority vote, without any other procedural protection, is itself sufficient to shift the burden of persuasion to the plaintiff under the entire fairness standard of review. The Court of Chancery found that "the plaintiffs themselves do not dispute that the majority-of-the-minority vote was fully informed and uncoerced, because they fail to allege any failure of disclosure or any act of coercion."

Both Procedural Protections Established

Based on a highly extensive record, the Court of Chancery concluded that the procedural protections upon which the Merger was conditioned—approval by an independent and empowered Special Committee and by a uncoerced informed majority of MFW's minority stockholders—had both been undisputedly established prior to trial. We agree and conclude the Defendants' motion for summary judgment was properly granted on all of those issues.

Business Judgment Review Properly Applied

We have determined that the business judgment rule standard of review applies to this controlling stockholder buyout. Under that standard, the claims against the Defendants must be dismissed unless no rational person could have believed that the merger was favorable to MFW's minority stockholders.[41] In this case, it cannot be credibly argued

---

[41]   E.g., In re Walt Disney Co. Deriv. Litig., 906 A.2d 27, 74 (Del. 2006) "[W]here business judgment presumptions are applicable, the board's decision will be upheld unless it cannot be 'attributed to any rational business purpose.' " (quoting Sinclair Oil Corp. v. Levien, 280 A.2d 717, 720 (Del. 1971))).

(let alone concluded) that no rational person would find the Merger favorable to MFW's minority stockholders.

Conclusion

For the above-stated reasons, the judgment of the Court of Chancery is affirmed.

———————

QUESTIONS

1. Why was the court not bothered by the fact that MFW's share price had been trading in the $20—$24 range in May, and Perlman's June offer followed a closing price of $16.96. Wasn't Perlman taking advantage of a market decline that might have been short-term? If you were representing Perlman, what might you say to defend such a decision?

2. MacAndrews & Forbes' financial advisor, Moelis and Company, had valued MFW at between $10 and $32 per share. Did Schwartz and Bevins, directors of MFW who were also directors of MacAndrews and Forbes, have any obligation to disclose the Moelis numbers to the MFW board or the Special Committee? Why or why not?

3. Why does the court insist on approval by both the independent directors and a majority of the non-controlling shareholders? Why is shareholder approval alone not sufficient, if the proxy disclosures are sufficiently candid?

4. Why does the court not refer to Section 144? How would the results differ if it had been applied?

5. As noted earlier in these materials, the Delaware General Assembly amended the section 251, governing mergers, to add a new subsection (h), authorizing short form mergers by majority shareholders. After reviewing this section, if MacAndrews & Forbes acquired sufficient shares to control a shareholder vote, would this section apply to allow a merger without a shareholder vote? What standard of review would govern this merger? See Glassman v. Unocal Exploration Corporation, which follows.

———————

NOTE

The Delaware Chancery Court has taken the requirements of Kahn v. M & F Worldwide quite literally. In In re Cornerstone Therapeutics Inc. Stockholder Litig., 2014 Del. Ch. LEXIS 170 Vice Chancellor Glasscock refused to dismiss a complaint against independent directors in a parent-subsidiary merger, even though the complaint did not contain any specific allegations that would overcome their presumed good faith and exculpate them from liability. While the merger was approved by over 80% of the minority shareholders, the merger was not conditioned on approval by a majority of the minority shareholders.

NOTE ON SOLOMON V. PATHE COMMUNICATIONS CORP.

The Delaware Supreme Court has held that a controlling shareholder owes no fiduciary duties of fairness to public shareholders of a target company in a tender offer, Solomon v. Pathe Communications Corp., 672 A.2d 35 (Del. 1996). In affirming the Chancery Court's dismissal of the complaint, the court stated:

"In the case of totally voluntary tender offers, as here, courts do not impose any right of the shareholders to receive a particular price. Lynch v. Vickers Energy Corp., Del. Ch., 351 A.2d 570, 576 (1976), rev'd on other grounds, Del. Supr., 383 A.2d 278 (1977); Weinberger v. U.O.P., Inc., Del. Supr., 457 A.2d 701, 703 (1983). Delaware law recognizes that, as to allegedly voluntary tender offers (in contrast to cash-out mergers), the determinative factor as to voluntariness is whether coercion is present, or whether there is "materially false or misleading disclosures made to shareholders in connection with the offer." Eisenberg v. Chicago Milwaukee Corp., Del. Ch., 537 A.2d 1051, 1056 (1987) (citations omitted). A transaction may be considered involuntary, despite being voluntary in appearance and form, if one of these factors is present. *Id.* There is no well-plead allegation of any coercion or false or misleading disclosures in the present case, however.

"Moreover, in the absence of coercion or disclosure violations, the adequacy of the price in a voluntary tender offer cannot be an issue. Weinberger, 457 A.2d at 703; Lynch, 351 A.2d at 576. Solomon has plead no facts from which there could be drawn a reasonable inference that there was coercion or lack of complete disclosure. The amended complaint focuses mainly on a conclusory allegation that coercion was present."

C. AVOIDING THE WEINBERGER DOCTRINE

Glassman v. Unocal Exploration Corporation

777 A.2d 242 (Del. 2001).

■ BERGER, JUSTICE.

In this appeal, we consider the fiduciary duties owed by a parent corporation to the subsidiary's minority stockholders in the context of a "short-form" merger. Specifically, we take this opportunity to reconcile a fiduciary's seemingly absolute duty to establish the entire fairness of any self-dealing transaction with the less demanding requirements of the short-form merger statute. The statute authorizes the elimination of minority stockholders by a summary process that does not involve the "fair dealing" component of entire fairness. Indeed, the statute does not contemplate any "dealing" at all. Thus, a parent corporation cannot satisfy the entire fairness standard if it follows the terms of the short-form merger statute without more.

Unocal Corporation addressed this dilemma by establishing a special negotiating committee and engaging in a process that it believed would pass muster under traditional entire fairness review. We find that such steps were unnecessary. By enacting a statute that authorizes the elimination of the minority without notice, vote, or other traditional indicia of procedural fairness, the General Assembly effectively circumscribed the parent corporation's obligations to the minority in a short-form merger. The parent corporation does not have to establish entire fairness, and, absent fraud or illegality, the only recourse for a minority stockholder who is dissatisfied with the merger consideration is appraisal.

I.   Factual and Procedural Background

Unocal Corporation is an earth resources company primarily engaged in the exploration for and production of crude oil and natural gas. At the time of the merger at issue, Unocal owned approximately 96% of the stock of Unocal Exploration Corporation ("UXC"), an oil and gas company operating in and around the Gulf of Mexico. In 1991, low natural gas prices caused a drop in both companies' revenues and earnings. Unocal investigated areas of possible cost savings and decided that, by eliminating the UXC minority, it would reduce taxes and overhead expenses.

In December 1991 the boards of Unocal and UXC appointed special committees to consider a possible merger. The UXC committee consisted of three directors who, although also directors of Unocal, were not officers or employees of the parent company. The UXC committee retained financial and legal advisors and met four times before agreeing to a merger exchange ratio of .54 shares of Unocal stock for each share of UXC. Unocal and UXC announced the merger on February 24, 1992, and it was effected, pursuant to 8 Del. C. § 253, on May 2, 1992. The Notice of Merger and Prospectus stated the terms of the merger and advised the former UXC stockholders of their appraisal rights.

Plaintiffs filed this class action, on behalf of UXC's minority stockholders, on the day the merger was announced. They asserted, among other claims, that Unocal and its directors breached their fiduciary duties of entire fairness and full disclosure. The Court of Chancery conducted a two day trial and held that: (i) the Prospectus did not contain any material misstatements or omissions; (ii) the entire fairness standard does not control in a short-form merger; and (iii) plaintiffs' exclusive remedy in this case was appraisal. The decision of the Court of Chancery is affirmed.

II. Discussion

The short-form merger statute, as enacted in 1937, authorized a parent corporation to merge with its wholly-owned subsidiary by filing and recording a certificate evidencing the parent's ownership and its merger resolution. In 1957, the statute was expanded to include parent/subsidiary mergers where the parent company owns at least 90% of the stock of the subsidiary. The 1957 amendment also made it possible, for the first time and only in a short-form merger, to pay the minority cash for their shares, thereby eliminating their ownership interest in the company. In its current form, which has not changed significantly since 1957, 8 Del. C. § 253 provides in relevant part:

> (a) In any case in which at least 90 percent of the outstanding shares of each class of the stock of a corporation . . . is owned by another corporation . . . , the corporation having such stock ownership may . . . merge the other corporation . . . into itself . . . by executing, acknowledging and filing, in accordance with § 103 of this title, a certificate of such ownership and merger setting forth a copy of the resolution of its board of directors to so merge and the date of the adoption; provided, however, that in case the parent corporation shall not own all the outstanding stock of . . . the subsidiary corporation[ ], . . . the resolution . . . shall state the terms and conditions of the merger, including the securities, cash, property or rights to be issued, paid delivered or granted by the surviving corporation upon surrender of each share of the subsidiary corporation. . . .

* * *

> (d) In the event that all of the stock of a subsidiary Delaware corporation . . . is not owned by the parent corporation immediately prior to the merger, the stockholders of the subsidiary Delaware corporation party to the merger shall have appraisal rights as set forth in Section 262 of this Title.

* * *

The next question presented to this Court was whether any equitable relief is available to minority stockholders who object to a short-form merger. In Stauffer v. Standard Brands Incorporated,[49] minority stockholders sued to set aside the contested merger or, in the alternative, for damages. They alleged that the merger consideration was so grossly inadequate as to constitute constructive fraud and that Standard Brands breached its fiduciary duty to the minority by failing to set a fair price for their stock. The Court of Chancery held that appraisal was the stockholders' exclusive remedy, and dismissed the complaint. This Court affirmed, but explained that appraisal would not be the exclusive remedy in a short-form merger tainted by fraud or illegality:

---

[49] Del.Supr., 187 A.2d 78 (1962).

[T]he exception [to appraisal's exclusivity] . . . refers generally to all mergers, and is nothing but a reaffirmation of the ever-present power of equity to deal with illegality or fraud. But it has no bearing here. No illegality or overreaching is shown. The dispute reduces to nothing but a difference of opinion as to value. Indeed it is difficult to imagine a case under the short merger statute in which there could be such actual fraud as would entitle a minority to set aside the merger. This is so because the very purpose of the statute is to provide the parent corporation with a means of eliminating the minority shareholder's interest in the enterprise. Thereafter the former stockholder has only a monetary claim.

The Stauffer doctrine's viability rose and fell over the next four decades. Its holding on the exclusivity of appraisal took on added significance in 1967, when the long-form merger statute—§ 251—was amended to allow cash-out mergers. In David J. Greene & Co. v. Schenley Industries, Inc.,[51] the Court of Chancery applied Stauffer to a long-form cash-out merger. Schenley recognized that the corporate fiduciaries had to establish entire fairness, but concluded that fair value was the plaintiff's only real concern and that appraisal was an adequate remedy. The court explained:

> While a court of equity should stand ready to prevent corporate fraud and any overreaching by fiduciaries of the rights of stockholders, by the same token this Court should not impede the consummation of an orderly merger under the Delaware statutes, an efficient and fair method having been furnished which permits a judicially protected withdrawal from a merger by a disgruntled stockholder.

In 1977, this Court started retreating from Stauffer (and Schenley). Singer v. Magnavox Co.[52] held that a controlling stockholder breaches its fiduciary duty if it effects a cash-out merger under § 251 for the sole purpose of eliminating the minority stockholders. The Singer court distinguished Stauffer as being a case where the only complaint was about the value of the converted shares. Nonetheless, the Court cautioned:

> [T]he fiduciary obligation of the majority to the minority stockholders remains and proof of a purpose, other than such freeze-out, without more, will not necessarily discharge it. In such case the Court will scrutinize the circumstances for compliance with the Sterling [v. Mayflower Hotel Corp., Del. Supr., 93 A.2d 107 (1952)] rule of "entire fairness" and, if it finds a violation thereof, will grant such relief as equity may require.

---

[51] Del.Ch., 281 A.2d 30 (1971).
[52] Del.Supr., 380 A.2d 969 (1977).

Any statement in Stauffer inconsistent herewith is held inapplicable to a § 251 merger.

Singer's business purpose test was extended to short-form mergers two years later in Roland International Corporation v. Najjar.[55] The Roland majority wrote:

The short form permitted by § 253 does simplify the steps necessary to effect a merger, and does give a parent corporation some certainty as to result and control as to timing. But we find nothing magic about a 90% ownership of outstanding shares which would eliminate the fiduciary duty owed by the majority to the minority.

* * *

As to Stauffer, we agree that the purpose of § 253 is to provide the parent with a means of eliminating minority shareholders in the subsidiary but, as we observed in Singer, we did "not read the decision [Stauffer] as approving a merger accomplished solely to freeze-out the minority without a valid business purpose." We held that any statement in Stauffer inconsistent with the principles restated in Singer was inapplicable to a § 251 merger. Here we hold that the principles announced in Singer with respect to a § 251 merger apply to a § 253 merger. It follows that any statement in Stauffer inconsistent with that holding is overruled.

After Roland, there was not much of Stauffer that safely could be considered good law. But that changed in 1983, in Weinberger v. UOP, Inc., when the Court dropped the business purpose test, made appraisal a more adequate remedy, and said that it was "return[ing] to the well established principles of Stauffer . . . and Schenley . . . mandating a stockholder's recourse to the basic remedy of an appraisal." Weinberger focused on two subjects—the "unflinching" duty of entire fairness owed by self-dealing fiduciaries, and the "more liberalized appraisal" it established.

With respect to entire fairness, the Court explained that the concept includes fair dealing (how the transaction was timed, initiated, structured, negotiated, disclosed and approved) and fair price (all elements of value); and that the test for fairness is not bifurcated. On the subject of appraisal, the Court made several important statements: (i) courts may consider "proof of value by any techniques or methods which are generally considered acceptable in the financial community and otherwise admissible in court . . . ;" (ii) fair value must be based on "all relevant factors," which include not only "elements of future value . . . which are known or susceptible of proof as of the date of the merger" but also, when the court finds it appropriate, "damages, resulting from the

---

[55] Del.Supr., 407 A.2d 1032 (1979).

taking, which the stockholders sustain as a class;" and (iii) "a plaintiff's monetary remedy ordinarily should be confined to the more liberalized appraisal proceeding herein established. . . ."

By referencing both Stauffer and Schenley, one might have thought that the Weinberger court intended appraisal to be the exclusive remedy "ordinarily" in non-fraudulent mergers where "price . . . [is] the preponderant consideration outweighing other features of the merger." In Rabkin v. Philip A. Hunt Chemical Corp.,[64] however, the Court dispelled that view. The Rabkin plaintiffs claimed that the majority stockholder breached its fiduciary duty of fair dealing by waiting until a one year commitment to pay $25 per share had expired before effecting a cash-out merger at $20 per share. The Court of Chancery dismissed the complaint, reasoning that, under Weinberger, plaintiffs could obtain full relief for the alleged unfair dealing in an appraisal proceeding. This Court reversed, holding that the trial court read Weinberger too narrowly and that appraisal is the exclusive remedy only if stockholders' complaints are limited to "judgmental factors of valuation."

Rabkin, through its interpretation of Weinberger, effectively eliminated appraisal as the exclusive remedy for any claim alleging breach of the duty of entire fairness. But Rabkin involved a long-form merger, and the Court did not discuss, in that case or any others, how its refinement of Weinberger impacted short-form mergers. Two of this Court's more recent decisions that arguably touch on the subject are Bershad v. Curtiss-Wright Corp.[68] and Kahn v. Lynch Communication Systems, Inc., both long-form merger cases. In Bershad, the Court included § 253 when it identified statutory merger provisions from which fairness issues flow:

> In parent-subsidiary merger transactions the issues are those of fairness—fair price and fair dealing. These flow from the statutory provisions permitting mergers, 8 Del. C. §§ 251–253 (1983), and those designed to ensure fair value by an appraisal, 8 Del. C. § 262 (1983) . . . ;"

and in Lynch, the Court described entire fairness as the "exclusive" standard of review in a cash-out, parent/subsidiary merger.

Mindful of this history, we must decide whether a minority stockholder may challenge a short-form merger by seeking equitable relief through an entire fairness claim. Under settled principles, a parent corporation and its directors undertaking a short-form merger are self-dealing fiduciaries who should be required to establish entire fairness, including fair dealing and fair price. The problem is that § 253 authorizes a summary procedure that is inconsistent with any reasonable notion of fair dealing. In a short-form merger, there is no agreement of merger

---

[64] Del.Supr., 498 A.2d 1099 (1985).
[68] Del.Supr., 535 A.2d 840 (1987).

negotiated by two companies; there is only a unilateral act—a decision by the parent company that its 90% owned subsidiary shall no longer exist as a separate entity. The minority stockholders receive no advance notice of the merger; their directors do not consider or approve it; and there is no vote. Those who object are given the right to obtain fair value for their shares through appraisal.

The equitable claim plainly conflicts with the statute. If a corporate fiduciary follows the truncated process authorized by § 253, it will not be able to establish the fair dealing prong of entire fairness. If, instead, the corporate fiduciary sets up negotiating committees, hires independent financial and legal experts, etc., then it will have lost the very benefit provided by the statute—a simple, fast and inexpensive process for accomplishing a merger. We resolve this conflict by giving effect the intent of the General Assembly. In order to serve its purpose, § 253 must be construed to obviate the requirement to establish entire fairness.[71]

Thus, we again return to Stauffer, and hold that, absent fraud or illegality, appraisal is the exclusive remedy available to a minority stockholder who objects to a short-form merger. In doing so, we also reaffirm Weinberger's statements about the scope of appraisal. The determination of fair value must be based on all relevant factors, including damages and elements of future value, where appropriate. So, for example, if the merger was timed to take advantage of a depressed market, or a low point in the company's cyclical earnings, or to precede an anticipated positive development, the appraised value may be adjusted to account for those factors. We recognize that these are the types of issues frequently raised in entire fairness claims, and we have held that claims for unfair dealing cannot be litigated in an appraisal.[72] But our prior holdings simply explained that equitable claims may not be engrafted onto a statutory appraisal proceeding; stockholders may not receive recessionary relief in an appraisal. Those decisions should not be read to restrict the elements of value that properly may be considered in an appraisal.

Although fiduciaries are not required to establish entire fairness in a short-form merger, the duty of full disclosure remains, in the context of this request for stockholder action.[73] Where the only choice for the minority stockholders is whether to accept the merger consideration or seek appraisal, they must be given all the factual information that is material to that decision.[74] The Court of Chancery carefully considered

---

[71] We do not read Lynch as holding otherwise; this issue was not before the Court in Lynch.

[72] Alabama By-Products Corporation v. Neal, Del.Supr., 588 A.2d 255, 257 (1991).

[73] See: Malone v. Brincat, Del.Supr., 722 A.2d 5 (1998) (No stockholder action was requested, but Court recognized that even in such a case, directors breach duty of loyalty and good faith by knowingly disseminating false information to stockholders.)

[74] McMullin v. Beran, Del.Supr., 765 A.2d 910 (2000).

plaintiffs' disclosure claims and applied settled law in rejecting them. We affirm this aspect of the appeal on the basis of the trial court's decision.[75]

III. Conclusion

Based on the foregoing, we affirm the Court of Chancery and hold that plaintiffs' only remedy in connection with the short-form merger of UXC into Unocal was appraisal.

QUESTIONS

1. Does this decision encourage parent corporations to engage in tender offers to reach the 90% ownership level in order to avoid fairness challenges?

2. In view of the addition of Delaware GCL § 251(h) in 2013 to permit short form mergers when the parent controls a majority of the stock under certain conditions, what effect will this case have on the likely future application of the entire fairness doctrine on parent-subsidiary mergers?

3. In light of the new breadth of the short form merger statute, if you were advising MacAndrews & Forbes about a takeout of minority shareholders in MFW, would you advise a different course of action that taken in 2011?

NOTE ON BERGER V. PUBCO CORPORATION

In Berger v. Pubco Corporation, 976 A.2d 132 (Del. 2009) Justice Jacobs addressed the question of the appropriate remedy for minority shareholders in a short form merger where the disclosures made were defective. He wrote:

> Under Glassman v. Unocal Exploration Corporation, the exclusive remedy for minority shareholders who challenge a short form merger is a statutory appraisal, provided that there is no fraud or illegality, and that all facts are disclosed that would enable the shareholders to decide whether to accept the merger price or seek appraisal. But where, as here, the material facts are not disclosed, the controlling stockholder forfeits the benefit of that limited review and exclusive remedy, and the minority shareholders become entitled to participate in a "quasi-appraisal" class action to recover the difference between "fair value" and the merger price without having to "opt in" to that proceeding or to escrow any merger proceeds that they received.

---

[75] In re Unocal Exploration Corporation Shareholders Litigation, Del.Ch., 2001 WL 823376 (2000).

PART IV

REGULATION OF ACQUISITIONS

CHAPTER TEN.   Securities Law Issues in Seller Financing and Mergers

CHAPTER ELEVEN.   The Williams Act

The Federal securities laws overlay virtually all fundamental corporate transactions. In the area of mergers and acquisitions they affect both buyers and sellers in important ways. Chapter Ten deals with the Securities Act of 1933. It arises in two settings. In some cases the buyer may be using its own securities as full or partial payment for the acquisition. This is sometimes called "seller financing." Here the buyer has disclosure obligations that arise primarily under the '33 Act. Where the buyer is distributing its securities to a widely dispersed group of shareholders, it may encounter registration obligations under the '33 Act. Even where the buyer is acquiring a privately owned business, the buyer, in order to find an exemption from the registration process, must comply with exemptions, some of which are briefly described in this chapter. And where a stock for stock merger is employed, it is treated as an offer of the buyer's shares to the seller's shareholders, and is subjected to the same requirements. This chapter briefly explores the restrictions on resale that may face those accepting the buyer's securities.

Chapter Eleven deals in more detail with the disclosure requirements of the William Act, which apply to any transaction involving a class of equity securities registered under the Securities Exchange Act, that is, held by 500 or more shareholders. Here the disclosure requirements focus on the protection of shareholders of the target firm (although some critics view them as target management protection statutes), and begin before any tender offer is made. This chapter introduces the reader to the subtleties of the disclosure requirements under the securities laws.

CHAPTER TEN

SECURITIES LAW ISSUES IN SELLER FINANCING AND MERGERS

The Federal securities laws overlay virtually all fundamental corporate transactions. In the area of mergers and acquisitions they affect both buyers and sellers in important ways.

The Securities Act of 1993 was adopted within the first 100 days of the New Deal, and thus illustrates the importance that Congress and the President attached to reforming the securities markets. A principal justification for the Securities Act was to fill in the gap left by state regulation, that could not reach transactions that occurred across state lines very effectively. Congress used the state laws (as well as certain provisions of the English Companies Act) as a model for the Securities Act. But Congress had to decide which model of state regulation to use: (1) merely prohibiting fraud in offering and selling securities; (2) requiring a registration and full disclosure to investors, or (3) providing that the government would judge the merits of offerings, and determine which could be sold to the public. Congress chose a combination of (1) and (2). The philosophy was one of full disclosure. The Securities Act contains an Appendix that states what a registration statement must contain, and it is a long and detailed list of disclosures about a business. These requirements were drawn from the "best practices" of reputable Wall Street underwriting firms of the time.

In privately negotiated acquisitions of closely held businesses, the use of seller financing has long been commonplace. The selling shareholders may be asked to take common stock of the buyer, and perhaps other instruments, such as promissory notes. Where the sellers may want an all cash sale, buyers may well offer a cash down payment combined with a series of promissory notes due periodically, perhaps over three to five years. Where buyer and seller have resolved their differences over value with a payment structure that is contingent on the performance of the business, additional notes or options on stock may be contingent on meeting certain performance goals (earn-outs). In all of these cases, selling shareholders are, to a large extent, simply exchanging securities in the target for those of the bidder. When a merger is proposed that involves the issuance of the acquiring corporation's shares to the target shareholders, these shareholders can be viewed as "selling" their target company shares and "buying" the acquiring corporation's shares.

The following materials deal with the obligations of buyers when issuing securities, and some of the resale problems that target shareholders may encounter with these securities.

1.   COVERAGE OF THE SECURITIES LAWS

Securities Act of 1933, Section 2(a)(1).

Section 5 of the Securities Act of 1933 requires the filing of a registration statement before any security or offering not exempt from registration can be offered. Section 2(a)(1) defines a security to include, except as the context may otherwise require, "any stock, . . . note, . . . or investment contract. . . ." In the context of business acquisitions, the most compelling question is when does the "context otherwise require" a note not to be a security?

Reves v. Ernst & Young

494 U.S. 56, 110 S.Ct. 945, 108 L.Ed.2d 47 (1990).

■ JUSTICE MARSHALL delivered the opinion of the Court.

This case presents the question whether certain demand notes issued by the Farmer's Cooperative of Arkansas and Oklahoma are "securities" within the meaning of § 3(a)(10) of the Securities Exchange Act of 1934. We conclude that they are.

I

The Co-Op is an agricultural cooperative that, at the time relevant here, had approximately 23,000 members. In order to raise money to support its general business operations, the Co-Op sold promissory notes payable on demand by the holder. Although the notes were uncollateralized and uninsured, they paid a variable rate of interest that was adjusted monthly to keep it higher than the rate paid by local financial institutions. The Co-Op offered the notes to both members and nonmembers, marketing the scheme as an "Investment Program." Advertisements for the notes, which appeared in each Co-Op newsletter, read in part: "YOUR CO-OP has more than $11,000,000 in assets to stand behind your investments. The Investment is not Federal [sic] insured but it is . . . Safe . . . Secure . . . and available when you need it." Despite these assurances, the Co-Op filed for bankruptcy in 1984. At the time of the filing, over 1,600 people held notes worth a total of $10 million.

After the Co-Op filed for bankruptcy, petitioners, a class of holders of the notes, filed suit against Arthur Young & Co., the firm that had audited the Co-Op's financial statements (and the predecessor to respondent Ernst & Young). Petitioners alleged, inter alia, that Arthur Young had intentionally failed to follow generally accepted accounting principles in its audit, specifically with respect to the valuation of one of the Co-Op's major assets, a gasohol plant. Petitioners claimed that

Arthur Young violated these principles in an effort to inflate the assets and net worth of the Co-Op. Petitioners maintained that, had Arthur Young properly treated the plant in its audits, they would not have purchased demand notes because the Co-Op's insolvency would have been apparent. On the basis of these allegations, petitioners claimed that Arthur Young had violated the antifraud provisions of the 1934 Act as well as Arkansas' securities laws.

Petitioners prevailed at trial on both their federal and state claims, receiving a $6.1 million judgment. Arthur Young appealed, claiming that the demand notes were not "securities" under either the 1934 Act or Arkansas law, and that the statutes' antifraud provisions therefore did not apply. A panel of the Eighth Circuit, agreeing with Arthur Young on both the state and federal issues, reversed. We granted certiorari to address the federal issue, . . . and now reverse the judgment of the Court of Appeals.

II

A

This case requires us to decide whether the note issued by the Co-Op is a "security" within the meaning of the 1934 Act. Section 3(a)(10) of that Act is our starting point:

> "The term 'security' means any note, stock, treasury stock, bond, debenture, certificate of interest or participation in any profit-sharing agreement . . . but shall not include currency or any note, draft, bill of exchange, or banker's acceptance which has a maturity at the time of issuance of not exceeding nine months, exclusive of days of grace, or any renewal thereof the maturity of which is likewise limited." 48 Stat. 884, as amended, 15 U.S.C. § 78c(a)(10).

The fundamental purpose undergirding the Securities Acts is "to eliminate serious abuses in a largely unregulated securities market." In defining the scope of the market that it wished to regulate, Congress painted with a broad brush. It recognized the virtually limitless scope of human ingenuity, especially in the creation of "countless and variable schemes devised by those who seek the use of the money of others on the promise of profits," and determined that the best way to achieve its goal of protecting investors was "to define 'the term 'security' in sufficiently broad and general terms so as to include within that definition the many types of instruments that in our commercial world fall within the ordinary concept of a security.'" Congress therefore did not attempt precisely to cabin the scope of the Securities Acts. Rather, it enacted a definition of "security" sufficiently broad to encompass virtually any instrument that might be sold as an investment.

* * *

A commitment to an examination of the economic realities of a transaction does not necessarily entail a case-by-case analysis of every instrument, however. Some instruments are obviously within the class Congress intended to regulate because they are by their nature investments. In Landreth Timber Co. v. Landreth, 471 U.S. 681 (1985), we held that an instrument bearing the name "stock" that, among other things, is negotiable, offers the possibility of capital appreciation, and carries the right to dividends contingent on the profits of a business enterprise is plainly within the class of instruments Congress intended the securities laws to cover. * * *

While common stock is the quintessence of a security, and investors therefore justifiably assume that a sale of stock is covered by the Securities Acts, the same simply cannot be said of notes, which are used in a variety of settings, not all of which involve investments. Thus, the phrase "any note" should not be interpreted to mean literally "any note," but must be understood against the backdrop of what Congress was attempting to accomplish in enacting the Securities Acts.[2]

Because the Landreth Timber formula cannot sensibly be applied to notes, some other principle must be developed to define the term "note." A majority of the Courts of Appeals that have considered the issue have adopted, in varying forms, "investment versus commercial" approaches that distinguish, on the basis of all of the circumstances surrounding the transactions, notes issued in an investment context (which are "securities") from notes issued in a commercial or consumer context (which are not).

The Second Circuit's "family resemblance" approach begins with a presumption that any note with a term of more than nine months is a "security." Recognizing that not all notes are securities, however, the Second Circuit has also devised a list of notes that it has decided are obviously not securities. Accordingly, the "family resemblance" test permits an issuer to rebut the presumption that a note is a security if it can show that the note in question "bear[s] a strong family resemblance" to an item on the judicially crafted list of exceptions, or convinces the court to add a new instrument to the list.

---

[2] An approach founded on economic reality rather than on a set of per se rules is subject to the criticism that whether a particular note is a "security" may not be entirely clear at the time it is issued. Such an approach has the corresponding advantage, though, of permitting the SEC and the courts sufficient flexibility to ensure that those who market investments are not able to escape the coverage of the Securities Acts by creating new instruments that would not be covered by a more determinate definition. One could question whether, at the expense of the goal of clarity, Congress overvalued the goal of avoiding manipulation by the clever and dishonest. If Congress erred, however, it is for that body, and not this Court, to correct its mistake.

[The court reviewed and rejected cases analyzing whether notes are securities under the so-called "investment contract" or "Howey" test in two circuits.]

The other two contenders—the "family resemblance" and "investment versus commercial" tests—are really two ways of formulating the same general approach. Because we think the "family resemblance" test provides a more promising framework for analysis, however, we adopt it. The test begins with the language of the statute; because the Securities Acts define "security" to include "any note," we begin with a presumption that every note is a security. We nonetheless recognize that this presumption cannot be irrebuttable. As we have said, Congress was concerned with regulating the investment market, not with creating a general federal cause of action for fraud. In an attempt to give more content to that dividing line, the Second Circuit has identified a list of instruments commonly denominated "notes" that nonetheless fall without the "security" category (types of notes that are not "securities" include "the note delivered in consumer financing, the note secured by a mortgage on a home, the short-term note secured by a lien on a small business or some of its assets, the note evidencing a 'character' loan to a bank customer, short-term notes secured by an assignment of accounts receivable, or a note which simply formalizes an open-account debt incurred in the ordinary course of business (particularly if, as in the case of the customer of a broker, it is collateralized)"). . . .

We agree that the items identified by the Second Circuit are not properly viewed as "securities." More guidance, though, is needed. It is impossible to make any meaningful inquiry into whether an instrument bears a "resemblance" to one of the instruments identified by the Second Circuit without specifying what it is about those instruments that makes them non-"securities." Moreover, as the Second Circuit itself has noted, its list is "not graven in stone," ibid., and is therefore capable of expansion. Thus, some standards must be developed for determining when an item should be added to the list.

An examination of the list itself makes clear what those standards should be. In creating its list, the Second Circuit was applying the same factors that this Court has held apply in deciding whether a transaction involves a "security." First, we examine the transaction to assess the motivations that would prompt a reasonable seller and buyer to enter into it. If the seller's purpose is to raise money for the general use of a business enterprise or to finance substantial investments and the buyer is interested primarily in the profit the note is expected to generate, the instrument is likely to be a "security." If the note is exchanged to facilitate the purchase and sale of a minor asset or consumer good, to correct for the seller's cash-flow difficulties, or to advance some other commercial or consumer purpose, on the other hand, the note is less sensibly described as a "security." Second, we examine the "plan of distribution" of the instrument, to determine whether it is an instrument in which there is "common trading for speculation or investment." Third, we examine the reasonable expectations of the investing public: The Court will consider instruments to be "securities" on the basis of such public expectations, even where an economic analysis of the circumstances of the particular transaction might suggest that the instruments are not "securities" as used in that transaction. Finally, we examine whether some factor such as the existence of another regulatory scheme significantly reduces the risk of the instrument, thereby rendering application of the Securities Acts unnecessary.

We conclude, then, that in determining whether an instrument denominated a "note" is a "security," courts are to apply the version of the "family resemblance" test that we have articulated here: a note is presumed to be a "security," and that presumption may be rebutted only by a showing that the note bears a strong resemblance (in terms of the four factors we have identified) to one of the enumerated categories of instrument. If an instrument is not sufficiently similar to an item on the list, the decision whether another category should be added is to be made by examining the same factors.

B

Applying the family resemblance approach to this case, we have little difficulty in concluding that the notes at issue here are "securities." Ernst & Young admits that "a demand note does not closely resemble any of the Second Circuit's family resemblance examples." Nor does an examination of the four factors we have identified as being relevant to our inquiry suggest that the demand notes here are not "securities" despite their lack of similarity to any of the enumerated categories. The Co-Op sold the notes in an effort to raise capital for its general business operations, and purchasers bought them in order to earn a profit in the form of interest. Indeed, one of the primary inducements offered purchasers was an interest rate constantly revised to keep it slightly above the rate paid by local banks and savings and loans. From both sides, then, the transaction is most naturally conceived as an investment in a business enterprise rather than as a purely commercial or consumer transaction.

As to the plan of distribution, the Co-Op offered the notes over an extended period to its 23,000 members, as well as to nonmembers, and more than 1,600 people held notes when the Co-Op filed for bankruptcy. To be sure, the notes were not traded on an exchange. They were, however, offered and sold to a broad segment of the public, and that is all we have held to be necessary to establish the requisite "common trading" in an instrument.

The third factor—the public's reasonable perceptions—also supports a finding that the notes in this case are "securities". We have consistently identified the fundamental essence of a "security" to be its character as an "investment." The advertisements for the notes here characterized them as "investments," and there were no countervailing factors that would have led a reasonable person to question this characterization. In these circumstances, it would be reasonable for a prospective purchaser to take the Co-Op at its word.

Finally, we find no risk-reducing factor to suggest that these instruments are not in fact securities. The notes are uncollateralized and uninsured. Moreover, unlike the certificates of deposit in Marine Bank, *supra*, at 557–558, which were insured by the Federal Deposit Insurance Corporation and subject to substantial regulation under the federal banking laws, and unlike the pension plan in Teamsters v. Daniel, 439 U.S. 551, 569–570 (1979), which was comprehensively regulated under the Employee Retirement Income Security Act of 1974, 88 Stat. 829, 29 U.S.C. § 1001 et seq., the notes here would escape federal regulation entirely if the Acts were held not to apply.

The court below found that "[t]he demand nature of the notes is very uncharacteristic of a security," on the theory that the virtually instant liquidity associated with demand notes is inconsistent with the risk ordinarily associated with "securities." This argument is unpersuasive. Common stock traded on a national exchange is the paradigm of a security, and it is as readily convertible into cash as is a demand note. The same is true of publicly traded corporate bonds, debentures, and any number of other instruments that are plainly within the purview of the Acts. The demand feature of a note does permit a holder to eliminate risk quickly by making a demand, but just as with publicly traded stock, the liquidity of the instrument does not eliminate risk all together. Indeed, publicly traded stock is even more readily liquid than are demand notes, in that a demand only eliminates risk when and if payment is made, whereas the sale of a share of stock through a national exchange and the receipt of the proceeds usually occur simultaneously.

We therefore hold that the notes at issue here are within the term "note" in § 3(a)(10).

QUESTIONS

1. Suppose a bidder proposes to issue debt in a takeout merger for the remaining shares of the target, which is a widely held public company. Will these notes be subject to the federal securities laws?

2. Suppose a prospective buyer in a negotiated transaction for a family-owned business, of the type described in Bowers v. Columbia General Corporation, *infra*, asks the family members if they are willing to accept promissory notes paid over five years for 50% of the purchase price. Will these notes be treated as securities?

3. Suppose, given the facts in Question 2, the buyer proposes to enter into an executory purchase contract, under which the purchase price will be paid over five years after a large down payment, and the sellers will give the buyer their irrevocable proxies to vote the shares until the price is fully paid?

---

2. THE TIMING OF REGISTRATION AND DISCLOSURE

Read Securities Act § 5 and Securities Act Rules 134, 135, 145, 165 and 166, and Securities Exchange Act 13(d) and Schedule 13D-1, Item 6.

The Securities Act of 1933 was written in contemplation of new offerings of securities by issuers into public markets for financing purposes. Indeed, for a long time the SEC took the position, in former Rule 133, that a stock-for-stock merger did not involve an offer and sale of securities subject to registration. The theory was that individual shareholders of a target company were not making an individual investment decision requiring the disclosures of the '33 Act. The SEC took the position that the merger occurred through "corporate action" authorized by state law, which incidentally required approval of both the board of directors and shareholders of the constituent corporations. In this setting, shareholders being asked to approve a merger in which they would receive shares in the surviving corporation or its parent got their protections from the fiduciary duties of their directors, under state law. This triumph of form over substance was reversed in 1972 with the adoption of Securities Act Rule 145, which treated most business combinations that resulted in target shareholders owning securities of the surviving corporation or its parent as involving the offer and sale of securities, and requiring registration under the Securities Act.

With the older model of offerings to finance a business in mind, the rules found in section 5 of the Securities Act made some sense, particularly in 1933. Section 5(c) prohibited any offers, broadly defined, until a registration statement had been filed with the SEC. This created the so-called "quiet period," which was thought to begin at the time the issuer first made initial arrangements for a securities offering, probably at the time it contacted prospective underwriters. The purpose of this rule was clear—it prevented the issuer from conditioning the market for its securities at a time when investors lacked full information about the issuer—later called "gun-jumping."

The approach of the SEC to disclosures in the context of offerings that must be registered has been extremely restrictive. While the SEC has permitted issuers to disclose hard facts that were "news" to the press and financial markets during the quiet period, one ruling suggested that privately held companies were not "newsworthy" prior to an initial public offering. In re Carl M. Loeb, Rhoades & Co. and Dominick & Dominick,

38 S.E.C. 843 (1959). Securities Act Rule 135 provided some modest relief from this silence, permitting an extremely restrictive disclosure about a forthcoming offering, that permitted disclosure of little more than "the title, amount, and basic terms of the securities proposed to be offered, the amount of the offering, if any to be made by selling security holders, the anticipated time of the offering and a brief description of the manner and purpose of the offering without naming the underwriters." Securities Act Rule 135.a.2.v. In 2005 the SEC engaged in comprehensive amendments to these rules. For issuers subject to periodic reporting under the Securities Exchange Act, Securities Act Rule 168 now permits not only announcements of factual business information, but also forward-looking information (projections), provided that information about a forthcoming offering is not included in the same communication, and that the information is consistent with previous releases in terms of timing, manner and form. "Well-known seasoned issuers"—defined as companies able to file registration statements on short form S-3 (see the discussion of integrated disclosure below) with a market value of securities in excess of $700 million—may make exempt offers before filing a registration statement, provided they caution readers to read the prospectus that is ultimately filed, under Rule 163. Even issuers not subject to reporting requirements under the Exchange Act can release factual business information (but not projections) subject to the same conditions as reporting companies must meet, under Securities Act Rule 169.

The filing of a registration statement with the SEC includes the filing of a "preliminary prospectus"—a disclosure document that complies with the SEC's requirements, except that it can omit information related to the offering price, which is ordinarily not determined until the SEC has completed its review and actual sales are imminent. Once the registration statement has been filed, the issuer can make written offers of the subject securities, but only by means of the preliminary prospectus. Securities Act section 5(b)(1). A "free writing prospectus" that provides supplemental information may also be employed, provided it is filed with the SEC and meets other conditions, under Rules 164 and 433. In a contractual sense, these are not "offers," because the essential price term is missing, and thus the preliminary prospectus could not create a power of acceptance in offerees. Once the preliminary prospectus is available, the SEC permits the use of an expanded notification to the public— similar to that in the pre-filing period, except that the notification must identify persons from whom a preliminary prospectus can be obtained. Securities Act Rule 134.

This regulatory regime requires a wait before sales can begin. Section 5(a) provides that it is illegal to make use of the mails or means or instruments of interstate commerce (the "jurisdictional means") to sell securities, or to carry them for purposes of sale or delivery after sale until a registration statement is "in effect." Effectiveness occurs primarily through an SEC declaration of effectiveness, after staff review of the preliminary prospectus. Under Securities Act section 5(b)(2), it is illegal to carry securities through the jurisdictional means unless accompanied or preceded by a "full statutory" prospectus that meets the requirements of section 10(a) of the act—one that has been approved by the SEC staff where the missing price terms have been filled in.

This process involves a highly structured disclosure system, beginning with an issuer's bare bones announcement that it intends to engage in a financing, generally followed by a quiet period while it prepares a registration statement for filing. Once filed, the issuer or underwriters can make a somewhat expanded announcement to alert the market that a preliminary prospectus is available, and they can provide the preliminary prospectus and a free writing prospectus. During this "waiting period," or "cooling-off period," no sales are permitted. Investors cannot be rushed into a hasty decision. After a waiting period and approval by the SEC staff, issuers are finally permitted to sell, but only after or in connection with delivery of a final statutory prospectus.

This system remained intact until around 1980. The system was focused on the initial public offering of a previously private issuer, about which investors knew nothing prior to the filing of the registration statement and distribution of the preliminary prospectus. The model assumed the primary market for offerings involved individual retail customers, rather than the sophisticated financial institutions that constitute the dominant buyers in today's markets. From the middle of the 1960s on, commentators and practitioners had begun to question this system. Financial economists found evidence supporting the Efficient Capital Markets Hypothesis ("ECMH"), at least in its semi-strong form (see Chapter Two, Part 2), which holds that market prices rapidly reflect all publicly available information about a company's value in its stock price. For companies making subsequent public offerings, where there was an active trading market, this quiet period approach made little sense. Indeed, it ran counter to requirements of markets such as the New York Stock Exchange, which require listed companies to disseminate all business news as rapidly as possible. Starting around 1980, the SEC introduced its "integrated disclosure" system, which recognized that markets received and processed a continuing flow of information about firms with widely traded securities. The basic reforms shortened the quiet period and the waiting period for new offerings by these firms. The 2007 reforms went further, as described above. The SEC authorized the use of shortened forms of registration statements that incorporated by reference the previous filings with the SEC for these companies, so that the registration statement and the prospectus would contain primarily information about the particulars of the subject offering—price, underwriting commissions, identity of the underwriters and use of proceeds. This reduced the time required to prepare a registration statement, and eliminated much of the need for SEC review, because so little was now contained in the registration statement.

Similarly, in mergers where stock or other securities are being issued by the surviving or acquiring corporation, the issuer may incorporate previous '34 Act filings by reference. But these reforms had little impact on simplifying disclosures in mergers or speeding up the preparation process, because the accounting disclosures required in a merger are more complex and burdensome than in straightforward securities offerings. Item 5 of Form S-4, applicable to "business combinations," required pro forma financial statements for the issuer whenever the business combination is "significant" for the issuer. Regulation S-X, Rule 11–01, 17 CFR 210.11–01. Issuers must provide a pro forma balance sheet of the combined businesses for the most recent fiscal year for the issuer, and must provide pro forma combined income statements for the most recent fiscal year of the issuer and for any interim unaudited financial statements that are required. Regulation S-X, Rule 11–02. Because of the risk of fraud liability, auditors will review the books to make certain there is nothing in the unaudited financials that would suggest prior misleading statements or omissions in the audited financial statements. When this is coupled with the requirement for filing pro forma statements for the combined companies, the regulatory burden becomes heavy, and the delays may be considerable.

The result, of course, is that it is possible that a lengthy period may exist between the time the boards of directors of two corporations agree to merge and the time when a registration statement and proxy statement is presented to shareholders. Chris-Craft Industries, Inc. v. Bangor Punta Corporation, 426 F.2d 569 (2d Cir. 1970), illustrated the difficulties created by this system. Piper Aircraft Corporation became the target of a struggle for control between the Piper family, which held 31% of Piper's stock, and Chris-Craft. Chris-Craft acquired 34% of Piper's stock through a combination of open market purchases and an exchange offer. It then filed a registration statement for another exchange offering that would have given it a majority of Piper's shares. During the waiting period Piper management began negotiations with Bangor Punta Corporation, a conglomerate, that resulted in an agreement by which the Piper family would exchange its shares for specified Bangor Punta securities, and Bangor Punta would make an exchange offer of its securities for the remaining Piper shares. The agreement described the exchange offer as one "under which such holders will be entitled to exchange each share of Piper common stock held by them for Bangor Punta securities and/or cash having a value, in the written opinion of The First Boston Corporation, of $80 or more." This was followed by a press release announcing the agreement, and describing the exchange offer as one "for a package of Bangor Punta securities to be valued in the judgment of The First Boston Corporation at not less than $80 per Piper share."

The SEC took the position that this statement constituted an offer of its securities by Bangor Punta, and sued to enjoin Piper and Bangor

Punta from further violations, and a consent decree was entered. Chris-Craft sued to enjoin completion of the merger following Bangor Punta's successful exchange offer, and lost in the trial court. On appeal, the Court of Appeals held that Bangor Punta had indeed violated section 5 of the Securities Act with its announcement, holding that Rule 135 was an exclusive means of communicating about a forthcoming securities offering, and that the statement about the value of the package of securities was outside the permitted list of disclosures in Rule 135.

The consequences of this approach seemed to be that companies facing similar circumstances were constrained about communicating with their shareholders. If a company is the subject of a takeover bid and agrees to a merger with a "white knight," what can it disclose? Rule 135 permitted only the barest of disclosures; hardly enough to persuade shareholders to resist an attractive tender offer or exchange offer. Similarly, where a company has entered into a stock-for-stock merger agreement and a second bidder wishes to make a competing exchange offer for its shares, Rule 135 only permitted similarly uninteresting information, which would be unlikely to cause shareholders to turn down a tender offer. When stock-for-stock mergers became more popular than cash tender offers, this led to a practice where firms agreeing to a business combination that will require registration have made a fairly complete public announcement and then gone silent during the "quiet period." Similarly, where a bidder for control has made an exchange offer to compete with an existing merger agreement, the bidder's initial announcement has been relatively complete, and is followed by a "quiet period."

The contrast with the regime for cash tender offers, to be covered in Chapter Eleven, was striking. Hostile bidders could make full announcements of their intention to begin a tender offer, provided they filed all communications with the SEC and the target on the same date, under Exchange Act Rule 14d–2. As the rule exists now, the bidder can announce all the terms of an intended tender offer before filing, provided it does not provide a means of acceptance. The tender offer, and the duty to file schedule TO (see Chapter 11, Part 3.A. (iv)), do not begin until the bidder gives target shareholders the means to accept, through instructions or a transmittal form under Rule 14d–3(a). There is no period of review of these disclosures with the SEC; the bidder is free to solicit tenders from the date of initiation of the tender offer, subject only to the shareholders' withdrawal rights under Exchange Act Rule 14d–7(a). Further, under the tender offer rules target management is required to disclose its recommendation to shareholders and its reasons therefor within ten business days of the start of a tender offer. Exchange Act Rule 14e–2.

In late 1999 the SEC proposed revisions to the disclosure limitations connected with mergers requiring registration designed to equalize the disclosure restrictions. SEC Securities Act Release No. 7760, 1999 SEC LEXIS 2291 (Oct. 22, 1999). These changes became effective January 24, 2000. The following discussion covers only the changes in the disclosures connected with securities offerings, whether in an exchange offer or a stock-for-stock merger or other business combination involving securities, leaving discussion of changes in the disclosures for tender offers for Chapter Eleven.

Rule 135(a)(2)(viii), which specifies the limited information that can be released about an offering in advance of filing a registration statement, now permits, in the case of exchange offers, publication of the basic terms of the exchange offer, the name of the subject company, and the class of the subject company's securities to be sought in the exchange offer. Similarly, in a proposed stock-for-stock merger or other business combination for securities, the bidder can now briefly describe the proposed transaction, including its basic terms, and the date, time and place of the meeting of securities holders to vote on the transaction. This presumably would have allowed Bangor Punta to make the disclosure it made involving Piper Aircraft.

Before a registration statement is filed for a business combination transaction, Rule 166 exempts communications made in connection with the transaction from Section 5, so long as participants, such as analysts or major shareholders of the target, take reasonable steps to prevent further distribution of their communications until either the first public announcement of the transaction or the filing of a registration statement.

Rule 165 goes further, and permits the acquiring firm in a business combination subject to the registration requirements, whether a business combination requiring a shareholder vote under Rule 145 or an exchange offer, to offer to sell its securities in its first public announcement before the filing of the registration statement, subject to the conditions that any written communication is filed with the SEC. Once a registration statement for such a business combination is filed, the bidder is no longer limited to the use of the preliminary prospectus or the limited disclosures of Rule 134, but can continue to make offers by any other document, so long as those documents are filed with the SEC.

The document soliciting shareholder approval of a merger is both a proxy statement and a registration statement, if shareholders are to receive the securities of another company in the merger. Under Exchange Act Rule 14a–12, a company may solicit shareholder proxies in advance of furnishing the definitive proxy statement, so long as shareholders are not given the forms of proxy or consent until such time as the definitive proxy statement is furnished. These rules fit with Rule 135, as amended, governing pre-filing disclosures in advance of the filing of a registration statement.

3. EXEMPTIONS FROM REGISTRATION

Read Securities Act Sections 3, 4(1) and 4(2).

The registration process is a slow and costly one. The difficulties in part stem from the issuer's need to disclose the effect of the acquisition on it—in effect, to project what the combined corporation and its businesses will look like. This process requires the preparation of "pro forma" financial statements, showing the effect of the combination of the two enterprises on the financial statements of the acquiring firm. If the issuer has been a publicly held company filing periodic reports under the Securities Exchange Act for a period of at least one year, and has a public "float" (trading securities, not including those held by insiders or large shareholders) of at least $75 million, many of the disclosures are simplified by the issuer's ability to incorporate much of the information in these reports by reference. Typically the SEC staff's review of documents filed by such issuers is accelerated, since the staff can rely on the issuer's experience with the disclosure system to assure generally high quality disclosures. But where the issuer is not a '34 Act reporting company of such long standing, more detailed disclosures and more extensive staff review can extend the time for preparation and review considerably. The process includes road shows to introduce sophisticated investors to the company, can take months, and cost millions.* Where the seller's financial records are unsatisfactory, or where the seller's statements have not been audited, review by accountants can add to the time and expense. These disclosure rules also apply to "business combinations" under form S-4.

Because of the time and expense involved in registration, the Securities Act offers a series of exemptions from registration (but not from the antifraud protections of the Act). A series of classes of securities are exempted under Section 3(a), largely because other regulatory systems, such as banking regulation, insurance regulation, public utility regulation, and the supervision of the bankruptcy courts, provide sufficient protection for investors. The fiduciary duties of corporate directors under state law are relied on to exempt transactions by an issuer solely with its own security holders, where no commissions are paid to any intervening underwriters.

For purposes of acquisitions, exemptions of certain types of transactions are more important. Section 3(a)(11) exempts transactions that are subject to complete state regulation, where the issuer, if a corporation, is incorporated in and doing business within the state, and offers and sales are made solely to residents of the state. Since most

---

* A 2012 survey by the accounting firm PWC reported that underwriting fees ranged between 5% and 7% of the gross proceeds of the offering. Other costs, such as legal, accounting and printing costs were more fixed, averaging $3.7 million. PWC, CONSIDERING AN IPO? THE COSTS OF GOING AND BEING PUBLIC MAY SURPRISE YOU (Sept. 2012) at http://www.pwc.com/us/en/deals/publications/assets/pwc-cost-of-ipo.pdf (last visited 3/11/2016)

states have regulatory schemes as extensive as federal law, investors are thought to obtain adequate protection from this source. The usefulness of this exemption is limited, however, by the fact that all offers and sales that are part of the same issue must be made solely to residents of the state. Thus the presence of a single non-resident offeree precludes the use of this exemption.

In 1973 the SEC adopted Rule 147, which was designed to provide a "safe harbor" from registration under the intrastate offering exemption, if all of its terms and conditions were complied with. The rule provided certain bright line tests of when a company was "doing business" in a state, requiring that 80% of assets and sales be within the state, and that 80% of the proceeds of the offering be used there as well. The SEC staff has exhibited some flexibility in permitting utilization of Rule 147 in acquisitions. Pittsburgh Bancshares, a bank holding company, proposed to acquire all of the outstanding shares of common stock of City National Bank of Pittsburgh (Kansas). Both the holding company and the bank were Kansas corporations. The proposed transaction was to take the form of a stock for stock exchange of bank shares for bank holding company shares. Fifteen stockholders of City National Bank, holding less than 4 percent of the outstanding stock, were non residents of Kansas. It was proposed that the holding company or its officer-shareholders, or the bank's officer-shareholders would acquire the nonresidents' shares in a cash transaction, and thereafter utilize Rule 147 to complete the acquisition. The SEC staff advised the participants that it would take no action against them if they proceeded in this manner. Pittsburgh Bancshares, Inc., SEC Div. Corp. Fin., available 5/30/90.

In addition to prohibiting direct sales to nonresidents, the exemption has been interpreted to preclude the use of residents as mere conduits for sales in the interstate markets. Thus, for a period of time after completion of the offering, all resales must be to residents until the offering is deemed to have "come to rest" in the hands of resident "investors." Rule 147 provides a bright line safe harbor if resales to non residents are restricted for nine months after the last sale by the issuer.

Historically perhaps the most important exemption from registration was provided by Section 4(2), which exempts "transactions by an issuer not involving any public offering." Unfortunately, the Act provides no definition of a "public offering," and this so-called "private offering" exemption has provided considerable difficulties for practitioners attempting to utilize it. Development of the "private" offering doctrine began with SEC v. Ralston Purina Corp., which held that offerings of company stock to several hundred company employees could not use the private offering exemption. After holding that the burden of proof was on the issuer to prove the availability of an exemption, the court held that an offering could be public "whether to few or to many," thus rejecting any numbers test. The purpose of the act was investor protection, and thus the test of the availability of the exemption was the ability of investors to "fend for themselves." Later cases have made clear that the ability to fend for one's self is a two-part test—that one must have access to information of the kind that a registration statement would have supplied, and that one must be sufficiently experienced in business and financial affairs to be able to assess the risks and merits of the investment. In dicta the court noted that an offer and sale to a single buyer might not comply with the exemption if the issuer intended to solicit many others if not successful with the first offeree. The court also suggested that the offeree group must be limited in some logical way in advance, so that general solicitations were forbidden.

The difficulties that developed under the private offering exemption center around the issuer's burden of proof with respect to each element of the exemption. First, the issuer must carry the burden with respect to each person to whom an offer is made, regardless of whether each offeree becomes a purchaser. As a result, a mistaken solicitation of a single person lacking sufficient business and financial experience ("sophistication") destroys the exemption, even if that person is not permitted to purchase, once the error is discovered. See, e.g., Henderson v. Hayden, Stone, Inc., 461 F.2d 1069 (5th Cir.1972), where a sophisticated plaintiff recovered from his broker because the broker was unable to prove the total number of offerees, and that they all qualified as sophisticated and with relationships that gave then access to information about the issuer. Second, the requirement that each offeree have "access" to the same information that registration would provide was interpreted to mean that each offeree should have an opportunity for personal contact with officers of the offeree, so the offeree could ask additional questions and request additional information necessary to verify the information previously furnished. See, e.g., Woolf v. S.D. Cohn & Co., 515 F.2d 591 (5th Cir.1975), where the buyer delegated the factual investigation to her financial advisor, and had no personal contact with representatives of the issuer. But see Doran v. Petroleum Management Corp., 545 F.2d 893 (5th Cir.1977), taking a more liberal approach toward these same standards in view of the regulatory safe harbor provided by the predecessor of Securities Act Rule 506. Given these strict requirements, the presence of a few shareholders lacking sophistication, or some shareholders at such a distance that they are not afforded an opportunity for personal contact, made the use of the private offering exemption risky.

Bowers v. Columbia General Corporation

336 F.Supp. 609 (D. Del.1971).

■ STAPLETON, DISTRICT JUDGE.

This action seeks injunctive relief, rescission and damages for violations of the Securities Act of 1933 and the Securities Exchange Act of 1934, breach of contract and fraud. The matter is currently before me on plaintiffs' motion for a preliminary injunction.

Prior to October 29, 1970, plaintiffs owned all of the outstanding capital stock of Fibre-Metal Products Company, a Pennsylvania corporation engaged in the manufacture and sale of welding and industrial safety supplies ("Fibre-Metal"). Fibre-Metal's business was founded in 1905 by Frederick M. Bowers. Plaintiff Naomi Bowers is his widow. Plaintiffs John Bowers and Charles Bowers, Sr. are his sons and plaintiff Charles Bowers, Jr., is his grandson; as of the fall of 1970, each of these three had occupied executive positions with Fibre-Metal for approximately 25 years. Up until that time Fibre-Metal had always been owned and operated by members of the Bowers family.

Defendant Columbia General Corporation, a Delaware corporation, ("CG") was organized in October of 1968 as a result of an amalgamation of two other enterprises. In the period between October 1968 and the present, CG has had serious acquisition discussions with approximately 25 business entities. These discussions resulted in 10 consummated acquisitions.

In the spring of 1970, Fibre-Metal and CG began merger discussions. After several months of negotiations, the acquisition of Fibre-Metal by CG was closed on October 29, 1970. For the purpose of effecting the acquisition, CG formed a wholly owned subsidiary, CGA, Inc., a Delaware corporation. Fibre-Metal was merged into CGA, Inc. whose name was contemporaneously changed to Fibre-Metal Products Company ("FM"). Immediately prior to the merger, CG transferred to CGA, Inc., as a contribution to capital, the capital stock and rights of CG necessary to consummate the merger. Upon the effective date of the merger, the capital stock in Fibre-Metal was converted into 200,000 shares of CG Common Stock, 200,000 shares of CG Series C Cumulative Convertible Preferred Stock, 7,000 shares of CG Series D Cumulative Preferred Stock,[1] and certain "participation units" evidenced by "Participation Certificates". In addition, the holders of the common stock of Fibre-Metal were given the right to receive up to 233,334 shares of CG Common Stock from an escrow agent in the event that the business of FM, measured by its "net income" as defined in the agreement, exceeded certain specified levels during fiscal 1971, 1972 and 1973. Under the participation certificates, additional shares of CG Common Stock are issuable in the event that the CG shares become issuable under the escrow agreement but have an aggregate market value of less than a specified amount.

Pursuant to the Plan and Agreement of Reorganization, Charles Bowers, Jr. was employed as the Chief Executive Officer of FM and Charles Bowers, Sr. and John W. Bowers were employed as consultants of FM, all for a period of five years. The Board of Directors, however, was

---

[1] The holders of Fibre-Metal's only class of preferred stock received solely Series D Cumulative Preferred Stock of CG.

to consist, and does consist, of four nominees of the former Fibre-Metal management and five nominees of CG management.

The complaint in this action sets forth seventeen claims. In connection with their application for preliminary relief, however, plaintiffs stress the five of these claims which they believe entitled them to rescission of the above-described transaction. In plaintiffs' First claim, it is alleged that the offer and sale of CG stock to plaintiffs violated Sections 5 and 12(1) of the Securities Act of 1933 in that no registration statement was in effect with respect to the CG stock issued to plaintiffs and no exemption from the Act's registration requirements was available.

* * *

III. THE PROBABILITY OF PLAINTIFFS' SUCCESS.

    A.   *Section 12(1) Recovery For A Section 5 Violation.*

    1.   *The Fibre-Metal Acquisition Considered As A Separate Offering.*

Section 12(1) of the Securities Act of 1933, 15 U.S.C.A. § 77l(1), states:

Any person who—

(1)   offers or sells a security in violation of section 77e of this title * * *

    shall be liable to the person purchasing such security from him, who may sue either at law or in equity in any court of competent jurisdiction, to recover the consideration paid for such security with interest thereon, less the amount of any income received thereon, upon the tender of such security, or for damages if he no longer owns the security.

Subsection 5(a) and (c) of the Securities Act of 1933, 15 U.S.C.A. § 77e, provide:

    (a)   Unless a registration statement is in effect as to a security, it shall be unlawful for any person, directly or indirectly—

    (1)   To make use of any means or instruments of transportation or communication in interstate commerce or of the mails to sell such security through the use or medium of any prospectus or otherwise; or (2) to carry or cause to be carried through the mails or in interstate commerce by any means or instruments of transportation, any such security for the purpose of sale or for delivery after sale.

* * *

    (c)   It shall be unlawful for any person, directly or indirectly, to make use of any means or instruments of transportation or communication in interstate commerce or of the mails to offer to sell or offer to buy through the use or medium of any prospectus or otherwise any security, unless a registration statement has been filed as to such security * * * .

Defendants CG and FM concede that there was no registration statement in effect as to any of the securities issued by CG in the Fibre-Metal acquisition and that interstate facilities were utilized in connection with this transaction. Defendants . . . contend, in the alternative, that the transaction came within the private offering exemption found in Section 4(2) of the Act.[17] 15 U.S.C. § 77d(2).

Turning to defendants' contention that the offering of the CG securities was not a public offering, I find that the following facts can fairly be inferred from the record:

1.   There were no offerees other than those who purchased and those who purchased did not purchase with a view to redistribution. The relevant class is, accordingly, limited to the actual purchasers. This group, consisting of four individuals and a testamentary trust,[19] were all closely related by family ties and by their common interest as the sole stockholders of Fibre-Metal.

2.   Those who negotiated the transaction on behalf of Fibre-Metal, Charles Bowers, Sr., John Bowers and Charles Bowers, Jr.,[20] each had at least 25 years experience in the active management of a business with a substantial manufacturing operation and a nationwide sales distribution.[21] As plaintiffs describe it, Fibre-Metal was "one of the oldest and most respected manufacturers and distributors of industrial safety supplies in the world." While the experience of these gentlemen was with a business enterprise somewhat different in character from portions of CG's operations, it did provide them with a background which enables them to understand the importance of and to analyze financial and other operating data. This is apparent not only from the successful history of the Fibre-Metal enterprise but also from affidavits submitted in this case which interpret financial and operating data of CG and its subsidiaries.

3.   Fibre-Metal and the Bowers were advised during the acquisition negotiations by a law firm and an accounting firm of acknowledged

---

[17]   Assuming that there has been a sale, it is clear that plaintiffs will be able to establish a prima facie case at trial and that the burden will be on the defendants to establish that the transaction came within the Section 4(2) exemption. Hill York Corp. v. American International Franchises, Inc., 448 F.2d 680 (5th Cir.1971). While this is a factor to be taken into consideration in determining the probability of plaintiffs' success, it does not relieve plaintiffs at this stage of the burden of establishing such a probability.

[19]   One of the purchasers was a testamentary trust established under the will of Frederick M. Bowers. Naomi T. Bowers, Charles Bowers, Sr. and Charles Bowers, Jr. are the trustees along with The Philadelphia National Bank.

[20]   Paul Scott, the chief financial officer of Fibre-Metal, also participated in the negotiations on behalf of Fibre-Metal.

[21]   Fibre-Metal, before the acquisition, had yearly sales of approximately $7,000,000.

expertise in their respective areas. While both disclaim that they gave any investment advice per se, the law firm advised with respect to the information which should be obtained from CG and the accounting firm was available to assist in the interpretation of that data.

4.   The Fibre-Metal management had the opportunity to, and did in fact, meet with the CG management on several occasions to discuss their respective businesses and the transaction. The Fibre-Metal management had the opportunity to, and did, make personal inspections of several of CG's physical facilities.

5.   The management of Fibre-Metal, both from the standpoint of personal contact with the top management of CG as well as from the standpoint of bargaining leverage, was in a position, as a practical matter, to insist upon access to relevant CG data.

6.   A substantial portion, though probably not all, of the information which a registration statement would have revealed was provided by CG to the Fibre-Metal management. Some of this information was solicited by the Fibre-Metal management and some was provided without a request. No request for information was denied.

7.   The transaction itself was a negotiated and relatively complex one. The terms thereof, both from the standpoint of the amount of consideration to be given for the acquired corporation and from the standpoint of the character of the securities to be issued, were tailored to this specific transaction and indicate some degree of business sophistication on the part of Fibre-Metal's management.

8.   The transaction was negotiated and consummated without utilizing the facilities of public securities distribution.

9.   Each of the stockholders of Fibre-Metal warranted at the time of the closing that he considered himself to be "a knowledgeable and sophisticated investor" and confirmed that "prior to the purchase of the subject securities he . . . [had] made an independent investigation of the business and financial condition of Columbia General Corporation".

Plaintiffs' case must be evaluated in this context. They rely primarily upon the disputed contention that they did not have knowledge of much of the information which would have been provided in a registration statement and the undisputed fact that those negotiating the transaction on behalf of Fibre-Metal had relatively little prior experience with the purchase and sale of securities. If established at trial, plaintiffs' actual knowledge and their lack of experience with similar transactions may well be relevant to the ultimate disposition of the issues raised. These factors do not, however, establish the probability of plaintiffs' success in the context of the current record.

The cases, the secondary authorities, and the legislative history indicate that the crucial issue here is whether the offerees had, or had access to, the information about the issuer and its business which would be disclosed by a registration statement. S.E.C. v. Ralston Purina Co., 346 U.S. 119, 73 S. Ct. 981, 97 L. Ed. 1494 (1953). . . . I believe plaintiffs probably did not have actual knowledge of all significant information which would have been revealed by a registration statement. Lack of actual knowledge, however, does not by itself preclude the application of the Section 4(2) exemption. If offerees have access to the relevant data as a matter of practical business reality, are reasonably equipped to deal with the information available to them, and choose not to take full advantage of their opportunity, I do not think that they are within the class which Congress sought to protect by enacting the Securities Act.

Plaintiffs insist that both "access" and "sophistication" on the part of the offerees must be established before the Section 4(2) exemption is available. I need not pass upon whether lack of sophistication is of crucial importance or upon the relative importance of these two factors. Plaintiffs' case on the "sophistication" point rests primarily upon the affidavits of the three Bowers who negotiated this transaction which explain that the experience of each with respect to the purchase and sale of securities has been limited to the purchase of a few blue chip securities listed on the New York Stock Exchange. Each affidavit further states, "I have never studied a prospectus, nor any other detailed financial or operational information for the purpose of considering an investment in a company." (Emphasis supplied) I do not think this is sufficient to establish a lack of sophistication on their part. If sophistication or lack thereof is relevant, the focus must be not so much upon prior experience with the purchase and sale of securities, but rather upon whether the offerees knew what to look for in, and how to interpret, the available information concerning the issuer's business and its profit potential. There are, of course, degrees of sophistication and the men who negotiated the transaction for Fibre-Metal may not be as sophisticated as some other business executives. The term must be given a realistic construction, however. Based upon the business background of these gentlemen it appears more likely than not that they will ultimately be found to possess the degree of sophistication required under the cases relied upon by the plaintiffs.

I do not hold that the facts recited in the nine numbered paragraphs above establish as a matter of law that the Section 4(2) exemption is applicable to this transaction. I conclude only that plaintiffs have failed to demonstrate a reasonable probability of ultimate success on this claim.

* * *

Conclusion

In short, having considered the relevant criteria, I conclude that plaintiffs have not demonstrated that they are entitled to preliminary relief.

Submit order.

___

QUESTIONS

1. Would the result be the same if there had been more distant family members involved in ownership of Fibre-Metal? What if there had been cousins and nieces and nephews who held small amounts of Fibre-Metal stock, and had little contact with Charles Bowers, Sr., Charles, Jr. and John Bowers?

2. Would the result be the same if Fibre-Metal were being acquired by a conglomerate corporation, engaged in a variety of manufacturing and marketing activities?

___

NOTE

Section 3(b) of the Securities Act authorizes the SEC to exempt offerings not exceeding $5 million from registration by rule-making. For a long time the only significant exemption under this authority was Regulation A, which presently exempts offerings up to $5 million. To secure this exemption the issuer must file a notification and offering circular with the appropriate regional office of the SEC, on Form 1-A. This document resembles a simplified registration statement. One of its principal attractions is that it does not require the issuer's financial statements to be audited and certified by independent public accountants. For some closely held acquirers that have not kept financial records that make audits possible, this may provide an attractive means of issuing relatively small amounts of securities where other exemptions are unavailable. The filings are reviewed by the regional staff during a waiting period, in much the same manner, although generally more rapidly, than a registration statement. The principal difficulty with this exemption is the $5 million limit.

In 2012 Congress passed the Jumpstart Our Business Startups (JOBS) Act to provide some regulatory relief for small businesses seeking capital. Part of it added § 3(b)(2) of the Securities Act to allow lower cost offering procedures for public offerings up to $50 million (Regulation A+). The SEC adopted authorizing regulations in 2015, which created two tiers: Tier 1 covers offerings up to $20 million, and Tier 2 covers offerings up to $50 million, each in a 12-month period. Disclosure requirements are more stringent for Tier 2 offerings, but the law preempts state laws for Tier 2 offerings, leaving smaller offerings with the burdens of compliance with state registration requirements.

In the late 1970's there was considerable dissatisfaction with the cumbersome nature of the exemptions from registration. The SEC conducted hearings on small business financing that led to the adoption of Regulation D, and Congressional adoption of Section 4(6), allowing offers and sales to "accredited investors", including financial institutions and affluent investors, defined in terms of annual income in excess of $200,000 or net worth exceeding $1 million, excluding personal residences. Regulation D provides a standardized set of disclosures resembling registration statement requirements for offerings over $1 million. The disclosure requirements increase in complexity with the size of the offering: up to $5 million, compliance with Regulation A's requirements is sufficient; beyond $5 million and up to $10 million, a small business issuer with revenues of less than $25 million can utilize a simplified registration form, Form SB-1 (a simplified small offering registration) is sufficient; thereafter, small business issuers raising more than $10 million can utilize Form SB-2. The extent of the financial statements depends upon the size of the issuer, and incorporates some of the same requirements as for registered public offerings.

Two of the exemptions under Regulation D are derived from the SEC's authority to exempt small offerings under Section 3(b) of the Act. Rule 504, covering offerings of $1 million or less, relies more or less completely on state law registration requirements for investor protection. Thus, if the offering is registered under a state law requiring registration, no special disclosure requirements are imposed by Rule 504. The only restriction is that the shares sold are deemed "restricted securities" of the type sold in a private offering under section 4(2). Under Rule 505, offerings up to $5 million are exempt, if sold to no more than 35 investors plus an unlimited number of "accredited investors." The disclosure requirements parallel those of Regulation A. The securities sold are also deemed to be restricted securities. In the ordinary business acquisition, few of the target's shareholders are likely to qualify as accredited investors, so that the 35 investor limit becomes the practical limitation.

Rule 506 of Regulation D was adopted under the authority of section 4(2), the private offering exemption, rather than the small offering exemption of section 3(b). Consequently, it imposes no dollar limits on the size of the offering. The disclosure requirements are those imposed by the registration statement forms that would be applicable, and the securities sold are deemed restricted securities. The securities may only be sold to 35 buyers, plus accredited investors. In addition, consistent with the requirements of the Ralston Purina case, all buyers must be able to fend for themselves, by being sufficiently experienced in business and financial affairs to be able to judge the risks and merits of the offering. Amendments to Amendments to Rules 502(c) and 506(c) now permit offerings to investors without concern over the manner of offering, provided that all the purchasers are accredited investors.

Persons who receive securities in a private offering cannot immediately resell these securities, for to allow them to do so would permit them to be conduits to the public markets for the issuer. Persons who take securities from an issuer with a view to distribution are "underwriters" under Section 2(a)(11) of the Securities Act. Normally selling shareholders are exempt from Section 5 registration requirements by virtue of Section 4(1), which exempts transaction by persons other than an "issuer, underwriter, or dealer." An issuer availing itself of the private offering exemption must take reasonable precautions to assure that the buyers are not underwriters. Typically issuers obtain so-called "investment letters" from buyers, in which the buyers represent that they are taking for investment and not for resale. To back up these representations, buyers are asked to consent to the placement of a legend on their stock certificates, which notifies any third party that might buy from them that the shares are not transferable unless certain conditions are met. Typically these legends will permit transfer only when a registration statement is in effect, or the issuer's counsel is satisfied that an exemption is available to the selling shareholder—in short—that the selling shareholder has held the securities for a sufficiently long time to dispel any inference that the shareholder bought with a view to distribution. Where the issuer's shares are not publicly traded, various practitioners will require a holding period of from two to five years.* Where the issuer is registered under the Securities and Exchange Act and files periodic reports, Securities Act Rule 144 permits persons taking "restricted securities" in private offering transactions to resell after a six-month holding period, but only if the issuer is a reporting company under the 1934 Act.

Additional complications may develop where relatively large amounts of securities are issued by the acquiring company to a single shareholder of the seller. This person may become a person deemed to be in "control" of the buyer, in which case this shareholder's sales will be treated as virtually identical to sales by the issuer for purposes of registration and the availability of exemptions.

The final area of difficulty involves unregistered sales by corporate insiders. Section 2(a)(11) defines "underwriter," which is a group excluded from the use of the section 4(1) exemption for resales. While the definition of underwriter is a person "who has purchased from an issuer with a view to [distribution], or offers or sells for an issuer in connection with, the distribution of any security . . . ", the problem is complicated by a peculiar definition of issuer, which includes "any person directly or indirectly controlling or controlled by the issuer, or any person under direct or indirect common control with the issuer." This group of persons are also called "affiliates" of the issuer under Securities Act Rule 405. Thus controlling shareholders, directors and executive officers are generally classified as "affiliates," and one reselling their securities into the public markets may be treated as an underwriter. In these cases, registration may be required, unless an exemption is found. Rule 144, briefly described above, is one such exemption.

----

* A selling shareholder who has not met the holding period requirements can sometimes satisfy the requirements of section 4(1) by assuring that the shareholder's resale will not result in a distribution for the issuer; in short, that had the second buyer been an original buyer from the issuer, her presence would not have destroyed the issuer's section 4(2) exemption. For the selling shareholder, practitioners sometimes refer to this as the "§ 4(1–1/2) exemption". In 2015 this exemption was codified and to some extent clarified in Securities Act § 4(a)(7) and 4(d).

4. RULE 145 AND REGISTRATION RIGHTS OF CONTROL PERSONS

Securities Act, § 4(1); Securities Act Rule 145.

The SEC's position on whether a corporate merger involved an offer or sale subject to the registration requirements of the Securities Act of 1933 has been inconsistent. For many years, under former Securities Act Rule 133, the SEC took the position that a merger in which target shareholders received the bidder's securities did not involve "offers" or "sales" to the target shareholders that required registration. The rationale was that individual shareholders did not make decisions to buy the acquiring firm's securities in the merger. The decision was made through "corporate action," which, under state law, required approval of both the board of directors of the target and a specified majority of its voting Stockholders. At the same time the SEC took the position that a "sale" was involved for purposes of Rule 10b–5. A further breakdown in the "no sale" theory developed when mergers began to be used in attempts to "launder" securities of restrictions imposed by virtue of their original issuance in a private offering under § 4(2) of the '33 Act, so that recipients of securities in the reorganized corporation could claim that they had not taken "restricted securities" in a private offering, but free-trading securities in a corporate reorganization. Because it was controlling shareholders of companies who utilized this means of creating free-trading securities, the SEC developed the doctrine that control shareholders of a constituent corporation were deemed to be underwriters in the surviving corporation, thus forcing them to avoid public resales in order to avail themselves of the exemption for "transactions by any person other than an issuer, underwriter or dealer" in section 4(1) of the Securities Act . . . "

In 1972 the SEC reversed its position on mergers, and held that a merger in which shareholders of constituent corporation received securities of the surviving corporation involved a "sale." Rule 145 codified this position, and old Rule 133 was repealed. Thus, if no exemption were available for the sale, registration was required. Selling shareholders in a merger that has been registered will be able to utilize the § 4(1) exemption for transactions by persons other than an issuer, underwriter or dealer for resales, unless one of the companies is a shell corporation.

5. STATE REGULATION

State securities laws generally bear a strong resemblance in their structure to the Securities Act of 1933, requiring registration of offers and sales unless an exemption from registration is available. This is hardly surprising, since they predated federal law, and to some extent served as the model for the Securities Act of 1933. Many states base their statutes on the Uniform Securities Act. That Act provides exemptions from registration for securities listed on certain stock exchanges (or in some jurisdictions on the National Association of Securities Dealers Automated Quotation system (NASDAQ)), for limited offerings, involving sales to no more than 25 (or fewer in some jurisdictions) persons. Most states also have a version of the Uniform Limited Offering Exemption, which coordinates with Regulation D under Federal law, and permits persons relying on it to file the same Form D as they file with the SEC.

Section 18 of the Securities Act of 1933 preempts the registration requirements of state law for offerings registered with the SEC, or for securities of issuers registered under the Securities Exchange Act. "Covered securities" under Section 18 are defined as those that either are, or will be at the close of the offering, listed or authorized for listing on the New York Stock Exchange, the American Stock Exchange, or the NASDAQ National Market system, or are securities equal in seniority or senior to those so listed or authorized. In addition, the act preempts state regulation of certain offerings that are exempt from federal registration. This covers offerings exempt under section 3(a) (except for intrastate offerings exempt under § 3(a)(11)), subsections (1) and (3) of section 4, with respect to issuers that are reporting companies under the Securities Exchange Act of 1934, subsection (4) of section 4, and under SEC rules issued under section 4(2) (of which Rule 506 is currently the only example).

6. SHORT SWING PROFITS

Section 16(b) of the Securities Exchange Act provides that any profits earned by an insider described in § 16(a) (officers, directors, and 10% shareholders) from any purchase and sale within six months of each other belong to the company, and may be recovered for the company in a derivative suit. These provisions represent a trap for the unwary, and most litigation involves either fringe transactions or transactions where the insider has options or other rights that must be exercised to take advantage of their benefits. The rule has been strictly enforced to provide the maximum incentive to avoid short-swing trading. For example, courts will determine profits by matching the highest sale price and the lowest purchase price during any six months, then the next highest sale price and lowest purchase, etc. It does not matter that the net effect of a series of purchases and sales involves no net profit to the insider, as long as some transactions can be matched to produce a profit. Smolowe v. Delendo Corp., 136 F.2d 231 (2d Cir.1943).

While the act expressly covers officers, directors and 10% shareholders, it has been interpreted more broadly to preclude possible evasion. Thus, the courts have indicated that a brokerage partnership could be deemed an insider where one partner is deputized by the partnership to serve as its representative on a corporate board. Cf., Blau v. Lehman, 368 U.S. 403 (1962). Even resignation from the board will not exempt a sale that follows within 6 months a purchase made while a person was a director. Feder v. Martin Marietta Corp., 406 F.2d 260 (2d Cir.1969) The SEC has ruled that shares owned by a spouse or minor children of a statutory insider are also covered by these rules. Exchange Act Release No. 175; see also Whiting v. Dow Chemical Co., 523 F.2d 680 (2d Cir.1975). On the other hand, where one is a 10% shareholder, § 16(b) provides that it "shall not be construed to cover any transaction where such beneficial owner was not such both at the time of the purchase and sale, or the sale and purchase. . . ." This has been interpreted to mean that a 10% shareholder can sell off shares until he or she has reduced holdings to less than 10% (accounting for profits on those sales) without any obligation to account for profits on additional sales. Reliance Electric Co. v. Emerson Electric Co., 404 U.S. 418 (1972). Similarly, the purchase that pushes one over the 10% limit is not a purchase subject to the statute. Foremost-McKesson, Inc. v. Provident Securities Co., 423 U.S. 232 (1976).

Since the adoption of Rule 145 it has been settled law that a merger involves the offer and sale of securities of the surviving corporation, if it issues securities as consideration in the merger, and, reciprocally, the sale by shareholders of the acquired corporation of their shares. Beginning with Kern County Land Co. v. Occidental Petroleum Corp., 411 U.S. 582 (1973), the Supreme Court has taken a "pragmatic" approach to the definition of a purchase and sale in the context of § 16(b), noting that " . . . the courts have come to inquire whether the transaction may serve as a vehicle for the evil which Congress sought to prevent— the realization of short-swing profits based upon access to inside information. . . ." 411 U.S. at 594–95. Thus, where a 10% shareholder which obtained that position through a hostile tender offer became a forced seller in the target's merger with a white knight corporation, no dangers of trading on inside information were deemed to be present. The courts have also held that execution of a letter of intent and definitive merger agreement do not constitute a sale of the target's shares, where the hostile bidder consented to the target's merger with a white knight, because there were sufficient conditions precedent to a closing that a sale was not a certainty. The SEC has exempted securities disposed of in short-form mergers with a parent owning 85% or more of its shares from the short-swing trading rules in Rule 16b–7.

Options present some of the most difficult problems in determining whether § 16(b) applies. Lock-up options may be obtained by bidders that ultimately fail to acquire control of the target corporation. Before the bidder can profit from the option, it must exercise the option, unless the option contains protection against destruction or dilution through merger, which most options will contain. Many decisions hold that the acquisition of an option to purchase more than 10% of the stock of a corporation does not constitute the purchase of 10% of the common stock. Colan v. Monumental Corp., 713 F.2d 330 (7th Cir.1983); Colan v.

Continental Telecom, 616 F.Supp. 1521 (S.D.N.Y.1985). But if the optionee makes such a large option payment that exercise seems likely, the courts have held that an option is equivalent to a purchase. Bershad v. McDonough, 428 F.2d 693 (7th Cir.1970) (option payment equal to 14% of total exercise price). See also Newmark v. RKO General, Inc., 425 F.2d 348 (2d Cir.1970) (option held to be a purchase where there was an opportunity to profit on unrevealed information).

Executives holding options on stock that must be exercised or canceled at the time of a merger face complex rules governing these transactions, set out in Rule 16b–3, and SEC interpretations of these rules. One way an officer or director can use this exemption is to sell target securities back to the target as part of the merger transaction, if approved by the target's board of directors or a committee of "non-employee directors" or the target's stockholders. The SEC initially took the position that this required provisions for the purchase of insider securities to be included in the merger agreement. This meant that the exemption was only available for cash mergers, since it would be difficult for the acquiring corporation's securities to come from the target. A 1999 SEC staff "no-action" letter has relaxed these restrictions to permit sale of insiders' securities directly to the acquiring corporation. Skadden, Arps, Meagher & Flom LLP (Jan. 12, 1999).

7. INVESTMENT COMPANY ACT ISSUES

A company selling its assets for stock of the acquiring corporation may find itself subject to the provisions of the Investment Company Act of 1940, 15 U.S.C. § 80a–1 et seq. Since this act requires registration of investment companies with the SEC, and observance of certain rules designed to prevent certain kinds of conflicts of interest, it is important that a transaction be analyzed in advance to determine whether registration will be required, or whether the transaction can be structured to avoid the coverage of the Act. Section 3(a)(3) defines an investment company as any issuer which "is engaged or proposes to engage in the business of investing, reinvesting, owning, holding, or trading in securities, and owns or proposes to acquire investment securities having a value exceeding 40 per centum of the value of such issuer's total assets (exclusive of Government securities and cash items) on an unconsolidated basis." Thus if the seller receives notes of the buying corporation that are treated as securities, or if the seller receives stock in the buyer, it could become an inadvertent investment company. Rule 3a–2, 17 C.F.R. § 270.3a–2, provides an escape for many selling corporations, by providing that a company will not be deemed an investment company for a period of one year, provided that it has a bona fide intent to be engaged primarily in a business other than being an investment company. Similarly, Rule 3a–1 provides that a company will not be deemed to be an investment company if no more than 45% of its total assets consist of securities and no more than 45% of its total income for the past four quarters is derived from securities. These rules mean that a company may hold substantial securities for a brief time without being subject to registration, but a company should plan either on reinvesting the proceeds in a going business or in distributing them to its stockholders. Reinvestment, of course, requires a sale of the securities, which may be difficult if they were received in a transaction not involving a public offering, or in a Regulation D transaction. Similarly, distribution to shareholders may create problems with restricted securities.

CHAPTER ELEVEN

THE WILLIAMS ACT

1. FEDERAL DISCLOSURE REGULATION

The Federal securities laws provide a variety of regulations that cover the process of gaining control of a company. If a bidder decides to offer an exchange of its securities for the shares of the target company, that constitutes an offer and sale of its securities that will be subject to the disclosure requirements of the Securities Act of 1933, as discussed in Chapter Ten. Similarly, if the bidder proposes a merger that involves a similar exchange of its securities for the stock of the target, disclosure requirements will apply. Absent an exemption, this process, required by Section 5 of the Securities Act of 1933, involves preparing a registration statement, the major part of which is a prospectus, disclosing all material facts the SEC believes investors should know about the company before buying its securities. The issuer can make a public announcement of its offer, if filed with the SEC, before filing the registration statement that must be filed with the SEC. Only after review by the SEC staff is completed and the registration statement has been amended and distributed to target shareholders may the bidder actually sell its securities, or, in the case of the merger, allow target shareholders to vote on the transaction. This process may be a lengthy one, taking several months. The legal rules governing this area are briefly described in Chapter Ten, Part 2.

Another way of gaining control of a corporation is through a proxy fight, in which a dissident shareholder seeks proxies from other shareholders to authorize election of the dissident's slate to the board of directors. Because proxy fights generally involve one shareholder group that seeks to displace management, these materials will not provide a detailed examination of the proxy rules. For a discussion of why proxy fights are not generally employed as a means to change management, see Henry Manne, Mergers and the Market for Corporate Control, in Chapter One, Part 2, *supra*. But the proxy rules do play a role in mergers and acquisitions, and should be described at least briefly here. The Securities Exchange Act of 1934 contains two sections dealing directly with requirements about providing information to shareholders. Section 13 authorizes the SEC to require registered companies (those with more than 500 shareholders) to provide periodic reports to investors. Regulations under Section 13 now require annual reports, with audited financials, on Form 10-K; quarterly income statements, unaudited but with "Management's Discussion and Analysis" of the results of operations on Form 10-Q, and reports upon the occurrence of specified major events, on Form 8-K.

Section 14 regulates the solicitation of proxies from shareholders. Section 14(a) prohibits the solicitation of proxies except in compliance with SEC rules. Rule 14a–3 provides that no proxies may be solicited unless accompanied or preceded by a "proxy statement" in the form specified in Schedule 14A (or a Securities Act registration statement for a merger vote). The proxy statement must either contain an offer to furnish each shareholder without charge a copy of the company's annual report to the SEC on Form 10-K, or be accompanied or preceded by an annual report containing financial statements and other specified information. Preliminary proxy materials must be submitted to the SEC for review at least ten days before delivery to stockholders, under Rule 14a–6. Rule 14a–2 contains a series of exemptions from these proxy rules. One of the most important exemptions is in Rule 14a–2(b)(1), which exempts from most of the proxy rules any solicitation by or on behalf of any person who does not (at any time during the solicitation) seek the power to act as a proxy for a security holder, or request a form of revocation of a proxy. This exemption excludes the subject company, its officers, directors, nominees for directors, affiliates, and anyone opposing a merger or other business combination who proposes or intends to propose an alternative transaction, plus some others. Thus it permits expression of opinion by shareholders, and recommendations, but not effective solicitations of shareholder action. Rule 14a–2(b)(2) exempts "any solicitation made otherwise than on behalf of the registrant where the total number of persons solicited is not more than ten," This is intended to allow large investors, typically institutions, to carry on discussions about replacing management or instituting other reforms through shareholder votes without the delay and expense of a filing with the SEC (and without notice to corporate management).

The restrictions on the types of persons who can use the Rule 14a–2(b)(1) exemption were largely relaxed with the adoption in 1999 of Rule 14a–12, which permits solicitations "before furnishing security holders with a proxy statement" if the definitive proxy statement is sent before or at the same time as the forms of proxy or consent are sent to shareholders. The soliciting material must be filed with the SEC, which is consistent with the requirements of Rule 165 that communications before filing a registration statement for a merger must be filed with the SEC. The effect is that a proxy campaign in support of or in opposition to a merger can begin with the first announcement of a merger or other transaction requiring shareholder approval.

There is an interesting intersection between proxy regulation and discussions of takeover bids that will be exposed in the materials that follow.

The material in Parts 3.A and 3.B of this Chapter focuses primarily on the process of bidding for shares for cash, which is the subject of the Williams Act amendments to the Securities Exchange Act described in

Part 2. The inquiry in these sections necessarily concerns why sellers should care about buyer's disclosures. If the offer is all cash, and is for all shares of the target, selling shareholders will have no particular need to know about the sources of the cash or the quality of the buyer's management after the takeover is completed. Selling shareholders will no longer have any economic interest in the target, and all the risks of owning and operating the target will be borne by the buyer and its shareholders. If the offer is a cash tender offer and the bidder explains that acceptance of the shares is contingent upon completion of financing arrangements, debt financing is typically obtained from commercial banks and other financial institutions such as insurance companies, which would, after investigation and negotiations, issue a binding commitment letter indicating the terms upon which they would be willing to finance an acquisition, in exchange for a commitment fee. Since this commitment fee might be ½ of 1% of the entire purchase price, many bidders declined to pay the commitment fee until they knew whether the tender offer was likely to succeed. For an example of an agreement dealing with this issue see the Merger Agreement in Appendix D, Article 5.13. The obtaining of financing for the deal is not a condition of the buyer's obligation - sometimes called a "come Hell or high water" clause. Even if the commitment fee were paid and the commitment letter issued, lenders frequently hedged their obligations sufficiently to add to uncertainty about financing.

The risk that the bidder might not secure financing is a relatively short term one, given the withdrawal rights granted to tendering shareholders by the Williams Act. The financial risk is generally limited to the bid's premium over the pre-bid market price, since tendering shareholders will receive their shares back if the bid fails for want of financing.

Target shareholders face greater risk if the bid is a partial, or two-tier bid. In these cases, as in Grace Bros. v. Farley Industries, Inc., *supra* Chapter Nine, part 3.E, the bidder may lack funds to complete the acquisition, or may decide not to acquire 100%, because it has learned that it overpaid, and finds further ownership unattractive. Thus, when Farley Industries succeeded in obtaining 95% of the shares of West Point-Pepperell, Inc., Farley was unable to obtain funds to acquire the remaining 5%, due to the collapse of the junk bond market in the wake of the bankruptcy of Drexel Burnham Lambert in 1989. As a result, minority shareholders remained in West Point-Pepperell for over two years after the takeover. In these cases target shareholders may have an interest in learning about the bidder's management and financing. But will the information do them any good? Remember that despite the fact that they did not tender, the bidder has gained control. Indeed, disclosures about the bidder may have a perverse effect: if target shareholders believe the bidder's management team is inferior, but that the tender offer price is high enough to give it a good chance of success, target shareholders may prefer to bail out rather than be subject to the risks of the bidder's management skills, or its later ability to secure financing for the takeout.

When the bidder's acquisition is to be financed by the sellers through the exchange of the bidder's securities, perhaps in the second stage takeout merger, then, of course, sellers have a much clearer interest in the buyer's existing businesses, management skills, and financial condition. As discussed in Chapter Ten, the bidder will be treated as offering its securities for sale, will be subject to the registration requirements of the Securities Act of 1933, and will be required to file a registration statement on Form S-4, which, among other things, will contain "pro forma" financial statements showing what the combined companies would have looked like had they been combined for recent financial reporting periods. Where the bidder's securities are already traded, information about their value, and about the bidder will be readily available. Indeed, the effect of the proposed acquisition on the value of the bidder's common stock should be reflected promptly in the stock price, if the securities are traded in efficient markets.* The only qualification is that the stock price of the bidder will be adjusted for the chances of success of the bid, so the price will not necessarily reflect 100% of the expected change in value of the bidder's stock. Recall that Securities Act Rule 165 allows a bidder to announce the terms of its offer before filing a registration statement and to continue making such communications until filing a registration statement, at which time the preliminary prospectus becomes the offering document. This is an attempt to level the playing field between cash tender offers on the one hand and exchange offers and stock mergers on the other.

If the bidder proposes to issue new classes of securities that have not been previously traded and for which no market price exists, valuing them becomes more complex. The securities may be "bundled," i.e., each target shareholder may receive a package of bidder securities, which might include some debt securities, some preferred stock, and perhaps even options on the bidder's common stock. Finally, in some cases the precise terms governing these securities may not be fully revealed (or even determined) at the time of a cash tender offer. Opinions about the value of these securities may vary, and the bidder will find that such an exchange offer is less clear-cut, and therefore less attractive, than an all-cash offer.

Where a bidder proposes to issue its own preferred or debt securities as part of the consideration in a takeover, the amount of new leverage

---

* Sometimes markets, even for large companies can become inefficient when deals have complexities. The stock of Gilead Science, Inc. fell substantially when it announced its acquisition of a small biotech with its only drug still in FDA clinical trials, for $11 billion. Apparently most traders thought Gilead was overpaying. Within two years the drug turned out to be a blockbuster, with its annual sales exceeding the purchase price. Gilead's stock more than doubled in that period.

introduced into the bidder's capital structure may have an adverse effect on its credit-worthiness, thus reducing the ratings these securities receive from independent rating services, depressing their market price, which results in higher interest costs for the bidder. It is often difficult to predict in advance how much prices of the bidder's securities will be depressed by these factors, and thus difficult to value its new securities. In the late 1980s new solutions to this information problem were devised. Bidders began to offer debt securities with "reset" provisions. With a reset bond, the interest rate was initially set at a rate calculated to have bonds trade at par. Periodically the bond indenture called for the interest rates to be increased if the bonds were not trading at par at certain measuring dates, and the increase was required to be large enough to cause the bonds to trade at par. In effect, the bonds carried a variable interest rate. Unlike other variable rate instruments, the interest rate increases would reflect not only general interest rate increases in the financial markets, but also any increased risk associated with holding these bonds. None of this, of course, protects against the ultimate risk of issuer bankruptcy.

2. OVERVIEW OF THE WILLIAMS ACT

Securities Exchange Act, Sections 13(d) and (e) and 14(d), (e) and (f).

Initially, before the adoption of the Williams Act in 1968, one of the principal advantages of a tender offer from the bidder's perspective was the speed with which the tender offer could be accomplished. It was epitomized by the so-called "Saturday night special"—a tender offer announced without warning, on a first-come, first-served basis. In this offer a bidder offered a premium over the market for sufficient shares to constitute control, and announced that those tendered first would be accepted, and all others rejected. Little time was available for target management to shop for a better offer, or to advise their shareholders on whether to accept or reject the offer. Since the bidder was typically not an insider in the target firm, no insider trading rules required any particular disclosures by the bidder, and the bid could be made without any disclosure other than the offering price and the identification of a location to which shares should be tendered. The Williams Act amendments to the Securities and Exchange Act changed these rules in several important respects. First, they require the bidder to provide substantial disclosures about the source of its funds, the background of the bidder, its plans and proposals for the target should it succeed in gaining control, and other information. Second, they require that bids be left open for certain minimum periods of time (now 20 days under Rule 14e–1), that shareholders be given the right to withdraw their shares at certain times at the beginning and end of a bid (now expanded by Rule 14d–7 to cover the entire bid period), and that if a bid is oversubscribed, the bidder must take pro rata from all tendering shareholders. These rules have the effect of providing basic information about the bid, providing target management with time to seek other bids and alternative courses of action, and to communicate with target shareholders. Third, they require that whenever a bidder increases its tender offer price it must pay the increased amount to any shareholder who has previously tendered. These rules reduce the pressure to tender early, and give target shareholders time to await developments. They also force bidders to reveal valuable information or insights about how to create more stockholder value, which can be utilized both by competing bidders and target management. In the hands of management resistant to a takeover, these regulations are powerful weapons to defeat or at least delay a hostile bid.

The Williams Act added subsections (d) and (e) to § 13 and sections (d) and (e) to § 14 of the Securities Exchange Act in 1968.* Section 13(d), as originally enacted, required the filing of a disclosure report with the SEC whenever any person or group of affiliated persons acquired more than 10% of a class of equity security of a company registered under the Securities Exchange Act. The 10% threshold was also used in section 16(a) of the Act as the threshold at which statutory insiders must file reports on their trading activity in a company's stock. In 1970 section 13(d) was amended to reduce the threshold to 5%. Section 13(d) requires one reaching the 5% threshold to file Schedule 13D within 10 days after acquiring the securities. The disclosures required by statute, which are elaborated in Schedule 13D, discussed in Part 3.A.v of this Chapter, call for identification of the buyers, their sources and amount of funds, their plans or proposals for the company if they intend to gain control, the number of shares owned, and information about any contracts entered into with respect to the securities.**

Section 13(e) is an antifraud statute with respect to issuer repurchases of securities. The authority given the SEC to engage in rule-making has been used to require issuers proposing to engage in repurchases during a third party's tender offer to file a disclosure document with the Commission (Rule 13e–1), and to require issuers engaging in self-tender offers to file disclosures on Schedule 13E-4. In

---

*   Subsection (f), which requires institutional investors to report their stock holdings, was added to section 13 in 1975, P.L. 94–29; while subsections (g) and (h), which require additional reports from 5% owners and reporting of large trades, were added in 1977. P.L. 95–213. Section 13(g) provides a short form of report for certain 5% purchasers, primarily financial institutions purchasing for investment rather than to effect control changes in the issuer. In most cases these filings must be made only after the close of a calendar year in which the investor still owns 5%, although filings must be made more promptly if such an investor acquires more than 10%.

**   Section 13(d)(6) provides an exemption for acquisitions made pursuant to a registration statement, which would presumably involve an exchange offer, and for acquisitions of beneficial ownership which, together with all other acquisitions by the person within the preceding 12 months do not exceed 2% of the class. Note that this exemption from the obligation to file Schedule 13D will not affect the obligation to file under section 13(g), described in the preceding footnote.

addition, the Commission requires separate disclosures when an issuer takes corporate action to "go private," under Rule 13e–3.

Section 14(d), governing tender offers, was added to the section governing proxy solicitations. Any person beginning a tender offer (which is not defined in the Act) which would result in the bidder becoming the beneficial owner of 5% or more of a class of equity securities of a company registered under the Exchange Act must file disclosures similar to those required by section 13(d), on Schedule TO (formerly Schedule 14D). Section 14(d) provides for some substantive regulation of the form of any tender offer. Under section 14(d)(5) bidders must permit tendering shareholders to withdraw their shares during the first seven days of the bid, and after 60 days from the beginning of the bid. The SEC has expanded the withdrawal rights to the entire period of the bid under Rule 14d–7. Whenever a bidder makes a partial tender offer—for less than all outstanding securities of the class, and the bid is oversubscribed, section 14(d)(6) requires that all shares tendered during the first ten days must be taken pro rata. Rule 14d–8 extends the pro rata requirement to all shares tendered during the tender offer period. Section 14(d)(7) provides that whenever the terms of a tender offer are improved, the improved consideration must also be paid to those who have already tendered their shares.

Section 14(e) is an antifraud provision. The Commission has used its authority to regulate the timing of offers—requiring all bids to remain open at least twenty business days, and requiring any changes in the terms of a bid to remain in effect for at least ten business days (Rule 14e–1). Rule 14e–2 mandates that target management must disclose to shareholders whether and why it recommends acceptance or rejection of the bid or remains neutral, as the case may be, while Rule 14e–3 is the so-called "insider trading" rule, that prohibits trading on nonpublic information about a forthcoming tender offer. Rule 143–4 prohibits "short tendering" of shares not currently owned by the tendering person, in order to obtain a greater proportion of shares than pro rata rules would otherwise provide, while Rule 14e–5 prohibits a bidder from acquiring shares outside the tender offer.

Section 14(f) is designed to secure disclosures about potential board members when the bidder proposes to elect its own nominees after gaining control without a proxy solicitation.

Toward a More Perfect Market
for Corporate Control

William J. Carney.
9 Del. J. Corp. L. 593, 597–601 (1984).

A. *The Dubious Benefits of Disclosures*

Under the Williams Act, a bidder must make rather full disclosures about its own background, sources of financing for the bid, and plans if the takeover is successful.[12] The results of this disclosure can be perverse, in terms of getting the most efficient management team in control of the target. If no takeouts were possible, for example, shareholders who believed that the bidder would do a better job of managing the target would be tempted to hold on to their shares, since they would expect the post-acquisition value of their stock to be higher than the bid price.[14] This makes perfect sense, since they would not expect the bidder to pay a premium price in the tender offer unless the bidder thought the shares would be worth more later on. Target shareholders would be tempted to free ride on the bidder's efforts.[15] The very act of retaining their shares would defeat the bid, if all shareholders acted in this manner.

B's Strategies:

A's Strategies:	Tender	Don't Tender
Tender	$35 for A	$35 for A
	$35 for B	$40 for B
Don't Tender	$40 for A	$30 for A
	$35 for B	$30 for B

On the other hand, if target company shareholders believe the bidder would be an inferior manager from the Williams Act disclosures, they would expect the success of the bid to mean the value of target shares not

---

[12] Section 14(d) requires a tender offeror to file Schedule 13D, 17 C.F.R. § 240.13d–101, as modified by SEC regulations, at the time a tender offer begins. Schedule 14D–1, 17 C.F.R. § 240.14d–101 (1984), Item 4, requires the bidder to disclose any plans or proposals which the bidder has which relate to such activities as mergers, reorganizations, liquidations, asset sales, management changes and other material changes involving the target.

[14] See Grossman & Hart, Takeover Bids, the Free-Rider Problem, and the Theory of the Corporation, 11 Bell J. Econ. & Mgmt. Sci. 42 (1980).

[15] The outcome of this situation is indeterminate. The problem can be illustrated with a game theory matrix using a two-person game. Assume a stock currently trading at $30 per share, with a tender offer at $35 for any or all of the shares of the firm, with an expected post-bid value of $40 for the firm's shares, because of the expectation of improved management. We can diagram the outcomes available for shareholders A and B as follows:

Each shareholder's choices may lead collectively to a suboptimal result, where no one tenders. Thus, for A, if B tenders A will receive more by not tendering. Thus, if all shareholders share a belief in the bidder's superior management abilities, none will tender. If, on the other hand, A believes B will not tender, he can maximize his own position by tendering.

tendered would be lower. They could avoid this by tendering to the inefficient bidder. Thus a disclosure that demonstrated the inferiority of the bidder as a manager could lead to the success of the bid, if enough shareholders believed the bid might be successful.[16] That is also a perverse result.

B's Strategies:

A's Strategies:	Tender	Don't Tender
Tender	$35 for A $35 for B	$35 for A $25 for B
Don't Tender	$25 for A $35 for B	$30 for A $30 for B

In the real world, of course, we do not have this problem. Bidders do their best to make all of the Williams Act disclosures irrelevant by threatening a takeout merger at a price below the cash tender offer price. The effect of the two-tier bid is to persuade shareholders to tender now rather than run the risk of getting the lower takeout price.[18] The bidder tells target shareholders in advance of the prices at which shares will be purchased in the takeout. By doing this the bidder assumes all of the risk of management of the target.[19] Target company shareholders then have no interest in information about the quality of the various management teams. Two-tier bids thus cure all of the incentive problems that the

---

[16] Given a pre-bid market price of $30, a tender offer at $35 for any or all of the shares of the firm, and an expected post-bid market price of $25, because of expected inferior management (which might take the form of looting the target corporation for the benefit of a parent), the situation would be as follows:

> Thus, if A assumes B will tender, A will prefer to tender, while if A assumes B will not tender, A will also prefer to tender. Since B faces the same situation, the success of the bid is guaranteed. This perverse result was recognized in the perspicacious opinion of Judge Tjoflat in Liberty Nat'l Ins. Holding Co. v. Charter Co., 734 F.2d 545, 569 n. 47 (11th Cir.1984), which concluded: "Therefore, non-tendering shareholders will be damaged by control moving to, or staying in, those hands less likely to increase the value of the firm. This is a curious result for a piece of legislation that is intended to help shareholders."

[18] This is the coercion imposed by a non-communication game, the "prisoner's dilemma." See, e.g., Carney, Shareholder Coordination Costs, Shark Repellents, and Takeout Mergers: The Case Against Fiduciary Duties, 1983 Am. Bar Found. Res. J. 341, 349 n.39 [hereinafter cited as Carney]. The problems of a target company shareholder are illustrated id. at 351–52 n.47. Two-tier bids are coercive only if the second stage, the takeout merger, carries with it a price below the current market price. The OCE study, *supra* note 17, indicates that the average takeout premium over the pre-bid market price is 47.1%. Release No. 21,079, *supra* note 17, at 86,916 n.7. Further, "shark repellent" amendments that impose supermajority requirements for shareholder votes on takeout mergers, or impose "fair price" conditions on such mergers protect target shareholders against this form of coercion. Carney, *supra*. Thus the only coercion generally appears to be that target shareholders will miss out on the first stage of the bid, which carries an average first-tier premium of 63.5%. *Id.*

[19] While a two-tier bid may be "coercive" in one sense, it shifts to the bidder, as sole owner of the firm after a successful takeover all risks associated with the future performance of the target firm.

Williams Act disclosures might create. Takeover defenses that assure everyone of the same price, whether they tender or await the cash-out merger, restore a form of free rider problem, by relaxing the incentives to tender.

B. *Equal Treatment Under the Williams Act*

The other major goal of the Williams Act is to protect investors from missing out on the best offer. They can miss out in any market if they don't respond promptly before offers are withdrawn. But we regulate tender offers and leave other markets alone, for reasons that are not obvious. The method used to protect target shareholders is to create incentives not to sell or to tender. In doing so the rules again alter investor incentives in a perverse manner.

Market traders are persuaded to hold out once a bidder acquires five percent of a target's shares and files its schedule 13D. They will now wait for the expected tender offer at a premium, which raises the bidder's costs.[23] Next, the SEC has done its best to make sure that once a bid has begun, everyone gets the same amount. Bidders are forbidden by the statute to make a "first-come, first-served" offer, with its incentives to respond quickly. Instead, shareholders who tender within a fixed period of time can all participate in the proration pool.[24] This creates an incentive to hold out until the last day to see if something better comes along. The SEC has extended the tender offer period from the statutory minimum of seven to ten days to twenty days, apparently on the theory that anything less is fraudulent and manipulative.[25] Under Rule 14d–8, the proration pool for a partial bid is extended for the entire period of the tender offer.[26]

---

[23] Since the schedule 13D requires disclosure of a bidder's plans and proposals with respect to a target, it necessarily discloses valuable new information that will have an impact on the target's stock prices. This, in turn, may raise the reservation price of existing shareholders, force the bidder to share the results of its research with them, and dissipate the profits for the bidder that otherwise would be generated by its research. Economic Effects, *supra* note 10.

[24] Exchange Act, § 14(d)(6), 15 U.S.C. § 78n(d)(6) requires the bidder to prorate all shares tendered within the first ten days of a tender offer. But see Rule 14d–8, *infra* note 26.

[25] The Williams Act did not specify a minimum offering period, but periods of seven days for "any or all" bids and 10 days for partial bids were implicit in the requirements that target shareholders be given withdrawal rights for seven days and proration rights for 10 days under § 14(d)(5) and (6), respectively. The minimum 20 day offering period only appeared explicitly in Exchange Act Rule 14e–1, 17 C.F.R. § 240.14e–1 (1984). Since this rule was adopted under the authority of the antifraud provisions of Section 14(e) of the Exchange Act, the SEC must have concluded that short two-tier bids were inherently fraudulent. C.f., SEC Exchange Act Release No. 16384, Special Bulletin No. 835, Part II, FED. SEC. L. REP. (CCH), 60–64 (Nov. 29, 1979). But see Radol v. Thomas, 534 F.Supp. 1302 (S.D.Ohio 1982).

[26] Exchange Act Rule 14d–8, 17 C.F.R. § 240.14d–8 (1984).

3. BUYERS' OBLIGATIONS

Securities Exchange Act Section 13(d) and Regulation 13D

A. SCHEDULE 13D FILINGS

Rule 13d–1.

Not all takeovers begin with an announcement of a hostile tender offer or an approach to target management to negotiate a friendly acquisition. Both tactics alert the market to the bidder's intentions, and are likely to raise stock prices in anticipation of the bidder's willingness to pay a high price for target shares. There are several advantages to the quiet acquisition of shares. If the market is not alerted, the price will be lower. If target management is not alerted, they cannot begin to consider defensive responses.

Prior to 1968 the only reporting obligations of shareholders were under § 16(a) of the '34 Act, and applied only to 10% shareholders. Reports under § 16(a) must be filed within 10 days after a person becomes a 10% shareholder, (Form 3), and before the end of the second business day following the day when any such person has changed his or her holdings (Form 4).

Section 13(d)(1) is consistent with Section 16's initial timing. It provides that any person who, after acquiring the beneficial ownership of any class of equity security registered with the SEC is the beneficial owner of more than 5% of that class, shall file a disclosure document with the SEC within 10 days after such acquisition, and deliver a copy to the issuer. Once a bidder owns 10%, it becomes subject to section 16(a), and its two-day filing requirement for changes of ownership, rather than the more general requirement to file an amendment "promptly" under Rule 13d–2.

The essential elements of section 13(d) involve (i) defining a person; (ii) specifying the purposes of an acquisition; (iii) defining beneficial ownership; (iv) calculating 5% of a class; and (v) specifying the required disclosures. Each of these items is examined in the following subparts.

i. WHAT IS A "PERSON"?

Securities Exchange Act, § 13(d)(3); Rules 13d–3, 13d–5.

A bidder's obligations to make disclosures after acquiring beneficial ownership of more than 5% of a class of equity securities could be avoided by arranging with others to each separately buy less than 5%, with a commitment to sell to the bidder. This practice, originally called "warehousing," (called "parking" more recently) was popular prior to 1968. A bidder could arrange with several financial institutions to each acquire a few percent, without alerting the target. Since the market was not alerted to an impending takeover, the market price would not necessarily rise in anticipation of a bid. The bidder would commit to take the shares after it began a tender offer, which would then be for a smaller percentage of the remaining publicly owned stock, necessitating less of a premium than would otherwise have been the case. The cooperating institutions would generally receive "most favored shareholder" protection, and would be assured they would receive the highest price paid by the bidder in the acquisition. This practice is discussed in Aranow & Einhorn, TENDER OFFERS FOR CORPORATE CONTROL, 25 (1973).

The Williams Act addressed this problem directly. Section 13(d)(3) of the Act provides:

> "When two or more persons act as a partnership, limited partnership, syndicate, or other group for the purpose of acquiring, holding, or disposing of securities of an issuer, such syndicate or group shall be deemed a 'person' for the purposes of this subsection."

GAF Corporation v. Milstein

453 F.2d 709 (2d Cir.1971).

■ KAUFMAN, CIRCUIT JUDGE:

This appeal involves the interpretation of section 13(d) of the Securities Exchange Act, hitherto a largely unnoticed provision added in 1968 by the Williams Act. We write, therefore, on a relatively tabula rasa, despite the burgeoning field of securities law. Essentially, section 13(d) requires any person, after acquiring more than 10% (now 5%) of a class of registered equity security, to send to the issuer and the exchanges on which the security is traded and file with the Commission the statement required by the Act. Although the section has not attracted as much comment as section 14(d), also added by the Williams Act and requiring disclosure by persons engaging in tender offers, the section has potential for marked impact on holders, sellers and purchasers of securities.

GAF Corporation filed its complaint in the United States District Court for the Southern District of New York alleging that Morris Milstein, his two sons, Seymour and Paul, and his daughter, Gloria Milstein Flanzer, violated section 13(d) of the Securities Exchange Act first by failing to file the required statements and then by filing false ones. The complaint also alleged violation of section 10(b) based on the same false statements and, in addition, market manipulation of GAF stock. The Milsteins moved for dismissal under Rule 12(b) (6), F.R.Civ.P., on the ground that the complaint failed to state a claim on which relief could be granted or, in the alternative, for summary judgment under Rule 56. Judge Pollack aptly framed the issues involved:

> The ultimate issue presented by the defendants' motion to dismiss the first count is whether, organizing a group of stockholders owning more than 10% of a class of equity

securities with a view to seeking control is, without more, a reportable event under Section 13(d) of the Exchange Act; and as to the second count, whether in the absence of a connected purchase or sale of securities, the target corporation claiming violation of Section 10 and Rule 10b(5), has standing to seek an injunction against a control contestant for falsity in a Schedule 13D filing. (Footnote omitted.)

Judge Pollack granted the Milsteins' motion to dismiss under Rule 12(b)(6), and GAF has appealed. We disagree with Judge Pollack's determination that GAF failed to state a claim under section 13(d) and Rule 13d–1 promulgated thereunder, and thus reverse his order in this respect, but we affirm the dismissal of the second claim of the complaint on the ground that GAF, as an issuer, has no standing under section 10(b).

* * *

The four Milsteins received 324,166 shares of GAF convertible preferred stock, approximately 10.25% of the preferred shares outstanding, when The Ruberoid Company, in which they had substantial holdings, was merged into GAF in May, 1967. They have not acquired any additional preferred shares since the merger.

* * *

The complaint alleged that initially the Milsteins sought senior management and board positions for Seymour Milstein with GAF. When this sinecure was not forthcoming, the Milsteins allegedly caused Circle Floor Co., Inc., a company in their control, to reduce its otherwise substantial purchases from GAF. It also charged that the Milsteins thereafter undertook a concerted effort to disparage its management and depress the price of GAF common and preferred stock in order to facilitate the acquisition of additional shares. On May 27, 1970, the Milsteins filed a derivative action in the district court, charging the directors, inter alia, with waste and spoliation of corporation assets. A companion action was filed in the New York courts. GAF further alleged that these actions were filed only to disparage management, to depress the price of GAF stock and to use discovery devices to gain valuable information for their takeover conspiracy.

In the meantime, the complaint tells us, Paul and Seymour Milstein purchased respectively 62,000 and 64,000 shares of GAF common stock. When GAF contended that the Milsteins were in violation of section 13(d) because they had not filed a Schedule 13D as required by Rule 13d–1, the Milsteins, although disclaiming any legal obligation under section 13(d), filed such a schedule on September 24, 1970. In their 13D statement (appended to the complaint), the Milsteins disclosed their preferred and common holdings and stated they "at some future time [might] determine to attempt to acquire control of GAF. . . ." They also stated that they had "no present intention as to whether or not any additional securities of

GAF [might] be acquired by them in the future. . . ." Indeed, within the next two months, commencing with October 2, Paul and Seymour each purchased an additional 41,650 shares of common. The Milsteins thereafter filed a Restated and Amended Schedule 13D on November 10 to reflect these new purchases.

Then, on January 27, 1971, the Milsteins filed a third Schedule 13D, disclosing their intention to wage a proxy contest at the 1971 annual meeting. Although the statement again disclaimed any present intention to acquire additional shares, Paul purchased 28,300 shares of common stock during February, 1971. These last purchases, which brought the Milsteins' total common holdings to 237,600 shares having a value in excess of $2 million and constituting 1.7% of the common shares outstanding, were reflected in a February 23 amendment to the January 27 Schedule 13D.

The last essential datum for our purposes is the proxy contest. On May 10, 1971, it was announced that GAF management had prevailed at the April 16 meeting by a margin of some 2 to 1.

* * *

I.

At the time the conspiracy allegedly was formed, section 13(d) (1) in relevant part provided:

> Any person who, after acquiring directly or indirectly the beneficial ownership of any equity security of a class which is registered pursuant to section 12 of this title . . . , is directly or indirectly the beneficial owner of more than 10 per centum of such class shall, within ten days after such acquisition, send to the issuer of the security at its principal executive office, by registered or certified mail, send to each exchange where the security is traded, and file with the Commission, a statement. . . .

This section, however, exempts from its filing requirements any acquisition which, "together with all other acquisitions by the same person of securities of the same class during the preceding twelve months, does not exceed 2 per centum of that class." Section 13(d) (6) (B). Section 13(d) (3), which is crucial to GAF's claim, further provides that "[when] two or more persons act as a partnership, limited partnership, syndicate, or other group for the purpose of acquiring, holding, or disposing of securities of an issuer, such syndicate or group shall be deemed a 'person' for the purposes of [section 13(d)]." On the assumption that the facts alleged in the complaint are true, we cannot conclude other than that the four Milsteins constituted a "group" and thus, as a "person," were subject to the provisions of section 13(d). We also are aware of the charge that the Milsteins agreed after July 29, 1968, to hold their GAF preferred shares for the common purpose of acquiring control of GAF.

Furthermore, the individuals collectively or as a "group" held more than 10% of the outstanding preferred shares—a registered class of securities. Since the section requires a "person" to file only if he acquires more than 2% of the class of stock in a 12-month period after July 29, 1968,[12] the principal question presented to us is whether the complaint alleges as a matter of law that the Milstein group "acquired" the 324,166 shares of preferred stock owned by its members after that date. We conclude that it does and thus that it states a claim under section 13(d).

The statute refers to "acquiring directly or indirectly the beneficial ownership of securities." thus, at the outset, we are not confronted with the relatively simple concept of legal title, but rather with the amorphous and occasionally obfuscated concepts of indirect and beneficial ownership which pervade the securities acts.

The Act nowhere explicitly defines the concept of "acquisition" as used in section 13(d). Although we are aware of Learned Hand's warning "not to make a fortress out of the dictionary," some light, although dim, is shed by Webster's Third International Dictionary. It tells us that "to acquire" means "to come into possession [or] control." If the allegations in the complaint are true, then the group, which must be treated as an entity separate and distinct from its members, could have gained "beneficial control" of the voting rights of the preferred stock[13] only after its formation, which we must assume occurred after the effective date of the Williams Act. Manifestly, according to the complaint, the group when formed acquired a beneficial interest in the individual holdings of its members. We find ourselves in agreement with the statement of the Court of Appeals for the Seventh Circuit in Bath Industries, Inc. v. Blot, 427 F.2d 97, 112 (7th Cir.1970), that in the context of the Williams Act, where the principal concern is focused on the battle for corporate control, "voting control of stock is the only relevant element of beneficial ownership." Thus, we hardly can agree with Judge Pollack that the language of the statute compels the conclusion that individual members must acquire shares before the group can be required to file.

* * *

The legislative history, as well as the purpose behind section 13(d), bear out our interpretation. Any residual doubt over its soundness is obviated by the following clear statement appearing in both the House and Senate reports accompanying the Williams Act:

> "[Section 13(d) (3)] would prevent a group of persons who seek to pool their voting or other interests in the securities of any issuer from evading the provisions of the statute because no

---

[12] The Milsteins concede that their group would have been required to file if the individual members had acquired additional preferred shares after the effective date of the Williams Act and within a 12-month period which amounted to more than 2% of the outstanding shares.

[13] The convertible preferred stock votes share-for-share with the common stock. Each share of preferred is convertible into 1.25 shares of common stock.

one individual owns more than 10 percent of the securities. The group would be deemed to have become the beneficial owner, directly or indirectly, of more than 10 percent of a class of securities at the time they agreed to act in concert. Consequently, the group would be required to file the information called for in section 13(d) (1) within 10 days after they agree to act together, whether or not any member of the group had acquired any securities at that time."

Indeed, Professor Loss, one of the foremost scholars of securities law, reached the same interpretation in his treatise, citing this passage. 6 L. Loss, Securities Regulation 3664 (Supp.1969).

The Senate and House reports and the Act as finally enacted, contrary to appellees' contention,[15] are entirely consistent in our view. This conclusion is buttressed by a consideration of the purpose of the Act. The 1960's on Wall Street may best be remembered for the pyrotechnics of corporate takeovers and the phenomenon of conglomeration. Although individuals seeking control through a proxy contest were required to comply with section 14(a) of the Securities Exchange Act and the proxy rules promulgated by the SEC, and those making stock tender offers were required to comply with the applicable provisions of the Securities Act, before the enactment of the Williams Act there were no provisions regulating cash tender offers or other techniques of securing corporate control. According to the committee reports:

"The [Williams Act] would correct the current gap in our securities laws by amending the Securities Exchange Act of 1934 to provide for full disclosure in connection with cash tender offers and other techniques for accumulating large blocks of equity securities of publicly held companies."

Specifically, we were told, "the purpose of section 13(d) is to require disclosure of information by persons who have acquired a substantial interest, or increased their interest in the equity securities of a company by a substantial amount, within a relatively short period of time." Otherwise, investors cannot assess the potential for changes in corporate control and adequately evaluate the company's worth.[16]

That the purpose of section 13(d) is to alert the marketplace to every large, rapid aggregation or accumulation of securities, regardless of technique employed, which might represent a potential shift in corporate control is amply reflected in the enacted provisions. Section 13(d)(1)(c)

---

[15] Appellees in their brief "concede" that the 1968 committee reports are "against" them. Professor Loss, co-counsel for the Milsteins both in this and the lower court, informed us at the argument that the view set forth in his treatise was "a mistake" and that this passage is "diametrically opposed to the text of the statute" and the purpose and intent of the Williams Act.

[16] The committee reports make it clear that the Act was designed for the benefit of investors and not to tip the balance of regulation either in favor of management or in favor of the person seeking corporate control.

requires the person filing to disclose any intention to acquire control. If he has such an intention, he must disclose any plans for liquidating the issuer, selling its assets, merging it with another company or changing substantially its business or corporate structure. It is of some interest, moreover, that section 13(d)(6)(D) empowers the Commission to exempt from the filing requirements "any acquisition . . . as not entered into for the purpose of, and not having the effect of, changing or influencing the control of the issuer or otherwise as not comprehended within the purpose of [section 13(d)]." (Emphasis added.)

The alleged conspiracy on the part of the Milsteins is one clearly intended to be encompassed within the reach of section 13(d). We have before us four shareholders who together own 10.25% of an outstanding class of securities and allegedly agreed to pool their holdings to effect a takeover of GAF. This certainly posed as great a threat to the stability of the corporate structure as the individual shareholder who buys 10.25% of the equity security in one transaction.[17] A shift in the loci of corporate power and influence is hardly dependent on an actual transfer of legal title to shares, and the statute and history are clear on this.

In light of the statutory purpose as we view it, we find ourselves in disagreement with the interpretation of Bath Industries, *supra*, that the group owning more than 10%, despite its agreement to seize control, in addition, must agree to acquire more shares before the filing requirement of section 13(d) is triggered. The history and language of section 13(d) make it clear that the statute was primarily concerned with disclosure of potential changes in control resulting from new aggregations of stockholdings and was not intended to be restricted to only individual stockholders who made future purchases and whose actions were, therefore, more apparent.[18] It hardly can be questioned that a group holding sufficient shares can effect a takeover without purchasing a single additional share of stock.

* * *

The Milsteins also caution us against throwing our hook into the water and catching too many fish—namely, hundreds of families and other management groups which control companies with registered securities and whose members collectively own more than 5% of a class of the company's stock. Although this problem is not part of the narrow issue we must decide, we cannot close our eyes to the implications of our decision. Upon examination, however, the argument while superficially

---

[17]   The appellees correctly argue that section 13(d) was not intended to be retroactive—that is, all persons who held 10% of an outstanding class before July 29, 1968, are not required to file unless they acquire an additional 2% after that date. Compare § 16(a). But, the Milstein group is not a "person" who held its stock before the effective date of the Williams Act, if the allegations of the complaint are to be accepted. The crucial event under section 13(d) was the formation of the group, which allegedly occurred after the effective date and the purpose of which was to seize control of GAF.

[18]   Section 13(d) (3) refers to groups formed "for the purpose of acquiring, holding, or disposing of securities." Bath Industries would read out "holding" and "disposing."

appealing proves to be totally without substance. Management groups per se are not customarily formed for the purpose of "acquiring, holding, or disposing of securities of [the] issuer" and would not be required to file unless the members conspired to pool their securities interests for one of the stated purposes.[20]

QUESTIONS

1. Why does Section 13(d) apply to the Milstein's ownership of the preferred stock that they received in the merger of their company, Ruberoid, with GAF? Isn't common stock the usual target of takeover bids?

2. If the Milsteins acquired their preferred stock by a merger in May of 1967, why did they not become obligated to file a Schedule 13D on the effective date of the Williams Act, on July 29, 1968?

3. If § 13(d)(6) of the Williams Act exempts acquisitions which, in the course of the preceding 12 months, do not exceed 2% of the class, why did the Milstein's acquisition of 1.7% of the common stock of GAF matter?

4. Was it the Milsteins' decision to acquire more common stock that triggered their filing obligation under Section 13(d)?

5. Who was obligated to file a Schedule 13D?

NOTE ON GROUP FORMATION

In Bath Industries, Inc. v. Blot, 427 F.2d 97 (7th Cir. 1970) several large shareholders, each holding less than the triggering 10% of Bath shares, discussed the need for a replacement of Bath's CEO. When the board of directors rejected the idea of replacing the CEO, some members of the group began buying more Bath stock, and ultimately one representative presented a request for a new CEO signed by holders of nearly 50% of the stock. A formal request for a shareholders list and meeting to pack the board by increasing its size followed, and management sued the members of the group, alleging 13(d) obligations. The court held that 13D filing obligations were not triggered until members of the group purchased additional securities, pursuant to agreement.

The rationale was that the Williams Act was designed to protect target company shareholders, not management. "It does not proscribe informal

---

[20] The more difficult question, and a question we need not decide on this appeal, is whether management groups which expressly agree to pool their interests to fight a potential takeover are subject to section 13(d). Nor do we intimate any view on whether an insurgent group which has filed under section 13(d) and subsequently is successful in its takeover bid remains subject to the section. In any event, as we have already indicated, the Commission can forestall any untoward effects under the exemptive power conferred upon it by section 13(d) (6) (D).

discussion among existing shareholders concerning the performance of current management. Nor does it proscribe legitimate cooperation among existing shareholders to assert their determination to take over control of management, *absent* an intention to acquire additional shares for the furtherance of such purpose." 427 F.2d at 110.

The court discussed the relationship between the proxy rules and the Williams Act, and noted that compliance with the proxy rules was excused if less than 10 persons were solicited, under Rule 14a–2(a) (now 14a–2(b)(1)). The court argued that its construction of § 13(d)(3) was consistent with the proxy rules. The decision was followed in Ozark Air Lines, Inc. v. Cox, 326 F.Supp. 1113 (E.D.Mo.1971).

While ordinarily such a split in the circuits might leave the matter in doubt, the SEC has resolved the matter by rule-making. Rule 13d–5(b)(1) adopts the rule of GAF v. Milstein with respect to agreements to vote shares.

Evidence of Group Formation

Once the GAF rule was adopted as the applicable rule by the SEC, the remaining question was when a group would be treated as formed. .Lane Bryant, Inc. v. Hatleigh Corp, [1980 Decisions] Fed. Sec. L. Rep. (CCH) ¶ 97,529, at 97,766 (S.D.N.Y. 1980) stated the general rule:

> "Section 13(d) seems carefully drawn to permit parties seeking to acquire large amounts of shares in a public company to obtain information with relative freedom, to discuss preliminarily the possibility of entering into agreements and to operate with relative freedom until they get to the point where they do in fact decide to make arrangements which they must record under the securities laws. By requiring the existence of a 'group', the law is designed to avoid discouraging and making risky that kind of preliminary activity."

Thus the analysis involves a determination of when shareholders have reached an "agreement," which involves analysis similar to that used to determine the existence of a contract, or, in other settings, creation of a partnership. An example of this treatment occurs in Cook United, Inc. v. Stockholders Protective Committee, [1979 Decisions] Fed. Sec. L. Rep. (CCH) ¶ 96,875 (S.D.N.Y. 1979), where an insurgent group unhappy with present management called a meeting of some major shareholders for March 21 to discuss the possibility of conducting a proxy contest. Most expressed an interest in such a contest, and one member was authorized to contact a law firm to represent the contestants. At a meeting the next day an agreement was prepared for the signatures of those who wished to become part of the committee. Not all present at the meeting joined, and those who did join signed between March 27 and April 18, with the second member signing April 9. The 13D was filed April 12. The court rejected plaintiff's argument that a group was formed at the March 21 meeting, noting that some members met each other for the first time, and that several people expressed indecision about joining the fight. There were subsequent telephone calls prior to executing the agreement, so the court was not persuaded that any "group" was formed at the March 21 meeting.

In Texasgulf, Inc. v. Canada Development Corp., 366 F.Supp. 374 (S.D.Tex.1973), the court rejected the suggestion that a group had been created where Canada Development approached a major Texasgulf shareholder about a joint venture to acquire Texasgulf, and the shareholder furnished information to Canada Development to assist in its analysis of Texasgulf, and indicated a willingness to obtain a shareholders' list for Canada Development, but never committed to purchasing further shares of Texasgulf. One court held that a group was not formed by the distribution of a private placement memorandum offering interests in and a confidentiality agreement in connection with the solicitation of limited partners for a limited partnership organized for the purpose of acquiring stock in a Bank holding company. Hubco, Inc. v. Rappaport, 628 F.Supp. 345 (D.N.J.1985).

Discussions by an unhappy shareholder with an insurgent who began a proxy fight over what course the unhappy shareholder should follow, accompanied by advice from the insurgent to ride things out did not constitute an agreement in National Home Products, Inc. v. Gray, 416 F.Supp. 1293, 1322–23 (D. Del. 1976), although the court did not discuss the applicability of the language in § 13(d)(3) concerning groups formed for the purpose of "holding" securities. In contrast, where one investor had prepared a report describing a corporation as mismanaged and undervalued if management were changed, which was circulated to a group of investors who quickly made purchases through a common broker, a meeting that "discussed, among other things, changing IBC's management, 'get[ting] together [to influence management]' and a proxy contest," was held sufficient to form a group, even though it was another nine days before they formally agreed to form a shareholders' committee to act together to change management. International Banknote Co. v. Muller, 713 F.Supp. 612 (S.D.N.Y.1989).

The holding of GAF v. Milstein seems to be that an agreement to act in concert is enough; that no further acts are required. That is the express holding of Jewelcor Inc. v. Pearlman, 397 F.Supp. 221, 250 (S.D.N.Y. 1975). But in Nicholson File Co. v. H. K. Porter Co., 341 F.Supp. 508, 518 (D.R.I. 1972), the court declined to find a group where one individual had controlled over 5% of the stock for several years prior to the events in question, through control of two corporate shareholders, and no actions had been taken for two years after the purchases and creation of the "group." Since the group took no action for over two years, the court held no 13D filing was required, holding that "it hardly seems a group which was formed to 'acquire, hold, or dispose of Nicholson's stock, as required by section 13(d)(3)." 341 F.Supp. at 518. Query: would the court have been able to reach the same conclusion if the failure to file a 13D had been challenged shortly after the corporate purchases? Should a Schedule 13D be filed that disclaims group formation for the specified purposes?

In General Aircraft Corp. v. Lampert, 556 F.2d 90, 95 (1st Cir. 1977), the court held that a group had been formed where "[t]he evidence upon which the District Court predicated its finding included: the 150,485 shares of GAC common stock were acquired simultaneously in identical transactions (except for amount) by all three appellants; Scuderi's shares were held in Lampert's [one of the three purchasers] name from the time of purchase; a single Schedule 13D was filed on behalf of all three appellants [more than 10 days later] and signed by all three; copies of correspondence with GAC from any one appellant were sent to the others." In Financial General Bankshares, Inc. v. Lance, [1978 Decisions] Fed. Sec. L. Rep. (CCH) ¶ 96,403, at p. 93,425–26 (D.D.C. 1978), the court inferred the existence of a group of four shareholders from their mutual dissatisfaction with incumbent management, efforts to interest a foreign bank in a takeover, meetings and discussions about the possibility of purchasing the company's stock, the subsequent rapid acquisition of shares, and statements by group members that they had the power to influence management.

But in Financial Federation, Inc. v. Ashkenazy, Fed. Sec. L. Rep. (CCH) ¶ 91,489 (C.D.Cal. 1983), the court declined to hold that purchases of stock by friends and acquaintances of one who sought control brought the buyers within the group. They testified that they bought the stock because they knew Ashkenazy had purchased the stock, and they trusted his business judgment and acumen. While Ashkenazy had offered to purchase options to buy their shares before their purchases, no agreements were entered into until after their purchases, and the shareholders did not give Ashkenazy proxies to vote their shares, nor would he be able to exercise the options until he had obtained regulatory approval for their exercise. All of the defendants testified that they had entered into no agreement about buying, holding or voting their shares. A similar result was reached in Corenco Corp. v. Schiavone & Sons, Inc., 488 F.2d 207 (2d Cir.1973), where a broker assisted a customer in purchasing just under 5% of the stock of Corenco, without specific knowledge that the customer was purchasing for any purpose other than investment, while the broker also acquired nearly 5%, without the customer's knowledge. The court declined to infer a conspiracy.

Membership in a Group

A number of cases raise the question of whether brokers or financial advisers are members of groups where their clients purchase shares. In Camelot Industries Corp. v. Vista Resources, Inc., 535 F.Supp. 1174, 1178–79, 1182 (S.D.N.Y. 1982), the court rejected a charge that a broker was a member of a 13(d)(3) group formed to effect a tender offer where the broker had done no more than initially inform the client that the target's stock was undervalued, and represented a good investment. But where an investment adviser is sufficiently influential or active, that adviser may be a member of the group. The SEC staff has taken the position that where several mutual funds share common management, and collectively hold more than 5% of a company's stock, they constitute a 13(d)(3) group. Stewart Fund Managers, Ltd., [1974 Decisions] Fed. Sec. L. Rep. (CCH) ¶ 80,047 (8/9/74). See also Equity Funding Corp. Securities Litigation, MDL No. 142 (D.C.Cal. Apr. 16, 1976) reported in 1 Lipton & Steinberger, TAKEOVERS AND FREEZEOUTS Sec. 2.2.5.4, at 98 (1978). And where the investors are aware of the activities of a broker in soliciting a small group of buyers to obtain control, one court has found a group, even in the absence of a formal agreement among the investors. Champion Parts Rebuilders, Inc. v. Cormier Corp., 661 F.Supp. 825 (N.D.Ill.1987).

Advisers without a stock position of their own, and not controlling the voting, acquisition or disposition of the securities of others appear to be excused from 13D filings by Transcon Lines v. A.G. Becker, Inc., 470 F.Supp. 356 (S.D.N.Y.1979). Rubenstein, owner of interests in a trucking line, had been approached by a firm to develop takeover targets for a prospective bidder. While that bidder was not interested in his suggestion of Transcon, A.G. Becker was. Rubenstein was disqualified by his interest in one trucking company from participating in the purchase of Transcon by ICC rules, but while actively advising the bidder about the takeover, he sought to dispose of his other trucking interests, without success. He testified that he had no agreement about compensation or participating in the ownership of Transcon with the bidder, but expected to be fairly treated. The court held that his contingent interest, if any, in Transcon stock was not a right to acquire it, and then squarely addressed the issue of his participation in the acquisition:

> "One may therefore state, as plaintiff does, that there is no *requirement* that all members of a group own shares of the subject company. Nevertheless, we believe that, in light of the purpose of Section 13(d) as evidenced by the legislative history and as interpreted by other courts in analogous cases, the better rule is that one who is not the beneficial owner of any shares of the subject company is not a member of a group within the meaning of Section 13(d)(3)." 470 F.Supp. at 373.

Control Persons

In SEC v. Zimmerman, 407 F.Supp. 623, 630 (D.D.C. 1976), affirmed in part & modified in part sub nom. SEC v. Savoy Industries, Inc., 587 F.2d 1149 (D.C.Cir. 1978), cert. denied 440 U.S. 913, the trial court appeared to hold that a control person of a group had an independent obligation to file as a group member, stating that "[s]ince Zimmerman was both a member of the group . . . and controlled another member of the group . . . , he, either separately or as a part of that group, was required to file a report with the Commission under Section 13(d). . . ." The difficulty with the opinion is that Zimmerman was also both a shareholder in the target in his own name and an active participant in planning a change in control. Where a control person deals with the broker executing trades and allocates the purchases to the controlled corporation, several employee benefit trusts of which he served as trustee, and to his personal account, the court held a group was formed even absent an agreement. Twin Fair, Inc. v. Reger, 394 F.Supp. 156 (W.D.N.Y.1975).

See also In re Teledyne, Exchange Act Release No. 14022 (Oct. 4, 1977), which indicates the SEC staff believes a schedule 13D filed on behalf of several subsidiaries of a holding company should disclose that the CEO of the holding company makes the investment and voting decisions with respect to the securities owned by the subsidiaries. Query: Does this mean the CEO has power to direct the voting, and is thus a member of the control group?

Selling Shareholders

Normally a bidder's purchase of target shares from a third party will not make the seller a member of a group. In Globe-Union, Inc. v. U.V. Industries, Inc., Civ. No. 77–C711 (E.D.Wis. May 18, 1978), described in 1 Lipton & Steinberger, TAKEOVERS AND FREEZEOUTS, 99 (1978), the court rejected the notion of a group where there was no indication of a common objective between buyer and seller. Complaints arguing such a theory are listed. *Id.* at 100. But where a raider agrees to purchase securities from an ally, a group is formed. SEC v. Madison Square Garden Corp., [1969–70 Dec.] Fed. Sec. L. Rep. (CCH) ¶ 92,649 (S.D.N.Y. 1970).

In Torchmark Corp. v. Bixby, 708 F.Supp. 1070 (W.D.Mo.1988), the court declined to hold that a group composed largely of family members that signed a non-binding "statement of intention" that they were not interested in selling to a bidder constituted a group. The mere fact that they were related by blood, marriage, business or social relationships was insufficient to find a group, But in Nottingham Partners, [1984–85 Dec.] Fed. Sec. L. Rep. (CCH) ¶ 77,862 (SEC, 1984), the SEC staff refused to issue a no-action letter to a shareholder proposing to communicate with other shareholders to determine if they would be willing to sell their shares at a specified price, in order to communicate to the market that the company could be acquired. The SEC staff refused to conclude that shareholders responding to the inquiry would not constitute a group, even though they were not asked to commit to sell their shares at that price.

In Telco Marketing Services, Inc. [1976–77 Decisions] Fed. Sec. L. Rep. (CCH) ¶ 81,007 (Div. Corp. Fin., avail. 4/4/77), the SEC staff took the position that a group of banks receiving warrants as part of a loan transaction need not file a Schedule 13D, because they had entered into no agreements with respect to the warrants or the underlying shares. On the other hand, where a bank borrower had disclosed his interest in acquiring sufficient shares to wage a control battle to bank officers, who were then introduced to the borrower's brokers for the purpose of personally purchasing shares in the target company, and who continued to cause the bank to advance funds to the borrower for additional purchases, and who accompanied the borrower to meetings with the target's management about changes in management, a group was formed with a common objective to acquire control, even though no formal agreement was entered into. SEC v. Levy, 706 F.Supp. 61, 70 (D.D.C.1989).

PROBLEM

Assume that you represent an investor who has identified a company he believes is both undervalued because it has "hidden value" in appreciated real estate and the potential for better management of its core business. The investor lacks the funds to engage in a 100% purchase of control of the company, and thus needs allies in obtaining voting control to replace management and sell off appreciated real property not essential to the business. Further assume that your investor has purchased 4.95% of the target's common stock. The target is relatively free of takeover defenses at the present time; it lacks a staggered board, a "dead hand" poison pill, or any shark repellent amendments to make a takeout merger more costly. Further, it is incorporated in a state that has not adopted antitakeover provisions. The investor seeks your advice about how she can quietly work with others to accumulate voting control without disclosing these efforts. Your investor is regularly in touch with other large investors capable of purchasing significant positions; indeed, four of them already hold just over 5% each of the target's stock, and have separately filed Schedule 13Gs several years ago.

1.   Who can file Schedule 13G? (See Rule 13d–1(b).)

2.   Can your client contact other major shareholders to determine their interest in seeking a change of control of the target? (Note: Review Securities Exchange Act Rules 14a–2(b)(1) and (2) and 14a–3 in connection with your answer.) Suppose the contact were initiated by a financial institution with the other major shareholders?

3.   Can your client contact other investors that own smaller amounts of the target's stock to urge them to acquire stock in the target because he believes it has strong potential for appreciation?

4.   Can your client, in the contacts mentioned in question 3, mention that he believes there is a potential for a change of control that would unlock hidden asset values and result in improved management?

5.   Can your client urge these investors to buy so they can later cooperate with him in a change of control transaction? (Note: Review Exchange Act Rule 14e–3.)

---

ii.   PURPOSES OF GROUP FORMATION

Exchange Act Section 13(d)(3); Rule 13d–5.

Section 13(d)(3) refers to formation of groups "for the purpose of acquiring, holding, or disposing of securities of an issuer." The statute has been interpreted broadly in this respect. Rule 13d–5 expands the purposes to include "voting."

The purpose of acquiring shares

While most cases involve a purpose of acquiring additional shares, Scott v. Multi-Amp Corp., 386 F.Supp. 44 (D. N.J. 1974) held that a group of major shareholders negotiating with the board for a purchase of all of the assets of the firm were required to file a 13D schedule. The opinion notes that there was doubt among SEC staff members about the filing obligation. While this position seems to be a dubious interpretation of the statute, it indicates the dangers in a literal reading of the statute if the SEC staff determines to take an aggressive position about the extent of the filing obligations under the Williams Act.

The purpose of disposing of securities

The Williams Act's purpose language refers to groups formed for "disposing" of an issuer's securities. Wellman v. Dickinson, 682 F.2d 355 (2d Cir. 1982) infra, Part 3.B of this chapter, involved persons who wanted to sell out to a bidder, and thus were not personally attempting to control the target. Nevertheless, the court held that where major shareholders, collectively holding more than 5% of the stock of Becton, Dickinson & Co., joined together to find a buyer interested in obtaining control of the company, they were a 13(d)(3) group. The court wrote: "Section 13(d) was designed to alert investors in securities markets to potential changes in corporate control and to provide them with an opportunity to evaluate the effect of these potential changes. The power to dispose of a block of securities represents a means for effecting changes in corporate control in addition to the possession of voting control." 682 F.2d at 366.

The purpose of voting securities

Soliciting the vote of other shareholders is covered by the proxy rules adopted under the authority of section 14(a) of the Securities Exchange Act, which makes it illegal to solicit proxies in contravention of SEC rules. Rule 14a–2(b)(1) provides an exemption where the solicitor does not seek the power to act as proxy on behalf of shareholders, and Rule 14a–2(b)(2) exempts solicitations where the number of persons solicited for proxies is not more than ten. The presence of the proxy soliciting rules raises the question of whether the proxy rules and the Williams Act filing rules under § 13(d) are mutually exclusive; whether one complies with either one or the other. One unanswered question is which rules, if either, apply, where the proxy rules provide an exemption. In Bath Industries, Inc. v. Blot, 427 F.2d 97, 110 (7th Cir. 1970), the court emphasized the need to construe § 13(d) in harmony with the proxy rules, and noted the exemption from SEC filings for solicitation of fewer than 10 shareholders, a result clearly inconsistent with GAF v. Milstein, *supra*.

Calumet Industries, Inc. v. MacClure, 464 F.Supp. 19, Fed. Sec. L. Rep. ¶ 96,434 (N.D.Ill. 1978) followed the controlling Bath v. Blot decision, and held that " . . . the additional requirement of an agreement to acquire, hold or dispose of shares cannot be satisfied by an agreement to solicit proxies. The plaintiff has argued that solicitation of a proxy should be considered as the acquisition of a security under Section 13(d). Although *Bath* did hold that investment and banking firms which exercised continuous control over the votes of their clients' shares enjoyed 'beneficial ownership,' 427 F.2d at 103, that holding does not extend to the possession of a revocable proxy to vote at a single meeting." *Id.* at 93,568–69.

In 1978 the SEC adopted Rule 13d–5(b), which provides that "persons [who] agree to act together for the purpose of . . . voting . . . equity securities . . . shall be deemed to have acquired beneficial ownership. . . ." The SEC took the position in proposing the rule that this did not change the prior law:

> "Minor word changes have also been made from the predecessor of Rule 13d–5(b). The most significant of these is the addition of the word 'voting' to the list of actions to which an agreement must relate in order for the rule to apply. The Commission considered 'voting' to be subsumed within the term 'holding' but has decided to make this express to avoid any misunderstanding." Exchange Act Release No. 14692 (April 21, 1978), 43 Fed. Reg. 18484, 18492.

At least one observer disagreed, and characterized this as a major change in the law. Wander, Proxy Contests—The Presolicitation Phase, 10th ANN. INST. SEC. REG. 197, 200 (1979).

Opposition to Takeover Bids

When a management team acts to resist a takeover bid, and thus to preserve the control of management and any shareholders with which it works, does it become a "group" for purposes of section 13(d)? Jewelcor Inc. v. Pearlman, 397 F.Supp. 221 (S.D.N.Y. 1975), centered around a proxy contest, and the complaint of the insurgents that target management had acted with three other individuals, including the estate of the largest shareholder "for the purpose of perpetuating themselves in office and in opposition to all efforts to limit or restrict defendant's control over [the target firm]." 397 F.Supp. at 243. The court held that "Jewelcor must establish that the defendants agreed to act in concert, but it need not establish that they took any affirmative steps in furtherance of that agreement." 397 F.Supp. at 250. Later purchases by some group members were used only as evidence of the existence of an agreement or conspiracy to prevent a takeover. *Id.* at 251. Some decisions have held that management groups were not required to file Schedule 13Ds when they opposed tender offers, because other filing requirements governed under section 14(d). The Jewelcor decision held that this did not necessarily preclude application of section 13(d) where no tender offer had been made, especially where management groups include some nonmanagement members. *Id.* at 244.

To the same effect is Warner Communications, Inc. v. Murdoch, 581 F.Supp. 1482 (D.Del.1984), where a bidder charged that Warner management formed a group with a white knight to preserve its control. While the white knight did purchase securities, the dicta in the case goes beyond that:

"If a management group, however, engages in a voting or pooling arrangement with third parties, the arrangements should be subject to the disclosure provisions of § 13(d). See Jewelcor, Inc. v. Pearlman, 397 F.Supp. at 243–44. Such an arrangement might significantly alter the control structure of a company and effectively enlarge the contours of the management group beyond the scope that investors would ordinarily presume." 581 F.Supp. at 1499.

But where directors joined with a large shareholder to propose a purchase of all the corporation's assets, which was disclosed immediately to the board, and where all the details were disclosed in a proxy statement to the shareholders, the court declined to hold that a group was created, both because a Schedule 13D filing would duplicate the proxy materials, and because it believed the purpose of the Williams Act was to disclose potential or existing changes in control, which were not present here since management was part of the proposal. Scott v. Multi-Amp Corp., 386 F.Supp. 44 (D.N.J.1974).

Where a shareholders' committee was organized to oppose a transaction in which another corporation became a 53% shareholder, and which retained counsel to file suit and wrote to shareholders explaining the reasons for the suit, the court held that this was not the formation of a group for the purposes specified in the Williams Act. "In our view, Congress did not intend section 13(d) to apply to shareholders who attempt to raise funds for a lawsuit challenging the validity of existing corporate stock." Portsmouth Square, Inc. v. Shareholders Protective Committee, 770 F.2d 866, 872 (9th Cir.1985). Although the result of the lawsuit might be a change in control, the shareholders' committee would not have effected a "takeover," in the view of the court. The court was concerned with the possible use of the Williams Act as a club by management to discourage shareholders' litigation. A similar result was reached in Southwest Realty, Ltd. v. Daseke, [1990–91 Dec.] Fed. Sec. L. Rep. (CCH) ¶ 95256 (N.D. Tex. 1990), where the court noted that plaintiffs could seek money damages under section 18(a) of the Securities Exchange Act.

The SEC staff has taken the position that whenever managers act in concert to acquire shares they constitute a § 13(d)(3) group, even if they already own a controlling interest in the company. There was no exemption because the purchase was not for control; as long as the joint purchases accounted for more than 2% of the outstanding shares within the previous twelve months, a 13D filing was required. Tony Lama Company, Inc., [1974–75 Decisions] Fed. Sec. L. Rep. (CCH) ¶ 79,901 (1974).

CSX Corporation v. The Children's Investment Fund

562 F.Supp.2d 511 (S.D. N.Y. 2008),
remanded for further findings 654 F.3d 276 (2d Cir. 2011).

■ LEWIS A. KAPLAN, UNITED STATES DISTRICT JUDGE.

Some people deliberately go close to the line dividing legal from illegal if they see a sufficient opportunity for profit in doing so. A few cross that line and, if caught, seek to justify their actions on the basis of formalistic arguments even when it is apparent that they have defeated the purpose of the law.

This is such a case. The defendants—two hedge funds that seek extraordinary gain, sometimes through "shareholder activism"— amassed a large economic position in CSX Corporation ("CSX"), one of the nation's largest railroads. They did so for the purpose of causing CSX to behave in a manner that they hoped would lead to a rise in the value of their holdings. And there is nothing wrong with that. But they did so in close coordination with each other and without making the public disclosure required of 5 percent shareholders and groups by the Williams Act, a statute that was enacted to ensure that other shareholders are informed of such accumulations and arrangements. They now have launched a proxy fight that, if successful, would result in their having substantial influence and perhaps practical working control of CSX.

Defendants seek to defend their secret accumulation of interests in CSX by invoking what they assert is the letter of the law. Much of their position in CSX was in the form of total return equity swaps ("TRSs"), a type of derivative that gave defendants substantially all of the indicia of stock ownership save the formal legal right to vote the shares. In consequence, they argue, they did not beneficially own the shares referenced by the swaps and thus were not obliged to disclose sooner or more fully than they did. In a like vein, they contend that they did not reach a formal agreement to act together, and therefore did not become a "group" required to disclose its collaborative activities, until December 2007 despite the fact that they began acting in concert with respect to CSX far earlier. But these contentions are not sufficient to justify defendants' actions.

The question whether the holder of a cash-settled equity TRS beneficially owns the referenced stock held by the short counterparty appears to be one of first impression. There are persuasive arguments for concluding, on the facts of this case, that the answer is "yes"—that defendants beneficially owned at least some and quite possibly all of the referenced CSX shares held by their counterparties. But it ultimately is unnecessary to reach such a conclusion to decide this case.

Rule 13d–3(b) under the Exchange Act provides in substance that one who creates an arrangement that prevents the vesting of beneficial ownership as part of a plan or scheme to avoid the disclosure that would have been required if the actor bought the stock outright is deemed to be a beneficial owner of those shares. That is exactly what the defendants did here in amassing their swap positions. In consequence, defendants are deemed to be the beneficial owners of the referenced shares.

* * *

I. Parties

Plaintiff CSX Corporation ("CSX") is incorporated in Virginia and headquartered in Jacksonville, Florida. Its shares are traded on the New York Stock Exchange, and it operates one of the nation's largest rail systems through its wholly owned subsidiary, CSX Transportation, Inc. Its chairman, president, and chief executive officer is Michael J. Ward, who is named here as an additional defendant on the counterclaims.

Defendants The Children's Investment Fund Management (UK) LLP ("TCIF UK") and The Children's Investment Fund Management (Cayman) LTD. ("TCIF Cayman") are, respectively, an English limited liability partnership and a Cayman Islands company. * * * These five defendants are referred to collectively as TCI.

Defendants 3G Fund L.P. ("3G Fund") and 3G Capital Partners L.P. ("3G LP") are Cayman Islands limited partnerships. * * * These four defendants are referred to collectively as 3G.

II. Proceedings

TCI and 3G currently are engaged in a proxy fight in which they seek, *inter alia,* to elect their nominees to five of the twelve seats on the CSX board of directors and to amend its by-laws to permit holders of 15 percent of CSX shares to call a special meeting of shareholders at any time for any purpose permissible under Virginia law. The CSX annual meeting of shareholders, which is the object of the proxy fight, is scheduled to take place on June 25, 2008.

CSX brought this action against TCI and 3G on March 17, 2008. The complaint alleges, among other things, that defendants failed timely to file a Schedule 13D after forming a group to act with reference to the shares of CSX and that both the Schedule 13D and the proxy statement they eventually filed were false and misleading. It seeks, among other things, an order requiring corrective disclosure, voiding proxies defendants have obtained, and precluding defendants from voting their CSX shares. TCI Master Fund, 3G Fund, 3G LP, and 3G Ltd. filed counterclaims against CSX and Ward asserting various claims under the federal securities laws.

* * *

III. Total Return Swaps

A. The Basics

The term "derivative," as the term is used in today's financial world, refers to a financial instrument that derives its value from the price of an underlying instrument or index. Among the different types of derivatives are swaps, instruments whereby two counterparties agree to "exchange cash flows on two financial instruments over a specific period of time." These are (1) a "reference obligation" or "underlying asset" such as a security, a bank loan, or an index, and (2) a benchmark loan, generally with an interest rate set relative to a commonly used reference rate (the "reference rate") such as the London Inter-Bank Offered Rate ("LIBOR"). A TRS is a particular form of swap.

The typical—or "plain vanilla"—TRS is represented by Figure 1.

Figure 1

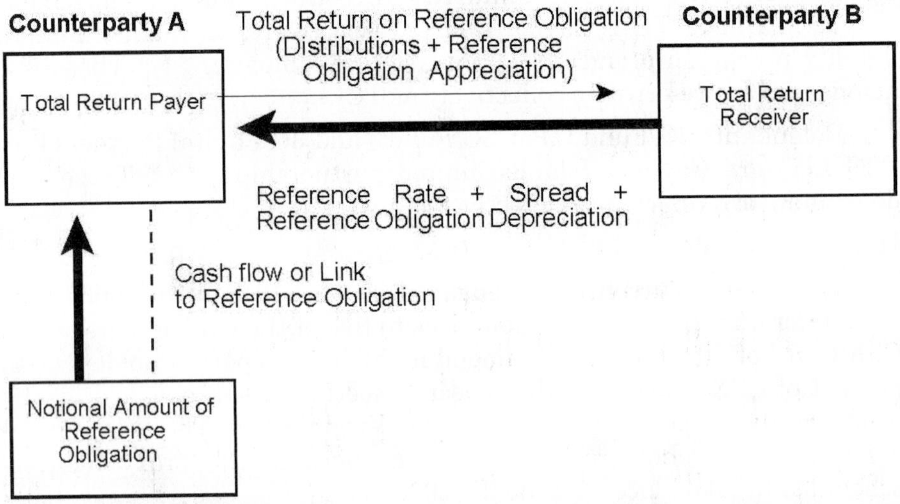

Counterparty A—the "short" party—agrees to pay Counterparty B—the "long" party—cash flows based on the performance of a defined underlying asset in exchange for payments by the long party based on the interest that accrues at a negotiated rate on an agreed principal amount (the "notional amount"). More specifically, Counterparty B, which may be referred to as the "total return receiver" or "guarantor," is entitled to receive from Counterparty A the sum of (1) any cash distributions, such as interest or dividends, that it would have received had it held the referenced asset, and (2) either (i) an amount equal to the market appreciation in the value of the referenced asset over the term of the swap (if the TRS is cash-settled) or, what is economically the same thing, (ii) the referenced asset in exchange for its value on the last refixing date prior to the winding up of the transaction (if the TRS is settled in kind). Counterparty A, referred to as the "total return payer" or "beneficiary," is entitled to receive from Counterparty B (1) an amount equal to the interest at the negotiated rate that would have been payable had it actually loaned Counterparty A the notional amount,[13] and (2) any decrease in the market value of the referenced asset.

For example, in a cash-settled TRS with reference to 100,000 shares of the stock of General Motors, the short party agrees to pay to the long party an amount equal to the sum of (1) any dividends and cash flow, and (2) any increase in the market value that the long party would have realized had it owned 100,000 shares of General Motors. The long party in turn agrees to pay to the short party the sum of (1) the amount equal to interest that would have been payable had it borrowed the notional amount from the short party, and (2) any depreciation in the market value that it would have suffered had it owned 100,000 shares of General Motors.

In practical economic terms, a TRS referenced to stock places the long party in substantially the same economic position that it would occupy if it owned the referenced stock or security. There are two notable exceptions. First, since it does not have record ownership of the referenced shares, it does not have the right to vote them. Second, the long party looks to the short party, rather than to the issuer of the referenced security for distributions and the marketplace for any appreciation in value.

The short party of course is in a different situation. It is entitled to have the long party place it in the same economic position it would have occupied had it advanced the long party an amount equal to the market value of the referenced security. But there are at least two salient distinctions, from the short party's perspective, between a TRS and a loan. First, the short party does not actually advance the notional amount to the long party. Second, it is subject to the risk that the referenced asset will appreciate during the term of the TRS. As will appear, the institutions that make a business of serving as short parties in TRSs deal with this exposure by hedging, a fact pivotal to one of CSX's claims here.

The swap agreements at issue in this case are cash-settled TRSs entered into by TCI with each of eight counterparties, most significantly Deutsche Bank AG ("Deutsche Bank") and Citigroup Global Markets Limited ("Citigroup"), and by 3G with Morgan Stanley.

B.   The Purposes of TRSs

[While normally TRSs are employed by a long party's desire to reap the benefits of an equity position without purchasing the equity, in

---

[13] The notional amount typically is the value of the referenced asset at the time the transaction is agreed and may be recalculated periodically. Subrahmanyam Report P 63. The difference between the reference rate and the negotiated interest rate of the swap depends on (1) the creditworthiness of the two parties, (2) characteristics of the underlying asset, (3) the total return payer's cost of financing, risk, and desired profit, and (4) market competition. *Id.* P 64.

exchange for an interest payment to the short counter-party. Counterparties are willing to bear the risk of their short position either because they are already long in that asset and want to hedge their position or, in the case of financial institutions such as Deutsche Bank and Citigroup, counterparties here, expecting an economic return from the interest payments. If they are not already long in the asset, as they were not here, they will purchase the referenced securities in amounts sufficient to hedge their positions.

Hedged counterparties are record holders of shares with voting rights. Generally they will be indifferent on voting issues because they have no economic risk in the stock, but they may vote the shares as they believe their long counterparties might prefer, in order to please a customer. If the long party wins the bet and gains on the referenced stock, the parties may settle up in cash, in which case the short counterparty will sell the referenced stock into the market, or the short party may simply deliver the shares to the long party.]

* * *

IV. *The Events of Mid-2006 Until Late 2007*

The events preceding this lawsuit are best understood by first considering the conduct of TCI and 3G separately. The Court then will analyze the relationship between TCI and 3G and their conduct in order to determine whether they in fact acted independently.

A. *TCI*

1. *TCI Develops a Position in CSX*

TCI began to research the United States railroad industry in the second half of 2006 and rapidly focused on Norfolk Southern and CSX, the two largest railroads in the eastern portion of the country. It decided to concentrate on CSX because it "had more legacy contracts that were below market value prices" and, in TCI's view, "ran less efficiently" than did Norfolk. In short, it felt that changes in policy and, if need be, management could bring better performance and thus a higher stock price. That insight, if insight it was, however, would be worthless or, at any rate, less valuable if CSX did not act as TCI thought appropriate. So TCI embarked on a course designed from the outset to bring about changes at CSX.

TCI made its initial investment in CSX on October 20, 2006, by entering into TRSs referencing 1.4 million shares of CSX stock. By the end of that month, it was party to TRSs referencing 1.7 percent of CSX shares.

TCI almost immediately contacted CSX and informed it that TCI had accumulated approximately $100 million of CSX stock. Two weeks later, it advised CSX that it had $300 million invested in CSX, "with the potential to scale that further," and sought a meeting with senior management at the Citigroup Transportation Conference, which was scheduled to take place on November 14, 2006.

In the meantime, TCI continued accumulating TRSs referencing CSX throughout November, engaging in seventeen swap transactions with various financial institution counterparties. By the middle of the month, it had increased its exposure to approximately 2.7 percent.

On November 14, 2006, TCI's Hohn and Amin attended the Citigroup conference. During the course of the day, they approached CSX representatives, including David Baggs, the assistant vice president of treasury and investor relations. Amin later told Baggs that TCI's swaps, the only type of investment exposure TCI then had in CSX, could be converted into direct ownership at any time.

Following the conference, TCI continued to build its position through additional swaps throughout December, reaching 8.8 percent by the end of 2006.

2. TCI's Leveraged Buyout Proposal

TCI's belief that it could profit substantially if it could alter CSX's policies or, if need be, management manifested itself when, during December 2006, it began to investigate the possibility of a leveraged buyout ("LBO"). It explored this possibility with Goldman Sachs, sending its LBO model. Its email "re-iterate[d]" the need to keep the communication highly confidential, as TCI "ha[d] not taken the idea to anyone else, nor [was its] holding publicly disclosed so any leakage of our conversations with you would be damaging for our relations with the company."

On January 22, 2007, by which date TCI had amassed TRSs referencing 10.5 percent of CSX, TCI met with one of CSX's financial advisors, Morgan Stanley, to discuss the LBO proposal. It noted during its presentation that a " 'perfect storm' of conditions makes a private equity bid [for a major U.S. railroad] nearly inevitable" and that "CSX [was] logically the prime candidate" because of its "valuation, size, [and] quality of franchise." TCI urged Morgan Stanley to back the plan and suggested that CSX "formally hire an investment bank to proceed urgently."

Morgan Stanley relayed the substance of its conversation to CSX. TCI then approached CSX directly about the issue on February 8 at an investor conference organized by J.P. Morgan. Amin asked Baggs for CSX's views on the LBO proposal. Baggs confirmed that Morgan Stanley had relayed the proposal but said that CSX was not in a position to respond.

[When CSX management declined to discuss the proposal and responded with an announcement of its plan to buy back about $2 billion of its shares, TCI began to contact other hedge funds and recommended that they buy CSX stock. This was followed by further attempts to persuade CSX financial advisers to consider TCI's LBO proposal, and exploration of possible individuals who would be willing to serve as offices and directors of CSX. 3G also began to explore interest in a proxy fight at CSX, even before it had purchased any CSX stock. By December 10, 2007 TCI had entered into agreements with several individuals to stand for election to the CSX board, and at least one of them had purchased shares of CSX stock in order to qualify for election. On December 19, 2007, TCI, 3G, and three nominees (the "Group") filed a Schedule 13D with the SEC. CSX filed a preliminary proxy statement on February 21, and on March 10 CSX and 3G proposed a slate of five directors for the CSX board and circulated their own proxy solicitation.]

* * *

VI. The Positions of the Parties

CSX contends that (1) TCI violated Section 13(d) of the Exchange Act by failing to disclose its beneficial ownership of shares of CSX common stock referenced in their TRSs and (2) TCI and 3G violated Section 13(d) by failing timely to disclose the formation of a group. It argues further that TCI and 3G violated Section 14(a) of the Exchange Act because their proxy statements were materially false and misleading. Its state law claim contends that defendants' notice of intent to nominate directors failed to comply with CSX's bylaws in violation of Section 13.1– 624 of the Virginia Stock Corporation Act.

* * *

Discussion

Section 13(d)

* * *

The heart of the dispute presently before the Court concerns whether (1) TCI's investments in cash-settled TRSs referencing CSX shares conferred beneficial ownership of those shares upon TCI, and (2) TCI and 3G formed a group prior to December 12, 2007.

A.   Beneficial Ownership

The concept of "beneficial ownership" is the foundation of the Williams Act and thus critical to the achievement of its goal of providing transparency to the marketplace.[153] Although Congress did not define the term, its intention manifestly was that the phrase be construed

---

[153] *See Takeover Bids: Hearing Before the Subcomm. on Commerce and Finance of the H. Comm. on Interstate and Foreign Commerce*, 90th Cong., 2d Sess. 40–41 (1968) (statement of Manuel F. Cohen, Chairman, Securities and Exchange Commission) ("[B]eneficial ownership is the test. [The acquiring entity] might try to get around it, and that would be a violation of law, but the legal requirement is beneficial ownership.").

broadly.[154] The SEC did so in Rule 13d–3, which provides in relevant part:

> "(a) For the purposes of sections 13(d) and 13(g) of the Act a beneficial owner of a security includes any person who, directly or indirectly, through any contract, arrangement, understanding, relationship, or otherwise has or shares:
>
>> "(1) Voting power which includes the power to vote, or to direct the voting of, such security; and/or,
>>
>> "(2) Investment power which includes the power to dispose, or to direct the disposition of, such security.
>
> "(b) Any person who, directly or indirectly, creates or uses a trust, proxy, power of attorney, pooling arrangement or any other contract, arrangement, or device with the purpose of [sic] effect of divesting such person of beneficial ownership of a security or preventing the vesting of such beneficial ownership as part of a plan or scheme to evade the reporting requirements of section 13(d) or (g) of the Act shall be deemed for purposes of such sections to be the beneficial owner of such security."

The SEC intended Rule 13d–3(a) to provide a "broad definition" of beneficial ownership so as to ensure disclosure "from all those persons who have the ability to change or influence control." This indeed is apparent from the very words of the Rule. By stating that a beneficial owner "includes" rather than "means" any person who comes within the criteria that follow, it made plain that the language that follows does not exhaust the circumstances in which one might come within the term. The phrases "directly or indirectly" and "any contract, arrangement, understanding, relationship, or otherwise" reinforce that point and demonstrate the focus on substance rather than on form or on the legally enforceable rights of the putative beneficial owner. It therefore" is not surprising that the SEC, at the very adoption of Rule 13d–3, stated that the determination of beneficial ownership under Rule 13d–3(a) requires

> "[a]n analysis of all relevant facts and circumstances in a particular situation . . . in order to identify each person possessing the requisite voting power or investment power. For example, for purposes of the rule, the mere possession of the legal right to vote securities under applicable state or other law . . . may not be determinative of who is a beneficial owner of such securities inasmuch as another person or persons may have the power whether legal, economic, or otherwise, to direct such voting.

---

[154] *See, e.g.,* Wellman v. Dickinson, 682 F.2d 355, 365–66 (2d Cir. 1982) (rejecting narrow construction of § 13(d)(3) in light of legislative history), *cert. denied* 460 U.S. 1069, 103 S. Ct. 1522, 75 L. Ed. 2d 946 (1983).

Nor does Rule 13d–3(a) exhaust the Commission's efforts to cast a very broad net to capture all situations in which the marketplace should be alerted to circumstances that might result in a change in corporate control. Rule 13d–3(b) was adopted so that Rule 13d–3(a) "cannot be circumvented by an arrangement to divest a person of beneficial ownership or to prevent the vesting of beneficial ownership as part of a plan or scheme to evade the reporting requirements of [S]ection 13(d)."

With these considerations in mind, the Court turns to CSX's contentions. It first considers whether TCI had beneficial ownership, within the meaning of Rule 13d–3(a), of the shares of CSX stock referenced by its swap agreements and held by its counterparties by considering the facts and circumstances surrounding those contracts. It then turns to the question of whether TCI, assuming it were not a beneficial owner of the hedge shares under Rule 13d–3(a), nevertheless would be deemed a beneficial owner under Rule 13d–3(b) because it used the TRSs as part of a plan or scheme to evade the disclosure requirements of Section 13(d) by avoiding the vesting of beneficial ownership in TCI.

1.   Rule 13d–3(a)

The contracts embodying TCI's swaps did not give TCI any legal rights with respect to the voting or disposition of the CSX shares referenced therein. Nor did they require that its short counterparties acquire CSX shares to hedge their positions. But the beneficial ownership

> "inquiry focuses on any relationship that, as a factual matter, confers on a person a *significant ability to affect* how voting power or investment power will be exercised, because it is primarily designed to ensure timely disclosure of market-sensitive data about changes in the identity of those who are able, as a practicable matter, to influence the use of that power."

It therefore is important to consider whether TCI's TRSs contemplated that its counterparties would hedge their positions with CSX shares and, if so, whether TCI had "a significant ability to affect how voting power or investment power will be exercised."

a.   Investment Power

TCI acknowledges, as it must, that its swaps contemplated the possibility that the counterparties might—indeed would—hedge by acquiring physical shares. It emphasizes, however, that they were under no contractual obligation to do so and, indeed, had other means of hedging their short positions. Moreover, TCI asserts that it had no influence over how its counterparties disposed of physical shares used to hedge a swap, if any, at the time of termination. TCI therefore maintains that it had no investment power over any shares used to hedge its swaps.

TCI correctly describes the legal instruments constituting the swaps. They do not require the counterparties to hedge their positions by purchasing CSX stock and do not in terms address the question of how the counterparties will dispose of their hedges at the conclusion of the swaps. But the evidence is overwhelming that these counterparties in fact hedged the short positions created by the TRSs with TCI by purchasing shares of CSX common stock. As the charts set forth in Appendix 1 show, they did so on virtually a share-for-share basis and in each case on the day or the day following the commencement of each swap.

This is precisely what TCI contemplated and, indeed, intended. None of these counterparties is in the business, so far as running its swap desk is concerned, of taking on the stupendous risks entailed in holding unhedged short (or long) positions in significant percentages of the shares of listed companies. As a practical matter, the Court finds that their positions could not be hedged through the use of other derivatives. Thus, it was inevitable that they would hedge the TCI swaps by purchasing CSX shares.

TCI knew that the banks would behave in this manner and therefore sought at the outset to spread its TRS agreements across a number of counterparties so as to avoid pushing any counterparty, individually, across the 5 percent threshold that would have triggered an obligation on the counterparty's part to disclose its position under Regulation 13D. This would have been a cause for concern only if TCI understood that its counterparties, although not legally obligated to do so, in fact would hedge by purchasing CSX shares equal or substantially equal to the shares referenced by the TCI swaps.

Moreover, TCI understood that there were advantages to TCI of its short counterparties hedging with physical shares. The fact that these are nominally cash-settled TRSs does not necessarily mean that they all will be settled for cash. TCI and its counterparties have the ability to agree to unwind the swaps in kind, i.e., by delivery of the shares to TCI at the conclusion of each transaction, as indeed commonly occurs. That simple fact means that the hedge positions of the counterparties hang like the sword of Damocles over the neck of CSX. Once the Hart-Scott-Rodino waiting period expired, nothing more was required to move the legal ownership of the hedge shares from the banks to TCI than the stroke of a pen or the transmission of an email. This greatly enhances TCI's leverage over CSX, even if it never settles any of the TRSs for cash, as indeed has been the case to date. And TCI so views the realities as evidenced by Amin's statement to CSX that TCI's swap position could be converted to shares at any time as well as his assertion on February 15, 2007, that TCI "owned" a quantity of shares that clearly included the shares held by its counterparties.

The corollary to the bank's behavior at the front end of these transactions, viz. purchasing physical shares to hedge risk, is that the banks would sell those shares at the conclusion of the swaps (assuming cash settlement) so as to avoid the risk that holding the physical shares would entail once the downside protection of the swap was removed. And that is exactly what happened here. With very minor exceptions, whenever TCI terminated a swap, the counterparty sold the same number of physical shares that were referenced in the unwound swap and it did so on the same day that the swap was terminated. Citigroup, Credit Suisse, Deutsche Bank, Goldman, and Morgan Stanley did precisely this, as did Merrill Lynch and UBS save that (1) Merrill Lynch's sales on a few occasions involved slightly different numbers of shares, and (2) UBS on five occasions sold on the day following the termination of a swap.

To be sure, there is no evidence that TCI explicitly directed the banks to purchase the hedge shares upon entering into the swaps or to sell them upon termination. Nor did it direct the banks to dispose of their hedge shares by any particular means. But that arguably is not dispositive.

On this record, it is quite clear that TCI significantly influenced the banks to purchase the CSX shares that constituted their hedges because the banks, as a practical matter and as TCI both knew and desired, were compelled to do so. It significantly influenced the banks to sell the hedge shares when the swaps were unwound for the same reasons.

b.   Voting Power

There is no evidence that TCI and any of its counterparties had explicit agreements that the banks would vote their hedge shares in a certain way. Moreover, the policies and practices of the counterparties with respect to voting hedge shares vary. But these are not the only pertinent considerations.

(1)   Deutsche Bank

Between October and November 2007, TCI moved swaps referencing 28.4 million and 18.0 million shares into Deutsche Bank and Citigroup, respectively, while leaving swaps referencing 1,000 shares with each of its remaining six counterparties. Hohn offered two reasons for doing so.

* * *

. . . [I]t is entirely clear that the move into at least Deutsche Bank was made substantially out of Hohn's belief that he could influence the voting of the shares it held to hedge TCI's swaps. As an initial matter, Hohn was well aware that Austin Friars, a hedge fund within Deutsche Bank, held a proprietary position in CSX common stock. From at least March 2007, when Austin Friars invited TCI to submit questions for and listen in on the John Snow call, the two funds shared a common interest in taking a railroad private. Nor was this the first time that they had shared detailed information about positions or plans. Hohn believed that TCI could exploit this relationship to influence how Austin Friars, and in turn how Deutsche Bank, voted its CSX shares. * * *

(2) *All of the Counterparties*

The Court is not persuaded that there was any agreement or understanding between TCI and any of the other banks with respect to the voting of their hedge shares. But the SEC has made plain that a party has voting power over a share under Rule 13d–3(a)(1) if that party has the "ability to control or *influence* the voting . . . of the securities."[182] So the question of influence must be considered with respect to all of the banks.

As an initial matter, TCI, which knew that the banks would hedge the swaps by purchasing physical shares, could and at least to some extent did select counterparties by taking their business to institutions it thought would be most likely to vote with TCI in a proxy contest. D.F. King's "Preliminary Vote Outlook" presentation concerning the proxy contest indicates that certain types of investors adhere to particular voting patterns in contested elections and are influenced by the recommendations made by institutional proxy advisory firms such as RiskMetrics (formerly ISS). Although D.F. King was clear that it could not guarantee the manner in which a particular investor would vote, patterns of behavior made it possible for TCI to predict the likelihood of that vote and place its swap transactions accordingly.

Further, some of the banks' policies gave TCI the power to prevent a share from being voted. Credit Suisse, for example, appears to follow a policy of not voting its hedge shares if it is solicited by its counterparty in a contested situation. In such instances, then, TCI could ensure that that bank's hedge shares would not be voted against it by the simple expedient of soliciting its counterparty. Thus, by entering into a TRS with Credit Suisse, TCI was in a position to ensure that Credit Suisse would purchase shares that otherwise might have been voted against TCI in a proxy fight and then to ensure that those shares would not be so voted. While this would not be as favorable a result as dictating a vote in its favor, it would be better than leaving the votes of those shares to chance.

Finally, the fact that TCI thought it could influence Citigroup at least suggests that its relationship with Citigroup permitted it to do so. Nevertheless, the proof on this point is not sufficient to find that TCI in fact had that ability.

c. *Synthesis*

In the last analysis, there are substantial reasons for concluding that TCI is the beneficial owner of the CSX shares held as hedges by its short counterparties. The definition of "beneficial ownership" in Rule 13d–3(a) is very broad, as is appropriate to its object of ensuring disclosure "from all . . . persons who have the ability [even] to . . . influence control." It

---

[182] Interpretive Release on Rules Applicable to Insider Reporting and Trading, Exchange Act Release No. 34–18114, 46 Fed. Reg. 48,147 (Oct. 1, 1981) (emphasis added). *See also* Wellman, 682 F.2d at 365 n.12 (beneficial ownership not defined by Rule 13d–3 "solely as present voting power").

does not confine itself to "the mere possession of the legal right to vote or direct the acquisition or disposition of] securities," but looks instead to all of the facts and circumstances to identify situations in which one has even the ability to influence voting, purchase, or sale decisions of its counterparties by "legal, economic, or other[ ]" means.

On this record, TCI manifestly had the economic ability to cause its short counterparties to buy and sell the CSX shares. The very nature of the TRS transactions, as a practical matter, required the counterparties to hedge their short exposures. And while there theoretically are means of hedging that do not require the purchase of physical shares, in the situation before the Court it is perfectly clear that the purchase of physical shares was the only practical alternative. Indeed, TCI effectively has admitted as much. It did so by spreading its swap transactions among eight counterparties to avoid any one hitting the 5 percent disclosure threshold and thus triggering its own reporting obligation—a concern that was relevant only because TCI knew that the counterparties were hedging by buying shares. And it did so in closing argument, where its counsel said that the banks' purchases of CSX shares were "the natural consequence" of the swap transactions. Thus, TCI patently had the power to cause the counterparties to buy CSX. At the very least, it had the power to influence them to do so. And once the counterparties bought the shares, TCI had the practical ability to cause them to sell simply by unwinding the swap transactions. Certainly the banks had no intention of allowing their swap desks to hold the unhedged long positions that would have resulted from the unwinding of the swaps.

The voting situation is a bit murkier, but there nevertheless is reason to believe that TCI was in a position to influence the counterparties, especially Deutsche Bank, with respect to the exercise of their voting rights.

* * *

The focus on TCI's legal rights under its swap contracts, while those rights certainly are relevant, exalts form over substance. The securities markets operate in the real world, not in a law school contracts classroom. Any determination of beneficial ownership that failed to take account of the practical realities of that world would be open to the gravest abuse. Indeed, this Court is not alone in recognizing that abuses would be facilitated by a regime that did not require disclosure of the sort that would be required if "beneficial ownership" were construed as advocated by CSX.[191]

---

[191] *See, e.g.*, Henry Hu & Bernard Black, *Equity and Debt Decoupling and Empty Voting II: Importance and Extensions*, 156 U. PENN. L. REV. 625, 735–37 (2008) (assuming that equity swaps do not give the long party beneficial ownership, they can be used to secure effective control without disclosure otherwise required by § 13(d)). Similarly, professor and former SEC commissioner Joseph Grundfest and other academics have written that "[i]n the context of this case, the . . . integrity of the stock market was undermined and an uneven playing field was

* * *

In this case, it is not essential to decide the beneficial ownership question under Rule 13d–3(a). As is discussed immediately below, TCI used the TRSs with the purpose and effect of preventing the vesting of beneficial ownership of the referenced shares in TCI as part of a plan or scheme to evade the reporting requirements of Section 13(d). Under Rule 13d–3(b), TCI, if it is not a beneficial owner under rule 13d–3(a), therefore is deemed—on the facts of this case—to beneficially own those shares. The Court therefore does not rule on the legal question whether TCI is a beneficial owner under Section 13d–3(a).

2. *Rule 13d–3(b)*

In construing any statute or rule, the Court is governed by well-established principles. It first must examine "the language of the provision at issue," which governs " 'unless that meaning would lead to absurd results.' " In addition, the provision "should be construed so that effect is given to all its provisions, so that no part will be inoperative or superfluous, void or insignificant, and so that one section will not destroy another unless the provision is the result of obvious mistake or error."

We begin with the language. Rule 13d–3(b) provides:

"Any person who, directly or indirectly, [1] creates or uses a trust, proxy, power of attorney, pooling arrangement or any other contract, arrangement, or device [2] with the purpose of [*sic*] effect of divesting such person of beneficial ownership of a security or preventing the vesting of such beneficial ownership [3] as part of a plan or scheme to evade the reporting requirements of section 13(d) or (g) of the Act shall be deemed for purposes of such sections to be the beneficial owner of such security."

Thus, the Rule by its plain terms is triggered when three elements are satisfied:

- the use of a contract, arrangement, or device

- with the purpose or effect of divesting such person of beneficial ownership of a security or preventing the vesting of such beneficial ownership

- as part of a plan or scheme to evade the reporting requirements of Section 13(d) or (g).

It is undisputed that TCI's cash-settled TRSs are contracts. The first element therefore concededly is satisfied.

The evidence that TCI created and used the TRSs, at least in major part, for the purpose of preventing the vesting of beneficial ownership of CSX shares in TCI and as part of a plan or scheme to evade the reporting

---

created." *See* Letter from Joseph Grundfest, Henry Hu, and Marti Subrahmanyam to Brian Cartwright, General Counsel of the SEC (June 2, 2008), at 13.

requirements of Section 13(d) is overwhelming. Joe O'Flynn, the chief financial officer of TCI Fund told its board, albeit not in the specific context of CSX, that one of the reasons for using swaps is "the ability to purchase without disclosure to the market or the company." TCI emails discussed the need to make certain that its counterparties stayed below 5 percent physical share ownership, this in order to avoiding triggering a disclosure obligation on the part of a counterparty. TCI admitted that one of its motivations in avoiding disclosure was to avoid paying a higher price for the shares of CSX, which would have been the product of front-running that it expected would occur if its interest in CSX were disclosed to the market generally. NCI Indeed, TCI acquired only approximately 4.5 percent in physical CSX shares to remain safely below the 5 percent reporting requirement until it was ready to disclose its position.

* * *

This leaves us with the [SEC's Division of Corporate Finance's] more likely position [in its amicus brief], viz. that Rule 13d–3(b) is satisfied only where the actor intends to create some false appearance, albeit not necessarily a false appearance of non-ownership. But false appearance of what?

The goal of Section 13(d) "is to alert the marketplace to every large, rapid aggregation or accumulation of securities ... which might represent a potential shift in corporate control." In consequence, the natural reading is that the Division refers to a false appearance that no such accumulation is taking place. Put another way, Rule 13d–3(b) applies where one enters into a transaction with the intent to create the false appearance that there is no large accumulation of securities that might have a potential for shifting corporate control by evading the disclosure requirements of Section 13(d) or (g) through preventing the vesting of beneficial ownership in the actor.

If that is what the Division means, then its proposed standard is more than satisfied in this case. TCI intentionally entered into the TRSs, with the purpose and intent of preventing the vesting of beneficial ownership in TCI, as part of a plan or scheme to evade the reporting requirements of Section 13(d) and thus concealed precisely what Section 13(d) was intended to force into the open. And if this is not what the Division means, the Division's argument would be unpersuasive. After all, there is not one word in Section 13(d) or in Rule 13d–3 that supports a requirement of an intent to create a false appearance of non-ownership if that term requires anything more than concealment of the sort of secret market accumulations that went on here.

Undaunted, TCI argues that it did not trigger Rule 13d–3(b). It relies in part on a letter from Professor Bernard Black to the SEC in which the professor argued that "it must be permissible for an investor to acquire equity swaps, rather than shares, in part—or indeed entirely—*because* share ownership is disclosable under § 13(d) while equity swaps are not."

He bases this argument on the premise that "the underlying [i.e., evasive] activity must involve holding a position which is 'beneficial ownership' under the *statute* (Exchange Act § 13(d) or (g)), but would otherwise fall outside the *rule*—outside the SEC's effort to define the concept of beneficial ownership elsewhere in Rule 13d–3." With respect, the Court finds the argument unpersuasive.

As an initial matter, the SEC, in the Court's view, has the power to treat as beneficial ownership a situation that would not fall within the statutory meaning of that term. Section 23(a) of the Exchange Act grants the Commission the "power to make such rules and regulations as may be necessary or appropriate to implement the provisions of this chapter for which [it is] responsible . . . " The validity of a rule or regulation promulgated under such a grant of authority will be sustained so long as it is "reasonably related to the purposes of the enabling legislation."

The purpose of Section 13(d) is to alert shareholders of "every large, rapid aggregation or accumulation of securities, regardless of technique employed, which might represent a potential shift in corporate control." Rule 13d–3(b) was promulgated to further this purpose by preventing circumvention of Rule 13d–3 with arrangements designed to avoid disclosure obligations by preventing the vesting of beneficial ownership as defined elsewhere—in other words, where there is accumulation of securities by any means with a potential shift of corporate control, but no beneficial ownership. As Rule 13d–3(b) therefore is reasonably related to the purpose of the statute, it is a perfectly appropriate exercise of the Commission's authority even where it reaches arrangements that otherwise would not amount to beneficial ownership.

Second, while it may be debated whether the term "beneficial ownership" as used in the Williams Act is broader than or coextensive with the same language as used in Rule 13d–3(a),[213] one thing is quite clear. If Rule 13d–3(b) reaches only situations that involve beneficial ownership, then it reaches only situations that are reached by Rule 13d–3(a). Professor Black's view thus would render Rule 13d–3(b) superfluous.

* * *

In sum, the Court finds that TCI created and used the TRSs with the purpose and effect of preventing the vesting of beneficial ownership in TCI as part of a plan or scheme to evade the reporting requirements of Section 13(d). Under the plain language of Rule 13d–3(b), it thus is

---

[213] The language of the Rule defines the term "[f]or the purposes of sections 13(d) and 13(g) of the Act." 17 C.F.R. § 240.13d–3(a). While the use in the Rule of the term "includes," *inter alia*, makes clear that Rule 13d–3(a)(1) and (2) are not the only criteria that define "beneficial ownership," Rule 13d–3(a) as a whole appears quite plainly to reflect the Commission's intent to define the term exhaustively for purposes of the statute. Curiously, however, the Division's *amicus* letter, without citation of authority, states that the Division "believes that Rule 13d–3, properly construed, is narrower in coverage than the statute."

deemed to be a beneficial owner of the shares held by its counterparties to hedge their short exposures created by the TRSs.

[The court determined that TCI and 3G formed a group as part of their plan or scheme to evade the reporting requirements of section 13(d), and that they did not disclose their joint ownership within ten days as required by the Act. The court denied CSX's request for an injunction that would prohibit the voting of any of the shares owned by the defendants at the 2008 annual meeting on the basis that CSX failed to show irreparable harm.]

NOTE

The district court declined to enjoin the Funds from voting their CSX shares, because their ownership was fully disclosed for other shareholders to consider. The Court of Appeals affirmed this decision. 292 F. App'x 133 (2d Cir. 2008). On further appeal, the Court of Appeals declined to decide whether the Total Return Equity Swaps must comply with section 13(d), because of disagreements on the panel. Instead it remanded to the District Court the question of group formation involving TCI and 3G. Judge Newman's opinion for the court did not discuss the swaps issue, but in a concurring opinion Judge Winter summarized his lengthy opinion as follows:

> In my view, cash-settled total-return equity swaps do not, without more, render the long party a "beneficial owner" of such shares with a potential disclosure obligation under Section 13(d). However, an agreement or understanding between the long and short parties to such a swap regarding the short party's purchasing of such shares as a hedge, the short party's selling of those shares to the long party upon the unwinding of the swap agreements, or the voting of such shares by the short parties renders the long party a "beneficial owner" of shares purchased as a hedge by the short party.

654 F.3d at 288–89.

PROBLEM

You represent a corporation that has just discovered that an investor has purchased a block of stock in excess of 10%, and it has filed an appropriate Schedule 13D. But the investor has tripped the trigger in a poison pill adopted by the company. Because the time has not yet run after which the rights become non-redeemable, and the client can still amend its rights plan, it proposes to except this investor from the definition of "Acquiring Person" under the Rights Plan, to the extent of its existing holdings. The client proposes that in exchange for this action, the investor will enter into a "standstill" agreement with the client, by which the investor will agree not to purchase any more client stock for ten years, and will further agree to vote its shares as instructed by the client. Does this create any filing obligations under the Williams Act? By whom? If the client doesn't want to create any schedule 13D filing obligations, how could you alter the stand-still agreement to achieve that result?

---

iii. WHAT IS "BENEFICIAL OWNERSHIP?"

Securities Exchange Act Rules 13d–1, 13d–3, 13d–4, and 13d–5.

Rule 13d–3(a) provides that a beneficial owner includes "any person who . . . has or shares: (1) voting power . . . ; and/or (2) investment power, which includes the power to dispose, or to direct the disposition of such security. . . ."

Rights to Acquire Shares

There may be several beneficial owners of the same security under Rule 13d–3(d)(i), which provides that a person will be deemed to be beneficial owner of a security if that person has the right to acquire beneficial ownership within 60 days pursuant to the exercise of options, warrants, or rights, the conversion of a security, through the power to revoke a trust or discretionary account, or when the trust or discretionary account is about to expire automatically.

Note that in GAF Corp. v. Milstein, the 10.25% convertible preferred triggered a 13D filing obligation; under this rule, the same shares must also be calculated as if converted, to determine whether, when added to any existing holdings of the common, they reach the triggering amount. The result is that one could hold less than 5% of a class of convertible security, and less than 5% of the common, and still have a 13D filing obligation if upon conversion the common stock would equal 5% or more of the outstanding common stock. The convertibles must be treated as if converted for purposes of calculating beneficial ownership of the common.

Transcon Lines v. A.G. Becker, Inc., 470 F.Supp. 356 (S.D.N.Y. 1979) held that an adviser to a takeover group, who expected to be treated fairly by the advisees if he became eligible to hold shares in the target (currently forbidden by ICC rules because of his ownership of another trucking line), did not have a right to acquire shares within 60 days. Even if he had a firm contract right under an oral agreement or implied contract, the court held that since it was contingent on his disposal of his current holdings, he lacked a right to acquire within the meaning of the rule.

Power of Sale

Wellman v. Dickinson, 682 F.2d 355 (2d Cir. 1982), infra, Part 3.B of this chapter, held that a brokerage firm holding target shares in discretionary accounts had the power to dispose of the shares, and was thus the beneficial owner of the shares, even though the voting rights belonged to the beneficial owner of the discretionary account. (A discretionary account is an account for which the customer has given the broker a power of attorney to buy and sell securities for the customer.)

The SEC staff takes the position that there may be several levels of beneficial ownership in employee stock ownership plans. San Jose Water Works [1977–78 Decisions] Fed. Sec. L. Rep.(CCH) ¶ 81,196 (April 7, 1977) dealt with a TRASOP (a specialized form of Employee Stock Ownership Plan created by the Tax Reduction Act of 1975). The trustee was to be the record owner of shares, with power to retain or dispose of securities held by the TRASOP. While the trustee was to vote employer shares as instructed by the participants with respect to the shares allocated to them, the power to sell was enough to constitute the trustee a beneficial owner. A mere record owner, with no ability to vote or dispose of stock without direction from a third party is not a beneficial owner. Calvary Holdings, Inc. v. Chandler, 948 F.2d 59 (1st Cir.1991); Second National Bank of Warren and The Raymond John Wean Foundation, [1988–89 Dec.] Fed. Sec. L. Rep. (CCH) ¶ 78,833 (Div. Corp. Fin. 1988).

Power to Vote

The TRASOP plan of San Jose Water Works, *supra*, was to be administered by an administrative committee consisting of two persons appointed by the employer. The administrative committee had the power to instruct the trustee how to vote unallocated shares. If those securities exceed 5% of the class, the administrative committee was obligated to file Schedule 13D. Employees had the power to instruct the trustee how to vote shares allocated to them. The SEC ruled that this constituted beneficial ownership, and these shares must be aggregated with any other shares of the same class for purposes of determining percentage ownership.

Where incumbent management decided to adopt an ESOP as a defensive tactic, the shares allocated to management were treated as acquired pursuant to an agreement, thus creating a section 13(d)(3) "group", with a Schedule 13D filing obligation if their total holdings, including ESOP shares allocated to their accounts, over which they had voting control, exceeded 5%. Podesta v. Calumet Industries, Inc., [1978 Decisions] Fed. Sec. L. Rep. (CCH) ¶ 96,433 (N.D. Ill. 1978).

This reasoning suggests that where a corporation owns 5% of the stock in another firm, the directors who control the corporation may also have a Schedule 13D filing obligation as "beneficial owners" because of their power to direct the voting of shares. 3B Bloomenthal, SECURITIES AND FEDERAL CORPORATE LAW § 13.20[2]. This may create inadvertent section 13(d) violations by management of bidders. It can create several levels of beneficial ownership of the same securities. In Wellman v. Dickinson, 475 F.Supp. 783, 828–30 (S.D.N.Y. 1979), *infra*, Part 3.B of this chapter, the CEO of a brokerage firm was treated as a beneficial owner of shares held in firm discretionary accounts, as well as of shares in mutual funds where the firm served as investment adviser through a subsidiary.

Investment advisers advising clients may also be treated as beneficial owners, if it is customary for the owners to follow their advice in voting their shares. In Bath Industries, Inc. v. Blot, 427 F.2d 97 (7th Cir. 1970), an investment adviser was treated as beneficial owner of shares of various advisee accounts. The court stated:

> "If a mutual fund, bank, trustee, broker or anyone else can guarantee a block of votes, the legal title to such shares would appear irrelevant. So far as the actual practice is concerned, [plaintiff's witnesses] testified that the usual practice is for an account to permit the investment bank that advised it to buy the stock to vote the stock. Thus, we conclude that the district court properly found that, for the purposes of the Williams Act, [the investment advisers] are the beneficial owners of Bath shares which they have the right to vote." 427 F.2d at 112.

In Jacobs v. Pabst Brewing Co., 549 F.Supp. 1050 (D.Del. 1982), an investment adviser, Torray Clark & Co., which had clients with holdings in Pabst, talked to an insurgent group, and directed its clients to vote with the insurgents. After further discussions with management, Torray Clark directed its clients to vote for management, and found itself sued by the insurgents for failure to file a 13D. While its clients apparently held shares in their own names, Torray Clark had informed both sides of its power to direct the voting of their shares as a block, and the court held that it had a filing obligation.

Rule 13d–3(b) deals explicitly with evasions:

> "(b) Any person who, directly or indirectly, creates or uses a trust, proxy, power of attorney, pooling arrangement or any other contract, arrangement or device with the purpose or effect of divesting such person of beneficial ownership as part of a plan or scheme to evade the reporting requirements of Section 13(d) or 13(g) shall be deemed for purposes of such sections to be the beneficial owner of such security."

Where doubt exists about the beneficial ownership of securities, one safe tactic is for the putative beneficial owner to file a Schedule 13D, while disclaiming beneficial ownership of the securities in the filing. See Rule 13d–4. This technique has been used by persons who were concerned about membership in § 13(d)(3) groups.

The SEC takes the position that *any* acquisition of 5% of the securities of an issuer is covered, whether through purchase, inheritance, gift, or otherwise. Rule 13d–5(a) provides that executors and administrators of a decedent's estate do not acquire beneficial ownership until they are qualified under local law to perform their duties. *But see* Ozark Air Lines, Inc. v. Cox, 326 F.Supp. 1113 (E.D.Mo.1971), where a court held that the receipt of shares by inheritance by a trustee was not the kind of acquisition covered by the Act, which was focused on acquisitions which have the effect of changing or influencing the control of the issuer or affecting the market.

A pledgee under a bona fide pledge agreement is not deemed the beneficial owner and does not have the power to vote, direct the vote, dispose, or direct the disposition of the securities (except in margin account agreements). Rule 13d–3(d)(3). The implication is that when foreclosure occurs, or perhaps even an event of default that gives the pledgee the power to dispose of the collateral, or direct its disposition, the pledgee becomes the beneficial owner at that time. Even if the securities were sold within the 10-day period allowed for filing Schedule 13D, the SEC staff has taken the position that the filing obligation remains. American Pepsi Cola Bottlers, Inc., [1971–72 Decisions] Fed. Sec. L. Rep.(CCH) ¶ 78,765 (Mar. 23, 1972).

The single exception to this rule is that where an issuer's repurchase activities raise one's holdings over the 5% threshold by the reduction in the number of outstanding shares, no Schedule 13D filing obligation is triggered. Drico Industrial Corp., [1977–78 Decisions] Fed. Sec. L. Rep. (CCH) ¶ 81,270 (May 25, 1976). Accord: Aranow, Einhorn & Berlstein, DEVELOPMENTS IN TENDER OFFERS FOR CORPORATE CONTROL, 37 (1977).

PROBLEM

Your client has accumulated 4.99% of the stock of a target. Your client has previously invested in several takeover targets, and has customarily used a single broker for its acquisitions. In many of these acquisitions, the CEO of the client has asked the broker to acquire shares in its own name, with the understanding that the client may "call" the shares at any time at the broker's purchase price plus interest, and that the broker may "put" the shares to the client on the same basis. This has the effect of not revealing any record ownership in the client prior to the time the 5% level is reached, and a Schedule 13D must be filed. Now your client wants the broker to engage in purchases that, if combined with the client's, would amount to more than 5%. The purchase of more than 500 shares would trigger this obligation.

1. Can your client tell the broker to purchase target shares on the usual put and call basis without filing a Schedule 13D once the broker acquires 500 shares?

2. Can your client simply suggest to the broker that the purchase of target stock in large amounts would be a very good investment in the short term?

See S.E.C. v. First City Financial Corp., Ltd., 890 F.2d 1215 (D.C.Cir.1989).

---

iv.   CALCULATING 5% OF A CLASS OF EQUITY SECURITY

Securities Exchange Act, Section 3(a)(11).

Rule 13d–1(d) provides:

> "(d) For the purpose of this regulation, the term 'equity security' means any equity security of a class which is registered pursuant to Section 12 of that Act, or any equity security of any insurance company which would have been required to be so registered except for the exemption contained in Section 12(g)(2)(G) of the Act, or any equity security issued by a closed-end investment company registered under the Investment Company Act of 1940; provided, such term shall not include securities of a class of non-voting securities."

Securities Exchange Act Rule 3a–11 defines equity securities broadly, to include "stock or similar security ... or any security convertible, with or without consideration into such a security, or carrying any warrant or right to subscribe to or purchase such a security, or any such warrant or right, or any put, call, straddle, or other option or privilege of buying from or such a security from or selling a security to another without being bound to do so."

Such a class of equity securities is only subject to registration under the '34 Act if it is held by 500 or more shareholders of record under § 12(g)(1), or is traded on a national securities exchange under § 12(b), or is a newly public issuer with a filing obligation under § 15(d) of the '34 Act. GAF Corp. v. Milstein, 453 F.2d 709 (2d Cir.1971), held that § 13(d) covered the "acquisition" of 10.25% of the convertible preferred stock of GAF, even though, if converted into common, it would not have represented the triggering 10% of that class. The only trap is that a "class" is defined in § 12(g)(5) to include all securities of the issuer "which are of substantially similar character and the holders of which enjoy substantially similar rights and privileges." One authoritative treatise concludes that convertible securities are not to be treated as part of the same class as the shares into which they are convertible. See 3E Harold Bloomenthal and Samuel Wolff, SECURITIES AND FEDERAL CORPORATE LAW, § 25:7 (Supp. 1998). This result is contrary to similar decisions dealing with § 16(b) calculations. Chemical Fund, Inc. v. Xerox Corp., 377 F.2d 107 (2d Cir.1967). Query: How would the courts treat a situation where a buyer purchased less than 5% of a class of convertible preferred shares, if it carried the right to conversion into more than 5% of the common stock? How would the courts treat a situation where a buyer held preferred shares convertible into 3% of the target's common stock and also owned another 3% of the common stock itself?

While generally § 13(d) applies only to classes of equity securities registered under the '34 Act, it also covers insurance company stocks that are otherwise exempt from '34 Act registration and stocks in some investment companies. Rule 13d–1(e) provides that, in determining the outstanding shares of the class, any person may rely upon the issuer's most recent quarterly or annual report and any current report subsequent thereto filed with the SEC, unless he knows or has reason to believe that the information in the filing is inaccurate.

v.   DISCLOSURE OBLIGATIONS

Those acquiring shares have a natural reluctance to reveal information about their acquisitions. Normally trading in publicly held securities is anonymous. At common law buyers generally are under no obligation to reveal to sellers why they find these securities more valuable than the sellers believe them to be, except in the special case of buyers in a fiduciary relationship with sellers. Typically buyers subject to the Williams Act are not insiders, and, absent Williams Act disclosure requirements, need not reveal the information that motivates them to buy under more general antifraud provisions such as Rule 10b–5. Revelation of that information may, of course, cause current shareholders to raise the reservation price they demand for their shares, increasing the buyer's costs, and perhaps making the planned acquisition of control so costly that the project will be abandoned. All studies of market activity prior to the announcement of a tender offer show upward movement in the target's share price, as information about a forthcoming bid leaks to traders.

What follows is an attempt to examine disclosure obligations under major parts of Schedule 13D, with sample disclosures and a discussion of problems that have arisen under each item.

In late 1999 the SEC revised the disclosure requirements for tender offers, in Schedule TO, 17 C.F.R. 240.14d–100. SEC Securities Act Release No. 7760, 1999 SEC LEXIS 2291 (Oct. 22, 1999). This replaced former Schedule 14D–1, but left the disclosures of Schedule 13D unchanged. In the case of tender offers, which may in some cases be exchange offers, the purpose was to integrate the disclosure requirements with those for mergers, in Regulation M-A, 17 C.F.R. 229.1000. Because much of the case law predates these changes, the following table compares the headings of the two schedules. In most cases the language of the disclosure requirements is substantially the same:

Disclosure title	Schedule 13D	Schedule TO
Summary Term Sheet		Item 1
Security and Issuer (of the target)	Item 1	Item 2 (Reg. M-A, Item 1002)
Identity and Background (of the bidder)	Item 2	Item 3 (Reg. M-A, Item 1003)
Source and Amount of Funds or Other Consideration	Item 3	Item 7 (Item 1007, Reg. M-A)
Purpose of Transaction	Item 4	Item 6 (Item 1006, Reg. M-A)
Interest in Securities of the Issuer	Item 5	Item 8 (Item 1008, Reg. M-A)
Contracts, Arrangements, Understandings or Relationships With Respect to Securities of the Issuer	Item 6	n/a
Terms of the Transaction	n/a	Item 4 (Item 1004, Reg. M-A)
Past Contracts, Transactions, Negotiations and Agreements (between bidder & target)	n/a	Item 5 (Item 1005, Reg. M-A)
Persons/Assets Retained, Employed, Compensated or Used (by bidder)	n/a	Item 9 (Item 1009, Reg. M-A)
Financial Statements (of bidder, or issuer in self-tender offer)	n/a	Item 10 (Item 1010, Reg. M-A)
Additional Information (about arrangements between bidder & target)	n/a	Item 11 (Item 1011, Reg. M-A)
Exhibits (these requirements overlap, but are not identical)	Item 7	Item 12 (Item 1016, Reg. M-A)
Information Required by Schedule 13E–3 (going private)	n/a	Item 13

The following material treats disclosures on Schedule 13D.

Item 3. Source and Amount of Funds or Other Consideration

"State the source and amount of funds or other consideration used or to be used in making the purchases, and if any part of the purchase prices is or will be represented by fund or other consideration borrowed or otherwise obtained for the purpose of acquiring, holding, trading, or voting the securities, a description of the transaction and the names of the parties thereto. Where material, such information should also be provided with respect to prior acquisitions not previously reported pursuant to this regulation. If the source of all or any part of the funds is a loan made in the ordinary course of business by a bank, as defined in Section 3(a)(6) of the Act, the name of the bank shall not be made available to the public if the person at the time of filing the statement so requests in writing and files such request, naming such bank, with the Secretary of the Commission. If the securities were acquired other than by purchase, describe the method of acquisition."

Sample Disclosure:

"As of the close of business on June 25, 1982, Securities owned 499,000 shares of Common Stock which it purchased for an aggregate consideration of $14,552,762.50 (excluding brokerage commissions). As of the close of business on June 25, 1981, Associates owned 323,900 shares of Common Stock which it purchased for an aggregate consideration of $10,017,337.50 (excluding brokerage commissions). The funds used by each Reporting Person for its purchase of such shares were obtained from such Reporting Person's working capital and from the proceeds of demand loans made by one or more banks in the ordinary course of business. Such loans bear interest at the brokers' 'call rate' from time to time in effect. Although no shares of Common Stock are now pledged, from time to time in the past Common Stock and other securities had been pledged and Common Stock and other securities may be pledged from time to time in the future to secure borrowings."

Schedule 13D of O'Connor Securities and O'Connor Associates with respect to The Trane Company, in Trane Co. v. O'Connor Securities, 561 F.Supp. 301, 302–03 (S.D.N.Y. 1983).

This disclosure was sustained as adequate by District Judge Carter in the following language:

"Nor am I persuaded that Item 3 of the Schedule 13d is improper. Defendants are not required to describe, in the detail plaintiff suggests, the financial transactions which defendants undertook to secure funds to buy the Trane Stock. [cite omitted] There is no need for O'Connor to describe the terms of the loans, dates taken out, the collateral utilized to secure them, etc. These are private details which would be of no interest to a shareholder. Moreover, the details of the loan arrangements are probably confidential business information which O'Connor should not be required to expose as a matter of course. Naturally, if such information became essential to vindicate plaintiff's right, exposure might be warranted. Moreover, plaintiff does not need this information for this litigation. It does not question the fact that the money O'Connor secured to finance the Trane transactions was secured in legitimate business dealings with defendants' bank and other financial institutions." 561 F.Supp. at 309.

In one sense, all borrowings indirectly enable a purchaser to acquire the shares in question. One court has rejected this notion of the required extent of disclosure, and held that a group needs to disclose only borrowing for the specific purpose of acquiring stock. Standard Metals Corp. v. Tomlin, 503 F.Supp. 586, 604 (S.D.N.Y.1980). In Purolator, Inc. v. Tiger International, Inc., 510 F.Supp. 554, 557 (D.D.C. 1981), the court similarly excused disclosure of an issue of debentures that were not directly used to finance the acquisition, citing the Standard Metals decision. In Management Assistance, Inc. v. Edelman, 584 F.Supp. 1021 (S.D.N.Y.1984), Asher Edelman had disclosed that three partnerships he controlled had acquired MAI stock, and that "in each case such shares were purchased with the respective partnership's partnership funds. . . ." MAI claimed that Edelman should have disclosed that the purchases were financed with the $12 million proceeds from loans from Citibank made six months before the first purchase of MAI stock. The court noted that these loans refinanced the purchase of stock of another company, which was pledged as collateral for the loans, and that the purpose of the loans, according to the lending documents, was to increase the trading ability and liquidity of the partnerships. The court noted that in the intervening six months the partnerships had actively traded hundreds of millions of dollars of securities in thousands of transactions, and that thus borrowings for the purpose of acquiring stock are loans for the purpose of carrying on their ordinary business activities. For MAI to argue that any borrowings for such purpose were for the purpose of acquiring MAI stock "would essentially be a requirement that they disclose all corporate borrowings regardless of whether they had any relationship to the purchase of MAI stock." 584 F.Supp. at 1030. The court found no violation of the disclosure requirements. Hubco, Inc. v. Rappaport, 628 F.Supp. 345 (D.N.J.1985) held that the source and amount of funds used to purchase shares below the 5% trigger need not be revealed unless it was material.

Item 4. Purpose of Transaction

"State the purpose or purposes of the acquisition of securities of the issuer. Describe any plans or proposals which the reporting persons may have which relate to or would result in: . . . "

"(a) The acquisition by any person of additional securities of the issuer, or the disposition of securities of the issuer."

Sample Disclosure:

"The shares of the Issuer's Common Stock covered by this Statement were purchased and are being held for investment. Bliss & Laughlin intends to continually assess the Issuer's financial position and operations and the market for the purchase and sale of the Issuer's securities. Depending upon such continuing assessment and future developments, Bliss & Laughlin may determine, from time to time or at any time, to increase its investment in the Issuer's Common Stock, or sell or otherwise dispose of some or all of its holdings. In making any such determination, Bliss & Laughlin will also consider other business opportunities available to it, prospects for its own business, and money and stock market conditions."

Kirsch Co. v. Bliss & Laughlin Industries, Inc., 495 F.Supp. 488, 492–93 (W.D.Mich.1980). The facts developed at trial indicated that Bliss & Laughlin (BLI) had a history of negotiated acquisitions, but that negotiations had become difficult recently because BLI had two major shareholders who were prominent takeover actors. The company also had surplus cash it needed to invest so it would be a less attractive target, and needed to obtain at least a 20% interest in any company in which it invested in order to be able to use the equity method of accounting, which allows the owner to take in a pro rata share of the earnings of the target in its own income statement, rather than the much smaller amount of dividends typically paid. (See Chapter 3, Part 2.B, "Partial Acquisitions".) This need was developed through an expert witness for Kirsch, and was supported by the fact that BLI's accounting firm had explained the operation of the equity method to BLI officials. As the court said, "This method of accounting is based on the presumption that, absent facts to the contrary, a shareholder who owns 20 percent or more of an issuer's securities has the ability to control or exercise significant influence over the issuer." 495 F.Supp. at 495 (emphasis the Court's). The court observed that BLI was, by its history and corporate motives, acquisition-oriented, had acquired many other companies meeting certain criteria; that Kirsch met the criteria, and that the history of purchases indicated an intent to acquire at least 20%. Further, rough drafts of the Schedule 13D indicated that BLI had reserved the right to seek control, propose a merger, etc., but this was deleted. The court concluded that this demonstrated that counsel thought such disclosure would be prudent and held that the Schedule 13D failed to make adequate disclosure of its purposes. The earlier drafts of the Schedule 13D were viewed as convincing proof that BLI had seriously considered other alternatives, when coupled with the other evidence. But see Saunders Leasing System, Inc. v. Societe Holding Gray D'Albion S.A., 507 F.Supp. 627 (N.D.Ala. 1981) (holding that where a family group owned 56% of the stock, a bidder's intention to acquire 25% of the stock did not constitute control, especially where cumulative voting does not exist.) The court rejected the conclusions of the decision in Dan River, Inc. v. Unitex Ltd., 624 F.2d 1216, 1219 (4th Cir.1980), that acquisition of 25% per se involved control, at least in these circumstances.

Sample Disclosure:

The Shares owned by Pennzoil have been acquired as a long-term investment. See the accompanying letter to Pennzoil shareholders filed as Exhibit 1 hereto. In addition to the expected benefits from ownership of the Shares, including potential appreciation in the value of the Shares and the potential receipt of dividends and distributions payable or made on the Shares, Pennzoil believes that its investment in the Shares may provide Pennzoil the opportunity to defer for an indefinite period a portion of the federal income taxes that would otherwise be payable currently on the litigation settlement proceeds which Pennzoil received from Texaco in 1988.

Pennzoil may decide to continue to expend up to an amount equal to the original Texaco settlement net proceeds (approximately $2.6 billion) to purchase additional shares for investment from time to time. Such additional purchases, if any, will be dependent upon, among other factors, prevailing market prices for the Shares and prevailing market and economic conditions generally.

Pennzoil will monitor on a regular basis its investment in the Shares and the Issuer's business affairs and financial position, as well as the market value of the Shares, conditions in the securities markets and general economic and industry conditions. Depending on the results of Pennzoil's ongoing review, Pennzoil may in the future take such actions in respect of its investment in the Shares it deems appropriate in light of circumstances existing from time to time.

Although Pennzoil has for analytical purposes considered the hypothetical effect of higher percentage levels of investment up to as much as 18% and the effect of accounting for such an investment using the cost method and the equity method of accounting, Pennzoil has no current plans or proposals other than those set forth above in the second paragraph of this Item 4 which relate to or would result in (i) the acquisition by any person of additional securities of the Issuer, or the disposition of securities of the Issuer, (ii) an extraordinary corporate transaction such as a merger, reorganization or liquidation, involving the Issuer or any of its subsidiaries, (iii) a sale or transfer of a material amount of assets of the Issuer or any of its subsidiaries, (iv) any change in the present board or directors or management of the Issuer, (v) any material change in the present capitalization or dividend policy of the Issuer, (vi) any other material change in the Issuer's business or corporate structure, (vii) changes in the Issuer's charter, bylaws or instruments corresponding there to or other actions which may impede the acquisition of control of the Issuer by any person, (viii) causing a class of securities of the Issuer to be delisted from a national securities exchange, (ix) a class of equity securities of the Issuer becoming eligible for termination of registration pursuant to Section 12(g)(4) of the Exchange Act or (x) any action similar to those enumerated above.

Chevron Corp. v. Pennzoil Co., 974 F.2d 1156 (9th Cir.1992). Pennzoil, having received $3 billion in settlement of its litigation with Texaco over tortious interference with its contract (letter of intent) to acquire an interest in Getty Oil, was attempting to make an investment comparable to that it had obtained in Getty Oil, in order to defer federal income taxes. Pennzoil executives testified that their tax position would be enhanced if Pennzoil had board representation in Chevron, and Chevron's expert witness testified that Pennzoil would have great difficulties with sustaining its tax position absent such board representation (contrary, of course, to Pennzoil's expert). The Court of Appeals reversed the trial court's dismissal of Chevron's claim on summary judgment, holding that there was a triable issue of fact:

> "The Supreme Court has stated that where" the factual context renders [a] claim implausible—if the claim is one that simply makes no economic sense—[the claimants] must come forward with more persuasive evidence to support their claim than would otherwise be necessary. "Matsushita Elec. Indus. Co. v. Zenith Radio, 475 U.S. 574, 587, 106 S.Ct. 1348, 1356, 89 L.Ed.2d 538 (1986). While in this case we need not go so far as to find Pennzoil's Section 13(d) claim—that its purchase of Chevron stock was simply a good investment that might provide some tax benefit—economically implausible—it is significant that Chevron's analysis makes better economic sense in light of the enormous tax liability Pennzoil will face if the deferral is denied. Pennzoil admits that it has now invested $2.2 billion of the settlement proceeds in approximately 9.4% of Chevron's outstanding stock. Pennzoil will be forced to pay in excess of $800 million in federal taxes if it cannot demonstrate, to the Internal Revenue Service's satisfaction, that the Chevron

investment is sufficiently similar to the Getty investment. On the basis of the record in this case, Pennzoil's argument that, in purchasing Chevron stock it merely sought a solid long term investment and did not intend to make every effort to obtain the tax deferral, is subject to serious doubt. Under these circumstances, Chevron's affidavits were sufficient to raise a genuine issue of material fact. A reasonable trier of fact, drawing the inferences most favorable to Chevron, could conclude from the affidavits and other cognizable evidence before the court that Pennzoil more probably than not sought control." 974 F.2d at 1161.

Sample Disclosure:

"The Reporting Persons have acquired their shares of common stock for investment. The Reporting Persons' objective is to sell such shares, together with any additional shares they may acquire, at a profit.

"The Reporting Persons may acquire additional shares if to do so would represent an opportunity for profit. The Reporting persons may sell their shares to any person, including the issuer.

"If the Reporting Persons have not sold their shares in the near term, they may attempt to interest the Issuer or other parties in a transaction that could result in disposition of the Reporting Persons' shares at a profit. Although no decision has been made to do so, the Reporting Persons may utilize a tender offer or other means to seek control of the Issuer in order to achieve their investment objective. If the Reporting persons were to seek and acquire control of the Issuer, they would undertake to sell their shares, sell or merge the issuer or otherwise pursue their investment objective. They would not attempt to influence or change the Issuer's on-going business.

"Except as set forth in this Item 4, neither the Reporting Persons nor the General Partners have any plans or proposals nor are they aware of any, which would result in any of the events enumerated in clauses (a)–(j) of Item 4 of Schedule 13D. In the future, however, the Reporting Persons may formulate such plans or proposals."

Schedule 13D of O'Connor Securities and affiliates, reported in Trane Co. v. O'Connor Securities, 561 F.Supp. 301, 303 (S.D.N.Y. 1983)

Two days after filing the Schedule 13D, O'Connor Securities made additional purchases of shares. The amendments to the 13D filed as a result of these purchases did not change these disclosures of purposes. The day after filing the amendment, O'Connor made an offer to buy a block representing approximately 18% of the target's securities, and a few days thereafter succeeded in buying about 5% of the issuer's shares. The court held that once O'Connor made the decision to acquire more than 5%, it is inconceivable that O'Connor was not committed to further large accumulations, in view of its determination that Trane was a likely takeover target, and the purchase of a large block by O'Connor would attract attention to the stock, which would more quickly assure their goal of a profit on a resale. The court held the filing was misleading, emphasizing the rapid acquisition of additional shares shortly after the filing as negating a lack of intent, if not a plan, to make further acquisitions. 561 F.Supp. 307–08.

The court also held that the statement suggesting the possibility of a tender offer was misleading under the circumstances, where they were not consistent with the buyers' past pattern as risk arbitrageurs, where no discussions had been undertaken with financial institutions concerning underwriting a tender offer, and no discussions had been undertaken with brokerage firms, counsel or other partners about a tender offer. The court concluded that it could not believe that an investment partnership that had never run a publicly owned company was seriously interested in a tender offer for control, and that the statement was thus misleading. 561 F.Supp. at 308.

The Form

"(b) An extraordinary corporate transaction, such as a merger, reorganization or liquidation, involving the issuer or any of its subsidiaries;"

Sample Disclosure:

"The Company intends through this Offer to acquire control of Specialty. It does not presently have any plans or proposals to liquidate Specialty, to sell its assets or to merge it with any persons (other than the Company or its subsidiaries), or to make any other change in its business or corporate structure. . . . Upon completion of this Offer the Company will give consideration to a merger between itself or a subsidiary and Speciality."

Schedule 14D–1 of International Controls Corp. filed in connection with tender offer for Electronic Speciality Co., in Electronic Specialty Co. v. International Controls Corp., 295 F.Supp. 1063, 1079–80 (S.D.N.Y. 1968). (Note that Schedule 14D–1, governing tender offers, has disclosure requirements that parallel those of Schedule 13D.)

Electronic Specialty sued to enjoin the tender offer on the ground that ICC had failed to disclose its firm intent to merge with ELS, despite the fact that ICC had arranged for bank credit to provide sufficient funds for a merger. ELS made this argument in part because ICC had initially approached ELS management with a proposal of merger talks. Affirming the district court on this issue, Judge Friendly wrote:

"As we read the record, ICC put forward merger early in the game as an alternative that, perhaps because of tax considerations to the stockholders, might be more acceptable to ELS than a tender offer, which ICC's directors then insisted could be made only if ELS agreed. Nothing in this committed ICC to propose a merger as a consequence of a successful 'overhead' tender offer or evidenced a firm intention that it would. If ICC acquired control as a result of a tender offer, the circumstances might or might not suggest a merger—an issue that could and presumably would be explored with the deliberation then possible. The statement in the August 19 offer that ICC would 'give consideration' to a merger in the event of success thus seems entirely accurate and the subsequent elaboration [by an amendment to the 13D that a merger would be considered on the basis of the relative market prices of the shares] unnecessary."

Electronic Specialty Co. v. International Controls Corp., 409 F.2d 937, 948–49 (2d Cir. 1969). Judge Friendly's tolerance for generality in this case was inspired by a detailed record showing disagreement between the CEO of ICC and its board over the course of action to pursue, and documented changes of policy by the board over the appropriate course to pursue. Further, the board had explicitly rejected a hostile tender offer at an early stage in its deliberations, only to change its mind at the urging of the CEO. Ironically, the CEO whose honest disclosures were vindicated in this case was Robert Vesco, now a fugitive from U.S. justice after being accused of massive frauds in connection with his management of another company.

Sample Disclosure:

"In this case the only statement of such purpose set forth in the 13D filing is a disclaimer of any plans or proposals 'to liquidate the Issuer, sell its assets, merge it with any other person or persons, or make any other major change in its business or corporate structure.' "

Schedule 13D of Carl C. Icahn in Marshall Field & Co. v. Icahn, 537 F.Supp. 413 (S.D.N.Y. 1982).

Icahn had engaged in a thorough analysis of the value of Marshall Field, and that thorough analysis included such alternatives as liquidation. The presence of the studies indicated to the Court that a serious disclosure issue existed, justifying issuance of a temporary restraining order. The court's opinion discussed not only the evidence, but the balance between disclosure of plans and proposals:

"There is some substantial proof in the evidence submitted after a few days of hasty discovery to the effect that the defendants have formulated tentative purposes which would include extraordinary corporate transactions, material sales of assets and material changes in Marshall Field's business. The evidence, although sketchy and incomplete, suggests that the motivation for the sudden attempt to acquire effective control of Marshall Field (involving the investment of what may well run to $70,000,000) may be a perception that the real estate assets of the company are worth far more on a liquidation basis than the going business value of the retailing concern. This is the conclusion expressed in a study prepared for Mr. Icahn last year. There is also sketchy evidence that the purchasing group has already formulated some tentative plans as to how cash raised in the liquidation of certain real estate assets might be invested, including the acquisition of undervalued companies." 537 F.Supp. at 415.

Turning to the questions of premature disclosure of proposals, the court stated:

"Although mindful of the Court of Appeals' warning that Congress did not intend 'to impose an unrealistic requirement of laboratory conditions that might make [the Williams Act] a potent tool for incumbent management to protect its own interest against the desires and welfare of the stockholders,' Electronic Specialty Co. v. International Controls Corp., 409 F.2d 937, 948 (2d Cir. 1969), and of the warning of the Fifth Circuit that a registrant should not be required to make predictions of future behavior which may result in unjustified reliance by a public investor, Susquehanna Corp. v. Pan American Sulphur Co., 423 F.2d 1075, 1083–84 (5th Cir. 1970), I nonetheless question whether an acquirer of control whose acquisition is motivated primarily by plans, however tentative, which would seriously alter the structure and business of the acquiring company [sic], is not obligated under the statute and regulations to inform the marketplace of the kind of plans being considered. Such advice can and should when appropriate be written in properly tentative language to avoid creating unjustified reliance." 537 F.2d at 416.

Sample Disclosure:

"Shortly before deciding to make this [Tender] Offer United had preliminary discussions with the management of the Company with respect to the possibility of a merger or similar combination of the businesses of the Company and United. These discussions were terminated when United was advised that the Board of Directors of the Company did not wish at that time to entertain a proposal by United with respect to such a combination. There is no agreement or understanding between United and the Company to the effect that any proposal will be made with respect to such a combination or that any such transaction will be consummated and United has not formulated any plan or proposal to merge the Company with United or with any other person or to cause the Company to sell its assets or liquidate or to make any other major change in the Company's business or corporate structure. United intends, however, if it purchases Shares pursuant to the Offer to continue to study the Company and its business and, if it determines that such a transaction is advisable, to propose the terms thereof to the Company and to seek to have the Company consummate such a transaction."

Schedule 13D of United Technologies Corp. in Otis Elevator Co. v. United Technologies Corp., 405 F.Supp. 960, 962–63 (S.D.N.Y.1975).

Prior to approaching target executives to propose a friendly merger, United Executives had their staff prepare extensive documentation about the terms of a proposed merger. The merger proposal involved a combination of cash, United Common and United convertible preferred, structured to create a tax-free exchange for those Otis shareholders who preferred it, with cash for those who wanted to sell. After the rebuff by Otis executives, United management considered a tender offer, which included the same merger plan as previously proposed. That plan involved a cash tender offer for 40% of the Otis stock, followed an exchange offer of United common for 30% of Otis's stock, and an exchange offer of a United convertible preferred stock for the remaining common. During the preparation of the tender offer documents, the merger documents that were previously prepared were updated to reflect changes in relative stock prices. No executive decision was made about a merger prior to the tender offer, and while the basic merger plan was explained to United's Board prior to the tender offer, it was not discussed by the board when it approved the cash tender offer. Counsel for United insisted these documents were presented to the board because they contained a great deal of financial data on Otis. Held: plans or proposals are not inchoate but material if there is evidence of its adoption by high corporate officers over a period of time. The court did not rely on board approval for its decision, but then went on to state that "it strains credulity to believe that the United Board did not realize that its officers had placed before it the first step in a two-step merger plan." 405 F.Supp. at 972.

Sample Disclosure:

"Susquehanna does not plan or propose to liquidate Pan American, to sell its assets or merge with it, any other person, or to make any other major change in its business or corporate structure. However, if, at some subsequent time, it should appear the interests of the Pan American stockholders would be better served by any of the foregoing courses of action, Susquehanna may propose or adopt such course."

Schedule 13D of the Susquehanna Corporation, in Matter of the Susquehanna Corporation, [1969–70 Decisions] Fed. Sec. L. Rep. ¶ 77,741 (Hearing Examiner's decision, SEC, 1969), aff'd *Id.* at ¶ 77,842, 44 S.E.C. 379 (1970).

Prior to the initial filing of a Schedule 13D at the beginning of a tender offer, Susquehanna officers had met with investment and commercial banks to seek financing for the offer, and had pointed out that the target, Pan American Sulphur Co. (PASCO), had approximately $60 million cash that could be used for the acquisition of other companies. During the pendency of the tender offer the president of Susquehanna approached the officers of American Smelting and Refining Co. (ASARCO) and proposed using PASCO as the vehicle for a business combination. The Schedule 13D was amended in other respects thereafter, but not with respect to this item. Susquehanna argued that it had not violated the Schedule 13D requirements because his intentions were "amorphous . . . merely ideas and hopes . . . " ¶ 77,741, at p. 83,698, and that no formal corporate action had been taken approving the ideas of the president, the second ranking corporate official. *Id.* at 83,699. Both the hearing examiner and the SEC concluded that the president's intentions were a plan or proposal within the meaning of the statute. The SEC cited the language of the hearing examiner, that " . . . the energy, aggressiveness and persistence of the Korholz efforts to bring to fruition his intentions to put the cash assets to use by acquisition or merger give to his intentions the substance, quality and character of a plan, as the term is used in this statute." ¶ 77,842, at 83,986–87.

Sample Disclosure:

"The purpose of Mannip's purchasing Shares is to acquire an equity investment in the Company. The Filing persons intend continuously to evaluate Mannip's position in the Company and the Company's business and industry. The Filing Persons presently intend for Mannip to make additional purchases of shares in open-market or private transactions, the extent of which will depend upon such evaluation and upon prevailing market and other conditions. Neither Mannip nor Unitex presently intends to seek to acquire control of the Company, to seek representation on the Company's Board of Directors, to seek joint ventures on other business relationships with the Company or to propose a merger of similar transaction with the Company. In addition, depending upon the results of such evaluation and upon prevailing market and other conditions, Mannip may dispose of all or a portion of its Shares.

"Since the Filing Persons could determine to seek to acquire control of the Company, seek representation on the Company's Board of Directors, seek joint ventures or other business relationships with the Company or propose a merger or similar transaction with the Company, Mannip should not be considered solely as a passive investor. However, it should not be assumed that a plan will in fact be formulated to do any of the foregoing." Dan River, Inc. v. Unitex Ltd., 624 F.2d 1216, 1219 (4th Cir.1980).

This disclosure was an amended Schedule 13D in response to a district court order for fuller disclosure. Even then the plaintiff amended its complaint to allege further inadequacies, and the trial court refused to dismiss in the face of complaints that the Schedule 13D failed to disclose the purpose of control persons of one of the bidders to control Dan River to be able to purchase its scarce output at favorable prices, and general allegations that it fails "to disclose fully the 'non-passive' role defendants intend to play in Dan River, or to identify the 'long-term relationship' that defendants may seek to establish with Dan River. . . ." Thus, any general language may become the focus of a complaint that will allow the plaintiff to stay in court through some preliminary hearings. See Dan River, Inc. v. Icahn, 701 F.2d 278 [1982–1983 Decisions] (Fed. Sec. L. Rep. (CCH) ¶ 99,043) (4th Cir. 1983) for an example of how to reserve all options in a Schedule 13D.

The Form

"(c) A sale or transfer of a material amount of assets of the issuer or any of its subsidiaries;"

Sample Disclosure:

"In its Schedule 13D, Tiger stated that its purpose in buying the shares was 'to acquire a significant minority interest in Purolator' and announced that Tiger was 'prepared to explore with the management of Purolator the possibility of Tiger acquiring Purolator's Services Group.' "

Purolator, Inc. v. Tiger International, Inc., 510 F.Supp. 554, at 555 (D.D.C. 1981).

Does this adequately disclose an intent to acquire control of Purolator and its air courier service? The District Judge thought there was no evidence that Tiger had determined to acquire control, and that the disclosure of the interest in the courier service was adequate, holding that no plan or intent yet existed. Judge Gesell stated:

"Absent a present plan or intent to acquire control of Purolator, the Court must nonetheless consider whether the disclosures made by Tiger are adequate properly to inform investors. Tiger's expressed hope of acquiring Purolator's courier division is made plain in the second paragraph of Item 4 of its 13D statement, in which Tiger announces that it 'is prepared to explore with the management of Purolator the possibility of Tiger acquiring Purolator's Services Group. . . .' This statement cannot be read in isolation, but must be read together with the preceding paragraph in which Tiger declares its present purpose 'is to acquire a significant minority interest in Purolator.' The only fair inference of Item 4 read as a whole is that Tiger's purchase of a significant minority interest in Purolator is being undertaken in an attempt to enhance its ability to gain the attention of Purolator's management, thus opening an opportunity to negotiate for the purchase of the courier operations." 510 F.Supp. at 556–57.

Sample Disclosure:

"The Purchaser currently anticipates that it will sell certain of the Company's businesses as going concerns. In this connection, although the Purchaser has analyzed, based on limited information, the effect of potential sales of various of the Company's businesses, no final determination as to the sale of any particular business has been made."

Schedule 14D of Samjens Partners in Burlington Industries, Inc. v. Edelman, 666 F.Supp. 799 (M.D.N.C.1987). The Plaintiff argued that Samjens had, in fact, made a final decision with respect its divestiture plans. Samjens officials had prepared memorandums which identified the divisions to be divested in the proposed takeover and which stated that "the success of the transaction may be dependent upon the completion of a divestiture program" and which refer to the asset sale as part of "the Dominion/Edelman plan."

"The court does not find these to be material misstatements. The Offer To Purchase clearly and fully states that Samjens anticipates selling assets after the acquisition. Plaintiff's evidence fails to indicate that defendants have made a final decision to sell certain assets. The fact that defendants have formulated plans as to which assets they might sell if divestiture becomes necessary for 'the success of the transaction' does not lead to the conclusion that defendants have finally determined to implement the 'divestiture strategy' contained in 'the Dominion/Edelman plan.'"

The Form

"(d) Any change in the present board of directors or management of the issuer, including any plans or proposals to change the number or term of directors or to fill any existing vacancies on the board;"

Sample Disclosure:

"Sun stated that its acquisitions were for investment; that it had no present intention of seeking control of Chromalloy; that it presently intended to continue to increase its holdings; that the amount of such increase had not been determined; that Sun had been discussing with certain directors and members of

Chromalloy's management the possible increase in Sun's holdings; and that Sun might 'at any time determine to seek control of Chromalloy.' Later amendments disclosed its unsuccessful attempt to gain representation on the Chromalloy board."

Chromalloy American Corp. v. Sun Chemical Corp., 611 F.2d 240 (8th Cir.1979).

The Court of Appeals held that "Sun's desire to influence substantially the policies, management and actions of Chromalloy amounts to a purpose to control Chromalloy." 611 F.2d at 246, citing the '34 Act definition of control from Rule 12b–2(f). The court held that a fixed plan was not a prerequisite for disclosing control, distinguishing a "purpose" which need not be specific and firm from a "plan."

In Energy Ventures v. Appalachian Co. [1984 Decisions] Fed. Sec. L. Rep. (CCH) ¶ 91,556 (D. Del. 1984) the court held that a Schedule 13D gave adequate notice of an intention to seek control by disclosing the bidder's intent to seek board positions.

The Form

"(e) Any material change in the present capitalization or dividend policy of the issuer;"

Sample Disclosure

"Madison Fund and Schwartz expressly stated in the Schedule 13D that the purpose of their purchases is to make significant investments in Todd and to seek to influence the deployment of excess liquid assets and future cash flows not directly required by or employed in Todd's current business. They further stated therein that although they have no specific plans, recommendations or proposals regarding the future conduct of Todd's business, they intend to discuss with its management the ways in which Todd's liquid assets and future cash flows not directly required by or employed in Todd's current business may be deployed, with the object of enhancing the value of the shareholders' investment in Todd, including among the alternative possibilities such transactions as selective acquisitions or repurchases of all or a portion of the outstanding shares."

Schedule 13D of Madison Fund, Inc. and Bernard L. Schwartz, as described in Todd Shipyards Corp. v. Madison Fund, Inc., 547 F.Supp. 1383, 1386 (S.D.N.Y.1982). The court held this was adequate disclosure of possible plans to go private, where the bidders had not formulated any plan or policy, or reached any agreement between themselves. The court stated: "Regarding the existence of an agreement to take the company private, plaintiff has failed completely to present any evidence that this intention was held by the purchasers. While some early memoranda were put into evidence in which it was noted that Todd had adequate cash to repurchase shares, these memoranda were prepared to evaluate the investment potential of Todd. They did not represent fixed plans of the purchasing group." 547 F.Supp. at 1390.

PROBLEM

These are times of consolidation and takeovers in the banking industry. Not only are huge banks gobbling up other huge banks, but acquisitions are occurring across the nation, as regional banks attempt to extend or consolidate their market positions, often by acquiring small community banks and thrifts. You represent an investment limited partnership, with a stated purpose of emphasizing investments in the stocks of selected savings & loan associations ("thrifts"), banks and savings banks which the general partners believe to be undervalued or that they believe represent "special situation" investment opportunities. Past investments have often resulted in putting banks and thrifts "in play." The limited partnership is somewhat leveraged, using borrowed funds to finance part of its purchases. The partnership is considering a purchase of slightly more than 5% of the stock of a local thrift, at a price that would yield a return of less than the partnership's cost of capital, if it were simply to hold the stock as a long-term investment. Your client has made it clear that it does not wish to announce any intention to gain control of the thrift. Which of the following statements should (should not) be included in your client's response to Item 4?

(1) "The primary purpose of the Partnership's purchase of shares of the Issuer is for investment."

(2) "The Partnership's stated purpose emphasizes investments in the stocks of selected savings & loan associations ('thrifts'), banks and savings banks which the general partners believe to be undervalued or that they believe represent 'special situation' investment opportunities."

(3) "The Partnership has, in the past, engaged in activities that have caused the sale or merger of some banks or thrifts in which it has invested."

(4) "The Partnership intends to continue to evaluate the Issuer and its business prospects, and may make further purchases of shares of Common Stock or may dispose of any or all of its shares of Common Stock at any time."

(5) "The Partnership's cost of capital for the funds used to acquire the Issuer's stock is higher than the currently anticipated return on the issuer's shares, which will make it difficult for the Partnership to hold the Issuer's stock for the long term."

(6) "The Partnership intends to consult with management of the Issuer regarding corporate governance matters relating to the 1999 Annual Meeting of stockholders of the Issuer."

(7) "If management of the Issuer exhibits no interest in a transaction to maximize the value of the Issuer's shares for its shareholders, the Partnership may consider seeking positions on the Issuer's board of directors."

(8) "At present, the Partnership has no specific plans or proposals which relate to, or could result in, any of the matters referred to in paragraphs (a) through (j), inclusive, of Item 4 of Schedule 13D."

(9) "The Partnership intends to continue to explore the options available to it."

(10) "The Partnership may, at any time or from time to time, review or reconsider its position with respect to the Issuer and formulate plans with respect to matters referred to in Item 4 of Schedule 13D."

B. BEGINNING A TENDER OFFER AND SCHEDULE TO FILINGS*

Securities Exchange Act, Section 14(d)(1); Exchange Act Rules 14d–1 to 14d–3.

The beginning of a tender offer requires the filing of a Tender Offer Statement on Schedule TO, which includes much of the same information as Schedule 13D, discussed in Part 3.A.v. of this chapter, plus information about the bid. Rule 14d–2(b) provides that a prospective bidder can communicate with target company shareholders in advance of beginning a tender offer, provided that it does not include the means for shareholders to tender their shares into the offer, and that the bidder files its written communications with the SEC under cover of Schedule TO, and with the target company and any other bidders. Rule 14d–3 provides that Schedule TO must be filed with the SEC and delivered to the target company and to any competing bidders that have previously filed their own Schedule TO. Schedule TO need not be published or delivered to target shareholders, who need only receive the "tender offer materials," pursuant to Rule 14d–4(a)(2)(ii), if the bidder elects to "adequately" publish a summary advertisement of the tender offer in newspapers. Alternatively, the bidder may publish a long-form version of the tender offer in such newspapers. The "tender offer materials" are defined in Rule 14d–1(g)(9) to include the bidder's formal offer (the contract terms), the related transmittal letter, which is the form of acceptance to be used by target shareholders, and press releases, letters and other documents either published by the bidder or sent directly to

---

*   Prior to 1999 these disclosures were required on Schedule 14D–1, which was superseded by Schedule TO.

target shareholders, to persuade them to tender. We turn now to examine when these disclosure obligations apply.

The Williams Act contains no definition of a tender offer. A student note, The Developing Meaning of "Tender Offer" under the Securities Exchange Act of 1934, 86 Harv. L. Rev. 1250 (1973), was widely cited by the courts in the years immediately after its appearance. The note recommended that the courts look at the shareholder impact of particular methods of acquisition, and classify as tender offers "those found capable of exerting the same sort of pressure on shareholders to make uninformed, ill-considered decisions to sell which Congress found the conventional tender offer was capable of exerting." *Id.* at 1275. The note argued that special bids at a premium price, with a stated maximum number of shares to be purchased, imposed such pressures, because of the need to respond quickly. Rapid market accumulations would not involve such pressures, nor would negotiations with major shareholders that imposed no time limits. *Id.* at 1278–80.

In 1979 the SEC promulgated proposed amendments to Rule 14d–1(b)(1), which would have defined a tender offer as follows:

"(1) The term 'tender offer' includes a 'request or invitation for tenders' and means one or more offers to purchase or solicitations of offers to sell securities of a single class, whether or not all or any portion of the securities sought are purchased, which

"(i) during any 45-day period are directed to more than 10 persons and seek the acquisition of more than 5% of the class of securities, except that offers by a broker (and its customer) or by a dealer made on a national securities exchange at the then current market or made in the over-the-counter market at the then current market shall be excluded if in connection with such offers neither the person making the offers nor such broker or dealer solicits or arranges for the solicitation of any order to sell such securities and such broker or dealer performs only the customary functions of a broker or dealer and receives no more than the broker's usual and customary commission or the dealer's usual and customary mark-up; or

"(ii) are not otherwise a tender offer under paragraph (b)(1)(i) of this section, but which (A) are disseminated in a widespread manner, (B) provide for a price which represents a premium in excess of the greater of 5% of or $2 above the current market price and (c) do not provide for a meaningful opportunity to negotiate the price and terms."

SEC Exchange Act Release No. 16385 (1979). The proposal was never adopted. Only one case has cited this proposal, E.H.I. of Florida, Inc. v. Insurance Co. of N. America, 499 F.Supp. 1053 (E.D. Pa. 1980).

The Harvard Law Review note indicated an offer to purchase securities belonging to a control shareholder or a control group need not be classified as a tender offer because controlling shareholders can be presumed powerful enough not to be pressured into making uninformed decisions to sell. 86 Harv. L. Rev. at 1280. This approach was analogous to the "private offering" exemption from securities registration under Section 4(2) of the Securities Act of 1933. Citing the note, this rationale was employed in Nachman v. Halfred, Inc., [1973–74 Decisions] Fed. Sec. L. Rep. (CCH) ¶ 94,455, at 95,592 (N.D. Ill. 1973), where the court concluded that "To characterize Hurwitz' negotiations with a relatively small and powerful group of shareholders as a tender offer or tender offers would not serve the purposes of §§ 14(d) and (e)." Similarly, in D-Z Investment Co. v. Holloway, [1974–75 Decisions] Fed. Sec. L. Rep. (CCH) ¶ 94,771, at 96,563 (S.D.N.Y.1974), the court held that "telephone calls to 'sophisticated persons', some 'two dozen' in all, and the four actual purchases from financial institutions do not meet the test."

In 2000 the SEC issued a release on "mini-tender offers," in which the bidder acquires securities that leave the bidder's ownership below the 5% threshold for Williams Act disclosures, either on Schedule 13D or Schedule TO. While mini-tender offers do not appear to have been used as a prelude to bids for control, the SEC has been concerned that some investors may have been defrauded by these offers. In some cases bids are apparently made at prices close to the market price by bidders who intend to hold the tendered securities without paying for them, waiting for a market price, on which they can sell at a profit, and provide the funds to pay for the tendered securities. The SEC reminded such buyers that all tender offers, no matter how small, are subject to the antifraud provisions of Regulation 14E, which requires bidders to keep offers open for a minimum of 20 business days, and to pay for securities promptly at the end of the offer. The SEC reminded such buyers that they should disclose whether tendering shareholders would be able to withdraw their securities during the course of the bid, and whether tendered securities would be taken pro rata or on a first come, first served basis in the event of oversubscription. SEC Securities Exchange Act Release No. 34–43069 (July 24, 2000).

Wellman v. Dickinson

475 F.Supp. 783 (S.D.N.Y.1979), affirmed on other grounds,
682 F.2d 355 (2d Cir.1982).

■ CARTER, DISTRICT JUDGE.

I

Status of the Proceedings

This litigation stems from the acquisition by Sun Company, Inc. ("Sun"), a Pennsylvania corporation whose principal business is oil and gas, of roughly 34% of the stock of Becton, Dickinson & Company ("BD"), a New Jersey corporation which manufactures health care products and medical testing and research equipment. Sun's brilliantly designed, lightning strike took place in January, 1978, and gave rise to seven separate actions which were consolidated for trial.

*　*　*

[The SEC brought an enforcement action against those associated with the bid, and BD sued them and a class action was brought on behalf of the remaining BD shareholders. All alleged violations of the Williams Act and the antifraud provisions of the Securities Exchange Act, § 10(b) and § 14(e). This is the ruling on liability after the first phase of a bifurcated trial.]

II

Findings of Fact

[Fairleigh S. Dickinson, Jr. was the son of one of the founders of BD. He held the reins of the company from 1948 until 1973. In 1973 he became Chairman of the Board, and left active management to others, including Wesley Howe, Chief Executive Officer. In 1977 Dickinson began the process that led to a falling out with Howe. Management became interested in an acquisition about which Dickinson had doubts. He unilaterally retained two investment banking firms to analyze the proposed transaction. When their reports were negative, Dickinson sent them to the entire board, which then disapproved the proposed acquisition. A month later Howe organized a coup, and at the next board meeting Dickinson was deposed as Chairman. Convinced that the company was being badly managed, Dickinson met with representatives of Salomon Brothers and its counsel, Martin Lipton, to discuss what could be done. Ultimately, he concluded that the best course was to sell his shares to a company interested in a takeover of BD. Dickinson owned about 5%, but his views were shared by several former directors who, collectively could sell approximately 10–13% of the BD shares.

Salomon, which was joined by F. Eberstadt & Co., Inc. ("Eberstadt"), another investment banking firm with which Dickinson and BD had a long relationship, then searched for a prospective buyer. They located Sun, an oil and gas company seeking diversification, which had determined to invest $300–$400 million in each of three or four companies. Sun was not seeking control of these companies, but large minority positions. Horace Kephart, a Senior Vice President of Sun, was in charge of Sun's search for candidates. After an investigation Sun determined that BD was a suitable candidate, and the Sun board ultimately approved a significant investment in BD. The Sun study team concluded that the optimum percentage level for Sun to reach was over 33 1/3%. At that level, Sun could utilize equity accounting and would have sufficient holdings to have a significant voice in BD's future direction.]

On January 9, there was a meeting of lawyers at Salomon. The lawyers indicated that the law regarding tender offers was still murky and that the concept of a tender offer had not been precisely defined. The lawyers wanted to structure a "privately negotiated" transaction. Fogelson and Charles Nathan of Cleary, Gottlieb felt this required that those solicited be limited in number. One felt that up to 60 solicitees was safe; the other argued for an upper limit of 40, but within those limits the lawyers felt there would be no problem.

* * *

On January 10 and 11, Kephart and the study team, augmented by Salomon (Rosenthal, Lipper, Gutfreund), Eberstadt (Zeller), Fogelson, Howard Blum, Sun's staff counsel, and Nathan met in Sun's headquarters to devise final recommendations to present to the Sun Board. * * *

Four possible strategies were listed by Kephart on a blackboard and rated in terms of legal risk, quick control and price: (1) to seek shares sequentially, first from individuals, then from institutions; (2) to seek shares simultaneously from these two groups; (3) to tender immediately; and (4) to contact management.

Simultaneous acquisition was considered the most desirable in terms of quick control and price, although there was a measurable legal risk that the effort would be aborted. Sun was advised by its lawyers that the exact boundary line between a private purchase and a tender offer had not been defined in the law. Nonetheless, the lawyers believed simultaneous purchases from large individual and institutional shareholders, carried out off the market after the New York Stock Exchange had closed, and with as much secrecy as possible constituted the strategy best suited to meet Sun's needs. The tender offer approach was rated best in terms of legal risk, but disadvantageous in terms of price. It would also give BD a wide opportunity to make counter moves. The lawyers felt it necessary to keep the solicitees limited in number in order for the acquisition to be considered a private transaction. There were discussions of the possibility of attaining the objective with purchases from 4 individuals and 6 institutions, but approaching as many as 40 solicitees was discussed. * * *

On January 11, Fogelson, Nathan and Blum carefully considered the approach to be made to solicitees. When they learned that the strategy envisioned approaches to a number of individuals and institutions, they initially wanted Rosenthal to make all the solicitations. When he said that was impossible because there were too many solicitees, the lawyers decided on preparing two scripts: one for those soliciting individuals and a second one for those soliciting institutions.[214] The instructions stressed

---

[214] OUTLINE FOR MAJOR INDIVIDUAL INVESTORS

1. Stress Need for Absolute Confidentiality (a) To make transaction possible (b) To avoid liability under securities laws.

confidentiality and it was agreed that a lawyer would be at the side of each solicitor to monitor the latter's side of the conversation.

* * *

Rosenthal's two tiered price offer with a most favored nation clause was agreed upon. At his suggestion, solicitees were to be offered a top price of $45 per share with no recourse or $40 per share with the right to receive the highest price subsequently paid to any other solicitee. It was the understanding of Salomon, Sun and Eberstadt that all solicitees would get the benefit of the highest price paid.

Blum advised Rosenthal that the price should be negotiated, not fixed, and that if another price were suggested by solicitees, it should not be rejected but referred back to Sun. He told Rosenthal that there should be no specified time to respond, but Rosenthal said time deadlines would be set within time frame normally allowable in block trading. Rosenthal

---

2. Provide outline of proposed transaction, including—(a) Name of purchaser. (b) General nature and scope of purchase program. (c) Minimum number shares sought and ultimate goal.

3. Determine precise details of investor's shareholdings and those of his family, including how registered, where securities located, whose approval needed for sale. Way shares held may affect ability to buy, since May not make offers to more than 10 shareholders resident in New Jersey—Assume that each member of family and each trust will count as separate New Jersey shareholder. Same true holdings of close friend (FD)

4. Terms of Offer

(a) Purchaser not able to make absolute commitment until minimum investment is assured. Thus final commitment from Purchaser must await results of institutional contacts.

(b) Price being offered and "most favored nation clause" [N.B. If raised by seller, no discussion of any kind concerning installment notes. Have lawyers work out all details].

OUTLINE FOR INSTITUTIONS

I. MANDATORY SELLING POINTS

1. Emphasize that transaction cannot proceed unless absolute confidentiality is maintained by all parties. Also warn of risk of seller becoming member of a Williams Act group with filing responsibility if talks to others.

2. Emphasize that your principal will not finally commit to purchase until a block meeting its minimum requirements is assembled.

II. PERMISSIBLE SELLING POINTS

1. If institution expresses reluctance to agree because of future expectations, you may point out that its refusal to sell may preclude reaching minimum target and that your principal has no intention of going forward in such event. If this transaction is not consummated because principal can't assemble block, institution's expectations will be defeated.

2. As is customary in block transactions, you may state both the minimum size requirements for the block and the status of sellers' commitments at the time.

III. DON'TS

1. Do not characterize the price as a "take it or leave it" proposition. Be appropriately responsive to negotiating initiative by institution.

2. Do not impose a time constraint or institution's response shorter than is customary for institutional block purchases.

3. Do not disclose identity of principal unless absolutely necessary to consummate the transaction and, in any event, not before the minimum size requirement for the block has been reached. If identity of principal is disclosed, make clear that purchase contract will be executed by subsidiary of principal.

4. Do not go beyond language in draft purchase agreement prefacing the "most favored nation" provision in response to questions regarding the intent of your principal.

was told that the principal was not to be disclosed and that solicitees should be told to keep the matter confidential, lest a 13(d) group develop as a result of leaks.

* * *

At noon on January 16 there was a meeting at Salomon of those persons who were to solicit the institutions. In addition to Rosenthal, Gutfreund, Lipper and Zeller, those present were Morris Offit, a Salomon partner, and Pike Sullivan and Joy Gidley of Eberstadt. A Salomon partner in its Boston office, Joseph Lombard, was tuned into the meeting via telephone. At mid-afternoon, Fogelson, Nathan, and the other lawyers arrived. Each solicitor was given a script and it was dictated over the phone to Lombard. Nathan explained the purpose the script served, and the solicitors were told to specify that only shares held by discretionary accounts were desired. The institutions were then called to determine whether someone would be available after 4:00 P.M. to receive a proposal.

Nilsen of Chemical Fund was called at 3:45, and was offered the proposal before the offer was made to any other institution. Nilsen accepted the $45 price for the two Eberstadt funds, Chemical and Surveyor, and for Eberstadt's discretionary accounts.

At 4:00 P.M. all the persons assigned to do the solicitation met in the trading room of Salomon. Each solicitor had a script from which to read, and a lawyer was teamed up with each caller. Shortly after 4:00 P.M. the telephoning began. Some 30 institutions were contacted. The following [22] institutions accepted the offer and sold their BD shares at $45 per share: . . .

The following [six institutions] rejected the offer for various reasons: . . .

* * *

The callers followed the script. There were slight variations, but each solicitee was told that a non-disclosed purchaser, sometimes identified as in the top fifty of Fortune Magazine's 500, was looking for 20% of BD stock; that no transaction would be final unless 20% of the shares were acquired; that the $45 option was a top final price and the $40 option could be accepted with protection in the event shares were later bought at a higher figure; and that the desired 20% goal was within reach or that the order was filling up fast and a hurried response was essential. Each solicitee was asked to respond within one hour or less, although some were given until the next day. Sun was identified to a few institutions, but to most the purchaser's specific identity was not revealed.

The institutions solicited had to consult with their in-house officials hurriedly. By 4:45 Kephart advised Burtis that verbal commitments for 3.1 million shares had been obtained. At 5:35 P.M. the total had reached 20%, and Kephart was given authorization to seal the bargain with these institutions that had committed their shares. Those institutions were called again, and Kephart was put on the phone. He identified himself, and after confirming that the solicitees were interested in selling at $45 a share, he accepted on behalf of Sun's subsidiary L.H.I.W. The project had gone so well that Kephart was concerned that the total might far exceed 34%, and he called Sharbaugh and asked whether he was to pro rate the shares if the 34% figure was exceeded. Sharbaugh replied that there would be no problem unless the figure was over 50%. Before retiring for the night on June 16, Sun officials knew that they had obtained their objective in that there were verbal commitments for at least 30% of BD's outstanding shares. Indeed, there was some concern that they might have overreached their goal by a wide margin.

On January 17 and 18, couriers were dispatched all over the country with Sun's checks to pay for the stock, to obtain signatures or collect prepared purchase agreements, to take physical possession of the stock certificates and to have the solicitees sign powers of attorney to allow Sun to vote their proxies.

* * *

III

Determination

Threshold Considerations

* * *

[The court then considered whether this was analogous to a "private" rather than a public offering under § 4(2) of the Securities Act of 1933.]

Based on the decided case law distinguishing "public" from "private" transactions, defendants have failed to carry their burden of showing that Sun's acquisition was "privately negotiated." Nor were these agreements a series of separate, independent contracts. This was a single integrated project, planned and executed to secure for Sun some 33 1/3% of outstanding BD shares, secretly and quickly so that the acquisition could not be aborted or halted at mid-point by legal action or other countermoves by BD. The institutions were solicited on the 4th market which, as I understand it, is the designation given transactions effectuated during the hours when the NYSE is not operating. Except for Turner and Dickinson, the same offer was made to each solicitee. There were no individual features to distinguish one confirmed solicitation from another except that the number of shares held by each institution varied. Nor, of course, is there any contention that these were open market purchases. Accordingly, the transaction fits neither of the traditional exceptions to Section 14.

This is not the end but merely the beginning of the inquiry. The conclusion that this was a public solicitation does not necessarily mean that the pre-acquisition filing requirements of the Williams Act apply. We now proceed to consider that issue.

Section 14(d) Claims

The Senate subcommittee introduced its report on the proposed Williams Act with a brief description of a typical tender offer: "The offer normally consists of a bid by an individual or group to buy shares of a company—usually at a price above the market price. Those accepting the offer are said to tender their stock for purchase. The person making the offer obligates himself to purchase all or a specified portion of the tendered shares if certain specified conditions are met." S. Rep. No. 550, 90th Cong., 1st Sess. 2 (1967). Thus, the Senate report identified as attributes of a tender offer a bid, a premium price, tender by the solicitees, and the conditional nature of the buyer's obligation. The House subcommittee's definition of a tender offer was identical to that adopted by its Senate counterpart. H. Rep. No. 1711, 90th Cong., 2d Sess. 2 (1968).

The committee reports reflected statements made during the earlier committee hearings. For example, Commission Chairman, Manuel F. Cohen, had testified that a tender offer typically involved the solicitation by the buyer of options to purchase. The option would only be exercised up to the maximum number of shares desired and would not be exercised at all unless some minimum number of shares had been tendered. Chairman Cohen further indicated that the buyer usually gave the impression that an immediate response was necessary but did not disclose either what its intentions were with respect to the target company or what the consequences might be for the investor who failed to tender if the acquisition was successful. Ibid. Commission General Counsel Phillip Loomis added to this definition his observation that buyers frequently hurried the decision of the solicitees by indicating that shares would be taken up on a first come, first served basis. This general outline of the nature of a tender offer was reiterated by Senator Kuchel, co-sponsor of the Williams Act. Finally, in opening the floor debate on the bill, Senator Williams alluded to many of these same characteristics and added that buyers often hired investment bankers and took out newspaper advertisements to facilitate the transactions.

The buyer need not seek one hundred percent or even a majority of the stock of a company in order for its bid to qualify as a tender offer. The Williams Act was drafted to cover only those tender offers resulting in ownership of more than 10% (now 5%) of the stock of a corporation. Thus, the Act recognizes the possibility that a purchase of even less than 5% might be a tender offer, although exempted from regulation.

A second characteristic common to many tenders but not an essential element of Congress' definition is universal publicity of the offer. Although the Senate recognized that use of a newspaper advertisement was one common tactic in making a tender offer, it also understood that other means of publicity were sometimes used. For example, the Senate Report refers to offers that are "published or otherwise sent or given to security holders," and in response to a question by Senator Williams, Robert Haack, President of the National Association of Securities Dealers, indicated that solicitations were sometimes made by telephone. Indeed, the practice of using newspaper advertisements was apparently a phenomenon of recent origin that developed because the management of target companies had begun to make it difficult for buyers to obtain lists of shareholders which could be used to make direct individual solicitations.

* * *

All of these elements—bid, premium price, obligation to purchase all or a specified portion of the tendered shares if certain specified conditions are met (in this instance, if 20% of the outstanding shares are acquired)—are present here. The above definition is set forth in Kennecott [Copper Corp. v. Curtiss-Wright Corp.], *supra*, 584 F.2d [1195] at 2106 [(2d Cir.1978)], a case on which defendants rely as the "definition of a conventional tender offer [that] has received general recognition in the courts." (citations omitted). Defendants also assert, however, that publicity, the widespread solicitation of the general body of shareholders, and placement of the tendered shares in a depository are requisites for a conventional tender offer. However, there is no mention in Kennecott of these factors. The court there appeared to be concerned that the position taken by some courts and commentators would create an overlap between open market purchases and tender offers, thereby rendering § 14(d)(5)–(d)(7) unworkable. But there were open and off-the-market purchases involved in both Kennecott and Gulf and Western Industries, while there are no open market purchases involved in this case. This was a single cohesive transaction involving face to face transactions with Turner, Dickinson, Lufkin and Dunning, and 4th market telephone communication with institutional holders in which Sun received in hand roughly 6 ½ million shares and paid out 290 million dollars in about 5 days.

What is probably more important than the fact that this transaction has all the characteristics of a tender offer that were identified by Congress in the debates on consideration of the Williams Act is that Sun's acquisition is infected with the basic evil which Congress sought to cure by enacting the law. This purchase was designed in intent, purpose and effect to effectuate a transfer of at least a 20% controlling interest in BD to Sun in a swift, masked maneuver. It would surely undermine the remedial purposes of the Act to hold that this secret operation, which in all germane respects meets the accepted definition of a tender offer, is not covered by Section 14(d)'s pre-acquisition filing requirements because Sun's coup was not heralded by widespread publicity and because no shares were placed in a depository. Sun wanted no publicity. It deliberately chose to keep its moves hidden because as Kephart stated, Sun executives were fearful that they might have large sums of corporate funds committed before having in hand shares and proxies representing a 33 1/3% controlling interest in BD. Nor did Sun put trust in a depository. It wanted to have physical possession of the stock certificates purchased as quickly as possible.

The argument that the solicitees were sophisticated investors and therefore did not need Section 14 disclosure is no more convincing in this connection than it was in relation to the issue of whether this was merely a private transaction. Sophistication serves no purpose unless it can be applied to the particulars of an investment or sale decision. Therefore, sophistication and expertise cannot be relied on here to exempt this transaction from the reach of section 14(d). See Aranow, Einhorn & Berlstein, Developments in Tender Offers For Corporate Control 8 (1977).

* * *

Even if this transaction were not seen as a conventional tender offer, it would not necessarily fall outside the ambit of Section 14(d). As discussed above, the concept of a tender offer has never been precisely defined either in the Williams Act itself or by the Commission. Congress left to the Commission the task of providing through its experience concrete meaning to the term. The commission has not yet created an exact definition, but in this case and in others, it suggests some seven elements as being characteristic of a tender offer: (1) active and widespread solicitation of public shareholders for the shares of an issuer; (2) solicitation made for a substantial percentage of the issuer's stock; (3) offer to purchase made at a premium over the prevailing market price; (4) terms of the offer are firm rather than negotiable; (5) offer contingent on the tender of a fixed number of shares, often subject to a fixed maximum number to be purchased; (6) offer open only a limited period of time; (7) offeree subjected to pressure to sell his stock. These characteristics were recently accepted as appropriately describing the nature of a tender offer. See Hoover v. Fuqua Industries, Inc., [[1979–80 Decisions] Fed. Sec. L. Rep. (CCH) ¶ 97,107 (N.D. Ohio 1979)]. In that case, the Commission also had listed an 8th characteristic not included here—whether the public announcements of a purchasing program concerning the target company precede or accompany rapid accumulation of large amounts of the target company's securities. The reason this last characteristic was left out undoubtedly was because publicity was not a feature of this transaction.

At any rate, it seems to me that the list of characteristics stressed by the Commission are the qualities that set a tender offer apart from open market purchases, privately negotiated transactions or other kinds of public solicitations. With the exception of publicity, all the characteristics of a tender offer, as that term is understood, are present in this transaction. The absence of one particular factor, however, is not necessarily fatal to the Commission's argument because depending upon the circumstances involved in the particular case, one or more of the above features may be more compelling and determinative than the others.

There was certainly "active and widespread solicitation" involved. Defendants contend that there was no widespread public solicitation of the general body of shareholders. But institutional holdings accounted for roughly 40% of all BD's outstanding shares as of January 16, and there was surely widespread solicitation of this class of shareholders. In addition, there was solicitation of individual shareholders holding a considerable percentage of BD shares. Measured by the size of the holdings solicited (34%), the geographic dimensions of the effort (from New York to California and from Massachusetts to North Carolina) and by the number of solicitees approached (30 institutions and 9 individuals, not including 3 institutions that were approached earlier and either indicated no interest, as did Morgan Guaranty Co., or were forgotten, as was Allendale Insurance Co.), there was widespread solicitation of BD's shareholders.

The second characteristic, substantial percentage, does not move us very far, for unless the solicitation embraces at least 5% of the issuer's stock, the Act would not be called into play. The third element, premium over market, is regarded as one of the typical indicia of a conventional tender offer and was certainly present here.

The fourth element—the firm terms of the offer and the absence of opportunity for negotiation—is stressed by the Commission. Defendants argue that the solicitees were not told that negotiations were barred, but the price was so attractive that none sought to negotiate. No negotiation took place and indeed if any had occurred, the whole project would have been derailed. It is undisputed that the solicitors could not barter about the terms of the offer. Any desire by a solicitee to deviate from the proffered terms had to be referred to Kephart. He, in turn, had to call Radnor to obtain permission to accept such a variation. That time-consuming process would have slowed the project and increased the legal risk of BD's being able to abort the acquisition. This project was structured so that there would be no individualized negotiations. The hope and expectation were that the price would be so attractive that negotiation would be unnecessary.

The fifth, sixth, and seventh elements were also present. The offer was contingent on Sun's achieving a stated percentage of BD shares— another characteristic of a typical tender offer. Time constraints were placed on each solicitee, and although some were given additional time to respond, most felt that they had to reply within the time constraints imposed. The solicitors tried to exert a maximum amount of pressure on the solicitees they contacted. The latter were told that favorable responses were coming in fast, and it was implied that either they had better make a hurried acceptance of this attractive offer or their chance would be gone.

The one element missing is publicity. Lack of publicity, however, should be no deterrent to classifying this transaction as a tender offer since, as has been stated, a principal objective of the Williams Act was to prevent secret corporate takeovers. Congress intended the Williams Act "to be construed not technically and restrictively, but flexibly to effectuate its remedial objectives," S.E.C. v. Capital Gains Research Bureau, *supra*, 375 U.S. at 195; S.E.C. v. National Securities, Inc., 393 U.S. 453 (1969), and it has long been the rule that all the federal securities laws must be given a construction which effectuates their remedial purposes. While Piper v. Chris-Craft Industries, Inc., *supra*, may have narrowed the presumed scope of the Williams Act in respect to who may claim its protection, particularly in suits for damages, there is nothing in that opinion to indicate a retreat from the long accepted doctrine that the substance of the federal securities laws must be broadly construed. Public investors are the intended beneficiaries of the Williams Act. Accordingly, its provisions should be construed to facilitate their coverage.

* * *

In sum, Sun is liable for violation of Section 14(d) of the Williams Act for making a tender offer without the required pre-acquisition filing. * * *

———————

QUESTIONS

1. Suppose Sun had placed a "block" order for 33% of the shares of Becton-Dickinson with a brokerage firm at the current market price or no more than ½ point over the current market price. Would that have been a tender offer?

2. Assume the broker in question 1 used "Autex," an electronic system operated by Thompson Financial that disseminates information to subscribing institutional investors, which indicates for one day the broker's interest in purchasing Becton-Dickinson shares, without identifying the buyer. (Other services used by brokers are Bloomberg's Instant Message System, Reuters' Messaging and MindAlign, an enterprise system.) Would this constitute a tender offer?

3. Suppose the broker in question 2 solicited 50 institutional investors on the same basis?

4. Suppose Sun had simply announced in its Schedule 13D that it intended to acquire shares in market transactions until it owned 33% of Becton-Dickinson's shares. Would this constitute a tender offer?

5. Would it make a difference in your answer to question 4 if Sun had issued a press release containing the contents of its Schedule 13D filing?

6. Suppose Sun had announced in its Schedule 13D that it was considering a tender offer for Becton-Dickinson stock, and continued to acquire shares in the market. Would this constitute a tender offer?

7. Suppose Sun had demanded a shareholder list from Becton-Dickinson, and, in response to a requirement of state law that the requesting person have a proper purpose, had announced to the company that it wanted to be able to communicate with the shareholders in connection with a tender offer it was considering. Would continued purchases in the market constitute a tender offer?

8. What protections would a tender offer filing have provided the sellers in this case?

9. If Sun had been required to file tender offer disclosures before beginning these purchases, what was the likelihood that Sun would still have been interested in purchasing the BD shares?

The Aftermath of Wellman v. Dickinson

The settlement with the SEC and private litigants in Wellman v. Dickinson involved divestiture of Sun's holdings in Becton-Dickinson. 497 F.Supp. 824 (S.D.N.Y.1980). It called for Sun to make a public offering of debentures that may be exchanged for B-D shares at a price to be fixed by Sun at the time of the offering but not to exceed $60 per share. The debentures were to have a term of at least ten and not more than twenty-five years, and Sun was to be obligated to take all necessary actions to divest itself of all B-D holdings within 25 years after it first issued and sold the debentures. The holders of the debentures would have the right to vote the B-D shares by directions of an escrow agent who would hold Sun's B-D shares, and the escrow agent was to vote all of Sun's B-D shares in accordance with the majority instructions of the debenture holders. The debentures were subject to call by Sun at fixed prices, and to the extent B-D shares were not exchanged for debentures, Sun was permitted to designate one nominee for election to the B-D board on management's slate. The $60 exchange value for B-D shares meant that if all of the B-D shares were exchanged for debentures in the eleventh year at $60 per share, Sun would have realized a total return of less than 2¼% per year, based on an investment of $45 per share. In addition, Sun agreed to pay $2.6 million to the class plaintiffs as damages.

Hanson Trust PLC v. SCM Corporation
774 F.2d 47 (2d Cir.1985).

■ MANSFIELD, CIRCUIT JUDGE:

Hanson Trust PLC, HSCM Industries, Inc., and Hanson Holdings Netherlands B.V. (hereinafter sometimes referred to collectively as

"Hanson") appeal from an order of the Southern District of New York, Shirley Wohl Kram, Judge, grant SCM Corporation's motion for a preliminary injunction restraining them, their officers, agents, employees and any persons acting in concert with them, from acquiring any shares of SCM and from exercising any voting rights with respect to 3.1 million SCM shares acquired by them on September 11, 1985. The injunction was granted on the ground that Hanson's September 11 acquisition of the SCM stock through five private and one open market purchases amounted to a "tender offer" for more than 5% of SCM's outstanding shares, which violated §§ 14 (d)(1) and (6) of the Williams Act, 15 U.S.C. § 78n (d)(1) and (6) and rules promulgated by the Securities and Exchange Commission (SEC) thereunder. See 17 C.F.R. §§ 240.14(e)(1) and 240.14d–7. We reverse.

The setting is the familiar one of a fast-moving bidding contest for control of a large public corporation: first, a cash tender offer of $60 per share by Hanson, an outsider, addressed to SCM stockholders; next, a counterproposal by an "insider" group consisting of certain SCM managers and their "White Knight," Merrill Lynch Capital Markets (Merrill), for a "leveraged buy-out" at a higher price ($70 per share); then an increase by Hanson of its cash offer to $72 per share, followed by a revised SCM-Merrill leveraged buy-out offer of $74 per share with a "crown jewel" irrevocable lock-up option to Merrill designed to discourage Hanson from seeking control by providing that if any other party (in this case Hanson) should acquire more than one-third of SCM's outstanding share (66 2/3% being needed under N.Y. Bus. L. § 903(a)(2) to effectuate a merger) Merrill would have the right to buy SCM's two most profitable businesses (consumer foods and pigments) at prices characterized by some as "bargain basement." The final act in this scenario was the decision of Hanson, having been deterred by the SCM-Merrill option (colloquially described in the market as a "poison pill"),* to terminate its cash tender offer and then to make private purchases, amounting to 25% of SCM's outstanding shares, leading SCM to seek and obtain the preliminary injunction from which this appeal is taken. A more detailed history of relevant events follows.

* * *

The next development in the escalating bidding contest for control of SCM occurred on September 10, 1985, when SCM entered into a new leveraged buy-out agreement with its "White Knight," Merrill. The agreement provided for a two-step acquisition of SCM stock by Merrill at $74 per share. The first proposed step was to be the acquisition of approximately 82% of SCM's outstanding stock for cash. Following a merger (which required acquisition of at least 66 2/3%), debentures would be issued for the remaining SCM shares. If any investor or group other than Merrill acquired more than one-third of SCM's outstanding shares,

---

*   This is a misnomer.—Ed.

Merrill would have the option to buy SCM's two most profitable businesses, pigments and consumer foods, for $350 and $80 million respectively, prices which Hanson believed to be below their market value.

Hanson, faced with what it considered to be a "poison pill," concluded that even if it increased its cash tender offer to $74 per share it would end up with control of a substantially depleted and damaged company. Accordingly, it announced on the Dow Jones Broad Tape at 12:38 P.M. on September 11 that it was terminating its cash tender offer. A few minutes later, Hanson issued a press release, carried on the Broad Tape, to the effect that "all SCM shares tendered will be promptly returned to the tendering shareholders."

At some time in the late forenoon or early afternoon of September 11 Hanson decided to make cash purchases of a substantial percentage of SCM stock in the open market or through privately negotiated transactions. Under British law Hanson could not acquire more than 49% of SCM's shares in this fashion without obtaining certain clearances, but acquisition of such a large percentage was not necessary to stymie the SCM-Merrill merger proposal. If Hanson could acquire slightly less than one-third of SCM's outstanding shares it would be able to block the $74 per share SCM-Merrill offer of a leveraged buy-out. This might induce the latter to work out an agreement with Hanson, something Hanson had unsuccessfully sought on several occasions since its first cash tender offer.

Within a period of two hours on the afternoon of September 11 Hanson made five privately-negotiated cash purchases of SCM stock and one open-market purchase, acquiring 3.1 million shares or 25% of SCM's outstanding stock. The price of SCM stock on the NYSE on September 11 ranged from a high of $73.50 per share to a low of $72.50 per share. Hanson's initial private purchase, 387,700 shares from Mutual Shares, was not solicited by Hanson but by Mutual Shares official, Michael Price, who in a conversation with Robert Pirie of Rothschild, Inc., Hanson's financial advisor, on the morning of September 11 (before Hanson had decided to make any private cash purchases) had stated that he was interested in selling Mutual's Shares' SCM stock to Hanson. Once Hanson's decision to buy privately had been made, Pirie took Price up on his offer. The parties negotiated a sale at $73.50 per share after Pirie refused Price's asking prices, first of $75 per share and, later, of $74.50 per share. This transaction, but not the identity of the parties, was automatically reported pursuant to NYSE rules on the NYSE ticker at 3:11 P.M. and reported on the Dow Jones Broad Tape at 3:29 P.M.

Pirie then telephoned Ivan Boesky, an arbitrageur who had a few weeks earlier disclosed in a Scheduled 13D statement filed with the SEC that he owned approximately 12.7% of SCM's outstanding shares. Pirie negotiated a Hanson purchase of these shares at $73.50 per share after rejecting Boesky's initial demand of $74 per share. At the same time Rothschild purchased for Hanson's account 600,000 SCM shares in the open market at $73.50 per share. An attempt by Pirie next to negotiate the cash purchase of another large block of SCM stock (some 780,000 shares) from Slifka & Company fell through because of the latter's inability to make delivery of the shares on September 12.

Following the NYSE ticker and Broad Tape reports of the first two large anonymous transactions in SCM stock, some professional investors surmised that the buyer might be Hanson. Rothschild then received telephone calls from (1) Mr. Mulhearn of Jamie & Co. offering to sell between 200,000 and 350,000 shares at $73.50 per share, (2) David Gottesman, an arbitrageur at Oppenheimer & Co. offering 89,000 shares at $73.50, and (3) Boyd Jeffries of Jeffries & Co., offering approximately 700,000 to 800,000 shares at $74.00. Pirie purchased the three blocks for Hanson at $73.50 per share. The last of Hanson's cash purchases was completed by 4:35 P.M. on September 11, 1985.

In the early evening of September 11 SCM successfully applied to Judge Kram in the present lawsuit for a restraining order barring Hanson from acquiring more SCM stock for 24 hours. On September 12 and 13 the TRO was extended by consent pending the district court's decision on SCM's application for a preliminary injunction. Judge Kram held an evidentiary hearing on September 12–13, at which various witnesses, testified, including Sir Gordon White, Hanson's United States Chairman, two Rothschild representatives (Pirie and Gerald Goldsmith) and stock market risk-arbitrage professionals (Robert Freeman of Goldman, Sachs & Co., Kenneth Miller of Merrill Lynch, and Daniel Burch of D.F. King & Co.). Sir Gordon White testified that on September 11, 1985, after learning of the $74 per share SCM-Merrill leveraged buy-out tender offer with its "crown jewel" irrevocable "lock-up" option to Merrill, he instructed Pirie to terminate Hanson's $72 per share tender offer, and that only thereafter did he discuss the possibility of Hanson making market purchases of SCM stock. Pirie testified that the question of buying stock may have been discussed in the late forenoon of September 11 and that he had told White that he was having Hanson's New York counsel look into whether such cash purchases were legally permissible.

SCM argued before Judge Kram (and argues here) that Hanson's cash purchases immediately following its termination of its $72 per share tender offer amounted to a de facto continuation of Hanson's tender offer, designed to avoid the strictures of § 14(d) of the Williams Act, and that unless a preliminary injunction issued SCM and its shareholders would be irreparably injured because Hanson would acquire enough shares to defeat the SCM-Merrill offer. Judge Kram found that the relevant underlying facts (which we have outlined) were not in dispute, and concluded that . . . "SCM has demonstrated a likelihood of success on the merits of its contention that Hanson has engaged in a tender offer which violates Section 14(d) of the Williams Act." * * * From this decision Hanson appeals.

DISCUSSION

* * *

The typical tender offer, as described in the Congressional debates, hearings and reports on the Williams Act, consisted of a general, publicized bid by an individual or group to buy shares of a publicly-owned company, the shares of which were traded on a national securities exchange, at a price substantially above the current market price. * * * The offer was usually accompanied by newspaper and other publicity, a time limit for tender of shares in response to it, and a provision fixing a quantity limit on the total number of shares of the target company that would be purchased.

* * *

Although § 14(d)(1) clearly applies to "classic" tender offers of the type described above (pp. 54–55), courts soon recognized that in the case of privately negotiated transactions or solicitations for private purchases of stock many of the conditions leading to the enactment of § 14(d) for the most part do not exist. The number and percentage of stockholders are usually far less than those involved in public offers. The solicitation involves less publicity than a public tender offer or none. The solicitees, who are frequently directors, officers or substantial stockholders of the target, are more apt to be sophisticated, inquiring or knowledgeable concerning the target's business, the solicitor's objectives, and the impact of the solicitation on the target's business prospects. In short, the solicitee in the private transaction is less likely to be pressured, confused, or ill-informed regarding the businesses and decisions at stake than solicitees who are the subjects of a public tender offer.

These differences between public and private securities transactions have led most courts to rule that private transactions or open market purchases do not qualify as a "tender offer" requiring the purchaser to meet the prefiling strictures of § 14(d). * * * The borderline between public solicitations and privately negotiated stock purchases is not bright and it is frequently difficult to determine whether transactions falling close to the line or in a type of "no man's land" are "tender offers" or private deals. This had led some to advocate a broader interpretation of the term "tender offer" than that followed by us in Kennecott Copper Corp. v. Curtiss-Wright Corp., *supra*, 584 F.2d at 1207, and to adopt the eight-factor "test" of what is a tender offer, which was recommended by the SEC and applied by the district court in Wellman v. Dickinson, 475 F.Supp. 783, 823–24 (S.D.N.Y.), aff'd on other grounds, 682 F.2d 355 (2d Cir.1982), cert. denied, 460 U.S. 1069 (1983), and by the Ninth Circuit in SEC v. Carter Hawley Hale Store, Inc., *supra*. * * *

Although many of the above-listed factors are relevant for purposes of determining whether a given solicitation amounts to a tender offer, the elevation of such a list to a mandatory "litmus test" appears to be both unwise and unnecessary. As even the advocates of the proposed test recognize, in any given case a solicitation may constitute a tender offer even though some of the eight factors are absent or, when many factors are present, the solicitation may nevertheless not amount to a tender offer because the missing factors outweigh those present.

We prefer to be guided by the principle followed by the Supreme Court in deciding what transactions fall within the private offering exemption provided by § 4(1) of the Securities Act of 1933, and by ourselves in Kennecott Copper in determining whether the Williams Act applies to private transactions. That principle is simply to look to the statutory purpose. In S.E.C. v. Ralston Purina Co., 346 U.S. 119 (1953), the Court stated, "the applicability of § 4(1) [sic—§ 4(2)] should turn on whether the particular class of persons affected need the protection of the Act. An offering to those who are shown to be able to fend for themselves is a transaction 'not involving any public offering.' " Similarly, since the purpose of § 14(d) is to protect the ill-informed solicitee, the question of whether a solicitation constitutes a "tender offer" within the meaning of § 14(d) turns on whether, viewing the transaction in the light of the totality of circumstances, there appears to be a likelihood that unless the pre-acquisition filing strictures of that statute are followed there will be a substantial risk that solicitees will lack information needed to make a carefully considered appraisal of the proposal put before them.

Applying this standard, we are persuaded on the undisputed facts that Hanson's September 11 negotiation of five private purchases and one open market purchase of SCM shares, totaling 25% of SCM's outstanding stock, did not under the circumstances constitute a "tender offer" within the meaning of the Williams Act. Putting aside for the moment the events preceding the purchases, there can be little doubt that the privately negotiated purchases would not, standing alone, qualify as a tender offer, for the following reasons:

(1) In a market of 22,800 SCM shareholders the number of SCM sellers have involved, six in all, was minuscule compared with the numbers involved in public solicitations of the type against which the Act was directed.

(2) At least five of the sellers were highly sophisticated professionals, knowledgeable in the market place and well aware of the essential facts needed to exercise their professional skills and to appraise Hanson's offer, including its financial condition as well as that of SCM, the likelihood that the purchases might block the SCM-Merrill bid, and the risk that if Hanson acquired more than 33 1/3% of SCM's stock the SCM-Merrill lockup of the "crown jewel" might be triggered. Indeed, by September 11 they had all had access to (1) Hanson's 27-page detailed

disclosure of facts, filed on August 26, 1985, in accordance with § 14(d)(1) with respect to its $60 tender offer, (2) Hanson's 4-page amendment of that offer, dated September 5, 1985, increasing the price to $72 per share, and (3) press releases regarding the basic terms of the SCM-Merrill proposed leveraged buy-out at $74 per share and of the SCM-Merrill asset option agreement under which SCM granted to Merrill the irrevocable right under certain conditions to buy SCM's consumer food business for $80 million and its pigment business for $350 million.

(3) The sellers were not "pressured" to sell their shares by any conduct that the Williams Act was designed to alleviate, but by the forces of the market place. Indeed, in the case of Mutual Shares there was no initial solicitation by Hanson; the offer to sell was initiated by Mr. Price of Mutual Shares. Although each of the Hanson purchases was made for $73.50 per share, in most instances this price was the result of private negotiations after the sellers sought higher prices and in one case price protection, demands which were refused. The $73.50 price was not fixed in advance by Hanson. Moreover, the sellers remained free to accept the $74 per share tender offer made by the SCM-Merrill group.

(4) There was no active or widespread advance publicity or public solicitation, which is one of the earmarks of a conventional tender offer. Arbitrageurs might conclude from ticker tape reports of two large anonymous transactions that Hanson must be the buyer. However, liability for solicitation may not be predicated upon disclosures mandated by Stock Exchange Rules. See S.E.C. v. Carter-Hawley Hale Stores, Inc., *supra*, 760 F.2d at 950.

(5) The price received by the six sellers, $73.50 per share, unlike that appearing in most tender offers, can scarcely be dignified with the label "premium." The stock market price on September 11 ranged from $72.50 to $73.50 per share. Although risk arbitrageurs sitting on large holdings might reap sizeable profits from sales to Hanson at $73.50, depending on their own purchase costs, they stood to gain even more if the SCM-Merrill offer of $74 should succeed, as it apparently would if they tendered their shares to it. Indeed, the $73.50 price, being at most $1 over market or 1.4% higher than the market price, did not meet the SEC's proposed definition of a premium, which is $2.00 per share or 5% above market price, whichever is greater. SEC Exchange Act Release No. 16,385 (11/29/79) [1979–80] Fed. Sec. L. Rep. ¶ 82,374.

(6) Unlike most tender offers, the purchases were not made contingent upon Hanson's acquiring a fixed minimum number or percentage of SCM's outstanding shares. Once an agreement with each individual seller was reached, Hanson was obligated to buy, regardless what total percentage of stock it might acquire. Indeed, it does not appear that Hanson had fixed in its mind a firm limit on the amount of SCM shares it was willing to buy.

(7) Unlike most tender offers, there was no general time limit within which Hanson would make purchases of SCM stock. Concededly, cash transactions are normally immediate but, assuming an inability on the part of a seller and Hanson to agree at once on a price, nothing prevented a resumption of negotiations by each of the parties except the arbitrageurs' speculation that once Hanson acquired 33 1/3% or an amount just short of that figure it would stop buying.

In short, the totality of circumstances that existed on September 11 did not evidence any likelihood that unless Hanson was required to comply with § 14(d)(1)'s preacquisition filing and waiting-period requirements there would be a substantial risk of ill-considered sales of SCM stock by ill-informed shareholders.

There remains the question whether Hanson's private purchases take on a different hue, requiring them to be treated as a "de facto" continuation of its earlier tender offer, when considered in the context of Hanson's earlier acknowledged tender offer, the competing offer of SCM-Merrill and Hanson's termination of its tender offer. After reviewing all of the undisputed facts we conclude that the district court erred in so holding.

In the first place, we find no record support for the contention by SCM that Hanson's September 11 termination of its outstanding tender offer was false, fraudulent or ineffective. Hanson's termination notice was clear, unequivocal and straightforward. Directions were given, and presumably are being followed, to return all of the tendered shares to the SCM shareholders who tendered them. Hanson also filed with the SEC a statement pursuant to § 14(d)(1) of the Williams Act terminating its tender offer. As a result, at the time when Hanson made its September 11 private purchases of SCM stock it owned no SCM stock other than those shares revealed in its § 14(d) pre-acquisition report filed with the SEC on August 26, 1985.

The reason for Hanson's termination of its tender offer is not disputed: in view of SCM's grant of what Hanson conceived to be a "poison pill" lock-up option to Merrill, Hanson, if it acquired control of SCM, would have a company denuded as the result of its sale of its consumer food and pigment businesses to Merrill at what Hanson believed to be bargain prices. Thus, Hanson's termination of its tender offer was final; there was no tender offer to be "continued." Hanson was unlikely to "shoot itself in the foot" by triggering what it believed to be a "poison pill," and it could not acquire more than 49% of SCM's shares without violating the rules of the London Stock Exchange.

Nor does the record support SCM's contention that Hanson had decided, before terminating its tender offer, to engage in cash purchases. Judge Kram referred only to evidence that "Hanson had considered open market purchases before it announced that the tender offer was dropped" (emphasis added) but made no finding to that effect. Absent evidence or a finding that Hanson had decided to seek control of SCM through purchases of its stock, no duty of disclosure existed under the federal securities laws.

* * *

It may well be that Hanson's private acquisition of 25% of SCM's shares after termination of Hanson's tender offer was designed to block the SCM-Merrill leveraged buy-out group from acquiring the 66 2/3% of SCM's stock needed to effectuate a merger. It may be speculated that such a blocking move might induce SCM to buy Hanson's 25% at a premium or lead to negotiations between the parties designed to resolve their differences. But we know of no provision in the federal securities laws or elsewhere that prohibits such tactics in "hardball" market battles of the type encountered here. See Treadway Companies, Inc. v. Care Corp., 638 F.2d 357, 378–79 (2d Cir.1980) ("We also see nothing wrong in Care's efforts to acquire one third of Treadway's outstanding stock, and thus to obtain a 'blocking position'.").

Thus, the full disclosure purposes of the Williams Act as it now stands appear to have been fully satisfied by Hanson's furnishing to the public, both before and after termination of its tender offer, all of the essential relevant facts it was required by law to supply.

SCM further contends, and in this respect it is supported by the SEC as an amicus, that upon termination of a tender offer the solicitor should be subject to a waiting or cooling-off period (10 days is suggested) before it may purchase any of the target company's outstanding shares. However, neither the Act nor any SEC rule promulgated thereunder prohibits a former tender offeror from purchasing stock of a target through privately negotiated transactions immediately after a tender offer has been terminated. Indeed, it is significant that the SEC's formal proposal for the adoption of such a rule (Proposed Rule 14e–5) has never been implemented even though the SEC adopted a similar prohibition with respect to an issuer's making such purchases within 10 days after termination of a tender offer. See Rule 13e–4(f)(6). Thus, the existing law does not support the prohibition urged by SCM and the SEC. We believe it would be unwise for courts judicially to usurp what is a legislative or regulatory function by substituting our judgment for that of Congress or the SEC.

* * *

In the present case we conclude that since the district court erred in ruling as a matter of law that SCM had demonstrated a likelihood of success on the merits, based on the theory that Hanson's post-tender offer private purchases of SCM constituted a de facto tender offer, it was an abuse of discretion to issue a preliminary injunction. Indeed, we do not believe that Hanson's transactions raise serious questions going to the merits that would provide a fair ground for litigation. In view of this holding it becomes unnecessary to rule upon the district court's determination that the balance of hardships tip in favor of SCM and that absent preliminary relief it would suffer irreparable injury. However, our decision is not to be construed as an affirmance of the district court's resolution of these issues.

* * *

The order of the district court is reversed, the preliminary injunction against Hanson is vacated, and the case is remanded for further proceedings in accordance with this opinion. The mandate shall issue forthwith.

QUESTIONS

1. If the Hanson court had applied the SEC's eight-part test, would Hanson's activities have involved a tender offer?

2. What factors does the court apply in lieu of the SEC's proposed test?

3. What impact do Hanson's previous disclosures in connection with its now abandoned tender offer have on determination of whether the contested purchases constituted a tender offer?

4. Suppose Hanson had instructed its broker, on the afternoon of September 11, that on the following day it wanted to acquire 30% of SCM's shares at a price of $73.50 per share. Assume that the broker then contacted an arbitrageur who had previously contacted the broker, indicating his unhappiness with the Merrill offer, and willingness to sell to another bidder. Assume the broker informed the arbitrageur of his client's interest in acquiring 30% in one day at $73.50, and that his client was not interested in purchasing any less than 30%. Assume the broker contacted ten other brokerage firms with arbitrage departments with the same message, and imposed no restrictions on whether they could repeat the terms of his offer to others. If word of these conversations spreads rapidly to the floor of the New York Stock Exchange, has Hanson engaged in a tender offer? See Paine, Webber, Jackson & Curtis, Inc. [1982–83 Decisions] FED. SEC. L. REP. (CCH) ¶ 83,310 (SEC, 1982).

For commentary on definitions of a tender offer see Keany and Sussman, Securities Commentary: The Elusive Definition of Tender Offers, 46 Brooklyn L. Rev. 1045 (1980) and casenote on Field v. Trump, 62 Temple L. Rev. 1033 (1989).

C. DISCLOSURES AT THE TAKEOUT

Once a bid is successful, and the bidder owns a majority of the shares of the target corporation and controls its board of directors, the bidder is in control of the information flow to target shareholders about their corporation. This control becomes important if the bidder seeks to squeeze out the remaining shareholders through a merger or reverse stock split. The bidder may require their approval if the company has previously adopted a "shark repellent" charter amendment that requires either a supermajority vote to approve a merger with an "interested shareholder" or requires approval of holders of a majority of the shares not held by the interested shareholder. In any event, even if the controlling shareholder does not require the consent of minority shareholders to complete the merger, SEC proxy rules will require it to furnish minority shareholders with an information statement containing the same information as would be required by a proxy solicitation.* One court has held that any false or misleading information in such circumstances will violate Rule 10b–5, because it is issued in connection with the forced sale of the minority's shares. In response to defense arguments that the falsehoods could cause no harm, because the majority shareholder could outvote the minority, Judge Friendly stated that minority shareholders could seek to avoid the harm either by seeking their appraisal remedy or by seeking to enjoin the merger. Goldberg v. Meridor, 567 F.2d 209 (2d Cir.1977), cert. denied, 434 U.S. 1069 (1978). In Virginia Bankshares, Inc. v. Sandberg, 501 U.S. 1083 (1991), the Supreme Court declined to create a private right of action for plaintiffs in a going private merger where their votes were not required for approval, because the alleged proxy fraud did not deprive the plaintiffs of any state rights. In Grace v. Rosenstock, 228 F.3d 40 (2d Cir. 2000), cert. denied sub nom. Grace v. Genser, 121 S.Ct. 1362 (2001), the court held that plaintiffs alleging proxy fraud in a freeze-out merger had not proven transaction causation because their votes were not required for approval of the merger.

In 1977 the SEC proposed a rule dealing with going private transactions. Exchange Act Release No. 14185 (Nov. 17, 1977). The initial version of the proposed rule contained substantive regulation of going private transactions, providing that it would be a fraudulent, deceptive or manipulative act or practice to purchase securities in a going private transaction if it "is unfair to unaffiliated securityholders." After much debate a final version of the rule was adopted in 1979 which did not contain such substantive fairness requirements. As adopted, Rule 13e–3 was a disclosure rule. It requires issuers subject to the Exchange Act which are about to engage in a going private transaction to file Schedule 13E–3. Schedule 13E–3 requires the issuer to disclose to shareholders all of the conventional financial information about an issuer, but also requires a discussion of the fairness of the transaction (Item 8) and a disclosure of any reports, opinions or appraisals received by the issuer or its affiliates relating to the fairness of the transaction. The extent of the

---

*   Securities Exchange Act § 14(c); 17 C.F.R. 240, Regulation 14C.

disclosure obligation is illustrated in the following case. While the issue arises in the context of a tender offer, the approach is illustrative of what may be expected under Rule 13(e)–3.

Flynn v. Bass Brothers Enterprises, Inc.

744 F.2d 978 (3d Cir.1984).

■ ADAMS, CIRCUIT JUDGE.

This appeal concerns the adequacy under federal and state securities law of disclosure in a tender offer by defendant Bass Brothers Enterprises, Inc. (Bass Brothers) for the outstanding shares of defendant National Alfalfa Dehydrating and Milling Company (National Alfalfa).

Plaintiffs, former minority shareholders of National Alfalfa, charge in a class action that Bass Brothers and the management of National Alfalfa violated sections 10(b) and 14(e) of the Securities Exchange Act of 1934 (1934 Act), as well as Delaware common law by failing to disclose material information in conjunction with the tender offer. At the conclusion of plaintiffs' case the district court directed a verdict for defendants. As to the federal claims, the judge ruled that plaintiffs had failed to produce sufficient evidence of fraudulent nondisclosure to raise a question of fact for the jury. Regarding the state claim, the judge found the subsequent merger had a proper business purpose. This appeal followed.

I.

The essential facts of the case are undisputed. Bass Brothers is a closely held Texas corporation. At the time of the tender offer its principal business was oil exploration with subsidiary interests in hydrocarbon production, radio, television, ranching and cattle-raising. In 1974 Bass Brothers was approached by the president of Prochemco, Inc. (Prochemco), a Texas corporation engaged in ranching and cattle-feeding, as a possible source of financing for a purchase by Prochemco of a large block of National Alfalfa's stock. National Alfalfa, a Delaware corporation whose stock was traded on the American Stock Exchange, was engaged in farming, farm supply operations and the sale of animal feed. Its former president, Charles Peterson, was seeking to sell his controlling interest in the company in order to raise sufficient capital to repay a large personal debt. To present its proposal to Bass Brothers and other potential sources of funding, Prochemco prepared two reports on National Alfalfa's history and operations, including an appraisal of its assets based on alternative hypothetical valuations.

Although Bass Brothers declined to finance such a purchase by Prochemco, it indicated that it might consider proceeding as a principal should Prochemco fail to obtain the necessary funding. In late 1975 Prochemco informed Bass Brothers that it had been unable to obtain financing and that Peterson's block of National Alfalfa stock was still available. In return for providing the detailed information about National Alfalfa contained in the Prochemco reports and for assistance in analyzing National Alfalfa's current and potential performance, Bass Brothers agreed to pay Prochemco a $130,000 finders fee.

In December 1975 Bass Brothers entered into an option agreement for the purchase of Peterson's 52% share of National Alfalfa's outstanding common stock. Thereafter, Bass Brothers exercised its option and bought the approximately 1.3 million shares from Peterson for a price of $8.44 million or $6.47 per share. A short time later, in a private sale, Bass Brothers was able to acquire an additional 226,673 shares of National Alfalfa, representing 9.1% of the outstanding shares, at $6.45 per share. This acquisition increased Bass Brothers' holding to 61.2% of the outstanding shares of National Alfalfa.

On March 2, 1976, Bass Brothers made public its tender offer for "any and all" outstanding shares of National Alfalfa at $6.45 per share. The reports prepared by Prochemco for Bass Brothers were not appended to the tender offer, nor did the tender offer refer to Prochemco's appraisal of the overall values per share of National Alfalfa which stated that:

> $6.40 could be realized through "liquidation [of National Alfalfa] under stress conditions";

> $12.40 could be realized through "liquidation in an orderly fashion over a reasonable period of time";

> $16.40 represented National Alfalfa's value "as [an] ongoing venture."

Further, the tender offer did not refer to a second report prepared by Prochemco which gave two additional valuations: $17.28 representing the "Value per Peterson"; $7.60 representing the "Value per Prochemco." To the contrary, the tender offer stated in bold letters that "Offeror did not receive any material non-public information from [National Alfalfa] with respect to its prior acquisitions of shares nor . . . does it believe it presently possesses any such information. Offeror has not been able to verify independently the accuracy or completeness of the information contained in Appendices A through E [furnished by National Alfalfa] and assumes no responsibility therefor."

On March 15, 1976, Bass Brothers did, however, issue a supplement to the tender offer describing the book value of "certain land owned or leased by" National Alfalfa and advising the shareholders that:

> While the Offeror has made no independent appraisal of the value of the Company's land and makes no representation with respect thereto, in view of the foregoing factors the aggregate current fair market value of the Company's agricultural land may be substantially higher than its original cost as reflected on the books of the Company. Depending upon the respective market values for such land, stockholders could receive, upon

liquidation of the Company, an amount per share significantly higher than the current book value and possibly higher than the price of $6.45 per Share offered by Offeror in the Offer. The amount received by stockholders upon liquidation of the Company would also be dependent upon, among other things, the market value of the Company's other assets and the length of time allowed for such liquidation. The Offeror has no reason to believe that the Company's management has any present intention of liquidating the Company. As noted on page 8 of the Offer to Purchase under "Purpose of This Offer: Present Relationship of Company and Offeror", Offeror does not currently intend to liquidate the Company.

The supplement also extended the duration of the offer by one week "to afford stockholders an opportunity to evaluate" the new information. While the offer was in effect, the named plaintiffs tendered their shares to Bass Brothers for $6.45 per share. At the expiration of the extended offer, Bass Brothers owned more than 92% of the outstanding shares of National Alfalfa and took control of the company by removing the board of directors and electing a new board of directors. Shortly thereafter, a Delaware "short-form merger" was effected between National Alfalfa and Bass Brothers Farming Company, a wholly owned subsidiary of Bass Brothers. Emerging as the surviving entity, National Alfalfa became a wholly owned subsidiary of Bass Brothers.

* * *

III.

Plaintiffs allege that Bass Brothers and the management of National Alfalfa violated section 10(b) and 14(e) of the 1934 Act and rule 10b–5 of the Securities and Exchange Commission (SEC) by not disclosing certain information with the tender offer. Specifically, plaintiffs maintain that defendants had a duty to disclose certain asset appraisal values because such information would have aided National Alfalfa's shareholders in deciding whether or not to accept Bass Brothers' tender offer. We must determine whether the district judge committed reversible error when he ruled that defendants had no duty to disclose the asset appraisal values they possessed.

In 1968, Congress enacted the Williams Act as an amendment to the Securities and Exchange Act of 1934. The purpose of the Williams Act was to protect investors confronted by a tender offer for their stock. See Piper v. Chris-Craft Industries, 430 U.S. 1, 22–27 (1977). Presenting the bill to the Senate, Senator Williams, it's sponsor, stated:

> [t]his legislation will close a significant gap in investor protection under the Federal securities laws by requiring the disclosure of pertinent information to stockholders when persons seek to obtain control of a corporation by a cash tender

offer or through open market or privately negotiated purchases
of securities.[3]

Congress sought to ensure that public shareholders who are suddenly
faced with a tender offer will not be forced to respond without adequate
information regarding the qualifications and intentions of the offering
party. See Rondeau v. Mosinee Paper Corp., 422 U.S. 49, 58 (1975). To
that end, section 14(e) of the Williams Act prohibits the making of untrue
statements of material fact or the omission of material facts in tender
offers that could mislead the shareholders of a target company. Similar
in thrust to rule 10b–5, this broadly worded anti-fraud provision protects
target shareholders by subjecting tender offerors to advance disclosure
requirements. See Piper, 430 U.S. at 22–27.

   Where a "duty to speak" exists, therefore, federal securities law
requires the disclosure of any "material fact" in connection with the
purchase or sale of a security under rule 10b–5 or the tendering of an
offer under section 14(e). See Chiarella v. United States 445 U.S. 222,
235 (1980).[4] Bass Brothers does not deny that at the time of the tender
offer it was under a duty to make certain disclosures in its capacity as a
majority shareholder of National Alfalfa as well as in its capacity as a
tender offeror. Similarly, the management of National Alfalfa does not
deny that it owed a duty of disclosure to its shareholders. Our task, then,
is to determine whether the alleged nondisclosures were material
omissions, and thus breached the duty to disclose.

   This Court has previously noted that section 14(e) of the Williams
Act makes unlawful the failure to disclose any "material fact" in
connection with a tender offer. See Staffin, 672 F.2d at 1205. Rule 10b–5
similarly prohibits such omissions with regard to the purchase or sale of
a security. The Supreme Court defined materiality in the context of an
alleged violation of rule 14a–9, which governs disclosure requirements
for proxy statements, in the following manner:

> An omitted fact is material if there is a substantial
> likelihood that a reasonable shareholder would consider it
> important in deciding how to vote. * * *

---

[3]   Similarly, Manuel Cohen, the Chairman of the SEC when the Williams Act was enacted,
testified to the Senate Subcommittee on Securities that "the general approach . . . of [the
Williams Act] is to provide the investor, the person who is required to make a decision, an
opportunity to examine and to assess the relevant facts. . . ." Hearings on S. 510 before the
Subcommittee on Securities of the Senate Committee on Banking and Currency, 90th Cong., 1st
Sess., 15 (1967).

[4]   Because we hold that at the time in question National Alfalfa had no duty to disclose
the report prepared by Carl Schweitzer, a vice president of the company, we need not reach
plaintiff's allegation that Bass Brothers, as the majority shareholder of National Alfalfa, had a
duty to disclose the report. There is evidence in the record that Bass Brothers, although the
majority shareholder of the target company, purposely distanced itself from the target
management. App. at 323a. While not central to our decision in the present case, we note that
a policy of conscious ignorance cannot eliminate the fiduciary duty a majority shareholder owed
to the minority shareholders.

TSC Industries, Inc. v. Northway, Inc., 426 U.S. 438, 449 (1976). This definition of "material" has been adopted for cases involving rule 10b–5[7] and we see no reason not to utilize the same formulation for evaluating materiality in the context of a tender offer.

* * *

[The court noted that in the past the SEC and the courts had discouraged disclosure of appraisals and valuations as unreliable "soft" information, to which they feared investors would attach too much importance. The opinion noted changing attitudes toward such information, including income and earnings projects, and that the SEC now encouraged such projections by providing a safe harbor in Securities Act Rule 175.] And with respect to asset valuations, the SEC in 1980 authorized disclosure of good faith appraisals made on a reasonable basis in proxy contests in which a principal issue is the liquidation of all or a portion of a target company's assets. While SEC policy has not yet explicitly approved the disclosure of appraisal values when the target is to continue as a going concern rather than being liquidated, recent SEC promulgations herald a new view, more favorably disposed towards disclosure.

Part of the reason for this shift in policy is recognition of shareholders' need for such information.[16] One rationale for the initial prohibition of soft information was the fear that potential purchasers of securities would be misled by overly optimistic claims by management. An unintended by-product of such concern, however, was to keep valuable information from those shareholders who had to decide, within the context of a tender offer or merger, whether or not to sell their securities. The present spate of proxy contests and tender offers was not anticipated when the SEC initially formulated its policy of nondisclosure of soft information.

At least one court has recognized that disclosure of asset valuations may be required. In Radol [v. Thomas, 556 F.Supp. 586 (S.D. Oh. 1983)] plaintiffs challenged, among other things, the adequacy of disclosure in United States Steel's successful tender offer for Marathon Oil Company's stock in 1981. Rejecting the notion that "asset valuations are, as a matter of law, not material," the court held that such a determination was a matter for the jury to resolve in light of all the circumstances.

* * *

In order to give full effect to the evolution in the law of disclosure, . . . today we set forth the law for disclosure of soft information as it is to be applied from this date on. Henceforth, the law is not that asset appraisals

---

[7]   See. e.g., Healey v. Catalyst Recovery of Pennsylvania, Inc., 616 F.2d 641. 647 (3d Cir.1980). [The U.S. Supreme Court later adopted this formulation of materiality for 10b–5 in Basic Inc. v. Levinson, 485 U.S. 224 (1988)—Ed.]

[16]   See generally Brudney, Insiders, Outsiders, and Informational Advantages Under the Federal Securities Laws, 93 Harv. L. Rev. 322 (1979).

are, as a matter of law, immaterial. Rather, in appropriate cases, such information must be disclosed. Courts should ascertain the duty to disclose asset valuations and other soft information on a case by case basis, by weighing the potential aid such information will give a shareholder against the potential harm, such as undue reliance, if the information is released with a proper cautionary note.[17]

The factors a court must consider in making such a determination are: the facts upon which the information is based; the qualifications of those who prepared or compiled it; the purpose for which the information was originally intended; its relevance to the stockholders' impending decision; the degree of subjectivity or bias reflected in its preparation; the degree to which the information is unique; and the availability to the investor of other more reliable sources of information.

IV.

It is against the background set forth in Part III, *supra*, that we must determine whether the trial judge erred in ruling that Bass Brothers and the management of National Alfalfa had no duty to disclose the asset valuations at issue in this case. We note that despite our formulation of the current law applicable to corporate disclosure, we are constrained by the significant development in disclosure law since 1976 not to apply the announced standard retroactively,[19] but to evaluate defendants' conduct by the standards which prevailed in 1976.

Plaintiffs point to three sources of information that they believe should have been disclosed in the tender offer: the Prochemco reports; a report allegedly commissioned by Bass Brothers to corroborate the appraisals in the Prochemco reports; and an internal valuation prepared by National Alfalfa's accountant and vice-president, Carl Schweitzer.

A.

The shareholders contend that the Prochemco reports were material and should have been disclosed. However, employing the approach commonly followed by courts when Bass Brothers made its tender offer in early 1976, we do not find the Prochemco reports had sufficient indicia of reliability to require disclosure. Plaintiffs did not adequately establish that the reports were prepared by experts. Although Prochemco did have experience in acquisitions, there was scant evidence of the company's expertise in appraising the type of land involved in the present case. Moreover, plaintiffs did not establish that the reports had sufficient basis in fact to be reliable. Evidence introduced at trial demonstrated only that the first Prochemco report was based on a report prepared by one of the company's employees, but no basis for the reliability of this foundation

---

[17] Some courts have approved the release of appraisal values with an appropriate disclaimer. See, e.g. South Coast, 669 F.2d at 1269: Alaska Interstate, 402 F.Supp. at 573.

[19] Our reluctance to apply the new standard for disclosure retroactively is confined to the facts of this case. We do not intend to imply that in other cases based on actions occurring before the date of this opinion, the new standard necessarily is inapplicable.

report was established. The first Prochemco report itself merely stated that it "is our opinion, based on an evaluation by our staff as well as local interviews with those knowledgeable in farm real estate and with the Soil Conservation Service." App. at 843a. No basis was established for the second report.

The purpose for which the Prochemco reports were prepared—to attract financing for its proposed purchase of Peterson's controlling block of National Alfalfa shares—also diminishes the reliability of the reports. Further, at the time of the tender offer the valuations in the Prochemco reports were outdated.

Plaintiffs assert that the reliability of the reports was amply demonstrated by Bass Brothers' reliance on them and by the payment of $130,000 to Prochemco for them. The shareholders reason that "if the Prochemco reports were reliable and accurate enough for Bass Brothers to use . . . in deciding to [purchase Peterson's stock] then the existence of and valuations in the Prochemco reports were material and should have been shared with National Alfalfa's shareholders" through the tender offer. To bolster their argument, the shareholders note that after buying Peterson's stock, Bass Brothers chose not to examine any of National Alfalfa's internal asset valuations before making the tender offer.

Although it is not inconceivable that Bass Brothers may have relied on the Prochemco valuations, plaintiffs did not advance sufficient evidence to establish the point. Moreover, even if there had been some reliance on the reports, that alone would be insufficient to mandate disclosure in this case. The reports were not prepared by experts, had no adequately demonstrated basis in fact and were prepared to encourage financing to purchase Peterson's share. In light of the record before us, we cannot say that the district court erred in concluding that at the time of the tender offer Bass Brothers had no duty to disclose the Prochemco reports.

B.

Plaintiffs assert that Bass Brothers also should have disclosed its own internal valuations. To substantiate their belief that Bass Brothers commissioned a report to corroborate the information in the Prochemco report, the shareholders point to an informal typewritten list of "Items for Investigation" drawn up by Rusty Rose, a Bass Brothers consultant. The list sets forth a number of assignments to be performed by Rose. Item 2(a) states: "Have expert appraise farm land and equipment." A handwritten notation after this item states "Done—values confirmed." At trial it was revealed that Richard Rainwater, a Bass Brothers officer, had written the notation, although no evidence was produced concerning the circumstances under which the notation was made. The shareholders contend that this cryptic notation, without more, "confirms that Bass Brothers had obtained an 'expert' appraisal." Plaintiffs had ample opportunity during discovery to pursue this lead yet failed to turn up any additional evidence of a corroborating study. Presentation of this handwritten notation, alone, to the jury simply could not support a finding of fraudulent and material nondisclosure of information.

C.

The third piece of information that the shareholders claim should have been disclosed was a study prepared by Carl Schweitzer, a vice president of National Alfalfa, using various assumptions, such as the projected appreciation of National Alfalfa's land holdings, to arrive at a value per share of $12.95. At trial. Schweitzer's unrefuted testimony indicated that such a figure was, in fact, hypothetical because of the nature of the assumptions used in the calculation. Schweitzer stated that he used land values supplied by Peterson and some "unnamed people within or without of the company." Thus, plaintiffs have not established a sufficient factual basis for the valuations. Moreover, the purpose of some of these calculations was to help Peterson find a buyer for his stock. Schweitzer testified that the land values were inflated, or optimistic, so as to present the company in the best possible light to future investors. Moreover, Schweitzer admitted that neither he nor members of National Alfalfa's accounting staff had expertise with regard to land appraisal. Thus, plaintiffs were unable to produce evidence that the Schweitzer reports were sufficiently reliable to be material for shareholders confronted with the tender offer.

* * *

VIII.

After carefully examining the evidence presented by the shareholders in the light most favorable to them, we are persuaded that the district court's grant of a directed verdict for defendants was not error; therefore it will be affirmed.

NOTE ON DISCLOSURE DUTIES

The court's discussion of the disclosure duties of the Bass Brothers does not deal with the origins of those duties. In Chiarella v. United States, 445 U.S. 222 (1980), the Supreme Court addressed this issue for the first time. It reversed the insider trading conviction of a pressman at a financial printer, who had been convicted of trading on information stolen from his employer about forthcoming tender offers. The court noted that the instructions to the jury failed to instruct that it must find that the defendant owed a fiduciary duty to shareholders of the target corporation. The court stated that " . . . one who fails to disclose material information prior to the consummation of a transaction commits fraud [at common law] only when he is under a duty to do so. And the duty to disclose arises when one party has information 'that the other [party] is entitled to know because of a fiduciary relation of trust and confidence between them." Accordingly, it was generally held that hostile bidders for a company's shares, not being in a position of trust and confidence with respect to the target corporation and its shareholders, owed no disclosure duties to them as a result of the general strictures of Rule 10b–5.

In an opinion critical of Flynn v. Bass Brothers, the Sixth Circuit characterized Flynn as holding that "Courts should ascertain the duty to disclose asset valuations and other soft information on a case by case basis, by weighing the potential aid such information will give a shareholder against the potential harm such as undue reliance, if the information is released without the proper cautionary note." Starkman v. Marathon Oil Co., 772 F.2d 231, 242 (6th Cir.1985). Is this an accurate characterization of the holding in Flynn? In Basic Inc. v. Levinson, 485 U.S. 224 (1988), the Supreme Court held that duties to disclose are not a function of materiality. Since Flynn the idea of including cautionary language with disclosures of soft information has flowered, and become enshrined as the "bespeaks caution" doctrine, which, in the Securities Litigation Reform Act of 1996, became a safe harbor from liability for forward-looking statements. Securities Exchange Act § 21E.

The Flynn case arose before the SEC adopted Rule 13e–3, which now governs so-called "going private" transactions, however structured. Note that the Bass Brothers appeared to take particular care to not become "insiders" in National Alfalfa, in order to minimize their disclosure obligations in connection with the tender offer. The SEC viewed this as a "regulatory gap," and proposed alternative versions of Rule 13e–3, first in 1975 and again in 1977. The final rule was adopted in 1979. Securities Exchange Act Release No. 16075 (Aug. 2, 1979). The rule applies to so-called "going private" transactions, and has two prongs. First, there must be a "transaction," which includes issuer repurchases of its own securities, tender offers, either by the issuer for its own securities, or by an "affiliate" (a control person or person controlled by or under common control with the issuer), or a proxy solicitation in connection with a merger, recapitalization or sale of substantially all assets. Second, in order to be a "Rule 13e–3 transaction," the transaction must have the effect of taking the company's shares out of the public markets, which can be accomplished by reducing the number of holders of the issuer's stock to less than 300 persons (which allows termination of registration and reporting under the Securities Exchange Act), or causing the stock to be delisted on a national securities exchange or registered inter-dealer quotation system (NASDAQ). Under these conditions, the issuer or affiliate causing the transaction must comply with the disclosure requirements of the rule, some of which are described below.

QUESTIONS

1. If Bass Brothers bought information from Prochemco, why did they owe disclosure to others who didn't invest in such information?

2. When the Bass Brothers decided to acquire National Alfalfa, what obligations did they owe to its shareholders (including Peterson) under fiduciary principles?

3. When the Bass Brothers bought Peterson's 52% interest in National Alfalfa, did their obligations with respect to the information they purchased from Prochemco change under traditional fiduciary principles? If so, why?

4. Why didn't the Bass Brothers deny any disclosure duties in their capacity as majority shareholders?

5. Why does the Court hold that the Bass Brothers had no obligation to disclose the Prochemco reports that the Bass Brothers purchased?

6. Why didn't the Bass Brothers' verification of the Prochemco appraisals raise them to the level of certainty requiring disclosure?

7. Why weren't the studies of Schweitzer, a National Alfalfa vice president, regarded as material?

PROBLEM

Today the transaction in Flynn is governed by Securities Exchange Act Rule 13e–3, which applies to "going private" transactions such as that in the Flynn case. After reviewing the requirements of Items 8 and 9 of Schedule 13E–3, and Item 229.1015 of Regulation M-A, 17 C.F.R. § 229.1015, advise on how they would apply to the Flynn case.

1. How do these rules apply to the Prochemco reports?

2. How do these rules apply to the Bass Brothers' verification of these reports?

3. How do these rules apply to the studies of Schweitzer, National Alfalfa's vice president?

Howing Co. v. Nationwide Corporation

826 F.2d 1470 (6th Cir.1987), cert. denied, 486 U.S. 1059,
108 S.Ct. 2830, 100 L.Ed.2d 930 (1988).

■ MERRITT, CIRCUIT JUDGE.

Under § 13(e) of the Securities Exchange Act of 1934, a Williams Act provision enacted in 1968, a company that has issued publicly traded stock is prohibited from buying it back unless the issuer complies with rules promulgated by the SEC. This appeal raises issues concerning the existence of a private right of action under § 13e–3, the nature of the disclosure duty imposed by Rule 13e–3, and the interrelationship of this provision with other antifraud rules.

Pursuant to its authority under § 13e–3, the SEC has issued Rule 13e–3 and Schedule 13e–3, a long and detailed set of disclosure requirements governing such "going private" transactions. Schedule 13e–3 accompanying the Rule requires that numerous items of information about the transaction be filed with the Commission, including three items pertinent to this case, i.e., Items 7, 8 and 9. Item 7 covers the "reasons" for the transaction; Item 8 requires a statement concerning the fairness of the transaction; and Item 9 requires disclosure of appraisals and other information concerning the value of the stock. The Rule also provides that this same information be disclosed to the selling shareholders.

The basic questions presented in this case are: (1) whether the plaintiffs have a private right of action under § 13e–3 to police non-compliance with Rule 13e–3; (2) and if so, whether the disclosure requirements of Rule 13e–3 have been met; and (3) if those requirements have not been met, whether defendant's conduct in violating Rule 13e–3 also gives rise to liability under the antifraud provisions of Rules 10b–5 and 14a–9.

Parties and Summary of Disposition Below

Defendant Nationwide Corporation is one of the largest life insurance holding companies in the United States. Originally incorporated in 1947 as Service Insurance Agency, the company has enjoyed steady growth since its affiliation with the Nationwide group of insurance companies in September 1955. As a result of this affiliation, the company adopted its present name and issued a special class of common stock (Class B common) which was held entirely by two Nationwide companies: Nationwide Mutual Insurance Company and Nationwide Mutual Fire Insurance Company. The Class A common stock continued in the hands of individual shareholders.

* * *

Nationwide Mutual and Nationwide Mutual Fire began to eliminate public ownership of Nationwide Corporation in December 1978 when these companies made a tender offer to buy the Class A shares for $20.00 per share net in cash. By January 1979, Nationwide Mutual and Nationwide Mutual Fire had purchased 4,074,695 Class A shares through this offer. After the tender offer, Nationwide Mutual and Nationwide Mutual Fire continued to purchase shares in the open market at prices ranging between $22.50 and $24.62 per share. These transactions ultimately gave Nationwide Mutual and Nationwide Mutual Fire ownership of 85.6% of the Class A common stock formerly held by the public.

In November 1982, the Board of Directors of Nationwide Corporation approved a transaction in which Nationwide Mutual and Nationwide Mutual Fire would acquire the remaining Class A shares at $42.50 per share. As a result, Nationwide Corporation would become a wholly-owned subsidiary of the two mutuals, and would have no public ownership. This transaction was approved by 94.7% of the Class A shares. Plaintiffs in the present litigation abstained from voting their shares respecting the merger or seeking their appraisal remedy under state law.

The present class action began with an action by Belle Efros, a Nationwide shareholder, seeking a preliminary injunction with respect to a vote on the proposed merger. Following the denial of the Efros motion for a preliminary injunction, the merger was approved by 94.7% of the voted public shares. The District Court ultimately consolidated the Efros action with an action brought by the Howing Company and Douglas McClellan, two former shareholders of Nationwide. The District Court also later conditionally certified the case as a class action. The final amended complaint in this action raised claims under the Securities Exchange Act of 1934 §§ 10(b), 13(e), and 14(a) and rules promulgated thereunder as well as state law claims based on a breach of fiduciary duty.

The defendants moved for summary judgment and plaintiffs filed a cross-motion for partial summary judgment. The District Court granted defendants' motion, denied plaintiffs' cross-motion, and dismissed the amended complaint.

* * *

The District Court concluded overall that the proxy statement satisfied the requirements of Rule 13e–3. The District Court stated:

> Most important, there was sufficient information disclosed in the proxy statement to enable the stockholders to make an informed decision on what to do. It is the conclusion of the Court, therefore, that there is no genuine issue of material fact concerning the adequacy of the proxy statement when measured against the standards set forth in Rule 13e–3, and that any omissions pointed out by plaintiffs were not material as defined by the Court in TSC Industries, Inc. v. Northway, Inc., 426 U.S. at 449, 96 S. Ct. at 2132.

* * *

Rule 13e–3 Compliance

Going private transactions raise unique problems because of their inherently coercive nature: minority shareholders are forced to exchange their shares for cash or other consideration. The coercive effect of these transactions is reinforced by the fact that the majority shareholders control the timing and terms of the transaction.

* * *

Rule 13e–3 does not require that the issuer's Schedule 13e–3 filing with the Commission be reproduced in its entirety in the communication with shareholders. Most items from that Schedule may be summarized. However, Items 7, 8 and 9 must be disclosed verbatim. The rationale behind complete disclosure of these items is that they go to the essence of the transaction. Item 7 requires full disclosure of the purposes, alternatives, reasons, and effects of the transaction; Item 8 requires a statement as to the fairness of the transaction and the factors upon which such belief is based; and Item 9 requires disclosure of reports, opinions, appraisals and certain negotiations.

* * *

B.   *Item 8 Disclosure*

The instructions accompanying Schedule 13e–3 are quite definite in the level of specificity required in certain disclosures.[5] The Instruction to Item 8 states that "conclusory statements, such as 'The Rule 13e–3 transaction is fair to unaffiliated security holders in relation to net book value, going concern value and future prospects of the issuer' will not be considered sufficient disclosure in response to Item 8(a)." (emphasis added.)

The Commission has expressed special concern with disclosures under Item 8(b) of Schedule 13e–3, the Item concerning the factors underlying a belief as to the fairness of the transaction. The Commission has issued the following guidance to prospective issuers:

> The Division is concerned that in many instances the Item 8(b) disclosure being made to security holders is vague and non-specific and is therefore of limited utility to security holders. . . . Each such factor which is material to the transaction should be discussed and, in particular, if any of the sources of value indicate a value higher than the value of the consideration offered to unaffiliated security holders, the discussion should specifically address such difference and should include a statement of the bases for the belief as to fairness in light of the difference.

Exchange Act Release No. 34–17719, at 17, 245–42.

The most serious problem in defendants' proxy statement concerns Item 8(b) compliance. Our review of the proxy statement indicates that

---

[5] The Instructions to Item 8(b) of the Schedule identify the following factors to be discussed in the disclosure:

Instructions. (1) The factors which are important in determining the fairness of a transaction to unaffiliated security holders and the weight, if any, which should be given to them in a particular context will vary. Normally such factors will include, among others, those referred to in paragraphs (c), (d) and (e) of this Item and whether the consideration offered to unaffiliated security holders constitutes fair value in relation to: (i) Current market prices, (ii) Historical market prices, (iii) Net book value, (iv) Going concern value, (v) Liquidation value, (vi) The purchase price paid in previous purchases disclosed in Item 1(f) of Schedule 13e–3, (vii) Any report, opinion, or appraisal described in Item 9 and (viii) Firm offers of which the issuer or affiliate is aware made by any unaffiliated person, other than the person filing this statement, during the preceding eighteen months . . .

defendants have made precisely the kind of conclusory statements prohibited by the Rule. In describing the fairness of the transaction as required by Item 8(b), defendants have done nothing more than provide a laundry list of factors considered by their investment banker.[6]

This kind of non-specific disclosure runs counter not only to the SEC's position taken in the Commission release discussed above but also to the Instruction to Item 8(b) of Schedule 13e–3. The Instruction states that the issuer shall "discuss in reasonable detail the material factors upon which the belief stated in Item 8(a) is based and, to the extent practicable, the weight assigned to each factor." (emphasis added). Thus, the proxy statement is incomplete in that we are not provided with any indication of the weights given the various factors as required by Rule 13e–3, incorporating Schedule 13e–3. Moreover, we therefore have no indication as to whether any of the "sources of value indicate a value higher than the value of the consideration offered to unaffiliated security holders." Exchange Act Release No. 34–17719, at 17, 245–42.

Instead of providing this itemized disclosure called for by Rule 13e–3, defendants rely heavily on the First Boston opinion letter to discharge their disclosure obligations.[7] Indeed, the proxy materials state specifically, "Although the Evaluation Committee did not give specific weight to each of the various factors considered in evaluating the fairness of the proposed merger, particular emphasis was placed upon the receipt of the opinion of First Boston."

While the Commission has stated that an issuer in a going private transaction can rely on an investment banker's opinion to meet its disclosure obligations, such opinion itself must fully analyze the factors enumerated in Item 8(b) as well as be "expressly adopted" by the issuer. Exchange Act Release No. 34–17719, at 17, 245–42. The issuer in this case did not conduct its own investigation but chose to rely on the expertise of First Boston. The problem with defendants adopting the First Boston opinion letter as their disclosure to shareholders is that this one-page letter is itself woefully inadequate when measured against the specific disclosure requirements of the Rule. An issuer cannot insulate itself from 13e–3 liability by relying on an investment banker's opinion letter which itself does not comply with the specific disclosure requirements of the Rule. Therefore, defendants' conclusory statements are not cured by conclusory statements made by First Boston in its opinion letter.

Somewhere in the proxy materials the Nationwide shareholders should have received a reasonably detailed analysis of the various financial valuation methods discussed by the Rule and the weights attached thereto. Even if certain valuation methods were not particularly

---

[6]   See Appendix A for the relevant language from the proxy statement.

[7]   See Appendix B for the language from the First Boston opinion letter which appears in the proxy statement as Exhibit II.

relevant, this should itself have been noted and explained. See Exchange Act Release No. 34–17719, at 17,245–42. Without this disclosure, Nationwide shareholders did not possess the information necessary to make an informed decision concerning the going private transaction.

* * *

The Antifraud Claims

In addition to liability under subsection (b)(2) of Rule 13e–3, plaintiffs also contend that the defendants breached the antifraud provisions of Rules 10b–5, 13e–3(b)(1), and 14a–9. In essence, plaintiffs contend that a failure to disclose information required by Rule 13e–3 ipso facto constitutes an "omission" actionable under the antifraud provisions. They argue that Rules 10b–5 and 14a–9 incorporate Rule 13e–3 by reference in the going private context.

The three antifraud provisions at issue here spring from distinct statutes which have unique texts and histories. All three, however, parallel the common law of fraud and deceit. Absent special circumstances, an action for deceit would lie at common law for both falsehoods and half-truths, but not for a complete failure to disclose. See III L. Loss, Securities Regulation at 1433–35. As was noted by this circuit almost fifty years ago with regard to a similarly worded antifraud provision in the Securities Act of 1933:

> The statute did not require appellant to state every fact about stock offered that a prospective purchaser might like to know or that might, if known, tend to influence his decision, but it did require appellant not "to obtain money or property by means of any untrue statement of a material fact or any omission to state a material fact necessary in order to make the statements made, in the light of the circumstances under which they were made, not misleading.

Otis & Co. v. SEC, 106 F.2d 579, 582 (6th Cir.1939) (emphasis in original) (construing § 17(a)(2) of the Securities Act of 1933).

The second clauses of Rules 10b–5 and 13e–3(b)(1), and similar language in Rule 14a–9, adopt the common law rule and prohibit silence only where the omitted information is necessary to prevent inaccuracy in existing disclosure. As a result, these provisions have been considered by commentators and the courts alike to be concerned with half-truth rather than omissions per se. See Myzel v. Fields, 386 F.2d 718, 733 n. 6 (8th Cir.1967); Trussell v. United Underwriters, Ltd., 228 F.Supp. 757, 767 (D.Col.1964); Cochran v. Channing Corp., 211 F.Supp. 239, 243 (S.D.N.Y.1962); see also III L. Loss, Securities Regulation at 1439; A. Bromberg & L. Lowenfels, Securities Fraud & Commodities Fraud § 2.6(2).

The essence of plaintiff's claim is that a failure to provide items of disclosure required by Rule 13e–3(e) always constitutes a material omission under the antifraud rules. This is tantamount to incorporating the disclosure provisions of the securities laws into the antifraud provisions. No longer would omissions be actionable only where a half-truth resulted. Instead, any failure to comply with SEC disclosure obligations would be actionable by private litigants under the antifraud provisions.

Although the antifraud rules are the "catch-all" provisions of the securities laws, the Supreme Court has emphasized in the Rule 10b–5 context that they apply only where some fraud has been committed. See Chiarella v. United States, 445 U.S. 222, 234–35, 63 L. Ed. 2d 348, 100 S. Ct. 1108 (1980). Congress did not enact sections 10(b), 13(e), or 14(a) to give private litigants the same enforcement powers granted to the Commissioner of the SEC. Allowing private suits based on any non-disclosure, without regard to the "half-truth" limitation, would contravene the congressional intent behind these statutes. Therefore, we hold that omission of disclosure required by Rule 13e–3(e) will constitute a violation of the antifraud provisions of sections 10(b), 13(e), and 14(a) only where the information is necessary to prevent half-truth. The violations of Rule 13e–3, Item 8, itemized above, do not constitute "fraud" under sections 10(b) and 14(a) but should be considered as violations only of the specific rule in question.[11]

* * *

Accordingly, the judgment of the District Court is reversed and remanded for proceedings consistent with this opinion.

APPENDIX A

The proxy statement provides in pertinent part:

The members of the Evaluation Committee believe that, from a financial point of view, the terms of the proposed merger are fair to the public shareholders of the Corporation. The committee members considered important, as an indication of the fairness of the proposed merger, the receipt of the written opinion of First Boston. The committee members also considered important a number of other factors discussed with the representatives of First Boston. These factors are the current market price of the Class A Common shares as compared with stock prices of other comparable entities; past and current earnings of the Corporation; past and current price/earnings ratios of the Corporation and other companies having similar operations; past and current price/equity ratios of the Corporation (as computed in accordance with generally accepted accounting principles); and the premium over market price offered to the public shareholders in other similar transactions as well as in other recent acquisitions in the life insurance industry

---

[11] Under certain circumstances, violations of Rule 13e–3 may be indicative of a "scheme or artifice to defraud" which would violate the antifraud provisions. Such is not the case here, however, where non-disclosure is claimed to be a violation standing alone.

generally. In its discussions with the representatives of First Boston, upon whose opinion the Evaluation Committee has concluded that it is appropriate to rely, these representatives stated that in addition to the above noted factors they had also considered the current overall level of the stock market; historical market prices of the Class A Common shares as compared with market prices for the stock of other comparable entities; going concern value of the Corporation; net book value of the Corporation; liquidation value of the Corporation; various financial ratios; present revenues, expenses, earnings and dividends of the Corporation and trends with respect thereto; the purchase price paid to holders of Class A Common shares by Nationwide Mutual in connection with the December 1978 tender offer for the Class A Common shares; present value of projected future cash flows of the Corporation; replacement value of the Corporation; off balance sheet items of the Corporation; significant trends in the insurance business; competitive environment of the insurance industry; regulatory environment of the insurance industry; and the impact of inflation on the Corporation.

APPENDIX B

The First Boston opinion letter reads in its entirety as follows:

November 1, 1982

Board of Directors

Nationwide Corporation

One Nationwide Plaza

Columbus, Ohio 43216

Gentlemen:

You have asked us to advise you as to the fairness to the shareholders of Nationwide Corporation, other than Nationwide Mutual Insurance Company and Nationwide Mutual Fire Insurance Company, of the financial terms of a proposed merger whereby the owners of 685,545 publicly held Class A common shares would receive cash for their shares and Nationwide Mutual Insurance Company and Nationwide Mutual Fire Insurance Company would become the only shareholder of Nationwide Corporation. The terms of the merger transaction are that Nationwide Corporation shareholders will be entitled to receive $42.50 for each share of Nationwide Corporation Class A common shares.

In connection with our review, Nationwide Corporation furnished to us certain business and financial data concerning Nationwide Corporation. This information was furnished specifically for the purpose of our advising you as to the fairness of the financial terms of the proposed merger, and our Corporation's representation that the information is complete and accurate in all material respects. We have not independently verified the information. We have also reviewed certain publicly available information that we considered relevant and have had discussions with certain members of Nationwide Corporation's management.

In arriving at our opinion we have also considered, among other matters we deemed relevant, the historical financial record, operating statistics, current financial position and general prospects of Nationwide Corporation and the stock market performance of the Class A common shares of Nationwide Corporation. In addition, we have considered the terms and conditions of the proposed transaction as compared with the terms and conditions of comparable transactions.

Based on our analysis of the foregoing and of such other factors as we have considered necessary for the purpose of this opinion and in reliance upon the accuracy and completeness of the information furnished to us by Nationwide Corporation, it is our opinion that the financial terms of the proposed transaction are fair to the minority shareholders of Nationwide Corporation.

Very truly yours,

THE FIRST BOSTON CORPORATION

QUESTIONS

1. The court found that the proxy statement did not comply sufficiently with Item 8(b) of Schedule 13e–3. If you were advising corporate officials after this decision, what kinds of disclosures would you want to explore?

2. Why didn't the First Boston letter satisfy the obligations of the Board on fairness disclosures? Why can't you rely on the recommendation of experts concerning the fairness of the price offered? Suppose the Board really has no idea about what price is fair except the information they obtain from its investment bankers, who provide a letter like that provided by First Boston. What else can the Board say about fairness? Is there a reason why First Boston has provided such a short letter on a complex topic? Would a lawyer be well advised to provide a short opinion letter on a complex legal question?

3. If Rule 13e–3 had been in effect at the time of Flynn v. Bass Brothers, *supra*, what kind of fairness discussion would you recommend?

4. If First Boston relied primarily on revenue projections for future periods, why isn't disclosure of these projections required?

5. Why doesn't a failure to comply with Item 8(b) constitute fraud under Rule 10b–5 and related statutes?

6. If a failure to comply with the requirements of Item 8(b) does not automatically constitute fraud, what risk does a company run if it fails to comply?

PROBLEM

Analyze whether the following Item 8(b) is responsive to the requirements of the SEC and of the Howing court.

Schedule 13E–3 of Bowles Fluidics Corp., filed March 2, 1999.

ITEM 8. FAIRNESS OF THE TRANSACTION.

(b) In reaching their determination that the proposed reverse stock split and subsequent purchase of fractional shares are substantively and procedurally fair to unaffiliated stockholders of the Company, the Special Committee and the Board of Directors considered the following factors:

(i) The written opinion of Ferris, Baker Watts delivered to the Special Committee and the Board of Directors on December 8, 1998, to the effect that, based upon and subject to certain factors and assumptions stated therein, as of such date, the Purchase Price to be received by the shareholders of the Company as a result of the reverse stock split and purchase of resulting fractional shares was fair, from a financial point of view. The full text of Ferris, Baker Watts' fairness opinion is attached hereto as Exhibit 3.

(ii) The relationship of the Purchase Price to the current market price of the Company's Common Stock, as of December 4, 1998, which was at a bid price of $0.75 per share and an asked price of $1.0625 per share.

(iii) The relationship of the Purchase Price to the historical market prices of the Company's Common Stock, as described under Item 1(c) of this Schedule, taking into account that at certain times during the previous two full fiscal years of the Company the price of the Company's Common Stock exceeded the Purchase Price.

(iv) The book value of the Company's Common Stock, which was $0.67 per share as of October 31, 1998 (the end of the Company's 1998 fiscal year).

(v) The relationship of the Purchase Price to the intrinsic value of the Company based upon a discounted cash flow analysis prepared by Ferris, Baker Watts in its reports to the Board of Directors, copies of which are attached to this Schedule as Exhibit 4.

(vi) The relationship of the Purchase Price to the value of the Company based upon a comparison to the value of publicly traded comparable companies as analyzed by Ferris, Baker Watts in its reports to the Board of Directors, copies of which are attached to this Schedule as Exhibit 4.

(vii) The advantages of and benefits to the Company of not being required to file periodic reports with the Securities and Exchange Commission pursuant to §§ 15(d) of the Securities and Exchange Act of 1934, the direct and indirect cost savings to be realized by the Company from not having to file such periodic reports, and the benefits to be derived by the remaining Company stockholders from the transactions described in this Schedule.

(viii) The Company's financial projections as analyzed by Ferris, Baker Watts which, in the view of the Special Committee and the Board of

Directors, support their determination that the Purchase Price is fair to unaffiliated stockholders,

(ix) The purchase of fractional shares of New Common Stock at the Purchase Price will enable owners of less than 1,000 shares of Old Common Stock to sell such shares and receive a premium over the highest price derived after applying the foregoing valuation analysis for such shares, without paying brokerage fees and commissions and other expenses of selling such shares.

The Board of Directors did not consider the liquidation value of the Company in making its decision to recommend the reverse stock split, since the value of the Company as a going concern far exceeded any liquidation value and provided the best opportunity to maximize the Purchase Price.

In reaching its determination as to the fairness of the Purchase Price and in view of the variety of factors considered in determining the fairness of the Purchase Price, the Special Committee and the Board of Directors of the Company did not assign any relative or specific weights to the various factors considered by them.

In reaching their conclusion that the proposed reverse stock split and subsequent purchase of fractional shares are substantively and procedurally fair to unaffiliated stockholders of the Company, William Ewing, III, James T. Parkinson, III, and Frederic Ewing, II, adopted the analysis of the factors described above by the Board of Directors, did not assign any relative or specific weights to the foregoing factors, and did not obtain any other analysis of the fairness of the transaction.

NOTE

Traditional doctrine about materiality holds that there is no need to disclose omitted information that would not change the total mix of information given to investors. TSC Indus. v. Northway, Inc., 426 U.S. 438, 449, 96 S.Ct. 2126, 48 L.Ed.2d 757 (1976)). The general result of this rule is that disclosures about fairness opinions need not disclose all of the matters considered by the giver of the opinion, or the details of calculations employed to reach the opinion. But the SEC staff, in commenting on filings, tends to demand information not literally required by the strict interpretation of the materiality doctrine. A 2006 blog describing demands made in reviewing a fairness opinion in connection with a merger (not a going private transaction) stated that in various cases the SEC staff inquired about or demanded: (1) the reasons a board chose to have two financial advisers' (2) a copy of the board book presented by the investment bankers and the engagement letters; (3) if the bankers relied on internal company projections, those should be disclosed in the filing; (4) prior relationships of the banker that might constitute conflicts of interest; (5) "please revise the discussion of the various analyses used by [the financial adviser] so that recipients of the proxy statement/prospectus can understand exactly what each analysis indicates. What are they used to show?; (6) what observations or conclusions the board had with respect to each analysis.

Disclosure issues also arise under the rubric of allegations of breach of fiduciary duties under state law. In Turner v. Bernstein, 776 A.2d 530 (Del. Ch. 2000), the court granted summary judgment on a claim of breach of fiduciary duties by directors of GenDerm, a semi-public corporation, in failing to make adequate disclosures in a solicitation for written consents to a merger. The solicitation consisted of a one-page letter stating that the board approved and recommended the transaction, which was negotiated by a special committee, a copy of section 262 of the Delaware Act setting forth shareholders' appraisal rights, and a copy of the merger agreement. The stockholders had not regularly received financial statements from the company, and none were disclosed in connection with the merger, although one of the plaintiffs had, after repeated insistence, received copies of the last two annual financial statements, before the merger was announced. There was no disclosure concerning the advisability of the merger or the fair value of GenDerm's stock. The court noted that in the negotiations with the prospective buyer GenDerm had provided its most recent monthly income statement, as well as optimistic projections about sales for the coming two years. The court held that the directors failed to "discharge their obligation to provide the GenDerm stockholders with 'the available material facts that would enable them to make an informed decision . . . whether to accept the merger consideration or demand appraisal.'" 2000 Del. Ch. LEXIS at *32–*33. To the same effect is Morton v. American Marketing Industries Holdings, Inc., 1995 WL 1791090 (Del.Ch. 1995), where the company mailed an information statement to preferred shareholders asking them to accept a charter amendment reducing the redemption price they would be entitled to receive in the event of a merger, and waiving liability (and asking common shareholders to waive their appraisal) rights. At the time of the solicitation, the definitive merger agreement had not yet been drafted, and the disclosure document contained no disclosure of whether the board had determined that the merger price was fair to the shareholders. The court declined to conclude that the plaintiff had not stated a colorable claim of breach of fiduciary duty, and scheduled an accelerated hearing on the motion for preliminary injunction.

Such claims are much more difficult where a proxy-like statement complying with federal requirements is involved. In Skeen v. Jo-Ann Stores, Inc., 750 A.2d 1170 (Del. 2000) the controlling 77% shareholder, Fabri-Centers of America ("FCA"), which had just completed a cash tender offer at $4.25 per share, proposed a cash-out merger of the target, House of Fabrics ("HF") at the same price. It sent what the court described as an information statement, not soliciting shareholder votes, since it didn't need them, which contained "the type of information normally found in a merger proxy statement, including a description of the companies, the background of the merger, and relevant financial information," and disclosure of shareholders' appraisal rights in compliance with the Delaware appraisal statute. The plaintiffs complained that it did not disclose, inter alia: (i) FCA's plan for HF and the extent that the plan had been implemented; (ii) the reason the HF board decided to sell the company; (iii) the range of HF's fair value, and the methodologies used, by HF's investment banker; (iv) management's financial projections for 1998–2003; and (v) the prices discussed with others for the sale of HF. The court stated:

"Appellants allege that this added financial data is material because it would help stockholders evaluate whether they should pursue an appraisal. They point out that the $4.25 per share merger price is 20% less than the company's book value. Since book value generally is a conservative value approximating liquidation value, they wonder how DLJ could conclude that the merger price was fair. If they understood the basis for DLJ's opinion, appellants say they would have a better idea of the price they might receive in an appraisal. Projections, more current financials and information about prices discussed with other possible acquirors, likewise, would help them predict their chances of success in a judicial determination of fair value.

"The problem with appellants' argument is that it ignores settled law. Omitted facts are not material simply because they might be helpful. To be actionable, there must be a substantial likelihood that the undisclosed information would significantly alter the total mix of information already provided. The complaint alleges no facts suggesting that the undisclosed information is inconsistent with, or otherwise significantly differs from, the disclosed information. Appellants merely allege that the added information would be helpful in valuing the company."

Skeen was reinforced in McMullin v. Beran, 765 A.2d 910, 926 (Del. 2000), where the court stated: "In Skeen, it was argued that the minority shareholders should have been given all of the financial data they would need if they were making an independent determination of fair value. We decline to establish 'a new disclosure standard where appraisal is an option.' [citations omitted]".

Some decisions of the Chancery Court have observed this rule. In In re Siliconix Inc. Shareholder Litigation, 2001 Del. Ch. LEXIS 83, Vice Chancellor Noble, dismissed a complaint that the Schedule 14D–9 prepared by the subsidiary in response to a parent's tender offer did not disclose "details and assumptions" relating to projections. In rejecting this claim, the court noted that there was no substantial likelihood shown by plaintiffs that the details and assumptions would "significantly alter the total mix already provided" to shareholders. The court concluded that the plaintiff failed to show that these details and assumptions "justify overcoming the reluctance of courts to order disclosure of 'soft information.' Such information might be 'helpful,' but here it has not been shown to be material." *Id.* at *41–42.

A significant departure appears in the opinion of Vice Chancellor Strine in In re Netsmart Technologies, Inc. Shareholders Litigation, 924 A.2d 171 (Del. Ch. 2007). Vice Chancellor Strine's jurisprudence should be put in the context of his rejection of the Supreme Court's materiality standard in Skeen in his opinion in In re Pure Resources, Inc., Shareholders Litigation, 808 A.2d 421 (Del. Ch. 2002). Pure involved a transaction with a controlling shareholder that exercised its control. Unocal Corp. owned 65% of Pure's stock and controlled its board. When Unocal determined to acquire all minority shares, it simply announced the terms of an exchange offer, and never varied them. When Pure's board selected a special committee to evaluate the fairness of the terms, the board determined to limit the power of the special committee, so that it could not seek alternative transactions or resist the offer by adopting takeover defenses. 808 A.2d at 430–31. The court concluded that the special committee was unwilling to challenge Unocal as aggressively as it would have challenged a third-party bidder, *id.* at 431, but the special committee nevertheless recommended that shareholders reject the offer. *Id.* at 432. The Schedule 14D–9 did "not disclose any substantive portions of the work" of the investment bankers who served as advisors. Vice Chancellor Strine also stressed that in transactions with controlling shareholders, "they have large informational advantages that can only be imperfectly overcome by the special committee process, which almost invariably involves directors who are not involved in the day-to-day management of the subsidiary", so that the work of investment bankers becomes even more important, as does the need to disclose it in full detail. *Id.* at 450.

Vice Chancellor Strine's opinion disagrees with opinions of the Delaware Supreme Court, as he candidly concedes. *Id.* at 78–79. "Fearing stepping on the SEC's toes and worried about encouraging prolix disclosures, the Delaware courts have been reluctant to require informative, succinct disclosure of investment banker analyses in circumstances in which the bankers' views about value have been cited as justifying the recommendation of the board." *Id.* at 79–80. Vice Chancellor Strine claims an ambivalence in recent Delaware Supreme Court opinions which is less than obvious upon closer inspection. In Skeen v. Jo-Ann Stores, Inc., *supra*, plaintiff's complaints were similar to those involved here—the absence of a summary of methodologies used, ranges of values generated by the bankers and the absence of management's projections of future performance, *inter alia*. The Supreme Court rejected these claims on materiality grounds, stating that:

> "it ignores settled law. Omitted facts are not material simply because they might be helpful. To be actionable, there must be a substantial likelihood that the undisclosed information would significantly alter the total mix of information already provided. The complaint alleges no facts suggesting that the undisclosed information is inconsistent with, or otherwise significantly differs from, the disclosed information. Appellants merely allege that the added information would be helpful in valuing the company." 750 A.2d at 1174.

Perhaps because Skeen did not support Vice Chancellor Strine's conclusions in Pure, he claimed that McMullin v. Beran, 765 A.2d 910 (Del. 2000), offers a "conflicting" impulse on additional disclosure of investment banker analyses. McMullin involved a total abdication by a subsidiary's board in the face of its parent's efforts to sell the subsidiary. The subsidiary's board failed to determine whether the offer was fair. Neither the board members nor its nominal financial adviser possessed sufficient information to judge the fairness of the transaction, or to advise shareholders. Not surprisingly, under these circumstances the court refused to dismiss the complaint. As if to reaffirm Skeen and distinguish McMullan, the court stated "In Skeen, it was argued that the minority shareholders should have been given all of the financial data they would need if they were making an independent determination of fair value. We declined to establish 'a new disclosure standard where appraisal is an option.' *We adhere to our holding in Skeen.*" 765 A.2d at 925.

Like McMullin, Netsmart offers a conflict of interest situation, where a management team chose to sell to private equity investors in order to obtain a larger share of the enterprise. Vice Chancellor Strine did not cite the governing law of the Skeen opinion concerning additional disclosures, choosing instead to cite his own opinion in Pure Resources that was critical of the Skeen rule. Noting the informational advantage of management in a leveraged management buyout, he stated that "[i]t would therefore seem to be a genuinely foolish (and arguably unprincipled and unfair) inconsistency to hold that the best estimate of the company's future returns, as generated by management and the Special Committee's investment bank, need not be disclosed when stockholders are being advised to cash out. * * * The conclusion that this omission is material should not be surprising. Once a board breaches a topic in its disclosures, a duty attaches to provide information that is 'materially complete and unbiased by the omission of material facts." 924 A.2d at 203.

Other Chancery Court decisions have continued to follow Skeen. See, e.g., In re Check Free Corp. Shareholders' Litigation, 2007 Del. Ch. LEXIS 148 and Globis Partners, L.P. v. Plumtree Software, Inc., 2007 Del. Ch. LEXIS 169.

D. REGULATION OF BID STRUCTURES

Read '34 Act § 14(d)(7) and Rule 14d–10.

NOTE

The "best price" rule of Rule 14d–10 implements the statutory requirement of Section 14d–7 that "[w]here any person varies the terms of a tender offer . . . before the expiration thereof by increasing the consideration offered to holders of such securities, such person shall pay the increased consideration to each security holder whose securities are taken up and paid for pursuant to the tender offer. . . ." The phrase "pursuant to the tender offer" has created difficulties for the courts. The problem arose most frequently in connection to payments negotiated to be made to target company executives, whether in the form of newly adopted severance agreements (golden parachutes) upon a change of control or new employment contracts with the bidder, to take effect after the change of control. This resulted in a "form versus substance" split among the courts, as described in the following excerpt from Katt v. Titan Acquisitions, Inc., 244 F.Supp.2d 841 (M. D. Tenn. 2003), a case in which the bidder negotiated with the target before the tender offer, and approved adoption of "golden parachute" arrangements that would pay management certain sums after completion of the tender offer, in addition to what they would receive in a tender offer that began somewhat later:

"Applying Rule 14d–2(a) to the instant case, UTC's tender offer for ICP commenced on June 30, 1999, and ended on August 9, 1999. The parties do not dispute that the awards to top ICP executives that allegedly constituted improper consideration for their shares was promised before the tender offer commenced and paid after its expiration and ICP's merger into UTC's Carrier subsidiary. Accordingly, "the focus thus becomes what interpretation the Court should apply to the Rule 14d–10 language stating that the relevant time frame is 'during such tender offer.' " In re Digital Island Sec. Litig., 223 F.Supp.2d 546, 556 (D. Del. 2002). The Sixth Circuit has not squarely addressed the question whether awards to key executives in a merger following a successful tender offer may be considered to constitute additional consideration for their shares so as to trigger a right of recovery by other tendering shareholders under the Williams Act, and there is a split among other courts as to the interpretation of this phrase. See id.

"In Epstein v. MCA, Inc., 50 F.3d 644 (9th Cir. 1995), vacated on other grounds, 516 U.S. 367 (1996), the Ninth Circuit expansively interpreted the Williams Act and adopted a flexible test for the definition of 'tender offer' that focuses not on timing but on whether the transaction in question was an 'integral part of [the] tender offer.' The plaintiffs in that case alleged that two insiders of the target corporation received additional, improper consideration for their stock pursuant to separate agreements before the tender offer commenced. The Ninth Circuit ꞏrejected the defendants' contention that the agreements were not actionable because they occurred outside the tender offer period, holding that questions of fact as to whether the agreements were integral to the tender offer, though outside of it in time, precluded summary judgment. Thus, under Epstein, bonus payments made to executives of a target company pursuant to golden parachute or other employment agreements may violate the Best Price Rule if they are meant as a 'premium' to the executives 'as an inducement to support the tender offer and tender [their] own shares' and are 'integral' to the tender offer, even if the agreements were executed prior to the tender offer's commencement.

"At least one lower court outside the Ninth Circuit has followed Epstein's approach in an unpublished opinion. See generally Millionerrors Inv. Club v. Gen. Elec. Co., 2000 U.S. Dist. LEXIS 4803, 2000 WL 1288333 (W.D. Pa. March 21, 2000). The Second Circuit has cited Epstein for the proposition that the timing provisions of the Best Price Rule should be interpreted flexibly, see Gerber v. Computer Assocs. Int'l, Inc., 303 F.3d 126, 135 (2d Cir. 2002), but it has not endorsed the Epstein standard. Indeed, as the Court discusses at pages 20 and 21, supra, the Second Circuit's approach to the Best Price Rule seems at odds with that espoused by the Ninth Circuit.

"In contrast, the Seventh Circuit, in an opinion affirming a district court's dismissal of a case under the Williams Act, rejected the standard enunciated in Epstein[7] and held that transactions or agreements made before the commencement of a tender offer do not, as a rule, occur 'during the tender offer.' Lerro v. Quaker Oats Co., 84 F.3d 239, 243 (7th Cir. 1996). In Lerro, the plaintiff challenged benefits granted to a controlling shareholder in an agreement executed before the commencement of the tender offer. The Seventh Circuit rejected the plaintiff's argument that this constituted extra compensation in violation of the Williams Act, despite the court's assumption that the agreement was 'integral to the transaction.' According to the court, the provisions of Rule 14d–2(a), defining when a tender offer begins, set a temporal limit to Best Price Rule actions: 'before the offer is not 'during' the offer. Many cases . . . tell us to respect the language of the securities statutes and regulations. The difference between 'during' and 'before' . . . is not just linguistic. Because the contested agreement occurred before the commencement of the tender offer, the Seventh Circuit affirmed the lower court's dismissal of plaintiff's Williams Act claims.

"Thus, Lerro establishes the bright-line rule that 'the protections in Section 14(d)(7) and Rule 14d–10 apply only to transactions between the commencement and expiration of the actual tender offer period.' Walker, 145 F.Supp.2d at 1371. Applying that rule, the Seventh Circuit held that whether or not challenged consideration was integral to the tender offer was irrelevant for purposes of Rule 14d–10. See Lerro, 84 F.3d at 244."

The result of this approach favored mergers over tender offers because of doubts about the treatment of severance payments to executives. This division among the circuits lasted until late 2006. In order to put tender offers on a level playing field with mergers, the SEC resolved the dispute by adopting the Lerro court's approach in 2006. Rule 13e–4, governing issuer self-tender offers, and Rule 14d–10, governing third party tender offers were both amended.

Rule 14d–10(d) was amended to provide a safe harbor exception for certain payments to executives that have created much of the litigation in the past. Rule 13e–4 is a comprehensive regulation governing all aspects of a self-tender offer covering both disclosure requirements and structural

---

[7]   Indeed, the Seventh Circuit noted, "Epstein lacks precedential value; the Supreme Court vacated the judgment after concluding that the ninth circuit should not have reached the merits in light of a prior settlement of class litigation in Delaware." Lerro, 84 F.3d at 243.

requirements. Rule 13e–4(f) governs the structure of self-tender offers. For our purposes, the relevant sections are subsection (f)(8) and amended subsection (f)(12). Parallel language appears in Rule 14d–10(d), governing third party tender offers:

"(d)(1) Paragraph (a)(2)(ii) of this section shall not prohibit the negotiation, execution or amendment of an employment compensation, severance or other employee benefit arrangement, or payments made or to be made or benefits granted or to be granted according to such an arrangement, with respect to any security holder of the issuer, where the amount payable under the arrangement:

"(i) Is being paid or granted as compensation for past services performed, future services to be performed, or future services to be refrained from performing, by the security holder (and matters incidental thereto); and

"(ii) Is not calculated based on the number of securities tendered or to be tendered in the tender offer by the security holder.

"(2) The provisions of paragraph (d)(1) of this section shall be satisfied and, therefore, pursuant to this non-exclusive safe harbor, the negotiation, execution or amendment of an arrangement and any payments made or to be made or benefits granted or to be granted according to that arrangement shall not be prohibited by paragraph (a)(2)(ii) of this section, if the arrangement is approved as an employment compensation, severance or other employee benefit arrangement solely by independent directors as follows:

"(i) The compensation committee or a committee of the board of directors that performs functions similar to a compensation committee of the issuer approves the arrangement, regardless of whether the issuer is a party to the arrangement, or, if an affiliate is a party to the arrangement, the compensation committee or a committee of the board of directors that performs functions similar to a compensation committee of the affiliate approves the arrangement; or

"(ii) If the issuer's or affiliate's board of directors, as applicable, does not have a compensation committee or a committee of the board of directors that performs functions similar to a compensation committee or if none of the members of the issuer's or affiliate's compensation committee or committee that performs functions similar to a compensation committee is independent, a special committee of the board of directors formed to consider and approve the arrangement approves the arrangement; or

"(iii) If the issuer or affiliate, as applicable, is a foreign private issuer, any or all members of the board of directors or any committee of the board of directors authorized to approve employment compensation, severance or other employee benefit arrangements under the laws or regulations of the home country approves the arrangement.

"Instruction to paragraph (d): The fact that the provisions of paragraph (d) of this section extend only to employment compensation, severance and other employee benefit arrangements and not to other arrangements, such as commercial arrangements, does not raise any inference that a payment under any such other arrangement constitutes consideration paid for securities in a tender offer."

Instructions to the amended rules also provide guidance on "independence" standards for directors.

NOTE

The safe harbor applies only to payments to executives and other employees who are security holders. The instruction quoted above provides that it raises no negative inference with respect to other kinds of payments to shareholders. This leaves some transactions litigated in the past still subject to the split in the circuits mentioned above.

In Susquehanna Capital Group v. Rite Aid Corp., Fed. Sec. L. Rep. (CCH) ¶ 91,993 (E.D. Pa. 2002), the plaintiff, holder of convertible notes of Rite Aid, exchanged them for Rite Aid common stock at a ratio of 125 shares for each $1,000 principal amount note. Shortly thereafter, Rite Aid engaged in a tender offer for the remaining outstanding notes at a ratio of 140 shares for each note.

Lerro v. Quaker Oats Co., 84 F.3d 239 (7th Cir. 1996), involved a challenge to a distribution agreement entered into between Quaker, the acquiring corporation and Thomas H. Lee, a 35% shareholder in Snapple, the target, by which a company controlled by Lee was given a distribution agreement for certain territories in Snapple and Gatorade, which commenced upon completion of the tender offer.

Field v. Trump, 850 F.2d 938 (2d Cir. 1988) involved a question of whether a single negotiated purchase of shares from a family group holding 18.4% of the target's shares. The board approved a tender offer for its stock at $22.50, with the family representative dissenting. The bidder announced the tender offer, and subsequently announced to the target board that they were withdrawing their tender offer in order to negotiate with the dissident Stroum family. Those negotiations resulted in the Stroums giving the bidder an option to purchase their shares at $23.50, plus receiving $900,000 cash for their expenses. The Trumps then initiated a "new" tender offer for all shares at $23.50. This was challenged as violating the best price rule because if the cash payment to the Stroums were included, they would receive $25.00 per share.

Gerber v. Computer Associates, 303 F.3d 126 (2d Cir. 2002) involved a different, and perhaps more difficult, set of payments. The Founder, CEO and 25% shareholder of On-Line Software International, Inc., received a $5 payment in exchange for his covenant not to compete. At the same time, he not only agreed to the terms of a tender offer, he gave the buyer an option to purchase his shares at the tender offer price even if another bidder offered a higher price. The basic terms of the acquisition were announced by press release on August 16, 1991; Berdy, the founder, signed the non-compete agreement, and Computer Associates and On-Line signed an agreement for a tender offer and follow-up merger on August 21. On August 22, the companies announced the formal agreement and the coming tender offer, and Computer Associates filed its tender offer materials with the SEC. In response to the claim of a best-price violation, Computer Associates claimed that because the non-compete was signed on August 21 and the tender offer began on August 22, it was outside the tender offer.

Query: What result in each case under the Epstein and Lerro approaches?

----

4. TARGET'S OBLIGATIONS

A. DISCLOSURE OBLIGATIONS

Basic Incorporated v. Levinson
485 U.S. 224, 108 S.Ct. 978, 99 L.Ed.2d 194 (1988).

■ JUSTICE BLACKMUN delivered the opinion of the Court.

This case requires us to apply the materiality requirement of § 10(b) of the Securities Exchange Act of 1934, 48 Stat. 881, as amended, 15 U.S.C. § 78a et seq. (1934 Act), and the Securities and Exchange Commissions Rule 10b–5, promulgated thereunder, see 17 CFR § 240.10b–5 (1987), in the context of preliminary corporate merger discussions. We must also determine whether a person who traded a corporation's shares on a securities exchange after the issuance of a materially misleading statement by the corporation may invoke a rebuttable presumption that, in trading, he relied on the integrity of the price set by the market.

I

Prior to December 20, 1978, Basic Incorporated was a publicly traded company primarily engaged in the business of manufacturing chemical refractories for the steel industry. As early as 1965 or 1966, Combustion Engineering, Inc., a company producing mostly alumina-based refractories, expressed some interest in acquiring Basic, but was deterred from pursuing this inclination seriously because of antitrust concerns it then entertained. In 1976, however, regulatory action opened the way to a renewal of Combustion's interest. The "Strategic Plan," dated October 25, 1976, for Combustion's Industrial Products Group included the objective: "Acquire Basic Inc. $30 million."

Beginning in September 1976, Combustion representatives had meetings and telephone conversations with Basic officers and directors, including petitioners here, concerning the possibility of a merger. During 1977 and 1978, Basic made three public statements denying that it was engaged in merger negotiations.[4] On December 18, 1978, Basic asked the New York Stock Exchange to suspend trading in its shares and issued a release stating that it had been "approached" by another company concerning a merger. On December 19, Basic's board endorsed Combustion's offer of $46 per share for its common stock, and on the following day publicly announced its approval of Combustion's tender offer for all outstanding shares.

Respondents are former Basic shareholders who sold their stock after Basic's first public statement of October 21, 1977, and before the suspension of trading in December 1978. Respondents brought a class action against Basic and its directors, asserting that the defendants issued three false or misleading public statements and thereby were in violation of § 10(b) of the 1934 Act and of Rule 10b–5. Respondents alleged that they were injured by selling Basic shares at artificially depressed prices in a market affected by petitioners' misleading statements and in reliance thereon.

The District Court adopted a presumption of reliance by members of the plaintiff class upon petitioners public statements that enabled the court to conclude that common questions of fact or law predominated over particular questions pertaining to individual plaintiffs. See Fed. Rule Civ. Proc. 23(b)(3). The District Court therefore certified respondents' class. On the merits, however, the District Court granted summary judgment for the defendants. It held that, as a matter of law, any misstatements were immaterial: there were no negotiations ongoing at the time of the first statement, and although negotiations were taking

---

[4]   On October 21, 1977, after heavy trading and a new high in Basic stock, the following news item appeared in the Cleveland Plain Dealer:

"[Basic] President Max Muller said the company knew no reason for the stock's activity and that no negotiations were under way with any company for a merger. He said Flintkote recently denied Wall Street rumors that it would make a tender offer of $25 a share for control of the Cleveland-based maker of refractories for the steel industry." App. 363.

On September 25, 1978, in reply to an inquiry from the New York Stock Exchange, Basic issued a release concerning increased activity in its stock and stated that

"management is unaware of any present or pending company development that would result in the abnormally heavy trading activity and price fluctuation in company shares that have been experienced in the past few days." Id., at 401.

On November 6, 1978, Basic issued to its shareholders a "Nine Months Report 1978." This Report stated:

"With regard to the stock market activity in the Company's shares we remain unaware of any present or pending developments which would account for the high volume of trading and price fluctuations in recent months." Id., at 403.

place when the second and third statements were issued, those negotiations were not "destined, with reasonable certainty, to become a merger agreement in principle."

The United States Court of Appeals for the Sixth Circuit affirmed the class certification, but reversed the District Court's summary judgment, and remanded the case. The court reasoned that while petitioners were under no general duty to disclose their discussions with Combustion, any statement the company voluntarily released could not be " 'so incomplete as to mislead.' " In the Court of Appeals' view, Basic's statements that no negotiations were taking place, and that it knew of no corporate developments to account for the heavy trading activity, were misleading. With respect to materiality, the court rejected the argument that preliminary merger discussions are immaterial as a matter of law, and held that "once a statement is made denying the existence of any discussions, even discussions that might not have been material in absence of the denial are material because they make the statement made untrue."

The Court of Appeals joined a number of other circuits in accepting the "fraud-on-the-market theory" to create a rebuttable presumption that respondents relied on petitioners' material misrepresentations, noting that without the presumption it would be impractical to certify a class under Fed. Rule Civ. Proc. 23(b)(3).

We granted certiorari . . . to resolve the split, see Part III, *infra*, among the Courts of Appeals as to the standard of materiality applicable to preliminary merger discussions, and to determine whether the courts below properly applied a presumption of reliance in certifying the class, rather than requiring each class member to show direct reliance on Basic's statements.

II

* * *

The Court previously has addressed various positive and common-law requirements for a violation of § 10(b) or of Rule 10b–5. The Court also explicitly has defined a standard of materiality under the securities laws, see TSC Industries, Inc. v. Northway, Inc., 426 U.S. 438 (1976), concluding in the proxy-solicitation context that "[a]n omitted fact is material if there is a substantial likelihood that a reasonable shareholder would consider it important in deciding how to vote." Acknowledging that certain information concerning corporate developments could well be of "dubious significance," this Court was careful not to set too low a standard of materiality; it was concerned that a minimal standard might bring an overabundance of information within its reach, and lead management "simply to bury the shareholders in an avalanche of trivial information—a result that is hardly conducive to informed decisionmaking." It further explained that to fulfill the materiality requirement "there must be a substantial likelihood that the disclosure of the omitted fact would have been viewed by the reasonable investor as having significantly altered the 'total mix' of information made available." We now expressly adopt the TSC Industries standard of materiality for the § 10(b) and Rule 10b–5 context.

III

The application of this materiality standard to preliminary merger discussions is not self-evident. Where the impact of the corporate development on the target's fortune is certain and clear, the TSC Industries materiality definition admits straightforward application. Where, on the other hand, the event is contingent or speculative in nature, it is difficult to ascertain whether the "reasonable investor" would have considered the omitted information significant at the time. Merger negotiations, because of the ever-present possibility that the contemplated transaction will not be effectuated, fall into the latter category.

A

Petitioners urge upon us a Third Circuit test for resolving this difficulty. Under this approach, preliminary merger discussions do not become material until "agreement-in-principle" as to the price and structure of the transaction has been reached between the would-be merger partners. By definition, then, information concerning any negotiations not yet at the agreement-in-principle stage could be withheld or even misrepresented without a violation of Rule 10b–5.

Three rationales have been offered in support of the "agreement-in-principle" test. The first derives from the concern expressed in TSC Industries that an investor not be overwhelmed by excessively detailed and trivial information, and focuses on the substantial risk that preliminary merger discussions may collapse: because such discussions are inherently tentative, disclosure of their existence itself could mislead investors and foster false optimism. The other two justifications for the agreement-in-principle standard are based on management concerns: because the requirement of "agreement-in-principle" limits the scope of disclosure obligations, it helps preserve the confidentiality of merger discussions where earlier disclosure might prejudice the negotiations; and the test also provides a usable, bright-line rule for determining when disclosure must be made.

None of these policy-based rationales, however, purports to explain why drawing the line at agreement-in-principle reflects the significance of the information upon the investor's decision. The first rationale, and the only one connected to the concerns expressed in TSC Industries, stands soundly rejected, even by a Court of Appeals that otherwise has accepted the wisdom of the agreement-in-principle test. "It assumes that investors are nitwits, unable to appreciate—even when told—that mergers are risky propositions up until the closing." Flamm v. Eberstadt, 814 F.2d, at 1175. Disclosure, and not paternalistic withholding of accurate information, is the policy chosen and expressed by Congress. We have recognized time and again, a "fundamental purpose" of the various securities acts, "was to substitute a philosophy of full disclosure for the philosophy of caveat emptor and thus to achieve a high standard of business ethics in the securities industry." The role of the materiality requirement is not to "attribute to investors a child-like simplicity, an inability to grasp the probabilistic significance of negotiations," Flamm v. Eberstadt, 814 F.2d, at 1175, but to filter out essentially useless information that a reasonable investor would not consider significant, even as part of a larger "mix" of factors to consider in making his investment decision.

The second rationale, the importance of secrecy during the early stages of merger discussions, also seems irrelevant to an assessment whether their existence is significant to the trading decision of a reasonable investor. To avoid a "bidding war" over its target, an acquiring firm often will insist that negotiations remain confidential, see, e.g., In re Carnation Co., Exchange Act Release No. 22214, 33 SEC Docket 1025 (1985), and at least one Court of Appeals has stated that "silence pending settlement of the price and structure of a deal is beneficial to most investors, most of the time." Flamm v. Eberstadt, 814 F.2d, at 1177.[11]

We need not ascertain, however, whether secrecy necessarily maximizes shareholder wealth—although we note that the proposition is at least disputed as a matter of theory and empirical research—for this case does not concern the timing of a disclosure; it concerns only its accuracy and completeness.[13] We face here the narrow question whether information concerning the existence and status of preliminary merger discussions is significant to the reasonable investor's trading decision. Arguments based on the premise that some disclosure would be "premature" in a sense are more properly considered under the rubric of an issuer's duty to disclose. The "secrecy" rationale is simply inapposite to the definition of materiality.

The final justification offered in support of the agreement-in-principle test seems to be directed solely at the comfort of corporate managers. A bright-line rule indeed is easier to follow than a standard that requires the exercise of judgment in the light of all the circumstances. But ease of application alone is not an excuse for ignoring the purposes of the securities acts and Congress' policy decisions. Any approach that designates a single fact or occurrence as always determinative of an inherently fact-specific finding such as materiality,

---

[11] Reasoning backwards from a goal of economic efficiency, that Court of Appeals stated: "Rule 10b–5 is about fraud, after all, and it is not fraudulent to conduct business in a way that makes investors better off. . . ." Flamm v. Eberstadt, 814 F.2d, at 1177.

[13] See SEC v. Texas Gulf Sulphur Co., 401 F.2d 833, 862 (C.A.2 1968) (en banc) ("Rule 10b–5 is violated whenever assertions are made, as here, in a manner reasonably calculated to influence the investing public . . . if such assertions are false or misleading or are so incomplete as to mislead. . . ."), cert. denied sub nom. Coates v. SEC, 394 U.S. 976 (1969).

must necessarily be over—or underinclusive. In TSC Industries this Court explained: "The determination [of materiality] requires delicate assessments of the inferences a 'reasonable shareholder' would draw from a given set of facts and the significance of those inferences to him. . . ." After much study, the Advisory Committee on Corporate Disclosure cautioned the SEC against administratively confining materiality to a rigid formula.[14] Courts also would do well to heed this advice.

We therefore find no valid justification for artificially excluding from the definition of materiality information concerning merger discussions, which would otherwise be considered significant to the trading decision of a reasonable investor, merely because agreement-in-principle as to price and structure has not yet been reached by the parties or their representatives.

* * *

C

Even before this Court's decision in TSC Industries, the Second Circuit had explained the role of the materiality requirement of Rule 10b–5, with respect to contingent or speculative information or events, in a manner that gave that term meaning that is independent of the other provisions of the Rule. Under such circumstances, materiality "will depend at any given time upon a balancing of both the indicated probability that the event will occur and the anticipated magnitude of the event in light of the totality of the company activity." SEC v. Texas Gulf Sulphur Co., 401 F.2d, at 849. Interestingly, neither the Third Circuit decision adopting the agreement-in-principle test nor petitioners here take issue with this general standard. Rather, they suggest that with respect to preliminary merger discussions, there are good reasons to draw a line at agreement on price and structure.

In a subsequent decision, the late Judge Friendly, writing for a Second Circuit panel, applied the Texas Gulf Sulphur probability/magnitude approach in the specific context of preliminary merger negotiations. After acknowledging that materiality is something to be determined on the basis of the particular facts of each case, he stated:

"Since a merger in which it is bought out is the most important event that can occur in a small corporation's life, to wit, its

---

[14] "Although the Committee believes that ideally it would be desirable to have absolute certainty in the application of the materiality concept, it is its view that such a goal is illusory and unrealistic. The materiality concept is judgmental in nature and it is not possible to translate this into a numerical formula. The Committee's advice to the [SEC] is to avoid this quest for certainty and to continue consideration of materiality on a case-by-case basis as problems are identified."

Report of the Advisory Committee on Corporate Disclosure to the Securities and Exchange Commission 327 (House Committee on Interstate and Foreign Commerce, 95th Cong., 1st Sess.) (Comm. Print) (1977).

death, we think that inside information, as regards a merger of this sort, can become material at an earlier stage than would be the case as regards lesser transactions—and this even though the mortality rate of mergers in such formative stages is doubtless high." SEC v. Geon Industries, Inc., 531 F.2d 39, 47–48 (C.A.2 1976).

We agree with that analysis.

Whether merger discussions in any particular case are material therefore depends on the facts. Generally, in order to assess the probability that the event will occur, a factfinder will need to look to indicia of interest in the transaction at the highest corporate levels. Without attempting to catalog all such possible factors, we note by way of example that board resolutions, instructions to investment bankers, and actual negotiations between principals or their intermediaries may serve as indicia of interest. To assess the magnitude of the transaction to the issuer of the securities allegedly manipulated, a factfinder will need to consider such facts as the size of the two corporate entities and of the potential premiums over market value. No particular event or factor short of closing the transaction need be either necessary or sufficient by itself to render merger discussions material.[17]

As we clarify today, materiality depends on the significance the reasonable investor would place on the withheld or misrepresented information. The fact-specific inquiry we endorse here is consistent with the approach a number of courts have taken in assessing the materiality of merger negotiations. Because the standard of materiality we have adopted differs from that used by both courts below, we remand the case for reconsideration of the question whether a grant of summary judgment is appropriate on this record.

* * *

---

[17] To be actionable, of course, a statement must also be misleading. Silence, absent a duty to disclose, is not misleading under Rule 10b–5. "No comment" statements are generally the functional equivalent of silence. See In re Carnation Co., *supra*. See also New York Stock Exchange Listed Company Manual § 202.01, reprinted in 3 CCH Fed. Sec. L. Rep. ¶ 23,515 (premature public announcement may properly be delayed for valid business purpose and where adequate security can be maintained); American Stock Exchange Company Guide §§ 401–405, reprinted in 3 CCH Fed. Sec. L. Rep. paras. 23,124A–23,124E (similar provisions).

It has been suggested that given current market practices, a "no comment" statement is tantamount to an admission that merger discussions are underway. See Flamm v. Eberstadt, 814 F.2d, at 1178. That may well hold true to the extent that issuers adopt a policy of truthfully denying merger rumors when no discussions are underway, and of issuing "no comment" statements when they are in the midst of negotiations. There are, of course, other statement policies firms could adopt; we need not now advise issuers as to what kind of practice to follow, within the range permitted by law. Perhaps more importantly, we think that creating an exception to a regulatory scheme founded on a prodisclosure legislative philosophy, because complying with the regulation might be "bad for business," is a role for Congress, not this Court. See also id., at 1182 (opinion concurring in the judgment and concurring in part).

V

In summary:

1.   We specifically adopt, for the § 10(b) and Rule 10b–5 context, the standard of materiality set forth in TSC Industries, Inc. v. Northway, Inc., 426 U.S., at 449.

2.   We reject "agreement-in-principle as to price and structure" as the bright-line rule for materiality.

3.   We also reject the proposition that "information becomes material by virtue of a public statement denying it."

4.   Materiality in the merger context depends on the probability that the transaction will be consummated, and its significance to the issuer of the securities. Materiality depends on the facts and thus is to be determined on a case-by-case basis.

* * *

The judgment of the Court of Appeals is vacated and the case is remanded to that court for further proceedings consistent with this opinion.

It is so ordered.

––––––––––––

QUESTIONS

1.   What are the three rationales given for an "agreement in principle" test of when disclosure of merger negotiations should occur? How does the Supreme Court respond to them?

2.   How could corporate secrecy maximize shareholder wealth?

3.   Is it possible to maintain corporate secrecy during merger negotiations after the Basic opinion? If so, how?

4.   Once rumors about merger negotiations circulate, what is the difficulty with a "no comment" response to questions? Can you devise a solution to these problems?

5.   Who bears the costs of management's misleading disclosures?

––––––––––––

Phillips v. LCI International, Incorporated
190 F.3d 609 (4th Cir. 1999).

■ MOTZ, CIRCUIT JUDGE:

As of February, 1998, LCI International was the nation's seventh largest long-distance telecommunications company, providing voice and data transmission services to residential and business customers. LCI had a major customer base, operating system, and sales force, but lacked a substantial transmission network. Qwest, a rival telecommunications company, had built an extensive fiber optic network, but lacked a commensurate base of customers, systems, and sales force. By March, 1998, the two companies agreed that a merger would benefit both and announced that Qwest would acquire LCI in a stock for stock merger valued at over $4.4 billion, making the merged company the fourth largest long-distance company in the United States. The question presented here is whether a public statement by LCI's chief executive that "we're not a company that's for sale," made less than a month before Qwest acquired LCI, violated federal securities laws. Because we find that, in context, the statement was not a material misstatement made with the intent to defraud, we affirm the district court's dismissal of this action brought by dissatisfied former LCI stockholders.

I.

Relying on the proxy statement issued to LCI shareholders in connection with the merger and certain press statements, the complaint alleges the following facts.

In October, 1997, Joseph P. Nacchio, President and CEO of Qwest, approached H. Brian Thompson, Chairman of the Board and CEO of LCI, at an industry trade convention and proposed that Thompson consider a merger of the two companies. During October and November, Phillip F. Anschutz, Chairman of the Qwest Board, discussed with Thompson the concept of a merger between the two companies.

Starting at the end of October, officers from the two companies began meeting to further discuss a possible merger. On November 27, Anschutz proposed to Thompson that Qwest and LCI begin reciprocal due diligence and begin negotiating a merger of the two companies in which Qwest would acquire LCI in a stock for stock merger. Even though LCI was larger than Qwest, the market value of Qwest was substantially higher than LCI.

On December 8, LCI Executive Vice President of LCI Joseph Lawrence met with officers of Qwest and investment bankers representing each party. On December 11, Nacchio sent a letter to Thompson, stating that Qwest "was prepared to begin its due diligence investigation immediately in order to be in a position to sign a definitive merger agreement within two weeks." This letter also stated that Qwest would be prepared to offer each shareholder, subject to due diligence and satisfactory negotiation of a merger agreement, $36 worth of Qwest stock for each share of LCI stock.

The LCI Board met on December 15 to discuss the offer and concluded that Qwest's offer did not merit a substantive response. On December 16, LCI's Lawrence sent Qwest's Nacchio a letter advising him the LCI Board had considered the offer but that "LCI was not for sale." The letter further indicated that in order for the LCI Board to consider a sale of LCI, an offer would have to be substantially higher than $36 per share.

On February 17, 1998, LCI publicly reported its fiscal fourth quarter earnings. LCI's Thompson was interviewed by the Dow Jones News Service in connection with the earnings announcement. Thompson is quoted as stating that "we're not a company that's for sale." The article also states that "[Thompson] said [that LCI] was more of a buyer than a seller in a telecommunications industry that is rapidly consolidating."

Two days later on February 19, LCI received another letter from Anschutz at Qwest indicating that his company was prepared to offer $40 worth of Qwest stock for each share of LCI stock, subject to a due diligence investigation. As in December, Qwest stated that "it was prepared to begin its due diligence investigation immediately in order to sign a definitive merger agreement within two weeks." On February 23, LCI's Board of Directors, assisted by legal counsel and investment bankers convened via conference call to discuss the Qwest letter. At that meeting, the LCI board directed its legal counsel to negotiate a confidentiality agreement with Qwest pursuant to which each party would conduct due diligence of the other; that agreement was signed on February 26, 1998. During the next two weeks, representatives of LCI and Qwest undertook due diligence and negotiated the terms of the agreement.

On March 8, both Boards approved the final merger agreement. That agreement provided that Qwest would acquire LCI in a stock for stock merger, with LCI shareholders receiving as consideration $42 worth of Qwest stock for every share of LCI stock exchanged. At the LCI Board meeting, Thompson voted against the merger because he "believed that LCI could continue to prosper as an independent company under its current management." Thompson later announced that he wished to vote in favor of the merger, and consequently changed his vote.

After the Boards of LCI and Qwest approved the merger, the companies informed the public of the agreement. On March 9, Thompson and Qwest President Nacchio were interviewed on the Cavuto Business Report. The executives were asked "What got the talks going?" Nacchio stated that "We started talking a couple of months ago . . . on a sincere basis and I guess it accelerated about three weeks ago." Thompson immediately responded "Yes." On the same day, on CNN Moneyline with Lou Dobbs, the host questioned "You have been talking to each other for how long?" Thompson replied, "Talking to each other? It goes way back, but really in earnest for the last three or four weeks."

On April 3, 1998, Lionel Phillips and others (collectively, the stockholders) purportedly representing the class of LCI shareholders that sold their stock after Thompson's February 17 statement but before the public announcement of the merger on March 9, filed this action against LCI and Thompson. The stockholders allege that when on

February 17, Thompson stated that LCI was "not a company that's for sale," LCI was in fact in ongoing negotiations to be acquired by Qwest. They maintain Thompson's statement constituted a material misrepresentation designed to defraud the market by artificially depressing the value of LCI stock. As proof of the falsity of Thompson's statement and his intent to defraud, the stockholders cite the post-merger interviews in which Thompson and Nacchio admitted that the parties had been "talking" on a "sincere basis" for three or four weeks prior to the March 9 interview. (Thompson made the statement in question on February 17, exactly three weeks before the March 9 interview.) Finally, they allege that Thompson's statement had the effect he desired—artificially depressing the price of LCI stock—in violation of § 10(b) of the Securities Exchange Act, *15 U.S.C.A. § 78(j)(b)* (West 1997), and Rule 10b–5, 17 C.F.R. § 240.10b–5 (1998), and that the stockholders, based on the publicly available information that LCI was not for sale, sold their stock at the artificially depressed price.

The district court dismissed the stockholders' original complaint on July 20, 1998, and their amended complaint on September 30, 1998. The stockholders appeal.

II.

In order to prevail on a § 10(b) and a Rule 10b–5 claim, the plaintiff carries the burden of proving:

> (1) the defendant made a false statement or omission of material fact (2) with scienter (3) upon which the plaintiff justifiably relied (4) that proximately caused the plaintiff's damages.

Hillson Partners Ltd. Partnership v. Adage, Inc., 42 F.3d 204, 208 (4th Cir. 1994). If a reasonable investor, exercising due care, would gather a false impression from a statement, which would influence an investment decision, then the statement satisfies the initial element of a § 10(b) claim. See SEC v. Texas Gulf Sulphur Co., 401 F.2d 833, 862 (2d Cir. 1968) (en banc).

The district court held that the stockholders' complaint failed to meet this initial requirement. First, the court concluded that Thompson's statement was not false because the "merger" of LCI and Qwest did not constitute a "sale." The court explained that a sale "is generally considered to occur when cash is tendered to shareholders in exchange for their shares in order for one company to assume control over the other," while a merger is "the combination of two corporations after which one of the corporations carries on the combined business and the other ceases to exist in separate form." Because Thompson never stated that LCI was "not due to be acquired through a merger," the district court concluded that his statement was not false.

In so doing, the district court looked to the definitions of sales and mergers made in a corporate treatise. See 1 Byron E. Fox & Eleanor M. Fox, Corporate Acquisitions and Mergers § 2.02 [3] (Supp. 1988). Because Qwest had tendered no cash to LCI, the district court found Qwest's acquisition of LCI for stock did not constitute a sale. Therefore, even assuming Thompson knew LCI was actively engaged in merger negotiations, his statement that LCI was "not for sale" was held not to be false.

We do not believe that a violation of the securities laws should rest on such a technical and narrow definition of "sale," particularly in view of the stockholders' well founded allegations that LCI management itself used "sale" as a synonym for "merger." Both the proxy statement issued to LCI shareholders and the press reports of the merger relating statements by LCI officers interchangeably use the terms "sale" and "acquired by merger." Moreover, the Supreme Court has expressly held that, for the purpose of § 10(b)'s requirement that statements be made "in connection with a purchase or sale," the term "sale" includes an exchange of one company's stock for that of another in the course of a merger or exchange. See SEC v. National Sec., Inc., 393 U.S. 453, 467– 68, 89 S. Ct. 564, 21 L. Ed. 2d 668 (1969). Indeed, a narrow definition of "sale" would seem to run counter to the intent of the securities laws—to protect a "reasonable investor" from fraud. See Basic v. Levinson, 485 U.S. 224, 231, 99 L. Ed. 2d 194, 108 S. Ct. 978 (1988). For a court to look only to a corporate treatise to define an element of an allegedly fraudulent statement would transform the "reasonable investor" standard to that of a "reasonable corporate lawyer."

Nor do we find persuasive the district court's reasoning as to materiality. The court held that Thompson's statement was not material as a matter of law because "every investor knows or should know that at the right price, and under certain circumstances, any publicly-held company can be for 'sale.' Thompson's statement was not a guarantee that LCI was not for sale." This conclusion seems to us to be a variation on the infamous statement in Flamm v. Eberstadt, 814 F.2d 1169 (7th Cir. 1987). There the court held that misstatements about merger negotiations were immaterial as a matter of law because "at the right price, any corporation is for sale." Id. at 1179. Basic substantially undercuts the force of such aphorisms. Although in Basic the Supreme Court did not expressly disapprove of such rationales, it did clearly state that the materiality of statements involving merger negotiations required a "fact-specific" inquiry that "depends on the significance the reasonable investor would place on the . . . misrepresented information," and explicitly rejected the view adopted by the Flamm court that merger discussions do not become material until the merger partners have agreed in principle as to price and structure. Basic, 485 U.S. at 233–41.

Basic directs that materiality of statements as to mergers be assessed by evaluating the probability of the merger reaching fruition and the magnitude of the proposed merger. *Id.* at 238. Probability is to be ascertained by examining "indicia of interest in the transaction at the highest corporate levels"; magnitude is to be assessed by considering "the size of the two corporate entities and of the potential premiums over market value." *Id.* at 239–40. Here the stockholders allege high-level negotiations between named managers and directors from both companies, involvement of investment bankers by both parties, and an earlier offer by Qwest to acquire LCI for $36 per share. Moreover, the merger resulted in a $4.4 billion merged company. Thus, it appears that allegations similar to these could, in the appropriate case, satisfy the materiality requirement.

In sum, we do not believe the district court's rationale for dismissing this complaint withstands scrutiny.

III.

Nevertheless, we agree with the district court that the stockholders' complaint fails to allege a misrepresentation of material fact. The complaint rests on mischaracterizations of the public record, exaggeration of a single statement, and isolation of that statement from its context and from the wealth of other information publicly available when it was made. Of course, factual allegations must be true to provide the basis for a cause of action, see generally In re Verifone Sec. Litig., 11 F.3d 865, 868 (9th Cir. 1993); hyperbole and speculation cannot give rise to a claim of securities fraud. See Biechele v. Cedar Point, Inc., 747 F.2d 209, 216 (6th Cir. 1984) ("Mere speculation may not be the basis of section 10(b) liability."). Moreover, the Supreme Court has repeatedly cautioned that allegedly fraudulent corporate statements must be examined in context and in light of the "total mix" of information made available to investors. Basic, 485 U.S. at 231–32; TSC Indus., Inc. v. Northway, Inc., 426 U.S. 438, 449, 48 L. Ed. 2d 757, 96 S. Ct. 2126 (1976). If what Thompson actually said here is examined in the context of all of the information publicly available, we believe that a reasonable factfinder could not conclude that the contested statement constitutes a material misrepresentation.

The stockholders' essential claim, as alleged in their complaint, is that Thompson "unequivocally and publicly stated that LCI was not for sale," while in fact "LCI was, at the time of the statement, engaged in serious merger negotiations with Qwest Communications International, and had been for some time." The allegations that the stockholders make to support that claim are not based on any confidential or private information. Rather, they avow exclusive reliance on the public record. Unfortunately, perhaps because facts in the public record often undercut their fraud claim, they occasionally mischaracterize those facts.

The stockholders do recognize and allege that according to the proxy statement filed with the SEC and provided to LCI stockholders in December 1997 (two months before Thompson's assertedly fraudulent February statement), LCI in fact rejected Qwest's merger offer after some months of tentative negotiations, stating that "LCI was not for sale." This rejection, in language identical to the February statement, seems to undermine the stockholders' allegation of continuing negotiations between LCI and Qwest. Perhaps anticipating this, the stockholders further allege that "according to the Proxy Statement" in the letter in which LCI rejected Qwest's December merger offer, LCI told Qwest that "LCI would definitely consider a higher proposal given the strategic benefits of the proposed deal." In fact the proxy statement actually says:

> . . . by letter dated December 16, 1997, Mr. Lawrence [of LCI] advised Mr. Nacchio [of Qwest] that the LCI Board had given careful consideration to the December 11th Letter, but that LCI was not for sale. Mr. Lawrence's letter further indicated that in order for the LCI Board to consider a sale of LCI, an offer would have to be substantially in excess of the value indicated in the December 11th Letter in order to reflect LCI's long-term value. Mr. Lawrence also noted that the December 11th Letter was vague or silent with respect to a number of material terms, and that the LCI Board did not believe it was in the interest of the LCI Stock holders to comment further at that time.

Thus, contrary to the allegations in the complaint, according to the proxy statement, LCI's rejection letter does not mention the "strategic benefits" of a merger with Qwest or that LCI "would definitely consider a higher proposal" from Qwest.

In the paragraph immediately following this mischaracterization and immediately prior to the description of Thompson's allegedly fraudulent February statement, the complaint alleges that, again "according to the Proxy Statement, Qwest, through Anschutz, advised LCI, in response to LCI's concern that Qwest's original offer was too low, that Qwest was prepared to raise its $36 offer by at least $4 to a minimum of $40 per share of LCI common stock." The stockholders' placement of this information in their complaint leads a reader to infer that the offer to raise the share price occurred chronologically between the initial negotiations and the February statement; however, this inference is without support in the public record. Rather, the proxy statement actually relates that "by letter dated February 19, 1998 [two days after issuance of the allegedly fraudulent statement]," Qwest advised the LCI Board of Qwest's willingness to up the offer to $40 per share.

Furthermore, Thompson's statement itself belies the stockholders' contention that Thompson "publicly denied any negotiations were ongoing," and for this reason, the statements and "facts in Basic bear a striking resemblance to those here." The sole asserted basis for the claim of securities fraud in this case is the purportedly fraudulent statement that: "we're not a company that's for sale." That statement does not "publicly deny any ongoing negotiations." Nor does it "resemble" the Basic statements. In Basic, the defendant corporation issued three statements, which said (1) the corporate officers "knew no reason for the stock's activity and that no negotiations were underway with any company for a merger;" (2) "management is unaware of any present or pending company development that would result in the abnormally heavy trading activity and price fluctuation;" and (3) "we remain unaware of any present or pending developments that would account for the high volume of trading and price fluctuations in recent months." Basic, 485 U.S. at 227 n.4. Thus in Basic, the company flatly denied any "awareness" of any "developments"—present or pending—that would affect the price or volatility of the company's stock and specifically denied that the merger "negotiations were underway."

Similarly, in the only other case that the stockholders cite in which shareholders of a publicly-held corporation were found to have stated a securities fraud claim solely on the basis of asserted misrepresentations about merger negotiations, corporate officers had repeatedly "denied the existence of any merger negotiations" and stated that they "were not currently engaged in any" such efforts. In re Columbia Sec. Litig., 747 F.Supp. 237, 240 (S.D.N.Y. 1990). Thompson's "we're not a company that's for sale" statement contains no equivalent blanket denial of awareness of any merger negotiations, let alone, any explicit assertion that the company was not presently engaged in such negotiations.

Nor do the remarks Thompson made in the post-merger interviews on March 9 provide support for the stockholders' assertion that his February "not for sale" statement was materially false like the statements in Basic and Columbia. During the interviews, Thompson acknowledged that Qwest and LCI "started talking a couple months ago . . . on a sincere basis," which "accelerated about three weeks ago." That account tells us nothing about the truth or materiality of the "not for sale" statement. Although the post-merger remarks could be consistent with a hiatus in negotiations after the December rejection and renewal of them with announcement of LCI's strong fourth quarter earnings, if interpreted in the light most favorable to the stockholders, the remarks certainly could support their allegation that merger negotiations were "ongoing" when Thompson issued his February "not for sale" statement. But that is all the post-merger remarks could do and thus they add nothing to the stockholders' case because, for purposes of evaluating the complaint, we assume that the stockholders' allegation as to "ongoing" negotiations is true. The postmerger remarks simply do not transform Thompson's February statement into a flat denial of any merger negotiations like those in Basic and Columbia.

Indeed, the stockholders themselves actually seem to recognize that the situation here differs markedly from that in Basic and Columbia. First, they acknowledge in their complaint that at the time of Thompson's statement "the transaction had not yet been finalized and Thompson did not and could not have known whether Qwest would acquire LCI in exchange for cash, or Qwest common stock, or whether the transaction would take some other form"—or, one might add, in view of the December rejection and the yet to be performed due diligence inquiry, whether it would go forward at all. Second, in their reply brief, the stockholders concede that the "we're not a company that's for sale" statement was, as LCI maintains, equivalent to stating that the company was not "in play." See Reply Brief at 1 (stating that LCI "chose to speak about whether LCI was 'in play' "). A corporate officer's statement that the company was not "for sale" or "in play" is a good deal different from that officer's express denial of any merger negotiations.

Having stripped the stockholders' allegations of mischaracterizations and exaggeration, we focus on whether the exact statement in its true context constitutes a material representation. In arguing that it is, the stockholders do not assert that they actually relied on the statement, but rather they maintain that it had an artificial depressive effect on the market of LCI stock, and therefore was a fraud on the market. See Basic, 485 U.S. at 243–44.

Although this fraud-on-the-market theory primarily impacts § 10(b)'s reliance element—by eliminating any need to prove individual reliance on an assertedly false statement—the rationale behind this theory also affects the materiality element—by "shifting the critical focus of the materiality inquiry." Because in a fraud-on-the-market case the "reasonable investor" for materiality purposes is not an individual plaintiff, but the market itself, a statement cannot be material if the hypothetical reasonable investor—that is, the market-would not regard the statement, in context, as significant. The market may well take a more jaundiced view of corporate statements—both optimistic puffery and "holding pattern" statements like the one at hand—than an individual investor. See, e.g., id.; Raab v. General Physics Corp., 4 F.3d 286, 289–90 (4th Cir. 1993) ("The market price of a share is not inflated by vague statements predicting growth. . . . Analysts and arbitrageurs rely on facts in determining the value of security, not mere expressions of optimism."); Glazer v. Formica Corp., 964 F.2d 149, 155 (2d Cir. 1992) ("The mere fact that a company has received an acquisition overture or that some discussion has occurred will not necessarily be material.").

With this understanding in mind, we examine the other information that was publicly available to reasonable investors at the time Thompson made his February statement. We undertake this examination because "even lies are not actionable" when an investor "possesses information sufficient to call the misrepresentation into question." Teamster Local

282 Pension Trust Fund v. Angelos, 762 F.2d 522, 529 (7th Cir. 1985). After all, the securities laws impose liability only when there is a "substantial likelihood" that an alleged misrepresentation "significantly altered 'the total mix' of information" a reasonable investor (the market) possesses.

The Dow Jones article in which Thompson's "not for sale" statement is reported contains a summary of much of this information. We note that although the stockholders failed to attach that article to their complaint (LCI attached it to its motion to dismiss), a court may consider it in determining whether to dismiss the complaint because it was integral to and explicitly relied on in the complaint and because the plaintiffs do not challenge its authenticity. The short article reads, in its entirety:

> LCI 4Q Rev. Up 30%; Chairman Says Co.
> Not For Sale—LCI by Shaw Young

> NEW YORK (Dow Jones)—After reporting fourth quarter earnings in line with Wall Street expectations on revenue growth of 30%, H. Brian Thompson, Chairman and chief executive of LCI International Inc. (LCI) on Tuesday said his company isn't looking to grow by being bought out. "We're not a company that's for sale," Thompson told Dow Jones. He said the McLean, Va., long-distance company is more of a buyer than a seller in a telecommunications industry that is rapidly consolidating.

> At the end of December, LCI, the nation's seventh biggest long-distance carrier, closed a $331.8 million merger with USLD Communications Corp.

> Including charges from the merger and other nonrecurring items, LCI reported a pro forma fourth-quarter loss of $37 million, or 39 cents a share, on revenue of $446 million. Year-ago pro forma earnings were $23 million, or 23 cents a share, on revenue of $344 million.

> Excluding one-time items, the company earned 26 cents a share. On a stand alone basis, earnings were 27 cents, as analysts surveyed by First Call Corp. had expected.

> Thompson said he couldn't yet comment on analysts' predictions for upcoming quarters because those estimates don't yet reflect the merger.

> Goldman, Sachs & Co. analyst Richard Klugman said in a report earlier Tuesday that he sees the company "posting a sustainable internal growth rate of roughly 25%, a rate that could be augmented by further EPS-accretive acquisitions, similar to the USLD deal."

Thompson said he is very pleased with the company's revenue growth and the 31% increase in calling traffic it registered in the fourth quarter.

Investors, apparently satisfied with the results, boosted the company's NYSE-listed shares 1 1/8, or 4%, to 29 1/8, on volume of 730,000 shares. Average daily volume is 616,400 shares. The stock is just below the 52-week high of 31 7/16 set Dec. 30.

Hence the article demonstrates that reasonable investors would know that: (1) LCI had excellent fourth quarter earnings; (2) the company was trading at very near its year high of 31 7/16 per share; (3) the telecommunications industry was "rapidly consolidating;" (4) LCI had closed a $331.8 million merger with another telecommunications company less than two months earlier; and (5) an analyst believed LCI's continued revenue growth was "sustainable" and could be "augmented" by further acquisitions. Furthermore, reasonable stockholders would learn from this article that the author regarded Thompson's "we're not a company that's for sale statement" as an indication that the company "wasn't looking to grow by being bought out." They would also learn, however, that Thompson was not foreclosing further mergers—although he believed the company was "more a buyer than a seller."

In none of the cases on which the parties rely, or any other case that we have found, has a statement like that at issue here, made in a context at all similar to this, been found to be a misstatement of material fact. Most of the cases cited by the parties involve claims that the corporation made statements that too optimistically reported on corporate earnings, profits, growth, or other developments. In those cases, the asserted misrepresentation caused the plaintiff shareholders to buy stock at an inflated price and resulted in an immediate loss to them when the too rosy forecasts failed to materialize and the stock's price plummeted.

That scenario presents rather different concerns than the case at hand in which the stockholders claim that a corporate statement artificially depressed the value of publicly traded stock. On the one hand, "depressive" statements cannot be dismissed as mere "puffery"; on the other hand, the effect of such statements on the market may be more difficult to quantify than statements that are too optimistic, because, in themselves, "depressive" statements may cause no actual gain or loss. For example, here the stockholders make no claim the statement caused any actual loss to them or gain to others. And although the complaint does not reveal the price the plaintiff stockholders paid for LCI stock, it does disclose that they sold it in late February and early March 1998 at prices ranging from $33 5/16 to $30 per share. The fact that the stock's 52-week high was $31 7/16 a share as of February 17, 1998, strongly suggests that no plaintiff lost money on the sale of LCI stock. (The stockholders' theory apparently is that they did not realize as much profit as they would have absent the asserted misrepresentation.)

Of the more than 80 cases cited by the parties only seven concern allegations like those at issue here, that corporate statements or omissions artificially depressed a stock's value. None of these cases assist us because all involve vastly different facts, i.e., corporations flatly denying any merger possibility, see Basic and Columbia; or corporate insiders allegedly conspiring to drive down the price in order to obtain over $30 million in benefits for themselves, or judicial rejection of the plaintiffs' claim because merger negotiations were too tentative.

We are therefore left without any clear precedent on point. Hence, the strength of the complaint must be resolved simply by analyzing the contested statement in light of the relevant general legal principles set forth above. That analysis requires the conclusion that the "we're not a company that's for sale" statement in the context in which it was made—a report of high fourth quarter earnings and an almost record price for the stock—and in view of the mix of other information available to reasonable investors—including the "rapidly consolidating" nature of the industry and LCI's very recent merger with another company and an analyst's opinion that LCI revenues could be augmented by further acquisitions—was not a misrepresentation of material fact.

We recognize that this is a close question. But we cannot conclude that there is a "substantial likelihood that" this statement "significantly altered" the "total mix" of information available to the market as a whole. We find important the fact that in making the statement Thompson did not deny present or future merger negotiations as did management in Basic and Columbia. Rather, although he maintained LCI was not "in play"—"we're not a company that's for sale"—Thompson actually indicated that there would be mergers in the company's future; to be sure he said, according to a reporter, that LCI was "more a buyer than a seller," but Thompson did not foreclose the latter possibility. In an industry known to be "rapidly consolidating," there is no substantial likelihood that the statement, taken in its entirety, significantly altered the total mix of information available to reasonable investors.

For these reasons, the district court correctly held that the challenged statement did not constitute a misstatement of material fact.

* * *

V.

In sum, because the challenged statement, in context, does not constitute a material misstatement with intent to defraud, the judgment of the district court is

AFFIRMED.

QUESTIONS

1. Why did the district court conclude that a merger is not a "sale"? Why did the Court of Appeals reverse this holding? Do you agree with its reasoning?

2. When LCI rejected Qwest's $36 offer on December 16, saying that it was not for sale, and that in order for the LCI board to consider a sale of LCI, an offer would have to be substantially higher, did that clearly signal LCI's intent not place itself up for sale? Did Qwest treat it that way?

3. If LCI's intent, according to Thompson's February 17 statement, was not to be for sale, why did Anschutz indicate a willingness to pay $40 per share on February 19?

4. The opinion states that Thompson made no blanket denial of any merger negotiations nor any explicit assertion that the company was not presently engaged in such negotiations. Is it a reasonable inference from Thompson's "not for sale" remarks that LCI was not engaged in any merger negotiations, or that it had not been engaged in them recently?

5. Why does the court state that Thompson's post-merger remarks that negotiations began several months ago "on a sincere basis," and accelerated three weeks previously tell us nothing about the truth or materiality of the "not for sale" statement?

6. How is a "corporate officer's statement that the company was not 'for sale' or 'in play' . . . a good deal different from that officer's express denial of any merger negotiations"?

7. How does the statement that LCI was "more a buyer than a seller" reconcile with the "not for sale" statement? Is it an admission that under some circumstances LCI would consider being acquired?

Securities Exchange Act Rules 14d–9 and 14e–2; Schedule 14D–9.

Starkman v. Marathon Oil Company

772 F.2d 231 (6th Cir.1985).

■ MERRITT, CIRCUIT JUDGE.

Like Radol v. Thomas, 772 F.2d 244 (6th Cir.1985), this action arises out of U.S. Steel's November, 1981 acquisition and eventual merger with Marathon Oil Company. The plaintiff here, Irving Starkman, was a Marathon shareholder until selling his shares on the open market for $78 per share on November 18, 1981, the day before U.S. Steel's tender offer for 51% of Marathon's outstanding shares at $125 per share was announced. On October 31, 1981, Mobil Oil had initiated its takeover bid for Marathon, a bid which Marathon actively resisted by urging its rejection by Marathon shareholders and by seeking and eventually finding a "white knight" or alternative, friendly merger partner-tender offeror, U.S. Steel. Starkman claims that Marathon's board violated Rule

10b–5 and its fiduciary duty to him as a Marathon shareholder by failing to disclose various items of "soft" information—information of less certainty than hard facts—in its public statements to shareholders during the period after Mobil's hostile tender offer and prior to Steel's friendly tender offer. In particular, he says that Marathon should have told shareholders that negotiations were underway with U.S. Steel prior to the consummation of those negotiations in an agreement, and that internal and externally-prepared asset appraisals and five-year earnings and cash flow projections should have been disclosed to shareholders so that they could make a fully informed choice whether to sell their shares or gamble on receiving a higher price in a possible Steel-Marathon merger.

The District Court granted summary judgment for Marathon, finding that these items of soft information had either been sufficiently disclosed or were not required to be disclosed because their nondisclosure did not render materially misleading Marathon's other affirmative public statements. For the reasons stated below, we affirm the judgment of the district Court.

I.   BACKGROUND

We have discussed the background and structure of U.S. Steel's acquisition of Marathon Oil at some length in Radol v. Thomas, 772 F.2d 244 (6th Cir.1985), and our attention here will therefore be focused on the facts which are especially relevant to Starkman's Rule 10b–5 claims.

* * *

[In anticipation of becoming a takeover target, Marathon's management assigned employees to undertake a valuation of the value of Marathon's assets. A report by Jon Strong valued Marathon at between $276 and $323 per share. These values were based on aggressive assumptions about future oil prices and the value of Marathon's reserves. First Boston was hired for an outside valuation, and reported values between $188 and $225 per share. Independent analysts had estimated Marathon's value in the $200 range.] Marathon's market value, however, was well below these appraised values. On October 29, 1981, Marathon closed at $63.75 per share. The next day, Mobil Oil announced its tender offer to purchase up to approximately 68% of outstanding Marathon common stock for $85 per share in cash. Mobil proposed to follow the tender offer with a going private or freezeout merger in which the remaining shareholders of Marathon would receive sinking fund debentures worth approximately $85 per share.

On October 31, 1981, Marathon's board of directors met in emergency session and unanimously decided that the Mobil offer was "grossly inadequate" and approved a vigorous campaign to persuade Marathon shareholders not to tender to Mobil, and to simultaneously seek a "white knight." On November 11 and 12, Marathon's Board made public statements to the shareholders recommending rejection of Mobil's bid as "grossly inadequate" and against the best interests of the company. We explore these statements in more detail below, as they are a primary focus of Starkman's claims of inadequate disclosure. However, at the time these statements to shareholders were made, Marathon representatives had already contacted all of the 30 to 35 companies who could possibly undertake an acquisition topping Mobil's bid, and, in particular, had begun negotiations with U.S. Steel on November 10. The Strong and First Boston reports were given to Steel on that same day, on the condition that they be kept confidential, and on November 12, Marathon's vice president for finance delivered five-year earnings forecasts and cash flow projections to Steel in Pittsburgh.

On November 17, Hoopman [Marathon's President and CEO] and David Roderick, Steel's president, reached agreement on the terms of Steel's purchase of Marathon, and, after Board approval, an agreement was signed on November 18, 1981. Under the terms of the agreement, Steel would make a tender offer for up to 31 million shares (about 51%) of Marathon stock for $125 per share in cash, to be followed by a merger proposal in which each remaining Marathon shareholder would receive one $100 face value, 12 year, 12½ per cent guaranteed note per share of common stock. On November 19, Steel mailed its tender offer to Marathon shareholders, and Hoopman sent a letter to Marathon shareholders describing the two-stage deal and stating the opinion of Marathon's Board that the agreement was fair to Marathon shareholders. Steel's offer was successful, with over 91% of the outstanding shares tendered, and the second stage freezeout merger was approved by a two-thirds majority of the remaining shareholders in February, 1982.

II. MARATHON'S PUBLIC STATEMENTS AND DISPOSITION BELOW

There are three public statements by Marathon management at issue here. First, Marathon's November 11, 1981, press release, which states, in pertinent part, that:

> Our Board of Directors has determined that Mobil Corporation's unsolicited tender offer is grossly inadequate. The offer is not in the best interests of Marathon Oil or its shareholders. It doesn't reflect current asset values and it doesn't permit the long-term investor the opportunity to participate in the potential values that have been developed.
>
>   * * *
>
> We plan to do everything we possibly can to defeat this offer. We are determined to stay independent.

The next day, as required by Rule 14e–2, 17 C.F.R. § 240. 14e–2 (1984), Marathon mailed a letter to its shareholders stating its position regarding Mobil's tender offer. The letter urged rejection of the offer, stating that Marathon's Board was "convinced that the Mobil offer is grossly inadequate and does not represent the real values of the assets underlying your investment in Marathon." The letter described a number of alternative courses of action that were being considered by the Board, including "repurchase of Marathon shares, acquisition of all or part of another company, a business combination with another company, (and) the declaration of an extra ordinary dividend and a complete or partial liquidation of the Company," and concluded by again urging rejection of Mobil's attempt to "seize control of Marathon's assets at a fraction of their value," and stating that "we are convinced that you and our other shareholders would be well served if Marathon remains independent."

Attached to this letter was a copy of Marathon's Schedule 14D–9, filed pursuant to Rule 14d–9, 17 C.F.R. § 240.14d–9, in which the board informed the SEC that it had recommended rejection of the Mobil offer as "grossly inadequate." Item 4(b) (iv) of Marathon's Schedule 14D–9 listed as a factor supporting this recommendation the board's belief that based on current economic and market factors, "this is an extremely inopportune time to sell the Company and, in any event, that its shareholders would be better served if the Company were to remain independent." Item 7 of this same schedule described "Certain Negotiations and Transactions" by Marathon:

> At a meeting of the Board of Directors held on October 31, 1981, the Board considered and reviewed the feasibility and desirability of exploring and investigating certain types of possible transactions, including, without limitation, repurchases of Company Common Shares, the public or private sale of equity or other securities of the Company, a business combination between the Company and another company, the acquisition of a significant interest in or the entire Company or of one or more of its significant business segments by another company, a joint venture between the Company and one or more other companies, the acquisition by the Company of all or part of the business of another Company, a complete or partial liquidation of the Company or the declaration of an extraordinary dividend. After considerable discussion, the Board resolved that it was desirable and in the best interest of the Company and its shareholders to explore and investigate, with the assistance and advice of First Boston, such transactions, although the Board noted that the initiation or continuation of such activities may be dependent upon Mobil's future actions with respect to the Mobil Offer. There can be no assurance that these activities will result in any transaction being recommended to the Board of Directors or that any transaction which is recommended will be authorized or consummated.

Starkman argues . . . that Marathon not only failed to adequately disclose its search for a white knight and its negotiations with Steel but actually gave the false impression that the Board was endeavoring to preserve Marathon as an independent entity. He argues that the Strong and First Boston reports, the five-year cash and earnings projections, and the fact of ongoing negotiations with U.S. Steel were all material facts because knowledge of them would have affected a reasonable shareholder's evaluation of the likelihood that Marathon would succeed in negotiating a higher price takeover, and thereby affect such a shareholder's decision to sell his shares. He contends that shareholders were not adequately informed of Marathon management's search for a "white knight" and of the negotiations with Steel, and that failure to disclose more information regarding these negotiations rendered statements suggesting that Marathon might remain independent materially misleading. Similarly, Starkman contends that if he had been told of the Strong and First Boston reports and the five-year earnings and cash flow projections, and also that Marathon management was using these figures in seeking an alternative bidder, then he would have anticipated a much higher bid than he did, and that failure to release this information rendered materially misleading the affirmative statements Marathon did make.

* * *

As to disclosure of the negotiations with Steel, the District Court cited Reiss v. Pan American World Airways, Inc., 711 F.2d 11, 14 (2d Cir.1983), and Staffin v. Greenberg, 672 F.2d 1196, 1206 (3d Cir.1982), in ruling that Marathon's 14D–9 disclosure that the acquisition of all or part of another company, or merger with another company, was being considered as an alternative to the Mobil offer sufficed to meet whatever disclosure obligation may have existed.

III. DISCUSSION

A. *Introduction*

* * *

Despite occasional suggestions by commentators and the courts that Rule 10b–5 imposes an affirmative obligation on the corporation to disclose all material information regardless of whether the corporation has made any other statements, the established view is that a "duty to speak" must exist before the disclosure of material facts is required under Rule 10b–5. Provided that such a duty to speak exists, a further limitation on the duty to disclose is imposed by the requirement that only misstatements of material facts and omissions of material facts necessary to make other required statements not misleading are prohibited by Rule 10b–5. The Supreme Court's definition of "material" in the context of an alleged violation of Rule 14a–9, governing disclosure requirements in proxy statements, has been adopted for cases involving Rule 10b–5 in the tender offer context. * * *

In structuring the disclosure duties of a tender offer target, we begin therefore with the basic proposition that only material facts—those substantially likely to affect the deliberations of the reasonable shareholder—must be disclosed, and then only if the nondisclosure of the particular material facts would make misleading the affirmative statements otherwise required by the federal securities laws and SEC regulations.

Our adherence to this basic proposition ensures that target management's disclosure obligations will strike the correct balance between the competing costs and benefits of disclosure. The benefits of disclosure in ensuring that shareholders who are suddenly faced with a tender offer will not be forced to respond without adequate information are clearly recognized in Section 14(e) of the Williams Act, 15 U.S.C. § 78n(e), which somewhat broadens the reach of Rule 10b–5 to statements made "in connection with any tender offer" and which provides the statutory authority for SEC rules imposing affirmative disclosure obligations on tender offer targets. On the hand, tender offers remain essentially contests in which participants on both sides act under the "stresses of the marketplace," and "probably there will no more be a perfect tender offer than a perfect trial." Electronic Specialty Co. v. International Controls Corp., 409 F.2d 937, 948 (2d Cir.1969) (Friendly, J.). Under these conditions, imposing an "unrealistic requirement of laboratory conditions," id., would place target management under the highly unpredictable threat of huge liability for the failure to disclose, perhaps inducing the disclosure of mountains of documents and hourly reports on negotiations with potential tender offerors, a deluge of information which would be more likely to confuse than guide the reasonable lay shareholder and which could interfere with the negotiation of a higher tender offer and actually reduce the likelihood that a shareholder will benefit from a successful tender offer at a premium over the market. It is with these competing considerations in mind that we turn to the particular disclosure claims made here.

* * *

C.

Starkman's contention that Marathon should have disclosed more information regarding its search for a white knight and its negotiations with Steel are equally without merit. The SEC and the courts have enunciated a firm rule regarding a tender offer target's duty to disclose ongoing negotiations: so long as merger or acquisition discussions are preliminary, general disclosure of the fact that such alternatives are being considered will suffice to adequately inform shareholders; a duty to disclose the possible terms of any transaction and the parties thereto arises only after an agreement in principle, regarding such fundamental terms as price and structure, has been reached. See Item 7 of Schedule 14D–9, 17 C.F.R. § 240.14d–101 (1984). . . .

The rationale emerging from these cases is that when dealing with complex bargaining which may fail as well as succeed and which may succeed on terms which vary greatly from those originally anticipated, the disclosure of preliminary discussions could very easily mislead shareholders as to the prospects of success, and by making public an impending offer, push the price of the target's stock toward the expected tender price, thereby depriving shareholders of the primary inducement to tender—a premium above market price—and forcing the offeror to abandon its plans or greatly increasing the cost of the offer. See Staffin v. Greenberg, 672 F.2d [1196] at 1207 [(3d Cir.1982)].

In the instant case, Marathon's shareholder recommendation letter and its Schedule 14D–9 stated that the company was considering a number of alternatives, including a merger with another firm. These statements adequately informed the shareholders of Marathon's plans. Additional statements in these documents to the effect that Marathon's board believed the best result would be for Marathon to remain independent were not misleading when read in their full context, and at most expressed a sincere hope which the board found unrealistic under the pressure of Mobil's offer.

Finally, Starkman's claims for fraud and breach of fiduciary duty are completely unsupported by authority in his brief, and were similarly neglected in his arguments below. We therefore affirm and adopt the reasoning of the District Court finding that no claim for fraud has been made out because Marathon did not fail to disclose any information necessary to make its other public statements not misleading, and that the directors' statements, made at a time of extraordinary pressure on the board, comported in all respects with federal law and did not breach a fiduciary duty to Marathon's shareholders.

Accordingly, the judgment of the District Court is affirmed.

QUESTIONS

1. Does the court's reasoning in this case stand as good law after Basic Incorporated v. Levinson, *supra*? See Item 7 of Schedule 14D–9.

2. Does Item 7 of Schedule 14D–9 and Regulation M-A, Item 1006(d) correspond with the requirements of Basic?

Minzer v. Keegan

218 F.3d 144 (2d Cir. 2000).

■ WINTER, CHIEF JUDGE:

Leonard Minzer and Harry Schipper, on behalf of themselves and similarly situated shareholders, appeal from then-Chief Judge Sifton's dismissal of their complaint. It alleged that a proxy statement seeking shareholder approval of a proposed merger was materially misleading, in violation of Section 14(a) of the Exchange Act, see *15 U.S.C. § 78n*(a), and Rule 14a–9, see 17 C.F.R. § 240.14a–9(a). Appellants also alleged a breach of state law fiduciary duties. We affirm the dismissal of the federal claim on the ground that the allegedly material omissions in the proxy statement would not have induced any reasonable investor to be less likely to approve the objected-to merger. There was, therefore, no causal link between the omissions and any harm resulting from approval of the merger. We dismiss appellants' state law claims without prejudice.

BACKGROUND

In reviewing a dismissal under Rule 12(b)(6), we take as true the allegations of the complaint, here the second amended corrected complaint and the proxy statement, which is incorporated by reference.

In early 1997, Gerald Keegan, the president of Greater New York Savings Bank ("Greater New York"), began exploratory merger talks with the top management of Astoria Financial Corporation and its subsidiary Astoria Federal Savings and Loan Association (collectively, "Astoria"). On February 26, 1997, Thomas O'Brien, the Vice Chairman of North Fork Bancorporation, Inc. ("North Fork"), phoned Keegan and informed him of North Fork's interest in a merger with Greater New York. The negotiations with Astoria continued, and, on March 16, Astoria's Chief Executive Officer informed Keegan that Astoria would, subject to due diligence—essentially an inspection of Greater New York's books—be willing to pay approximately $18 per share in cash and stock for Greater New York's stock. The next day, John A. Kanas, North Fork's Chief Executive Officer, called Keegan and informed him that North Fork had acquired a significant stake in Greater New York and that he desired a face-to-face meeting to discuss a merger. Keegan declined the invitation, stating that Greater New York was not planning to merge and that he was unwilling to talk to North Fork under any circumstances. However, that same day, Keegan discussed both the Astoria offer and the North Fork expression of interest with his board. The board authorized Keegan to proceed with the Astoria transaction.

Also on the same day, Kanas drafted a strongly worded letter expressing his disappointment at Keegan's refusal to arrange a meeting and offering a 2-for-1 stock-for-stock merger, subject to "customary due diligence." This offer would have allegedly valued Greater New York's stock at approximately $19 per share. Kanas never sent that letter but did send a milder letter four days later. Either the same day or the next, Christopher Quackenbush, a principal at Sandler O'Neill & Partners, L.P., Greater New York's investment bank, suggested to Kanas that Greater New York "was willing to reconsider." The two arranged a telephone conversation for March 19.

Between March 19 and March 27, 1997, Quackenbush had a series of telephone calls with Kanas and O'Brien. Kanas asked to make a presentation to Greater New York's board, but no such opportunity was offered. O'Brien pressed for the opportunity to conduct due diligence and told Quackenbush that "in the absence of due diligence, North Fork did not know if everything was as it had modeled it or presumed it to be and that diligence was very important and was necessary before making any kind of final offer." North Fork was never given the opportunity to conduct due diligence and had to rely solely on publicly available information in determining Greater New York's financial condition. Astoria, however, was given an opportunity to conduct due diligence and acquire nonpublic financial information about Greater New York.

Greater New York convened a special meeting of its board on March 27, 1997. Kanas went to Greater New York's offices but was denied entry to the meeting. Nevertheless, Quackenbush informed Kanas by telephone that the board was interested in as many details as were available about North Fork's bid. Kanas offered a stock-for-stock merger in which North Fork would acquire Greater New York, exchanging .486 North Fork shares per Greater New York share (approximating the value of the offer to be $19.00 per share). Quackenbush asked if that was North Fork's best offer; Kanas replied, "that was our best bid until such time as we would be allowed to go in and . . . [conduct] due diligence." He informed Quackenbush that he had a team of bank officers prepared to work over the weekend to conduct due diligence, and that North Fork was "unwilling to raise [its] price or consider raising [its] price until such time as [it] had a chance to [conduct due diligence]." In refusing to increase North Fork's bid, Kanas told Quackenbush that "North Fork's bid included a substantial one-time charge to cover credit related issues," but that North Fork had "already factored that [charge] in so [its] price wouldn't go down." After Quackenbush pressed him as to whether the price would go up, Kanas replied, "it won't go down." Kanas was also asked whether Keegan would have a major role to play in any such merged enterprise, to which Kanas responded in the negative.

Quackenbush described his conversations with Kanas to Greater New York's board, which in turn requested Astoria to increase its bid. Astoria raised its stock and cash bid to $18.94. This price included a substantial premium over Greater New York's trading price. Two days later, on March 29, 1997, Greater New York's board unanimously approved a merger with Astoria. As a part of the merger agreement, Greater New York's board agreed to termination fees capped at $5 million (with a maximum aggregate profit capped at $10 million) in the event that the merger did not go through and a lock-up option allowing Astoria to purchase 19.9% of Greater New York's outstanding common shares under certain conditions. Also, Greater New York agreed not to entertain any other inquiries about a merger. Finally, it is alleged that Keegan was employed by Astoria as part of the merger agreement, and Greater New York's board members were given three-year contracts providing them a stipend and stock options in return for serving on the Astoria Advisory Board.

On March 31, 1997, Greater New York and Astoria publicly announced the merger. Within seventy-two hours of that announcement, appellants filed a New York state court action against Greater New York's board for alleged breaches of fiduciary duty. The parties subsequently consented to dismiss that state court action without prejudice.

On June 24, 1997, Astoria and Greater New York distributed proxy statements seeking their respective shareholders' approval of the transaction. The portions of Greater New York's proxy statement relevant to the present appeal are as follows:

> On March 17, 1997, Mr. Keegan received a call from the chief executive officer of another banking organization (the "Other Organization") expressing an interest in acquiring [Greater New York].

> Mr. Keegan reported the contact with the chief executive officer of the Other Organization to the [Greater] Board at a special meeting on March 17, 1997. . . .

> Subsequently, the chief executive officer of the Other Organization initiated a series of telephone calls with Mr. Keegan and [Greater New York's] investment bankers, Sandler O'Neill, regarding its interest in [Greater New York] and seeking the opportunity to make a proposal regarding a possible business combination with [Greater New York]. As part of these discussions and at the request of [Greater New York], the Other Organization submitted a letter intended to address its views on how an acquisition by it would impact the communities and customers served by [Greater New York] and its employees.

> . . . . At [a special] meeting, the [Greater New York] Board considered, among others, the strategic alternatives available to [Greater New York], the [Astoria] proposal and the alternatives to the [Astoria] proposal, including a possible combination with the Other Organization, and their feasibility.

> As part of the [Greater New York's] Board's deliberations, it instructed Sandler O'Neill to contact the Other Organization to inquire as to the consideration it would be willing to provide

to [Greater New York's] shareholders in a combination with [Greater New York] and its ability to move expeditiously to sign a definitive agreement with respect to such a transaction. The Other Organization responded with a proposal that involved a combination conditioned on "pooling of interests" accounting treatment and consideration consisting of a fixed exchange ratio of the Other Organization's common stock that had a value of $18.53 per share of [Greater New York] Common Stock based on the closing price of the Other Organization's common stock on March 27, 1997. Sandler O'Neill asked the Other Organization to increase its price and it declined to do so. The Other Organization also indicated that it could move expeditiously to enter into a definitive agreement. This proposal was immediately communicated to the [Greater New York] Board.

The proxy statement also contained a statement by Sandler O'Neill that the merger was "fair, from a financial point of view" and a recommendation of Greater New York's board that the shareholders approve the proposed Astoria merger.

On July 18, 1997, appellants initiated the instant lawsuit in the Eastern District of New York. Their complaint alleged that the proxy statement was materially misleading and that Greater New York's directors had breached state law fiduciary duties in negotiating and recommending the Astoria merger. On August 1, 1997, the shareholders of Astoria and Greater New York approved the merger. The district court reserved decision on appellees' motion to dismiss and ordered expedited discovery. Appellants obtained document discovery and deposed, inter alia, Keegan, Kanas, and Quackenbush. On September 2, appellants amended their complaint to reflect the fruits of that discovery.

On September 22, 1997, the district court issued a written decision denying appellants' motion for a preliminary injunction to block the merger, and the merger was subsequently effected. On June 1, 1998, the district court granted defendant's motion to dismiss the amended complaint without prejudice. Appellants thereafter amended their complaint again, and on January 25, 1999, the district court dismissed the second amended complaint. This appeal followed.

DISCUSSION

We review a Fed. R. Civ. P. 12(b)(6) dismissal de novo and may affirm only if it appears beyond doubt that appellants can prove no set of facts that would entitle them to relief.

Rule 14a–9, promulgated pursuant to Section 14(a) of the Exchange Act, states that:

No solicitation subject to this regulation shall be made by means of any proxy statement . . . containing any statement which, at the time and in the light of the circumstances under which it is made, is false or misleading with respect to any material fact, or which omits to state any material fact necessary in order to make the statements therein not false or misleading. . . .

17 C.F.R. § 240.14a–9(a). There is an implied private right of action under Rule 14a–9. See J.I. Case Co. v. Borak, 377 U.S. 426 (1964).

Appellants allege a violation of Rule 14a–9 as to the proxy statement's disclosure regarding three matters: (i) North Fork's attempts to negotiate a merger with Greater New York and the thwarting of those efforts; (ii) the Sandler O'Neill opinion as to the fairness of the terms of the Astoria merger; and (iii) the recommendation of Greater New York's board regarding the Astoria merger. We address each in turn.

a) North Fork's Efforts to Negotiate a Merger

With regard to North Fork's efforts to negotiate a merger and appellees' thwarting of those efforts, appellants catalog the following as material omissions in the proxy statement:

i) the competing offeror [North Fork] was a serious, motivated institution that already had a considerable stake in [Greater New York] and which had the wherewithal and interest to compete on a level playing field if allowed to do so;

ii) [North Fork] did not flatly decline to raise its price;

iii) [North Fork] was arbitrarily denied due diligence by [Greater New York] and/or Keegan which could have supplied information justifying a premium bid by [North Fork];

iv) [North Fork] remained interested in [Greater New York] even after declining to raise its bid, subject to due diligence;

v) [North Fork] proposed a better and higher offer than Astoria's, when scrutinized, even without the due diligence afforded Astoria;

vi) defendants were not even-handed and balanced with [North Fork] because they denied it the due diligence information needed in order to facilitate and elicit a competitive bid from [North Fork] but did furnish it to Astoria; and

vii) the Board may have entertained Astoria and not [North Fork] because [North Fork] was not prepared to offer employment to [Greater New York] Board members (including Keegan), but Astoria was.

We may assume that the omitted information would have been important to a reasonable shareholder in determining how to vote on the proposed merger with Astoria and thus meets the standard definition of materiality. See TSC Indus., Inc. v. Northway, Inc., 426 U.S. 438, (1976) (holding that an omitted fact is material "if there is a substantial likelihood that a reasonable shareholder would consider it important in deciding how to vote"). However, in the proxy context this definition of materiality assumes that the omitted information would have influenced a reasonable shareholder against the proposed transaction for which proxies were sought. Here, the omitted information would not have made a reasonable shareholder any less likely to favor the objected-to transaction, and such an omission, material or not, could not have caused the injury for which damages are sought.

In Virginia Bankshares, Inc. v. Sandberg, 501 U.S. 1083 (1990), the Supreme Court held that a materially misleading proxy solicitation was not actionable where the controlling shareholder had enough votes to approve the objected-to transaction without seeking proxies. The rationale of that holding applies equally to cases where the omissions would have caused a reasonable shareholder to favor rather than disfavor the transaction. In Virginia Bankshares, the omissions were not actionable because the disputed transaction would have occurred even if the proxy statement had been complete and accurate. That is also the case here. Had a reasonable Greater New York shareholder been fully informed, that shareholder would not have been any less likely to vote for the Astoria merger knowing of the cataloged information than being ignorant of it.

The matters omitted amount to the following: Greater New York's board and management were determined to reject a merger with North Fork and to bring about a merger with Astoria, at least in part because Astoria was offering future employment to the members of the board and Keegan. However, a reasonable shareholder would, upon learning such information, hardly be induced to vote against the merger with Astoria. At the time of the vote, a fully informed, reasonable shareholder would calculate that a defeat of the Astoria merger would leave Greater New York's shareholders with the existing management and corporate structure but without the substantial premium available in the Astoria deal. Such a shareholder would not believe, as appellants posit, that there was a substantial likelihood of a near-term and more favorable merger with North Fork after rejection of the Astoria merger.

The complaint alleged that North Fork continued to have an "interest" in Greater New York, but a reasonable shareholder would have grave doubts about whether that "interest" would ever culminate in a merger with Greater New York, at least in the near term. The termination fee and lock-up option in the Astoria merger agreement hardly made Greater New York a more tempting target for North Fork, and the complaint offers no concrete assurance that North Fork would have made an offer significantly better than Astoria's. More significantly, even if North Fork's desire for Greater New York led it to offer more favorable terms than Astoria's bid, a reasonable shareholder would anticipate that Greater New York's board and management would mount defensive measures effectively thwarting any offer by North Fork. The complaint alleged that the board and management did not want to talk with North Fork "under any circumstances," and there is little in New York law that would force them to abandon that stance. For example, there is no statutory law or caselaw requiring the board to consider merger offers or, in the presence of such offers, to conduct a fair auction. Indeed, there are New York statutes that allow management considerable leeway in defending against hostile takeovers, see N.Y. Bus. Corp. Law §§ 501(c), 505(a), 912(a)(10) (authorizing the creation by publicly traded New York corporations of shareholder rights plans that permit board to discriminate against "interested shareholders" who own 20% or more of company's stock), and there is no case law that would enable shareholders to compel Greater New York's board to negotiate with North Fork. Were New York courts to follow leading precedents from other states, see, e.g., Paramount Communications, Inc. v. Time Inc., 571 A.2d 1140 (Del. 1990) (holding in favor of board's "defense-motivated" actions against plaintiff Paramount's takeover attempts), it would not require much ingenuity on Greater New York's board or management's part to thwart North Fork's advances, however favorable they might seem to shareholders. At best, therefore, a reasonable shareholder would have foreseen a protracted struggle between North Fork and Greater New York's board, with the latter having a powerful advantage. Any North Fork deal would be perceived as being a marginally possible event of uncertain value in the distant future. The present value of such a deal, discounted by its improbability, would be viewed by a reasonable shareholder as considerably less valuable than the cash-in-hand Astoria deal. There is, therefore, no sense in which the omitted information, if available, would have diminished a reasonable shareholder's favorable view of the merger with Astoria.

b) The Sandler O'Neill Opinion

Appellants also challenge as materially misleading the proxy statement's incorporation of Sandler O'Neill's fairness opinion, which determined the Astoria merger to be "fair, from a financial point of view." Even assuming for purposes of analysis that, at the time the opinion was proffered, North Fork's offer was higher than Astoria's, the Astoria offer would not necessarily be deemed financially unfair from the perspective of Greater New York's shareholders. See Koppel, 167 F.3d 125 at 134 ("There is no § 14(a) violation for merely failing to inform shareholders that a proposed action is not subjectively the most beneficial to an entity's shareholders. . . ."). The fairness opinion did not purport to suggest that the Astoria merger was the highest potential price for Greater New York but only that the "consideration . . . [was] fair, from a financial point of view." The fairness opinion also stated that Sandler O'Neill had not "solicited indications of interest in a potential transaction from other third parties other than one third party specifically identified to us by [Greater New York's] Board of Directors," and specifically noted, in bold capitalized letters: "The Sandler O'Neill opinion . . . does not address the underlying business decision of [Greater New York] to engage in the merger and does not constitute a recommendation. . . ."

To attack the Sandler O'Neill opinion as materially misleading, therefore, appellants must allege with particularity, Fed. R. Civ. P. 9(b), "provable facts," see Virginia Bankshares, 501 U.S. at 1094, undercutting the statement that the merger was "fair from a financial point of view." An example of such a fact might be that the premium paid by Astoria over historic share price was substantially below that of comparable transactions. Another example of such a fact might be that the merger price did not adequately reflect the present value of expected future free cash flows to the shareholders. No such allegation or showing has been made here. The merger price included a significant premium over historical trading prices for Greater New York's stock. Appellants did allege that the transaction was priced lower than the average banking merger in terms of book value multiple, but such an allegation indicates nothing about the transaction's financial fairness absent allegations of facts suggesting that this ratio differential does not reflect appropriately priced risk variations. And the proxy statement clearly suggests that Greater New York's lower book value premium is explained by above-average risk. The proxy statement reports, inter alia, that the market-value-to-book-value ratio for Greater New York's stock was 1.48 compared to a company mean and median of 1.58; that Greater New York's ratio of nonperforming loans to total loans was 19.69%, compared with a 3.38% mean and 1.52% median for comparable companies; and that Greater New York's ratio of nonperforming assets to total assets was 7.91% compared with a 1.61% mean and 0.86% median for comparables. Thus, appellants have not alleged facts tending to suggest that the Sandler O'Neill opinion was materially misleading in opining that the transaction at issue was financially fair.

c)   The Recommendation of Greater New York's Board

Finally, appellants challenge the recommendation of Greater New York's board that the shareholders approve the Astoria merger. For the most part this challenge overlaps with the alleged omissions concerning North Fork's efforts to negotiate a merger that is discussed in part (a) above. As such, it suffers from the same flaw—a lack of causal link with the approval of the Astoria merger. To be sure, given the allegations of the complaint, Greater New York's board and Keegan may have deprived the shareholders of an opportunity to select a more profitable (for the shareholders) merger with North Fork and they may have done so to obtain a more profitable deal for themselves. However, knowing that management had a powerful self-interest in rejecting North Fork's advances would not have caused a reasonable shareholder to reject the Astoria deal, for reasons stated in part (a).

It may also be that the allegations amount to a breach of fiduciary duties under state law, but such conduct, without an accompanying materially misleading disclosure, does not state a claim under the federal securities laws. See Santa Fe Industries, Inc. v. Green, 430 U.S. 462, (1977) (refusing to extend federal securities laws to "overlap and quite possibly interfere with state corporate law"); Koppel, 167 F.3d 125 at 139 (reinstating state law claims because court concluded there was a federal claim to which state law claims could be appended). We also note that appellants have not alleged that the omissions caused them to lose state court rights. See RCM Sec. Fund, Inc. v. Stenton, 928 F.2d 1318, (1991) (explaining interplay between federal and state claims where such claims are "interdependent"). Indeed, given their bringing of a state court action upon announcement of the merger—an action that can be revived—no such claim could be made.

CONCLUSION

The alleged omissions to the proxy statement challenged by appellants cannot establish a claim under Rule 14a–9. Having determined that appellants' federal claim lacks merit, we decline to exercise pendent jurisdiction over their remaining state law claims. We therefore affirm.

―――――――

QUESTIONS

1. Judge Winter uses the Supreme Court's definition of "materiality," which asks whether a reasonable shareholder would have considered the information important in deciding how to vote, and then assumes the omitted information is material. How does that square with his conclusion that shareholders would not have changed their votes?

2. How would Delaware courts have judged the behavior of the Greater New York Board?

3. Judge Winter dismissed the complaint because plaintiffs could not plead that the alleged misstatements and omissions caused shareholders to behave differently than if they had received full disclosure. In part he relied on the absence of New York authority that boards of New York corporations are obligated to negotiate with firms such as North Fork. Does the adoption of a statute permitting the use of rights plans provide persuasive evidence of this lack of a duty?

4. Judge Winter cites Paramount Communications, Inc. v. Time, Inc., supra page 622 as evidence that Delaware law would permit the Greater New York board to thwart North Fork's advances. Do you agree?

5. Judge Winter also cited the existence of "deal protection" devices such as a break-up fee and lock-up option as evidence that shareholders would not have believed there was a reasonable prospect that North Fork would proceed with an acquisition. Does this mean that the board of a New York corporation can protect itself against an inadequate proxy

statement with a favored partner simply by providing sufficient deal protection?

6.   Is such deal protection possible for a Delaware corporation? If not, would this result in a different outcome for a Delaware corporation on the causation issue?

NOTE ON SEC DISCLOSURE REGULATIONS

Until 2004, absent insider trading or statements made misleading by omission, companies were required to disclose acquisition activity in a formal SEC filing on Form 8-K within fifteen calendar days after the occurrence of a specified event, or five business days in some instances. Item 1 covered changes of control that had occurred, and Item 2 covered cases where the company "has acquired or disposed of a significant amount of assets. . . ." Amendments to Form 8-K in 2004 have accelerated these filing requirements so they must be made within four business days, and applied them to a broader group of events. Item 1.01 requires a filing when a company enters into a "material definitive agreement" not in the ordinary course of business. Item 2.01 requires further disclosure of completion of an acquisition or disposition of assets, and Item 1.02 requires disclosure of termination of a material definitive agreement. It has always been the case that most issuers have felt an obligation to disclose these events as promptly as practicable, to keep markets informed about material events. They have always been able to use the catch-all provision of Form 8-K to file any announcement they deemed appropriate.

The adoption of Regulation FD, 17 C.F.R. 243.100–.103, by the SEC in 2000 also put pressures on companies to provide timely and equal access to important business news. It requires that whenever an issuer discloses material non-public information, it must disclose it simultaneously in the case of an intentional disclosure, and promptly in the case of a non-intentional disclosure. Today most companies provide advance notice of forthcoming announcements, and allow interested investors to listen in on a webcast.

NOTE ON STATE LAW DISCLOSURE DUTIES

Malone v. Brincat, 722 A.2d 5 (Del.1998) held, for the first time, that directors of Delaware corporations owe fiduciary duties with respect to disclosure outside the context of proxy solicitations. The complaint in Malone charged that the directors of Mercury Finance Corporation had overstated Mercury's earnings and assets over a four year period in its financial statements, to the ultimate detriment of Mercury and its shareholders. The court focused on the "breach" of fiduciary duties in this context, rather than on disclosure obligations more generally. But the case raises the more general question of when directors have disclosure duties, and to what they apply. Might these duties create affirmative disclosure duties even where Federal law does not impose them? See Berger v. Pubco Corp., 976 A.2d 132 (Del. 2009) involving a short form merger under Del. G.C.L. § 253, where the statute only requires the notice of the merger to include a copy of the appraisal statute, "and Delaware case law requires the parent company to disclose in the notice of merger all information material to shareholders deciding whether or not to seek appraisal." The parent company argued that since, in a short form merger it had no obligation to set a fair price, it had no obligation to explain how or why the price was set. Justice Jacobs responded, quoting the Chancery Court decision:

"Defendants' argument entirely misses the mark, however, because the issue is not about necessity—it is about materiality. In the context of Pubco, an unregistered company that made no public filings and whose Notice was relatively terse and short on details, the method by which Kanner set the merger consideration is a fact that is substantially likely to alter the total mix of information available to the minority stockholders. Where, as here, a minority shareholder needs to decide only whether to accept the merger consideration or to seek appraisal, the question is partially one of trust: can the minority shareholder trust that the price offered is good enough, or does it likely undervalue the Company so significantly that appraisal is a worthwhile endeavor? When faced with such a question, it would be material to know that the price offered was set by arbitrarily rolling dice. In a situation like Pubco's, where so little information is available about the Company, such a disclosure would significantly change the landscape with respect to the decision of whether or not to trust the price offered by the parent. This does not mean that Kanner should have provided picayune details about the process he used to set the price; it simply means he should have disclosed in a broad sense what the process was, assuming he followed a process at all and did not simply choose a number randomly."

B. LITIGATION STRATEGIES

Hostile takeover battles are fought in the courts as much as in markets. The mergers & acquisitions departments of a number of large law firms became litigation departments in the 1980's, as litigation became a tool in planning the strategy of both bids and defensive responses. A debate raged over whether defensive maneuvers by targets were good for target shareholders, in extending an auction, or bad, in protecting incumbent management. One study examined 100 takeover contests, and found shareholder gains (compared to the first bid) in 79 of 100 cases where the target was sold after litigation. In the other 21% of the cases examined, shareholders suffered from litigation because all bids were defeated. In the 79% of the cases where the company was sold, litigation was seen as permitting an auction to develop, which produced a 17% increase in target shareholder wealth. Jarrell, *The Wealth Effects of Litigation by Targets: Do Interests Diverge in a Merge?*, 28 Journal of Law & Economics 151 (1985).

The motives of bidders and target managers resisting a bid may or may not be congruent with those of target company shareholders. We begin with cases examining whether the contestants should be allowed to bring suit to vindicate the rights of others.

Two legal issues are somewhat intermixed in these cases. The first question is whether, when a statute is silent, Congress intended to confer a private right of action on private parties. The second question, more directly addressed in the following cases, is "if Congress intended to confer a private right of action, upon whom did it intend to confer it?" Students familiar with the development of private rights of action under Section 10(b) of the Securities Exchange Act will recall that lower courts began implying private rights of action for violations of Rule 10b–5 as early as Kardon v. National Gypsum Co., 69 F.Supp. 512 (E.D.Pa.1946). In this case of first impression, the court cited the general principles set forth in the Restatement of Torts § 286:

> "However, 'The violation of a legislative enactment by doing a prohibited act, or by failing to do a required act, makes the actor liable for an invasion of an interest of another if (a) the intent of the enactment is exclusively or in part to protect an interest of the other as an individual; and (b) the interest invaded is one which the enactment is intended to protect.' "

This holding was ultimately confirmed 25 years later in Superintendent of Insurance of the State of New York v. Bankers Life & Casualty Co., 404 U.S. 6 (1971), where, in a footnote Mr. Justice Douglas merely stated: "it is now established that a private right of action is implied under § 10(b)." 404 U.S. at 13, n. 9.

Similar results obtained under section 14 of the Securities Exchange Act. In a case brought by a shareholder to challenge a merger on the ground that the proxy statement soliciting shareholder consent was misleading, the Supreme Court held that a private right of action would be implied under section 14(a). J. I. Case Co. v. Borak, 377 U.S. 426, 84 S.Ct. 1555, 12 L.Ed.2d 423 (1964). The Court used sweeping language to affirm the existence of a private right of action. In support of its holding, the opinion cited section 27 of the Act, which provides that the district courts shall have exclusive jurisdiction over suits arising under the act. This reasoning would have supported a private right of action under every provision of the Act. Arguably, the Court limited this holding slightly by noting that the purpose of section 14(a) was to protect stockholders from misleading proxy statements (echoing the reasoning of Kardon v. National Gypsum and the Restatement of Torts). But this could be read to address the standing issue, rather than the appropriateness of private rights of action. The opinion went on to note that the SEC lacked the staff to review in detail every proxy statement submitted to it with respect to its truthfulness and completeness, and that it was up to the courts to fashion remedies that would effectuate the Congressional purpose. Accordingly, it concluded that "under the circumstances here it is the duty of the courts to be alert to provide such remedies as are necessary to make effective the congressional purpose." 377 U.S. at 433. These were words the Court would later reject in the cases that follow.

Piper v. Chris-Craft Industries, Inc.
430 U.S. 1, 97 S.Ct. 926, 51 L.Ed.2d 124 (1977).

■ MR. CHIEF JUSTICE BURGER delivered the opinion of the Court.

We granted certiorari in these cases, 425 U.S. 910 (1976), to consider, among other issues, whether an unsuccessful tender offeror in a contest for control of a corporation has an implied cause of action for damages under § 14(e) of the Securities Exchange Act of 1934, as added by § 3 of the Williams Act of 1968, 82 Stat. 457, 15 U.S.C. § 78n(e), or under Securities and Exchange Commission (SEC) Rule 10b–6, 17 CFR § 240.10b–6 (1976), based on alleged antifraud violations by the successful competitor, its investment adviser, and individuals constituting the management of the target corporation.

I. *Background*

The factual background of this complex contest for control, including the protracted litigation culminating in the cases now before us, is essential to a full understanding of the contending parties' claims.

The three petitions present questions of first impression, arising out of a "sophisticated and hard fought contest" for control of Piper Aircraft Corp., a Pennsylvania-based manufacturer of light aircraft. Piper's management consisted principally of members of the Piper family, who owned 31% of Piper's outstanding stock. Chris-Craft Industries, Inc., a diversified manufacturer of recreational products, attempted to secure voting control of Piper through cash and exchange tender offers for Piper common stock. Chris-Craft's takeover attempt failed, and Bangor Punta Corp. (Bangor or Bangor Punta), with the support of the Piper family, obtained control of Piper in September 1969. Chris-Craft brought suit under § 14(e) of the Securities Exchange Act of 1934 and Rule 10b–6 alleging that Bangor Punta achieved control of the target corporation as a result of violations of the federal securities laws by the Piper family, Bangor Punta, and Bangor Punta's underwriter, First Boston Corp., who together had successfully repelled Chris-Craft's takeover attempt.

The struggle for control of Piper began in December 1968. At that time, Chris-Craft began making cash purchases of Piper common stock. By January 22, 1969, Chris-Craft had acquired 203,700 shares, or approximately 13% of Piper's 1,644,790 outstanding shares. On the next day, following unsuccessful preliminary overtures to Piper by Chris-

Craft's president, Herbert Siegel, Chris-Craft publicly announced a cash tender offer for up to 300,000 Piper shares at $65 per share, which was approximately $12 above the then-current market price. Responding promptly to Chris-Craft's bid, Piper's management met on the same day with the company's investment banker, First Boston, and other advisers. On January 24, the Piper family decided to oppose Chris-Craft's tender offer. As part of its resistance to Chris-Craft's takeover campaign, Piper management sent several letters to the company's stockholders during January 25–27, arguing against acceptance of Chris-Craft's offer. On January 27, a letter to shareholders from W. T. Piper, Jr., president of the company, stated that the Piper Board "has carefully studied this offer and is convinced that it is inadequate and not in the best interests of Piper's shareholders."

* * *

Despite Piper's opposition, Chris-Craft succeeded in acquiring 304,606 shares by the time its cash tender offer expired on February 3. To obtain the additional 17% of Piper stock needed for control, Chris-Craft decided to make an exchange offer of Chris-Craft securities for Piper stock. Although Chris-Craft filed a registration statement and preliminary prospectus with the SEC in late February 1969, the exchange offer did not go into effect until May 15, 1969.

* * *

While Chris-Craft's exchange offer was in registration, Piper in March 1969 . . . entered into negotiations with Bangor Punta. Bangor had initially been contacted by First Boston about the possibility of a Piper takeover in the wake of Chris-Craft's initial cash tender offer in January. . . . [T]he Piper family agreed on May 8, 1969, to exchange their 31% stockholdings in Piper for Bangor Punta securities. Bangor also agreed to use its best efforts to achieve control of Piper by means of an exchange offer of Bangor securities for Piper common stock. A press release issued the same day announced the terms of the agreement, including a provision that the forthcoming exchange offer would involve Bangor securities to be valued, in the judgment of First Boston, "at not less than $80 per Piper share."

While awaiting the effective date of its exchange offer, Bangor in mid-May 1969 purchased 120,200 shares of Piper stock in privately negotiated, off-exchange transactions from three large institutional investors. All three purchases were made after the SEC's issuance of a release on May 5 announcing proposed Rule 10b–13, a provision which, upon becoming effective in November 1969, would expressly prohibit a tender offeror from making purchases of the target company's stock during the pendency of an exchange offer. The SEC release stated that the proposed rule was "in effect, a codification of existing interpretations under Rule 10b–6," the provision invoked by SEC officials against Mr. Siegel of Chris-Craft a month earlier. Bangor officials, although aware of the release at the time of the three off-exchange purchases, made no attempt to secure an exemption for the transactions from the SEC, as provided by Rule 10b–6(f). The SEC, however, took no action concerning these purchases as it had with respect to Chris-Craft's open-market transactions.

With these three block purchases, amounting to 7% of Piper stock, Bangor Punta in mid-May took the lead in the takeover contest. The contest then centered upon the competing exchange offers. Chris-Craft's first exchange offer, which began in mid-May 1969, failed to produce tenders of the specified minimum number of Piper shares (80,000). Meanwhile, Bangor Punta's exchange offer, which had been announced on May 8, became effective on July 18. The registration materials which Bangor filed with the SEC in connection with the exchange offer included financial statements, reviewed by First Boston, representing that one of Bangor's subsidiaries, the Bangor & Aroostock Railroad (BAR), had a value of $18.4 million. This valuation was based upon a 1965 appraisal by investment bankers after a proposed sale of the BAR failed to materialize. The financial statements did not indicate that Bangor was considering the sale of the BAR or that an offer to purchase the railroad for $5 million had been received.

In the final phase of the see-saw of competing offers, Chris-Craft modified the terms of its previously unsuccessful exchange offer to make it more attractive. The revised offer succeeded in attracting 112,089 additional Piper shares, while Bangor's exchange offer, which terminated on July 29, resulted in the tendering of 110,802 shares. By August 4, 1969, at the conclusion of both offers, Bangor Punta owned a total of 44.5%, while Chris-Craft owned 40.6% of Piper stock. The remainder of Piper stock, 14.9%, remained in the hands of the public.

After completion of their respective exchange offers, both companies renewed market purchases of Piper stock, but Chris-Craft, after purchasing 29,200 shares for cash in mid-August, withdrew from competition. Bangor Punta continued making cash purchases until September 5, by which time it had acquired a majority interest in Piper. The final tally in the nine-month takeover battle showed that Bangor Punta held over 50% and Chris-Craft held 42% of Piper stock.

II

Before either side had achieved control, the contest moved from the marketplace to the courts. Then began more than seven years of complex litigation growing out of the contest for control of Piper Aircraft.

A. *Chris-Craft's Initial Suit*

On May 22, 1969, Chris-Craft filed suit seeking both damages and injunctive relief in the United States District Court for the Southern District of New York. Chris-Craft alleged that Bangor's block purchases of 120,200 Piper shares in mid-May violated Rule 10b–6 and that

Bangor's May 8 press release, announcing an $80 valuation of Bangor securities to be offered in the forthcoming exchange offer, violated SEC "gun-jumping" provisions, 15 U.S.C. § 77e(c), and SEC Rule 135, 17 CFR § 230.135 (1976). Chris-Craft sought to enjoin Bangor from voting the Piper shares purchased in violation of Rule 10b–6 and from accepting any shares tendered by Piper stockholders pursuant to the tender offer.*

* * *

F.   Court of Appeals Decision on Liability March 16, 1973

Chris-Craft appealed, and the SEC sought review of the District Court's denial of injunctive relief against Bangor Punta. In the Court of Appeals, each member of the panel wrote separately. All three members of the panel agreed that Chris-Craft had standing to sue for damages under § 14(e) and that a claim for damages had been established. * * *

III.   The Williams Act

* * *

Besides requiring disclosure and providing specific benefits for tendering shareholders, the Williams Act also contains a broad antifraud prohibition, which is the basis of Chris-Craft's claim. Section 14(e) of the Securities Exchange Act, as added by § 3 of the Williams Act, 82 Stat. 457, [15 U.S.C. § 78n(e)], provides:

> "It shall be unlawful for any person to make any untrue statement of a material fact or omit to state any material fact necessary in order to make the statements made, in the light of the circumstances under which they are made, not misleading, or to engage in any fraudulent, deceptive, or manipulative acts or practices, in connection with any tender offer or request or invitation for tenders, or any solicitation of security holders in opposition to or in favor of any such offer, request, or invitation."

This provision was expressly directed at the conduct of a broad range of persons, including those engaged in making or opposing tender offers or otherwise seeking to influence the decision of investors or the outcome of the tender offer. Senate Report 11.

The threshold issue in these cases is whether tender offerors such as Chris-Craft, whose activities are regulated by the Williams Act, have a cause of action for damages against other regulated parties under the statute on a claim that anti-fraud violations by other parties have frustrated the bidder's efforts to obtain control of the target corporation. Without reading such a cause of action into the Act, none of the other issues need be reached.

---

*   The complaint also alleged violations of Section 14(e).—Ed.

IV

Our analysis begins, of course, with the statute itself. Section 14(e), like § 10(b), makes no provision whatever for a private cause of action, such as those explicitly provided in other sections of the 1933 and 1934 Acts. E.g., §§ 11, 12, 15 of the 1933 Act; §§ 9, 16, 18, 20 of the 1934 Act. This Court has nonetheless held that in some circumstances a private cause of action can be implied with respect to the 1934 Act's anti-fraud provisions, even though the relevant provisions are silent as to remedies. J. I. Case Co. v. Borak, 377 U.S. 426 (1964) (§ 14(a)); Superintendent of Ins. v. Bankers Life & Cas. Co., 404 U.S. 6 (1971) (§ 10 (b)).

The reasoning of these holdings is that, where congressional purposes are likely to be undermined absent private enforcement, private remedies may be implied in favor of the particular class intended to be protected by the statute. For example, in J.I. Case Co. v. Borak, *supra*, recognizing an implied right of action in favor of a shareholder complaining of a misleading proxy solicitation, the Court concluded as to such a shareholder's right:

> "While [§ 14(a)] makes no specific reference to a private right of action, among its chief purposes is 'the protection of investors,' which certainly implies the availability of judicial relief where necessary to achieve that result." 377 U.S., at 432. (Emphasis supplied.)

Indeed, the Court in Borak carefully noted that because of practical limitations upon the SEC's enforcement capabilities, "[p]rivate enforcement . . . provides a necessary supplement to Commission action." Ibid. (Emphasis added.) Similarly, the Court's opinion in Blue Chip Stamps v. Manor Drug Stores, 421 U.S. 723 (1975), in reaffirming the availability of a private right of action under § 10(b), specifically alluded to the language in Borak concerning the necessity for supplemental private remedies without which congressional protection of shareholders would be defeated.

Against this background we must consider whether § 14(e), which is entirely silent as to private remedies, permits this Court to read into the statute a damages remedy for unsuccessful tender offerors. To resolve that question we turn to the legislative history to discern the congressional purpose underlying the specific statutory prohibition in § 14(e). Once we identify the legislative purpose, we must then determine whether the creation by judicial interpretation of the implied cause of action asserted by Chris-Craft is necessary to effectuate Congress' goals.

A

Reliance on legislative history in divining the intent of Congress is, as has often been observed, a step to be taken cautiously. In this case both sides press legislative history on the Court not so much to explain the meaning of the language of a statute as to explain the absence of any express provision for a private cause of action for damages. As Mr. Justice Frankfurter reminded us: "We must be wary against interpolating our notions of policy in the interstices of legislative provisions." Ibid. With that caveat, we turn to the legislative history of the Williams Act.

In introducing the legislation on the Senate floor, the sponsor, Senator Williams, stated:

> "This legislation will close a significant gap in investor protection under the Federal securities laws by requiring the disclosure of pertinent information to stockholders when persons seek to obtain control of a corporation by a cash tender offer or through open market or privately negotiated purchases of securities."

* * *

The legislative history thus shows that Congress was intent upon regulating takeover bidders, theretofore operating covertly, in order to protect the shareholders of target companies. That tender offerors were not the intended beneficiaries of the bill was graphically illustrated by the statements of Senator Kuchel, cosponsor of the legislation, in support of requiring takeover bidders, whom he described as "corporate raiders" and "takeover pirates," to disclose their activities.

* * *

The legislative history thus shows that the sole purpose of the Williams Act was the protection of investors who are confronted with a tender offer. As we stated in Rondeau v. Mosinee Paper Corp., 422 U.S.[49] at 58: "The purpose of the Williams Act is to insure that public shareholders who are confronted by a cash tender offer for their stock will not be required to respond without adequate information. . . ." We find no hint in the legislative history, on which respondent so heavily relies, that Congress contemplated a private cause of action for damages by one of several contending offerors against a successful bidder or by a losing contender against the target corporation.

* * *

B

Our conclusion as to the legislative history is confirmed by the analysis in Cort v. Ash, 422 U.S. 66 (1975). There, the Court identified four factors as "relevant" in determining whether a private remedy is implicit in a statute not expressly providing one. The first is whether the plaintiff is " 'one of the class for whose especial benefit the statute was enacted. . . .' " As previously indicated, examination of the statute and its genesis shows that Chris-Craft is not an intended beneficiary of the Williams Act, and surely is not one "for whose especial benefit the statute was enacted." To the contrary, Chris-Craft is a member of the class whose activities Congress intended to regulate for the protection and benefit of an entirely distinct class, shareholder-offerees. As a party whose previously unregulated conduct was purposefully brought under federal control by the statute, Chris-Craft can scarcely lay claim to the status of "beneficiary" whom Congress considered in need of protection.

Second, in Cort v. Ash we inquired whether there was "any indication of legislative intent, explicit or implicit, either to create such a remedy or to deny one." Ibid. Although the historical materials are barren of any express intent to deny a damages remedy to tender offerors as a class, there is, as we have noted, no indication that Congress intended to create a damages remedy in favor of the loser in a contest for control. Fairly read, we think the legislative documents evince the narrow intent to curb the unregulated activities of tender offerors. The expression of this purpose, which pervades the legislative history, negates the claim that tender offerors were intended to have additional weapons in the form of an implied cause of action for damages, particularly if a private damages action confers no advantage on the expressly protected class of shareholder-offerees, a matter we discuss later. *Infra*, at 39.

Chris-Craft argues, however, that Congress intended standing under § 14(e) to encompass tender offerors since the statute, unlike § 10(b), does not contain the limiting language, "in connection with the purchase or sale" of securities. Instead, in § 14(e), Congress broadly proscribed fraudulent activities "in connection with any tender offer . . . or any solicitation . . . in opposition to or in favor of any such offer. . . ."

The omission of the purchaser-seller requirement does not mean, however, that Chris-Craft has standing to sue for damages under § 14(e) in its capacity as a takeover bidder. It may well be that Congress desired to protect, among others, shareholder-offerees who decided not to tender their stock due to fraudulent misrepresentations by persons opposed to a takeover attempt. These shareholders, who might not enjoy the protection of § 10(b) under Blue Chip Stamps v. Manor Drug Stores, 421 U.S. 723 (1975), could perhaps state a claim under § 14(e), even though they did not tender their securities. But increased protection, if any, conferred upon the class of shareholder-offerees by the elimination of the purchaser-seller restriction can scarcely be interpreted as giving protection to the entirely separate and unrelated class of persons whose conduct the statute is designed to regulate.

Third, Cort v. Ash tells us that we must ascertain whether it is "consistent with the underlying purposes of the legislative scheme to imply such a remedy for the plaintiff." We conclude that it is not. As a disclosure mechanism aimed especially at protecting shareholders of target corporations, the Williams Act cannot consistently be interpreted as conferring a monetary remedy upon regulated parties, particularly where the award would not redound to the direct benefit of the protected class. Although it is correct to say that the $36 million damages award indirectly benefits those Piper shareholders who became Chris-Craft shareholders when they accepted Chris-Craft's exchange offer, it is equally true that the damages award injures those Piper shareholders who exchanged their shares for Bangor Punta's stock and who, as Bangor Punta shareholders, would necessarily bear a large part of the burden of any judgment against Bangor Punta. The class sought to be protected by the Williams Act are the shareholders of the target corporation; hence it can hardly be said that their interests as a class are served by a judgment in favor of Chris-Craft and against Bangor Punta. Moreover, the damages are awarded to the very party whose activities Congress intended to curb; Chris-Craft did not sue in the capacity of an injured Piper shareholder, but as a defeated tender offeror.

Nor can we agree that an ever-present threat of damages against a successful contestant in a battle for control will provide significant additional protection for shareholders in general. The deterrent value, if any, of such awards can never be ascertained with precision. More likely, however, is the prospect that shareholders may be prejudiced because some tender offers may never be made if there is a possibility of massive damages claims for what courts subsequently hold to be an actionable violation of § 14(e). Even a contestant who "wins the battle" for control may well wind up exposed to a costly "war" in a later and successful defense of its victory. Or at worst—on Chris-Craft's damages theory—the victorious tender offeror or the target corporation might be subject to a large substantive judgment, plus high costs of litigation.

In short, we conclude that shareholder protection, if enhanced at all by damages awards such as Chris-Craft contends for, can more directly be achieved with other, less drastic means more closely tailored to the precise congressional goal underlying the Williams Act.

Fourth, under the Cort v. Ash analysis, we must decide whether "the cause of action [is] one traditionally relegated to state law. . . ." Despite the pervasiveness of federal securities regulation, the Court of Appeals concluded in these cases that Chris-Craft's complaint would give rise to a cause of action under common-law principles of interference with a prospective commercial advantage. Although Congress is, of course, free to create a remedial scheme in favor of contestants in tender offers, we conclude, as we did in Cort v. Ash, that "it is entirely appropriate in this instance to relegate [the offeror-bidder] and others in [that] situation to whatever remedy is created by state law," at least to the extent that the offeror seeks damages for having been wrongfully denied a "fair opportunity" to compete for control of another corporation.

C

What we have said thus far suggests that, unlike J.I. Case Co. v. Borak, *supra*, judicially creating a damages action in favor of Chris-Craft is unnecessary to ensure the fulfillment of Congress' purposes in adopting the Williams Act. Even though the SEC operates in this context under the same practical restraints recognized by the Court in Borak, institutional limitations alone do not lead to the conclusion that any party interested in a tender offer should have a cause of action for damages against a competing bidder. First, as Judge Friendly observed in Electronic Specialty Co. v. International Controls Corp., 409 F.2d 937 (C.A.2 1969), in corporate control contests the stage of preliminary injunctive relief, rather than post-contest lawsuits, "is the time when relief can best be given." Furthermore, awarding damages to parties other than the protected class of shareholders has only a remote, if any, bearing upon implementing the congressional policy of protecting shareholders who must decide whether to tender or retain their stock. Indeed, as we suggested earlier, a damages award of this nature may well be inconsistent with the interests of many members of the protected class and of only indirect value to shareholders who accepted the exchange offer of the defeated takeover contestant.

* * *

We therefore conclude that Chris-Craft, as a defeated tender offeror, has no implied cause of action for damages under § 14(e).

* * *

Accordingly, the judgment of the Court of Appeals is

Reversed.

QUESTIONS

1. Does the majority hold that there is no private right of action under § 14(e), or that bidders lack standing to bring such actions?

2. The majority opinion holds that a damage remedy for defeated bidders is not consistent with the investor protection purposes of the Williams Act. On net, if Piper shareholders had received shares in Chris-Craft and Bangor Punta respectively, how would a damage award affect them? Would your answer change if either Chris-Craft or Bangor Punta had issued debt securities instead of stock in the exchange offer?

3. Does the use of a cash tender offer by both parties alter who pays the damages?

4. When the majority opinion stated that while a damage remedy might not deter fraud, some tender offers might never be made, what does this imply about litigation costs and the ability of courts to screen out meritless claims at low cost to defendants?

5. What effect will a holding that bidders cannot challenge target management fraud under the Williams Act have on the number of suits brought against target management?

6. Is an action under Section 10(b) and Rule 10b–5 a good substitute for a Williams Act suit complaining of fraudulent behavior by target management? See Blue Chip Stamps v. Manor Drug Stores, 421 U.S. 723 (1975).

7. Are there common law suits that will substitute for Williams Act litigation by bidders, such as tortious interference with prospective advantage? Would such litigation be a satisfactory substitute, from a bidder's perspective?

8. Is the court influenced by who would bear the cost of a recovery by a bidder? Who would bear this cost?

NOTE ON IMPLIED RIGHTS OF ACTION UNDER THE WILLIAMS ACT

No Supreme Court decisions have held that an implied private right of action exists under Section 13(d). Rondeau v. Mosinee Paper Corp., 422 U.S. 49 (1975), involved a suit by a target corporation to enjoin the holder of more than 5% of its shares from voting the shares, acquiring additional shares, and to require the sale of shares already owned. The Court did not address the issue of whether a private right of action existed, but simply affirmed the District Court's dismissal of the injunction action because of the corporation's failure to show irreparable injury. The shareholder had filed corrections to his Schedule 13D form, making a showing of irreparable injury impossible.

A footnote to the Rondeau opinion gives some guidance about the Court's attitude at the time: "Because this case involves only the availability of injunctive relief to remedy a Section 13(d) violation following compliance with the reporting requirements, it does not require us to decide whether or under what circumstances a corporation could obtain a decree enjoining a shareholder who is currently in violation of Section 13(d) from acquiring further shares, exercising voting rights, or launching a takeover bid, pending compliance with the reporting requirements."

The Court's attitude about private rights of action has varied considerably over recent years. In J. I. Case Co. v. Borak, 377 U.S. 426 (1964), the Court held that "It appears clear that private parties have a right under Section 27 to bring suit for violation of Section 14(a) of the Act." Section 27 merely provides that "the district courts . . . shall have exclusive jurisdiction of violations of this title . . . and of all suits in equity and actions at law brought to enforce any liability or duty created by this title. . . ." Under that reasoning, private rights of action would exist for violations of all sections of the '34 Act, including Section 13(d). The court reasoned that private litigants would serve as "private attorneys general" to supplement the enforcement activities of the SEC, which lacked to resources to detect all violations.

The broad rationale of Case v. Borak was rejected in Piper v. Chris-Craft Industries, Inc., 430 U.S. 1, *supra*. Rather than follow the reasoning of Case v. Borak, that Section 27 created actions for all violations of the securities laws, the Court held that the doctrines of Cort v. Ash, 422 U.S. 66, 78 (1975), decided the same day as Rondeau v. Mosinee Paper Corp., *supra*, would govern. In this instance, it held that the Williams Act was adopted to protect investors, not defeated tender offerors, and that such bidders did not have a private right of action. The opinion limited its impact in a footnote that stated "[n]or is the target corporation's standing to sue in issue in this case." 430 U.S. at 42, n. 29. This language was cited in Dan River, Inc. v. Unitex Ltd., 624 F.2d 1216 (4th Cir.1980), cert. denied 449 U.S. 1101 (1981) for the proposition that Piper does not preclude actions by targets.

The approach of Case v. Borak was also expressly rejected in Touche Ross & Co. v. Redington, 442 U.S. 560 (1979), which involved an unsuccessful attempt to imply a private right of action under section 17(a) of the '34 act, which requires registered securities brokers and dealers to file reports with the SEC. The court held that the implied cause of action in Case v. Borak was derived from section 14, not section 27. The court stated "We do not now question the actual holding of that case, but we decline to read the opinion so broadly that virtually every provision of the securities acts gives rise to an implied private cause of action. * * * To the extent our analysis in today's decision differs from that of the Court in Borak, it suffices to say that in a series of cases since Borak we have adhered to a stricter standard for the implications of private causes of action, and we follow that stricter standard today."

The Touche Ross opinion even cast doubt on the vitality of the Cort v. Ash test, since the court said the four factors mentioned there were merely ways to determine Congressional intent. The court said: "Indeed, the first three factors discussed in Cort—the language and focus of the statute, its legislative history, and its purpose—are ones traditionally relied upon in determining legislative intent. Here, the statute by its terms grants no private rights to any identifiable class and proscribes no conduct as unlawful. And the parties as well as the Court of Appeals agree that the legislative history of the 1934 Act simply does not speak to the issue of private remedies under Section 17(a). At least in such a case as this, the inquiry ends there: the question whether Congress either expressly or by implication intended to create a private right of action, has been definitively answered in the negative." 99 S.Ct. at 2489.

Shortly thereafter the Court refused to create a private right of action for damages under the antifraud provisions of the Investment Advisers Act of 1940, in Transamerica Mortgage Advisors, Inc. v. Lewis, 444 U.S. 11 (1979), although it did allow equitable relief for rescission. The majority opinion focused on the legislative history and the language of the act exclusively, and rejected the suggestion in Cort v. Ash that it was relevant to examine the utility of a private remedy to the enforcement scheme as evidence of legislative intent. In dissent, Justice White argued that the decision could not be reconciled with earlier decisions.

In a case arising under the Commodity Exchange Act, the Court has taken a more generous approach toward implied causes of action, simply holding that where lower courts have implied private rights of action under general antifraud language in the statute prior to Congressional amendment of the statute, Congress has indicated its approval of an implied right of action. Merrill Lynch, Pierce, Fenner & Smith v. Curran, 456 U.S. 353 (1982). Four justices—Powell, Rehnquist, Burger & O'Connor, dissented from the holding, indicating the uncertainty surrounding rules in this area.

In Liberty National Insurance Holding Company v. The Charter Company, 734 F.2d 545 (11th Cir.1984), the court held that the target company, Liberty, was not authorized to sue a bidder under the Williams Act by alleging market manipulation by Charter. The allegations included filing a false and misleading Schedule 13D. Judge Tjoflat, writing for the majority, noted the lack of an express rights of action in the Williams Act, and proceeded to apply the Cort v. Ash test. The court concluded that giving a target corporation a remedy is not consistent with the underlying purposes of the legislation. The court held that Congress tried to avoid tipping the balance in favor of either side in a takeover contest, and permitting target management to bring costly litigation could impair takeovers. The remedy sought by the target was divestiture of Charter's shares, which would eliminate a large shareholder with a sufficient financial stake to discipline poor managers.

The Liberty National decision was followed in Polaroid Corp. v. Shamrock Holdings, Inc., 862 F.2d 987 (3d Cir.1988). Another, but divided, panel of the Eleventh Circuit Court of Appeals reached a somewhat different result in Florida Commercial Banks v. Culverhouse, 772 F.2d 1513 (11th Cir.1985). The majority opinion distinguished the Liberty National opinion on the basis that the relief sought by the target in Liberty National was to require the bidder to divest its shares, while in the instant case the target only sought injunctive relief to require the bidder to cure allegedly false statements in its tender offer materials, and to enjoin the tender offer until the disclosures were made. Under these circumstances the panel held that a target could seek relief.

Most court of appeals' decisions either assumed or affirmed the existence of a private right of action, without addressing the conflicts of interest that might be faced by target management. Wellman v. Dickinson, 682 F.2d 355 (2d Cir.1982); Treadway Companies, Inc. v. Care Corp., 638 F.2d 357, 380 (2d Cir.1980); Bath Industries v. Blot, 427 F.2d 97 (7th Cir.1970); Chromalloy American Corp. v. Sun Chemical Corp., 611 F.2d 240 (8th Cir.1979); Corenco Corp. v. Schiavone & Sons, Inc., 488 F.2d 207 (2d Cir.1973).

GAF Corp. v. Milstein, 453 F.2d 709, 719 (2d Cir.1971), cert. denied 406 U.S. 910 (1972) held that a private right of action existed under § 13(d), citing Case v. Borak, *supra* and held that an issuer has standing to enforce § 13(d). General Aircraft Corp. v. Lampert, 556 F.2d 90, 94, n. 5 (1st Cir.1977) dealt with the problem in a footnote:

> "Neither the availability of a private suit under Section 13(d) nor GAC's standing to bring such a suit are challenged by appellants. [citing Rondeau, GAF v. Milstein, and Piper.]"

Indiana National Corp. v. Rich, 712 F.2d 1180 (7th Cir.1983) expressly held that a private right of action exists. The court reasoned that the Williams Act was patterned after the protection provided by the proxy rules, where a private right of action had already been implied. Oddly, the court cited its own holding in Studebaker Corp. v. Gittlin, 360 F.2d 692 (2d Cir.1966), rather than J.I. Case Co. v. Borak, 377 U.S. 426 (1964), which was the authority for Studebaker. It is not clear whether this was done because the authority of Case had been weakened by subsequent Supreme Court decisions.

The policy argument made by the court closely follows that of J. I. Case Co. v. Borak, *supra*.

"Our conclusion is further bolstered by the fact that such an interpretation of the statutory provision at issue is the only construction which can make the Section 13(d) disclosure requirements effective at all. See Huddleston, 103 S. Ct. at 689–90. The filing required by Section 13(d) is sent to the S.E.C. and to the issuer corporation; it is not disseminated to the shareholders, for whose protection the information is required. The S.E.C., as friend of the court, has told us that it is unreasonable to expect the Commission to police possible Section 13(d) filing violations [noting that 1,574 Schedule 13D's were filed in 1982 with 3,673 amendments]. The only party with both the capability and incentive to pursue these violations is the issuer corporation. Our conclusion that Congress intended that a private right of action for an issuer corporation be implied under Section 13(d) is thus inescapable if the objectives of the statute are to be realized." 712 F.2d at 1184.

This analysis attempts to make an economic analysis of efficient enforcement of the Williams Act. Bureaucratic agencies lack the information available to the issuer to determine truthfulness of Schedule 13Ds, and also lack the incentives that move issuers to police the matter. Further, individual shareholders who receive only a small fraction of the payoff from enforcement (having to share it with their fellow shareholders while bearing all of the risk and costs of enforcement) also lack correct incentives. The group likely to receive the largest payoff from enforcement is target management; the difficulty is that since management can pass these costs on to investors, management is likely to overinvest in enforcement activities. The Court of Appeals recognized these arguments in a rudimentary way. The Liberty National opinion went further, and recognized the potential for perverse incentives of target management. The Fifth Circuit has followed this holding in Motient Corp. v. Dondero, 2008 U.S. App. LEXIS 1138, where the issuing corporation sued for damages alleged to have arisen from false statements in schedule 13D amendments filed by the defendant. Eschewing extensive analysis, the court simply stated that "[n]o other Circuit has found a private right of action for money damages under Section 13(d)." The court noted that a cause of action would lie for false SEC filings under section 18(a) of the Exchange Act.

Dan River, Inc. v. Unitex Ltd., 624 F.2d 1216 (4th Cir. 1980), cert. denied 449 U.S. 1101 (1981) did not focus on the line of Supreme Court decisions involving implied rights of action, but only on the significance of Rondeau and Piper, *supra*. Because Piper was a damage action, the court held it did not control an action brought by a target against a bidder to enjoin use of a false Schedule 13D, noting the footnote in the Piper opinion to the effect that the court did not decide that issue. The court held that Rondeau only involved the right of a target to equitable relief after the bidder had complied with the requirements of Schedule 13D. 624 F.2d at 1222. Other circuits have expressly held that targets have standing after acknowledging Judge Tjoflat's analysis in Liberty National. Gearhart Industries, Inc. v. Smith International, Inc., 741 F.2d 707 (5th Cir.1984) and Portsmouth Square, Inc. v. Shareholders Protective Committee, 770 F.2d 866 (9th Cir.1985).

In In re Dow Chemical Securities Bhopal Litigation, 2000 WL 1886612 (S.D.N.Y. 2000), the court held that shareholders of a bidder lacked standing to sue the bidder for alleged misstatements and omissions in its Schedule 13D filing. The court pointed out that the filing was required to be sent to the target corporation and the SEC, and that bidder shareholders were not the intended beneficiaries of this filing requirement.

In contrast, in E.ON AG v. Acciona, S.A, 468 F.Supp.2d 537 (S.D.N.Y. 2006), the court held that a bidder had standing to sue to enjoin the allegedly false 13D filing of a competing bidder. The court noted the lack of information possessed by most shareholders about false filings by bidders and their weak economic incentive to enforce the disclosure requirements, and wrote that "a tender offeror has not only the resources, but also the self-interest which the GAF Co. court identified as 'vital to maintaining an injunctive action.' " The court noted that the target had little incentive in the particular case to litigate because it apparently favored the second bidder. Against the Cort v. Ash argument that the statute was not adopted to protect bidders, the court responded that if targets had standing to challenge filings, the same logic would permit competing bidders to do so.

Most of the cases denying an issuer the right to raise Schedule 13D violations are district court opinions. Equity Oil Co. v. Consolidated Oil & Gas, Inc., 596 F.Supp. 507 [1983–84 Decisions] Fed. Sec. L. Rep. (CCH) ¶ 99,425 (D. Utah, 1983), applied the Cort v. Ash test to determine that no right of action exists. The opinion held that "[P]laintiff (target) is not a member of the class for whose especial benefit the statute was enacted, since the Williams Act is designed to protect investors." Id. at 96,435. Gateway Industries, Inc. v. Agency Rent A Car, Inc., 495 F.Supp. 92 (N.D.Ill.1980), also held no private right of action existed, but its reasoning was later rejected in Indiana National Corp. v. Rich, 712 F.2d 1180 (7th Cir. 1983), supra.

Other lower court opinions holding that there is no private right of action for targets under the Williams Act include Leff v. CIP Corp., 540 F.Supp. 857, 863–65 (S.D. Ohio 1982); Berman v. Metzger, [1981 Decisions] Fed. Sec. L. Rep. (CCH) ¶ 97,857 (D.D.C. 1981); Sta-Rite Industries, Inc. v. Nortek, Inc., 494 F.Supp. 358 (E.D.Wis.1980); American Bakeries Co. v. Pro-Met Trading Co. [1981 Decisions] Fed. Sec. L. Rep. (CCH) ¶ 97,925 (N.D. Ill. 1981) (rejecting the 7th Circuit's assumption of a private right of action in Bath Industries, Inc. v. Blot, 427 F.2d 97 (7th Cir.1970) as not binding in light of recent Supreme Court decisions); Holly Sugar Corp. v. Buchsbaum, [1981–82 Decisions] Fed. Sec. L. Rep. (CCH) ¶ 98,366 (D. Colo. 1981).

The Second Circuit has denied a private right of action to target shareholders. Kamerman v. Steinberg, 891 F.2d 424, 430 (2d Cir. 1989); see also Sanders v. Thrall Car Mfg. Co., 582 F.Supp. 945, 960 (S.D.N.Y. 1983); Schnell v. Schnall, 1981 WL 1618, at *2 (S.D.N.Y. 1981); Seagoing Uniform Corp. v. Texaco, Inc., 705 F.Supp. 918, 926 (S.D.N.Y. 1989); Wellman v. Dickinson, 497 F.Supp. 824, 835 (S.D.N.Y. 1980), aff'd on other grounds, 682 F.2d 355 (2d Cir. 1982); and Enterprises Myers v. American Leisure Time, 402 F.Supp. 213, 214–15 (S.D.N.Y. 1975).

A number of district court opinions have also held an implied right of action exists under § 13(d). Jacobs v. Pabst Brewing Co., 549 F.Supp. 1050, 1054–57 (D.Del.1982); Seilon, Inc. v. Lamb, [1983–84 Decisions] Fed. Sec. L. Rep. (CCH) ¶ 99,448 (N.D. Ohio 1983) (magistrate's decision); K-N Energy, Inc. v. Gulf Interstate Co., 607 F.Supp. 756 [1983–84 Decisions] Fed. Sec. L. Rep. (CCH) ¶ 99,423 (D. Colo. 1983) and Rorer Group, Inc. v. Oppenheimer & Co., Inc., [1982–83 Decisions] Fed. Sec. L. Rep. (CCH) ¶ 99,256 (S.D.N.Y. 1983).

Only one court of appeals has addressed the question of whether a private right of action exists under Section 13(e) for inadequate issuer disclosures when going private. Howing Co. v. Nationwide Corp., 826 F.2d 1470 (6th Cir.1987), cert. denied, 486 U.S. 1059, 108 S.Ct. 2830, 100 L.Ed.2d 930 (1988), *supra*, Part 3.C of this chapter, held that a private right of action did exist. It has been followed in Brewer v. Lincoln Int'l Corp., 148 F.Supp.2d 792 (W.D.Ky. 2000); Dowling v. Narragansett Capital Corp., 735 F.Supp. 1105 (D.R.I.1990); and Kahn v. Lynden Inc., 705 F.Supp. 1458 (W.D.Wash.1989).

NOTE ON REMEDIES

Damages

In Piper v. Chris-Craft Industries, Inc., 430 U.S. 1, 97 S.Ct. 926, 51 L.Ed.2d 124 (1977), *supra* Part 4.B of this chapter, a damage action brought by a defeated bidder under the antifraud provisions of § 14(e), the Court denied that a right to bring an action for damages existed, at least for such bidders. In responding to the dissent, the majority opinion argued that Chris-Craft was not suing as an ordinary shareholder in the target, but as a defeated contestant. 430 U.S. at 35. In a footnote the Court noted the issue of damages to nontendering shareholders was not presented in this case, and the Court expressed no view on it.

Fisher v. Plessey Co., Ltd., [1982–83 Decisions] Fed. Sec. L. Rep. (CCH) ¶ 99,246 (S.D.N.Y. 1983) allowed a private damage action by target shareholders. This case involved § 13(e), since the issuer was repurchasing its own shares, but the reasoning should be parallel to cases under § 13(d). The court concluded that the line of decisions including Cort v. Ash, Touche Ross v. Redington and Transamerica Mortgage Investors v. Lewis involves two levels of inquiry—first, the court should examine the statutory language, scheme and legislative history for legislative intent, and if the court finds an intent to provide a remedy, to then turn to the Cort v. Ash test to determine whether a remedy exists in the particular case. ¶ 99,246, at p. 96,072. In this case the court noted it was well accepted that investors have a private cause of action under § 14(e), citing two second Circuit opinions, and reading Piper as limited to the fact situation of a claim by a defeated bidder. *Id.* It found a parallel scheme of investor protection under § 13(e), and a legislative intent to protect investors, of the kind referred to in Piper. Turning then to the Cort v. Ash factors, the court found that an implied remedy would comport with the statutory scheme as a whole, since there were so many other implied rights of action under the securities laws. *Id.* at 96,073. The court noted that the SEC took the position in Release 14185 that a private right of action was consistent with the legislative scheme. The court found this was not an area traditionally relegated to state law, since tender offers have been primarily an area of federal concern. *Id.* at 96,074. Dicta in Hundahl v. United Benefit Life Ins. Co., 465 F.Supp. 1349 (N.D.Tex.1979) supports a private right of action for damages, although the court held the plaintiff lacked standing to bring it, since he knew of the falsity of the statements complained of. In dicta, the court in Treadway Companies, Inc. v. Care Corp., 490 F.Supp. 668, 684, n. 29 (S.D.N.Y.), aff'd in part, reversed in part on other grounds, 638 F.2d 357 (2d.Cir.1980) indicated it reached no conclusion about the potential liability of 13D filers to investors who bought or sold target stock, under § 13(d).

The two other cases sustaining shareholder damage actions predate Piper v. Chris-Craft, and are thus of limited precedential value. Grow Chemical Corp. v. Uran, 316 F.Supp. 891 [1969–70 Decisions] Fed. Sec. L. Rep. (CCH) ¶ 92,688 (S.D.N.Y.1970); Washburn v. Madison Square Garden Corp., 340 F.Supp. 504, 508 (S.D.N.Y.1972).

Cases holding that shareholders cannot sue for damages are more numerous. See, e.g., Gateway Industries, Inc. v. Agency Rent A Car, Inc., 495 F.Supp. 92 (N.D.Ill.1980); Leff v. CIP Corp., 540 F.Supp. 857 (S.D.Ohio 1982); Berman v. Metzger, [1981 Decisions] Fed. Sec. L. Rep. (CCH) ¶ 97,857 (D.D.C. 1981); Sta-Rite Industries, Inc. v. Nortek, Inc, 494 F.Supp. 358 (E.D.Wis.1980); American Bakeries Co. v. Pro-Met Trading Co, [1981 Decisions] Fed. Sec. L. Rep. (CCH) ¶ 97,925 (N.D. Ill. 1981); Holly Sugar Corp. v. Buchsbaum, [1981–82 Decisions] Fed. Sec. L. Rep. (CCH) ¶ 98,366 (D. Colo. 1981); Equity Oil Co. v. Consolidated Oil & Gas, Inc., 596 F.Supp 507 [1983–84 Decisions] Fed. Sec. L. Rep. (CCH) ¶ 99,425 (D. Utah 1983); and Sanders v. Thrall Mfg. Co., 582 F.Supp. 945 [1983–84 Decisions] Fed. Sec. L. Rep. (CCH) ¶ 99,500 (S.D.N.Y. 1983) Citations to numerous other cases so holding can be found in 2 Fed. Sec. L. Rep. (CCH) ¶ 23,710.26, and in the Sanders opinion, *supra.*

Disgorgement of Profits by Sellers

Wellman v. Dickinson, 497 F.Supp. 824, 834 (S.D.N.Y.1980), affirmed, 682 F.2d 355 (2d Cir. 1982), rejected disgorgement of Dickinson's profits on the basis of a theory of unjust enrichment. The district court noted that the offending stockholder had not violated any fiduciary duty to the other shareholders in accepting a control premium for his own shares, and thus had not been unjustly enriched. 497 F.Supp. at 835. The Court of Appeals affirmed. 682 F.2d at 367. Disgorgement is a remedy generally reserved for the SEC, to capture the unjust enrichment profits of a wrongdoer. See generally 5C Jacobs, LITIGATION AND PRACTICE UNDER RULE 10b–5 (2d ed., rev. 1984) § 261.03[b]. In SEC v. Bilzerian, 814 F.Supp. 116 (D.D.C.1993), the court held that the amount of profit to be disgorged is the amount of stock appreciation arising from the late and inaccurate Schedule 13D filing, or "the difference between the sale price of the securities and what their market price would have been but for defendant's untimely and inaccurate filing." *Id.* at 122.

Injunctions, Divestiture and Rescission Offers

The cases discussed below either assume or expressly hold that some form of relief is available to private litigants under § 13(d). A relatively small number of cases require defendants to divest their shares if they have violated section 13(d). Financial General Bankshares, Inc. v. Lance, [1978 Decisions] Fed. Sec. L. Rep. (CCH) ¶ 96,403 (D.D.C.1978) required defendants to offer rescission to shareholders who sold their shares to them in the open market. S-G Securities, Inc. v. Fuqua Investment Co., 466 F.Supp. 1114, 1130–31 (D.Mass.1978) ordered a rescission offer by the bidder. Hanna Mining Co. v. Norcen Energy Resources Ltd., 574 F.Supp. 1172 [1982 Decisions] Fed. Sec. L. Rep. (CCH) ¶ 98,878 (N.D. Ohio 1982) granted a preliminary injunction against a proposed tender offer based on an allegedly false prior Schedule 13D filing. The court indicated it would consider divestiture after a hearing on the merits, because it viewed the bidder's actions as involving a continuing and deliberate fraud.

General Steel Industries, Inc. v. Walco National Corp., [1981–82 Decisions] Fed. Sec. L. Rep. (CCH) ¶ 98,402 (E.D. Mo. 1981), involved a finding of false Schedule 13D filings prior to a tender offer. The bidder had acquired 29% of the target's shares prior to the tender offer. In this case the Schedule 13D failed to disclose the bidder's control purpose, while the tender offer filings failed to disclose securities law violations of the bidder and the background of the controlling shareholder of the bidder, which included adverse information about his character. With respect to the Schedule 13D violation, the court held that the target was irreparably harmed because the bidder was in a position to inhibit competing offers, and ordered the bidder to offer recision to all target shareholders that sold in the open market during the period of violation. The SEC filed an amicus brief in support of the court's broad equitable power to fashion any form of relief it believed appropriate. See SEC Litigation Release No. 9533, [1981–82 Decisions] Fed. Sec. L. Rep. (CCH) ¶ 98,387 (1981). Wellman v. Dickinson, 497 F.Supp. 824, 828–29 (S.D.N.Y.1980), affirmed 682 F.2d 355 (2d Cir.1982), *supra* Part 3.B of this chapter, called for divestiture of Sun's shares

Where the market price for the shares had declined significantly, the court declined to order divestiture, as an unduly harsh remedy and one that might depress the market price of the stock. In Electronic Specialty Co. v. International Controls Corp., 409 F.2d 937, 947–48 (2d Cir.1969), Judge Friendly rejected requiring a rescission offer where the stock purchased at

$39 had declined to $26–27. He further rejected depriving the bidder in a tender offer of its voting rights, since this would simply force it to sell out.

A number of courts have been willing to grant preliminary relief, in the form of temporary restraining orders and preliminary injunctions, against further market purchases where the target makes a showing of improper disclosures. These decisions also involve an implicit or explicit holding that targets have standing to seek such relief on behalf of their shareholders. Numerous cases grant injunctions or support their grant until a truthful filing is made. See, e.g., General Aircraft v. Lampert, 556 F.2d 90, 96–97 (1st Cir.1977); Chromalloy American Corp. v. Sun Chemical Corp., 611 F.2d 240, 243 (8th Cir.1979), affirming 474 F.Supp. 1341 (E.D.Mo.1979); Saunders Leasing v. Societe Holding Gray D'Albion S.A, 507 F.Supp. 627, 632 (N.D.Ala.1981); Kirsch Co. v. Bliss & Laughlin Industries, Inc., 495 F.Supp. 488, 502 (W.D.Mich.1980); Hoover v. Fuqua Industries, [1979–80 Decisions] Fed. Sec. L. Rep. (CCH) ¶ 97,107 (N.D. Ohio 1979); Chromalloy American Corp. v. Sun Chemical Corp., 474 F.Supp. 1341, 1347–48 (E.D.Mo.1979), affirmed 611 F.2d 240 (8th Cir.1979). But once a truthful filing is made, most courts refuse to further enjoin acquisitions. Rondeau v. Mosinee Paper Corp., 422 U.S. 49 (1975) held that no relief was available where corrective Schedule 13D amendments were filed, since no irreparable injury could be shown at that time. See also Chromalloy American Corp. v. Sun Chemical Corp., 611 F.2d 240, 249 (8th Cir.1979), affirming 474 F.Supp. 1341 (E.D.Mo.1979); Financial General Bankshares, Inc. v. Lance [1978 Transfer Binder] Fed. Sec. L. Rep. (CCH) ¶ 96,403, at 93,427 (D.D.C. 1978); Corenco Corp. v. Schiavone & Sons, Inc., 488 F.2d 207, 214–15 (2d Cir.1973) and University Bank & Trust Co. v. Gladstone, 574 F.Supp. 1006, 1010 (D.Mass.1983).

In Kirsch Co. v. Bliss & Laughlin Industries, Inc., 495 F.Supp. 488, 502 (W.D.Mich.1980), the court granted a 30 day cooling off period, which began from the filing of a curative Schedule 13D, during which time the bidder would not be allowed to acquire additional stock in the target. The opinion does not contain any discussion of the circumstances that prompted the grant of this unusual relief, except for a finding that the bidder's Schedule 13D was intended by one of its officers to be false and misleading with respect to its intention to seek control. San Francisco Real Estate Investors v. Real Estate Investment Trust of America, 701 F.2d 1000, 1009 (1st Cir.1983), suggested the following standards for imposing a cooling off period after corrective disclosure: "(1) whether a substantial number of shares were purchased after the misleading disclosures and before corrective disclosure, (2) whether the curative disclosure occurred simultaneously with or on the eve of a tender offer, and (3) whether the violation was egregious."

Injunctions Against Voting Shares

Permanent injunctions against voting shares already acquired are not likely to be granted. Judge Friendly rejected such relief in Electronic Specialty Co. v. International Controls Corp., 409 F.2d 937, 948 (2d Cir.1969) on the basis that disenfranchising a shareholder will force it to sell the shares, and thus becomes a harsh divestiture order. In University Bank &

Trust Co. v. Gladstone, 574 F.Supp. 1006, 1010 (D.Mass. 1983), the district court refused to enjoin a bidder from voting its shares or acquiring any more shares once it had made curative filings. See also Raybestos-Manhattan, Inc. v. Hi-Shear Industries, Inc., 503 F.Supp. 1122, 1133 (E.D.N.Y.1980). In Kirsch Co. v. Bliss & Laughlin Industries, Inc., 495 F.Supp. 488, 502 (W.D.Mich.1980), the court declined to prevent a bidder from voting its shares even where it found the Schedule 13D was misleading. But see Jacobs v. Pabst Brewing Co., 549 F.Supp. 1050, 1063–64 (D. Del. 1982).

But in Treadway Companies, Inc. v. Care Corp., 490 F.Supp. 660, 663, n. 5 (S.D.N.Y.1980), the court granted a temporary restraining order enjoining a major shareholder from acquiring additional shares, soliciting proxies or voting its shares. The court refused to grant permanent relief, however, since corrections had been made, but noted " . . . such relief may be proper in order 'to allow a corporation, its shareholders and investors— before a takeover might become a fait accompli—the opportunity to receive, and react to, information required to be disclosed under Section 13(d).' " 490 F.Supp. at 665. The Court of Appeals affirmed this ruling. 638 F.2d 357, 380 (2d Cir.1980). And in Spencer Companies, Inc. v. Agency Rent-A-Car, Inc., 542 F.Supp. 237, [1982 Decisions] Fed. Sec. L. Rep. (CCH) ¶ 98,668 (D. Mass.1982), the Court disenfranchised Spencer from voting shares it had acquired while its misleading Schedule 13D was filed. This order was a preliminary injunction.

Hallwood Realty Partners, L.P. v. Gotham Partners, L.P.

286 F.3d 613 (2d Cir. 2002).

■ CALABRESI, CIRCUIT JUDGE:

Appellant Hallwood Realty Partners, L.P. ("Hallwood") brought this action asserting a violation of § 13(d) of the Securities and Exchange Act, 15U.S.C. § 78m(d). Specifically, Hallwood alleged that the defendants formed a group to purchase and amass Hallwood units for the purpose of effecting a take-over of Hallwood and substantially altering its business and operations, without disclosing their group, its activities, or its intentions in public filings, as required under § 13(d). Hallwood sought (i) various forms of injunctive relief; (ii) a declaratory judgment that the defendants, by forming a § 13(d) group, had become an "Acquiring Person" under the terms of Hallwood's "poison pill"; and (iii) an award of monetary damages. Hallwood also requested a jury trial.

The district court struck Hallwood's demand for a jury trial after holding that § 13(d) provides no cause of action for money damages and that Hallwood was not entitled to a jury trial on its injunctive and declaratory claims. Following a bench trial, the district court dismissed these equitable claims because it concluded that Hallwood had not proved the existence of a group of investors under § 13(d).

Hallwood appeals both decisions, arguing (1) that the district court improperly rejected circumstantial evidence in determining whether a § 13(d) group existed, and (2) that the court erred in denying Hallwood's jury demand. We affirm the judgment and order of the district court.

BACKGROUND

Hallwood is a limited partnership that acquires, owns, and operates commercial real estate. Hallwood units are traded on the American Stock Exchange. The various defendants in this case were purchasers of Hallwood units.

The defendants began acquiring Hallwood units in the early to mid 1990s. Each individual defendant claims to have made an independent decision to purchase units, based on due diligence and a common understanding among knowledgeable investors that Hallwood units were undervalued.

[The opinion describes the acquisitions of each of the defendants, Gotham Partners, L.P., Gotham Partners III, L.P., and Gotham Holdings II, L.L.C. (collectively, "Gotham"); Interstate Properties; PMG; and EFO/Liberty, Inc. The trial court ruled that Hallwood had failed to establish an agreement among these parties to acquire Hallwood stock.]

* * *

DISCUSSION

I.

[The court affirmed the trial court's finding of a failure to establish an agreement to acquire Hallwood's shares.]

* * *

II.

With regard to Hallwood's request for a jury trial based on its claim for damages under § 13(d), the district court observed:

> Section 13 does not explicitly create a cause of action for damages. Courts repeatedly have held that no such right of recovery may be inferred under Section 13 in favor of shareholders who rely to their detriment on false or misleading statements contained in, or material omissions from, filings under that statute. While few cases address the availability of damages to issuers for Section 13 violations, they indicate uniformly that there is no such right to relief.

Accordingly, the court concluded that Hallwood had "no colorable claim for damages under Section 13 of the Exchange Act" and therefore no right to a jury.

Hallwood contends that this ruling was in error, because a private cause of action for damages to issuers is implied under § 13(d). This question is one of first impression for our court.

Over the years, the Supreme Court has come to view the implication of private remedies in regulatory statutes with increasing disfavor. In 1964, in J.I. Case Co. v. Borak, 377 U.S. 426 (1964), the Court held that the broad remedial purpose of § 14(a) of the Securities Exchange Act was sufficient to give rise to a private right of action for damages. This approach was narrowed a decade later in Cort v. Ash, 422 U.S. 66 (1975), in which the Court set forth four factors to be considered in determining whether a private right of action is implicit in any given statute: (1) legislative intent, (2) the consistency of the remedy with the underlying purposes of the legislative scheme, (3) whether the plaintiff was a member of the class for whose benefit the statute was enacted, and (4) whether the cause of action is one traditionally relegated to state law. *Id.* at 78. Later, in cases such as Transamerica Mortgage Advisors, Inc. v. Lewis, 444 U.S. 11 (1979) and Touche Ross & Co. v. Redington, 442 U.S. 560 (1979), the Court focused the analysis on the single question of whether congressional intent to create a private cause of action can be found in the relevant statute.[18]

Courts in this circuit have consistently declined to imply a cause of action for shareholders under § 13(d). See, e.g., Kamerman v. Steinberg, 891 F.2d 424 (2d Cir. 1989) ("One complaining of a false or misleading statement in a Schedule 13D may seek damages only under Section 18(a) of the Act."); Sanders v. Thrall Car Mfg. Co., 582 F.Supp. 945 (S.D.N.Y. 1983) (noting that "courts have consistently refused to imply private rights of action for damages under § 13(d)"), aff'd, 730 F.2d 910 (2d Cir. 1984) (per curiam). . . .

Courts have identified various reasons for denying shareholders a private cause of action under § 13(d). First, the relevant legislative history reveals "an absence of legislative intent to imply a right of action under § 13(d)," particularly for money damages. Sanders, 582 F.Supp. at 960 (internal quotation marks omitted). Second, § 13(d) does not contain rights-creating language; it simply requires investors to file certain statements, see id., and "statutes that focus on the person regulated rather than the individuals protected create 'no implication of an intent to confer rights on a particular class of persons.'" Sandoval, 532 U.S. at 289 (quoting California v. Sierra Club, 451 U.S. 287 (1981)). Finally, courts have found significant the existence of an express remedy under § 18(a) of the Williams Act, available to those shareholders who can prove reliance on misleading filings. 15 U.S.C. § 78r(a); see Sanders, 582 F.Supp. at 960 (citing the presence of an express private remedy for damages under § 18(a) as a reason not to infer a cause of action for damages under § 13(d)); Myers, 402 F.Supp. at 214 (same); see also Touche Ross, 442 U.S. at 574 (in holding that there is no private cause of action under § 17(a) of the Williams Act, stating that "we are extremely

---

[18] As this circuit has explained, the remaining Cort factors (other than congressional intent) now enter into the analysis only as possible indicia for legislative intent. See Health Care Plan, Inc. v. Aetna Life Ins. Co., 966 F.2d 738, 740 (2d Cir. 1992).

reluctant to imply a cause of action . . . that is significantly broader that the remedy Congress chose to provide," particularly as "there is evidence to support the view that § 18(a) was intended to provide the exclusive remedy for misstatements contained in any reports filed with the Commission"); Olmsted, 283 F.3d 429, 433 ("Congress's explicit provision of a private right of action to enforce one section of a statute suggests that omission of an explicit private right to enforce other sections was intentional.").

Hallwood attempts to distinguish these cases by noting, first, that they all involve damages claims by shareholders, not issuers, and, as such, can be viewed as having been premised on the existence of § 18(a), an explicit damages remedy that is available to shareholders but not to issuers. Second, and more significantly, Hallwood stresses that this circuit has expressly held that issuers have a private cause of action under § 13(d) for injunctive relief. See GAS Corp. v. Milstein, 453 F.2d 709 (2d Cir. 1971) (holding that the issuer has a private cause of action and standing to sue for injunctive relief).

Hallwood then highlights the Supreme Court's statement that once an implied right of action is found, "we presume the availability of all appropriate remedies unless Congress has expressly indicated otherwise." Franklin v. Gwinnett County Pub. Sch., 503 U.S. 60 (1992). According to Hallwood, the holdings of GAF Corp. and Franklin taken together require that, absent clear congressional indications to the contrary, there must be a damages remedy for issuers under § 13(d).

We hold today that there are sufficient congressional indications to the contrary, and that, therefore, there is no private damages remedy for issuers under § 13(d). Cf. Salute, 136 F.3d at 299 n.4 (declining to imply a damages remedy under Franklin when doing so would frustrate the purposes of the statute). As in Salute, we find those indications in the purpose for which the relevant statute was enacted.

The aim of § 13(d) is to ensure that investors will be informed about purchases of large blocks of shares. See H.R. Rep. No. 90–1711, at 8 (1968), reprinted in 1968 U.S.C.C.A.N. 2811, 2818 ("The purpose of section 13(d) is to require disclosure of information by persons who have acquired a substantial interest, or increased their interest in the equity securities of a company by a substantial amount, within a relatively short period of time."); GAS Corp., 453 F.2d at 717 ("The purpose of section 13(d) is to alert the marketplace to every large, rapid aggregation or accumulation of securities, regardless of technique employed, which might represent a potential shift in corporate control. . . .").

In GAF Corp., we found that this congressional purpose was furthered by providing issuers with the right to sue "to enforce [the] duties created by [the] statute," as the issuer "unquestionably is in the best position to enforce section § 13(d). The statute requires a copy of the statement to be sent by registered mail to the issuer . . . and the issuer, in the course of constantly monitoring transactions in its stock, better than anyone else will know when there has been a failure to file." 453 F.2d at 719. This court, however, expressly distinguished money damages from such injunctive relief, which furthers the object of § 13(d) by increasing honest disclosure for the benefit of investors without placing incumbent management in a stronger position than aspiring control groups. We noted that we were recognizing the rights of issuers "seeking equitable or prophylactic relief—not monetary damages—to take the necessary steps to effectuate the purposes of section 13(d)." *Id.* at 720 n.22 (emphasis added). In other words, in GAF Corp. we recognized that issuers have a private cause of action and standing to sue for injunctive relief because, inter alia, such relief increases the accurate information available to investors, while at the same time recognizing, in dicta, that monetary damages for issuers would not similarly benefit investors.[19]

Moreover, an implied cause of action for damages not only does not serve the same aim as a cause of action for injunctive relief, but it also may actually frustrate congressional purposes. The legislative history of the Williams Act, of which § 13(d) is a part, makes clear that the Act was intended to assist shareholders while at the same time remaining "evenhanded" in any struggle between the issuer and entity purchasing large quantities of stock. See e.g., Rondeau v. Mosinee Paper Corp., 422 U.S. 49 (1975) ("Congress expressly disclaimed an intention to provide a weapon for management to discourage takeover bids or prevent large accumulations of stock which would create the potential for such attempts."); GAF Corp., 453 F.2d at 717 n.16 ("[It is] clear that the [Williams] Act was designed for the benefit of investors and not to tip the balance of regulation in favor of management or in favor of the person seeking corporate control."). We think it manifest that a damages remedy granted to issuers is likely to "tip the balance" between the two sides, while the issuer's ability to sue for injunctive relief does not do anything of the kind.

In Salute, we held that once we have determined that there is an implied cause of action, the question becomes "whether the general rule that federal courts may award all appropriate relief should . . . nevertheless yield where necessary to carry out the intent of Congress or

---

[19] Notably, four other circuits have followed this court's holding in GAF Corp. and recognized that issuers have a cause of action for injunctive relief, and none of these courts have to date granted issuers a cause of action for damages. See Chevron Corp. v. Pennzoil Co., 974 F.2d 1156, 1158 (9th Cir. 1992); Gearhart Indus., Inc. v. Smith Int'l, Inc., 741 F.2d 707, 714 (5th Cir. 1984); Ind. Nat'l. Corp. v. Rich, 712 F.2d 1180, 1184 (7th Cir. 1983); Dan River, Inc. v. Unitex Ltd., 624 F.2d 1216, 1224 (4th Cir. 1980); see also CNW Corp. v. Japonica Partners, 874 F.2d 193 (3rd Cir. 1989) (implicitly assuming the existence of a cause of action for injunctive relief without discussion); Chromalloy Am. Corp. v. Sun Chemical Corp., 611 F.2d 240 (8th Cir. 1979) (same); Gen. Aircraft Corp. v. Lampert, 556 F.2d 90, 94 n.5 (1st Cir. 1977) (explicitly assuming the existence of such a cause of action without deciding). But see Liberty Nat'l Ins. Holding Co. v. Charter Co., 734 F.2d 545, 555–59 (11th Cir. 1984) (holding that issuers have no cause of action for injunctive relief or damages under § 13(d)).

to avoid frustrating the purposes of the statute involved." 136 F.3d at 299 (internal quotation marks and citation omitted). Thus the Franklin presumption in favor of the availability of all remedies is not absolute, and must not be applied irrespective of congressional intent and purposes. Because a damages remedy for issuers contravenes the congressional purposes underlying the statute of which § 13(d) is a part, the general rule that federal courts award all appropriate relief does not apply. Cf. Transamerica, 444 U.S. at 19–25 (holding that Congress intended an implied right of action for certain injunctive relief but not for damages under the Investment Advisors Act of 1940). Accordingly, we affirm the district court's striking of Hallwood's jury demand.[20]

III.

We conclude that the district court properly considered circumstantial evidence in determining whether a 13(d) group existed. We also hold that the court was correct in concluding that 13(d) does not provide a damages remedy to issuers. Accordingly, we AFFIRM both the court's order of January 22, 2001, striking Hallwood's demand for a jury trial, and its February 28, 2001 judgment dismissing Hallwood's remaining claims for injunctive and declaratory relief.

QUESTION

1.   Would the result have been different if the court had applied the Cort v. Ash test?

Schreiber v. Burlington Northern, Inc.

472 U.S. 1, 105 S.Ct. 2458, 86 L.Ed.2d 1 (1985).

■ CHIEF JUSTICE BURGER delivered the opinion of the Court.

We granted certiorari to resolve a conflict in the Circuits over whether misrepresentation or nondisclosure is a necessary element of a violation of § 14(e) of the Securities Exchange Act of 1934, 15 U.S.C. § 78n(e).

---

[20]   In declining to hold that issuers may obtain damages, we in no way intend to cast doubt on the continued validity of GAF Corp. with respect to injunctive relief. Notably, the Supreme Court has not sought to reconsider the existence of causes of action, such as the right to injunctive relief recognized in GAF Corp., that were implied under the now dubious analysis of Borak. Cf. Merrill Lynch, Pierce, Fenner & Smith, Inc. v. Curran, 456 U.S. 353, 378–79, 72 L. Ed. 2d 182, 102 S. Ct. 1825 (1982) (on the effects of congressional reenactments of statutes following courts' findings of implied causes of action); Cannon v. Univ. of Chi., 441 U.S. 677, 698–99, 60 L. Ed. 2d 560, 99 S. Ct. 1946 (1979) (same).

I

On December 21, 1982, Burlington Northern, Inc., made a hostile tender offer for El Paso Gas Co. Through a wholly owned subsidiary, Burlington proposed to purchase 25.1 million El Paso shares at $24 per share. Burlington reserved the right to terminate the offer if any of several specified events occurred. El Paso management initially opposed the takeover, but its shareholders responded favorably, fully subscribing the offer by December 30, 1982 deadline.

Burlington did not accept those tendered shares; instead, after negotiations with El Paso management, Burlington announced on January 10, 1983, the terms of a new and friendly takeover agreement. Pursuant to the new agreement, Burlington undertook, inter alia, to (1) rescind the December tender offer, (2) purchase 4,166,667 shares from El Paso at $24 per share, (3) substitute a new tender offer for only 21 million shares at $24 per share, (4) provide procedural protections against a squeeze-out merger[1] of the remaining El Paso shareholders, and (5) recognize "golden parachute"[2] contracts between El Paso and four of its senior officers. By February 8, more than 40 million shares were tendered in response to Burlington's January offer, and the takeover was completed.

The rescission of the first tender offer caused a diminished payment to those shareholders who had tendered during the first offer. The January offer was greatly oversubscribed and consequently those shareholders who retendered were subject to substantial proration. Petitioner Barbara Schreiber filed suit on behalf of herself and similarly situated shareholders, alleging that Burlington, El Paso, and members of El Paso's board violated § 14(e)'s prohibition of "fraudulent, deceptive or manipulative acts or practices . . . in connection with any tender offer." 15 U.S.C. § 78n(e). She claimed that Burlington's withdrawal of the

---

[1] A "squeeze-out" merger occurs when Corporation A, which holds a controlling interest in Corporation B, uses its control to merge B into itself for into a wholly owned subsidiary. The minority shareholders in Corporation B are, in effect, forced to sell their stock. The procedural protection provided in the agreement between El Paso and Burlington required the approval of non-Burlington members of El Paso's board of directors before a squeeze-out merger could proceed. Burlington eventually purchased all the remaining shares of El Paso for $12 cash and one quarter share of Burlington preferred stock per share. The parties dispute whether this consideration was equal to that paid to those tendering during the January tender offer.

[2] Petitioner alleged in her complaint that respondent Burlington failed to disclose that four officers of El Paso had entered into "golden parachute" agreements with El Paso for "extended employment benefits in the event El Paso should be taken over, which benefits would give them millions of dollars of extra compensation." The term "golden parachute" refers generally to agreements between a corporation and its top officers which guarantee those officers continued employment, payment of a lump sum, or other benefits in the event of a change of corporate ownership. As described in the Schedule 14D–9 filed by El Paso with the Commission on January 12, 1983, El Paso entered into "employment agreements" with two of its officers for a period of not less than five years, and with two other officers for a period of three years. The Schedule 14D–9 also disclosed that El Paso Deferred Compensation Plan had been amended "to provide that for the purposes of such Plan a participant shall be deemed to have retired at the instance of the Company if his duties as a director, officer or employee of the Company have been diminished or curtailed by the Company in any material respect."

December tender offer coupled with the substitution of the January tender offer was a "manipulative" distortion of the market for El Paso stock. Schreiber also alleged that Burlington violated § 14(e) by failing in the January offer to disclose the "golden parachutes" offered to four of El Paso's managers. She claims that this January nondisclosure was a deceptive act forbidden by § 14(e).

The District Court dismissed the suit for failure to state a claim. 568 F.Supp. 197 (D.Del. 1983). The District Court reasoned that the alleged manipulation did not involve a misrepresentation, and so did not violate § 14(e). The District Court relied on the fact that in cases involving alleged violations of § 10(b) of the Securities Exchange Act, (15 U.S.C. § 78j(b)), this Court has required misrepresentation for there to be a "manipulative" violation of the section. 568 F.Supp., at 202.

The Court of Appeals for the Third Circuit affirmed. 731 F.2d 163 (1984). The Court of Appeals held that the acts alleged did not violate the Williams Act, because "§ 14(e) was not intended to create a federal cause of action for all harms suffered because of the proffering or the withdrawal of tender offers." *Id.*, at 165. The Court of Appeals reasoned that § 14(e) was "enacted principally as a disclosure statute, designed to insure that fully-informed investors could intelligently decide how to respond to tender offer." *Id.*, at 165–166. It concluded that the "arguable breach of contract" alleged by petitioner was not a "manipulative act" under § 14(e).

We granted certiorari to resolve the conflict, 469 U.S. 815 (1984). We affirm.

II

A

We are asked in this case to interpret § 14(e) of the Securities Exchange Act, 48 Stat. 895, as amended, 15 U.S.C. § 78n(e). The starting point is the language of the statute. Section 14(e) provides:

> "It shall be unlawful for any person to make any untrue statement of a material fact or omit to state any material fact necessary in order to make the statements made, in the light of the circumstances under which they are made, not misleading, or to engage in any fraudulent, deceptive or manipulative acts or practices, in connection with any tender offer or request or invitation for tenders, or any solicitation of security holders in opposition to or in favor of any such offer, request, or invitation. The Commission shall, for the purposes of this subsection, by rules and regulations define, and prescribe means reasonably designed to prevent, such acts and practices as are fraudulent, deceptive, or manipulative." 15 U.S.C. § 78n(e).

Petitioner relies on a construction of the phrase, "fraudulent, deceptive or manipulative acts or practices." Petitioner reads the phrase "fraudulent, deceptive or manipulative acts or practices" to include acts which, although fully disclosed, "artificially" affected the price of the takeover target's stock. Petitioner's interpretation relies on the belief that § 14(e) is directed at purposes broader than providing full and true information to investors.

Petitioner's reading of the term "manipulative" conflicts with the normal meaning of the term. We have held in the context of an alleged violation of § 10(b) of the Securities Exchange Act:

> "Use of the word 'manipulative' is especially significant. It is and was virtually a term of art when used in connection with the securities markets. It connotes intentional or willful conduct designed to deceive or defraud investors by controlling or artificially affecting the price of securities." Ernst & Ernst v. Hochfelder, 425 U.S. 185, 199 (1976) (emphasis added).

Other cases interpreting the term reflect its use as a general term comprising a range of misleading practices:

> "The term refers generally to practices, such as wash sales, matched orders, or rigged prices, that are intended to mislead investors by artificially affecting market activity. . . . Section 10(b)'s general prohibition of practices deemed by the SEC to be 'manipulative'—in this technical sense of artificially affecting market activity in order to mislead investors—is fully consistent with the fundamental purpose of the 1934 Act' " to substitute a philosophy of full disclosure for the philosophy of caveat emptor. . . . "Indeed, nondisclosure is usually essential to the success of a manipulative scheme. . . . No doubt Congress meant to prohibit the full range of ingenious devices that might be used to manipulate securities prices. But we do not think it would have chose this 'term of art' if it had meant to bring within the scope of § 10(b) instances of corporate mismanagement such as this, in which the essence of the complaint is that shareholders were treated unfairly by a fiduciary." Santa Fe Industries, Inc. v. Green, 430 U.S. 462, 476–477 (1977).

The meaning the Court has given the term "manipulative" is consistent with the use of the term at common law,[2] and with its traditional dictionary definition.[3]

---

[2] See generally, L. Loss, Securities Regulation 984–989 (3d ed. 1983). For example, the seminal English case of Scott v. Brown, Doering, McNab & Co., [1982] 2 Q. B. 724, 724 (C.A.), which broke new ground in recognizing that manipulation could occur without the dissemination of false statements, nonetheless placed emphasis on the presence of deception. As Lord Lopes stated in that case, "I can see no substantial distinction between false rumors and false and fictitious acts." Id., at 730. See also, United States v. Brown, 5 F.Supp. 81, 85 (S.D.N.Y.1933) ("[E]ven a speculator is entitled not to have any present fact involving the subject matter of his speculative purchase or the price thereof misrepresented by word or act").

[3] See Webster's Third New International Dictionary 1376 (1971) (Manipulation is "management with use of unfair, scheming, or underhanded methods").

She argues, however, that the term manipulative takes on a meaning in § 14(e) that is different from the meaning it has in § 10(b). Petitioner claims that the use of the disjunctive "or" in § 14(e) implies that acts need not be deceptive or fraudulent to be manipulative. But Congress used the phrase "manipulative or deceptive" in § 10(b) as well, and we have interpreted "manipulative" in that context to require misrepresentation.[4] Moreover, it is a " 'familiar principle of statutory construction that words grouped in a list should be given related meaning.' " Securities Indus. Assn. v. Board of Governors, 468 U.S. 207, (1984). All three species of misconduct, i.e., "fraudulent, deceptive or manipulative," listed by Congress are directed at failures to disclose. The use of the term "manipulative" provides emphasis and guidance to those who must determine which types of acts are reached by the statute; it does not suggest a deviation from the section's facial and primary concern with disclosure or Congressional concern with disclosure which is the core of the Act.

B

Our conclusion that "manipulative" acts under § 14(e) require misrepresentation or nondisclosure is buttressed by the purpose and legislative history of the provision. Section 14(e) was originally added to the Securities Exchange Act as part of the Williams Act, 82 Stat. 457. "The purpose of the Williams Act is to insure that public shareholders who are confronted by a cash tender offer for their stock will not be required to respond without adequate information." Rondeau v. Mosinee Paper Corp., 422 U.S. 49, 58 (1975).[5]

It is clear that Congress relied primarily on disclosure to implement the purpose of the Williams Act. Senator Williams, the Bill's Senate sponsor, stated in the debate:

"Today, the public shareholder in deciding whether to accept or reject a tender offer possesses limited information. No matter what he does, he acts without adequate knowledge to enable him to decide rationally what is the best course of action. This is precisely the dilemma which our securities laws are designed to prevent." 113 Cong. Rec. 24664 (1967) (Remarks of Sen. Williams).

The expressed legislative intent was to preserve a neutral setting in which the contenders could fully present their arguments.[6] The Senate sponsor went on to say:

---

[4]   Santa Fe Industries, Inc. v. Green, 430 U.S. 462, 476–477 (1977); Piper v. Chris-Craft Industries, 430 U.S. 1, 43 (1977); Ernst & Ernst v. Hochfelder, 425 U.S. 185, 199 (1976).

[5]   For a more thorough discussion of the legislative history of the Williams Act, see Piper v. Chris-Craft Industries, *supra*, at 24–37.

[6]   The process through which Congress developed the Williams Act also suggests a calculated reliance on disclosure, rather than court-imposed principles of "fairness" or "artificiality," as the preferred method of market regulation. For example, as the bill progressed through hearings, both Houses of Congress became concerned that corporate stock repurchases

"We have taken extreme care to avoid tipping the scales either in favor of management or in favor of the person making the takeover bids. S. 510 is designed solely to require full and fair disclosure for the benefit of investors. The bill will at the same time provide the offeror and management equal opportunity to present their case." *Ibid.*

To implement this objective, the Williams Act added §§ 13(d), 13(e), 14(d), 14(e), and 14(f) to the Securities Exchange Act. Some relate to disclosure; §§ 13(d), 14(d) and 14(f) all add specific registration and disclosure provisions. Others—§§ 13(e) and 14(d)—require or prohibit certain acts so that investors will possess additional time within which to take advantage of the disclosed information.

Section 14(e) adds a "broad antifraud prohibition," Piper v. Chris-Craft Industries, 430 U.S. 1, 24 (1977), modeled on the antifraud provisions of § 10(b) of the Act and Rule 10b–5, 17 CFR § 240.10b–5 (1984). It supplements the more precise disclosure provisions found elsewhere in the Williams Act, while requiring disclosure more explicitly addressed to the tender offer context than that required by § 10(b).

While legislative history specifically concerning § 14(e) is sparse, the House and Senate Reports discuss the role of § 14(e). Describing § 14(e) as regulating "fraudulent transactions," and stating the thrust of the section:

"This provision would affirm the fact that persons engaged in making or opposing tender offers or otherwise seeking to influence the decision of investors or the outcome of the tender offer are under an obligation to make full disclosure of material information to those with whom they deal." H. R. Rep. No. 1711, 90th Cong., 2d Sess., 11 (1968) (emphasis added); S. R. Rep. No. 550, 90th Cong., 1st Sess., 11 (1967) (emphasis added).

Nowhere in the legislative history is there the slightest suggestion that § 14(e) serves any purpose other than disclosure,[11] or that the term

---

could be used to distort the market for corporate control. Congress addressed this problem with § 13(e), which imposes specific disclosure duties on corporations purchasing stock and grants broad regulatory power to the Securities Exchange Commission to regulate such repurchases. Congress stopped short, however, of imposing specific substantive requirements forbidding corporations to trade in their own stock for the purpose of maintaining its price. The specific regulatory scheme set forth in § 13(e) would be unnecessary if Congress at the same time had endowed the term "manipulative" in § 14(e) with broad substantive significance.

[11] The Act was amended in 1970, and Congress added to § 14(e) the sentence, "The Commission shall, for the purposes of this subsection, by rules and regulations define, and prescribe means reasonable designed to prevent, such acts and practices as are fraudulent, deceptive, or manipulative." Petitioner argues that this phrase would be pointless if § 14(e) was concerned with disclosure only.

We disagree. In adding the 1970 amendment, Congress simply provided a mechanism for defining and guarding against those acts and practices which involve material misrepresentation or nondisclosure. The amendment gives the Securities and Exchange Commission latitude to regulate nondeceptive activities as a "reasonably designed" means of preventing manipulative acts, without suggesting any changes in the meaning of the term "manipulative" itself.

"manipulative" should be read as an invitation to the courts to oversee the substantive fairness of tender offers; the quality of any offer is a matter for the marketplace.

To adopt the reading of the term "manipulative" urged by petitioner would not only be unwarranted in light of the legislative purpose but would be at odds with it. Inviting judges to read the term "manipulative" with their own sense of what constitutes "unfair" or "artificial" conduct would inject uncertainty into the tender offer process. An essential piece of information—whether the court would deem the fully disclosed actions of one side or the other to be "manipulative"—would not be available until after the tender offer had closed. This uncertainty would directly contradict the expressed Congressional desire to give investors full information.

Congress' consistent emphasis on disclosure persuades us that it intended takeover contests to be addressed to shareholders. In pursuit of this goal, Congress, consistent with the core mechanism of the Securities Exchange Act, created sweeping disclosure requirements and narrow substantive safeguards. The same Congress that placed such emphasis on shareholder choice would not at the same time have required judges to oversee tender offers for substantive fairness. It is even less likely that a Congress implementing that intention would express it only through the use of a single word placed in the middle of a provision otherwise devoted to disclosure.

C

We hold that the term "manipulative" as used in § 14(e) requires misrepresentation or nondisclosure. It connotes "conduct designed to deceive or defraud investors by controlling or artificially affecting the price of securities." Ernst & Ernst v. Hochfelder, 425 U.S.; at 199. Without misrepresentation or nondisclosure, § 14(e) has not been violated.

Applying that definition to this case, we hold that the actions of respondents were not manipulative. The amended complaint fails to allege that the cancellation of the first tender offer was accompanied by any misrepresentation, nondisclosure or deception. The District Court correctly found, "All activity of the defendants that could have conceivably affected the price of El Paso shares was done openly." 568 F.Supp., at 203.

Petitioner also alleges that El Paso management and Burlington entered into certain undisclosed and deceptive agreements during the making of the second tender offer. The substance of the allegations is that, in return for certain undisclosed benefits, El Paso managers agreed to support the second tender offer. But both courts noted that petitioner's complaint seeks only redress only for injuries related to the cancellation of the first tender offer. Since the deceptive and misleading acts alleged by the petitioner all occurred with reference to the making of the second tender offer—when the injuries suffered by petitioner had already been sustained—these acts bear no possible causal relationship to petitioner's alleged injuries. The Court of Appeals dealt correctly with this claim.

III

The judgment of the Court of Appeals is

Affirmed.

QUESTIONS

1. Why would Burlington agree to terminate one tender offer and submit a new one? Note that Burlington is purchasing the same number of shares at the same price as in the earlier offer, with the only difference being that it will purchase some of them from El Paso.

2. In Ernst & Ernst v. Hochfelder, quoted by the court, the opinion defined "manipulative" to include conduct "designed to deceive or defraud investors by controlling or artificially affecting the price of securities." Doesn't the restructured agreement, which requires Burlington to purchase fewer shares from shareholders at $24, artificially affect the price of Burlington shares?

3. Is there a conflict between Ernst & Ernst v. Hochfelder and Santa Fe Industries, Inc. v. Green over the meaning of "manipulation"?

4. What significance does the plaintiff claim for the use of the disjunctive phrase "deceptive or manipulative"? What significance does the Court's opinion give to the fact that these phrases are grouped together? Which interpretation is more consistent with correct grammatical usage?

5. Review Securities Exchange Act Rule 14e–2, which requires target management to comment on a third party tender offer within ten days. Does this rule deal with a fraudulent, deceptive or manipulative act or practice, given the decisions in Schreiber and Basic Inc. v. Levinson?

United States v. O'Hagan

521 U.S. 642, 117 S.Ct. 2199, 138 L.Ed.2d 724 (1997).

■ JUSTICE GINSBURG delivered the opinion of the Court.

This case concerns the interpretation and enforcement of § 10(b) and § 14(e) of the Securities Exchange Act of 1934, and rules made by the Securities and Exchange Commission pursuant to these provisions, Rule 10b–5 and Rule 14e–3(a). Two prime questions are presented. The first relates to the misappropriation of material, nonpublic information for securities trading; the second concerns fraudulent practices in the tender offer setting. In particular, we address and resolve these issues: (1) Is a person who trades in securities for personal profit, using confidential information misappropriated in breach of a fiduciary duty to the source of the information, guilty of violating § 10(b) and Rule 10b–5? (2) Did the Commission exceed its rulemaking authority by adopting Rule 14e–3(a), which proscribes trading on undisclosed information in the tender offer setting, even in the absence of a duty to disclose? Our answer to the first question is yes, and to the second question, viewed in the context of this case, no.

I

Respondent James Herman O'Hagan was a partner in the law firm of Dorsey & Whitney in Minneapolis, Minnesota. In July 1988, Grand Metropolitan PLC (Grand Met), a company based in London, England, retained Dorsey & Whitney as local counsel to represent Grand Met regarding a potential tender offer for the common stock of the Pillsbury Company, headquartered in Minneapolis. Both Grand Met and Dorsey & Whitney took precautions to protect the confidentiality of Grand Met's tender offer plans. O'Hagan did no work on the Grand Met representation. Dorsey & Whitney withdrew from representing Grand Met on September 9, 1988. Less than a month later, on October 4, 1988, Grand Met publicly announced its tender offer for Pillsbury stock.

On August 18, 1988, while Dorsey & Whitney was still representing Grand Met, O'Hagan began purchasing call options for Pillsbury stock. Each option gave him the right to purchase 100 shares of Pillsbury stock by a specified date in September 1988. Later in August and in September, O'Hagan made additional purchases of Pillsbury call options. By the end of September, he owned 2,500 unexpired Pillsbury options, apparently more than any other individual investor. O'Hagan also purchased, in September 1988, some 5,000 shares of Pillsbury common stock, at a price just under $39 per share. When Grand Met announced its tender offer in October, the price of Pillsbury stock rose to nearly $60 per share. O'Hagan then sold his Pillsbury call options and common stock, making a profit of more than $4.3 million.

The Securities and Exchange Commission (SEC or Commission) initiated an investigation into O'Hagan's transactions, culminating in a 57-count indictment. The indictment alleged that O'Hagan defrauded his law firm and its client, Grand Met, by using for his own trading purposes material, nonpublic information regarding Grand Met's planned tender offer. According to the indictment, O'Hagan used the profits he gained through this trading to conceal his previous embezzlement and conversion of unrelated client trust funds.[2] O'Hagan was charged with 20 counts of mail fraud, in violation of 18 U.S.C. § 1341; 17 counts of securities fraud, in violation of § 10(b) of the Securities Exchange Act of

---

[2] O'Hagan was convicted of theft in state court, sentenced to 30 months' imprisonment, and fined. See State v. O'Hagan, 474 N. W. 2d 613, 615, 623 (Minn.App.1991). The Supreme Court of Minnesota disbarred O'Hagan from the practice of law. See In re O'Hagan, 450 N. W. 2d 571 (Minn.1990).

1934 (Exchange Act),and SEC Rule 10b–5; 17 counts of fraudulent trading in connection with a tender offer, in violation of § 14(e) of the Exchange Act, and SEC Rule 14e–3(a); and 3 counts of violating federal money laundering statutes. A jury convicted O'Hagan on all 57 counts, and he was sentenced to a 41-month term of imprisonment.

A divided panel of the Court of Appeals for the Eighth Circuit reversed all of O'Hagan's convictions. 92 F. 3d 612 (1996). Liability under § 10(b) and Rule 10b–5, the Eighth Circuit held, may not be grounded on the "misappropriation theory" of securities fraud on which the prosecution relied. The Court of Appeals also held that Rule 14e–3(a)— which prohibits trading while in possession of material, nonpublic information relating to a tender offer—exceeds the SEC's § 14(e) rulemaking authority because the rule contains no breach of fiduciary duty requirement. * * *

Decisions of the Courts of Appeals are in conflict on the propriety of the misappropriation theory under § 10(b) and Rule 10b–5, see *infra* this page and n. 3, and on the legitimacy of Rule 14e–3(a) under § 14(e), see *infra*, at 25. We granted certiorari, 519 U.S. (1997), and now reverse the Eighth Circuit's judgment.

II

We address first the Court of Appeals' reversal of O'Hagan's convictions under § 10(b) and Rule 10b–5. Following the Fourth Circuit's lead, see United States v. Bryan, 58 F. 3d 933, 943–959 (1995), the Eighth Circuit rejected the misappropriation theory as a basis for § 10(b) liability. We hold, in accord with several other Courts of Appeals,[3] that criminal liability under § 10(b) may be predicated on the misappropriation theory.[4]

A

* * *

Liability under Rule 10b–5, our precedent indicates, does not extend beyond conduct encompassed by § 10(b)'s prohibition. See Ernst & Ernst v. Hochfelder, 425 U.S. 185, 214 (1976) (scope of Rule 10b–5 cannot exceed power Congress granted Commission under § 10(b)); see also Central Bank of Denver, N. A. v. First Interstate Bank of Denver, N. A.,

---

[3] See, e.g., United States v. Chestman, 947 F.2d 551, 566 (C.A.2 1991) (en banc), cert. denied, 503 U.S. 1004 (1992); SEC v. Cherif, 933 F.2d 403, 410 (C.A.7 1991), cert. denied, 502 U.S. 1071 (1992); SEC v. Clark, 915 F.2d 439, 453 (C.A.9 1990).

[4] Twice before we have been presented with the question whether criminal liability for violation of § 10(b) may be based on a misappropriation theory. In Chiarella v. United States, 445 U.S. 222, 235–237 (1980), the jury had received no misappropriation theory instructions, so we declined to address the question. See *infra*, at 17. In Carpenter v. United States, 484 U.S. 19, 24 (1987), the Court divided evenly on whether, under the circumstances of that case, convictions resting on the misappropriation theory should be affirmed. See Aldave, The Misappropriation Theory: Carpenter and Its Aftermath, 49 Ohio St. L. J. 373, 375 (1988) (observing that "Carpenter was, by any reckoning, an unusual case," for the information there misappropriated belonged not to a company preparing to engage in securities transactions, e.g., a bidder in a corporate acquisition, but to the Wall Street Journal).

511 U.S. 164, 173 (1994) ("We have refused to allow [private] 10b–5 challenges to conduct not prohibited by the text of the statute.").

Under the "traditional" or "classical theory" of insider trading liability, § 10(b) and Rule 10b–5 are violated when a corporate insider trades in the securities of his corporation on the basis of material, nonpublic information. Trading on such information qualifies as a "deceptive device" under § 10(b), we have affirmed, because "a relationship of trust and confidence [exists] between the shareholders of a corporation and those insiders who have obtained confidential information by reason of their position with that corporation." Chiarella v. United States, 445 U.S. 222, 228 (1980). That relationship, we recognized, "gives rise to a duty to disclose [or to abstain from trading] because of the 'necessity of preventing a corporate insider from . . . taking unfair advantage of . . . uninformed . . . stockholders.' " (citation omitted). The classical theory applies not only to officers, directors, and other permanent insiders of a corporation, but also to attorneys, accountants, consultants, and others who temporarily become fiduciaries of a corporation. See Dirks v. SEC, 463 U.S. 646, 655, n. 14 (1983).

The "misappropriation theory" holds that a person commits fraud "in connection with" a securities transaction, and thereby violates § 10(b) and Rule 10b–5, when he misappropriates confidential information for securities trading purposes, in breach of a duty owed to the source of the information. Under this theory, a fiduciary's undisclosed, self-serving use of a principal's information to purchase or sell securities, in breach of a duty of loyalty and confidentiality, defrauds the principal of the exclusive use of that information. In lieu of premising liability on a fiduciary relationship between company insider and purchaser or seller of the company's stock, the misappropriation theory premises liability on a fiduciary-turned-trader's deception of those who entrusted him with access to confidential information.

* * *

In this case, the indictment alleged that O'Hagan, in breach of a duty of trust and confidence he owed to his law firm, Dorsey & Whitney, and to its client, Grand Met, traded on the basis of nonpublic information regarding Grand Met's planned tender offer for Pillsbury common stock. This conduct, the Government charged, constituted a fraudulent device in connection with the purchase and sale of securities.

B

We agree with the Government that misappropriation, as just defined, satisfies § 10(b)'s requirement that chargeable conduct involve a "deceptive device or contrivance" used "in connection with" the purchase or sale of securities. We observe, first, that misappropriators, as the Government describes them, deal in deception. A fiduciary who "[pretends] loyalty to the principal while secretly converting the principal's information for personal gain," Brief for United States 17, "dupes" or defrauds the principal. See Aldave, Misappropriation: A General Theory of Liability for Trading on Nonpublic Information, 13 Hofstra L. Rev. 101, 119 (1984).

* * *

Deception through nondisclosure is central to the theory of liability for which the Government seeks recognition. As counsel for the Government stated in explanation of the theory at oral argument: "To satisfy the common law rule that a trustee may not use the property that [has] been entrusted [to] him, there would have to be consent. To satisfy the requirement of the Securities Act that there be no deception, there would only have to be disclosure." Tr. of Oral Arg. 12; see generally Restatement (Second) of Agency §§ 390, 395 (1958) (agent's disclosure obligation regarding use of confidential information).[6]

* * *

We turn next to the § 10(b) requirement that the misappropriator's deceptive use of information be "in connection with the purchase or sale of [a] security." This element is satisfied because the fiduciary's fraud is consummated, not when the fiduciary gains the confidential information, but when, without disclosure to his principal, he uses the information to purchase or sell securities. The securities transaction and the breach of duty thus coincide. This is so even though the person or entity defrauded is not the other party to the trade, but is, instead, the source of the nonpublic information. See Aldave, 13 Hofstra L. Rev., at 120 ("a fraud or deceit can be practiced on one person, with resultant harm to another person or group of persons"). A misappropriator who trades on the basis of material, nonpublic information, in short, gains his advantageous market position through deception; he deceives the source of the information and simultaneously harms members of the investing public.

The misappropriation theory targets information of a sort that misappropriators ordinarily capitalize upon to gain no-risk profits through the purchase or sale of securities. Should a misappropriator put such information to other use, the statute's prohibition would not be implicated. The theory does not catch all conceivable forms of fraud involving confidential information; rather, it catches fraudulent means of capitalizing on such information through securities transactions.

The Government notes another limitation on the forms of fraud § 10(b) reaches: "The misappropriation theory would not . . . apply to a case in which a person defrauded a bank into giving him a loan or embezzled cash from another, and then used the proceeds of the misdeed

---

[6]   Under the misappropriation theory urged in this case, the disclosure obligation runs to the source of the information, here, Dorsey & Whitney and Grand Met. Chief Justice Burger, dissenting in Chiarella, advanced a broader reading of § 10(b) and Rule 10b–5; the disclosure obligation, as he envisioned it, ran to those with whom the misappropriator trades. 445 U.S., at 240 ("a person who has misappropriated nonpublic information has an absolute duty to disclose that information or to refrain from trading"); see also id., at 243, n. 4. The Government does not propose that we adopt a misappropriation theory of that breadth.

to purchase securities." Brief for United States 24, n. 13. In such a case, the Government states, "the proceeds would have value to the malefactor apart from their use in a securities transaction, and the fraud would be complete as soon as the money was obtained." Ibid. In other words, money can buy, if not anything, then at least many things; its misappropriation may thus be viewed as sufficiently detached from a subsequent securities transaction that § 10(b)'s "in connection with" requirement would not be met. Ibid.

* * *

The misappropriation theory comports with § 10(b)'s language, which requires deception "in connection with the purchase or sale of any security," not deception of an identifiable purchaser or seller. The theory is also well-tuned to an animating purpose of the Exchange Act: to insure honest securities markets and thereby promote investor confidence. See 45 Fed. Reg. 60412 (1980) (trading on misappropriated information "undermines the integrity of, and investor confidence in, the securities markets"). Although informational disparity is inevitable in the securities markets, investors likely would hesitate to venture their capital in a market where trading based on misappropriated nonpublic information is unchecked by law. An investor's informational disadvantage vis-a-vis a misappropriator with material, nonpublic information stems from contrivance, not luck; it is a disadvantage that cannot be overcome with research or skill. See Brudney, Insiders, Outsiders, and Informational Advantages Under the Federal Securities Laws, 93 Harv. L. Rev. 322, 356 (1979) ("If the market is thought to be systematically populated with . . . transactors [trading on the basis of misappropriated information] some investors will refrain from dealing altogether, and others will incur costs to avoid dealing with such transactors or corruptly to overcome their unerodable informational advantages."); Aldave, 13 Hofstra L. Rev., at 122–123.

In sum, considering the inhibiting impact on market participation of trading on misappropriated information, and the congressional purposes underlying § 10(b), it makes scant sense to hold a lawyer like O'Hagan a § 10(b) violator if he works for a law firm representing the target of a tender offer, but not if he works for a law firm representing the bidder. The text of the statute requires no such result.[9] The misappropriation at issue here was properly made the subject of a § 10(b) charge because it

---

[9] As noted earlier, however, see *supra,* at 9–10, the textual requirement of deception precludes § 10(b) liability when a person trading on the basis of nonpublic information has disclosed his trading plans to, or obtained authorization from, the principal—even though such conduct may affect the securities markets in the same manner as the conduct reached by the misappropriation theory. Contrary to the dissent's suggestion, see *post,* at 11–13, the fact that § 10(b) is only a partial antidote to the problems it was designed to alleviate does not call into question its prohibition of conduct that falls within its textual proscription. Moreover, once a disloyal agent discloses his imminent breach of duty, his principal may seek appropriate equitable relief under state law. Furthermore, in the context of a tender offer, the principal who authorizes an agent's trading on confidential information may, in the Commission's view, incur liability for an Exchange Act violation under Rule 14e–3(a).

meets the statutory requirement that there be "deceptive" conduct "in connection with" securities transactions.

* * *

III

We consider next the ground on which the Court of Appeals reversed O'Hagan's convictions for fraudulent trading in connection with a tender offer, in violation of § 14(e) of the Exchange Act and SEC Rule 14e–3(a). A sole question is before us as to these convictions: Did the Commission, as the Court of Appeals held, exceed its rulemaking authority under § 14(e) when it adopted Rule 14e–3(a) without requiring a showing that the trading at issue entailed a breach of fiduciary duty? We hold that the Commission, in this regard and to the extent relevant to this case, did not exceed its authority.

The governing statutory provision, § 14(e) of the Exchange Act, reads in relevant part:

> "It shall be unlawful for any person ... to engage in any fraudulent, deceptive, or manipulative acts or practices, in connection with any tender offer.... The [SEC] shall, for the purposes of this subsection, by rules and regulations define, and prescribe means reasonably designed to prevent, such acts and practices as are fraudulent, deceptive, or manipulative." 15 U. S. C. § 78n(e).

Section 14(e)'s first sentence prohibits fraudulent acts in connection with a tender offer. This self-operating proscription was one of several provisions added to the Exchange Act in 1968 by the Williams Act, 82 Stat. 454. The section's second sentence delegates definitional and prophylactic rulemaking authority to the Commission. Congress added this rulemaking delegation to § 14(e) in 1970 amendments to the Williams Act. See § 5, 84 Stat. 1497.

Through § 14(e) and other provisions on disclosure in the Williams Act, Congress sought to ensure that shareholders "confronted by a cash tender offer for their stock [would] not be required to respond without adequate information." Rondeau v. Mosinee Paper Corp., 422 U.S. 49, 58 (1975); see Lewis v. McGraw, 619 F.2d 192, 195 (C.A.2 1980) (per curiam) ("very purpose" of Williams Act was "informed decisionmaking by shareholders"). As we recognized in Schreiber v. Burlington Northern, Inc., 472 U.S. 1 (1985), Congress designed the Williams Act to make "disclosure, rather than court-imposed principles of 'fairness' or 'artificiality,' ... the preferred method of market regulation." Section 14(e), we explained, "supplements the more precise disclosure provisions found elsewhere in the Williams Act, while requiring disclosure more explicitly addressed to the tender offer context than that required by § 10(b)."

Relying on § 14(e)'s rulemaking authorization, the Commission, in 1980, promulgated Rule 14e–3(a). That measure provides:

"(a) If any person has taken a substantial step or steps to commence, or has commenced, a tender offer (the 'offering person'), it shall constitute a fraudulent, deceptive or manipulative act or practice within the meaning of section 14(e) of the [Exchange] Act for any other person who is in possession of material information relating to such tender offer which information he knows or has reason to know is nonpublic and which he knows or has reason to know has been acquired directly or indirectly from:

"(1) The offering person,

"(2) The issuer of the securities sought or to be sought by such tender offer, or

"(3) Any officer, director, partner or employee or any other person acting on behalf of the offering person or such issuer, to purchase or sell or cause to be purchased or sold any of such securities or any securities convertible into or exchangeable for any such securities or any option or right to obtain or to dispose of any of the foregoing securities, unless within a reasonable time prior to any purchase or sale such information and its source are publicly disclosed by press release or otherwise." 17 CFR § 240.14e–3(a) (1996).

As characterized by the Commission, Rule 14e–3(a) is a "disclose or abstain from trading" requirement. 45 Fed. Reg. 60410 (1980).[15] The Second Circuit concisely described the rule's thrust:

"One violates Rule 14e–3(a) if he trades on the basis of material nonpublic information concerning a pending tender offer that he knows or has reason to know has been acquired 'directly or indirectly' from an insider of the offeror or issuer, or someone working on their behalf. Rule 14e–3(a) is a disclosure provision. It creates a duty in those traders who fall within its ambit to abstain or disclose, without regard to whether the trader owes a pre-existing fiduciary duty to respect the confidentiality of the information." United States v. Chestman, 947 F.2d 551, 557 (1991) (en banc) (emphasis added), cert. denied, 503 U.S. 1004 (1992).

* * *

In the Eighth Circuit's view, because Rule 14e–3(a) applies whether or not the trading in question breaches a fiduciary duty, the regulation

---

[15]   The rule thus adopts for the tender offer context a requirement resembling the one Chief Justice Burger would have adopted in Chiarella for misappropriators under § 10(b). See *supra*, at 10, n. 6.

exceeds the SEC's § 14(e) rulemaking authority. In support of its holding, the Eighth Circuit relied on the text of § 14(e) and our decisions in Schreiber and Chiarella. See 92 F. 3d, at 624–627.

The Eighth Circuit homed in on the essence of § 14(e)'s rulemaking authorization: "The statute empowers the SEC to 'define' and 'prescribe means reasonably designed to prevent' 'acts and practices' which are 'fraudulent.' " All that means, the Eighth Circuit found plain, is that the SEC may "identify and regulate," in the tender offer context, "acts and practices" the law already defines as "fraudulent"; but, the Eighth Circuit maintained, the SEC may not "create its own definition of fraud." Ibid. (internal quotation marks omitted).

This Court, the Eighth Circuit pointed out, held in Schreiber that the word "manipulative" in the § 14(e) phrase "fraudulent, deceptive, or manipulative acts or practices" means just what the word means in § 10(b): Absent misrepresentation or nondisclosure, an act cannot be indicted as manipulative. See 92 F. 3d, at 625 (citing Schreiber, 472 U.S., at 7–8, and n. 6). Section 10(b) interpretations guide construction of § 14(e), the Eighth Circuit added, see 92 F. 3d, at 625, citing this Court's acknowledgment in Schreiber that § 14(e)'s " 'broad antifraud prohibition' . . . [is] modeled on the antifraud provisions of § 10(b) . . . and Rule 10b–5," 472 U.S., at 10 (citation omitted); see id., at 10–11, n. 10.

For the meaning of "fraudulent" under § 10(b), the Eighth Circuit looked to Chiarella. See 92 F. 3d, at 625. In that case, the Eighth Circuit recounted, this Court held that a failure to disclose information could be "fraudulent" under § 10(b) only when there was a duty to speak arising out of " 'a fiduciary or other similar relationship of trust and confidence.' " Chiarella, 445 U.S., at 228 (quoting Restatement (Second) of Torts § 551(2)(a) (1976)). Just as § 10(b) demands a showing of a breach of fiduciary duty, so such a breach is necessary to make out a § 14(e) violation, the Eighth Circuit concluded.

As to the Commission's § 14(e) authority to "prescribe means reasonably designed to prevent" fraudulent acts, the Eighth Circuit stated: "Properly read, this provision means simply that the SEC has broad regulatory powers in the field of tender offers, but the statutory terms have a fixed meaning which the SEC cannot alter by way of an administrative rule." 92 F. 3d, at 627.

The United States urges that the Eighth Circuit's reading of § 14(e) misapprehends both the Commission's authority to define fraudulent acts and the Commission's power to prevent them. "The 'defining' power," the United States submits, "would be a virtual nullity were the SEC not permitted to go beyond common law fraud (which is separately prohibited in the first [self-operative] sentence of Section 14(e))."

In maintaining that the Commission's power to define fraudulent acts under § 14(e) is broader than its rulemaking power under § 10(b), the United States questions the Court of Appeals' reading of Schreiber.

Parenthetically, the United States notes that the word before the Schreiber Court was "manipulative"; unlike "fraudulent," the United States observes, "manipulative" . . . is "virtually a term of art when used in connection with the securities markets." Most tellingly, the United States submits, Schreiber involved acts alleged to violate the self-operative provision in § 14(e)'s first sentence, a sentence containing language similar to § 10(b). But § 14(e)'s second sentence, containing the rulemaking authorization, the United States points out, does not track § 10(b), which simply authorizes the SEC to proscribe "manipulative or deceptive devices or contrivances." Brief for United States 38. Instead, § 14(e)'s rulemaking prescription tracks § 15(c)(2)(D) of the Exchange Act, which concerns the conduct of broker-dealers in over-the-counter markets. Since 1938 § 15(c)(2) has given the Commission authority to "define, and prescribe means reasonably designed to prevent, such [broker-dealer] acts and practices as are fraudulent, deceptive, or manipulative." When Congress added this same rulemaking language to § 14(e) in 1970, the Government states, the Commission had already used its § 15(c)(2) authority to reach beyond common law fraud.[16]

We need not resolve in this case whether the Commission's authority under § 14(e) to "define . . . such acts and practices as are fraudulent" is broader than the Commission's fraud-defining authority under § 10(b), for we agree with the United States that Rule 14e–3(a), as applied to cases of this genre, qualifies under § 14(e) as a "means reasonably designed to prevent" fraudulent trading on material, nonpublic information in the tender offer context.[17] A prophylactic measure, because its mission is to prevent, typically encompasses more than the core activity prohibited. As we noted in Schreiber, § 14(e)'s rulemaking authorization gives the Commission "latitude," even in the context of a term of art like "manipulative," "to regulate nondeceptive activities as a 'reasonably designed' means of preventing manipulative acts, without suggesting any change in the meaning of the term 'manipulative' itself."

---

[16] The Government draws our attention to the following measures: 17 CFR § 240.15c2–1 (1970) (prohibiting a broker-dealer's hypothecation of a customer's securities if hypothecated securities would be commingled with the securities of another customer, absent written consent); § 240.15c2–3 (1970) (prohibiting transactions by broker-dealers in unvalidated German securities); § 240.15c2–4 (1970) (prohibiting broker-dealers from accepting any part of the sale price of a security being distributed unless the money received is promptly transmitted to the persons entitled to it); § 240.15c2–5 (1970) (requiring broker-dealers to provide written disclosure of credit terms and commissions in connection with securities sales in which broker-dealers extend credit, or participate in arranging for loans, to the purchasers). See Brief for United States 39, n. 22.

[17] We leave for another day, when the issue requires decision, the legitimacy of Rule 14e–3(a) as applied to "warehousing," which the Government describes as "the practice by which bidders leak advance information of a tender offer to allies and encourage them to purchase the target company's stock before the bid is announced." Reply Brief 17. As we observed in Chiarella, one of the Commission's purposes in proposing Rule 14e–3(a) was "to bar warehousing under its authority to regulate tender offers." 445 U.S., at 234. The Government acknowledges that trading authorized by a principal breaches no fiduciary duty. See Reply Brief 17. The instant case, however, does not involve trading authorized by a principal; therefore, we need not here decide whether the Commission's proscription of warehousing falls within its § 14(e) authority to define or prevent fraud.

472 U.S., at 11, n. 11. We hold, accordingly, that under § 14(e), the Commission may prohibit acts, not themselves fraudulent under the common law or § 10(b), if the prohibition is "reasonably designed to prevent . . . acts and practices [that] are fraudulent." 15 U.S.C. § 78n(e).

Because Congress has authorized the Commission, in § 14(e), to prescribe legislative rules, we owe the Commission's judgment "more than mere deference or weight." Batterton v. Francis, 432 U.S. 416, 424–426 (1977). Therefore, in determining whether Rule 14e–3(a)'s "disclose or abstain from trading" requirement is reasonably designed to prevent fraudulent acts, we must accord the Commission's assessment "controlling weight unless [it is] arbitrary, capricious, or manifestly contrary to the statute." Chevron U.S.A. Inc. v. Natural Resources Defense Council, Inc., 467 U.S. 837, 844 (1984). In this case, we conclude, the Commission's assessment is none of these.[19]

In adopting the "disclose or abstain" rule, the SEC explained:

"The Commission has previously expressed and continues to have serious concerns about trading by persons in possession of material, nonpublic information relating to a tender offer. This practice results in unfair disparities in market information and market disruption. Security holders who purchase from or sell to such persons are effectively denied the benefits of disclosure and the substantive protections of the Williams Act. If furnished with the information, these security holders would be able to make an informed investment decision, which could involve deferring the purchase or sale of the securities until the material information had been disseminated or until the tender offer has been commenced or terminated." 45 Fed. Reg. 60412 (1980) (footnotes omitted).

The Commission thus justified Rule 14e–3(a) as a means necessary and proper to assure the efficacy of Williams Act protections.

The United States emphasizes that Rule 14e–3(a) reaches trading in which "a breach of duty is likely but difficult to prove." Reply Brief 16. "Particularly in the context of a tender offer," as the Tenth Circuit recognized, "there is a fairly wide circle of people with confidential information," Peters, 978 F.2d, at 1167, notably, the attorneys, investment bankers, and accountants involved in structuring the transaction. The availability of that information may lead to abuse, for

---

[19] The dissent urges that the Commission must be precise about the authority it is exercising—that it must say whether it is acting to "define" or to "prevent" fraud—and that in this instance it has purported only to define, not to prevent. See post, at 18–19. The dissent sees this precision in Rule 14e–3(a)'s words: "it shall constitute a fraudulent . . . act . . . within the meaning of section 14(e). . . ." We do not find the Commission's rule vulnerable for failure to recite as a regulatory preamble: We hereby exercise our authority to "define, and prescribe means reasonably designed to prevent, . . . [fraudulent] acts." Sensibly read, the rule is an exercise of the Commission's full authority. Logically and practically, such a rule may be conceived and defended, alternatively, as definitional or preventive.

"even a hint of an upcoming tender offer may send the price of the target company's stock soaring." SEC v. Materia, 745 F.2d 197, 199 (C.A.2 1984). Individuals entrusted with nonpublic information, particularly if they have no long-term loyalty to the issuer, may find the temptation to trade on that information hard to resist in view of "the very large short-term profits potentially available [to them]." Peters, 978 F.2d, at 1167.

"It may be possible to prove circumstantially that a person [traded on the basis of material, nonpublic information], but almost impossible to prove that the trader obtained such information in breach of a fiduciary duty owed either by the trader or by the ultimate insider source of the information." Ibid. The example of a "tippee" who trades on information received from an insider illustrates the problem. Under Rule 10b–5, "a tippee assumes a fiduciary duty to the shareholders of a corporation not to trade on material nonpublic information only when the insider has breached his fiduciary duty to the shareholders by disclosing the information to the tippee and the tippee knows or should know that there has been a breach." Dirks, 463 U.S., at 660. To show that a tippee who traded on nonpublic information about a tender offer had breached a fiduciary duty would require proof not only that the insider source breached a fiduciary duty, but that the tippee knew or should have known of that breach. "Yet, in most cases, the only parties to the [information transfer] will be the insider and the alleged tippee." Peters, 978 F.2d, at 1167.

In sum, it is a fair assumption that trading on the basis of material, nonpublic information will often involve a breach of a duty of confidentiality to the bidder or target company or their representatives. The SEC, cognizant of the proof problem that could enable sophisticated traders to escape responsibility, placed in Rule 14e–3(a) a "disclose or abstain from trading" command that does not require specific proof of a breach of fiduciary duty. That prescription, we are satisfied, applied to this case, is a "means reasonably designed to prevent" fraudulent trading on material, nonpublic information in the tender offer context. See Chestman, 947 F.2d, at 560 ("While dispensing with the subtle problems of proof associated with demonstrating fiduciary breach in the problematic area of tender offer insider trading, [Rule 14e–3(a)] retains a close nexus between the prohibited conduct and the statutory aims."); accord, Maio, 51 F. 3d, at 635, and n. 14; Peters, 978 F.2d, at 1167. Therefore, insofar as it serves to prevent the type of misappropriation charged against O'Hagan, Rule 14e–3(a) is a proper exercise of the Commission's prophylactic power under § 14(e).

* * *

The judgment of the Court of Appeals for the Eighth Circuit is reversed, and the case is remanded for further proceedings consistent with this opinion.

It is so ordered.

■ JUSTICE SCALIA, concurring in part and dissenting in part.

I join Parts I, III, and IV of the Court's opinion. I do not agree, however, with Part II of the Court's opinion, containing its analysis of respondent's convictions under § 10(b) and Rule 10b–5.

* * *

■ JUSTICE THOMAS, with whom the CHIEF JUSTICE joins, concurring in the judgment in part and dissenting in part. * * *

QUESTIONS

1. Under the court's explanation of the misappropriation theory, who is defrauded by O'Hagan?

2. How is O'Hagan's fraud connected to a securities transaction? Does O'Hagan's law firm have a cause of action against him under the securities laws?

3. Why wouldn't an embezzler from a bank be liable for a 10b–5 violation if the embezzled funds were used to purchase securities?

4. Can an investor purchase target shares without disclosure if another investor has informed him that it intends to purchase over 5% of the target's shares and file a Schedule 13D, without stating any intent to make a tender offer? Aside from disclosure considerations under § 13(d)(3), if the two were treated as a group, would the recipient of such a "tip" have any other disclosure obligations, if not in a fiduciary relationship with either the target or the potential bidder?

5. Would it matter if the recipient of information in question 4 had received permission to use this information for his own trading? See footnote 17 in the majority's opinion.

6. The majority opinion states that the misappropriation theory is well-tuned to insuring honest security markets. As between O'Hagan and Grand Metropolitan, if both buy Pillsbury stock without disclosure, how does application of Rule 10b–5 to O'Hagan protect honest securities markets? Do Grand Metropolitan's market purchases offend honest securities markets? Why or why not?

7. Rule 10b–5, in such cases as Chiarella v. United States (classical theory) and O'Hagan (misappropriation theory), seems to require some breach of a pre-existing duty, whether to an employer, a prospective bidder, a target, or to target shareholders before liability attaches. Does Rule 14e–3 have the same requirement? Does the language of § 14(e) differ from that of § 10(b) in such a manner that makes it clear that no duty is required for a violation?

8. Does the court find that Rule 14e–3 directly addresses fraudulent conduct? Is any breach of duty required for a violation? Is any deceptive conduct required for a violation?

9. Suppose a brokerage firm learns that a buyer of stock (not a client of the broker) is rapidly accumulating an amount in excess of 5%, and correctly infers that the buyer is planning a tender offer. Can the broker purchase shares in anticipation of a tender offer at a higher price without disclosing that information?

10. Suppose that a person in an elevator hears part of a conversation that reveals that a tender offer will be made for a corporation. Can that person purchase the target's shares without disclosing this information?

11. Could O'Hagan, upon learning of Grand Metropolitan's plans, have sold that information to Pillsbury management without violating either Rule 10b–5 or 14e–3?

_____

PROBLEM

Your client has signed a confidentiality agreement with a potential target of an acquisition. The agreement simply provides that your client will treat non-public information revealed to it as confidential, and will return all documents to the potential target if an acquisition agreement is not reached within a specified amount of time. There is no provision prohibiting the acquisition of shares contained in the agreement. Your client learns of material information in this review, concerning research projects of the target and its new products plans. At the end of this process, the client is unable to reach agreement with the target's management about the terms of an acquisition.

Your client now wants to consider a hostile tender offer for the target. Can it do so?

APPENDIX A

GLOSSARY

Acquiring Person. A defined term in "rights agreements" (see "Poison Pill," *infra*) to describe a bidder once it acquires a specified percentage of target shares, and typically triggers "flip-in" rights (see below).

Any-and-All Bid. An offer to buy all of the shares tendered to a bid, which avoids the charge that a two-tier bid may be "coercive" because shares not taken by the bidder may be treated differently (worse). (See *"Two-tier bid," infra.*)

Arbitrageur. A professional investor that purchases stock in a target company with the expectation of tendering to a takeover bid and reselling at a profit. The arbitrageur, or "arb," bears the risk that the bid will fail and that there will be no resale at a higher price. This is called "risk arbitrage" to distinguish it from classic "riskless arbitrage," where an investor buys a security in one market and simultaneously sells the same security in another market at a higher price.

Bear Hug. A letter from a bidder to target management making an offer for its shares, generally without initial public disclosure.

Bidder. The prospective buyer of a controlling interest in another corporation (see *Target*), often through a tender offer.

Break-Up Fee. A fee paid by a party to be acquired by agreement (Target) in the event the Target is unable to complete the agreement because it is acquired by another buyer.

Bust Up Takeover. A takeover where the buyer intends to sell of all or a significant part of the Target's assets after the acquisition. Often used pejoratively by target managers and their representatives.

Continuing Directors. A defined term used both in shark repellents and poison pills (see Poison Pill, *infra*). Typically the directors in place at the time of adoption of a shark repellent amendment or a poison pill are the "continuing directors," as are those successors nominated by a majority of the continuing directors then in office. Where this term is employed, only Continuing Directors have the power to waive the barriers of the takeover defense for a bidder.

Crown Jewel. One of a target's most valuable or significant assets.

Dead Hand Poison Pill. A poison pill with a provision that it can only be redeemed by the affirmative vote of a majority of the "continuing directors." This means that even if a bidder engages in a successful proxy fight to remove and replace the board of directors, it cannot redeem the rights for the balance of their term.

Distribution Date. The date, in a rights agreement, upon which rights to purchase target shares separate from the common stock, and rights certificates are distributed to the target shareholders (excluding the bidder).

Dual Class Voting Plan. A plan by which some shares of common stock receive more votes than others. This requires a charter amendment. It may divide the shares into two classes, with management electing to obtain shares with more than one vote per share, while public shareholders elect shares with one vote, typically in exchange for a higher dividend. In some cases all shares begin with a large number of votes, but convert to single-vote shares upon transfer.

ESOP. An Employee Stock Ownership Plan. These plans invest only in the stock of the employer.

Fair Price Provision. Typically a charter amendment adopted by a target that forbids a merger with an "interested shareholder" (typically defined as owner of a specified percentage of target shares, sometimes as low as 10%) unless (i) a supermajority vote of shareholders is obtained or (ii) the price in the merger is at least as high as the price paid by the interested shareholder for any shares it owns (typically obtained in a tender offer). (See *Shark Repellent.*)

Fairness Opinion. An opinion of a financial expert, frequently an investment banker, that an offer for the company or its shares is fair from a financial point of view.

Financial Buyer. An entity considering an acquisition that is primarily a financial organization, such as a private equity fund, which has no experience with the operations of the prospective target or any business either as a supplier or customer of the target.

First Generation Takeover Statutes. A group of 37 state laws regulating takeovers adopted in the late 1960s and early 1970s. These laws frequently required disclosures more burdensome than those of the Williams Act, and at an earlier date. In some states securities officials were given authority to hold hearings and to determine whether the offer was unfair to local shareholders, and should be enjoined. These laws were declared unconstitutional in the 1970s.

Flip-In. Provisions of a poison pill that give shareholders, other than a bidder, the right to purchase target common stock at a bargain price.

Flip-Over. Provisions of a poison pill that give target shareholders the right to purchase bidder common stock at a bargain price, typically after a merger in which the target does not survive as a separate entity.

Freeze-Out. A merger or other similar transaction in which a controlling shareholder forces the remaining public shareholders to relinquish their shares in exchange for non-equity consideration, whether debt or cash. (See *Going private.*)

Going Private. A merger, share repurchase or other fundamental corporate change that has the effect of making the subject company ineligible for trading on recognized exchanges and permits it to terminate filing reports under the Securities Exchange Act, so that brokers generally will be unable to make a market in the stock. Typically these transactions reduce share ownership to a single shareholder, or a limited group of owners.

Golden Parachute. A severance agreement with a top executive, that assures the executive that if there is a change of control of the employer, whether through stock ownership or a change in the composition of the board through a proxy fight, if the executive's employment is terminated, severance payments will be made. Typically these payments are for at least three years's compensation. They usually apply whether the executive is fired or leaves voluntarily. Sometimes called "management retention" plans, because target management must stay with the target at least through the change in control to be entitled to receive the payments.

Go-Shop Provision is a term in an acquisition agreement or a preliminary letter of intent that precludes the target from talking to third parties (see *"No-Shop Provision")* while engaged in negotiations with a first bidder, and permitting active marketing once an agreement has been signed for a specified period.

Greenmail. Payments made by a target company to repurchase shares from a prospective bidder, typically at a premium over the current market price, and usually at a profit to the selling shareholder (the "greenmailer"). This price is not made available to other shareholders. It is frequently coupled with a "standstill" agreement. (See below.) Tax changes in 1987 eliminated this practice by imposing punitive tax rates on such payments.

"Highly Confident" Letter. A letter from an investment bank that it was highly confident that it could raise the funds to finance a takeover bid. These letters were used most prominently by Drexel Burnham Lambert, which dominated the junk bond business in the 1980s. A "highly confident" letter from Drexel Burnham was always honored, and thus became almost as credible in some circles as a firm loan commitment from a commercial bank.

Hostile Bidder. Any bidder not invited by the target board of directors.

Junk Bonds. Corporate bonds that carry a rating from a major bond rating service of less than "investment" grade, which covers only the top four grades at these rating firms. Junk bonds are regarded as riskier, and require higher interest rates in order to be sold.

Leveraged Buyout ("LBO"). Any acquisition of a company using large amounts of borrowings to finance the acquisition.

Lock-Up. Any transaction that is designed to either (i) preclude a competing bidder from acquiring a target or (ii) provide compensation to a first bidder that loses an auction for its efforts that created greater value for target shareholders. Most frequently it involves an option to purchase authorized but unissued target common stock if a competing bidder should acquire control, at a lower price than the competing bidder has paid. In other cases, it may involve an option to purchase the target's "crown jewels" (see above) at a bargain price should a competing bidder gain control

Management Buyout ("MBO"). A leveraged buyout structured by management, to leave management as major owners of the firm.

No-Shop Provision. A term in an acquisition agreement that precludes the target from seeking further bids from a third party.

No-Talk Provision. A term in an acquisition agreement that prevents the target from discussing terms with a second bidder unless the board determines that it is likely to generate a "superior offer." Typically these provisions also require the target to notify the first bidder if it actually receives a superior offer, and provides for a period in which the first bidder can meet or top that offer.

Parking. A transaction where a third party holds target company shares for a bidder. (See *Warehousing.*)

Partial Bid. A tender offer in which the bidder offers to purchase only a fraction of all of the outstanding shares of the target, typically the minimum amount necessary to gain control.

Poison Pill. A plan that grants to existing shareholders the right to purchase additional shares of common stock, normally at 50% of the then current market price. These purchase rights are triggered by significant ownership by a bidder, and provide that the rights are void in the hands of the bidder. The result, of course, is significant dilution for the bidder, both of its voting power and of the value of its investment in the target.

Poison Put. A rights plan that grants shareholders the right to "put" their shares to the company for repurchase at a specified price in the event a new bidder gains control. Typically this repurchase price is set at the highest value imaginable by an investment banker, to assure that any such repurchase will be costly to the bidder as the remaining shareholder (which will not have such rights).

Qualified Offer. A "qualified offer", used in some poison pills, is defined as a fully-financed, all-cash, all-shares offer which remains open for at least a specified number of business days, which results in the offeror owning shares representing a majority of the outstanding voting power and where, upon commencing the offer, the offeror agrees to complete a final all-cash transaction at the offer price to acquire the remaining shares. The pill, by its terms, will not be triggered by such an offer.

R & D. Research and development.

Raider. A hostile (not invited by management) bidder.

Rights Plan. See *Poison Pill.*

Saturday Night Special. A tender offer (before the Williams Act) designed to be completed as quickly as possible, before target management can react with defensive tactics.

Second Generation Takeover Laws. After *First generation takeover statutes* were declared invalid, states began adopting new statutes based on changes in corporate governance. Some adjusted voting rules in takeout mergers; others removed the votes of bidders unless they were restored by the other shareholders.

Shark Repellent. Amendments to articles of incorporation that make second stage "takeout mergers" more difficult for a bidder. They do this either by raising the voting requirement for such a merger to a supermajority, or by requiring approval by holders of a majority of the remaining shares not held by the bidder. In many cases these voting requirements are relaxed to allow normal (majority of all shares eligible to vote) voting rules if the price offered in the takeout merger is "fair," which is typically defined as the highest price paid by the bidder for any shares of the target, with a series of adjustments to prevent manipulation of the formula. (See *Fair Price Provision.*)

Slow Hand Poison Pill. A provision that new directors elected after a change in control without the consent of continuing directors (see above) cannot act to redeem a rights plan for a specified period of time.

Standstill Agreement. An agreement by which a prospective bidder agrees either to limit future purchases of shares or avoid them altogether for a specified period.

Strategic Buyer. An entity engaged in the same business as the prospective target, or in a related enterprise such as a supplier or customer of the target, that may anticipate operating synergies from the acquisition.

Street Sweep. A rapid accumulation of target company shares, through either open market or privately negotiated purchases or both. This is often facilitated by the fact that arbitrageurs have accumulated large blocks which they are willing to sell.

Squeeze-Out. See *Freeze-out.*

Sunset Provision. A provision in a poison pill calling for shareholder review every two or three years.

Takeout Merger. A merger following acquisition of voting control by a bidder, in which the remaining shareholders of the target corporation are removed as shareholders in the surviving corporation. These shareholders may receive cash or other securities of the surviving corporation or its parent for their stock.

Takeover Bid. A hostile bid, typically a tender offer, for control of a target.

Target. The object of a takeover bid.

Tender Offer. An invitation to the shareholders to tender their shares to the bidder. That is, to offer to sell their shares to the bidder on terms specified by the bidder. The bidder commits that it will purchase the shares if the bidder's conditions are met. Typically the bidder conditions its obligation on the tender of sufficient shares to obtain control of the target. The bid may also be conditioned on removal of certain takeover defenses of the target corporation.

TIDE Provision. "Three Year Independent Director Evaluation." A requirement in a poison pill that it be reviewed by independent directors after three years.

Tin Parachute. A plan providing severance benefits for lower level employees in the event of a change of control.

Topping Fee. A form of Break-Up Fee (see above) in an acquisition agreement, based on the gains to the target from selling to another bidder. The fee is usually based on a percentage of the gains the target shareholders receive from selling to a second bidder, compared to the price they would have received from the first bidder.

Top-Up Option. An option given by a target to a bidder in a negotiated two-tier acquisition to purchase shares directly from the target to reach the 90% ownership level, thus allowing completion of the transaction with a short-form merger (no shareholder vote, and in Delaware, no Weinberger fairness requirements, making appraisal the exclusive remedy).

Triangular Merger. A merger that occurs between a subsidiary of the acquiring corporation and the target corporation. Typically the shares of the acquired corporation are canceled and exchanged for consideration frequently paid directly by the parent corporation.

Two-Tier Bid. A combination of a tender offer and the announcement of a takeout merger on terms less favorable than those of the tender offer, designed to create pressure on shareholders to tender.

Warehousing. A transaction in which a third party holds shares for the benefit of a bidder, but without any contract binding it to sell them to the bidder. (See *Parking*.)

White Knight. A bidder selected by target management in preference to a hostile bidder.

White Squire. A bidder selected by management that may take a significant minority position to block acquisition of control by a hostile bidder.

Williams Act. The Williams Act amendments to the Securities Exchange Act of 1934, adding sections 13(d) and (e) and 14(d)–(f).

Window Shopping Provision. A weakened form of No-Shop provision (see above) in which the target is permitted to provide some information to other interested buyers, but may not actively solicit their bids.

Due Diligence Checklist

LIST OF WORK TO BE ASSIGNED FOR BUYER'S COUNSEL

A. Legal Reviews

    1.   State Corporation Statutes Governing Seller

        a.   Review must cover states of incorporation of Seller & all its subsidiaries, if separate corporate action is required of subs.

        b.   Do Shareholders have preemptive rights unless denied in articles of incorporation?

        c.   What notice is required for shareholder approval of a merger or asset sale?

        d.   What vote is required for shareholder approval? Will it increase if Buyer first acquires a significant holding? (Check state anti-takeover statute) If so, can it be waived by Seller's Board?

        e.   Will dissenting shareholders have appraisal rights?

        f.   Check the procedures for statutory mergers

        g.   Are there any special restrictions on mergers or consolidations with foreign corporations or corporations in different businesses? (This may apply to regulated industries such as insurance or banking).

        h.   What action is required by the Board of Directors to approve an asset sale or merger?

        i.   Is seller qualified to do business in all states where required?

            (1)   If seller is not qualified, are any of Seller's rights in those states subject to forfeiture or non-enforceability?

            (2)   What penalties will be imposed in states where Seller has not been properly qualified?

        j.   Get certificate of existence or good standing for state of incorporation of Seller and each subsidiary.

> k.   Any special statutes or court decisions regulating or preventing receipt of control premiums?
>
> l.   Any self-dealing aspects to transaction that threaten shareholder challenges? (e.g., are major shareholders or officers to be employed by buyer, or receive special consideration?)

2.   Securities Laws Governing Seller

     a.   Federal

> (1)   Does Seller have any contingent liabilities for previous sales of securities? (Review claims to exemptions for recent sales).
>
> (2)   Has Seller recently repurchased any securities under circumstances that may raise 10b–5 claims in connection with this sale?
>
> (3)   If Seller is a '34 Act company, has Seller taken precautions to make certain that its employees do not leak or trade on inside information concerning these negotiations?
>
> (4)   If Seller is a '34 Act company, does Buyer propose to work with major shareholders of Seller as co-owners, triggering creation of a 13(d)(3) group and a filing requirement?
>
> (5)   Will acquisition result in distribution of buyer's securities to seller's shareholders?
>
>   (a)   Is exemption from registration available?
>
> (6)   If seller was organized in past 5 years, will we need details of founders' transactions for SEC disclosures?

     b.   State

> (1)   Does Seller have any contingent liabilities for previous sales of securities? (Review claims to exemptions for recent sales).
>
> (2)   Is Seller governed by a state takeover statute? How will it affect this transaction?
>
> (3)   Are any permits required prior to negotiation or consummation of an agreement to purchase shares?

(4)   If the acquisition will result in distributions of buyer's securities to seller's shareholders, are permits required, or is an exemption available?

3.   State Creditor Protection Laws Governing Seller (in a Sale of Assets)

    a.   Bulk Sales Provisions of UCC

        (1)   Do they apply?

        (2)   Effect of noncompliance?

        (3)   Is escrow needed to protect from liability?

    b.   Fraudulent Conveyance Statutes

    c.   Will local law make buyer liable for products liabilities or other liabilities of seller?

4.   Review of Seller's Corporate Documents

    a.   Articles of Incorporation

        (1)   What notice is required for shareholder approval of a merger or asset sale?

        (2)   What vote is required for shareholder approval? Will it increase if Buyer first acquires a significant holding? Can it be waived by Seller's Board?

        (3)   What classes of securities have voting rights on mergers or asset sales? (Check corporation act as well as charter.)

        (4)   Will dissenting shareholders have appraisal rights granted by articles, if not by statute?

        (5)   Have preemptive rights ever existed, either by default under the corporation act or by charter, and not been honored? Are there records of waivers?

        (6)   Provide a summary description of the rights of each class of outstanding security.

        (7)   Any restrictions on the transfer or voting of stock?

b.   Bylaws

(1)   Any restrictions on the transfer or voting of stock?

(2)   What notice is required for shareholder approval of a merger or asset sale?

(3)   What vote is required for shareholder approval? Will it increase if Buyer first acquires a significant holding? Can it be waived by Seller's Board?

(4)   Any unusual provisions governing powers of officers, votes required for merger or sale, notice of shareholders' meetings, etc.?

c.   Minute Books

(1)   Any restrictions on the transfer or voting of stock?

(2)   Any powers of attorney outstanding with respect to voting securities?

(3)   Provide a summary description of the rights of each class of outstanding security approved by the board under any "blank preferred" authority, or of debt issues.

(4)   Are there outstanding warrants, options or conversion rights that must be honored, or can they be canceled or redeemed?

(5)   If preemptive rights ever existed, have they been honored? Are there records of waivers?

(6)   Was stock validly issued, fully paid and non-assessable?

(7)   Are there employment agreements that impose long-term obligations on seller, or provide for severance payments on a change in control?

(8)   Are there officer or employee benefit plans that impose long-term obligations on the seller?

(a)   Bonus plans?

(b)   Profit-sharing agreements?

          (c)   Retirement plans, and other fringe benefit agreements, such as life insurance, hospitalization, major medical?

    (9)   Any contracts providing special retirement payments to former officers or employees?

    (10)   Any contracts providing consulting payments or finders' fees in the event of a sale of the company?

    (11)   Union contracts?

    (12)   Voting trust agreements that restrict transfer or voting of stock?

d.   Stock Books

    (1)   Outstanding shares

    (2)   Number of shareholders

    (3)   Names & addresses of controlling shareholders and number of shares owned personally and by family.

    (4)   Number of shares held in treasury

    (5)   Were applicable taxes paid on original issue and transfer of shares?

    (6)   Were transfers from estates, trusts or other fiduciaries legal?

    (7)   Any record of pledges of outstanding shares?

    (8)   Evidence of compliance with exemptions from securities registration (within applicable statutes of limitation)?

          (a)   Legends on certificates?

          (b)   Investment letters?

          (c)   Location of all investors within state?

    (9)   Voting trusts or other agreements that restrict transfer or voting of stock? (Get copies of stock certificates to check for legends.)

e.   Bond Indentures

(1)   Prohibitions of mergers or asset sales?

(2)   Variable interest rates?

(3)   Restrictions on dividend payments?

(4)   Restrictions on new debt issues?

(5)   Procedures for surviving corporation to assume obligation?

(6)   Conversion rights?

(7)   Call provisions?

(8)   Other negative covenants that will restrict Buyer?

f.   Other Agreements

(1)   Are there any shareholders' agreements restricting the transfer of shares?

(2)   Are any shares subject to pledges that must be redeemed before transfer?

(3)   Are there any lending agreements that make a change in control of Seller an event of default?

(4)   Are there any employment contracts that trigger severance payments or defaults on a change in control?

(5)   Major contracts, such as union, distributorship, license, government, suppliers, insurance and consulting agreements should be reviewed for:

(a) Assignability

(b) Antitrust problems

(c) Enforceability

(d) Breaches or defaults (including pending or threatened grievances & arbitrations)

(e) Redetermination

(f) Escalation

(g) Term and renewability

(6)   Does seller have any contracts, leases or other arrangements with selling shareholders that are likely to cause difficulties in the future because of their ability to withhold consents, renewals, etc?

(7)   Any earn-out or profit-sharing agreements with prior owners?

(8)   Any rights agreements that would be triggered by either a tender offer or a purchase of shares? Are the restrictions in this agreement waivable by the current members of the board?

B.   Regulatory Review

   1.   Are regulatory approvals required for changes in control?

   2.   Are there prohibitions of certain kinds of ownership, such as corporate owners or foreign owners?

   3.   Are there any pending or threatened proceedings or investigations against seller?

C.   Tax and Accounting Review

   1.   Federal Tax Status

      a.   Last year audited.

      b.   Deficiency claims

      c.   Carrybacks and carryforwards

      d.   Status of current audit

      e.   Tax Credits

      f.   Effect of acquisition on tax status

      g.   Renegotiation

      h.   Recapture of accelerated depreciation or investment credit.

      i.   Liens filed

   2.   State and Local Tax Status

      a.   Applicable taxes (state, county, city, village, improvement district, school district, water, sewer, sales, excise, property, income, etc.)

      b.   Means of obtaining evidence of current payments of each (certificates issued by local authorities?)

      c.   Deficiency claims

      d.   Last year audited for each type of tax & government

      e.   Liens filed

      f.   Unemployment tax rate

      g.   Will real property be reassessed on transfer?

D.   **Financial Review**

    1.   Balance Sheet Items

      a.   Last three years audited statements plus auditor's letters.

      b.   Aged accounts receivable for most recent balance sheet, plus detail on methodology on allowance for doubtful accounts.

      c.   Schedule of deferred revenue calculation plus supporting documentation.

      d.   Accounts payable aging reports for most recent balance sheet.

      e.   Descriptions of any changes in accounting methods or procedures during the past three years.

      f.   Description of any off-balance sheet liabilities and financial derivative instruments held by or issued by the Company, if any.

E.   **Property Review**

    1.   Owned Real Property

      a.   List of major holdings and evidence of title in seller (title insurance, abstracts, title opinions). Will title insurance coverage survive closing or will new policies be required?

      b.   Encumbrances on property (mortgages, tax liens, mechanics' liens.

      c.   Recent surveys showing improvements within boundaries?

      d.   Are mineral rights severed?

e.   Easements, rights of way, restrictions or reversions?

f.   Zoning restrictions?

g.   Is condemnation pending or threatened?

h.   Is soil polluted with any hazardous waste?

i.   City or county water & sewer, or other assured sources?

2.   Leased Real Property

a.   List of major leaseholds, with name & address of landlord.

b.   Date, term and termination rights under lease.

c.   Who owns improvements at termination of lease?

d.   Renewal rights.

e.   Current rent & any provisions for periodic increases.

f.   Events of default, and waiver of past defaults before closing.

g.   Assignability.

h.   City or county water & sewer, or other assured sources?

3.   Personal Property

a.   List of all major machinery, equipment, office furniture, vehicles, etc., owned, and location, if not in state of principal place of business and the remaining useful life of each item.

b.   List of leased property and terms of lease.

c.   Security agreements, financing statements, tax, mechanics' or other liens. (Check UCC filings in each applicable jurisdiction.)

d.   Any property of third parties (government, contractors, etc.) in use and subject to return?

4.   Intangibles

a.   List of patents

b.   Patent search for validity and infringement of third party patents by patented products

c.   Infringement by third party of seller's patents

d.   Review of patent licensing agreements (antitrust problems?)

e.   Who has rights in employee inventions?

f.   Employee trade secret and nondisclosure agreements?

g.   List of trademarks

h.   Infringement of third party trademarks?

i.   Infringement by third parties of seller's trademarks?

j.   Trade secrets, how protected.

k.   List of copyrights.

l.   Any special benefits under contracts or government programs that might be threatened by acquisition?

   (1)   Government programs for small or minority owned businesses?

   (2)   Allocations which will disappear if seller is acquired by this buyer?

F.   Pending and Contingent Liabilities

1.   Litigation

   a.   Contract actions, including warranty claims

   b.   Products Liability

      (1)   Are insurance policies for products liabilities & toxic waste damage renewable?

   c.   Tort claims

   d.   Government actions

2   Antitrust

   a.   Consent decrees

   b.   Present activity with FTC, Justice Department or state officials

   c.   Past and present antitrust claims and litigation

   d.   Review and test facts on which any prior antitrust opinions were based.

e.   Review contracts with distributors for restrictive agreements.

f.   Are Hart-Scott-Rodino filings required?

3.   Brokerage in connection with this acquisition

a.   Name of any broker

b.   Whose agent?

c.   Who is to pay commission? (If buyer, will this be boot that will create tax problems?)

4.   Criminal

a.   Any RICO investigations that threaten ownership of seller?

G.   Risk Management Issues

1.   Complete copy of current worker's compensation policy.

2.   Complete copy of policies insuring buildings and fixtures.

3.   Copy of any directors' and officers' liability insurance policies.

4.   Copy of any umbrella insurance policies.

5.   Copies of any other insurance policies that are in force.

6.   Copies of files of any employees terminated for cause in the past three years.

AGREEMENT AND PLAN OF MERGER

Editor's Note: The regular type illustrates a recent strong form seller's agreement to acquire a public company. Some of it was deleted during negotiations. The deleted language is shown stricken through. The italicized type in brackets presents alternative language from a buyer's form of agreement added in the course of negotiations. Defined terms are underlined at their first usage.

AGREEMENT AND PLAN OF MERGER
Among [COMPANY], [PARENT]
and [MERGER SUB]

Dated as of _____

TABLE OF CONTENTS

Page

DEFINED TERMS

AGREEMENT AND PLAN OF MERGER

AGREEMENT AND PLAN OF MERGER (THIS "AGREEMENT"), DATED AS OF ◙, 2011, AMONG ◙, A DELAWARE CORPORATION (THE "COMPANY"), ◙, A DELAWARE CORPORATION ("PARENT"), AND ◙, A DELAWARE CORPORATION AND A WHOLLY-OWNED SUBSIDIARY OF PARENT ("MERGER SUB").

RECITALS

WHEREAS, THE RESPECTIVE BOARDS OF DIRECTORS OF EACH OF PARENT, MERGER SUB AND THE COMPANY HAVE APPROVED THE MERGER OF MERGER SUB WITH AND INTO THE COMPANY (THE "MERGER") ON THE TERMS AND SUBJECT TO THE CONDITIONS SET FORTH IN THIS AGREEMENT AND HAVE APPROVED AND DECLARED ADVISABLE THIS AGREEMENT; AND

WHEREAS, THE COMPANY, PARENT AND MERGER SUB DEEM IT ADVISABLE THAT THE MERGER SUB MERGE WITH AND INTO THE COMPANY PURSUANT TO SECTION 251(H) OF THE DELAWARE GENERAL CORPORATION LAW, AS AMENDED (THE "DGCL") AND UPON THE TERMS AND CONDITIONS HEREIN, AND

WHEREAS, THE COMPANY, PARENT AND MERGER SUB DESIRE TO MAKE CERTAIN REPRESENTATIONS, WARRANTIES, COVENANTS AND AGREEMENTS IN CONNECTION WITH THIS AGREEMENT;

NOW, THEREFORE, IN CONSIDERATION OF THE PREMISES, AND OF THE REPRESENTATIONS, WARRANTIES, COVENANTS AND AGREEMENTS CONTAINED HEREIN, THE PARTIES HERETO AGREE AS FOLLOWS:

ARTICLE 1.   The Offer and the Merger; Closing; Effective Time

ARTICLE 1.1.   The Offer

(a) *[Unless this Agreement shall have been terminated in accordance with Article 7,]* subject to the following sentence, Merger Sub shall (and Parent shall cause Merger Sub to), as promptly as practicable and in no event later than three (3) Business Days after the date hereof, commence (within the meaning of Rule 14d–2 under the Securities Exchange Act of 1934 (the "Exchange Act")), a tender offer to purchase all of the outstanding shares of common stock, par value $0.001 per share

("Common Stock"), of the Company (the "Shares") at a price of $◉ per Share in cash, net to the seller but subject to any required withholding tof Taxes (such tender offer and price, as they may from time to time be amended in accordance with this Agreement, (the "Offer" and the "Offer Price," respectively). The obligations of Merger Sub to (and of Parent to cause Merger Sub to) accept for payment and pay for any Shares validly tendered and not withdrawn pursuant to the Offer shall be subject to the satisfaction or waiver of the conditions set forth in Annex A (the "Tender Offer Conditions"), and no other conditions. The initial expiration date of the Offer shall be midnight (Eastern Time) on the date that is twenty (20) Business Days after the date on which the Offer was commenced (determined as provided in Rule 14d–1(g)(3) under the Exchange Act) (the initial "Expiration Time") and any expiration time and date established pursuant to an extension of the Offer in accordance with this Agreement, also an Expiration Time). Merger Sub expressly reserves the right (i) if the Minimum Tender Condition has not been satisfied or if a Change of Recommendation has been made, to increase the Offer Price and (ii) to waive any condition to the Offer or modify the terms of the Offer, except that, without the prior written consent of the Company, Merger Sub shall not (A) reduce the number of Shares subject to the Offer, (B) reduce the Offer Price, (C) waive the Minimum Tender Condition, (D) add to the Tender Offer Conditions or amend or modify any Tender Offer Condition in any manner adverse to the holders of Shares, (E) except as otherwise provided in this Section 1.1, extend the Expiration Time, (F) change the form of consideration payable in the Offer or (G) otherwise amend the Offer in any manner adverse to the holders of Shares. Notwithstanding the foregoing, Merger Sub may, without the consent of the Company, (x) extend the Expiration Time for one or more consecutive increments of not more than five (5) Business Days each, if at any otherwise scheduled Expiration Time any Tender Offer Condition has not been satisfied or waived, (y) extend the Expiration Time for the minimum period required by any rule, regulation, interpretation or position of the Securities and Exchange Commission (the "SEC") or the staff thereof applicable to the Offer, or (z) make available a "subsequent offering period" in accordance with Exchange Act Rule 14d–11. If at any otherwise scheduled Expiration Time any Tender Offer Condition has not been satisfied or waived. Merger Sub shall (and Parent shall cause Merger Sub to) extend the Expiration Time at the request of the Company for one or more consecutive increments of not more than five (5) Business Days each until the earliest of (1) the termination of this Agreement in accordance with its terms and (2) the Outside Date. In addition, Merger Sub shall (and Parent shall cause Merger Sub to), if requested by the Company, make available a subsequent offering period in accordance with Exchange Act Rule 14d—11 of not less than ten (10) Business Days; provided that Merger Sub shall not be required to make available such a subsequent offering period in the event that, prior to the commencement of such subsequent offering period, Parent and Merger Sub, directly or indirectly own more than ninety percent (90%) of the outstanding Shares. On the terms and subject to the conditions of the Offer and this Agreement, Merger Sub shall (and Parent shall cause Merger Sub to) accept for payment all Shares validly tendered and not withdrawn pursuant to the Offer as promptly as practicable after the Expiration Time (the time and date on which Merger Sub accepts such Shares for payment, the "Acceptance Time"), and pay for such Shares as promptly as practicable following the Acceptance Time. Parent shall (or shall cause Merger Sub or any other direct or indirect wholly—owned Subsidiary of Parent to) provide or cause to be provided to the Paying Agent on a timely basis the funds necessary to purchase any Shares that Merger Sub becomes obligated to purchase pursuant to the Offer. For purposes of this Agreement, the term "Business Day" shall have the meaning provided in Rule 14d–1(g)(3) under the Exchange Act, and the term "Subsidiary" means, with respect to any Person, any other Person of which at least a majority of the securities or ownership interests having by their terms ordinary voting power to elect a majority of the board of directors or other persons performing similar functions is directly or indirectly owned or controlled by such Person and/or by one or more of its Subsidiaries.

(b) On the date on which the Offer is commenced, Parent and Merger Sub shall file with the SEC, in accordance with Rule 14d–3 and Regulation M-A under the Exchange Act, a Tender Offer Statement on Schedule TO with respect to the Offer, which shall contain an offer to purchase and a related letter of transmittal and summary advertisement (such Schedule TO and the documents included therein, together with all amendments, supplements and exhibits thereto, the "Offer Documents"), shall make all deliveries, mailings and telephonic notices required by Rule 14d–3 under the Exchange Act, and shall cause the Offer Documents to be disseminated to holders of Shares as and to the extent required by the United States federal securities Laws and the rules and regulations of the SEC promulgated thereunder (collectively, the "Securities Laws"). Parent and Merger Sub shall cause the Offer Documents to comply in all material respects with the Securities Laws. Parent and Merger Sub shall deliver copies of the proposed forms of the Offer Documents (including any amendments or supplements thereto) to the Company within a reasonable time prior to the dissemination or filing thereof for review and comment by the Company and its counsel. Each of Parent, Merger Sub and the Company shall respond promptly to any comments of the SEC or its staff with respect to the Offer or the Offer Documents and promptly correct any information provided by it for use in the Offer Documents if and to the extent that such information shall have become false or misleading in any material respect or as otherwise required by the Securities Laws. Parent and Merger Sub shall amend or supplement the Offer Documents and cause the Offer Documents, as so amended or supplemented, to be filed with the SEC and to be disseminated to the holders of Shares, in each case as and to the extent required by the Securities Laws and subject to the terms and conditions of this Agreement. Parent and Merger Sub shall provide the Company and its counsel with copies of any written comments, and shall inform them of any oral comments, that Parent, Merger Sub or their counsel receive from the SEC or its staff with respect to the Offer Documents promptly after the receipt of such comments and shall give the Company a reasonable opportunity under the circumstances to review and comment on any written or oral responses to such comments. The Company hereby consents to the inclusion in the Offer Documents of the Company Recommendation as it may be amended or modified, and until but not after it is withdrawn, in each case as permitted by this Agreement.

ARTICLE 1.2.   Company Actions

(a)   On the date the Offer Documents are first filed with the SEC, the Company shall file with the SEC a Tender Offer Solicitation/Recommendation Statement on Schedule 14D–9 with respect to the Offer (together with all amendments, supplements and exhibits thereto, the "Schedule 14D–9"), which, subject to Section 5.2, shall contain the Company Recommendation. Parent shall cause the Schedule 14D–9 to be disseminated to the holders of Shares along with the Offer Documents, in accordance with Rule 14d–9 under the Exchange Act and the Securities Laws. The Company shall cause the Schedule 14D–9 to comply in all material respects with the Securities Laws. The Company shall deliver copies of the proposed forms of the Schedule 14D–9 (including any amendments or supplements thereto) to the Parent within a reasonable time prior to the dissemination or filing thereof for review and comment by the Parent and its counsel. Each of the Company, Parent, and Merger Sub and shall respond promptly to any comments of the SEC or its staff with respect to the Schedule 14D–9 and promptly correct any information provided by it for use in the Schedule 14D–9 if and to the extent that such information shall have become false or misleading in any material respect or as otherwise required by the Securities Laws. The Company shall amend or supplement the Schedule 14D–9 and cause the Schedule 14D–9, as so amended or supplemented, to be filed with the SEC and to be disseminated to the holders of Shares, in each case as and to the extent required by the Securities Laws. The Company shall provide Parent and its counsel with copies of any written comments, and shall inform them of any oral comments, that the Company or its counsel receive from the SEC or its staff with respect to the Schedule 14D—9 promptly after the receipt of such comments and shall give Parent a reasonable opportunity under the circumstances to review and comment on any written or oral responses to such comments.

(b) In connection with the Offer, the Company shall instruct its transfer agent promptly to furnish or cause to be furnished to Merger Sub (i) a list of the names and addresses of the record holders of Shares as of the most recent practicable date, as well as mailing labels containing such names and addresses and (ii) security position lists, computer files and any other information identifying the beneficial owners of Shares, in each case as of the most recent practicable date which the Company or ~~its~~the transfer agent have in their possession or control or can obtain without unreasonable effort or expense. The Company shall instruct its transfer agent to furnish or cause to be furnished to Merger Sub such additional information (including updates to the items provided pursuant to the preceding sentence) and such other assistance as Merger Sub may reasonably request in communicating the Offer to the record and beneficial owners of Shares. Subject to the requirements of applicable Law, and except for such steps as are necessary to disseminate the Offer Documents and any other documents necessary to consummate the Merger, Parent and Merger Sub and their agents shall hold in confidence the information contained in any such labels, listings and files, shall use such information only in connection with the Offer and the Merger and, if this Agreement shall be terminated, shall, upon request, deliver, and shall use their reasonable best efforts to cause their agents to deliver, to the Company all copies of such information then in their possession or control.

ARTICLE 1.3. Company Directors

(a) Promptly after the Acceptance Time and from time to time thereafter (but only for so long as Parent, Merger Sub and their Affiliates beneficially own at least a majority of the outstanding Shares), Merger Sub shall be entitled to elect or designate to the board of directors of the Company (the "<u>Company Board</u>") such number of directors, rounded up to the nearest whole number, as is equal to the product of the total number of directors on the Company Board (giving effect to the directors elected or designated by Merger Sub pursuant to this sentence) multiplied by the percentage of the outstanding Shares (determined on a fully diluted basis) that are then beneficially owned by Merger Sub and its Affiliates and to have such designees be elected or appointed to such classes of the Company Board so as to be as evenly distributed as possible among the three classes of directors on the Company Board. As used in this Agreement, the terms "<u>beneficial ownership</u>" (and its correlative terms), "<u>Affiliate</u>" and "<u>Associate</u>" shall have the meanings provided in Rule 13d–3 and Rule 12b–2 under the Exchange Act, respectively.* Upon any exercise of such right by Merger Sub, the Company shall use its reasonable best efforts to (i) elect or appoint to the Company Board the

---

* The author believes this definition of affiliate is problematic. Under Rule 12b–2 an "affiliate" is a person who, inter alia, directly or indirectly controls, or is controlled by, an issuer. Rule 13d–3 defines "beneficial ownership", so that referring to both of these as "affiliates" includes individual officers, directors and employees of the issuer.

individuals designated by Merger Sub and permitted to be so elected or designated by the preceding sentence, including by promptly filling vacancies or newly created directorships on the Company Board, increasing the size of the Company Board and/or securing the resignations of such number of its incumbent directors, and (ii) cause the directors so elected or appointed to constitute the same percentage (rounded up to the nearest whole number) of the members of each committee of the Company Board as such directors represent of the Company Board, in each case to the fullest extent permitted by applicable Law and the rules of the NASDAQ Stock Market ("NASDAQ"). The Company's obligations under this Section 1.3(a) shall be subject to Section 14(f) of the Exchange Act and Rule 14f–1 promulgated thereunder, and the Company shall include in the Schedule 14D–9 such information required by Section 14(f) and Rule 14f–1 as is necessary to enable Merger Sub's designees to be elected or appointed to the Company Board. Merger Sub shall timely furnish to the Company, and be solely responsible for, information with respect to Merger Sub's designees and Parent's and Merger Sub's respective officers, directors and Affiliates to the extent required by Section 14(f) and Rule 14f–1. The provisions of this Section 1.3(a) are in addition to and shall not limit any rights that any of Merger Sub, Parent or any of their respective Affiliates may have as a holder or beneficial owner of Shares as a matter of applicable Law with respect to the election of directors or otherwise.

(b) In the event that Merger Sub's designees are elected or appointed to the Company Board pursuant to Section 1.3(a), then, until the Effective Time (and subject to any further designations permitted to be made by Merger Sub pursuant to Section 1.3(a) from time to time), the Company and Parent shall allow (i) the remaining members of the Company Board to consist of individuals who were members of the Company Board on the date hereof (the "Existing Directors"), (ii) the Existing Directors who are members of the audit committee of the Company Board immediately prior to the date of this Agreement to remain as members of the audit committee of the Company Board and (iii) such audit committee to comply with all requirements of the Securities Laws and NASDAQ applicable thereto (collectively, the "Audit Committee Requirements"). If any Existing Director is unable to serve due to death, disability or resignation, then the remaining Existing Directors (or, if none of the Existing Director are then in office, the members of the Company Board) shall be entitled to elect or appoint another individual to fill each such vacancy, which individual shall not be an officer, director, employee or agent of, or otherwise affiliated with, Parent or Merger Sub, and each such individual shall be deemed to be an Existing Director for purposes of this Agreement.

(c) Notwithstanding anything in this Agreement to the contrary, at any time prior to the Effective Time when Merger Sub's designees constitute a majority of the Company Board, the affirmative vote of a majority of the Existing Directors, acting qua audit committee of the Company Board, shall be required and shall, to the fullest extent permitted by the DGCL, be sufficient to (i) amend, modify or terminate this Agreement on behalf of the Company or to amend or modify the terms or conditions of the Offer or the Merger, (ii) exercise or waive any of the Company's rights or remedies under this Agreement, (iii) extend the time for performance of Parent's or Merger Sub's obligations under this Agreement or (iv) enforce any obligation of Parent or Merger Sub under this Agreement. The Existing Directors, acting qua audit committee of the Company Board, shall have the authority to retain counsel (which may include current counsel to the Company) and other advisors at the expense of the Company as determined appropriate by the Existing Directors and shall have the authority, after the Acceptance Time and prior to the Effective Time, to institute any action on behalf of the Company to enforce the performance of this Agreement in accordance with its terms.

ARTICLE 1.4.   Top-Up Option*

(a) The Company hereby grants to Merger Sub an irrevocable option (the "Top-Up Option") to purchase from the Company up to that number of newly issued shares of Common Stock (the "Top-Up Option Shares") equal to the lowest number of shares of Common Stock that, when added to the number of Shares owned by Parent and Merger Sub at the time of exercise, shall constitute one Share more than the number of Shares necessary for Merger Sub to be merged into the Company pursuant to Section 253 of the DGCL (after giving effect to the issuance of the Top-Up Option Shares), for consideration per Top-Up Option Share equal to the Offer Price.

(b) The Top-Up Option shall only be exercisable once, in whole and not in part within ten (10) Business Days after the date on which Merger Sub accepts for payment and pays for Shares pursuant to the Offer (the "Purchase Date"); provided, however, that notwithstanding anything in this Agreement to the contrary, (i) the Top-Up Option shall not be exercisable and shall terminate on the Purchase Date if the number of Top-Up Option Shares issuable under the Top-Up Option would exceed the number of authorized shares of Common Stock that have not been issued, subscribed for, or otherwise committed to be issued, and (ii) the Top-Up Option shall terminate concurrently with the termination of this Agreement in accordance with its terms.

(c) In the event that Merger Sub wishes to exercise the Top-Up Option, Merger Sub shall give the Company written notice specifying the number of Shares that are or will be owned by Parent and Merger Sub immediately preceding the purchase of the Top-Up Option Shares and

---

*   The top-up option will not be necessary under Del. GGL § 251(h), but a similar provision may be necessary under the laws of other jurisdictions that only permit short-form mergers with 90% ownership.

specifying a place and a time for the closing of such purchase. The Company shall, promptly following receipt of such notice, deliver written notice to Merger Sub specifying the number of Top-Up Option Shares to be issued and the consideration due in exchange therefor, calculated in accordance with Section 1.4(a). At the closing of the purchase for the Top-Up Option Shares, Merger Sub shall pay the Company the consideration due in exchange for such Top-Up Option Shares either (i) in cash (by wire transfer or cashier's check) or (ii) by delivery of cash in an amount equal to the aggregate par value of such Top-Up Option Shares (by wire transfer or cashier's check) plus a promissory note for the balance due having full recourse to Parent, bearing interest at the rate of three percent (3%) per annum, maturing on the first anniversary of the date of execution and delivery of such promissory note and being pre-payable without penalty and having no other material terms, and the Company shall deliver to Merger Sub a certificate representing such Top-Up Option Shares. The Company Board has determined that such consideration for the Top-Up Option Shares is adequate in accordance with the DGCL and otherwise taken all steps necessary such that upon issuance and delivery in accordance with this Section 1.4(c) the Top-Up Option Shares shall be validly issued, fully paid and non-assessable.

(d) Notwithstanding anything to the contrary contained herein, each of Parent, Merger Sub and the Company acknowledges and agrees that, in any appraisal proceeding under Section 262 of the DGCL with respect to shares of Common Stock held by Dissenting Stockholders, the Surviving Corporation shall not assert that the Top-Up Option, the Top-Up Option Shares or any cash or promissory note delivered by Merger Sub to the Company in payment for such Merger Option Shares should be considered in connection with the determination of the fair value of the shares of Common Stock held by the Dissenting Stockholders in accordance with Section 262 of the DGCL.

ARTICLE 1.5.   The Merger

On the terms and conditions set forth in this Agreement, at the Effective Time, the Merger Sub shall be merged into the Company in accordance with Section 251(h) of the DGCL and the corporate existence of Merger Sub shall thereupon cease. The Company shall be the surviving corporation (the "Surviving Corporation") in the Merger, and th separate corporate existence of the Company, with all its rights, privileges, immunities, powers and franchises, shall continue unaffected by the Merger, except as set forth in Article 2. The Merger shall have the effects specified in the DGCL.

ARTICLE 1.6.   Closing

Unless otherwise mutually agreed in writing between the Company and Parent, the closing for the Merger (the "Closing") shall take place at the offices of Parent's outside legal counsel, at the address set forth in Section 8.5, at 9:00 A.M. (Eastern Time) on the first Business Day following the day on which the last to be satisfied or waived of the conditions set forth in Article 6 shall be satisfied or waived (excluding conditions that, by their terms, cannot be satisfied until the Closing, but subject to the satisfaction or waiver of such conditions at the Closing) in accordance with this Agreement.

ARTICLE 1.7. Effective Time

As soon as practicable following the Closing, the Company shall cause a Certificate of Merger (such certificate, or the certificate of ownership and merger referenced below, as applicable, the "Delaware Certificate of Merger") to be executed, acknowledged and filed with the Secretary of State of the State of Delaware in accordance with the DGCL. The Merger shall become effective at the time when the Delaware Certificate of Merger has been duly filed with the Secretary of State of the State of Delaware or at such later time as may be agreed by the parties hereto in writing in accordance with the DGCL and specified in the Delaware Certificate of Merger (the "Effective Time"). If Parent and Merger Sub own, directly or indirectly, a number of Shares sufficient to enable the Merger to be consummated without a meeting of stockholders of the Company in accordance with Section 253 of the DGCL, then the parties hereto agree that Merger Sub shall effect the Merger without a meeting of stockholders of the Company pursuant to Section 253 of the DGCL by filing a Certificate of Ownership and Merger with the Secretary of State of the State of Delaware in accordance with the DGCL.

ARTICLE 2. Certificate of Incorporation and Bylaws of the Surviving Corporation

ARTICLE 2.1. The Certificate of Incorporation

At the Effective Time, the certificate of incorporation of the Surviving Corporation (the "Charter") shall, by virtue of the Merger, be amended and restated in its entirety to read as set forth on Annex B, and such amended and restated Charter shall become the certificate of incorporation of the Surviving Corporation until thereafter amended in accordance with the applicable provisions of the DGCL.

ARTICLE 2.2. The Bylaws

The parties hereto shall take all actions necessary so that the bylaws of Merger Sub in effect immediately prior to the Effective Time shall be amended and restated in their entirety to read as set forth on Annex C and shall be the bylaws of the Surviving Corporation (the "Bylaws"), until thereafter amended as provided therein or by applicable Law.

ARTICLE 2.3. Directors of the Surviving Corporation

The parties hereto shall take all actions necessary so that the directors of Merger Sub immediately prior to the Effective Time shall, from and after the Effective Time, be the directors of the Surviving Corporation until their successors have been duly elected or appointed and qualified or until their earlier death, resignation or removal in accordance with the Charter and the Bylaws.

ARTICLE 3.   Effect of the Merger on Capital Stock; Exchange of Certificates

ARTICLE 3.1.   Effect on Capital Stock

At the Effective Time, as a result of the Merger and without any action on the part of the holder of any capital stock of the Company:

(a) Merger Consideration. Each Share issued and outstanding immediately prior to the Effective Time, other than (i) Shares owned by Parent, Merger Sub or any other direct or indirect wholly-owned Subsidiary of Parent, (ii) Shares owned by the Company or its Subsidiary and (iii) Shares that are owned by stockholders who properly demand appraisal of their Shares pursuant to Section 262 of the DGCL ("Dissenting Stockholders") (the Shares described in clause (i), (ii) or (iii) above, collectively, "Excluded Shares"), shall be converted into the right to receive an amount in cash equal to the Offer Price (the "Per Share Merger Consideration"). At the Effective Time, all of the Shares shall cease to be outstanding, shall be cancelled and shall cease to exist, and each certificate (a "Certificate") that immediately prior to the Effective Time represented any of the Shares (other than Excluded Shares) shall thereafter represent only the right to receive the Per Share Merger Consideration, without interest.

(b) Cancellation of Excluded Shares. Each Excluded Share shall, by virtue of the Merger and without any action on the part of the holder thereof, cease to be outstanding, shall be cancelled without payment of any consideration therefor and shall cease to exist, subject to any rights the holder thereof may have under Section 3.2(f).

(c) Conversion of Merger Sub Common Stock. At the Effective Time, each share of common stock, par value $0.001 per share, of Merger Sub issued and outstanding immediately prior to the Effective Time shall be converted into one share of common stock, par value $0.001 per share, of the Surviving Corporation, and such shares shall constitute the only outstanding shares of capital stock of the Surviving Corporation. From and after the Effective Time, all certificates representing the common stock of Merger Sub shall be deemed for all purposes to represent the number of shares of common stock of the Surviving Corporation into which they were converted in accordance with the preceding sentence.

ARTICLE 3.2.   Exchange of Certificates

(a) Paying Agent. At the Effective Time, Parent shall deposit, or shall cause to be deposited, with a paying agent selected by Parent with the Company's prior approval (such approval not to be unreasonably withheld or delayed) (the "Paying Agent"), for the benefit of the holders of Shares and pursuant to a paying agent agreement in customary form, cash in immediately available dollar-denominated funds in the aggregate amount necessary for the Paying Agent to make the payments contemplated by Section 3.1(a) (such cash, the "Exchange Fund"). Parent shall cause the Paying Agent to invest the Exchange Fund in direct short-term obligations of, or obligations fully guaranteed by the full faith and credit of, the United States of America or in commercial paper obligations rated A-1 or P-1 or better by Moody's Investors Service, Inc. or Standard & Poor's Corporation, respectively, or a combination of the foregoing, and, in each case, with maturities not exceeding three (3) months. To the extent there are losses with respect to such investments or the Exchange Fund diminishes for any other reasons below the level required to make prompt cash payment of the aggregate funds required to be paid pursuant to Section 3.1(a), Parent shall promptly replace or restore the cash in the Exchange Fund so as to ensure that the Exchange Fund is at all times maintained at a level sufficient to make such cash payments. Any interest and other income resulting from such investment shall become a part of the Exchange Fund, and any amounts in excess of the amounts payable under Section 3.1(a) shall be promptly paid to Parent.

(b) Exchange Procedures. Promptly (and in any event within three (3) Business Days) following the Effective Time, the Surviving Corporation shall cause the Paying Agent to mail to each holder of record of Shares (other than holders of Excluded Shares) (i) a letter of transmittal in customary form specifying that delivery shall be effected, and risk of loss and title to the Certificates shall pass, only upon delivery of the Certificates (or affidavits of loss in lieu thereof as provided in Section 3.2(e)) to the Paying Agent, such letter of transmittal to be in such form and have such other provisions as Parent and the Company may reasonably agree, and (ii) instructions for use in effecting the surrender of the Certificates (or affidavits of loss in lieu thereof as provided in Section 3.2(e)) in exchange for the Per Share Merger Consideration. Upon surrender of a Certificate (or an affidavit of loss in lieu thereof as provided in Section 3.2(e)) to the Paying Agent in accordance with the terms of such letter of transmittal, duly executed, the holder of such Certificate shall be entitled to receive in exchange therefor a cash amount in immediately available funds (after giving effect to any required Tax withholdings as provided in Section 3.5) equal to the product of (A) the the number of Shares represented by such Certificate (or affidavit of loss in lieu thereof as provided in Section 3.2(e)), multiplied by (B) the Per Share Merger Consideration, and the Certificate so surrendered shall forthwith be cancelled. No interest will be paid or accrued on any amount payable upon due surrender of the Certificates or affidavits of loss, as the case may be. In the event of a transfer of ownership of Shares that is not registered in the transfer records of the Company, a check for any cash to be exchanged upon due surrender of the Certificate may be issued to such transferee if the Certificate formerly representing such Shares is presented to the Paying Agent, accompanied by all documents required to evidence and effect such transfer and to evidence that all applicable transfer Taxes and other similar Taxes required to be paid in connection with such transfer of ownership of Shares have been paid or are not applicable.

(c) **Transfers.** From and after the Effective Time, there shall be no transfers on the stock transfer books of the Company of the Shares that were outstanding immediately prior to the Effective Time. If, after the Effective Time, any Certificate is presented to the Surviving Corporation, Parent or the Paying Agent for transfer, it shall be (subject to compliance with the exchange procedures of Section 3.2(b)) cancelled and exchanged for the cash amount in immediately available funds to which the holder thereof is entitled pursuant to this Article 3.

(d) **Termination of Exchange Fund.** Any portion of the Exchange Fund (including the proceeds of any investments thereof) that remains unclaimed by the stockholders of the Company for 180 days after the Effective Time shall be delivered to the Surviving Corporation. Any holder of Shares (other than Excluded Shares) who has not theretofore complied with this Article 3 shall thereafter look only to the Surviving Corporation for payment of the Per Share Merger Consideration upon due surrender of such holder's Certificates (or affidavits of loss in lieu thereof, and subject to compliance with the exchange procedures of Section 3.2(b)), without any interest thereon. Notwithstanding the foregoing, none of the Surviving Corporation, Parent, the Paying Agent or any other Person shall be liable to any former holder of Shares for any amount properly delivered to a public official pursuant to applicable abandoned property, escheat or similar Laws. For the purposes of this Agreement, the term "Person" shall mean any individual, corporation (including not-for-profit), general or limited partnership, limited liability company, joint venture, estate, trust, association, organization, Governmental Entity or other entity of any kind or nature.

(e) **Lost, Stolen or Destroyed Certificates.** In the event that any Certificate shall have been lost, stolen or destroyed, upon the making of an affidavit of that fact by the Person claiming such Certificate to be lost, stolen or destroyed and, if required by Parent, the posting by such Person of a bond in customary amount and on such terms as may be required by Parent as indemnity against any claim that may be made against it or the Surviving Corporation with respect to such Certificate, the Paying Agent will (subject to compliance with the exchange procedures of Section 3.2(b)) issue a check in the amount equal to the product of (i) the number of Shares represented by such lost, stolen or destroyed Certificate, multiplied by (ii) the Per Share Merger Consideration.

(f) **Appraisal Rights.** No Person who properly demands appraisal of his Shares pursuant to Section 262 of the DGCL shall be entitled to receive the Per Share Merger Consideration with respect to the Shares owned by such Person unless and until such Person shall have effectively withdrawn such demand or otherwise lost such Person's right to appraisal under the DGCL. Each Dissenting Stockholder shall be entitled to receive only the payment provided by Section 262 of the DGCL with respect to Shares owned by such Dissenting Stockholder. If, after the Effective Time, any such holder fails to perfect or effectively withdraws or loses such right, such Excluded Shares shall thereupon be treated as if they had been converted into the right to receive the Per Share Merger Consideration, and the Surviving Corporation shall remain liable for payment of the Per Share Merger Consideration for such Shares. The Company shall give Parent (i) prompt notice of any written demands for appraisal, attempted withdrawals of such demands, and any other instruments served pursuant to applicable Law that are received by the Company relating to stockholders' rights of appraisal and (ii) the opportunity to participate in all negotiations and proceedings with respect to demands for appraisal under Section 262 of the DGCL. The Company shall not, except with the prior written consent of Parent (such consent not to be unreasonably withheld, conditioned or delayed), voluntarily make any payment with respect to any demands for appraisal, offer to settle or settle any such demands or approve any withdrawal of any such demands.

ARTICLE 3.3.   Treatment of Stock Plans

(a) Options. Immediately prior to the Acceptance Time, each outstanding option to purchase Shares (a "Company Option") awarded under the Stock Plans, shall fully vest and be cancelled and shall only entitle the holder thereof to receive an amount in cash [*without interest*] as soon as practicable following the Acceptance Time equal to (i) the product of (A) the total number of Shares subject to a Company Option immediately prior to the Acceptance Time, multiplied by (B) the the excess, if any, of the Per Share Merger Consideration over the exercise price per Share under such Company Option, less (ii) applicable Taxes required to be withheld with respect to such payment.*

(b) Restricted Stock. Immediately prior to the Acceptance Time, any vesting conditions or restrictions applicable to any shares of restricted stock (each such share, a share of "Company Restricted Stock") granted pursuant to the Stock Plans shall lapse, and the holders thereof shall be entitled to tender any such shares of Company Restricted Stock for purchase in the Offer, provided that applicable Taxes shall be withheld with respect to the consideration payable or deliverable in accordance with Section 3.5.

(c) Actions. At or prior to the Acceptance Time, the Company, the Company Board and its compensation committee, as applicable, shall adopt any resolutions and take any actions that are necessary to effectuate the provisions of Sections 3.3(a) and 3.3(b).

---

*   If the Company has warrants outstanding, a similar provision will be required by a buyer.

ARTICLE 3.4.   Adjustments to Prevent Dilution

In the event that the Company changes the number of Shares or securities convertible or exchangeable into or exercisable for Shares issued and outstanding prior to the Effective Time as a result of a reclassification, stock split (including a reverse stock split), stock dividend, distribution or division, recapitalization, merger, issuer tender offer or issuer exchange offer or other similar transaction, the Offer Price and the Per Share Merger Consideration shall be appropriately and proportionately adjusted.

ARTICLE 3.5.   Withholding Rights

Each of the Paying Agent, Parent, Merger Sub, and the Surviving Corporation shall be entitled to deduct and withhold from the consideration otherwise payable or deliverable pursuant to this Agreement such amounts as it is required to deduct and withhold with respect thereto under the Internal Revenue Code of 1986 (the "Code") or any other applicable state, local or foreign Law relating to Taxes. To the extent that amounts are so deducted or withheld, such deducted or withheld amounts (a) shall be remitted to the applicable Governmental Entity as required by applicable Law, and (b) shall be treated for all purposes of this Agreement as having been paid to the Persons in respect of which such deduction or withholding was made.

[ARTICLE 3.6.   Lost Certificates

If any Certificate shall have been lost, stolen or destroyed, upon the making of an affidavit of that fact, the Person claiming such Certificate to be lost, stolen or destroyed and, if required by Parent, the posting by such Person of a bond, in such reasonable amount as Parent may direct, as indemnity against any claim that may be made against it with respect to such Certificate, the Per Share Merger Consideration to be paid in respect of the Shares formerly represented by such Certificate as contemplated under this Article 3.]

ARTICLE 4.   Representations and Warranties

ARTICLE 4.1.

(a) Representations and Warranties of the Company. *[No representation or warranty made by the Company in this Agreement contains any untrue statement of a material fact or fails to state a material fact necessary to make any such representation or warranty, in light of the circumstances in which it was made, not misleading.]* Except as set forth in (i) the Company Reports filed with or furnished to the SEC on or prior to the date hereof (excluding, in each case, any disclosures set forth in any risk factor section or in any other section to the extent they are forward-looking statements or cautionary, predictive or forward-looking in nature) *[; provided, however, that the exception provided for in this clause (i) shall be applied with respect to a particular representation or warranty only to the extent that it is apparent on the face of such* *disclosure that such disclosure is applicable to such representation or warranty*] or (ii) the disclosure schedule delivered to Parent by the Company prior to entering into this Agreement (the "Company Disclosure Schedule")* (with each exception set forth in the Company Disclosure Schedule being identified by reference to, or grouped under a heading referring to, a specific individual section or subsection of this Agreement and relating only to such section or subsection; provided, however, that a matter disclosed with respect to one representation or warranty shall also be deemed to be disclosed with respect to each other representation or warranty to which the matter disclosed reasonably relates, but only to the extent that such relationship is reasonably apparent on the face of the disclosure contained in the Company Disclosure Schedule), the Company hereby represents and warrants to Parent and Merger Sub that:

(b) Organization, Good Standing and Qualification. Each of the Company and its Subsidiary is a legal entity duly organized, validly existing and in good standing under the Laws of its jurisdiction of organization and has all requisite corporate power and authority to own, lease and operate its properties and assets and to carry on its business as presently conducted and is qualified to do business and is in good standing as a foreign corporation in each jurisdiction where the ownership, leasing or operation of its assets or properties or conduct of its business requires such qualification, except where the failure to be so organized, qualified or in good standing, or to have such power or authority, individually or in the aggregate with other such failures, has not had, and ~~would~~ *[is]* not ~~be~~ reasonably likely to have, a Company Material Adverse Effect. The Company has made available to Parent complete and correct copies of the Company's and its Subsidiary's certificates of incorporation and bylaws or comparable governing documents, each as amended as of the date hereof, and each as so delivered is in full force and effect. The Company has made available to Parent true and correct copies of the minutes [*(or, in case of minutes that have not yet been finalized, a brief summary of the meeting) of all meetings of stockholders, the Company Board and each committee of the Company Board since ◙.]***

As used in this Agreement, the term "Company Material Adverse Effect" means any event, change, effect, development, state of facts,

---

* Some buyers may object to this first exception, preferring that all disclosures be made in the schedules to the acquisition agreement.

** The Company will want to qualify this to protect information about the interest of other buyers, to protect itself from having this buyer lower its price to just above any other offers, in language such as this: "*provided, however,* that the Company shall not be obligated to make available any minutes of meetings related to other bidders in connection with any potential sale of the Company or any of its material assets or otherwise related to deliberations by the Company Board with respect to the consideration of strategic alternatives, except as my be required by law or regulation." The latter phase allows disclosure of shopping efforts by the company required in the Schedule 14D–9 recommending the acceptance of the tender offer.

condition, circumstance or occurrence that has a material adverse effect on the business, results of operations[, *Covered Assets, liabilities*], prospects, or financial condition of the Company and its Subsidiary, taken as a whole, except to the extent that such material adverse effect results from or is attributable to any of the following: (i) any changes in general United States or global economic conditions; (ii) any changes in conditions generally affecting the pharmaceutical or biotechnology industries, except in the event that such changes in conditions have a materially disproportionate adverse effect on the Company and its Subsidiary, taken as a whole, relative to the adverse effect that such changes have on other clinical-stage pharmaceutical companies (in which case ~~only~~ the incremental disproportionate impact may be taken into account in determining whether there has been a Company Material Adverse Effect); (iii) any decline in the market price or trading volume of the Shares on NASDAQ (*provided* that the exception in this clause (iii) shall not prevent or otherwise affect a determination that any change, effect, circumstance or development underlying such decline has resulted in or contributed to a Company Material Adverse Effect); (iv) any regulatory, legislative or political conditions or securities, credit, financial or other capital markets conditions, in each case in the United States or any foreign jurisdiction; (v) any failure, in and of itself, by the Company or its Subsidiary to meet any internal or published projections, forecasts, estimates or predictions in respect of revenues, earnings or other financial or operating metrics for any period (provided that the exception in this clause (v) shall not prevent or otherwise affect a determination that any change, effect, circumstance or development underlying such failure has resulted in or contributed to a Company Material Adverse Effect); (vi) the execution and delivery of this Agreement, the performance by any party hereto of its obligations hereunder, or the public announcement or pendency of the Offer, the Merger or any of the other Transactions, including the impact thereof on the relationships, contractual or otherwise, of the Company with its employees or with any other third party; (vii) changes or proposed changes in GAAP or in Laws applicable to the Company or the enforcement or interpretation thereof; (viii) any geopolitical conditions, the outbreak or escalation of hostilities, any acts of war, sabotage, terrorism or military actions, or any escalation or worsening of any such hostilities, acts of war, sabotage, terrorism or military actions threatened or underway as of the date of this Agreement; *[except to the extent that such events, acts or changes have a materially disproportionate adverse effect on the Company and its Subsidiary, taken as a whole, relative to the adverse effect that such changes have on other development-stage companies in the pharmaceutical or biotechnology industry (in which case the incremental disproportionate adverse impact may be taken into account in determining whether there has occurred a Company Material Adverse Effect),]*, (ix) any action required to be taken pursuant to or in accordance with this Agreement or taken at the request of Parent or Merger Sub; (x) actions taken, or not taken, with the express prior written consent of Parent or Merger Sub; (xi) any legal action commenced on behalf of the Company's stockholders and arising from this agreement or the transactions contemplated hereby (except as it relates to breaches by the Company; or (xii) any matter set forth in Section 4.1(a) or any other part of the Company Disclosure Schedule[, *but only if such relationship is reasonably apparent on the face of the disclosure in such other part of the Company Disclosure Schedule. As used in this Agreement, the term "Covered Assets" means the Company's assets associated with the Key Product.*]

(c) **Capital Structure.** The authorized capital stock of the Company consists of (A) ◙ Shares, of which ◙ were outstanding as of the close of business on ◙, and (B) ◙ shares of preferred stock, par value $0.001 per share, none of which were outstanding as of the close of business on ◙. All of the outstanding Shares have been duly authorized and are validly issued, fully paid and nonassessable. As of ◙, other than ◙ Shares reserved for issuance under the 1998 Stock Plan and the ◙ Equity Incentive Plan (together, the "Stock Plans"). Section 4.1(b) of the Company Disclosure Schedule sets forth a true and complete list of Company Options and Company Restricted Stock issued and outstanding as of the close of business on ◙, including the holder, date of grant, term, number of Shares and, where applicable, exercise price. Each of the outstanding shares of capital stock or other securities of the Company's Subsidiary is duly authorized, validly issued, fully paid and nonassessable and owned by the Company, free and clear of any lien, charge, pledge, security interest, claim or other encumbrance (each, a "Lien"). Except as set forth above and except for the Top-Up Option, there are no preemptive or other outstanding rights, options, warrants, conversion rights, stock appreciation rights, redemption rights, repurchase rights, agreements, arrangements, calls, commitments or rights of any kind that obligate the Company or its Subsidiary to issue or sell any shares of capital stock or other securities of the Company or its Subsidiary or any securities or obligations convertible or exchangeable into or exercisable for, or giving any Person a right to subscribe for or acquire, any securities of the Company or its Subsidiary, and no securities or obligations evidencing such rights are authorized, issued or outstanding. Upon any issuance of any Shares in accordance with the terms of the Stock Plans, such Shares will be duly authorized, validly issued, fully paid and nonassessable and free and clear of any Lien. Upon any issuance of Shares pursuant to the Top-Up Option, such Shares will be duly authorized, validly issued, fully paid and nonassessable and free and clear of any Liens. The Company does not have outstanding any bonds, debentures, notes or other obligations the holders of which have the right to vote (or convertible into or exercisable for securities having the right to vote) with the stockholders of the Company on any matter. Other than ◙, an English company, the Company has no Subsidiaries.

(d) Corporate Authority; Approval and Fairness.

(i) The Company has all requisite corporate power and authority and has taken all corporate action necessary in order to execute, deliver and perform its obligations under this Agreement and to consummate the Transactions, subject only, with respect to the consummation of the Merger, if required by the DGCL, to the adoption of this Agreement by the affirmative vote of the holders of a majority of the outstanding Shares entitled to vote on such matter at a stockholders' meeting duly called and held for such purpose (the "Company Requisite Vote"). This Agreement has been duly executed and delivered by the Company and, assuming this Agreement constitutes the valid and binding agreement of Parent and Merger Sub, constitutes a valid and binding agreement of the Company enforceable against the Company in accordance with its terms, subject to bankruptcy, insolvency, fraudulent transfer, reorganization, moratorium and similar Laws of general applicability relating to or affecting creditors' rights and to general equity principles (the "Bankruptcy and Equity Exception").

(ii) [*At a meeting duly called and held prior to the execution and delivery of this Agreement,*] the Company Board has adopted resolutions [*by the unanimous vote of all directors of the Company**] (A) approving and declaring advisable this Agreement and the Offer, the Merger and the other transactions contemplated hereby (collectively, the "Transactions"), (B) determining that the terms of the Offer, this Agreement, the Merger and the other Transactions are fair to and in the best interests of the Company and to the holders of the Shares and (C) subject to Section 5.2, recommending that the holders of Shares accept the Offer, tender their Shares into the Offer and [*to the extent required by applicable Law to Consummate the Merger, vote their shares in favor of*] adopt[*ing*] this Agreement (such recommendation, the "Company Recommendation"), and, as of the date hereof, none of the aforesaid actions by the Company Board have been amended, rescinded or modified. Assuming the accuracy of the representations and warranties set forth in Section 4.2(h), the Company Board has taken all actions necessary so that Parent and Merger Sub will not be prohibited by Section 203 of the DGCL from consummating the Transactions in the manner contemplated hereby and to ensure that Section 203 of the DGCL will not impose any additional procedural, voting, approval or other restrictions on the timely consummation of the Transactions or restrict, impair or delay the ability of (x) Parent or Merger Sub to engage in any of the Transactions with the Company or (y) Parent or Merger Sub, following the Acceptance Time and subject to the other provisions of this

---

* This relieves the buyer of any concerns that a majority of disinterested directors did not approve the transaction.

Agreement, to vote or otherwise exercise all rights as a stockholder of the Company. No other state takeover statute applies to this Agreement, the Merger or the other Transactions.

(iii) The Company Board has received the oral opinion of its financial advisor, ◙, to the effect that, as of the date hereof, the consideration to be received by the holders of the Shares in the Offer and the Merger is fair from a financial point of view to such holders. A written version of such opinion will be delivered to Parent promptly following its receipt by the Company, it being agreed and understood that such opinion is for the benefit of the Company Board and may not be relied on by Parent or Merger Sub.

[*(iv) The execution, delivery and performance of this Agreement by the Company, and the consummation by the Company of the transactions contemplated by this Agreement, including the Merger, do not and will not (A) contravene or conflict with, or result in any violation or breach of, the Charter or Bylaws of the Company or its Subsidiary, (B) subject to compliance with the requirements set forth in Section 3.03(d)(i) and, in the case of consummation of the Merger, obtaining the Company Requisite Vote, conflict with or violate any Law applicable to the Company, its subsidiary or any of their respective properties or assets, (C) result in any breach of or constitute a default (or an event that with notice or lapse of time or both would become a default under, or alter the rights or obligation of any third party under, or give to others any rights of termination, amendment, acceleration or cancellation, or require any consent under, any Contract to which the Company or its subsidiary is a party or otherwise bound as of the date hereof, or (D) result in the creation of a Lien on any of the properties or assets of the Company or its subsidiary, except, in the case of each of clauses (B), (C) and (D), for any conflicts, violations, breaches, defaults, alterations, terminations, amendments, accelerations, cancellations or Liens, or where the failure to obtain any consents, in each case, would not reasonably be expected to have, individually or in the aggregate, a Company Material Adverse Effect.*]

(e) Governmental Filings; No Violations.

(i) Other than (A) the filing of the Delaware Certificate of Merger, (B) compliance with applicable requirements of the Hart-Scott-Rodino Antitrust Improvements Act of 1976 (the "HSR Act"), (C) compliance with the applicable requirements of the Exchange Act, including the filing of the Schedule 14D–9 in connection with the Offer and the Proxy Statement, if applicable, in connection with the Company Requisite Vote, (D) compliance with the rules and regulations of NASDAQ and (E) the other filings, consents and/or notices set forth on Section 4.1(d)(i) of the Company Disclosure Schedule, no notices, reports or other filings are required to be made by the Company with, nor are any consents, registrations, approvals, permits or authorizations required to be obtained by the Company from, any domestic or foreign governmental or regulatory authority, agency, commission, body, court or other legislative, executive or judicial governmental entity (each, a "Governmental Entity"), in connection with the execution, delivery and performance of this Agreement by the Company and the consummation of the Offer, the Merger and the other Transactions, except those that the failure to make or obtain, individually or in the aggregate with other such failures, has not had, and is not reasonably likely to have, a Company Material Adverse Effect and would[is] not reasonably likely to prevent, materially delay or materially impair the consummation of the Transaction.

(ii) The execution, delivery and performance of this Agreement by the Company do not, and the consummation of the Offer, the Merger and the other Transactions will not, constitute or result in (A) a breach or violation of, or a default under, the certificate of incorporation or bylaws of the Company or the comparable governing instruments of its Subsidiary, (B) a breach or violation of, a termination (or right of termination) or a default under, the creation or acceleration of any obligations under, or the creation of a Lien on any of the assets of the Company or its Subsidiary pursuant to any lease, license, contract, note, mortgage, indenture, or other agreement (each, a "Contract") to which the Company or its Subsidiary is a party or, assuming compliance with the matters referred to in Section 4.1(d)(i) and (if applicable) receipt of the Company Requisite Vote, any Law to which the Company or its Subsidiary is subject, or (C) any change in the rights or obligations of any party under any Contract to which the Company or its Subsidiary is a party, except, in the case of clause (B) or (C) above, for any such breach, violation, termination, default, creation or acceleration that, individually or in the aggregate with other such matters, has not had, and is not reasonably likely to have, a Company Material Adverse Effect and is not reasonably likely to prevent, materially delay or materially impair the consummation of the Transactions.

(iii) Neither the Company nor its Subsidiary is a party to any non-competition Contracts or other Contract that purports to limit in any material respect either the type of business in which the Company or its Subsidiary (or, after giving effect to the Offer or the Merger, Parent or its Subsidiary) may engage or the manner or locations in which either of them may so engage in any business.

[(iv) Neither the Company nor its Subsidiary is a party to, nor has any commitment to become a party to, any joint venture, off-balance sheet partnership or any similar Contract (including any Contract or arrangement relating to any transaction or relationship between or among the Company, on the one hand, and any unconsolidated Affiliate, including any structured finance, special purpose or limited purpose entity or Person, on the other hand), or any "off-balance sheet *arrangements" (as defined in Item 303(a) of Regulation S-K promulgated by the SEC), where the result, purpose or intended effect of such Contract is to avoid disclosure of any material transaction involving, or material liabilities of, the Company in its published financial statements or other Company Reports.***

(v) Each of the balance sheets included in or incorporated by reference into the Company Reports (including the related notes and schedules) fairly presents or, in the case of Company Reports filed after the date hereof, will fairly present, the financial position of the Company as of its date and each of the statements of income, changes in shareholders' equity and cash flows included in or incorporated by reference into the Company Reports (including any related notes and schedules) fairly presents or, in the case of Company Reports filed after the date hereof, will fairly present, the results of operations, retained earnings (loss) and changes in financial position, as the case may be, of the Company for the periods set forth therein (subject, in the case of unaudited statements, to notes and normal year-end audit adjustments that will not be material in amount or effect); in accordance with U.S. generally accepted accounting principles ("GAAP") consistently applied during the periods involved, except as may be noted therein.

(vi) Except for (A) those liabilities that are reflected or reserved against on the audited consolidated balance sheet of the Company and its Subsidiary as of ◙ (the "Most Recent Balance Sheet"), (B) liabilities incurred in the ordinary course of business consistent with past practice since the date of the Most Recent Balance Sheet, and (C) obligations incurred pursuant to this Agreement, neither the Company nor its Subsidiary has incurred any liability of the type required to be set forth on a balance sheet prepared in accordance with GAAP that, individually or in the aggregate with other such liabilities, has had, or would reasonably be expected to have a Company Material Adverse Effect.

(f) Company Reports; Financial Statements.

(i) The Company has filed or furnished, as applicable, on a timely basis all forms, statements, certifications, reports and documents required to be filed or furnished by it with the SEC pursuant to the Exchange Act or the Securities Act of 1933 (the "Securities Act"), since ◙ [date] (the forms, statements, reports and documents filed or furnished since ◙ [date] and those filed or furnished subsequent to the date hereof, including any amendments thereto, the "Company Reports"). Each of the Company Reports, at the time of its filing or being furnished complied or, if not yet filed or furnished, will comply, in all material respects with the applicable requirements of the Securities Act, the Exchange Act and the Sarbanes-Oxley Act of 2002 (the "Sarbanes-Oxley Act"). As of their

---

*   This item in item was inspired by infamous off-balance sheet transactions by officials of Enron Corporation that created false transactions with the company that were not arm's length, and vastly exaggerated its profits.

respective dates (or, if amended, as of the date of such amendment), the Company Reports did not, and any Company Reports filed with or furnished to the SEC subsequent to the date hereof will not, contain any untrue statement of a material fact or omit to state a material fact required to be stated therein or necessary to make the statements made therein, in light of the circumstances in which they were made, not misleading.

(ii) The Company is in compliance in all material respects with the applicable listing and corporate governance rules and regulations of NASDAQ and the Sarbanes-Oxley Act.

(iii) The Company's system of internal control over financial reporting (as defined in Rules 13a–15(f) and 15d–15(f) of the Exchange Act) ~~are designed to provide~~ [*is effective in providing*] reasonable assurance (A) that the Company maintains records that in reasonable detail accurately and fairly reflect its transactions and dispositions of assets, (B) that transactions are recorded as necessary to permit preparation of financial statements in conformity with GAAP, (C) that receipts and expenditures are executed only in accordance with authorizations of management and the Company Board and (D) regarding prevention or timely detection of the unauthorized acquisition, use or disposition of the Company's assets that could have a material effect on the Company's financial statements. The Company has disclosed, based on the most recent evaluation of its chief executive officer and its chief financial officer prior to the date hereof, to the Company's auditors and the audit committee of the Company Board (A) any significant deficiencies in the design or operation of its internal controls over financial reporting that are reasonably likely to adversely affect the Company's ability to record, process, summarize and report financial information and has identified for the Company's auditors and audit committee of the Company Board any material weaknesses in internal control over financial reporting and (B) any fraud, whether or not material, that involves management or other employees who have a significant role in the Company's internal control over financial reporting. The Company has made available to Parent (x) a summary of any such disclosure made by management to the Company's auditors and audit committee since ◙ [date] and (y) any material communication since ◙ [date] made by management or the Company's auditors to the audit committee required or contemplated by listing standards of NASDAQ, the audit committee's charter or professional standards of the Public Company Accounting Oversight Board. Since ◙ [date], no material complaints from any source regarding accounting, internal accounting controls or auditing matters, and no concerns from Company employees regarding questionable accounting or auditing matters, have been received by the Company. The Company has made available to Parent a summary of all material complaints or concerns relating to other matters made since ◙ [date] through the Company's whistleblower hot-line or equivalent system for receipt of employee concerns regarding possible violations of Law. No attorney representing the Company or its Subsidiary, whether or not employed by the Company or its Subsidiary, has reported evidence of a violation of Securities Laws, breach of fiduciary duty or similar violation by the Company or any of its officers, directors, employees or agents to the Company's chief legal officer, audit committee (or other committee designated for the purpose) of the Company Board or the Company Board pursuant to the rules adopted pursuant to Section 307 of the Sarbanes-Oxley Act or any Company policy contemplating such reporting, including in instances not required by those rules.

(iv) Each of the balance sheets included in or incorporated by reference into the Company Reports (including the related notes and schedules) fairly presents or, in the case of Company Reports filed after the date hereof, will fairly present, the financial position of the Company as of its date and each of the statements of income, changes in shareholders' equity and cash flows included in or incorporated by reference into the Company Reports (including any related notes and schedules) fairly presents or, in the case of Company Reports filed after the date hereof, will fairly present, the results of operations, retained earnings (loss) and changes in financial position, as the case may be, of the Company for the periods set forth therein (subject, in the case of unaudited statements, to notes and normal year-end audit adjustments that will not be material in amount or effect); in each case in accordance with U.S. generally accepted accounting principles ("GAAP") consistently applied during the periods involved, except as may be noted therein.

(v) Except for (A) those liabilities that are reflected or reserved against on the Company Financial Statements, (B) liabilities incurred in the ordinary course of business consistent with past practice since ◙ [date], (C) obligations pursuant to any Contract existing as of the date hereof, (D) obligations to comply with applicable Laws and (E) obligations incurred pursuant to this Agreement or the Transactions, neither the Company nor its Subsidiary has incurred, since ◙ [date], any liability of the type required to be set forth on a balance sheet prepared in accordance with GAAP that, individually or in the aggregate with other such liabilities, has had, or is reasonably likely to have, a Company Material Adverse Effect.

[(vi) Neither the Company nor its Subsidiary is a party to, or has any commitment to become a party to, any joint venture, off balance sheet partnership or any similar Contract (including any Contract or arrangement relating to any transaction or relationship between or among the Company and its Subsidiary, on the one hand, and any unconsolidated Affiliate, including any structured finance, special purpose or limited purpose entity or Person, on the other hand, or any "off balance sheet arrangements" (as defined in Item 303(a) of Regulation S-

K under the Exchange Act), where the result, purpose or intended effect of such Contract is to avoid disclosure of any material transaction involving, or material liabilities of, the Company or its Subsidiary in ~~its~~the Company's or such Subsidiary's published financial statements or other Company Reports.]

(g) Information Supplied. None of the information supplied or to be supplied by the Company for inclusion or incorporation by reference in (i) the Offer Documents or the Schedule 14D–9 will, at the time such document is filed with the SEC, at any time it is amended or supplemented or at the time it is first mailed to the Company's stockholders, contain any untrue statement of a material fact or omit to state any material fact required to be stated therein or necessary to make the statements therein not misleading, or (ii) if required to be filed, the Proxy Statement will, at the date it is first mailed to the Company's stockholders or at the time of the Stockholders Meeting, contain any untrue statement of a material fact or omit to state any material fact required to be stated therein or necessary in order to make the statements therein, in light of the circumstances under which they are made, not misleading. The Schedule 14D–9 and the Proxy Statement will comply as to form in all material respects with the requirements of the Exchange Act and the rules and regulations promulgated thereunder, except that no representation or warranty is made by the Company with respect to statements made or incorporated by reference therein that are based on information derived from Parent's public SEC filings or supplied by Parent or Merger Sub for inclusion or incorporation by reference therein.

(h) Absence of Certain Changes.

(i)   Since the date of filing by the Company of the most recent form 10-Q or 8-K, other than in connection with the transactions contemplated by this Agreement, the Company and its Subsidiary have conducted their business only in, and have not engaged in any material transaction other than in accordance with, the ordinary course of such business consistent with past practice.

(ii) Since the date of the most recent balance sheet, there has not occurred: (A) any change, development, event or circumstance that, individually or in the aggregate with other such changes, developments, events or circumstances, has had, or is reasonably likely to have, a Company Material Adverse Effect; (B) any material damage, destruction or other casualty loss with respect to any material asset or property owned, leased or otherwise used by the Company or its Subsidiary, whether or not covered by insurance; (C) any declaration, setting aside or payment of any dividend or other distribution with respect to any shares of capital stock of the Company or its Subsidiary, or any

---

*   This might be called the "Enron" provision, after an earlier financial scandal noted above.

repurchase, redemption or other acquisition by the Company or its Subsidiary of any outstanding shares of capital stock or other securities of the Company or its Subsidiary (except for a two-for-one split of the Common Stock in the form of a stock dividend paid on August 31, 2011); (D) any material change in any method of accounting or accounting practice by the Company or its Subsidiary; or (E) except to the extent required by applicable Laws, (x) any increase in the compensation payable or to become payable to the officers or employees of the Company or its Subsidiary (except for increases in the ordinary course of business and consistent with past practice); ~~or~~ [(y) *payment to any Company director or officer of any material bonus, making to any Company officer or director of any material profit-sharing or similar payment, or grant to any Company officer or director of any rights to receive severance, termination, retention or tax gross-up compensation or benefits to (in any case except for increases in the ordinary course of business and consistent with past practice; (z) or*] any establishment, adoption, entry into, or amendment of any collective bargaining, bonus, profit-sharing, thrift, compensation, employment, termination, severance or other plan, agreement, trust, fund, policy or arrangement for the benefit of any director, officer or employee, except ~~as~~ to the extent required by applicable Laws.

(i) Legal Proceedings. Except for any action, claim, suit, investigation or proceeding by or before any Governmental Entity, arbitrator, mediator or other tribunal (collectively, "<u>Proceedings</u>") that, individually or in the aggregate with other Proceedings, has not had, and is not reasonably likely to have, a Company Material Adverse Effect, there is no Proceeding pending or, to the knowledge of the executive officers of Company, threatened~~,~~ against the Company or its Subsidiary [~~(other than disputes of a type as may arise from time to time in the Company's ordinary course of business and which would not, individually or in the aggregate, be material to the Company or its Subsidiary, taken as a whole).~~]*. Section 4.1(h) of the Company Disclosure Letter lists, as of the date of this Agreement, all material Proceedings that the Company or its Subsidiary has pending against other parties and, to the knowledge of the executive officers of the Company, all Proceedings that are pending against the Company or its Subsidiary. Except for any judgment, order, writ, injunction or decree (whether temporary, preliminary or permanent) of any Governmental Entity (an "<u>Order</u>") that, individually or in the aggregate with other such Orders, has not had, and is not

---

* This is a buyer's deletion from a seller's form. Given the materiality qualification, what does a buyer gain with this? [Hint: For a long time asbestos claims were deemed immaterial by many companies, until increasing volume forced a change. Ultimately a number of these companies entered bankruptcy protection. One can imagine similar problems with pharmaceutical companies, where a single claim may not be financially material, but may be the first of many.]

reasonably likely to have, a Company Material Adverse Effect, neither the Company nor its Subsidiary is subject to or bound by any Order.

(j) Employee Benefits.

(i)   All material benefit and compensation plans, contracts, policies or arrangements covering current or former employees (the "Employees") and current or former directors of the Company and its Subsidiary under which there is a continuing financial obligation of the Company, including "Employee Benefit Plans" within the meaning of Section 3(3) of the Employee Retirement Income Security Act of 1974 ("ERISA"), and deferred compensation, stock option, stock purchase, stock appreciation rights, stock based, incentive and bonus plans, severance, retention, change in control, employment or similar plans, programs, agreements or arrangement [whether written or unwritten] (the "Benefit Plans"), other than Benefit Plans that are maintained outside of the United States primarily for the benefit of Employees working outside of the United States ("Non-U.S. Benefit Plans"), are listed on Section 4.1(i)(i) of the Company Disclosure Schedule, and each Benefit Plan which has received a favorable opinion letter from the IRS has been separately identified. True and complete copies of all Benefit Plans listed on Section 4.1(i)(I) of the Company Disclosure Schedule [*(or, in the case of any unwritten Benefit Plan, a written summary of the material provisions of such plan), (ii) the most recent report on Form 5500 filed with the Internal Revenue Service ("IRS") with respect to each Benefit Plan in effect on the date hereof, to the extent any such report was required by applicable Law, (iii) the most recent summary plan description for each Benefit Plan for which a summary plan description is required by applicable Law and (iv) each currently effective trust agreement or other funding vehicle relating to any Benefit Plan*] have been provided or made available to Parent.

(ii) To the knowledge of the executive officers of Company, each Benefit Plan other than Non-U.S. Benefit Plans (collectively, "U.S. Benefit Plans") is in substantial compliance with ERISA, the Code and other applicable Law. Each U.S. Benefit Plan which is subject to ERISA (an "ERISA Plan") that is an "employee pension benefit plan" within the meaning of Section 3(2) of ERISA intended to be qualified under Section 401(a) of the Code, has received a favorable determination letter from the Internal Revenue Service (the "IRS") or has applied to the IRS for such favorable determination letter under Section 401(b) of the Code, and the Company is not aware of any circumstances likely to result in the loss of the qualification of such ERISA Plan under Section 401(a) of the Code. To the knowledge of the executive officers of the Company, neither the Company nor its Subsidiary has engaged in a transaction with respect to any ERISA Plan that could subject the Company or its Subsidiary to a tax or penalty imposed by either Section 4975 of the Code or Section 502(i) of ERISA in an amount that would be material.

(iii) No U.S. Benefit Plan is a "Multiemployer Plan", within the meaning of Section 4001(a)(3) of ERISA (a "Multiemployer Plan"), and neither the Company nor its Subsidiary has at any time sponsored or contributed to, or has or had any liability or obligation in respect of, any Multiemployer Plan.

(iv) Neither the Company nor its Subsidiary currently maintains or has ever maintained a "Single-Employer Plan", within the meaning of Section 4001(a)(15) of ERISA. Neither the Company nor any other Person that, together with the Company, is treated as a single employer under Section 414(b), (c), (m) or (o) of the Code or any other applicable Law, has sponsored, maintained, contributed to or been obligated to sponsor, maintain or contribute to, or has any actual or contingent liability under, any benefit plan that is subject to Title IV of ERISA or Section 412 of the Code or is otherwise a defined benefit pension plan or is a plan described in Section 3(40) of ERISA or Section 413 of the Code.

(v) No Benefit Plan that is an employee welfare benefit plan as defined under ERISA Section 3(1) provides benefits to, or on behalf of, any former Employee after the termination of employment except (A) where the full cost of such benefit is borne entirely by the former Employee (or his eligible dependents or beneficiaries) or (B) where the benefit is required by Section 4980B of the Code.

(vi) No Employee has received or is reasonably expected to receive any payment or benefit from the Company that would be nondeductible pursuant to Section 162(m) of the Code or any other applicable Law.

(vii) As of the date hereof, there is no material pending or, to the knowledge of the executive officers of the Company, threatened litigation relating to the Benefit Plans, other than routine claims for benefits.

(viii) Except as set forth in Section 4.1(i)(ivi) of the Company Disclosure Schedule, none of the execution of this Agreement, the adoption of this Agreement by the stockholders of the Company, if applicable, or the consummation of the transactions contemplated hereby will (A) entitle any Employee to severance pay or any material increase in severance pay upon any termination of employment after the date hereof, or (B) accelerate the time of payment or vesting or result in any payment or funding (through a grantor trust or otherwise) of compensation or benefits under, increase the amount payable or result in any other material obligation pursuant to, any of the Benefit Plans [or (C) entitle any "disqualified individual" (as such term is defined in Treasury Regulation Section 1.280G–1) with respect to the Company, to receive any gross-up payment for any excise tax liability pursuant to Section 280G or Section 4999 of the Code].

(ix) All Non-U.S. Benefit Plans comply in all material respects with applicable local Law. All Non-U.S. Benefit Plans are listed on Section 4.1(i)(ivii) of the Company Disclosure Schedule [*(or, in the case of any unwritten Benefit Plan, a written summary of the material provisions of such plan), the most recent report on Form 5500 filed with the Internal Revenue Service ("IRS").*]

(k) Legal and Regulatory Compliance.

(i)   Since ◙, the business of the Company and its Subsidiary has not been, and is not being, conducted in violation of any federal, state, local or foreign law, statute or ordinance, common law, or any rule, regulation, standard, Order, agency requirement, license or permit of any Governmental Entity (collectively, "<u>Laws</u>"), except for violations that, individually or in the aggregate with other such violations, have not had, and are not reasonably likely to have, a Company Material Adverse Effect.* No investigation or review by any Governmental Entity with respect to the Company or its Subsidiary is pending or, to the knowledge of the executive officers of the Company, threatened, nor has any Governmental Entity indicated an intention to conduct the same, except for those the outcome of which, individually or in the aggregate with the outcome of other such matters, has not had, and is not reasonaby likely to have, a Company Material Adverse Effect and is not reasonably likely to prevent, materially delay or materially impair the consummation of the Transactions.

(ii)   Each of the Company and its Subsidiary has all permits, licenses, certifications, approvals, registrations, consents, authorizations, franchises, variances, exemptions and orders issued or granted by any Governmental Entity ("<u>Licenses</u>") necessary to conduct its business as presently conducted, including all such Licenses of the United States Food and Drug Administration ("FDA") or any other applicable U.S. or foreign drug regulatory authority (collectively with the FDA, "<u>Regulatory Authorities</u>") necessary to conduct its business as presently conducted (collectively, the "<u>Regulatory Licenses</u>"), except those Licenses the absence of which, individually or in the aggregate with other such absences, has not had, and is not reasonably likely to have, a Company Material Adverse Effect and is not reasonably likely to prevent, materially delay or materially impair the consummation of the Transactions. There has not occurred any revocation or termination of any Regulatory License, or any material impairment of the rights of the Company or its Subsidiary under any Regulatory License, except for any such revocation, termination or impairment that, individually or in the aggregate with other such revocations, terminations and impairments, has not had, and is not reasonably likely to have, a Company Material Adverse Effect. Each of the Company and its Subsidiary has operated in compliance in all material respects with applicable Laws administered

---

*   Note that this representation is restricted to a current period. In the document from which this was drawn, it was the date the Company first went public. Earlier private offerings of securities can often raise questions of legal compliance. In this case no damages would have been available because of the rise in the value of the Company's stock. In other cases buyers would resist this, especially if the company had ever given stockholders preemptive rights that might have been inadvertently violated.

or enforced by the FDA or any other Regulatory Authority, except where the failure so to comply, individually or in the aggregate with other such failures, has not had, and is not reasonably likely to have, a Company Material Adverse Effect. [*As of the date of this Agreement, there are no, and have not been any, inspection observations, notices pursuant to 21 U.S.C. Section 305, warning letters, untitled letters or similar documents that assert a lack of compliance by the Company or its Subsidiary with any applicable Laws, Orders or regulatory requirements that have not been fully resolved to the satisfaction of the FDA or any other Regulatory Authority.*]

(iii) Since ◙, all preclinical studies and clinical trials, and other studies and tests conducted by or, to the knowledge of the executive officers of the Company, on behalf of the Company or its Subsidiary have been, and if still pending are being, conducted in compliance with all applicable Laws (including those pertaining to Good Laboratory Practice and Good Clinical Practice contained in 21 C.F.R. Part 58 and Part 312 and all applicable requirements relating to protection of human subjects contained in 21 C.F.R. Parts 50, 54, and 56), except for noncompliances that, individually or in the aggregate with other such noncompliances, have not had, and are not reasonably likely to have, a Company Material Adverse Effect. Since ◙, except for such exceptions that, individually or in the aggregate with other such exceptions, have not had, and are not reasonably likely to have, a Company Material Adverse Effect, no clinical trial conducted by or, to the knowledge of the executive officers of Company, on behalf of the Company or its Subsidiary has been terminated or suspended prior to completion for safety or other non-business reasons, and neither the FDA nor any other applicable Regulatory Authority, clinical investigator that has participated or is participating in, or institutional review board that has or has had jurisdiction over, a clinical trial conducted by or, to the knowledge of the executive officers of Company, on behalf of the Company or its Subsidiary has commenced, or, to the knowledge of the executive officers of Company, threatened to initiate, any action to place a clinical hold order on, or otherwise terminate, materially delay or suspend, any ongoing clinical investigation conducted by or, to the knowledge of the executive officers of Company, on behalf of the Company or its Subsidiary.

(iv) Since ◙, neither the Company nor its Subsidiary nor, to the knowledge of the executive officers of the Company, any of their executive officers or Employees at the "director" level or above has been convicted of any crime or engaged in any conduct that in any such case has resulted, or is reasonably likely to result, in debarment under 21 U.S.C. Section 335a [*or exclusion from participation in any Federal health are program pursuant to 42 U.S.S. Section 1320a–7*]. (v) The Company has made available to Parent complete and correct copies of each Investigational New Drug Application and each similar state or foreign regulatory filing made on behalf of the Company or its Subsidiary, including all related supplements, amendments and annual reports.

[*(vi) All material applications, reports, documents, claims, permits and notices required to be filed, maintained or furnished to the FDA or any other Regulatory Authority by the Company or its Subsidiary, including with respect to its Company Pharmaceutical Products, have been so filed, maintained or furnished. All such applications, reports, documents, claims, permits and notices: (i) have been made available to Parent; and (ii) were complete and accurate in all material respects on the date filed (or were corrected in or supplemented by a subsequent filing). Neither the Company nor its Subsidiary, nor, to the knowledge of the executive officers of the Company, any officer, employee or agent or distributor of the Company or its Subsidiary, has made an untrue statement of a material fact or a fraudulent statement to the FDA or any other Regulatory Authority, failed to disclose a material fact required to be disclosed to the FDA or any other Regulatory Authority, or committed an act, made a statement, or failed to make a statement that, at the time such disclosure was made, would reasonably be expected to provide a basis for the FDA or any other Regulatory Authority to invoke its policy respecting "Fraud, Untrue Statements of Material Facts, Bribery, and Illegal Gratuities", set forth in 56 Fed. Reg. 46191 (September 10, 1991) or any similar policy. As used in this Agreement, the term "Company Pharmaceutical Product" shall mean ◙, ◙, ◙ and ◙.*

(vii) To the knowledge of the executive officers of Company, all manufacturing operations conducted for the benefit of the Company with respect to any Company Pharmaceutical Product being used in human clinical trials have been and are being conducted in accordance, in all material respects, with GMP Regulations. As used in this Agreement, the term "GMP Regulations" means the applicable laws and regulations, as may be amended from time to time, for current Good Manufacturing Practice, which have been promulgated by (i) the FDA under the United States Federal Food, Drug and Cosmetic Act, 21 C.F.R. § 210 et seq., (ii) the European Medicines Agency or under the European Union guide to Good Manufacturing Practice for medical products and (iii) any other applicable Governmental Entity in each jurisdiction where the Company, or a third party acting on its behalf, is undertaking or has undertaken a clinical trial or any manufacturing activities as of or prior to the Effective Time.]*

(l)   Material Contracts.

(i)   Except for this Agreement and except for Contracts filed as exhibits to the Company Reports as of the date hereof, neither the

---

*   This representation is not absolute, but depends upon the actual knowledge of company officers.

Company nor its Subsidiary is a party to any Contract (or group of related Contracts with the same party or an Affiliate of such party):

(A) that would be required to be filed by the Company as a "material contract" pursuant to Item 601(b)(10) of Regulation S-K under the Securities Act;

(B) that purports to limit or otherwise restrict in any material respect the ability of the Company or its Subsidiary to compete in any business or geographic area (or that, following the Offer or the Merger, would by its terms apply such limits or other restrictions to Parent or its Subsidiary);

(C) containing any standstill, or similar agreement pursuant to which the Company or its Subsidiary has agreed not to acquire assets or securities of another Person, or (y) containing a put, call, right of first refusal or similar right pursuant to which the Company or its Subsidiary could be required to purchase or sell, or otherwise acquire or transfer, as applicable, any equity interests of any Person or assets that have a fair market value or purchase price of more than [$500,000 *$300,000 or relating to the acquisition or disposition of any business or any material assets other than in the ordinary course of business consistent with past practice (whether by merger, sale of stock or assets or otherwise)*] .

(D) that would prevent, materially delay or materially impede the Company's ability to consummate the Offer, the Merger or the other Transactions;

(E) that is between the Company or its Subsidiary and any of their respective directors or officers or any Person beneficially owning five percent (5%) or more of the outstanding Shares;

(F) that involves the payment or receipt by the Company or its Subsidiary of royalties or other amounts of more than [$500,000 *$300,000*] in the aggregate calculated based on the revenues or income of the Company;

[*(G) for the furnishing of services or the sale of products which involves, or would reasonably be expected in the future to involve, consideration in excess of $300,000 in any twelve (12) month period, for the receipt of services by a third party or for the purchase of raw materials, commodities, supplies, products, or other personal property, which involves payment by the Company of consideration in excess of $300,000 in any twelve (12) month period or which would reasonably be expected to involve payment by the Company of consideration in excess of $300,000 in any future twelve (12) month period during the term of such agreement or (z) that provides for future payment* *obligations by the Company of either $300,000 or more related to clinical trials of Company Pharmaceutical Products;*

(H) under which any the Company is a lessee of, or holds or uses, any equipment, machinery, vehicle or other tangible personal property owned by a third Person which requires future annual payments in excess of $300,000;

(I) pursuant to which the Company has entered into a partnership, joint venture, collaboration or other similar arrangement with any Person other than the Subsidiary;

(J) for capital expenditures or the acquisition or construction of fixed assets which requires aggregate future payments in excess of $300,000;

(K) entered into other than in the ordinary course of business pursuant to which the Company agrees not to make use of any material right in any Intellectual Property owned by the Company;

(L) pursuant to which the Company has outstanding indebtedness, or provides a guarantee in a principal amount in excess of $300,000;

(M) which requires future payments by the Company in excess of $300,000 per annum containing "change of control" or similar provisions; or

(N) pursuant to which the Company or any other party thereto has material continuing obligations, rights or interests relating to the distribution, supply, manufacture, marketing or co-promotion of, or collaboration with respect to any Company Pharmaceutical Product.]

Each such Contract described in clauses (A) through (N) above is referred to herein as a "Material Contract."

(ii) Each of the Material Contracts (and those Contracts that would be Material Contracts but for the exception of being filed as exhibits to the Company Reports), ~~but in any event excluding Benefit Plans and Company Leases, are (ii) Each of the Material Contracts~~ is valid and binding on the Company or its Subsidiary and, to the knowledge of the executive officers of the Company, each other party thereto and is in full force and effect, except for such failures to be valid and binding or to be in full force and effect that, individually or in the aggregate with other such failures, hasve not had, and [~~would~~ *are*] not reasonably ~~be expected~~[*likely*] to have, a Company Material Adverse Effect. None of the Company, its Subsidiary or, to the knowledge of the executive officers of the Company, any other party, is in default under any Material Contract, in each case except for such defaults that, individually or in the aggregate with other such defaults, have not had, and [~~would~~ *are*] not reasonably be expected [*likely*] to have, a Company Material Adverse Effect.

([~l~*m*]) Properties.

(i)   Neither the Company nor its Subsidiary owns any real property.

(ii)   [*Section 4.1(l)(ii) of the Company Disclosure Schedule sets forth a list of all of the leases and subleases pursuant to which the Company or its Subsidiary holds a leasehold or a subleasehold estate in real property (the "Company Leases"). The Company has delivered or made available to Parent true, correct and complete copies of the Company Leases, including all amendments, supplements and modifications thereto.*] With respect to the real property leased to the Company or its Subsidiary (the "Leased Real Property"), each lease or sublease for such property is valid, legally binding, enforceable and in full force and effect, and neither the Company nor its Subsidiary is in breach of or default under any such lease or sublease, and no event has occurred that, with notice, lapse of time or both, would constitute a breach or default by the Company or its Subsidiary, permit termination, modification or acceleration by any third party thereunder, or prevent, materially delay or materially impair the consummation of the Transactions except, in each case, for such invalidity, failure to be binding, unenforceability, ineffectiveness, breaches, defaults, terminations, modifications, accelerations or repudiations that, individually or in the aggregate with other such matters, have not had, and [~~would~~ *are*] not reasonably ~~be expected~~ [*likely*] to have, a Company Material Adverse Effect.

([~mn~*n*]) Environmental Matters. Except for such exceptions that, individually or in the aggregate with other such exceptions, have not had, and [~~would~~ *are*] not reasonably ~~be expected~~ [*likely*] to have, a Company Material Adverse Effect: (i) the Company and its Subsidiary ~~are in compliance with and~~ have complied at all times with all applicable Environmental Laws~~, which compliance includes obtaining, maintaining and complying with the terms of any consents, registrations, approvals, permits or authorizations required to be obtained from any Governmental Entity~~; (ii) [*to the knowledge of the executive officers of the Company,*] no property (including soils, groundwater, surface water, buildings or other structures) currently operated by the Company or its Subsidiary is contaminated with any Hazardous Substance [*requiring reporting or remediation by, or as could reasonably be expected to result in liability to, the Company or its Subsidiary*]; (iii) no property formerly owned,[*leased*] or operated by the Company or its Subsidiary was contaminated with any Hazardous Substance during or prior to such period of ownership or operation [*requiring reporting or remediation by, or as could reasonably be expected to result in liability to the Company or its Subsidiary*]; (iv) neither the Company nor its Subsidiary has incurred any liability [*or alleged to be liable*] for any Hazardous Substance disposal or contamination on any third-party property[*including any sites to which the Company or its Subsidiary have or may have sent Hazardous Substances, now or in the past*]; (v) neither the Company nor its Subsidiary has released any Hazardous Substance other than in compliance with Environmental Laws; (vi) neither the Company nor its Subsidiary has received since ◙ any written or, to the knowledge of the executive officers of the Company, oral notice, demand, letter, claim or request for information alleging that the Company or its Subsidiary is in violation of, or has incurred liability under any Environmental ~~Laws;~~ (ii)Law; (vii) [*to the knowledge of the Executive Officers of the Company there are no other circumstances or conditions involving the Company or its Subsidiary that would reasonably be expected to result in any claim, liability or investigation pursuant to any Environmental Law; (viii)*] neither the Company nor its Subsidiary is subject to any Order or any indemnity or other agreement with any third party relating to liability under any Environmental Law or relating to Hazardous Substances; ~~(viii) there are no other circumstances or conditions involving the Company or its Subsidiary that are reasonably likely to result in any claim, liability, investigation, cost or restriction on the ownership, use, or transfer of any property pursuant to any Environmental Law~~; and (ix) the Company has delivered to Parent copies of all environmental reports, studies, assessments, sampling data and other environmental information in its possession relating to the Company or its Subsidiary or their respective current and former properties or operations.

As used herein, (A) the term "Environmental Law" means any Law concerning (i) the [*pollution or*] protection, investigation or restoration of the environment, health, safety [*as it relates to Hazardous Material exposure*], or natural resources, (ii) the handling, use, presence, disposal, release or threatened release of[, *or exposure to,*] any Hazardous Substance or (iii) noise, odor, indoor air, employee exposure, [*surface water, groundwater, land,*] wetlands, pollution, contamination or any injury or threat of injury to persons or property relating to any Hazardous Substance, [*(iv) endangered or threatened species of fish, wildlife and plants, or the mitigation of adverse environmental effects on environment,*] and (B) the term "Hazardous Substance" means [*any chemical, pollutant, contaminant, waste, material or*] any substance that is: (x) listed, classified or regulated pursuant to any Environmental Law; (y) any petroleum product or by-product, asbestos-containing material, lead-containing paint or plumbing, polychlorinated biphenyls, radioactive material or radon[, *fungus, mold or mycotoxins*]; or (z) any other substance which may be the subject of regulatory action by any Government Entity in connection with any Environmental Law.

([no]) Taxes.*

(i) The Company and its Subsidiary (i) have prepared or will prepare in good faith and have duly and timely filed or will duly and timely file (taking into account any extension of time within which to file)

---

*   This provision demonstrates the need for inclusion of tax specialists on the buyer's M & A team.

all material Tax Returns required to be filed by[, *with respect to, or on behalf of*] either of them at or prior to the Effective Time, and all such Tax Returns are or will be [*true, correct and*] complete ~~and accurate~~ in all material respects; (ii) have timely paid or will timely pay all material Taxes[, *whether or not shown on any Tax Return,*] that are required to be paid by either of them at or prior to the Effective Time; (iii) have timely withheld and paid all material Taxes required to have been withheld and paid by either of them in connection with amounts paid or owing to any employee, creditor or other third party, except with respect to matters contested in good faith [*by appropriate proceedings*]; ~~and~~ (iv) have not waived any statute of limitations with respect to any material Taxes or agreed to any extension of time with respect to the assessment or collection of a material Tax [*and have not entered into a closing agreement or other similar agreement with a Taxing Authority relating to material Taxes of the Company or its subsidiary with respect to a taxable period for which the statute of limitations is still open*]. As of the date hereof, there are not pending or, to the knowledge of the executive officers of the Company, threatened in writing, any audits, examinations, investigations or other proceedings in respect of Taxes or Tax matters. There are not, to the knowledge of the executive officers of the Company, any unresolved questions or claims concerning the Company's or its Subsidiary's Tax liability that, individually or in the aggregate with other such questions or claims, have had, or are reasonably likely to have, a Company Material Adverse Effect. The financial statements included in or incorporated by reference into the Company Reports reflect adequate reserves in accordance with GAAP for all Taxes payable by the Company for all taxable periods (and portions thereof) through the dates of such financial statements. [*There are not pending or, to the knowledge of the executive officers of the Company, threatened in writing, against the Company or its Subsidiary any audits, examinations, investigations or other proceedings in respect of Taxes or Tax matters. All deficiencies asserted in writing or assessments made in writing for material amounts of Taxes with respect to the Company or its Subsidiary have been fully paid, and neither the Company nor its Subsidiary has received written notice that any material assessments, audits, claims, suits, proceedings relating to Taxes of the Company or its Subsidiary are in progress, or pending. Neither the Company nor its Subsidiary (x) has constituted either a "distributing corporation" or a "controlled corporation" within the meaning of Section 355(a)(1)(A) of the Code within the last two (2) years; (y) has participated in a "listed transaction" within the meaning of Treasury Regulation Section 1.6011–4(b)(2) (or similar provision of state, local or foreign law); or (z) is required to include in income any material adjustment pursuant to Section 481(a) of the Code or any similar state, local, or foreign Tax Law by reason of a change in accounting method. The Company has provided to Parent true and complete copies of all income Tax Returns and other material Tax Returns of the Company and its*

Subsidiary filed for tax years that are still open. The net operating loss and credit carryovers, if any, available to the Company as of ◙ are set forth in Section 4.1(n) of the Company Disclosure Schedule. To the knowledge of the executive officers of the Company as of ◙, during the period between ◙ and ◙ there was no "change in control" of the Company within the meaning of Section 382 of the Code. There are no agreements relating to allocating or sharing of Taxes to which the Company or its Subsidiary is a party except for any such agreements between the Company and the Subsidiary. Neither the Company nor its Subsidiary is liable for Taxes of any other Person, or is currently under any contractual obligation to indemnify any Person with respect to any amounts of such Person's Taxes or is a party to or bound by any Contract providing for payments by the Company or its Subsidiary with respect to any amount of Taxes of any other Person except for agreements entered into in the ordinary course of business.]

[(ii) The Company has made available to Parent complete and accurate copies of all federal, state and foreign income, franchise and other material Tax Returns filed by or on behalf of the Company or its Subsidiary for any tax period ending after ◙.]

(iii) As used in this Agreement, (x) the term "<u>Tax</u>" (including, with correlative meaning, the term "<u>Taxes</u>") shall mean any and all U.S. federal, state, local and foreign income, profits, franchise, gross receipts, environmental, customs duty, capital stock, severances, stamp, payroll, sales, employment, unemployment, disability, use, property, withholding, excise, production, value added, occupancy, gains, alternative minimum, estimated, social security, welfare, license, ad valorem, transfer, workers' compensation, windfall and net worth taxes, and other taxes, duties, fees, levies, customs, tariffs, imposts, obligations, charges and assessments of the same or a similar nature, together with all interest, penalties and additions imposed with respect to such amounts and any interest in respect of such penalties and additions and (y) the term "Tax Return" shall mean any and all returns, statements, certificates, bills, documents, claims for refund and reports (including elections, declarations, disclosures, schedules, estimates and information returns) supplied to or required to be supplied to a Governmental Entity relating to Taxes, and any and all attachments, amendments and supplements thereto[*; and (z) the term "<u>Taxing Authority</u>" means any and all U.S. federal, state, local and non-U.S. governments, agencies, and political subdivisions of any such government having jurisdiction over the assessment, determination, collection, imposition or administration of any Tax*].

[(iv) No claim has ever been made in writing by any taxing authority in a jurisdiction where the Company and its Subsidiary does not file Tax Return s that the Company or its Subsidiary is or may be subject to Tax in that jurisdiction.]

[(v) *Neither the Company nor its Subsidiary (A) has been a member of a group filing Tax Returns on a consolidated, combined, unitary or similar basis, (B) has any material liability for Taxes of any Person (other than the Company or its Subsidiary) under Treasury Regulation section 1.1502–6 (or any comparable provision of local, state or foreign law), as a transferee or successor by Contract, or otherwise, or (c) is a party to, bound by or has material liability under any Tax sharing, allocation or indemnification agreement or arrangement (other than the customary Tax indemnifications contained in credit or other commercial agreements the primary purpose of which agreements does not relate to Taxes).*]

[(vi) *Neither the Company nor its Subsidiary has agreed to make, nor is required to make, any adjustment under Section 481(a) of the Code or any comparable provision of state, local or foreign Tax laws by reason of a change in accounting methods or otherwise.*]

(ep) Labor Matters. Neither the Company nor its Subsidiary is a party to or otherwise bound by any collective bargaining agreement or other Contract with a labor union or similar labor organization. Neither the Company nor its Subsidiary is the subject of any material proceeding asserting that the Company or its Subsidiary has committed an unfair labor practice or seeking to compel it to bargain with any labor union or labor organization. There is no labor strike, dispute, slowdown, stoppage or lockout involving the Company or its Subsidiary pending, or to the knowledge of the executive officers of the Company, threatened against the Company or its Subsidiary. [*To the knowledge of the executive officers of Company, no employee of the Company or its Subsidiary is in any material respect in violation of any term of any employment agreement, nondisclosure agreement, common law nondisclosure obligation, fiduciary duty, noncompetition agreement, assignment of invention covenant, restrictive covenant or other obligation to (i) the Company or its Subsidiary or (ii) a former employer of any such employee relating (A) to the right of any such employee to be employed by the Company or its Subsidiary or (B) to the knowledge or use of trade secrets or proprietary information. All current and former officers and employees of the Company who are or have been involved in the creation or development of Company Intellectual Property material to the manufacture, use, sale, offer for sale or importation of any Company Pharmaceutical Products have executed and delivered to the Company an agreement providing for the protection of proprietary information and the assignment to the Company of such Intellectual Property. All current and former consultants and independent contractors to the Company who are or have been involved in the creation or development of Company Intellectual Property material to the manufacture, use, sale, offer for sale or importation of any Company Pharmaceutical Products have executed and delivered to the Company an agreement providing for the protection of proprietary information and the assignment to the Company of such Intellectual Property. As of the date of this Agreement, to the knowledge of* *the executive officers of the Company no current employee of the Company or its Subsidiary above the level of Vice President, with an annual salary in excess of $200,000, or who is a member of the clinical development team who intends to terminate his or her employment.*]*

([pq]) Intellectual Property.

(i) Section 4.1(p)(i) of the Company Disclosure Schedule lists all material (A) Patents that are owned, solely or jointly, by the Company or its Subsidiary and (B) Trademarks owned by the Company or its Subsidiary that are the subject of a registration or a pending application for registration (collectively, the "Registered Intellectual Property"). To the knowledge of the executive officers of the Company, the Registered Intellectual Property is valid, subsisting and enforceable, and is not subject to any outstanding order, judgment or decree adversely affecting the Company's or its Subsidiary's use thereof or rights thereto, except for such exceptions that, individually or in the aggregate with other such exceptions, have not had, and are not reasonably likely to have, a Company Material Adverse Effect.

(ii) [*The Company or its Subsidiary owns, or has a valid right to use all Intellectual Property used in or necessary to conduct, the Company's or its Subsidiary's business ("Company Intellectual Property"), except for such failures to own or have a valid right to use that, individually or in the aggregate with other failures, have not had, and are not reasonably expected to have, a Company Material Adverse Effect.*] To the knowledge of the executive officers of the Company, since ◉ [date], (A) neither the Company nor its Subsidiary has infringed or otherwise violated the Intellectual Property rights of any third party, [*and there has been no claim asserted or threatened in a writing directed to the Company (including in the form of written offers or invitations to obtain a patent license) that the Company or its Subsidiary is infringing, misappropriating, or otherwise violating the Intellectual Property of any third party;*] and (B) no Person is infringing, misappropriating, or otherwise violating the Intellectual Property rights owned by or exclusively licensed to the Company or its Subsidiary, except in each case, for such exceptions that, individually or in the aggregate with other such exceptions, have not had, and are not reasonably likely to have, a Company Material Adverse Effect.

(iii) Section 4.1(p)(iii) of the Company Disclosure Schedule lists all (x) material IP Contracts [*pursuant to which the Company Pharmaceutical Products, or any Company Intellectual Property covering the Company Pharmaceutical Products, are developed or licensed, (y) IP*

---

*   Buyers may want assurance about key employees below the vice president level being willing to continue their employment. Some may add a provision to the effect that "None of the individuals identified on Schedule __ shall have ceased to be employed by the Company, or shall have expressed an intention to terminate his or her employment with the Company or to decline to accept employment with Parent or Merger Sub." In other cases buyers may wish to obtain new conditional employment agreements with key officers or other employees.

Contracts pursuant to which preclinical toxicity studies or formulation development are performed with respect to the Key Product and PSI–938, and (z) CRO agreements with respect to the Key Product]. Each of the material IP Contracts and the agreements described in the foregoing clauses (y) and (z) is valid and binding on the Company or its Subsidiary and, to the knowledge of the executive officers of the Company, each other party thereto, and is in full force and effect, except for such failures to be valid and binding or failures to be in full force and effect that, individually or in the aggregate with other such failures, have not had, and are not reasonably expected to have, a Company Material Adverse Effect.

[(iv) No Company Intellectual Property owned or exclusively licensed by the Company or its Subsidiary is subject to any outstanding injunction, judgment, order, decree, ruling, charge, settlement, or other disposition of a dispute.]

(v) The Company and its Subsidiary have taken commercially reasonable measures to protect the confidentiality of material Trade Secrets that are owned by the Company or its Subsidiary and such Trade Secrets have not been disclosed by the Company or its Subsidiary to any Person except pursuant to written non-disclosure agreements, except for any disclosures that, individually or in the aggregate with other such disclosures, have not had, and are not reasonably expected to have, a Company Material Adverse Effect.

(vi) The consummation of the Transactions will not result in the loss or impairment of or payment of any additional amounts with respect to, nor require the consent of any other Person in respect of, the Company's or its Subsidiary's right to own or use any of the material Company Intellectual Property owned by the Company or its Subsidiary.

(vii) The Company has not received any written notice from any third party challenging or threatening to challenge the right, title or interest of the Company in, to or under the Company Intellectual Property, or the validity, enforceability or claim construction, as applicable, of any material Company Intellectual Property.

(viii) There is no IP Contract under which the Company or its Subsidiary has granted a license under Company Intellectual Property to any Person to commercialize any Company Pharmaceutical Product.

(ix)] As of the date of this Agreement, the Company's President and Chief Executive Officer and Vice President, Senior Counsel and Secretary believe in good faith that the Company has made available to Parent through the Company's data site relating to the Transactions and/or through oral or telephonic presentations all material information in the Company's possession relating to the matter described in Section 4.1(p)(ix) of the Company Disclosure Schedule, other than information and documents as to which the Company (x) is entitled to assert a legal

privilege (including attorney-client privilege), (y) is entitled to claim work product immunity or (z) owes a duty of confidentiality to a third party.]

(x) For purposes of this Agreement, the following terms have the following meanings:

"Intellectual Property" means all [*registered and unregistered intellectual property and industrial property rights of any kind or nature throughout the world, including all U.S. and foreign*] (A) trademarks, service marks, corporate names, trade names, Internet domain names, logos, slogans, trade dress, and other indicia of source or origin, any applications and registrations for the foregoing and the renewals thereof, and all goodwill associated therewith and symbolized thereby (collectively, "*Trademarks*"); (B) patents (including utility and design patents and utility models), and patent applications, including any divisionals, revisions, supplementary protection certificates, continuations, continuations-in-part, reissues, re-examinations, substitutions, extensions and renewals thereof (collectively, "*Patents*") [*and inventions*]; (C) trade secrets, know-how, and any other proprietary confidential information, including processes, formulae, models and methodologies (collectively, "*Trade Secrets*"); (D) copyrights and copyrightable subject matter, including all published and unpublished works of authorship and the registrations and applications, and renewals, extensions, restorations and reversions thereof; [*(E) rights in computer programs (whether in source code, object code, or other form), algorithms, databases, compilations and data, technology supporting the foregoing, and all documentation, including user manuals and training materials, related to any of the foregoing; and (F) all rights in the foregoing and in other similar intangible assets*].

"*IP Contracts*" means (i) all Contracts in force as of the date hereof, the primary subject of which is the licensing, of Intellectual Property, under which the Company or its Subsidiary has obtained or granted any express license or other right to use, or which by their terms expressly restrict the Company's or its Subsidiary's right to use any Company Intellectual Property, other than (A) Contracts involving Intellectual Property that is generally available on a commercial basis from third parties; [~~and~~] (B) Contracts providing for the license of software that is generally available on a commercial basis[, *and (ii) all Contracts in force as of the date hereof, the primary subject of which is the assignment or other conveyance of Intellectual Property, under which the Company or its Subsidiary has obtained or granted any ownership right in any Company Intellectual Property, other than Contracts entered into in the ordinary course of business, such as Contracts with employees, material transfer agreements, and CRO* agreements*].

---

*   "CRO" stands for Contract Research Organization, which was not defined in this agreement.

(r) Insurance. Except as, individually or in the aggregate with other similar exceptions, has not had, ~~or would~~ and [*is*] not reasonably ~~be expected~~ [*likely*] to have, a Company Material Adverse Effect, all insurance policies maintained by the Company and its Subsidiary are in full force and effect, all premiums due and payable thereon have been paid, and the Company and its Subsidiary are otherwise in compliance with the terms and conditions of such policies. Section 4.1(q) of the Company Disclosure Schedule (i) lists all material insurance policies maintained by or on behalf of the Company and its Subsidiary as of the date hereof and (ii) includes a description of any self-insurance arrangements in effect as of the date hereof with respect to the Company and its Subsidiary. Neither the Company nor its Subsidiary has received any notice of cancellation[, *termination*] or non-renewal of any such policy or arrangement [*or any notice of material adjustment in the amount of the premiums payable with respect to any such policy*], and there is no material claim pending under any of such policies or arrangements as to which coverage has been questioned, denied or disputed by the underwriters of such policies or arrangements.

(s) Rights Agreement. As of the date hereof, [*neither*] the Company [*nor its Subsidiary*] is [~~not~~] a party to any ~~stockholder~~shareholder rights agreement, rights plan, "poison pill" or other similar agreement or plan.

(t) Brokers and Finders. Except for ◙, [*to which fees are payable according to an engagement letter listed in the Company Disclosure Schedule, a complete and correct copy of which has been provided to Parent,*] there is no investment banker, broker or finder that has been retained by or is authorized to act on behalf of Company who would be entitled to any fee or commission in connection with the Offer, the Merger or the other Transactions.

[*(u) Key Product Event. Since the date of this Agreement, there has not occurred any Key Product Event. As used in this Agreement, "Key Product Event" means any Serious Adverse Event (an "SAE") that (i) is determined by an independent safety review committee overseeing the safety of the relevant clinical study to be directly related to the Key Product (not predominantly related to any compound with which the Key Product is co-administered) and to have (a) resulted in death, (b) been life-threatening, (c) required inpatient hospitalization or a significant prolongation of existing hospitalization, (d) resulted in persistent or significant disability or incapacity, (e) resulted in a congenital anomaly or birth defect, or (f) required significant intervention to prevent permanent impairment or damage; and (ii) (x) results in the FDA's placing a clinical hold on the development program of the Key Product or (y) is likely to result in a significant delay to the development timeline of the Key Product as of the date of this Agreement. As used in this Agreement, "Key Product" means (describe the product)]*

[(v) *Related Party Transactions*. *No executive officer or director of the Company or its Subsidiary or any Person owning 5% or more of the Company Common Stock (or any of such Person's immediate family members or Affiliates or Associates) is a party to any Contract with or binding upon the Company or its Subsidiary or any of their respective assets, rights or properties or has any interest in any property owned by the Company or its Subsidiary or has engaged in any transaction with either of the foregoing within the last twelve (12) months.]*

(w) No Other Representations or Warranties. The Company acknoweledges and agrees that the only representations, warranties, covenants and agreements made by Parent, Merger Sub or any of their Affiliates or representatives are the representations, warranties, covenants and agreements made in this Agreement. The Company acknowledges and agrees that none of Parent, Merger Sub or any of their representatives has made any representation or warranty, whether express or implied, as to the accuracy or completeness of any information regarding Parent or Merger Sub or their respective Affiliates furnished or made available to the Company and its representatives except as expressly set forth in this Agreement, and none of Parent, Merger Sub or any other Person shall be subject to any liability to the Company or any other Person resulting from Parent's or Merger Sub's making available to the Company or the Company's use of such information, or any information, documents or material made available to the Company in any due diligence materials provided to the Company.

ARTICLE 4.2.   Representations and Warranties of Parent and Merger Sub

Except as set forth in (i) the forms, statements, certifications, reports and documents filed with or furnished to the SEC since ● by Parent pursuant to the Exchange Act or the Securities Act (excluding, in each case, any disclosures set forth in any risk factor section or in any other section to the extent they are forward-looking statements or cautionary, predictive or forward-looking in nature) [*; provided, however, that the exception provided for in this clause (i) shall be applied with respect to a particular representation or warranty only to the extent that it is reasonably apparent on the face of such disclosure that such disclosure is applicable to such representation or warranty*] or (ii) the disclosure schedule delivered to the Company by Parent prior to entering into this Agreement (the "<u>Parent Disclosure Schedule</u>") (with each exception set forth in the Parent Disclosure Schedule being identified by reference to, or grouped under a heading referring to, a specific individual section or subsection of this Agreement and relating only to such section or subsection; provided, however, that a matter disclosed with respect to one representation or warranty shall also be deemed to be disclosed with respect to each other representation or warranty to which the matter disclosed reasonably relates, but only to the extent that such relationship is reasonably apparent on the face of the disclosure contained in the Parent Disclosure Schedule), Parent and Merger Sub each hereby represent and warrant to the Company that:

(a) Organization, Good Standing and Qualification. Each of Parent and Merger Sub is a legal entity duly organized, validly existing and in good standing under the Laws of its respective jurisdiction of organization and has all requisite corporate power and authority to own, lease and operate its properties and assets and to carry on its business as presently conducted and is qualified to do business and is in good standing as a foreign corporation in each jurisdiction where the ownership, leasing or operation of its assets or properties or conduct of its business requires such qualification, except where the failure to be so organized, qualified or in good standing, or to have such power or authority, ~~would~~[*is*] not individually or in the aggregate with other such failures, reasonably ~~be expected to prevent or, materially impede, interfere with, hinder or delay~~[*likely*] to prevent, materially delay or materially impair the ability of Parent and Merger Sub to commence the Offer or to consummate the Offer, the Merger or the other Transactions contemplated by this Agreement~~, in each case in a timely manner~~ (a "Parent Material Adverse Effect"). Parent has made available to the Company a complete and correct copy of the certificate of incorporation and bylaws of Parent and Merger Sub, each as amended as of the date hereof, and each as so delivered is in full force and effect.

(b) Corporate Authority. The board of directors of each of Parent and Merger Sub has approved this Agreement and the Offer, the Merger and the other Transactions, and no vote of holders of capital stock of Parent is necessary to approve this Agreement or the Offer, the Merger and the other Transactions. Each of Parent and Merger Sub has all requisite corporate power and authority and has taken all corporate action necessary in order to execute, deliver and perform its obligations under this Agreement and to consummate the Transactions, except for the adoption of this Agreement by Parent in its capacity as the sole stockholder of Merger Sub (which Parent covenants to effect immediately following the execution of this Agreement). This Agreement has been duly executed and delivered by each of Parent and Merger Sub and, assuming this Agreement constitutes the valid and binding agreement of the Company, constitutes a valid and binding agreement of Parent and Merger Sub enforceable against each of Parent and Merger Sub in accordance with its terms, subject to the Bankruptcy and Equity Exception.

(c) Governmental Filings; No Violations.

(i) Other than (A) the filing of the Delaware Certificate of Merger, (B) compliance with applicable requirements of the HSR Act [*or any other applicable antitrust or competition Law,*] (C) compliance with the applicable requirements of the Exchange Act and (D) compliance with the rules and regulations of [*NASDAQ or FINRA,*], no notices, reports or other filings are required to be made by Parent or Merger Sub with, nor are any consents, registrations, approvals, permits or authorizations required to be obtained by Parent or Merger Sub from, any Governmental Entity in connection with the execution, delivery and performance of this Agreement by Parent and Merger Sub, and the consummation of the Offer, the Merger and the other Transactions, except those that the failure to make or obtain, individually or in the aggregate with other such failures, has not had, and ~~would~~ [*is*] not reasonably ~~be expected~~ [*likely*] to have, a Parent Material Adverse Effect.

(ii) The execution, delivery and performance of this Agreement by Parent and Merger Sub do not, and the consummation of the Offer, the Merger and the other Transactions will not, constitute or result in (A) a breach or violation of, or a default under, the certificate of incorporation or bylaws of Parent or Merger Sub or the comparable governing instruments of any of Parent's Subsidiaries, or (B) with or without notice, lapse of time or both, a breach or violation of, a termination (or right of termination) or a default under, the creation or acceleration of any obligations under, or the creation of a Lien on any of the assets of Parent or any of its Subsidiaries pursuant to, any Contracts to which Parent or any of its Subsidiaries is a party or, [(C)] assuming compliance with the matters referred to in Section 4.2(c)(i), [*a violation of*]any Law to which Parent or any of its Subsidiaries is subject, or [(D~~C~~)] any change in the rights or obligations of any party under any Contract to which Parent or any of its Subsidiaries is a party, except, in the case of clauses (B) or [(~~D~~C)] above, for any such breach, violation, termination, default, creation or acceleration that, individually or in the aggregate with other such matters, has not had, and ~~would~~ [*is*] not reasonably ~~be expected~~ [*likely*] to have, a Parent Material Adverse Effect.

(d) **Legal Proceedings.** As of the date of this Agreement, there are no Proceedings pending or, to the knowledge of the executive officers of Parent, threatened against Parent or Merger Sub that seek to enjoin, or ~~would~~ [*is*] not reasonably ~~be expected~~ [*likely*] to have the effect of preventing, making illegal, or otherwise interfering with, any of the Transactions, except for those that, individually or in the aggregate with other such Proceedings, have not had, and ~~would~~ [*are*] not reasonably ~~be expected~~ [*likely*] to have, a Parent Material Adverse Effect.

(e) **Information Supplied.** None of the information supplied or to be supplied by Parent or Merger Sub for inclusion or incorporation by reference in (i) the Offer Documents or the Schedule 14D–9 will, at the time such document is filed with the SEC, at any time it is amended or supplemented or at the time it is first published, sent or given to the Company's stockholders, contain any untrue statement of a material fact or omit to state any material fact required to be stated therein or necessary to make the statements therein not misleading, or (ii) if required to be filed, the Proxy Statement will, at the date it is first mailed to the Company's stockholders or at the time of the Stockholders Meeting, contain any untrue statement of a material fact or omit to state any material fact required to be stated therein or necessary in order to make the statements therein, in light of the circumstances under which they are made, not misleading. The Offer Documents will comply as to form in all material respects with the requirements of the Exchange Act and the rules and regulations promulgated thereunder, except that no representation or warranty is made by Parent or Merger Sub with respect to statements made or incorporated by reference in the Offer Documents based on information derived from the Company's public SEC filings or supplied by the Company for inclusion or incorporation by reference therein.

(f) Financing. Parent has delivered to the Company a true, complete and correct copy of the executed commitment letter, dated as of [◉ (date)], among Parent and [◉, *the "Lead Commitment Parties" and, together with any person who executes a joinder to such commitment letters or who otherwise commits to provide any portion of the Financing (as defined below), "Commitment Parties" and, together with their respective shareholders, partners, members, affiliates, directors, officers, employees and agents, the "Financing Sources")*], which are attached hereto as Annex D (the "Financing Commitments"), pursuant to which the lenders party thereto [*severally*] have committed, on the terms and subject to the conditions set forth therein, to lend the amounts set forth therein for the purposes of financing the Transactions (the "Financing"). The Financing Commitments have not been amended or modified prior to the date hereof, no such amendment or modification is contemplated, and, as of the date hereof, the respective commitments contained in the Financing Commitments have not been withdrawn or rescinded in any respect. Except for a fee letter relating to fees [*and related arrangements*] with respect to the Financing (a true, complete and correct copy of which has been provided to the Company, with only fee amounts and certain economic terms of the market flex (none of which is reasonably likely to adversely affect the amount or availability of the Financing) redacted), as of the date hereof there are no side letters or other Contracts or arrangements altering the terms or conditions of the funding of the Financing other than as expressly set forth in the Financing Commitments delivered to the Company prior to the date hereof. Parent has fully paid any and all commitment fees or other fees in connection with the Financing Commitments that are ~~due and~~ payable on or prior to the date hereof, and, as of the date hereof, the Financing Commitments are in full force and effect and are the legal, valid, binding and enforceable obligations of Parent and Merger Sub, as the case may be, [*in each case subject to the Bankruptcy and Equity Exception and any legal limitations on the enforceability of provisions requiring indemnification against liabilities under securities laws in connection with any offering,* *sale or issuance of securities,]* and, to the knowledge of the executive officers of Parent, each of the other parties thereto. There are no conditions precedent or other contingencies related to the funding of the full amount of the Financing, other than as expressly set forth in the Financing Commitments. Assuming the accuracy of the representations and warranties set forth in Section 4.1 in all material respects [*(except to the extent already qualified as to Company Material Adverse Effect)*], as of the date hereof, no event has occurred that, with or without notice, lapse of time or both, has constituted or ~~would~~[*is*] reasonably [*likely*] ~~be expected~~ to constitute a default or breach under any of the Financing Commitments by Parent or Merger Sub or, to the knowledge of the executive officers of Parent, any other party thereto. [*Assuming the accuracy of the representations and warranties set forth in Section 4.1 in all material respects (except to the extent already qualified as to Company Material Adverse Effect) and assuming compliance by the Company with its obligations herein in all material respects,*] Parent has no reason to believe that any of the conditions to the Financing contemplated by the Financing Commitments will not be satisfied. Parent and Merger Sub will have available to them at and immediately prior to the Acceptance Time cash in an aggregate amount sufficient to pay the aggregate Offer Price, assuming all issued and outstanding Shares are tendered in the Offer and not withdrawn. Parent and Merger Sub will have available at and immediately prior to the Effective Time cash in an aggregate amount sufficient to pay the Per Share Merger Consideration. Parent and Merger Sub will have at and after the Closing funds sufficient to (i) pay any and all fees and expenses required to be paid by Parent, Merger Sub and the Surviving Corporation in connection with the Transactions and the Financing, (ii) pay for any refinancing of any outstanding indebtedness of the Company contemplated by this Agreement or the Financing Commitments and (iii) satisfy all of the other payment obligations of Parent, Merger Sub and the Surviving Corporation contemplated hereunder.

(g) **Capitalization of Merger Sub.** The authorized capital stock of Merger Sub consists solely of 100 shares of common stock, par value $0.001 per share, all of which are validly issued and outstanding. All of the issued and outstanding capital stock of Merger Sub is, and at the Acceptance Time and at the Effective Time will be, owned by Parent or a direct or indirect wholly—owned Subsidiary of Parent. Merger Sub has outstanding no option, warrant, right, or any other agreement pursuant to which any Person other than Parent may acquire any equity security of Merger Sub. Merger Sub was formed solely for the purpose of engaging in the Transactions and has not engaged in any business other than those incidental to its formation and pursuant to this Agreement, the Offer and the Merger and the other Transactions.

(h) **No Interested Stockholder.** None of Parent, Merger Sub or any of their "~~a~~Affiliates" or "~~a~~Associates" is, or has been within the last three (3) years, an "interested stockholder" of the Company, in each case as those terms are defined in Section 203 of the DGCL. Within the last three (3) years, none of Parent, Merger Sub or any of their Affiliates has beneficially owned, directly or indirectly, any Shares.

(i) **Brokers and Finders.** Except for ◙, there is no investment banker, broker or finder that has been retained by or is authorized to act on behalf of Parent or Merger Sub or any of their respective Subsidiaries who would be entitled to any fee or commission in connection with the Offer, the Merger or the other Transactions.

(j) **No Other Representations or Warranties.** Parent and Merger Sub each acknowledges and agrees that the only representations, warranties, covenants and agreements made by the Company or any of its Affiliates or representatives are the representations, warranties, covenants and agreements made in this Agreement. Parent and Merger Sub each acknowledges and agrees that none of the Company, its Subsidiary or any of their representatives has made any representation or warranty, whether express or implied, as to the accuracy or completeness of any information regarding the Company or its Affiliates furnished or made available to Parent or Merger Sub and its representatives except as expressly set forth in this Agreement, and none of the Company, its Subsidiary or any other Person shall be subject to any liability to Parent or Merger Sub or any other Person resulting from the Company's making available to Parent or Merger Sub or Parent's or Merger Sub's use of such information, or any information, documents or material made available to Parent or Merger Sub in any due diligence materials provided to Parent or Merger Sub, including in the "data room," management presentations (formal or informal) or in any other form in connection with the Transactions. Without limiting the foregoing, the Company makes no representation or warranty to Parent or Merger Sub with respect to any financial or operating projections or forecasts relating to the Company.

ARTICLE 5.   Covenants

ARTICLE 5.1.   Interim Operations

(a) From the date hereof until the Acceptance Time, except (A) as may be required by applicable Law, (B) with the prior written consent of Parent (which consent shall not unreasonably be withheld, conditioned or delayed), (C) as expressly contemplated by this Agreement, or (D) as set forth in Section 5.1(a) of the Company Disclosure Schedule, (x) the Company shall cause the business of the Company and its Subsidiary to be conducted in the ordinary course consistent with past practice and, to the extent consistent therewith, the Company shall use reasonable best efforts to [(i)] preserve intact its and its Subsidiary's present business organization and maintain ~~the current~~satisfactory relationships with Governmental Entities and other Persons having business dealings with the Company and its Subsidiary, [(ii) *prepare and file any requisite regulatory filings with any Regulatory Authority on a timely basis and consistent with their respective past practices and (iii) obtain and maintain quantities of each finished Company Pharmaceutical Product and related raw materials and components that the Company reasonably expects to be required for use in the ongoing and anticipated phase 2 and phase 3 clinical trials of each Company Pharmaceutical Product]* and (y) without limiting the generality of clause (x) above and in furtherance thereof, the Company shall not and shall not permit its Subsidiary to:

(i)   amend its certificate of incorporation, bylaws or comparable governing documents;

(ii)   merge or consolidate the Company or its Subsidiary with any other Person, except for such transactions between the Company and its Subsidiary, or dissolve or completely or partially liquidate;

(iii)   *[form any Subsidiary or]* acquire assets from any other Person with a value or purchase price in the aggregate in excess of $~~3~~500,000 in any transaction or series of related transactions, other than acquisitions in the ordinary course of business consistent with past practice with a value or purchase price in the aggregate not in excess of $~~3~~500,000 or pursuant to Material Contracts in effect as of the date hereof;

(iv)   issue, sell, pledge, dispose of, grant, transfer or encumber, or authorize the issuance, sale, pledge, disposition, grant, transfer or encumbrance of, any shares of capital stock of the Company or its Subsidiary, or securities convertible or exchangeable into or exercisable for any shares of such capital stock, or any options, warrants or other rights of any kind to acquire any shares of such capital stock or such convertible or exchangeable securities other than (A) issuance or sales of Shares upon exercise of the Company Options or the vesting of Company Restricted Stock or (B) as permitted under Section 5.1(a)(xv);

(v)   other than in the ordinary course of business consistent with past practice, create or incur any Lien on *[(i)]* any assets *[(other than Company Intellectual Property)]* of the Company or its Subsidiary having a value in excess of $~~500,000~~ *[$300,000, (ii) any material Intellectual Property of the Company or its Subsidiary, or (iii) material Intellectual Property licensed to the Company or its Subsidiary]*;

(vi)   make any loans, advances, guarantees or capital contributions to or investments in any Person (other than the Company or its Subsidiary) in excess of *[$300,000]*~~500,000~~ in the aggregate;

(vii)   *[(A)]* declare, *[accrue,]* set aside, make or pay any dividend or other distribution payable in cash, stock, property or otherwise, with respect to any of its capital stock (except for dividends paid by the Company's Subsidiary to the Company), *[(B) repurchase, redeem or otherwise reacquire any shares of capital stock or other securities, or subdivide, reclassify, recapitalize, split, combine or exchange or enter into any similar transaction with respect to any of its capital stock or other securities or issue or authorize or propose the issuance of any other securities in respect of, in lieu of or in substitution for shares of its capital stock or other securities, except for any split, combination or reclassification of capital stock of a wholly owned Subsidiary of the Company, or any issuance or authorization or proposal to issue or authorize any securities of a wholly owned Subsidiary of the Company to the Company or another wholly owned Subsidiary of the Company, or (C)]* or enter into any agreement with respect to the voting of its capital stock;

(viii) incur any indebtedness for borrowed money or assume, guarantee, endorse or otherwise become liable or responsible for (whether directly, contingently or otherwise) any other Person's indebtedness for borrowed money, or issue or sell any debt securities or warrants or other rights to acquire any debt security of the Company or its Subsidiary, except for indebtedness for borrowed money incurred in the ordinary course of business consistent with past practices not to exceed [$*300,000*]500,000 in the aggregate;

(ix) except as contemplated in capital budgets furnished to Parent prior to the date of this Agreement, make any capital expenditures in excess of [$*300,000*]500,000 in the aggregate;

(x) make any changes with respect to accounting policies or procedures other than as required by changes in GAAP;

(xi) or as advised by the Company's regular independent public accountant;

(xi) other than in the ordinary course of business consistent with past practice, settle any litigation for an amount in excess of [$*300,000*]500,000;

[*(xii) other than as reasonably necessary to facilitate the research and/or clinical operations of the Company in a manner consistent with the Company's operating budgets furnished to Parent prior to the date of this Agreement,*[$*300,000*]500,000;

(xii) enter into any Contract that would have been a Material Contract had it been entered into prior to this Agreement;

(xiii) [*other than as reasonably necessary to facilitate the research and/or clinical operations of the Company in a manner*] other than in the ordinary course of business consistent with [*the Company's operating budgets furnished to Parent prior to the date of this Agreement*] past practice, amend, modify or terminate any Material Contract;

(xiv) other than pursuant to Contracts in effect prior to the date hereof, transfer, sell, lease, license, mortgage, pledge, surrender, encumber, divest, cancel, abandon or allow to lapse or expire or otherwise dispose of any material assets, licenses, operations, rights or businesses of the Company or its Subsidiary, except for (A) sales, transfers or dispositions of obsolete or worthless assets, (B) sales, transfers, leases, licenses or other dispositions of assets with a fair market value not in excess of $500,000 in the aggregate and (C) any of the foregoing actions taken with respect to Intellectual Property in the ordinary course of business;

(xv) except as required by applicable Law or otherwise required pursuant to existing Contracts or Benefit Plans in effect as of the date hereof, (A) increase the salaries or wages of any Employee, except in the ordinary course of business, (B) pay any bonus to any Employee in excess of the amount earned based on actual performance (as determined by the Company or its Subsidiary, as applicable, in the ordinary course of business), (C) enter into or establish any new employment agreement or change in control severance agreement with any Employee, other than with any new Employee hired to replace an Employee who is party to any such agreement, (D) make any severance payments to any Employee in excess of what they are contractually entitled to, except for severance payments in the ordinary course of business and consistent with past practice to Employees who are not party to employment agreements or change in control severance agreements, (E) make any new equity awards to any Employee, except in the ordinary course of business or (F) other than in accordance with Section 5.1(a)(xv)(C), establish, adopt, terminate or materially amend any Benefit Plan;

(xvi) outside the ordinary course of the Company's administration of its Tax matters, adopt or change any material method of Tax accounting, make or change any material Tax election or file any amended material Tax Return; or

(xvii) enter into any Contract to do any of the foregoing.

(b) Each of Parent and Merger Sub agrees that, except as otherwise provided in this Agreement, after the date hereof and prior to the Effective Time, it shall not knowingly take or knowingly omit to take any action that is reasonably likely to prevent or delay the consummation of the Offer, the Merger and the other Transactions in accordance with the terms of this Agreement. Without limiting the generality of the foregoing, each of Parent and Merger Sub agrees that, after the date hereof and prior to the Effective Time, it shall not consummate or agree to consummate any purchase or other acquisition of any assets, licenses, operations, rights or businesses that, individually or in the aggregate with any other such purchase or acquisition, is reasonably likely to (i) prevent or delay the parties hereto from obtaining any consents, registrations, approvals, permits or authorizations required to be obtained from any Governmental Entity in connection with the consummation of the Offer, the Merger and the other Transactions, (ii) result in the imposition of a condition or conditions on any such consents, registrations, approvals, permits or authorizations, or (iii) otherwise prevent or delay any party hereto from performing its obligations hereunder or consummating the Offer, the Merger and the other Transactions.

[(c) *The Company shall promptly notify Parent and Merger Sub of any significant data relating to the Key Product, including information related to any significant adverse events with respect to the Key Product.**

(d) *Each party hereto shall promptly advise the other parties hereto of any Proceeding or material claim threatened, commenced or asserted against or with respect to any such party relating to the Transactions and promptly provide the parties hereto with copies of all material complaints, pleadings and filings related thereto.*

(e) *From the date hereof until the Acceptance Time, the Company shall (i) consult with Parent in connection with any proposed meeting with the FDA or any other Governmental Entity relating to any Company Pharmaceutical Product, (ii) promptly inform Parent of, and provide Parent with a reasonable opportunity to review, any material filing proposed to be made by or on behalf of any of the Company or its Subsidiary, and any material correspondence or other material communication proposed to be submitted or otherwise transmitted to the FDA or any other Governmental Entity by or on behalf of any of the Company or its Subsidiary, in each case relating to any Company Pharmaceutical Product, (iii) keep Parent promptly informed of (A) any communication (written or oral) with or from the FDA and any other Governmental Entity and (B) any material communications (written or oral) received from any Person relating to the Company Intellectual Property and (iv) promptly inform Parent and provide Parent or Merger Sub with a reasonable opportunity (but no more than three (3) Business Days) to comment, in each case, prior to making any material change to any study protocol, adding any new trial, making any material change to a manufacturing plan or process, making any material change to a development timeline or initiating, or making any material change to, promotional or marketing materials or activities relating to any Company Pharmaceutical Product.*

(f) *Notwithstanding the above, the delivery of any notice pursuant to Section 5.1(b), 5.1(c), 5.1(d) or 5.1(e) shall not limit or otherwise affect the representations, warranties, covenants or agreements of the parties hereto, the remedies available hereunder to the party hereto receiving such notice or the conditions to such party's obligation to consummate the Offer, the Merger or any of the other Transactions.*]

(g) Nothing contained in this Agreement shall give Parent or Merger Sub, directly or indirectly, the right to control the Company or its Subsidiary or direct the business or operations of the Company or its Subsidiary prior to the Effective Time. Prior to the Effective Time, the Company shall exercise, consistent with the terms and conditions of this

---

*   "Significant Adverse Events" is a term of art in clinical drug trials, signifying an adverse effect on patients taking the drug, sufficiently material to be reported to the Food & Drug Administration, which may result in either suspending or terminating the trial or a warning label on the drug container if the drug is approved (a so-called "black box").

Agreement, complete control and supervision over its operations and the operations of its Subsidiary. Nothing in this Agreement, including any of the actions, rights or restrictions set forth herein, shall be interpreted in such a way as to place the Company, Parent or Merger Sub in violation of any rule, regulation or policy of any Governmental Entity, including any applicable Law.

ARTICLE 5.2.   Acquisition Proposals

(a) The Company shall immediately cease and cause to be terminated any discussions or negotiations pending as of the date hereof regarding any Acquisition Proposal and shall instruct the Person who made such Acquisition Proposal to return to the Company or to destroy any confidential information provided by the Company to such Person in connection with such Acquisition Proposal. The Company shall promptly (and, in any event, within [*twenty-four*]~~thirty-six~~ ([*24*]~~36~~) hours) notify Parent if any Acquisition Proposal is received by the Company (which notification shall include the name of the Person making such Acquisition Proposal and the material terms and conditions thereof) and shall thereafter keep Parent reasonably informed on a current basis of any material change to the terms of such Acquisition Proposal. Subject to the following sentence, neither the Company nor its Subsidiary nor any of [*their respective*] ~~its~~ officers or directors shall, and the Company shall instruct and use its reasonable best efforts to cause its and its Subsidiary's employees, investment bankers, attorneys, accountants and other advisors or representatives (such officers, directors, employees, investment bankers, attorneys, accountants and other advisors or representatives, collectively, "<u>Representatives</u>") not to, (i) initiate, solicit or knowingly encourage the making of any proposal or offer that constitutes an Acquisition Proposal, or (ii) engage in any discussions or negotiations regarding, or provide any [*non-public*] ~~confidential~~ information to any Person in connection with, any Acquisition Proposal, except to notify such Person of the existence of this Section 5.2. Notwithstanding anything to the contrary set forth in this Agreement, prior to the Acceptance Time the Company may (A) provide [*non-public*] ~~confidential~~ information in response to a request therefor by a Person who has made an unsolicited written Acquisition Proposal; and/or (B) engage in any discussions or negotiations with any Person who has made such an Acquisition Proposal, if prior to taking any action described in clause (A) or (B), (x) the Company receives from such Person an executed confidentiality agreement containing nondisclosure provisions that are substantially similar to those contained in the Confidentiality Agreement, dated ◙, between Parent and the Company (the "<u>Confidentiality Agreement</u>"); it being understood that such confidentiality agreement need not contain any "standstill" provisions or otherwise prohibit the making or amendment of any Acquisition Proposal), (y) the Company Board determines in good faith after consultation with its [*outside*] legal counsel and its financial advisor that such Acquisition Proposal either constitutes a Superior Proposal or could reasonably be expected to result in a Superior Proposal, and (z) the Company Board determines in good faith after consultation with its outside legal counsel that the failure to take such action would be inconsistent with the directors' fiduciary duties under applicable Law. With respect to any non-public information regarding the Company provided to any other Person that was not previously provided to Parent, the Company shall provide such non-public information to Parent [*simultaneously with*] ~~promptly (and in any event within thirty-six (36) hours) following~~ the ~~date of~~ provision of such information to such other Person. The Company shall keep Parent reasonably informed on a current basis of the status and terms of any Acquisition Proposal (including any material changes to the key terms thereof) and the general status of any discussions and negotiations with respect thereto.

(b)   Subject to Section 5.2(C) and Section 5.2(d), the Company Board shall not: (i) withhold, withdraw, qualify or modify, in a manner adverse to Parent, the Company Recommendation (a "<u>Change of Recommendation</u>") (it being understood that the Company Board may refrain from taking any position with respect to an Acquisition Proposal until the close of business on the tenth (10th) Business Day after the commencement of such Acquisition Proposal pursuant to Rule 14d–2 under the Exchange Act without such action being considered a Change of Recommendation); (ii) approve, recommend or declare advisable any Acquisition Proposal; or (iii) cause the Company to enter into any Contract (other than a confidentiality agreement entered into in compliance with Section 5.2(a)) concerning an Acquisition Proposal (an "<u>Alternative Acquisition Agreement</u>").

(c)   Notwithstanding anything to the contrary set forth in this Agreement, ~~if (i) the Company receives an unsolicited written Acquisition Proposal, (ii) the Company Board determines in good faith after consultation with its financial advisor that such Acquisition Proposal constitutes a Superior Proposal, and (iii) the Company Board determines in good faith after consultation with its outside legal counsel that a failure to do so would be inconsistent with the directors' fiduciary duties under applicable Law, then, prior to the Acceptance Time,~~ the Company Board may make a Change of Recommendation in response to an Acquisition Proposal and/or ~~(B) (x) approve, recommend or declare advisable the Superior Proposal, and/or (y)~~ cause the Company to enter into an Alternative Acquisition Agreement concerning ~~the Superior~~ [*such Acquisition*] Proposal [*at any time prior to the Acceptance Time if, and only if: (i) such Acquisition Proposal did not result from a material breach of this Section 5.2; (ii) the Company Board determines in good faith, after consultation with its outside legal counsel and after consultation with its financial advisor, (A) that such Acquisition Proposal would, if this Agreement or the Offer were not amended or an alternative transaction with Parent were not entered into, constitute a Superior Proposal and (B)*] *that in light of such Acquisition Proposal, a failure to make a Change of Recommendation and/or enter into such Alternative Acquisition Agreement would be inconsistent with the Company Board's fiduciary obligations to the Company's stockholders under applicable Law; (iii) the Company delivers to Parent a written notice (the "Superior Proposal Notice") stating that the Company Board intends to take such action and (in the event the Company Board contemplates causing the Company to enter into an Alternative Acquisition Agreement) including a copy of such Alternative Acquisition Agreement; (iv) during the three (3) Business Day period commencing on the date of Parent's receipt of such Superior Proposal Notice, the Company shall have made its Representatives reasonably available for the purpose of engaging in negotiations with Parent (to the extent Parent desires to negotiate) regarding a possible amendment of this Agreement or the Offer or a possible alternative transaction so that the Acquisition Proposal that is the subject of the Superior Proposal Notice ceases to be a Superior Proposal; (v) after the expiration of the negotiation period described in clause "(iv)" above, the Company Board shall have determined in good faith, after consultation with its outside legal counsel and after consultation with its financial advisor, and after taking into account any amendments to this Agreement and the Offer that Parent and Merger Sub have irrevocably agreed in writing to make as a result of the negotiations contemplated by clause "(iv)" above, that (A) such Acquisition Proposal constitutes a Superior Proposal and (B) the failure to make a Change of Recommendation and/or enter into such Alternative Acquisition Agreement would be inconsistent with the Company Board's fiduciary obligations to the Company's stockholders under applicable Law; and (vi) if the Company enters into an Alternative Acquisition Agreement concerning such Superior Proposal, the Company terminates this Agreement in accordance with Section 7.1(f); provided, however, that, in the event of any amendment to the financial or other material terms of such Acquisition Proposal, the Company shall be required to deliver to Parent a new Superior Proposal Notice (including as attachments thereto a copy of any new Alternative Acquisition Agreement relating to such amended Acquisition Proposal, if any), and the negotiation period described in clause "(iv)" above shall be extended by an additional two (2) Business Days from the date of Parent's receipt of such new Superior Proposal Notice.]* ; provided that, concurrently with the taking of any action described in this clause (B), the Company terminates this Agreement pursuant to Section 7.1(f)(ii) and pays to Parent the Initial Fee pursuant to Section 7.2(b).

(d) Nothing contained in this Agreement shall prohibit or restrict the Company or the Company Board, in circumstances not involving an Acquisition Proposal, from effecting a Change of Recommendation prior to the Acceptance Time if the Company Board determines in good faith after consultation with its outside legal counsel that thea failure to take

~~such action~~do so would be inconsistent with the Company ~~Board's~~directors' fiduciary obligations to the Company's ~~stockholders~~duties under applicable Law. [*Notwithstanding anything to the contrary set forth in this Agreement, the Company may also make a Change of Recommendation not related to an Acquisition Proposal at any time prior to the Acceptance Time if: (i) an event, fact, circumstance or occurrence or combination or series thereof, that was not known to the Company Board as of the date of this Agreement, becomes known to the Company Board (an "Intervening Event"); (ii) the Company Board determines in good faith, after consultation with its outside legal counsel, that, in light of such Intervening Event, a failure to effect a Change of Recommendation would be inconsistent with the Company Board's fiduciary obligations to the Company's stockholders under applicable Law; (iii) such Change of Recommendation is not effected prior to the third (3rd) Business Day after Parent receives written notice from the Company confirming that the Company Board intends to effect such Change of Recommendation; (iv) during such three (3) Business Day period, if requested by Parent, the Company engages in good faith negotiations with Parent to amend this Agreement or the Offer or enter into an alternative transaction; and (v) at the end of such three (3) Business Day period, the Company Board determines in good faith, after consultation with its outside legal counsel and after taking into account any amendments to this Agreement and the Offer that Parent and Merger Sub have irrevocably agreed in writing to make as a result of the negotiations contemplated by clause "(iv)" above, that, in light of such Intervening Event, a failure to effect a Change of Recommendation would be inconsistent with the Company Board's fiduciary obligations to the Company's stockholders under applicable Law.*]

(e)   Nothing contained in this Agreement ~~through the Acceptance Time, the Company~~ shall ~~not terminate, amend, modify or waive any provision of any confidentiality, "standstill" or similar agreement entered into by the Company or its Subsidiary prior to the date of this Agreement, unless~~prohibit or restrict the Company or the Company Board from (i) disclosing to its stockholders a position contemplated by Rules 14d–9 and 14e–2(a) promulgated under the Exchange Act, or from issuing a "stop, look and listen" statement pending disclosure of its position thereunder, or (ii) making ~~any~~]*accurate*] disclosure to ~~its~~ [*the Company's*] stockholders ~~if the Company Board determines in good faith, after consultation with its~~the Company's outside legal counsel, that the failure of the Company Board to ~~take~~make such ~~action~~disclosure would be inconsistent with the Company Board's~~directors'~~ fiduciary obligations under applicable Law or (iii) making accurate disclosure to the Company's stockholders under applicable Law. (b) Subject to Section 5.2(c) and Section 5.2(d),of any factual information regarding the business, financial condition or results of operations of the Company, Parent or Merger Sub or the fact that an Acquisition Proposal has been made, the identity of the party making such Acquisition Proposal or the material terms of such Acquisition Proposal (and no such disclosure shall be deemed to be a Change of Recommendation); provided, however, that the Company Board shall not~~: (i) withhold, fail to include in the Schedule 14D-9, withdraw, qualify or modify, in a manner adverse to Parent and Merger Sub, the Company Recommendation, (ii) approve, recommend or declare advisable any Acquisition Proposal (any such action described in clauses (i) or (ii) of this Section 5.2(b), a "Change of Recommendation"); or (iii) cause the Company to enter into any Contract (other than a confidentiality agreement entered into in compliance with Section 5.2(a)) concerning an Acquisition Proposal (an "Alternative Acquisition Agreement"). (c) Notwithstanding anything to the contrary set forth in this Agreement, the Company Board may~~ make a Change of Recommendation ~~in response to an Acquisition Proposal and/or cause the Company to enter into an Alternative Acquisition Agreement concerning such~~except in accordance with Section 5.2(c) or Section 5.2(d).

(f) For purposes of this Agreement:

"Acquisition Proposal" means (i) any proposal, ~~or~~ offer, [*inquiry or indication of interest, whether written or otherwise,*] with respect to a merger, joint venture, partnership, consolidation, dissolution, liquidation, tender offer, exchange offer, recapitalization, reorganization, share exchange, business combination or similar transaction involving the Company or (ii) any acquisition by any Person of, or proposal or offer which if consummated would result in any Person becoming the beneficial owner of ~~twenty-five~~ [*fifteen*] percent (~~2~~[*1*]5%) or more of the total voting power of the equity securities of the Company, or ~~twenty-five~~ [*fifteen*] percent (~~2~~[*1*]5%) or more of the total assets of the Company, in each case other than the Transactions.

"Superior Proposal" means an [*unsolicited, bona fide written offer made by one or more Persons (none of whom is an Affiliate of the Company) constituting an*]Acquisition Proposal ~~at any time prior to the Acceptance Time if, and only if: (i) such Acquisition Proposal did not result from a material breach of this Section 5.2; (ii)~~that[, *if consummated,*] would result in any person becoming the beneficial owner of [*(i)*] ~~more than fifty percent (50%)~~ [*a majority*]of the assets [*of the Company and its subsidiary, taken as a whole*], or ~~more than fifty percent (50%)~~ [*(ii) a majority*] of the [*outstanding*] total voting power of the equity securities of the Company, which the Company Board determines in good faith, after consultation with its outside legal counsel and after consultation with its financial advisor, ~~(A) that such Acquisition Proposal would, if this Agreement or the Offer were not amended or an alternative transaction with Parent were not entered into, constitute a Superior Proposal and (B) that in light of such Acquisition Proposal, a failure to make a Change of Recommendation and/or enter into such Alternative Acquisition Agreement would be inconsistent with the Company Board's~~

~~fiduciary obligations~~ would result in a transaction more favorable to the Company's stockholders ~~under applicable Law; (iii) the Company delivers to Parent a written notice (the "Superior Proposal Notice") stating that the Company Board intends to take such action and (in the event the Company Board contemplates causing the Company to enter into an Alternative Acquisition Agreement) including a copy of such Alternative Acquisition Agreement; (iv) during the three (3) Business Day period commencing on the date of Parent's receipt of such Superior Proposal Notice~~from a financial point of view than the Transactions.~~,~~*[, taking into account the terms and conditions of such offer and (y) reasonably capable of being completed, taking into account the material financial, legal and regulatory aspects of such offer; provided, however that any such offer shall not be deemed to be a "Superior Proposal" if any financing required to consummate the transaction contemplated by such offer is not committed or, in the good faith judgment of the Company Board after consultation with its financial advisors, is not reasonably capable of being obtained by such third party.]*

ARTICLE 5.3.   Stockholders Meeting

(a)   If after the Acceptance Time the adoption of this Agreement by the Company's stockholders is required by applicable Law in order to consummate the Merger, the Company shall ~~have made its Representatives reasonably available~~take all action necessary in accordance with applicable Law and the Company's certificate of incorporation and bylaws to convene a meeting of the holders of Shares for the purpose of ~~engaging in negotiations with Parent (to the extent Parent desires to negotiate) regarding a possible amendment of this Agreement or the Offer or a possible alternative transaction so that the Acquisition Proposal that is the subject of the Superior Proposal Notice ceases to be a Superior Proposal; (v) after the expiration of the negotiation period described in clause "(iv)" above, the Company Board shall have determined in good faith, after consultation with its outside legal counsel and after consultation with its financial advisor, and after taking into account any amendments to this Agreement and the Offer that Parent and Merger Sub have irrevocably agreed in writing to make as a result of the negotiations contemplated by clause "(iv)" above, that (A) such Acquisition Proposal constitutes a Superior Proposal and (B) the failure to make~~obtaining the Company Requisite Vote (the "Stockholders Meeting") as promptly as practicable and shall not postpone or adjourn the Stockholders Meeting unless the Company determines that it is advisable to do so in order to solicit additional proxies in order to obtain the Company Requisite Vote or to comply with applicable Law. Unless a Change of Recommendation ~~and/or enter into such Alternative Acquisition Agreement would be inconsistent with the Company Board's fiduciary obligations to~~shall have occurred, (i) the Company shall solicit from the holders of the Shares proxies in favor of the adoption of this Agreement, and (ii) the Proxy Statement shall include the Company

Recommendation [,*the fairness opinion of ◙ and a summary and copy of Section 262 of the DGCL*]. Parent and Merger Sub agree to cause all Shares beneficially owned by Parent or Merger Sub or any of their Affiliates to be present at the Stockholders Meeting and to be voted at the Stockholders Meeting in favor of adoption of this Agreement.*

(b) If the adoption of this Agreement by the Company's stockholders ~~under applicable Law; and (vi) if the Company enters into an Alternative Acquisition Agreement concerning such Superior Proposal, the Company terminates this Agreement~~is not required by applicable Law in order to consummate the Merger, the parties hereto shall take all necessary and appropriate action to cause the Merger to become effective as soon as practicable after the Acceptance Time in accordance with Section [*253 of the DGL*]. ~~7.1(f); provided, however, that, in the event of any amendment to the financial or other material terms of such Acquisition Proposal, the Company shall be required to deliver to Parent a new Superior Proposal Notice (including as attachments thereto a copy of any new Alternative Acquisition Agreement relating to such amended Acquisition Proposal, if any), and the negotiation period described in clause "(iv)" above shall be extended by an additional two (2) Business Days from the date of Parent's receipt of such new Superior Proposal Notice.~~

ARTICLE 5.4.   Efforts; Filings; Other Actions; Notification; Antitrust Matters

(a) If the adoption of this Agreement by the Company's stockholders is required by applicable Law in order to consummate the Merger, then, as promptly as practicable following the Acceptance Time, the Company shall prepare and file with the SEC in preliminary form a proxy statement (such proxy statement, including any amendment or supplement thereto, the "Proxy Statement"). The Company agrees that the Proxy Statement will comply in all material respects with the applicable Securities Laws. The Company shall promptly notify Parent of the receipt of all comments of the SEC with respect to the Proxy Statement and of any request by the SEC for any amendment or supplement thereto or for additional information and shall promptly provide to Parent copies of all written correspondence between the Company and/or any of its Representatives and the SEC with respect to the Proxy Statement. The Company and Parent shall each use its reasonable best efforts promptly to provide responses to the SEC with respect to all SEC comments received with respect to the Proxy

---

* As previously noted, the author believes this definition of affiliate is problematic. Under Rule 12b–2 an "affiliate" is a person who, inter alia, directly or indirectly controls, or is controlled by, an issuer. Rule 13d–3 defines "beneficial ownership", so that referring to both of these as "affiliates" includes individual officers, directors and employees of the issuer. Thus this provision requires the Company to cause all officers, directors and employees to vote their shares in favor of the acquisition. Does this unlawfully force all these shareholders to vote without their consent?

Statement and shall cause the definitive Proxy Statement to be mailed as promptly as practicable after the date the SEC staff advises that it has no further comments thereon or that the Company may commence mailing the Proxy Statement.

(b)   Subject to the terms and conditions set forth in this Agreement, the Company and Parent shall cooperate with each other and shall use (and shall cause their respective Subsidiaries to use) their respective [*reasonable*]* best efforts to take or cause to be taken all actions, and do or cause to be done all things, reasonably necessary, proper or advisable on its part under this Agreement and applicable Law to consummate the Offer, the Merger and the other Transactions as soon as practicable, including (i) the obtaining of all necessary actions, waivers, consents and approvals from any Governmental Entity [*or from any third parties*] and the preparation and making of all necessary registrations, notices, reports and other filings and the taking of all steps as may be necessary to obtain an approval or waiver from, or to avoid an action or proceeding by, any Governmental Entity; and (ii) the execution and delivery of any additional instruments necessary to consummate the Transactions; provided, however, that in no event shall the Company or its Subsidiary be required to pay, prior to the Effective Time, any fee (except for customary fees to Governmental Entities), penalty or other consideration to any Person for any consent or approval required for the consummation of the Transactions. [*Without limiting the generality of the foregoing, each party hereto shall make or cause to be made, in cooperation with the other parties hereto and to the extent applicable and promptly, (i) an appropriate filing of a Notification and Report Form pursuant to the HSR Act with respect to the Transactions and (ii) any other necessary filings, forms, declarations, notifications, registrations and notices with other Governmental Entities under any applicable antitrust or competition Laws relating to the Transactions.*] Subject to applicable Law relating to the exchange of information, Parent and the Company shall have the right to review in advance, and to the extent practicable each shall consult with the other on and consider in good faith the views of the other in connection with, all of the information relating to Parent, the Company or any of their respective Subsidiaries, as the case may be, that appears in any filing made with, or written materials submitted to, any Governmental Entity in connection with the Offer, the Merger and the other Transactions (including the Offer Documents, Schedule 14D–9 and the Proxy Statement). In exercising the foregoing rights, each of the Company and Parent shall act reasonably and as promptly as practicable. Notwithstanding the foregoing, nothing in this Agreement

---

* This qualification is probably not necessary in this case, given the nature of the Seller's assets and business, but is important for buyers where antitrust issues arise that can be solved by the buyer's sale of some of its assets. Without this qualification, the clause becomes a "come Hell or High Water" obligation of the buyer. In some cases a buyer may expressly limit the amount of divestiture it is willing to engage in.

shall require any party hereto to provide the other parties hereto with a copy of its HSR Act filing or any exhibits thereto.

(c)   The Company and Parent each shall, upon request by the other, furnish the other with all information concerning itself, any of its respective Subsidiaries, directors, officers and stockholders and such other matters as may be reasonably necessary or advisable in connection with the Offer Documents, the Schedule 14D–9 and the Proxy Statement or any other statement, filing, notice or application made by or on behalf of Parent, the Company or any of their respective Subsidiaries to any third party and/or any Governmental Entity in connection with the Offer, the Merger and the other Transactions.

(d)   Subject to applicable Law and as required by any Governmental Entity, the Company and Parent each shall keep the other reasonably apprised of the status of matters relating to completion of the Transactions, including by Parent and the Company promptly furnishing the other with copies of notices or other communications received by Parent, the Company or any of their respective Subsidiaries, as the case may be, ~~that appears in any filing made with, or written materials submitted to, any Governmental Entity in connection with the Offer, the Merger and the other Transactions (including the Offer Documents, Schedule 14D–9 and the Proxy Statement). In exercising the foregoing rights, each of the Company and Parent shall act reasonably and as promptly as practicable. Notwithstanding the foregoing, nothing in this Agreement shall require any party hereto to provide the other parties hereto with a copy of its HSR Act filing or any exhibits thereto.~~ from any third party and/or any Governmental Entity with respect to the Offer, the Merger and the other Transactions. The Company shall give prompt notice to Parent of any change, fact or condition that has had or would reasonably be expected to have a Company Material Adverse Effect or any failure of any of the Tender Offer Conditions impossible or unlikely. Parent shall give prompt notice to the Company of any change, fact or condition that has had or would reasonably be expected to have a Parent Material Adverse Effect. [*None of the parties hereto shall independently*] ~~Neither the Company nor Parent shall permit any of its officers or any other representatives or agents to~~ participate in any meeting, [*or engage in any substantive conversation,*] with any Governmental Entity in respect of any filings [*or inquiry without giving the other parties hereto prior notice of the meeting and, unless prohibited by such Governmental Entity*], ~~investigation or other inquiry relating to the Offer, the Merger and the other Transactions unless it consults with the other party in advance and, to the extent permitted by such Governmental Entity, gives the other party~~ the opportunity to attend and/or participate. [*The parties hereto shall consult and cooperate with one another in connection with any information or proposals submitted in connection with proceedings under or relating to any antitrust or competition Laws.*]

(e)   Subject to the terms and conditions set forth in this Agreement, without limiting the generality of the undertakings pursuant to this Section 5.4, each of the Company (in the case of clauses (ii) and (iii)) and Parent (in the case of clauses (i), (ii) and (iii)) agrees to take or cause to be taken the following actions:

(i)   the prompt provision to each and every federal, state, local or foreign court or Governmental Entity with jurisdiction over enforcement of any applicable antitrust or competition Laws ("Government Antitrust Entity") of non-privileged information and documents requested by any Government Antitrust Entity or that are necessary, proper or advisable to permit consummation of the Transactions;

(ii)   the prompt use of its [*reasonable*]* best efforts to avoid the entry of any permanent, preliminary or temporary injunction or other order, decree, decision, determination or judgment that would delay, restrain, prevent, enjoin or otherwise prohibit consummation of the Transactions, including, without limitation, the defense through litigation on the merits of any claim asserted in any court, agency or other proceeding by any Person or entity, including, without limitation, any Governmental Entity, seeking to delay, restrain, prevent, enjoin or otherwise prohibit consummation of such Transactions and the proffer and agreement by Parent of its willingness to sell, lease, license or otherwise dispose of, or hold separate pending such disposition, and promptly to effect the sale, lease, license, disposal and holding separate of, such assets, rights, product lines, licenses, categories of assets or businesses or other operations, or interests therein, of the Company, Parent or any of their respective Subsidiaries (and the entry into agreements with, and submission to orders of, the relevant Government Antitrust Entity giving effect thereto) if such action should be reasonably necessary or advisable to avoid, prevent, eliminate or remove the actual, anticipated or threatened (x) commencement of any proceeding in any forum or (y) issuance of any order, decree, decision, determination or judgment that would delay, restrain, prevent, enjoin or otherwise prohibit consummation of the Offer by any Government Antitrust Entity; and

(iii) the prompt use of its [*reasonable*] best efforts to take, in the event that any permanent, preliminary or temporary injunction, decision, order, judgment, determination or decree is entered or issued, or becomes reasonably foreseeable to be entered or issued, in any proceeding or inquiry of any kind that would make consummation of the Offer in accordance with the terms of this Agreement unlawful or that would delay, restrain, prevent, enjoin or otherwise prohibit consummation of the Offer or the other Transactions, any and all steps (including, without limitation, the appeal thereof, the posting of a bond

---

*   This relates to a buyer's concern that it might be forced to divest assets in order to satisfy antitrust authorities. In some cases, where the parties expect some antitrust difficulties because of overlapping operations, buyers may choose to limit the amount of any divestitures required to obtain antitrust approval.

or the taking of the steps contemplated by clause (ii) of this paragraph) necessary to resist, vacate, modify, reverse, suspend, prevent, eliminate or remove such actual, anticipated or threatened injunction, decision, order, judgment, determination or decree so as to permit such consummation on a schedule as close as possible to that contemplated by this Agreement.

[*(f) Notwithstanding anything to the contrary in this Agreement, Parent shall not be required to sell, divest, hold separate, license or agree to any other structural or conduct remedy with respect to, any operations, divisions, businesses, product lines, customers, assets or relationships of Parent or any of its Subsidiaries (other than the Company and its Subsidiary following the Merger), on the one hand, or the Company or its Subsidiary, on the other hand, which (A) would materially and adversely affect the business of Parent and its Subsidiaries, taken as a whole, or (B) would require the sale, divestiture, holding separate or license of the Key Product, ◙ or ◙ to any third party or materially impair the benefits expected by Parent as of the date of this Agreement to be derived by Parent from the acquisition of the Key Product, ◙ or ◙ (any such action, a "Non-Required Remedy").]**

(g)   Prior to the Expiration Time, the Company (acting through the Company Board and its compensation committee) shall take such actions as may be required to cause any agreements, arrangements or understandings that have been or will be entered into by the Company, Parent or any of their respective Affiliates with current or future directors, officers or employees of the Company pursuant to which payments are made or to be made or benefits are granted or to be granted according to such arrangements to be approved as an "employment compensation, severance or other employee benefit arrangement" within the meaning or Rule 14d—10(d)(1) under the Exchange Act and to satisfy the requirements of the non-exclusive safe harbor set forth in Rule 14d—10(d) under the Exchange Act.

ARTICLE 5.5.   Access and Reports

(a)   Subject to applicable Law, upon reasonable notice, the Company shall (and shall cause its Subsidiary to) afford Parent's officers and other authorized Representatives reasonable access, during normal business hours throughout the period prior to the Effective Time, to its employees, properties, [*assets,*] books, Contracts, [*Tax Returns,*] and records, and, during such period, the Company shall (and shall cause its Subsidiary to) furnish promptly to Parent all information concerning its business, properties, [*finances, operations, assets, litigation matters, environmental compliance, cash-flow reports*] and personnel as may reasonably be

---

*   This indicates a case where the buyer does not believe there are any serious antitrust problems, and makes clear its unwillingness to divest any material assets. The buyer was developing a drug to address the same disease, which it hoped to combine with the Company's Key Product.

requested. All requests for information made pursuant to this Section 5.5 shall be directed to the executive officer or other persons designated by the Company. All such information shall be governed by the terms of the Confidentiality Agreement. No investigation pursuant to this Section 5.5 or by Parent or its Representatives at any time prior to or following the date hereof shall affect or be deemed to modify any representation or warranty made by the Company herein[, *the covenants or agreements of the parties hereto or the conditions to the obligations of the parties hereto under this Agreement*].

(b)   This Section 5.5 shall not require the Company or its Subsidiary to permit any access, or to disclose (i) any information that, in the reasonable, good faith judgment (after consultation with [*outside*] counsel, ~~which may be in-house counsel~~) of the Company, would reasonably be expected to result in any violation of any Law or any Contract to which the Company or its Subsidiary is a party or cause any privilege (including attorney-client privilege) that the Company or its Subsidiary would be entitled to assert to be undermined with respect to such information and such undermining of such privilege could in the Company's good faith judgment (after consultation with [*outside*] counsel, which may be in-house counsel) adversely affect in any material respect the Company's position in any pending or, what the Company believes in good faith (after consultation with [*outside*] counsel~~, which may be in-house counsel~~) could be, future litigation or (ii) if the Company or any of its Affiliates, on the one hand, and Parent or any of its Affiliates, on the other hand, are adverse parties in a litigation, any information that is reasonably pertinent thereto; provided, that, in the case of clause (i), the parties hereto shall cooperate in seeking to find a way to allow disclosure of such information to the extent doing so (A) would not (in the good faith belief of the Company (after consultation with [*outside*] counsel, ~~which may be in-house counsel~~)) be reasonably ~~be expected~~[*likely*] to result in the violation of any such Law or Contract or be reasonably ~~be expected~~[*likely*] to cause such privilege to be undermined with respect to such information or (B) could reasonably (in the good faith belief of the Company (after consultation with [*outside*] counsel, ~~which may be in-house counsel~~)) be managed through the use of customary "clean-room" arrangements pursuant to which non-employee Representatives of Parent could be provided access to such information.

(c)   The information provided pursuant to this Section 5.5 shall be used solely for the purpose of the Transactions, and such information shall be kept confidential by Parent and Merger Sub in accordance with, and shall otherwise abide by and be subject to the terms and conditions of, the Confidentiality Agreement.

ARTICLE 5.6.   Stock Exchange Delisting

The Surviving Corporation shall use its ~~reasonable~~ best efforts to cause the Shares to no longer be quoted on NASDAQ and to be deregistered under the Exchange Act as soon as practicable following the Effective Time.

ARTICLE 5.7.   Publicity

The initial press release regarding the Transactions shall be a joint press release by the Company and Parent. Thereafter, provided that the Company Board shall not have made a Change of Recommendation, the Company, and Parent and Merger Sub each shall consult with the other prior to issuing any press releases or otherwise making public announcements with respect to the Transactions and prior to making any filings with any third party and/or any Governmental Entity (including any national securities exchange or interdealer quotation service) with respect thereto, except [*(i) in any case in which the management of any such party hereto shall have determined in good faith (after consultation with its outside legal counsel) that such disclosure is*] as may be required by applicable Law or by obligations pursuant to any listing agreement with or rules of any national securities exchange or interdealer quotation service or by the request of any Governmental Entity [*or (ii) in any case in which such disclosure is made in connection with any dispute between the parties hereto regarding this Agreement or the Transactions*].

ARTICLE 5.8.   Employee Benefits

(a) Parent and Merger Sub agree that, during the period commencing at the Effective Time and ending on the eighteen (18) month anniversary following the Effective Time, the employees of the Company and its Subsidiary who continue to be employed by Parent or an Affiliate following the Acceptance Time ("Continuing Employees") shall be provided with (i) base salary or wage rate and bonus opportunities (including annual bonus opportunities[, *but excluding equity-based compensation*] and long-term incentive opportunities) that are no less than the base salary or wage rate and bonus opportunities provided by the Company or its Subsidiary, as applicable, immediately prior to the [*Acceptance*]* Effective Time, (ii) pension and welfare benefits that are no less favorable in the aggregate than those provided by the Company or its Subsidiary, as applicable, immediately prior to the [*Acceptance*] Effective Time and (iii) severance benefits that are no less favorable than those set forth in Section 5.8(a) the Company Disclosure Schedule.[*Following the Effective Time, Continuing Employees shall be eligible to participate in the equity compensation plans of Parent on the same terms as similarly situated Parent employees (including with respect to the grant of any awards (to be made at the discretion of Parent's board of directors) under such equity compensation plans and the terms and conditions of such awards). Parent shall have no obligation and the Company shall take no action that would have the effect of requiring*

---

*   This protects the Buyer from post-acceptance opportunistic compensation increases before the closing.

Parent or the Surviving Corporation to continue any specific plans or to continue the employment of any specific Person.]

(b)   Parent and Merger Sub shall cause any employee benefit plans in which the Continuing Employees are eligible to participate following the ~~Effective~~ [*Acceptance*] Time to take into account for purposes of eligibility, vesting, level of benefits and benefit accrual thereunder, service by such employees to the Company or its Subsidiary, as applicable, as if such service were with Parent, to the same extent such service was credited under a comparable plan of the Company or its Subsidiary, as applicable (provided, however, that the foregoing shall not apply with respect to benefit accrual under any defined benefit pension plan or to the extent that its application would result in a duplication of benefits).

(c)   To the extent permitted under applicable Law, with respect to any employee benefit plans maintained for the benefit of the Continuing Employees following the ~~Effective~~ [*Acceptance*] Time, Parent and Merger Sub shall, and shall cause the Surviving Corporation and any successor thereto, to (i) cause there to be waived any eligibility requirements or pre-existing condition limitations or waiting period requirements to the same extent waived under comparable plans of the Company or its Subsidiary, as applicable, and (ii) give effect, in determining any deductible, co-insurance and maximum out-of-pocket limitations, amounts paid by such employees during the calendar year in which the Effective Time occurs under similar plans maintained by the Company or its Subsidiary, as applicable.

(d)   Parent shall, and shall cause the Surviving Corporation and any successor thereto to, honor, fulfill and discharge the Company's obligations under the agreements identified in Section 5.8(d) of the Company Disclosure Schedule.

[*(e)   If directed in writing by Parent prior to the Effective Time, the Company shall take (or cause to be taken) all actions reasonably determined by Parent to be necessary or appropriate to terminate, effective immediately prior to the Effective Time, any Employee Plans that contain a cash or deferred arrangement intended to qualify under Section 401(k) of the Code.*]

[*(f)*]/~~[(e)]~~ Regardless of the calendar year in which the [*Acceptance*] ~~Effective~~ Time occurs, the Company and its Subsidiary, [*as applicable, shall pay to each eligible Employee, immediately prior to the Acceptance Time, a pro rata bonus for the Company's 2012 fiscal year*] shall be permitted to ~~(i)~~ pay annual bonuses for 2011 in an amount equal to the [*product of (x) the Employee's 2012 fiscal year target bonus, multiplied by (y) the ratio of such Employee's actual bonus received for the Company's 2011 fiscal year to the Employee's target bonus for the Company's ◉ fiscal year, multiplied by (z) the ratio of the number of calendar days elapsed between ◉ and the Acceptance Time to 365 days.*] ~~annual bonus earned by~~

~~participants for the 2011 calendar year and (ii) to establish bonus targets and performance objectives for 2012 in the ordinary course of business consistent with past practice.~~

(f)[(g)] The provisions contained in this Section 5.8 are included for the sole benefit of the Company and Parent and nothing in this Section 5.8, whether express or implied, shall ~~(i)~~ create any third-party beneficiary or other rights (i) in any other Person, including any current or former employees, any participant in any Benefit Plan, or any dependent or beneficiary thereof*[, (ii) be construed as an amendment, waiver or creation of or limitation on the ability to terminate any Benefit Plans or benefit plan or agreement of Parent or (iii) limit the ability of Parent, the Company, the Surviving Corporation or any of their respective Subsidiaries to terminate the employment of any Continuing Employee at any time]*.

ARTICLE 5.9.   Expenses

Parent or the Surviving Corporation shall pay all charges and expenses, including those of the Paying Agent, in connection with the transactions contemplated in Article 3. Except as otherwise provided in this Agreement, whether or not Shares are purchased pursuant to the Offer, all costs and expenses incurred in connection with the Transactions shall be paid by the party ~~hereto~~ incurring such expense.

ARTICLE 5.10. Indemnification;   Directors'   and   Officers' Insurance

(a) From and after the Effective Time, Parent and the Surviving Corporation shall indemnify and hold harmless, to the fullest extent permitted under applicable Law, each present and former director and officer of the Company or its Subsidiary (in each case, when acting in such capacity) determined as of the Effective Time (the "Indemnified Parties"), against any and all costs or expenses (including reasonable attorneys' fees), judgments, fines, losses, claims, damages, liabilities and amounts paid in settlement incurred in connection with any Proceeding arising out of matters existing or occurring at or prior to the Effective Time, whether asserted or claimed prior to, at or after the Effective Time, including the Offer, the Merger and the other Transactions; and Parent or the Surviving Corporation shall also advance to the Indemnified Parties all reasonable costs and expenses incurred in such Proceeding to the fullest extent permitted under applicable Law, provided that the Person to whom expenses are advanced provides an undertaking to repay such advances if it is finally determined by a court of competent jurisdiction that such Person is not entitled to indemnification.

(b) Any Indemnified Party wishing to claim indemnification under Section 5.10(a), upon learning of any such claim, action, suit, proceeding or investigation, shall promptly notify Parent thereof, but the failure to so notify shall not relieve Parent or the Surviving Corporation of any liability it may have to such Indemnified Party except to the extent such failure materially prejudices the indemnifying party. In the event of any such claim, action, suit, proceeding or investigation (whether arising before or after the Effective Time), (i) Parent or the Surviving Corporation shall have the right to assume the defense thereof and Parent and the Surviving Corporation shall not be liable to such Indemnified Parties for any legal expenses of other counsel or any other expenses subsequently incurred by such Indemnified Parties in connection with the defense thereof, except that if Parent or the Surviving Corporation elects not to assume such defense or counsel for the Indemnified Parties advises that there are issues which raise conflicts of interest between Parent or the Surviving Corporation and the Indemnified Parties, the Indemnified Parties may retain counsel satisfactory to them, and Parent or the Surviving Corporation shall pay all reasonable fees and expenses of such counsel for the Indemnified Parties promptly as statements therefor are received; provided, however, that Parent and the Surviving Corporation shall be obligated pursuant to this Section 5.10(b) to pay for only one firm of counsel for all Indemnified Parties in any jurisdiction unless the use of one counsel for such Indemnified Parties would present such counsel with a conflict of interest; provided that the fewest number of counsels necessary to avoid conflicts of interest shall be used; (ii) the Indemnified Parties shall cooperate in the defense of any such matter, and (iii) Parent and the Surviving Corporation shall not be liable for any settlement effected without their prior written consent; provided, further, that Parent and the Surviving Corporation shall not have any obligation hereunder to any Indemnified Party if and when a court of competent jurisdiction shall ultimately determine, and such determination shall have become final, that the indemnification of such Indemnified Party in the manner contemplated hereby is prohibited by applicable Law.

(c) Prior to the Acceptance Time, the Company shall use its reasonable best efforts to (and if the Company is unable to, Parent shall cause the Surviving Corporation as of the [*Effective*] ~~Acceptance~~ Time to) obtain and fully pay for "tail" insurance policies (providing only for the Side A coverage for Indemnified Parties where the existing policies also include Side B coverage for the Company) with a claims period of at least six (6) years from and after the Acceptance Time from an insurance carrier with the same or better credit rating as the Company's current insurance carrier with respect to directors' and officers' liability insurance and fiduciary liability insurance (collectively, "<u>D & O Insurance</u>") with benefits and levels of coverage at least as favorable as the Company's existing policies existing or occurring at or prior to the Acceptance Time (including in connection with this Agreement or the Transactions or actions contemplated hereby); provided, however, that such "tail" insurance policies shall not require the payment of an aggregate premium in excess of three hundred percent (300%) of the aggregate annual premium most recently paid by the Company prior to the date hereof to maintain the D & O Insurance. If the Company and the Surviving Corporation shall for any reason fail to obtain such "tail" insurance policies as of the Acceptance Time, the Surviving Corporation shall, and Parent shall cause the Surviving Corporation to, continue to maintain in effect for a period of at least six (6) years from and after the Acceptance Time the D & O Insurance in place as of the date hereof with benefits and levels of coverage at least as favorable as that provided under the Company's existing policies as of the date hereof, or the Surviving Corporation shall, and Parent shall cause the Surviving Corporation to, use reasonable best efforts to purchase comparable D & O Insurance for such six (6)-year period with benefits and levels of coverage at least as favorable as provided under the Company's existing policies as of the date hereof; provided, however, that neither Parent nor the Surviving Corporation shall be required to pay an aggregate annual premium for such D & O Insurance or comparable D & O Insurance in excess of three hundred percent (300%) of the aggregate annual premium most recently paid by the Company prior to the date hereof to maintain the D & O Insurance.

(d)   If Parent or the Surviving Corporation or any of their respective successors or assigns (i) shall consolidate with or merge into any other corporation or entity and shall not be the continuing or surviving corporation or entity of such consolidation or merger or (ii) ~~shall~~ shall transfer all or substantially all of its properties and assets to any Person, then, and in each such case, proper provisions shall be made so that the successors and assigns of Parent or the Surviving Corporation shall assume all of the obligations set forth in this Section 5.10.

(e) The provisions of this Section 5.10 shall survive the consummation of the Offer and the Merger and are intended to be for the benefit of, and shall be enforceable by, each of the Indemnified Parties, each of whom is an intended third-party beneficiary of this Agreement. The obligations of Parent and Merger Sub under this Section 5.10 shall not be terminated or modified in such a manner as to adversely affect the rights of any Indemnified Party to whom this Section 5.10 applies unless (i) such termination or modification is required by applicable Law or (ii) the affected Indemnified Party shall have consented in writing to such termination or modification.

(f)   The rights of the Indemnified Parties under this Section 5.10 shall be in addition to any rights such Indemnified Parties may have under the certificate of incorporation or bylaws or comparable governing documents of the Company or its Subsidiary, or under any applicable Contracts or applicable Law. Parent and Merger Sub hereby agree that the Charter and Bylaws shall contain provisions for indemnification, advancement of expenses and exculpation of directors no less favorable to the Indemnified Parties (and employees and agents of the Company and its Subsidiary to the fullest extent indemnification and advancement of expenses are afforded to such persons under the Company's and its Subsidiary's certificate of incorporation and bylaws or comparable governing documents) than such provisions as are presently contained in the certificate of incorporation and bylaws or comparable governing documents of the Company and its Subsidiary.

ARTICLE 5.11. Takeover Statutes

If any takeover statute is or may become applicable to the Offer, the Merger or the other Transactions, the Company Board shall grant such approvals and take such actions as are necessary so that such Transactions may be consummated as promptly as practicable on the terms contemplated by this Agreement and shall otherwise act to eliminate or minimize the effects of such statute or regulation on such Transactions.

ARTICLE 5.12. Parent Vote

If a Stockholders Meeting is held, Parent shall vote or cause to be voted any Shares beneficially owned by it or any of its Subsidiaries or with respect to which it or any of its Subsidiaries has the power (by agreement, proxy or otherwise) to cause to be voted, in favor of the adoption of this Agreement at any meeting of stockholders of the Company at which this Agreement shall be submitted for adoption and at all adjournments or postponements thereof. [*From and after the Acceptance Time until the Effective Time, Parent, Merger Sub and their Affiliates shall at all times maintain ownership of Shares equal to at least a majority of the then outstanding Shares.*]

ARTICLE 5.13. Financing

(a) Notwithstanding anything herein to the contrary, Parent and Merger Sub acknowledge and agree that obtaining the Financing or any Alternate Financing is not a condition to consummation of the Transactions, and that, irrespective and independently of the availability of the Financing or any Alternate Financing, Parent and Merger Sub shall be obligated to pay for the tendered Shares and consummate the Merger and the other Transactions as provided herein, subject to the satisfaction or waiver of the Tender Offer Conditions or the conditions set forth in Article VII[*6*], as applicable.

(b) Each of Parent and Merger Sub shall use its reasonable best efforts to take, or cause to be taken, all actions and to do, or cause to be done, all things necessary, proper or advisable to arrange and obtain the Financing on the terms and subject to the conditions described in the Financing Commitments[, *shall not, until after the Effective Time, permit, effect or cause to be effected any voluntary or mandatory termination, prepayment or reduction in the aggregate amount of the Financing or the respective commitments contained in the Financing Commitments,*] and shall not permit any amendment or modification to be made to, or any waiver [*by Parent or Merger Sub*] of any provision or remedy under the Financing Commitments if such amendment, modification or waiver would (i) reduce the aggregate amount of the Financing (including by changing the amount of fees to be paid or original issue discount of the Financing), or (ii) impose new or additional conditions, or otherwise amend, modify or expand any conditions, to the receipt of the Financing in a manner that, individually or in the aggregate with other such amendments, modifications or waivers, ~~would~~ [*is*] reasonably ~~be expected~~ [*likely*] to (A) have a Parent Material Adverse Effect ~~or~~, (B) delay or make the funding of the Financing (or satisfaction of the conditions to obtaining the Financing) less likely to occur or (C) adversely impact the ability of Parent or Merger Sub to enforce their rights against the other parties to the Financing Commitments or the definitive agreements with respect thereto[; *it being understood and agreed that, notwithstanding the foregoing provisions of this sentence, Parent or Merger Sub may reduce (through voluntary or mandatory terminations or otherwise) the aggregate amount of the Financing in connection with any cash received by Parent or Merger Sub from other sources (including by reason of a capital market or other financing transaction) that is available to satisfy the obligations of Parent or Merger Sub under this Agreement*]. Subject to the limitations set forth in Section 4.2(f), Parent and Merger Sub may replace or amend the Financing Commitments to add [*agents, co-agents,*] lenders, lead arrangers, [*joint*] bookrunners, [*managers,*] syndication agents or ~~other~~similar entities that have not executed the Financing Commitments as of the date hereof, if the addition of such additional parties, individually or in the aggregate with other such additions, ~~would~~ [*is*] not reasonably ~~be expected~~ [*likely*] to prevent, delay or impair the availability of the financing under the Financing Commitments or have a Parent Material Adverse Effect. For purposes of this Section 5.13(b), references to "<u>Financing</u>" shall include the financing contemplated by the Financing Commitments as permitted to be amended or modified by this Section 5.13(b) and references to "<u>Financing Commitments</u>" shall include such documents as permitted to be amended or modified by this Section 5.13(b). Without limiting the foregoing, Parent and Merger Sub shall use their reasonable best efforts to (u) maintain in effect the Financing Commitments until the Offer, the Merger and the other Transactions are consummated, (v) satisfy [*(or have waived)*] all conditions and covenants applicable to Parent and Merger Sub in the Financing Commitments at or prior to the Acceptance Time or the Closing, as applicable, and otherwise comply with their obligations under the Financing Commitments, (w) enter into definitive agreements with respect to the Financing Commitments on the terms and subject to the conditions (including the flex provisions) contemplated by the Financing Commitments, (x) consummate the Financing at or prior to consummation of the Offer, the Merger or the other Transactions, as applicable, (y) enforce their rights under the Financing Commitments, [*including any rights to cause the Financing Sources*] ~~lenders~~ and other

Persons providing[, *on the terms and conditions set forth therein, the*] Financing to fund, on the day of the consummation of the Offer, the Merger or the other Transactions, as applicable, the Financing contemplated to be funded on such day by the Financing Commitments (or such lesser amount as may be required to consummate the Offer, the Merger and the other Transactions) [*and (y) consummate the Financing at or prior to consummation of the Offer, the Merger or the other Transactions, as applicable.*] ~~Without limiting the generality of the foregoing,~~ Parent and Merger Sub [*shall keep the Company informed on a reasonably current basis in reasonable detail of the status of its efforts to arrange the Financing (or replacement thereof) as the Company may reasonably request, and*] shall give the Company prompt notice [*of any development with respect*]: ~~(1) of any breach or default (or any event or circumstance that, with or without notice, lapse of time or both, is reasonably likely to give rise to any breach or default) by any party~~ to the Financing [*that would reasonably be expected to have a Parent Material Adverse Effect;*] ~~Commitments or definitive document related to the Financing of which Parent or its Affiliates becomes aware; (2) of the receipt of any written notice or other written communication from any Person with respect to any: (i) actual or potential breach, default, termination or repudiation by any party to the Financing Commitments or any definitive document related to the Financing or any provisions of the Financing Commitments or any definitive document related to the Financing or (ii) material dispute or disagreement between or among any parties to the Financing Commitments or any definitive document related to the Financing; and (3) if for any reason Parent or Merger Sub believes in good faith that it will not be able to obtain all or any portion of the Financing on the terms, in the manner or from the sources contemplated by the Financing Commitments or the definitive documents related to the Financing;~~ provided that in no event will Parent or Merger Sub be under any obligation to disclose any information that is subject to attorney-client or similar privilege if Parent and Merger Sub shall have used their reasonable best efforts to disclose such information in a way that would not waive such privilege.

(i) ~~As soon as reasonably practicable, but in any event within five (5) days of the date on which the Company delivers to Parent or Merger Sub a written request, Parent and Merger Sub shall provide any information reasonably requested by the Company relating to any circumstance referred to in clause (1), (2) or (3) of the immediately preceding sentence.~~ If any portion of the Financing becomes unavailable on the terms and conditions (including the flex provisions) contemplated in the Financing Commitments, Parent shall use its reasonable best efforts to arrange and obtain alternative financing from alternative sources on terms and subject to the conditions that are no less favorable, in the aggregate, to Parent (taking into account the flex provisions set forth in the Financing Commitments) than those set forth in the

Financing Commitments, in an amount sufficient to consummate the Offer, the Merger and the other Transactions as promptly as practicable following the occurrence of such event.

[*(ii) Parent shall have the right from time to time to substitute other debt or equity financing for all or any portion of the Financing from the same and/or alternative financing source, in each case, in a manner not materially less beneficial to the Company, Parent and Merger Sub as compared to the Financing Commitments (and no less beneficial in terms of confidentiality or the aggregate amount of funds available under the Financing); provided, however, that any such financing arranged in accordance with this Section 5.13(b)(ii) shall be subject to the same limitations that apply to the Financing Commitments as set forth in the first sentence of this Section 5.13(b). For purposes of this Agreement: (A) any financing arranged in accordance with Section 5.13(b)(i) above or this Section 5.13(b)(ii) shall be referred to as the "Alternate Financing"; (B) the term "Financing" shall be deemed to include the debt financing contemplated by the Financing Commitments as permitted to be amended or modified by this Section 5.13(b) and/or any Alternate Financing; and (c) the term "Financing Commitments" shall be deemed to include such Financing Commitments as permitted to be amended or modified by this Section 5.13(b) and/or any new commitment letter (the "New Financing Commitments") entered into with respect to any Alternate Financing (it being understood and agreed that any Alternate Financing shall be subject to the terms and conditions hereof that apply to Financing Commitments). Parent and Merger Sub shall provide the Company with a copy of any New Financing Commitments obtained by Parent or Merger Sub in connection with an Alternate Financing as promptly as practicable following the execution thereof (other than fees and other information customarily redacted from such agreements).*]

(c)   Prior to the Acceptance Time, the Company shall (and shall cause its Subsidiary to) provide to Parent and Merger Sub, and shall use reasonable best efforts to cause Representatives of the Company and its Subsidiary to provide to Parent and Merger Sub, at Parent's sole expense, all cooperation reasonably requested in writing by Parent and Merger Sub as compared to the Financing Commitments (and no less beneficial in terms of confidentiality or the aggregate amount of funds available under the Financing) that is necessary in connection with the Financing, including using reasonable best efforts to, in each case to the extent reasonably requested, (i) [*cooperate with the marketing efforts of Parent and lenders for any of the Financing, including using reasonable best efforts to cause its Representatives to be available, during normal working hours and upon reasonable notice,*] participate in meetings, presentations, road shows, due diligence sessions and sessions with rating agencies, and (ii) assist with the preparation of materials for rating agency presentations, offering documents, private placement memoranda, bank information memoranda, prospectuses [, *road show presentations; (iii) provide to Parent and Merger Sub, and use reasonable best efforts to cause Representatives of the Company and its Subsidiary to provide to Parent and Merger Sub all financial information regarding the Company and its Subsidiary required to be delivered pursuant to Section 2 of Exhibit B of the Financing Commitments or required in connection with the preparation of the Offering Documents referred to in Section 8 of Exhibit B of the Financing Commitments; (iv) obtain consent from its certified independent auditors to SEC filings and offering memoranda that include or incorporate Company consolidated financial information (with such changes as the Company and its auditors deem necessary or appropriate), in each case, to the extent such consent is required, together with auditors' reports and comfort letters with respect to financial information relating to the Company and its Subsidiary in customary form; (v) provide information regarding the Company and its Subsidiary reasonably required to assist in the preparation of pro forma financial statements by Parent and Merger Sub; provided that it is understood that assumptions underlying the pro forma adjustments to be made are the sole responsibility of Parent and/or Merger Sub; (vi) provide assistance in the preparation of definitive financing documents and providing any sources of Financing (subject to confidentiality) with reasonable access to the properties, books and records of the Company and its Subsidiary; (vii) provide other information regarding the Company and its Subsidiary reasonably required by Parent and Merger Sub in connection with preparation of the Offering Document referred to in Section 8 of Exhibit B of the Financing Commitments (it being understood that preparation of the Offering Document is the responsibility of Parent and Merger Sub); (viii) provide reasonable cooperation with the Financing Sources, other potential financing sources and their respective agents with respect to their due diligence, including access to documentation reasonably requested by persons in connection with capital markets transactions; and (ix) provide all documentation and other information required by any Governmental Entity with respect to the Financing under applicable "know your customer" and anti-money laundering rules and regulations, including the PATRIOT Act, and in any event at least five (5) days prior to the Acceptance Time.]* ~~and similar documents necessary, proper or advisable in connection with the Financing; provided, however, that any such financing arranged,~~[*Notwithstanding the foregoing,*] (A) ~~irrespective of the above,~~ no obligation of the Company or its Subsidiary under any certificate, document or instrument shall be effective until the Acceptance Time (or such later time set forth in such certificate, document or instrument), and neither the Company nor its Subsidiary [*nor any of its representatives*] shall be required to take any action under any certificate, document or instrument that is not contingent upon the consummation of the Offer (including the entry into any agreement that is effective before consummation of the Offer) or that would be effective prior thereto, (B) nothing herein shall require such cooperation to the extent that it would interfere unreasonably with the business or operations of the Company or its Subsidiary and (C) neither the Company nor its Subsidiary shall be required to issue any offering or information document. [*The Company hereby consents to the use of the logos of the Company and its Subsidiaries in connection with the syndication or marketing of the Financing; provided that such logos are used in a manner that is not intended to harm or disparage the Company, its Subsidiaries or their marks; provided, further, that such logos are used solely in connection with a description of the Company, its business and products or the Transactions and shall not appear on the cover of any rating agency presentations, offering documents, private placement memoranda, bank information memoranda, prospectuses, road show presentations and similar documents used in connection with the Financing.*] Neither the Company nor its Subsidiary shall be required to bear any cost or expense or to pay any commitment or other similar fee or make any other payment in connection with the Financing or any of the foregoing prior to the Acceptance Time. Parent shall [, *promptly upon request by the Company, reimburse the Company for all reasonable out-of-pocket costs incurred by the Company or its Subsidiary in connection with such cooperation and*] indemnify and hold harmless the Company, its Subsidiary and their respective Representatives from and against any and all costs or expenses (including reasonable attorneys' fees), judgments, fines, losses, claims, damages, liabilities and amounts paid in settlement incurred in connection with any claim, action, suit, proceeding or investigation, whether civil, criminal, administrative or investigative, arising out of the arrangement of the Financing (including any action taken in accordance with this Section 5.13(b)(ii) shall be c)) and any information utilized in connection therewith (other than historical information relating to the Company or its Subsidiary provided by the Company in writing specifically for use in the Financing offering documents). Notwithstanding anything to the contrary, the Tender Offer Condition set forth in clause (iv) of Annex A, as it applies to the Company's obligations under this Section 5.13(c), shall be deemed satisfied unless there has occurred a willful and intentional material breach of its obligations under this Section 5.13(c). Parent shall, promptly upon request by the Company, reimburse the Company for all reasonable out-of-pocket costs incurred by the Company or its Subsidiary in connection with this Section 5.13(c).

[*5.14. **Litigation.** The Company shall provide Parent with prompt notice of, and copies of all pleadings and correspondence relating to, any Proceeding against the Company or any of its directors or officers by any holder of Shares arising out of or relating to this Agreement or the Transactions. The Company shall give Parent the opportunity to participate in the defense, settlement, or compromise of any such Proceeding, and no such settlement or compromise shall be agreed to without the prior written consent of Parent, which consent shall not be* *unreasonably withheld, conditioned or delayed. For purposes of this paragraph "participate" means that Parent will be kept apprised of proposed strategy and other significant decisions with respect to the Proceeding by the Company (to the extent that the attorney-client privilege between the Company and its counsel is not undermined or otherwise affected), and Parent may offer comments or suggestions with respect to the Proceeding but will not be afforded any decision-making power or other authority over the Proceeding except for the settlement or compromise consent set forth above.*

*5.15. **Rights Agreement**. From the date hereof until the earlier of the Acceptance Time and the date this Agreement is terminated in accordance with its terms, the Company shall not, and shall cause its Subsidiary not to, enter into any stockholder rights agreement, rights plan, "poison pill" or other similar agreement, unless such plan or agreement exempts from its application the acquisition of Shares by Parent and Merger Sub pursuant to this Agreement, the Offer and the Merger.*

*5.16. **Payoff Letters**.*

(a) At least three (3) Business Days prior to the anticipated Acceptance Time, the Company shall deliver a notice of termination in accordance with Section 2.3(b) of the Venture Loan and Security Agreement (the "Loan Agreement") to ▣ and ▣ under the Loan Agreement.

(b) Prior to the Acceptance Time, the Company shall use reasonable best efforts to (i) either (A) terminate or otherwise cause the release of the Liens securing the Loan Agreements or (B) obtain a customary payoff letter from the lenders under the Loan Agreement (and other outstanding indebtedness for borrowed money, if any) which (1) confirms the full outstanding amount then outstanding, along with accrued interest thereon and all fees and other obligations of the Company accrued under the Loan Agreement (or such other indebtedness) (the "Payoff Amount"), (2) contains payment instructions, and (3) evidences the agreement by such lenders to release all Liens upon the payment of such amount in accordance with the payment instructions, and (ii) obtain documents, including an authorization to file UCC termination statements, executed terminations and releases of outstanding mortgages, as are reasonably necessary to release such Liens.

(c) At or prior to the Closing, the Company shall repay the Payoff Amount to the lenders under the Loan Agreement and terminate such agreements at or prior to the Closing.]

ARTICLE 6.   Conditions

ARTICLE 6.1   Conditions to Each Party's Obligation to Effect the Merger

The respective obligations of each party hereto to effect the Merger is subject to the satisfaction or waiver (to the extent permitted by applicable Law) by such party at or prior to the Effective Time of each of the following conditions:

(a) Stockholder Approval. If required by the DGCL to effect the Merger, this Agreement shall have been adopted by the Company Requisite Vote.

(b) No Order. No Order by ~~any~~a United States court of competent jurisdiction that restrains, enjoins or otherwise prohibits the consummation of the Merger shall have been entered and shall continue to be in effect. No Law or Order shall have been enacted, issued, entered, promulgated or enforced by any Governmental Entity that prohibits or makes illegal consummation of the Merger and shall continue to be in effect.

(c) Purchase of Shares in Offer. Merger Sub shall have accepted for payment and purchased, or caused to be accepted for payment and purchased, all Shares validly tendered and not withdrawn pursuant to the Offer (provided that the purchase of Shares pursuant to the Offer shall not be a condition to the obligations of Parent and Merger Sub hereunder if Merger Sub fails to accept for payment and pay for Shares pursuant to the Offer in violation of the terms of this Agreement or the Offer).

[*(d) Representations and Warranties. Each of the representations and warranties made by the Company in this Agreement shall have been accurate in all respects as of the date of this Agreement, and shall be accurate as of the Closing as if made on the date of the Closing.*]

ARTICLE 7.   Termination

ARTICLE 7.1.   Termination

This Agreement may be terminated and the Transactions may be abandoned at any time prior to the Acceptance Time:

(a) by mutual written consent of Parent, Merger Sub and the Company;

(b) by either Parent or the Company, if the Acceptance Time shall not have occurred on or before ◙ (the "Outside Date"); provided, that the right to terminate this Agreement pursuant to this Section 7.1(b) shall not be available to any party hereto that has breached its obligations under this Agreement in any manner that shall have proximately contributed to the failure of the Acceptance Time to have occurred prior to the Outside Date;

(c) by either Parent or the Company, if any Order permanently enjoining, restraining or otherwise prohibiting the making or the consummation of the Offer exists and such Order shall have become final and non-appealable; provided that the right to terminate this Agreement pursuant to this Section 7.1(c) shall not be available to any party hereto that has breached its obligations under this Agreement in any manner that shall have that shall have been the primary cause of such Order;

(d) by Parent, (i) if the Company Board shall have effected a Change of Recommendation or if following the public announcement of an Acquisition Proposal the Company Board shall have failed to publicly confirm the Company Recommendation within ten (10) Business Days of its receipt of a written request by Parent that it do so; or (ii) if there has been a breach of any representation, warranty, covenant or agreement made by the Company in this Agreement, other than Section 5.2, or any such representation or warranty shall have become untrue or incorrect on any date subsequent to the date hereof, in any such case in a manner that will cause any Tender Offer Condition not to be satisfied at any scheduled Expiration Time, and such breach or failure to be true or correct either is not curable or, if curable, has not been cured prior to the earlier of (x) the Outside Date and (y) the thirtieth (30th) calendar day after written notice thereof has been given by Parent or Merger Sub to the Company;

(e) by the Company, (i) if Parent or Merger Sub breaches or fails to perform in any material respect any of its representations, warranties, covenants or agreements contained in this Agreement, which breach or failure to perform has had, or is reasonably likely to have, a Parent Material Adverse Effect and is not curable or, if curable, has not been cured prior to the earlier of (A) the Outside Date and (B) the thirtieth (30th) calendar day after written notice thereof has been given by the Company to Parent or Merger Sub; or (ii) if Merger Sub fails to commence the Offer on or prior to the tenth (10th) Business Day following the date hereof or if Merger Sub fails to consummate the Offer in accordance with the terms of this Agreement; or

(f) by the Company, if the Company Board shall have effected a Change of Recommendation [*in response to a Superior Proposal or causing the Company to enter into an Alternative Acquisition Agreement concerning a Superior Proposal if the Company and the Company Board shall have complied in all material respects with the notice, negotiation and other requirements set forth in Section 5.2(c) with respect to such Superior Proposal.*

Any party hereto desiring to terminate this Agreement pursuant to Sections 7.1(b) through 7.1(f) shall give written notice of such termination to the other parties hereto, and the date and time on which written notice of such termination is delivered shall be the "Termination Date."] ~~or if, following the public announcement of an Acquisition Proposal or the commencement of a tender offer or exchange offer for the Shares,~~, or (ii) if the Company Board shall have ~~failed to publicly confirm the Company Recommendation (and, in the case of a tender offer or exchange offer, failed to publicly recommend that the holders of Shares reject such tender offer or exchange offer) upon Parent's written request within ten~~

(10) Business Days after the Company's receipt of any such request (or, in the case of a tender offer or exchange offer, such commencement) (or, if the Outside Date is fewer than ten (10) Business Days after the Company's receipt of such request from Parent or, in the case of a tender offer or exchange offer, such commencement, by the close of business on the Business Day immediately preceding the Outside Date), or (ii) if there has been a breach of any representation, warranty, covenant or agreement made by the Company in this Agreement or any such representation or warranty shall have become untrue or incorrect on any date subsequent to the date hereof, in any such case in a manner that will cause any Tender Offer Condition not to be satisfied at any scheduled Expiration Time, and such breach or failure to be true or correct either is not curable or, if curable, has not been cured prior to the earlier of (x) the Outside Date and (y) the thirtieth (30th) calendar day after written notice thereof has been given by Parent or Merger Sub to the Company;

(e) by the Company, (i) if there has been a breach of any representation, warranty, covenant or agreement made by Parent or Merger Sub in this Agreement or any such representation, or warranty shall have become untrue or incorrect on any date subsequent to the date hereof, which breach or failure to perform has had, or would reasonably be expected to have, a Parent Material Adverse Effect and is not curable or, if curable, has not been cured prior to the earlier of (A) the Outside Date and (B) the thirtieth (30th) calendar day after written notice thereof has been given by the Company to Parent or Merger Sub; or (ii) if Merger Sub fails to commence the Offer on or prior to the tenth (10th) Business Day following the date hereof or if Merger Sub fails to consummate the Offertaken any of the actions contemplated by clause (B) of Section 5.2(C) in accordance with the terms of this Agreement; or

(f) by the Company, in connection with the Company Board's effecting a Change of Recommendation in response to a Superior Proposal or causing the Company to enter into an Alternative Acquisition Agreement concerning a Superior Proposal if the Company and the Company Board shall have complied in all material respects with the notice, negotiation and other requirements set forth in Section 5.2(C) with respect to such Superior Proposal.

ARTICLE 7.2.   Effect of Termination and Abandonment; Termination Fee

(a) In the event of termination of this Agreement and the abandonment of the Offer and the Merger pursuant to this Article 7, this Agreement shall become void and of no effect, with no liability to any Person on the part of any party hereto (or of any of its Representatives or Affiliates); provided, however, that (i) no such termination shall relieve any party hereto of any liability or damages to the other party hereto resulting from any willful and intentional breach of this Agreement, it being acknowledged and agreed that the failure by Parent or Merger Sub to consummate the Offer, the Merger and the other Transactions after the respective conditions thereto have been satisfied or waived shall constitute a willful and intentional breach of this Agreement, and (ii) the provisions set forth in this Section 7.2 and the second sentence of Section 8.1 shall survive the termination of this Agreement. For purposes of this Agreement, "willful and intentional breach" means a material breach or failure to perform that is a consequence of an act or omission undertaken by the breaching party with the knowledge that the taking of, or failure to take, such act would, or would reasonably be expect to, cause a material breach of this Agreement.

(b)(i) In the event that this Agreement is terminated by the Company pursuant to Section 7.1(f) or by Parent pursuant to Section 7.1(d)(i) or 7.1(f), then:

(A) the Company shall pay to Parent, within two (2) Business Days following the date of such termination, all reasonable and documented out-of-pocket expenses of Parent and Merger Sub incurred in connection with this Agreement and the Transactions, not to exceed $10,000,000 (the "Expense Reimbursement");* and

(B) if, within one (1) year following such termination, the Company consummates a Subsequent Transaction, the Company shall pay to Parent, no later than two (2) Business Days following the date of such consummation, a termination fee equal to $◙ (the "Termination Fee"), minus the Expense Reimbursement paid.**

(ii) In the event that (A) an Acquisition Proposal shall have been made known to the Company Board or shall have been publicly announced (and such Acquisition Proposal shall not have been unconditionally terminated or withdrawn at least three (3) Business Days prior to the Outside Date), (B) this Agreement is terminated by either Parent or the Company pursuant to Section 7.1(b), and (c) prior to the date that is 12 months after the date of any such termination, the Company or its Subsidiary consummates a Subsequent Transaction, then the Company shall pay to Parent, no later than two (2) Business Days following the date of such consummation, the Termination Fee. Solely for purposes of this Section 7.2(b)(ii), the term "Acquisition Proposal" shall have the meaning assigned to such term in Section 5.2(f) except that all references to "fifteen percent (15%) or more" therein shall be deemed to be references to "a majority."

(iii) As used in this Agreement, "Subsequent Transaction" means (i) a merger, joint venture, partnership, consolidation, dissolution, liquidation, tender offer, exchange offer, recapitalization, reorganization,

---

*   In this instance the Company lacked the liquidity to pay a full termination fee at the time of termination, prior to consummation of a Superior Proposal or successful financings.

**   In 2014 target break-up fees averaged 3.4% of deal value. ABA Business Law Section, Market Trends Subcommittee of the Mergers & Acquisitions Subcommittee, Strategic Buyer/Public Target M & A Deal Points Study (2014), slide 97.

share exchange, business combination or similar transaction involving the Company, or any acquisition by any Person, which results in any Person becoming the beneficial owner of fifty percent (50%) or more of the total voting power of the equity securities of the Company or fifty percent (50%) or more of the total assets of the Company, in each case other than the Transactions, or (ii) any license (whether exclusive or non-exclusive) pertaining to commercialization rights for the Key Product. In any situation where this Agreement has been terminated pursuant to Section 7.1(d)(i) or 7.1(f) or the Company is required to pay the Termination Fee pursuant to this Section 7.2(b), Parent's right to receive the Expense Reimbursement and/or the Termination Fee, as the case may be, shall be the sole and exclusive remedy of Parent and Merger Sub against the Company and its Representatives for any and all losses and damages suffered in connection with this Agreement or the Transactions or as a result of the failure of the Transactions to be consummated. The agreements contained in this Section 7.2(b) are an integral part of the transactions contemplated by this Agreement and without these agreements none of the Company, Parent or Merger Sub would enter into this Agreement. Payment of the Expense Reimbursement Fee and/or the Termination Fee, as the case may be, shall be made by wire transfer of immediately available funds if Parent shall have furnished to the Company appropriate wire payment instructions prior to the date of payment or, otherwise, by certified or official bank check. In no event shall the Company be required to pay the Expense Reimbursement Fee or the Termination Fee more than once.

(c) If the Company fails to pay when due any amount payable under Section 7.2(b), then (i) the Company shall reimburse Parent for all reasonable and documented costs and expenses (including fees and disbursements of outside legal counsel) incurred in connection with the collection of such overdue amount and the enforcement by Parent of its rights under this Section 7.2, and (ii) the Company shall pay to Parent interest on such overdue amount (for the period commencing as of the date such overdue amount was originally required to be paid and ending on the date such overdue amount is actually paid to Parent) at a rate per annum equal to the "prime rate" (as announced by Bank of America or any successor thereto) in effect on the date such amount was originally required to be paid.

ARTICLE 8.   Miscellaneous and General

ARTICLE 8.1.   Survival

Article 3, this Article 8 and the agreements of the Company, Parent and Merger Sub contained in Sections 5.8 (Employee Benefits), 5.9 (Expenses) and 5.10 (Indemnification; Directors' and Officers' Insurance) shall survive the consummation of the Merger. This Article 8 and the agreements of the Company, Parent and Merger Sub contained in Section 5.9 (Expenses) and Section 7.2 (Effect of Termination and Abandonment;

Termination Fee) and the Confidentiality Agreement shall survive the termination of this Agreement. None of the other representations, warranties, covenants or agreements in this Agreement shall survive the consummation of the Merger or the termination of this Agreement.

ARTICLE 8.2.   Amendment; Extension; Waiver

Subject to applicable Law, this Agreement may be amended by the parties hereto at any time prior to the Effective Time by an instrument in writing signed by each party hereto, provided, that Sections 8.2, 8.4, 8.6 and 8.7, which Sections (and the related definitions and other provisions of this Agreement to the extent a modification or waiver or termination would serve to modify the substance or provisions of such Sections) may not be amended or modified in any manner adverse to any Financing Source without the Lead Commitment Parties' prior written consent (such consent not to unreasonably withheld, conditioned or delayed). At any time prior to the Effective Time, each of Parent and Merger Sub, on the one hand and the Company, on the other hand, may (but shall not be under any obligation to) (a) extend the time for the performance of any of the obligations or other acts of the other, (b) to the extent permitted by applicable Law, waive any inaccuracies in the representations and warranties of the other contained herein or in any document delivered pursuant hereto or (c) to the extent permitted by applicable Law, waive compliance with any of the agreements of the other or any of the conditions for its benefit contained herein. Any agreement on the part of a party hereto to any such extension or waiver shall be valid only if set forth in an instrument in writing signed by such party. The failure of any party hereto to assert any of its rights hereunder or under applicable Law shall not constitute a waiver of such rights and, except as otherwise expressly provided herein, no single or partial exercise by any party hereto of any of its rights hereunder shall preclude any other or further exercise of such rights or any other rights hereunder or under applicable Law.

ARTICLE 8.3.   Counterparts

This Agreement may be executed in any number of counterparts, each such counterpart being deemed to be an original instrument, and all such counterparts shall together constitute the same agreement. Delivery of an executed counterpart of a signature page to this Agreement by facsimile or other means of electronic transmission (such as via portable document format (.pdf)) shall be as effective as delivery of a manually executed counterpart.

ARTICLE 8.4.   Governing Law and Venue; Waiver of Jury Trial; Specific Performance

(a)   This Agreement shall be deemed to be made in and construed in and in all respects shall be interpreted, construed and governed by and in accordance with the law of the State of Delaware without regard to the conflicts of law principles thereof. The parties hereto hereby irrevocably submit to the personal jurisdiction of the Court of Chancery of the State of Delaware or, if such Court of Chancery shall lack subject matter jurisdiction, the Federal courts of the United States of America located in the County of New Castle, Delaware, solely in respect of the interpretation and enforcement of the provisions of (and any claim or cause of action arising under or relating to) this Agreement and of the documents referred to in this Agreement, and in respect of the transactions contemplated hereby, and hereby waive, and agree not to assert, as a defense in any action, suit or proceeding for the interpretation or enforcement hereof or of any such document, that it is not subject thereto or that such action, suit or proceeding may not be brought or is not maintainable in said courts or that the venue thereof may not be appropriate or that this Agreement or any such document may not be enforced in or by such courts, and the parties hereto irrevocably agree that all claims with respect to such action or proceeding shall be heard and determined exclusively in such courts. The parties hereto hereby consent to and grant any such court jurisdiction over the person of such parties and, to the extent permitted by law, over the subject matter of such dispute and agree that mailing of process or other papers in connection with any such action or proceeding in the manner provided in Section 8.5 or in such other manner as may be permitted by law shall be valid and sufficient service thereof. [*Notwithstanding anything herein to the contrary, each of the parties hereto agrees that any claim, action or proceeding against the Financing Sources arising out of or relating to this Agreement or the transactions contemplated hereby or in connection with the Financing, or the performance of services by the Financing Sources with respect to the foregoing, shall be governed by, and construed in accordance with, the laws of the State of New York applicable to contracts executed in and to be performed entirely within such State (provided, however, that, for purposes of the foregoing, (i) the interpretation of the definition of "Company Material Adverse Effect" (and whether or not a "Company Material Adverse Effect" has occurred) and (ii) the determination of the accuracy of any representations and warranties of the Company herein and whether as a result of any inaccuracy thereof the Parent or Merger Sub have the right to terminate its (or their) obligations under this Agreement, in each case shall be governed by, and construed and interpreted in accordance with, the laws of the State of Delaware, without regard to the principles of conflicts of law), and shall be subject to the exclusive jurisdiction of New York State or United States federal courts sitting in the Borough of Manhattan, City of New York and no party hereto shall, nor shall it permit any of its Affiliates to, bring or support anyone else in bringing any claim, action or proceeding against the Financing Sources in relation hereto in any other court.*]

(b) EACH PARTY HERETO ACKNOWLEDGES AND AGREES THAT ANY CONTROVERSY WHICH MAY ARISE UNDER THIS

AGREEMENT IS LIKELY TO INVOLVE COMPLICATED AND DIFFICULT ISSUES, AND THEREFORE EACH SUCH PARTY HEREBY IRREVOCABLY AND UNCONDITIONALLY WAIVES ANY RIGHT SUCH PARTY MAY HAVE TO A TRIAL BY JURY IN RESPECT OF ANY LITIGATION DIRECTLY OR INDIRECTLY ARISING OUT OF OR RELATING TO THIS AGREEMENT, OR THE TRANSACTIONS CONTEMPLATED BY THIS AGREEMENT; INCLUDING ANY LITIGATION AGAINST ANY FINANCING SOURCES ARISING OUT OF THIS AGREEMENT OR THE FINANCING COMMITMENTS. EACH PARTY HERETO CERTIFIES AND ACKNOWLEDGES THAT (i) NO REPRESENTATIVE, AGENT OR ATTORNEY OF ANY OTHER PARTY HERETO HAS REPRESENTED, EXPRESSLY OR OTHERWISE, THAT SUCH OTHER PARTY WOULD NOT, IN THE EVENT OF LITIGATION, SEEK TO ENFORCE THE FOREGOING WAIVER, (ii) EACH PARTY HERETO UNDERSTANDS AND HAS CONSIDERED THE IMPLICATIONS OF THIS WAIVER, (iii) EACH PARTY HERETO MAKES THIS WAIVER VOLUNTARILY, AND (iv) EACH PARTY HERETO HAS BEEN INDUCED TO ENTER INTO THIS AGREEMENT BY, AMONG OTHER THINGS, THE MUTUAL WAIVERS AND CERTIFICATIONS IN THIS SECTION 8.4.

(c) The parties hereto agree that irreparable damage would occur if any provision of this Agreement were not performed in accordance with the terms hereof (and, more specifically, that irreparable damage would likewise occur if any of the Transactions were not consummated and the Company's stockholders did not receive the aggregate consideration payable to them in accordance with the terms and subject to the conditions of this Agreement), and, accordingly, that the parties hereto shall be entitled to an injunction or injunctions to prevent breaches of this Agreement or to enforce specifically the performance of the terms and provisions hereof (including the obligation of the parties hereto to consummate the Transactions and the obligation of Parent and Merger Sub to pay, and the Company's stockholders' right to receive, the aggregate consideration payable to them pursuant to the Transactions, in each case in accordance with the terms and subject to the conditions of this Agreement) in the Court of Chancery of the State of Delaware or, if said Court of Chancery shall lack subject matter jurisdiction, any Federal court of the United States of America located in the County of New Castle, Delaware, this being in addition to any other remedy to which such party is entitled at law or in equity. In the event that any action is brought in equity to enforce the provisions of this Agreement, no party hereto shall allege, and each party hereto hereby waives the defense or counterclaim, that there is an adequate remedy at law. Each party hereto further agrees that no other party hereto or any other Person shall be required to obtain, furnish, or post any bond or similar instrument in connection with or as a condition to obtaining any remedy referred to in this Section 8.4(c), and each party hereto irrevocably waives any right it may have to require the obtaining, furnishing, or posting of any such bond or similar instrument.*

[(d) Each party hereto agrees, on behalf of itself and its stockholders, Affiliates and Representatives, that the Financing Sources shall be beneficiaries of all limitations on remedies and damages in this Agreement that apply to Parent and Merger Sub.]

ARTICLE 8.5.   Notices

Any notice, request, instruction or other communication hereunder by any party hereto shall be in writing and delivered personally or sent by registered or certified mail, postage prepaid, by facsimile or overnight courier (such as Federal Express) to the other parties hereto at the following addresses:

If to Parent or Merger Sub:

[Name]

[Street Address]

[City, State, Zip]

Attention: [Name]

fax: [Number]

with a copy (which shall not constitute notice) to:

[Attorney's Name]

[Street Address]

[City, State, Zip]

Attention: [Name]

fax: [Number]

If to the Company:

[Name]

[Street Address]

[City, State, Zip]

Attention: [Name]

fax: [Number]

with a copy (which shall not constitute notice) to:

[Attorney's Name]

[Street Address]

[City, State, Zip]

Attention: [Name]

fax: [Number]

---

* Specific performance remedies against buyers have become almost universal, included in 98% of deals in 2014.

or to such other Persons or addresses as may be designated in writing by the party hereto to receive such notice as provided above. Any notice, request, instruction or other document given as provided above shall be deemed given to the receiving party upon actual receipt, if delivered personally; three (3) Business Days after deposit in the mail, if sent by registered or certified mail; upon confirmation of successful transmission if sent by facsimile (provided that if given by facsimile such notice, request, instruction or other document shall be followed up within one (1) Business Day by dispatch pursuant to one of the other methods described herein); or on the next Business Day after deposit with an overnight courier, if sent by an overnight courier.

ARTICLE 8.6. Entire Agreement

This Agreement (including the Annexes), the Company Disclosure Schedule, the Parent Disclosure Schedule and the Confidentiality Agreement constitute the entire agreement, and supersede all other prior agreements, understandings, representations and warranties, both written and oral, among the parties hereto with respect to the subject matter hereof. [*EACH PARTY HERETO AGREES THAT, EXCEPT FOR THE REPRESENTATIONS AND WARRANTIES CONTAINED IN THIS AGREEMENT, NEITHER PARENT AND MERGER SUB NOR THE COMPANY MAKES ANY OTHER REPRESENTATIONS OR WARRANTIES, AND EACH HEREBY DISCLAIMS ANY OTHER REPRESENTATIONS OR WARRANTIES, EXPRESS OR IMPLIED, OR AS TO THE ACCURACY OR COMPLETENESS OF ANY OTHER INFORMATION, MADE BY, OR MADE AVAILABLE BY, ITSELF OR ANY OF ITS REPRESENTATIVES, WITH RESPECT TO, OR IN CONNECTION WITH, THE NEGOTIATION, EXECUTION OR DELIVERY OF THIS AGREEMENT OR THE TRANSACTIONS CONTEMPLATED HEREBY, NOTWITHSTANDING THE DELIVERY OR DISCLOSURE TO THE OTHER OR THE OTHER'S REPRESENTATIVES OF ANY DOCUMENTATION OR OTHER INFORMATION WITH RESPECT TO ANY ONE OR MORE OF THE FOREGOING.*]

ARTICLE 8.7. Third-Party Beneficiaries

Except as provided in Section 5.10 only, each party hereto hereby agrees that its representations, warranties and covenants set forth herein are solely for the benefit of the other parties hereto, in accordance with and subject to the terms of this Agreement, and this Agreement is not intended to, and does not, confer on any Person other than the parties hereto any rights or remedies hereunder, including the right to rely on the representations and warranties set forth herein. Notwithstanding the immediately preceding sentence, (i) following the Effective Time the provisions hereof shall be enforceable by stockholders of the Company to the extent necessary to receive the Per Share Merger Consideration to which each such stockholder is entitled pursuant to Article 3, [*and (ii) the Financing Sources shall be third-party beneficiaries with respect to the terms and provisions of Sections 8.2, 8.4, 8.6 and 8.7.]*

ARTICLE 8.8.   Obligations of Parent

Whenever this Agreement requires Merger Sub or a Subsidiary of Parent (including, after the Closing, the Surviving Corporation) to take any action, such requirement shall be deemed to include an undertaking on the part of Parent to cause Merger Sub or such Subsidiary to take such action. Parent and Merger Sub shall be jointly and severally liable for the failure by either of them to perform and discharge any of their respective covenants, agreements or obligations hereunder.

ARTICLE 8.9.   Severability

The provisions of this Agreement shall be deemed severable, and the invalidity or unenforceability of any provision shall not affect the validity or enforceability of the other provisions hereof. If any provision of this Agreement, or the application thereof to any Person or any circumstance, is invalid or unenforceable, (a) a suitable and equitable provision shall be substituted therefor in order to carry out, so far as may be valid and enforceable, the intent and purpose of such invalid or unenforceable provision and (b) the remainder of this Agreement and the application of such provision to other Persons or circumstances shall not be affected by such invalidity or unenforceability, nor shall such invalidity or unenforceability affect the validity or enforceability of such provision, or the application thereof, in any other jurisdiction.

ARTICLE 8.10. Interpretation; Construction

(a) The table of contents and headings herein are for convenience of reference only, do not constitute part of this Agreement and shall not be deemed to limit or otherwise affect any of the provisions hereof. For the convenience of the parties hereto, each of the terms set forth in the table following the table of contents is defined in the Section of this Agreement set forth opposite such term. Where a reference in this Agreement is made to an Article, Section or Annex, such reference shall be to such Article or Section of, or Annex to, this Agreement unless otherwise indicated. The Company Disclosure Schedule, Parent Disclosure Schedule and the Annexes identified in this Agreement are incorporated into this Agreement by reference and made a part hereof. The terms "include," "includes" or "including" are not intended to be limiting and shall be deemed to be followed by the words "without limitation" or words of like import. The use of the masculine, feminine or neuter gender, or the singular or plural form of words used herein (including defined terms) shall not limit any provision of this Agreement. Reference herein to a particular Person includes such Person's successors and assigns to the extent such successors and assigns are permitted by the terms of any applicable Contract. Reference to a particular Contract (including this Agreement), document or instrument means such Contract, document or instrument as amended or modified and in effect from time to time in accordance with the terms thereof. Any reference to a particular Law means such Law as amended, modified or supplemented (including all rules and regulations promulgated thereunder) and, unless otherwise provided, as in effect from time to time. The terms "cash", "dollars" and "$" mean United States Dollars. The use of the terms "hereunder," "hereof," "hereto" and words of similar import shall refer to this Agreement as a whole and not to any particular Article, Section, paragraph or clause of, or Annex to, this Agreement. [*Except as provided in Section 4.1(p)(ix), the Company shall be deemed to have "made available" a document or item of information to Parent only if such document or item was actually delivered by the Company to Parent or its legal counsel or publicly filed in unredacted form with the SEC prior to the execution and delivery of this Agreement or was, prior to the execution and delivery of this Agreement, posted in the electronic data room organized by the Company in connection with the due diligence investigation conducted by Parent.*]

(b)   The parties hereto have participated jointly in negotiating and drafting this Agreement. In the event that an ambiguity or a question of intent or interpretation arises, this Agreement shall be construed as if drafted jointly by the parties hereto, and no presumption or burden of proof shall arise favoring or disfavoring any party hereto by virtue of the authorship of any provision of this Agreement.

(c)   No reference to or disclosure of any item or other matter in the Company [*Disclosure Schedule or the Parent*] Disclosure Schedule shall be construed as an admission or indication that such item or other matter is material or that such item or other matter is required to be referred to or disclosed in this Agreement. Without limiting the foregoing, no such reference to or disclosure of a possible breach or violation of any Contract, Law or Order shall be construed as an admission or indication that a breach or violation exists or has actually occurred.

ARTICLE 8.11.   Assignment; Binding Effect

Neither this Agreement nor any of the rights, interests or obligations hereunder shall be assignable by any of the parties hereto (by operation of law or otherwise) without the prior written consent of the other parties hereto [*; provided, however, that Parent may designate, by written notice to the Company, another wholly-owned direct or indirect Delaware Subsidiary of Parent, with a certificate of incorporation and bylaws identical (other than the corporate name) to the correlative instruments of Merger Sub as in effect on the date hereof, in which case all references herein to Merger Sub shall be deemed to be to such other Subsidiary; provided, further, that any such designation shall not impede or delay the commencement or consummation of the Offer, the Merger or the other Transactions.*] Subject to the preceding sentence, this Agreement shall be binding on and shall inure to the benefit of the parties hereto and their respective successors and assigns. Any purported assignment in violation of this Agreement is void.

[Signature page follows, which is omitted]

ANNEX A

TENDER OFFER CONDITIONS

Notwithstanding any other provision of this Agreement or the Offer, Merger Sub shall not be obligated to accept for payment or, subject to the rules and regulations of the SEC, including Rule 14e–1(C) under the Exchange Act relating to Merger Sub's obligation to pay for or return the tendered Shares promptly after termination or withdrawal of the Offer, pay for any Shares validly tendered and not withdrawn pursuant to the Offer, if:

(i) prior to the Expiration Time there shall not be validly tendered (not including Shares tendered pursuant to procedures for guaranteed delivery and not actually delivered prior to the Expiration Time) and not properly withdrawn a number of Shares that, together with the Shares beneficially owned by Parent and Merger Sub, constitute at least a majority of the total number of then outstanding Shares on a fully diluted basis (which total number shall be the number of Shares issued and outstanding plus the number of Shares which the Company would be required to issue pursuant to any then outstanding warrants, options, benefit plans or obligations or securities convertible or exchangeable into Shares or otherwise, but only to the extent then so exercisable, convertible or exchangeable or exercisable, convertible or exchangeable as a result of the consummation of the Offer) (the "Minimum Tender Condition");

(ii) the applicable waiting period under the HSR Act shall not have expired or been terminated;

(iii) as of the date of this Agreement and as of the Acceptance Time (in each case, except for any representation or warranty that is expressly made as of a specified date, in which case as of such specified date), (A) any representation or warranty of the Company contained in this Agreement that is qualified as to Company Material Adverse Effect shall not be true and correct in all respects, (B) any representation or warranty of the Company contained in Section 4.1(a), Section 4.1(b) or Section 4.1(c) shall not be true and correct in all respects, or (c) any other representation or warranty of the Company contained in this Agreement that is not qualified as to Company Material Adverse Effect shall not be true and correct in all respects except where the failure of such representations and warranties referred to in this clause (c) to be true and correct, individually or in the aggregate with other such failures, has not had, and is not reasonably likely to have, a Company Material Adverse Effect;

(iv) the Company shall not have performed in all material respects those obligations under this Agreement required to be performed prior to the Acceptance Time, and such failure to perform shall not have been cured prior to the Acceptance Time;

(v) the Company shall have failed to deliver to Parent a certificate signed by an officer of the Company and certifying as to the satisfaction of the conditions described in paragraphs (iii) and (iv) above;

(vi) there shall be in effect an Order by a court of competent jurisdiction restraining, enjoining or otherwise prohibiting consummation of the Offer or making the acceptance of Shares pursuant to the Offer illegal; or

(vii) this Agreement shall have been terminated in accordance with its terms.

The foregoing conditions (except for the Minimum Tender Condition) may be waived by Parent or Merger Sub in whole or in part at any time and from time to time, subject in each case to the terms of this Agreement.

CONFIDENTIALITY AGREEMENT

THIS AGREEMENT, entered into as of ___, by and between PROSPECTIVE SELLER, a _____ corporation, ("Seller") and the PROSPECTIVE BUYER, a _____ corporation ("Buyer").

WHEREAS, Buyer has expressed its interest in holding discussions concerning the possible acquisition of the business and assets of Seller, and Seller has made a determination to explore various options concerning its future, without committing that it will sell its assets and business,

NOW THEREFORE, in consideration of the mutual covenants contained herein, the parties hereto agree as follows:

1. *Seller's Disclosure of Confidential Information.* Representatives of Seller and Buyer plan to meet from time to time for discussions concerning the possible purchase and sale of Seller by Buyer, during which time Seller may reveal to Buyer, either orally or in writing or by inspection, confidential information as to its business that would be helpful in evaluating such acquisition or business combination. Such "Confidential Information" to be disclosed or inspected, as the case may be, might include financial statements, cost and expense data, budget and financial projections, production data, trade secrets, technology, marketing and customer data, employee relations records and such other information as may be supplied by Seller that is not generally ascertainable from public or published information or trade sources. Because of the broad inspection rights granted to Buyer hereunder, it shall be presumed that all information to which access is granted hereunder is confidential, unless Buyer has access to it through public sources, or is informed in writing by Seller either that such information is not confidential or may be released. It is understood that the unauthorized release of such Confidential Information might cause irreparable injury to Seller or to its relationships with its members, customers, suppliers, employees, regulatory agencies, or the communities in which it serves. It is agreed and understood that such Confidential Information shall not include information which (i) is or becomes generally available to the public other than as a result of a disclosure by you or your Representatives, (ii) was within your possession prior to its being furnished to you by or on behalf of Seller pursuant hereto, provided that the source of such information was not known by you to be bound by a confidentiality agreement with or other obligation of confidentiality to the Company or any other party with respect to such information, (iii) becomes available to you on a non-confidential basis

from a source other than the Company or any of its Representatives, provided that such source is not bound by a confidentiality agreement with or other obligation of confidentiality to the Company or any other party with respect to such information, or (iv) was independently developed by you without reference to the Confidential Information, provided such independent development can be proven by you by contemporaneous written records.

2. ·*Inspection Rights*. Seller will afford to Buyer, its principals, officers, directors, employees or agents (collectively, "Affiliates") reasonable opportunity and access, during normal business hours, to inspect, investigate and audit the assets, liabilities, contracts, operations and businesses of Seller. Seller, its employees and agents will cooperate fully with Buyer in granting such access, provided that such cooperation shall not interfere with the daily operations of Seller, or any rights granted by Seller to other entities to engage in a similar inspection and examination. Seller reserves the right to deny access to records of negotiations with other parties concerning the possible acquisition of Seller, studies of the possible restructuring and reorganization of Seller, Seller's documents concerning its negotiations with Buyer, and all documents, evaluations, appraisals, memoranda and minutes related thereto.

3. *Confidentiality of Seller's Information*. Buyer covenants and agrees neither it nor any of its principals, officers, directors, employees or agents shall at any time, without Seller's prior written consent, communicate, divulge or use for Buyer's or their benefit or the benefit of any other person, firm, association, corporation or other entity, any information or data concerning marketing, equipment, business methods, research, customers, contacts, suppliers, contracts or finances of Seller or related to Seller, or other Confidential Information possessed, owned or used by Buyer, that may be communicated to or acquired or learned by Buyer or any of its principals, officers, directors, employees or agents in the course of the negotiations, investigations undertaken pursuant to this Agreement or otherwise. Buyer agrees to disclose the Confidential Information only to its directors, officers and employees who need to have the information in connection with the evaluation and negotiation of any proposed acquisition, and that all such persons will agree to be bound by the terms of this Agreement. All records, files, financial statements, client and customer lists, brochures, documents and the like relating to Seller or its business that shall come into Buyer's possession shall remain and be deemed to be the sole property of Seller and shall promptly be returned to Seller upon the earlier of its request or the termination of any discussions or negotiations between Buyer and Seller concerning a possible acquisition (without retaining copies thereof). Buyer also agrees that any analyses, compilations, studies or other documents which may be prepared for internal use by Buyer or its agents, and which reflect the Confidential Information, will be kept

confidential by Buyer to the same extent as the Confidential Information and Buyer will promptly destroy all such analyses, compilations, studies or other documents in the event it is decided that Buyer will not make a proposal, its proposal is not accepted by Seller, or if accepted, a sale is not consummated. Buyer further agrees and covenants that Buyer shall not at any time, directly or indirectly, do or omit to do any act that would in any way diminish or impair the business or future business prospects of Seller or which is prejudicial to the best interest of Seller and its members.

4. *Consultants and Advisers.* Buyer agrees that it will require any consultants, advisers, or professional representatives and agents who need to have any of Seller' Confidential Information in order to advise or assist Buyer in evaluation or negotiations connected with the purchase of Seller to observe the terms of this Agreement in the same manner as Buyer is required to.

5. *No Public Statements.* Buyer shall not, without the prior written consent of Seller, make any statements or public announcements or any release to trade publications or to the press, or make any statement to any competitor, customer, or any other third party, with respect to such discussions, except as may be necessary in the written opinion of Buyer's counsel, furnished to Seller in advance of such release, to comply with the requirements of any law, governmental order or regulation. Should Buyer receive such an opinion of counsel or become legally compelled (by deposition, interrogatory, request for documents, subpoena, civil investigative demand or other legal process) to disclose any of the Confidential Material, then Buyer shall provide Seller with prompt prior written notice of such request or requirement so that Seller may seek a protective order or other appropriate remedy and/or waive compliance with the terms of this Agreement. In the event that such protective order or other remedy is not obtained, or that Seller waives compliance with the provisions hereof, Buyer agrees to furnish only that portion of the Confidential Information which it is advised by written opinion of counsel it is legally required to disclose and to exercise best efforts to obtain assurance that confidential treatment will be accorded to such Confidential Information.

6. *Negotiations with Creditors.* It is understood and agreed that Buyer will not carry on discussions concerning the assumption or alteration of Seller' current long-term indebtedness with Seller' creditors, without the express written permission of Seller. Seller covenants and agrees that if it should enter into any preliminary agreements concerning the restructuring of its indebtedness that it will inform Buyer, on a non-exclusive basis, of the results of such negotiations.

7. *Application to Prior Disclosures.* Buyer confirms that any information disclosed by Seller, or any discussions held between Seller

and Buyer, prior to the execution of this agreement, shall be subject to the terms of this Agreement.

8. *Termination of Obligations.* The confidentiality obligations of this Agreement shall terminate with respect to any Confidential Information which shall become a matter of public knowledge, other than through disclosure by Buyer or any of its principals, officers, directors, employees, consultants, advisers or professional representatives or agents or others bound by this Agreement.

9. *Covenant Not to Purchase.* Because Buyer recognizes that any attempt by Buyer to publicly offer to purchase Seller prior to an indication from Seller that it was ready to receive an offer could interfere with the full consideration of all alternatives by Seller in the course of its present review, Buyer covenants and agrees that it will make no offer to purchase, nor publicly announce its willingness to purchase, Seller until it receives written notification from Seller that it is willing to receive such offers. Buyer further covenants that for a period of three years from the termination of this agreement it will make no such offers to purchase nor public announce a willingness to purchase Seller or its shares, unless Seller shall have first received a firm offer in writing from a third party.

10. *Fiduciary Duties.* Buyer recognizes and acknowledges that the Board of Directors of Seller is under a fiduciary obligation to consider all alternatives that may be available to Seller in achieving the maximum value for Seller, and that this may require furnishing similar Confidential Information to other parties that may be interested in negotiating for the purchase of Seller. In exercising its rights of inspection and examination hereunder, Buyer covenants and agrees that it will not unreasonably interfere with the rights of others to undertake similar activities.

11. *No Offers to Employees.* For a period of three years from the date of termination of this Agreement, neither Buyer nor any of its Affiliates will solicit to employ or hire, nor enter into any consulting agreement with, any of the current officers or employees of Seller with whom Buyer has had contact or who was specifically identified to you during the period of Buyer's investigation of Seller, so long as they are employed by Seller without obtaining Seller's prior written consent.

12. *Costs.* Each party shall bear its own costs in connection with their activities conducted in accordance with this Agreement; provided, however, that Seller may charge Buyer for the cost of copying any documents for Buyer.

13. *Survival of Covenants.* The covenants of Buyer concerning the treatment of Confidential Information and concerning offers to Seller's employees shall survive the termination of the investigation and possible negotiations contemplated hereby, and the return of documents to Seller by Buyer.

14. *Termination.* This Agreement shall continue in effect for so long as Buyer is pursuing the investigation of Seller and negotiating with Seller as described above. If at any time either party determines that further investigation or negotiation is not in that party's best interest, it may terminate this Agreement and any activities in connection therewith.

15. *No Representations or Warranties.* Seller is not making, nor will it make at the time of delivery of any Confidential Information, any representation or warranty, express or implied, as to the accuracy or completeness of the Confidential Information, and neither Seller nor any of its members, directors, officers, agents or employees will have any liability to Buyer or any other person resulting from the use of the Confidential Information.

16. *Remedies.* Buyer agrees to indemnify Seller for any loss or damage resulting from its violation of this Agreement related to the Confidential Information. The parties agree that remedies at law for any actual or threatened breach by them of the covenants contained in this Agreement would be inadequate and that Seller shall be entitled to equitable relief, including injunction and specific performance, in the event of any breach of the provisions of this Agreement, in addition to all other remedies available at law or in equity. Buyer also hereby irrevocably and unconditionally consents to submit to the jurisdiction of the courts of the State of_____ and of the United States of America located in _____. The parties hereby irrevocably and unconditionally waive any objection to the laying of venue of any action, suit or proceeding arising out of this Agreement or the transactions contemplated hereby, in the courts of the State of_____ or in the United States Courts located in _____.

17. *No Further Commitments.* Except for this Agreement, neither Buyer nor Seller shall be committed in any way with respect to the matters to be discussed by them, unless and until a formal agreement is executed, pursuant to the due authorization of their respective companies, by the appropriate officers of both Buyer and Seller, or by both such officers and members, as the case may be.

18. *Severability.* It is the intention of the parties hereto that the provisions of this Agreement shall be enforced to the fullest extent permissible under the laws and public policies of each state and jurisdiction in which such enforcement is sought, but that the unenforceability (or the modification to conform with such laws or public policies) of any provision hereof shall not render unenforceable or impair the remainder of this Agreement which shall be deemed amended to delete or modify, as necessary, the invalid or unenforceable provisions. The parties further agree to alter the balance of this Agreement in order to render the same valid and enforceable.

19. *No Waivers.* It is further understood and agreed that no failure or delay in exercising any right, power or privilege hereunder will operate as a waiver thereof, nor will any single or partial exercise thereof preclude any other or further exercise thereof or the exercise of any right, power or privilege hereunder.

IN WITNESS WHEREOF, this Agreement has been duly executed by the parties hereto under their respective corporate seals as of the day and year first above written.

SELLER

By _____

Title: _____

BUYER

By _____

Title: _____

INDEX

References are to Pages